VERDI

Frontispiece: Verdi, photograph by André Adolphe Disderi, Paris, *c.* 1855.

VERDI

A BIOGRAPHY

MARY JANE PHILLIPS-MATZ

With a Foreword by
ANDREW PORTER

Oxford   New York
OXFORD UNIVERSITY PRESS

Oxford University Press, Great Clarendon Street, Oxford OX2 6DP

Oxford New York

Athens Auckland Bangkok Bogota Bombay
Buenos Aires Calcutta Cape Town Dar es Salaam
Delhi Florence Hong Kong Istanbul Karachi
Kuala Lumpur Madras Madrid Melbourne
Mexico City Nairobi Paris Singapore
Taipei Tokyo Toronto

and associated companies in
Berlin Ibadan

Oxford is a trade mark of Oxford University Press

Published in the United States
by Oxford University Press Inc., New York

British Library Cataloguing in Publication Data
Data available

Library of Congress Cataloging in Publication Data
Phillips-Matz, Mary Jane.
Verdi: a biography / Mary Jane Phillips-Matz; with a foreword by Andrew Porter.
Includes bibliographical references and index.
1. Verdi, Giuseppe, 1813–1901. 2. Composers—Italy—Biography.
I. Title.
ML410.V4P43 1996 782.1'092—dc20 [B] 92-37841
ISBN 0-19-313204-4 (cloth)
ISBN 0-19-816600-1 (pbk)

Printed in Great Britain
Biddles Ltd
Guildford & King's Lynn

To my children

Mary Ann Margaret
Catherine Eleanor
Margaret Spencer
Clare Ann
Carlino

in gratitude, faith and love

1992

Foreword

Mary Jane Phillips-Matz's *Verdi* is the latest, longest, and most thoroughly informed of the many Verdi biographies in English. One of the earliest was Giannandrea Mazzucato's—32 close-printed columns in the first edition of Grove's *Dictionary of Music and Musicians* (1890). Three years before that, Arthur Pougin's *Verdi: An Anecdotic History* had appeared; this was an English translation of the edition in which Pougin had incorporated material that Verdi himself—in an uncharacteristic flood of reminiscence to Giulio Ricordi—had provided for an amplified Italian translation (by 'Folchetto', the pen-name of Jacopo Caponi) of Pougin's original *Vie anecdotique*. Pougin also had the collaboration of Emanuele Muzio, Verdi's daily companion of several years and lifelong friend, whose 'very lively and very accurate recollections' supplied 'much information of great accuracy on a crowd of facts entirely unknown'.

Thus, Mazzucato said, 'through the combined shrewdness and skill of "Folchetto" and M. Giulio Ricordi we are enabled to present to our readers the most important period of Verdi's career in words that are almost the great composer's own'. Those words, their authority accepted without question, set the pattern for subsequent Verdi biographies. They were used by Ferruccio Bonavia, who wrote the Verdi entry for the third *Grove* (1927), and whose *Verdi* appeared in 1930; and by Francis Toye, whose *Verdi*—the 'standard' English biography for many years—appeared in 1931. To those authors other—and more accurate—words of the great composer were now available. His *Copialettere*—the volumes containing copies of his voluminous correspondence—were published in 1913. Verdi's letters to Antonio Somma, the poet of *Un ballo in maschera* and of the *King Lear* whose libretto was fully written but never composed, had been published back in 1902; they form a veritable correspondence course on the art of libretto writing.

Subsequent landmarks were the composer's frank, informal correspondence with his friend Count Arrivabene, and Muzio's letters to Antonio Barezzi—Verdi's father-in-law, and his and Muzio's 'second father'—which were both published in 1931. Carlo Gatti's two-volume *Verdi*, with new information, also appeared that year. Alessandro Luzio's four volumes of *Carteggi verdiani* (1935–47) and a miscellany of letters published in various periodicals nearly doubled the tally of 'the composer's own words' available to his biographers. Franco Abbiati's four-volume *Verdi* (1959) took account of them and—for he had access to unexplored archives—gave us many more.

But no one really questioned the authenticity of the 'official portrait' until Frank Walker wrote the Verdi entry for the fifth *Grove* (1954), reviewed Abbiati, and then in 1962 published his own *The Man Verdi*. Walker, as Mary Jane Phillips-Matz puts it in her preface, 'had the courage to look squarely at some of the problem areas of Verdi's life that other writers had avoided'. He had read hundreds of documents overlooked by earlier biographers and had noticed that the plain historical facts were not always in accord with the official story promulgated in the first place by the composer himself. Meanwhile, Mary Jane had been similarly attentive; in her paper 'The Verdi Family . . . Legend and Truth' delivered at the first International Congress of Verdi Studies (1966) and in its successors she quietly undermined foundations on which the legend had been erected, exploded one bombshell after another. In the Verdi entry for the sixth *Grove* I could take stock of her discoveries.

Let me be personal for a paragraph. Frank Walker—I'm writing this in a London room suddenly filled again with his presence as I recall his visits here—was at once a scholar-detective, a brilliant researcher, and a romantic: learned, entertaining, and eccentric; scrupulous in his written presentation of evidence but sometimes swayed in his interpretation thereof, I felt, by emotional identification with the protagonists of his researches (Verdi and Giuseppina Strepponi and Teresa Stolz, Hugo Wolf and Melanie Köchert), even by a fusing of their problems with his own romantic impasse, which led him to take his life in a flamboyant gesture of devotion. Mary Jane is a survivor of personal tragedy, quick as Frank was to identify and suffer, but perhaps more in touch with the way that other people—and especially Italian people—really think and feel and act. I met her first over a cheerful dinner at a Spoleto Festival thirty years ago (and learned, usefully, that drinking a bottle of mineral water could help to stave off a morning-after hangover). At the Verdi congresses I heard her startling papers. In New York we then lived for fifteen years in the same Broadway building, ten floors apart. There she shared with me her latest discoveries, tested on me her speculations, was patient with my insistence that bold leaps of thought, imaginative deductions, likely but not necessary connections needed documentary underpinning or, if that were not forthcoming, a frank declaration of probability, not proof.

FOREWORD

During those years Verdi scholarship had been transformed. The Istituto di Studi Verdiani, founded in Parma in 1959, gathered and ordered under one roof copies of documents that could previously be consulted only by much travel. The American Institute of Verdi Studies, founded in 1976, soon acquired (thanks largely to Mary Jane Phillips-Matz) an even richer archive than its sister institute. Verdi's works and all that bears on them began at last to receive close, serious attention such as Josquin's, Mozart's, Beethoven's, Wagner's had long received. A new biography was needed. And in amassing the materials for it Phillips-Matz ranged far beyond the readily available resources.

When not in New York, she lived in Venice and, after 1975, in Busseto, Verdi's town, where she became the friend and trusted confidante of people for whom Verdi was only a generation away. She explored Verdi's lodgings and houses, walked his fields and farms, got to know families descended from his relations, colleagues, neighbours, tenants. Memories passed on through generations can be revealing, they can be distorted, and often they can be checked. In towns and villages, for thirty years and more, Mary Jane has been discovering and scanning documents of all kinds: parish registers, civil lists, municipal rolls, orphanage ledgers, minutes and archives of the many local organizations, public libraries, private libraries. As a result, she has been able to give us a fuller account than ever before of the composer in context: as 'son, suitor, father, husband, family patriarch, musician, man of theatre, farmer, patriot, parliamentarian, and philanthropist'.

In a time when 'the latest operatic work is *Aida*' and 'amateurs and enthusiasts are anxiously waiting for *Othello*'—Mazzucato declared, 'Of Verdi as a man . . . little or nothing can be said'. He did, however, provide some details of the composer's daily life in the villa that 'stands far from the high road, concealed almost entirely by large trees. Adjoining it is a large and beautiful garden, and this again is surrounded by the farm. Verdi himself looks after the farming operations, and an Englishman will find there all the best agricultural implements and machines of modern invention.' Rising at 5, after a cup of hot black coffee Verdi visits the garden and the stables; coffee with milk at 8, *déjeuner* with his wife at 10.30, a walk in the garden; then dealing with the post, which arrived at 2; dinner at 5 in summer, 6 in winter; and after cards or billiards, to bed at 10.

Even after many, many letters had been published—even after Walker's book—the man Verdi remained mysterious. New puzzles,

FOREWORD

paradoxes, contradictions appeared: among them, his frequent expression of a resolve never to compose another opera, coupled with his evident eagerness to do so once a suitable subject could be found; his disgust with everything that the Paris Opéra stood for, coupled with his determination to win a Paris triumph (*Don Carlos*, from which he hoped much, flopped; the Opéra *Aida*, then the Paris *Otello* and *Falstaff*, at last provided his triumph); the Shylock-strict exaction of any monies due to him, coupled with his bounteous charity to individuals and institutions; his persistent, profound unhappiness; the strange mixture of warmth and generosity with unforgiving harshness (towards his father at times, towards some former close friends); his repeated insistence, while honours were heaped upon him and his operas were played the world over, that no one understood or even appreciated his music. . . .

Mary Jane Phillips-Matz has not glibly explained Verdi away; she has sought to understand him. By revealing so many new details of his life; by taking us to the places where he lived and worked, and introducing us year by year to the people among whom he lived and worked, who influenced and were influenced by him; by setting her new information in the context of what was known (and correcting what was wrongly believed), she has brought us closer than ever before to the complicated, important man whose operas have been the delight and admiration of the world for a hundred and fifty years.

ANDREW PORTER

London, December 1992

Preface

I love the land because it gives us grass and grain, food for people
and for animals, if indeed there is some difference between them.

Verdi to Ercolano Balestra, *c.* 1880

I adored and I adore this art; and when I am alone and am wrestling
with my notes, then my heart pounds, tears stream from my eyes, and
the emotions and pleasures are beyond description.

Verdi to Francesco Maria Piave, 3 November 1860

Verdi's view of biography

Verdi has been the subject of countless biographical studies, although he
himself was reserved and fiercely aggressive in defence of his privacy,
asking to be left alone, 'in oblivion'. One invaluable manuscript, in which
he certainly did have a hand, was written in the 1840s and 1850s by
Giuseppe Demaldè, Verdi's staunch paladin in many battles of the early
years. This is the 'Cenni biografici', the notes for which are almost as
important as the final version. This sketch has the ring of authenticity, for
its author knew Verdi as a boy and may even have been present at his
baptism. Demaldè, the first cousin and intimate friend of Antonio Barezzi,
Verdi's patron and father-in-law, was also the father of Caterina Demaldè,
who married Verdi's notary Angiolo Carrara. Their son Alberto Carrara
married Filomena Maria Verdi, the composer's second cousin and
universal heir. Beyond that, Demaldè fought harder than anyone to get
Verdi the scholarship that made possible his studies in Milan; as the
Treasurer of the Monte di Pietà he could and did use his power to further
Verdi's cause.

We do not know whether Verdi helped Ercole Cavalli, another Busseto
native, as he was writing *José Verdi*, published in Madrid in 1867 and
dedicated to Verdi's friend, the tenor Gaetano Fraschini; but he may
have, for the Cavallis, who sold Verdi their palazzo in the 1840s, were
also Verdi's partisans in his early struggles. Verdi sent Ercole Cavalli off
to Genoa with a personal letter of recommendation to Settimio Malvezzi,
launching him in his career in commerce and journalism.

xi

PREFACE

Verdi also helped Michele Lessona with the section on his life in *Volere è potere* (1869) and dictated to Giulio Ricordi a memoir of his early years for use in the Italian edition of Pougin's biography of him (1881). Both of these, though, like the statements Verdi made to Countess Clara Maffei in the 1860s for her biographical notes, are misleading, containing errors and misinformation that the documents refute. Verdi's mistrust of biographers was reflected in his fury at the Venetian publisher Luzzati, who hoped to release a study of his life in the 1850s. On another occasion he deplored the proposed publication of some of Bellini's letters, expressing his belief that the public examination of private papers was an offence against the subject of such scrutiny.

Recent biographies

Since the Second World War many substantial biographical studies have been published, each important in its own way. Carlo Gatti's magisterial biography, in its one-volume edition (1951), opened fields of inquiry for every scholar who followed him. Gatti's own *Revisioni e rivalutazioni* (1952) forced a re-examination of several important areas of Verdi studies. Massimo Mila's *Giuseppe Verdi* (1958) proved to be, as its author predicted, a 'work-in-progress that will never end'. It was followed by Mila's invaluable *La giovinezza di Verdi* (1974), with its examination of the composer's childhood, youth, and early operas. Franco Abbiati's four-volume *Giuseppe Verdi* (1959) was the result of decades of collaboration with several helpful families, Natale Gallini, the Museo Teatrale alla Scala, other major Italian opera-houses, and a large number of private collectors. For all its faults, it still remains the best source for Verdi's letters, especially those in private collections, many of which are closed to scholars. Thanks to the work of Dr Pierluigi Petrobelli, Dr Marcello Conati, and Marisa Di Gregorio Casati at the Istituto di Studi Verdiani, Parma, many of Abbiati's errors of dating and transcription have been corrected, so his *Giuseppe Verdi* and the notated cards at the Istituto are the most important source for Verdi's correspondence.

Frank Walker, a pioneer in post-war Verdi studies, asked many questions that are still unanswered, for he had the courage to look squarely at some of the problem areas of Verdi's life that other writers had avoided. His *The Man Verdi* (1962), based on thousands of documents he had gathered during his studies, is the most critical and significant modern work in the field. George Martin's *Verdi: His Music, Life and*

PREFACE

Times showed Verdi as a man of his century, of the Italian Risorgimento, as no other author had done. In Martin's pages, history and the biographer's subject are in perfect balance: we see Verdi large and small, composer, farmer, parliamentarian, patriot, head-of-family, brilliantly portrayed.

Two other books, although they are not strictly biographies, must be mentioned here. One is Marcello Conati's 1981 edition of Aldo Oberdorfer's *Verdi: autobiografia dalle lettere*, which had already become an essential Verdi handbook after it was reissued in 1951. The other is William Weaver's *Verdi: A Documentary Study* (1977), in which documents, commentary, and illustrations combine to give us an unmatched portrait of Verdi, the man and the composer.

Principles behind this biography

I wanted from the start to base my work only on original documents. Carlo Gatti, author of the books mentioned above and of *Verdi nelle immagini* (1941), was particularly important to my project because he gave me specific guidelines for research and convinced me that there was a great deal more to be said about Verdi's life and how those around him managed their relationships with 'the Bear of Busseto', as Verdi called himself.

I was soon struck with the many discrepancies between what Verdi said and wrote and the facts revealed in the documents. Like Lincoln, who spoke of his own childhood in terms of 'the short and simple annals of the poor', the composer emphasized his family's poverty; but, as I learned, the Verdis were not as badly off as Verdi would have had people believe. Carlo Verdi, the composer's father, has been described as a shiftless ne'er-do-well; but he owned land and a house and had under lease from the diocese many small parcels of land and the 'master's house', the Casa Padronale which had been the Verdi home in Roncole since the 1790s. He managed his property with some skill and seems not to have any major problems until the late 1820s, when he had been helping to underwrite his son's education for more than five years. In 1846 and in 1849 he sold his house and land in Roncole, turning the entire proceeds over to Verdi, who bought the farm Il Pulgaro in Roncole, Palazzo Cavalli in Busseto, and the farm at Sant'Agata. When Verdi and his father reached a final settlement of their obligations on 29 April 1851, after months of bitter dispute, Verdi owed Carlo Verdi 2,305 lire. That figure speaks for itself.

PREFACE

During my second visit to Italy, I again worked in Milan, Venice, Parma, and Busseto, where someone told me that Verdi always said he was not born in the house in Roncole that was declared his birthplace and a national monument in 1901. So even the question of where he was born remained open to investigation. As I examined the evidence I gathered from many public and private archives, I had to re-evaluate much of what had been accepted for decades as 'truth'. Few efforts in my life have brought me such pain, because I had to weigh intellectual honesty against loyalty to friends and possible damage to the composer's reputation, which was founded as much on legend as on truth. Sometimes the conclusions I reached seemed almost beyond belief, yet I think that the documents justify those conclusions.

Although Verdi's letters often seem to have come from the pen of an unforgiving person, a gentle, passionate, oddly dependent, defensive, and dangerously vulnerable man lay behind them. His countless acts of charity, and those of his second wife, are revealed in the many letters in collections that testify to their gifts to the ill, the poor, the hungry, and those often undefended members of a seemingly uncaring society: children.

The composer's feelings about women are important, beginning with the complex issue of his relationship with his mother. They are given all possible consideration here, although we have almost no letters from his hand that cast light on his feelings for his first or second wives or any other women he may have loved. But I have tried to show all aspects of his character, dealing with the son, suitor, father, husband, family patriarch, musician, man of theatre, farmer, patriot, parliamentarian, and philanthropist. Behind the image of the rich, honoured artist was an extremely difficult man who fought with himself, his friends and relatives, his colleagues, his community, and fate. Affliction and tragedy were often his lot, perhaps reinforcing in him that hearty scepticism that ranged toward pessimism. His anticlericalism and refusal to believe in God or any higher power brought him close to atheism. 'I won't say he is an "atheist", but certainly not much of a believer', Giuseppina Strepponi wrote of her husband. He laughed at her expressions of faith and said she and other believers were 'all mad'. He put his faith in land, gold, and his compositions. After the traumatic events of 1851, which shook his family to its very foundations, he led a highly organized life centred on his music, his nation, his estate, and his friends, protecting their privacy and his own.

PREFACE

In this biography, I have not tried to provide any musical examples or analysis, because Julian Budden's three-volume *The Operas of Verdi* answers almost every question that one might ask about them. Nor have I chosen more than a few illustrations for this book because Gatti's *Verdi nelle immagini* and Weaver's *Verdi: A Documentary Study* give us a comprehensive iconography.

M.J.P.-M.

New York City, 1992

Sources and Acknowledgements

The generosity of institutions and families and their hospitality to scholars over the last eighty years have made possible the serious study of Verdi's life and work, and without the core documents in the archive at Sant'Agata most of the books about him could not have been written. From the moment when plans were made for the publication of his letter-books, the *Copialettere*, in 1913, Verdi's heirs endorsed many scholarly projects and contributed their time and energy as active participants in the ongoing work. Gaetano Cesari, Alessandro Luzio, and Carlo Gatti, among many others, had the help of Filomena Maria Verdi, the wife of Alberto Carrara. Taken first into Verdi's father's house as a foster-daughter, then into his own, educated to become a schoolteacher, and chosen as his universal heir, she, with her daughter Peppina and son Angiolo, made Verdi comfortable during the last years of his life.

It was Angiolo, the father of the present heirs, who carried on the family tradition, opening the doors of Sant'Agata to Franco Abbiati, who worked for about fifteen years on his four-volume *Giuseppe Verdi*, helped Luzio with the essential *Carteggi verdiani*, and offered the resources of the collection to other scholars who were preparing to publish Verdi's correspondence with his colleagues and friends. The openness of the local families was a factor in convincing the Barezzi heirs to agree to the publication of the letters of Emanuele Muzio to Antonio Barezzi. Gatti was the editor of that book.

After the Second World War several English and American scholars came to the Verdi territory, among them Richard Repass, Frank Walker, Andrew Porter, William Weaver, and George Martin. In 1956 Gatti took me to Busseto, where I met his close friends. He also directed me to important civil and parish archives nearby, including those of the Monte di Pietà in Busseto. On Ascension Day 1956 Gatti introduced me to people from all walks of life in Piacenza, where we first stopped in the car he had rented for the day, so that he could show me and an American soprano living in Milan that part of Italy he knew and loved so well. We went on to Busseto, where I met several people who had been his collaborators over many years of his research and writing.

SOURCES AND ACKNOWLEDGEMENTS

Urged by Gatti to continue writing about Verdi and helped by The Metropolitan Opera Guild, Mrs August Belmont, Lauder Greenway, Mrs Carolyn Allen Perera, and Mario Del Monaco and his wife, I began a serious exploration of the major archives in several Italian cities and towns, relying all the while on conversations and correspondence with Gatti, Abbiati, several archivists and other scholars for clarification of material that I did not understand. Both Mrs Perera and I contributed to Frank Walker's research for *The Man Verdi* as well. My family and I were ever more frequently welcomed by colleagues as this work went on. It is no exaggeration to say that the support offered by Mrs Perera, Mrs Mary Ellis Peltz, the archivists of many Italian archives, the librarians of many public libraries and university collections, those working in many Italian and American opera companies, and a host of collectors and my writing colleagues made this book possible.

Access to parish church archives was made easier by the late Don Adolfo Rossi, the parish priest of the church of San Michele in Roncole. His nephews, the Reverend Monsignor Stefano Bolzoni, Provost, and the Reverend Don Tarcisio Bolzoni, Vicar and Co-Adjutant, both of the Collegiate Church of San Bartolomeo in Busseto, arranged for me to rent their former parish house, giving me a permanent base in the heart of Verdi country. After 1976 I was able to make regular use of dozens of archives to which I would not otherwise have had access. I also was able to spend about twelve hours a week in the Busseto library, my 'second home', where its former director, the late Professor Almerindo Napolitano, and its present director, Professor Corrado Mingardi, became my mentors and valued colleagues. The library is now the Biblioteca della Cassa di Risparmio di Parma e del Monte di Credito su Pegno di Busseto. Its major archive is that of the Monte di Pietà, which also holds the records of the Società Filarmonica of Busseto. Invaluable insight on the history of Busseto and the adjacent Province of Piacenza was provided by Lino Baratta and his wife and children.

I have also been fortunate in the resources of the Istituto di Studi Verdiani in Parma, where in the 1960s and 1970s I worked with the late Mario Medici, its original director, and Dr Pierluigi Petrobelli, its present director. I could never have finished this book without them and such good friends as Professors Marcello Conati, Gustavo Marchesi, and Gaspare Nello Vetro; Marisa Di Gregorio Casati, Lina Ferretti Re, and Daniela Mazzoli. Assistance in many archival matters was offered by Professor Marcello Pavarani, director of the Music Division of the

SOURCES AND ACKNOWLEDGEMENTS

Biblioteca Palatina of Parma. I have also used private collections and the major civil and church archives in Piacenza, Milan, Venice, Bologna, Cremona, Florence, Turin, and Trieste, as well as in the Diocesan Archives of Fidenza, helped by its archivist, Don Amos Aimi, and in the Seminario Vescovile of Fidenza, directed by the Reverend Monsignor Pier Giacomo Bolzoni. Don Enrico Gallarati and Don Oreste Bionda of Saliceto di Cadeo, Don Ugo Uriati of La Madonna dei Prati, and the Reverend Monsignor Giovanni Ferrari of Cortemaggiore kept me from losing my way in their records. The Reverend Monsignor Dante Caifa provided access to important holdings in the Cathedral of Cremona and other archives there. In the Seminario Vescovile of Cremona, I was helped by the Reverend Monsignor Maurizio Galli, its director, who helped to locate Barberina Strepponi's collection.

Study in the United States was made easier by the American Institute for Verdi Studies, begun by Claire Brook, Martin Chusid, Andrew Porter, and myself after the International Congress for Verdi Studies in Chicago in 1974. Centre College in Danville, Kentucky, where Dr Floyd Herzog was the Director of the Kentucky Regional Arts Center, helped by hosting an important Verdi Congress in 1977. Knowing that I had collected material for the Toscanini Memorial Archive in the 1960s, those in charge of several collections agreed to let me oversee the project of microfilming their archival materials for the American Institute for Verdi Studies. In my family the original impetus for this project was provided by my mother Hazel Spencer Phillips, a museum director who had supervised the microfilming of the court records of Warren County, Ohio, in the 1950s. She also lent financial support over many years. In 1977 and 1978 I was able to photocopy about 1,000 documents that were to be added to the collection of the American Institute for Verdi Studies. The filming project, funds for which were provided by grants from the Martha Baird Rockefeller Fund for Music and the Ford Foundation, was a natural next step, for the American Institute for Verdi Studies had begun to organize an important microfilm library. On a hot July Sunday in 1978 John Nadas, the archivist of the American Institute, and I set up the portable microfilm camera on the work-table in the historic Busseto Library. As I compiled my handlist of the collection and Nadas, and, later, Luke Jensen, filmed, I began to realize how little we knew about many critical aspects of Verdi's life. The microfilming went on for three summers; after it ended I continued to work on my catalogue and surname index of the

SOURCES AND ACKNOWLEDGEMENTS

significant documents and on my transcription of hundreds of parish register and civil record entries in northern Italy.

Essential to Verdi's professional life was the publishing house of G. Ricordi, which was instrumental in the 1950s, 1960s, 1970s, and 1980s in helping me find documents in its archives. I would like to mention Dr Guido Valcarenghi, who first welcomed me there; Dr Luciana Pestalozza, Dr Carlo Clausetti, and Dr Kathleen Hansell, all of whom helped as I completed my research on the Ricordis, their employees, and their relations with their celebrated, cantankerous composer. I owe Kathleen Hansell a special debt of gratitude for her careful research on the Uttinis in Stockholm.

I have had unfailing support from Anthony Mulgan, Bruce Phillips and David Blackwell of Oxford University Press and am particularly indebted to Mr Mulgan for his final editing of this book. Andrew Porter has seen me through some of the most difficult moments of my life and has remained a faithful mentor and supporter, as has William Weaver, a trusted friend and colleague. Andrew read the manuscript at least twice; Bill read many chapters of it. Guidelines for the book were given by Dr Hans Busch and Julian Budden, who made suggestions that led me to make important changes in it. The Metropolitan Opera Guild made possible my first trip to Italy and one of my most recent trips. Alton E. Peters, its president, and Patrick J. Smith, Editor-in-Chief of *Opera News*, the late Gerald Fitzgerald, John Freeman, Jane Poole, Gregory Downer, and Brian Kellow helped me to resolve some of the most critical issues of Verdi biography. Mr Lawrence D. Lovett, Honorary Director of the Metropolitan Opera Association; Mrs John Barry Ryan, Jr., and Mrs Dorle J. Soria have offered special assistance as well.

I am enormously grateful to Norman Mailer, who took an interest in this book and helped through a time of confusing transition; and Gian Carlo Menotti, a dearly loved friend, the godfather of one of my daughters. In Italy I was shown constant concern by Dr Giacomo Donati and the Amici di Verdi, Busseto; Dr Gianfranco and Katie Stefanini; Rina and Remo Costa; Romano Bergamaschi and his family, with particular thanks to Giovanni Bergamaschi; Ines Bigna Faroldi, Nello Faroldi, Anna Maria Faroldi; Ivo and Bruno Gavazzi and their families; Lino, Anna Maria, Enrica, and Riccarda Baratta; the late Wally Toscanini, Countess Castelbarco, who provided me and my family with our first house in Venice; and Olga Rudge, who welcomed me to 'the hidden nest' in Calle Querina for weeks at a time.

SOURCES AND ACKNOWLEDGEMENTS

The examination of many documents was made possible by J. Rigbie Turner of the Pierpont Morgan Library in New York; the staff of the Music Division and Music Special Collections of the Library for the Performing Arts at Lincoln Center (New York Public Library); Robert Tollett and the late Natale Gallini; Dr Giampiero Tintori, Museo Teatrale alla Scala; Dr Giuseppe Pugliese, Sergio Fontanin, the late Dr Sandro Della Libera, and Antonio Busetto at the Teatro La Fenice; and Dr Maria Teresa Muraro at the Fondazione Cini in Venice. Advice on editorial and business matters was freely given by the late Elizabeth Otis and Shirley Fisher of McIntosh and Otis, Inc. Julie Fallowfield of that firm helped to see this project to the end.

I owe my passion for history to my parents, especially my father William Mason Phillips, a historian who encouraged both his daughters to become serious professionals and watched, sometimes with surprise, as I started writing about Italian opera and my half-sister Evelyn Phillips Harper became America's only woman boxing-manager. From the Stivanello family, Agostino, Anthony, and Eugene, I learned about backstage life and absorbed most of my Italian, over a forty-year friendship.

My closest collaborators have always been my children; and I am fortunate in having had editorial assistance from Catherine, Margaret, Clare, and Carlino, who checked hundreds of notes against their sources. Their knowledge of Italian, Venetian, French, Spanish and English also proved invaluable as they read many of the original documents from photocopies and microfilm.

In addition, I am grateful to the following people for help in the research for this book: Don Carlo Abbiati, church of S. Agata, Cremona; Don Albino Aglio, church of S. Imerio, Cremona; Archivio della Curia Arcivescovile, Milan; Dr Franco Armani, Teatro alla Scala; Possidio Artoni; William Ashbrook; Evan Baker; Sandro Balestra and family; Dr Egidio Bandini, Assessore del Comune di Cortemaggiore; the late Dr Guglielmo Barblan, Conservatorio Giuseppe Verdi, Milan; Carlo Bavagnoli; the late Cina Orlandi Barezzi; Lalla Bellingeri, Comune di Busseto; Carlo Bergonzi and family; Anna Maria Berlingeri, Comune di Cadeo-Roveleto; Don Franco Berti, church of Santa Maria della Passione, Milan; Dalmazio and Ferdinando Besagni; Luciana Bevilacqua, Orphanage of Santa Maria della Pietà, Venice; Biblioteca Nazionale, Florence; Biblioteca dell'Archiginnasio, Bologna; Don Gian Carlo Biolzi, church of Santa Maria delle Grazie, Cortemaggiore; Don Sisto Bonelli; Luciano Bonini and family; Don Lorenzo Boselli, church of S. Lorenzo, Lusurasco;

SOURCES AND ACKNOWLEDGEMENTS

Don Mario Boselli, church of S. Pietro, San Pietro in Cerro; the late Don Ferruccio Botti; Don Paolo Botti, Vigolo Marchese; Jean Bowen, Chief, Music Division, The New York Public Library, and her staff at the Library for the Performing Arts at Lincoln Center, New York; Antonio Brasini, Director, Biblioteca Civica, Ancona; Patricia Brown; Don Angelo Busi, church of S. Giorgio, San Giorgio Piacentino; Don Albino Buzzetti, Frescarolo; Aristide Buzzetti and family; Professor Francesco Cafasi; Mario Caffarra and family; Gianfranco Cammi, Comune di Busseto; Dr Frank Campbell; Monsignor Ernesto Cappellini; church of S. Pietro, Cremona; Alba Caraffini; Fortunato Carbognani and family; Dr Maurizio Marchetti, Director, Cassa di Risparmio di Parma, succursale di Busseto, and his staff; Stephen Casale; Emilio Casali; Sauro Casoni; Dr Pietro Castignoli, Director, Archivio di Stato, Piacenza; Don Attilio Cavalli, church of Santa Maria della Passione, Milan; Valentino Cavalli; Don Cristoforo Cavedon, church of S. Carlo al Corso, Milan; Andrea Cawelti who helped to organize the Bibliography; Adriana Cerati, Assistant Archivist, Diocesan Archive, Cremona; Schuyler Chapin; James Chapman; Don Giovanni Cigala, church of S. Fiorenzo, Fiorenzuola; the late Fausto Cleva and family; Dr Franco Colombo; Donatella Fiorenzi, Princess Colonna; Licia Conati; Mario Concari and family, with special thanks for help in Besenzone and Busseto; Antonaldo Conforti; Franco Cordani and family; Dr Maria Luisa Corsi, Archivist, Archivio di Stato, Cremona; William Crawford; Don Pio Daprà, church of Santa Maria della Pietà, Cremona; Professor Marcello De Angelis; Raffaele De Banfield; Emanuele De Checchi; Roberto De Janna, Office of the City Engineer, Comune di Busseto; Viviana Pecci-Blunt, Countess Della Porta; Dr Marzio Dell'Acqua, Director, Archivio di Stato, Parma; the late Luigi Demaldè and Angioletta Demaldè, Roncole; Don Adriano Dodi, Villanova sull'Arda; Dismo Dondi and family; Dr Pier Paolo Dorsi, Director, Archivio di Stato, Trieste; Linda Beard Fairtile, American Institute for Verdi Studies; Pietro Fanchin and family; Dr Mario Fanti, Director, Diocesan Archive, Bologna; Donatella Fioni, Archivist, Ospedale Civile, Cremona; Dr Adelfo Fragni, Comune di Villanova sull'Arda; Bruno Freddi and family; Don Alceo Frepoli, Church of Santa Maria della Grazie, Chiavenna Landi; Paolino and Ida Frondoni; Don Luigi Galluzzi, church of S. Martino, San Martino in Olza; Carlo Garbi; Maria Adele Garioni, Comune di Busseto; Camilla Gavazzi, Archivio Storico del Comune, Milan; Vera Giannini; Professor Giuseppe Godi; Dr Philip Gossett; Mrs Rhea Guard and staff, Lebanon Citizens National Bank, Lebanon, Ohio; Don Rino Guerreschi,

SOURCES AND ACKNOWLEDGEMENTS

church of S. Michele Arcangelo, Roncole; David Hamilton; Dr James Hepokoski; Barbara Heymann for her careful reading and scholarly criticism of an early draft of this book; Alice Hudson, Chief, Map Division, New York Public Library; Nancy Kandoian, Map Division, New York Public Library; Thomas Kaufman; Dr David Kimbell, Dr Antonietta Lamour, Saliceto di Cadeo; Dr David Lawton; Ernesto Macchidani; the family of Alessandro and Rina Macchiavelli; Ada Maestri; Don Francesco Magnani, Cadeo; Count Carlo Emanuele Manfredi, Director, Biblioteca Passerini Landi, Piacenza; Dr Rosalia Manno-Tolù, Sovrintendente dei Beni Archivistici, Archivio di Stato, Florence; Charles A. Matz, jr.; Don Arturo Melloni, church of San Gaudenzio, Crusinallo; Dr Marina Messina, Director, Sovrintendenza Archivistica per la Lombardia; The Metropolitan Opera Guild and Thomas J. Hubbard, Chairman of the Board of Directors; Dr Philip Miller; Professor Marisa Napolitano, with special thanks for the use of the Muzio materials; Carolyn Johnson Nolan; Dr Grant O'Brien; Gabriella Peca, Director, Biblioteca Civica, Cortemaggiore; Countess Camilla Pecci-Blunt; the Pedretti family of Piantadoro; Giovanna Pegoiani, Archivist, Ospedale Civile, Cremona; the late Mary Ellis Peltz; Mario Peracchi, Monte di Pietà, Busseto; the late Argent Phillips of St Margaret's, Westminster; the late Don Cesare Picciotti, Busseto; Sergio Pinto and family, TWA, Milan; Sheila Porter, with my thanks for her friendship and concern; Don Giuseppe Radole, Trieste; Jesse Rosenberg, American Institute for Verdi Studies, New York; Maria Rich; Dr John Rosselli; Gabriella Ruggeri, archivist, Comune di Besenzone; Don Primo Ruggeri, church of San Vitale, Besenzone; Dr Anna Rosa Rugliano, Director, Biblioteca Civica, Trieste; Francesca Scarmiglia, Segretario Comunale, Besenzone; the late Anthony Schippers and family; Gianfranco Scognamiglio; Giovanni Secchi; William Seward, a mine of information about the late 1800s; Avv. Corrado Sforza-Fogliani, President, Banca di Piacenza; John Shepard, Curator, Toscanini Memorial Archives; the late Henry Simon; Susan Sommer, The New York Public Library; Dario Soresina; the late Mary Smith Spencer; Gianni Spigaroli, Comune di Busseto; Dr Orio Susani and family; Antonella Pedretti Tagliaferri, Sant'Agata; Dr Severino Tagliaferri, Banca di Piacenza; G. Tarchini, TWA, Milan; Cav. F. Tosi; Dr Romeo Trabucchi, Maria Teresa Orlandi Trabucchi, and their son Andrea Trabucchi; Paola Usberti; Don Italo Uttini; Nella, Bruno and Renzo Uttini; Dr George Van Harlingen and family; Ninetto and Noemi Vanoli; Dr Giuseppe Vecchi, Director, Accademia Filarmonica, Bologna; Claudio

SOURCES AND ACKNOWLEDGEMENTS

Vela, Archivio di Stato, Piacenza; Don Gandolfo Venturini, church of Santa Maria Maggiore, Trieste; Guglielmo Veroni and family, Roncole; Dr Gianfranco Viglioli, Vice-Segretario Comunale, Busseto, and Luisa Carra Viglioli; Alessandra Rosenberg Visconti; and Don Giuseppe Zolla, collegiate church of Sant'Ambrogio, Omegna. I owe a special debt to Don Giovanni Ghisoni, Arciprete of the parish church of Sant'Agata, Don Adriano Dodi of Santa Maria Assunta in Villanova sull'Arda, and Don Aimi, diocesan archivist, for use of parish registers and *Status animarum* during the summer of 1992. I am very grateful to J. Rigbie Turner, the Mary Flagler Cary Curator of Music Manuscripts and Books at The Pierpont Morgan Library, who made available the letters and documents in The Frederick R. Koch Foundation Collection and The Mary Flagler Cary Collection. These are particularly important in the study of Verdi's correspondence with Francesco Maria Piave. I am also grateful to Josephine Inzerillo; the Italian Cultural Institute and the Italian Government Tourist Office, New York City. Loredana Groppi and Silvana Contini provided invaluable help in compiling the index of this book. I owe particular thanks to Alan Schrager and to the late Fausto Cleva and his family.

Contents

CONTENTS

List of Illustrations

(between pp. 480–481)

ILLUSTRATIONS

ILLUSTRATIONS

Abbreviations

Abbiati	Franco Abbiati, *Giuseppe Verdi* (Milan, 1959)
BMP-B	Biblioteca del Monte di Pietà, Busseto
BN-F	Biblioteca Nazionale, Florence
Cavalli	Hercules Cavalli, *José Verdi, maestro de musica* (Madrid, 1867)
C	G. Cesari and A. Luzio (eds.), *I copialettere di Giuseppe Verdi* (Milan, 1913)
CV	A Luzio, *Carteggi verdiani*, i and ii (Rome, 1935); iii and iv (Rome, 1947)
Demaldè	Giuseppe Demaldè, 'Cenni biografici del Maestro Giuseppe Verdi' (MS in the BMP-B)
Di Ascoli	Arturo Di Ascoli [pseud.], *Quartetto milanese ottocentesco: lettere di G. Verdi, G. Strepponi, C. Maffei, C. Tenca e di altri personaggi del mondo politico e artistico dell'epoca* (Rome, 1974)
Garibaldi	Luigi Agostino Garibaldi, *Giuseppe Verdi nelle lettere di Emanuele Muzio ad Antonio Barezzi* (Milan, 1931)
Gatti (1931)	Carlo Gatti, *Verdi* (Milan, 1931)
Gatti (1951)	Carlo Gatti, *Verdi* (Milan, 1951)
Grove	*The New Grove* (London, 1980)
ISV	Istituto di Studi Verdiani
ISV-P	Photograph or photocopy in the Istituto di Studi Verdiani, Parma
LAN-BN-F	Lanari Archive, Biblioteca Nazionale, Florence
Napolitano	Almerindo Napolitano, 'Emanuele Muzio e Giuseppe Verdi', 2 vols., typescript, Private collection.
Pougin	Arthur Pougin, *Giuseppe Verdi: vita aneddotica con note e aggiunte di Folchetto* (Milan, 1881)
SAA	Villa Verdi Sant'Agata Archive
TLF-V	Teatro La Fenice, Venice
Walker (Eng. edn.)	Frank Walker, *The Man Verdi* (London, 1962)
Walker (It. edn.)	Frank Walker, *L'uomo Verdi* (Milan, 1964)

BOOK I

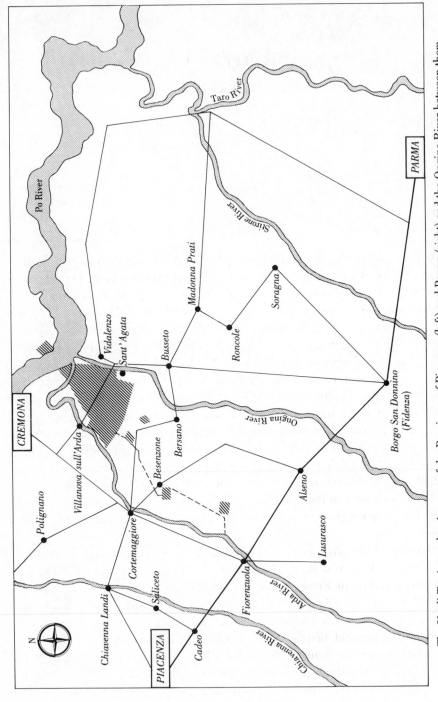

The Verdi Territory, showing part of the Provinces of Piacenza (left) and Parma (right) and the Ongina River between them. Hatched areas show approximate boundaries of Verdi's most important holdings of farm lands in the area.

1571–1813

The Province of Piacenza, a lozenge of plains and mountains lying south of the Po River in northern Italy, is a stable, productive land. Only flood, drought, war, or pestilence can break the quiet rhythm of its daily life. Then, in time of crisis, migrations carry some of its families away. During one turbulent period at the end of the eighteenth century and the beginning of the nineteenth, two Piacentine families emigrated from their rural villages into the nearest reaches of the Duchy of Parma, which lay across the Ongina River to the south.[1] These were the Uttinis of Saliceto di Cadeo and the Verdis of Sant'Agata. Country taverners, they had small groceries in their inns, where they were licensed to sell government monopoly commodities and everyday household needs.[2] Both families lived in the *contado* or rural district of Cortemaggiore, the Uttinis having come there in 1705 from an Alpine hamlet near Switzerland and the Verdis having settled in Sant'Agata, where they farmed, operated taverns, and sold groceries in the 1600s and 1700s. On market-day, these families met in Cortemaggiore, where the Respighis and the Toscaninis also lived.[3]

Between 1781 and 1805 the families of Carlo Uttini and Giuseppe Antonio Verdi moved into the territory of Parma.[4] The former began to operate a tavern in Busseto, which, like Cortemaggiore, had once been the capital of a small independent state. A seat of the noble Pallavicino family, Busseto lies 14 kilometres from Saliceto, where the Uttinis still had their store and tavern.[5] The Verdis' move was shorter, from their riverside hamlet at Sant'Agata to the village of Roncole, a parish that included an important pilgrimage church at La Madonna dei Prati, 3 kilometres south of Busseto.[6] Soon after moving the Uttinis became

3

friendly with the Carrara-Barezzi family, of the prosperous middle class then rising in Italy, and asked Donna Margherita Carrara, the godmother of Antonio Barezzi, to be the godmother of one of their own babies.[7] The Barezzis were Bonapartist and anticlerical. In Roncole and at La Madonna dei Prati the Verdis made a connection at the other end of the political scale as they supported and were helped by the parish and diocesan clergy.[8] They also knew the affluent Demaldès and Casalis, landholders with large holdings in the neighbourhood and solid connections at the ducal court in Parma.[9] In 1805 Carlo Verdi, the young taverner of Roncole, married Luigia Uttini, a spinner by trade, whose parents and brothers ran the Busseto tavern.[10] From their union the composer Giuseppe Verdi was born in October 1813.

The Uttinis of Crusinallo and the Val d'Ossola

Verdi's mother's family originated in mountain hamlets in the Alps, east of the *grand massif* of Monte Rosa and south of the Swiss border. They are probably Swiss in origin, having moved from the Canton of Valais into the Val d'Ossola about 1400. From the valleys of the Strona and Toce Rivers they emigrated in three waves to Bologna and Cortemaggiore between 1656 and 1705, working first as blacksmiths, bakers, and taverners. In the mid-1700s the branch that settled in Bologna in 1656 could boast two singers, Elisabetta and Brigida Uttini, and a composer, Francesco Antonio Uttini, who married Alessandro Scarlatti's niece. Another member of this family, a tenor, sang in an opera that Mozart attended at the Teatro Scientifico in Mantua in January 1770 and performed with him in concert at the Accademia Reale Filarmonica there. Mozart, writing about the tenor's love for ornamentation, called him 'Otini', but the records of the Accademia have his name right: 'Professor Uttini'. Verdi is descended from the branch of the family that emigrated in 1705 from Cranna Superiore, near Crusinallo and Omegna, to Cortemaggiore.[11]

The Uttinis enjoyed the stability that came from being in trade and from holding the *appalto* or licence to sell restricted commodities. They served the public. Respected, they provided educations for their sons and some of their daughters, who became teachers. Two of Verdi's great-uncles from his mother's family were parish priests; others were directors of schools.[12] In the composer's own generation, four of his Uttini cousins won recognition for their pioneering effort in the nursery-school movement, winning national awards for work in Piacenza, Parma, and several towns in the area. Verdi's grandfather Carlo Uttini succeeded his own father Lorenzo as the innkeeper, grocer, and postmaster in Saliceto di Cadeo, a village spread along several country roads just east of the highway that runs from Milan to Bologna. Among the chief monuments of Saliceto are the church of San Pietro, where Verdi's mother was baptized; the nursery-school and kindergarten founded by the Uttinis; the great estate called Lo Zamberto, where they served as farm managers; and the Uttini inn where on 28 September 1787 Luigia Uttini was born, the daughter of Carlo Uttini and his wife Angela Villa.[13]

Carlo Uttini's tavern stands at a once-important crossroad. Still known as the Palta Vecchia, or 'Old Store', it has now been restored as a private house. When Verdi's grandparents lived there, it was a centre of village life, serving at once time as post house, town hall, inn, and seat of government administration.[14] Now marked with a commemorative stone, the inn is a long, large, clean-lined structure with raftered ceilings, red terracotta floors, solid plank doors, big fireplaces, and some early, fine hardware from the seventeenth and eighteenth centuries. Like many young women of her time, Luigia Uttini became a spinner, or *fileuse*, as the French records of Napoleonic times describe her.[15] Paid for work done at home, she took raw material such as hemp, silk, wool, or flax and spun thread from it. Her occupation was common among women of her class in her time as the decades of the cruel cloth mills still lay ahead. Tradition has it that Luigia Uttini spun and wove in one of the upstairs rooms at the Palta Vecchia where in the 1960s some of the tools of the spinner's trade were still to be found. One of her brothers, Lorenzo Uttini, served in Napoleon's troops in the war against Austria.[16] It was he who, with his brother Antonio, moved to Busseto to operate a tavern, taking his parents and sister with him, between 1800 and the beginning of 1805.[17] Some of the Verdis from Sant'Agata were already there.[18] Sometime before 1821 Carlo Uttini, his wife Angela, and their oldest son Lorenzo returned to the Palta Vecchia. But by then Luigia Uttini was married and some of her brothers had moved away.

The Verdis of Sant'Agata

A hamlet of about thirty houses, Sant'Agata lies along the north bank of the Ongina River, just above its junction with the Po. Here the Verdi family lived for about 300 years before Giuseppe Verdi was born. The earliest direct Verdi ancestor is Vincenzo, born in the early 1600s.[19] By 1695, a Giovanni Verdi, also in the composer's direct line, held leases to farms owned by the Marquis Pallavicino; among them were La Possessioncella at Sant'Agata, a small property in Bersano, which adjoins Sant'Agata, and the Colombarola del Leone and San Bernardino near Busseto. Marcantonio Verdi, the composer's great-grandfather, was the last of Verdi's direct line to be born and die in the village;[20] but many in the family remained there. The land survey map (Mappa Catastale) commissioned by Napoleon I and finished in 1819 shows that one of the family owned a large section of Sant'Agata di Sopra that is called Possessione dei Verdi; and in 1848 a farmhouse by the river, three tenant houses, and the land around them, surrounded by Verdis, became the core of Giuseppe Verdi's estate.

Marcantonio Verdi's son Giuseppe Antonio Verdi emigrated to Roncole, where he operated a tavern and farmed land leased from the church of La Madonna dei Prati. The composer's grandfather, he was born at Sant'Agata in 1744, and married Francesca Bianchi, who was born in Villanova. Three years younger than he, she bore him twelve children, seven of whom were born before the move to Roncole. In the parish records of Sant'Agata, a priest has inserted a note into the volume: 'From Sant'Agata they emigrated, they went to Roncole to open an inn; but Sant'Agata was the cradle of the Verdi family, the oldest family of Sant'Agata [*illegible word*] to be small landowners.'[21] When Giuseppe Verdi and Francesca Bianchi moved to Roncole in the 1780s, he was about 40. In his new home, he followed family tradition and became an innkeeper-grocer, selling salt, flour, lard, cured meats, coffee, sugar, spices, wine, and perhaps liqueurs and brandy. They also had interests at La Madonna dei Prati, to which long columns of pilgrims came, some from nearly a hundred miles away, seeking the blessing of the Virgin. On a direct road from Busseto to Parma, La Madonna dei Prati, like Roncole, was busier and more accessible than secluded Sant'Agata, where the rest of the immediate family remained, close to the ancient Cittadella.[22]

After the move to Roncole, Giuseppe and Francesca had five more children. Among them were Carlo Verdi, the composer's father, and Marcantonio Verdi. It was Marcantonio's granddaughter who later became the composer's foster-daughter and universal heir.[23] Here the Verdis prospered, raising their family in the ancient house they leased on 11 February 1791 from the treasurer of the sanctuary church of La Madonna dei Prati. In the centre of Roncole, it was the Casa Padronale, a fine house with a fresco of the Virgin Mary, a coat-of-arms, and the date 1695 over the portico. It was known as the Osteria Vecchia, or Old Tavern, and had six rooms downstairs and three rooms upstairs that could be used for the storage of grain or (as now) for bedrooms. Behind were a stable, wine cellar, barnyard, well, pigsty, chicken yard, and outbuildings. On the half of the house that still stands, its function as a tavern is verified in the sign visible over the windows on the front façade: 'VENDITA DI VINO' ('Wine sold'). It is now the home of Guglielmo Veroni. With it, the Verdis leased 18 hectares of land in several parcels scattered through Roncole and at La Madonna dei Prati; a tenant house had originally also come with the property.[24] Their first lease ran for nine years; it was regularly renewed until 1830. Because it stipulated that they could not sublet without written permission, which they seem never to have requested, the Verdis were the only occupants of this Osteria Vecchia in Roncole. The composer's uncles, Giulio and Isidoro Sivelli, owned a small farm adjacent to this property.[25]

The family owed some of their well-being to the clergy of the parish, whom they always served. Giuseppe Verdi, the composer's grandfather, was a loyal member of the Confraternity of the Holy Conception, a men's organization affiliated with the parish church. It met in the rectory and helped raise funds for the parish. To this group the composer's father also belonged after he reached his majority.[26] The Verdis made substantial contributions to it for many years.[27] In 1796 the Bishop's Court in Borgo San Donnino granted the Verdis the right to hold a church pew in Roncole and put their name on it.[28] Equally important was their bond with the Franciscan friars in Busseto, a community of teaching religious who had a rich library and promoted scholarship and music education.[29] The Franciscans ran a small school and trafficked regularly with Roncole and other villages, where they bought provisions and wine. Their church and cloister, Santa Maria degli Angeli, is one of the finest monuments in Busseto, an example of Lombard Gothic style.

The Verdi family's economic stability was shaken on 1 March 1798, when Giuseppe Verdi had a heart attack as he was walking along the road outside Santa Maria degli Angeli. He died instantly. This 'unexpected death',[30]—he was an apparently healthy man of 54—left Francesca Bianchi Verdi a widow with the Osteria, grocery, and land to manage while she had four children still at home.[31] It says a lot for her courage that Verdi's grandmother continued to run the family business herself and went on managing the farmlands and buildings acquired under the lease, bidding them in at a public auction on 17 May 1800. The auctions were nerve-wracking events where winning bids were determined by the Provost, who decided whose voice was the last heard just before a burning candle-flame went out. Bidders watched the flame, judged other bidders' potential, then spoke.[32] Francesca Bianchi Verdi had help especially from her son Carlo, who was sufficiently mature to have become his mother's partner in 1804.[33]

At La Madonna dei Prati, the Verdis became friendly with Don Paolo Costa, their landlord, the curate of the sanctuary and music-master to the boys of the Roncole–Prati neighbourhood. The Verdis were special tenants for, in addition to the fields they leased and the house in Roncole, they held the two fields adjacent to the church at La Madonna dei Prati. On one of them a tavern called The Pilgrims' Restaurant was later built. Although we cannot be certain that the Verdis ever operated it, it seems more than likely that they did so, probably also using it for the dinners they served for the country clergy.[34]

Carlo virtually took over the tavern in Roncole before he was 19. Known as a strict, church-going, observant Catholic who heard Mass every day, he was fined once for leaving a pack of playing cards on the table in the Osteria, where authorities found several village men playing cards. In his defence, Carlo Verdi claimed that he had not encouraged gambling and that he had been at La Madonna dei Prati with his mother when the incident happened. A testimonial written for him stated that he was poor and struggling, still supporting his mother and his little brother Marco; but it did not save him from having to pay the fine.[35]

The Marriage of Carlo Verdi and Luigia Uttini

Because he bought provisions in Busseto, Carlo Verdi probably met his future wife there. On 30 January 1805, at the altar of the Blessed Virgin in the chapel of Santa Maria, he and Luigia Uttini were married.[36] The little church stands just outside the medieval walls of Busseto, near the old market-place, where farmers brought feed and livestock to be sold in one of the region's most important exchanges. On one side was a convent of Poor Clares, the Franciscan nuns; on the other was a tavern that was probably the Uttini inn. A few yards beyond the church is the Carrara villa called Il Paradiso, which in 1800 was also the name of the entire quarter.[37] After their marriage, the couple lived with Carlo Verdi's mother in the Osteria Vecchia in Roncole; but they often were chosen as god-parents for Uttini children and appeared as witnesses for Uttini weddings in Saliceto di Cadeo and Chiavenna Landi, where Luigia's father may have operated the historic roadside inn.[38] When Francesca Bianchi Verdi died on 21 September 1807 in the Osteria Vecchia in Roncole, her son and son-in-law were at her side.[39] Carlo Verdi had, in fact, already taken over the tavern, which he and his wife now ran. After nearly three years of marriage they were still childless; Marco Verdi, then in his early twenties, lived with them.

At this moment, as in many years to come, this family enjoyed a certain importance in their small world. To understand the composer Verdi and his passion for this land, we have to remember the single-mindedness of his people as they pursued respectability and nurtured their modest patrimony of fields, houses, taverns, and country stores, preserving them even through the ruin of the Napoleonic Wars. Like their parents and grandparents, Carlo Verdi and Luigia Uttini continued to uphold the traditions that had been taught them. Although family unity was some-times threatened, it survived across the generations. The composer's relationships with his family ran the gamut from love and respect to dislike and mistrust; but the clan's bonds proved stronger than any emotion of the moment. We must discard the common clichés about the poverty and ignorance that afflicted this clan. We have heard far too much about the 'poor and miserable village called Roncole', the 'poor *osteria* with its narrow, wretched rooms, badly ventilated and badly lighted',[40] and 'the squalid building where Verdi's father kept a tavern of sorts'.[41] These misstatements only serve to keep alive the legend of 'poor boy grown rich'. Some biographers' errors were honest enough, for Verdi himself spoke of the meanness of his family's circumstances and the lack-lustre monotony of his childhood. The now-familiar tradition of the Verdi's straitened circumstances was sanctified by publication in Michele Lessona's *Volere è potere*,[42] a handbook for the self-made man that was cherished by the new Italy. The image of the disadvantaged boy who walks barefoot from Roncole to Busseto to save shoeleather resembles the popular, sentimentalized image of Saint Pius X, the boy from Riese who goes to school with his shoes slung over his shoulder. The 'poor boy Verdi' idea flowered into full-scale historical biography, partly because Verdi, later a national hero and totem of the Italian spirit, fostered it himself. But a study of the land-map of Roncole and La Madonna dei

BOOK I

Prati reveals the very substantial holdings of the Verdis and their relatives there.[43] Carlo Verdi went on with his land deals through the decades, as his brothers-in-law and sisters did. Like all businessmen, he had his ups and downs; but in spite of occasional reverses, he conducted his affairs reasonably well and was sufficiently respected to have been named the secretary and treasurer of the vestry at Roncole, where he held the office from 7 September 1825 until 14 June 1840, when he resigned in favour of his friend and notary Ercolano Balestra.[44] In a period when more than ninety per cent of the population could not read or write, Carlo Verdi could. In a province where in 1833 there was only one school-attender for every forty-seven people, the Verdis had their son in school.[45] While it is true that Verdi's father sometimes made errors in his letters, invoices, and memoranda, they are perfectly clear, and his handwriting was not much worse than that of the clerk who drew up his lease for the Osteria Vecchia in 1827. He submitted his work-records and accounts, paid his rent, and kept his properties in repair. To farm the 54 *biolche* of land at Roncole, he would also have had to use paid farm-hands. Like other taverners, he trafficked with travellers, coachmen, carters, vendors, and clients and negotiated with them. He heard news from outside the village and was often the first to learn of events in far-away places. Going to market was a broadening, weekly experience. The Verdis never sank into the 'profound ignorance of the peasant class' that was marked by superstition and fear, nor were they scarred by the 'tragic and desperate isolation' of the rural poor.[46] Seeing them in proper perspective makes it possible for us to understand better some of the most significant developments of Verdi's life.

1813–1823

The eleventh of October 1813 was a joyful day for the Verdis of Roncole. Marcantonio Verdi, the younger brother, married Maria Angelica Giuditta Picelli, a young woman from Besenzone in the Commune of Cortemaggiore, in a traditional rite that included a Solemn High Mass, celebrated by several priests and sung.[1] Given the local custom of having instrumental music during the service, the organ may also have been supported by strings and winds. Carlo Verdi, the older brother, then 28, brought for baptism the first child born to Luigia Uttini in almost nine years of marriage. Giuseppe Verdi, their son, had been born one or two days before.[2] Presiding over the ceremonies was Don Carlo Arcari, the Provost, middle-aged and ill. Verdi's godparents were Barbara Bersani, whose husband Gaetano Mussi owned property in Roncole,[3] and Pietro Casali, a prosperous landowner whose title of 'Dominus' signified money and power.[4] The baby was named Giuseppe (after his father's father, who had been dead for fifteen years), Francesco (after Francesca Bianchi, his father's mother), and Fortunino, which was a traditional Verdi name around Sant'Agata and Vidalenzo. According to an account of this baptism by Giuseppe Demaldè of Busseto, Pietro Casali had hired a band of local musicians to play that day. They struck up a lively tune as they accompanied the guests back to the Verdis' tavern, where Marco and Carlo laid the feast for the double holiday. The mother of the new-born put her baby to the breast, for she neither wanted nor needed a wet-nurse.[5] Because they were taverners, it was no chore for the Verdis to serve large numbers of people, for they catered many banquets for laymen and clergy.[6] Some descendants of Marco Verdi still operated a restaurant and bar in Roncole until the mid-1960s, when they finally gave up the 'Bar Verdi' and opened a hotel in a spa above Fidenza.[7]

11

BOOK I

The composer Verdi was born during the fair week of the Feast of San Donnino, the patron saint of the diocese to which Roncole belongs, but we cannot be sure where or when. For about 140 years everyone has believed that he was born on 10 October in the 'Verdi Birthplace' that was declared a national monument in 1901, just after Verdi died. But to his family, Verdi denied that he was born there and always said that he was born on 9 October in 1814. He told Filomena Maria Verdi (his foster-daughter and heir) and her husband and son: 'That is not my birthplace. The house where I was born was burned by the Russians.'[8] None the less, he hung a large oil painting of the 'Verdi Birthplace' in the salon of his villa at Sant'Agata. Apparently he saw no contradiction between hanging the painting and denying that he had been born in the house it represented. It is now beyond dispute that the Verdis lived in the present Veroni house (the Osteria Vecchia) from 11 February 1791 until 11 November 1830; it was Carlo Verdi's Casa Padronale (as described in his lease), where he had to live.[9] About the precise date of Verdi's birth, there is still lingering confusion. The two available birth records are in absolute agreement. One, the church's document, is in the archive of San Michele Arcangelo in Roncole. The other, the civil record, is in the city archive in Busseto.[10] The former, entered by Don Carlo Arcari under the date 11 October 1813, records the fact that the priest baptized 'this morning' a male child born 'yesterday' at the 'eighth hour' of the day. The civil record, dated 12 October 1813 at nine in the morning, states that Verdi was born on 10 October at the eighth hour. Both depend on Carlo Verdi's declaration about his son's birth. Verdi, though, always refused to accept 10 October as his birthday. 'My mother always told me that I was born at nine in the evening on the ninth day of October in 1814. Which of the dates is correct, I do not know, nor do I care to know.' he wrote once to the subprefect of Borgo San Donnino.[11] Yet in 1876 he asked to see his birth certificate. He said he was surprised to learn that there was some confusion about the *year* of his birth, as he wrote to Countess Clara Maffei, the Milanese noblewoman who was his friend for nearly forty years:

Do you know? I was really born in 1813, and a few days ago I completed 63 years. My mother had always told me that I was born in '14 and I naturally believed her, and have deceived everybody who has asked me about my age; but a few months ago, I had them get out my birth certificate, from which—although it is written in Latin—I was able to understand that on the ninth of October in this very year, I completed 63 years.[12]

Because he refers to a Latin document, we know which certificate he saw: the record from Roncole. He seemed to feign ignorance about a set of facts that he must have known, having been required to present his birth or baptism certificate many times in his life, to get passports, and to marry twice. Giuseppe Demaldè, who knew Verdi better than almost anyone, got the composer's age right.[13] So did Hercules Cavalli, the early biographer.[14] The commemorative stone that was set into the façade of the official birthplace in 1872 also has the correct date: 10 October 1813. But Verdi held to his own ways. He and history remained at odds on this point.

Among the accounts associated with Verdi is that of the wandering musicians who, according to biographers, assembled under Luigia Uttini Verdi's window when her son was born.[15] Knowing now of the Solemn High Mass that was celebrated for Marco Verdi's wedding that day, we understand why they were there. Demaldè noted on a scrap of paper that served him for his notes that 'the nobleman Pietro Casali, a man of good will, who was the godfather, wanted the new-born to be accompanied to the Holy Font with signs of joy and the playing of a brigade of musicians.'[16] Knowing that members of local amateur music societies very frequently played for such events, and knowing that several of these societies existed in the neighbourhood (including the important one in Busseto), we can understand that the 'brigade' was probably hired from one of them. This meant that they, too, also joined the banquet guests at the Verdi tavern, for it was customary that they be wined and dined after the ceremonies where they played. It was common then for musicians of these philharmonic societies to travel in big, horse-drawn omnibus coaches that brought them from their town to the country church where they had been hired. As they rode through the fields to and from such engagements, they played and sang, making a merry company indeed.

Another familiar story, dating from the first year of Verdi's life, concerns the invasion of 1814, when the Duchy of Parma was overrun by troops of the Holy Alliance, ranged against Napoleon. The traditional tale is this: when foreign soldiers reached Roncole, sowing destruction and bloodshed in the land, Luigia Verdi and other women of the village took refuge in the parish church. Blood ran in the aisles. Peasants were slain at the doors of their houses.[17] A stone commemorating the incident was set into the south wall of the church in 1914. Verdi told a German writer about the adventure in 1883:

'Up there', Verdi said, pointing to the old bell tower, 'my mother, carrying me in her arms, saved herself in 1814 from the Russians, whose outrages brought grief and terror to the people of Roncole for twenty-four hours; and during this whole time, she hid herself up in the middle of the tower, which was reached by one single ladder, terrified that I with my cries could betray our hiding place. Luckily, though, I slept almost all the time and when I awakened I smiled contentedly.'[18]

There is no reason to doubt that Roncole was invaded, although no one was killed there by foreign soldiers.[19] It may even be possible to set an approximate date for the incident, for on 11 February 1814 the French prefect abandoned Parma to the Austrians; three days later French troops retook the city; scarcely more than two weeks later it was lost again.[20] The official historian of Busseto, Emilio Seletti, stated that the territory was 'overrun with Napoleon's enemies: Austrians, English, and Neapolitans'; but he does not mention Russians.[21] A major engagement of the Parma campaign was fought at Ponte Taro, about 15 kilometres south of Roncole. If any date can be set for Luigia Uttini's dramatic escape from the invading soldiery, it must be at this time. On the morning of 2 March 1814 French and Italian troops under General Grénier moved south through Roncole with three columns of men to engage the rear guard of the Austrian forces.[22] Verdi was not quite 5 months old. Foreign troops of any stripe were a real danger to the Po Valley farmers: they all raided barns, plundered stores, and commandeered wagons, food, and animals. It would have been perfectly natural for Don Arcari to take the women of the parish into the church. At San Michele, a second-floor platform in the belfry makes a small room there that is accessible only from the rectory. Verdi's mother may have hidden in it as she sought safety, carrying her infant son with her.

The years between 1814 and 1820 were particularly hard in rural areas of the duchy, where the death rate from typhoid fever during the epidemic of 1816–18 was matched by loss in the animal population as raiding soldiers carried off or slaughtered more than half of the farm horses, seventeen per cent of the cattle, and forty per cent of the hogs. A general recovery was not registered until 1831.

The Child Verdi

Called 'Peppino' by his friends and members of his family, Verdi seems to have had plenty of attention in his childhood, although he was not the only baby in the family, as his uncle Marco and aunt Giuditta were raising their children in Roncole too. A close friend of the Verdis was the farmer/schoolmaster/organist Pietro Baistrocchi, Aide to the Provost of the parish church, a native of Sant'Agata. Baistrocchi adored Peppino Verdi, dandling him constantly on his knees and paying special attention to him 'from the time he was in swaddling clothes'.[23] With his thick, chestnut-brown hair, coarse, wavy, and somewhat unruly, and his intense blue-green eyes, Verdi was a handsome boy, although he was thin, introverted, and painfully shy. When he learned to speak, he used the dialect of the region. This sweet language has lilting rhythms and marked cadences, coloured by French sounds, although even within the former Duchies of Piacenza and Parma there are variations from town to town. Growing up as his parents had, in the village Osteria, Verdi met everyone in the community, as men came for a glass of wine at the tavern tables, where they also transacted their business, and the women gathered to shop. In country taverns people often sang, for group singing of folk-songs was a common evening and holiday pastime. Travellers and vagabonds were the 'newspapers' of the place. As the central exchange for information, commerce, music, jokes, and food, the Osteria was busy from dawn until late at night. Carlo and Marco Verdi served customers, kept accounts, and replenished their supplies from nearby markets. Their wives cooked, cleaned, spun, wove, and sewed, helping in the inn as well. From Demaldè, we learn that Verdi 'did the little chores of the tavern', even when he was small.[24]

A contemporary description of life in a country village near Parma tells of a perhaps somewhat romanticized household where 'the mother is a true housewife, filled with concern for her family', keeping a house where everything was 'peaceful, tranquil, and happy'; 'the sober food, the cleanliness, the simplicity of their ways, their habits, their very life, contributes to the good health and the robustness of these fine people'.[25] As for the programme of the day,

the mother after the main meal at noon, sits down to weave at the loom, making the cloth that will protect her loved ones from the bitter cold of the winter. She makes fabrics . . . that cost very little. But although she is busy with her work, she never loses sight of her children, who play around her feet all the time. She sings to them while they play.[26]

This glimpse into the life of a family of the Po Valley might have been written about any household like the Verdis'. We even know what Luigia

BOOK I

Uttini wove at her loom, for Verdi kept a fine wool coverlet made by her among his linens at Villa Sant'Agata. Luigia and her son were often alone together in Roncole; she told Hercules Cavalli that she had virtually raised Verdi herself because his father was away all the time, managing the family's business and lands.

Just as the folk music of the region was Verdi's first introduction to secular music, so the first church music he heard was played at Roncole and La Madonna dei Prati. Roncole hired its first full-time organist, Carlo Anelli, in 1810. As Don Arcari noted in his Day-Book, 'It is cheaper than looking for an organist from outside of town every time there is a ceremony, and sometimes finding one and sometimes not, then paying a lot of money and getting no service in return.'[27] Baistrocchi went on playing occasionally.

When Verdi was not quite 3, his parents had another child, Giuseppa Francesca, their first and only daughter.[28] Like Verdi himself, and like Marco Verdi's first daughter, she was named after her Verdi and Bianchi grandparents. Demaldè said that there was a strong bond between Giuseppe Verdi and his sister: 'Verdi loved her as much as he loved himself.' Demaldè added that the two children were adored beyond all measure by their parents. Carlo Gatti, in his Verdi biography, suggested that Giuseppa was retarded or deficient in some way; but the only evidence for this is Gatti's footnote, which cites a family tradition handed down from Verdi's heir and cousin Filomena Maria Verdi. Apart from this note, there seems to be no evidence that Giuseppa Verdi was anything other than normal. Demaldè wrote that she was a 'handsome girl, with excellent manners and beautiful hopes for the future'. This does not sound as if she were ill or retarded; there was no reason for Demaldè to evade an uncomfortable truth, for he could have omitted all reference to her had he wished to do so. There is no information about any abnormal condition in the confidential 'Personal Statistics File' in the Monte di Pietà in Busseto, where Demaldè described the family of 'Verdi Carlo, taverner in Roncole di Busseto'.[29] There are observations on the 'probity, morality, talents, knowledge, zeal, and activity' of the taverner, his wife, and their children. Giuseppa appears to have been normal and active, working as a seamstress and dressmaker, perhaps helping her cousin Gaetano Bianchi, the tailor. Her civil death record of August 1833 describes her as if she were in employment.[30] She and Verdi lived at home together until he was 10; after 1823, though, he lived in Busseto and came home only on Sundays and holidays and during summer vacations. Still Giuseppa may have been her brother's only close companion.

Men from Roncole, some of whom knew Verdi as a child, recalled him as

quiet, all closed within himself, sober of face and gesture, a boy who kept apart from happy, loud gangs of companions, preferring rather to stay near his mother or alone in the house. There lingered about him an air of authority; and even when he was a boy, the other children pointed him out as someone different from the rest of them; and they admired him in a certain way.[31]

The cautious use of the words 'in a certain way' suggests strongly that Verdi, even as a child, was respected rather than loved, and that he was, for better or worse, somewhat beyond the reach of his contemporaries, even in his native village.

The Education of the Prodigy

Peppino Verdi appears to have been precociously intelligent. Before he was 4, the boy was sent to study with Baistrocchi, who taught him both Latin and Italian in private lessons.[32] These must have begun some time between the autumn of 1816 and the autumn of 1817, according to Demaldè. Putting the child to study shows that the Verdis considered their son's education important, for that particular year was difficult. A typhoid epidemic had run through the region; in Roncole alone, twenty-three people had died in just a few weeks. Among them were parishioners, vagrant paupers, and even the young priest sent to help Don Arcari minister to victims of the disease.[33] Carlo Verdi persisted even then in trying to launch his son's education; his ambitiousness was remarked upon by Demaldè.[34]

When Verdi turned 6, he attended the regular village school, which Baistrocchi directed. This schoolmaster, described by Don Arcari as 'magister parvulorum Roncularum ac etiam organicus', the first person to train the boy Verdi in letters, may also have been the first to introduce Verdi to the organ. The most frustrating of all Demaldè's notes refers to this period. It reads: 'When the boy was just past the age of 5, he wanted at any cost to put . . .': here the note breaks off. There is nothing in any of Demaldè's manuscripts to give us the slightest clue to what this child wanted 'to put' 'at any cost'. Yet the remark has its own value, because Demaldè could obviously discern in Verdi a determination even at this early age.[35] Verdi later spoke of being in ecstasy when he heard Bagasset, a wandering musician, play in Roncole; and his mother told Hercules Cavalli that when Verdi heard the sound of a hand-organ, he pestered her until she let him go outside to stand near it. He was so captivated by music that his parents decided to give him an instrument of his own, a little spinet that belonged either to Baistrocchi or to Don Paolo Costa, the curate at La Madonna dei Prati. Don Costa, who died in December 1820, was succeeded by Don Domenico Morelli, who may have taught Verdi some of the rudiments of music. Verdi's gift for music was apparent then, even by 1820 or 1821: Demaldè noted that the sound of any instrument hypnotized him. The long wooden case and keyboard, humble as it is, was a remarkable acquisition, for few children in Italy even today have their own piano at home, and conservatory students still practise at the rectory or at school. Verdi's love for his spinet was proved beyond all doubt, for he kept it for eighty years. At Sant'Agata it stood near the door that leads from the composer's bedroom-study into the main part of the house. When he died, he left 'my spinet that is at Sant'Agata' to the Casa di Riposo, the home for aged and infirm musicians that he built in Milan.[36] It is now in the museum of the Teatro alla Scala. Some time after the spinet was brought to Roncole, Carlo Verdi asked Stefano Cavaletti, of a well-known family that manufactured and repaired organs, to repair it. The craftsman left a record of his visit on a scrap of paper attached to the instrument. It reads:

By me, Stefano Cavaletti, these hammers were repaired and lined with leather, and I fitted the pedals, which I gave as a gift, just as I also gave my labour for fixing the hammers, seeing the good disposition that the youth Giuseppe Verdi has toward learning to play this instrument, which is enough to satisfy me completely. Year of Our Lord 1821.

In 1888 Verdi showed the spinet to the same German writer he took to Roncole, saying: 'Yes, I did my first lessons on the old spinet, and for my parents it was a large sacrifice to get me this wreck, which was already old at that time; having it made me happier than a king.' He showed his guest the rough card and inscription that Cavaletti had written.[37] Because the Cavalettis were important organ-makers in the region, the spinet may have been repaired while they were restoring the organ in the church of the Carmine (Oratorio di San Rocco) at nearby Soragna, where they also left a record of their effort.[38]

Whatever time Verdi did not spend at home, practising on his spinet or working around the Osteria, he spent at church, where he served as altar boy, sang in the choir, studied in Baistrocchi's classes, and learned his catechism. He also took organ lessons and may have helped to coach the choir, in which his cousin Gaetano Bianchi sang. Here he learned something about art; here he took first communion. At San Michele Arcangelo were laid the foundations of that bitter anticlericalism that later coloured Verdi's views and stayed with him throughout his life. Even when he was in his seventies and eighties, he continued to express his mistrust of the clergy. 'Stay away from priests', he warned Filomena Maria Verdi's son, Angiolo Carrara, 'Sta lontan dai pret'.[39] Against this backdrop we must read the familiar account of Verdi's childhood that concerns his being kicked or pushed down the altar steps of San Michele by an angry priest. One day in his seventh year, Verdi was serving Mass, waiting upon the celebrant, Don Giacomo Masini. Momentarily distracted by the sound of music from the organ loft, the boy failed to hear the priest ask him for the ampules of water and wine. Don Masini, exasperated at Verdi's lack of attention, pushed the boy, throwing him off balance and toppling him from the altar. Publicly embarrassed, Verdi, in his humiliation, cursed the priest: 'Dio t' manda 'na sajetta!' ('May God strike you with lightning!') This sounds like the curses of carters and peasants of that expanse of open land, where lightning is a feared natural phenomenon that turns the fairest day into a hell of noise, fire, wind, and torrential rain. (Verdi said that the story of the boy cursing a priest on the altar during Mass caused a scandal.) It gave Verdi some satisfaction as well, for it seems to have been one of the few stories from his childhood that he recalled and often retold. At Sant'Agata, the Verdi family grew accustomed to hearing it.[40]

The boy's curse was fulfilled. This fact undoubtedly lent importance to the event, which might otherwise perhaps have been forgotten. Eight years after Verdi cursed Don Masini at Roncole, the priest was struck by lightning and killed at the church of La Madonna dei Prati, at three-thirty in the afternoon of a religious holiday, the Sunday within the Octave of the Feast of the Nativity of the Virgin. Verdi was to have sung in the choir or done some chore for his parents, who had been engaged to serve a banquet for the clergy after the ceremony, which celebrated the Holy Name of Mary. Having stopped with friends, perhaps the Michiaras, as he made his way across the fields, he was delayed and thus saved from possible injury or even death.[41] When the storm struck La Madonna dei Prati, lightning killed one dog, a puppy, a mare, four priests, and two lay members of the choir, one of whom was Verdi's cousin Gaetano Bianchi.

When Verdi reached the church, this—according to his own account—is what he saw: 'that miserable priest, sitting where he had been when the lightning struck, as he was taking snuff: his thumb was still pressed against his nostril, as if it were glued there. His blackened face was terrifying, but the other victims were not so frightening.'[42] Their deaths were marked by widespread mourning in the duchy as a commemorative broadside with the headline 'TRAGIC EVENTS' let the populace know the details. At the foot of the poster was a prayer to the Holy Virgin, imploring her protection from 'Storms, Hail, Lightning, and Earthquakes'.[43] Given the circumstances, the planned banquet did not take place, but Carlo Verdi got paid for it all the same. Many decades later Verdi said 'I can still remember it, and it still seems like a dream.'[44]

Changes of Direction

In the early 1820s Verdi's life changed as the priests who had guided him through childhood died or were retired. As we have seen, Don Costa died at La Madonna dei Prati in 1820; Baistrocchi, ill, left Roncole and died in 1823; and Don Arcari died in 1824.[45] In a sense, Verdi's childhood ended at this time, for he was never again to lead the old, sheltered existence he had known. Another change in the Verdis' life came in 1821, when Carlo Uttini died at the Palta Vecchia in Saliceto. Bedridden and ill, he called the notary on 20 November and in the upstairs east-facing bedroom, before three witnesses, dictated his will. First, he acknowledged that he owed his son Lorenzo the sum of 4,000 old Parma Lire, money that had been lent out of Lorenzo's military pension on different occasions, so that the family's 'shop and Osteria' could be kept open; he ordered that his son remove from the inn enough furniture to cover that debt. The heirs were Lorenzo himself, who—with his wife Luigia Rizzi—was living with his parents in the Osteria; Maria Uttini Da Parma, living in San Giorgio Piacentino; Gaetano Uttini, living in Piacenza; Antonio Uttini, living in Parma; Luigia Uttini, 'married to Carlo Verdi of Roncole in the Duchy of Parma'; and Giuseppe Uttini, married to a Sichel and living in Polignano, near Cortemaggiore. 'All are brothers and sisters, my beloved children, by my wife Angela Villa.' He also left an equal portion to his granddaughter Andreana Mosconi, 'wife of Luigi Ghisoni of Chiavenna Landi'; she was the daughter of his late daughter

Paola Uttini. Lorenzo was to have an additional portion and to care for
Carlo Uttini's wife 'as a reasonable and obedient son must do' and always
show her 'the highest respect'.[46] Lorenzo carried out his father's wishes,
taking over the Osteria and store, managing the family affairs, and caring
for his mother.

The inheritance from her father's estate may have helped Luigia Uttini
and her husband as they prepared to send their son away to Busseto
to school. Verdi had become the part-time organist at San Michele
Arcangelo some time around 1823 after old Baistrocchi left. At this time
the vestry hired as principal organist Donnino Mingardi, a blind youth
from Busseto who was something of a local celebrity;[47] but in 1825 the
vestry dismissed him and gave young Verdi the full-time job. Verdi
recalled this moment years later, when he said: 'My greatest ambition
was to become the successor of my teacher [Pietro Baistrocchi] some
day; and in three years I had truly reached the point where I could take
his place, which filled my parents and me with much pride.'[48] Because
Verdi's lessons in Latin, Italian, and arithmetic had stopped when
Baistrocchi left, his parents, unwilling to have his education end, sent
him to Busseto, perhaps two or three times a week, to continue Latin with
yet another priest, Don Giuseppe Bassi, known as a scholar.[49] This was
the first step toward the big move that Verdi made in the autumn of 1823,
'when my father took me to Busseto, so that I could get a better education.
Every Sunday I walked the road back to Roncole to carry out my office as
organist, which had been entrusted to me for a fee of 40 lire [a year] after
the death of old Baistrocchi.'[50] For Carlo and Luigia Verdi, the venture
represented a considerable sacrifice, for their son would no longer be
available to help with the tavern chores, the grocery, and the household.
To the inconvenience of not having him at home was added the financial
burden of keeping him in Busseto. Schoolbooks had to be bought; room
and board provided. The boy lived with one of the Michiara family from
La Madonna dei Prati who was living in Busseto. This interesting clan,
which had the great farm called La Separata at La Madonna dei Prati,
were Austrians who had changed their name from Mickler. Fond of music,
they, like the Biazzis in Roncole, bought scores and had a piano. One
of the Mickler/Michiaras who was Verdi's age was celebrated for his
beautiful voice. Instead of going into the theatre, he became a priest after
studying at the Seminary in Borgo San Donnino and won fame as a soloist
at religious functions all over the diocese. He was perhaps the first trained
singer Verdi knew.[51] It is entirely possible that he and Verdi lived in the

same house, across from the old barracks in Busseto. Pietro Michiara, sen., served in Busseto on the city council. He was Verdi's host.

Verdi was 10 when he left his village; but because he returned one or more times every week, the move did not represent a complete break with Roncole. This part of his life, at least, did not change. We have his own account of his nearly drowning when he fell into an irrigation canal during one of these treks: 'In the winter these journeys were often very unpleasant, and once in the darkness, I fell in a deep ditch, in which I probably would have drowned, if a peasant woman who was passing that way and heard my cries for help had not pulled me to safety.'[52] During the summers he came home to help, as all country boys did; but each autumn the Verdis sent their son away again. All things considered, he was fortunate. Years later, though, he told writers that his youth was hard. To Onorato Roux, he said: 'About my childhood, I would not know what to say, even if I wanted to say something, because I spent it in poverty and obscurity.'[53] To a French biographer, Camille Bellaigue, he said: 'My youth was very hard.'[54] Yet he was particularly lucky to have been born in a place where the gift of music was highly prized, and to have had parents who were determined to educate him. They could just as easily have put him into one of their rented fields as a labourer or kept him in the Osteria, where Marco Verdi's children were raised. So we must give credit to his parents, who wanted their son to be educated at a time when only a very small number of children were able to go to school at all and most country people were illiterate. This, then, is the story of a village prodigy whose family and teachers recognized his gifts when he was scarcely more than a child. Those around him did all they could to help him within the frame of his native village. At home, he was able to practise on his own instrument, the spinet. And when every resource in Roncole was exhausted, Carlo and Luigia Verdi did not hesitate to send their gifted son away, first to La Madonna dei Prati for music, then to Busseto for a humanistic education in the best nineteenth-century tradition. At 10 he was a shy, reticent, and perhaps overly mature child, a wage-earner with a stipend. Organist, student, tavern boy, he lived under pressure that might not have been brought to bear on a less precocious, less intelligent child. But together with the pressure, he came to know the satisfaction of making music that many considered remarkable.

3

Autumn 1823–Summer 1832

Ten is normally an age of considerable stability in children. Verdi had just reached this best of birthdays when his father took him to Busseto to study. The boy's spinet, too, made the move to the Michiara house, which can now be identified as 17–19 Via Piroli. His landlord, Pietro Michiara, sen. was the only member of his family then living in Busseto.[1] Verdi was enrolled in the Ginnasio, an upper school for boys, where he studied the regular curriculum. Latin lessons continued under two Franciscan friars, Father Lorenzo Da Terzorio and Father Lorenzo Gagliardi, both from the monastery at Santa Maria degli Angeli. Terzorio, the master of the Franciscan elementary school, owned a fine spinet. A musician of modest skill, he was drawn to the boy Verdi, whom he invited to practise at the school.[2] This may have been the only musical guidance Verdi had between 1823 and 1825.[3] As if all these projects and lessons were not enough, the boy returned regularly to cover the services at Roncole. Demaldè says that Verdi was 'non amante del divertimento' (not fond of diversions) and that he practised at his own spinet 'all night' and 'studied night and day'.[4] Gradually he became known as the boy who slept little, worked constantly, and earned from his post as organist. His fee of 40 lire a year did help to cover some of his room and board, which cost 30 centesimi a day. Because the house where he was boarding, perhaps with the Michiara boy who had such a fine voice, was across the narrow street from the guardhouse where the local soldiery was quartered, Verdi's practising sometimes kept the men awake at night. Once Captain Giovanelli pounded on the Michiaras' door long after midnight. Sword in hand, he demanded that the boy stop making a noise.[5] This incident, the subject of local gossip, also drew people's attention to young Verdi, who was gradually becoming a familiar figure, at least in his neighbourhood.

Busseto and its Culture

Designated a city in the sixteenth century, Busseto was a little fortress of culture and commerce, walled and turretted, when Verdi was brought there to live. Its citizens boasted a 700-year tradition of art, music, literature, philosophy, architecture, and science. Between the Middle Ages, when it was the capital of the Stato Pallavicino, and Verdi's era, many distinguished Bussetans had made local and larger reputations as the Pallavicino nobles put money into the city and its institutions, building their Rocca or fortress, the hospital, bank, Franciscan church of Santa Maria degli Angeli, monastery, and the elegant Villa Pallavicino.[6] Busseto had public schools before 1533. It was known for two libraries, one at the Franciscan monastery, and one in the centre of town. The latter had become a public institution in 1768, after the suppression of the Jesuits. In Verdi's youth, it had 10,000 volumes and was open every Thursday.[7] He was one of its users. The erudite, versatile priest Don Pietro Seletti, his schoolmaster, was its librarian.[8] Prominent in a family of professors and historians, Seletti took a natural pride in the city's schools; and when they were suppressed and closed by order of the rulers of Parma in 1806, he continued to teach privately. Finally the Duchess Marie Louise agreed in 1820 to let the Ginnasio reopen, with classes in elementary and advanced grammar, reading, writing, rhetoric, and history. Seletti was named its director. Housed in the airy seventeenth-century buildings that had once belonged to the Jesuits, it had rooms in the former monastery and also had use of the church of Sant'Ignazio, which was built into the complex. It stands on the main street, just around the corner from the house where Verdi was then living.[9]

When Verdi first entered his classes in 1823, Seletti was 53, a shrewd, balding, sharp-tongued epigrammatist with boundless intellectual curiosity. Author of critical works on Greek and Hebrew language and literature, he was also a Latinist, an archaeologist of no mean skill, a historian, numismatist, and astronomer. As an amateur musician, he had played the viola in the church orchestra in the collegiate church of San Bartolomeo, where he had also directed the music. Several evenings a month Seletti played a role in the literary academy or club, founded for the study of Greek literature. Its members, the most educated men in the city, continued a tradition begun in Busseto in the eighteenth century, when the first such Accademia was founded.[10] On the nights when the literary club did not meet, many of its members turned out for the meetings of the local Società Filarmonica, or Philharmonic Society, a group of seventy-odd amateur musicians. This 'new' Società Filarmonica had been established on 12 August 1816 as a continuation of an older, similar organization. Responsible for its popularity were two men of anticlerical, free-thinking persuasion: Ferdinando Provesi, the organist of San Bartolomeo, teacher of music and the humanities, and his friend Antonio Barezzi, a wholesale grocer and distiller who at 29, was emerging as an important merchant in town. It was Barezzi's godmother Donna Margherita Carrara who had befriended the Uttinis in 1806; and while it is by no means certain that Barezzi knew the boy Verdi in 1823, it is likely that the gifted child organist from a nearby village would not have gone unnoticed by the town's ardent amateur musician.

Provesi, the outsider in this set, had a tainted reputation, having come to Busseto from the prisons of Parma. A librettist and composer, he had worked in the town of Sissa, near Parma, as organist of the parish church there and had become a protégé of the wealthy Cavalli family. He had been left behind when they moved to Busseto in the late 1790s.[11] In 1799 Provesi committed a crime, stealing from the parish treasury of the church where he played. When the theft was discovered, Provesi was carried away in chains. For two years he lay in prison in Parma, regularly sending appeals for clemency to the Duke, and awaiting trial. Finally, he was convicted and condemned to exile. Like many other criminals, he was sent to forced domicile at Compiano in the Appennines.[12] Soon he fled and escaped to Busseto, where he could seek the Cavallis' protection and, if necessary, slip across the Po into Lombardy. He found a promising situation, with the Cavallis in possession of a grand town house and substantial temporal power. Had he not been able to profit from their influence, he might have been taken back to prison. Instead, he was given an apartment for himself, his wife, and child, in the house of a Jewish family where Antonio Barezzi's widowed mother had raised her family. Provesi was also made director of the drama academy and the municipal music school, and organist of the church of San Bartolomeo. To make way for the Cavallis' candidate, a church-sponsored organist was ousted from his post and reduced to playing occasional concerts around the city. In spite of his record, Provesi was an asset to Busseto. He had grown up in

Parma, which was known as 'The Athens of Italy' and studied at the music school of Alessandro Rolla, conductor of the Ducal Orchestra, the teacher of Paganini and Paër. Provesi wrote operas, masses, songs, symphonies, and cantatas. He became the maestro di cappella in Busseto in 1813, and soon afterward he began to direct the rehearsals of the Philharmonic Society; he also presided over a poetry society, which he founded.[13] There was a distinct breach between some members of these organizations and the leading clergymen of the area, although some priests belonged to the societies. The fact that the Philharmonic Society played many opera scores and took part in theatrical productions widened a rift between it and the church. Matters were not helped by the fact that Provesi had something of a reputation as a Jacobin. Priests in general mistrusted the men of the Philharmonic and held them responsible for disorders that erupted in Busseto.

In the very year that Provesi took over church music at San Bartolomeo, a small-scale civil war had broken out between the supporters of two rival sopranos who were singing at the local theatre. Sonnets were composed and circulated. Posters appeared mysteriously, and without the required legal permit, on walls around the city, carrying scurrilous attacks on various heroes in the struggle. At night, fist fights took place outside cafés where members of the factions gathered.[14] After this, both the government and the clergy grew more suspicious than ever of those who loved secular and theatrical music. By their definition, this extended to anyone who had ever admired Napoleon or had had a Bonapartist in the family, anyone who was pro-French, went to the theatre, or expressed anticlerical sentiments. In the years after the Congress of Vienna, reaction rode particularly high.

The Barezzis and the Demaldès

A modern man of his period, Antonio Barezzi was a wholesale grocer and distiller. Raised by his widowed mother Donna Giuseppa Carrara Barezzi, he was the godson of Donna Margherita Carrara. His other aunt was Donna Agata Carrara, the mother of Giuseppe Demaldè, who later became Verdi's ardent supporter. The Barezzis seemed to have a genuine gift for music and art. Antonio Barezzi's daughter Margherita, who studied piano with Provesi and later taught it, had a fine voice. His niece Teresa Barezzi Tessoni became a protégée of the Monte di Pietà and soprano soloist for local concerts. His brother Orlando and son-in-law Pietro Garbi were said to have been the first in the area to play key trumpets or piston trumpets. Another brother, Stefano Barezzi, born two years after Antonio in 1789, became a celebrated painter, sculptor, and art conservator. Having studied in Busseto and Cremona, he went on to graduate from the Accademia delle Belle Arti in Milan. During the Napoleonic Wars Stefano served as a map-maker with the French army; but when the Austrians retook northern Italy he left Busseto, where one of his children was born, and went to work in Milan under Giuseppe Bossi, an art historian and scholar who was a Leonardo expert, trying to make a copy of *The Last Supper*, which was then decaying on the walls of Santa Maria delle Grazie and was not expected to last a decade.[15] Stefano, who became obsessed with the idea of trying to save the work, perfected the method of removing frescos from walls in sections and mounting them on wooden panels to preserve them. He was said to have been the first conservator to lift frescos from any walls, flat or curved, and restore them without repainting. Periodicals of the time wrote of his work, first on the Bernardino Luini frescos at Villa la Pelucca in Monza, then on *The Last Supper*. He was also recognized as a fashionable portraitist. A frequent visitor to Busseto, he let fellow-townspeople stay with him when they came to Milan.

Antonio Barezzi's closest collaborator in the Philharmonic Society was his first cousin Giuseppe Demaldè. Crippled, perhaps having lost all or part of his left leg in an accident, Demaldè was witty, tireless, and ferociously anticlerical, an amateur musician and historian, the Secretary of the Philharmonic and Treasurer of the Monte di Pietà e d'Abbondanza, a charitable foundation that made loans to the poor and gave grants to disadvantaged students. Demaldè had been playing the double bass since 1815. Others in the orchestra had been playing at least that long. Barezzi, whom Demaldè described as a 'maniac dilettante' of music, had mastered several instruments, among them the flute, clarinet, and ophicleide, which he played regularly in the orchestra. He also made the salon of his handsome town house available to the Philharmonic, which rehearsed several times a week and also gave concerts there.[16]

Because it was large and serious, the Philharmonic provided much of the music heard in Busseto and surrounding towns. With Provesi in charge, it also played important services at the church of San Bartolomeo and led all local parades, religious and secular. In addition to a repertory taken from the works of past composers, it played pieces by men like

Seletti and Provesi as well. In fact, it was a matter of honour for the Philharmonic to offer new works. The merits of its compositions sometimes provoked noisy arguments and even an occasional fist-fight. The organization jealously guarded its music library, lending scores to the church as needed.[17]

Verdi's Studies at the Ginnasio and at Provesi's Music School

Young Verdi was not lucky enough to move into this circle at once. His introduction was perhaps accomplished in 1825, when he was 12; then Father Da Terzorio suggested to Carlo Verdi that they boy ought to be enrolled in Provesi's music school.[18] Verdi had graduated with honours from the first two-year course at the Ginnasio. Following the friar's advice, Carlo Verdi took his son to Provesi, who accepted him. But Verdi continued studying at the Ginnasio, where he passed into the advanced humanities and rhetoric classes and had as his classmates a group of boys who would later become important professionals in their chosen fields.[19] Working harder than he had before, he had to get assignments in on time and complete his music practice. Yet he also had to find time to prepare the weekly services for Roncole, where sometimes he had to go for extra rehearsals. Burdened with far too many duties, he faltered. For the first time, it seems that his ambition and others' ambitions for him overwhelmed him. Under Provesi, Verdi was working on harmony and composition and teaching himself piano from self-help manuals. Under Seletti and his other teachers, Carlo Curotti and Don Giacinto Volpini,[20] he studied Virgil, the expurgated Juvenal, Cicero's *Orations*, Pliny, and an anthology of rhetoric and the humanities. He read history and philosophy at the library. From Demaldè we learn that the docile, respectful, timid boy began to be a bit short-tempered and capable of an occasional sharp remark; his teachers noticed that he was shirking his Ginnasio assignments and leaving things incomplete.

Soon Seletti called him in, for Verdi was too good a student to be allowed to slide. The schoolmaster advised him to give up either the Ginnasio or the music school, since he could not serve two gods at once. Fearful of being expelled from the Ginnasio, Verdi then began to neglect his music lessons, missing some and doing imperfect work in others. Because he had originally been Provesi's best student, the music-master was concerned over the boy's fall from grace. When he asked Verdi why he had let so much work go, the boy replied, not without embarrassment, that Seletti had urged him to give up music and pay closer attention to his other studies.[21] Verdi may have been caught between his two teachers, between whom there seems to have existed a genuine rivalry. Provesi was 'not friendly to [the priests]', whom he constantly mocked with 'little comedies, satires, and texts that stung them'.[22] Provesi's chief target was Seletti, who had a mean tongue of his own and responded as best he could. Because Provesi taught rhetoric in the Ginnasio, he was capable of becoming Verdi's tutor, and was not simply a music-teacher—Verdi learned much of what he knew about drama at this time from Provesi. Seletti began to fear that he might indeed lose his gifted pupil; so he and the other teachers stopped hounding Verdi, who continued in both schools.

Verdi finished his courses at the Ginnasio, where he graduated with honours in 1827, a particularly difficult year for his family because Carlo Verdi had decided to give up his lease on the Casa Padronale and his lands, which were to be surrendered in November. Behind with his rent, he gave notice in April; but when the properties were put up at auction in May, he bid for them again and won. Perhaps not having enough cash for the overdue rents, he had earlier taken small 'peace offerings' to the Bishop. Among these were funds for a part-time preacher and the organists of the cathedral, one of whom was Ottorino Respighi's grandfather. The Bishop hounded Carlo Verdi constantly, to no avail, and the family remained where it was.

After graduation, Verdi was free to go on with his music, which many already considered his life work. His decision to choose music was determined in part by an incident, recalled by Verdi himself,[23] that happened in 1826 or 1827. Captain Luigi Soncini, a former member of the military guard of the Infante of Parma, had been engaged to play a special service for the school in the church of Sant'Ignazio in the Ginnasio. Soncini, who was then 61, was an important landowner and a *gonfaloniere* (standard-bearer) of the parish, prominent in church affairs. When, for some reason, he could not play, Seletti asked Verdi to take his place. No more than 13 at the time, the boy played with such virtuosity that those who heard him were genuinely surprised. This, the first public performance Verdi ever gave in Busseto, was a great success.

'Whose music were you playing?' Seletti asked.

'My own, Signor Maestro. I just played it as it came to me,' Verdi replied, blushing.

'Go on with it, son. Go on always. Study music. You are right. I will not be the one to tell you to stop. Not after today.'

Verdi's Early Compositions and the Società Filarmonica

Studying with Provesi, Verdi composed all kinds of pieces:

From my thirteenth to my eighteenth year . . . I wrote a wide variety of music, marches by the hundred for the band, perhaps hundreds of little works to be played in church, in the theatre, and in private concerts; five or six concerti and variations for piano, which I played myself in private concerts; many serenades, cantatas (arias, duets, many trios), and several religious compositions, of which I remember only a Stabat Mater.[24]

At 14, he was teaching Provesi's pupils, studying music, and giving occasional concerts at those private evenings called *accademie*, some of which gave him the chance to play Barezzi's new grand piano.

He was, at this age, already old enough to perform with great ease and skill, reading at sight any of the most difficult works, whether fantasias, capriccios, variations, or concertos for that instrument, of which he was the finest champion, although he was self-taught from printed manuals. But no one of us [from the Philharmonic] could rival him.[25]

It was about at this time that Verdi wrote an overture for Rossini's *Il barbiere di Siviglia*, which was played before a performance of an opera company visiting Busseto. It seems that the young musician wanted to surprise his teacher with this work, although he did show it to some of his supporters in the Philharmonic, who judged it worthy of inclusion on the programme. 'The applause and ovations given by the public for that first score were long and extremely noisy.'[26] Thus Verdi made his public début as a composer, hearing his score played by a familiar, well-rehearsed ensemble as part of a professional evening of opera.

The Philharmonic was his workshop. In 1829 and 1830, according to Demaldè, he devoted himself to 'the study of classical composers'.[27] He also explored the works of three writers who later influenced his development: Shakespeare, Vittorio Alfieri, and Alessandro Manzoni. Of Manzoni, the great Lombard writer, Verdi knew *Il conte di Carmagnola*, and set a chorus from *Adelchi* and *Il cinque Maggio*, an ode on the death of Napoleon.[28] He considered *I promessi sposi* a national treasure, writing nearly forty years later to Countess Clara Maffei of its impact on him:

You well know how much and how I venerate that man who, in my opinion, has written not just the greatest book of our time, but one of the greatest books ever to come from the human brain; and it is not just a book, but a consolation for humanity. I was 16 when I read it for the first time. . . . [M]y enthusiasm has never changed; rather, as I have come to know men better, it has grown even greater, for this is a *true* book, true as *truth* itself.[29]

Of equal importance in Verdi's development was his discovery of Alfieri, some of whose dramas were thought to be dangerous and daring. He was a poet of uncompromising ideals: 'His purpose was to promulgate those great principles of liberty that inspired his own life. A deep, uncompromising hatred of kings is seen in each of his plays. . . . Alfieri was the first [Italian] to speak of a fatherland, a united Italy; he practically founded the patriotic school of literature.'[30] Verdi was drawn to his nationalism and his use of Old Testament stories; one of the youth's first major compositions was a cantata in eight movements called *I deliri di Saul*, based on Alfieri's drama *Saul*. The protagonist, a mad king, was a baritone; the role was almost certainly sung in Busseto by café-owner Giuseppe Guarnieri, an amateur musician and avid Verdi partisan. The work was at once a political essay, being derived from Alfieri, and a sort of trial run for other important works that would come later. Demaldè wrote: 'That composition is a real jewel, a precious stone, something that any creditable maestro would be happy to call his own.'[31] The score was played several times when Verdi was 16 and 17, attracting people from nearby towns who came to hear and praise it. The cantata brought Verdi a certain kind of fame in the area. Barezzi recorded his own impressions of it in his Day-Book, noting that it was 'for full orchestra and solo baritone voice, the first work of some significance [that Verdi has done], composed at the youthful age of fifteen, in which he shows a vivid imagination, a philosophical outlook, and sound judgement in the arrangement of the instrumental parts'.[32] Other compositions of the period include a Domine ad adiuvandum for orchestra, tenor, and flute soloist, played by the Philharmonic with Barezzi as the solo flautist and the local pharmacist Luigi Macchiavelli as tenor soloist; and a Stabat Mater with 'an enchanting trio'. In the former work, Verdi set Psalm 70: 'Make haste, O God, to deliver me'. Although Barezzi, Demaldè, and others praised these works, Verdi declared later that they were of no merit. Hardly any of them have been found, because of the composer's own determination to destroy them.[33]

As it developed, young Verdi's career was being built on the soundest possible foundation. He composed, revised, transcribed, asked others their opinion of his work,[34] rehearsed, and performed with an orchestra and band that were virtually at his personal disposal. The excellence of Provesi's school proved enormously helpful. It was singled out for praise in a book that was written about 1830 as a history of the Duchies of Parma, Piacenza, and Guastalla:

a music school that continually trains young people and produces players of the highest quality. [It is] the excellent result of the knowledge and zeal of the Maestro di Cappella Ferdinando Provesi, well known for his learned compositions in sacred music, and of the extraordinary concern of the amateur Antonio Barezzi; [both] can be considered the founders of this fine and useful institution.[35]

We know that in 1834 the Busseto Philharmonic had thirty-eight members: six violins, one cello, one viola, two double basses, eight clarinets, five trumpets, four horns, one bass drum, six other percussion instruments, two oboes, two flutes, and other small instruments.[36] In addition to his musicians, Verdi could draw on two first tenors, two second tenors, two basses, and one or more sopranos, with a full chorus.[37] Because Demaldè records the fact that some of these men had been playing for nineteen years, we have to conclude that some sort of regular organization had been in existence since about 1815, even before its formal founding, shortly after Provesi took over the music in church. Steadily, then, over a period of nearly ten years, Verdi was able to write for this experienced amateur organization, while drawing on the knowledge of men like Don Seletti and Don Ubaldo Neri, who had once also belonged to it. The young maestro's own position changed rapidly from that of apprentice and copyist to that of leader.

His talent opened many doors, none more important than the iron grilles and massive, polished portals of Casa Barezzi. The grand salon was used by the Philharmonic as early as 1830 and perhaps even earlier.[38] Richly decorated with frescoes and fine, carved woodwork, the house had yards of lace to curtain the French windows in the summer, while cut velvet hangings kept out the winter cold. The dining-table seated twelve, but it, like the grand piano, was dwarfed by the dimensions of the room. Generous to a fault, Barezzi and his wife Maria Demaldè represented the best of the city's lay society. She was a seamstress by trade. The Demaldès lived in an imposing town house that adjoined Palazzo Cavalli.[39] The relationship between Antonio Barezzi and Verdi was virtually like that of father and son; in 1828 Verdi was a musically and intellectually mature 15, while Barezzi was 41. When Verdi first knew him, Barezzi was the father of Margherita, who was 7 months younger than Verdi; Marianna; Giovanni; Amalia; and Teresa. Another son, Demetrio, was born in 1830. Of these children, Verdi would become intimate with two: Margherita, who later became his wife; and Giovanni, called Giovannino, the companion of his youth, consolation of his years as widower, and supporter through the early years of his career. In this family, so passionately devoted to music, Verdi was respected and at home. Margherita, a singer, had also been Provesi's pupil. Her cousin Teresa Barezzi sang the soprano parts in Verdi's early compositions. Pietro Garbi, a shopkeeper who became Margherita's brother-in-law by marrying Marianna, played the trumpet and violin in the Philharmonic orchestra. Orlando Barezzi was also a trumpeter, while Antonio, normally a flautist, could also substitute on other instruments. Demaldè remained the company's double-bass player.

Young Verdi was not Barezzi's only protégé, for one of the Ghezzi boys had already been sent to Milan to study at his expense in the 1820s, rooming and boarding with Giuseppe Seletti, a professor and man of letters who was the nephew of Don Pietro and the father of the historian Emilio Seletti, whose work has already been cited here, for he was the author of the three-volume history of Busseto that remains the definitive work on the city. Giuseppe Seletti also had the responsibility for overseeing the education of Giovannino Barezzi, who was sent to a boarding school at Rhò, outside Milan, in 1828. Another of Barezzi's favourites was Luigi Martelli, a music student who went to Milan with Verdi in 1835. A year after settling Giovannino in school, Barezzi decided to send Margherita to Milan Conservatory to study voice. Quite naturally, he asked his brother Stefano if he could help. On 28 January 1829, while Verdi was still a 15-year-old music student, Stefano wrote that he was delighted to learn that Margherita, his niece, would be coming to Milan and that he would do what he could for her: 'Everything depends on her good will, since nature has favoured her with a voice and heart.'[40] We do not know whether Margherita Barezzi did study voice in Milan, but we know that she later became a music-teacher in her own right, for one of her pupils was Emanuele Muzio, who later became Verdi's student.

The close relationships among these families led also to one between the Milan Selettis and Carlo Verdi, who perhaps deliberately, perhaps through error, involved them all in a tangle with the customs agents in Cremona in 1828. These friends and relatives were always sending parcels as they shipped clothing, bed-linen, books, music, musical instruments, combs, and food in and out of the Duchy of Parma and Lombardy-Venetia. Two key customs depots were at Piacenza, where formidable searches with dogs took place at La Carossa, and Cremona, where Seletti and Barezzi used a mutual friend's house as an exchange point. Confusion and delay were frequent, leaving Seletti to send letters of complaint and Barezzi to answer in his four-square language. In 1828 Seletti ordered a large shipment of pork products—about 60 pounds in all—to be sent to Milan. Carlo Verdi was asked to get it to Cremona and was given a letter from Seletti that constituted a sort of customs declaration. Instead of having it hauled by the person agreed upon, he shipped it in the wagon of a professional carter. In Cremona, the customs officers seized the entire shipment and sequestered the carter's wagon and oxen. To get them back, his wife had to deposit a bond. The pork butts and shoulders were then to be sold at auction. Naturally, Seletti's wrath fell on Carlo Verdi; to Barezzi, the professor raged:

All this trouble happened because of Verdi's ignorance and recklessness, for if he had acted differently, or if he had taken the things and delivered them with care just outside Porta San Luca as I wished, he could have got them to Cremona. But even after they were judged to be contraband, if he had taken the letter to Casa Peroni instantly, he could have saved the entire situation; and the damage is beyond repair because he was three and a half hours late. . . . Tell Verdi, too, that I kept my mouth shut about his name, so as not to do him more harm; but the director of the Customs Office told Canon Mussi that if he finds out who put the salami in Angelo Agosti's wagon, he wants to send him to prison. You see what a cheat Verdi is! . . . Here everyone is saying that Verdi was imprudent and stupid; now think of a way to cover me for my loss.[41]

Later the same day, apologizing for his abrupt tone, Seletti again said that everyone thought Verdi had acted like a 'beast' because he could have prevented the seizure.[42] All Seletti's string-pulling did not spare him the pain of having to buy the pork at public auction. After giving Barezzi further orders about recovering the money from Carlo Verdi, he went back to the old familiar topics. Among other news sent from Milan that year, Seletti confided to his friend that whenever Giovannino Barezzi was heard speaking Busseto dialect at school the masters made him miss dinner! He also reported on Giuditta Pasta:

a woman who knows how to act in the style of Vestri and Damarini, rendering the passions with gestures and facial expressions, having been taught by the late Talma; her veiled voice, though, can create a furore only in a small theatre. Yet the Milanesi are mad for her: women imitate her hairstyle; they carry parasols with her picture on them; men have her image on their handkerchiefs. All in all, if she were in Borgo San Donnino, the Bishop would have her portrait on his mitre![43]

Apart from his concern for Margherita's voice lessons in Milan and Giovannino's plight in Rhò, Barezzi continued to show interest in Verdi. Because Carlo Verdi lacked the means to send his son to the University of Parma, where he could study to become a teacher, the youth decided to return to Roncole; but Barezzi intervened: 'You are born for something better than that,' he said.[44] But Verdi also tried other solutions. On 29 October 1829, acting perhaps on his own, he wrote to the vestry of the church of San Giacomo in Soragna, a town near Roncole, to apply for the post of organist, which was about to fall vacant:

Illustrious Sirs, Giuseppe Verdi, resident of the village of Roncole, knowing that the position of organist of the parish church in Soragna will soon be vacant because of the voluntary resignation of Signor Frondoni, offers himself in place of the one who is leaving, subject, however, to whatever inquiries, whether private or public, are necessary to determine the petitioner's ability to perform the sacred offices. Therefore, he asks that the said Illustrious Gentlemen admit him among the competitors for the aforementioned [post], assuring them of the most attentive and conscientious service and every possible effort to merit the approval of everyone. In the mean time, full of confidence and declaring respectful consideration, [I am] your most devoted and obliging servant, Giuseppe Verdi. Roncole, 24 October 1829.[45]

Provesi also sent along his letter of recommendation; but Verdi did not get the post, perhaps because of his youth. When the candidate from the Piacentine town of Monticelli d'Ongina was chosen, Verdi returned to Busseto for the winter.

He had hardly settled in when Provesi began to prepare an ambitious concert of Verdi's works, which the Philharmonic planned to present in February 1830. Scores were examined, rehearsals begun. A co-sponsor, the Poetry Society, was found. Finally invitations went out, asking important families to applaud and encourage 'that genius who today is rising and will soon become the most beautiful ornament of this city'.[46] The date was 19 February. Several weeks later, on Good Friday, always the occasion for a long procession, accompanied by the Philharmonic, four new marches by Verdi were played; in his Day-Book, Barezzi described them as 'beautiful'. Verdi composed his *Le lamentazioni di*

Geremia for that same Holy Week; it was a cantata for baritone and orchestra. 'Che portentoso lavoro,' Barezzi noted, 'What an imposing work.'[47]

The Three 'Lost Years' of Verdi's Youth

Having graduated from the Ginnasio's four-year programme with honours in 1827 and from Provesi's four-year music school in June 1829, Verdi might have left Busseto to go on to higher studies, either at the University of Parma or at one of the conservatories nearby. Milan Conservatory was the most likely choice, especially since Antonio Barezzi had intended to send Margherita to the city that year. Yet another option would have been private study, perhaps in Parma or Cremona. Yet Verdi stayed on in Busseto, where his only choice was to go on learning from Provesi, although Provesi had already said that that would be pointless. As a manuscript biography had it:

At the beginning of the third year [of his lessons with Provesi], the teacher declared that there was nothing more he could teach him; that boy knew more already than he did. At 16 the student not only frequently substituted for his teacher in directing the rehearsals and concerts of the Philharmonic Society; . . . but he also played the organ in [church]. Beyond that, he wrote concert pieces and military marches for the band. To score these compositions, to reduce and copy the scores and parts, to get them rehearsed, to conduct performances of them—these were the responsibilities of Antonio Barezzi's young shop-boy.[48]

There was clearly some exploitation here. The only men who could profit from it were Provesi and Barezzi, who found their young musician useful in making the Philharmonic a polished ensemble with a living repertory of works that Verdi was composing on a day-to-day, month-to-month basis. This situation put Carlo Verdi at a tremendous disadvantage, for he and his wife were losing money every day their son postponed further training or the search for work. Some of the tasks Verdi was doing, without pay, ought to have been Provesi's, for the City of Busseto was paying him to perform them. It seems that his health was so poor that he could cover about half of what he had contracted to do; Verdi may thus have saved him from embarrassment or forced retirement. No one would deny that Verdi learned from this experience, especially that of writing for the collegiate church, but in terms of daily progress toward a diploma that would let him earn a living, these were three wasted years.

The exploitation did end, finally. Provesi 'asked that people work to send him to Milan for he could conclude his studies better in that conservatory of music.'[49] But in the years between 1829 and 1832 Verdi had gradually come to be almost a member of the Barezzi family and had won the heart of Margherita as well. Because Verdi was so reserved, no one in Casa Barezzi realized that he and Margherita were in love; not even 'the many people who frequented the house' were aware of it, Demaldè said. But in 1830, when Verdi was 17, Maria Demaldè Barezzi discovered that the two young people had fallen in love, and 'that was why the freedom that they had previously enjoyed was taken away from them'. Clearly their shared love of music was a bond. 'They thought about a way to make Verdi finish his studies away from Busseto, where he could also go on learning about the theatre.'[50] Milan was chosen. Apart from Seletti and Stefano Barezzi, Provesi had friends in Milan on whom he thought he could count. Alessandro Rolla, former director of the Ducal Orchestra in Parma, had moved there and had become director of the orchestra at La Scala, a post he held from 1802 until 1808 and then left to become a professor at Milan Conservatory. Although Rolla was no longer young, Provesi felt that he could help Verdi.

But first there was a purgatory to be passed through. During the 1820s, Carlo Verdi had found it ever more difficult to pay the rent on the house and land he leased. Between 1806 and 1827 he was sometimes as much as eighteen months in arrears, partly because he kept repairing the buildings on the property and partly because he often made contributions to the parish and Confraternity in Roncole, the cathedral organist, and one of the diocese's preachers. None the less, he renewed his lease in 1827, bidding it in at an auction overseen by Don Ballarini, the Provost of Busseto. In Verdi's favour was the fact that Ballarini had made a tour of the properties and found them in good condition. But the Bishop, Monsignor Luigi Sanvitale, kept pressing Ballarini to get Verdi to pay his rent arrears; if he could not, he should be thrown out ('cacciato via'). On 5 February 1830, at Ballarini's request, the court in Busseto issued an eviction order against Carlo Verdi, who, 'together with his family', had to move before 11 November of that year. On that day the Verdis left their home, where they had lived since 1791, and moved to the tavern which is now the national monument 'Verdi Birthplace'. They rented it from Marquis Pallavicino. A new tenant took over their Casa Padronale on 29 November.[51] Carlo Verdi then began to pay his rent arrears in instalments; although he could not make a payment every month, he did manage at least three in 1831. In 1832 he was able to pay only once, in January. Just a few months earlier, in the spring of 1831, Marco Verdi and Giuditta Picelli had moved from Roncole and gone back into the Piacentino, having children and becoming taverners in Besenzone, where they leased the old inn at Bersano, a short distance from Sant'Agata.[52] Verdi's cousin, Giovanni Uttini, and his wife, Anna Maria Bersani, were also having children there at that time. If we can set a date for the move from the Osteria Vecchia in Roncole to the present 'Verdi Birthplace', which then belonged to the Pallavicinos, it is the autumn of 1830. Until now, no document has been found to suggest that the Verdis left the Osteria Vecchia earlier than 11 November 1830 when, in debt to the priest of La Madonna dei Prati, they gave it up.

On 14 May 1831 Carlo Verdi addressed himself to the president and administrative council of the Monte di Pietà in Busseto, asking for a scholarship for his son Giuseppe Verdi, 'so that he can perfect himself in every way in the art of music, in which he has demonstrated extraordinary talent, both in performance and in composition'. That favourite phrase 'ornament of this *patria*', so dear to Provesi, makes one suspect that his was the hand behind the letter, which Carlo Verdi signed.[53] On the same day Verdi was taken into the Barezzi house as a lodger. Two nights before, a murder had been committed during a robbery in the house where Provesi had lived, just next to Barezzi's, when Isacco Levi, a prominent member of Busseto's large Jewish community, was killed. His niece Rina Muggia, then 13, was stabbed and left for dead in a corner of the room. Levi's wife, who had hidden, escaped. Maria Demaldè Barezzi, whose oldest son was at school in Rhò, may have felt safer with another teenager in her house; so Verdi was invited in, presumably because everyone in town knew that he worked in his room most of the night and would thus be awake to hear an intruder. It says a lot for the Barezzis that they kept him there, for it was soon discovered that the murderer was Francesco Mezzadri, nicknamed 'Cantaben' ('Sings Well'), whose mother, like Verdi's grandmother, was a Bianchi from Sant'Agata! Mezzadri, Levi's steward, had also known the Provesis, who lived on the top floor of the house. Knowing that Levi had the money from a land sale in the house that night, he solicited the help of an accomplice and committed the murder, for which he was later hanged.[54]

Verdi's very comfortable back bedroom-sitting room was on the first landing of the Barezzi house, but because it was completely exposed to anyone coming up the stairs, its position was somewhat public. This room was kept exactly as it had been when Verdi lived there well into the 1960s. Handsomely furnished, it had a bed at one end and a little living area at the other, with a sofa, two armchairs, and several straight chairs.[55] Its walls were covered with French paper; the one window was hung with heavy draperies. On the ochre plaster wall over the door, someone, perhaps Verdi, had written 'G. Verdi'. At one time, the signature had a little plate of glass over it. This move was a decisive step upward in the progress that, by then, everyone had come to expect of Verdi. As Provesi coped less and less, the younger man took on more of his work; but in Roncole he still served as organist, while composing regularly for the Philharmonic. During the summer of 1831 the Barezzis and the Verdis waited for an answer to the scholarship application; but nothing came. In December Carlo Verdi appealed to the highest authority in the duchy writing to 'Her Majesty' the Duchess Marie Louise on behalf of 'his only son Giuseppe, student of the music school in Busseto'. He cited the public ovations Verdi got when he played or presented his own compositions 'of every kind of music, whether vocal or instrumental'. He then stated that he could not continue to give money to his son and asked the ruler to help.[56] On 22 December the Duchess's Minister for Internal Affairs ordered the administrative council to consider the application and advise him of the outcome. Carlo Verdi further strengthened his position by sending the Monte di Pietà written letters of recommendation and getting a statement from Barezzi to the effect that he would underwrite Verdi's studies himself for one year 'being asked to do so by Carlo Verdi'.[57] At the Monte di Pietà, Verdi had strong support for his case, with Antonio Accarini, the Podestà of Busseto, on his side, bolstered by Provesi's patron Contardo Cavalli. It was Accarini who wrote sometime in January 1832 that he was of the opinion that the foundation could grant Verdi a scholarship, 'all the more because the young man behaves in an exemplary fashion and is extremely diligent and has parents of very limited means who absolutely cannot underwrite the studies of the young man, who will some day be the sole supporter of his poor family'.[58] On 14 January the Monte di Pietà agreed that Verdi should have a scholarship of 300 lire each year for four years, provided he was willing to audition for a well-known musician, Giuseppe Alinovi, in Parma, 'to provide stronger justification for the commission's having acted in favour of the aforesaid Verdi'.[59] One month later Carlo Verdi and Antonio Barezzi were told that the Minister of the Interior had approved the award. Barezzi agreed to advance the money for one year, in response to Carlo

BOOK I

Verdi's request that he do so, in order to get Verdi to Milan as quickly as possible. Both men answered at once: Carlo Verdi with 'inexpressible joy', adding that his son will 'never forget the generous benefactors'; and Barezzi, declaring his 'sweet' satisfaction over the outcome and the assistance to this 'singular genius in music'.[60]

With that, letters began to leave Busseto for Milan to arrange for a hearing with the Conservatory admissions board. Giuseppe Seletti agreed to take Verdi in as a lodger, giving him a room of his own in his house in Contrada di Santa Marta. Barezzi also asked Seletti to investigate the possibility that Verdi might work as a music copyist or transcriber in the flourishing publishing-house Casa Ricordi. The answer was not encouraging: 'as for writing or working for Ricordi, it will not be hard because he gives work to anyone who falls in his clutches but pays them badly.'[61] At the end of May passports were requested from the Minister of the Interior. Three men would travel from Parma to Lombardy-Venetia: Provesi, Carlo Verdi, and his son 'Giuseppe, by profession a student of music, native of Roncole, residing in Busseto, who goes to Milan to be admitted in that Conservatory of Music.'[62] During the summer of 1832 Verdi prepared to leave the city that had nurtured him for nearly ten years.

June 1832–June 1834

From Small City to Large

The high expectations of the loyal Philharmonic clique in Busseto were fastened on Verdi when he went off to Milan in the summer of 1832, for community money and its members' energy had been invested in him. In fact, he owed Busseto much, for it had prepared him to pass from its small, walled cultural enclave to the larger stage of the Lombard centre. Already a Bussetan, he had acquired tastes that he could not have satisfied in the Osteria in Roncole. Born for something better, as Barezzi had said, Verdi had adopted the style of his patron's world. When he did eventually return to Busseto as a famous composer and buy a house of his own, he tried to reconstruct Barezzi's world within its walls, then bring his parents away from their village so they could share his *vita signorile*. Not quite 19, Verdi was tall; he had a high forehead, grey eyes, black eyebrows, and chestnut brown hair, a small mouth, thick beard, aquiline nose, and a pale skin pitted with smallpox scars.[1] He left Busseto accompanied by his father and Provesi.

When their coach rolled into Milan, they entered a city where medieval houses still stood beside Roman ruins. Salted through the city were dozens of churches, monasteries, and convents, some of them, abandoned since Napoleonic times, falling into ruin. The hand of commerce was shown in the banks and exchange offices. The stamp of 'Theresan' architecture had been added to the mix with its ornate, scrolled coats-of-arms; wrought-iron balconies; and Austrian government emblems. The large private houses almost all had inner courtyards with fountains and inviting trees. Some evidence could be seen of the Napoleonic renovations. And by 1832 the new architecture of Italy was beginning to leave its mark, although the spacious piazzas and boulevards were to come later, as the newly rich Milanese bourgeoisie made room for its own expansion.[2] The total impression was one of crowding and noise. In front of La Scala there was a slight widening of the rather narrow street that was called the Corsia del Giardino (present Via Manzoni). A clutter of houses there, including the old Palazzo Marino, dated from the 1500s. That square was not cleared until the late 1850s. The Milan of 1832 was in a state of flux and growth, for the city had lived through three decades of increasing productivity. The metals and fabrics industries flourished; capital accumulated. To the clamour of human voices and wooden clogs on the streets was added the racket of carriage wheels, the clatter of horses on the stones, and the tolling of church bells. Vendors shouted their wares as pedestrians cursed at passing carts and chaises. Elegant clothing was important, especially to the rich *arrivistes*. The best shops had already learned to shade their windows with awnings that hung out over the walkways.[3] Only in the side-streets could one find what people loved to call 'Old Milan'; and it was toward one of these quiet side-streets that Verdi, his father, and Provesi made their way. Giuseppe Seletti lived behind what is now Piazza Cordusio, in Contrada di Santa Marta.[4] Just a few steps away was one of the remaining medieval quarters of the city, clustered around the church of Santa Maria Podone, the Borromeo palace, and the church of San Giorgio al Palazzo. In Seletti's well-run house, books were everywhere; good clothes and linen meant a great deal; and meals were served on time. A professor at the Ginnasio di Santa Marta, Seletti wrote essays, sonnets, hymns, and elegies. He published a life of Scipio, an important text on geography, a Greek grammar and text that went into six editions, an edition of the letters of Cato, with commentary, several comedies and tragedies, a translation of the *Iliad*, a history and geography of Russia, a history of Italy, and an anthology of humanistic studies.[5]

When Verdi settled in the professor's house in June he was a boarder for the third time in nineteen years. His stay in the city began badly, partly because of the animosity Seletti felt toward Carlo Verdi. Whatever else he was, Seletti was not a forgiving man, although he did sometimes show sympathy to young Verdi. Shortly after Verdi, his father, and Provesi arrived, the two older men were robbed in Piazza del Duomo. Short of funds, they appealed to Seletti for a loan of 2 gold sovereigns, which he gave them, being assured that he would be repaid at once.

Unfortunately, he did not get his money back and at the end of August was beginning to suspect the worst, having heard from neither Provesi or Carlo Verdi. Although they had asked him not to do so, he notified Barezzi, suggesting that some 'trick' had been played on him. He was sure they had not been honest at the outset, when Carlo Verdi told him that their pockets had been picked.[6] Before leaving for home, Provesi had, though, shown young Verdi the city and had taken him to the Conservatory to introduce him to Rolla, Provesi's former teacher, whom they asked to help.

Milan Conservatory and Verdi's Application for Admission

Verdi made formal application to the Conservatory on 22 June:

Giuseppe Verdi has begun the study of music, but, not having the means in his own *patria*, Busseto in the State of Parma, to reach that perfection to which he aspires, would like for that purpose to be admitted as a pupil paying room and board in the Imperial Royal Conservatory of Music in Milan.

Therefore he addresses his application to the Imperial Royal Government, confident that in the examinations that he will take at the said Conservatory of music there will be recognized in him the talent covered in Article 10 of the regulations of that same Institution so that he can get a dispensation, which he needs as he has passed the normal age, now being 18 years old.[7]

There followed a promise to produce the necessary documents and letters of recommendation. This shows clearly that Verdi knew he was well over age, but believed that his special gift for music would secure him entry, under Article 10 of the regulations.

He appeared before the examining board one day at the end of June. Before him were Alessandro Rolla; Francesco Basily, head of the conservatory; Gaetano Piantanida, his assistant, who was a professor of counterpoint; and Antonio Angeleri, the professor of piano and inventor of a new method of keyboard technique that placed emphasis on the position of the pianist's hands. It was hot. Rolla expected to leave for his summer vacation within a week or ten days. Verdi appeared with some of his own compositions and a score of a well-known caprice by the Viennese composer Heinrich Herz. He played it as the first part of his examination and composed a four-part fugue for the second part. He then left the Conservatory and returned to Seletti's house. A terrible week followed, a week of rumours. Then silence, capped by more rumours. Seletti arranged for Verdi to practise in a friend's house, as he had no piano of his own; then the friend's daughter fell ill, forcing Verdi to suspend his practice. He went for walks occasionally and studied in his room. But much of the time he waited alone for an answer that did not come.

Seletti was a bit more informed than Verdi on what had happened; and, although he did not tell the student what he knew, he confided some of the forewarnings of disaster to Barezzi: '*Do not become alarmed*, but keep cool and read what I have to write to you.'[8] From friends he had received the worst possible news:

The censor . . . answered that Verdi is weak at the cembalo. Maestro Angeleri told me Monday that, having sought from the censor his honest view . . . he answered that Verdi does not know how to play the cembalo, nor will he ever learn. Rolla's son, however, had said from the first day to Dr Frigeri [one of Seletti's friends] that Verdi lacked emphasis, but that that was no great problem for someone who wants to study *composition*. . . . Count Sormani, questioned by my friend, told him on *Monday* that . . . he would have said nothing about Verdi's age, but that he would have spoken out instead about the lack of space. . . . The elder Rolla can protect Verdi somehow, but . . . on Tuesday he had a fight with the censor . . . and almost gave him a punch in the face. . . . Coccia said that at the age of 18 it is difficult to make oneself into a great player but that he did not find it as impossible as Angeleri, if the young student is committed. Yesterday . . . Rolla said beautiful things to Verdi, but I don't trust him. . . . I warn you, too, that Verdi does not know about Angeleri's answer, and I will never tell him, so as not to depress him. . . . If the affair of the Conservatory goes badly, I will have to move him somewhere else. In spite of the failure of all our hopes, . . . I would advise you to say nothing to the Bussetani, so as not to have aggravations from anyone.[9]

After eight days Verdi went to see Rolla, as planned. The old man simply told him not to think any further about the Conservatory, but to 'choose a maestro in the city; I advise either Lavigna or Negri'.[10] When Seletti himself went to the Conservatory, he was told that 'there is no place to lodge him, and he is the wrong age. Piantanida's opinion is *that he will turn out to be a mediocrity*.' The underlined words seem to be a quote from Piantanida. Because the 'Conservatory affair' had turned into a rout, Seletti urged Barezzi to hitch up his little *chaise* and come to Milan, where they could settle Verdi's future together. He said that he would keep Verdi one week beyond the date already stipulated, provided Barezzi paid him for doing so. 'Verdi knows I am writing to you, and he greets you with his whole soul, and he is waiting for your decisions.'[11] Seletti also warned that even 600 francs could not cover the student's needs, if he were to go to a private teacher and live in private lodgings.

Verdi was bitter about the Conservatory. At some later date he wrote across the envelope that held his application:

In the year 1832 22 June Giuseppe Verdi's request to be admitted to the Milan Conservatory was rejected[12]

He kept this application in the front corner of his writing-desk at Sant'Agata next to his letter-paper.

Verdi's own 'authorized' view of his failure to get into Milan Conservatory was published in 1883 by Emilio Seletti, Giuseppe's son, in *La città di Busseto*:

Having come to Milan in June 1832 in the hope of going to the celebrated Conservatory, [Verdi] was to suffer his first disillusionment. Those maestri, judging him by the imperfect standards of their examinations, decreed that young Verdi was incapable and not fit to be admitted. Turned away from that school, Verdi risked being lost completely, had his generous protector or had Verdi himself lost faith on hearing this verdict.[13]

When Verdi received his copy of Seletti's book, he wrote to its author:

I have to thank you for having wanted to bother with my poor self. It was not worth the trouble. But I am very happy that you have spoken out honestly about the events that happened at the Conservatory. Asked about this many times I never wanted to, nor was able to say, just what happened. The truth, coming from my mouth, would have sounded like revenge, taken years later.[14]

A few further details were added by the librettist Antonio Ghislanzoni, who asked Verdi about the incident:

He remembers the event without rancour, and, speaking to me about it, seemed in a certain way to justify the strange verdict. Angeleri had his own special method of teaching the students, a method that was excellent, judging from results achieved. So he liked to teach only those who had not yet adopted the schools of the other teachers. Verdi, presenting himself to give an example of his ability as a pianist, seemed, as it happened, to be spoiled by the teaching he had received in Busseto, so that [Angeleri] did not want to bother to teach him again from the start. It was a question of the mechanics [of playing] and perhaps this good man, seeing the boy reading music at sight and performing it on the piano, going against all the rules, despaired of getting from him the subordination and patience needed for him to change his method.[15]

BOOK I

Advised by Rolla to choose a maestro in the city, Verdi waited for Barezzi's authorization. His patron, who had advised the Monte di Pietà that Verdi had been rejected because of his age and because he was a foreigner in Lombardy,[16] agreed to underwrite the private study. Verdi was placed with Vincenzo Lavigna, one of Rolla's old acquaintances. Born in 1777, he had studied in Naples with the composer Paisiello, who had then helped him get established in the north. In 1802 one of Lavigna's operas was presented at the Teatro alla Scala with considerable success. Later Lavigna was named the maestro al cembalo at the theatre, a post he held for about thirty years, during which he also composed and presented his own operas and ballets. The first performance of *Don Giovanni* was given at La Scala under Lavigna in 1814. He closed his career there with *Norma* in 1832. His was an altogether distinguished tenure.[17] When Verdi went for his first lessons in July, he found his teacher old, affable, and still very much a part of the world of the theatre in Milan. Something of a pedant, but 'fortissimo'[18] in counterpoint, he knew every path and byway of the professional world. After welcoming Verdi, Lavigna asked to see some of his compositions, which, he said, 'impressed' him. 'He, like everyone else, found it quite unbelievable' that Verdi had been turned away from the Conservatory. By 8 August he had given his new pupil five lessons of one and a half hours each and was 'enormously concerned' about Verdi and pleased, for he found him 'very promising'.[19]

Lavigna insisted that Verdi get a subscription to La Scala, so that he could go to the theatre. To fill the days, he enrolled Verdi at a musical library so he could bring scores home. Exercises in counterpoint and composition completed the routine; Verdi later said that he did 'canons and fugues, fugues and canons of all kinds'.[20] When there was nothing on at La Scala, Verdi sometimes went back to Lavigna's, where conversation revolved around music and theatre. At the end of the visit, the maestro could take a score from the shelves and run through it with his pupil.[21] On many occasions Lavigna invited friends in and, rarely, presented his own pupils' works. It is possible that Verdi also got to know Angelo Boracchi at this time. The theatrical agent and impresario, who was eight years older than Verdi, lived next door to the Selettis in Contrada di Santa Marta with his four younger sisters. Born in Monza, he was in business with two other agents, Leopoldo Robbia, a crippled writer, and Camillo Cirelli, both of whom shared an office in Piazza dei Filodrammatici with Boracchi, just across the street from La Scala. They lived nearby. Slowly

Verdi got to know a grand, lively Milan, from the fashionable Galleria de Cristoforis, which had just opened, with its twenty-four beautiful shop-windows and its bookshops and antique dealers, to the cafés around the Teatro dei Filodrammatici and the Cannobiana. Apart from the Selettis, the Parma-born cellist Vincenzo Merighi was also active in Milanese opera circles at this time, living near the Conservatory and playing in the orchestra at La Scala.[22]

From what Seletti wrote to Barezzi, it seems that Verdi began to find the professor's home somewhat boring, as he changed into a rather more independent and somewhat truculent young man. But this change came slowly. At the outset, Verdi was utterly dependent on Seletti for every-thing; even his pocket-money was doled out by the older man. Scarcely six weeks after Verdi got to Milan, Seletti began urging him to have his own bed shipped from Roncole so that a room could be prepared for guests from Busseto. Arguments about the bed went on until December, as both Carlo Verdi and Barezzi seemed unwilling to take care of the matter. Finally, Seletti used some of Verdi's money and bought a bed, mattress, and linen, all of 'first quality'.[23] Seletti also raised the issue of Verdi's clothes, for he found the young man so shabbily dressed that he could not be introduced to 'other people' outside Seletti's intimate circle. 'He must have clothes, because of his absolute need and because he must make a decent appearance.'[24] At the very least, an overcoat, a pair of new trousers, and a vest. Seletti was not sure that Verdi should go to the opera as often as he wished.

Finally Verdi went home in June 1833, his first trip outside the city in a year. Lavigna, very pleased with his student, had said that Verdi was doing 'very, very well'; Seletti reported with satisfaction that he was working long hours, at least some of the time.[25] But a falling-off came in the month before his visit home, as Verdi was composing a Mass for the Busseto Philharmonic. When he got back to Milan, he fell ill with the flu, then suffered two personal losses, the first with the death of Provesi on 26 July, and the second the death of his sister Giuseppa on 9 August. Barezzi noted in his Day-Book his own regret over Provesi: 'Maestro di musica, spontaneous poet, died, forgotten by fortune.'[26] Giuseppa may have succumbed to cholera or typhoid. It is certain that her family expected her to die, for she made confession and took Holy Communion one day before her death; one of the chaplains from San Michele Arcangelo administered Extreme Unction. The girl died in the national monument now marked as Verdi's birthplace, which, as her death record states, belonged to the Marquis Pallavicino, from whom the Verdis then rented it.[27]

These losses depressed Verdi at a time when he was sick and under pressure. Seletti blamed Barezzi for having been 'wrong to keep him so long in Busseto',[28] for Verdi was nearly 20, yet he had about half of his formal training still ahead of him. He could not afford to lose a day. Provesi's death came as a double shock, personal and professional, for Verdi had fully expected to take the place of his former maestro, but was obviously far from being qualified to do so. Stalled in his lessons in Milan, he became very difficult to live with. Seletti, insistent and self-righteous, ever ready with a pungent remark, urged Verdi to work harder and advised Barezzi to drive his young protégé harder himself, even as he offered suggestions to the Philharmonic on how to preserve Provesi's post for Verdi. Also under pressure to find other quarters for Verdi, he began to warn Barezzi that he could not keep him much longer. These and other problems relating to Verdi came up in Seletti's letters to Barezzi of 1833 and 1834: he was undisciplined; he kept impossible hours; he refused to listen to criticism of his behaviour; worse, he sometimes seemed not to care whether he finished his course or not. In April 1834 matters came to a head when Seletti announced that he could no longer offer the room in his house, perhaps because the young man was flirting with Seletti's daughter (a situation at which the professor hinted in a letter of 4 May).[29] Seletti and Lavigna found lodgings for Verdi and his spinet with a family named DuPuy who lived in Contrada di San Paolo not far from La Scala. Seletti took the room for a year, but neither he nor Lavigna had the courage to tell this difficult pupil that they were moving him! Finally Seletti broke the news and on 15 May Verdi moved. The change of landlord apparently did not improve his disposition for the DuPuys began to complain and even Lavigna registered some concern, urging his pupil to study harder and get on with his course, which Verdi no longer seemed to care about finishing. Sounding a note of warning, Seletti said that it was hard to know whether he really wanted to study or not. He perhaps wanted to finish his course, but also liked what Seletti ominously referred to as 'Milan'—the exciting city outside the professor's doors.

The 'Milan' that attracted a young, lively crowd was that of the theatres, cafés, and shops within easy walking reach of the Cathedral. The Galleria de Cristoforis boasted the popular pastry-shop of Carlo De Albertis, where hot meals and 'black coffee from the Levant' were also served, the coffee at 25 centesimi a cup; the offices of the Società degli Editori degli Annuali

Universali delle Scienze e dell'Industria, the lighthouse of modern minds; several antiques dealers and booksellers; a shop that advertised 'fine razor strops of best leather for sharpening razors'; and a unisex hairdresser who copied his styles from Paris. On 10 February 1834 the Galleria de Cristoforis was the scene of a tumultuous masked ball that the police commissioner, Luigi Torresani-Lanzfeld, had agreed to allow. It was later reported that 6,000 people joined the celebration there, when the Galleria was transformed into a huge theatre where crowded shops looked like boxes filled with spectators. Men had to attend in evening clothes (something Verdi may even have owned that year) and wear white ties, hats, berets, and masks that could be any colour other than black, which was forbidden. Women were costumed as theatrical or historical characters, with a scattering that came as pine trees or flowers. The event was so popular that the Corsia dei Servi had to be closed at three in the afternoon; after nine that evening no carriage was allowed beyond the stone lion of Porta Orientale. Thousands of lamps created 'an immense light that blinded the eyes of all who walked in the . . . magnificent passageway'. During the night the Vice-Regent Ranieri, the Austrian ruler's delegate, came with his wife to slaughter three wild stags with his own knife as the crowd shouted. After strolling through the full length of the Galleria four times and visiting two cafés and a shop, they left. The celebration ended at about eight the next morning, but places that had been open all night went on serving until noon.[30] Although this was not an annual affair, it was held at least twice while Verdi was studying in the city. With men and women 'dancing, strolling, and having a good time' exchanging kisses, vows, and rings, the *ballo in maschera* in the Galleria de Cristoforis stood for the 'Milan' that Seletti feared Verdi might come to like too well.

Verdi's First Public Performance in Milan: April 1834

A new circle of professional and amateur musicians had become Verdi's friends some time during this Carnival season as he began to attend the rehearsals of the Milanese Società Filarmonica, which Pietro Massini directed, although he was 'not very knowledgeable' but was 'tenacious and patient, just what was needed for a Society of Amateurs'.[31] Born in Brescia on 15 November 1796, he always lived close to the Teatro dei Filodrammatici, just across the street from La Scala. Here Massini's

49

troupe performed and here he had his home when Verdi first knew him. Later Massini moved to the Contrada dei Clerici, in the house next to Cirelli's.[32] With his pupils and amateurs, he was organizing a production of Haydn's *Creation*.

The Teatro dei Filodrammatici, founded in the eighteenth century as the Teatro Patriottico, had opened with Alfieri's *Filippo II*, playing to an audience so liberal that it was called 'The Scarlets'. Among other plays offered later were Alfieri's *Virginia* and *Bruto*. The theatre had something of a reputation as a gathering-place for free-thinkers. After the Austrian Restoration, radical and liberal currents were suppressed. Yet some of Massini's circle were against Austrian rule. One was Count Pompeo Belgioioso. His sister-in-law, daringly anti-Austrian, had a reputation for controversial behaviour second to almost none in Italy. Count Pompeo, less flamboyant, was an amateur singer of some fame, an Italian patriot, a close friend of Rossini, and one of Massini's mainstays.[33]

Verdi got his chance to work with the Filarmonica through Lavigna, who had introduced him to Massini during one of his soirées. Lavigna and Verdi attended rehearsals at the theatre; and it was at one of these that Verdi was asked to help. The regular maestro al cembalo was absent on an evening when Verdi seemed more prepared to take over than anyone else there, Lavigna having declined the honour. Many years later Verdi recalled that engagement to his publisher Giulio Ricordi:

I was fresh from my studies and certainly did not feel uncomfortable when faced with an orchestral score; I accepted, sat down at the pianoforte to begin the rehearsal. I remember very well some ironic little smiles on the faces of the gentlemen-amateurs, and it seems that my young figure, thin and not very fancily dressed, was one that would inspire very little faith in them. Anyway, we began to rehearse, and little by little I caught fire and became excited by the music, and did not just limit myself to accompanying them, but also began to conduct with my right hand, playing with my left. I was really very successful, all the more so because no one expected it. When the rehearsal ended, I got compliments and congratulations from all sides, and especially from Count Pompeo Belgioioso and Count Renato Borromeo. Finally, whether because the other maestri, whom I mentioned before, had too much to do and could not take on the work, or whether for other reasons, they ended up by entrusting the whole concert to me. The public performance took place and was such a success that it was repeated afterward in the grand salon of the Casinò de' Nobili, in the presence of the Archduke Raineri and all the high society of that time.[34]

These performances, for which Verdi was maestro al cembalo and chorus-master, were conducted by Michele Rachelle, who was mentioned in the theatrical journal *Il barbiere di Siviglia* of 16 April 1834, where the reviewer praised Verdi for his handling of the chorus: he was not, however, mentioned when the second performance of the *Creation* took place.[35] This was excellent experience for this young musician, just past 20. The distinguished amateur musicians of Massini's Filarmonica, who had the support of important Milanese professionals, had founded the society in the spring of 1833 just to give young people exposure such as this. Reviews in papers such as *Il barbiere di Siviglia* and *Il censore teatrale* attracted an audience, helped to bring beginners and aspiring artists to the attention of agents and impresarios, and also won them encouragement from rich, dilettante composers and performers in the ranks of Lombard nobility. They were considered worthy of having librettos printed and circulated at their performances, just as professional productions had.[36] Massini was so pleased with Verdi's work that he promised him that he could perform again with the Filarmonica, which he did the following year. Verdi also won a commission to compose a cantata for Count Renato Borromeo, which he described as having been written to celebrate a wedding. It was, though, nothing of the sort; the Cantata, written to Borromeo's own text, was an *hommage* to Ferdinand I, the Emperor of Austria, offered on his birthday. It was performed in Milan on 19 April 1836.[37]

Encouraged by his success, Verdi began to think in terms of a career in Milan, of patronage, and of influential acquaintances. At the Filodrammatici, the members of the Società Filarmonica were planning a performance of *Roberto il Diavolo*. But Verdi was compelled to return to Busseto, where his obligations were: Carlo and Luigia Verdi, now alone in Roncole, with their daughter dead and their son living in the city; Antonio Barezzi and Giuseppe Demaldè, who had invested so much in him; and Margherita, Barezzi's high-spirited, redheaded daughter, whose love for him had been known for years. All the Philharmonic members in Busseto were waiting for him to finish his studies so that he could legitimately claim the chair left empty by Provesi and had been acutely embarrassed because Verdi had not been ready when his old maestro died. Two parties had already strung their ranks along the margins of the controversy: the Codini or conservative clerical faction, headed by Don Gian Bernardo Ballarini, Provost of San Bartolomeo, a large, beefy priest; and the

Coccardini, the liberal Philharmonic faction, headed by Barezzi and Demaldè. It got its name from the cockades of French Revolutionaries. Ballarini, a mountain of a man, had disliked Provesi. Stung by the barbed epithets Provesi had launched against him, he was already opposed to Verdi.[38] Critical of Verdi's conduct in Milan and outraged by what he considered the scandals and unseemly behaviour of loose city people, he had accepted applications for Provesi's post, among them one filed in November 1833 by Giovanni Ferrari, the temporary maestro di cappella in Guastalla and candidate favoured by the Bishop.[39]

Ferrari was in Busseto; at the suggestion of Don Ballarini, he had paid a call on Antonio Barezzi and the members of the Philharmonic Society, which had performed a Requiem Mass for Provesi during his visit. At that moment Ferrari was operating from strength, for the interim organist appointed by Ballarini had proved a failure. The people of Busseto, used to hearing good music in church, were angry. On some Sundays there was no music at all. On 22 November 1833 Ferrari had given the Monte di Pietà his application for the post of new maestro di cappella and organist. As it happened, neither the church nor the Monte could move without the other, for the vestry of the church paid its organist such a small stipend that the Monte had to supplement it. Their grant, though, was contingent on the organist's filling the posts of municipal music-master and director of the Philharmonic. The administrative council of the Monte, playing for time, had understood that there was to be an open competition for the post; there was yet a third candidate; and Verdi had not officially applied for the job, for he, too, was waiting for the competition to be announced. Having provided the Monte di Pietà with a certificate of progress in November, he offered yet another letter from Lavigna in February 1834. The second letter altered or falsified the date of Verdi's first lessons with Lavigna to make it seem that he had been studying in Milan longer than he actually had, for the first attestation gives 'August 1832', while the later one gives 'June'. With the crisis in Busseto, even the gift of a couple of months might help.

Verdi's candidacy had been in trouble from the start. In Ballarini and the Bishop of Borgo San Donnino, he had two powerful enemies who were willing to try almost anything to keep a theatre-oriented musician from getting the post. Torn between his studies and Busseto's hopes for him, Verdi was also troubled by the knowledge that his Mass, perhaps that written for the Philharmonic, had not been particularly successful. Lavigna may have urged him to rework it, but he seems to have had no time.[40] No longer the obedient scholar who obeyed his elders and got compliments on his behaviour, Verdi had—according to Seletti—become a somewhat secretive person. He complained about the DuPuys' house, although Seletti said his own could not compare with it, and became suspect for what Seletti called his *maniere villane* (coarse manners). Griping about having to climb the stairs at DuPuys', he had behaved uncivilly when his landlord spoke to him, turning his back on DuPuy as he 'always' had on Seletti and walking out of the building to go for a long walk alone. In a final burst of indignation, Seletti stated flatly that Verdi was a person 'whom I would never have wanted to know'.[41]

At the height of the crisis in June 1834, Carlo Verdi came unannounced to Milan to take his son home. Saying nothing to anyone, Verdi left without telling either Seletti or Lavigna that he was going, leaving his maestro to wait in vain for his pupil. Under pressure from DuPuy, Verdi admitted that 'he was being taken back to Busseto forever by his father'.[42] The landlord was outraged: who indeed were these Verdis, who acted as if his home were an *osteria*? What about the ten months' room and board? Seletti, uninformed, defended himself as best he could. Barezzi's letter, assuring him that Verdi would be back in Milan in two weeks, meant little in the face of the young man's abrupt departure and abandoned lessons. If anyone doubted that Carlo Verdi held the *patria potestà* in the family, his actions made it clear: 'He is being taken back to Busseto forever by his father,' Seletti had written. But Carlo Verdi had good reasons for calling his son home, for Provesi's successor was about to be named. Without Verdi there, the post was lost to him; but with him in town, the Philharmonic, Barezzi, Demaldè, and Carlo Verdi might win the day after all.

June 1834–February 1836

The Busseto Civil War

Disappointment awaited Verdi at home, for instead of being greeted with news of his own appointment, he learned that the vestry of San Bartolomeo had just confirmed Ferrari's nomination as maestro di cappella and organist.[1] It was assumed that he would take over the local music-school as well, for Verdi had not completed his studies. To prevent the pro-Verdi faction from blocking Ferrari's nomination, the church had apparently acted while Carlo Verdi and his son were on their way home. The fabric of clerical conspiracy, said Demaldè, was woven by Ballarini, 'an ambitious, vindictive, and Machiavellian man'.[2] When Verdi's name came up in the vestry meetings, Ballarini deliberately turned away from the speaker, pretending not to hear arguments on Verdi's behalf. Because he had the full support of Monsignor Luigi Sanvitale, the Bishop of Borgo San Donnino, Ballarini wielded considerable power, both locally and in Parma. Sanvitale defended Ferrari as 'more experienced' and referred to Verdi's 'voluble character' and 'youthful hotheadedness', which were 'perhaps not balanced with prudence'. As for Ballarini, he was 'the best of my vicars'. Many of Verdi's adult supporters were dismissed patronizingly as 'boys'.[3] All evidence points to the vestry and the Bishop trying to prevent an open competition in which Ferrari would be defeated.

'Verdi was astonished to hear that the post for which he had worked for years, encouraged by Provesi, his old maestro, [the post] for which he undoubtedly had more talent and more qualifications than were necessary, was destined for someone else.'[4] But Verdi's disappointment seemed mild compared to the fury of the Philharmonic Society members, whose rage grew out of and bred decades of anticlerical sentiment.

When he was asked to explain Ferrari's nomination, Don Ballarini feigned regret, saying that it was a pity that Verdi had not won the post; but because he had never presented a formal petition, the vestry had not considered him. The Bishop took a similar tack; writing to the President for Internal Affairs at the ducal court in Parma, he said:

As for Verdi (protected by the head of the Philharmonic, Signor Antonio Barezzi, who, it is said, wants to give him one of his daughters as a wife, and therefore hopes to wreck Ferrari's nomination by using Signor Molossi), he [Verdi] turned his back on [the nomination]. Verdi did not present a petition; and the afore-mentioned Mayor Signor Galluzzi, before coming to the meeting, asked Barezzi whether he would speak in Verdi's favour; and Signor Barezzi declined several times.[5]

In fact, Barezzi's situation was difficult for Verdi *had* sent an application and letters of recommendation to his patron earlier. It is not sure why Barezzi did not submit them, though he may have thought a competition would be held. It is even possible that his faith in his protégé was shaken by a shocking letter from Seletti denouncing Verdi as ignorant, ill-bred, uncouth, rude, arrogant, dishonest, 'asinine', and 'a rogue'. Seletti wrote:

You, who live with the delusion that Verdi is another Rossini, will be mortified to hear me speak of him in these terms; but you must understand that being a good musician does not make him an honest man; and even if Verdi were to turn out a thousand times better than Rossini himself, I would still say that I found him rude, uncivil, proud, and acting like a scoundrel in my house. I write this to you because he is not yet your son-in-law; and when he becomes that, I will keep my mouth shut rather than lie to you about him. . . . I cannot tell you how much damage he has done to my family, because it is [too indecent] to write about. . . . Don't ever speak to me again about Verdi, nor ask me to do anything for him. Just his name alone is too disgusting to me; I pray to God that I may forget him forever.

Rather ominously Seletti also added: 'And he can be happy that I don't tell you even more.'[6] On the very day that Seletti was writing this, Verdi was in nearby Polesine conducting the Philharmonic orchestra and band in a concert.

No matter how much confidence Barezzi had in his protégé, he must have been shocked by this letter from a man he had known and trusted all his life. Seletti's anger seems to have been fired by Verdi's courting

BOOK I

Dorina Seletti, the professor's daughter, who had left Milan with Verdi in June 1833 to visit the Barezzis in Busseto. The matter was particularly serious as it came when Verdi was understood by everyone, even the Bishop, to be Margherita Barezzi's fiancé. Yet Barezzi remained loyal, joining Demaldè and the Philharmonic in their campaign to get Verdi a post. Soon the partisans put into effect their programme of sanctions against the church, refusing to go to San Bartolomeo or play for any service there so long as Ferrari was organist in Busseto. All the Philharmonic music was removed from San Bartolomeo; eventually some of these scores became part of the collection of the Biblioteca Civica in Busseto.[7] The civil war was on. With the opening skirmishes, Busseto was divided into two parties, involving many of the town's families. Certain shops and taverns became 'headquarters' for the factions and places of rendezvous for partisans.

In the summer of 1834 Verdi began again to work with the Philharmonic, which had suffered from his absence and from Provesi's bankruptcy and long illness. Provesi had despaired for its future, writing to Lorenzo Molossi of Parma, secretary of the Parma Philharmonic Society and member of the ducal government:

This poor Philharmonic Society, which boasts three hundred years of life, is now on its death-bed. That is how things go in the world. Time destroys everything! Poor Busseto Philharmonic Society! It is about to be laid in the tomb. Ignorant people attack it and want it destroyed forever. . . . But let us do everything so that music, at least, does not die.[8]

But Verdi, not Molossi, would save the day. Rehearsals got under way; scores were examined; parts were extracted; the amateur musicians rehearsed in their homes and in Barezzi's grand salon. From Barezzi's Day-Book we learn that on 22 June 1834 Verdi conducted at Polesine, with 'musica e banda'; on 12 October he took part in a grand concert; and on 16 November he performed at Villanova sull'Arda, near Sant'Agata, with his burly baritone Giuseppe Guarnieri; his one-eyed tenor, Luigi Macchiavelli; and Antonio Barezzi himself as his soloists.[9] Verdi was so busy that he had not even had time to write to Lavigna, nor notify the Milan authorities of his change of domicile. Working under great pressure, he also had to face the possibility that he had lost permanently the post of organist in Busseto. The problems associated with his apparently unsuccessful Mass were responsible, at least in part, for his losing the post.[10]

The Campaign for Verdi's Appointment

At least some of the young composer's time was taken up calling on influential people, a task for which he was ill-suited. His supporters at the Philharmonic had, as the Bishop saw, set their sights on several government officials, on whom they hoped to bring pressure to get Ferrari's nomination revoked. Their targets were the ducal bureaucracy in Parma and the local officials in Borgo San Donnino. Letters were sent; and soon Verdi was asked to fight for his own cause, something he appeared to be reluctant to do. On 3 July, at the request of members of the Philharmonic, he called on the Commissioner and his secretary, presenting a letter on his arrival.[11] But Verdi, reticent and shy as he was, was not cut out to pay court to officials. After a short conversation with the man to whom Demaldè had referred him, he left for Busseto, apparently without offering an apology or an explanation. Nor, apparently, would he discuss his visit when he got home. Demaldè then went to Borgo San Donnino himself to repair fences and press Verdi's cause in person, armed with plenty of ammunition, for Ferrari, who had been persuaded by Don Ballarini to move his whole family to town, had given an organ recital at the Franciscan church of Santa Maria delle Grazie and had played so badly that even some of his partisans in the clergy had been embarrassed by it. Demaldè called Ferrari a 'bad organist and worse maestro', an inexperienced musical illiterate, 'Beast, beastliest of all beasts'.[12]

To bolster the petitions being addressed to the Duchess Marie Louise, both Verdi and Demaldè went to Parma on 16 July. After hours wasted in attempting to find out where, exactly, their petitions were and how good Verdi's chances were, the two men were assured that 'a competition will take place'.[13] But only two days later it was rumoured that the competition was a mere formality to seal Ferrari's appointment. Ferrari was pressing Busseto and the Monte di Pietà for his salary, which the Monte refused to pay, claiming that no competition had yet taken place. The priests had hired Ferrari, the pro-Verdi faction claimed. Let the priests pay him. Ferrari went to Parma, together with Don Andrea Pettorelli, whom Demaldè was still calling 'Father Fart-o-relli' in his correspondence.[14]

Tensions were heightened as the annual Feast of San Bartolomeo approached. This was Busseto's liveliest fair and one of its holiest religious holidays, celebrating the saint in whose honour the collegiate church was named. On this occasion, Don Ballarini had engaged 'foreign' musicians from Parma, to take the Philharmonic's place. This, of course, set off a protest, as citizens nursed their wounded civic pride and Busseto was disgraced at having to pay an ensemble from outside the *patria*. The Philharmonic fought back, scheduling a concert of its own; but the clergy was not to be beaten on home ground. It tried to prevent the Philharmonic from playing, as Barezzi and Demaldè sought out the Podestà to ask for a written guarantee that they could appear. This was refused at first. The Philharmonic went on with its plans, until a permit for this lay event was given; members, though, had to promise not to engage in name-calling and fighting, even if they were provoked. This was a lot to ask of a faction that had been embattled for months. September found Verdi still waiting impatiently for the competition to be announced. Some of his works, played by the Philharmonic, had been heard by Ferdinando Savazzini, a respected composer from Parma who appears to have been the impresario for Carnival in Piacenza. He stated that 'in the whole Duchy of Parma there is no musician who can match him; and the spontaneity of his works gives promise of great things to come'.[15] Knowing that Ferrari had gone to Parma, soliciting support at court, Verdi was finally forced to ask the Duchess for a private audience or audition.

To celebrate Verdi's twenty-first birthday, the Philharmonic concert of 12 October featured him as both composer and piano soloist. To ensure its success, the society engaged the conductor Vincenzo Morganti for the programme, in which he also was first violinist. With this, the Philharmonic also took an important step in furthering Verdi's career. Morganti, who lived in Parma, had been engaged by Bartolomeo Merelli, the impresario of La Scala, to act as maestro for the 1834–5 Carnival season of opera at the Teatro Concordia in Cremona. He was later re-engaged by Merelli for spring and autumn 1835. Morganti also played in other theatres, halls and churches.[16] As the first violin for the birthday concert, Morganti rehearsed and heard seven of Verdi's compositions, among them two overtures, one romanza, an original theme for clarinet, two recitatives and arias, and a capriccio for pianoforte. The soprano was Teresa Barezzi Tessoni, like Verdi the recipient of a Monte di Pietà grant; the tenor was the local pharmacist Luigi Macchiavelli; the clarinetist was one of the Philharmonic members; and Verdi performed his own Capriccio. Morganti played his own *Variazioni per violino*. An oboist from the court of the Duchess Marie Louise was the soloist in a fantasia he had written on a Rossini aria. This was the beginning of a solid friendship between Verdi and a major conductor, whom Verdi later called 'my dear

Morgantello'. Later that month, the Philharmonic concluded a three-year contract with Morganti, making him its first violin and orchestral conductor. At the same time, they freed Verdi to go back to Milan.

The clergy was having a hard time promoting Ferrari that autumn, although it had begun an initiative to have him named music master of Busseto. To be paid, he had to teach; but because he had not attracted many pupils, his sponsors 'manufactured' some, bringing in a nephew of a priest who, Demaldè swore, was a usurer, along with an altar boy and someone from Genoa. None was needy, so none was qualified for a scholarship from the Monte di Pietà, although another young music student, Emanuele Muzio, had been granted one. Ferrari, who had a wife and six children to provide for, began to press for payment, thus setting Demaldè off with a claim that the priests were 'trying to steal 357 lire from us, to pay out to an animal [Ferrari]. . . . Since the Provost brought him here, let the Provost pay him.'[17] As no money was being paid out to have the Philharmonic in church, it was Ballarini's responsibility to use the money he had in his till.

With all this, Busseto became a hotbed of strife, with the police constantly on the alert for fights. A report called the tavern of Verdi's baritone Guarnieri 'extremely dangerous' and another *osteria* a site of brawls. Giovannino Barezzi and his mother were involved in an altercation in November 1834, arguing with one of Verdi's enemies, Luigi Seletti, who was so outraged that he wrote to the Podestà to protest. While he was standing by a shop in the piazza, talking to a priest, Don Ubaldo Neri, he was set upon by Giovannino, who called him 'Infamous Old Man' and accused him of talking against Verdi to Don Neri. 'Can't you just mind your own business and look straight ahead?' Giovannino said; 'You said bad things about Verdi to Don Ubaldo; I heard you now, you filthy old tongue, old idiot, old hypocrite!' When Luigi Seletti swore he did not know what Giovannino was talking about, young Barezzi threatened to hit him, and would have done so, had several persons not pushed him aside. At that point Maria Demaldè Barezzi rushed in, insulting him in the same terms, adding: 'You even hate your own children, o, you infamous old man!' By this time a small crowd had gathered, as shopkeepers ran from their counters in time to hear Seletti called a slanderer. His remarks about Verdi, which triggered the entire fracas, concerned the big October concert with Verdi and Morganti: Seletti had observed that while Verdi was good at counterpoint and would become a fine performer, he had gone too far in presenting so many of his compositions to the public without having his maestro go over them first. That, to the Barezzis, was heresy. Had bystanders not intervened, Maria Barezzi and her son would have thrashed him.[18]

During the same week Verdi's staunch supporter Francesco Silva was accused of writing and circulating an insulting sonnet about Don Andrea Pettorelli, whom the anonymous sonneteer called Father Hog.[19] Swearing that he did not know who had written it, and that he did not know who it described, Silva tried to get the accusation lifted, in spite of the fact that he had been overheard reading it to friends. The Podestà Accarini was put on the alert because his own son Ferdinando, a staunch Verdian, had been present when the sonnet was read. But Don Pettorelli was not to be placated; he brought charges against persons unknown, driving the police to question and take statements from six Bussetan tradesmen—this, in spite of the fact that Silva himself was the chancellor of the district court that sat in Busseto! At the end of the inquiry it was determined that not one but two libellous poems about Don Pettorelli were circulating in town. The more insulting one accused him of being a swine who was sleeping with his maid, while preaching public and private morality from the pulpit. Silva's letter to Accarini, written tongue-in-cheek, claimed that a dirty sonnet (*sonnettaccio*) that names no one and is read in private to a few friends cannot injure anyone. Yet the matter got as far as the director of police for the Duchy of Parma, as Accarini lamented the deplorable condition of the city:

Every day here the ruptures and hostility are growing over futile controversies among the good residents of this place. For several months there has continued a very heated dispute between the Clergy and the Philharmonic Society over the choice of a maestro of music. The Philharmonic party is larger. Both can have perfectly sound reasons [for believing as they do], so [they] cannot be budged from their positions. Up to now, my attempts to bring them together in harmony have not achieved anything positive; and they get angry and erupt like volcanoes over nothing.[20]

At one point, even a priest was cursed in surprisingly strong terms as an ignorant hog; his attacker shouted 'God damn you and that bishop who gave you the Mass.' There was also an outcry for Don Pettorelli to dismiss his pretty maid Mariannina, 'in whom he shows a great deal of interest'. The issue, though, was not just the priests, the maid, the sonnets. The real insult was that hurled at Barezzi and at his protégé by Don Ballarini, who invited the Podestà to offer Verdi the post of maestro di cappella and 'be satisfied with the honorarium from the Monte, which is 357 lire a year'. Barezzi, to whom the offer was conveyed, was told that Verdi could manage on that, being single. Barezzi reminded Accarini that Verdi needed to help his parents and had no intention of remaining a bachelor; furthermore, even if Verdi had more money, Barezzi would never advise him to accept 'such a vile insult'.[21]

Ferrari, equally unhappy about this turn of events, thought that half of his position would be taken away from him. No wonder he was writing about 'bad luck' and 'shattered hopes'.[22] The government in Parma finally agreed to announce a competition; and in the mean time the church would have to pay 'the organist chosen by whim'; to ask the Monte to pay seemed 'impertinent'. Molossi counselled Demaldè to tell the Philharmonic members to gossip less and have confidence in the government.[23] But the tumult did not subside. Daring fate, the Philharmonic had presented another grand concert on 17 November, again with Verdi and Morganti. In response, Ferrari announced that he would offer one of his own compositions, a Tantum Ergo, in San Bartolomeo on Christmas Eve. At the beginning, there was a respectful silence in the crowded church, but soon whispers were heard, then mumbling, then laughter, for the 'panthers' of the Philharmonic had recognized in Ferrari's music passages plagiarized from a farce called *Pianella perduta nella neve* that had been given in the theatre in Busseto a year earlier. During the solemn benediction, one irrepressible Verdi partisan made a rude remark that provoked a Ferrarian into attacking him, saying that the church became 'a Theatre of Shame'. The two enemies were separated by bystanders, Demaldè reported, but had someone not intervened promptly, a riot would have followed.[24] Several fights had broken out in the streets. Again, the Podestà Accarini had to answer to the higher authorities, whose attention was drawn to Busseto yet again just a few days after Christmas when one of Ferrari's supporters defrauded Barezzi's clerk out of 7 lire worth of cakes and liquor by presenting a falsified credit slip. He carried off enough loot to feed a large party of pro-church celebrators on New Year's Eve. Dining in Ferrari's house, the revellers created such an uproar that the neighbours protested, as bawdy songs about Barezzi and the Philharmonic rang out in the night. Gossip around town the next day spread the news that Ferrari should have been in deep mourning because of the death of his grandfather only a few days before. Then it got about that the man who cheated Barezzi had just been released from prison. After that, Ferrari's stock went far down.

Verdi's Return to Milan

As early as November 1834 Barezzi had decided to send Verdi back to Milan and take an apartment in Contrada San Pietro all'Orto for him. But this time Verdi was not to be alone, for another of Barezzi's music students was to be his companion and was to be taught by him. This was Luigi Martelli, whom Barezzi had also agreed to support. The apartment, in the palazzo of a Countess De Capitani, was free from 1 January 1835. On 5 January Barezzi, Verdi, and Martelli left for Milan together, on the kind of trip that shows why Demaldè later called the older man a 'maniac' music-lover.[25] After crossing the Po at Piacenza, they went on to Lodi, where they stayed overnight, perhaps with friends, since they did not go to an inn or lodging. They also went to the theatre there. In 1835 Francesco Strepponi was the chief spokesman for music in the city and thus was Barezzi's counterpart as head of the local Philharmonic Society. A composer, organist, and teacher, Francesco had lost his brother Feliciano, who had died in Trieste in 1832 after launching what had promised to be a successful career as an opera composer. Francesco had been left with a certain responsibility for his niece, Giuseppina Strepponi, who was later to play a large part in Verdi's life. She was then 19, a recent graduate of Milan Conservatory, the institution that educated several members of this family. Francesco had launched Giuseppina's career the previous autumn, when he presented her in two concerts in Lodi under Philharmonic sponsorship. When Barezzi, Verdi, and Martelli visited the city, Giuseppina may have been there herself. She was expected in Trieste for her début in opera on 19 January.[26]

Barezzi and the two young men went on to Milan the next day. While he was in the city, Barezzi went twice to La Scala, once to the Teatro alla Canobbiana, and once to the Teatro Carcano. From his expense record, we know that he stayed there more than a week and went out to dinner only three times. Verdi and Martelli, for whom he was providing,[27] moved into the apartment in Countess De Capitani's house; and Barezzi returned to Busseto, banking his high hopes on Verdi. His absolute devotion to Verdi and his control over him were a commonplace in Busseto: writing to the President for Internal Affairs, Accarini described Verdi as being 'young, and, they say, very promising and of extraordinary merit, the creature of Signor Barezzi'.[28] At that time, Barezzi's 'creature' had already begun negotiating through Massini to find a libretto and write his first opera. The previous August while he was at home, Verdi had asked

Lavigna to contact Massini for him, reminding the impresario about 'the libretto that Tasca' was to have written.[29] The librettist was Count Ottavio Tasca, a well-known literary figure in Milan. If Tasca wrote something for him, we do not know what it was. In the mean time Verdi had to get on with his lessons and teach Martelli, who lived with him. As before, Seletti administered all the funds; the two young men, Verdi past 21 and Martelli 20, knocked fairly frequently on Seletti's door, as the expenses soared. Verdi was far from happy with the arrangement and with his student's progress, for he wrote to Barezzi that Martelli was doing badly. This remark infuriated Martelli's relatives, who claimed that Verdi was jealous of the younger man's gifts, at which Verdi protested: 'Eternal God! What gifts?—What if he is not even a beginner in the study of music? That's how it is, and if Signor Barezzi can relieve me of this [burden] I will be half-way happy', he wrote to Demaldè.[30] But he did not get free then, and Martelli caused even more trouble later on.

It seems that by the beginning of 1835 Barezzi was of two minds about Verdi's future. On one hand, he should continue his lessons with Lavigna, the frequency of which Seletti monitored and reported to Barezzi. The chief purpose of these lessons was certification, which would permit Verdi to apply for the late Provesi's post. And on the other hand, the family's position, as represented at least twice by Margherita Barezzi, was that Verdi should not stay in Busseto. In the summer of 1834, when the new mayor asked her about her fiancé's future, she said:

Never, absolutely never would Verdi settle in Busseto; first of all, because if he did that, he would have to interrupt his course of study; second, because having dedicated himself to theatre music, he will succeed in that and not in music for the Church; finally, any commitments he had made to his advantage [in the city] would be useless, and he would even compromise his relations with any [of his] patrons.[31]

Seven months later Ballarini reported to the President for Internal Affairs in the government in Parma that even in Barezzi's shop people talked about Verdi's plan to move to Milan permanently; and 'even Signor Barezzi's own daughter, Verdi's fiancée, stated clearly that once she was married, she would go to live in Milan'.[32]

A conflict between Verdi's needs and those of the Philharmonic developed along these lines at a time when the composer did indeed have 'patrons' in Milan and had agreed to write an opera for the Filo-drammatici. The prospect of life in the city seemed ever more appealing

BOOK I

as local strife in Busseto flared once more. Shortly after the Christmas Eve argument in the parish church, a much more serious brawl broke out after a young organist played a concert in the Franciscan church, as one of Verdi's partisans—one of the ever-faithful Macchiavellis—and a Ferrarian got into an argument. Soon Ferrari intervened directly, then yet another of his supporters ran after Macchiavelli and 'injured him seriously', leading Verdi's supporter to file charges. The lieutenant in charge of the local Dragoons said that Ferrari himself was largely responsible and that he should suspend his activities 'until the matter is finally settled'.[33] It was recommended that Ballarini and his vestrymen be officially warned of the damage they were doing to their own cause. The police intervened, as the Bishop swore that the clergy feared violence: 'Then the two parties will grow and will start a kind of revolution.'[34] A report from the police headquarters in Parma to the Podestà of Busseto named two Verdians and two Ferrarians as fomentors, but added that people in the municipal government were equally culpable. It named cafés and *osterie* that were hotbeds of trouble and warned that the strongest possible measures would be taken to prevent violence.[35] Finally Marie Louise had no alternative but to order all instrumental music excepting that of the organ forbidden in the churches of Busseto. The Philharmonic was limited to its private concerts. Thus a part of Busseto's rich musical tradition was lost.

Verdi and Martelli were well out of Busseto at this time, but they had problems of their own, for Martelli got in some kind of scrape while he was living with Verdi in the new apartment Barezzi had provided for them. That it was serious is clear from his frightened letter to Verdi:

Dearest Verdi and my benefactor,

Lacking enough courage to speak directly to you, I have taken the liberty of writing this letter of mine, in which you will get the answer you expected from me. As you well know, and as I have already told you, I do not want to go home because you can imagine the curses and beatings I would rightly get because of having betrayed my family. So I said that if you have a bit of compassion and pity for me, even though I do not deserve it, because I know that I have offended you—and because of that I beg a thousand thousand pardons—I would ask you to make it possible for me to stay on in Milan. . . . Find me a miserable room and a broken-down piano . . . and go on with our lessons . . . and find a friend who could take me in. . . . Do not abandon me. I can no longer stay in this house because I see that I am no longer worthy to stay with you. . . . Be kind enough to act as you have in the past. [Or] at least keep me in this house until I get a trade of my own. . . . You see that I am 20 years old and, as you see, don't have even

64

the hope of being able to say that I have a profession from which I could live. . . . If you see that I can contribute to your well-being with my lessons (because I cannot do anything more than just the lessons) and with loving you, then we will go on; but if you see that I have not done what I have promised to make you happy, you can throw me out. . . . Oh, my dear Verdi, pity me. At least do that, after so very, very much sorrow that my family (and my friend Barezzi, too) have suffered. . . . If you abandon me, I am lost, utterly lost.[36]

This curious letter throws light on a period in Verdi's life about which we formerly knew almost nothing. Among other things, it shows that Emanuele Muzio was not Verdi's only pupil, as was later claimed; just as it proves that Barezzi, having established his two protégés in an apartment in Countess De Capitani's house, was putting additional money into Verdi's pocket by paying for Martelli's lessons. All evidence points to Verdi's having forgiven his pupil for whatever sins he had committed, for in July they planned to meet in Cremona and return to Busseto together. Sixteen years later they were neighbours, when Verdi moved to Sant'Agata and Martelli, married, was living in San Martino in Olza, on a farm nearby.

While in Milan, Verdi went on studying with Lavigna, although he was not as assiduous as his teacher and Seletti thought he should be. Again he began to spend time with Massini and Merighi and the members of their circle, which was still performing at the Teatro dei Filodrammatici. Although the cellist from Parma played regularly at La Scala, he filled in for Massini on occasion and had a chance to work with Verdi, watching him change from a humble, badly dressed boy to a more worldly musician. At this time his expenses were so large that Barezzi, writing in July, felt that he had to say something about them:

My dearest friend, I want you to know that in the time you have been in Milan, I have paid out 1425.76 lire, a sum far larger than that I spent when you were in Seletti's house: do you remember that you told me that if you were alone, you could make some economies? Now the facts prove that this is not so. But let us forget these sad thoughts for now.[37]

No wonder Barezzi was concerned! The Monte di Pietà grant was for 300 lire a year; but Verdi had spent nearly five times that amount in just over six months, as he adopted what Seletti called Milanese habits, going to cafés, buying books, going to concerts and opera, and, by Barezzi's own choice, living in an apartment in a noblewoman's *palazzo*. We do not know what Verdi saw at La Scala; but in 1834–5 he could have heard

Giuditta Pasta in *Norma*, or Malibran in *Otello*, *La sonnambula*, *I Capuleti e Montecchi*, or *Norma*. Verdi's recollection of Malibran was that she was 'very, very great but not always equal! Sometimes sublime and sometimes baroque. [*He used the word 'baroque' to refer to exaggeration.*] Her style was not always perfectly pure, her action not always correct, her voice strident on top! In spite of everything, she was a very, very great artist, marvellous.'[38] He might also have seen her at La Scala in 1834–5. Works by Bellini, Ricci, Mercadante, and Donizetti made up much of the repertory there in this period. Among the ballets in 1833–4 was *Una festa da ballo in maschera*, which followed very closely the plot that Verdi later used in his own *Un ballo in maschera* more than twenty years later. We do not know what scores he rented while he was a student. Through Massini, he may also have obtained a libretto that spring or summer of 1835, for he seemed busy with matters other than his lessons. Seletti reported to Barezzi that Verdi went to his lessons irregularly, scarcely more than once a week: Lavigna 'did not want to say outright that Verdi was negligent, but . . .'.[39] He had had only thirty-six lessons in seven months.

From Verdi himself (writing much later) we learn that he was again rehearsing works for Massini at the Filodrammatici: 'After Haydn's *Creation*, I helped him many other times, preparing and conducting various productions [among them *La cenerentola*].'[40] The Rossini work earned Verdi his second review in the Milan press: 'Praise to Massini and to Maestro Verdi, who conducted it; praise to the singers who performed it, to the orchestra, to the chorus, to everyone', wrote the critic of the theatrical paper *Figaro* on 8 April 1835.[41] During this same period Verdi composed a Tantum Ergo for Macchiavelli and the Busseto Philharmonic; Demaldè described the concert as 'enormously successful' and Verdi's new piece as combining 'the expertise of the composer, good taste, freshness, elegance, thought, and, all in all, it inspires devotion. The many people from other towns [who heard it] were convinced by it and admire a successful man [Verdi], who is almost polished in his profession'.[42] Don Ballarini's continued opposition, though, provoked Verdi into referring to him that same month as 'that monstrous, black soul',[43] as Demaldè railed: '[Ballarini was] raised in a Dominican cloister where, alas, he sucked that milk that once made the idiots of the world tremble! Oh, how many victims these despicable wretches [of priests] had! Read about the Spanish Inquisition, and then make up your mind!'[44] No wonder Don Ballarini (to use Verdi's phrase) wanted 'to make war on us under any conditions'.[45] Verdi was pleased that his Tantum Ergo had been well received. Fortunately Ferrari had wisely not pronounced judgement on it, as he was 'a man of little heart; and when a man has no heart, even if he were the best man on earth, he will always be base and evil'.[46]

When Verdi did get a libretto, Massini was responsible, according to Verdi's account of 1881:

'Massini, who seems to have had confidence in the young maestro, then proposed that I should write an opera for the Teatro Filodrammatici, which he was directing, and [he] handed me a libretto that later, in part modified by Solera, became *Oberto, conte di San Bonifacio*. I accepted the offer with pleasure and returned to Busseto, where I was engaged as organist.[47]

The author was Antonio Piazza, a writer for the *Gazzetta privilegiata di Milano* and the *Rivista europea*, had also served as tutor to sons and daughters of some of Milan's important families. His own daughter was a linguist.[48]

Unfortunately, Verdi's description of himself is not quite correct, for he was never 'organist' in Busseto; his account sounds as if he had been given Ferrari's post. The truth was quite different. When Verdi came home that summer, he faced yet another long, exhausting struggle. Some time would pass before he won any official endorsement at all. Given his scanty attendance at lessons, he might even have been criticized by his teacher, had his gifts not encouraged Lavigna to remain his mentor. On 15 July 1835, after the end of the performances at the Filodrammatici, Verdi won the certification that he had come to Milan to obtain, as Lavigna wrote:

Signor Giuseppe Verdi of Busseto in the State of Parma studied counterpoint under my direction and has commendably finished his studies of two-, three-, and four-part fugues, as he has also studied canons, double counterpoint, etc. I therefore believe him to be ready to practise his profession at the level of any accredited maestro di cappella. I also add that his behaviour toward me in this period has been extremely docile, respectful, and temperate, even in his habits. I declare that this is the absolute truth.[49]

With this document, Verdi could now legitimately fight for Provesi's former post.

Just as his partisans were overjoyed that their champion had completed his formal studies, so his enemies feared his return. Again controversy shook even the walls of the closed chambers of the city council, where a tumultuous meeting ended as an argument over the Philharmonic Society led members to walk out *en bloc*. Among those voting for Verdi in that crucial session were Accarini, Demaldè, and Pietro Michiara, sen. What the Bishop called 'the fire of discord' continued to blaze.[50] Demaldè, misled by an all-too-brief instant of peace, wrote 'Triumph!. . . There are still hotheads about; but some of the dispositions or measures taken by the police will make that damned gang pull back.'[51] His optimism proved unfounded. Just one month after Demaldè had his hopes raised, the Duchess Marie Louise, angered by the 'scandals in the Temple of God', issued a decree ordering that 'In all the Churches of Busseto, music shall remain forbidden forever.'[52]

Verdi, fortunately, had his mind on something else, as he wrote to Massini that he was at work on the opera: 'I am writing the opera (as you know), and I hope to have sketched out all the numbers before I come back to Milan.'[53] He asked Massini to let him know who would be singing it, so he could compose music suited to the soloists' ranges. Yet he was still drawn sometimes into the local strife; in mid-September a horn-player from a nearby town dared to criticize Verdi's Mass, provoking the composer into challenging him to a duel in 'music theory, practice, and sight reading of any piece of music he might choose'. At this, the critic retracted, declaring that Verdi's compositions 'left nothing to be desired' and that he was 'an extremely capable composer'.[54]

Some of Verdi's supporters, perhaps doubting that he would ever find a niche in Busseto, suggested to him that he ought to seek another position, as he was not even sure of having something to do in town that winter. One post that was proposed, perhaps by Lavigna, perhaps by Massini, who came from Monza, was that of maestro di cappella in the Cathedral there. An important centre of commerce, Monza had just had Feliciano Strepponi as its maestro di cappella; he had left the post to go on to the successful career in opera that was cut short by his untimely death in January 1832. Two years later Lavigna and Basily had served as judges of a competition that still remained open.[55] On 11 October, one day after Verdi's twenty-second birthday, he sent his official application for the post.[56] Because the basilica of San Giovanni was an important church, the salary was 2,000 lire a year, which was supplemented with a house, wood, and oil for light. Further income could come from teaching private pupils. Urged by Lavigna, who believed that Verdi had a good chance at the nomination, he got his documents in order. Knowing that none of the other applicants was willing to submit to an examination, which he would do, he had reason to be optimistic. Lavigna sent word through Seletti that once Verdi got to Milan, 'the business can be concluded in a short time'.[57] Yet neither Verdi nor Barezzi seemed about to leave Busseto. On 14 December Seletti sounded a more desperate note, saying that Lavigna had 'a thousand reasons' for having Verdi in Milan.[58] And Lavigna himself turned on Verdi, who had written him a letter in which there was no mention of the proposed trip or the post: 'I do not understand how you could ever have written me your last note, without saying anything to me about whether you feel like coming to Milan.' At the beginning of his letter, he told Verdi that the vestry in Monza was 'extremely impatient' to see his documents: 'yes or no!!! So make up your mind . . . so I, too, can let those men in Monza know what you have decided.'[59]

But Verdi was virtually a prisoner in his own city, for as soon as the Philharmonic members learned that he and Barezzi were about to leave for Milan, they came out in open opposition to the trip. The incredible tale is told in two letters. The first is from Verdi to Lavigna; it opens with a quotation from Dante:

Esteemed Sig. Maestro,

'Nuovi tormenti e nuovi tormentati' (*New torments and new people tormented*). Just as I thought I was about to get out of so many of my difficulties, and earn an honest income, and [be] comfortable, I again find myself thrown back down into an abyss, from which I can see only darkness. Last Saturday was the day set for me to come to Milan, and because of this I sent an express letter to Parma the day before, to get a passport, when—as word of my leaving got around Busseto— such a protest broke out as you cannot imagine. The party that is against the Philharmonic was overjoyed, and they insulted the [Philharmonic] party, which— in its turn—became angry and hurled insulting words at me and at Sig. Barezzi. Finally the affair got down to the point where the Philharmonic members, after reminding me of [their] commitment made [to me], and [of] the injuries they have suffered, and the benefits I have received from my *patria*, and the new obligation they had taken on to get me 1,000 francs a year, irritated by my refusal to stay here, started to scare me with threats, and—finally—to force me to stay in Busseto, were I to be seen leaving. If my benefactor Barezzi were not (because of me) to suffer the almost general hatred of the whole town, I would have left at once; and neither the reproach about benefits received nor the threats would have had any effect on me, since even though I received a modest amount from the Monte di Pietà to support me in Milan, this grant should not have bought my humiliation and my enslavement; otherwise I would be forced to think that this benefit was not a generous act, but a vile one. For this reason alone I have remained in Busseto; and to this very great sacrifice of mine a new aggravation has been added: that of having committed you and of not being able to respond to all of your many concerns for me; this alone hurts me; and if I could set this right, no matter what the cost, I would do it with much, much pleasure. Having said this, I have nothing to add to my apology. But I assure you that my appreciation and gratitude will be eternal, and if you deign to answer me, I will write you from time to time; and it will be a great honour for me. Perhaps I can come to Milan during the Carnival season, and then we can talk at length about this matter. If at any time I can lend you my services in any way, I will consider it an honour. I beg you to give my good wishes to all your family and I assure you of my esteem and gratitude. I greet you with my whole heart. Your affectionate friend and servant, Giuseppe Verdi.[60]

Barezzi sent Seletti his report a week before Christmas:

I don't know when I have ever found myself so embarrassed or so disgusted as today, because of Verdi. You know all about this business, and the intrigues on his behalf and against him, so he could be settled honourably in the city. . . . A few days ago the government approved a decision of the city council to limit the maestro's stipend to only 687 lire [a year], which made both me and Verdi nauseated; and as soon as I received yours of the seventh, I got Verdi's passport and last Saturday was the day set for our departure to Milan.

As soon as this got around Busseto, such a hubbub erupted as you cannot imagine. Our opponents were overjoyed; and were slandering me as well. Everyone said that it was the blackest ingratitude to put Verdi's interests ahead of the constant sacrifices and the generosity of so many poor souls of the Philharmonic toward him and me . . . [and] through this long struggle, I never had any other goal than that of begin useful, that of the public good. . . . This craziness has reached the point where I am threatened physically, but [the threats] did not frighten me; but if I did not cave in before them, I have to, and Verdi has to, give up in the face of the many, many demonstrations [of support] he has had in the city, and which this very outburst of rage proves. We have had to surrender to this insane will of our friends; and all the more are we compelled to do so because they have opened a voluntary subscription to get an annual stipend for Verdi of 1,000 lire. Verdi and I know how much this sacrifice is costing; but honour demanded that it be made. You yourself will now see the motive that made me refuse the well-paid post in Monza, and understand the bitterness at not being able to take advantage of your efforts and those of Signor Lavigna, to whom Verdi will write about this. It is now certain that Her Majesty has ordered the President for Internal Affairs that both Verdi and Ferrari must go through an examination in Parma, the first to be maestro, the second to remain organist. This is all I can tell you about this, and I beg you to do what you can to make up for this unexpected disaster.[61]

Verdi was thus condemned to stay on in Busseto to wait until Marie Louise would see fit to announce the competition. A pathetic figure indeed, he was a prisoner of his supporters' goodwill; at 22 he could only see further delay in launching himself, getting established in his profession, marrying his fiancée.

On 6 January 1836 he enjoyed a tremendous success when he played an organ recital, his first in the Franciscan church of Santa Maria degli Angeli. Demaldè, whose loyalty never flagged for an instant, boasted that: 'No one ever saw that church as crowded as it was yesterday, and the collegiate church empty. The wretched Provost was astonished and was beating his head against the wall. . . . An enormous crowd came . . . even our opponents.'[62] Two weeks later Verdi saw the posters go up announcing the competition for the post of maestro di musica. The conditions of employment were very strict, for the maestro could not take trips out of the city except during his regular summer vacation, which fell when the music business in Milan was at a dead stop. He was to give five lessons a week to *each* of his pupils, working every day excepting Thursday and Sunday, teaching cembalo, piano, organ, voice, counterpoint, and composition. With a dozen students, all his days and some of his evenings would be filled. Whatever free time he had was committed in advance to the Philharmonic members, whom he would continue to coach, rehearse, and conduct in private and public concerts. Moreover, the maestro had to furnish an instrument of his own for his pupils.[63] Busseto had indeed ensured his virtual enslavement.

Another 'new torment' followed when Barezzi tried to collect his unpaid scholarship money from the Monte di Pietà, so he could recoup a part of what he had spent in educating his 'creature'.[64] Payments of the scholarship had stopped in January 1836, after only a total of 650 lire had been paid of the 1,200 owed; justification for stopping was that Verdi had finished his studies. Barezzi protested, saying that he had begun covering Verdi's expenses about eighteen months before the grant went into effect. He said that Verdi had worked thirty-two months with Lavigna. (This was not quite true, as he had stayed in Busseto for two extended periods during his studies.) The Monte di Pietà answered that they were delighted that Verdi had done so much in such a short time: so much the better for him and for the foundation, which was saving money. The matter remained unresolved temporarily.

Verdi went to Parma during the last week in February, accompanied by Demaldè, who stood by him during the competition. Also at his side was

Ferdinando Accarini, the Podestà's son. At the end of a private concert given on 23 February, Molossi swore 'that he had never heard such a formidable pianist'.[65] The competition on 27 and 28 February found Verdi being judged by Giuseppe Alinovi, a court organist and celebrated local maestro. A Signor Rossi from Guastalla was the only competitor. The result was an absolute triumph for Verdi, who wrote to Barezzi describing the test:

On Saturday afternoon about three o'clock, I went to Alinovi, who examined me in the following fields: piano; singing, accompanying from a score, and sight-reading. First I played my own Variations, which I repeated a little later because Alinovi liked them a lot and wanted to hear them better. Then he gave me operatic pieces, which I declined to play because I already knew them. I then played the accompaniment to a Donizetti duet that was full of mistakes (and I believe they were made on purpose) so that I would correct them as I played; and it went well and Alinovi was very satisfied. To assure the maestro that I was playing even the new pieces at sight, I asked him for something of his own, and he gave me a Laudate that was very beautiful, which I played without any difficulty. With Alinovi I played a Herz sonata for four hands; and he was very happy.[66]

If Verdi's Saturday ended well, his Sunday went even better. Molossi wrote to Barezzi about the examination that day. At eight in the morning Verdi was back in Alinovi's studio to get the theme he was to develop into a four-part fugue. By six in the evening he had it ready. After reading it through, Alinovi rose from his chair and told Verdi how impressed he was:

Up to now, I have carried out my role of vigorous examiner; but now I am your admirer. This fugue is worthy of a consummate maestro, good enough to be published. You are sufficiently knowledgeable to be a maestro in Paris, in London,—not in Busseto. I confess that I would not have been able to accomplish in a whole day what you did in a few hours.[67]

Alinovi called him 'the Paganini of the pianoforte', comparing him to one of the masters of Italian music.[68]

Ferdinando Accarini, the son of the Podesta, wrote:

Our patriot Verdi has finally been chosen. Evviva! Justice will finally put an end to the grave political scandal that erupted in our Busseto . . . You would have thought they were fighting for a kingdom! So let the flags come down; and let hatreds be put aside. That fine young man passed the examination. . . . I am very happy that the factions will be [broken up] and his true merit will be recognized and rewarded.[69]

72

It is entirely possible that Verdi met Paganini while he was in Parma and that he is the brilliant young composer that Paganini recommended to Alessandro Lanari, the Florentine impresario, in a letter of 11 March 1836. From Verdi's (and Molossi's and Accarini's) letters on 29 February, it is clear that he did not expect to leave Parma at once. He was to learn of the unofficial confirmation of his victory on the evening of 29 February, when he returned to Alinovi's house. But Alinovi, who had called Verdi 'the Paganino of the pianoforte', had left little doubt that Verdi would win. On 1 March he sent the official document of confirmation to the Minister for Internal Affairs. During that same week, at the end of February and the beginning of March, Paganini accepted the nomination as head of the Ducal Orchestra, engaging Vincenzo Morganti for the first violin section. And on 11 March he wrote to Lanari, asking him to produce the opera of 'a fortunate young man who is gifted with an extensive understanding of the arts and sciences, and especially of music, in which he is a trained, elegant composer, who hopes only to win a name for himself and hopes you will be the one to help him in his first step in that direction.' Paganini went on to describe the 'new opera', 'which this gifted young man from Parma will create', as being set in England in the 1400s. From Verdi's letters to Massini, we know that he was sketching out the pieces for either *Lord Hamilton* or *Rochester* at the end of 1835 and the beginning of 1836. But Lanari evidently was not interested, perhaps because Paganini said that the young composer 'wanted to keep the ownership of the score for himself' and that he wanted to finish his composition after he knew who his singers would be.—Two Verdi trademarks! Nothing came of the project.[70]

6

Spring 1836–September 1838

An Appointment, an Engagement, and a Marriage

Verdi was named maestro di musica on 5 March 1836.[1] The peace that some hoped that nomination might bring was slow in coming, though, for Sanvitale, the Bishop-Nemesis of Verdi and the Philharmonic, persisted in his harassment of the organization's members, whom he described as

bad-mannered people in general, and some [of them] not examples of the true Christian morality; this comes . . . from the fact that they saw from the outset that they were being treated well and constantly had the support of some authority. Because of that they became overbearing; first they demanded one thing, then another; and then they got to the point where they gave orders in church, saying 'We do not want this music, we want this other [music]'.

He was far along toward his stated goal of killing forever any hope that the Philharmonic might cherish of performing in the churches of Busseto. 'The Seculars today are bad for [holy places]; and Blessed God cannot welcome singing from their profane lips.'[2] But not even the Bishop could dull the enthusiasm of the boisterous men of the Philharmonic, whom Verdi continued to direct, while working on his opera for Massini. He declared to the Podestà,

I have been an impassive spectator in this long battle. Immersed in my chosen study of music; and, almost forgetting the battles, I awaited Justice, which finally came. . . . I put my faith in the magistrates' wisdom, in the integrity of a legal decision . . . Everyone knows that I did not get mixed up with the factions, that I never fomented trouble, nor went against any of them, that I have never been so evil as to take pleasure in these battles. . . . Neither my adversaries not my competitors ever had, or shall ever have, any reason to suspect that I intrigued against them.[3]

His good name and character were attested to by Pietro Frignani, a local physician, who, writing to Marie Louise's chamberlain, Baron Bianchi, described Verdi as 'a young man of the highest quality, enormously honest and worthy of esteem, who has perhaps sacrificed his only chance for success and fortune because of the goodness of his character, his love for his *patria*, and his loyalty to his friends'. It is a glowing recommendation, but Frignani also knew the other side of the coin: the 'friend' who had supported Verdi for so long—Antonio Barezzi—could 'get tired' of such a burden.[4] It seemed that he might indeed have to go on, for Verdi's salary, which might have been adequate for a bachelor, might not prove enough for a young married man.

As everyone expected, Verdi and Margherita Barezzi became officially engaged on 16 April 1836.[5] Four days later Verdi signed his contract as maestro.[6] At the office where Verdi and Margherita made their Declaration of Intent to Wed, they had her parents and his father with them: 'Verdi Carlo, innkeeper, property owner, age 50, living at Roncole; and Signor Barezzi Antonio, son of the late Giovanni, age 48; and his wife Signora Demaldè Maria, daughter of the late Francesco, age 48, property-owners and shopkeepers, both living in Busseto'.[7] Verdi's mother stayed at home because she was ill.

Verdi and Margherita, or Ghita, as he called her, were married on 4 May 1836, the bride's birthday, by that wicked and sprightly Ferrarian, Don Pettorelli, who was writing *Gli uccelli accademici* ('The Birds of the Accademia', referring to the Philharmonic's private concerts, or *accademie*), a jocular poem about Barezzi, Demaldè, Verdi, and their friends.[8] Edging toward the salacious, Don Pettorelli cast Barezzi as The Great Blackbird, Verdi as a Parrot, Margherita as a Dove, and the lesser Philharmonic members as Sodomite-Blackbirds. Not even Maria Demaldè escaped, for she was described as the seamstress-mother who hastily added 'four rags' to her daughter's dower-chest; the marriage was, Pettorelli said, delayed because Ghita's dowry was not complete. Some of the clothes were made of scraps of cloth bought on the cheap. Demaldè was the Weaver of Conspiracies. The hapless Ferrari was a Cuckoo; Pettorelli, in his long black cassock, was the Owl. The dangerous left-wingers at the wedding-party left 'the door open' for Mazzini!

As soon as the ceremony ended, the entire Philharmonic Society and their 'relatives and friends were invited to Casa Barezzi for the wedding celebration. The newly weds sat at the head of the table. . . . It was a day of true jubilation and universal satisfaction.'[9] A married man, Verdi left for his honeymoon with his bride and his father! Their destination was Milan, where the wary Seletti opened his house to what Barezzi called 'my daughter and her company'. To say that the Verdis were welcome would be an overstatement, for Seletti had written to Barezzi: 'I shall never be able to like Verdi; but your daughter and all the others in your family are dear to me, as you can imagine. But although I did say that I do not like Verdi, I did not say that I never wanted to see him again.' He added that his 'bed will be fine for the newly weds'.[10] The arrival of Carlo Verdi too may have been hard to take, given Seletti's past troubles with him. At the end of the trip, Verdi, his wife, and his father came home, so the new maestro could get back to his musical troops, who saw him as a living, local legend, a cause. It is not hard to imagine that his young students held him in some awe, for a struggle that lasted three years had been fought over him. His music school, which could have been an oasis of peace in a small market city, was instead a field of triumph, cleaned up after the battle.

According to his contract, Barezzi had the right to evaluate the students seeking admission and pass judgement on them. Verdi, overburdened from the start, had to provide a 'decent house', keep a ledger and records on all students, test them with written exercises, and make up missed lessons if a national or religious holiday fell on one of his work-days, giving up his own free day or days to compensate for the lost time. He was extremely lucky to have a music-teacher and singer for a wife, and luckier still to have a father-in-law who provided the couple with a fine apartment in Palazzo Tedaldi, a noble building that still stands (recently restored) near the Busseto Library and the building where Verdi had attended Ginnasio.[11] Because Stefano Barezzi's charcoal portraits of Margherita and Verdi probably date from their wedding, we can see the young couple as they were: he, serious and vulnerable; and she, alert, with lively eyes and a touch of humour in her expression.[12] Verdi had perhaps taken on too much work: besides his professional duties, he had to carry out the duties of head of family, and keep records on the help and his personal expenses as well of those required by his profession. Hercules Cavalli left an account of the young music-teacher:

During the three years when Verdi was maestro di musica, almost every Sunday after Vespers, the band [of the Philharmonic Society] played Verdi's music in the public square in Busseto, to the immense joy of the people, who were proud of their maestro and adored him. As maestro, paid by the Monte di Pietà, he wrote Masses, Vespers, and Benedictions, taught his own music to his chorus and orchestra, and even found a way to [get round the church's ban] and get his compositions played, to spite his rival. The Month of Mary [May] was celebrated with Verdi's music at a little chapel called the Madonnina Rossa, a chapel that was in fact completely independent of the Provost and the collegiate church, belonging to the Franciscan friars . . . and there on Sunday mornings were performed the young composer's motets. Afterward the band assembled in the piazza; sometimes when the band appeared in the piazza, [Verdi's partisans] would set off fireworks.

In the Franciscan church, the most beautiful Gothic monument [in the city], which then belonged to the Pallavicini family, Verdi's Masses and other important works were performed. When he went to play the organ in this church, and when he played his own compositions, the collegiate church was empty, and all the faithful attended Benediction and Mass in the Franciscan church. The Franciscans, opposing the clergy of the city, openly took the side of Barezzi's protégé.

Verdi's fame was so great that he was in demand everywhere. All the cities and towns around Busseto—Soragna, Monticelli d'Ongina, Castell'Arquato—wanted him at any cost. They would send omnibus carriages for Verdi, his singers, and his instrumentalists, to take them to whatever city had managed to get him for the day. There they would play Masses and Vespers, and the band would then play and accompany the solemn processions. Crowds of people from the country would pour into the towns, enormous gatherings came together, the response was tremendous. Unheard-of triumphs resulted. What a welcome they gave Verdi and those who went with him![13]

Verdi thus enjoyed a remarkable popularity and regional celebrity. His new marriage was somewhat tried, though, shortly after he and Margherita settled in Palazzo Tedaldi, when a fresh quarrel broke out over Barezzi's claim against the Monte di Pietà. All through the previous autumn and winter, friction over it had troubled everyone involved, for Barezzi had at one point threatened to sue Carlo Verdi for the money that was owed him by the Monte. Over these families there still hung what Verdi's father referred to as the threat of legal action. The idea that his father and father-in-law might face each other in a court of law was indeed troubling, for Barezzi was claiming a very large sum from the Monte di Pietà, saying that he had spent 2,572 lire and 68 centesimi to keep young Verdi in Milan.[14] Carlo Verdi, too, had helped with his son's expenses, and was still struggling to pay his delinquent rent account to the church of La Madonna dei Prati. To Verdi's humiliation, the entire controversy was made public when the Monte appointed a mediator to examine the several claims, thus inviting gossip about the matter. A summary of Verdi's activities was drawn up, and it was favourable to him: he had made remarkable progress in his lessons and had had glowing endorsements from both Lavigna and Alinovi; he was an excellent piano-teacher, surpassed by none in the Duchy; he was teaching thirteen pupils instead of the six or seven that had been anticipated; they were making praiseworthy progress; he was also teaching members of the Philharmonic; he was tireless in his profession and had completed an opera that might perhaps be heard at the Ducal Theatre in Parma; he had also written countless other works, all of which were worthy to be played anywhere, even before Marie Louise; his manners and morals were beyond reproach; his father, who had petitioned the Monte di Pietà, had financial problems, given the large debt he had incurred with Barezzi for the musical instruction of his son; the salary now paid to Verdi was so small that now that he was married, and now that he was forbidden to play in church and could not count on that extra source of revenue, he was unable to put aside any money to give to his father; he could not furnish his house or buy the instruments he was required to provide. If this debt were not set to rights, the Monte di Pietà would not 'have the honour of calling Verdi its own, *which it will very much want to do, when he reaches the heights.*'[15] All the glorious words came to little: it was agreed that Carlo Verdi would be paid 550 lire at the end of 1837, for the commission was sure that Barezzi, who was described as 'Carlo Verdi's creditor', would not mind the delay.

Although he had scarcely begun the first three-year contract of his nine-year term, Verdi was already at the end of his patience with his home town. Complaining to Massini that he was 'wasting' his youth 'in a void', he asked in October whether the post in Monza was still open, as he hoped to escape from 'a little city where there are no resources for anyone who wishes to make music his profession, no hopes for advancement, far from the city [of Milan]'.[16] He must have been desperate indeed to have opened the old, embarrassing matter of the Monza fiasco; but he was much burdened, for Margherita was expecting a child in the spring. With his meagre stipend, he could not even meet his present obligations; with a baby, new expenses would have to be covered. In September he had finished his opera composed to Piazza's libretto *Lord Hamilton*, which may have had as its source a work by Sir Walter Scott about James Hamilton, the Earl of Arran. Verdi wanted to see it produced; but Massini replied that he could do nothing. Lavigna had died in September 1836 in Milan. Despairing, as he replied to Massini's answer, Verdi acknowledged that

'We will not be able to do anything this year.'[17] Two weeks later the school term began again, with thirteen scholars, sixty or more lessons every week, and the Philharmonic concerts to be rehearsed and conducted. Verdi may have got another libretto from Piazza. Called *Rochester* (as Demaldè spelled it) or *Rocester* (as Verdi spelled it), it may be *Lord Hamilton* under another name. By this time certain of his supporters from the Philharmonic Society were putting pressure on him to get out of Busseto, as 'they urged him to stop being so obsessed with isolation and solitude and not to sacrifice himself as maestro to a few pupils and as director of a little orchestra'.[18] This touches on a very real inner struggle between his desire to achieve fame, to be someone, as he said, and his own shyness and the difficulty he had when he was expected to be outgoing. Now that he had a completed score, why not try to get it produced in Parma, if it could not be given in Milan? Suggestions were made along these lines, for Demaldè enjoyed some influence in the Ducal capital.

During the first spring of his marriage, Margherita had a child, a daughter, on 26 March 1837. She and Verdi named the baby Virginia, after Alfieri's tragedy of the same name. It was a republican drama. To name a child after its leading female role was to make a statement that no one could misunderstand. Verdi was still making his own declaration with his Mazzini-style beard, which was the object of admiration in the city.[19]

On his twenty-fourth birthday Verdi went to Parma, as he had told Massini he was going to do, bolstered by Demaldè's supportive acquaintances, to see officials who might bring pressure on an impresario to produce his opera, after they heard all or part of it in some salon of the city. But even after a full week of campaigning, he had to admit that he had failed. Toward the end of his visit, he even tried to write to the sovereign herself, although 'my name and my humble talent are perhaps unknown to Your Majesty; but I have faith and confidence that I can please Your Majesty'.[20] No audience, accademia, or private hearing was planned, so Verdi turned to the impresario of the Teatro Regio, who said straightforwardly that he could not gamble on a new score by an unknown composer. Verdi was so surprised at not being able to arouse any enthusiasm that he thought at first that some of his enemies had got to the theatre before him and turned the impresario against him; but finally he had to acknowledge that he simply could not convince anyone to take such a risk. Again he turned to Massini: 'Tell me, couldn't you possibly talk to Merelli to see whether [the opera] could be produced in some theatre in Milan? . . . Perhaps you could haul me out of this vacuum, and I will be eternally obliged to you. Get together with Piazza and discuss it.'[21]

Merelli, who then ran La Scala, was also a director of the Kärntnerthor Theatre in Vienna. Born in Bergamo in 1793, he had been the private pupil of Simone Mayr, Donizetti's teacher. Three years older than Donizetti, Merelli served as his librettist, agent, friend, and producer. He also wrote librettos for other composers as well. While Verdi was studying with Lavigna, Merelli ran a theatrical agency near the office of Cirelli, Boracchi, and Robbia in the Piazza del Teatro dei Filodrammatici. By 1834 Merelli had become an associate of Duke Carlo Visconti di Modrone at La Scala; in the autumn of 1836 he became the impresario there, and, later, employed the lame Robbia ('that infernal cripple', wrote Boracchi) as his aide. Verdi seems never to have met Merelli and perhaps had not even met his librettist, Piazza. Having formed the habit in adolescence and youth of letting others act in his behalf, perhaps because of his shyness, he managed everything through Massini, who became his eyes and ears in Milan; but in spite of Massini's professionalism, nothing seemed to bring Verdi's problems to resolution. December passed as he continued to give lessons and direct concerts, filling the winter evenings with the Philharmonic rehearsals for Carnival–Lent concerts in Busseto.[22] The programmes, some of which were given at the Teatro Comunale in the old Rocca, included works by Rossini and Meyerbeer as well as Verdi's own new compositions. As in the past, his usual soloists were Guarnieri and Macchiavelli.

Although Verdi seemed to have given up on Parma, Demaldè still hoped that something might be accomplished there; unwilling to let the matter slide, he still pressed the case for Verdi's opera at Court and among men like Molossi, his trusted friend. In April, though, another rebuff came from the Teatro Ducale: '[They] cannot say anything definite because the impresario does not want to produce [Verdi's opera] and is in bad humour because he cannot pay his bills,' Molossi wrote.[23] Marie Louise planned to be away for the summer, so there was no point in another appeal to her. Molossi advised Demaldè to let the matter drop. Easter came and went in Busseto with the Philharmonic still forbidden to take part in Good Friday rites; 'Poor Busseto', Molossi wrote, tongue-in-cheek, 'what ever happened to your Miserere, your illuminations of the city, your bands, and your night-time procession on Good Friday'?[24]

Verdi's *Sei romanze*, six songs composed during January and February

1838 for voice with piano accompaniment were somehow fitted into his crowded schedule. A new sinfonia by him was played at a Philharmonic concert on 4 February; another sinfonia and other compositions were played in another concert on 18 February; it was followed by a third *accademia* one week later, during which the composer again presented his own works.[25] Perhaps a trip to Milan in May was connected to his *Sei romanze*. The six songs, written to poetry by Vittorelli, Bianchi, Angiolini, and Goethe, were done while Verdi was collaborating with the local doctor Luigi Balestra, who provided Italian translations of the German poems. They are: 'Non t'accostare all'urna', 'More Elisa lo stanco poeta', 'In solitaria stanza', 'Nell'orror di notte oscura', 'Perduta ho la pace', and 'Deh pietoso, o Addolorata'. They were published the same year by the Milanese house of Giovanni Canti.[26] While he was in the city, Verdi probably pushed once more for a production of his opera, perhaps through Count Opprandino Arrivabene, an influential journalist he had met in 1836 or 1837.[27]

Margherita stayed at home, awaiting their second child. This was a son, Icilio Romano, named—as his sister had been—after a character in Alfieri's *Virginia*. Again the couple made a liberal and patriotic statement with the names. Their joy of July turned to grief in August, when Virginia, then 16 months old, died. They were helped and consoled in mourning by Pasquale Dinelli, Margherita's uncle, who also did errands and may have paid some of their bills. With Verdi's annual vacation at hand, they decided to visit Milan together, leaving the new-born with a wet-nurse. Dinelli took care of things in their absence. Lacking funds for the trip, Verdi again appealed to Barezzi, to whom he wrote on 5 September:

Dearest Father-in-law,

Since I have been in Busseto, I have always tried to inconvenience you as little as possible, and I believe that I have never been troublesome. Now, against my wishes, I must bother you. You know that Ghita and I are going to Milan, and not just for pleasure, but for business relating to my profession. I will have to stay there the entire period of my vacation, and the money I have in hand is not enough to keep us there. All things taken into account, I would have to have between 129 and 130 francs. If you were to give me this sum, I will, on my return, have my monthly stipends to use, and I will give you a note for that much, and keep the remainder for myself. This would be just a simple advance [on your part] and not a long loan. If you will give me this, I beg you to tear up this letter, keeping the thing a secret between us. Rather, for maximum secrecy, you could refrain from entering this debt in your Day-Book, because I am very, very, very anxious to repay you, as your daughter is also. I salute you with all my heart, your son-in-law G. Verdi.[29]

The composer's request that Barezzi destroy his letter and keep the loan a secret suggests that someone in the family or in the shop may have been troubled over the large amount of money that Verdi's patron had already spent and had not yet begun to recover. It is odd, too, that the composer, not wanting anyone to know that he was asking for help, wrote to his father-in-law rather than simply walking two blocks down the street and speaking to him directly. This he could easily have done, unless he was too embarrassed to do so. Barezzi did not destroy the letter, which his heirs later found in a packet with other early letters from the composer to him. He must have lent the money for the trip, for Verdi and Margherita left Busseto a few days later, putting their maid Gigia in charge of the house, the spinning, and the wet-nurse who was taking care of their new-born son. The trip, which took one day, was made on 8 September 1838, when Verdi's fortunes finally began to change.

7

Autumn 1838–Autumn 1839

Milan

Festive Milan, its churches hung with scarlet and gold silks for the visit of the Emperor and Empress of Austria, was crowded and noisy when Verdi and Margherita Barezzi arrived. Reviews of troops, military parades, bands, plays, ballets, grand balls, and banquets kept the city alive by day and by night. As always, the established theatrical scenery designers were commissioned to produce decorative illuminations in their workshops. Among these was Scenografie Sormani, founded that year and still in existence. The firm produced sets for Verdi's works throughout his life and was the first to build scenery in Italy, under his direction, for important tours of his works abroad.[1] La Scala was already open for the autumn season with operas by Rossini and other composers on the programme. Also scheduled was a ballet with a biblical setting: *Nabucodonosor*, with Domenico Ronzani as Nabucco and the celebrated Antonia Pallerini as Abigaille. It was a time of rejoicing among Italian patriots in Lombardy, for the Emperor had granted pardons to some of their co-conspirators who had been sentenced to long or life terms in Austrian prisons. Although the amnesty was not wholly unexpected, it evoked expressions of gratitude and joy from many Italians. One of these, Temistocle Solera, a librettist and composer who was two years younger than Verdi, had been told that his father had been amnestied and would be set free. Solera's hymn *L'amnistia* was given at La Scala, where Verdi may have heard it.[2]

When Verdi and his wife arrived in the city on the evening of 8 September, they could find neither a room for themselves nor a stable for their horse. In desperation, they appealed to Seletti, who took them into his house and gave them what the composer called 'an apartment with a lot of freedom', welcoming them as he had during their honeymoon.[3] Verdi may have again been in an awkward situation in the capital, with little or no money; he was waiting for funds from Barezzi, who forwarded two packets of money to his daughter and son-in-law. For Verdi, as for his musical wife, this was a business trip. We know that the composer expressed a desire to go to La Scala, but have no way of knowing whether he actually got tickets. It is clear, though, that he was promoting his interests, yet even after ten days in the city, he had no news that he could send to Barezzi about the 'very, very important business' that had brought him there.[4] We do not know exactly whom he saw, but Massini and the cellist Merighi were likely sources of help. So was Francesco Pasetti, an acquaintance of Massini, a Milan-born engineer and man of property who was then 40 and was living with his sister near the Conservatory.[5] Passionately fond of opera, Pasetti became one of Verdi's early supporters and, over many years, acted as his advocate in dealings with Merelli and the publisher Giovanni Ricordi, as the composer was gaining in reputation. After Pasetti married, his wife and daughter became Verdi's friends.

Verdi wrote home to his partisans on 6 October, to squelch rumours that were circulating in Busseto to the effect that his opera was going to be given in Milan very soon:

What the devil has got into your heads, that you think my opera is to be staged on the fifteenth of this month? I never said nor wrote that. This is one of the usual beauties! Oh, what daydreamers you are! I will tell you frankly that I came here to make a deal about the opera, but the season was too far along, and, since three operas had [already] been given, with a cantata and three other operas still to come [and] already promised to the audience (an immense job), there is no longer enough time to get mine produced in a dignified way, as is required. Perhaps it will be given in the next [Carnival] season; but it is a matter of a new work, written by a new maestro, to be shown in nothing less than the foremost theatre in the world; I want to think about it a great deal more.[6]

Before the end of their stay, Verdi had received enough encouragement to convince him that he might be able to make a career in Milan. The fact that someone in Busseto learned that his opera might be produced at La Scala reinforces the belief that he had support at the highest levels of his profession, otherwise it would have been impossible to aspire to a début in such a theatre. He had been given the courage to make a drastic change in his life, for he decided to cancel his contract with the City of Busseto and move his whole household to Milan, just as Margherita Barezzi had declared to the Podestà of Busseto he would do. She was about to carry through the plan Provost Ballarini had described in 1835 and 'go to live in Milan' as Verdi's wife.[7] Indeed, it even seemed difficult for them to leave Milan that autumn, for they postponed their departure, although Verdi was already late in reopening the music school. But Busseto would not contain him and his ambitious wife much longer. Although his contract did not expire until the following spring, they planned to leave permanently as soon as he could get free.

Soon after they got home, Verdi wrote a bitter letter to the Podestà:

I see clearly that I cannot be useful to this wretchedly unhappy home town of mine; and I am sorry that circumstances do not let me show what I want to accomplish in this place, where I was first given the chance to make progress in that art that I profess. The need to earn an income large enough to cover my family's needs forces me to decide to look somewhere else for what I cannot have in *patria*.[8]

He gave notice of resignation on 28 October, resolved to leave Busseto for a precarious future, the riskiest imaginable for a man of 25 who had a wife and child to support, large debts to repay, expectant parents hoping to see him in a steady job, and a troupe of partisans at his elbow. At a time when he had scarcely begun to earn a living as the head of a small, city music school, where he could have remained in reasonable security for nine full years, he left to follow the hope that his opera might be produced.

Early that winter Verdi began to disentangle himself from the music school and from the Philharmonic Society. After Christmas packing began; and on 6 February 1839 Verdi and his wife and son moved to Milan, to a future that held some faint hope for success. He described the event many years later:

I stayed in Busseto about three years; with the opera [*Oberto, conte di San Bonifacio*] finished, I started out for Milan again, taking with me the complete score in perfect order, having gone to the trouble of copying out the score and extracting all the vocal parts myself. But here the problems began: Massini was no longer the director at the Teatro Filodrammatico, so it was no longer possible [for him] to give my opera. However, either because Massini really had confidence in me, or because he wanted to show his gratitude to me in some way—for after Haydn's *Creation* I had helped him on several other occasions, rehearsing and conducting various performances (including *Cenerentola*) without ever asking to be paid at all—he was not discouraged by the difficulties, but told me that he would do all he could to have my opera performed at La Scala, at the benefit performance for the Pio Istituto [Filarmonico].[9]

Of *Oberto*, Verdi also wrote: '*Oberto, conte di San Bonifacio* was altered and added to by Solera, on the basis of a libretto entitled *Lord Hamilton* by Antonio Piazza, a government employee [who was] then a writer of *feuilletons* for the *Gazzetta [privilegiata] di Milano*.'[10]

Demaldè, although he does not mention *Lord Hamilton* by name, does refer to two operas Verdi had written before the spring season of 1839.

A friend of his wrote for him a libretto called *Rochester* [*sic*] and [Verdi] finished the score in the spring of 1838. What became of that work one cannot say. However, it seems that the librettist was not sufficiently pleased with the poetry and that he therefore stood in the way of the production, since he was making his début in the great Teatro alla Scala with the opera *Oberto, conte di S. Bonifacio*, which, as his first work, won deserved praise from the cultivated Milanese audience.[11]

The fate and indeed the existence of *Rocester* has been argued by scholars for decades.[12] We know that Verdi referred to one of his operas as *Rocester* in his letter of 21 September 1837 to Massini;[13] we know that he said that *Lord Hamilton* became *Oberto*. The current consensus is that *Rocester* and *Oberto* are closely linked, and that Verdi wrote just one opera, modifying it as time went on; but it is also possible that Demaldè had it right.

In this period of his 1839 residence in Milan, he succeeded in getting more of his music published. His three songs with piano accompaniment were an aria called 'L'esule', to Solera's verses, on the then-popular theme of the loneliness of the exile; a romanza called 'La seduzione', written, as some of Verdi's earlier songs were, to a text by Dr Luigi Balestra; and a 'Guarda che bianca luna: notturno', to a text by Vittorelli for soprano, tenor, and bass, with flute obbligato. A short review of these works appeared in *the Gazzetta privilegiata* on 13 April: 'Maestro Giuseppe Verdi has added to his other admired compositions a new work that is an inspiration and an enchantment of delicate sound.'[14] The notice, perhaps inserted by Piazza, was helpful to the young composer in his new situation. It was a short step forward; yet Verdi still had no firm commitment for *Oberto*, as we see from the letter he wrote to Demaldè, for he had entered into negotiations far enough to have a company of singers proposed to him; but they did not suit him:

The advice you offer about my opera is absolutely right and as soon as I got to Milan and heard what the singers were like, I got out of the affair at once, although it cost me a great deal of disappointment. In my place, Maestro Speranza of Parma will write. Poor young man! I wish him good luck, but I doubt very much that he will find it. My score is still packed away, but it is not asleep. In confidence I will tell you just these few words: *Perhaps it will be given at the Teatro alla Scala with Moriani, Ronconi, la Strepponi, and la Kemble.* I cannot be sure of this, but I hope for it. . . . That's enough. I will write to you about it straight away, perhaps within the week.[15]

We have no way of knowing what theatre Verdi had been offered or who the singers might have been, for it might not even have been in Milan. Demaldè remained in constant contact with Parma and, as we know from a later letter, was involved in negotiations with the major theatre in Piacenza as well. But it is clear from his letter that Verdi was opposed to compromise. Better to have his score at home in his desk than to have his chances for success endangered by a poor company. On this, at least, he and Demaldè were in perfect agreement. But his decision left him with little or no income. Unless either he or Margherita was teaching music, they must have been dependent on Barezzi for everything.

Oberto, conte di San Bonifacio at La Scala

Verdi's fortunes took an upward turn very shortly after this hopeful letter was sent to Demaldè. In the late spring, the composer got a firm commitment from La Scala. The singers' parts were then distributed; and, nearly three years after he first tried to get one of his works staged in Milan, rehearsals began.[16] If, as Demaldè wrote, Piazza had prevented Verdi from producing *Rocester* because he was preparing to present an opera composed to the better of his two librettos, then it seems that *Oberto* was taken from *Lord Hamilton,* as Verdi said it was. Both he and Piazza were working in Milan, where Piazza, a government employee writing for the most important newspaper, was helping Verdi. The younger man, an untried composer, would have been foolish to defy someone who could have done him harm. He may at some point have inserted pieces from *Rocester* in the score of *Oberto,* making use of the earlier work in that way. This would account for the fact that traces of *Rocester* are found in the *Oberto* score.

His opera was, as he had expected, to be put on for the benefit of the

Pio Instituto Filarmonico, a foundation established in 1782 by Count Ercole Castelbarco and two other noblemen to provide financial aid to widows and surviving children of professional musicians and music teachers of the city of Milan. The work chosen for the annual benefit was given several times during the regular season of La Scala, most frequently during the important season of Lent. On the evening of the Pio Instituto Filarmonico benefit, the orchestra of La Scala played for nothing; and the musicians' fees, plus the box-office returns, were given over to needy widows and orphans. Because the charity was popular among the Milanese, a composer need not fear that he would not have a good box-office for his première. Massini undoubtedly had taken all this into consideration before deciding to press the case of Verdi's *Oberto*.

Verdi could never have hoped for better singers than Merelli offered him. For that particular stagione, La Scala had two very famous artists under contract: the tenor Napoleone Moriani and the baritone Giorgio Ronconi, both of whom were at the peak of their careers. Moriani, the handsome 'Swan of the Arno', was 33, and a veteran of scores of performances. Unlike other colleagues, who had made their débuts in the provinces, the Tuscan Moriani had made his début in 1832 at La Scala itself. By 1839 he was an important interpreter of Donizetti, called 'il tenore della bella morte', whose death scenes drove audiences to frenzy. It was said that he also boasted a strong high C in full voice.[17] Ronconi, no less an artist, was born in Milan into a large theatrical family; he was one of three brothers who sang professionally, all having been taught by their father Domenico, a tenor and voice-teacher of considerable reputation. Giorgio Ronconi was justly celebrated for the beauty of his voice, his sensitive phrasing, and his acting skills. For Verdi, as for Donizetti, he proved an important asset, a powerful, dramatic artist who brought melodrama to life. Like Moriani, he often sang in Donizetti's operas; like him, he sometimes worked through the impresario Alessandro Lanari in Florence.[18]

The third member of the cast proposed to Verdi was the most vulnerable at that time. Giuseppina Strepponi was driving herself to the limits of her resources in 1839 and finding that stress, overwork, and pregnancies were already taking a toll on her voice. A full account of her early life is given in the chapter on *Nabucco*. Here it is enough to note that the soprano was caught in a tangle of personal problems that must at times have seemed beyond solution. Her father's premature death had thrust on her the burden of helping to support her mother, who had had five children, some of whom were living with her at 105 Contrada della Guastalla in the Parish of Santa Maria della Passione. One daughter had been placed in the Lodi Orphanage before 1834. Davide, 22, was studying medicine at the University of Pavia. Maria Antonietta, then 20, lived with her mother Rosa, who was described in Milan civil records as 'a woman of property' and 'well-off'.[19] Strepponi was already being managed by Cirelli, Boracchi, and Robbia, who had a valuable singer in this intelligent, gifted young woman; but their greed and her need and popularity kept her singing almost constantly. When she did interrupt her schedule of performances, it was for childbirth or recovery from break-down. When the management of La Scala was giving out the parts of Verdi's opera to its singers, Strepponi was recovering from the birth of her second child, Giuseppa Faustina, who had been born during the second week in February 1839 in Florence, just six hours after her mother finished singing *Il giuramento* at the Teatro Alfieri. Because she had sung literally until the day the baby was born, everyone knew that Strepponi had been pregnant; but because she, Cirelli, and Lanari's employees hid the fact of Giuseppa Faustina's birth, no one knew that she had survived. The baby was put in the turnstile for abandoned infants of the Ospedale degli Innocenti in Florence just before her mother left the city to keep a singing engagement in Venice.[20] Cirelli, not at all sure that he was the father, eventually accepted paternity.[21] He also believed that he was the father of the soprano's first child, Camillo, who had been born in Turin in January 1838. Strepponi, then, went into rehearsal at La Scala weakened and suffering from post-partum problems that Cirelli did not hesitate to air with Lanari; her condition was aggravated by the fact that she had given birth twice in less than thirteen months.

The soprano made her début at La Scala on 20 April in *I Puritani* and was handed her music for *Oberto, conte di San Bonifacio* at about the same time. Although she was still ill, she was, Cirelli said, 'much better' though afflicted with 'the consequences of the *last unfortunate accident*, which has left her with problems that are hard to cure'.[22] In spite of everything, she proved again that she was the mistress of her art, an excellent musician and fine actress. Because of its stars' reputations, expectations ran high for that season at La Scala, where it seemed that Verdi's promise was about to be fulfilled.

BOOK I

The 1839 Spring Season at La Scala

When Merelli announced the schedule, Bellini's *I Puritani* was the most important production on the programme.[23] Rehearsals for it were barely under way when Ronconi's father died, casting a pall over the artists, for the old man was a beloved, familiar figure in the house.[24] But grief was not the impresario's major concern, for Moriani, his first tenor, was suffering from throat trouble that threatened the entire season. After some difficulty, he agreed to go on singing.[25] Merelli reported to Lanari, with whom he corresponded regularly, that the first two acts of *I Puritani* were 'immensely successful', but that Moriani's voice failed in the third act.[26] During the second performance, the tenor had to withdraw after the first act, forcing Merelli to close the theatre. It seemed that as soon as one singer's problem was solved, another arose. Because of casting problems, Merelli substituted *Lucia di Lammermoor* for *I Puritani*, which was not restored to the programme until the end of April. Moriani, who had returned to the cast, pleaded indisposition during the performance and refused to sing his last duet with Strepponi. One day later Ronconi fell ill and had to be replaced. After the impresario patched a new cast together, Strepponi had to miss performances. On 30 April she declared that she could not sing that night, but Merelli convinced her to go on; one day later, she, too, was in bed sick. Although we do not know exactly when Verdi's rehearsals for *Oberto, conte di San Bonifacio* began, we do know that some were held; but Moriani's continuing illness finally forced Merelli to change his plans for the new opera. His season was beginning to turn into a financial rout. 'The signori are beginning to leave for the country', he lamented to Lanari,[27] referring to the annual exodus of Milanese families to their villas to the north and east of the city. Not even the success won by Strepponi and Ronconi in *L'elisir d'amore* generated enough enthusiasm to make the patrons change their plans. Merelli described the opera as 'Ne plus ultra', but added 'It does me no good because it is a success that comes too late.'[28] Too late for him meant too late for Verdi as well, for no impresario could stage a benefit for the charitable institution called the Pio Istituto Filarmonico at a time when its rich patrons were out of the city.[29] Worse, Merelli had no dependable tenor, for Moriani had fled in mid-season. He did return to sing the final performances of *Lucia di Lammermoor*, but even these did not go as planned, for the soprano Adelaide Kemble pleaded illness at the last moment and Strepponi was substituted for her.

In spite of all the adversity, Strepponi scored a real triumph at La Scala. In *L'elisir d'amore*, her vein of humour gave her an absolute mastery of the role; she emerged as a comic actress, supported by Ronconi.[30] After this opera, she received offers from impresarios, Merelli said, adding that among these was his own bid, a two-year contract at 40,000 lire a year, plus the expenses of travel and lodging.[31] Even this did not satisfy the soprano, who felt the two impresarios—Merelli and Lanari—were exploiting her.[32] She later refused all future engagements in Milan, advising Lanari that she did not wish to be booked there again. Because she was not booked that autumn at La Scala, she did not continue to rehearse *Oberto, conte di San Bonifacio* and therefore did not sing its world première.[33] But in learning Verdi's music, she had come to like it and had 'spoken very favourably' about it, as Verdi later recalled. Ronconi, too, had been impressed with it.[34] Thus Verdi's name and his style were fixed in their minds, winning him two important advocates, even though Merelli decided that he would not produce Verdi's opera that season.[35]

This meant the collapse of Verdi's hopes, for with La Scala closed and summer approaching, he knew that he would not see his opera staged in Milan. In despair, he prepared to take his family back to Busseto, where the old, painful strife still raged on.[36] In February 1839 the recently appointed bishop, Giovanni Neuschel, had written to the President of Internal Affairs to complain that 'the departure of Signor Verdi from Busseto' had not brought tranquillity to the town. The Philharmonic members, he said, were still profaning 'church music' by turning it into 'theatrical music' and substituting 'profane words' for the 'Holy words' of the text. He also kept up his campaign to prevent the Philharmonic from performing anywhere except in theatres and private homes, in the hope of excluding them from the popular open-air events for which they were justly famous.[37] In March he had tried to enforce a rule preventing music in any chapels or oratorios where the Philharmonic appeared; he also had to forbid the playing of opera overtures in church before or after the Mass, after the Epistle, during the Offertory, Elevation, or Benediction. The music during Vespers must not be taken from operatic scores! Nor should the Philharmonic be paid, as it regularly was; it should play 'for the honour of God', the Bishop said. He also mentioned the ongoing scandals and unrest.[38] In April, angrier still, the Bishop railed to the Duchess herself about 'sacrilege' and 'evil practice' that were raging to such an extent that not even 'Divine and human laws' could end them. Verdi is referred to as 'il noto soggetto' (the well-known person) whose accession to Provesi's post had meant additional 'injury' and 'villainy' directed at the clergy.[39] The Philharmonic men 'fomented discord' and committed 'indecent, daring, and irreligious acts' against public order. Offensive posters were still going up; Silva, who was still the Chancellor of the Court, was accused, together with other Verdi partisans, of being responsible. As this continued, Verdi was in the process of abandoning his career in Milan and returning home in defeat.

The Première of *Oberto, conte di San Bonifacio*

What the composer did not know, apparently, was that Merelli had not rejected *Oberto* out of hand, but had simply decided to postpone the production until autumn. When the confusion of the spring season's closing subsided, he sent for Verdi to talk about producing the opera later.[40] As Verdi recalled in 1881:

I was truly stuck and was getting ready to return to Busseto when one morning I saw come to my door a member of the staff of the Teatro alla Scala, who said to me in a gruff tone of voice: 'Are you that maestro from Parma who was supposed to give an opera for the Pio Istituto? Come to the theatre; the impresario is calling for you.' 'Really?' I cried. 'Yes, Sir, he ordered me to call the maestro from Parma who was supposed to give an opera. If it is you, come.'

And I went.

The impresario then was Bartolomeo Merelli: one evening backstage in the theatre he had heard a conversation between Signora Strepponi and Giorgio Ronconi [and] she was speaking very favourably about the music of *Oberto*, and Ronconi agreed with her.

I presented myself then to Merelli, who told me in no uncertain terms that because of the favourable information he had had about my music, he wanted to produce it during the next season. If I accepted his offer, I would have to make some changes in the tessitura because he no longer would have all four of the same artists that he had had earlier.

It was a good offer. Young, unknown, I happened to meet an impresario who dared to put a new work on stage without asking me for any kind of underwriting, underwriting which, in any case, I could not possibly have given [him]. Merelli, taking the risk of covering all the expenses of the staging out of his own funds, only offered to divide half and half with me the money that he would get if, in case of a success, he could sell the opera.—Nor should anyone think that he made me a hard proposition: it was an opera by a beginner![41]

It was indeed a very advantageous proposition. He had not only Merelli's help, but also his practised hand in the revision of *Oberto*, to make it more stage-worthy. The impresario, a librettist himself, made certain suggestions about the Piazza libretto and sent Verdi to Solera, who was then living in Casa de Marchi, across from La Scala in Corsia del Giardino.[42] The second-act quartet was added at Merelli's suggestion; Solera wrote the words for this new number, which, Verdi later admitted, was the most successful of all the pieces in the opera. The collaboration of librettist–impresario and poet–librettist–composer helped *Oberto* toward success.[43] Verdi and Solera may also have worked together on other projects that spring, as Verdi's song 'L'esule', was written to a Solera text, Encouraged by the interest in him and his music, Verdi looked for another, perhaps better, house in Milan. He took an apartment at 3072 Contrada di San Simone, in the Parish of Sant'Ambrogio, not far from Seletti's.[44] But rent had to be paid, and Verdi had no funds. On 4 September he appealed to Barezzi for money for it and 'other things I need' because 'having to write for the Opera, I cannot get money anywhere else'.[45] He asked for 350 lire.

If I could get by without asking this, I would. I swear it. You know what my hopes and goals are. Not, certainly, the hope of accumulating wealth, but that of being something among men, and not being a useless tool like the others. If I were not to get from you what I ask, I would be like a man swimming in water and seeing the bank that he is trying to reach, and is just about to reach, but . . . his strength fails and he dies. Confident of your generosity, I thank you in advance; and, hoping to embrace you soon, I send you my regards.[46]

Although his father-in-law responded promptly, it was not with money of his own. Barezzi appealed to Baroness Eroteide Soldati, the wife of a prominent government official who was later the President of the Council of State in the restoration government of Carlo II of Parma. The Baroness, who had a villa at Sant'Andrea near Busseto, knew both Barezzi and Verdi; the composer was later reported to have had an affair with her.[47] Verdi moved on 29 September.

Soon after this crisis, the Verdis' infant son Icilio Romano came down with a disease that even Milanese doctors could not diagnose. He lingered between life and death for three weeks, during which money was again short. By 20 October Verdi and Margherita had exhausted all their financial resources. A new debt was then incurred when the composer signed a promissory note to Marianna Barezzi Garbi, his sister-in-law, for

55 lire, 2 gold Parmese Napoleons.[48] Two days later on 22 October the child died of bronchial pneumonia. He was not quite 18 months old. Surprisingly, he is entered in the Stato Civile of 17–24 October 1839 as 'Giuseppe Verdi, age 1 year and 2 months'. 'The poor little boy, languishing, died in the arms of his utterly desolate mother', Verdi said in 1879.[49] Icilio was buried from the ancient Milanese basilica of Sant'Ambrogio. The death of their second and last child left the young couple alone with their grief at a time when Verdi was facing his first real trial in the theatre, burdened with debt. He may have asked Pasetti to cover the cost of having the *Oberto* parts copied, when they were prepared by Ricordi's copyists earlier that month.

Oberto, conte di San Bonifacio had its première at La Scala less than one month later, on 17 November 1839, more than three years after the date Massini and Verdi had hoped to give one of his works at the Filodrammatici. Merelli gave Verdi three first-rank singers, Antonietta Raineri-Marini, who sang Leonora; her husband Ignazio Marini, bass, who sang the title role; and the tenor Lorenzo Salvi, who sang Riccardo. The composer's own appraisal of the event, made more than thirty years later, was: 'It won a success, which, if not very notable, was at least great enough to warrant a certain number of performances, which Merelli thought he might increase by giving a few beyond those of the subscription.'[50] On 26 November Giovannino Barezzi, Demaldè, and other Verdi partisans from the Philharmonic came to the opera, vindicated at last by seeing their friend's work on the stage of Italy's most important theatre.[51] For them, as for Margherita Barezzi and her parents, the première was the culmination of their long, shared, expensive battle to establish Verdi in the ranks of operatic composers. Although the opera was not, as Verdi observed, an absolute triumph, it was stage-worthy, bearing his own accent, that voice of his that would keep his works alive long after those of many of his contemporaries had sunk into oblivion. Even so, he was criticized for certain aspects of it. In the *Gazzetta privilegiata* one critic remarked on the lack of fire and creative imagination, observing also that Verdi should pay more attention to the quality of his melody and distinguish more clearly which melodies are suited to Church music and which are right for the theatre.[52] The critic of *La moda*, writing after the fourth performance, gave the opera a very favourable review, saying that he felt the music had sometimes touched upon the sublime. The composer had won his artistic battle with his own weapons and had nothing to fear.[53] The opera's success can also be measured by two extraordinary reviews in foreign papers, one in the *Allgemeine Musikalische Zeitung*, which was published in Leipzig, the other in the *Revue et gazette musicale de Paris*. The critic of the former even declared that Verdi had established a turning-point in music with his opera, although he faulted Piazza, 'a local journalist' who had created a 'barren plot'; and Solera, who was dismissed as an 'apprentice man-of-letters' who had also been composing music.[54] The success of this opera can be measured by its fourteen performances that season and by the many curtain-calls Verdi got during the première. While it did not make him a celebrity overnight, it did establish him as a valid composer who was supported by a cadre of Piazza's and Solera's friends as well as by his old body of enthusiasts from Massini's Società Filarmonica.

According to Verdi's recollection, Merelli made him a generous offer on the morning after the première,

a proposition that was lavish at that time: he offered me a contract for three operas to be written at eight-month intervals, to be performed either at La Scala or in Vienna, where he was also the impresario; in return he would pay me 4,000 Austrian lire per opera, afterward dividing the profit from the sale of the scores half and half with me. I accepted the contract at once; and soon afterward Merelli left for Vienna, commissioning the poet [Gaetano] Rossi [librettist of Rossini's *Semiramide* and Mercadante's *Il bravo* and *Il giuramento*] to furnish me with a libretto, and this was *Il proscritto*.[55]

The impresario also seems to have mentioned the composer's gifts to Giovanni Ricordi, the head of the great Milanese publishing-house. Tito Ricordi, Giovanni's son, wrote about *Oberto* just eight days before the première; 'Soon we are going to hear another opera, which a certain Maestro Verdi is writing.'[56]

After the première Ricordi secured the rights to the new opera for 2,000 lire, which Verdi, according to the agreement he had made, divided half-and-half with Merelli. This established Verdi with Casa Ricordi, the house that published almost all of his operas and represented him until his death.[57] The bond between composer and publisher spanned the tenure of Giovanni Ricordi, his son Tito, his grandson Giulio, and his great-grandson Tito II or Titino, bringing Verdi into a correspondence that continued until 1901. It also brought him whatever little protection was offered to authors' rights in the middle of the nineteenth century, for even as early as 1839 Ricordi was paying for notices in theatrical papers, warning pirates that the firm would sue if their composers' scores were illegally copied. Casa Ricordi was by the 1830s the largest music publishing house in southern Europe. Giovanni Ricordi, its founder, had left his father's occupation of glass-making to study the violin. Later he had become a first violinist and maestro concertatore at the small Teatro Fiando in Milan, working to supplement his income by acting as a music copyist under the portico of the Palazzo della Ragione. Born in 1785, he was about the age of Verdi's father. By 1804 he had negotiated an important contract with the Teatro Carcano, where he was also a copyist. When the contract was renewed in 1806, it carried a clause that was to turn the fortunes of Italian composers: 'NB The orchestra scores will be Signor Ricordi's property when the performances are finished.' On this was built the firm's huge music library; Giovanni Ricordi learned some of his trade in Leipzig, where he studied the publishing techniques used at Breitkopf and Härtel. He returned to Milan with a press that reproduced scores from engraved copper plates. By 1811 Ricordi was the official publisher for Milan Conservatory; by 1813 he owned 800 scores. In 1814 Giovanni Ricordi published his first catalogue and became official prompter and copyist at La Scala, having signed a contract that stipulated that he could make commercial use of the scores of new works presented there. Two years later he signed a similar contract with the Teatro Re. He bought the complete archives of La Scala in 1825, a treasury of unimagined proportions. With a new shop opposite La Scala, another in Piazza del Duomo in Florence, and a third in London, he was in business at an international level, selling not just music but portraits of musicians and books and instruments as well. In 1827 Ricordi provided twelve illustrations for Manzoni's novel *I promessi sposi*. Affluent and respected, he also showed a concern for composers that led musicians to trust him at a time when exploitation of composers by plagiarism was common. He even asked the Austrian governor of Milan to enter negotiations with other governments for authors' rights. Verdi found in Casa Ricordi a valuable source of support. As early as the third week in November 1839, one piece from *Un giorno di regno* had been assigned to one of Ricordi's engravers; before the end of the month, five other pieces had been assigned. These were for the vocal score; three of them were published on 9 December. Others followed later in 1839. Piano solos were assigned in 1839 as well. As Luke Jensen has pointed out in 'The Early Publication History of *Oberto*: An Eye toward *Nabucco*', work on the vocal score began 'almost immediately after the première.' Further, 'Ricordi's decision to continue publication of works based on *Oberto* attest to its continued success.'[58]

With the production of *Oberto*, Verdi was plucked from the middle-class world of the Barezzis and Selettis and thrust into the theatre, a crude place that was sometimes considered barely better than a circus-arena or carnival field. Few singers were invited into the houses of the titled and the rich; socially they almost never were included in what was thought of as respectable circles, although they were asked to perform for private musicales and were given gifts such as jewellery as payment. Liaisons among theatrical people were frequent; it was sometimes difficult for a young woman to make her way without becoming the mistress of an agent, conductor, or impresario. The theatre, like a monastery or convent, had an idiom all its own. It was driven by money from many sources, among them the box-office and the payoffs and kickbacks from those who worked in or around it. Rich patrons were a steady source of income. In this tough world, a young composer had to consider the critics, claqueurs, stagehands, wardrobe mistresses, stage-door guards, and a small army of lesser lights who could make or break his opera. At times the composer ranked far down in the hierarchy, which was ruled by the all-powerful impresario and controlled to a surprising extent by theatrical agents. Famous singers merited consideration because they filled the box-office till. Front-desk instrumentalists who also taught at major conservatories were respected by all. But some composers were grouped with the maestro al cembalo and the maestro concertatore as journeymen. Into this rather corrupt empire of the stage came Verdi, wanting—as he said—to be something among men. To survive he would have to become resilient and strong. Later he learned to impose his will on the theatre and turned out to 'be something' beyond even the wildest dreams of his partisans. Yet he was able to conduct his sixty-year adventure with the theatre without ever being completely assimilated into it. Aloof, reserved, he managed never to be turned into a true-blood denizen of backstage. Just as he had remained above the disorder in Busseto, often by letting others act for him, so he stayed remarkably clear of the turmoil of the boards. Although, as John Rosselli has pointed out, he was not entirely alien to 'that old opera world', he was able to emerge as the

composer who could not only dictate terms but could impose himself as an autonomous artist, entitled to his privacy and able to create away from the world of the theatre. That was the difference between the young Rossini, who stayed at his impresario's house and composed the opera with the opera company laughing, talking, singing around him, and Verdi, who insisted on staying at an hotel and kept the impresario at arm's length.[59]

BOOK I

To live fully in the theatre was quite beyond this difficult, reclusive man; but it did not take him long to learn all he needed to know about earning his living there.

At least one fairly objective reviewer believed that Verdi might look forward to a significant career. This was the Milan correspondent for the *Allgemeine Musikalische Zeitung*, whose report on *Oberto* appeared in February 1840. Although it is too long to reproduce here, it is worthy of some notice.

The second [new work of the season] (17 November), called *Oberto conte di San Bonifazio* [*sic*], by Maestro Giuseppe Verdi was unusually well received and created a certain kind of small sensation here; how long it will stay in the repertory, only time will tell. . . . [The librettists were] a local journalist [Piazza] and an apprentice writer who has been composing for some time [Solera]. These gentlemen are mentioned here also because both, through their many friends, were able to contribute significantly to the good reception given to this opera. . . . [*A review with musical examples follows.*] This opera, commissioned originally for the Pio Istituto dell'Orchestra of La Scala, has made its author's fortune for now. It is said that Sig. Merelli . . . has signed a contract with Sig. Verdi to compose two other operas for Milan and one for Vienna. . . . Those who disparage Mercadante have got to the point of asserting that he, Mercadante, —God forbid!—ought to take lessons from Sig. Verdi. . . . It remains to be seen whether [Verdi] will be able to push himself even higher; we hope very much that he will, because he could surpass all his colleagues.[60]

8

January 1840–Autumn 1841

Bereavement

1840 began well with news that both the Teatro Regio in Turin and the Carlo Felice in Genoa wanted to give *Oberto*, which Merelli also planned to produce in Vienna. Verdi wrote to Demaldè on 5 January:

After half a century I finally get news from you and am happy to hear you are completely well again. You advise me to go to Turin [where the Carnival season had already begun] and I think I will stay in Milan, in spite of my desire to see Turin, get to know [Felice] Romani and pocket 10 or 12 *zecchini*, net, after all expenses are paid. These are all good, but I do not want to spoil the impresarios.

Nor did he readily accept Demaldè's suggestion that he produce *Oberto* in Piacenza; he would only go there, he said, if the impresario commissioned him to write a new work, as his former pupil Luigi Martelli had told Barezzi he might. As for Parma, the Teatro Regio 'would go from bad to worse because that impresario does not know his business. An impresario must never leave the choice of the operas to the singers.'[1]

After Merelli handed him Gaetano Rossi's *Il proscritto*, Verdi found, perhaps to his surprise, that inspiration did not come as he might have expected. As we shall see, he may have given it to Solera to revise. Merelli, returning from Vienna, learned that nothing had been done on it. According to Verdi's account to Ricordi, he said he was dissatisfied with it. In mid-May Merelli advised the management of the Imperial Royal Theatres that he would give Verdi's *Oberto*, Nicolai's *Il templario*, and a comic opera by Nini in the coming autumn season. The programme was soon approved; but within weeks it was changed, as Verdi had been asked to write a comic work to be substituted for *Oberto*. That plan, too, was approved.[2] Merelli asked Verdi to choose among several librettos, all of which he found unsatisfactory for one reason or another. Forty years later he recalled that he had chosen the 'least bad', *Il finto Stanislao*, later called *Un giorno di regno*.[3] For the second time in a matter of months, he faced a work that he found unsatisfactory. This opera had already been composed unsuccessfully by Adalbert Gyrowetz in 1818. As Roger Parker has pointed out, we need not assume that Verdi 'felt alienated from his subject matter and consequently produced a mediocre score', for 'considerable alterations' were made to the old libretto. 'Unless very strong evidence appears to the contrary, we must assume that Verdi himself had a hand in these alterations' and that he was perhaps helped by Solera. Parker suggests that the work 'might well be placed more firmly in the mainstream of Verdian development and be seen as a coherent, logical step in his progress as a dramatic composer' rather than as a special case.[4]

Because so little evidence is available, and because so much of what Verdi said to Lessona and Giulio Ricordi is questionable, little indeed is known about the composition of *Un giorno di regno* and *Nabucco*. But by comparing other early accounts and Verdi's own, we can perhaps understand something of what happened.

Verdi's account to Giulio Ricordi describes—according to what Verdi said—the events of late April or early May 1840.

As soon as I began to work, I was struck down with a severe sore throat, which kept me in bed for many long days. I was just beginning to get well when I remembered that the rent was due in three days, and I needed 50 *scudi*. At this time, even if this amount was not small, it was not a large sum either; but my painful illness had prevented me from taking care of it in time, nor did the communications with Busseto (the post went twice a week) give the chance to write to my excellent father-in-law to get that amount of money quickly. I wanted to pay the rent on the date it was due, no matter what the cost, so, even though it troubled me to have to ask a third party, I still decided to give the engineer Pasetti the job of asking Merelli for the 50 *scudi* needed, whether as an advance on my contract or as a loan for eight or ten days, that is [for] as long as it took to write and get the money back from Busseto. It is useless to go into the reasons why Merelli, through no fault of his own, did not advance me the 50 *scudi*. I was furious at letting rent-day come and go without paying, even if the delay were only a few days; and my wife, seeing my distress, takes the few gold things of her own, and leaves the house. Somehow she manages to get together the amount we need, and she gives it to me. I was deeply affected by this loving act, promising myself that I would repay everything to my wife, which I was quickly able to do, given the contract that I already had.[5]

As often happens when we try to reconcile Verdi's narrative with the facts, it is difficult to establish a chronology of events. Because he and Margherita were living at 3072 Contrada di San Simone, in an apartment filled with furniture brought from Busseto, it is likely that their rent was paid either in quarterly or in semi-annual payments. Their lease began on 29 September 1839, the Feast of San Michele, with at least a quarter (if not a half) paid in advance out of the 350 lire Verdi had borrowed from Barezzi. Subsequent payments would have been due on 29 December, 29 March 1840, 29 June, and 29 September. Verdi does not say which payment was about to fall due when Margherita made a loan against her gold jewellery; but it can only have been 29 March, as she did not live until the end of June. This cannot be made to fit with what we know about the composition of *Un giorno di regno*. His account does reflect his anguish at being too poor to pay his rent, of having to appeal to Pasetti to act as his go-between with Merelli, and of having to promise himself that he would repay Margherita, who had become yet one more of his creditors in the Barezzi family.

He then suffered another devastating personal loss, when she was stricken with a disease that, according to the civil records, was 'rheumatic fever'.[6] She must have been ill for at least five or six days, for Barezzi was notified and was able to get to Milan just before she died. In his Day-Book, he wrote:

From a dreadful disease, perhaps not known to the doctors, there died in Milan at noon on the Feast of Corpus Domini, in her father's arms, my beloved daughter Margherita in the very flower of her youth and at the peak of her fortune because [she was] the faithful companion of the excellent young man Giuseppe Verdi, maestro di musica. I beg for peace for her pure soul, even as I weep over this tragic loss.[7]

Of himself, Verdi said: 'A third coffin goes out of my house. I was alone! Alone!'[8] Funeral services were held at the basilica of Sant'Ambrogio, from which Verdi's and Margherita's son Romano had been buried just eight months before. Soon afterward Barezzi and Verdi went back to Busseto together, arriving there four days after Margherita died.[9] Masses for her continued to be said in Milan.

Demaldè described Verdi as being so severely depressed that 'his profound sorrow led him to give up everything completely and forever. He thought of nothing but hiding himself in some dark place and living out his miserable existence.'[10] He swore that he would give up his career, leaving *Un giorno di regno* unfinished. The 'dark place' was perhaps his old room in the courtyard of Barezzi's house, where he raged against his fate until those who knew him thought he was going mad. He let Merelli know that he had no intention of returning to Milan and finishing the opera, which was scheduled to go into rehearsals in August. But Merelli, in a difficult position, would not release Verdi from his contract. Verdi had to go back to Milan.[11] There he returned to his little apartment near the Carrobbio, to a world that was irretrievably lost. There were the prim walnut sofa and side-chairs, the empty beds, all the furnishings of the home he had shared with his wife and son. Some months later, in November, he had these shipped back to Busseto,[12] but he seems to have kept in Milan the spinet made by Gualtiero Anelli, that his father-in-law had given him, with its inscription: 'To Giuseppe Verdi from Antonio Barezzi 1832.'[13] His purpose in coming to the city was to break his agreement with Merelli. Perhaps if the impresario had been less pressed, or if Verdi had not finished part of the opera, Merelli might have released him; but *Un giorno di regno* was already announced. Verdi had no choice but to go on. According to Demaldè, there were at least four strong pieces in it.[14] The rest of the score may have been written in as little as six weeks as Verdi, distraught with grief, worked on.

Un giorno di regno was the second opera of the season, preceded by Nicolai's *Il templario*. As was customary, the composer helped with rehearsals, which cannot under any circumstances have been easy. Two members of his cast, Salvi and Raineri-Marini, had sung in his *Oberto* the year before; but as they prepared *Un giorno di regno* the soprano was—as Merelli described her to the authorities—recovering from an unspecified illness. It was rumoured that she did not want to sing at all and was not as committed to it as she might have been.[15] On the night of the première, 5 September 1840, both she and Salvi sang somewhat spiritlessly, at some points just mouthing the words in an undertone while the orchestra played. They thought it safest to 'spare their voices', said one critic, and 'they reduced by half the effect of some of the pieces that were perhaps not entirely bad'.[16] In spite of everything, Verdi got some applause; among his singers, the best was the young soprano Luigia Abbadia, then 22, blessed with a fresh, beautiful voice. An occasional laugh came in response to the basses, Agostino Rovere and Raffaele Scalese. Verdi liked Scalese a great deal and, when they were both old, supported him and his family with regular gifts of money.[17] But on the whole, his singers seem not to have done the best they could for his opera. Some of the numbers were received with catcalls and whistles: he never forgot the pain of the experience. The next day Merelli announced that *Un giorno di regno* would not be performed again, giving Raineri-Marini's illness as the official reason for the closing. Verdi, called to the impresario's office, expected to be criticized; but Merelli urged him to take heart. Understandably the critics noted Verdi's failure, saying that his opera was derivative and barren of humour and sparkle. 'A real mess', said one important critic.[18] Only two writers mentioned the 'sad events suffered in [the composer's] family life'[19] and 'the cruel and unexpected misfortunes that came without pity to destroy him'.[20] But their compassion could not make up for the agony. Words written nearly twenty years later show how deeply he was hurt: the audience

abused the opera of a poor, sick young man, harrassed by the pressure of the schedule and heartsick and torn by a horrible misfortune! . . . Oh, if the audience then had—I do not say applauded, but had borne that opera in silence, I would not have had words enough to thank them.[21]

He continued more generally:

I admit the severity [of the audience]; I accept its whistles, on the condition that I am not asked to give back anything in exchange for its applause. We poor gypsies, charlatans, and whatever-you-want-to-call-us are forced to sell our efforts, our ideas, our ravings, [getting paid in] gold. For 3 lire the audience buys the right to whistle or applaud us. Our destiny is to resign ourselves to the situation; that is the whole story.

In another letter recalling this fiasco, he wrote:

At 25 I already knew what 'the public' meant. From then on, successes have never made the blood rush to my head, and fiascos have never discouraged me. If I went on with this unfortunate career, it was because at 25, it was too late for me to do anything else and because I was not physically strong enough to go back to my fields.[22]

Giovannino Barezzi, who was with Verdi in Milan on the night of the première, took back to Busseto the news that *Un giorno di regno* had failed. Among the anti-Verdians there, Don Pettorelli described the fiasco in lines seemingly added to *Gli uccelli accademici*. In this section, Parrot-Verdi dies, killed by the Duck (Teresa Barezzi Tessoni) because he laughed out loud during a concert when her voice cracked on a high note.

Dove-Margherita survives him and stands dry-eyed at her husband's coffin while the Owl reads a funeral oration. Verdi's fall is commemorated by the epitaph Don Pettorelli wrote:

> Here lies the Parrot, who, among his peers,
> Was glory, honour, genius—so they say.
> With his rare—indeed, unique—gifts
> He left the world a precious memory.
> He reigned alone as King and scorned his enemies,
> But his reign lasted but a day, one may say.
> Unable to survive, he died,
> Miserable wretch, in the flower of his youth and talent,
> Laid low by the rage of the Duck.
>
> . . .
>
> Oh, Traveller, bow your head
> And pray for him, as he lies here in his grave.[23]

The reference to the one-day reign, 'un giorno di regno', was a parting shot. Don Pettorelli closed by having the Sodomite-Blackbirds of the Philharmonic gather after 'their grief over the Parrot had worn off'. Barezzi, the Great Blackbird, exhorted them to swear revenge for the Parrot's death; but as they were swearing their oath, Jove turned them all into insects, so that Cuckoo-Ferrari could swoop down and fill his belly with 'a Blackbird Dinner'. At last he had disposed of the feared 'Patriots', the Church's nemesis.

Curiously, it was the failure of *Un giorno di regno* that kept Verdi in his profession and guaranteed, in a way, the continuation of his career, for Merelli, looking for another work to put on the programme in its place, remembered that he still had scenery for *Oberto* in the warehouse and that he had two of its singers under contract. By scheduling it, he opened the door for Verdi to stay on in Milan and oversee it. The opera came back to La Scala on 17 October and was welcomed by the same audience that had whistled *Un giorno di regno*. It got seventeen performances. According to Verdi's (often unreliable) account of 1881, after the failure of his second opera, he did resolve to stop composing and to get his contract back from Merelli. Demaldè's statement that he did this because he had been forced to go on with *Un giorno di regno* suggests that there may have been bad feeling on both sides at this time. Verdi again asked Pasetti to act as his agent. He was supposed to be working on the third opera of his contract and had been told by Merelli to put *Il proscritto* aside. In September the impresario offered it to Nicolai. Verdi's new work should have been delivered in January 1842, in time for Carnival; but Verdi (according to his account to Ricordi) did not have the heart to go on:

With my soul torn apart by my family tragedies, exacerbated by the failure of my work, I convinced myself that I would never again be consoled by Art, and I decided never to compose again! Merelli sent for me and treated me like a capricious boy. He would not let me be defeated by one unhappy experience; . . . but I stood my ground, so that Merelli, giving me back my contract, said to me: 'Listen, Verdi, I cannot force you to compose! [But] my faith in you remains unshaken. Who knows whether you may or may not decide some day to begin to write again? Just let me know two months before a season, and I promise you that your opera will be given.'[24]

If this is accurate, one cannot help respecting the impresario for his management of the bereaved composer. Sensing that Verdi might have a future, he offered him yet another chance to succeed. A very different version of these events, though, is given in Hercules Cavalli's account, quoted later in this chapter.

The La Scala revival of *Oberto* carried Verdi into the autumn; a production of that opera was also scheduled for Carnival 1840–1 in Genoa. Verdi gave up his apartment in Contrada di San Simone on 9 November and took a room in Contrada degli Andegari, near Solera's house and near La Scala. Among his personal possessions at that time was a small packet with Margherita's locket, her wedding-ring, and a strand of her hair. These he wrapped together and put with a handwritten note of his own that read: 'Souvenirs of my poor family.'[25]

The Creation of *Nabucco*

About this period, there is no truth written in stone, for each of the four accounts that survive has some credible elements; two of them, Demaldè's and Hercules Cavalli's, pre-date Verdi's accounts to Lessona and Ricordi; in the case of Demaldè, perhaps by as much as thirty years; in the case of Cavalli, by as much as twelve or perhaps fifteen years. Both come out of the Busseto tradition and out of the Barezzi-Demaldè clan, which expanded later to include Adele Cavalli, Giovannino Barezzi's wife. Hercules is her brother; had Margherita lived, he would also have been her brother-in-law. Both cast suspicion on Verdi's later narratives.

To Ricordi, he said that in the winter of 1840, he had no faith in anything, and was no longer thinking about music, when one winter evening, as he was coming out of the Galleria De Cristoforis, he ran into Merelli. At that time the impresario lived at 864 Contrada del Monte, just at the end of the Galleria.[26] Merelli was on his way to the theatre.

Large snowflakes were falling; and he, taking me by the arm, invited me to come with him to the director's office at La Scala. As we walked along, we chatted and he told me that he was in a terrible situation because of the new opera he had to present. He had given the assignment to Nicolai, who was unhappy with the libretto.

'Imagine', Merelli said, 'a libretto by Solera, stupendous, magnificent! extraordinary! effective dramatic situations, grand, beautiful lines; but that crank of a composer refuses to look at it, saying that it is an impossible libretto! I don't know where to look to find him another one right away.'

'I'll get you out of that problem', I volunteered. 'Didn't you have *Il proscritto* written for me? I haven't composed a note of it! You can use it.'

'Oh, bravo! that is a stroke of good luck!'

As we were discussing this, we reached the theatre. Merelli called Bassi, who was a librettist, stage-director, bouncer, librarian, etc., and gave him the job of looking right away in the archive to see whether he could find a copy of *Il proscritto*: the copy is there. But at the same time Merelli took another manuscript in his hand and, showing it to me, exclaimed:

'See, here is Solera's libretto! Such a beautiful plot! . . . Imagine turning it down! Take it. Read it.'

'What in the devil must I do with it? No! No! I have no desire to read librettos!'

'Well, it's not going to hurt you. Read it and then bring it back to me.' And he handed me a huge sheaf of papers written in big letters, the kind they used then. I rolled it up; and, saying goodbye to Merelli, I went off to my house. As I was walking along, I felt a kind of indefinable, sick feeling all over, an immense sadness, an agitation that made my heart swell! I went to my place and, with an almost violent gesture, I threw the manuscript on the table, and stood straight in front of it. The bundle of pages, falling on the table, opened by itself: without knowing why, I stared at the page before me and saw the line 'Va pensiero sull'ali dorate'. I ran through the lines that follow and get a tremendous impression from them, all the more moving because they were almost a paraphrase of the Bible, which I always loved to read. I read one section; I read another; then, firm in my decision not to compose again, I forced myself to close the manuscript and go to bed. But YES! *Nabucco* was racing through my head! I could not sleep: I got up and read the libretto, not once, not twice, but three times, so that in the morning, you might say, I knew Solera's whole libretto from memory. In spite of all that, I still did not feel that I wanted to go back on my resolution not to compose, and the next day I went back to the theatre and gave the manuscript back to Merelli.

'Beautiful, eh?' he said to me.

'Very, Very beautiful.'

'All right, then, set it to music!'

'Not a chance! I would not even dream of it. I don't want anything to do with it.'

'Set it to music! Set it to music!'

And, saying this, Merelli took the libretto, stuck it in the pocket of my overcoat, took me by the shoulders, and, with a big shove, rushed me out of his office.—Not just that: he closed the door in my face and locked it!

What was I to do?

I went back home with *Nabucco* in my pocket. One day, one line; one day, another; now one note, then a phrase . . . little by little the opera was composed.[27]

In 1876, however, a few years earlier than this account, Verdi gave yet another version of this critical moment in his career to his friend Michele Lessona. According to this, Verdi lived in a furnished room from October 1840 to January 1841, almost never going out during the day and reading cheap novels, one after another. After Merelli gave him the libretto of *Nabucco*, he threw it in a corner, where it stayed five months as he went on with his reading.

One fine day at the end of May [1841], that blessed drama popped up again; he read the last scene, of Abigaille's death, which was later removed; he went almost mechanically to the piano, that piano that stood silent for so long, and set that scene to music. The ice was broken. Like a man emerging from a dark, dank jail to breathe the pure country air, Verdi again found himself in the atmosphere he adored. Three months from then, *Nabucco* was finished, composed, and exactly as it is today.[28]

Verdi told his friend Arrivabene that this was 'my true, true, true story'.[29]

As we have seen, Demaldè had said that Verdi had asked to be freed from his contract with Merelli because of having been 'forced' to write *Un giorno di regno*. This account goes on to say that Verdi's 'friends' then pledged that he would write one more *opera seria* for La Scala, fulfilling his contract; thus he would be free 'of any obligation to the impresario'. The librettist Solera was *then* [*italics mine*] chosen to write the poetry, which he was perfectly suited to do, 'because of Verdi's strong feeling for it'.[30] Here a note of realism is introduced: Merelli had a synopsis or (as Verdi called it) *programma* of *Nabucco*; this was shown to Verdi, who liked it. At that point Solera began to write the libretto. Demaldè does not mention either Nicolai or any exchange of *Il proscritto* for *Nabucco*.

Neither does he identify the 'friends', but one of them must have been Pasetti, who was negotiating for him at this time.

Hercules Cavalli knew Verdi well. He wrote that after Margherita's death, Verdi spent 'a few' months in 'sorrow and retirement', then overcame his grief, 'which, at first, he could not control'. Becoming somewhat more calm and resigned, he decided to go back to Milan and try to make up for what 'had been lost'. Bound in the closest possible friendship to Solera, in such an intimacy that 'it seemed that they had been born for each other', he found that the librettist had been

charged with writing two dramas at the same time, one for Verdi and the other for Nicolay [sic], the composer of Il templario. He wrote Nabuco [sic] and marked it for Nicolay, and afterward wrote Il proscritto and meant it for Verdi. Without knowing it, the poet had committed an error that the composers themselves set to rights. . . . As a friend of Nicolay, [Verdi], discussing with him the [composers'] respective works, [found that] neither of them was satisfied with his assignment; and they reached an agreement. Nicolay showed Verdi the Nabuco; and, as for Verdi, he ceded Il proscritto to his colleague, because it seemed to him more suited to his gifts. With this exchange confirmed, Verdi made an effort to make more beautiful the drama that he . . . [enriched] with his music; and at the end of 1841, he finished his job.

Cavalli went on to describe the several failures of the Carnival season of 1841–2, the irritated public, and Verdi, who 'had his Nabuco ready [and] saw the right moment' to get it on the programme of La Scala.

But the problem in being able to present it [was due to the fact that] the first contract had been cancelled. Merelli had no confidence [in Nabucco] and did not want to risk the money; all this forced [Verdi] to produce it on his own and at his own risk [italics mine], agreeing with Merelli that if the result was a success the management would reimburse him for the expenses; and if it were a failure, he would bear the loss himself.[31]

Although there is some discrepancy between the two accounts in the matter of the contract—Demaldè stating that Nabucco was written to satisfy the original one, and Cavalli saying that the original one had been terminated—much in these two early sources demands serious consideration.

Verdi had not in fact been away from the theatre very long, if, indeed, at all. The seventeen performances of Oberto had kept his name before the Milanese public for much of the autumn season. Some pieces from Un giorno di regno had been published, so even it was not a total loss. As for

Nabucco, he may have been familiar with the ballet *Nabucodonosor* at La Scala and may have known Don Pettorelli's epic version of the story called *Il sogno di Nabucco*. And, as he said, he often read the Bible.

During this same winter, Verdi went to Genoa to supervise the production of *Oberto* at the Teatro Carlo Felice. He and Giovannino Barezzi left Milan on 31 December, ending what Verdi called 'the accursed year'. While there, he helped to get his own work ready, heard Mercadante's *La vestale* and saw the city and the sea for the first time. One of the pieces Verdi had set to music and later cut from the score was a duet, written to a text by Dr Luigi Balestra of Busseto. According to the composer himself, it was replaced with a shorter duet because the soprano Raineri-Marini found it too hard to sing.[32] *Oberto* had its first performance in Genoa on 9 January 1841. As at La Scala, it was neither a failure nor a notable success. It was given only six times, although it had a good cast. This time, Verdi blamed the Genoese audience for not understanding his work. They had applauded in the wrong places, he said, while greeting coldly the numbers that he preferred. The opening aria went best of all, but the added band instruments had 'made a hellish racket'. Before leaving Genoa, he sent Massini a report on the cold reception his opera had got. Even the new duet between the soprano Raineri-Marini and the baritone Raffaele Ferlotti had passed unnoticed, as had the chorus, duet, trio, and finale that followed, even though the soprano had never sung so well and with such commitment. Verdi also wrote to Demaldè, saying that he probably would not come to Busseto that spring because getting a passport was 'too much trouble'. He fired off his opinion of Alberto Mazzucato's opera *I due sergenti*, which was playing at the Teatro Re in Milan. It was, he said, 'born of a lunatic mind: it is a madness. [Mazzucato] deserves to be put in a madhouse, out of pity. Imagine the poor audience! It howled, cursed, whistled. There were also a few who applauded; a few friends who wield a lot of power.'[33] The remark about the passport is curious, for within a matter of months, Demaldè (deformed and crippled—according to Pettorelli's description of him—and one-legged—according to his passport) was able to make several trips to Milan when he felt it was important to be there for the rehearsals of *Nabucco*.

From Verdi's letters, it seems that he had got back into the mainstream of Milanese life. His confidence restored, he worked with Solera on *Nabucco*. During this collaboration, their second (or perhaps even their third, if Verdi had him working on *Il proscritto*), Solera listened to the composer and followed his wishes, at least in some matters, apparently impressed by the conviction that Verdi had about this work. When Verdi found something which did not suit him, he made Solera change it. In the third act, he came upon an insignificant love duet for Fenena and Ismaele. According to Verdi's own account:

I did not like it because it chilled the action and seemed to me to take away a bit of the grandeur of the Bible which marked that drama. One morning when Solera was at my place, I told him what I thought, but he did not want to take me seriously, not so much because he did not think me right, but because it bored him to go over work already done. We argued both sides of the question: I stuck fast, and so did he. He asked me finally what I wanted in place of the duet; and I suggested to him a prophecy for the Prophet Zaccaria: he did not think this was such a bad idea, and then he said, 'But . . .' and 'Well . . .' and said that he would think about it and then write it. But that was not what I wanted, because I knew that days and days would pass before Solera decided to write a line. I locked my door, put the key in my pocket, and—half-seriously, half-teasing— said to Solera: 'You are not going to leave here until you have written the Prophecy. Here is the Bible, you already have the words, beautiful and written there!' Solera, who had an impetuous character, took this badly; a fire of rage burned in his eyes. I had an ugly moment then, for the poet was a large man who could quickly have done away with that obstinate composer; but after a moment he sat down at the writing table; and fifteen minutes later the Prophecy was written.[34]

Wanting the advice and, perhaps, the endorsement of others, he acted somewhat as he had in Busseto when he had summoned men like Francesco Silva to listen to his fresh compositions. In Milan, he turned to other mentors, some of whom he met through Pasetti. One of these was, surprisingly, Teresa Saporiti, the celebrated prima donna, the first Donna Anna in *Don Giovanni*, who had served Mozart so well. Living in Milan with her daughter Fulvia, Saporiti let Verdi give salon concerts in her house, where he, together with the Bussetan Francesco Mingardi, was her guest. In 1841 he dared to try out the music of *Nabucco* on Teresa Saporiti. As we know from her daughter's later, warm letters to Verdi, he was 'received as a welcome and delightful [guest] when he came to play *Nabucco*'.[35] Comparing the vocal challenge of Donna Anna with that of Abigaille, one cannot help wondering whether the famous, old soprano made suggestions to Verdi about how to write the music, especially as we know that Strepponi later did exactly this for Verdi and we may suppose that Margherita, who was also a singer, did so too. In these months before he got *Nabucco* staged the composer was also the honoured guest of Pasetti and his family, who invited him to play at private concerts and asked important Milanese to hear him: during the soirées 'in the home of the Signor Engineer Pasetti', he showed the first examples of that genius that [later] showed itself so great and so lustrous', in the days 'before the audience was allowed to applaud it at La Scala'.[36] He finally finished *Nabucco* in the early autumn of 1841, well in time, he thought, to get it on the programme for the Carnival season of 1841–2. Verdi said that, score in hand, he sought out Merelli at La Scala and learned that the opera would indeed be staged but that it was too late to have it included in the coming season, for the impresario had already announced three new operas. Adding a fourth might be dangerous. The impresario asked Verdi to wait until the spring season, when no new works were scheduled; he promised that only first-rank singers would be engaged for it.

'But I refused', Verdi said of that interview.

During Carnival or never. . . . And I had good reasons of my own, for it would not be possible to find two artists suited to my operas as Strepponi and Ronconi were; and I knew that they were under contract at that time. Merelli, although he wanted to keep me happy, was not exactly wrong. . . . Four new operas in one single season was a great risk. But I had good artistic reasons to put against his argument. Anyway, between the yesses and the noes, the embarrassments, and the half-promises, the *cartellone* of La Scala went up, but *Nabucco* was not announced on it.[37]

Once again, it seemed that Verdi would be kept out of La Scala.

9

〜

December 1841 – March 1842

The Production of *Nabucco*

Giovannino Barezzi was staying with Verdi in their apartment when the composer came in, dejected and angry, after seeing the La Scala poster without *Nabucco* on it. As Verdi recalled his feelings, describing them to Ricordi decades later, 'I was young; my blood was boiling. I decided to write a nasty letter to Merelli, letting out all my resentment—I confess that as soon as I sent it, I felt a kind of remorse! And I was afraid that because of it, everything would be ruined!'[1]

Another account, far more reliable than Verdi's has proved to be, is found in a letter from Giovannino Barezzi to his father, dated 26 December 1841. It is lent validity by a notary, Lino Carrara, who in 1926 wrote: 'Its authenticity is beyond dispute and is absolute because at the bottom it is also signed by Verdi.' He goes on to show which words from the letter are cited in the article where it was published; they are in quotation marks:

then he decided to write to Merelli in rather sharp terms. Merelli took offence and showed the letter to Pasetti and said to him 'Look how Verdi has mis-understood; I did not mean that; but I did it because when we got to the end of Carnival, I would put out another *cartellone* announcing his opera; and by doing that I would get some credit from the subscribers [for adding it]; anyway, tell Verdi that he should have Strepponi look at her part; and if she wants to sing it, I will gladly give it.' Pasetti sent for Verdi and they went to Strepponi's: they told her what was happening: and she very willingly agreed to do the opera, and added 'Come tomorrow at one-thirty, so I can see my part.' The next day, then, 23 [December] 1841, Verdi and Pasetti went at the hour set by Strepponi; she went over her part with Verdi at the piano and then said to him: '*I like this music very much and want to do it for my début opera* [of the season]' and then firmly added 'Let's go and see Ronconi.' [*Italics in original.*] They got into Pasetti's carriage, which was waiting at the door, and went to Ronconi's. Strepponi showed him *the beautiful parts of the opera* and Verdi told him the plot. Ronconi, having heard everything, said: 'Well, this evening I will speak with the impresario and I will tell him that I do not want to do Nini's opera but want to sing yours.'[2]

Lino Carrara wrote that the report is in a letter from Giovannino to 'his own father'. Other correspondence of the period shows that two people often used the same letter to send news; they signed two names at the bottom. To cite but a few examples: letters of Ferdinando Accarini and Verdi; Antonio Barezzi and Demaldè; Verdi and Strepponi; Giovannino and Verdi; and Muzio and Carlo Verdi. It was a common practice.

Verdi himself seems never to have included the anecdote in conversations or letters. In Lessona, this same period of his life is covered differently.

Merelli gladly welcomed that new score [*Nabucco*], but showed very little interest in producing it that next winter [1841–2]: the management already had three operas on its hands, Donizetti's *Maria Padilla*; Pacini's *Saffo*, new to Milan; and another work by Maestro Nini. Verdi fought hard, so that—in spite of everything—*Nabucco* would be staged that very season; and there were very serious disputes [about it]. Still, it came out all right finally: [but] there were those who said that the intervention of certain important people fighting for his cause was responsible [for the production]; but that is not true. He succeeded because he wanted to accomplish something and to persevere with all his soul. *Nabucco* was given at La Scala on the evening of 8 [*sic*] March 1842.[3]

The reference to 'certain important people' is perhaps to Strepponi and Ronconi.

Hercules Cavalli, whose account of this period was mentioned in the previous chapter describes only the events after Merelli asked Verdi to use his own funds to produce the opera; but he says nothing about Strepponi and Ronconi bearing in any way upon its outcome. Demaldè says simply that Verdi was so taken with the historical subject and poetry that the opera became reality and finally reached the stage at La Scala, where the public was pleasantly surprised, for it did not expect such a grand and magnificent work.[4] Unlike Cavalli, Demaldè does not mention money. Rumours of some sort of transaction were current, though, during Verdi's lifetime and after his death. Barezzi was said to have guaranteed to Merelli that he would underwrite *Nabucco* himself, to be sure that it would be produced. Although Verdi denied this, the Barezzis continued to claim, even in this century, that their father had made *Nabucco* possible, with his offer of underwriting.[5]

According to Verdi's account to Ricordi, things went smoothly after Pasetti and Merelli met.

Merelli sent for me, and, seeing me, explained angrily: 'Is this any way to treat a friend? Never mind. You are right. We will give this *Nabucco*, but you will have to realize that I have to spend a lot of money on the other new operas. I cannot make new sets and costumes for *Nabucco*; and we will have to throw something together as best we can from what we can find in the warehouse.' I agreed to everything, because I wanted so much to have the opera performed. A new *cartellone* came out, and on it I finally read: NABUCCO.[6]

We will perhaps never know whether he had to advance money for the production. It is certain, though, that Demaldè made several trips to Milan at the beginning of 1842, as his passport at Sant'Agata proves. If anyone were to have come from Busseto with money from home, it would have been the Treasurer of the Monte di Pietà. Tito Barezzi later actually named a figure, when he said that 10,000 lire had been deposited with Merelli as a guarantee.[7]

All these events had to have taken place after 21 December, when the first *cartellone* went up. According to the Venice newspaper, Strepponi left that city that day; she would have got to Milan the next day. On 26 December Giovannino and Verdi wrote to Antonio Barezzi about the meetings with her. But she went on to Genoa about a week later, to cover her engagement for Carnival season, leaving the composer without a prima donna soprano for rehearsals. January and early February were taken up with mounting the production. Verdi, in his account to Ricordi, said that he began rehearsals at the end of February, which fits with Strepponi's return to Milan about the fifteenth of the month. *Nabucco* is a big opera to prepare in such a short time.

In his account to Ricordi, he described these preparations:

The costumes, patched together haphazardly, are proving splendid! The old sets, retouched by the painter Perroni, have an extraordinary effect: the first scene of the temple in particular produces such a great effect that the audience's applause lasts for a good ten minutes! At the final dress rehearsal, no one knew how and when to have the band come on stage: Maestro Tutsch was embarrassed: I show him a bar: and at the first performance the band entered so in time on the crescendo that the audience bursts into applause![8]

This victory was torn from the jaws of defeat. The refurbished scenery had probably served for the grand ballet *Nabucodonosor*, choreographed by Antonio Cortesi and given thirty-five times at La Scala in the autumn of 1838. (It is entirely possible, as we have seen, that Verdi attended one of those performances during his long stay in the city that year.) The cast, which included some veterans, was an asset to the composer; but Strepponi had been singing almost steadily for seven years, taking time off only for the births of three (or four) children. While Verdi was overseeing the assembly of sets and costumes, she was on stage in Genoa. Ill—indeed, on the brink of collapse—she faced an exceedingly taxing leading role, Abigaille, at a time when it was by no means certain that she could get through it.

Verdi's librettist Solera can only have been a help in such a chaotic time, for his background had prepared him to solve the kinds of problem that arise at the last minute. After years of discipline in lower and upper schools in Vienna and Milan, he knew at least two languages, had studied singing and composition, had given some of his own works at La Scala and other theatres and had perhaps even directed the orchestra at the important Teatro Real in Madrid. A published poet, he had also worked, however briefly, as a circus hand and performer. His friendship with Verdi went back at least three years, if not more, for one of Solera's poems served Verdi for the text of the song 'L'esule' (1839); he had also reworked Piazza's libretto for *Oberto* and may have revised *Il proscritto* as well. We know something of his collaboration with Verdi on the libretto of *Nabucco*. And, as we have seen, his 'friends' were believed to have been responsible, at least in part, for the success Verdi had won with *Oberto*; this meant that he could muster support for *Nabucco* even before the opening night. This was a man-of-theatre valuable to Verdi on many fronts.[9] He was a braggart and garrulous, but helpful.

At home, the composer could count on Giovannino Barezzi, who seems to have been with him much of the time after June 1840; Demaldè, during his visits to the city; Pasetti; and a contingent of Bussetans—the Selettis and Mingardis, among others—who lived in Milan. In the orchestra of La Scala itself, there was Vincenzo Merighi, a staunch Verdian. Through the weeks when *Nabucco* was in preparation and in rehearsal, Verdi had support when he needed it.

Apart from the general confusion Verdi mentioned in connection with the last dress rehearsal, we know only that he was troubled by Strepponi's vocal problems, which threatened the production. Donizetti, who was in Milan at the time, sent a message (through his brother-in-law Antonio Vasselli) to a Roman impresario—probably Vincenzo Jacovacci—that described the soprano's problems in no uncertain terms: 'Tell him that this singer, who [was reported to have] created such an uproar here in *Belisario*, was the only one who got no applause at all, [and] that her Verdi did not want her in his opera and the management forced him to take her.'[10] The dress rehearsal must have gone fairly well, though, for Verdi later remembered that the stagehands shouted their approval, then beat on the floor and sets with tools to create an even noisier demonstration. That changes were being made even at the last minute is shown by the fact that Verdi, perhaps at the suggestion of Giovannino Barezzi, added an overture just before the first performance.[11] As Parker notes, this was not an uncommon practice, for it required no stage rehearsal. 'The *Nabucco* overture is a potpourri, based on themes from the opera, and it would be absurd to imagine that these themes were first invented in an orchestral setting. Finally, the paper type on which the Sinfonia is written unquestionably belongs to a later layer of the autograph.'[12] It was perhaps composed during the rehearsal period; but Giovannino Barezzi reported that Tito Ricordi had taken him aside *after* the final dress rehearsal and urged him to persuade Verdi to write an overture. Verdi refused at first, and then sat down to compose it.[13] This anecdote, like many others, cannot be documented; but it does come, though indirectly, from a man who said he was at Verdi's side when it was written and was living with him. Everything that we know about this period indicates that he and Verdi shared the excitement and the anxiety over *Nabucco* just as brothers would have—months of anticipation and twelve days of rehearsal.

On 9 March, the night of the première, Verdi, according to the custom of the time, went to take his seat in the orchestra, between the cembalo and the violoncello al cembalo, purportedly to turn the pages for these two unimportant collaborators, but really to share in his own triumph or defeat. The cellist Merighi said to him: 'Maestrino, I wish I were in your place this evening.'[14] According to Verdi's account to Ricordi, applause broke out when the curtain first went up. A long ovation apparently followed the stretta of the first finale; but Verdi was so nervous that when everyone in the chairs and in the platea stood up at once, shouting and screaming, he mistook the demonstration for a protest. 'At first, I believed that they were making fun of the poor composer, and that they were about to jump on me and do me harm.'[15] But he was wrong. As one reviewer wrote afterward in the Gazzetta privilegiata di Milano, it was a 'noisy, enormously well-received' première, one of the few occasions when 'the universal agreement of the audience' was beyond dispute. He said that after the first act, 'the Maestro, and, with him, the singers were called out repeatedly by the applause; . . . [and even after the end of the opera] the ovations did not end, [for they] were long and often [the singers came out for calls, time after time] and for Maestro Verdi they were particularly and truly triumphant.'[16]

The critic of Il Figaro wrote that Verdi 'had employed throughout this opera of his a grand and severe style' and had struck the audience with 'a surprising effect that moves listeners and, in some pieces, causes them to applaud and shout with enthusiasm'.[17] The Corriere delle dame described applause during Verdi's curtain-calls, some taken alone and some with his artists, as 'loud, endless', and offered by an ecstatic audience.[18]

Lessona, writing three decades after the event, and with Verdi's approval, said that

the great success of Nabucco aroused tremendous enthusiasm such as had never been seen before. The night [after the première] no one in Milan slept; the next day the new masterpiece was the sole topic of conversation. Everyone was talking about Verdi; and even fashion and cuisine borrowed his name, making hats alla Verdi, shawls alla Verdi, and sauces alla Verdi. From every city in Italy impresarios hurried to beg the new maestro to write something just for them, and made him the biggest possible offers.[19]

Verdi, in his account to Ricordi, recalled that night:

We [gave] the first performance, which took place on 9 March and had Strepponi, Bellinzaghi, Ronconi, Miraglia, and Dérivis in the cast. With this opera, you can truly say that my artistic career began. And although I had to fight against many obstacles, it is certain all the same that Nabucco was born under a lucky star, so lucky that even all the things that could have gone wrong [did not do so, but] helped to make it a success.[20]

He had no chance to reflect on the première until he and Giovannino Barezzi were walking home together, having got free of the last of the well-wishers who had come to congratulate him. As they started off for Contrada degli Andegari, Verdi, silent at first, finally confessed that he had not expected such a triumph, even though he had been encouraged by the dress rehearsal. As he later observed, *Nabucco* marked the beginning of a very long career.

Among the problems that troubled him while the opera was in rehearsal, the most worrisome concerned Strepponi's voice. Although it did not fail her during the première, it came close to doing so. For the rest of her life, she was to be closely associated with Verdi, as colleague, mistress, and wife, so some account of her earlier life is called for; it is briefly covered here.

Giuseppina Strepponi

The daughter of a musical family, she grew up in a home where her father and uncle were composers and organists; others in the family studied at Milan Conservatory, then played or taught music.[21] Her aunt Giovanna Strepponi was a schoolmistress at a time when Maria Hadfield Cosway, Thomas Jefferson's friend, was teaching at the convent school in Lodi. The soprano Teresa Brambilla, who said that she was Strepponi's schoolmate, seems to have attended this popular school as well.

Feliciano Strepponi, born in 1797, studied at Milan Conservatory, where he was awarded a special prize for composition. When he was married on 3 November 1814 to Rosa Cornalba, also from Lodi, he was just 18. Their first child, Giuseppina, was baptized Clelia Maria Josepha Strepponi on 9 September 1815, when she was 1 day old.[22] Feliciano finished his studies in Milan in 1820 and was named maestro di cappella at the Cathedral in Monza.

Feliciano Strepponi had his operas performed at major theatres in Turin, Milan, and Trieste between 1822 and 1830, launching what promised to be a solid career in theatre. Appointed assistant to Giuseppe Farinelli, the director of the Teatro Grande in Trieste in 1828, he left Monza and his post as organist. In 1830 he personally introduced his daughter Giuseppina at Milan Conservatory, where she was admitted as a paying pupil, having been granted exemption to the age rule, for she was just over 15. Basily noted that the young soprano had shown an unusual degree of skill in her entrance examinations and that she was well advanced in her studies,[23] as one might expect from the daughter of such a family.

Giuseppina was in Milan when her father died in January 1832, at the age of 35 in the Parish of Santa Maria Maggiore in Trieste. As Milan

Conservatory records show, his widow had help from Triestine friends, who gave her the proceeds from a benefit concert given in the Teatro Mauroner less than two weeks after her husband's death. After she moved back to Lodi with her children, she was helped by her Cornalba brothers, so that Giuseppina could go on studying; but by June 1834 the family had fallen on such hard times that the authorities in Lodi had to report to Milan Conservatory that Rosa Cornalba Strepponi had had to sell her furniture and her husband's clothes and had put one of her daughters in the Lodi city orphanage, keeping two boys and another girl at home.[24] From then on, Giuseppina studied as a non-paying pupil in Milan Conservatory, from which she graduated in the autumn of 1834, after singing in a school concert that won her a review in the *Gazzetta privilegiata di Milano*, in which she was praised for her dramatic flair and her voice, which was 'neat and agile' in the upper register.[25] One month later Strepponi was back with her family in Lodi, singing two concerts in Palazzo Modigliani under the baton of Francesco, her uncle, who conducted the orchestra of the Istituto Filarmonico and presented his niece in excerpts from popular operas of the day. Again the young soprano got good reviews, this time in the local papers such as *the Corriere dell'Adda* and the *Gazzetta di Lodi e Crema*. As we have seen, it is entirely possible that Giuseppina Strepponi was still in Lodi in the first week of January 1835, when Barezzi, Verdi, and Martelli stopped to attend an opera there as they were on their way to Milan.

Sometime during that year Rosa Cornalba Strepponi's financial situation improved remarkably so that she was able to move to Milan with at least two of her daughters and take an apartment at 105 Contrada della Guastalla in the Parish of Santa Maria della Passione. The Ruolo della Popolazione of 1835 describes her as 'a woman of property and well-off'.[26] In Milan the Strepponis were at the heart of the music business; and soon Giuseppina got her first important engagement, a contract to sing in the Carnival season in Trieste at the Teatro Grande, where her father was working at the time of his death and a loyal public had provided part of the funds for her education.

After singing the title role in Rossini's *Matilde di Shabran* and Jane Seymour in *Anna Bolena*, she went on to Vienna for the spring season at the Kärntnerthor Theatre and the summer and autumn seasons in Udine, Gorizia, Verona, and Venice, where she appeared for the first time at Antonio Gallo's Teatro San Benedetto.[27] During the Carnival season of 1835–6 she sang at the Teatro Grande in Brescia, Cirelli's native city.

BOOK I

The spring season of 1836 found her again in Venice, this time at the Teatro La Fenice, where she stayed until May. She spent June and part of July at the Teatro Sociale in Mantua, then sang in Piacenza in July and August before beginning the autumn season at the Teatro della Concordia in Cremona, where Cirelli had been the impresario several times in the 1820s and 1830s. As we have seen, Verdi's friend and colleague Morganti was working there at that time and playing for the Busseto Philharmonic Society as well. In October she returned to Venice, appearing at the Teatro Apollo, and then to Trieste, where she began the Carnival season of 1836–7. This extraordinary record of uninterrupted performing speaks for her ability and that of her agents, Boracchi and Cirelli and their partner Robbia, Merelli's crippled secretary. One can only speculate at the strain it imposed on her voice.

Gifted, intelligent, and attractive, Strepponi soon came to the attention of Alessandro Lanari of Florence, 'the Napoleon of impresarios', with whom she signed up in the spring of 1837.[28] She had scarcely taken this important step when she found that she was pregnant. Her first performance under Lanari's banner was at the Teatro Comunale in Bologna in April with Moriani and Ronconi. The young Bolognese tenor Francesco Luigi Morini, a colleague with whom Strepponi often sang during the five years that followed, also signed up with Lanari that year.[29] With her early successes, the soprano laid the foundation for a promising career. But from the beginning of her association with Lanari, when she most needed to have everything go well, she was faced with the embarrassment of having to sing through at least three pregnancies. As a result, she defaulted on engagements, paid forfeits and fines to impresarios, created problems for opera companies that had to keep to schedule, and—more seriously—progressively damaged her voice.

The first of her children, mentioned in a previous chapter, was Camillo Luigi Antonio Strepponi, born in Turin in January 1838 and entered in the civil registers as 'Sterponi'. Delivered by the King's surgeon, he was baptized on 16 January.[30]

The boy's father was Camillo Cirelli. His godfather was Luigi Vestri, the famous actor of the Compagnia Reale Sarda, whom the soprano may even have known when she was a girl,[31] his godmother Antonietta Dupin Donzelli, daughter of a celebrated choreographer and wife of the tenor Domenico Donzelli.[32] Strepponi stopped singing during the first week of December 1837, but returned to the stage in concerts when her baby was less than 2 months old. She got back on the Lanari circuit with

Moriani, Morini, and Ronconi, gradually building her repertory and getting generally good reviews, although at least one critic faulted her for singing too often.

In Rome the soprano opened the spring season at the Teatro Argentina in *Lucia di Lammermoor*, with Moriani, Ronconi, and Antonio Superchi, the Parma-born baritone whom Verdi later favoured. When, before the end of the engagement, Cirelli went back to Milan, leaving his mistress alone, she took another lover, who, she thought, got her pregnant. She went on singing in Florence, appearing in concerts and in *Norma*, *La straniera*, and *La sonnambula* at the Teatro Alfieri and in *Lucia di Lammermoor* and *Betly* at the Cocomero, where her partner was Morini. Cirelli, who contemptuously referred to her lover as 'the Sergeant', finally accepted paternity late in January, when it became evident that the baby would be born more than a month before it was expected. The soprano's health began to deteriorate and she frequently suffered from bouts of coughing that, during performances, forced her to turn her head toward the wings.

Agents and impresarios soon learned the bad news, Lanari in November 1838, Merelli just after New Year's Day 1839. When asked whether it was true that Strepponi was five months pregnant, Lanari at first denied it, then admitted it. Still, he said, his soprano would be in Milan on 20 April and make her début at La Scala at the end of the month. In spite of everything, she was still enormously popular, as Pietro Romani reported to Lanari. Everyone could see that she was pregnant and no one cared.[33]

Cirelli expected to take the soprano away to some quiet place when her time came; but the baby was born several weeks earlier than expected, after a chaotic costume fitting and a successful performance of *Il giuramento* at the Teatro Alfieri. On 9 February 1839 Strepponi was delivered of a baby girl. She nursed the baby for almost three weeks. On 28 February at 11.45 p.m. the new-born was left in the turnstile for abandoned infants at the Ospedale degli Innocenti under the name of 'Sinforosa Cirelli'.[34] We do not know whether Strepponi ever saw her again.

The baby became a statistic in the registers of the hospital and orphanage, where, as in much of Italy at that time, a rigid system of classification divided orphans, foundlings, and abandoned children into three separate classes. The 'upper class' was orphans, and, within it, children whose fathers had died in the service of their country. Below it were foundlings or *trovatelli*, children who could not be identified as belonging to a particular parent. The lowest rank was that of the *esposti*, society's trash, who had been 'exposed' in the turnstile.

After her March engagement in Venice, the soprano went on to Milan, where she sang with Moriani and Ronconi in the regular spring season of 1839. Merelli assigned her a role in the production of Verdi's *Oberto*, which he scheduled and later removed from the programme. She then sang in other major theatres and returned to Verona, where she became ill in the winter of 1840–1 and may even have been pregnant again. She and Lanari became involved in a series of angry exchanges, during which she asked to be released from her contract and Lanari refused to free her.[35] At some time before March 1840 Strepponi, still living with Cirelli, who, as Lanari himself said, was passing himself off as her husband in the theatre and outside it, became engaged to a man whom Boracchi, writing to Lanari, described as 'the fiancé Monti', the cause of the uproar that was disrupting the season.[36] It is possible that a child was born while Strepponi was in Milan, for the pattern of the time taken out of her schedule corresponds exactly to other such periods of recovery from pregnancies. A stillborn child, a girl, born in her parish of Santa Maria della Passione in Milan on 22 March 1840 to parents who abandoned her, would fit into such a pattern.[37] Strepponi returned to the stage in June at the Pergola in Florence then went on to Venice for the autumn season and to Rome for the Carnival season of 1840–1 at the Teatro Apollo, where she was to sing in the première of Donizetti's *Adelia*.[38]

After an attack of German measles, she prepared the new opera under Donizetti's direction. The première went badly. The impresario Vincenzo Jacovacci sold more tickets than he had seats to offer, and there was a riot.[39] With this season behind her, Strepponi returned to Florence, where she and Moriani sang in *I Puritani* and Ricci's *Michelangelo e Rolla*. At some time in February or March 1841, either in Rome or in Florence, Strepponi again got pregnant. The father of this child is unknown, but it was not 'the fiancé Monti', who was single, while the father of this child was married and the father of a family.[40] About this time she attracted the attention of a wealthy nobleman, Count Filippo Camerata dei Passionei, Lanari's close friend and supporter, who became her lover.[41] This relationship might have been useful to Strepponi; but once again her career was interrupted as it became impossible for her to hide her new pregnancy after July or August 1841.

Vocally the soprano must have been in poor condition, for Merelli warned Lanari not to try to offer her to the audience of La Scala as a leading soprano. She could be engaged only as a substitute or cover, he said. As her pregnancy progressed, she had to let Lanari know that she could sing only a few of her performances at the Teatro Grande in Trieste, where she was engaged from September through the autumn season. Ill and depressed, she wrote that she would nevertheless have to arm herself 'with patience and avoid sad thoughts'.[42] Singing through the late summer fair season at the Teatro Riccardi in Bergamo, she fought utter despair. At one point the fact that she had been in good voice for *three consecutive days* was a cause for rejoicing. She and Salvi arrived in Trieste on 21 September, and, under the composer Fabio Campana, began rehearsing *Giulio d'Este* with the baritone Cesare Badiali. At this time Lanari let the soprano know that she would be singing at La Scala again, five performances a week, during the next Carnival season, which would begin just after Christmas. She let Lanari know that she had written to Count Camerata, 'the person you know in Ancona', to break off completely with him.[43] She had hoped that Camerata would support her, but when he answered, he sent her nothing. The nobleman's involvement with Strepponi is proved by the fact that when someone sent him an anonymous letter saying that she was making love with Salvi, he left Ancona and took the steamer to Trieste, where his arrival on 30 September was reported in the *Osservatore triestino*. Furious, he confronted the soprano in her dressing-room at the Teatro Grande and accused her of being Salvi's mistress, as she later confided to Lanari, although she was more than eight months pregnant with someone else's child at that time.

The Trieste season opened on schedule with *Giulio d'Este*, in which Salvi scored a tremendous personal triumph. Both Campana and Strepponi came off rather badly in the press, the composer for his lack of originality and the soprano for her poor performance. The reviewer in the *Osservatore triestino* remarked on the 'temporary impediment' that prevented her from demonstrating her 'full command' of her means. He did have the grace to mention her mastery of her art, which distinguished her among her colleagues. At the very end of her pregnancy, the impresario let her sing a concert for own benefit, for her sister had died in Milan that week.

On 4 November 1841 Strepponi gave birth to another daughter, Adelina Rosa Maria Theresia Carolina Strepponi.[44] Although the soprano had written to tell Lanari that she was going to take her new baby to Venice, where she could get better care for her, she left the new-born with a working-class couple in Trieste. Andrea Vianello and his wife lived at 58 Piazza Vecchia, next to the evangelical church, where they were raising a family of their own and taking in illegitimate children as well. Cirelli, who came to help Strepponi in Trieste, picked up the soprano and left with her that same day on the steamer for Venice. So far as we know Strepponi never saw her daughter again. Known as Adele Strepponi, she died of dysentery on 4 October 1842, just two weeks after one of Vianello's own children died. Adelina was given a third-class funeral at Santa Maria Maggiore.[45]

When Strepponi got to Venice on 21 November, the *Gazzetta privilegiata di Venezia* reported that she was staying at the Hotel Danieli, then as now one of the finest in the city. She spent a month there, with Cirelli at her side. This was perhaps when Strepponi sent Verdi a token of her friendship: a portrait of herself in operatic costume, signed with an enigmatic dedication: 'Nell'arduo tuo calle, reggesti i miei passi, alma Vinegia.' ('In your narrow street, you guided my steps, life-giving Venice.')[46] It is signed 'Giuseppina Strepponj' (*sic*), an early signature. The suggestion of strength or guidance found in the lagoon city is indeed puzzling. Strepponi seems to allude to her own condition.

On 21 December, according to the *Gazzetta*, Strepponi left Venice for Milan, *en route* to Genoa. As we have seen, it was during her short stay, that she met Verdi and Pasetti, went over the part of Abigaille in *Nabucco* with its composer, and persuaded Ronconi to perform it with her. While in Genoa, the soprano lamented to Lanari that she had never been able to manage her personal affairs:

I have always been cheated and deceived; and for every bad thing [that I have done], I have always had to pay an enormous penitence. Let us hope that it will all be over soon, for after Vienna [the season that followed the La Scala season] I will never again see that ghastly, pale face that made my head spin.[47]

This phrase apparently refers to one of her lovers, perhaps Donizetti, whose mistress Gatti thought she had been.

This, then, was Verdi's grand prima donna soprano: the 26-year-old mother of three or four illegitimate children, the oldest of whom had just turned 4; the veteran singer who considered herself lucky when she was in good voice on three consecutive days; the artist whom Merelli had been reluctant to hire for leading roles in his theatre; the woman with a former common-law husband in Milan, two or more former lovers who had fathered her children, a possible future prospect in Count Camerata, and, as she revealed to Lanari, a prospective husband—perhaps 'the fiancé Monti'—who wanted to marry her if she would give up her career. Beset by personal problems that she admitted she could not manage, she left Genoa, as we have already seen, and began to rehearse *Nabucco*.

Verdi must have shared the worst fears of many in the music trade about Strepponi, who had by then received many bad notices in theatrical papers. Donizetti, reporting on her poor showing in *Belisario*, added that the Austrian government had refused to have her in Vienna and that Raineri-Marini was going to take her place.[48] Strepponi let Lanari know that she could not sing the Vienna performances.[49] To cover himself, Merelli asked her to get a complete medical examination and give him the certificates he had to have before she could be released. On 3 March 1842, just six days before the première of *Nabucco*, the examination took place in Cirelli's office in Piazza dei Filodrammatici. The doctors stated that since 1839 Strepponi had been afflicted with respiratory and stomach ailments, that her career had been interrupted at least twice, that she had lost weight and that her once beautiful voice was weak, covered, and inadequate to the strain placed upon it. She could not perform, even when she put all her physical energy into singing. Although she was young, she had reached the limits of her endurance. The doctors certified that unless she gave up her career, she would undoubtedly become a consumptive.[50]

With this document legalized, Strepponi was free to leave the stage. But first there was *Nabucco*. Verdi must have been aware of what was happening, and apprehensive over the outcome. His score made extraordinary demands on the range, colour, control, and interpretive skills of his artists; Abigaille, above all, requires a power that very few sopranos can muster. It is certain that Strepponi could not possibly have given Verdi what he needed. As he said, *Nabucco* was born under a lucky star, for she managed to get through all eight performances. In her own words to Lanari: 'Then I sang, or rather, I dragged myself to the end of the performances, so as not to reduce the return from the Lenten [season]. For that, you have to be grateful to me.'[51] She added that there was a slight chance she might be getting married to a man who was not very well-off and

would be forced to take on the burden of my small and large families [her children, her mother, brother, and surviving sister], a man completely outside the theatre, [who] would not want to marry me (if indeed this should happen) unless I had settled my remaining [contractual] affair that I have with you. The greater probability, *rather, the virtual certainty*, is that this marriage will not take place; but in any case, I have to put my soul at peace, and I turn to you with perfect frankness.[52]

She described herself incorrectly as 'the mother of two children', Camillino and Adelina. These, and other letters to Lanari, reflect the depth of her despair, for she was too ill to go on: 'I have no health. I am earning nothing. The doctors, medicines and food for myself and my family are forcing me to use the funds I had.'[53] As we shall see, it took her more than a year to recover.

Nabucco and 'The Run of the Show'

The reviews of the opera, briefly mentioned earlier, all attest to Verdi's honestly won victory. Ricordi's *Gazzetta musicale di Milano* declared that 'an indication of a very remarkable progress in the art of melodrama' could be seen in *Nabucco* and praised Solera's cohesive libretto and Verdi's gift in understanding the poet's intentions. 'Audaciously sure of himself,' Verdi worked to interpret Solera's dramatic ideas just as he was making noteworthy progress in his own art. The opera was not a perfect model of 'true tragic opera'; but the composer had undeniably taken a great step forward.[54] In *Il Figaro*, the critic described the 'serious, powerful, imaginative subject [of the opera], the struggle between religion and one man's pride' and added that Verdi had infused the work with something 'grand and severe. . . . [Ronconi] is still the most believable actor and most polished singer now before us.' In sum, the review praised the work yet did intimate that Verdi had not quite risen to the challenge posed by Solera's libretto. He might later care to 'come back to it', the article suggested.[55] A critic in *Glissons, n'appuyons pas*, whose article was reprinted in the widely read *Teatri, arti e letteratura*, proclaimed the 'triumph', the 'victory', the appropriate distribution of the roles, the clarity of the music, and 'the stamp of grandeur [set] on the whole drama'. It acknowledged that Ronconi was magnificent, singing with commitment and intelligence, while Strepponi, though weak of voice, 'worked miracles' as an actress and musician. She was clearly in need of rest, the writer added. Prospero Dérivis, the Zaccaria, was praised for his full, robust voice, although he seemed unable to shade the phrases just as the composer required. Giovannina Bellinzaghi, the young Milanese who sang Fenena, was welcomed as a promising artist; the tenor Corrado Miraglia did well with his minor role.[56]

As we know from these reviews, Verdi did make changes in *Nabucco*, for after the first two performances, Abigaille's death scene was dropped.

It had been 'treated lovingly', but was ineffective, and a 'useless pro-longation of the action; for this reason the score now ends with the ensemble piece ['Immenso Jeovha'], nor could Verdi more solemnly conclude his fine composition.'[57] (This observation was made ten days after the première.) In allowing the piece to be omitted, Verdi removed from the score the music that, according to his account to Lessona, was the first that he composed for the opera. When all critical opinion was in, the consensus was that Verdi could boast of having composed a work that was certain to stay on the boards for years to come.

BOOK II

10

March 1842–February 1843

Society in Milan

After the première of *Nabucco*, Verdi, settled firmly in influential, liberal circles in Milan, lived in his lodgings in Contrada degli Andegari. This was at the centre of one of the city's most aristocratic quarters, the Porta Nuova. At its south-east corner stood La Scala, facing the Contrada del Teatro Grande. Diagonally across from it, in the first reach of Corsia del Giardino, stood the Caffè Martini, almost a patriotic institution during the first half of the nineteenth century. A few steps away, Manzoni lived at the corner of Contrada del Morone and Piazza Belgioioso. At the corner where Contrada degli Andegari joined the Corsia del Giardino stood the Gothic church of Santa Maria del Giardino. To the north of the house where Verdi lived was the historic Contrada del Monte di Pietà, where a row of noble residences was a reminder of the heroic anti-Austrian struggles of the early Risorgimento. Here had lived Baron Teodoro Arese, one of the subversive Carbonari; Count Federico Confalonieri, who was arrested, condemned to death, then pardoned and sent into exile in 1837; and Marquis Luigi Porro Lambertenghi, who in 1820 was arrested with his guest, the patriot Silvio Pellico. Like Porro and Confalonieri, Pellico was condemned as 'guilty of having conspired for the independence of Italy'. During his imprisonment, he wrote *Le mie prigioni*, which became a holy book of the Italian revolt against Austrian rule.[1] Among others who lived in the street were Stefano Barezzi; two of Verdi's closest friends, Countess Clara Carrara-Spinelli Maffei and her husband Andrea Maffei; and Carlo Tenca, who was emerging as a leader in the revolt against Austria. Tenca wrote of the Porros' house that he had gone there 'every day' and that after

BOOK II

1842 the most active and ingenious young men of his time gathered there. 'It was in that house that the revolution of Forty-Eight was planned.[2] Substantial risks were run by those who espoused the cause, among them harassment by censors and police; sequestration of assets; closing of theatres; impounding of passports; mutilation of dramas, libretto texts, and musical scores; and the ultimate, dreaded danger: arrest and imprisonment or a sentence of death.

'Among the friendships that the happy circumstances [of *Nabucco's* success] offered Verdi, he preferred those with men who had distinguished themselves for their literary or scientific merits,' wrote Cavalli.[3] The influence of the Piacentine writer Melchiorre Gioia and of Gian Domenico Romagnosi, a native of Salsomaggiore, near Fidenza, weighed heavily in such circles, where French ideas were gradually being transformed into the economic, social, and political base of the Italian revolution. Although it is clear that no one in Verdi's circle was an extravagant revolutionary in 1842, many of his closest friends had taken anti-Austrian positions. A few already had friends or relatives whom the Austrian authorities had condemned. Among those was Countess Maffei, whose celebrated salon began to draw its first adherents in 1834.[4]

She was almost of an age with Verdi, having been born near Bergamo in the spring of 1814. Her father Count Giovanni Battista Carrara-Spinelli was an idealistic dramatist and poet with many friends among the ruling Austrian nobility in Milan. Her mother was Countess Ottavia Gàmbara, daughter of a Brescian liberal family that counted in its ranks two zealots who had thrown family coats-of-arms on a Revolutionary bonfire in 1789. Several of the Gàmbara women were poets. In 1832 Clara married Andrea Maffei, a poet, translator, essayist, and journalist who was sixteen years older than she. This cosmopolitan gentleman from Molina Val di Ledro, near Trent, was more conservative than his wife, but had many friends from liberal circles. A Maffei scholar recently described him as 'a person difficult to classify within traditional frameworks; he was not an enemy of the Italian Risorgimento but was not its enthusiastic supporter either', at least in the early 1840s; but he later distinguished himself in the revolt of 1848.[5]

The Maffeis lived at 1 Contrada del Monte di Pietà until 1842, when they moved to Piazza Belgioioso, becoming the neighbours of Manzoni and his son-in-law Massimo d'Azeglio.[6] Although Maffei served as a functionary in an Austrian court, where his uncle was an official and an appointee of the Emperor, Clara Maffei provided a meeting-place for free-thinking intellectuals for more than twenty-five years. She was reluctant to call on or to receive many of the Austrian officials with whom her husband worked.[7] But in her salon, she gathered an ever broader group of Italian and foreign literary and artistic figures.

Among those who came to the salon in the evenings were Verdi's friend Arrivabene; the patriot Luciano Manara, not yet 20; Giulio Carcano, poet and translator; the painter Francesco Hayez; and the critic Luigi Toccagni, a librettist for the ballet and mime-theatre of the time. These formed the core of Verdi's group of acquaintances immediately after the première of *Nabucco*. Some had met Verdi at least casually before 1842. Others had met him during the rehearsals of the opera and admired him as a new voice for nationalist sympathies.[8] The writers and artists who belonged to the Maffeis' circle gathered in the afternoons at the Caffè San Carlo, the Caffè Martini, the Caffè Cova, or in the bookshops under the arcades. In the evenings they went either to La Scala or to the Maffeis', and sometimes to both when there was an important event in the theatre. Through the Maffeis Verdi met members of liberal movements whom he might not otherwise have known; among them were partisans of Mazzini's Giovine Italia—the Young Italy movement, to which Verdi seems not to have belonged, being naturally opposed to joining any organization. His Mazzini beard, though, was a badge of political commitment that had drawn the fire of the Codini at home; and his later involvement with Mazzini himself in London points to a possible connection with Mazzinians.

One of the more important voices in the Maffei salon was that of Opprandino Arrivabene, whom Verdi had met in the mid-1830s. A junior member of an ancient, noble Mantuan family that was suffering harassment at the hands of the Austrians,[9] Arrivabene figured with others of his clan in Atto Vannucci's hagiography of the Italian revolt, *I martiri della libertà italiana*.[10] Young Count Giovanni Arrivabene, arrested and condemned to death with Pellico, later escaped hanging and fled into exile with the Maffeis' friend Giuseppe Arconati-Visconti. Opprandino's friendships with literary and musical figures of the time had proved helpful to a shy and reticent Verdi when he was trying to launch his own career.[11] As an editor and writer, working with the critic Francesco Regli on the important theatrical periodical *Il barbiere di Siviglia*, he was in a position to influence other journalists and (as he did later) call Verdi's attention to dramas and operas that he considered right for him. As we have seen, *Il Figaro* (as *Il barbiere* was later retitled) praised *Nabucco* in fulsome terms.[12] Later Arrivabene contributed to *L'indicatore lombardo*, the first weekly published in Italy, a forum for philosophical and political views that Tenca edited.[13]

Another of Verdi's closest friends was Giulio Carcano, who had already begun his life-task, the translation of the complete works of Shakespeare into Italian.[14] By sending Verdi his translations, as they appeared over the years, and by discussing his work with the composer, he engaged in the same kind of intellectual give-and-take that Verdi had with Maffei over Schiller.[15] Tommaso Grossi, one of the most important literary figures in Italy at the time, served as a counsellor on law to the Maffeis, being a notary as well as a writer. His *Ildegonda*, written in 1820, had provided Solera with the subject for his opera of the same name. He won recognition as a serious poet with *I Lombardi alla prima crociata*, written between 1821 and 1826.[16] Another favourite at the Maffei salon was Manara, a disciple of Cattaneo, who was 17 when Verdi met him.[17] Thin, with a dark moustache and neat goatee, he cut a fine figure in Milanese society and was known as the Young Lord, 'il Milordino'.

Verdi usually stopped by Clara Maffei's salon during the early part of the evening, after each day's work. This was the hour when the Countess's intimates gathered to talk and to play *tresette* at her card table. Tenca describes this group coming together every evening to discuss the artistic and political news of the hour. Verdi loved both cards and billiards, and was good at both. Tenca describes him as fighting hard for his winnings and arguing over disputed points (*bisticciando*) with his cards gripped in his hand.[18]

Defensive and aggressive by turns, Tenca, the only member of the Maffei circle to have been born in real poverty, was the son of a portress.[19] He had risen from the servant class by educating himself and tutoring children. Something of a poet, he left an unforgettable portrait in words of Clara Maffei, seated in her little armchair, withdrawn, tired, resigned, and brooding over her concealed feelings.[20] Francesco Hayez caught another side of her in his troubling portrait, painted in this same period.

Other Milanese noblewomen in the circle of Verdi's friends remained close to him for decades. In some cases, they and their children and even grandchildren could be counted among his intimates. Prominent among them were Countess Gina Della Somaglia, the first to invite him for a long stay at her family's country home; Donna Giuseppina Strigelli Appiani, a patrician devotee of music and art; Donna Emilia Zeltner Morosini; and the Morosini daughters.[21] Giuseppina Appiani, the daughter-in-law of the artist Andrea Appiani, and daughter of Antonio Strigelli, the Counsellor of State, counted Bellini and Donizetti among her celebrated lodgers. Known as a patroness of composers, she was also Hayez's trusted companion and the intimate of the poet Giovanni Prati, the bard of the Risorgimento. One patriot who lived with her was Giuseppe Sandrini, whom Verdi knew. Sandrini was constantly under police surveillance; in 1848 the Austrians drove him into exile because of his pro-unification sympathies.[22] At the time that Verdi wrote *Nabucco*, Appiani was a grandmother in her forties whose house overflowed with family and friends. *La sonnambula* had been composed here in the first months of 1831; *Linda di Chamounix* was written here in 1842. Donizetti was also staying with Appiani as he was staging *Maria Padilla* and *Belisario* at La Scala in the season that marked Verdi's return to the stage in *Nabucco* and Strepponi's unfortunate performance in *Belisario*. She provided a family circle for some of the creative geniuses of her time, as she and her daughters crocheted house-slippers and made suspenders for—among others—her two widower-guests, Verdi and Donizetti.

Of the other friends that Verdi made at this time, one deserves mention. Donna Emilia Zeltner Morosini, nine years Verdi's senior, was the daughter of a Swiss diplomat and the wife of Giovanni Battista Morosini, a man born in 1782 who was old enough to be her father. She and her children enjoyed a special intimacy with Verdi. They lived in the palazzo at 870 and 870A Contrada del Monte. The fashionable Casinò dei Nobili, scene of one of Verdi's earliest triumphs in Milan, was next door, near the Galleria de Cristoforis.[23] Verdi's friendship with the Morosinis endured until the end of his life and extended from the mother to the daughters Luigia (Bigetta), Marianna (Annetta), Giuseppina, and Carolina, and the son Emilio, who was born in 1831. Among the many friends Verdi and the Morosinis had in common was Toccagni, who, twenty-five years older than Verdi, was an important source of support for him. The Morosinis were at the very heart of the Italian revolt against Austria. Many of the movement's fugitives and exiled patriots found a sanctuary in Donna Emilia's villa at Vezia, near Lugano. Verdi visited the family at Casbeno, where they had a summer house. It is possible that Verdi was in love with Donna Emilia, whose husband's move from the family *palazzo* to other quarters (documented in Milanese population rolls) would appear to indicate a separation from his wife. Although Verdi was so reserved that one can hardly say that he wrote 'love letters', he certainly expressed love in letters to her in the 1840s. Fifteen of these still survive in some form;

most are in the Museo Teatrale alla Scala. In them Verdi uses words like *tenero, tenerissimo, tenerezza,* and phrases that express something more than just a platonic friendship.

[21 July 1842] I am perhaps the last to write to you, but that does not mean that I am the least affectionate. . . . I hear that you are having a wonderful time [away from Milan] and that the amusements, and the waters [of the spa at Recoaro] are doing you a great deal of good. I am happy in my heart about that. Send all your domestic worries to the Devil and you will be even better. . . . I have not yet begun to write the new opera because I don't have the libretto, and I am extremely unhappy about the revival of *Nabucco.* What is the lovable Peppina doing? and my dear Bigettina? A kiss to the second and nothing to the first. I have some important accounts to settle with Peppina. She won't get away from me. You are very, very cruel! As you are riding on donkey-back and letting your thoughts roam in the Third Sphere of Heaven perhaps you do not ever remember the miserable mortals who are desperate about you! . . . A thousand greetings to . . . (shall I say it or not) Peppina, and Bigettina, and to her travelling companion. For you I wish a sea of health, and remember that I am all *tenerezza.* I am dying of *tenerezza.*

[12 April 1843] Pardon me, pardon me, if I did not write to you as soon as I got back from Vienna, and if I did not answer your very, very kind [letter] immediately. I thought that I could surprise you and express to you all my *tenerezza* and my love; but unfortunately you had already left for Varese. Cruel one! I got to Milan the morning of the eleventh after having helped with *Nabucco* and conducted it with my baton. It came off well, and better than I hoped after having seen the scheming there of a certain person. I am packing to leave for Parma, or, rather, for Busseto, where I will celebrate the holiday with my family; afterward I will go to Parma to hear a performance of *Nabucco,* then I will go to Bologna to hear the *Linda* performed by the Poniatowskis, and then I will come back to Milan; where I hope that we will meet. Happy moment! . . . Toccagni will do *everything possible . . . to come to Varese.* I kiss your hands with a lot more pleasure than I would have kissing the hands of the Holy Father. Your S[ervant] and friend

G. Verdi.

PS Today I am unhappy!

[11 July 1844] I have just come back from your house where Carolina, even more kind than usual . . . , read me some parts of your letter that had to do with me; I am writing to you immediately and I am sorry to fulfil a sacrosanct duty of friendship [in so brief a letter]. You will understand how happy I was to have your news and how much I envy you and that lovable *Traitor* [Peppina?] who is near you as you enjoy that healthy place, while I am forced to get consumption here, shut in these four walls with one hand on the keyboard and the other on a sheet of paper, writing music. . . . Please tell Count Barbò [why I cannot compose the cantata *Flavio Gioja* for the Nobile Società]. I know that my very, very close friend Soldati from Venice is at Recoaro. . . . To you, my trust and friendship.

[12 August [1844] from Bergamo] *Ernani* was given last night and turned out very, very mediocre. I am leaving tomorrow morning for home, via Cremona. I will wait for your letter. A thousand wishes to your family and, in a hurry, I say that I am your *tenerissimo*

G. Verdi.

[14 July 1846 from Recoaro] I am blessedly happy to have your news and at the same time mortified not to have written to you. It is partly the fault of Venice, partly Maffei's, who, I know, wrote to you. . . . One dies of boredom here; it is very crowded. . . . I, too, find this valley beautiful, but what is it, compared to Como, Varese, etc.? . . . I am very, very happy that Carolina is better, and sorry that Peppina is not well. Now why not come to Recoaro? Then we will all be happy; we would make up a little society and, in spite of Recoaro, we would have a good time. The good thing here is that you do not hear or make music. It was truly an inspiration not to have a cembalo sent here. I now no longer seem myself, and I cannot believe that I know music, know how to compose so many beautiful and ugly things, and I don't know how I will be able to go back to my work. Who knows whether one day I shall not wake up a millionaire! What a beautiful word, full of meaning! Beautiful! And how empty by comparison are *fame, glory, Genius.* . . . I will leave Recoaro probably on Thursday. Will I find you in Milan? I hope so. For now, I think I will say the most affectionate things to your daughters, to my friend Toccagni. I kiss one of your hands, and then the other, and then the first one again. Believe that I am your affectionate

G. Verdi.

In one of these letters, written in September or October of 1842, Verdi wrote an explicit expression of love. 'I am always loving, passionate, on fire, half-dead over you. . . . How many things I would like to say to you!'[24] For a man as shy as Verdi, phrases like this and those in the letters cited above must have meant something. At the time that the first of these was written, Verdi was almost 30, Donna Emilia was 38 or 39. His two years of mourning had just ended. Whether he was in love with Donna Emilia we do not know, but these letters certainly indicate something more than casual friendship. Fortunately for posterity, we know how Donna Emilia looked in 1852, when Hayez painted her, showing her as a distinguished matron. His portraits also include Countess Della Somaglia,

Countess Maffei, Giuseppina Negroni Prati Morosini, Antonietta Negroni Prati Morosini, and Giuseppina Appiani.[25]

The Progress of *Nabucco*

Nabucco was so successful that the publisher Canti issued new portraits of Verdi, together with his songs. As for the opera, negotiations for various productions were under way; but the course of Verdi's business affairs did not run smoothly at this time. As we know from Demaldè's notes, Verdi was tempted by offers made by Francesco Lucca and his wife, the imposing Giovanna Strazza, who was Strepponi's friend.[26] But after the première of *Nabucco*, Merelli sold his half of the rights to Ricordi, who paid Verdi for the right to publish the score. Also sold were the rights to Solera's libretto.[27] Perhaps acting on advice given him by Strepponi, Verdi sold his half of *Nabucco* to the ambitious Luccas.[28] This transaction, which took place on 13 March 1842, was to cost Verdi much anguish later. Lucca and Ricordi began to argue over the rights, quarrelling through the summer of 1842 and delaying plans for performances outside of La Scala for one of the most successful operas of the century. The composer, who needed to have the work produced as quickly as possible, was inevitably drawn into the dispute. Demaldè wrote of the matter that the opera was 'half his, yet not his'.[29]

In May 1842 Verdi wrote a song for voice and piano called 'Chi i bei di m'adduce ancora', from a text translated from Goethe's 'Erster Verlust', which Dr Luigi Balestra of Busseto translated as 'Prima perdita'. It was inscribed by the composer into three pages of the album of Sofia de' Medici, the Marchioness of Marignano.[30]

During that summer Verdi chose his next subject for an opera, Grossi's *I Lombardi alla prima crociata*, to fulfil his next obligation to La Scala. By July the Maffei salon was closed for the summer, Clara having gone to her family's villa at Clusone, near Bergamo. Many of Verdi's other friends also left the city for their villeggiature, as he waited for Solera to begin the new libretto.[31] Donna Emilia and her daughters had gone to take the waters at Recoaro, in the mountains near Vicenza. Verdi kept up with her through friends and through letters of his own. 'I am neither well nor ill', he said, adding that he had not yet begun the new opera because he did not have the text and that he was very unhappy about matters relating to *Nabucco*.[32]

Verdi went home to Busseto for the first time since the *Nabucco* première, probably arriving there in June. As Cavalli recalled the visit,

His friends and relatives wanted very much to see him in town again, to pay homage to him with the obligatory demonstrations, because he, with his [fame], had exalted the name of a town that had been very little known before then. . . . It is impossible to describe how [magnificently] his return to Busseto was celebrated; but he behaved exactly as he had when he was an unknown maestro, and neither the honours [of the city] nor the applause . . . changed him in the slightest.[33]

Later he spent five days in Bologna, where he may have gone to try to arrange for a production of *Nabucco*. There he met Rossini for the first time and was welcomed by the older composer with great kindness, as Verdi reported to Donna Emilia.[34] Rossini, who later lived in the heart of the city in an apartment in the house of his friend and colleague Domenico Donzelli, had returned from Paris with his mistress Olympe Pélissier and had given up his own town house on the Strada Maggiore. At the request of the city government, he had undertaken the reorganization of the Liceo Musicale, where he had once studied.[35] We do not know what Verdi and Rossini discussed, but we know that Verdi was impressed by the older composer and 'very, very happy' about the meeting. 'When I think that Rossini is the living celebrity of the world, I could kill myself and kill all the imbeciles with me', he wrote to Donna Emilia. 'Oh, it is a magnificent thing to be Rossini.'[36]

The contrast between his life and Rossini's must have seemed marked at a time when *Nabucco* was caught in a mesh of disputes. Nor that summer could Verdi be sure that this triumph would be repeated. Given in Milan as a tremendously successful repeat in the autumn season of 1842, it achieved a record run that still stands at La Scala, with fifty-seven performances;[37] but as he was writing to Donna Emilia, that lay in an uncertain future, especially because Merelli's financial problems were acute. Nevertheless, Verdi began to provide for his parents. 'Up to then, his precarious state had not allowed him to help his parents, who went on living in the village where he was born; but as soon as he was able to do so, he bought land and a house that he made over to them [1844] so that they could profit from the investment', Cavalli wrote.[38] Other beneficiaries of his generosity were the Michiaras, who had lodged and fed him in Busseto from 1823 until 1832. Pietro Michiara, sen. had died, leaving his widow in poverty, being assisted by the City. He helped her and, 'when he was richer, supported her in a dignified way until her death'. These are the first items in what later became Verdi's remarkable record of alleviating suffering and assisting the poor and the ill.

When he got back to Milan, he had to prod Solera about the libretto for *I Lombardi*, as they faced the challenge of producing a work to match or surpass their astonishing *Nabucco*, which opened again in Milan in mid-August.

I Lombardi alla prima crociata

From Pougin's biography of Verdi and from its notes, which Verdi approved, we know his version of how he came to get the commission for the new opera.

The enormous success of [*Nabucco*] had established Verdi in the ranks of the most fashionable composers, those who, like Donizetti, Mercadante, Pacini, Luigi Ricci, could be asked to write the *opera d'obbligo* for the important Carnival season. On the evening of the third performance [of *Nabucco*], Merelli had Verdi come to his office and let him know . . . the decision that the administration had reached about him:

'Dear Verdi, the decision has been made to engage you to write the *opera d'obbligo* for next season. Here is a blank contract. After a success like yours, I cannot dictate conditions; it is up to you to set them. Fill out this contract; whatever you write there will be yours.'

Verdi was very embarrassed and did not know what to do. Having gone to Strepponi's box [*sic*] and told her what Merelli had said to him, he asked her advice. She answered that, on the one hand, he had to profit from his good luck, but on the other hand, he could not reasonably ask to be paid more for his next opera than Bellini had got for *Norma*. For *Norma*, Bellini had been paid 8,000 Austrian lire. Verdi asked Merelli for that amount, which was granted him without any questions being asked.[39]

A note to this text states that 'Merelli gave the contract to Verdi, leaving blank the space for the fee. Verdi himself wrote 9,000 Austrian lire there.'[40]

The Pougin account goes on: 'His friend Solera had taken the libretto of [*I Lombardi*] from the poem of the same name by Tommaso Grossi, and, in spite of its defects—one might say, in spite of its pecularities—this libretto, which is generally very moving, contained scenes that were beautiful enough to arouse the composer's imagination.'[41] Solera and

Verdi worked on it between mid-March and late June 1842, sometimes in harmony and sometimes in strife. Solera later told one historian how hard it was to please Verdi. Here is his account of this period.

Verdi, or *The Tyrant*, as Solera called him, was complaining of the lack of fire in the duet between the prima donna and the tenor:

'Here I need a warm phrase, an expression of love, with something in it to suggest the Orient, Palestine, or something like that. You find it: sit down and think and write; I'll run over to the theatre and come back later.'

And he took his hat and left, turning the key once in the lock from the outside. His idea of locking me in the room was a real fixation with him. I fiddled around for a while, jotting down half of a line, then another half, and getting very angry because I was a prisoner in [Verdi's] room; I wanted to take my mind off the work, and—with the idea of playing a joke on my friend—I opened a cupboard. A half-dozen bottles of wine were lined up there, seeming to invite me to taste them. I took one and opened it. Getting back to work, I toasted every line I wrote, welcoming it with a good swig of wine. When Verdi came back, it looked as if my eyes were shining rather brightly; so when he spoke to me, he was overjoyed:

'You have inspiration written all over your face. I'll bet you have found something beautiful.'

The poor man was not aware that something else had put the shine in my eyes. But when he picked up the scribbled sheet, where there were more things crossed out than finished, he seized my arm and shouted:

'You wretch! You villain! Why did you stop here?'

And he, carried away with excitement, read aloud the last two legible lines, which were (and still are) 'Sarà talamo l'arena | Del deserto interminato'.

'—*Interminato.... arena....* wait a minute...' and gesturing like an actor in a cheap theatre, right then he improvised those other lines that close the strophe, and remain in the libretto: '*Sarà l'urlo della jena | La canzone dell'amore!*'[42]

Solera's reference to Verdi's mania for locking him in the room to try to force him to write lends some credence to another anecdote, told by Verdi himself, about the librettist being locked in Verdi's rooms to write Zaccaria's Prophecy for *Nabucco*.[43]

Verdi was ready to begin composing *I Lombardi* at the beginning of July, even as he sought information from Parma on the young soprano Teresa De Giuli Borsi, whom he was considering for the role of Abigaille for the autumn season *Nabucco* at La Scala.[44] Cavalli says that he spent most of the summer in Busseto that year, 'to the great satisfaction of his relatives and friends', composing *I Lombardi*, to which he added 'the final touches' in Milan in the autumn.[45] There *Nabucco* was breaking all records at La Scala, where it held the stage until December.

The theme of his new opera was religio-patriotic; it was a spectacle of heroic dimensions with an important role for the chorus. It was specifically Milan-centred, showing the Lombards on the First Crusade to the Holy Land. A Milanese shrine, beloved by everyone, was shown on stage: the piazza and basilica of Sant'Ambrogio. From that church, as we have seen, Verdi's son and wife had been buried. As was customary, Austrian censors asked to review the libretto. Among those concerned with it were two powerful men who wielded influence with the censors. One was the archbishop, the other the chief of police.

Count Gaetano Gaisruck, the Austrian-born prelate, worldly, cynical, and witty, had ruled the diocese for almost thirty years. 'He did not like religious life,' one chronicler wrote of him.[46] Yet Gaisruck was fair, and not without courage. Defending his seminarians' right to read Prati's controversial *Ermenegarda*, Gaisruck overruled his own clergy's decree condemning the work. When the reformer Carlo Porta exposed the misconduct of certain priests in the diocese, Gaisruck dealt with them at once and praised Porta publicly.[47] His role was that of a buffer between petty bureaucrats in the Austrian government and the Milanese people who were, after all, his flock. Because of his high station, he wielded immense power at Court; and sometimes he used it to defend Milan, in a period when restrictions of all kinds were applied to keep the people in order. Among them were rules governing even small public gatherings and demonstrations, even those in the theatre, where, it was feared, an excess of enthusiasm or hostility might provoke a riot. At La Scala, for example, one noisy ovation for the soprano Erminia Frezzolini so alarmed the authorities that a notice was posted to advise the audience and singers that 'singers are forbidden to take more than three curtain-calls during an act to encourage the public's applause; and if the audience insists on calling [the singer] on stage again, the curtain will be run down and the singers will not be allowed to appear on stage again.'[48] This, like the ordinances prohibiting public gatherings, affected the response to every composer's work and reflected the authorities' fear of the powerful emotions music could generate.

Gaisruck, though, may even have helped clear the way for *I Lombardi*, although at first he opposed it. Soon after Merelli announced that La Scala would produce the opera, Gaisruck wrote a letter of protest to the Chief Commissioner of Police, Baron Carlo Luigi Torresani-Lanzfeld, whose persecution of the Italian liberal upper classes had made him hated by the patriots of the day. Gaisruck said that he had heard that the staging of Verdi's new work required religious processions, churches, the Valley of Jehosaphat, a religious conversion, and a baptism. These would be sacrilegious. Suggesting to Torresani that he forbid performances of the opera, he said that he would write to the Emperor directly and denounce the Imperial Theatres for licentiousness and failure to show respect for the faith.[49] One day later the police sent a notice to Verdi, Merelli, and Solera, warning that *I Lombardi* could not be given unless substantial changes were made. They were summoned to appear before Torresani so that they could decide where the changes would fall. According to his own much later account, Verdi refused to go. To Merelli and Solera, he said: 'You go. The rehearsals are well along; the opera is going well; and my position is this: I will not change a word or a note. *It will be performed as it is or it will not be performed at all.*'[50] Merelli and Solera reported to police headquarters, where Torresani showed them Gaisruck's letter. Making his case, Merelli said that the costumes were ready, the scenery painted, and the rehearsals almost over. He added that the cast and orchestra were enthusiastic about the music and that because Verdi refused to make any changes, Torresani himself would be held responsible for the cancellation of what seemed to be a masterpiece. Torresani listened, then rose and said that he would never be 'the one to clip the wings of this young man, who promises so much to the art of music. Go on. I will take responsibility for what happens.' He asked only that the words 'Ave Maria' be changed to 'Salve Maria', 'a trivial concession to the Archbishop's scruples'.[51] This first important victory over the Austrian authorities, significant in itself, reinforced Verdi's position *vis-à-vis* the censors. It is significant that Gaisruck, who had raised major issues at the outset, also gave way. To give Torresani and Gaisruck credit is only fair; but there is another side to the picture, for the authorities would surely have run a risk in closing La Scala or forbidding the production of a work about which certain expectations had been raised. In allowing the production, after only one single word had been changed, the Austrian rulers of Milan admitted tacitly the extent of this risk.

Although he had won, Verdi was still uneasy, mistrusting the capriciousness of the public, which he never ceased to regard as a potential enemy. His excellent cast included Frezzolini, the soprano, and Carlo Guasco, who had made his début in 1839 and was becoming one of Italy's leading tenors. Frezzolini was the darling of Milan, where she had sung a brilliant *Lucrezia Borgia* for Donizetti in 1840 and sealed that triumph with *La sonnambula*, in a performance where she was so overcome with emotion that she was said to have wept on stage. A pupil of her father, who was the first Dulcamara in *L'elisir d'amore*, she continued to study with Tacchinardi, the elder Ronconi, and the younger Manuel Garcia, becoming an ever more polished artist.[52] Dérivis, the Zaccaria of *Nabucco*, sang Pagano; the Arvino of the première was Giovanni Severi, who became one of Verdi's close friends. Later he was replaced by Raffaele Monti, a tenor from Leghorn.

When the dress rehearsal of *I Lombardi* did not meet Verdi's expectations, his nervousness increased. In his account of events, he says that on the evening of the première, 11 February 1843, Frezzolini reassured him when he stopped in her dressing room to ask how she felt. She was fine, she said. '"Take courage, then", Verdi advised her. "Don't worry, Maestro. If necessary, I will die on stage tonight; but your opera will be triumphant."'[53]

At the last minute she was warned about getting the words of the prayer right, 'Salve Maria', so as not to bring the censors' wrath down on the theatre. The house was full when the curtain rose at seven. *I Lombardi alla prima crociata* embodied the highest ideals of Lombard patriotism and courage, depicting them in the frame of war against a pagan infidel. Its success was compared to that of *Nabucco*, with the audience hailing the composer and artists.

Verdi's former librettist Antonio Piazza reviewed *I Lombardi* for the heavily censored *Gazzetta privilegiata di Milano*, saying that 'The work's success surpassed even the advance expectations for it, which were superlative.'[54] Perhaps it is difficult for us now to understand the passions Verdi's works raised. The point was made, though, by an early biographer, who wrote:

Foreigners can never realize how much influence . . . was exercised by the burning, impassioned melodies that Verdi composed when [dramatic] situations or even single passages of poetry reminded him of Italy's unhappy condition or of its hopes. The audience saw allusions everywhere; but Verdi perceived them even before the audience did; and he adapted to them his most inspired music, which often had the end result of bringing revolution into the theatre. . . . Let us be aware . . . of the fact that the Austrian censors (and later the censors of petty tyrants in Italy) began with *I Lombardi* their patient efforts, their [persecutions], which later they always carried on, so as to clean up the librettos Verdi chose . . . [and] make popular demonstrations impossible.[55]

The particular appeal of *I Lombardi* was described in 1847 by Eugenio Montazio, writing for *La rivista di Firenze*.

The plot, if not so grand as that of *Nabucco*, was perhaps even more popular, more loaded with passion, and more likely to satisfy the local pride of the Lombards, who saw in [the opera] the poetic ideas of one of the best contemporary poets [Grossi]. That libretto, too, offered Verdi a vehicle for showing his listeners a new aspect of himself . . . [for it contained] Christian and pagan elements, the love for one's country, the [passions] of vengeance and of religion—the most exquisite feelings in human nature.[56]

He emphasized the partisan sentiments particularly, 'lo spirito di parte', and stressed Verdi's genius at handling such a complicated work, predicting for it a long life in the repertory.

Another early writer, in a sketch in *Il Fuggilozio* in 1857, singled out *I Lombardi* because it depicted 'the piety of our ancestors and the greatness of the Lombard cities' and their citizens.[57] The chorus 'O Signore dal tetto natio' became a popular hymn of the revolt in Lombardy, as did 'Va pensiero'; both are still taught as patriotic anthems in the elementary schools of northern Italy.

Before the première of *I Lombardi*, Verdi had written to Count René De Bombelles, the morganatic husband of Marie Louise of Parma, asking to be allowed to pay homage to 'Our August Sovereign' by dedicating the opera to her.[58] Two days after the première he wrote again. 'My gratitude will be eternal and the benefit to me immense, if I can be honoured by the generosity of the venerated Sovereign with some symbol [of her esteem], which would mean everything for the security of a splendid career.'[59] This was the first letter he wrote from his new lodgings at 601 Corso Francesco (the present-day Corso Vittorio Emanuele).

As he learned, the honour did not come easily. At least one of his letters failed to reach De Bombelles; and Verdi had to appeal to Demaldè to help. He seemed uneasy in the role of petitioner, claiming that Giovannino Barezzi and Solera had 'orchestrated [the appeal], almost without my knowing it'.[60] Later he solicited the honour in Parma himself, after Demaldè had intervened. There was a quid pro quo attached; for De Bombelles asked Verdi to write three pieces of music for him; but Verdi apparently declined to do so.[61] He did eventually get an audience with the Duchess. He presented to her the first fascicles of *I Lombardi*, and she gave him a gold pin set with diamonds. It was valued at 522 Lire, according to her record of works offered to her. Marie Louise accepted the dedication, which was published in 1843, when the vocal score was published. Long before that, Verdi had lost patience with the whole affair. 'I am not longing for anything; I do not want anything,' he wrote, with some evident exasperation, to Demaldè.[62]

In the decades after its première *I Lombardi alla prima crociata* proved extremely popular. Verdi offered it to the difficult Paris public as his début opera in France, where, modified, it played under the title *Jérusalem*. In the late autumn of 1843 Count Ottavio Tasca, who years before had agreed to write a libretto for the then-unknown Verdi, published a poem extolling the merits of 'the fervid, good maestro in whom knowledge and genius abound', the Paladin of Italy who would fight for his native land and defend it against 'foreign jealousy' that hurls at Italy the accusation that it has nothing more to offer the world of art. Tasca saw in *Nabucco* and *I Lombardi* the two tiers of Verdi's 'double crown' that he would wear as he conquered the world. 'Onward, O young man, on this difficult path. . . . Fearless, you must dare to risk everything and hurry to climb the highest peak of fame, where immortality is found. . . . Do not let unanimous acclaim make you proud . . . May you live in peace and happiness.'[63]

Winter 1843–Spring 1844

On 20 March 1843 Verdi set out for Vienna on the first long trip of his life. He was on his own, leaving behind the reassuring comfort of family, friends, and colleagues. To a person as shy as he, the uncertain life of a theatrical composer meant coping with uncertainty, anxiety, and even pain, for the demands of the opera world kept him exposed to a sometimes savage professional milieu. His drive to succeed, which dominated these years as he rose to power, led him to make extraordinary efforts to further his career and play a game of calculated risk. Sometimes he fell into depression, and he was often ill with throat infections and stomach trouble. As he told Demaldè, he was 'very, very well off in Milan'.[1] But his trip to Vienna was the first leg of a six-year odyssey that took him to many Italian cities and several European countries. The journey was marked by defeats and triumphs; at times it resembled a political campaign, with the candidate fêted at banquets and hailed by shouting fans carrying banners. As Verdi pushed himself from theatre to theatre, scores in hand, he came to rule his world, even as he became ever more impoverished in physical well-being and peace of mind. Between the winter of 1842–3 and the summer of 1849, when he took up residence in Busseto, he spent hectic years fighting fatigue and illness, as his life became a cacophony of conflicting motives. He was ready to pay a high price for the fame he so desired. And he did.

The Fortunes of *Nabucco*

When he set out for Vienna, he may have believed, as Donizetti did, that *Nabucco* would open the season there. As musical director, Donizetti had had word from Merelli 'that we will begin here with *Nabucco*, and [Merelli] has done the right thing because [the soprano] Tadolini, who will come to us from far away, will be quite tired when she gets here and thus she will be able to rest. *Nabucco* first, then, and *Linda* [*di Chamounix*] afterward.'[2] Later the order of the programme was reversed so that *Nabucco* followed Donizetti's opera. The company included well-known artists such as the tenor Carlo Guasco, the soprano Teresa De Giuli, and the bass Dérivis. Both De Giuli and Dérivis had sung in Verdi's opera at La Scala. Conducted by the composer himself, *Nabucco* went on stage on 4 April. 'It was a greater success than I had expected, after having watched the intrigues of a certain person there,' Verdi wrote to Emilia Morosini.[3] That 'certain person' was perhaps Otto Nicolai, whose career and Verdi's had curiously crossed over a period of years. Verdi had his first great triumph with *Nabucco*, which Nicolai had refused to compose, while Nicolai had come to grief with *Il proscritto*, the opera Verdi had been unable to write for Merelli. Whether Nicolai was the 'certain person' we do not know; but in his *Tagebücher* he wrote that *Nabucco* was impossible to set to music, raging, bloody, vile, and black with murder. Of Verdi himself he wrote: 'His operas are truly awful and utterly degrading for Italy.'[4]

Donizetti, by contrast, helped Verdi as much as he could. In an extraordinary letter to Donna Giuseppina Appiani, written on 22 January 1844, he acknowledged that Verdi's time had come:

I approve your passion [for Verdi]; just so much as you shall love artists of great gifts, just so much I shall esteem you; I cannot be angry about it—my time for pre-eminence has passed, someone else must certainly take my place. The world wants something new; others gave up their place to make way for us; we have to make way for others. I am still very, very happy to give way to people of talent like *Verdi*. Friends are always fearful, but you may be very sure about the success of this young man. The Venetians will appreciate him as much as the Milanese . . . [Nothing] will prevent the good Verdi from soon reaching one of the most honourable positions in the cohort of composers.[5]

Verdi, who was expected in Parma, did not stay long in Vienna. From Udine, as he was on his way back to Milan, he wrote to Count Mocenigo of the Teatro La Fenice in Venice about an offer from that theatre. After a stop in Milan, he expected to go on to the Ducale: 'On the fourteenth I will be in Parma, where I will stay until the end of the month.'[6] On the way he stopped in Busseto and visited his parents, who were still living in Roncole, operating the Osteria, tending two small properties that they owned, and paying off the rent owed to the priest of La Madonna dei Prati and to the diocese.

The prima donna in Parma was Strepponi, who had been in retirement since her last appearance in *Nabucco* at La Scala. With a year of rest behind her, she was ready to return to the stage, again as Abigaille. During her illness the soprano had been under the care of a very famous physician, Giacomo Tommasini, who lived in Parma and treated her there and in Milan in the spring of 1842, then entrusted the further cure to a colleague.[7] She recovered sufficiently to be able to risk a return to the stage. Also in the cast were the baritone Filippo Colini, the tenor Enrico Rossi-Guerra, and the bass Giuseppe Miral.[8] The conductor Nicola Di Giovanni had relieved Verdi in Vienna, after the composer conducted the first two performances of *Nabucco*.

In Parma the entire company shared the triumph of the opera at its first performance at the Teatro Regio on 17 April. Verdi, presented with a laurel crown, was called on stage again and again. It was an unforgettable experience, particularly for Carlo Verdi, who came from Busseto for the opera and sat in the box of a local gentlewoman. Overcome, he wept with emotion at the ovation tendered to his son.[9] The first-night audience even called the scenery designer and the impresario out for bows. The sovereign Marie Louise 'deigned to honour the theatre with Her August Presence'.[10] The opera was given twenty-one times. An odd incident occurred on the second evening, when the Duchess was again in the audience. A craftsman described as 'the gilder Baroncini', who was perhaps related to Barezzi's mother-in-law, incited his friends to interrupt Strepponi's singing with a demonstration and was arrested for causing a disturbance. A second uproar broke out when two ballerinas came to blows, presumably backstage. They were detained and later released.[11]

After that, the opera ran smoothly. In late April Verdi went to Bologna to hear an expertly produced private performance of *Linda di Chamounix*, staged by Prince Giuseppe Poniatowski in the theatre of the Società del Casino with his brother and sister and himself in leading roles.[12] The performances at the Teatro Comunale were something of a disappointment, Verdi said. After them, he returned to Parma, where *Nabucco* was still doing well. In spite of her illness, Strepponi's voice did not fail; the public remained loyal to her. On 31 May she sang in her own benefit; on 5 June, grateful for the favour the city had showered on her, she offered a charity concert for the local Pio Istituto degli Asili all'Infanzia. The *Gazzetta di Parma* remarked on the completely sold-out house for the benefit, full beyond anyone's hopes, and on Strepponi's 'noble modesty' as she, learning that men in the audience intended to unhitch her horses and pull her carriage back to her hotel themselves, managed to avoid that homage. The charity concert began with the overture to *Nabucco* and ended with Strepponi singing the cavatina from it in costume as flowers fell on to the stage. The soprano was hailed as 'a fine singer, certainly, [and] extremely fine in *Nabucco*. . . . So every evening [she got] applause and, unfailingly, many curtain calls; then some garlands of flowers, . . . sonnets, and so many bouquets of flowers and garlands and wreaths that she laughed with joy'.[13] After what she had suffered in 1841 and 1842 her reception in Parma was gratifying.

Verdi had intended to leave the city after the première, go to Bologna, visit his family at home, and then return to Milan. On 17 May he wrote to Count Alvise Francesco Mocenigo of La Fenice that he would leave five days later;[14] but on 25 May he was still there, telling Mocenigo to write to him by return of post to Parma.[15] The composer's delay in leaving Parma as scheduled may be attributed in part to his desire to remain near Strepponi, who may have been his mistress at this time, for she herself dated their intimacy from 1843,[16] but it is far more likely that he stayed on to await the return of Marie Louise, who was out of the city in May and returned in time to hear *Nabucco* again on 27 May and receive the composer in audience, during which she gave him a gold pin. Given the number of friends and supporters he had in the city, and given his father's business connections there, he may simply have had affairs of his own that required his attention. It is certain that Verdi enjoyed an immense personal triumph. One periodical noted that he was treated like an idol, showered with praise, having remained with his 'lucky child [*Nabucco*] even to the last night of the engagement, [so that] he will remember this past season in Parma for a long time, having enjoyed the sweetest and most exquisite pleasures, where he heard himself honoured so many times with the frenetic applause of the entire audience. Lucky Verdi! His life ought to be a river of honey!'[17] While he was in the city, he was again able to meet Rossini, who was passing through on his way from Bologna to Paris.[18] He then returned to Milan himself.

In May 1843 Donna Emilia Morosini had tried to persuade Verdi to take an unfurnished place and decorate it to his own taste, but he declined. 'I do not feel like spending thousands of lire to furnish it for the short time I could probably spend there,' he said.[19] However, he did move later to a place almost next to hers in Contrada del Monte.

He spent June in Milan then visited Senigallia, which had an important fair and theatre season, in July. Under Lanari's aegis he staged *I Lombardi* at the recently reopened Teatro La Fenice (like its Venetian counterpart, risen from the ashes of a fire). The Florentine impresario had been producing opera and ballet there since 1831, using the season as a showcase for many stars, among them Ronconi, Ungher, Tadolini, Rubini, Moriani, Strepponi, and Ivanov. He had also engaged some of the most famous dancers of the century.[20] Here, too, was Lanari's supportive friend Count Camerata, whose summer residence served as Lanari's temporary headquarters.[21] Verdi conducted his opera with Erminia Frezzolini as his soprano and her husband Antonio Poggi in the leading tenor role. While he was busy with this production the composer negotiated with Venice and the librettist Francesco Maria Piave for his next opera, which was to be given there; and when his work was finished at the beginning of August, he returned to Milan and continued his negotiations with Venice.[22]

Verdi and Strepponi may have worked together again that late summer or autumn, as the Teatro Comunale in Bologna was producing *Nabucco*, in which Strepponi sang Abigaille. Although one reviewer, writing in *Teatri, arti, e letteratura*, criticized the opera as 'a little too noisy and truly deafening even in some of the recitatives', he did admit that it was extraordinary for its 'vigorous instrumentation' and its 'abundance of melodies'. One of the most successful pieces in *Nabucco* was 'the aria of Abigaille (La Strepponi) in the second part [of the opera], especially the adagio recently written expressly for her by the composer'.[23] The soprano was praised for her clear voice, secure stage action, and appropriateness of expression. The baritone Cesare Badiali won praise for his imposing, moving Nabucco. The opera was given thirty-two times, exceeding everyone's expectations. Strepponi was also the Elisabetta in *Roberto Devereux*, which opened on 19 October but was so coolly received that on the second and third evenings the impresario mounted a pastiche of two acts of *Nabucco* and single pieces from *Roberto Devereux* instead of substituting another work. Later in the season Fraschini returned in the complete *Devereux*.

Apart from the fact that the critic in Bologna said that Verdi had 'recently' written the adagio for Strepponi, we know little of the relationship between the composer and the soprano at this time, save that they had both been in Milan in the weeks after the Parma *Nabucco* and after Verdi's return from Senigallia. A letter from Cirelli to Lanari, written on

11 October, just three days after the opening of *Nabucco* in Bologna, refers to the older agent's concern about Strepponi's 'buggering love affairs' (*buggerate amorose*) that 'compromise her' and threaten her career. He hoped that she might 'give up' this self-defeating behaviour.[24] It is entirely possible that Verdi was involved seriously with her at this time. Later in the season, when Fanny Maray was called to Bologna to replace her, Strepponi went back to Milan. Less than three months later she and Verdi were together again in Verona, where she was singing Abigaille and Verdi was looking for a tenor for his new opera.

Venice and *Ernani*

Negotiations with the Teatro La Fenice, begun in 1842, brought Verdi into contact with several men with whom he would be associated for many years to come. His ties with that theatre spanned decades and brought La Fenice five premières of his operas. After La Scala, the Teatro La Fenice was the most important stage for his career; he came to count on it and on a smaller house, the Teatro San Benedetto, for premières and successful revivals of his works. The management of La Fenice had begun asking for the right to give *Nabucco* as early as May 1842, and it was finally given as the opening programme of the Carnival season of 1842–3, playing for twenty-five evenings.[25] After that, Count Mocenigo, the Venetian nobleman who oversaw La Fenice as presidente agli spettacoli, offered Verdi the opportunity to produce *I Lombardi alla prima crociata* there and to compose a new opera for the theatre.[26] This was an important step for the composer, his first première away from La Scala and his first exposure to the difficult, knowledgeable Venetian audience. To establish his own position at once, he rejected several of the terms of the contract offered him. Counter-offers followed, to be met by the protests of a wary composer: 'I believe that it is useless for me to repeat what I wrote to you' and 'I cannot accept the sum' and 'I absolutely will not go below my figure'.[27] Verdi's profile as an astute businessman was already taking on its hard lines. Even when the final contract was sent, Verdi wrote: 'In it I seem to see several points that could be questionable; and, since surely neither you nor I want to argue [over these], I am thus making some changes, which (it is understood) you will be free to accept or reject.'[28] These changes were in fact accepted.

Once the terms were settled, the composer and the management began to discuss the dramas from which a libretto could be taken. Verdi, busy as he was, had left himself little enough time to compose such an important work. 'If I had an artist with Ronconi's power, I would choose either *Re Lear* or *Il corsaro*,' he wrote. 'No matter what, I would choose a subject that would have no relationship at all to the subject of any other opera.'[29] Apart from Shakespeare's *Lear* and Byron's *The Bride of Abydos* and *Corsair*, other choices were considered: *Catterina Hovvard*, the tragedy of Catherine Howard, which both the Austrian censors and the composer thought unsuitable; *Cola di Rienzi*, and *La Caduta dei Longobardi*, both risky because of the censors' opposition to inflammatory or allusive historical works. 'I do not know whether they could be put on,' Verdi wrote. 'Perhaps the police would not approve.'[30] In July, just before leaving for Senigallia, he proposed *I due Foscari*,[31] which the censors rejected because some Venetian families, the surviving Foscaris among them, might take offence. *Cromwell* or *Cromvello* also came under consideration, but the composer decided that the situations, as outlined in the scenario, were lifeless as sketched. Finally at the beginning of September Count Mocenigo was told of a subject that had truly captured Verdi's imagination: Victor Hugo's *Hernani*. 'Oh, if *Hernani* could be done, it would be a great and beautiful thing! . . . [It would] certainly have the biggest effect possible on the audience', he wrote.[32] Fully satisfied with the story, he feared nevertheless that it might prove almost impossible to get approved by the censors. Yet by the third week in September Mocenigo and his management had asked the librettist Piave to prepare a treatment or rough draft, using the sketch of the drama that Verdi said he was sending. At the outset, the composer had considered using either Solera, the Neapolitan Salvatore Cammarano, or 'a very, very distinguished poet from Milan'[33] who might wish to write under a pseudonym. This was probably Maffei. But, having been in communication with Piave since June, when *Cromvello* had been under examination, the composer decided to accept the Venetian, although he had little enough experience as a librettist, and Verdi asked Mocenigo to help get the censors' approval.

Francesco Maria Piave, born in Murano and Venetian to the core, was the son of a local official who owned a glass factory on the lagoon island and boasted 'a solid and wide culture'. The family's friends included Pope Gregory XVI. When he fell on hard times, the elder Piave and his son moved to Pesaro, then to Rome, where Francesco Maria, a former seminarian, soon established himself in literary circles, becoming a corresponding member of the Accademia Tiberina in 1831. Later admitted to full membership because of his translations and original works, he was also welcomed into the house of Jacopo Ferretti, a distinguished poet and writer who was one of Donizetti's close friends and helped Verdi win a following in Rome. Piave's friends called him 'the Goth Checcomaria' and 'Teutonic Piave', joking about his mop of unruly hair and the raucous voice he raised in night-time serenades outside their windows.[34] After his father died, Piave returned to Venice, where he arrived in 1838, happy indeed to be with his mother, brothers, and friends again. He was employed as a proof-reader and editor for the publisher Giuseppe Antonelli, where he had perhaps worked as a boy. Piave sent Ferretti news of a new project, a libretto for Verdi, in August 1843. The opera, he said, would be given at La Fenice with Sofia Löwe as the prima donna, Carolina Vietti as the contralto, Carlo Guasco as the tenor, and Antonio Superchi as the baritone. Later, he said, it seemed that the tenor Conti might take over Guasco's role. Verdi and the librettist had not met, but the friendship that grew out of their long collaboration was soon reflected in their letters. It lasted until the end of Piave's life.

By the end of October the Austrian police in Venice had vetoed many details in the sketch of the 'subversive' drama *Ernani*, as well they might have done, given the uproar the original play had caused in Paris.[35] The Romanticism of Hugo was politically dangerous; and many aspects of his *Hernani* had offended defenders of the status quo. Its language was considered rough and coarse; its glorification of the bandit Hernani and its attack on authority were held to be an endorsement of anarchy. In reactionary, Austrian-held Venice in 1843, the very words 'Hugo' and '*Hernani*' were suspect. The Habsburg Emperor was perhaps too much like the 'Vieillard stupide' ('the stupid old man') of the play, the symbol of the Old Regime.[36] While the censors continued their opposition to the opera, Verdi came to love it and feel himself completely committed to it. 'I am fully satisfied with it,' he wrote to the theatre management.[37] But the imperial censors had already begun to weaken the drama and under-mine some of its most effective moments, demanding that a conspiracy scene be changed, that no swords be drawn on-stage, that the dialogue between Ernani and his sovereign be modified, that the Emperor's proclamation of clemency be expanded into a scene, that the bandit-hero address the sovereign respectfully, that the words 'blood' and 'vengeance' be stricken from the text, and, finally, that the work be called *L'onore castigliano*, (Castilian Honour), to discourage that segment of the public that might respond too fervently to the title *Ernani*. If Verdi didn't like their title, he could choose from two others: *Il bandito* and *D[on] Gomez de Silva*.[38] None satisfied the composer, who stood firm as he had in Milan during the controversy over *I Lombardi alla prima crociata*.

Piave had completed all but the fourth act of the work by 15 November.[39] In Verdi's name he handed it to the directors of La Fenice, while Verdi went on with his composition, which he had begun some time before. He wanted further changes in the libretto, which Piave resisted, drawing from Verdi a fine letter written to the management of La Fenice on the strengths and weaknesses of opera librettos:

As for me, I would never want to trouble a poet [by asking him] to change a single line; and I have written the music to three librettos by Solera; and, comparing the original, which I have, with the printed librettos, one would not find more than a very, very few lines changed, and these by Solera himself. But Solera has already written five or six librettos and knows the theatre, [its] effects, and musical forms. Signor Piave has never written [for the opera stage], and thus it is natural that he falls short in these matters. What soprano, in fact, will sing (one right after the other), a big cavatina, a duet which ends with a trio, and an entire finale, as [Piave has] written in this first act of *Ernani*? Signor Piave will have good explanations to offer me, but I have others, and I answer that the [singer's] lungs cannot hold up under this strain. What maestro, without boring people, will set 100 lines of recitative to music, as in this third act? In the whole four acts of *Nabucco*, or *Lombardi*, you will surely not find more than 100 lines of recitative. . . . Even though I myself have very limited experience, I go to the theatre all year round, just the same, and I pay very careful attention: I have seen as clear as day that so many works would not have failed, had there been a better distribution of the set pieces, if the effects had been better calculated, if the musical forms had been clearer . . . in a word, if poet and composer had been more experienced. So many times a recitative that is too long, a phrase or a sentence that would be exquisite in a book, and even in a play, make people laugh in an opera.[40]

Armed with his convictions and apprehensive over certain shortcomings in the company hired by La Fenice, Verdi left Milan on 1 December 1843 and arrived before dawn on the lagoon, taking lodgings near the theatre. Piave, at Verdi's request, came to his room that morning. In Venice, he served as the composer's guide and companion. The city aroused mixed emotions in Verdi at the start. 'Venice is beautiful, is poetic, is divine, but . . . I would not stay here of my own will,' he wrote to Giuseppina Appiani.[41] The climate was very bad for a man who suffered from chronic throat infections; after experiencing some of the worst Venetian weather,

Verdi swore that he could get consumption if he stayed there too long. While there, he became a 'lion' of Venetian society, his entry into it having been facilitated by Countess Teresa Mosconi Papadopoli, Clara Maffei's closest friend. She lived in a fine *palazzo* behind San Marco, near Santa Maria Formosa. Through her, Verdi met Francesco Venturi, her legal adviser and close friend, whose long friendship with the composer is documented in many letters. Venturi, a declared enemy of Austria, was born in Avio near Rovereto. After the Revolution of 1848 and the founding of the Venetian Republic, Daniele Manin chose Venturi to represent the new state as its diplomatic envoy to the rulers of Tuscany, the Piedmont, and Rome. Another of Verdi's acquaintances in Venice was Galeazzo Fontana-Pini, a writer who, like Venturi, welcomed the composer into his home. Countess Soranzo, a descendant of one of the oldest patrician families, also entertained in Verdi's honour.

The composer's first assignment was to produce his *I Lombardi* to the best of his ability, for it had been given in September at Lanari's Teatro della Pergola in Florence and had had only a fair reception there. The Venetian rehearsals had scarcely begun when Verdi became involved in a discussion with the management of the Teatro La Fenice over a remark he was said to have made during an evening in a private home. When someone asked him how the rehearsals were going, he replied 'Not bad', a phrase that seemed to offend the powers at the theatre, perhaps because of his tone, perhaps because he spoke laconically. But his answer was reported back to the directors of La Fenice, who took Verdi's remark as criticism of the theatre. They protested directly to the composer, who defended himself: '"Not bad", I said. That is the whole story. I do not think that you can argue over that phrase.'[42] But the rehearsals, two each day, were not going particularly well. Of the cast, only Sophia Löwe seemed adequate. 'The others are doing what they can,' he said. He was especially worried over the tenor, Domenico Conti.[43]

He was not wrong to be alarmed. *I Lombardi*, which opened the important Carnival season at La Fenice on 26 December, was an almost total failure. Every set piece in it was either whistled or tolerated in silence. 'One of the truly classic fiascos,' Verdi wrote to Giuseppina Appiani.[44] Hurt, bitter, angry, he went back to his hotel just minutes after the curtain came down, facing what seemed to be a complete rout. He wrote to Luigi Toccagni, a Milanese journalist and friend: 'You, who love me as a father loves his own son, will be impatient to hear the news of *I Lombardi*. *I Lombardi* was a fiasco. There. I have told you everything.'[45] Only one short cabaletta, sung by Löwe, had been applauded. Under the circumstances, Verdi was lucky that the audience didn't shout the opera off the stage.

Slightly recovered by 29 December, Verdi took a hard line with the theatre, refusing to give *Ernani* with Conti in the cast. He protested that the tenor could not meet the demands of the role, and asked for a postponement of the première until another tenor—preferably Carlo Guasco—could be engaged. Otherwise, he said, 'I propose to dissolve the contract between us. Let us break this agreement; give me my passport; and I will leave at once.'[46] But the theatre management refused to let Verdi go. Like all other houses of the time, La Fenice held the passports of its contracted artists as security; Verdi could not leave the city without the theatre's release. Negotiations followed, and on the last day of the year, Verdi agreed to produce *Ernani* 'one way or another'. But he was far from satisfied; so on 4 January he left Venice, with the blessing of La Fenice, to go to Verona, in search of a tenor.[47] There, Strepponi and the tenor Raffaele Vitali were rehearsing *Nabucco* for the production at the Filarmonico. He helped with the last rehearsals and saw the opera through its first performance. The interests of La Fenice, too, were served; Verdi went to hear the *Nabucco* tenor, thinking that he might serve for *Ernani*; but Vitali, like Conti, could not satisfy Verdi, who decided finally that Carlo Guasco would have to sing.

Verdi wrote again to Toccagni:

I am writing to you with tears in my eyes, and I cannot wait to leave here. Add to this a slight fever that strikes me every evening, and you will see how 'well' I am. . . . I have a reasonably comfortable place to stay, and I stay in the house a lot, that is, I stay in bed. I am writing my poor *Ernani*, and I am not unhappy. In spite of my apparent indifference [to the success of *Ernani*], if it were to fail, I would blow out my brains; I could not bear the idea, all the more because these Venetians expect God-knows-what. . . . Night is coming, my desperation. Say hello to all my men and women friends, and tell them to think of me. Love me, but really love me.'[48]

On 28 January the finished vocal score of *Ernani* was delivered to the theatre management, which, in turn, gave it to the copyists. Three days later the Secretary of La Fenice, Guglielmo Brenna, reported to Count Mocenigo that 'the copyists say that this, too, is a masterpiece.'[49] But because of the confusion which prevailed at La Fenice, and because of the unruliness of the Venetian public, Verdi was frightened and depressed. Pacini's opera *La fidanzata corsa* had been shouted off the stage in mid-January, during a demonstration directed at the singers and at Mocenigo, who resigned his post in protest. (He later resumed it.) Verdi was in his loneliest, most dispirited state. Yet he did persist, through difficult circumstances. Guasco did not arrive in Venice until the last week in February; and when he did, Verdi discovered that he did not yet know his music. The scenery and costumes were late. But *Ernani* was finally presented to the Venetian public on 9 March 1844 with Guasco, Löwe, the baritone Antonio Superchi, and the bass Antonio Selva.[50]

From Giovannino Barezzi, who came for the last rehearsals and early performances, we know that Verdi was still orchestrating the score as late as 28 February, writing 'at full speed'.[51] The handicap of staging without proper scenery added to the confusion. Yet there was an air of success in the theatre. Venice was waiting hopefully for *Ernani*, as large groups of enthusiasts had begun to arrive from Padua, Trieste, Bologna, Treviso, and Milan. One group of young Paduans, members of one of the many societies of amateur musicians and writers that honoured Verdi, had tendered him an honorary banquet in Venice. Talk of gold wreaths, ovations, and triumph raised everyone's spirits. Even the composer must have been heartened by the dress rehearsal, which the cast performed in fine style.[52] 'This will be a night of triumph, of the coronation of Verdi as the foremost composer in the world',[53] Giovannino exulted, on the afternoon before the première. At the fashionable Caffè Florian in Piazza San Marco, everyone was talking about *Ernani*; and even before the first performance, the principal melodies were being sung in the city. Giovannino's letter captures Verdi's own excitement on that afternoon, which was crucial to his future.

Yet even a much more experienced composer would have found the first night utterly daunting. Disorder reigned at La Fenice, with Guasco shouting and raging, as he protested against the bad management in the theatre. His tirade went on for an hour, Giovannino reported, until he finally was seized with an attack of hoarseness and swore he could not sing. Some of the scenery had still not been delivered. Many costumes were missing. Improvisation was the order of the hour. Löwe, dissatisfied with her role, wished for more opportunities for personal vocal display. As the critical hour approached, Verdi must have despaired for his *Ernani*.[54]

But the opera was so good that not even a mediocre performance could ruin it. Löwe sang flat; Guasco, his voice perhaps damaged by his shouting, barely got through; Selva appeared to be too young for his role.

But in spite of everything, *Ernani* survived to become one of Verdi's most popular works. At the première, almost all the set pieces were generously applauded as their composer was called out for bows at the end of each act. The first night, though, was not nearly as successful as those of *Nabucco* or *Lombardi* had been. Even Giovannino Barezzi had to admit that. 'If the score had not been as good as I told you yesterday, the opera would never have been allowed to finish,' he wrote to his father.[55] Verdi, writing to Giuseppina Appiani, gave her what he called 'the real story'. '*Ernani*, which had its première last night, was fairly successful. If I had had singers—I will not say sublime singers, but just singers who would sing—*Ernani* would have come off as well as *Nabucco* and *Lombardi* in Milan.'[56]

Yet his personal triumph was beyond dispute, as he continued to be entertained in the great *palazzi* of Venice and was accompanied back to his rooms by a band that followed him home after the opera, playing his music and shouting his name. He also became the hero of an influential circle of intellectuals, poets, journalists, and professional men such as Venturi, Fontana-Pini, and, later, Dr Cesare Vigna, a pioneer in humane care of the mentally ill. Because of the hospitable welcome given him, Verdi gradually came to like Venice, which, he said, he would regret leaving. While there, he became involved with a woman friend in whom he was interested for at least seven years. Referring to her in letters to Piave between 1844 and 1851, he called her 'that Angel whom you know' ('quel Angiolo che tu sai') and 'the woman I like' ('la mia simpatia') in letters of 15 March and 2 April 1844. On 25 March 1851 he again called her 'the Angel whom you know' ('l'Angelo che sai'). She may have been a singer such as Geltrude Bortolotti, whom Verdi liked a great deal and often mentioned in letters, or the Cadiz-born Antonietta Del Carmen Montenegro; but it is more likely that she was a Venetian woman. In the letter of 2 April 1844 Verdi asked Piave about the *Lionesse* or 'Gentlewomen' of Venice; but in the previous sentence he mentioned 'la cara Valmarana', who is perhaps identifiable as Countess Giuseppina Valmarana, daughter of the ducal family Valier, whom he and Piave both knew. The composer referred to her on at least one other occasion. It is equally possible that the woman Verdi loved was the daughter of one of the city's other old families, the Soranzos, the Papadopolis, or the Venturis. As we shall see, after the traumatic events that shattered his peace of mind in the winter and spring 1850–1, he never mentioned 'that Angel' again.[57]

The Return Home and the Purchase of Il Pulgaro

The bloom of satisfaction left Verdi as soon as he began to travel. From Cremona at dawn on 15 March he wrote back to Piave: 'I tremble as I get near my home!! What a tremendous fate is mine!! Never a single joy without sorrows!! . . . My health is fair, but I have no strength. I feel as if I have no blood at all.' He added that perhaps a few weeks of rest in the country would get him back on his feet.[58] While he was at home, he signed an agreement to buy the farm called Il Pulgaro near La Madonna dei Prati. He also gave his father powers of attorney to manage his affairs and to bid the farm in at the 'burned candles' auction where it was sold by Sabatino Sacerdoti, a gentleman from Parma. Thus Verdi became the owner of 80 *biolche* of first-quality farm land and a farmhouse and other outbuildings near Il Pulgaro, not far from Le Piacentine, which was the setting for Bernardo Bertolucci's film *1900*; it virtually adjoined some of the land that Carlo Verdi had leased from the priest of La Madonna dei Prati and had given up in 1830. The Verdis had not been without property in those fourteen years, though, for Carlo Verdi owned land in his own name in Roncole during that time. With its meadows, cultivated fields, vineyard, and dwelling, Il Pulgaro perhaps was Verdi's parents' primary residence after 8 May 1844, the day Verdi bought it. The price was 29,800 lire in gold and silver, to be paid in four instalments, 8,000 gold lire at once, the second of 4,000 lire at the end of November 1844, the third of 8,900 due at the end of December 1845; and the fourth due on 31 December 1846, also of 8,900 lire. The deed was drawn up by the notaries Giovanni Biazzi and Giuseppe Rivi and filed in the Archivio Notarile in Parma on 8 May. With this farm, described in the deed as having about 25 hectares or 62 acres, the composer became a man of property in his own name.[59] As we have seen from Cavalli's account, it was believed in Busseto that he had made the farm over to his parents. From some of Carlo Verdi's letters to Sacerdoti in 1846 and 1847, it seems Verdi had overreached himself financially.

When he set out for Milan, Verdi had with him a young musician whom he had known for years, Emanuele Muzio. Eight years Verdi's junior, Muzio was a former protégé of Provesi and the Busseto Philharmonic Society. Born in the village of Zibello, near Busseto, he was the son of Genovese emigré parents; his father was a cobbler. Muzio had studied at the city music school, perhaps even when Verdi was master there, and had been a student of Margherita Barezzi, who also taught music. He and

Verdi probably met in 1828 and may have worked together even before Provesi's death. Planning to become a priest, Muzio had been helped by Don Pettorelli in a modest career as an organist. His life as a seminarian was said to have come to an end when he paraded around Busseto with the family cat, which he had decked out with a clerical collar. But Muzio did study with Ferrari, Verdi's rival for the post of organist in Busseto, and had played and sung in country parishes such as Sant'Agata and Vidalenzo. At the beginning of 1844 the Monte di Pietà gave him a grant, similar to the one awarded earlier to Verdi, to study music in Milan. The same foundation had refused to assist him with study in the seminary.[60] As Barezzi's protégé, he fared better. To be sure that he did not go astray, Barezzi entrusted him to Verdi's care.

On 10 April 1844, 'a fine, beautiful, sunny day', as Barezzi noted in his Day-Book, he gave Muzio a cash advance of 180 lire and 80 centesimi in Milanese currency. Three days later, on a 'day with some rain and sun afterwards', Verdi and his charge left for Milan.[61] For both men a new chapter of life had begun, Muzio entering the large, cosmopolitan world of the international music business and Verdi assuming responsibility for another person, someone who was vulnerable, naïve, and susceptible.

12

April 1844 – Autumn 1846

More 'Years in the Galleys'

Verdi's new arrangement with Muzio helped him to manage overwork and strain in the post-*Ernani* years, for the younger man virtually lived to serve his Signor Maestro. Adapting to each other's ways, the two men developed a bond that grew stronger daily and endured, in spite of the many stresses to which it was subjected over the decades. Between the première of *Ernani* and that of *La battaglia di Legnano* in January 1849, Verdi composed constantly; in that period only *Jérusalem* was a reworking of an earlier score. He had to deal with contracts, deadlines, correspondence, composition, orchestration, singers, conductors, publishers, impresarios, enemies, and well-wishers, keeping all the while to an exhausting schedule of travel. Understandably, he paid his toll with bouts of illness, one of which was life-threatening. When he wrote to Clara Maffei in 1858 complaining of the drudgery of his 'years in the galleys', he was referring to his entire career up to that year and was not exaggerating.[1] Muzio helped to relieve at least some of it, even when he and Verdi were separated from each other by the Atlantic Ocean. When the two men started working together as teacher and student, Verdi was already committed to new works for Rome, Milan, and Naples, with the first commission on his calendar an opera for Lanari's son Antonio (Tonino), who was then the impresario at the Teatro Argentina in Rome.[2] *Ernani*, which Gallo was producing at the Teatro San Benedetto in Venice in mid-May 1844, was also on the programme of the Argentina. Genoa and Florence were getting ready to give it and secondary houses all over Italy were adding it to their summer and autumn schedules.[3] Verdi and

Piave, reviewing possible subjects for the opera for Rome, had settled, with Ricordi's approval, on *Lorenzino de' Medici*; but it was vetoed by the papal censors.[4] The two men then had to look for another drama.

In Vienna that spring the important first Austrian production of *Ernani* was on the calendar, although Verdi was unable to oversee it himself. At this juncture, when impresarios were vying to give it, and were planning productions of *Nabucco* and *I Lombardi*, it was important to the composer to have his music played as he wished, so he sometimes sent written instructions to those in charge. To Leone Herz in Vienna he wrote:

I could not tell you which tenor would be best suited for the role of Ernani because I do not know Ivanoff. [Eugenia] Tadolini would be appropriate, all the more because there is a cavatina. [Antonietta] Montenegro absolutely could not do that role. The part of Carlo would be just right for Ronconi; and Selva's [role is right] for him, but Selva will not come because he is singing in Venice now and is enormously successful. The tempos are all marked in the score as clearly as possible. If you pay attention to the dramatic situation and to the words, [you] could hardly make a mistake with a tempo. I only point out that I do not like slow tempos; it is better to sin on the side of liveliness than to drag. I again thank you for your concern, and for wanting to perform *Ernani* correctly. Thus I ask that you see that the roles are entrusted to singers that the audience likes the most and that the performance be accurate. . . . I beg you not to allow cuts. There is nothing to remove, and one could not take out the smallest phrase without damaging the whole. I ask again that the conspiracy [scene] of the third act not be either too slow or too fast. The tempo is exactly the same as that of the Prophecy in *Nabucco* at the words 'pietra ove sorge l'altro, etc.'. Furthermore, I ask you to press a bit at the end. You will be good enough to tell me when the rehearsals begin, to whom the roles will be assigned, and about the outcome of the first night: I will be very, very grateful to you.[5]

He was happy to hear from Giacomo Pedroni in May that Donizetti had taken over the production himself. In the older composer's hands, Verdi's work was safe. Even before the end of May, Muzio reported, more than twenty theatres in Italy and others in Paris and London had asked for *Ernani*.[6] During the next three years the opera was produced from Constantinople and Corfu to Rio de Janeiro and Havana, from Copenhagen to Algeria. Marcello Conati has identified 32 theatres that gave the work in 1844, 60 in 1845, and at least 65 in 1846, not including revivals in houses that had already presented it.[7] As Conati notes, *Ernani* was more than a success; it became the fashion, keeping Verdi's name before the public month in and month out. His popularity was reflected in the press of people who tried to see him. Muzio found that even when Verdi tried to shut himself in his apartment, he could not escape. Among those who sought him out were publishers who hoped to profit from his rapidly developing career.[8] Ricordi appeared likely to go on publishing Verdi's works; but that did not discourage others from trying to lure him to their houses. Francesco and Giovanna Strazza Lucca, who had entertained Verdi in their home in Milan, were particularly persistent. Muzio described the humorous scene when Giovanna came to Verdi's apartment to plead the Lucca cause. She began to cry, declaring that her husband was ill with frustration because Verdi would not enter into a contract with him. '"When we are in bed, all he does is sigh," she said. At this, the Signor Maestro said to her: "Sigh? Is that all he does?" and began to laugh and turned it all into a joke, to get rid of her quickly.'[9] However, this formidable woman and her husband did not give up. Eventually Verdi did agree to write for the Luccas, but his relationship with them was far from cordial.

Among other supporters Verdi could count the Milanese noblemen and gentlemen who had travelled to Venice with Luciano Manara for his *Ernani*: Count Bernardo Tolomei, Marquis Giulio Sommariva, the Marquises Giovanni and Carlo d'Adda, and Marquis Mainoni. It is perhaps to them that Verdi owed an offer that came to compose a cantata for a very important congress of scientists of the day.[10] The Società de' Nobili, which congregated in its private club, the Casinò de' Nobili in Verdi's street, was divided into two factions over the choice of a poet to write the text. One group supported Andrea Maffei, the other, the critic and librettist Felice Romani. Maffei won the assignment. But, in spite of Verdi's previous associations with the Casinò de' Nobili, where he had performed with Massini's troupe in the 1830s, he was unwilling to write this *pièce d'occasion*. It seems that he did not decline at the outset, though, for—finding the text unsuitable—he asked Maffei to revise it. The poet refused, although Verdi's unquestioned authority in matters of music should have carried weight with the older poet. At that, Verdi wrote to the Società de' Nobili, refusing to compose the music for Maffei's text, which he described as impossible to set. But when Romani's better poem was presented to him, he praised it.[11] A few days later the story came out in *Il Figaro*, causing the composer considerable embarrassment. Angry at the airing of a private matter in the press, he protested that he was a close friend of Maffei. To prove it, he returned the Romani text to the gentlemen of the Società and refused the commission because of having, as he said, limited time, too many pressing commitments, and precarious health. At one point, he used Donna Emilia Morosini to communicate his position directly to the head of the Società. He then turned to mending his fences with Maffei, one of his closest friends.

To salve the poet's wounded feelings, Verdi wrote to him at Riva del Garda, where Maffei was holidaying, offering to write the music to the *Inno* as soon as possible and to have it performed and published, 'to prove to the public that I extricated myself from that assignment not because your poetry was poor, but for other reasons'.[12] At this point, Verdi seemed genuinely interested in doing the *Inno*, but because of the pressure of his other contractual obligations, he never wrote the work. His inherent dislike of such pieces undoubtedly played a role in his decision not to compose it. To his chagrin, the incident remained a matter of discussion in the city, for such a controversy loomed large in the world of Milanese intellectuals. Muzio says that Maffei had been chosen over the better-known Romani perhaps because he was Verdi's friend. The verses were 'decidedly impossible to set to music: sometimes free verse, sometimes *terzine*, sometimes *quartine* . . . and the Signor Maestro could not divide this poetry into pieces to be sung by the chorus and the soloists. . . . He wanted it to be dramatic.'[13]

Maffei was not Verdi's only close friend at this time. Among the older men of his circle, he trusted Toccagni, with whom he had a kind of father–son relationship. And among the younger men, he was particularly fond of Manara, who remained one of Verdi's staunchest supporters between 1844 and 1847. Manara was 17 and Verdi 31 when they met.[14] Both advocated Italian independence from Austria and were influenced by the fervour of Carlo Cattaneo. The two men may have met through the Maffeis or Donna Emilia Morosini, whose son, as we have seen, became one of Manara's followers.[15] With his energy and great physical beauty, Manara spoke for the Italy that was ready four years later to leap to the barricades and rush to the battlefields. The composer described him as his intimate friend; unfortunately, although they corresponded, their letters do not survive.

In these first months of Muzio's stay in Milan, he was with Verdi daily; through his eyes, we see Verdi at 31, generous, open, courteous, and surrounded by the Milanese gentlemen who revered him. At times he became angry, impatient, or nervous; he was often ill, rarely free of pressure, and always volatile. 'For several days now the Signor Maestro has been giving me lessons in counterpoint', Muzio informed Barezzi on 22 April, shortly after he settled in the city.

No one can go to the Conservatory, neither local people nor foreigners; and if, eventually, I shall be able to go, it will be as a special favour conferred by the Viceroy and Governor of Milan on the Signor Maestro Verdi. Moreover, he will be kind enough to give me a certificate as well, which—as soon as I have it—I will send to you. Many music students would pay 2 or even 3 *talleri* a lesson if the Signor Maestro wished to give them; but he does not give them to anyone excepting a poor devil to whom he has proffered a thousand advantages, even that of giving him a lesson every morning, rather than two or three times a week. I am overwhelmed; and furthermore, sometimes when he gets me to do [something] for him, he even gives me my dinner. He, my Signor Maestro, has a breadth of spirit, a generosity, a wisdom, a heart that (to draw a comparison) one would have to set beside yours and say that they are the most generous hearts in the whole world.[16]

At this time Muzio was living in a furnished room in Contrada dei Frustagnani in the Parish of Santa Maria Segreta, but Verdi, wanting him nearby, found him a room just across the street from his own new apartment in Contrada del Monte. With this new physical closeness came still greater collaboration, with Muzio serving Verdi rather as a younger brother might have done, going far beyond any role of pupil, copyist, or secretary. Sometime in 1844 the younger man met Strepponi, probably through Verdi. The soprano had been with Verdi in Verona during the Carnival season at the Teatro Filarmonico before Muzio came to Milan; after that engagement, though, she seemed to have no contracts for opera until August and September, when she sang *Ernani* in Bergamo, again with Verdi present. Between March and August she sang only once, a concert in Turin in May. It is likely, therefore, that she and Muzio first met that spring or summer, for in the autumn and winter she sang the Carnival of 1844–5 at the Teatro Carolino in Palermo in an engagement that kept her away from Milan almost six months.

By May Barezzi was getting regular dispatches from Muzio about life with Verdi, with detailed accounts of the composer's meetings with friends, enemies, and acquaintances. On one occasion, Muzio described an encounter with a writer:

Signor Vitali, a contributor to the *Gazzetta musicale di Milano*, wanted to demonstrate a method of establishing precise tempos, and he said that . . . where a composer writes 'adagio' and 'allegro' he should also put the number of minutes that the piece should last; and he said that the Signor Maestro approved this system and would adopt it in his next opera; the Signor Maestro, though, says that he would not dream of doing this, and that [Vitali] is an *old prick*. See what a wretched fool Signor Vitali is, to compromise the name of a maestro like Signor Verdi, who is so fine and good![17]

As it happened, Verdi later did give the minutes and seconds that some of his pieces should last.

In this same letter, Muzio said he had seen Seletti and some of the Busseto Carraras; Verdi had gone with him to look at rooms and to try to locate a piano for him.

How good he is! . . . I sometimes have headaches. The Signor Maestro tells me that they are caused by the study of counterpoint, for I sometimes have to rack my brain for an hour to bring out one bar; and because today I have an extremely difficult bass, the Signor Maestro said this has caused it; and when he says that something is so, you can be sure that it really is.[18]

Verdi was coaching him in exercises by Fenaroli, Lavigna's teacher; these were perhaps the same ones he had used when he was a student in Milan. Soon Muzio was ready to go on to Palestrina, Corelli, and other masters whom Verdi considered the cornerstones of musical education. The lessons were a challenge and a joy:

When I begin a lesson, the Signor Maestro says to me: 'Remember that I am inexorable.' You can imagine how frightened I am; but the fear goes away little by little, when he says 'Well done.' Understand, though, please, Signor Barezzi, that he does not let a single note pass unless it is perfect; he wants things perfect. . . . You may be sure that he has made me write some great basses; I will always keep everything I write, as if it were a precious pearl. . . . So far I have studied harmony; and you may be sure that if I had been with some other maestro, apart from the fact that he would never have taught me so well, so perfectly, it would have taken at least a year, surely. These mercenary teachers do not teach with the Signor Maestro Verdi's love and zeal. . . . And then other teachers do not explain things so well or in such detail as the Signor Maestro Verdi does; so even the student is fired with enthusiasm. I can truly say that I was born very, very lucky! First because I found an incomparable Maecenas [Barezzi], who cares for me; second, because I have a maestro who is so celebrated, and famous all over Europe, as the Signor Maestro Verdi is—the idol of the Milanese.[19]

At Verdi's insistence, Muzio began to go to performances at the various Milanese theatres—'and I must go only when he tells me to himself, and when there is good music.'[20] On the morning before a performance, Verdi told Muzio what to listen for.

Inevitably, Muzio heard much of Verdi's music as it was being composed. Thus we have frequent, detailed accounts from the period of the composition of *I due Foscari*, *Giovanna d'Arco*, and other works of these years. Muzio thought much of it glorious; each opera was the greatest of all of Verdi's works, certain to drive every other composer from the stage. Muzio's *naïveté* takes away nothing from the beauty of their relationship, for Muzio served Verdi well, even though he could never have been objective about him. When things went badly, he was supportive. When Verdi was ill, Muzio cared for him. And when things went well, the letters to Barezzi are filled with the joy that both the composer and his protégé felt.

Oh, Signore, if you had been in Signor Maestro Verdi's house on the day that news came of the enormous success [of *Ernani* in Vienna], to see people coming in for more than an hour, now someone who had had a letter from Donizetti, now another who had had news from a count, I don't remember his last name, then another who had something written by Merelli, and so many others; . . . and [if you could] hear the beautiful things that they wrote about the Signor Maestro and about his *Ernani*, you would surely have cried, oh Signore, because you are so sensitive, and then to see them all sitting there, side by side, now one reading his letter, now another, and with all these letters in their hands they looked like a lot of youngsters in school, and the Signor Maestro there in their midst, sitting at his writing-table, looking like their teacher; and I there in a corner, watching so carefully that I looked like the beadle of the school. It was something that gave both pleasure and delight.[21]

So it was throughout the middle years of the 1840s, Verdi giving Muzio his piano and getting another for himself; Verdi calling out of the window to the young man across the way; Muzio measuring Verdi's medicine and massaging his back when he suffered one of his frequent bouts of rheumatism, laryngitis, or neuralgia; Muzio accompanying Il Signor Maestro on day-long excursions to the country that were regular events in the men's circle in which Verdi moved; Muzio running beside Verdi to see the great Milan fire of September 1846 and Verdi climbing over the wall of the city gardens, when he got caught inside; and the two men bowling and playing cards and billiards. Verdi bought his student a complete wardrobe and fed and sheltered him. The extent to which this relationship enriched them both is reflected in the lifelong friendship that followed. Although Muzio always referred to the composer in his letters to Verdi and others in the most formal usage possible, choosing the 'Egli' and 'Lui' that one might use in addressing nobility,[22] there developed between them a remarkable trust that Verdi shared with almost no one else in his life. Muzio repaid the many favours with almost fifty years of unshakable loyalty, promoting Verdi's interests on three continents and giving his music the widest possible exposure everywhere he could.

Rome and *I due Foscari*

The question of a suitable subject for the Teatro Argentina arose in Verdi's correspondence with Piave during the first half of May 1844, as the composer put steady pressure on his librettist to get a scenario to him and begin the text of *I due Foscari*, a drama that Verdi found extremely moving. Earlier that year Demaldè had urged him to consider *Marion Delorme*, which the composer found distasteful: 'I know the subject you suggest. The protagonist is a character I do not like. I do not like women who are whores on stage. As for everything else, it would be a very, very beautiful subject if it were not for this obstacle.'[23] *I due Foscari*, though unacceptable for Venice, because of the possible objections of the Foscaris, Loredans, and Barbarigos, proved a much safer subject, the first of Byron's works that Verdi seems to have considered for the stage. Byron was still something of a hero in the 1840s, although he had been dead for twenty years. In spite of his enthusiasm for this 'sensitive and extremely touching' drama, Verdi noted that 'in Byron there is not found that theatrical grandeur that is nevertheless needed for operas', as he begged Piave to send him the scenario or treatment as quickly as possible.[24] When he got it, he was truly impressed: 'A beautiful drama, very beautiful, superlatively beautiful.' Yet he was far from satisfied with all Piave's work, although he could praise the first scene as 'fine' and the poetry as 'superb'. Making suggestions for the structure and arrangement of the scenes and set pieces, he urged brevity, as he often did while working with Piave.[25] Keeping *Lorenzino de' Medici* in mind, with the idea that he and Piave might do it later, he also let Piave know that he had concluded an agreement with Lanari to compose for Venice in the Carnival season of 1845-6, provided the impresario could secure the Teatro La Fenice that year; otherwise he would write for Florence under the same contract.

Verdi was into the composition of *I due Foscari* for Rome when another composer, Francesco Cannetti of Vicenza, wrote begging him not to finish the opera, for he himself was setting *I due Foscari* at that time. He apparently feared that he would share the fate of Alberto Mazzucato, whose *Ernani* disappeared from the stage as Verdi's opera on the same subject swept from one theatre to another. His appeal fell on deaf ears: Verdi went on with the opera, as indeed he was obliged to do.[26] Work was slowed at times by recurrences of his old illnesses, throat infections, a bronchitis that kept him short of breath, and—as always—stomach trouble. Planning to finish *I due Foscari* in Busseto, he made arrangements to go home. He also went to Bergamo, where Strepponi was singing *Ernani* during the annual summer fair season, and conducted it at the Teatro Riccardi on 11 August. From there Strepponi wrote to Giovanna Lucca on Verdi's behalf about the contract Verdi had agreed to sign with Casa Lucca:

At Verdi's request I am answering your husband's letter of 10 August, in which he acknowledges receipt of the agreement issued on the first of the month, approving all of it. That is fine, and when I get back from Bergamo, I will carry out the duties of *Correspondent*, which I have assumed, and the regular contract will be drawn up. I warn you, however, of one thing: Verdi intends to do as he has done [in the past], that is: when the two parties agree on the terms, the contract must be written and signed without any lawyers having a part in this, because they are absolutely useless. This is what he told me to write to you, and this is what I am writing. I am sending this letter to you because I know your husband less well than I know you. . . . My health is very, very good. I hope that you will stay wonderfully beautiful, as always. Love me, and believe that I am [yours], in haste,

Giuseppina Strepponi.[27]

While Verdi was in Busseto, complaining that he was not feeling well, Strepponi went back to Milan, where he arrived two days after she did. On the thirtieth he and Piave left for Rome, where they directed rehearsals for *I due Foscari*. Its première at the Teatro Argentina was on 3 November with Marianna Barbieri-Nini, the bass Achille De Bassini, and the tenor Giacomo Roppa. On the first night it got a rather disappointing reception. Muzio attributed part of the problem to the exorbitant prices of the first-night tickets; but the singers themselves seem not to have done complete justice to their roles.[28] For the composer, though, there were impressive personal ovations and the theatre was sold out for all the early performances.[29] Verdi's entry into the highest social and intellectual circles was facilitated by Piave and Ferretti, who was by then the 60-year-old dean of Roman poets and the author of many librettos. He wrote a long poem in Verdi's honour and read it at a banquet given by Prince Alessandro Torlonia. A medal bearing Verdi's image was struck by the government.

He and Piave stayed in Rome for the first performances of *I due Foscari*, and then returned north by land, perhaps because the sea journey from Leghorn to Civitavecchia in October had discouraged them from trying it again in winter weather. In Bologna they separated, as Piave went to Venice and Verdi made for Milan. He had serious second thoughts about his opera, as he confided to Toccagni and others. Writing to Piave in 1848, Verdi referred to it: 'In subjects that are inherently sad, you end up in the mortuary, as—for example—in the *Foscari*; [these works] have one single tint from start to finish.'[30]

In November, when Ferretti sent him a copy of the verses written in his honour, Verdi sent him a note of thanks that reflects something of his discouragement at that time. Piave, he wrote, was 'very sad'; the trip had been long and trying; and they had separated in Bologna 'almost without speaking' to each other. Verdi let Ferretti know that he had received one of the medals with his image from Cardinal Antonio Tosti, the Vatican Treasurer. He promised to stop in Rome the next summer, when he would be on the way home from Naples.[31]

Giovanna d'Arco

Suffering from a cold and exhaustion after the difficult trip from Rome,[32] Verdi was forced back into his routine as Merelli waited for the new opera for La Scala. Casting about for a libretto, he chose Joan of Arc as his subject; it was perhaps suggested originally by Solera,[33] who drew his historically incorrect drama at least in part from Schiller. Verdi wrote *Giovanna d'Arco* in about four months. Perhaps because of his haste, it fell short of what it might have been. While he was composing it, he also directed the revival of *I Lombardi*, which Merelli offered for the opening night of the 1844–5 season.[34] Muzio's description of the rehearsals shows how much energy Verdi invested in these productions. 'I am sorry to see him wear himself out; he shouts desperately; he stamps his feet so hard that it looks as if he is playing the pedals of an organ; he sweats so much that drops of perspiration fall on his score . . . Collini [*sic*] is doing a tremendously good job . . . Poggi, good; Frezzolini is incomparable'.[35]

But as the rehearsals went on, the singers developed problems that compromised the opera. Erminia Frezzolini, one of the finest performers of her age, found that her powers were diminished and cried over her shortcomings. Poggi the tenor, her husband, was afraid of being shouted off the stage because of his suspected pro-Austrian sympathies and his involvement with a notorious noblewoman. Colini seemed ill-suited to his role, being too sweet of temperament and too slight of voice.[36]

Verdi, composing *Giovanna d'Arco*, rehearsing *I Lombardi*, and carrying on his usual schedule of business correspondence and interviews, was working from eight in the morning until after midnight. His only break was at midday, when he and Muzio took about two hours off. All this labour was rewarded, for *I Lombardi* ran for fifteen nights; but Verdi did not go to the theatre, avoiding even the opening performance, as Muzio reported. *Giovanna d'Arco* had its première on 15 February 1845. It was a turbulent season at La Scala. Poggi and Merelli were fighting with each other over *I Lombardi*; the orchestra seemed mean and small; the audience was restless.[37] At the height of the season, Antonietta Raineri-Marini broke her contract and left Milan, forcing Merelli to find a substitute for her.[38] 'A cat', Muzio called one singer who stepped in. Solera's wife, the soprano Teresa Rosmini, ignored Verdi's advice and sang Donizetti's *Gemma di Vergy*, which proved to be a fiasco of such proportions that it was taken off the programme after only two performances. She then left the company.[39]

In spite of these unfavourable circumstances, Verdi seemed happy with his *Giovanna d'Arco*, about which Muzio, understandably, raved. Although critical reception was cool, and Verdi uneasy about the reviews, the opera had a respectable run of seventeen performances at La Scala and proved popular with the audience. Its most accessible pieces were taken up at once by bands and barrel-organs[40] which passed them along to the people, who embraced them. Verdi confided to Piave that *Giovanna d'Arco* was a great success in spite of an organized opposition to it and that it was without doubt the best of his operas. His popularity was confirmed by the fact that three of his operas were on the programme at La Scala that year, the third being a revival of *Ernani*. This once again proved a triumph for him, but the level of performance was uneven and Verdi's dissatisfaction great because the cast, which included Rita Gabussi, De Bassini, and two débutante singers, had had insufficient rehearsal. Verdi told Piave that it was very badly performed but popular with the audience.

The day after the first performance of *Ernani* Verdi, ready to leave for Venice, asked Muzio to stay in Milan and monitor the performances that followed. He arranged for Piave to meet him in Padua, where they had dinner and stayed overnight before going on. Verdi had taken rooms near Gallo's Teatro San Benedetto, where he oversaw the final rehearsals of *Ernani*, which had its first performance on 24 March, and *I due Foscari*, which followed six days later. His soprano was Bortolotti, the baritone Badiali, a substitute for Celestino Salvatori, who was ill. While he was in Venice, Verdi wrote a long letter to Pietro Romani, the maestro concertatore who was preparing *Giovanna d'Arco* for Lanari's spring season at the Teatro della Pergola in Florence. It is quoted here as an example of the anxious care he took over productions which he could not supervise.

Dearest Romani,

I thank you for the regards sent to me by Bortolotti. Do you want me to point out for you some things about *Giovanna*? You don't need them and know how to interpret [it] by yourself; but if you will be happy to have me tell you something, here I am at your service. First of all, take care about the overture. . . . The first section of the overture is an allegro agitato vivo ma non troppo. The adagio is an andantino non troppo mosso (which should be pastoral in feeling). The last section is a marziale that should be played at the same tempo as the first all[egr]o. The introduction is an and[ante] piùttosto mosso. The adagio of the tenor aria lies well forward for the voice. The chorus in C minor very fast. The cabaletta larga and cantabile. I won't tell you anything about Giovanna's cavatina, which takes care of itself. The Chorus of Demons is a graceful and sensuous little waltz, rather adagio: the Chorus of Angels goes on in the same tempo with the same movement as the waltz. The woman's cabaletta ('Son guerriera') as lively as you like. The adagio trio for solo voices largo and precise in its tempo. . . .

Chorus of the first act in C [should be] presto. The bass aria has the same exact tempos as the bass aria in *Ernani*, both in the adagio and in the cabaletta. I beg you to take care with the duet between the tenor and the woman. Let the tempos be lively in the orchestra, largo in the sung parts. The adagio in G minor should be largo and very movingly sung by Giovanna, particularly when it gets to the words 'Sia maledetta'. There should be a great deal of contrast between the two pieces. The chorus that comes next should be fast, and the cabaletta cantabile, and the mixed Chorus of the Demons presto. All the rest is clear by itself. In the adagio of the finale I beg you to keep the chorus singing staccato and sotto voce.

The last act begins with a description of a battle. I want it to be played pianissimo, sotto voce, as if from far away, like an echo. The adagio of the duet largo. . . . The cabaletta in four tempos, but very, very lively and passionately. It must be very strongly marked also by the cor anglais and the cello. The final scene: adagio the 6/8 in G minor and the notes for the violin leggere a punta d'arco, which makes a great effect.

Rec[itativ]o: largo. The clarinet solo should be very precise and all 'sotto voce', with the exception of the trill with the cadenza. [. . .] The rest largo.

Here is a lot of chatter for you, and no use to you. I put everything in your hands; but I don't even have to say this because I know how friendly you feel toward your friend, G. Verdi.[41]

Writing to Piave, perhaps even on the day he got back, the composer said that he was looking forward to the arrival of fresh fish and oysters that the librettist was sending him.

I won't tell you to say hello to Bortolotti because now that I am no longer there, you will no longer be spending your time *between the theatre and the prima donna's house*. Nevertheless, if *by chance* you should meet that dear, dear woman, tell her the nicest possible things for me and also give my regards to her family. Addio, dear Tom Cat, love me a lot, for—to tell you the truth—even though I don't show it, I do love you a little.[42]

Verdi, who had a visit from Solera as soon as he got home, also spoke to Andrea Maffei about writing a sketch or scenario of *Attila* for his new opera for the Teatro La Fenice. Intending to have Piave set it in verse, he was also planning to send the librettist a copy of Zacharias Werner's play *Attila, König der Hunnen*, from which it would be taken. Less than two weeks later, the scenario was on its way to Piave, although Verdi then suggested that he look for the Werner drama in Venice to save time and read Madame de Staël's *De l'Allemagne* for background. With Gallo's successful season behind him and *Attila* on schedule, at least for the moment, he could give his attention to yet another work, *Alzira*, which he had agreed to write for the Teatro San Carlo in Naples. Its libretto was by Salvatore Cammarano, a Neapolitan poet then in his forties, who had written *Lucia di Lammermoor*, *Roberto Devereux*, and *Belisario* for Donizetti; *La vestale* for Mercadante; and *Saffo* for Pacini. He could offer Verdi extensive knowledge and experience for the new venture, far beyond anything Solera or the novice Piave possessed.

Naples and *Alzira*

Ill with stomach trouble, severe headaches, and rheumatism, Verdi suffered through the spring of 1845, sometimes staying in his apartment to avoid drafts and wind, sometimes staying in bed. He watched the post daily for letters from Busseto, hoping to hear from Barezzi, Demaldè, or Giovannino. In Muzio's letters, the composer is seen as anxious, angry, and depressed. 'What the devil are they doing, that they don't write? Are they dead?' he asked.[43] Once, when Verdi waited in vain for Barezzi's letters, he boiled over because the post brought him 'just nothing', 'un bel niente'. He appears to have been genuinely lonely and even homesick, in spite of his fame. His attachment to Busseto endured, even when things went badly. Money may have been something of a problem, for the composer had had to make one of his 3,000-lire payments on the farm Il Pulgaro in December 1844. Verdi and Muzio were constantly in touch with the other Bussetani in Milan, the Selettis, Francesco Mingardi; one of the Corbellinis, who, like Muzio, was on a scholarship from the Monte di Pietà; Stefano Barezzi, with whom Muzio stayed briefly in 1845; and some of the Carraras, from Barezzi's mother's clan. As in the past and future, they exchanged goods and gossip. New irritations and insults from Busseto seemed never to be lacking, nor did Verdi's fame discourage certain Bussetans from annoying him.

During the spring of 1845 Muzio had composed some marches for the Busseto Philharmonic and had asked Verdi to look over them and criticize them before he turned them over to the organization at home. Instructions for their performance accompanied the scores, and it even seems that Verdi had a hand in their orchestration. But to his and Muzio's dismay, the men of the Philharmonic said they were difficult to play and to understand. Muzio was called home to help with the concerts, very much as Verdi had been nearly ten years earlier; but Verdi forbade it, as he was planning to leave for Venice and wanted Muzio to remain in the city and send his usual bulletins on what went on there. About the marches, Muzio wrote: '[Verdi] says that if he had not thought them good, he would not have let me send them, and that since he revised them himself, [the musicians of the Philharmonic] will find that all the notes could not be in better order. The Signor Maestro has just played them over and over again and he says that they are good.'[44]

This, like many other conflicts in Busseto, had its origin in friction between the clergy and the anticlerical faction. Yet another nomination aroused fresh rivalries as Enrico Landi, then the organist of the collegiate church of San Bartolomeo, tried to have himself appointed to Verdi's former position as maestro di musica. The Monte di Pietà, though, acted as it had in the early years of the 1830s, by trying to get the post held open until Muzio could finish his studies with Verdi in Milan. This new strife divided Busseto into a Muzio faction and a Landisti party; but this time there was a difference, for Landi had succeeded in winning some of the most important Philharmonic members to his own side. This was the group that objected to Muzio's marches. The irony of the situation lay in the fact that Verdi, Muzio, and Landi had all been launched by Barezzi. Verdi reacted angrily: 'These Landisti believe they know more than I do! Bravi! Bravissimi! What asses! What asses!'[45] Another controversy, which raged in Busseto for decades, concerned the new theatre that the Bussetani wished to build in place of the old Teatro Comunale where Verdi and the Philharmonic Society had often performed. The Philharmonic members and their partisans hoped that Verdi would write a new opera for the inauguration and bring famous singers from Milan to appear. But as early as 1845 Verdi warned Barezzi not to count on him, even though he had tentatively given his word to help with the project. In June 1845 Barezzi sent the composer a précis of the plan drafted by Bussetan officials, businessmen, and amateur musicians. Verdi's angry answer went back by return:

I have read the theatre project and, with my usual frankness, I will tell you that I am very, very unhappy over it. To tell you the truth, it is a very risky business to guess at what may happen and to put me in a compromising position with the [City] Authorities, because of a word [I said] to friends and a confidential letter [I wrote]. Everywhere in the world theatres are built without having someone to write [expressly] for them and get singers to sing in the opera; and if Busseto enjoys the advantage [of having a composer] they still ought to have managed it without counting on me. I will not withdraw my pledged word; but you know that I have to write two operas for Naples and for the publisher Lucca; I do not have a stomach of bronze so that I can stand up under the additional burden of work. As for the two singers, how can I promise anything? I said to your brothers exactly these words: '*Maybe, [just] maybe, we could have Frezzolini and Poggi.*' In an enthusiastic moment (for I admit that I liked the idea of a theatre a great deal) I dared to say this because—apart from the friendship that exists between me and those artists—the last time I saw Frezzolini she said to me: 'This autumn we are going to rest. You come and visit us for two weeks in the country, and we will come and visit you in Busseto, where we will sing a benefit for your poor.' And I answered her: 'I take you at your word, but not this year because I do not have a house. But next year I will expect you there without fail.' But if Frezzolini should have a contract in hand (which means 40 or 50 thousand francs) in the year when the theatre is to be inaugurated, what madman would propose that she come to sing for nothing in Busseto?

I repeat that they should not under any circumstances have used my name in their request, all the more because it makes me sound like an ambitious man who wants to have a theatre named after him and a bust [in the foyer]. And most Italians know from experience that I oppose this publicity whenever I can.

I beg you to stop them sending me the proposal for me to endorse and secure their position, because I would answer telling them that I am now used to putting my name in contract next to a figure of 20 or 30 thousand francs.[46]

Again and again the theatre project returned to infuriate Verdi over many years. But these skirmishes in his long battle with his home town did not deter him from wanting to have a home there. In the spring of 1845, though, he apparently was having financial problems, for he had to borrow money from his father, who, in turn, was soon forced to sell a field he owned in Roncole. Carlo Verdi gave the 1,000 lire from the sale to his son. As we shall see, Verdi did not repay the loan for many years, and then only during a family crisis.[47] As he did when he bought his first farm, he may have been attempting too much; for in 1845 he also began to negotiate to buy Palazzo Cavalli, the former mayor's huge town house on the main street in Busseto.

As far as his professional commitments were concerned, Verdi seemed most worried about conditions in Naples that boded ill for the success of his *Alzira*, the opera he had agreed to write for the Teatro San Carlo. The librettist assigned to him, Salvatore Cammarano, proved to be an asset to Verdi, who was about to venture south of Rome for the first time. The soprano Verdi wanted, Eugenia Tadolini, whom Muzio considered one of the greatest artists of the time, had been in temporary retirement following the birth of a child. Anna Bishop, who sang virtually the entire season 1844–5, was offered as a substitute but was unacceptable to Verdi, who hoped that his première could be postponed until Tadolini returned. When he fell ill in April 1845, work on the opera went very slowly; at one point he stopped composing altogether, as Muzio confided to Barezzi.[48] On his doctor's advice, Verdi decided not to go to Naples as planned and asked the management of the San Carlo to postpone the production until July or August. Medical certificates were sent with return receipts requested; but Vincenzo Flaùto, representing the theatre, tried to persuade the composer to come anyway:

The illness from which you suffer is a minor matter, and no other remedies are needed than tincture of wormwood and a quick trip to Naples. [I can assure you] that the air here and the high spirits of our Vesuvius will get all your functions moving again, especially your appetite. Make up your mind, then, to come soon and leave behind that crowd of doctors, who can only aggravate the illness from which you are suffering. You will have to recover in the Neapolitan air, on the basis of the advice which I will give you, once you are here, since I, too, was a doctor and now I have given up that fraud.[49]

The letter made Verdi angry, for he was genuinely ill and, in any case, unwilling to let others direct his life. To Flaùto, he wrote:

I am terribly, terribly sorry to have to advise you that my illness is not an insignificant matter, as you think; tincture of wormwood does nothing for my condition. As for the high spirits of Vesuvius, I assure you that I do not need to get all my functions going again, but I do need calm and rest. I cannot leave quickly for Naples, as you ask; if this were possible, I would not have sent you the doctor's certificate. I advise you of all this, so that you can take whatever steps you think necessary, while I think seriously about restoring my health.[50]

At the time Muzio was running from place to place in Milan getting signatures on the certificates, while Verdi, who was being bled, was still confined to bed, in constant pain, and under heavy medication. He could not eat and had lost weight. As late as 14 May 'the Signor Maestro is not doing anything yet'.[51]

The trip to Naples, begun on 20 June, followed twenty days of uninterrupted composing, during which Verdi finished all of *Alzira* except the second act finale. He allowed himself six days for the orchestration. But even with the opera finished, Verdi could not be certain of what awaited him at the San Carlo. When he had tried to force Flaùto to give him written guarantees that Tadolini would sing and that the opera would not be given until it was adequately prepared, Flaùto had refused. 'What a cheat!' wrote Muzio, undoubtedly echoing Verdi's words. Verdi wrote to the superintendent of theatres setting forth his conditions.[52]

The composer was given a warm reception in Naples, where his fame had preceded him. When word spread through the city that he had finally arrived and that he would attend a performance of *I due Foscari* at the San Carlo, crowds of people swarmed in the piazza before the royal palace to catch a glimpse of him. During this performance, the audience in the sold-out house cheered him enthusiastically, calling him on stage, where he took many bows.[53] Gratified and happy, he said that no other city, not even Rome or Venice, had given him such a warm welcome. Having said that he would remain in Naples only for the three obligatory performances, he planned to leave as soon as he could; 'four days later he will be in Milan', Muzio noted.[54] But first he had to get his opera staged.

Alzira, composed under severe pressure, was certainly not as good as Verdi would have wished it. As he learned while he was in Naples, he was also faced with powerful opposition. He heard of conspiracies woven by rival composers' factions, threats of the evil eye, and newspaper campaigns mounted against him. The anti-Verdi cabal in the city drew strength from supporters of an older, classical tradition. The conservative audience clung to an entrenched taste and supported its favourite, Mercadante, who also headed the Conservatory. Sought out by young musicians who hoped for his advice and protection, Mercadante had just had a month-long visit from Angelo Mariani, a promising protégé of Rossini who was beginning to make his way as a composer and Maestro concertatore. Born in Ravenna in 1821 Mariani had been engaged for the autumn and Carnival seasons in Messina for 1844–5. When that ended, he left for Naples about the same time that Verdi arrived to finish scoring *Alzira* and oversee its production, Verdi's situation was made worse by the fact that the small but very vocal pro-Verdi faction had aroused the champions of the Neapolitan 'school' to a resentment they might perhaps otherwise not have felt. To add to the composer's problems, he was told that the soprano Bishop, Tadolini's rival, had increased her monthly bribes to local journalists. This did not bode well for his opera. On 15 July, just after he began rehearsing, Verdi wrote somewhat naïvely to Antonio Tosi, the editor of *La rivista dei teatri*, a theatrical journal with offices in Rome:

I do not think that I will have to put up with cabals and intrigues; at least, that is what I believe; the [Neapolitan] audience is very much on my side. It is certain that the newspapers will say all kinds of bad things [about *Alzira*], all the more because now La Bishop has increased her monthly payments to those gentlemen, since I do not want her in my opera. I will also give you news of the première, and you can be sure that it will be the truth.[55]

In fact, *Alzira* was not successful, although it was not a fiasco. The opera profited from the artistry of three major singers: Eugenia Tadolini, whose arias were applauded; Gaetano Fraschini, one of the greatest tenors of the nineteenth century; and Filippo Coletti. The major set pieces passed muster, but much was received without applause on the night of the première, 12 August 1845. It was greeted with shouts and whistles on later evenings. Journalists gloated over the 'bitter lesson' Verdi had been taught in Naples. From Vincenzo Torelli of *L'omnibus* came a warning: 'No human talent is capable of producing two or three grand operas a year'.[56]

BOOK II

To add to Verdi's distress, a contemptuous, irreverent song about him became popular in Naples, its lyrics echoing Torelli's warning about striving too hard for success:

> First you wrote *Nabucco*
> And left your audience thunderstruck;
> Next you wrote *Lombardi*
> And people were just as impressed.
> Your third opera was *Ernani*,
> And with it, applause stopped.
> You wrote *I due Foscari* for Rome.
> Do you remember what a fiasco it was?
> *Giovanna* was produced in Milan
> And she was burned yet again and thrown out.
> For the San Carlo you composed *Alzira*;
> And [Naples], trembling with rage,
> Asked: 'Who is this threadbare beggar
> That brought *Alzira* to the San Carlo?'
>
> .   .   .
>
> At the San Carlo, people want melody,
> Accompanied by harmony.
> The audience wants dramatic singing,
> Not wretched howls that take away the singers' breath
> And force them to sing flat.
> What could Fraschini do [to save such a work]?[57]

Apart from having to read attacks like these, Verdi was also offended at having his privacy invaded at every moment as journalists followed him and commented in his clothing, his diet, his habits and those of his friends, his schedule, and his character. He railed against the Neapolitans' curiosity, deeming it unworthy of a great city. At the same time, though, he convinced himself that *Alzira* might survive. He wrote to Giovanna Lucca that '*Alzira* was fairly successful the first night, less the second.'[58] But he felt it might do better, at least in Naples, and that it would eventually be vindicated. To Piave he confided his hope that 'from now on it will be better liked and will remain in the repertory. . . . If I am not wrong, it will make the usual rounds soon, for it seems to me more effective than *Foscari*.'[59]

At this time, Verdi was so depressed that he said he was planning to abandon the theatre altogether. He had written to Demaldè in April about *I due Foscari*: 'So they like *Foscari*? Fine. . . . Let them think whatever they want about it; I am happy, no matter what reception it gets, and am utterly indifferent to everything. I cannot wait for these next three years to pass. I have to write six operas, then addio to everything.'⁶⁰ He expressed similar sentiments in other letters, even referring to his work as a career that he abhorred. In May 1845 the French publisher Marie Escudier, who was in Milan on other business, had paid Verdi a visit at the apartment in Contrada del Monte and had written an article about it, giving his readers information on 'this young composer' in 'his home'. He wrote:

I had been given a wholly misleading idea of [Verdi's] character, which was said to be that of a cold, uncommunicative man who was always absorbed in his art. Verdi welcomed me very affably; and he showed a completely French gracious-ness as he received several friends who came to visit him while I was with him; we spoke a lot about French music and the composers now writing for the theatres in Paris; he knows all our musical works that are worth knowing and shows a lively understanding of everything that comes from France. . . . Verdi is a handsome young man about 28 or 29 years old. He has brown hair, blue eyes, and an expression that is both sweet and vivacious at the same time. When he speaks, his face lights up; the constant shifting of his gaze reflects all the variety of his feelings; everything about him suggests an honest heart and a sensitive soul. . . . I asked Verdi to let me hear a piece from *I Lombardi*, which has always seemed to me the best in this work, the 'Ave Maria'. He sat right down at the piano and sang very expressively; he himself considers [it] one of his best creations. The works of the young and already celebrated composer are very much sought after in Italy, and are paid for with their weight in gold. He has a substantial fortune, but his tastes are marked by the most modest simplicity. In his workroom are only four or five chairs, a grand piano, his statuette, and, above the piano, three wreaths with gold ribbons, hung on a picture frame in which we found—imagine what? the French caricature 'The Road to Posterity'. I can sketch in a few words the physical and spiritual image of the young maestro: he is very natural, [he has] a fine physique; in his form and height, he resembles Donizetti; and in the gentleness of his speech, Bellini. Verdi is passionately fond of all the arts. He took me to the studio of the famous sculptor [Pompeo] Marchesi, who is one of his closest friends, and showed me every detail of the atelier, which is the largest and richest in Europe.⁶¹

This laudatory interview reflects little of the pressure Verdi was under at this time. Just a few weeks later, writing to Andrea Maffei, Verdi wrote of *Alzira*: 'I did it almost without knowing I was composing it and without effort; for this reason, even if it were to fail, I would not feel very sorry.'⁶² He thus feigned indifference to the opera, which, he later acknowledged, was a failure. Yet the very modest reception given the work in an old and famous theatre was embarrassing. Some thought was given to a planned production of *Alzira* at the Teatro Argentina in Rome, where it was on the autumn programme. At first the composer considered revising it, then concluded that his effort was useless. To Ferretti he wrote in November that it was 'sick in the guts and touching it up would only make it worse'.[63] He said that even before its première in Naples, he had become aware of its shortcomings, 'and you cannot imagine how I studied them. . . . I was hoping that the overture and the last finale would make up in large measure for the defects of the rest of the opera.'[64] A production in Milan fared no better. Many years later, in a letter to Giuseppina Negroni Prati Morosini, who had asked him about *Alzira*, he said 'That one is really ugly.'[65]

Settled again in Milan, he turned to *Attila*, the sketch of which, written by Maffei, had been sent to Piave in the spring. Later, though, the composer had persuaded him to give it back so that Solera could write it, offering the Venetian librettist other projects for the future. Solera had dawdled over *Attila*, forcing Muzio to enlist the help of Toccagni and Andrea Maffei in prodding 'that big, lazy poet' to get on with the job.[66] The libretto was not finished in first draft until 26 August, just as Verdi got back from Naples. Verdi asked Solera to polish it and make some changes. He then decided to go to Busseto with Muzio and work there,[67] for in Milan he was constantly interrupted. Among those who came to his apartment was a messenger from La Scala, who asked Verdi to come to the theatre and oversee the dress rehearsal of *I due Foscari*, but the composer refused to go, saying that he did not care whether the opera was a fiasco or not because it had already been so successful in other theatres that it was constantly being sought by impresarios.[68] The insult to Merelli came at a time when Verdi was angry at what he considered the impresario's underhand dealings and the poor quality of the productions at La Scala. In February 1845, without letting Verdi know what he was doing, Merelli had opened negotiations with Ricordi for the sale of his rights in *Giovanna d'Arco*, to help him through a financial crisis. From reports in the files of the Presidenza del Governo, we learn that the impresario had bought an expensive villa in the country near Lentate and furnished it with luxurious fittings, incurring debts that put him in an 'extremely critical situation' later.[69] Verdi vowed to break with him and never do business with La Scala again so long as he was there.

The visit to Busseto that autumn was planned to let the composer rest and write. 'Get his bed ready and the things he will need for composing,'

Muzio asked Barezzi, who was to provide two pianos, for both master and pupil would be working every morning.[70] While there, he wrote to Andrea Maffei of the peace he found in the country. At home nothing happened, he said, as he ate, drank, and slept all day. On 11 September he began to write *Attila*. During the first week in October he reached final agreement with Contardo Cavalli, the former podestà, to buy his town house, once known as Palazzo Dordoni, one of the finest residences in the city. Cavalli had raised his family there.[71] Verdi made the first payment on 6 October, adding another asset to his real estate holdings and going further into debt. After taking care of their business at home, he and Muzio left for Milan together in driving rain.[72]

Again besieged by visitors, he was also feeling pressure from Madrid, London, Paris, and even St Petersburg. He left Milan almost at once for another trip to the country, this time to Clara Maffei's villa at Clusone. There he stayed on more than a week beyond the date of his planned return,[73] for he found there what he called a true paradise. He had had good news of the success of *Nabucco* in Paris and was looking forward to going to London eventually, having been invited there by Benjamin Lumley. Yet when he got back to Milan, he had to go on with *Attila*. Solera had left for Spain, following his wife there but letting no one know he was leaving. His defection left Verdi with the libretto unfinished. He sent it to Piave as Solera had suggested, with instructions for writing the final scene of the third act. Solera had wished to close with a choral hymn. Verdi, though, had ideas of his own and wanted to use the soloists instead. When Piave's finished text was sent to Solera with the suggestion that he make changes if he wished, Solera protested that the scene was a parody. But he acknowledged that Verdi had the right to do what he wanted with it. The incident ended his long friendship with Solera and, of course, his professional association as well. This rupture paralleled the end of Verdi's relationship with Merelli and La Scala and, in a certain way, sealed it.

Clearly the composer had other plans, as he told a long-time admirer, Baroness Eroteide Soldati: 'At the beginning of next spring I will go to London to write an opera; and on the way back I will stay several months in Paris.'[74] He did, though, expect to be in Busseto in the autumn of 1846. The Escudiers in Paris and Lumley in London swore to protect his interests and promote him. To the Escudiers, Marie and Léon, he assigned the French rights to his operas, and sought their help in getting one of his major works produced in Paris. In September 1845 he told them that he would like to see *Attila* at the Paris Opéra in about two years; if he could guarantee such a production, he would not accept other commissions in Italy. To Lumley he said that he would give one opera in London.[75] Planning for his trips abroad, he also asked Piave to help him find a tutor to teach him French while he was in Venice to prepare the new opera.

Attila at the Teatro La Fenice

Even while he was in Naples, the composer was looking forward to returning to Venice and the growing numbers of his admirers there. He wrote to 'Dear Monster' Piave as early as September about his planned return, reporting on his visits with their Venetian friends, the Venturis and Fontanas, in Milan: 'Addio, addio, keep well and go and get fucked! Let's be happy! Let's be happy! Will you come to meet me in Padua? Be careful not to leave Venice during Carnival: [or] by God, I will strangle you. Regards to the *Lions*.'[76] Verdi's letters to Piave in this period include a familiar tone that he used with almost no one else and a surprising number of obscenities, as he addressed the librettist with the Venetian term 'mona' and the Lombard 'potta', both meaning 'cunt'. Piave, keeping watch until Verdi could get to Venice, kept Verdi informed about another man's *Attila*, on the programme of the Teatro Apollo; this was by Francesco Malipiero, the ancestor of the twentieth-century composer Gian Francesco Malipiero. At the San Benedetto Verdi's *Un giorno di regno* had been unusually successful under the title *Il finto Stanislao*.[77] Ahead lay Verdi's *Attila*, about which Piave was enormously enthusiastic. As Verdi had hoped, his librettist did meet him in Padua. Piave had also found a good piano. The French teacher was hired for one hour a day, including Sundays. Verdi arrived in December 1845, expecting to begin work, take care of the cold that had been plaguing him in Milan, and enjoy his 'good room, good fire, and good little supper'.[78] Soon, though, he was ill again and unable to attend rehearsals for *Giovanna d'Arco*, which was to be given at La Fenice in December; he did, though, compose a cavatina for Sofia Löwe. He was sorry, he wrote to Giuseppina Appiani, that he could not help in preparing it for he loved it very much; he also found *Attila* thoroughly satisfying as he finished it and began the orchestration.

When *Giovanna d'Arco* opened the Venice season on a gala Christmas

Eve, the Tsar of Russia was in the imperial box, having just come from Milan, where he and his Tsarina had attended *I due Foscari* at La Scala. As Muzio proudly told Barezzi, the rulers had even postponed their departure for Venice so that they could hear another performance of it.[79] Verdi, reporting to Clara Maffei on the first night of *Giovanna d'Arco* at La Fenice had to admit that it had been very coldly received: 'fredda, fredda', he said, greeted with 'perfect silence from the first note to the last'. A better reception could be reported after the second night, when several numbers were applauded but 'the overture and the last finale, which are the best pieces of the opera' passed without notice.[80] Kept in bed in Venice over Christmas, he had to concentrate on getting well. Later, he described the frightening experience of being 'in bed and almost dying' and of having to live up to his pledge and finish the opera.[81] At one point it was even rumoured in newspapers that he had died; but after nearly three weeks, he was able to get up and move around his room. On 21 January he saw real hope of recovery, although his doctors told him he needed six months of rest.

The pressure of his business affairs required him to keep in touch with Lucca to settle details of his London engagement. He hoped that Piave would go to England with him, for he had chosen him to write *Il corsaro* for Her Majesty's Theatre; in case Piave did not go, the Anglo-Italian poet Manfredo Maggioni could 'fix up those little details that circumstances may demand', as he also had written a libretto of *Il corsaro* and was familiar with the drama. But Verdi asked Lucca to write to Lumley to postpone the date of the première by one month.[82] He found that he was improving very slowly and had almost no strength. By February he was again confined to bed and putting further pressure on Lucca, all the while reassuring his Venetian friends that he would not fail to produce *Attila* before the end of the season at La Fenice. The première, though, was truly in jeopardy on 24 February. '*Attila* (even if I shall be able to finish it) will be on the programme only for the last three or four evenings', he advised Giovanna Lucca, whose husband was planning to come for the opening.[83]

The first night was 17 March 1846. Verdi was fortunate in having the moral support of Giovannino Barezzi and Luciano Manara and others from Milan who had joined him. The cast included Löwe, Guasco, Ignazio Marini, and Costantini. Verdi directed it himself. Given its subject and its setting, *Attila* might have proved as successful on its first night as it did in the years that followed. But Guasco was hoarse; Costantini had had influenza; and a stage mishap, when the smoke from the many candles caused people in the audience to choke, weighed against it. The many ovations Verdi got in the opening scenes preceded an ever cooler reception as the evening wore on. The third act got almost no applause at all. Yet its composer seemed pleased with the evening, writing to both Clara Maffei and Countess Gina Della Somaglia that it had gone well, although he admitted to the latter that he had perhaps expected too much: 'Either I deceived myself or the audience did not understand', he said, adding that he was hoping for better luck for the second performance.[84] He was right. The second night created a furore, while the third performance brought him the triumph he had hoped for; he was escorted back to his apartment with a torchlight parade, led by a military band as Marini, at his side, supported him 'with so much love, with so much tenderness that you would have taken him for a father or a brother', wrote one reviewer.[85] In time *Attila* was to prove to be a favourite as it was produced in one theatre after another. Many years later Verdi, writing to Giuseppe Perosio in Genoa, said that he had been 'rummaging among my rags', looking for *Attila*, but that he could not find it. 'I wanted to see what there is and what there is not in this old score, but perhaps it is better than I did not find it.'[86]

Painfully thin and weak, but with 'a lively expression in his eyes' and 'high colour' in his cheeks, Verdi led a quiet life in Milan after more than two months of illness that put him in real danger. 'Rest will get him back on his feet', Muzio wrote to Barezzi; but Verdi was still far from well.[87] Even as he asked for a postponement of his London engagement, he had to delay signing a contract with Léon Pillet, the director of the Paris Opéra, whose offer he had had to decline in February, while he was still bedridden in Venice. To professional concerns was added some personal worry over the imminent separation of Clara and Andrea Maffei. Like the couple's other friends, he had observed the gradual disintegration of their marriage over the previous four years. As to the causes, the poet is reported to have been a gambler. Clara Maffei was said to have flirted with Balzac and other guests of the salon. For many years she was the mistress of the revolutionary Tenca. But her final rupture with Maffei was perhaps owed in part to politics. We know that Maffei asked her to call on Austrian dignitaries in Trieste and, when she refused, tried to persuade her, observing that no one would know she had made the call because she was far from Milan. But Clara's own convictions made the visit impossible. In June 1846 the document of separation was drawn up by Tommaso

Grossi, notary and author of the poem *I Lombardi alla prima crociata*. Verdi and Giulio Carcano were witnesses to the act. The terms of the agreement were that Clara, 'for reasons of health', would retire to her villa at Clusone on 16 June 1846 and would 'cease cohabiting with her husband'.[88]

Maffei was extremely unhappy. But in a diary entry, written on the day she left for Clusone, Clara wrote:

I leave my husband's house with a desolate heart, but with a clear conscience. . . . If God helps me, this fatal step will be nothing more than the first step toward a tranquil life; and I will be able to become a loving sister to my husband, toward whom I will always feel esteem and affection. And you, my adored friends . . . Carcano [and] Verdi, . . . who so completely share my grief, who so carefully protected me, may my life prove to you that your loving appraisal of me was not a mistake; may I always be worthy of your friendship, which, in the future, will be my only comfort.[89]

Verdi's letter of 24 June to Clara reflects his understanding: 'I absolve you, and even the Just One will absolve you.'[90] He was apparently chosen to give Clara's note of farewell to Andrea Maffei. He was 'beyond consolation', Verdi said.[91] In spite of the separation, the composer remained close to both Andrea and Clara Maffei, their friendship continuing for decades.

During this period in the spring of 1846 Verdi's career was flourishing. After its tentative start, *Attila* was steadily gaining ground, its success in Florence in April auguring well for future scheduled productions in Leghorn, Rovigo, Vicenza, Trieste, and Cremona.[92] The opera would probably be given at La Scala as well, Muzio told Barezzi, because Löwe and Marini, both from the original cast, were engaged there. Verdi learned that *I Lombardi* had also been successful in London.[93] *Ernani*, after its productions in Venice and Milan, had done well in Parma and gone on to other houses. Yet the composer's health still posed serious problems for him. After the rumour that he had died was published in Leipzig[94] and reprinted by Italian papers, he had to go on reassuring people about his recovery for months; Demaldè and Carlo Verdi went on worrying, and with good reason, for much of the spring. Verdi seemed to long for letters from Busseto as he expressed his sense of isolation and loneliness. Muzio commented on the way he watched the post: 'Today is Thursday, one of the days when either the Signor Maestro or I usually get letters from you,' he wrote to Barezzi, 'but I went to the post office twice yet found no letter. . . . Did you perhaps have some kind of accident that keeps you from writing?'[95] At one point, Verdi even begged Barezzi's shop assistant to write to him when his father-in-law could not.

Surrounded by the men Muzio called his 'satellite nobles',[96] who were constantly currying favour with him and trying to keep him amused, the composer was still unhappy. Oppressed by the summer heat, he and Andrea Maffei decided to go to Recoaro, a favourite retreat of Donna Emilia Morosini, where Verdi hoped that his health would improve more rapidly.[97] Because rumours about him continued to circulate, Carlo Verdi's fears were again aroused, leading him to write to his son at the spa—he was convinced that Verdi was dying of gastric fever, poison, or consumption.[98] As expected, the slow cure at Recoaro helped, so that Maffei, who returned to Milan briefly on business, could report that the composer had put on weight, looked better, and was feeling 'very, very well'.[99] At the end of July Verdi and Maffei went home. Soon he was studying three possible subjects for the opera he was to write for Lanari and Florence. Abroad, *I Lombardi* was scheduled for Paris, where it would be given in a French translation. It was also staged at the Teatro Carcano, where Mariani's violin solo was the only saving grace in an otherwise bad production. *Ernani* was also directed there by Mariani, who had just completed a successful run of *I due Foscari* at the important Teatro Re.

An early identification of Verdi's music with Italian nationalist politics dates from the summer of 1846 when a major demonstration took place in Bologna during a performance of *Ernani*. A number of slogans about Pope Pius IX had come to be used politically that year; and on 13 August Muzio let Barezzi know that the words of the finale of the opera were changed from 'O sommo Carlo' to 'O sommo Pio': 'The name of Carlo was changed to Pio, and there was such a furore that the piece had to be repeated three times; and when they came to the words "Pardon for everyone", shouts of "Evviva" burst forth from all over [the theatre].'[100] Everyone associated this amnesty in the opera with the Pope's amnesty for political prisoners, granted shortly after his elevation to the papacy. Later, the words 'A Carlo Quinto sia gloria ed onor' were changed by patriots in the audience to 'A Pio Nono sia gloria ed onor'. The identification of Verdi with Italian nationalist aspirations became firm.

One sign of Verdi's emancipation from Milan came with his determination to cut himself off from La Scala. Merelli, his former mentor and supporter, found himself at an ever greater disadvantage, where Verdi was concerned. We have seen the friction of the summer of 1845.[101] Fifteen months later, in October 1846, Merelli, with his fortunes faltering, asked Verdi to stage *Attila* at La Scala; 'but he doesn't want anything to do with it; if the opera goes well, the Signor Maestro will not earn anything [from it]; if it goes badly, he will not lose anything; he does not care at all whether it goes well or fails.'[102] Muzio added that Merelli had antagonized Verdi by saying in public that *Attila* was 'a miserable opera, that it is not beautiful at all' and that Merelli had been forced by public opinion to ask Verdi to direct it for him. After Verdi heard what Merelli had said, he sent word to Lucca, 'the owner of the score', saying that he wanted 3,000 francs for its rental. 'No one ever paid so much for any score, for a simple rental, in any theatre, ever,' Muzio said.[103] Lucca apparently went even beyond Verdi's demands and asked for 5,000 francs. Merelli appealed to the authorities for relief from such an exorbitant demand; the matter was eventually settled when the police ordered Lucca to lower the fee. Because of incidents like this, and because he deplored the level of productions at La Scala, Verdi became persuaded that the theatre could never give his operas the kind of presentation he demanded. To protect himself, he told Ricordi to prevent La Scala from producing his next work *Macbeth*, at least 'until things change for the better. I think I ought to tell you also that these stipulations, made now for *Macbeth*, will apply from this time forward, for all my operas.'[104]

During the mid-1840s Verdi's stature as a national figure steadily increased. Italians had no other visible, tangible, accessible, forceful lay person to symbolize their growing nationalist fervour. Between 1830 and 1840, wrote the historian Luigi Anelli, 'All Italy was quiet, the revolutions put down, the people forced into a blind obedience.'[105] But from 1840 onward there was a great deal of discontent, particularly in Lombardy, where mounting corruption in the Austrian government dismayed ordinary citizens, while patriots, who had been working underground, became more daring. 'Hatred, diffidence, and the shame of our degradation proved sharp stimuli to those who cared the most.'[106] The critic and baritone Antonio Ghislanzoni, who later became Verdi's collaborator, confirms that before 1842 there were few patriots in Milan.

Most people were unaware that Italy existed; yet there were those who worked in secret; those who wrote [patriotic tracts]; those who took on the dangerous job of circulating leaflets written by Mazzini [who was in exile]. At that time it was tremendously risky to speak of politics. These passions were beginning to be felt toward 1842.[107]

BOOK II

Verdi's choruses in *Nabucco* and *I Lombardi* began to give this movement a voice. The association of Pius IX and the chorus from *Ernani*
roused audiences to demonstrations even at a time when the police were
forbidding them. *Attila*, too, spoke for patriotism, with emotion-laden
lines. When these works were beginning to be heard from the stages of
Italy, the misery and desperation of the poor were beginning to cause the
upper classes to take notice of their condition and to help them. The
meagre harvest and resulting famine in 1846 and 1847 brought these two
classes together, especially in Lombardy, where 'the best people among
the Milanese patricians put their whole hearts into alleviating the suffering with their charitable efforts. . . . The Austrian government became
suspicious at this and were afraid of the most committed agitators for
freedom whom they saw gathering support from the masses.'[108]

The Austrians' fear of these masses was reflected in edicts forbidding
crowds to gather. In 1846, for example, the government enforced the law
and tried to disperse the groups that stopped to listen to a large street
organ that day and night played music from Verdi's *Giovanna d'Arco*. The
instrument stopped traffic and attracted crowds that the police could not
control, even after they prevented it from being played after dark.[109]

By the spring of 1846 Verdi had emerged as a kind of idol. This is
reflected in a sonnet by Andrea Maffei in a national annual, the *Strenna
teatrale europea*:

> TO GIUSEPPE VERDI   THE GLORY OF ITALY
> New is the sweet, angelic magic [of your music];
> New is the tender, pure melody . . .
> You bring joys and delights to the soul . . .
> Already you are the heart of Italian music.
> You live and reign in every heart;
> And when you interpret fiery emotions,
> Because of you, new leafy fronds are woven . . .
> What do you fear? You are at the Apex of Glory.
> The words *Verdi* and *Victory* ring out together.[110]

The political impulse here is clear, especially coming from a conservative
who still had close relatives among the highest ranks of the Austrian
government in Milan. These lines also show where Verdi's supporters
believed that his strength lay. Phrases like 'Italian music' and 'Italian art'
were charged with political intent in this period. Giuseppe Giusti and
Mazzini prayed for the emergence of a young, Italian artist who would give

voice to the aspirations of a nation that did not yet exist. In a letter to Verdi, Giusti called for the artist to express 'the sorrow of a people that feels that it needs a higher destiny, . . . a people that had fallen and wishes to stand erect again, . . . that wants to be regenerated.'[111]

From an article written in 1843 by the journalist Francesco Regli we learn just *how* Verdi's message reached the people:

[The important melodies are passed along from one person and one group to another]. . . . The Milanese public . . . went around and is still going around the streets singing the main themes. When an opera becomes *popular*, so to speak, it must of course possess supreme merits. Everyone will not be touched, will not be moved, will not feel rapture unless there are good reasons for this to happen.[112]

In Verdi's case, the 'good reasons' carried his music through the populace. Age 33 in 1846, the former master of Busseto's city music school was becoming an important figure in the struggle for Italian identity. From the obscurity of 1839 he had moved into the glare of fame.

13

⌁

Autumn 1846–Spring 1847

Towards *Macbeth*

After more than two years at Verdi's side, Muzio was changing, becoming more urbane and sophisticated and losing his country manners. Even as his brother took over the family's cobbler shop in Busseto and kept his old nickname of 'Giulio Il Genovese', Emanuele was becoming Maestro Muzio and by 1847 addressing Antonio Barezzi as 'mio caro' and writing about international affairs, art, and fine food as well as music. Working for Ricordi and Lucca and moving in Verdi's circle, he had acquired a voice of his own, although his loyalty to 'the Signor Maestro' never flagged. As Verdi's assistant at home, he became more than a friend, going far beyond even Giovannino Barezzi, Pasetti, and Toccagni in his closeness to the composer. From 1836 until 1840 Verdi had always had a musician at his side in Margherita Barezzi; after her death, he had lived almost four years without that support before Muzio came to fill the gap. The relationship between the two men elevated Muzio and softened Verdi, whose material help to his protégé and other friends is recorded in Muzio's letters as gifts of money, clothing, meals, and loans of gold napoleons.[1] Virtually inseparable from early morning until evening, they worked together side by side at Verdi's long table.

When Muzio was invited to compete for the post of maestro di musica in Busseto in November 1846, he wrote to Barezzi that it would be

a very sad thing to have to abandon the Signor Maestro now that he has given me a second life and is always trying to make me appear at my best in society in the homes of all the Signori. . . . If you could see us, I seem more like a friend, rather than his pupil. We are always together at dinner, in the cafés, when we play cards (but just for one hour from twelve to one); all in all, he doesn't go anywhere without me at his side; in the house he has a big table and we both write there together, and so I always have his advice; as for myself, I absolutely will not be able to abandon him. . . . If it were not for the Signor Maestro, what would I be? A poor devil who would not know how to do anything; and now that he has taught me, now that—thanks to his teaching—I can live well enough, now when he will eventually do something more, must I leave him? No, I will never, never do it. Let people say what they want; I don't care. It is enough for me just to be beside by Signor Maestro; and may he never say to me: 'Now that I have taught you, you abandon me, you ingrate!' I would die of remorse if I were to give him a reason for saying this.[2]

This same letter emphasizes that Verdi still intended to leave the theatre soon: 'one more year at most', then his career would be over. As he had told Demaldè on 21 April 1845, he expected to give up composing in the spring of 1848;[3] as he wrote to his friend L. Masi on 5 November 1845, he hated the 'accursed notes' he had to write and would find relief 'only when I shall have finished this career that I abhor'.[4]

Yet Verdi's growing popularity and the continuing success of his operas put ever greater pressure on him to produce, creating a tension that Muzio helped to defuse as he and his Signor Maestro faced professional and social challenges together. Of particular importance to Verdi was the new opera he was to write for the historic Teatro della Pergola in Florence, under a contract that had originally been arranged between him and Antonio Lanari for the Teatro Sociale in Mantua. When Alessandro Lanari acquired the contract from his son, the change in site resulted. The idea of doing *Macbeth* probably grew out of Verdi's friendship with Andrea Maffei, with whom he had holidayed in Recoaro in July 1846, although even in May Verdi and the elder Lanari had agreed that the new work would be in the *genere fantastico* or 'imaginative genre',[5] with 'all its witches, apparitions, soothsayings, sabbaths, wires, trapdoors, Bengal lights, phantasms, gnomes, sylphs, undines, *willis*', and wild settings.[6] On historical, political, and aesthetic grounds, such subjects offended many Italians, above all because the genre was considered foreign.

Writing an opera based on Shakespeare constituted a risk in its own right, because no Shakespeare play had been produced in a public theatre in Italy until 1842, when *Othello* was given in Milan. Even though the leading actor was the celebrated Gustavo Modena, the work was a fiasco, with the audience first whispering, then laughing and howling with derision,[7] forcing the company to ring down the curtain and end the performance.

The Shakespeare cult, far from being widespread, was the mark of an intellectual and 'liberal' elite. As for the countless *Giulietta and Romeos*, *Amletos*, *Macbets*—whether plays, operas, or ballets—that entertained Italian audiences from the later eighteenth century onwards, they bore only a vestigial resemblance to their Shakespearean prototypes.[8]

Thus the very act of setting *Macbeth* took courage, but Verdi was determined to try his hand, having chosen the Shakespeare work over two other subjects—Schiller's *Die Räuber* and Grillparzer's *Die Ahnfrau*. In August 1846, as Muzio told Barezzi, Verdi still had not decided: 'If he has Fraschini, he will do *l'Avola* [*Die Ahnfrau*]; if they give him Moriani instead of Fraschini, as it seems, he will then do *Macbeth*, and a powerful tenor is not needed. If Moriani were still in voice, he could be given a leading role, but they say that he is burned out.'[9] Muzio added that the composer would decide for himself when he went to Bergamo to hear Moriani in the regular season there. Yet even before he made the trip, Verdi was thinking of writing an opera that would not require an important tenor, for he urged Lanari to do everything he could to engage Felice Varesi: 'Varesi is the only artist now in Italy who could do the role I have in mind, because of his singing, his sensitivity, and even his actual appearance.'[10] One day later he took it upon himself to write to the great baritone directly, urging him to set the most reasonable terms possible. 'If you want it, I will compose *Macbeth* for you.'[11] When he got an answer almost by return post, Verdi said he would do all he could to get Varesi a fair fee. For Lady Macbeth, he was considering Löwe.

Although Lanari was somewhat slow in responding to the composer's urgency, Verdi committed himself to sending Piave his sketch of *Macbeth*, describing the drama in passionate terms as 'one of the greatest creations of man'. He begged his librettist to stand by him as they made 'something extraordinary' out of it. The lines should be short—the shorter the better—to make a dramatic impact; 'Oh, I beg you not to neglect this *Macbeth*, I beg you on my knees, if for no other reason, treat it well for me and my health, which is not excellent but will soon turn bad, if you upset me.'[12] With Moriani ruled out and Varesi's engagement 'almost sure',[13] Verdi could write to Clara Maffei at the end of September that he would compose *Macbeth* for Lanari and *I masnadieri* for Lucca.[14]

Verdi and Muzio were living comfortably that autumn, although correspondence about the new opera annoyed the composer, as did Piave's wordy text, parts of which he was beginning to receive from Venice. As he asked for a revision of Lady Macbeth's Cavatina and the first scene with the witches, he said that he hoped Piave could find a more poetic and mysterious tone for the libretto and that he would keep it as short as possible. In capital letters, he admonished: 'ALWAYS KEEP [THIS] IN MIND: USE FEW WORDS . . . FEW WORDS . . . FEW BUT SIGNIFICANT' and 'I REPEAT FEW WORDS.'[15] At the beginning of October Piave came to Milan where he and Verdi could work together; on the fourth they visited the Fontana-Pini family at their villa near Como.

A day or two later, Verdi gave Strepponi a letter that she valued highly. She had been passing through an extremely difficult period. In 1843, about six months before Muzio first met her, the soprano had been reduced to advertising in theatrical trade papers for work:

Among the few artists of true distinction now available in Milan for the forth-coming autumn and Carnival seasons is the worthy Signora Giuseppina Strepponi, who, although she recently refused several engagements that were offered to her, has not suffered the slightest indisposition and is in perfect health, now finding herself even better off vocally and in the full vigour and glory of her powers, perhaps even better off than ever before. . . . This Signora is now disposed to accept new contracts, providing they are appropriate to her decorum and position.[16]

She had sung *Nabucco* and *Roberto il Diavolo* in Verona and had done one concert in Turin and several performances of *Ernani* at the Teatro Riccardi in Bergamo during the fair. Her advertisement brought an offer for the autumn and Carnival in Palermo, where she was frequently ridiculed, received little applause, and sometimes whispered her way through her role. One critic said that she seemed to have forgotten everything she knew about stagecraft; another attacked her as 'unrecognizable'; a third remarked on her 'useless efforts of a dying voice'; and a fourth claimed that she had mimed her part in Donizetti's *Belisario* because her voice had failed her completely.[17] As she left Sicily in the spring of 1845, her career was virtually over, although she did appear in productions of *Nabucco* in Alessandria in the autumn of that year and in Modena at the beginning of 1846.

In Milan she again lived with her mother and sister Barberina in their apartment at 358 Contrada della Cerva in the Parish of Santo Stefano near Piazza San Babila.[18] The family was not utterly alone, for Strepponi's uncle Giuseppe Cornalba, a furniture-polisher, lived nearby with his daughter, who remained the soprano's friend. Strepponi continued to be Verdi's supporter, promoter, unofficial adviser, and occasional secretary as she prepared to settle in Paris, where she wanted to establish a singing school for young gentlewomen. Just before she left, Verdi made a serious commitment to her, giving her a letter expressing his love. This letter is still at Sant'Agata, in its envelope, sealed. On it, Strepponi wrote: '5 or 6 October 1846. They shall lay this letter on my heart when they bury me!' ('5 o 6 ottobre 1846. Questa lettera la metteranno sul mio cuore quando mi seppellirano!')[19] When she died at Sant'Agata fifty-one years later, Verdi, who knew that his wife wished to have this letter buried with her, had the house searched for it, but it could not be found. Later, it was discovered among her papers. By agreement within the circle of the family, it has never been opened. There can, though, be no doubt about its importance, for Strepponi considered this her most precious possession. When she made her will, she left her wedding-ring to Barberina, together with the gold bracelet Verdi had given her in 1872; but she wanted this letter with her in the grave.[20] Shortly after writing it, she left for France. Verdi asked the Escudiers to watch over 'la mia raccomandata', 'the woman I entrust to your care'.[21] By mid-October Strepponi was settled in Paris, where the Escudiers carried out Verdi's mandate, helping her with publicity about the concerts she intended to give in Salle Herz. In their theatrical journal, she ran an advertisement for her singing lessons.

Verdi was looking for a suitable situation for Muzio that autumn, because he was getting ready to 'abandon Italy' himself and was negotiating to write *I masnadieri* for Her Majesty's Theatre in London and produce it there in July 1847.[22] Muzio's description of the composer's plans suggests that something longer than a brief stay was planned as, with finality, Verdi was about 'to put the seal on all the good he has done for me'.[23] If Verdi intended to go on living in Milan, Muzio did not mention it; the words 'abandon Italy' sound as if he were about to make a major change in his life. As he had gone on with *Macbeth*, Verdi had sent a sketch or scenario of the opera to Lanari, whom he begged to pay particular attention to the chorus and stage machinery, two important elements of the production that he feared the impresario might economize on. Confident that Lanari would stage the work as magnificently as he could, he asked that nothing be spared. He would bless the impresario 'a thousand times a day' with blessings that were almost as powerful as those of the Pope, he said. 'But all joking aside, I truly urge you to see that everything goes well and that I will not have to worry about other people. If you want me to have sketches of the scenery and costumes done, I will, though not in any rush, for now I have to get on with composing and have no time to lose.'[24] Muzio reported that Verdi was working very, very slowly but was well.[25] Faithful to the Signor Maestro, he did not mention Strepponi in his letters, although he had known her for more than two years. At the end of October Verdi asked Piave to get in touch with Lanari directly about the scenery, props, costumes, and supers for the *Macbeth* production, which the librettist described to the Florentine impresario in the most glowing terms imaginable, 'the great thing', with the role of Lady Macbeth one of the most impressive parts ever heard in opera on the Italian stage. 'I believe that if the public likes this opera, it will give new directions to our music and open new roads to present and future maestros', Piave declared.[26] *Macbeth* proved difficult for both the librettist and the composer, as Verdi grew ever more dissatisfied with Piave's work, criticizing and asking for revisions of the text right through December 1846.

Lanari had problems of his own, as Löwe, whom Verdi wanted, became pregnant that autumn. Not wanting to risk miscarriage or abortion, as Muzio reported, she cancelled engagements and temporarily left the stage. Lanari, who then turned to Barbieri-Nini, was at home ill when the soprano's answer came: she demanded 12,000 Austrian lire, which he considered an outrageous amount:

My God, your demand terrified me, and if I were to give you what you ask, the remedy would be worse than the disease. . . . I am sending you a contract for 9,000 lire. . . . Addio, dear Marianna, remember that Ungher, Duprez, Moriani, so many other artists elevated by me to the peak of their professions helped me in similar circumstances; and I hope that you will wish to do the same, all the more because I have granted you twice the fee that [other] theatres could give you.[27]

While these negotiations between the impresario and the soprano were still in progress, Verdi believed that Barbieri-Nini was already engaged; but she did not accept Lanari's offer until mid-November. According to Muzio, she was a poor second choice, for 'the Signor Maestro is sorry about [her] because in the role of the Lady in *Macbeth*, no other woman singing today could get the same effect that Löwe can.'[28] While he was still waiting to learn whether Barbieri-Nini would indeed be his soprano, the composer kept up pressure on Piave and went over the scenario of the opera with Varesi, when the baritone was in Milan. He promised to give him half of his music—'the first and second act[s]'—as soon as possible.[29] Varesi even asked someone to write to London and Edinburgh for details about the period of *Macbeth* and the appropriate costumes for it. When Verdi contacted Pietro Romani, who was still Lanari's maestro concertatore, he said that the company would be doing something extraordinary in producing the opera. From Milan, he sent his specifications for many sets, as he went on writing; but he was far from satisfied with the text Piave was sending him. At the beginning of December, wondering how to 'do something better' with the second act, he copied out much of one scene and asked the librettist to find 'strong and concise' lines 'in the manner of Alfieri'.[30] He wanted them 'quickly, quickly' and asked to have 'the rest at once'. Almost as an afterthought, he ordered Piave to be sure that all the loose ends were tied off and that no disasters would ensue.[31]

Unhappy and ill in December, Verdi did manage to send Muzio off to Casa Ricordi on the fourteenth with 'almost one act' of *Macbeth*, for which the publisher's copyists were waiting. Praising the opera to Barezzi, Muzio wrote that when Verdi played it for him, he was stunned at its beauty. '[W]hat sublime music! I tell you that there are things in it that make your hair stand on end! Writing this music is taking a great deal out of him, but it is coming out very, very well.' They were working from nine in the morning until midnight, one at each end of Verdi's long study table. When Verdi gave Varesi two scenes of his part to study, the baritone told everyone that this was Verdi's 'most beautiful and most dramatic music' and went around 'shouting like a madman' that he had the composer's finest score in his hands.[32]

Three days before Christmas the composer again had to urge Piave to get on with the last act and wrote to Lanari about staging the appearance of Banquo's ghost during the banquet, insisting that the singer who played the role had to be the ghost as well. He would rise from beneath the stage through a trapdoor, as Verdi had been advised 'from London',[33] and should have an ashen face, rumpled hair, and several wounds on his neck. A few weeks later, writing about the setting for the apparitions of the kings, he said that the designer Alessandro Sanquirico recommended using a phantasmagoria as the stage machinery to get the greatest possible effect. 'By God, if this thing works well, as Sanquirico described it to me, it will be astonishing stunning, and make a great many people run just to see it.'[34] He even said that he would enlist Hayez to design the costumes. Working right through Christmas and New Year's Day of 1847, he was also collecting historical information on the period of *Macbeth* and sending it along to Tito Ricordi, Giovanni's son, who was to relay it to the scenic designer who, Verdi feared, was wrong about the era.[35]

Ever more troubled about Piave's dilatoriness and the quality of his work, Verdi asked Andrea Maffei to help revise the libretto. When Piave learned of this, perhaps from Verdi himself, perhaps from a third party, the composer wrote him a brusque letter:

Oh, you certainly have done nothing wrong, except for having neglected these last two acts in an unbelievable way! But never mind! Saint Andrea [Maffei] has helped you and me; and me even more [than you], because, I must tell you frankly, I could not have set them to music, and you see what a mess I would have found myself in. Now everything is fixed up, with almost everything changed, however. I will send the libretto to Lanari myself, and now there is no need for your orders for the staging.[36]

In this abrupt way, Piave was relieved of his duties. His attempt to get his own preface inserted in the printed libretto came to naught. Nevertheless, his friendship with Verdi survived. Late in January Verdi sent him news (which later proved incorrect) of the death of Gina Fontana-Pini, the wife of their Venetian friend Galeazzo Fontana, whom they had visited at their villa in Como a few months earlier. He wrote as if the problems with the *Macbeth* libretto had never existed.[37] Piave, who took his dismissal badly at first, came to accept the situation and let Verdi know that. He then received a conciliatory letter from the composer: 'I am happy that you have understood the other side of this. I assure you that I would not want to harm you [*non vorrei il tuo danno*] for all the gold in the world. I am leaving tomorrow! Addio! I have a lot to do! Addio!'[38]

During January 1847 Verdi sent parts of the score to both Varesi and Barbieri-Nini, so they would be ready when they all met in Florence. With his music went detailed instructions for interpretation of the character. To Varesi, he said: 'I will never stop urging you to study the dramatic situation and the words; the music will come by itself. In a word, I would be happier if you serve the poet better than the composer.'[39] And to Barbieri-Nini,

it would be a profanation to change such a character so great, so energetic, so original as this one created by the great English tragedian. I believe I told you already that this is a drama that has nothing in common with the others, and we all must make every effort to render it in the most original way possible. I also believe that it is high time to abandon the usual formulas and procedures, and I think that by doing so one could make much more of it, especially with you, who have so many resources.[40]

To be sure that the Macduff role was understood, Verdi sent his views on it to Lanari: it was 'not a big part, but still an important character; besides, I again say that he has the aria, which, for example, if it were sung by Guasco would cause a furore.'[41] Careful even about the fabrics for the costumes, he warned that silk and velvet would be inappropriate. Muzio reported at the end of January that the opera was finished and that Verdi had begun to score this 'modern opera' which he believed was the grandest and most impressive spectacle of his time.[42]

As the two men got ready to leave for Florence, Verdi was given several important letters of introduction, among them one to the sculptor Bartolini and another to the poet Giusti. Giuseppina Appiani wrote on 14 February:

Dear Bartolini,

the man who will bring you these lines is Maestro Verdi, who is coming to your beautiful Florence to cheer it up with his sweet melodies. It is not necessary to write praise of him, for you will know him, you will judge him, and you will love him. He wanted to get to know you because he highly esteems and honours you; and now I am happy to make this possible for him; when he is [there], admiring the marvels you have created with your chisel, God knows how grateful he will be to me![43]

A former Jacobin and Bonapartist, the sculptor was a close friend of Rossini, Giusti, Moriani, the sopranos Grisi and Ungher, the actor Vestri, and Lanari himself. Living very near the Teatro della Pergola, Bartolini was a regular there; he had become one of the city's most acute dilettante critics, a former musician and singer who had played as a professional in several of the city's orchestras in his youth. A self-declared enemy of baroque and neo-classical art, he had made his own daring personal statement in 1839 when, newly appointed as professor of sculpture at the Accademia delle Belle Arti, he had invited a hunchback to pose nude for his first sculpture class, setting off a scandal. At the time, Bartolini declared: 'Everything in nature is beautiful and the person who understands how to copy nature will know how to do everything.'[44] On his personal insignia, he drew the figure of the deformed man, who is shown wrestling with a large serpent; around him runs the motto: 'THE HUNCHBACK WHO STRANGLES IGNORANCE AND ENVY.'[45] When Verdi asked to be introduced to Bartolini, he was hoping to visit the sculptor's studio to see his famous kneeling female nude figure, *Fiducia in Dio* (Faith in God), which dated from 1835 and had inspired Andrea Maffei to write a canto in its honour.

The letter presenting Verdi to Giusti was provided by Manzoni, who wrote: 'Two lines, and useless ones. Maestro Verdi wishes, and in this he is right, but along with many others, to make your acquaintance; and he imagines, and in this he is wrong, that he needs a recommendation to you. But [these lines] will not really be pointless because they will recall to you Your Sandro.'[46] The introduction, which Clara Maffei got for Verdi, was helpful in getting the composer a meeting with the poet, even though Manzoni's and Giusti's relationship had not always gone smoothly and even then was not well established. In 1845 Manzoni had had the poet as his house-guest for a month in his home in Contrada del Morone; after the visit, Giusti wrote his famous poem *Sant'Ambrogio*, with its evocation of Verdi's *I Lombardi*. Yet Manzoni's admirers Niccolò Tommaseo and Cesare Cantù remarked that Giusti had made derisive remarks about Manzoni and that Manzoni had spoken ungraciously about Giusti.[47] Later cordial exchanges between the two men do not sound a note of hostility, although members of the Manzoni family were involved in disputes with Giusti.[48]

With these introductions and his score in hand, and with Muzio beside him, Verdi set off for Florence on 15 February, stopping in Piacenza to see some of his family, perhaps his parents, perhaps Don Carlo and Egidia Uttini.[49] He spent three hours with them before going on to Bologna, where he and Muzio began the Appennine crossing that the composer always dreaded,[50] through the Passo della Futa into Tuscany, where he faced the daunting task of convincing the sophisticated Florentine audience that his opera was worthy of their stage.

Macbeth

Verdi had to test himself against the Florentines' knowledge of six of his own works, which had been produced at the Teatro della Pergola between 1843 and 1846, and of Meyerbeer's *Robert le Diable* and Weber's *Der Freischütz* as well. Through its Società Filarmonica, founded in 1834, Florence had become familiar with symphonic and chamber music by composers from north of the Alps. Indeed, 'the Florentine musicians and critics of this period considered themselves to be an elite, an inner circle of specialists with more refined perceptions.'[51] In the city there existed

two factions, the Verdians and Anti-Verdians, even before *Macbeth* went
into rehearsal.

The composer declared his independence as soon as he got to the city,
declining Lanari's invitation to stay in his house. 'I have someone with me
and cannot take advantage of it, but be sure that I am grateful for it all the
same', he wrote.[52] That 'someone' was Muzio; but later the two men were
joined by Andrea Maffei, Giovannino and Antonio Barezzi, and several of
Verdi's Milanese friends, Manara among them. Strepponi came from Paris
for the première, bringing her sister Barberina. The soprano was already
convinced that *Macbeth* had 'every probability of being a great success in
Italy' and was 'one of the subjects that is best suited to the French stage',
as she had written to Giovannina Lucca in February.[53] Then, as in recent
years, she was defending Verdi's interests, protesting at the exorbitant
rental fees the Luccas were asking for the opera *I masnadieri*, which
Verdi was writing under contract to them. Comparing their fees with those
of Casa Ricordi, she said she could not believe that the Luccas could
profit from damaging Verdi's chances; she also referred to the 'odious'
personal friction between the composer and the Luccas and advised them
to reach an agreement with the Escudiers about the opera. In the same
letter, Strepponi thanked Giovannina Lucca for her kindness to Camillino
Strepponi, who was perhaps in Milan at the time, although he was not
staying with his father, who had his legitimate daughter Giulia Cirelli
at home, or with his grandmother Cornalba in the Strepponi house in
Contrada della Cerva.[54] Strepponi may very well have seen her daughter
Giuseppa Faustina in Florence. Eight years old at the time, she was living
in Via Toscanella near Palazzo Pitti with the Stefanis, who were passing
as her 'true' parents.[55]

While Verdi awaited the Barezzis, Muzio kept them and other Bussetans
informed about rehearsals, writing from the Hôtel Suisse, where they had
a 'magnificent apartment with the air of paradise and *food fit for a king*
and the Maestro is taking care of the bill, that is to say, the impresario
is.'[56] Because Verdi always liked to revive one of his earlier operas first
in a city where he had not previously produced a première, he planned
Attila at the Pergola and turned the rehearsals over to Muzio. Barbieri-
Nini got to Florence on the twenty-fourth and began rehearsing *Macbeth*
three days later. During his visit there, Verdi's time away from the theatre
was taken up with the famous men who admired him and came to
seek him out. Among them were the Tuscan dramatist Giovanni Battista
Niccolini, the poet Giusti, the sculptors Bartolini and Giovanni Dupré,

and the painter Giulio Piatti. Both Piatti and Bartolini had strong ties
to the Bonapartes and the nationalist movement; Piatti's brother used
his printing-house as an outlet for Italian patriots and also backed the
women's movement in Italy—his sister Rosalia Piatti later became the
first Italian woman to win a major prize for literature.[57] Giulio Piatti had
worked as a painter in the opera-house in Leghorn and had completed his
huge, vivid canvas *I vespri siciliani*, which is now in the Pistoia Museum.
He punctuated his letters with patriotic slogans such as 'Death to the
Germans' (with skulls and crossbones drawn in the margins) and 'VIVA
L'INDIPENDENZA D'ITALIA'.[58] Verdi had long-standing ties with the Piattis,
reaching back to their connections in Busseto and Piacenza and forward to
his term in Parliament.[59] Piatti shared a studio in Florence with Dupré,
Bartolini's pupil, who sculpted Verdi's hand while the composer was
preparing *Macbeth*.

Dupré's recollections of Verdi's visit include remarks on his partisans
and enemies in the city.

The enemies said that as an artist he was terribly vulgar and a corrupter of Italian
bel canto, and they said that as a man he was a real bear, filled with arrogance
and pride, and that he kept himself aloof from everyone. I wanted to find out the
truth at once; I wrote a note as follows: 'Giovanni Dupré would like to request the
eminent Maestro G. Verdi to deign at his convenience to visit his studio, where
he is finishing his *Cain* in marble, and he would like to show it to him before
sending it off. But to see just how much of a bear he was, I wanted to deliver the
letter myself and introduce myself as a young man from the professor's studio. He
welcomed me very politely, read the letter, and then, with an expression that was
neither smiling nor serious, he said to me:

'Tell the professor that I thank him very much, and I will go to see him as soon
as I can, since I already had intended to get to know personally the young
sculptor who . . . etc.'

I replied: 'Signor Maestro, if you want to meet that young sculptor as soon as
possible, you may do so at once, for I am he.'

He gave a pleasant smile and, grasping my hand, said: 'Oh, you managed that
like a true artist.'

We spoke for a long time, and he showed me some letters of introduction that
he had for Capponi, Giusti, and Niccolini; the one for Giusti was from Manzoni.
We saw each other almost every day during the whole time he stayed in Florence;
we made some short excursions into the surrounding country, for example to the
Ginori factory, to Fiesole, and to Torre del Gallo. We were a group of four or five:
Andrea Maffei, [Luciano] Manara (who died later in Rome), Giulio Piatti, Verdi,
and I; in the evenings he let one or another of us attend the *Macbeth* rehearsals;

in the mornings he and Maffei very often came to my studio. He was extremely fond of painting and sculpture and spoke about them with an uncommon acuteness; he especially favoured Michelangelo. . . . He seemed pleased with my *Cain*; that almost savage pride went straight to his heart, and I recall that Maffei tried to persuade him that from Byron's tragedy *Cain*, which in fact he was then translating, a drama could be drawn that would be effective because of situations and contrasts such as Verdi's genius and natural disposition loved to explore.[60]

Sometime during the composer's stay in Florence, an unknown artist, perhaps one of Piatti's circle, made three miniatures, one of the composer, one of Giuseppina Strepponi, and one of a woman who is shown sketching the head of a child. Two of these, that of Verdi and that of the woman sketching, were used as models for two fine portraits that were said to be Verdi and Giuseppina.[61] The sepia drawing of the witches' cavern scene from *Macbeth*, later presented to Verdi by Clara Maffei, may have been done, perhaps by Piatti, from the Florence production.[62]

Attila, the first of Verdi's works to go on stage at the Pergola, was completely successful, generating rousing enthusiasm for its composer. One evening when Verdi stayed away from the theatre, the performance was brought to a stop as the audience shouted for him, even trying to get him brought from his hotel. Finally on 8 March Muzio tricked the composer into coming to the theatre by telling him that Barbieri-Nini and the bandmaster needed some of the music rewritten. The two men entered the Pergola by a secret door that led directly backstage. When Muzio let some of their friends in the audience know that Verdi was in the house, they mounted a noisy demonstration. Hearing it, Verdi wanted to leave but was finally persuaded to take a curtain-call. 'He had to come out eight times in the midst of the wildest applause,' Muzio told Barezzi, saying that he felt 'as happy as a prince' at having tricked Verdi into going to the theatre. 'After the finale, he was called out again and they threw an immense bouquet of flowers. At the end, he . . . said "*I am angry with you*", but it was not true. I have never seen him angry with me. This morning as soon as he awakened, I asked him whether he was angry with me. And he said to me: "*You are really crazy!*" That is the story.'[63] Verdi told Clara Maffei that he was in excellent health and that he liked Florence more and more every day. 'The opera continues to go well at the rehearsals; everyone thinks highly of it, but that does not mean much because at rehearsals everyone feels obliged to find everything one's written beautiful, as opposed to the audience, which normally feels obliged to find everything awful.'[64] He promised to keep her informed and added that he hardly ever saw Maffei excepting at meals.

While *Attila* was being performed, Verdi rehearsed his company during the day as often as possible, then stepped up his schedule when he had the whole theatre for the new production. Barbieri-Nini recalled much later that the cast endured more than 100 rehearsals in all; and although that is materially impossible, it suggests that the composer probably demanded three or four rehearsals a day instead of his usual two, keeping his company at the Pergola virtually all the time. According to Barbieri-Nini, the whole company was gradually forced to bend to the composer's 'iron will', as the concertatore, Pietro Romani, had to go over and over the passages that did not satisfy Verdi. Nor did he spare his chorus and orchestra, by whom he was not 'too well liked, because a word of encouragement never escaped his lips', not even when they all thought they had done their best to please him. Some of them cursed their pitiless taskmaster for his lack of response to their effort. The soprano recalled that Verdi considered the sleepwalking scene and the duet between her and Varesi the climactic moments of the opera and that he even called the two principals out into the foyer of the theatre for one final run-through on the night of the final dress rehearsal, while the invited audience was already seated in the auditorium, the orchestra was in the pit, and the chorus was in place on-stage. When the soprano protested that she was already in costume, Verdi told her to throw a cloak over her dress and hurry. Varesi,

fed up with this extraordinary request, tried raising his voice a little, saying: 'For God's sake, we've already rehearsed it a hundred and fifty times!' [And Verdi answered] 'You won't be saying that in half an hour's time: it will be one hundred and fifty-one by then.' We were forced to obey the tyrant. I still remember the threatening looks Varesi shot at him all the way to the foyer; with his fist on the hilt of his sword, he seemed to be about to slaughter Verdi, as he would later slaughter King Duncan. However, he yielded, resigning himself too; and the one hundred and fifty-first rehearsal took place, while the impatient audience created an uproar in the theatre.[65]

The première of *Macbeth* on 14 March was preceded by so much publicity that the Teatro della Pergola had to open its doors at four in the afternoon, four hours before curtain time. Within a few minutes it was so full that even Antonio and Giovannino Barezzi had to pay an extra premium for their reserved seats. On that first night, they had the joy of seeing Verdi take about thirty curtain-calls and bows. His protagonists were rewarded for their effort, as the first part of the duet 'Fatal mia donna' had to be repeated before the opera could go on. The opening witches chorus and one other piece were also encored. Barbieri-Nini, who described the duet's reception as unbelievable and unprecedented, said that she waited in the wings before the sleepwalking scene while the composer prowled nervously around her. Like the duet, it was greeted with a storm of applause. Verdi came to her dressing-room at once, gesturing with his hands and unable to speak at all. She was laughing and crying, also speechless. Verdi's eyes were red, she said, with tears. He grasped her hands tightly between his own and then rushed out without saying a word. When they left the Pergola a huge crowd accompanied their carriage back to the Hôtel Suisse, about a mile away. Verdi could feel confident about the success of *Macbeth*. Three days later Varesi called its reception extraordinary, confirming that the crucial second performance had gone even better than the première, at which he felt the audience had not fully understood the work. On the second night Verdi was called out 'countless times' and followed home by a crowd of people who 'yelled like the damned'. The baritone felt that Verdi had met the challenge of the new style and had composed a score that was the most carefully and 'artistically beautiful' of all his works. Varesi's own personal triumph was, he said, the most important of his career.[66]

The reviews of the opera were mixed. Piave, whose name was not on the printed libretto, as he was to discover later to his own dismay, was widely blamed for having written poetry that was mediocre at best; the singers were praised. Like Varesi, the critic Enrico Montazio felt that *Macbeth* was the finest of Verdi's works in its musical philosophy and its rich, beautiful instrumentation, although he criticized the opera in long articles published two weeks after its première, declaring that Verdi had not made his mark in the 'genere fantastico' and lagged far behind Weber, Meyerbeer, and other composers. He did, though, praise many pieces from the work and admitted the 'presence of genius' and the 'crucible' of the composer's 'glowing imagination'.[67] At least one of the critics emphasized the support Verdi got from the coterie of young men around him.[68] Verdi was 33; Giusti, 37; Dupré, 30; and Manara, 21. They were emerging as symbols of Italian hope, although they were poles apart in background and appearance: Giusti, the rugged *popolano*, risen from the ranks of the poor; Dupré, elevated by his more cosmopolitan background and honours bestowed on him by foreign governments; Verdi, out of the Emilian middle class; and the handsome Manara, the Young Lord.

Verdi and his friends were treated affectionately by Baron Bettino Ricasoli, who took to the composer at once. Two days after the première he sent his carriage at seven in the morning for Verdi, Muzio, and the Barezzis, who were treated to an all-day tour of Florence and the hill-towns nearby. Antonio Barezzi's widely appreciated record of support for his protégé and son-in-law earned him the respect of everyone and made him the most popular figure in the composer's entourage. The growing success of the opera was heartening. On the evening of the seventeenth, during the third performance, a group of Verdi's admirers, headed by Prince Giuseppe Poniatowsky, honoured him with a gold crown inscribed: 'THE FLORENTINES TO G. VERDI'. Barbieri-Nini presented it to him during a curtain-call in the second-act interval, when he was tendered yet another ovation by the public. At the end of the opera, a crowd of well-wishers unhitched the horses from his carriage and pulled it back to the Hôtel Suisse by hand.

Verdi left the city the next day. As soon as he reached Milan, he had a letter from Giusti, who had been out of Florence for several days and had not had a chance to say goodbye personally. Saying that he was sorry not to have found Verdi in when he called, he offered his view of *Macbeth* with some advice to its creator:

The more your work is performed, the more it will be understood and enjoyed; the excellence of certain things is not grasped at once. Continue, for you cannot help but be successful. But, if you will trust someone who loves both art and you, do not lose the chance to express with your music that sweet sadness in which you have shown you can achieve so much. You know that the tragic chord is the one that resounds most in our soul, but sorrow takes on a different character according to the times and according to the nature and the condition of this or that nation. The kind of sorrow that now fills the souls of us Italians is the sorrow of a people who feel the need of a better future; it is the sorrow of one who has fallen and wants to get himself back on his feet; it is the sorrow of one who feels regret, and is awaiting and willing his regeneration. My Verdi, accompany this lofty and solemn sorrow with your noble harmonies; nourish it, fortify it, direct it to its goal. . . . I would like all Italians of genius to contract a strong and full marriage to Italian art and shun the wanton lust of foreign liaisons.[69]

Responding warmly from Milan, Verdi thanked him and said that he would certainly follow the suggestions that the great artist had sent. 'Oh,' Verdi lamented, 'if we had a poet who knew how to devise a drama such as you have in mind! But unfortunately (you will agree yourself) if we want something that is at least effective, then we must, to our shame, resort to things that are not ours.'[70]

Just after he got home Verdi also wrote to Barezzi to send him the dedication of *Macbeth*, fulfilling a desire he had harboured at least one year before, when he first discussed with Ricordi the idea of dedicating one of his operas to his father-in-law. On 25 March the composer wrote:

For a long time I have been thinking of dedicating an opera to you, who have been my father, benefactor, and friend. It was a duty that I ought to have taken care of before now, and I would have done it if overriding circumstances had not been an obstacle. Now here is this *Macbeth*, which I love more than my other operas and thus believe is more worthy of being presented to you. The heart offers it; may the heart accept it, and may it be a witness to the eternal memory, the gratitude, and the love felt for you by your affectionate G. Verdi.[71]

Cavalli later recalled the moment when Barezzi got this letter.

Few men will ever have the chance to feel the joy of gratitude in such a personal way as did the good, old Barezzi when he read such sweet words; and, weeping profusely and deeply moved, he exclaimed: 'I recognized his goodness and talent [even] when he was a boy and protected him as best I could, and he has not let me down.'[72]

But Barezzi's curious answer to Verdi suggests that his tears may not have come only from sheer gratitude.

Dearest Son-in-Law, if my heart were not unfortunately immensely troubled, I would have died at the consolation of reading your very dear letter of the twenty-fifth of the month! Your gift is extremely precious to me: your recognition of me will always remain engraved in my heart. Deign to receive in exchange the hot tears of love that I shed for you, the only tribute that I can offer you. Love me, O my adored son of my heart, as I love you; and receive a thousand kisses. Addio! Your Antonio Barezzi.[73]

Barezzi's letter probably reached Verdi before the end of March.

Its puzzling reference to Barezzi's being 'immensely troubled' cannot be explained by any documents that have come to light in the civil and private archives that are relevant to a study of this period. But it is entirely possible that Barezzi had learned for the first time of the intimacy that existed between Verdi and Strepponi while they were all in Florence together before the *Macbeth* première. One published document does lend credibility to that explanation. Before the première, a printer's boy named

Salvatore Landi, who worked for the Tipografia Galletti in Via delle Terme, was sent to Verdi's rooms in the Hôtel Suisse with the proofs of the libretto. There he found 'Verdi and his wife'. Verdi gave him an extraordinarily large tip, he said. Because Landi took the trouble to report this in a letter to Giulio Piccini, the Florentine journalist known as 'Jarro', we have no reason to doubt him.[74] Further, we have every reason to believe that Barezzi, given his background and character, would have hoped that his beloved son-in-law would find a socially acceptable second wife. As later events proved, Strepponi was not considered acceptable, although Barezzi did embrace her as his daughter after 1852. But her presence in Florence may have come as a surprise to the Barezzis, who got to the city on the afternoon of the eleventh and stayed about a week. If Verdi's father-in-law was 'immensely troubled' by something connected to *Macbeth*, his anguish may perhaps be explained by what he discovered that March.

Verdi, in Milan, settled his debt to an unhappy Piave, who was paid in full for the libretto, which was printed without his preface and without his name. Maffei was thanked with a fine gold watch and chain; but he seemed uncomfortable about what had happened, as he apologized for the patches he had added to the text. He also acknowledged Verdi's payment for the libretto of *I masnadieri*, which Verdi planned to produce in London that summer.

Macbeth marked the first time that Verdi was paid a fee that was considerably larger than any paid to Bellini. John Rosselli, who has worked out a formula for translating the currencies of the time into francs, contrasts the 10,440 francs paid to Verdi for *Ernani* with the 10,825 francs he received for *Alzira*, while noting that the 24,000 francs Lucca paid to the composer for *Il corsaro* did not represent an important step forward, for Verdi ceded all his rights to the publisher. With *Macbeth*, however, he did begin to explore new ways of earning from his work by using his popularity to win ever larger concessions from impresarios and publishers. It was a time when he and other composers could hope to benefit from agreements and laws that established new protection for authors' rights.[75] As he was already beginning to learn how to use land and houses for profit, so he came to use his music.

14

April 1847–Spring 1848

London

Satisfied and happy over their experience in Florence, Verdi, Muzio, and the Barezzis started home. Having given Muzio leave to stop in Busseto, for about two weeks in late March and early April, the composer went on alone. But he was busy in Milan, so that when Muzio got back on 11 April, he found the Signor Maestro somewhat angry that he had stayed away too long. Encouraging signs of the continuing success of *Macbeth* came regularly as Italian cities vied with each other to give it. Padua, Vicenza, and Venice were rivals for the honour of being the first to produce it in Venetia, where the impresarios of all three theatres were discovering that the new, convenient railway brought them larger audiences than they had seen before. Lanari hoped to schedule *Macbeth* in Mantua; Brescia and Bergamo were also clamouring for it. Lumley wanted to give the opera at Her Majesty's Theatre; but Covent Garden had already secured the rights for the English première, in which Ronconi was to sing the title role. Lumley was expecting Verdi to keep his postponed appointment in London. The delay of 1846 had been granted because of absolute need; but in 1847 Verdi, clearly recovered, had to appear. Given all this pressure, Verdi and Muzio worked frantically in adjacent rooms in Verdi's apartment—as the younger man was besieged by Ricordi's engravers, who were hounding him for the vocal score of *Macbeth*.[1] Although Verdi again fell victim to one of his chronic throat infections, he was in fair health and was intending to go to London as planned. Just after his return from Florence he accepted 250 gold napoleons from Lucca as the first payment on his fee for composing the new work for Her Majesty's Theatre. To

Demaldè he confided that he could earn a fortune composing for foreign theatres; instead of getting 20,000 or 24,000 francs for a new opera, as he did in Italy, he might make as much as 80,000 or even 100,000.[2]

The subject he had chosen for London was *I masnadieri*, taken from Schiller's *Die Räuber*, a powerful drama of violence and cruelty coloured by such Romantic themes as freedom from authority, angry rebellion against reason, and the glory of desperate heroism. Early in August, just after Verdi and Maffei returned from their stay in Recoaro, Verdi wrote Clara Maffei that it was likely Andrea would write the libretto for him. Even then, he had a clear idea of the singers he hoped to secure. According to Muzio, Verdi wanted '[Caterina] Hayez or Barbieri, Fraschini, Varesi, and old Lablache' for his company.[3] In choosing Maffei as his librettist, he relied on an old friend and respected poet to whom he gave work at a moment when Maffei was lonely and desperate. A Schiller scholar, he seemed suited for the task at hand. The libretto must have been delivered to Verdi early in the autumn, for he let Lucca know on 3 December that he had finished one third of *Masnadieri*; by 17 May 1847 the opera was virtually complete.[4] But it was not clear sailing ahead, for there were rumours of trouble with the London company. Verdi wrote to Lucca to warn him that he would not tolerate 'the slightest slip-up'. If the opera were not to be produced at the time agreed upon, with the staging planned, he could not let it be performed.[5] Indeed, he was right to be alarmed, for Lumley faced a hectic season. In his memoir *Reminiscences of the Opera* the English impresario wrote of the turmoil in his professional life that year. Jenny Lind, his prima donna soprano, whom Verdi had formally accepted in November 1846, was being threatened with legal action by a rival impresario who had claims on her. Gossip raged about whether the Swedish Nightingale would come to England at all: 'Jenny Lind had signed with me at Darmstadt on 17 October 1846, . . . but the position of the celebrated prima donna with respect to this engagement was fraught with complications, some of them hazardous to herself and certainly perplexing to [me].'[6] Letters about Lind's contract appeared in London newspapers as the public asked when and whether she would come. When Her Majesty's Theatre opened, Lumley printed the names of several famous singers on his posters, but, as he soon discovered, this did not guarantee an orderly season. Verdi was shocked to learn that *I due Foscari* was given with a comprimaria (second-ranked singer) in the leading role, because all three of Lumley's leading sopranos were ill. When Lind finally got to London in mid-April, she was too exhausted to

211

sing. It was also rumoured that she did not wish to learn new operas. In fact, *I masnadieri* was only the second new work of her entire career. Given the situation, Verdi's wariness was justified.

The confusion of that spring in Milan added to the problems, as rising liberal and nationalist hopes caused unrest that the police met with ever more severe repressive measures. The death of the 75-year-old Cardinal Gaisruck in November 1846 had brought to an end the Austrian nobleman's thirty-year rule over Milanese religious and cultural life. Patriots then demanded that an Italian be named to this important see, warning that the nomination of yet another Austrian count would be met with rebellion. Responding to popular pressure, the Church elevated an Italian nobleman, Bartolomeo Romilli, the Bishop of Cremona. Named in April 1847, he was to make his official entry in September to claim the Cathedral of this seething city. As always in times like these, the theatres were targets of heightened police surveillance. At the Teatro Carcano in the spring of 1847, the company conducted by Mariani risked closure when a scheduled opera, Uranio Fontana's *I Baccanti*, could not be produced as planned. The other operas of the repertory were Verdi's *Giovanna d'Arco* and Ricci's *Michelangelo e Rolla*; *Nabucco* was substituted when it became clear that the Fontana opera could not be performed adequately and when the baritone Ghislanzoni failed to report for work on the night of the première. The *Nabucco* set off a political demonstration that turned into a near-riot after which Ghislanzoni was arrested and Mariani was threatened with jail. The season was allowed to continue; but with the passionately conducted *Nabucco* perceived as an incitement to revolt, audiences at the Carcano were more carefully monitored than they had been before. The repression in the theatre was but a microcosm of greater severity and more diligent enforcement of rules everywhere in Milan, for circumstances were right for revolution. Prices were rising; work was scarce; farmers that spring were already aware that the first harvest would be scanty; promise for the second one was no better; hunger was growing.

This, then, was the situation when Verdi and Muzio set out for London in May. They travelled by coach, train, and boat, making their way through Switzerland, Germany, Belgium, and France. They saw Lugano, the Saint Gotthard Pass (where there was so much snow that they had to put on overcoats and capes), Lucerne, Basle, Strasburg, Baden-Baden, Karlsruhe, Mannheim, Mainz, Coblenz, Bonn, Cologne, and Brussels on their way to Paris. Among other sites they visited William Tell's house, the chapel where he had worshipped, and the place where he had killed Gessner. They saw the Gutenburg monument and several monuments to Napoleon's generals and even stood on the Plain of Waterloo. Muzio wrote to Barezzi that they had seen waterfalls, cathedrals, vineyards, and wheatfields; that they had ridden through twenty-four railway tunnels between Cologne and Brussels, one of them 3 miles long. The two men talked with other travellers about the price of grain. Muzio reported their surprise as they saw that in all of 'these provinces and kingdoms' no one ever looked at their passports. Their luggage was inspected only once, at the Belgian customs. Such freedom of movement came as a surprise, especially to Muzio who had risked arrest just six weeks before when he ran foul of the customs at the check-point at the Carossa near Piacenza. A dog sniffed at his luggage, where he had hidden the salami and pork shoulders that he was carrying from Busseto to Milan on his return trip after *Macbeth*. 'How different from travelling in Italy,' he said, 'where it is inconvenient because you have to let someone see your passport all the time and always have to have your trunks ready to let someone see what is in them.'[7] Verdi, who was impressed with Mainz, Cologne, and Brussels, declared that he had had a good time.

Paris

When the two men got to Paris, they used the Escudiers as their guides. Muzio told Barezzi that Verdi did not wish to see anyone, although the tenor Guasco and other Italian singers were in the city then. Although Muzio did not mention Strepponi, Verdi probably saw her, for she was preparing to give a concert of Verdi's music to an invited audience in her home. The soprano had been in Paris for more than seven months, having left France only to attend the *Macbeth* première. As a voice-teacher, she was promoting the new, Verdian style of singing. Given Verdi's letter to the Escudiers, she may have had their help as she settled in France, for she visited their shop and even discussed Verdi's affairs with them. Strepponi lived at 13 Rue de la Victoire, where another famous tenant was the soprano Rosine Stoltz, who was just a few months older than Strepponi and was then the mistress of Léon Pillet, director of the Opéra since 1840. Stoltz won her celebrity in *La Juive*, *Dom Sébastien*, *La favorite*, and other repertory works of the period. When Strepponi moved to Paris, Stoltz was two years away from retirement. Rue de la Victoire is just north of the present Boulevard Haussmann, not far from the Théâtre des Italiens and the Opéra. The 'Coin de Lorette', as the quarter was called, took its name from the church of Notre Dame de la Lorette, which was a stone's throw from Strepponi's house. This part of Paris was then known as 'La Nouvelle Athènes' because so many writers and artists lived there. Here in 1833 the elder Dumas had staged his masked ball; here Sand and Chopin had lived. This setting seemed proper for Strepponi, as she was on her way to becoming what one of the Escudiers called 'the Perfect Parisienne'. Their theatrical journal had announced her arrival in October 1846; her classes opened on 15 November for ladies, professional women, and amateurs. She conducted lessons from three to five on Tuesdays and Fridays for 40 francs (eight lessons a month) or 100 francs for three months. Her concert of Verdi's music was planned for June 1847, just as he arrived.

Verdi was still fearful over the situation at Her Majesty's Theatre. On 2 June he sent Muzio ahead to London to find out whether Lind would sing or not, for he had heard in Paris that she had refused to learn his opera. With Muzio went the composer's angry letter, announcing that he would not cross the Channel without further guarantees. Muzio was ordered to deliver the letter, assess the situation, and send Verdi a report to Boulogne, where the composer would wait for it.[8] Lumley, under pressure from the competition at Covent Garden, offered Verdi the confirmation he demanded, swearing that Lind was waiting impatiently to get her music and start learning it. Muzio, reporting to Barezzi, said that Lumley was 'mortified', 'mortificato', that he had not yet seen Verdi in London.[9] The composer arrived finally on 5 June.

In London, which Muzio described as 'a chaos' and 'a Babylonia', the most expensive city in the world, and the noisiest and most confused, he and Verdi were like two lost souls. Verdi kept to the three-room apartment, very near the theatre, that Muzio had rented. Their quarters were so small that if a warm spell came, they would suffocate. They were unable to communicate with their English-speaking servants, whom Muzio described as 'rougher than rocks'. They discovered to their dismay that no one knew French, which, they had been assured, was commonly spoken in England. Their language problem was 'a desperation', Muzio said. The food was loaded with too much spice and pepper. It was served cold. The wine was so alcohol-laden that it tasted like rum. The rain and fog depressed the two men. The climate was the worst in the world, with the air poisoned by smoke. The only time they could breathe, Muzio said, was in the early morning hours, before the English stoked up for the day. At other times, the smoke burned their eyes; it 'softens and blackens the skin'. They were 'two poor devils who are not all right and are not comfortable'.[10]

Verdi and Muzio kept to a tight schedule, getting up at five in the morning, beginning work at six and working twelve hours, with scarcely a break. After the evening meal, they often went to the theatre, where Lumley had given Verdi a box among the ranks of the nobility. 'Every evening the Ambassadors of Russia, France, etc. and all the Lords come to pay him a visit,' Muzio said, adding that Lumley declared that Verdi was very likeable and that he had never found anyone more pleasant.[11] From Muzio's letters, it seems that he coached the singers while Verdi worked at the composition. The end of June was almost at hand and more than three weeks had passed since Verdi had begun the final draft of the opera. 'He has not yet finished, and still has to do the instrumentation as well,' Muzio reported on 29 June. The first piano rehearsals were scheduled to begin on the following day.[12]

Verdi's excellent cast included Jenny Lind, the most famous soprano in the world at that time; the tenor Italo Gardoni, whom Lumley described as 'young, handsome, gifted, with a lovely voice, belonging to a 'good school [of singing]';[13] and the celebrated bass Luigi Lablache, the brother-in-law of Camillo Cirelli, Strepponi's former manager and common-law husband. Lablache was cast as Massimiliano Moor, a role that he had sung in Mercadante's opera I briganti at the Théâtre des Italiens in Paris in 1836. Muzio compared his voice to the tones of a great organ. Filippo Coletti, the Francesco Moor and the leading baritone of the cast, was singing so much better than he had when he and Verdi had worked together in Naples in Alzira that Verdi revised the cabaletta 'Tremate, o miseri' for him, making major changes to show Coletti's voice to better advantage.[14]

Jenny Lind, naturally, was the singer who impressed Muzio most favourably.

I have found La Lind very good, kind, full of good manners and charm. She is a perfect and profound musician; she sight-reads any piece of music whatever. Her face is ugly, serious, and there is something Nordic about it that makes it very unattractive to me; she has a huge nose; . . . the Nordic complexion; very, very large hands and feet. . . . She leads a very, very private life: she receives no one (and is right not to do so, so as not to be annoyed); she lives alone; they tell me that she hates the theatre and the stage; she says that she is unhappy and that she will find happiness and a little bit of pleasure when she no longer has to deal with people in the theatre and with the theatre itself. In this, she is very much in agreement with the Maestro [Verdi], who also hates the theatre and cannot wait for the moment when he can leave it.[15]

About Lind's voice, Muzio wrote that he had heard her in *La figlia del reggimento*, *La sonnambula*, and *Roberto il Diavolo*, and that she was

an artist, in every sense of that word. She is great in all three of the operas mentioned above. Her voice is a bit sharp at the top, weak at the bottom, but through study she has reached the point where she is able to make it flexible at the top, so that she can perform the most difficult passages. No one can match her trill; she has an agility like no other singer, and generally, in order to let people hear her bravura in singing, she sins in performing too many fioriture, gruppetti, [and] trills, things that were pleasing to audiences in the last century, but are not [acceptable] in 1847.[16]

He added that Lind was not particularly successful in *Norma*.

Work on *Masnadieri* went forward slowly. As late as 27 June Verdi wrote to Giuseppina Appiani that he had not yet begun rehearsals 'because I have no desire to do anything. Understand clearly: no desire *to do anything*. And that is that.'[17] He blamed the English weather, the cold, the fog, the wine, and everything around him for his condition. 'Long live our sun, which I loved so much, which I now worship—now that I am in these fogs and in this smoke, which suffocates me and blinds my spirit.'[18] His humour grew worse as the weeks wore on, driving even Muzio to make a remark about it to Barezzi. 'The humid, heavy air acts very powerfully on his nervous system and makes him crazier and more melancholy than usual.'[19] Verdi briefly considered taking a house in the country near London, but he gave up the idea because he would have had to travel nearly three hours a day and pay high rentals for carriages and horses. Although Verdi was richer than he had ever been, money was still a matter of concern. 'Oh, if I could just stay here for a couple of years, I would carry off a bag of these *holy*, *holy* coins', he wrote to Appiani.[20] Muzio made frequent remarks about the high prices.

Yet neither of them could complain about Verdi's reception in London, for the English gave him all the honour due him. When he went to the theatre, every eye was turned in his direction. Newspapers invented countless stories about his comings and goings, reporting his presence at many soirées and dinners he did not even attend. 'I go out very, very rarely in society'; he said.[21] But Verdi was not entirely alone. In Lumley's company that year were Fraschini, Coletti, and Superchi, whom Lumley described as 'a protégé of the composer Verdi'.[22] He may also have known Lablache. During his visit, Verdi also met the Italian patriot Giuseppe Mazzini, exiled in London since 1837. This meeting must have been gratifying to both men, for they had many mutual friends, common acquaintances, and a common cause. By 1847 Verdi was among the foremost representatives of Italian art. His fame was beginning to surpass that of other artists of his time. As we know from later correspondence, Mazzini asked Verdi to compose a national hymn for Italy. Also in exile, and in London, was Prince Louis Bonaparte, whom Verdi met at a banquet that Lumley gave in his honour. Had he wished, the composer could also have met the Queen, who summoned Lablache to an audience and sent word through him that she wished to meet Verdi personally. 'But he does not want to go there,' Muzio reported, in a letter of 17 July.[23] Verdi also refused to help Giorgio Ronconi by coaching him in the leading role of *I due Foscari*, which the baritone was to sing at Covent Garden. Given the tight schedule at Her Majesty's Theatre, it would have been almost impossible for Verdi or Muzio to take on this task as summer approached and the Queen, who was pregnant, planned to leave London. Muzio blamed the delay on Gardoni, who, he said, was slow to learn his role.

The date for the première was fixed finally by order of the Queen, who chose 22 July, the same day that Parliament closed. Verdi had often been asked to conduct the opera, but as late as the eighteenth he was still refusing to do it. Finally he capitulated, and conducted the first two performances. Excitement over the production infected the whole theatre-going public in London, but the gala attracted travellers from abroad as well. Muzio reported that three people from Havana had crossed the ocean just to hear Jenny Lind. The gala brought out the Court and all London society. The Queen, the Prince Consort, the Duke of Cambridge, and 'an infinity of lords and dukes' attended. 'From the prelude to the last finale, there was nothing but applause, [shouts of] "Evviva", curtain-calls, and encores.'[24] There were also cries of 'Viva Verdi' and 'Bietifol' (Muzio's spelling). From the moment the orchestra filed into the pit, a great tumult rocked the theatre. Verdi, who was honoured with an ovation as he appeared at the conductor's chair, was later offered flowers and was called out for many solo bows. Lumley said that the house was filled to overflowing, and that Jenny Lind acted admirably and sang her music exquisitely.

With so many factors working in its favour, *I masnadieri* should have been a triumph for all. In fact, it was, as Lumley said, 'given with every appearance of a triumphant success, the composer and all the singers receiving all the highest honours'.[25] Muzio declared that Lumley's earnings at the box-office were larger than the total annual revenues of many Italian city-states. Lind told him that she had never heard music more beautiful than that of *I masnadieri* and that she had never had a role fit her so well. But in spite of all the factors favouring it, the opera did not enter the repertory and was rarely given after the end of the London engagement. Lumley attributed its lack of success to the fact that the work was 'singularly ill-suited' to Her Majesty's Theatre. 'The interest which ought to have been centred in Mademoiselle Lind was centred on [the tenor] Gardoni; whilst Lablache, as the imprisoned father, had to do about the only thing he could not do to perfection—having to represent a man nearly starved to death,'[26] referring to the singer's large size and great height. He also faulted the libretto for being poorly constructed. After Verdi left London, Lind went back to the roles that had made her famous; as Lumley said, it was impossible to hope that Verdi's new work would attract the paying audience. Having seats to fill, he did not turn to the Verdi repertory, in spite of the substantial success of *Nabucco*; instead he added *Le nozze di Figaro* and cast Lind as Susanna.

Verdi made no attempt to explain what was seen as the failure of *I masnadieri*. After the first night, though, he wrote to Clara Maffei: 'It went well; and, although it did not create a furore, it did have a success that brought me a lot of money.'[27] The opera eventually proved one of his least successful works. It may have got off to a poor start because it had its première so late in the season—Verdi had expressed his fears about the date, even while he was still in Milan. Further, it was compared unfavourably with the successful *I due Foscari* which had played at Covent Garden with Ronconi, Giulia Grisi, and the tenor Mario. During this run, a cabaletta that Verdi had written earlier for Mario became the subject of a dispute between the composer and the tenor, who, Verdi thought, had no right to it and was using it against his wishes. Muzio, reporting on the production of *I due Foscari*, said that its success was 'so extraordinary that no one in London has ever seen anything like it. About half of the opera had to be encored.'[28] Compared to this triumph and those of the popular *Nabucco*, of *I Lombardi*—which had been produced with Ronconi, Grisi, Mario, and Luciano Fornasari, a Verdi stalwart (and distant relative of the composer)—and *Ernani*, the new opera was disappointing. But it brought him the cachet of a London première and an offer to return there, as Lumley proposed that he compose and conduct for Her Majesty's in the future. Verdi did not announce his terms then. Something might indeed have come of the offer, for he was impressed with London, in spite of the pollution. He wrote to Emilia Morosini that it was 'not a city, but a world; nothing can be compared to its size, its wealth, the beauty of its streets, the cleanliness of its houses'.[29] For the third performance, Verdi handed over the baton to Michael Balfe, feeling gratified at the honours tendered him in England and resentful that—as he saw it—Lucca had refused to release him from his contract (for which Verdi said he would pay 10,000 francs) and let him write for 1848 for Lumley at Her Majesty's. With Muzio, he left England and started for France.

Paris, *Jérusalem*, and Strepponi

While Verdi was away, Strepponi had given her concert in Paris.[30] Soon after he got to Paris, he sent Muzio back to Milan and began to negotiate to produce *I Lombardi* at the Opéra. In return for arranging the music to fit a new French translation of the libretto, he was to be paid his rights fee exactly as if this were a new work. With the première tentatively set for early November, he set to work on the task, which was more than a simple revision. Muzio, who kept in touch with Verdi by post very frequently, even when they were apart for months or years, noted that five or six new numbers would be added and that the distribution of the pieces would be completely different from that in the old score. Verdi, during his London sojourn, also received an attractive offer from the Théâtre des Italiens, which asked to produce *I masnadieri* and *Macbeth*, also offering to pay him full fees for the work. In spite of being so sought after, the composer gave little indication of wishing to stay long in Paris. On 27 June he had written to Giuseppina Appiani: 'I cannot wait to go to Paris, which has no particular attraction for me but will surely make me very happy, because there I can lead the life I wish.'[31] Also from London, he had told Clara Maffei that he intended to stay a month in Paris, if he liked it.[32] And to Emilia Morosini, shortly after he got back to France, he said: 'I have been here two days, and if I go on being bored like this, I will soon be back in Milan.'[33] Muzio believed that Verdi would return to Italy at the end of November;[34] but the days lengthened into weeks and the weeks into months. Verdi stayed on, living in an apartment in Rue Saint-Georges, around the corner from Strepponi's house.

Tired from illness and from years of pushing himself far beyond his resources, the composer had clearly found a comfortable niche in Paris. He was far from idle, though, as he worked on *Jérusalem*, as the French version of *I Lombardi* was called, with his French colleagues. 'Two poets, two impresarios, two music publishers. . . . Get a prima donna under contract, settle the subject of the libretto. . . . Tell me that this is not enough to drive me mad!' he complained to Appiani.[35] He said, though, that he was in better health in Paris than he had been in London, yet he had 'a real hatred for the boulevards.'[36] There, he explained, he saw 'friends, enemies, priests, friars, soldiers, spies, beggars. . . . In other words, a little of everything; and I do my best to avoid them. . . . [In Paris] no one bothers me; no one points to me.'[37] Quite naturally, he did not tell his Milanese women friends that he had visited Strepponi; but the news got back to Italy all the same, when Giulia Tillet-Torriglioni let Tenca know that Verdi had been seen '*chez* Strepponi'.[38] He may have asked Strepponi's advice about terms for the proposed London contract, as the Tillet-Torriglioni letter is dated just one day before Verdi sent Lumley his demands. On 2 August he wrote:

I could accept this contract [for Her Majesty's] . . . and pledge myself to compose one new opera every year for three consecutive years, 1849, '50, '51; and, at the same time, conduct all the other operas of the season from mid-February to mid-August, if you will pay me the sum of 90,000 francs for each season, that is to say 60,000 for the new opera and 30,000 for conducting all the operas presented, plus a house in the country and a carriage.[39]

Lumley did not answer at once; Verdi made other commitments; and the proposed future collaboration came to nothing.

In writing the new music for *Jérusalem* and adapting the rest of the score to the French text, he had the help of Strepponi, whose handwriting appears in alternate lines with his in a love duet. Found by Ursula Günther and described by Andrew Porter as 'one of the more romantic discoveries of recent years', the passage reads:

[Strepponi's hand]: Alas! Hope is banished. My glory has faded!
                     Family . . . fatherland . . . all I have lost!
[Verdi's hand]:   No, I am still left you! And it will be for life!
[Strepponi's hand]: Angel from heaven! . . . May I die in the arms of a husband!

[Verdi's hand]:   Let me die with you! My death will be . . .
[Strepponi's hand]:   . . . sweet.[40]

This shared effort lends support to the belief that the letter Verdi had given her during the first week of October 1846 was indeed a pledge of love; but given the course of subsequent events, we must be careful not to exaggerate its importance, for the course of their love did not run smoothly. Still, at this moment in 1847, when both were abroad and Strepponi was undoubtedly helpful to him, Verdi depended on her for professional advice and moral support, as he sometimes had in the previous six or seven years.

Verdi said that he did want Muzio in Paris that autumn, though there were rumours that the two men had quarrelled, which Muzio vehemently denied.[41] Messages were sent through Marquis Giuseppe Arconati-Visconti, Clara Maffei's friend, who was in exile. In fact, Muzio was given ample reason to leave when the Lombard Revolt of September 1847 erupted during Bishop Romilli's formal entry into the Archdiocese of Milan. As the dead and wounded were counted, the people rose up against police provocation and brutality. Muzio considered fleeing to Busseto or France,[42] but then decided to stay where he was. Verdi could have used his help with *Jérusalem*, at a time when he had such a low opinion of the Opéra. There in June he had criticized 'the worst singers and the most mediocre chorus' he had ever heard, accompanied by an orchestra that was no better than they.[43] Muzio let Barezzi know that the composer had already given the chorus and singers their parts before 16 October and had written 'a new scene for [the tenor Gilbert] Duprez.[44]

While producing *Jérusalem*, the composer was also planning to give it in Italian as *Gerusalemme*. To Ricordi in the middle of the month he stipulated that no one could add anything to his score or 'mutilate' it, although the ballet music could be cut. He said that he would demand that Ricordi pay a 1,000-franc fine whenever the opera was altered in first-rank theatres. 'In second-rank theatres, the clause will apply just the same, and you will seek in every way to have the fine paid if my terms are violated.'[45] However, he did add that if Ricordi could not get the fine paid by lesser theatres, the publisher would not have to pay him.

At this point Verdi still had obligations to Lucca (one opera) and to the Teatro San Carlo (one opera); but his first services were owed to the Opéra, where he sometimes oversaw rehearsals and sometimes left them to theatre employees. Unlike Italian opera-houses, where rehearsals were concentrated into a short period, they went on at the Opéra for more than two months, exhausting the composer. He did, though, praise the scenery, which, he said, was 'absolutely splendid; and here they pay no attention to saving money'.[46] Yet all the money lavished on it could not create a success for *Jérusalem*, which had its première on 26 November 1847. Verdi seems to have taken this disappointment badly, for he wrote to Clara Maffei: 'Now it is too late to talk about [my opera]. And I am so tired of hearing this word *Jérusalem* that I do not want to share my boredom and bad humour with you.'[47] Under normal circumstances he would have started home after the third performance of the opera; but his situation in that late fall and winter differed from any he had known before. Remaining out of Italy, he preserved that valued privacy and independence that seemed to him his most precious assets in France. He lived in Rue Neuve Saint-Georges, near Strepponi's house. Eventually he may have moved into either her own apartment or a separate apartment in her building.

His friendship with her was no secret. Sometime between the middle of November and Christmas 1847 Antonio Barezzi came to Paris to pay his son-in-law a long-delayed visit, for he had not been able to get to London, as planned. While there he was entertained by Strepponi and treated graciously by her and her students. From Busseto, after he got home, he and Demaldè wrote to Verdi:

Since my arrival in Busseto from Paris, I have not let one single day go by without telling people about the great things I saw during my trip, and the welcome I got there from you, from Signora Peppina, and from your other friends; and I assure you that those memories will always remain engraved in my heart . . . I am always very, very eager to have word of your theatrical activities, and thank you for the news you sent me; just as I am also always wanting to know about your health, and how you are getting along there . . . You give me hope that I will get a letter from Signora Peppina, and I have to tell you that I am waiting anxiously for it, and in the mean time give her my regards, and her women too, whom I found so kind. Your father and your mother are in Busseto [in Palazzo Cavalli], in the very best of health, and they have asked me to give you their regards, since I gave them news of you. Here is a kiss with my whole heart, and I am your very loving father-in-law, Antonio Barezzi.[48]

In Demaldè's part of the letter, he thanks Strepponi for her regards sent to him, presumably through the letter just received from Verdi, and expresses his appreciation of her 'talents', her 'fine spirit', and 'her virtues' ('*le sue doti, il suo bell'animo, e le sue virtù*'). He also shows how

Verdi heard of political developments at home. In more than a thousand words, cast into tight prose and crowded on to three pages of letter-paper, Demaldè reviewed for Verdi the political history of Parma and Piacenza since the Treaty of Vienna in 1815. At the end he warned Verdi that there was a great deal of unrest in Italy, that Rome was a hive of disorder, that Tuscany supported Rome in its revolutionary foment, that Lucca was likely to revolt, and that the reforms granted by the King of Naples were futile.

Absolute monarchy serves no purpose now . . . Lombardy, which wanted to stand up for itself, is in chains, a [prisoner of the Austrian] Eagle. The uprisings in Milan at the beginning of the year cost five lives and left fifty-four wounded. That kingdom is flooded with Germans . . . Pius IX is the pivot, not just of Europe, but of the whole world.

Demaldè went on to describe the effects of 'the good and bad' of parliaments and told Verdi about the activities of Giuseppe Piroli, Verdi's former schoolmate and friend, who was already launched in his political career. All this was sent in response to 'Caro Peppino', who had asked for news of his native land.[49]

Verdi, who had said that he would return to Italy in November 1847 and again in January 1848, had been prevented from doing so, first by business matters and then by illness. But he certainly was not unhappy. On 9 March 1848 he wrote Giuseppina Appiani a letter that rings with a joy that had often been alien to him.

I cannot hide from you the fact that I am having a very good time and that nothing [in the political situation] has prevented me from sleeping, up to now. I go for walks; I hear a lot of stories; I buy about twenty newspapers every day (it goes without saying I do not read them) to keep newspaper vendors from hounding me; thus when they see me with a bundle of newspapers in hand, they don't try to sell me any, and I laugh, and I laugh, and I laugh. If nothing important calls me back to Italy, I will stay on here through all of April to see the National Assembly. I have seen everything that has happened so far, both serious and funny (and I beg you to understand that I mean *seen* with my own eyes); and I also want to see the twentieth of April'.[50]

This Verdi is in high spirits, sounding little or nothing like the chronically ill, depressed composer of the previous years. We cannot doubt that his optimism and good feelings were owed, at least in part, to political developments and to the personal freedom he was obviously enjoying. He also had Strepponi's support at this time. She, who had paid such an appalling price for what she once called the 'bad' she had done, found in him a man she could trust. He saw in her a knowledgeable, intelligent woman with the sophistication he never learned. Having depended on her advice for years, he continued to do so and, as she later remarked, entrusted some of his most important matters to her. In 1847, though, there was no suggestion that they intended to live together all the time, for she had, she said, settled permanently in France. He, having bought Il Pulgaro at Roncole and Palazzo Cavalli in Busseto, was about to acquire property at Sant'Agata, the Verdis' and Bianchis' ancestral village. There he expected to settle his parents at least during the summers. When Carlo Verdi and Luigia Uttini moved there in 1849, the Verdis' sixty-year sojourn in the Duchy of Parma ended and they returned to their Piacentine terrain. Although the composer stayed on in France in 1848 and through much of 1849, he seemed to have no intention of cutting himself off from his home and his people.

15

~

Spring 1848–September 1849

Il corsaro and The Revolution of 1848

Early in 1848 Verdi, living in Paris, sometimes seemed happier with his lot than he had been for many years; but in a letter to his old friend Toccagni, he admitted to a certain restlessness.

What do you want me to tell you about myself? I am the same as ever, always unhappy about everything. When I have good luck, I would like to have things go against me; when things go badly, I want good luck; when I am in Milan, I would like to be in Paris; now that I am in Paris, I would like to be . . . where? I don't know . . . on the moon. As for everything else, I enjoy all the personal freedom here that I have always wanted and have never been able to have. I don't go anywhere, I don't receive anyone, and I don't have the annoyance of seeing people point to me, as they do in Italian cities. I am in good health, I write a lot; my business affairs are all going well; but my frame of mind, which I always hope will change, never changes.[1]

Among other professional concerns, two loomed large. The first was the continuing friction between Verdi and Lucca; the second was the composer's determined attempt to prevent impresarios, conductors, and singers from making changes and cuts when they performed his operas. In January he sent Piave a tirade about Lucca.

You are talking to me about things that can never be to my liking. You have an interest in Signor Lucca? Don't you know how I have been treated by this gentleman, after I acted so generously toward him, forcing myself to finish *Attila* in my deplorable physical condition, and after fulfilling the contract for London, even though I was not obliged to do so? He has been insensitive, mean, demanding toward me. I forgive a slap in the face, because if I can I will give

225

back twenty, and then will kill the person who slapped me, even on the altar; but I cannot pardon an insult to which I cannot respond. And he, thinking to placate me, has the idea of sending me a cheque for a thousand francs.—Buy me off with a thousand francs? Imbecile! But that is enough about Signor Lucca, and I hope you will never speak to me again about him.[2]

Verdi also wrote to others, including Giuseppina Appiani, about the 'odious and insensitive' publisher, 'this ingrate', with whom he had, none the less, to deal.

Verdi's battles with singers, theatre directors, and impresarios over protection of his scores also went on. In March 1848 he wrote to Ricordi to try to stop the

insolent licence taken by conductors and singers. Our lot is very hard: How can an opera ever win out over the ignorance and arrogance of those who, under the pretence of adapting it to suit their respective audiences, allow themselves to make any kind of change, without ever, ever understanding (not even by accident) the composer's ideas? . . . I beg you to provide, in your contract with impresarios, for the operas to be ruined as little as possible.[3]

In the summer of 1847 Verdi tackled the problem of how he would fulfil his contract with Lucca and, after considering other subjects, settled on *Il corsaro*, which he had commissioned from Piave in 1845. At that point, he had been familiar with Byron's *The Corsair* for at least a year and loved it for its passions, which he thought would be easy to convey in music. In August 1846, when he had written some of it—at least the prison duet and the trio of the last act—Piave asked to have it back. Verdi refused, claiming that he had always found it fascinating. But by December of that year he was confiding to Lumley that after Piave set it in verse, he found it cold and lacking in theatrical effects. With that, he put it aside. Yet the work fitted neatly into these years, with its rebellious pirate hero, living outside society as the bandits in *Masnadieri* did, as the earlier *Ernani* had done. *Il corsaro* also suited its time, being composed on the eve of the Revolution of 1848. But, given the friction between Verdi and Lucca, and given certain changes in Verdi's way of life in 1847 and 1848—his move to Paris, his new circle of friends there, his new professional terrain at the Opéra—the outcome was not certain. He was also composing without knowing where or when the opera would be given or by whom it would be sung.

The finished score was sent from Paris in February 1848, but it is clear that Verdi had intended to return to Italy himself at that same time. His plans were so firm that he had even given Muzio a date for his arrival and did not let Muzio know until that very day that he had decided to stay in France. Verdi asked his assistant to get 1,200 gold napoleons, his fee, from Lucca and send it to Paris through a bank. He also gave Muzio instructions on how the music should be performed. 'And I (if Lucca will pay me well) will go to get it staged,' Muzio informed Barezzi.[4] At the same time Verdi sent Lucca a letter stating that upon payment of 1,200 gold napoleons the publisher would become 'absolute owner' of the score. 'I repeat that Signor Lucca may do anything he likes with the libretto and with the music, in Italy as well as in other countries, either for publication, with all possible arrangements for any instrument whatever, or for rental [of the score] to all theatres'.[5]

Lucca, to his credit, assigned *Il corsaro* to the Teatro Grande in Trieste, one of Italy's finest houses, and secured a cast that was almost as good as anyone could have mustered in Europe at that time. The tenor was Fraschini; the baritone Achille De Bassini; the soprano, Verdi's Lady Macbeth of his 1847 première of *Macbeth* in Florence, Barbieri-Nini. To her, his prima donna, he wrote careful instructions for singing the role of Gulnara. He wanted, he said, 'to tell you a few things about your pieces' and went on to provide details on her music.

The cavatina is easy to interpret: you must sing it simply, and you can do that; take the adagio slowly and sing it mezza voce. Don't take the cabaletta too fast, and accelerate on the three or four notes of passagework, with which it ends. . . . Be sure that the finale is well staged. The first agitato could be ridiculous if it is not effectively staged. The adagio should be slow and declamatory, and the stretta not too fast . . . You know better than I that anger is not always expressed in shouting, but sometimes in a suffocated voice; and that is the case here. Sing the whole movement sotto voce, then, except for the last four notes; wait until bass has almost left the stage before exploding with a shout, accompanied by a terrifying gesture, almost a premonition of the crime you are about to commit. . . . The dramatic situation of the whole duet is stupendous, as you will see . . . [In the final trio], don't forget that you have killed a man, and in all of your words, even when you comfort Medora, let your remorse show all the time . . . The last movement should be performed largo, like the trio in *Lombardi*. Be sure you keep together. Let it be sung by all with extreme passion, and I'm sure that you will find it effective.

One final suggestion [or warning]: take care to see that the opera is divided into just two acts [and not three]. The first act will close with the end of the [concertato] finale; the second [act] with the trio [Medora, Gulnara, Corrado]. It will gain in interest, brevity, in everything.[6]

This splendid letter proves that Verdi cared about *Il corsaro* and did not simply cast it off like an orphan shipped away on the operatic sea. As we read it we cannot help wondering whether Verdi wrote others like it to singers who were presenting his operas in important engagements in theatres where he could not direct the production himself.

Il corsaro was produced in a year of revolution, counter-revolution, fear, and upheaval. 1848, greeted by liberals as a year of miracles, brought to some the realization of their aspirations, to others, defeat. Like many others who held his political convictions, Verdi welcomed the news of spreading revolts. Those in February in Paris and in March in Milan meant most to him because of his personal associations with those cities.

The Revolution of 1848 came to Paris on the heels of uprisings in Bohemia, Hungary, Berlin, and Vienna. Louis Philippe, the 'Citizen-King' of France, was overthrown, his rule giving way to the Second Republic in the last week in February. Prince Louis Bonaparte, whom Verdi had met in London, returned from exile to his homeland. In this new state Verdi could see at first hand how the revolutionary dream could be translated into reality. As he confided to Giuseppina Appiani, he was pleased to have '*seen* everything *with my own eyes*'.[7] She already had one of her own family engaged in revolutionary agitation in Milan, while her friend Sandrini remained under the surveillance of Austrian spies. Verdi, who had planned to go back to Italy during the third week in February, let her know that he expected to stay on in France until the end of April unless something important called him back to Italy. As he was writing to her, Milan was under martial law as its citizens resisted the restrictions imposed on them. Patriots gave out leaflets to the populace in the streets, demanding a boycott of La Scala on the nights when the Austrian ballerina Fanny Elssler danced. One broadside urged 'One more sacrifice!' and 'Let the Germans have the theatre!' Some Milanese went to La Scala to agitate; and not all of them were in the audience. On 17 March, when Elssler danced, the chorus conspired to wear revolutionary emblems on their costumes. Seeing them, and hearing patriots hooting and Austrian officials cheering in the auditorium, she fainted.[8] Eventually the authorities closed the theatre. Fresh troops were brought in; many were billeted in *palazzi* where Italian patriots were planning the revolt against them.

During the first three months of 1848 Verdi also wrote four letters to Emilia Morosini which dealt at length with her plan to buy an Erard pianoforte for her daughter Giuseppina. Verdi negotiated with Erard for almost three months about the purchase, sending his reports back to

Milan, together with his impressions of the celebrated Conservatoire orchestra, which he heard play a Beethoven symphony. They played the Adagio better than he had heard it in Italy, he said; the Minuet was enormously effective and the last movement extremely loud— almost louder than the music he wrote himself!—And that says it all, he remarked. He had also seen a ballet at the Opéra, which he described as the most indecent thing that anyone could possibly see: 'almost' because the performance at the Opéra-Comique was the same or worse. In a letter of 9 March (the same day that he wrote to Appiani), he described the events of the Revolution of 1848: 'At this moment you will know about everything that has happened in Paris; and I can only say that after the twenty-fourth the only sign of insurrection is the *funeral procession* of last Saturday that accompanied the dead from the Madeleine to the Bastille. It was a stupendous, sublime spectacle!' He hoped to see the Assembly and continue to follow events at least through the twentieth of April. 'I would blame myself if I were to abandon Paris now, after having been a witness to all, or almost all, of the serious and funny scenes that have taken place.'[9]

While he was still in Paris, the bloody, historic Five Days (Cinque Giornate) rocked the city of Milan. On 18 March, when Austrian soldiers fired into a group of citizens outside the Governor's Palace, peaceful protest gave way to violence. Barricades thrown up in the streets were defended by men, women, and children who attacked their oppressors with any weapon at hand. The commoners of Milan fought their improvised war at the doors of their houses and shops, in narrow streets where the parade-ground trained Austrian regulars could neither hold ranks nor regroup. Theirs was a triumph of popular passion over organized strength.

Verdi had helped feed that fire. With *Nabucco*, *Lombardi*, *Ernani*, *Giovanna d'Arco*, and particularly *Attila*, he forged weapons of his own. Learning of the revolt, he returned to Milan, where he arrived on 5 April, as Ricordi's *Gazzetta Musicale di Milano* announced: 'Arrivò a Milano questa mattina il celebre Maestro Verdi.' He had every right to play a hand in this revolution. The friend of Giusti, Capponi, and Niccolini in Florence; of Mazzini in London; of Prince Louis Bonaparte, who had attended the dinner in Verdi's honour in London, he found himself in a newly created country, where the Chief of State was Cattaneo, Giuseppe Seletti's former neighbour and colleague from the Ginnasio di Santa Marta. Verdi may even have had a title in the new ruling structure; and as Mazzini and other exiles hurried back, so he returned to seek out friends.

The language of revolt came readily to his lips. Piave, whom Verdi had called the Lion-Cat, Big Tom-Cat, Toad, and Lazy Beast of Venice, became Citizen Francesco Maria Piave of the new Venetian Republic of San Marco. In these glorious weeks Verdi seemed to be the only Italian composer with a valid national voice in music and theatre circles, for Donizetti had died before the Milan revolt and Rossini had fallen out of favour with the liberals.[10] After his marriage to Pélissier in 1846, Rossini moved back to Bologna with his wife and rented an apartment in Donzelli's house, so he and the famous tenor could be neighbours, as we know from one of Donzelli's letters at La Scala. He also acquired a town house of his own. Ill and suspicious, he became frightened of the rabble on the Left, who accused him of pro-Austrian leanings. In 1848 he was jeered by a band of volunteers who, ready to leave for Lombardy and the field of war, had stopped beneath his windows and called to him. After hearing their catcalls, he decided to leave Bologna.[11]

Like Mazzini, Verdi became a prophet of a people, of the force of nationalism that was carrying Italy in its tide. When he composed music to patriotic phrases in his librettos, he evoked a cultural and philosophical idea that was to become a political reality in his lifetime. Words like 'liberty', 'the people', and 'Italy' were not mere catchwords, but rather the vehicles of Verdi's nationalistic message. In his music, Messianic nationalism found a voice that aroused Italians to the cause of the *Patria*.

A letter from Verdi to Citizen Piave of the Venetian Republic echoes the hopes of both men for their country. Dated 21 April 1848, it was written from a free Milan, where Verdi could see all around him the effects of the battle in which he had not actually fought.

Dear Piave,

You can imagine whether I wanted to stay in Paris, after hearing about the revolution in Milan. I left there immediately after hearing the news; but I only got to see these stupendous barricades [and not the fighting]. Honour to these heroes! Honour to all of Italy, which is now truly great!

The hour of her liberation is here; be sure of that. The people want it: and when the people want it, there is no absolute power that can resist. Those who want to impose themselves on us by sheer force can do what they want, they can conspire as much as they like, but they will not succeed in cheating the people out of their rights. Yes, yes, a few years more, perhaps a few months, and Italy will be free, united, and republican. What else should she be?

You talk to me about music!! What has got into you? Do you think that I want to bother myself now with notes, with sounds? There cannot be any music welcome to Italian ears in 1848 except the music of cannon! I would not write a note for all the money in the world: I would feel an immense remorse, using music-paper, which is so good for making shells. Bravo, my Piave, bravi all the Venetians, put aside all local concerns. Let us all lend each other a brotherly hand, and Italy will again become the foremost nation in the world!

You are a national guard? I am happy that you are not just a plain soldier. What a fine soldier! Poor Piave! Where do you sleep? How do you eat? Had I been able to enlist, I, too, would [have wanted] to be just a soldier; but now I can only be a tribune, and a wretched tribune, because I am only occasionally eloquent.

I have to go back to France because of obligations and business. You can imagine that—in addition to having to write two operas—I have a lot of money to collect there, and other money to collect in bank drafts.

I abandoned everything there; but I cannot ignore a sum of money which is, to me, quite large; and I have to be there in person to salvage at least a part of it, given the present crisis. As for everything else, no matter what happens, I will not be troubled by this. If you could see me now, you would not recognize me. I no longer have that long face that scared you! I am drunk with joy! Imagine that there are no more Germans here!! You know what kind of feelings I had for them! Addio, addio, say hello to everyone. A thousand good wishes to Venturi and Fontana. Write to me soon, for [even] if I leave, I shall not do so right away. Of course, I will come back![12]

This letter testifies to Verdi's joy. Here he expresses a pure Mazzinian faith in the people: if the people will something, they will get it, for they carry the destiny of the nation. Here, too, may be found a hint of a possible political role that Verdi might play in the new Italy. His reference to being 'a tribune' and 'a wretched tribune at that, for I am only occasionally eloquent' may be a reference to a specific position in a republican government, the government that he believed would rule in Milan 'in a few years or a few months'. There would be triumvirs under Cattaneo's plan, as there were later in Italy and as there had been in ancient Rome. Beside them, representing that sacred body the People, would stand the tribunes. This seems almost to be taken directly from Roman history, or from Alfieri's drama *Virginia*. Its protagonist was Icilio Romano, tribune of Rome, for whom Verdi's only son had been named. He was the proud, plebeian, fierce defender of the virgin Virginia, after whom Verdi's daughter was named. In the play Icilio Romano proclaims himself 'tribune' and 'defender' of republican Rome, enemy of tyrants. When the composer announced that he too could 'be a tribune', he may have had Alfieri's dramatic scene in mind.[13] He may have been offered a new office, a new rostrum, by either Cattaneo, who was elected Chief of State and head of the Milanese Council of War, or Mazzini. Of the two, Mazzini seems the more likely, for he had actually assigned Verdi the job of writing the hymn of the new nation. Italy was not to survive as a country in 1848; for Austria soon regained power; but when it was born through unification, Verdi was indeed a tribune, a deputy in the Assembly, the first governing body of the democratic Parma Provinces, and in the first Italian Parliament.

Many friends of Verdi were committed to the revolt and had a role in it. One of the Strigellis was Cattaneo's right hand. The Morosinis gave both money and lives. The Arrivabenes were on the field in Venetia. Tenca, both before and after 1848, was among the most determined agitators. Manara was on the barricades and went on to become a general. Even the apolitical Andrea Maffei had begun to express patriotic sentiments; later he became an outspoken enemy of Austria with firm ties to Trentine exiles and unificationists. Clara Maffei opened her house to liberals; when citizens were wounded in an early round of skirmishes, she was one of fifty-two noblewomen who hurried to serve as a nurse in Palazzo Borromeo and organize a relief fund.[14] Among others who had returned from exile was Princess Cristina Belgioioso, a friend of the Strepponis, who entered the city on 6 April at the head of a volunteer corps of 160 men whom she had mustered in Naples and brought north by sea. She 'entered the free city to cheering crowds' and appeared on the balcony of the provisional seat of government at the side of Count Casati, the brother of Count Confalonieri's widow, and of Count Borromeo.[15] It was reported that when Princess Cristina reached Milan she was dressed as Joan of Arc.

Verdi, having spent April in the city, saw Mazzini there and then went on to Busseto to visit his family and the Barezzis. He also concluded the purchase of his new farm. On 8 May 1848, just four years to the day after he acquired Il Pulgaro at Roncole, he bought his first acreage at Sant'Agata.[16]

Disillusionment lay ahead, for the new, provisional government of Milan did not become republican, as the Venetian government had, nor did it have the spirit or the structure that Verdi believed it might have. Indeed, there was a conflict between Mazzini republicans, who wished to integrate the entire peninsula into one, single, republican state, and the more conservative liberals, who believed that the safest course lay in a constitutional monarchy and felt that Milan should be unified with the Piedmont, if only on a temporary basis. Its king, Carlo Alberto, was fighting for the Milanese cause as his army kept the Austrian troops at bay in Lombardy and Venetia. Mazzini was dismayed and shocked at what he considered the intrigue and treachery of some members of the Milanese provisional government.

Verdi appeared not to be involved directly with the governors of the city at that time. After his visit to Busseto, he returned to France, arriving there sometime after the middle of May.[17] He was thus spared the pain of seeing Milan handed back to the Austrians on 5 August, when Carlo Alberto, defeated, was forced to accept the return of the oppressors and let the heroic Milanese resistance be crushed. The Austrian troops and their rulers drove many Milanese into exile: Carcano, Tenca and his mother, Princess Cristina Belgioioso, and several of the Borromeos. Even Muzio fled. He moved to Mendrisio, not far from Locarno, where knots of Lombard refugees clustered[18] and did not even have money to get home to Busseto. When he went, finally, he had to make a long detour around the part of Lombardy where the Austrian army was encamped in full force.[19] Even outside the city, though, he went on working for Ricordi and Verdi, who remained in Paris. Soon after the Austrians re-entered Milan, Verdi was expecting Muzio in Paris. To Clara Maffei, Verdi wrote: 'Emanuele wrote me that he could not stay any longer in Milan and that he will be here tomorrow or later.'[20] But instead of going to France, he stayed close to the Ricordi office in Mendrisio. In 1847 and 1848 he had been active in promoting Verdi's operas and had conducted *Macbeth* in Lodi and *Macbeth* and *Ernani* in Mantua, as we know from his reports to Ricordi. Verdi continued to depend on him to take care of the most intimate matters while he and Strepponi stayed on in France.

As the composer's reputation grew in Italy and the rest of Europe, his works were also beginning to be heard in the United States, where the Barili-Patti company had offered *I Lombardi* in New York in March 1847, the first production of a Verdi opera in this country. With Sanquirico and Pogliani, the troupe later inaugurated the new Astor Place Opera House in November, with *Ernani* as the opening bill. This work was not new to New York, having been given by the Arditi-Badiali company earlier that year. In Philadelphia in March the company offered *Ernani* before returning to give *Nabucco* at the Astor Place. When it failed in mid-April the company's managers decided to try Boston, where on 23 June it gave Mercadante's *Il giuramento*, which it advertised as 'VERDI'S IL GIURAMENTO', 'Verdi's favourite and celebrated opera' in playbills and newspaper notices for the Howard Athenaeum.

BOOK II

A Battle-Hymn and Two Battle-Operas

Verdi had taken to heart Mazzini's and perhaps even Giusti's exhortations about continuing as a composer of patriotic music, working on a war hymn or anthem by Goffredo Mameli, the text of which Mazzini sent to him. He also began to consider two operas. The first was *La battaglia di Legnano*, a patriotic work that celebrated the victory of the Lombard League over the Germans, an allegorical treatment of contemporary affairs that had a certain specific bearing on the history of the day.[21] The other, which was destined to remain uncomposed, was *Ferruccio*, its protagonist an iron man of Italian history, the hero of the novel *L'assedio di Firenze* by the Leghornese patriot Francesco Domenico Guerrazzi.[22] It too reflected the upheaval of 1848 and 1849. France, to which Verdi returned, was torn by internal struggles. Workers, believing that the Second Republic would not allow them to reach their goals, rioted and threw up barricades in June 1848. In bloody battles the government of France put down this new uprising and voted a dictator's powers to General Cavaignac. Peace was restored, but at a terrible price, with the Archbishop of Paris killed, together with many citizens. Many were arrested, held without trial, and deported. It was at this period that Verdi and Strepponi took a villa at Passy.

On 22 July Verdi wrote to Piave:

I don't know whether you know that I have been in Paris more than a month; and I don't know how long I will stay in this chaos. Have you heard about this latest revolt? How many horrors, my dear Piave! and pray to Heaven that it is all over! And Italy? Poor country!!! I read and reread the newspapers, always hoping for some good news, but . . . And you, why don't you ever write to me? It seems that these ought to be the real moments when friends remember friends! In the middle of all these world-wide upheavals, I have neither the mind nor the will to get busy with my own business (it seems to me even ridiculous to work on . . . music); however, I have to think about it and think seriously. Tell me, then, if I were to propose to you that you write me a libretto, would you do it? The protagonist should be an Italian, and free; and if you don't find anything better, I propose *Ferruccio*, a gigantic figure, one of the greatest martyrs of Italian liberty. *L'assedio di Firenze* by Guerrazzi could offer you grand scenes; but I would want you to stay close to history. I believe that the four principal characters should be Ferruccio, Lodovico Martelli, Maria Benintendi, [and] Bandini Giovanni. . . . There is the Florentine senate. What do you think? If you find that this is a good subject, make me a draft sketch of it and send it to me. Don't forget that I like a very general draft-sketch because I have to make my own comments, not that I believe that I am able to judge such a work, but because it is impossible for me to write good music if I have not understood the drama thoroughly and an not convinced of its validity. Be sure not to be boring!. . . . Addio, addio! Let's hope for happier times. But I am afraid when I look around France and then at Italy. . . . Russia is even taking steps toward Constantinople. If we let the Russians take Constantinople, we will all become Cossacks in a few years! Christ!!![23]

L'assedio di Firenze is one of Verdi's most important uncomposed works, like *Cola di Rienzi*, another symbol of insurrection that Verdi once had under consideration. Guerrazzi, a friend of Giusti and others from Verdi's circle of Tuscan friends, was, like Giusti, a poet, former law student, and disciple of Byron, whom he had met in Pisa and whose memory he had honoured with verses of his own. Guerrazzi published *L'assedio di Firenze* in the 1830s and won critical acclaim, particularly from Mazzini, who considered the work a masterpiece. 'Guerrazzi has a titan's soul', Mazzini wrote of him.[24] He was an editor and publisher of *L'indicatore livornese*, a periodical similar to *L'indicatore lombardo*, for which so many of Verdi's acquaintances wrote. Later his career paralleled Verdi's in its political development as Guerrazzi became a deputy and, eventually, the minister of internal affairs in Tuscany. After the flight of the Grand Duke, he moved into the provisional government and became dictator in February 1849, as Farini did in Parma. It is not surprising that Verdi was attracted to his work. Impatient to get to work on a scenario of *L'assedio di Firenze*, Verdi wrote a long sketch of what he hoped the plot might be. With Piave a foot-soldier and the war going badly, nothing could be done, so Verdi put it aside, only to return to it later.

He then turned to *La battaglia di Legnano*, another patriotic piece. This subject had been suggested by Cammarano, who wrote: 'If there burns in you, as in me, the desire to illuminate the most glorious epoch of Italian history, that of the Lombard League, [we could do] *La battaglia di Legnano*.'[25] Matching living and dead history, they could re-create the struggle of the Lombards against Frederick Barbarossa as the Lombardy of 1848 and 1849 fought Austria. Verdi soon accepted the plan and asked his collaborator to get the libretto ready as quickly as possible; but the librettist delayed in sending the text. Verdi waited, chafing, through June and July and tried in vain to prod the overworked librettist, who, in addition to other duties at the San Carlo, was helping to produce *Ernani*, *Attila*, *I masnadieri*, and *Gerusalemme* there.[26] When parts of the libretto finally arrived, Verdi found that he could not work as easily as he had wished. He changed certain scenes and characters, as was his custom,[27] but the turn of events in Italy proved too depressing and made it difficult for him to work. Ricordi wrote in July from Milan to describe the military engagements near Verona, Vicenza, and Legnago: 'bad news from the field . . . this disaster . . . mobilization'.[28] Milan was again threatened by Austria, which intended to return as master of Lombardy. Giulio Carcano, who had left Milan earlier, reached Paris in August as a member of an Italian delegation seeking to persuade the French government to intervene and save the situation. On 8 August this group directed a noble petition to General Cavaignac and to his government: 'Messieurs, we have just received news from Milan dated 4 August. There a desperate defence is being prepared. . . . Lombards are dying with the cry "Long live Italy!" on their lips.'[29] But for all their effort, nothing came of this attempt to get aid from France. An angry Verdi wrote to Clara Maffei, who had set up a ménage in exile with Tenca at Ambrì in Switzerland.

Everyone who is not against us is indifferent. I will say more: the idea of Italian unity frightens these little nobodies who are in power. France most certainly will not mount an armed intervention unless it is dragged in unwillingly by some event that we cannot foresee. The Anglo-French diplomatic intervention can only be iniquitous; and it is ruinous for us. In fact, the intervention would tend to provide for Austria to abandon Lombardy and be content just to have Venetia. Even if Austria were induced to leave Lombardy (at this moment Austria is bombarding it; and before pulling out they would sack and burn everything); then we would have the devastation of Lombardy and one additional disgrace: one more extra prince left in Italy. No, no, no: we can expect nothing from either France or England; and—as for me—if I hope for something, . . . do you know where I put my hopes? In internal upheavals within Austria itself. Something serious has to develop there; and if we know how to seize the right moment, and make war as we should have done, [with] an insurrection, Italy can yet be free. But God save us from putting our faith in kings or foreign countries. . . . Italian diplomats from everywhere are arriving here. . . . They will accomplish *nothing*; it seems beyond belief that they still hope for help from France. In a word: France does not want Italy to be a nation.[30]

He added that Carcano had already left for Switzerland. All hope was dead as Verdi was writing to Clara Maffei, for the armistice of 9 August had sealed Lombardy's fate.

'What a wretched time we live in,' Verdi exploded to Clara Maffei. 'What a pygmy time! Nothing great: not even great crimes!'[31] Yet the air of unrest again hung over Paris, he observed. Another upheaval there would, as he said, destroy 'this poor republic'. He hoped that it would not happen, but had every reason to believe that it would.

He dashed off his Italian battle-hymn in the early autumn of 1848. This was the work Mazzini had first asked him to do in Milan in May, when he requested a musical setting for Mameli's *Suona la tromba*. Mazzini had then actually solicited the text from Mameli, to whom he wrote on 6 June 1848, as the poet was fighting with the troops: 'Seize the first moment of inspiration; let it not be inspired by the Graces but by a warlike, popular spirit; and send me a hymn that will become "La Marseillaise" of Italy, a hymn that—to use Verdi's phrase—will make the people forget both the poet and the composer.'[32] Mameli, already known for his 'Fratelli d'Italia', answered at once. Verdi, when he sent his composition to Mazzini, wrote: 'I am sending you the hymn; and even though it is a little late, I hope it will arrive in time. I have tried to be as popular and easy as possible. Do with it what you want: even burn it if you think it unworthy.' After some instructions to Mameli about changes, he concluded: 'May this hymn soon be sung on the Lombard plains, to the music of cannon.' He closed the letter with an expression of his 'total veneration' for Mazzini.[33] But the hymn came too late for the soldiers, too late for the people, and 'Fratelli d'Italia' remained the Italian national song.

As they saw their revolution fail, Italians watched the return of the hated Austrian troops and police to their cities and towns. Among the Maffei circle, many were still in exile. To Clara Maffei Verdi wrote on 3 October:

I don't know what consoling words I can say to you! Lucky you, who still have some hope. I don't have any. What can come from all these diplomatic intrigues and from the extension of the armistice? When it ends, it will be winter; and then they will say: 'You can't try anything in winter.' In the mean time Lombardy will become a wasteland, a cemetery, [and] afterward they will say that the weakened nation, every resource exhausted, can call itself happy to belong to the paternalistic Austrian government.[34]

La battaglia di Legnano and the Battle for Italy

The revolutionary abandon of 1848 had found expression in the theatre even in Venetia, as Muzio found out when he conducted in Mantua. *Ernani* in January of that year was performed under police rules as the audience refused to let the words 'Glory and honour to Charlemagne' be sung because of Charlemagne's German identification. 'You can imagine what an uproar they made', Muzio told Ricordi, adding that the police 'want the opera to be given again, just to make their point.'[35] In the struggle, the authorities had obviously won. But soon afterward the public answered in kind and refused to go to the theatre when *Macbeth* was being done. He also reported on the killing of two Austrian soldiers in a skirmish in which no Italians were lost. While Verdi was composing *La battaglia di Legnano*, he seemed torn between wanting to return to Italy and having to stay in France. As he dealt with Naples and Rome from abroad, he was cantankerous. A dispute with the management of the Teatro San Carlo is reflected in a September 1848 letter to Cammarano, written when Verdi became upset over the use of the word 'obliged' by the correspondence:

I cannot convince myself that your letter of the ninth is serious! What? *I am still obliged to compose and to deliver the music four months after receiving the libretto?* So . . . I should always be obliged to be the very humble servant at the disposition of the Management? So I should give up all other projects until the Management deigns to send me the libretto? Oh, tell me that you were not serious when you wrote!![36]

He was equally offended when the Teatro Argentina mentioned that they were 'doing a favour' for him by producing *La battaglia di Legnano* in Rome. To Colini he wrote: 'I have never made anyone accept [my] scores, nor have I ever had *favours* or *charity* from anyone, not even six years ago, when I needed them terribly: you can imagine whether now I would want to put up with any humiliation, no matter how slight.'[37] And to the Roman sculptor Vincenzo Luccardi:

you are talking about a matter that has made me very unhappy because of the way it has been handled. You tell me that the [Roman] Senate has accepted my score? Accepted? but whoever offered it? . . . No, no: I cannot, I must not put up with this. Because of an old contract, I owe Ricordi a score: once it is written, Ricordi will pay me and that is the end of it. At Ricordi's request, I agreed to come to Rome, taking a personal loss, because the thousand francs that I asked are not enough to cover the trip from Paris to Rome and from Rome to Paris. . . . I did not want anyone to be obliged to me; I did not want to be obliged to anyone. I thought it was a matter of shared interest, but I would never have thought that anyone wanted to do me a favour. . . . I cannot accept this favour and this effort.[38]

At this point, Verdi said he probably would not go to Rome as previously planned. Finally, though, he did agree to go, having been offered an excellent cast, which included Teresa De Giuli, who had sung Abigaille in the successful *Nabucco* revival of 1842 at La Scala; Fraschini, who had created the role of Zamoro in *Alzira* under Verdi's direction at the San Carlo; and Colini, who had created Giacomo in *Giovanna d'Arco* at La Scala.

Verdi finished *La battaglia di Legnano* in December in Paris and left for Rome before Christmas. Here he was at the apex of his career as a composer of patriotic music, just as Rome was ready for revolt.[39] Pius IX, once hailed as a liberal and herald of freedom, had disappointed those who believed in him when he turned coat and fled the city in November; some said that he had escaped dressed as a simple abbot, while others claimed that he wore the cloak of a housemaid. Having taken refuge in Gaeta, he had the opprobrium of liberals heaped upon him; by many, he was regarded as a traitor to the Italian cause.[40] On 9 December the Roman Council of Deputies approved establishment of a constituent assembly; three weeks later the way was paved for free elections as Mazzini arrived from Switzerland. The unimaginable had happened: Rome was becoming a republic.

At the beginning of 1849 Verdi was busy preparing his company. As he had witnessed free elections in Paris the year before, so he saw them in Rome on 21 January. More than 250,000 citizens of the former Papal States voted. One observer noted that the voters were drawn to the polling seats by 'music, flags, processions, and songs'.[41] The Roman people, drunk on liberty, demanded that the Teatro Argentina open the dress rehearsal of *La battaglia di Legnano*, threatening to assault the theatre were this concession not made. Quite naturally, Verdi was hailed as the composer-patriot of the hour. When he walked along the street, crowds gathered around him. The Argentina was virtually in a state of siege, with all tickets sold out before the event. Muzio sent Barezzi the news of the dress rehearsal: 'The people wanted to attend at any cost; and they broke into the theatre, packing it as full as an egg. Maestro [Verdi] was called on stage twenty times. The next day there was not a box seat, a ticket, or a libretto of the opera to be found anywhere; everything was sold out!'[42] *La battaglia di Legnano* was intended to inflame, and it did. The first and last words hail the nation: Italy. Martial choruses, trumpet-calls, and vows of liberty or death abound. In a time when patriots were already coming on stage with revolutionary cockades attached to their costumes, at a time when the words of Verdi's operas—as rewritten by patriots—kept large forces of police in theatres that they sometimes had to close down in reprisal, the high patriotic passion of the opera filled a need.

On 27 January 1849, the day of the première, people flooded the streets around the Argentina, waving flags and wearing liberty symbols on their hats. The theatre was filled as soon as the doors opened. A veritable pandemonium broke out as the first bars of the men's opening chorus were played:

'Viva l'Italia! Sacro un patto tutti stringe i figli suoi!' ('Long live Italy! A sacred pact unites all its children!') The sacred pact united liberals and radicals in a country that had groaned too long under tyrant's yokes. Verdi had found just the right note in a city where the Roman Republic was proclaimed ten days later. The new opera matched and may even have heightened the fever that infected Rome for his music rallied the people as no other art could. Patriots' harangues and leaflets proved not nearly as inflammatory as dramas accompanied by music in an hour when Italy's political situation could be interpreted on stage. When it was a crime to agitate openly for freedom the people found that music offered them a way to defy the authorities. A labourer or shopkeeper cannot walk through the streets declaiming a speech from a play or an excerpt from a pamphlet; but to sing a piece of music from an opera score is another matter. Because they brought the people freedom of expression and a means of defying the authorities, the patriotic operas and certain scenes and pieces from the earlier works became a weapon against the occupying forces that held the peninsula in bondage. *La battaglia di Legnano* came providentially to Rome when the hour of freedom struck. It was such a success that the delirious audience came close to rioting during the first performance and demanded that the entire last act be repeated. The opera's final, inspiring chorus carried a message that was unambiguous: Whoever dies for the *patria* is pure of soul.

The Return from France

'Verdi will have gone on to France, believing that a revolution [there] is imminent and fearing that some accident might happen to the people who are there,' Muzio wrote to Ricordi on 8 February. In a postscript he added:

I have just this minute received a letter from Verdi, dated the third. He travelled four days and four nights over the Appennines, a very, very tiring trip, and when he got to Pontremoli he decided to go ahead to Paris, so as not to have to pass through the German lines to get to Busseto. As soon as I have finished all the arrangements [of the score], I will have to go there myself in his place, for very, very urgent family business matters that are closely related to the interests of Verdi himself.[43]

Muzio urged Ricordi to send him the score of *Gerusalemme*, which was for Strepponi. He would see that it reached her at once. Because Muzio was short of money, both the publisher and Verdi sent him funds. Verdi's came with a personal word: the money was given to 'get him out of the red, only, though, if he promises to keep on being my Red-head for ever.'[44] As he had in the past and would continue to do for many years, Muzio acted as the composer's personal emissary.

It was clear by then that Verdi intended to come home. On 15 January, while *La battaglia di Legnano* was in rehearsal, the composer had written to Charles Duponchel and Nestor Roqueplan, the directors of the Paris Opéra, stating that he was cancelling his contract with them because they had not lived up to its terms. He told them to send his signed copy to 'la Signora Strepponi' in Rue de la Victoire 13a, so that she could return their signed copy to them.[45] Although it is not certain that Verdi was living at this address, he may have moved to her building by then. In January 1849 Escudier had published a song, 'L'abandonnée', that Verdi had dedicated to her. Its appearance in *La France musicale* and the dedication of *Gerusalemme*, mark a kind of public acknowledgement of his love for her. Verdi said that he 'left Rome feeling sad' but hoped to return there soon. To Piave, writing in February from Paris, he said that he would 'fly to Italy' as soon as he could. He sent kind words of admiration for the courage the Venetian troops had shown in the war. While regretting the disaster of Milan and Venetia, he nevertheless saw some hope that Italy might all be free for things were going well in Rome, the Romagna, and Tuscany. 'There is nothing to hope for from France, now less than ever,' he lamented.[46] His mistrust of the clergy was not diminished, as we know from his remarks about the patriot-priest Vincenzo Gioberti, who had won high office in the Piedmont.[47]

In May he received a synopsis of a new opera from Cammarano; then called *Eloisa Miller*, it was intended for the Teatro San Carlo in Naples. Its source was Schiller's *Kabale und Liebe*, chosen after the Neapolitan censors unconditionally rejected *L'assedio di Firenze*, on which Verdi had spent much time and energy.[48] The censors had also begun to attack *La battaglia di Legnano* as well. To have it produced in other cities, the composer had to agree to change the title to *L'assedio di Arlem* and let Barbarossa become the Duke of Alba. The Lombard League ceased to exist, at least on stage, as Milan became Haarlem! Proving more successful than some earlier operas, it began to make the rounds of theatres as Verdi was working on *Luisa Miller*.

The late summer of 1849 brought an end to hopes of liberty in the Papal States. Manara, who had emerged as a military hero in the Lombard uprising, had gone with Enrico and Emilio Dandolo and Emilio Morosini to Rome, to offer help to the Roman Republic. Against overwhelming odds, they and Garibaldi's troops fought on through the spring. Manara proved so courageous that Garibaldi offered him the rank of chief of the high command, although he was only 24. He, Enrico Dandolo, and Morosini were killed in June; Dandolo was 21; Morosini, 18. Also among the dead was Mameli, another youth. Mazzini was driven into one more exile. Garibaldi's retreat across the peninsula began on 3 July as Rome was reoccupied. Verdi was desolate at this tragedy. To Luccardi he said: 'Let us not talk about Rome!! What good would it do? Force still rules the world! And Justice? What can Justice accomplish against bayonets? We can only weep over our misfortunes and curse those who are responsible for so many disasters. . . . I have an inferno in my heart.'[49]

In Paris that spring he had corresponded with Cammarano after learning of the Neapolitan censors' rejection of *L'assedio di Firenze*, which had been submitted under the innocuous title *Maria de' Ricci*. On 1 June he confirmed that he had received the libretto of *Luisa Miller*, which had been sent from Naples on 3 May, but protested that it was too early to think about the cast, although he thought that it was 'almost certain that we will have to take [Marietta] Gazzaniga for the woman, and Bettini for the tenor';[50] at the same time he said that he thought he might be able to finish the opera at the end of September. Five days later he was asking Ricordi to give Muzio 387 gold napoleons that the publishing house owed him. Some of these were to be taken to Carlo Verdi so he could take care of some of his son's obligations at home. In June the composer provided for further repairs on the farmhouse at Sant'Agata and let people know the paint colours he wanted for it.[51] Verdi's parents had moved from Palazzo Cavalli on 12 May; and Carlo Verdi could write to let his son know that they were settled: 'Your mother is very, very happy to be in the country; and she would never again want to go back to Busseto. She also brought your bed to Sant'Agata, so that if you come, you will—I hope—want to live with us and enjoy it in the midst of your beautiful possessions.'[52] He assured his son that he had been given the three wine casks and four vats that the former owners of Sant'Agata had agreed to deliver. Almost all the cows had successfully calved, but he was still waiting for one calf to be born. He was about to get the stables in order and would send his son the account sheets, as requested.

Muzio was with Carlo Verdi in Busseto then, having served as courier when Verdi's father went to Piacenza to pick up the money that was sent to him. Adding a few lines to Verdi's father's letter, he said that he was truly out of luck for he could not hope to get the post of maestro di musica in town because the man who was then the podestà had told him he would not be invited to compete in the examination. All the old reactionaries who had been driven from their posts by the uprising of 1848 in Parma were then back in place. 'Corrupt men are all enemies of freedom', Muzio said; and they were all against him. Rather wistfully he signed off: 'Give my best regards to Signora Peppina but remember E. Muzio.'[53] From this letter it is clear that Verdi's parents were not sure that he would live with them at Sant'Agata, yet hoped that he would. His father appeared to have few illusions about his son's state of mind. When he wrote to Ricordi to confirm that he had received the funds sent to Piacenza, he thanked the publisher for the 'kind words' in a previous letter then added a moving expression of his own: 'Heaven made me a father, and a courageous and happy father of a son who is an honour to me and to his country. I thank Heaven for this every day; and I pray to God to set him on the road that leads to happiness!'[54] For a conservative, church-going man like Carlo Verdi, 'happiness' meant living reasonably and respectably, and, if possible, staying at Sant'Agata, sleeping in the bed that had been moved there. Concerned with his son's happiness, he looked forward only to the moment when Verdi would return home.

'The Celebrated Maestro Verdi', as newspapers called him, had to look to the political situation and to his own professional estate at that time, for he had had to tally up failures in the years after *Macbeth*. One of the most painful was the fiasco of *Il corsaro* at its première, which had taken place at the Teatro Grande in Trieste on 25 October 1848. In spite of an excellent cast, made up of Barbieri-Nini, Fraschini, and De Bassini, all of whom were apparently at the top of their form, the opera got a glacial reception. The critic of *Il costituzionale* said that 'if the audience was kind and did not whistle, that happened only because of its innate kindness'.

He advised Verdi to 'stay in Paris a long time (now that he has pocketed a fine dose of English guineas and many gold napoleons from Lucca)' and start studying the great composers of the past and present. Art, the critic said, does not consist only of 'knowing how to work out some good cabaletta or some beautiful chorus' but in creating music that will not force the singers to strain their voices and a duet 'that is not always sung in unison' and concertato finales that pass muster with the audience. 'After [Verdi] has studied and has had a long rest, we hope with all our heart that he will come back to Italy with a new masterpiece.'[55] After three performances of *Il corsaro*, which Luigi Ricci had prepared, the opera was taken off the programme and replaced with *Macbeth*, which was very successful. 'No one could ever guess that this music was written by the same composer who wrote *Il corsaro*, which was stillborn here in this city', wrote the critic of *Il Telegrafo*.[56] The acclaim given to *La battaglia di Legnano* just three months after this fiasco somewhat redeemed Verdi's situation, which he might perhaps have improved had he been willing to produce *Il corsaro* in Trieste himself. In any case, he needed a triumph. Dealing with Ricordi from France was not always easy either, as is proved by a letter he wrote on 14 March 1849, one of two letters in which he protested at the 'colossal' mistakes he found in his published works.[57] He may have hoped that it would be easier to deal with Ricordi at closer reach. By 26 July he was ready to go back to Italy. Advising Flaùto in Naples of his terms for going there to produce *Luisa Miller*, he said that he would be leaving Paris in three days, but that he did not intend to stay long in Busseto, although he did not say where he wanted to go from there.

Strepponi, who had lived in Paris for almost three years, also went back to Italy that summer. As she had told Pietro Romani in 1848, she had not felt able to give up her new way of life in France, even though the Revolution had cut into her income. She had been reluctant to sell her furniture and move. 'Where should I have gone to earn good money? To Italy?' She added that had she had enough to live on without working, she would have stayed on in France because of 'the freedom one enjoys here',[58] which she evidently felt she could not find at home. One year later she changed her mind. After having borne the burden of pregnancies, of caring for Barberina and their eccentric mother and helping to educate her brother, she had emerged as a person of some dignity and was no longer the abject creature whose conduct Moriani had deplored. As she found stability with Verdi she discovered that they both liked privacy and a simple life and disliked the soirées, galas, receptions, and banquets that were almost obligatory for celebrities of Verdi's stature. In that, they were ideally suited to each other. But when they left Paris that summer, he made straight for Busseto to wait for her there, while she went to Florence, perhaps after stopping in Pavia to see her family. For both, a long, self-imposed absence from Italy ended.

BOOK III

16

Summer 1849 – November 1850

Busseto

Giving up Paris and the freedom he enjoyed there, Verdi came home to a world he knew all too well. Behind Busseto's shaded arcades and the façades of shops and cafés lived the families that had fed for almost twenty years on gossip about the Philharmonic Society and its favourite son. Verdi confided to Giovanni Ricordi that he hoped to find peace, if nothing else, in his home town. But he was soon disappointed, for the same strife that had blighted his youth raged on, with him, the Barezzis, and Muzio in the eye of the storm.

From the day of his arrival, about 10 August, people in the community tried to engage him in local affairs. Those approaching him were intimates— his relatives, in-laws, and Demaldè, his next-door neighbour. Many former schoolmates from the Ginnasio now held important positions in Busseto, Fidenza, Parma, Cremona, Piacenza, and Milan. It would have been natural for him to renew his long-standing bonds with them and to take up again with Giovannino Barezzi, his brother-in-law and closest friend in town. Intimacy came naturally to the two men, one unmarried and one a widower. Soon after Verdi got home he was reported to have wanted to resume an old friendship with Baroness Eroteide Soldati, whose lover he was rumoured to have been before he left Italy. She, the wife of a minister of State of the Duchy of Parma, was spending the summer of 1849 at her villa near Sant'Andrea, just outside Busseto. As Tito Barezzi recalled in an article in the newspaper *Il presente* (1 September 1913), Verdi ordered his horses hitched to his carriage, called for Giovannino, and drove out to visit the Baroness. But when the two men got to the villa, they found her with a lover, the Marquis Malaspina. It was, Barezzi said, the composer's last visit to the woman who had helped him with loans or gifts of money as he struggled to establish himself in Milan.

Verdi was not entirely free that summer, for Strepponi, who had gone to Florence on business, was about to join him at Palazzo Cavalli. There is no solid evidence, though, that he intended to go on living with her. His brusque attitude toward her, for which she reproached him (as we shall see), suggests that he was not entirely happy with her imminent visit. He believed that she might not stay in Busseto, as he anticipated having someone accompany her when she left.

In Florence, she had first contacted Lanari and asked him to help her find Livia Zanobini, her former maid and friend. She also asked Lanari's son Antonio to call on her at the Albergo della Luna. Although we do not know whether she saw her daughter Giuseppa Faustina, we do know that she found what she believed was a suitable arrangement for Camillino, who was then 11, placing him in Bartolini's studio so he could study sculpture.[1] She probably asked the Zanobinis and Filippo Pagliai, Livia's brother-in-law, to care for the boy, for she gave this family gifts of money from the 1840s until the 1880s, suggesting that a large debt existed there.[2] The Zanobini-Pagliais also boarded one of Camillino's friends, who later studied medicine with him in Florence.[3] Strepponi also contacted several people about her investments in commercial firms. Although we do not know where her money came from (and the issue of how she got it later became a subject of gossip in Busseto), we know that she had risen from virtual bankruptcy in 1842 and had managed to get together enough to live well in Paris; once there, she had been able to return to Italy at least once, for the première of *Macbeth*. Possible sources of her funds were Lanari, Cirelli, Count Camerata, or even Verdi himself, perhaps through a loan from Casa Ricordi.[4] In 1851 Verdi was able to negotiate such a loan from his publisher; the transaction then was handled entirely by Strepponi.[5] Her business interests in Florence centred on wholesale foodstuffs and cloth; advice on investments may have been offered by Lanari himself or his agent Montier.[6] She had her earnings as well.

On 3 September, as she got ready to leave for Busseto, she wrote to Verdi to let him know her plans. Her letter is somewhat abrupt.

I will have finished my chores on Wednesday and will perhaps even have left for Parma on Wednesday evening. Don't come, though, to get me before Friday evening or Saturday morning, because I would be sorry if you were to have to wait in vain for me in Parma. When I tell you who has taken the responsibility for Camillino's artistic education, you will just be astonished! For now, it is enough for you [to know] that I kissed the hands of the illustrious man who said to me: 'Do you want to entrust him to me?' I saw very few people in Florence; but [they were] people who worked enthusiastically [on my behalf]; and you must realize that [they were] *mere acquaintances* [and not close friends]!! No aristocrat, it goes without saying. Truly, we sometimes find a heart where we expect to find only indifference—and vice versa. Addio, my joy! Now that I have almost finished my business, business too important to neglect, I would like to be able to fly to you. You tell me about the ugly countryside, the bad service, then you say: 'If you don't like it, I will have you accompanied' (NB. *I will have you!!!*) 'wherever you want to go.'—What the devil! In Busseto do people forget how to love and how to write with a little affection? I am not yet there; but I still know how to write to you to tell you what I feel—that is that the country, the service, and everything will be just fine for me, so long as you are there, you ugly, wretched monster! Addio . . . addio. I barely have time to tell you that I detest you and I embrace you.

Peppina.

She added a postscript: 'Do not send anyone else, but come to Parma yourself for me, for I would be terribly embarrassed to be introduced in your house by others instead of by you.'[7]

Both she and Verdi seem justifiably nervous, for it would have been difficult for him to present his mistress, this mother of illegitimate children who had sung in public through to the very end of three pregnancies, to the Busseto families that had supported him for so long. Many of these people, fixed in their bourgeois morality, did become angry that Verdi should flaunt Strepponi before the family of Margherita Barezzi, to say nothing of his conservative, respectable parents. While it is true that both Demaldè and Barezzi knew Strepponi, meeting her in Milan or Paris was different from having her in Busseto.

Verdi's feelings about his home town were reflected in an ironical letter written on Sunday 9 September to Giuseppina Appiani.

Dear friend, I am still moved by the deep feelings I have experienced in my utterly charming home town! '*Ah, what miracles the warm affection of one's own native land can accomplish!*' I could do with some miracles, too: for example. . . . Ah, but the time of miracles is past. Anyway (please understand that I am talking seriously)—Busseto and Paris! This blessed, blessed Busseto! How beautiful! How elegant! What a place! What society! I am enthralled, and I don't know whether I can tear myself away from here soon!!! I found my father and mother in excellent health and certainly happier than I am.—But what am I saying? Today is a holiday [and] I don't want to talk of depressing things. So let's be happy. I will come to Milan as soon as I can. Send me your news.[8]

But he did not go to Milan; his next visit was postponed for twenty years.

To Piave on 11 September he wrote a desolate letter.

Perhaps you wrote to me in Paris after our last upheavals, but I have been gone from there for more than a month. I again ask you to write to me: tell me a lot about yourself, about your poor country, and about our friends. As for myself, I can only tell you that my heart is torn to pieces by a thousand troubles. Addio! Write to me soon, for I do not know whether I shall stay on here after the end of this month. Addio! Always think of me as your very, very close friend.[9]

The tone of desperation may betray a bad situation at home, if Verdi was thinking of leaving just one month after having settled in his fine *palazzo*.

As Strepponi had asked, he went to Parma to get her. On Friday 14 September 1849 she made what Muzio later called her 'famous triumphal entry' into Busseto. He had run into the country to meet Verdi's coach and was waiting for it on the road to Borgo San Donnino. When the couple arrived, Strepponi turned to Verdi and said 'Emanuele can walk'. As Muzio later recalled, he had 'good legs' and followed on foot as they drove on.[10]

The kind of life they had in Palazzo Cavalli was described by Verdi in a letter to Piave the following May:

This holiday spot has no entertainments. We eat here, we sleep, we work: I have two young horses to take us for a drive—and that is all. The life that I lead is an extremely solitary one. I do not visit anyone's house; and I receive no one excepting my father-in-law and my brother-in-law. You, however, can do whatever you want!!! You can go to the café, to the bar, wherever the devil you like. Maybe Giovannino will go with you.[11]

Muzio, again at his mentor's side, was helping as he had in the past. Verdi also had to deal with his family and townspeople, many of whom believed that they had made him who he was. His return home was the realization of Barezzi's and Verdi's parents' fondest dream, for he was the living justification of everything that they had invested in him. But Verdi's mother, who had had his bed moved from Palazzo Cavalli to Sant'Agata earlier that summer, in the hope that he would live in the country with his parents, may have felt some disappointment that he did not choose to do so, particularly after such a long absence.

As for Strepponi, she wanted to retire from the world and live away from society, which she said she detested. But one obstacle to her being accepted in Busseto was the fact that no one there—not even Barezzi—knew whether she was or was not Verdi's wife. As we know from her diaries of the 1860s and from his letters of the 1840s and 1860s that are transcribed there, the city's ostracism of her made itself felt everywhere, even at night, when people shouted epithets from the arcades and cafés below. It is a local tradition that someone threw stones at the windows of Palazzo Cavalli. According to the Barezzi descendants, Giovannino reproached his brother-in-law for having brought home a prostitute. We do not know whether she was able to go to the local parish church or had anyone, apart from Verdi, Muzio, and the servants, to whom she could speak on a daily basis. Her later indictment of the place, which she described as utterly without culture, a place where no one could discuss current affairs or intellectual matters, suggests that she was lonely there and without recourse. She was perhaps being made to pay for her past and for the resentment the Bussetans felt against Verdi for bringing her there. But he, at least, had a freedom of movement which was denied to her; and he had the release of his music, while her career was over and her voice a ruin. In Paris, she had had the dignity of being a respected voice-teacher. In Busseto, she was Verdi's companion housekeeper, and secretary.

Luisa Miller and the Return to Naples

Cammarano sent Verdi the complete libretto on 13 August. Luisa Miller was written in about six weeks, as Muzio waited for him to finish each piece so that he could begin the reductions of it. Happy to be at Verdi's side again, he had decided not to seek work from Ricordi in Milan. By the beginning of October the composer was ready to leave for Naples, taking Antonio Barezzi with him. Reflecting perhaps more tranquillity than he had felt earlier, he wrote to Escudier from Naples about his life in his home town: 'I have lived all this time [since leaving Paris] in a country place, far from every human contact, without news, without reading any newspapers, etc. It is a life that turns men into animals, but at least it is quiet.'[12] In this same letter he expressed concern over Muzio's future. A suitable situation would have to be found for him. Strepponi had left for

253

Pavia, where she visited her mother, Barberina, who was then 21, and her brother Davide, who was about to turn 33 and was starting his professional life as the *medico condotto*, the city physician, at Locate Triulzi. The family may have had help from Verdi in the spring of 1849, when he told Ricordi to pay 3,000 lire to 'Rosa Strepponi of Pavia'.[13]

After spending several days in Genoa, Verdi and Barezzi went to Rome, where they were detained fifteen days in quarantine. They reached the Hotel de Rome in Naples at the end of the month. There they behaved much as tourists might, at least when Verdi was not rehearsing his company at the San Carlo. From Barezzi's Day-Book we get a glimpse of the two earnest explorers in this southern land:

The Royal Palace, Capo di Monte, the Gardens, the Hermitage, San Gennaro, the Gesù Nuovo, Santa Chiara, the Campo di Marte, two large obelisks; San Severo [Chapel] with its surprising [sculpture of] *The Dead Christ beneath a Veil* [by Sammartino]; . . . and in the evening with Verdi to watch the sunset from Chiaia . . . Toured the port in a boat, visited . . . one of the largest steamers, and [went] in the evening with Verdi and the Signora [Marietta] Gazzaniga to the Teatro Fiorentini. . . . With Verdi to Herculaneum, and saw the excavation of the big theatre, and the Palace of Portici. . . . With Verdi and [the Bussetan, Marco] Arati to Camaldoli on donkeys. . . . With Verdi to Pompeii by train. . . . To Caserta, by train, alone. . . . Again to Pozzuoli with Verdi; saw the Grotto of the Cumean Sybil, Nero's [Baths], the Temple of Serapis, the amphitheatre of Pozzuoli, and the remains of Caligula's famous mountain. . . . With Verdi by steamer to Procida, Ischia, Casamicciola, Cuma, and the Grotto of Fusaro. . . . In the evening the sunset again.[14]

The two did all this touring in about three weeks. Barezzi enjoyed himself in the light of Verdi's glory as he had in Florence and Paris.

The composer rehearsed between his tourist jaunts and staged *Luisa Miller* on 8 December 1849, but not without great difficulty. There were problems with the singers, among them the tenor Bettini, whom Verdi had authorized for the leading role. Because he was singing badly, the theatre management wished to take legal action against him but later replaced him with the Roman tenor Settimio Malvezzi. In financial difficulties, the San Carlo seemed so close to insolvency that it could not pay Verdi even the first of the three instalments of his fee. When he demanded that Flaùto deposit his 3,000 ducats in the hands of a trusted third party, he also threatened to renege on his contract if guarantees could not be given.[15] At this point the Duke of Ventignano, a member of the governing board of the San Carlo, threatened Verdi, saying that he would prevent him from leaving the city. Ever sensitive to anything he considered a personal insult, the composer, who could not leave without his passport, said he would ask for political asylum on a French warship that was standing in Naples harbour, taking his score with him. The San Carlo then let him know that he could count on being paid, perhaps not on schedule, but eventually. Mollified, he was persuaded to get on with the production. *Luisa Miller* had a fair cast that included Gazzaniga, De Bassini, Malvezzi, Arati, and Antonio Selva. Although the opera was a success, people talked of the disappointments Verdi had suffered in Naples. He himself referred to gossip passed to him as a clique of his enemies tried in every way to cause *Luisa Miller* to fail, but he declared that he knew that no conspiracy could bring down any good opera. As he considered this subtle opera, he showed that he cared for it. This affection moved him later to write to Varesi, who had asked him to come to help out with another Neapolitan production of the opera:

Do you want me to leave my fields, my deep solitude to come to the opening of *Miller*? I surely would be gratified by the pleasure of hearing you and your colleagues; but . . . you understand! You know my tastes! You know how much I love . . . the theatre . . . *when I am far away from it*!! I wish you and myself a success and goodnight to *La Miller*, which, I confess to you, I love very much.[16]

With *Luisa Miller* behind him, he looked to the future. One of the works he was considering that December was *El trovador*, a Spanish drama by García Gutiérrez that Verdi may have been reading as early as 6 December, when he asked Giovanni Ricordi to send him a Spanish-Italian dictionary. Less than a month later he was proposing it to Cammarano, saying that he thought it was extremely beautiful, highly dramatic, and a good showcase for two women, the most important of whom was a gypsy, after whom he intended to name the opera.

Re Lear and *Stiffelio*

On the trip back from Naples, Verdi caught a heavy cold that kept him in the house in Busseto, where he also once more had to face financial problems. On 4 December 1849 Carlo Verdi had sold his house and field in Roncole so that he could give his son 2,200 lire that were needed to get through the winter. Like the money Verdi borrowed from his father in 1846, this sum was not repaid until 1851. The fact that Carlo Verdi had to provide these funds suggests that the family was in some difficulty, for by December the harvest is in, the rents of San Martino for 11 November, have been paid, and the landlord's coffers should be full. The first week in December is traditionally the week when the family's notary comes round with the cash. In Verdi's case, many of the rents were paid directly by the shopkeepers and tradesmen on the ground floor of his Palazzo Cavalli; Carlo Verdi would have brought the harvest money in from Sant'Agata himself. Verdi's account sheets for 1851 show that he and his father were contributing jointly to their enterprise; and it is even possible that the farm at Sant'Agata was saved when Carlo Verdi sold his Roncole property to meet the payments on it.

Verdi began to work on two important projects, *Re Lear*, taken from Shakespeare's tragedy, and the new opera for Venice. He asked Piave to provide a draft scenario for either *Le Roi s'amuse*, *Stradella*, or *Kean* from the drama by Dumas père. Verdi clearly was taking the Hugo play seriously for he had also asked Ricordi to have Cammarano do a sketch of it. These were not the only works under consideration. Sometime in 1849 the composer drew up a list of other possible subjects. In the printed *Copialettere* as plate XI, it includes *Hamlet* and *The Tempest*, Byron's *Cain*, Hugo's *Marion Delorme* and *Ruy Blas*, Grillparzer's *Die Ahnfrau*, Racine's *Phèdre*, Calderón's *A secreto agravio secreta venganza*, Dennery's *Marie Jeanne ou La Femme du peuple*; Chateaubriand's *Atala*, which Verdi spelled with two 'Ts'; *Guzmán el Bueno* by Moratín; *Ines di Castro*; *Buondelmonte*, and other works.[17] When Verdi wrote to Piave about the new libretto, he also mentioned a version of Alfieri's *Filippo*, which Piave had just rendered as *Elisabetta di Valois*.[18] Verdi would later compose the same subject as *Don Carlos*.

When he answered, Piave suggested several possible works, among them *Stifellius*, translated into Italian by Gaetano Vestri, Luigi's son, from a French play by Emile Souvestre and Eugène Bourgeois, which Verdi said he did not know. He then asked the librettist to write a synopsis of it; but he was still fascinated by *Re Lear* and was studying a long, detailed scenario of it. In a letter to Cammarano dated 28 February 1850, he admitted the difficulty of writing an opera on such a long, complicated drama, although he had also had it in mind in 1843, 1845, and 1846. To Cammarano he said 'At first glance *Re Lear* appears so vast, so intricate, that it seems impossible to get an opera out of it; however, after having gone over it thoroughly, I feel that the difficulties are undoubtedly great but not insuperable.' He thought it could be staged in eight or nine scenes, but, like *Macbeth* it would demand new forms, 'different from those normally used up to now', and 'an entirely new style'.[19] Yet work on *Re Lear* was put aside and was not to be considered again for several years. Verdi declared that he was not really eager to work and wrote to let Escudier know that he had refused 'a contract [with the Paris Opéra] that I had in my hand'.[20] In March 1850 he agreed to write a new opera for La Fenice, although no subject was chosen at that time.

Stiffelio, a difficult drama about a Protestant pastor who absolves his adulterous wife, was an unconventional work that posed particular problems, because of its plot and because of the financial crisis faced by northern Italian theatres in the years after the Revolution of 1848. Its staging raised the issue of the contemporary costumes it required, as men and women were to be dressed in street clothes. The men were to have Mazzini beards, which Piave later ordered changed, so that they finally appeared clean-shaven.[21] When the librettist came to work in Busseto in the summer of 1850, he and Verdi fashioned the libretto, the scenario for which had been sent to the composer in May. The protagonist, Verdi thought, should be a Lutheran or the head of some other Protestant sect. The opera, which Ricordi was to place with an Italian theatre, was assigned to the Teatro Grande in Trieste, perhaps because *Macbeth* had done so well there.

Work perhaps went forward more slowly than Verdi had anticipated, with some of the delay being owed to Piave's late delivery of the libretto. In mid-July a storm destroyed almost the entire harvest of grapes and corn.[22] Damaged outbuildings and the supports for the vines would have to be repaired. Verdi also worried about Muzio, whose first opera, *Giovanna la pazza*, written about Juana la Loca of Spain, was ready to be given at the Italian opera-house in Brussels, where Muzio had been engaged as a conductor. As Verdi had done in 1839, he had given up hope of serving Busseto as *maestro di musica* and turned his back on their city.[23]

Verdi himself went to Bologna, with Piave. One of the company, Marianna Barbieri-Nini, had sung in the world premières of both *Macbeth* and *Il corsaro*.[24] Two of the other singers had had recent experience in interpreting *Macbeth* roles: G. Ferri had sung Macbeth in Barcelona in 1848; Biondi was the Macduff in a production in Senigallia in 1850. But they would all have to be coached. Verdi threw himself into the productions and was rewarded with success and a substantial personal triumph as well; but the effort told on him. He returned ill to Busseto, his old stomach disorder having come back to plague him.

Apologetically, Verdi wrote to Ricordi that he could not leave for Trieste at once. There, the theatre had been taken over by Domenico Ronzani, a former primo ballerino, mime, and choreographer, who—although a veteran of a lifetime on stage—was not an experienced administrator. At Verdi's request, Ricordi arranged for Luigi Ricci to take the composer's place at rehearsals;[25] but this cannot have been a satisfactory solution. Even in ideal circumstances, Ricci would have found it difficult to replace Verdi in preparing a controversial opera in a reactionary city, especially during such parlous times. Trieste, a seat of Austrian power, had become a target of pro-Italian nationalist revolutionaries who, in the years after 1848, had been driven underground. Agitation threatened the constituted authorities, whose reports reflect conditions in the city at the time. On 13 February 1850 the director of the police wrote to Francesco Wimpffen, the civil and military governor, that 'nationalist and separatist sympathies' were popular 'even in the cultivated, moneyed class', and that 'among the common people, anti-patriotic songs are sung everywhere'.[26] He warned two days later of 'unpleasant incidents such as the singing of anti-patriotic songs and verses [and] the use of three-coloured Italian flags . . . in public [gathering places] of the poor, in public dance halls, and here and there in the streets'.[27]

Unrest was not limited to Trieste. Muzio had reported from Piacenza in July that the police were 'doing nothing but searches [of houses and people]. Saturday, on the fireworks that they are preparing for [a celebration on] the fifteenth, they found a tricolour flag 15 yards long.'[28] In such an atmosphere, an appearance by two self-declared Italian patriots represented a clear danger. Verdi was greeted as a voice of Italian freedom, while Piave had been a volunteer soldier in the revolutionary army that had driven Austria out of the Veneto and established the Republic of Venice just two years before. The two men could count on finding like-minded friends in Trieste, where two 'hot patriots' rallied to their side at once. Michele Buono was a conspirator in the 1848 uprising, a volunteer in Garibaldi's armies, a poet and journalist who persisted in his anti-Austrian political activities until in 1860 he was condemned to ten years in prison.[29] Like Piave, Buono was a librettist who also wrote novels. The other Verdiano was Vincenzo Poiret, a painter who in 1848 had been described by the police as 'a shameless enemy of Austria, politically very dangerous'.[30] An activist in the revolt in Zara, he later moved on to Milan and Turin. Buono celebrated Verdi's arrival by publishing an ode in his honour; Poiret published a lithograph portrait of the composer.

Among other friends there were the trustworthy tenor Fraschini and Giovanni Severi, a former actor who had made his début as an opera tenor in Trieste in 1840 and then gone on to Turin and La Scala. There he had sung in 1842 and 1843, appearing in *Maria di Rudenz*, and the world première of *I Lombardi*. In Trieste, Severi was in trade, having given up the professional stage. Verdi's and Piave's friendship with him was demonstrated when they collaborated in writing the words and music to a *barcarola* for Severi's 6-month-old son. 'AL TUO BAMBINO', the title of the piece, heads the manuscript page. 'Fiorellin che sorge appena' begins Piave's text.[31] When Verdi and Piave, accompanied by Ricordi, reached Trieste at the end of October, the production was still rough. They had scarcely settled into their quarters in the Grand Hotel de la Ville, facing the city's busy port, when rumours began to circulate about possible censorship of *Stiffelio*. Worse, it was said that the censor Giuseppe de Lugnani might forbid all performances of the opera, having already placed severe restrictions on a theatrical company that was giving another play by Emile Souvestre at the same time, in the Teatro Filodrammatico.[32] The critic Francesco Hermet, an enemy of the censor and a former colleague of Severi in the local Filodrammatici, wrote that '*Stiffelio*, as it stands, cannot be staged without endangering the public morals and Catholic, apostolic, Roman doctrine . . . and a decree [will be issued] prohibiting absolutely any performances of *Stiffelio*.'[33]

A document in the archive of the Teatro Grande (now Teatro Verdi) in Trieste records the meeting of the theatre commission on 13 November 1850.

The president [of the theatre], Ángelo Vivante, described what was done today to overcome the obstacles raised by the local authorities about the production of *Stiffelio*. . . . A discussion was undertaken about how to change the libretto and the plot. It was agreed that the poet and the composer should be summoned at once. Both being called, then, Maestro Verdi and Piave appeared; and the seriousness of the emergency was conveyed to them; they agreed, after some remarks about this, to try to make the changes that were ordered. Piave promised then to bring the changes they will try to make [by] tomorrow morning, so that they can be approved and be corrected, as far as possible, in the librettos, which are already printed. As they left, they were thanked by all. Afterwards, it was decided not to change the proposed date of the première of *Stiffelio*, given the fact that the changes are to be made.[34]

BOOK III

It is not hard to understand why the authorities felt that this drama about a Protestant sect and its leader's adulterous wife would be offensive to a Catholic culture. As it happened, they also felt it would offend members of the evangelical sects there, one of which had its church in Piazza Vecchia, next to the building where Adelina Strepponi had lived and died. Curiously the registers of Santa Maria Maggiore, where Adelina's baptism and death records are entered, show that a family named Stankar actually lived in the parish at that time; the censors may have noted that, as they read the list of characters for the opera. As Verdi and Piave conceived it, *Stiffelio* was to be a contemporary drama. Its preacher-protagonist leaves home to evangelize. His wife betrays him. When he learns what she has done, he forgives her, speaking from his pulpit. Trieste, like Udine and other cities of north-east Venetia, was a seat of entrenched Catholic power, where religious rites and customs bound a formalistic society together under the banner of piety. Daily attendance at Mass was the sign of true commitment. In Venetia the morning Masses were crowded, as most people—men and women—believed that there was no other way to start the day. Verdi and his kind offended the imperial censors and their allies, the priests.[35]

Stiffelio, with its unusual subject, contained almost every element likely to arouse the censors: its protagonists were Protestants; verses from the Bible were sung on-stage; a religious rite was depicted; a pastor preached a sermon; an adulteress was portrayed sympathetically by her husband, who spoke of forgiveness and divorce; the score contained what the censors called 'sacred music'; an altar, pulpit, and church benches were among the props; and, as a final insult, the singers were dressed in the common, everyday clothes of their time. Here was a bold political and social statement. Just by stripping away the familiar trappings of historical drama, Verdi and Piave had run a dangerous course; but the choice of subject went beyond a rejection of theatrical convention and threw down a challenge to custom and practice.

With only a few days left to revise both the libretto and the score, Piave and Verdi set to work. The words 'Evangelico pastore' had to be changed to 'La purezza dell'amore'. The last scene, in which the adulterous Lina asks her husband to hear her confession was gutted: her line 'Ministro, confessatemi' was changed to 'Rodolfo, ascoltatemi'. Stiffelio, the protagonist, had to be transformed from the leader of a congregation into a simple 'member of a sect' without authority. With his stature diminished, Stiffelio could not persuade anyone in the audience that he had power. He had no title that would authorize him to hear confession or offer pardon. Deprived of his pulpit, cross, and altar, he had to sit in a plain armchair for even his Gothic throne was vetoed. He could not even be a preacher addressing his sermon to the flock.[36] As Piave and Verdi originally planned it, this finale was different from all of the composer's earlier works. It was cast in a quiet tone; it lacked triumphalism and the panoply of the insistent finales of other operas. Stiffelio, with his people gathered, was to go to his pulpit and open his Bible to the text of Christ forgiving the adulteress. He read. Lina begged him to pardon her. He did. The scene was a remarkable understatement. Piave and Verdi worked carefully on this finale, only to see it ravaged by the censor. Even the sex of the person pardoned is changed from female to male.

On 19 November the president of the Teatro Grande informed Ronzani that the 'local superior political authorities' had 'enjoined' the heads of the theatre to notify Ronzani that the singers 'performing *Stiffelio* absolutely must keep to the words printed in the libretto [that has been] approved, and not sing anything else,' under threat of dire consequences to all concerned. Ronzani was ordered to convey the warning to the singers in writing, formally, within the day and before the evening's performance.

Verdi later wrote angrily to denounce what he called the castration of his opera.[37] Like *La traviata*, it was a criticism of the written and unwritten laws of the time and a daring moral statement. In producing it, he and Piave needed all the help they could get, even after the 16 November opening night, when their friends carried on with the battle. Foremost among them was Hermet. But their effort went for nothing, for De Lugnani remained unmoved and proved even more difficult after the opening night than before it, continuing to threaten the composer, the librettist, and Ricordi, who had come from Milan. Some of the singers may have done their part by singing some of the forbidden text. Through chance or by plan, some librettos were sold without the censors' changes, bringing new warnings from De Lugnani to Ronzani and the company. It is clear that there was no definitive version of the opera even on opening night. Verdi seems to have written the overture in his suite at the Grand Hôtel de la Ville one or two days before the première. Handed to Giuseppe Scaramelli, the concertmaster, perhaps as late as the morning of the première, while the singers were still trying to learn the new words and music, it may have been read through only once or twice by the orchestra.

Whatever could be salvaged from such a shambles was a genuine accomplishment. Some good came from the singers, especially Fraschini and Colini. The soprano was Marietta Gazzaniga, who had disappointed Verdi in *Luisa Miller* in Naples but was a distinguished artist whose repertory later included no fewer than eleven Verdi operas. In spite of the havoc wrought by the censors, *Stiffelio* was not a failure. In the review in *La favilla* the censors were attacked for 'the ruin of the score'; but the opera itself was hailed as a masterpiece.[38] 'Verdi succeeded utterly' in his difficult task of finding 'new ways' and 'new forms' of operatic expression. The critic of *L'osservatore triestino* noted that one duet was repeated and that even though the opera did not enjoy the 'authentic triumph' that the music deserved, Verdi had done an excellent job with it. The censors were blamed for whatever problems it had.[39] Verdi, surrounded and supported by loyal friends, was congratulated for his efforts. Soon after he got back to Busseto, he was invited to produce *Stiffelio* at La Scala. As he considered this offer, he noted that the opera must be done with great care.

The censors must be persuaded that there is nothing in the libretto that is dangerous to the political situation or to religion, and that they must leave the original libretto with every word and all the setting and action intact as well; it must be performed without any change whatever, without being castrated. . . . I will stage it myself in any theatre that gives me a free hand and a suitable company [of singers].[40]

This important letter proves that Verdi was ready to return to Milan and to La Scala as early as January 1851, although he still had reservations about the management. Merelli had left at the end of November 1850, perhaps raising the composer's hopes for better quality productions there in the future. But just then he learned that *Gerusalemme* at La Scala had been cut drastically. Scenes that had passed untouched in 1843, when *I Lombardi* had been given, were being cut in 1850. The Ave Maria, for which Verdi had fought, was taken out entirely. Fulminating against this new outrage against his creative integrity, he returned to Venice, where he and Piave were to prepare his next opera.

November 1850–Spring 1851

Towards *Rigoletto*

Verdi's interest in Victor Hugo's *Le Roi s'amuse* dated back at least to 1849, when he had considered the drama for Naples, only to have Cammarano raise the issue of censorship. But the composer, convinced of the play's potential as an opera, had entered it on his list of works for future consideration[1] and, at one point, hoped to have Frezzolini and De Bassini sing 'the two magnificent roles'.[2] When his Neapolitan friend Cesare De Sanctis advised him that the opera could not be done at the San Carlo, it was set aside. The scenario of *Re Lear* was left with Cammarano as Verdi began to look to other theatres that were less affected by budget constraints and changes of management than the San Carlo. He began to negotiate through Piave to write again for the Teatro La Fenice, hoping to conclude something for the Carnival season of 1850–1, and was expecting some kind of offer soon after his return from Naples. Irritated when he learned that Ricordi, with whom he had been negotiating for yet another work, had visited the Venetian management himself, Verdi told Piave that he had heard nothing from the theatre and was afraid that Ricordi might have confused the issue: 'I would not want him to have messed up this business. Let me be clear: I would not want him to offer in his own name an opera by me for next year. . . . [T]he impresario must in that case come to terms directly with me.'[3] Verdi got his way; within a few days he got a letter from the directors of La Fenice that led him to write to Piave again: 'I will keep the score for myself; I will have the libretto written; I cede [to the theatre] the right to give all the performances at La Fenice for all of the season 1851; and I have asked

6,000 Austrian lire.' He suggested to Piave that he look at 'a Spanish drama (*Gusmano il Buono*)' and asked him to get on with the negotiations.[4] Representing the theatre, Carlo Marzari and Guglielmo Brenna sent Verdi their official proposition on 9 March, agreeing to let him retain ownership of the opera, which La Fenice would produce under a rental agreement—'a titolo di nolo'.[5] This suited Verdi, who wrote back to stipulate his conditions and the fee of 6,000 Austrian lire. He would own the score and pay the librettist, as he had originally proposed.[6] The theatre, which, like many houses in northern Italy, had fallen on hard times after the Revolution of 1848, made a counter-offer of 3,000 lire, which Verdi refused,[7] but he said that he would allow La Fenice to make a copy of the score for its own archives and to perform it after the Carnival season without paying additional rentals. He did, though, state clearly that he could 'not even accept 5,000 Aus[trian lire]'[8] and was not very happy about the company of singers that had been suggested. Even in an earlier letter, he had said that he would not sign a final contract until he knew the names of the leading artists; several letters to Piave protested at the low terms, the company, and the sacrifice he would be making in accepting such a proposal. And to Marzari, the director of La Fenice, he pointed out that he had taken into consideration the circumstances and the time in his own offer: 'Two or three years ago, I would have refused 10,000 Aus[trian] l[ire], retaining the rights to the score myself, just as I refused to accept 30,000 Aus[trian] l[ire] offered to me in Paris to write an opera for La Fenice. . . . I am terribly sorry to have to tell you that I cannot accept the conditions you offer me.'[9] Two weeks later the directors of the theatre gave in to many of the composer's demands. As Regli had declared in *Strenna teatrale* in 1847, Verdi's music had become indispensable to any theatre that wanted to fill its seats and the prestige of a première added lustre to the impresario's programme.

The composer agreed to get to Venice no later than the end of January 1851, to begin rehearsals on 1 February, and to stage the new opera as soon as possible.

I don't lose a lot of time in doing the instrumentation and rehearsals, so the directors can be sure that if the rehearsals proceed normally, we can [present the première] about 20 February. The directors will have the right to perform the opera only at the Teatro La Fenice in the following seasons [as in 1851], and for that reason can have a copy of my original score and preserve it in the archive of the . . . theatre, meticulously kept.[10]

The final contract was drawn up in Venice, dated 23 April 1850. Verdi signed one copy five days later and sent it back to Marzari with urgent recommendations about the libretto and singers. At the end of the month several possibilities were under consideration, among them *Stradella*, Dumas's *Le Comte Hermann* and *Kean*, and *Stiffelius*.

As to the subject, let it be grandiose, passionate, fantastic; just so long as it is beautiful, I don't care. Nevertheless, the passionate [genre] is most certain to succeed. . . . I might have yet another subject, which, if the police were to permit it, would be one of the greatest creations of modern theatre. Who knows! they allowed *Ernani*; maybe they [the police] would permit this too; and here there are no conspiracies. Have a try! The subject is grand, immense, and there is a character that is one of the greatest creations that the theatre can boast of, in any country and in all history. The subject is *Le Roi s'amuse*, and the character I am telling you about is *Tribolet*, which—if Varesi is engaged—could not be better for him and for us. Addio. Addio!

G. Verdi.

PS As soon as you get this letter, get yourself four legs: run all over the city, and try to find an influential person who can get the permission for *Le Roi s'amuse*. Don't go to sleep: get moving: hurry. I will expect you in Busseto, but not now; after we have chosen the subject.[11]

Unwilling to let Piave delay their project, he wrote again on 8 May to his librettist, boiling with enthusiasm.

Oh *Le Roi s'amuse* is the greatest plot, and perhaps the greatest drama of modern times. *Tribolet* is a creation worthy of Shakespeare!! . . . It is a subject that cannot fail. You know that six years ago, when Mocenigo suggested *Ernani* to me, I exclaimed: 'Yes, by God, that's the right one.' Now, reviewing several subjects again, when—like a bolt of lightning, like an inspiration—I thought of *Le Roi s'amuse*, I said the same thing . . . 'Yes, by God, that's the right one.' . . . Turn Venice upside down to make the censors permit this subject.[12]

He added observations about several singers and some remarks about *Stiffelius*, which, as we have seen, he and Piave completed in 1850 and produced in Trieste. Piave, slightly more cautious and more realistic about the censors, answered Verdi and raised his own doubts about the divided stage of the last act, the sack which holds Gilda's body, and other matters of stage business.[13] An Italian title also had to be chosen for the opera.

Piave, through an error, had sent this letter of 14 May in an envelope addressed to the Neapolitan composer Vincenzo Capecelatro, and had sent his letter to Capecelatro to Verdi. The letter intended for Verdi finally reached him at the end of the month: but because both letters passed through Muzio's hands (at Verdi's insistence) and because the Neapolitan musician had perhaps read Piave's letter about *Le Roi s'amuse*, Verdi's privacy was violated and one of his important professional matters was probably the talk of Naples.[14]

He dressed Piave down in Venetian slang:

Dear Piave,

Sior Mona a real *mona* . . . By mistake you sent me a letter with G. Verdi at the top, and I think (as it seems to me from the contents) intended for Capecelatro. I sent it to Emanuele, so that he can exchange it for mine, since I suppose that Capecelatro will have received one addressed to me. . . . *Mona*! a real *mona*!! Do you feel like coming to Busseto? Now we can really work hard . . . If you decide to come, please come at once, because perhaps I will go away later on.[15]

When Verdi finally read what Piave had written in mid-May, he answered:

There is no problem, neither about the divided stage nor about the sack [for Gilda's body]. Just stick to the French and you cannot go wrong. As for the title, if we cannot keep *Le Roi s'amuse*, which would be perfect, the title has to be *La maledizione di Vallier* or—to keep it shorter—*La maledizione*. The whole theme lies in that curse, which also becomes [the] moral. An unhappy father who weeps over his daughter's honour, which has been stolen; mocked by a court jester, whom the father curses; and this curse strikes the jester in the most terrifying way, [all] this seems moral to me and great, stupendously great. Be sure that La Vallier [*sic*] should appear only twice (as in the French [play]) and say a very, very few, strong, prophetic words. I say again that the whole theme lies in that curse. Come to Busseto and we will settle it all. Please propose the subject to the directors and the police. Hurry, really hurry. Come here, because maybe I will have to have you do another work, but we have to be very careful and keep it secret.[16]

This letter was written from Cremona on 3 June. Piave may have spent as much as two months with Verdi in Palazzo Cavalli that year, working on *Stiffelio* and other projects.[17] In mid-June Verdi read in a theatrical journal that the Teatro La Fenice had not received its government funds and would have to close during 1850–1 and offer its singers to other impresarios. At once he wrote to ask Marzari whether this was true and, if it were, 'what dispositions and intentions you have toward me'.[18] He was reassured in July that the theatre was not closing.[19]

On 5 August, writing from Busseto, Piave sent the director of La Fenice the scenario of the new opera: 'Verdi would like to call it *La maledizione*, but I confess that I am against that and would prefer something else.' He noted that the subject 'is taken from the celebrated drama by Victor Hugo, *Le Roi s'amuse*, the approval for which on the stage [of La Fenice], I was assured in a conversation, would not cause difficulty.'[20] If the librettist believed this, he must have been shocked to hear from Marzari that 'some problems could be found' in what Piave called 'my new libretto'.[21] Among these were the cruelty and violence of the story; the portrayal of King Francis I of France; the King's violation of Blanche; and the general immorality of the drama. Piave defended himself on all of these points, particularly the last:

As for the plot as a whole, it seems to me, as it does to Verdi, very, very moral, when one sees the awful effects of Saint-Vallier's curse unleashed against Triboletto, who lets himself insult a miserable father who comes to seek justice for the stained honour of his daughter, and at the cost of his own blood. More moral, certainly, than *Ernani*, the *Foscari*, etc.'[22]

Yet *Le Roi s'amuse* did raise issues of morality. The original drama, a five-act play in verse, had become notorious as a work in which a reigning monarch, Francis I of France, was portrayed as a lecher and debauchee. Other aspects of the play were equally offensive to the authorities. At one point Triboulet, the jester, comes on stage, desperately looking for his daughter Blanche. When the courtiers jeer at him and tell him she is with the King, he begs them to save her. They believe that Blanche is his mistress. When they refuse to help him, the jester Triboulet, blind with anger, and realizing that his daughter's honour is lost, curses them: 'Bastards! Your mothers slept with their lackeys.' This scene and the violation of Blanche caused outrage when Hugo's play was first given; they were not likely to pass the Austrian censors unscathed. (As late as the 1920s some women sitting in boxes at the Metropolitan Opera turned their chairs around to protest at the scene when Gilda emerges from the bedroom where the Duke had raped her. And as late as the 1950s the expression 'Bastard! Your mother slept with her servants' was a good backstage curse in American opera-houses where Italian was the first language.) Added to these offences was the preposterous idea of having a hunchbacked jester as the protagonist of a tragedy. Quite beyond the moral issues the play raised were the political considerations. A king was shown as a libertine; his antagonist was a court jester. At a time when men like Demaldè were denouncing absolute monarchy as an anachronism and absolute rulers were under siege in many countries, the censors would have seen in *Rigoletto* a threat to divine order.

On 24 August Verdi addressed Marzari himself:

I myself have asked Piave to come back to Venice just to carry this letter personally to you, and to speak to you at length about everything that I can only write about briefly. The doubt about the permission for *Le Roi s'amuse* puts me in a serious position. I was assured by Piave that there were no obstacles to this subject, and I, having faith in what he said, set myself to studying it, to meditate deeply on it, and the idea and the musical tint were in my mind. I can tell you that the main—and the hardest—work was done. If I now were forced to take on another subject, I would not have enough time to undertake such a study, and I could not write an opera which would satisfy my conscience.[23]

He urged Marzari to intervene personally to get permission for the opera to be performed, and to find a better singer than the soprano Sanchioli to sing the prima donna role. He added that if these two matters could not be settled to his satisfaction, he proposed that the contract between him and the Teatro La Fenice be cancelled.

Some reassurance came from the theatre, in communications from Piave and Guglielmo Brenna, the secretary of La Fenice. 'Piave will have already let you know that we will not have any obstacles put in our path, not even by the authorities.'[24] Had Brenna and Piave not misled the composer, the history of opera would be quite different today. They really had no official approval at all from censors and police. Now the management of the theatre asked Piave to approach the authorities formally as it went on with the search for a soprano who would satisfy Verdi. Unaware of the true situation, Verdi assumed that the way had been cleared for his new opera.

At the end of the summer of 1850 he went to Bologna to direct *Macbeth* and attend at least one performance of *Luisa Miller*, during which he was given more than ten curtain calls. From there he wrote to Brenna on 5 October, expressing his view of sopranos who were 'caricatures of Malibran, who have only her extravagant ways without having any of her genius.'[25] With that, he suggested that Teresa Brambilla, then a mature artist, might be the best choice for the leading role that would later be called Gilda. As we know from a desperate letter to Ricordi, Verdi's chronic stomach trouble was plaguing him and he was worn out from rehearsing; he had only been able to score one number of *Stiffelio* in fifteen days and was worried about Venice: 'Whatever did I do when I accepted that contract?'[26] To Piave, who had been in Bologna, he wrote later in October to say that he had received the last part of the new libretto, *La maledizione*. He then authorized Ricordi to pay the librettist his fee. Some revision of *Stiffelio* was also under way as Verdi prepared to leave for Venice, to meet Piave there and continue on to Trieste with him.[27] While the two men were fighting another battle with the Austrian censor, trying to get *Stiffelio* staged, Verdi had a letter saying that the central directors for public order in Venice had asked to see the complete libretto that he was setting to music for the Teatro La Fenice. The management let him know that the police had made this demand in response to rumours that 'the drama *Le Roi s'amuse* was badly received in Paris, as in Germany, because it is loaded with immorality. The central directors, none the less, believe in good faith that, given the poet's honesty and the Maestro's prudence, the plot will be developed in a reasonable way.'[28] The composer answered by return to say that he and Piave would be in Venice on 20 November and that he hoped that the theatre would have got formal approval by then. He added that he would send the completed libretto at once. 'Don't lose a minute', he added.[29] On 16 November he had begged Brenna to see that the directors sent the libretto as soon as possible 'so I can know the decision as soon as I get to Venice'.[30] Unfortunately the theatre did not act in time, leaving Verdi to return to Busseto still not knowing whether he would or would not be allowed to write the opera.

The lack of official authorization did not stop him from composing. On 25 November he wrote to Piave that he had been at home for two days and was expecting a letter from Venice about the new opera.

I have looked carefully at the second act, and I find that everything will work well, if we can find a place for Francesco's aria; you think about it and I, too, will think about it, and [you] write to me about it. We have to find something more decent [and] take out this *fottisterio*, which is too obvious. Take away the key, which suggests the idea of [the Duke's intercourse with Gilda], etc. etc. Oh, God! These are simple, natural things, but the Patriarch [of Venice] can no longer enjoy them!!! . . . Peppina sends you many regards, thanks you for your letter, and will write to you when she has a free moment. Addio, addio.[31]

Four days later he went on:

I am not losing any time, and am going ahead with writing [the music]; but I am not calm. Please keep after the directors and make them write to me as soon as possible. Don't treat this casually as you always do, because this is a serious matter, and very serious indeed. Be careful not to let yourself be persuaded to make deals that will lead to changes in the characters, the plot, the dramatic situations: if it is a matter of words, you can do that: if it is also a matter of changing the scene where Francesco enters Bianca's [Gilda's] room with a key, you can also do that, as I too believe (as I said in my last letter) that we will have to find something better there: but be sure to leave unchanged the scene where Francesco goes to the house of Saltabadil [Sparafucile]; without this, the drama will no longer exist. We also have to leave the stage business with the sack: this cannot matter to the police; as to the effect it will make, it is not up to them to think about it.

Addio. Write to me more often: it seems to me that we must not let this thing drag on, *and if I were the poet* I would be very, very concerned, all the more because you would have a great deal of responsibility if by chance (may the Devil not make it happen) they should not allow this drama [to be given]. So speak to the director: take whatever steps are necessary; and all of this as quickly as possible.[32]

But the situation was not as simple as Verdi hoped. On 1 December Carlo Marzari wrote to Verdi, to say that although he had had no official report, he had learned that 'in spite of all the efforts of the directors and of the poet', the public order office 'absolutely refused' to allow *Le Roi s'amuse* to be performed, and that even changes of any kind were 'prohibited'. He went on to say that Piave hoped to change Francis I of France into 'a feudal lord of the same period', take out some of the 'obscene indecencies that permeate it' and get the authorities to approve the sanitized version. 'But the directors, after taking soundings, does not have any illusions about its success.'[33] Just as Marzari was writing this, the official decree arrived in his office. Sent in the name of His Excellency the Signor Military Governor Cavalier de Gorzkowski, it stated that he

deplores the fact that the poet Piave and the famous Maestro Verdi did not know how to choose some other field to display their talents and [chose] such a repugnant [example of] immorality and obscene triviality as the plot of the libretto called *La maledizione*. . . . [His] Excellency has therefore found that he must absolutely prohibit this production and, at the same time, wants me to warn the directors [of the Teatro La Fenice] not to insist further on this matter.[34]

This notification was signed by Luigi Martello, the director of the public order office.

Verdi reacted at once to say that the decree, which he received from the director of La Fenice, had been 'unexpected' and had made him 'go crazy'. Piave was to blame, he said, for he had assured the composer 'in several letters' over the previous eight months that the opera would be approved.

Because of this I set to music a good part of the drama and made the greatest possible commitment to finish it on time as agreed. The rejection drives me to desperation because now it is too late to choose another libretto, which would be impossible for me. It was [sic] the third time that I had the honour of writing for Venice, and the Noble Directors know how carefully I have always fulfilled my obligations. You know that I gave my word that I would finish *Attila* when I was in bed and almost dying; and I finished it. Now on my honour I say again that it is impossible for me to set a new libretto, even if I wanted to do it, [even] to the point of ruining my health over it. To show all my good faith I offer the only thing I can. *Stiffelio* is a new opera for Venice. I suggest it, and I myself would come to direct it . . . in the Carnival season of 1850–1. In this opera there is one very big problem (this, too, because of the censors); and that is the last scene. As it stands it cannot be played; however, if authorization to perform it as I conceived it cannot be got from Vienna, then I would be disposed to change the end of it, which would be new for Venice. I beg the directors to accept my good faith and believe that the damage and the unhappiness resulting from this veto are so great that I have no words to describe them.[35]

He wrote to Brenna on the same day: 'Anyway, I tell you particularly, and in a friendly way, that even if they shower me with gold, or throw me in prison, I absolutely cannot set a new libretto.'[36] At this point he also reported to Ricordi: 'Very big problems in Venice over the new opera. It is a serious matter! perhaps I won't write any more [for them]; the censors haven't approved the new [libretto]. What will the impresario do? It is a serious matter, serious, very, very serious!!!'[37]

The director and impresario of La Fenice, undaunted by the censors' veto, worked with Piave to make some changes in the libretto. By 9 December the new title was *Il duca di Vendôme*; the revised libretto 'observed all the proper concerns that are required for decency on-stage'.[38] It satisfied the censors, who gave their official approval almost at once. On 11 December Marzari sent the revised text to Verdi. If he expected compliance, he was soon disappointed. On 14 December Verdi wrote a long letter, saying that he had not had much time to study the new libretto:

I have seen enough, however, to understand that [it], revised as it is, lacks character, importance, and finally the *punti di scena* [most important scenes] have become very, very cold. . . . The old man's curse, so original and sublime in the original, becomes ridiculous here because the motive that drives him to utter the curse no longer has its original importance, and because he is no longer a subject who speaks so boldly to the king. Without this curse, what purpose, what meaning has the drama? The Duke becomes a useless character and the Duke absolutely must be a libertine; without that, we cannot justify Triboletto's fear about his daughter leaving her hiding-place, without that, this drama is impossible. In the last act, why in the world does the Duke go to a far-off tavern alone, unless he has been invited there, for a rendezvous with a lover? I do not understand why they have taken away the sack: what difference did the sack make to the police? Are they afraid of the effect it has? But I allow myself to say, Why do they think they know more about this than I do? Who is the Maestro? Who can say this will be effective, and that will not be? This same kind of difficulty came up about the *horn* in *Ernani*: well, who laughed when they heard that horn? If you take away the sack, it is unlikely that Triboletto would talk for half an hour to a corpse, without having a flash of lightning show him that it is his daughter. Finally, let me note that they have avoided making Triboletto ugly and a hunchback!! What is their motive? Someone may say 'A hunchback that sings!'—And why not? Will it be effective? I don't know, but if I don't know—I repeat—the person who proposed this change does not know either. I find it really a very, very beautiful thing to portray this character who is deformed and ridiculous on the outside, and passionate and full of love inside. I chose this very subject just because of all these qualities and these original traits if they are taken out, I cannot write the music for it. If someone says to me that the notes can work equally well for this drama, I answer that I cannot understand such reasoning, and I say frankly that my notes—whether beautiful or ugly—are not written haphazardly, and that I always manage to give them a character all their own. To sum up, they have made an ordinary, commonplace, and cold thing out of an original, powerful drama. . . . I can only repeat [what I said before] because in my conscience as an artist I cannot set this libretto to music.[39]

He wrote the same day to Piave in a sharp, brusque tone:

Thank you for the powder and the *baicoli* [Venetian biscuits], for which I will pay you. Spare yourself the trouble of getting the fish because I cannot send to Cremona [for it]. I am writing to the directors about the new libretto. I am not sending the *200* Austrian lire because our contract is naturally cancelled, as I will not write the opera for Venice, because I gave you the commission [to write the libretto of] *Le Roi s'amuse* on the condition that you get the clearance from the police, and [the police] are not allowing it to be performed (and are damaging me a great deal). So you may keep *200* lire of the *500* that I sent you for *Le Roi s'amuse*, to arrive at a total of 1,000 Austrian lire: the price we agreed upon for the libretto of *Stiffelio*; and you will pay me back the remaining *300*. Addio, addio.[40]

When he wrote this, the season at the Teatro La Fenice was to open in two and a half weeks! As we know from Piave's letter of 19 December to the directors, the all-important *cartellone*, the official poster announcing the season, was about to be printed.[41]

At La Fenice, everyone involved in this difficult matter reacted with consternation to Verdi's angry letter. Under considerable pressure, Marzari and Piave then sought out Maurizio De Hepsky, a lieutenant-colonel in the imperial office of the 'military authorities responsible for oversight of the theatre'.[42] The three men met Luigi Martello, director of public order, to hammer out a compromise, the terms of which were sent to Verdi on 23 December.

[T]he colours and the original characters that you want will be kept. . . . The character substituted for Francesco . . . can be a libertine and absolute ruler of his state. The buffoon can be deformed, as you want. There will be no problem about the sack, and [the only reservation] is that we will have to treat the kidnapping of the buffoon's daughter in a way that conforms to the demands for [decency] on stage.[43]

At about this time the opera was given the name by which we know it. *Rigoletto* was still *La maledizione* on the twenty-third; four days later it was *Il duca di Vendôme*, just a few hours before Brenna and Piave—acting on Marzari's orders—left for Busseto to review the situation personally with Verdi, who first referred to *Rigoletto* in his 14 January 1851 letter to Piave. The title was taken from *Rigoletti, ou Le dernier des fous*, a parody of Hugo's original play. Marzari's decision to send his two emissaries to Busseto in the holiday week meant that three principals could sit down together. 'It is a matter of persuading Verdi to agree to the changes we have agreed upon; that will be easier to do in a conversation, where views and objections can better be aired than in letters . . . Delay in this case would rob [Verdi] of the actual time needed to finish the work of writing the music.'[44]

Verdi, aware that the two men were coming, wrote to Piave on 29 December:

I will send you my little carriage to bring you and Brenna to Busseto. The servant (Giacomo) will be on this side of the Po because he has no passport [to leave the Duchy]. So don't be upset if you have to take those few steps on foot and cross the Po at la Croce, where Giacomo will be on the river bank. He will wait for you until ten tomorrow morning (Monday), so get ready to leave Cremona about eight.

Piave was warned that he and Brenna would have to share a bedroom because Verdi's mother was 'living in her room'. Otherwise they could go to the nearby hotel.[45] He did not mention Strepponi.

Verdi, Piave, and Brenna must have set to work at once, for an agreement signed by the three men is dated the same day of their arrival. It stipulates that the setting will be changed from the court of France to a small, independent duchy; that the 'original kinds of characters of the Victor Hugo drama' will be kept, changing their names to fit the period and setting chosen; that the scene in which the King 'declares that he is determined to profit from the key. . . . to let himself into the room of the kidnapped Bianca' will be 'avoided completely'; that another scene, which will 'preserve the necessary decency' will be substituted; that the ruler will be lured to the tavern by a ruse, so that the drama would not suggest that he had gone to keep a rendezvous with a lover; that Verdi would decide how to handle the sack and the corpse of the jester's daughter; and that he would not be forced to produce the new opera before the end of February or the first of March.[46]

With this in hand, Brenna returned to Venice, leaving Piave with Verdi. But a new warning to them both went out from Marzari on 4 January 1851: 'I cannot urge you strongly enough, and Piave especially, to avoid everything in your new work that could offend decency on stage, so that we will not have new obstacles raised by the authority for public order.'[47] One week later Piave, back in Venice, gave Marzari the revised libretto, which met the censors' guidelines. 'I hope not to encounter any further obstacles', Marzari wrote to Verdi, adding remarks about several of the singers under consideration. The composer, working at top speed, was considerably inconvenienced by having no one to help him, for Muzio, after an engagement in Trent in 1850, had gone on to Brussels for the winter season. Although he kept in touch through Verdi's letters to him and through theatrical journals, for some of which he even served as an anonymous correspondent, his absence left Verdi without a secretary, clerk, and copyist during one of the most trying periods of his life.

Marzari's letter of 4 January had proposed that Verdi be in Venice no later than the third or fifth of February.[48] Again on the fourteenth he pushed for an arrival on the fourth or fifth.[49] Not having heard anything from Venice in more than a week, Verdi wrote to Piave on the fourteenth, just as Marzari was writing to him. 'I hope you will have got authorization from the police!' Verdi said. 'And I hope that the directors will agree to what I asked because *time* is needed, more than anything; yet I don't want to throw the theatre off balance. In the mean time this infernal *Rigoletto* is getting on—between one curse and another. Even the Duke's aria is done, and it was very difficult because . . . I must call some things to your attention' and he went on to ask for changes in some of the poetry and concluded: 'I need these changes right away and I need to know my fate! *You* have patience, for I . . . ah, I am putting up with too much, and I don't know whether I will still have a lot of [patience] in my storeroom.'[50] Less than a week later on 20 January he let Piave know that the second act was almost finished: 'I say *almost* because the stretta of the last duet was ineffective because of Gilda's aside. I realize that two actors who tell their business, one [speaking] in one direction, the other in the other direction, are ineffective, particularly in the fast sections. I have therefore decided to redo this stretta, but I need your help.' He then outlined the entire duet between Gilda and Rigoletto with the text 'Sì, vendetta', which later became one of the most dramatic moments in the opera. 'Write to me soon and send me the verses at once so that we can finish.'[51]

On that same day Piave was writing to Verdi from Venice to say that he would not have final approval for another two days. He had also not had time to change the verses Verdi had requested earlier. 'Oh, this *Rigoletto* will be a milestone in my life,' he said.[52] The next day he let Verdi know that he had ordered the 'magnificent' scenery and that he would return to the censors and 'get back to hammering on them' as he reassured Verdi: 'Be calm, though, because they need you too much to risk annoying you again. You can and must consider the thing done.'[53]

Just a few days earlier Verdi had written a memorandum sketching out his master plan:

Pro Memoria per Piave

1. Make my apologies to the directors if there is not enough time for me to compose—

2. Get the authorization for the new libretto from the police as quickly as possible and write me an official notification—

3. Get the directors to grant me the time we have lost: that is, make my opera the last one of the season: leave me at home in peace until the last moment: You can write to me three or four days before Malipiero's opera is staged, via the post through Parma [Borgo S. Don[nino] *cancelled*]: then another letter two days before the première [of the Malipiero opera], to Poste Restante in Cremona. I will leave here the very day that Malipiero's opera is staged and I will be in Venice the [the second *cancelled*] morning of the second day in time to direct the first rehearsal—the parts will be sent ahead before that—

4. Decide whether the role of Magellona [Magdalena] must be a contralto and . . . write to me about it at once—
5. Good secondary singers, and not taken from the chorus—See that the [singer for] old Castiglione [Monterone] is a beautiful, strong baritone voice: not a second-rate singer—
6. It will be good if the first and second scenes and the last scene are got ready right away.[54]

Piave's letter of 24 January was still in the post when Verdi wrote urgently:

Well? Do I have to come to Venice or stay in Busseto? I am not joking! I see that you go on treating this matter very casually, but I again tell you that I am not joking and am taking it very seriously! I've had enough of staying here and working myself to death with this damned opera; I don't want to come to fight with the censors in Venice. Here is my last word: if the police have approved the new libretto, then I will come to Venice as agreed with you, that is after Malipiero's opera [*Fernando Cortez*]; if the police do not give their formal approval, it is useless for me to make the trip and I am staying here. Answer me immediately.

He added a short postscript: 'If the police do approve the libretto, I beg you [to have] the directors leave me here in Busseto as long as possible. I am waiting for the verses I asked you for.'[55]

Piave's good news came in a letter of 24 January in which he let the composer know that Malipiero might be delayed as late as mid-February and perhaps beyond.

You need time . . . and this is a break for you. Today I finally got the signature of the general director of the public order [office] for *Rigoletto*, without any changes in the text; I just had to change the name of *Castiglione* to *Monterone* and that of *Cepriano* [*originally Cavriano*] to *Ceprano* because those families exist. We also had to omit the name of *Gonzaga* and just say in the cast of characters: *The Duke of Mantua*. That cannot be very important to us because everyone knows already who was ruling at that time. . . . The Colonel told me that he would get the signature of the Governor no later than tomorrow, and then we won't hear any more about this. Then the directors will give you the official notification.

In a second section of this letter, perhaps added later on the twenty-fourth, Piave let Verdi know that Martello

had got it in his head to change the period and the setting as well as the characters. I was finally successful, a little because of *graciousness*, a little because of *desperation*, a little by saying *I could not*, etc. etc., . . . I swear to you that it seems like a dream. So let's celebrate. The wind has changed, and our ship will get to port safely.[56]

Hearing this, Verdi wrote to Ricordi to reconfirm his understanding with the publisher, for terms very favourable to him:

You will pay me fourteen thousand (14,000) francs in 700 gold napoleons of 20 francs each, in addition to the rights that I kept for myself for the rentals [of scores] and the sales, exactly as with *Stiffelio*. You will have to pay me 300 of the 700 gold napoleons (and not 400) immediately after the above-named opera [*Rigoletto*] is staged, and you will make this amount available to me at the Poste Restante in Cremona as I return from Venice; you will pay me the rest in monthly payments of 50 napoleons beginning on the first of next April and continuing in the same way on the first of each month until it is all paid.[57]

The composer reminded Ricordi that the score was his own 'absolute property' but that the Teatro La Fenice had the right to make a copy of it and to give *Rigoletto*, but only at that theatre, in the following seasons. He added that there was not time to have the score copied in Milan, and that Ricordi should send one of his employees to Venice to meet Verdi there on the day of his arrival and oversee the copyists. As it happened, the score was to be entrusted in Venice to Verdi's friend and supporter, Antonio Gallo, and later to the theatre.

Another letter from Piave, dated 26 January, sounded the trumpets of victory:

Dear Verdi
Te Deum laudamus!
Gloria in excelsis Deo!
Alleluja, Alleluja!
At last yesterday at three in the afternoon our *Rigoletto* reached the directors safe and sound, with no broken bones and no amputations.[58]

Verdi responded, first to the director of La Fenice with reassuring words, saying he had only the final duet left to write and that he would have finished this had he not been suffering with a bad stomach ache in recent days. He agreed to get to Venice two days after Malipiero's opera had its première, but again asked to be left in Busseto as long as possible. He expected to complete the scoring in five or six days. To Piave he exulted:

Praise be to Heaven! *Rigoletto* will go on?! . . . and we hope it will go well. I am happy about this. From the time you left here you can't believe how much work I have done. I have only the final duet left. It is true that in recent days I have had such a terrible stomach ache that I was afraid of being really ill. Goodbye to *Rigoletto*. I rested three days and today I am fine.[59]

He sent further instructions about the scenery and the special effects for the storm scene of the last act and asked to have rooms at the Hotel Europa on a high floor so he could have air and sunshine; fewer pests would come up there to bother him. He also asked for a grand piano in his rooms, and sent final admonitions about finding a good Monterone because a second-rate one could ruin the first scene of the opera. He wrote to Piave on 5 February: 'today I finished the opera'.[60] He also told the librettist to meet the coach coming from Cremona, which would bring 'two-thirds of the opera'. Piave was to give the nine pieces to Gallo and get the parts copied so they could be given out. He said he would bring the rest of the opera with him and do the instrumentation during rehearsals. Even so, the production was still at risk five days later, when Verdi threatened the management, saying that he was really ill and would send doctors' certificates to prove it if anyone at La Fenice tried to hold him strictly to his contract. He did, though, promise Piave that he would send more of the music of Act III and bring the last act with him. Operating from a position of strength, for he still had about one third of his score in Busseto, he could make or break the faltering Venice season.

Separations

It is surprising that Verdi could work at all during the winter of 1850–1, for he was under extraordinary pressure, at odds with his parents and engaged in a struggle with them and his community. In January he did the unthinkable, breaking off relations with his parents. This rupture came just after Piave and Brenna left for Venice; Verdi's mother rejoined his father at Sant'Agata at about the same time. When the break finally came, Strepponi had been living in Palazzo Cavalli off and on for about sixteen months, leaving occasionally for trips to Florence or Pavia to take care of her personal affairs. From her Letter-Books and correspondence, we know that she was treated very badly there. In fact, the situation in Busseto worsened steadily. No one was sure of her legal status, for Verdi apparently told no one whether he was married to her or not. He lived in virtual seclusion; as he told Piave, he received no one except Antonio and Giovannino Barezzi. His only guests, as far as we know, were Piave and

Brenna. Muzio was counted as a member of the family, as he reported to Ricordi. But Verdi and Strepponi were wretchedly unhappy, offended by the neighbours' prying. They developed a siege mentality, fending off attacks from all sides. Verdi's anger seems to have been directed chiefly toward his father, although he never forgot the insults other Bussetans directed toward him. Carlo Verdi had every reason to protest, for a wrenching family crisis arose just as he and his son were arguing over the management of Verdi's property, some of which could not have been acquired and held without Carlo Verdi's help.

It was perfectly natural that Verdi's devout father, whom Strepponi later described going to daily Mass and returning to church in the evening to recite the rosary, would have been troubled at having a woman with a tainted reputation in the house, whether Verdi was married to her or not. Strepponi's past, which was no secret to those who worked in the opera business and those who went to the theatre for entertainment, would have made marriage extremely difficult. In the years after the births of Camillino, Giuseppa Faustina, and Adelina, the soprano had found only one man who had made her a serious proposal and offered to assume the burdens of what she called her large and small families. She was evidently not looked upon as a marriageable woman. As we have seen, Moriani had described her as being considered 'abject in the eyes of society' and Cirelli had deplored her 'buggering love affairs'. Her conduct put her beyond the pale of bourgeois society of the time and was a matter of gossip even decades later.

Verdi decided to cut himself off from his parents in January 1851, when he engaged the notary Ercolano Balestra to draw up a document of legal separation from them. (Twenty years later, when he urged the soprano Teresa Stolz to do the same, he called the act 'emancipation'.) He ordered his father and mother out of the farmhouse at Sant'Agata, asking them to leave within about eight weeks so that he could move there himself at the end of February. Such an acrimonious controversy arose that he and his parents stopped speaking to each other and communicated only through Balestra. Not even the notary could arrange a settlement, because of Carlo Verdi's opposition. On 21 January, while Verdi was struggling with *Rigoletto*, he let Balestra know how unhappy he was over the situation.

From a trusted source I have heard that my father is going around peddling the story that things have been settled between us in one of the two following ways:

that I would grant the administration of my properties to my father, or that I would lease them to him. I do not believe that there has been any misunderstanding between you and me, Sig. Doctor, nor do I believe that you have proposed [either] one of these two things; nevertheless, for my greater peace of mind, I want to repeat to you that I will never agree to these two proposals. I intend to be separated from my father in my residence and in my business. To sum up, I can only repeat what I told you yesterday in person: *as far as the world is concerned, Carlo Verdi has to be one thing, and Giuseppe Verdi something else.*[61]

The situation worsened some ten days later. Again Verdi wrote to Balestra:

A man from Roncole nicknamed *Piga* had someone speak to me about a debt of about 22 francs that my father owes him. I told him to give you the information, and, if the debt is legal, it will be paid. So, Sig. Doctor, I ask you to have a look at this little matter. I will also ask you to pay my father whatever amount you think right for the month of February. I want him to resign himself to accepting one of the proposals offered to him, because if things are not definitely settled when I get back from Venice, I will choose one of the offers that perhaps will not be to his advantage. I would very much like my father to be convinced that the decision to separate myself from him *in my residence and in business* will not change because it was made after serious and considered thought.

PS I also beg you to advise my father that Agostino Garbi sent me a [note] about an old debt of his and that I paid it.[62]

At this point, both Verdi and his father owed each other money. Their affairs were far from settled.

By 5 February another serious problem had come up. To Balestra he wrote:

I am sorry about this misunderstanding! I let my mother have the rights to the chicken-yard while we were together; now that we are separated it is quite natural that this right should revert to me. About fifteen days ago the Brunelli woman asked me to whom she should bring the produce from the chicken-yard, I answered: *Here in the house in Busseto.* That is the whole story! I did not give this order out of stinginess, but because I do not want to let my parents have any rights, either small or large. Anyway, what do they lack? Aren't 195 francs and 4 gold napoleons that I gave them myself—in addition to wine, a house, and wood—enough for a few days? Tell my father frankly too that I am tired of the scenes that he is going around making; and all his violence will only lead to making me choose a solution ruinous for me and for him. I will sell everything at any price whatever, and I will abandon this place forever! Sig. Doctor, I am desolate that you have to deal with such a painful and shameful matter; but I am not to blame.[63]

This is Verdi at his worst; but, as we shall see, he was driven to the wall. On the same day that he wrote this to Balestra, he was asking Piave to meet the Cremona coach and collect most of *Rigoletto*, while assuring his Venetian colleagues that he would bring the rest of the score with him and have it ready for production. Shortly before this, he and Strepponi had written to Piave together. On 8 February Piave answered, thanking Strepponi for her 'gracious letter', which had so touched him.[64] In fact, this was her postscript to Verdi's letter of 5 February about sending the score:

Dear Signor Piave, called 'The Gracious One'!

[I have] The terrible suspicion that Verdi *always* leaves my regards to you in his pen, even though I *always* ask him to say the friendliest things for me. This time, to be surer, I [myself] send you my many greetings, past, present, and future. Please also let me again send you expressions of my consideration for that *Grace* [of yours] that is famous *in the Universe and in other places*! I beg you to put a lot of effort into educating Verdi, so that he comes back to Busseto a little bit less of a Bear!!! All joking aside, do not forget that in Busseto the Bears and the Gracious Ones will always have the greatest pleasure any time at all that you want to make the sacrifice of leaving Venice and coming to bury yourself in this *Hole*. Verdi is yelling that he wants to have the letter, so I don't have time to do more than grasp your hand and say that I am your friend

G. Strepponj [*sic*].[65]

On 7 February Verdi wrote to Piave again. This letter is postmarked Cremona. The composer gave Gallo and Piave his instructions for the distribution of the parts to the singers, while asking that the rehearsals begin the day after Malipiero's opera opened. He was planning to come to Venice when he had final information from Piave.[66]

One day later he was expressing his satisfaction with the agreement Balestra had forced on his father and mother:

If you had read my heart, you could not have done anything that could have pleased me more in this situation. Anyway, while you were drawing up the draft that I just got, I was trying to cancel Article 5 and a part of [Article] 7 that offended me mightily and that, as you so wisely observe, could have caused acts of revenge later. As for [Giuseppe] Galanti, Sig. Doctor, let us look together for a way to satisfy my father without my having to become the odious tool of his revenge. My father never had any right over the chicken-yard; and if you persuade my mother to accept for the moment a gift of money to compensate her [for losing her income from the chicken-yard], it would be absolutely improper and ridiculous for my father to come forward with some claim over this, too. Finally I would like to ask you not to forget to tell my parents that if they will leave the farmhouse at Sant'Agata before the beginning of March, I will give them an additional gift of (8 or 10) eight or ten gold napoleons; I could move [to Sant'Agata] to enjoy the country even sooner, and I would avoid the inconvenience of having Giovannino [Barezzi] take care of my affairs.[67]

The Draft of Compromise, drawn up by Balestra, reads:

Draft of Compromise
between Giuseppe and Carlo Verdi

The undersigned, to provide for his own peace of mind and at the same time for the needs of his parents, from whom he intends to separate himself in residence and in business, pledges himself to them:

1. to pay in valid currency an annual allowance in new currency of one thousand and eight hundred lire in trimestral payments, in advance, beginning with the first of March of this year;
2. to provide them with a good horse;
3. to let them stay in the house that he owns in the country [at Sant'Agata] until 11 March or, at the latest, 11 May of this year; and if the latter date [applies], the administration and control of his properties will be entrusted to his brother-in-law Giovanni Barezzi.

The rejection or alteration of even one of the above-written clauses will release the signatory from all [his obligations].

G. Verdi.[68]

The composer's note to Giovannino Barezzi reads: 'Dearest Giovannino, I beg you, and I empower you, to administer my properties at Sant'Agata for all the time that I will be in Venice.'[69]

On 8 February, then, Verdi and his parents were still not speaking. He was very heavily in debt to his father; although no mention is made of a settlement of their affairs at this time, Carlo Verdi had every reason to want to see his son pay his debts, for he was not able to meet his own needs. Between January and the end of April 1851 he borrowed from several people around Busseto, and, on at least two occasions, asked them to ask Verdi to cover these obligations, knowing how much his son owed him.

We do not know whether Carlo Verdi and Luigia Uttini accepted Verdi's Draft of Compromise, but it seems that they did not, for friction between father and son continued well into the spring. After nearly thirty-eight years of sacrifice and of sharing their son's life, they were about to be evicted from Sant'Agata, which they had helped him to buy, at a time when he was overwhelmed by debts and behind schedule on the stipulated payments he had contracted to make on these properties. Now his parents were in serious financial straits themselves and were unable to pay the rent on Pietro Allegri's little house in Vidalenzo, where they intended to move. Smaller than Verdi's tenant houses, it still stands at the end of the Stradello, a dirt-road at the edge of the hamlet, about 2 kilometres down the Ongina from Sant'Agata.[70] Verdi lent them the money they needed to secure the lease, but in April he demanded his money back and was repaid. At the time, Carlo Verdi was 65; Verdi's mother was 63 and ill. At an age when they might have hoped to share their son's fame and enjoy it with him, they saw him getting ready to move his mistress into Sant'Agata, even as Carlo Verdi, stripped of his power of attorney, was going deeper into debt daily. During these difficult weeks, Verdi was finishing his new opera.

Rigoletto

Verdi travelled from Busseto to Cremona and on to Padua by coach. From there to Venice he could take the train, using the new railway line that had been opened in 1846. The fourth line in Italy, and one of two in northern Italy, it had already served him well, even when he was not producing his own works in Venice, for it carried organized groups of listeners from one city to another as opera fans learned to use the trains. Arriving on the lagoon on 19 February, he moved into his two warm sunny rooms on the Grand Canal. They were the finest in the Hotel Europa, which Piave had reserved for him. There the 'best piano' from Camploy's music-shop was ready.[71] Earlier that year the librettist had written to say that the new opera was 'awaited here as the salvation of this theatre';[72] now it was up to Verdi and his troops to see whether they could save an otherwise disappointing season. In his cast were Teresa Brambilla as Gilda, Varesi as Rigoletto, Raffaele Mirate (who, Piave said, sounded like a young Moriani) as the Duke, Annetta Casaloni as Maddalena, and the bass Feliciano Pons as Sparafucile. Verdi even got his way about Monterone, which was sung by Paolo Damini, rather than by a friend of Varesi whom the baritone wanted to see in the role.

BOOK III

Verdi's own opinion of the opera was expressed in a later letter to Piave in 1854, when he was trying to get it produced instead of *Ernani*, which was still enormously popular.

Why not *Rigoletto* instead of *Ernani*? Listen to me: *Rigoletto* will live longer than *Ernani*. I know perfectly well that all the wise men, the doctors of music, who ten years ago were running around furious over *Ernani*, will now say that it is better, just because it is eight years older than its brother; but *Rigoletto* is a somewhat more revolutionary opera, and therefore newer, both in its form and style.[73]

The challenge that Verdi faced in Venice in 1851 was getting his 'revolutionary' work ready in the three weeks of rehearsal that were left before the première.

Rigoletto was given on 11 March 1851. As the box-office figures show, it was a great success,[74] playing for thirteen nights, although the reviews reflect confusion about the score and the moral issues it raised. The critic of the *Gazzetta Previlegiata di Venezia* said:

An opera like this cannot be judged in one night. Yesterday we were overwhelmed by the novelty, or, rather, the oddness of the subject; novelty in the music, in the style, in the very form of the pieces, and we did not get a complete idea of it. . . . All in all, it is Victor Hugo's *Le Roi s'amuse*, pure and simple, with all its sins. The composer, or the poet, seized with a late-blooming love for the satanic [in art], which is now out of style and passé, are [*sic*] looking for ideal beauty in deformity, in horror: They are looking for effects, not in the usual areas of pity and terror, but in the soul's torment and in destruction. We cannot, in good conscience, praise such taste. In spite of that, the opera was a complete success, and the composer was hailed, called out, acclaimed after almost every piece, and two numbers even had to be repeated. To tell the truth, the instrumentation is stupendous, admirable; the orchestra speaks to you, cries out to you; it instills passion in you; . . . it strikes you with sweet, ingenuous passages; . . . There was never such powerful eloquence in sound.[75]

Although he had some reservations about some of the vocal writing, he concluded that several arias and duets were 'very, very beautiful' and well executed and remarked that as the audience left the theatre, people were already beginning to sing the Duke's aria 'La donna è mobile' to themselves.

One critic wrote in *Il Lombardo Veneto* that the music was 'of a truly new kind. It is an unbroken fabric of instrumentation, easy, flowing, spontaneous, which either speaks softly to your soul, or awakens you to pity, or horrifies you, according to the development of the drama.'[76] He added that because journalists had been kept out of the dress rehearsal, contrary to custom, he would have to hear it again to understand it thoroughly. But it was clearly a masterpiece.

Unfavourable reviews appeared in *Il vaglio*, published in Venice, and in *L'Italia musicale*, Lucca's theatrical journal, published in Milan. The former attacked Piave on grounds of immorality and bad taste, claiming that he had wanted to copy *Le Roi s'amuse* and 'make a gift to the honourable House of the Dukes of Gonzaga' by making their ancestor 'a new Don Giovanni' and accusing him of licentiousness, abductions, rapes, and acts of violence. The anonymous writer reproached the librettist for forgetting that some of the Gonzagas still lived in Venice. He conceded, however, that Piave knew how to 'inspire the composer' to write beautiful music. Several pieces from the opera were singled out for praise, especially the 'masterfully composed quartet' in the last act. Verdi had 'returned to simplicity' and turned his back on his usual 'grandiose ensembles, big arias, noisy finales'. The singers were praised for their 'perfect execution' of the score. But the last phrase of the review was: '[It will] send [the audience] away [from the theatre] empty and disgusted at such a horrendous and nauseating spectacle.'[77] One had to read carefully to understand that Verdi was not the reviewer's chief target.

Lucca, who had a personal grudge against Verdi and remained the chief rival of Casa Ricordi, published an anonymous critic's review that described *Le Roi s'amuse* as one of the 'most grotesque abortions of French dramatic literature'. The insult to the Gonzagas drew fire. The original title *La maledizione*, was considered appropriate, for the work was indeed a curse, because of its immorality and offences against taste, its 'ugly images and clumsy lines'. The libretto was 'a real California'—a gold mine—of transgressions. Some of the music was deemed unfailingly effective; Verdi had changed his ways and given up brutally noisy instrumentation. But even this praise involved a charge against the composer: he had taken his new style from Beethoven and Meyerbeer! Verdi did, however, win praise for 'setting us on the right track', even though there was a 'lack of ensembles' and a debt to Rossini and Bellini in the score. The conclusion was that Verdi would surely incorporate these 'different schools' and emerge with one of his own, one that would answer the needs of the art and society of his time. Many reviews took Piave to task. Almost every article said something about the ugliness of the subject, which was variously denounced as monstrous, horrible, indecent, horrifying, and a veritable textbook for crime. But this criticism unsurprisingly, did not keep the public away from most theatres. After a disastrous second production at the Teatro Riccardi in Bergamo in March 1851 (with Muzio conducting and Piave in charge of the stage), *Rigoletto* brought its composer and librettist a great deal of satisfaction as it entered the repertory and sometimes, with its undisputed popular success, pulled other Verdi operas in its wake. Produced in Rome, Trieste, Verona, Bergamo, and Treviso in 1851, it went on to Turin, the Pergola in Florence, the Kärntnerthor in Vienna, Padua, Genoa, Bologna, and Parma the next year. Gallo brought *Rigoletto* back to Venice in 1852, conducting it at the Teatro San Benedetto. It was also seen the same year in other Italian cities such as Faenza, Leghorn, Fabriano, and Ascoli Piceno, and at the important fair in Senigallia, where it was given thirteen times. Abroad, in 1852, the opera played in Budapest and Corfu. By 1853 it was being given in Malta, Austria, Germany, Russia, Portugal, Spain, England, Poland, and Greece and in Italian cities all over the peninsula. It reached Alexandria, Bucharest, Constantinople, and San Francisco in 1854; and Havana, New York City, Montevideo, Gibraltar, and Edinburgh in 1855. There was even a reported performance at Astrakhan![78]

One of the voices raised in praise of *Rigoletto* was that of the conductor Angelo Mariani, who wrote in Ricordi's *Gazzetta musicale di Milano* of 15 August 1852:

I do not hesitate at all to declare that this most recent Verdi work [is] the best, as regards novelty, knowledge, and musical beauty. I say this to you honestly: I have no words to express the wonder that such a noble work aroused in me. . . . I am immensely pleased especially that people admire true beauty. From my heart, I congratulate the man who wrote it, who is justifiably renowned.[79]

At this time most published criticism of *Rigoletto* was unfavourable or only partly favourable. Mariani's dispatch was published in the same issue of the *Gazzetta* as an article from the reviewer in Padua, giving Verdi some credit for the music but denouncing the opera as a monstrosity—'one cannot determine whether the score belongs to opera seria, buffa, or whatever'—an opera with no characters that would fail without a Varesi to keep it alive.[80] But *Rigoletto* survived. Sometimes censored or given under such titles as *Viscardello*, *Lionello*, or *Clara di Pert*, it brought Verdi a steady income and kept his name before the public in dozens of theatres. After several failures or half-failures, he could celebrate this opera as a kind of Italian homecoming, his first big triumph on the peninsula since the 1847 *Macbeth* in Florence. *Rigoletto*, which kept gaining momentum while he was planning and composing *Il trovatore* and *La traviata*, gave him a sense of accomplishment at a time when he sorely needed it.

The Return to Busseto

On his way home from Venice, Verdi collected 200 gold napoleons from Ricordi that had arrived in his name at the coach office in Cremona. With his payment in hand he left for Busseto, to face his continuing family crisis and prepare to entertain Giovanni Ricordi and his mistress Marietta Ventura, who spent several days in Palazzo Cavalli. Verdi went as far as Cremona with them when they started back to Milan on 11 April. Things were far from calm at home, as he had written to Piave at the end of March:

My father-in-law will not come to Venice; he has an armour of steel that your bombs cannot pierce!! I am glad that *Rigoletto* is doing well, I am only sorry that the newspapers are against you because of the choice of subject. . . . My mother . . . is still sick! I foresee new disasters with my father! I am not well!! I feel tired, as exhausted as if they had drained off half my blood; I still have a bit of stomach ache and cough. Hurrah! And beyond that, beyond that, beyond that . . . An infinity of moral problems!! Poor artists!! Write to me, write to me. Be sure that you have a letter at the Poste Restante in Cremona; I will be there on 2 April; and tell me everything. Give my greetings to the Angel you know about. Addio addio.[81]

From this troubled letter to Piave, we learn that Verdi was still interested in the woman with whom he had first become involved in 1844. 'The Angel', as Verdi called her, evidently had expectations of her own about her relationship with the composer, believing that she could visit him at home. This, of course, was not possible. Verdi's life in Busseto had become unusually difficult at this time. His mother's illness, coming just as she and her husband were being moved from Sant'Agata to Vidalenzo, added one further complication. In the culture in which he lived, a man's concern for his parents was a measure of his character. The bass Marco Arati, for example, was anathema in Busseto because of his neglect of his mother, for which he was never forgiven. Verdi's conduct toward his own parents was something his society would have found hard to dismiss. Signs of disapproval from the Barezzis may be seen in Antonio

Barezzi's refusal to go to Venice to hear *Rigoletto* and in Giovannino's failure to set foot at Sant'Agata even once during Verdi's absence, even though he had a power of attorney to handle Verdi's affairs. As Abbiati described the composer's situation, he was 'tired, infuriated, sickly, even when he [had] to hide a tear for the hurt being inflicted on him and for the hurt he [was] inflicting'.[82] After the violent break with his parents, Verdi was left alone with Strepponi, who (in her words) had regularly to bear unpleasantness directed at her. Carlo Verdi was refusing to accept defeat gracefully and was still airing his outrage and dismay. While the break with Antonio Barezzi came more gradually than the legal separation between Verdi and his parents, it came all the same, although it was not characterized by the bitterness that marked the ruinous dissension within the Verdi family. Still it was a rupture with a man whose devotion, though sometimes tried, had survived unshaken until 1851. Barezzi was left puzzled and hurt.

As Verdi said, he had to 'lower a curtain' between him and the outside world.[83] Strepponi wrote later that he let a 'veil' fall to protect their privacy. Among those who were shut out was Verdi's Venetian woman friend, about whom he wrote to Piave on 15 and 28 April 1851.

Since you are so good, please be kind enough to give this letter to *Sior Toni*. I swear to you that among the many miseries that I have, the knowledge that this matter is being kept the deepest secret is something that brings me immense pleasure! I want this mystery to continue; I beg this with all my heart; I even implore you, although I am sure there is no need whatever to do so. Tell me, when do you see her, and how do you speak to her?

My affairs are up in the air, sometimes happy, sometimes [there are] awful storms; and I am afraid of them. My mother is still in bed, but her fever has gone; but my father is still being obstinate, in yet another way: it seems that he absolutely does not want to leave me free and in peace. I assure you that I am at a fork in the road that is so dreadful that I do not know how to get out of it. But it is better not to mention certain things to you, and it is useless for me to tell you about my troubles, [for] you cannot help me. My strength of will is great, you know that; but I assure you . . . Enough! Enough![84]

One way out of the dilemma led to secluded Sant'Agata. That was the route Verdi chose at the beginning of 1851. But some of his problems seemed insoluble and, as time proved, took years to resolve. The proof of an ongoing, agonizing situation lay in the fact that Carlo Verdi continued to launch his attacks on his son, whom he did not intend to leave 'free and in peace'. The old man had not been bought off with gifts of money, a horse, and the promise of a pension, for the moral issues between the two men were graver than anything a notary's settlement could mend.

On 28 April Verdi wrote another letter to Piave:

As Peppina [says], I hope to move to the country about seven or eight days from now. As soon as I settle in and get a little room fixed up, I shall beg you to come and be bored at Sant'Agata, [and] note that Sant'Agata is even worse than Busseto. Nothing could be worse than to have *Sior Toni* pay me this hasty visit in Busseto: certainly there are things that we say but do not do; but even showing that she has the idea [of coming] is really very daring. . . . So I beg you to be *prudent*. Anyway, she knows my situation, I did not deny it to her, you can talk to her openly about it whenever you feel like it.[85]

Even though this was being written at a time when Strepponi was planning to be in Florence for about three weeks in May, it would have been inconceivable for Verdi to have yet another lover visit him, whether at Sant'Agata or at Busseto. He correctly counted on Piave to keep his woman friend from coming there while he tried to deal with a tangle of conflicting loyalties and manage the crisis.

The Child at La Rabbiosa

There was perhaps yet another problem which Verdi had to face at this time. On 14 April 1851 a baby girl was born to unidentified parents who had her delivered at nine-thirty that same night to the turnstile for abandoned babies at the Ospedale Maggiore in Cremona.[86] There the nuns, hearing the bell ring, found her. As the register of abandoned infants shows, she was identified as 'Santa Streppini' when she was left and was thus spared the humiliation of having the authorities give her a surname. The senior adjutant priest of the church of Santa Maria della Pietà baptized her the next morning and entered her into the records of the institution's in-house parish. Her godmother was Domenica Ghio, a woman who worked in the hospital and often held foundlings at the font.[87] Because of the circumstances of Verdi's and Strepponi's lives that spring, because of Strepponi's custom of abandoning her children, and because of what later happened to this baby, it appears possible that she was Giuseppina Strepponi's daughter, although there is a chance that she was born to a local woman to whom Strepponi lent her name. It has also been suggested that she might have been Barberina Strepponi's child. This, however, does not seem likely for Barberina at that time was living in

Locate Triulzi with her mother and her brother, who was the municipal doctor there.

Santa Streppini is not the first abandoned child to be associated with Verdi's household. A boy, called Giuseppe, had been born late in May 1850 and he, too, had been put in the turnstile in Cremona hospital, where his records still can be found. He was placed in Busseto with Giovanni Belli and his wife, Giuseppa Fulcini, who later became his permanent foster parents. An employee and, later, the steward or farm-agent for Luca Orlandi, he was told by the Orlandi-Barezzis that he was Verdi's illegitimate son and that his mother was one of the maids in Palazzo Cavalli (now, of course, known as Palazzo Orlandi). As for this, one can say that the Orlandi-Barezzis would have been likely to know of the pregnancy, but no proof exists that this was Verdi's child, though this was local tradition.

Santa Streppini's mother got pregnant around the end of June or the beginning of July in 1850 and could not have hidden her condition much before the end of the year, which is just when an abyss opened between Verdi and his parents. Santa's history closely parallels that of Strepponi's second child, Giuseppa Faustina, who, as we have seen, was abandoned in the turnstile of the foundling home in Florence in 1839, baptized under the institution's auspices, and later released to a couple that claimed her, swearing that she was their daughter. Her history also resembles that of Adelina Strepponi, left with a taverner in Trieste in 1841, when Giuseppina Strepponi and Cirelli boarded the steamer for Venice, and that of Strepponi's own sister, who was left in the Lodi foundling home to become a ward of the city. Camillino, the soprano's son, had fared slightly better, although he had not lived with his mother beyond the first weeks of his life and had not been entrusted to either of his grandmothers. Foster-parents also raised him. He, Giuseppa Faustina, and Adelina all died as charity cases, he as a *gratuito* in Siena in 1863, Giuseppa Faustina in a charity hospital for the insane in Florence in 1919, and Adelina in Trieste, where she was given a third-class funeral in 1841.

Santa Streppini, a ward of the Congregazione della Carità in Cremona, was assigned under the false name 'Santa Stropellini' to a family living almost at the edge of Verdi's lands. Marco Uggeri and Luigia Bassini, Santa's foster-parents, were smallholders living on the farm called 'La Rabbiosa', which his family had owned for decades.[88] Some of the Bassinis lived a few doors away from Verdi at Sant'Agata; one later worked in his garden. The correct name of this new baby was not given to either the Uggeris or the parish priest of San Martino in Olza, which includes La Rabbiosa, for she appears in the parish census or Status animarum in 1852, 1853, and 1854 as 'Santa *Stropellini*'.[89] In 1855 she was listed simply as 'Abandoned child from Cremona, Santa, [age] 4'. In 1857 she was 'Santa of the Cremona Hospital, [age] 6'. With appropriate changes of age, she was described in this same way until 1859, the last surviving volume of the Status animarum in the San Martino archives. Never recognized by any parent, she remained the ward of the Congregazione della Carità and went on living with the Uggeris until she was fifteen. In 1865 the Uggeris' daughter Brigida, with whom Santa had grown up, married Antonio Zilioli, whose mother had grown up with Verdi in Busseto. Zilioli himself had been brought up with the composer's Verdi and Uttini cousins at San Pietro in Cerro. On 18 April 1866 Santa Streppini was 'definitely assigned' to Brigida Uggeri and Zilioli.[90] They all continued to live at La Rabbiosa on the family land, just at the edge of Verdi's fields. Again, no proof exists that she was Verdi's child.

If Strepponi was pregnant, then this might have been the cause of the upheaval in Verdi's family life in 1850 and 1851, shattering long-established, stable relationships and leading the composer to cut himself off completely from his parents even as he became estranged from the Barezzis. He had brought home a woman whose past lived on in her children. The clearances required for marriage, had they wished to marry, would have raised the issue of where her own children were, who was providing for them, and who held the *patria potestà* over them. Working in a profession that fed more on gossip than on food, Verdi could not have afforded any occasion for scandal that opened a door on Strepponi's past and reflected on him. By 1851 he was an international celebrity, who, under the law of the time, would also have become the stepfather and holder of the *patria potestà* of her illegitimate children, only one of whom (Giuseppa Faustina) had been assigned (on the basis of falsified documents) to a couple who lied when they claimed to be her 'true and legitimate parents'. Even if third parties had conducted all the negotiations concerning Giuseppa Faustina, someone beside her parents must have known whose child she was, just as someone later insisted that Strepponi had 'had a child in the Cremonese', as Carlo Gatti stated in 1956, when he also said he had learned that 'the boy' was a carpenter. Decades later Maurizio Chierici was told that 'the young man from San Pietro in Cerro', a carpenter, was somehow connected to Strepponi. He was given this information by a couple in Cortemaggiore.[91]

BOOK III

Situations such as these offered unscrupulous people the chance for blackmail, a problem Chierici also considered.[92] While I am not suggesting that the Zanobinis and Pagliais in Florence were blackmailing Strepponi, it is true that their letters triggered off payments from her, as she herself remarked after she had been sending them money and doing favours for them for decades. And it is equally true that the controversy over Strepponi's past never really died out. It returned again and again to plague her, as we know from her Letter-books and random memoranda. As late as 1873 a family crisis was brought on when one of the maids, Zeffirina Braibanti, of whom Strepponi was fond, spread the word that even then Verdi and Strepponi were 'not husband and wife' and that she had had 'a very promiscuous youth' and 'had really been in some messy situations'.[93] At that time it was Barberina Strepponi who heard the gossip and became upset over the affront to her sister. When this happened, Verdi and Strepponi had been married for fourteen years.

When it came to marriage, it was also a question of Verdi's freedom. As his wife, Strepponi would have the right to go anywhere with him. As his mistress, she could be told to stay at home and often was asked or told to do so. Verdi's refusal to take her with him became a matter of dispute between them; she cajoled and compared him to Dionysius, the tyrant of Syracuse; but he refused to give in. In Busseto, and particularly at Sant'Agata, she was all but invisible, living almost as cloistered as a nun. No one could see her as she came and went, getting in and out of Verdi's carriage in the enclosed central courtyards of Palazzo Cavalli and Sant'Agata, and riding, as many people did, with the blinds drawn. So long as she remained in the house and was not seen in public around Busseto, Verdi was safe, entrenched behind his four walls.

Every document relating to Santa Streppini leads one to believe that she was yet another of Strepponi's 'settled' but abandoned children. The use of the falsified names 'Streppini' and 'Stropellini' suggests that this child's parents wanted her real name kept a secret. These are invented surnames that do not appear in any large-city telephone book nor in any civil records of the provinces of Parma, Piacenza, or Cremona from 1806–65. The 'Stropellini' calls to mind one of Strepponi's 1840 letters to Lanari, in which she asks him to write to her under an assumed name, 'Erminia Spillottini'.[94] Camillino was, as we have seen, entered in the Turin records as 'Sterponi'. It seems that the misrepresentation from 'Streppini' to 'Stropellini' is not a mere clerical error, for the registers of San Martino in Olza are models of correct spelling and clear handwriting.

As to the matter of whether Santa was indeed Strepponi's daughter, we must consider in this context Strepponi's letter to Verdi dated 3 January 1853. This was written while she was in Leghorn, waiting for him, and he was in Rome overseeing the première of *Il trovatore* and composing *La traviata*: 'We will not have children (since God perhaps is punishing me for my sins by preventing me from enjoying any legitimate joy before I die)! Well, not having children by me, I hope you will not hurt me by having any by another woman.'[95] Her choice of the future tense and of the word 'legitimate' gives us pause, for when she wrote this she had about eight years ahead during which she could have had children. 'Legitimate' children and marriage were apparently not an issue for this 37-year-old woman. She and Verdi could, of course, have married and had 'legitimate' children, had they wished to have him assume the *patria potestà* of any children she already had. When she wrote this, Camillino Strepponi, who was then living in Florence, was 14; Giuseppa Faustina, 13.

The circumstances of their lives between December 1850 and May 1851 suggest the possibility that Santa Streppini was Strepponi's daughter. The fact that Verdi gave his father a very large sum of money (232 new Parma lire, as we learn from their settlement on 29 April) 'when he went to Cremona' lends credence to this view; the sum was roughly one-tenth of the price of a house and a small piece of land. Once Santa was put in the turnstile, it would have been impossible for any man as famous as Verdi to recognize her. Indeed, the hatred the general public felt toward parents of *esposti* was expressed in no uncertain terms in a first-page article in *Il Lombardo-Veneto* on the same day that the newspaper announced the date of the *Rigoletto* première.[96] In such an atmosphere, with the parents of *esposti* under attack for adding a burden to the charity system while unmarried mothers were also an object of contempt, it was extremely difficult, almost impossible, for people of the upper and middle classes to recognize their *esposti*. Records in Cremona, Milan, Trieste, and Venice show that a few parents of *esposti*, often poor and sometimes unmarried, came to the institutions to recognize the children they had left; these 'recognitions' usually came when the child was old enough to work (before the age of 7) and before permanent placement took effect. These children could then contribute to the family enterprise.

The fact that the Uggeris were assigned Santa Streppini on a temporary basis and that Brigida Uggeri and Antonio Zilioli became her permanent foster-parents suggests that this family was chosen to care for her before she was born, perhaps by being given a token (a half-coin or note) of identification.

Given the upheaval in the lives of the Verdis, Strepponi, and the

Barezzis between December 1850 and the end of 1851, it is not surprising that the composer felt as if he had been drained of half of his blood, as he confided to Piave just twenty days before Santa Streppini was left in the turnstile of the Cremona hospital.[97] He wrote to his librettist about the dreadful fork in the road just one day after the baby was abandoned. As for Strepponi, people in Busseto, Antonio Barezzi among them, were not even certain about where she was or whether she was living in Verdi's house. These were clearly not normal times. The events of this winter changed the very course of Verdi's life.

He reached an agreement with his father when the notary Balestra drew up a final settlement after months of acrimony and dispute. Dated 29 April 1851, this tally of their accounts shows that Carlo Verdi had given his son the money from the sale of two properties in Roncole to save Sant'Agata and cover Verdi's debts to Carlo Bonini.[98]

The first of these was the sale of a field on 3 March 1846, for 1,000 new lire. The second was the sale of a house and land in Roncole on 4 December 1849 for 2,900 new lire. Both deeds were drawn up by notaries. And it was Carlo Verdi who carried the gold to Piacenza to pay Bonini and his mother Annunciata Morosoli.

Carlo Verdi's debts toward his son totalled 1,594.75 new Parma lire, which meant that Verdi owed his father 2,305.25 new Parma lire. The tally shows the father's indebtedness as follows (all amounts in new Parma lire):

Exact sum remaining from the wine:	41.25
Exact sum remaining from cheese:	36.95
Extra money actually given in January and February 1851:	26.20
Money actually given when he went to Cremona	232.00
Debt paid to Luca Orlandi (not agreed on)	410.00
Debt paid to Tommaso Riva [of Frescarolo]	217.00
Debt paid to Agostino Garbi	16.46
Debt paid to the pharmacist [Giovanni] Ghezzi	1.89
Debt paid to [Antonio] Cocchi, café-owner	22.50
Money actually paid for the advance for the rent to Pietro Allegri	1,000.00

The last line of the document reads 'Accounts settled between the above-mentioned father and son', for Verdi paid his debt to his father. Separated legally from his parents, he could finally say, as he wished, 'Carlo Verdi has to be one thing and Giuseppe Verdi something else'; but his victory came at considerable cost to himself. He even lost Antonio Barezzi's support briefly, as Strepponi's hatred of Giovannino and Demetrio Barezzi opened a breach between the composer and his brothers-in-law. Verdi's actions also cost him the respect of his community, as he himself complained, for so much suspicion and animosity was generated that even the few Bussetans invited to his country house became objects of the townspeople's scorn. Because of these drastic changes in his and his family's lives, Verdi and Strepponi became ever more isolated from the community around them while Sant'Agata became their primary residence and refuge.

18

∾

May 1851 – January 1853

Sant'Agata

A gentleman of property and landowner on his own small farm, Verdi was 'padrone in casa mia', as he described himself,[1] surrounded by his fields, 'le possessioni di Sant'Agata'.[2] The hamlet, with its church, tavern, and one-room store, lay about half a kilometre away, down a country road that was virtually impassable when it rained. The Ongina River, which often flooded in the spring, marked the border between the duchies of Parma and Piacenza and ran along the eastern line of the property. A narrow wooden bridge, spanning it, led to Verdi's house. Busseto, on the Parma side, was 3 kilometres away. Villanova sull'Arda, more than 3 kilometres to the north-west, was the seat of the municipal government; but the courts and tax offices were at Cortemaggiore.[3] Between Sant'Agata and the Arda River lay the farms at La Rabbiosa, Gerbida, Canale, the mill and land of Castellazzo, Il Giardino, Possessione and Possessioncella, and other parcels, most of which Verdi later bought. To the north were Vidalenzo, where his parents had settled on the property called Stradello Secchi, and the broad reaches of the huge estate called Piantadoro, which also became his. Nearby were the simple dwellings of farm-labourers and boatmen, several of them Verdi by name. The composer, who had lived in the country village of Roncole but had never lived on a farm, found himself isolated and perhaps surprised at 'questa profonda quiete' and 'questo silenzio', this deep stillness and this silence.[4] Almost 38 years old, he had learned to manage the various productions of his operas and earn from them, making them a substantial asset. At Sant'Agata was his second important asset, the landed estate, which he continued to improve.

It was, he said, 'in the middle of a horrible, abandoned village, sur-rounded by yokels and oxen'.[5] Apart from the horses, to which he always devoted particular attention, he owned the livestock needed to keep the farm going. By the end of 1853 he had four oxen, sixteen cows, ten bulls, eleven calves, and six rams;[6] over the coming decades, as he traded, bought, and sold, he became a familiar figure at the market in Cremona, where he also later used the library, met friends, and exchanged greetings with boys who recognized him on the street. The Hotel Cappello became his centre of operations there, perhaps because it was next to the stage-coach and (later) post offices.

Soon after the move to Sant'Agata at the beginning of May 1851, Strepponi went to Florence to take care of her own affairs, leaving Verdi alone at the farm. He must have visited or had visits from some of his family, leading her to beg him not to turn again to the very people she considered her enemies, for she wrote to him on 18 May, saying that she hoped to be home at the end of the month.

I hear that Piave has written . . . [and I shall show him] just as much friendship, because, to tell the truth, Piave is an excellent person whom I love for his kindness and because you love him.

If you are looking forward to my arrival, I am burning to come back. I say again that I am counting on being home on Ascension Day at the latest.

I urge you, beg you not to be too intimate *with your heirs*, and that not out of a feeling of malice, I swear to you, but because it would be impossible for me to put up with new miseries of the sort I have borne for almost two years! Human nature has shown itself so foul in the vicissitudes of the past that it is better for us to take all possible precautions so that the veil with which you chose to cover it may never again be lifted.

Addio, my Wizard. I won't make an effort to express myself [in words], reserving the right to do it with many kisses when I get back. Addio addio,

Peppina.

She added a postscript about Lanari, saying that he had done everything possible to make himself ridiculous and to make everyone hate him.[7]

Strepponi may have persuaded Verdi to keep his distance from those she called his 'heirs', in whose ranks were his parents, uncles, aunts, cousins, and in-laws; but it cannot have been easy for him to do this, for they were all nearby. Available evidence leads us to believe that neither Antonio nor Giovannino Barezzi was welcomed at Sant'Agata that year; but it is hard to imagine that Verdi did not visit his parents, for his mother was still ill.

BOOK III

The first weeks at Sant'Agata were marred by an unpleasant incident when the house was broken into and robbed one night. Curiously, Verdi was not there when the thieves came; but he described the event to Piave in a letter sent from Cremona on 2 June:

about midnight they climbed a ladder and broke a window and, once in the rooms upstairs, broke into my writing-desk, they stole some gold napoleons that I kept for everyday use. Beyond the damage done during the theft, there is the bother of visits from the magistrates, marshals, police, etc., etc.; and you can imagine how angry I am. Will I never be able to have a little peace?!! I am expecting you in Busseto, but I would like you to delay a bit. For about a month I, to my misfortune, have had bricklayers, carpenters, and others like them in my house; they have not finished yet; and you would not know where to find a corner to hide in anyway. So wait a bit and bring your good humour with you, because you will need it a lot here in this frightening solitude. Addio addio. Give my greetings to *Sior Toni* and believe that I am your [G. Verdi].[8]

At the time, Verdi thought the burglars were strangers; later he found that they were in fact his own servants, whom he then dismissed.[9] This letter shows that he was still interested in his Venetian woman friend.

One month after the robbery Verdi's mother died in Vidalenzo. With her were her husband and her brother Giuseppe Uttini, a blacksmith then living in the village of San Nazzaro, north-west of Sant'Agata on the Po. Her death apparently sent Verdi into a kind of emotional shock—he sobbed and raved, perhaps torn by guilt or remorse as well as by sorrow. Muzio, who had by then returned from Brussels and was at Verdi's side, wrote to Ricordi: 'I cannot describe his grief, for it is too great, Peppina is suffering, watching him weep, and I have the sad task of making arrangements for the funeral, priests, etc. I had persuaded him to leave and come [to Milan], but he has changed his mind and does not want to leave his house.'[10] Luigia Uttini Verdi is buried at Vidalenzo.[11]

After remaining in seclusion for weeks, Verdi finally welcomed Piave to Sant'Agata as his first guest, after warning him of the inconvenience and clutter he would find.[12] In Strepponi, the librettist, and Muzio, he had beside him those few intimates on whose support he could count. The composer had already begun to get into the routine of country habits that ruled his life for decades to come: the physical labour of gardening; the long rides and tramps in the fields, where he oversaw his workers; hunting; arranging for brick-laying and stone-setting; supervision of the horses and the once-contested chicken-yard; the safe delivery of calves; the sale of livestock; tree-planting, the care of fruit and vine; irrigation and water control; the rental of fields and farm tenant houses; and the frequent trips to market in Cortemaggiore, Cremona, and other towns nearby. Gradually life at Sant'Agata made him well and strong.

Verdi was also following the fortunes of *Rigoletto* that summer and was considering *Il trovatore*, about which he had written to Cammarano earlier that year. Muzio and Piave had been together in Bergamo, overseeing the production of *Rigoletto* there in the important September fair season, where Muzio was engaged to conduct. Surprisingly the opera failed, where Verdi had often enjoyed some notable successes. Verdi said he did not care, Muzio reported. He had expected it. But another failure, this time in Rome, drew from Verdi an angry letter to his publisher:

So *Rigoletto* went to the devil in Rome too! With the changes and mutilations that were made [ordered by the censors], any success is impossible. The audience wants things that interest them: writers do everything they can to find them: if the censors take them away, *Rigoletto* is no longer my opera. If the words, the scenes had been different, I would not have written the music of *Rigoletto*. On the Rome poster, it should have said:

> RIGOLETTO
> words and music
> by
> Father ———
> (put the censor's name here).[13]

In spite of the stress of moving and the shock of his mother's death, Verdi went on with his professional life, working on *Il trovatore* and negotiating through Francesco Regli for a contract to compose an opera for Madrid.[14] This engagement did not work out, nor did an offer to write for Venice and the Teatro La Fenice bring him a contract at that time.[15] Instead, Verdi decided to leave Italy and visit Paris. To do this, he had to borrow money. He did not go to Milan himself to ask Ricordi for the loan, but sent Strepponi in his place, armed with a note to the publisher, confirming that she was coming specifically to 'arrange a business matter with you on my behalf'.[16] Earlier that same October he had again arranged for Ricordi to pay a sum of money to Strepponi's former maid Livia Zanobini in Florence, perhaps for Camillino Strepponi's care; certain confidential matters were understood between composer and publisher. Verdi asked for 10,000 francs (500 gold napoleons) and got it, at five per cent interest. Strepponi was evidently the right person for the errand. From Pavia, where she had gone to visit her mother, sister, and brother, she wrote to reassure him: 'Dearest . . . the matter about which you care so much is settled, without severe terms being imposed upon you.'[17] With a final word to 'My Wizard', she also let Verdi know that Ricordi had invited her to visit his villa at Blevio. She returned to Sant'Agata through Piacenza, where Verdi met her, in driving rain, and picked up 11,000 francs (550 gold napoleons) from Ricordi at the mail-coach office. Ten thousand were a loan to cover a mortgage payment.

Together at Sant'Agata, Verdi and Strepponi prepared for the trip to Paris, then left home without fanfare. Even Piave did not know they had gone, for he was planning to send Verdi fresh fish from Venice for Christmas Eve. On 11 December Muzio closed the house for the winter. Paris was a dangerous place, with Louis Napoleon's coup of 2 December barely accomplished and his troops firing on the people, even on the crowded Boulevard des Italiens on the fourth.

Verdi and Strepponi had been in Paris for some weeks when there came a 'cold' and 'stinging' letter from Antonio Barezzi. From Verdi's answer, we learn something of the composer's relations with his father-in-law in that critical period that preceded the move to Sant'Agata. On 21 January 1852 he wrote to his 'Carissimo Suocero'.

Dearest Father-in-Law,

After such a long wait, I did not expect to get from you such a cold letter, in which, if I am not mistaken, there are some very stinging phrases. If this letter were not signed 'Antonio Barezzi', which means my benefactor, I would have answered very sharply, or I would not have answered at all; but since it bears that name, which I will always have a duty to respect, I will try as best I can to convince you that I do not deserve any kind of reproach whatever. To do this, I have to go back over things that have passed, talk about others, about our town, and my letter will become a bit long and boring, but I will try to be as brief as I can.

I do not believe that you, acting alone, would have written me a letter that you know could only make me unhappy; but you live in a town that has the bad habit of often getting mixed up in other people's business, and disapproving of everything that does not conform to its ideas. It is my habit not to get mixed up in others' affairs, unless I am asked, precisely because I demand that no one meddle in mine. From this come the gossip, the complaints, the disapproval. This freedom of action, which is respected even in less civilized countries, is certainly my right to demand, even in my own town. You be the Judge, and be a severe but cool and objective judge: What is bad about my living in isolation? if I think it right not to pay calls on titled people? if I do not share in the festivities and the joys of others? if I administer my lands because I like to do it and it amuses me. I repeat: what is bad about this? In any case, no one is damaged by it.

Having said this, I come to the phrase in your letter: '*I understand perfectly that I am not the man to take care of [important matters], because my time has already run out; but I could still handle little things.*' If you mean by that that I once trusted you with serious things and now I use you for unimportant matters, referring to the letter [to a third party] that I enclosed with the one for you, I cannot find any excuse for my having done this; but anyway, I would do the same for you [and pass the letter on] in similar circumstances. I can only say that this will be a lesson for me in the future. If the phrase is a reproach [to me], because I did not entrust my affairs to you during my absence, let me ask you: How could I ever be so inconsiderate as to entrust such a heavy burden to you, when you never set foot on your own lands, because your shop business is already too much for you to handle? Should I have given Giovannino [Barezzi] the responsibility?— But is it not true that last year, while I was in Venice, I gave him a wide-ranging, written power of attorney, and that he never set foot even once in Sant'Agata? Nor do I reprove him for this. He was perfectly right. He had his own affairs, which are quite important, and because of that, he could not take care of mine.

This has revealed to you my views, my actions, my wishes, my public life—I might say. And since we are now revealing things, I have no difficulty whatever in raising the curtain that hides the mysteries shut behind my four walls, and telling you about my private life. I have nothing to hide. In my house there lives a free, independent lady, a lover—like me—of the solitary life, with means that cover her every need. Neither I nor she owes any explanation for our actions to anyone at all; but on the other hand, who knows what relationship exists between us? What business connections? What ties? What rights I have over her, and she over me? Who knows whether she is or is not my wife? And if she were, who knows what particular motives, what reasons we have for not making that public? Who knows whether it is good or bad? Why could it not also be good? And if it were bad, who has the right to hurl curses at us? But I will say that in my house people owe to her the same respect owed to me, or even greater [respect], and that no one is allowed to fall short in that, for any reason whatever; that really she has every right [to that respect] because of her behaviour, her spirit, and because of the special concern she never fails to show for others.

The point of this long letter is just to say that I demand my freedom of action, because everyone has the right to it, and because my nature rebels against doing as others do; and that you, who are basically so good, so just and have such a good heart, should not let yourself be influenced [by others] and not absorb the ideas of a town that—I have to say this—as far as I am concerned, did not find me worthy enough to be its organist and now complains wrongly against my actions and my own business. That cannot go on; but if it were to continue, I am man enough to stand up for myself. The world is so big, and the loss of 20 or 30 thousand francs will never stop me from finding another patria somewhere else. In this letter there can be nothing offensive to you; but if, by chance, something should offend you because it has not been said, then I swear to you on my honour that I have no intention of giving you any kind of unhappiness. I have always considered you and I consider you my benefactor, and I am honoured by that and I boast of it. Addio, addio! With the usual friendship.[18]

This letter raises some thorny issues. It seems that from September 1849 until 1 May 1851 Strepponi had lived in Palazzo Cavalli without having been seen by the Barezzis, two of whom (at least) she knew. Verdi's letters to Piave show that he did receive Antonio and Giovannino Barezzi there; but it is by no means sure that they met Strepponi during their visits. We wonder, given Verdi's deep-seated anticlericalism and his conflict with the local clergy, whether she was able to go to church in Busseto or had to leave town to attend Mass, make Confession, or take Holy Communion. One of the couple's pets at Sant'Agata was named 'Pretin' (Little Priest) and another 'Prevost' (dialect for 'Provost', a shot at Don Andrea Pettorelli). Such names were taken as an offence against the church. So it is even possible that Strepponi could not practise her faith in Busseto; we have a lot of evidence that she did not practise it at the parish church at Sant'Agata.

The 'mysteries shut behind my four walls' were no mystery to Muzio and the servants. But it is not at all sure that anyone else had actually seen Strepponi in Verdi's house before Piave's and Brenna's visit of late December 1850, when they may or *may not* have seen her. What we know of Barezzi's letter to Verdi of January 1852 and Verdi's answer suggests that Strepponi was virtually an invisible partner in Verdi's enterprises, an invisible companion in his battle for privacy. He clearly took seriously the 'motives' and 'reasons' for *not* letting people know whether they were married or not. Her odd reference to the 'passions, (good and bad) that will keep us from enjoying there [at Sant'Agata]' that peace of mind that would lift her 'anxiety'[19] has been cited in the previous chapter; but even now we do not know what the 'mysteries' were and what kept her and Verdi in a state of 'anxiety'. We ask ourselves what would happen in 'eight or ten years' to liberate them. She cannot have been referring to the eventual deaths of Carlo Verdi or Antonio Barezzi, nor to a husband, had she had one. (In discussions some scholars have suggested that she might have married someone after Adelina was born at the end of 1841.)

As far as Strepponi's children were concerned, the only events that might have taken place 'in eight or ten years' were Camillino's likely entry into some profession or trade; Giuseppa Faustina's coming-of-age, which would take place in February 1860; and Santa's permanent placement with a foster family, which would normally have taken place between 1858 and 1861, before her tenth birthday. Because Strepponi was apparently referring to something that would happen at or near Sant'Agata, she may indeed have been thinking of Santa's placement or 'consegno definitivo'. 'Eight or ten years' from the date of Strepponi's letter to Verdi would have been January 1861 to January 1863. Permanent custody was given to Antonio Zilioli and Brigida Uggeri in April 1866; but under standard procedure Santa should have been placed earlier. With Camillino independent and Giuseppa Faustina and Santa legally assigned to foster-families, there was no chance that the role and burdens of a stepfather would be forced on Verdi. Whatever the problem was, Strepponi felt that it would be with them for about another decade. In the mean time they would have to manage as best they could in an imperfect world.

Paris was a refuge compared to Sant'Agata, particularly for Strepponi. Muzio let Ricordi know how grateful she was for her passport, which the publisher had got for her—a means of escape from the 'hole' (as she called the farm). She and Verdi lived quietly in Paris in a rented apartment at Rue de la Fontaine Saint-Georges 24, as he took care of business with agents and impresarios, having several projects under consideration at that time, among them a French translation of *Macbeth*; a new opera for Venice, as Verdi responded to Gallo's earlier approach to him; and a première for the opening of the new Italian theatre in Vienna. A French production of *Luisa Miller* also claimed some of his time, as did his next opera, *Il trovatore*. He also agreed to write a new work for the Paris Opéra.

While in Paris, he and Strepponi did go to the theatre. The tradition in the Carrara-Verdi family is that the couple attended a performance of Dumas fils's *La Dame aux camélias*, which opened at the Théâtre du Vaudeville in Paris on 2 February 1852 with Eugénie Doche as Marguerite Gautier and Charles Fechter as Armand Duval. Verdi himself was said to have told Filomena Maria Verdi that he began to compose the music for what would later become *La traviata* immediately after seeing the play, without either a scenario or a libretto. She, in turn, passed this information on to her son, who repeated it to his children, the present heirs. The composer had a copy of *La Dame aux camélias* sent to him some time in late summer or early autumn of 1852 and thanked Marie Escudier for sending it.

Strepponi and Verdi left Paris for Sant'Agata in March 1852, taking twelve days of leisurely travel for the trip. They got home on 18 March and were met by Muzio, who was getting ready for their name-day, San Giuseppe, which both celebrated on 19 March. The three of them 'spent the day together in the intimate joy of the family, not disturbed by any unpleasantness', Muzio wrote to Giovanni Ricordi.[20] Later that spring, when Carlo Verdi became ill and seemed in danger of dying, Verdi had to put aside his own business and take care of him. In March he also became involved in a bitter dispute with Ricordi that was later resolved. Verdi, angry and aggressive toward the publisher, accused him of bad faith and of acting legally but not properly in his regard. At issue was a French translation of the libretto of *Luisa Miller* and its eventual sale; but the larger problem was Ricordi's attempt to hold Verdi to agreements, and forcing him to look at signed documents, the commas and full stops of earlier contracts. Muzio was busy correcting the proofs of pieces from *Rigoletto*, which Ricordi was publishing. 'My sad, sad state', Verdi complained, while he was considering committing himself to staging *Stiffelio* in Bologna that autumn.[21] The project, which would have brought him a good fee, interested him, and later it pained him to refuse it. Writing about his problems to Clara Maffei, he said: 'For some time now, troubles have followed one upon the other with a terrifying rapidity. I, who would give anything for a little peace, who do everything to find it, cannot succeed. I run crazily from one place to another, from noisy cities to virtually uninhabited country fields, [but] it is all useless.' He added a sad reflection on the fact that his friendship with Gina Della Somaglia had ended, and said that the fault was his 'or, rather, of fate, which, through strange coincidences, is taking away from me, one by one, all the things that make me happy'.[22]

The Creation and Production of 'Our' *Trovatore*

On 29 March 1851, when Verdi had got *Rigoletto* behind him and was facing the 'dreadful fork in the road' and difficult ethical decisions that had to be resolved, he had been considering *El trovador* for more than a year. His chief concern that spring was that his librettist Cammarano might not be sufficiently enthusiastic about the work. 'Does he like it or not?' Verdi asked De Sanctis, confessing that he was furious at Cammarano for dragging his heels. 'He thinks nothing about time, which is extremely precious to me.'[23] Cammarano's delay was not the only problem, for the composer and the librettist were somewhat at odds over the style of the opera. Cammarano, the highly skilled professional was prudent, while Verdi wanted to press on to something fresh. 'The more novel and free the forms, the better I will compose. Let him do anything he wants: the more daring it is, the better I will like it.'[24]

In writing to Cammarano on 4 April, he outlined in greater detail his hopes for creating something new:

If in operas there were no more cavatinas, no more duets, no more trios, no more choruses, no more finales, and if the whole opera were one single piece, I would find that more reasonable and right. For this reason I tell you that it would be a good thing if, in the beginning of this opera, the chorus could be left out (every opera begins with a chorus); if Leonora's cavatina could be left out; and we begin right off with the Troubadour's song, and make one single act out of the first two acts; for these isolated pieces and the changes of scene . . . make me feel that they are numbers from a concert rather than an opera. If you can do it, *do it*.[25]

The end result speaks for itself. The opera has an early chorus and includes the set pieces that the composer hoped to avoid. Cammarano also feared the censors, as he had when *Rigoletto*, as *Le Roi s'amuse*, had been proposed to him, and had reservations about a convent scene for *Il trovatore* in which Leonora would voluntarily go off with Manrico. That 'the Nun', as she was called, would be swept away by passion, and choose the way of shame, was too dangerous. Verdi agreed to have Leonora unconscious as she was carried away. 'If you do not want the Nun to escape of her own free will, then make the Troubadour (with many followers) carry her off when she faints', he instructed.[26] This was the sort of concession Verdi had to make. Yet Cammarano wanted to cut the scene entirely; Verdi refused, saying that it was too original to be thrown out and that he wanted to extract every possible effect from it. Still, the danger lay in showing the convent itself, the nuns in habits, the praying on-stage, and the invasion of the sacred precinct by two rival bands of conspirators. As the work went on Verdi had to explain the characters' inner motivations to his librettist, telling Cammarano why Azucena let slip to Manrico the hint that he was not her son and why, in the final scene, she did not save herself and Manrico by telling Di Luna in time that Manrico was his own brother. 'Because at the stake her mother had cried out to her "Avenge me"', Verdi said.[27]

BOOK III

The composer's impatience with Cammarano is reflected in his letters. 'It is true that I do not have a noose around my neck (and thus do not have to hurry); nevertheless, I do want to start.'[28] At one point he seemed genuinely worried. 'If you did not like [the subject] why didn't you tell me?' he asked.[29] In April 1851 he threatened to give it up entirely. 'Let us drop *Il trovatore* if you don't like it.'[30]

It was at this point in the development of the opera that the controversy over Strepponi, the move, and the death of Luigia Uttini Verdi took up all his energy. Not until late summer did he again contact Cammarano and begin to think about the opera. 'A lot of terrible misfortunes have kept me from thinking seriously about *Il trovatore*', he wrote on 9 September. 'Now that I am beginning to regain [my] spirits, it is right that I think about my art and my business affairs.'[31] But when the Teatro San Carlo seemed not to be eager for the opera, Verdi warned his collaborator that it would have to be sold in a way that in no way offended his dignity as a man and as an artist.[32] The lessons he had learned earlier at the San Carlo had not been forgotten. Even in a year when, as we have seen, he was short of money and had had to borrow from Ricordi, he would not let any theatre take advantage of him if he could prevent it.

In December 1851 Verdi and Strepponi went to Paris, as we have seen. Two months before leaving he again wrote to Cammarano: 'I beg you with all my soul to finish this *Trovatore* as quickly as you possibly can.'[33] In February 1852 he learned that Cammarano was ill and responded thoughtfully to De Sanctis, saying that he hoped he was better.[35] On that same day he started home. Another interruption came when Carlo Verdi became ill; but when the old man recovered some of the pressure was lifted. He was 'out of danger; the fear that he will die is past', Muzio informed Ricordi on 2 May.[36] One day later Verdi wrote to De Sanctis to try to find out why he had had no news of Cammarano.[37] Believing, though, that it would come, he began to investigate the possibility of giving *Il trovatore* under Jacovacci's aegis in Rome. The impresario, who had originally approached Verdi in November 1851, had learned of the composer's terms some months later. He was willing to meet them. If the censors approved the libretto, and if Verdi would be satisfied with the two prima donnas that the opera company offered, *Il trovatore* could be given at the Teatro Apollo around 15 January 1853.[38]

Meanwhile, though, Cammarano's condition had worsened, though Verdi did not know this. 'I suppose that he is completely recovered,' he had written on 3 May to De Sanctis. 'Ask him to send me the rest of the libretto as quickly as possible; and tell him that when this is finished, if he wants to do another for me, I will be blissfully happy.'[39] De Sanctis, after a delay, did write to Verdi on 24 May, while Cammarano was still alive, but apparently sent no further bulletins. The librettist died on 17 July, unknown to Verdi, who learned of the death from a theatrical paper. The news, he told De Sanctis, came as a complete shock,

a bolt of lightning. . . . It is impossible to describe to you my deep sorrow over this! I read of this death not in a friend's letter but in a stupid theatrical journal!!! You, who loved him as much as I, you will understand all the things that I cannot bear to say to you. Poor Cammarano!!! What a loss!!! How does it happen that you did not get my letter of 19 July? How does it happen that you did not find at the post office a cheque, sent by Ricordi in my name, for our poor friend?[40]

Cammarano had finished Manrico's 'Di quella pira' just eight days before he died. Verdi asked De Sanctis to find another poet to make the usual last-minute changes that would be required for the libretto. '[We must] not change, even in the smallest way, the creation of our poor friend whose memory I, first of all, wish to have respected.'[41] Verdi also asked De Sanctis to locate and return to him his own long scenario for *Re Lear*. When asked to help Cammarano's widow and six orphaned children, Verdi sent the family everything that was owing for the libretto and added a gift of money as well. The libretto was later polished by a young Neapolitan poet, a friend of both Cammarano and De Sanctis, Leone Emanuele Bardare, who 'cannot contain himself for joy at working for Verdi' but was waiting to be paid 'for the time spent on this work of yours, since he set aside other [opera librettos] to do it'.[42] Bardare also worked on the adaptation of *Rigoletto* that was done in December 1857, when it was given as *Clara di Pert* at the Teatro Nuovo in Naples. A teacher and journalist about seven years younger than Verdi, he wrote more than fifteen librettos between 1851 and 1880. His collaboration with Verdi, then, came near the start of his career. It was to the composer's advantage that he was a professional writer, to his disadvantage that Bardare's great gift was for comic opera.[43]

Apart from last-minute changes in the text, and the work of composition, there was the cast to be considered. Once Verdi had thought of Teresa De Giuli-Borsi for the role of Leonora, but now that the opera was to be given in Rome, he weighed Rosina Penco's shortcomings and merits, as De Sanctis outlined them for him. Under Verdi's direction she would be satisfactory, for, although she had some defects, she also had many strong points; she was very attractive, but a demon to deal with. It was absolutely sure that she would come to blows with the other prima donna, the Azucena, the mezzo-soprano Emilia Goggi, a hardy veteran of Lanari's stable who had sung often in secondary theatres with Raffaele Monti. Instead of the tenor Raffaele Mirate, whom Verdi had wanted as Manrico, he accepted Carlo Baucardé. Giovanni Guicciardi, a baritone who had made his début a few years earlier in Reggio Emilia, was the Count Di Luna.

Arranging for his lodgings, Verdi asked for two or three rooms at the Hotel Europa. 'I will be in Rome around 20 December. . . . Never mind whether [the rooms] are on a high floor; but I want *sun*: now, after having been in the country for two or three years, walls *suffocate* me! Sun! Sun! Sun!!!' he told his Roman friend Luccardi.[44] He also wanted a piano in his apartment, so that he could—as he said—write the opera for Venice without wasting a minute. While he was producing *Il trovatore* he would be composing *La traviata*.

He left Sant'Agata with Strepponi, who went with him to Genoa and on to Leghorn, where she took a hotel room as he went on alone by steamer to Civitavecchia and Rome. He began to work on both *Il trovatore* and *La traviata* as soon as he got to the city, but was confined to his rooms by illness. As De Sanctis had predicted, Penco and Goggi began to argue; the soprano and Guicciardi had both sung badly earlier in the season; and disputes arose about where rehearsals would be held, for Verdi, ill, was confined to his hotel. Somewhat irritated with the confusion, he was not over-optimistic about *Il trovatore*. But when it finally had its première on 19 January 1853, it was successful beyond anything he had hoped. At the end of the evening, he was honoured with the presentation of a crown of laurel leaves intertwined with embroidered red ribbons. He brought this trophy home and presented it as a gift to Antonio Barezzi, a tangible symbol of their reconciliation.[45]

On the night of the third performance of *Il trovatore*, Verdi was taken home in the midst of a mob of Romans carrying lighted torches. Beneath the balcony of his suite, a band played music from his operas until the early hours of the morning. To show his appreciation, he announced that he would not leave Rome after the third performance, as he usually did, but would stay on until the fourth *Trovatore*. Then the theatre was decorated as if for royalty, with white banners and flowers. 'Total triumph', Demaldè wrote in his notes at home.[46] Verdi, as always, was careful with words. '*Il trovatore* did not go badly', he wrote somewhat laconically to De

Sanctis.[47] 'It would have been better if the cast had been [better]', he told Clara Maffei. He also told her that people had criticized the opera for being too sad and too gloomy. 'But after all, in life isn't everything death? What else exists?'[48] Yet he had, as he intended, poured melodramatic passion into this work. The public repaid him by clamouring for it, as it was also doing for *Rigoletto*, making it a staple of the repertory. More than nine years later the composer, writing to Arrivabene, remarked on its success. 'When you go to the Indies or the middle of Africa, you will hear *Il trovatore*.'[49]

Strepponi's Letters

Very few letters survive from Strepponi to Verdi; and only a few telegrams and the fragments of two late letters survive from him to her. Hers are valuable when they illuminate the story of Verdi's life. To read a group of them together is to gain special insight into Strepponi's complex character, and the way in which she encouraged Verdi in his work.

When in December 1852 Verdi went to Rome to produce *Il trovatore*, he had originally agreed to take Strepponi with him. She had arranged to have her mail sent there. For whatever reason, she did not go. As we have seen, she and he went as far as Leghorn, where she remained in a hotel, waiting for news. This group of letters was written at that time, when she was recovering from an illness that Verdi's former schoolmate Dr Pietro Frignani had treated earlier. Excerpts from them are given here, beginning with the letter dated 2 January and added to the following day, when it was sent to 'Signor Giuseppe Verdi, Compositore di Musica a Roma'.[50]

Tomorrow I expect news from you, and pray God that it will not fail to come, needing it so much as I do. I hope that you had a better New Year than I did. If our arms and legs lose their flexibility from lack of exercise, then I'm afraid I will have lost the use of my tongue when you get back, having observed virtually the silence of a Trappist since Tuesday! I go out very rarely, because I am bored with dragging myself around the streets, and also Leghorn is not sufficiently big to go out absolutely freely, without being recognized very frequently.

You know that Frezzolini spent two months in this hotel, with a servant from the Piedmont, a French maid, and *Monsieur Polichinelle* [Poggi]. I asked the maid who serves me who was more likeable, Frezzolini or De Giuli; she said that she liked the latter more, which surprised me a lot.—Enough of that; when I get [your] letters from Rome, I will go over to Florence and listen and judge with my own ears, which are not a donkey's ears. [Angelo] Mariani, although he has much better ears than a donkey's, and although he is a million times better and greater musician than I, although I fear that *sex*, emotion, friendship, vanity, and age make him a judge who is sometimes not wholly loyal nor devoted to the laws of Themis [the goddess of justice]; not because of [his] bad faith but because of passion.

I have not gone nor will I go to the Giardinetto [restaurant], because, when I looked carefully at the entrance, I felt it was not right for me to go through the curtains at a time when I have usually finished eating; that is a little too late. This means that some meals will cost more, but it is a necessary sacrifice for me, completely isolated as I now am. I am still content with my little room, but in general the service in this hotel (which must be excellent during the spa season) is now bad [and] the main meal is awful—so much so that I complained about it, and you know that I am not very hard to please in that. But these are trivial matters, all the more because we are talking about [only] a short stay.

You can't imagine how impatiently I am awaiting your return! I have started reading, and I read, read, read until my eyes are red; but I am afraid that sadness and boredom will attack me violently during these days when you have condemned me to a *cell.* You will say '*Spend money and have a good time.*' First of all, I do not like you to tell me '*Have a good time,*' when I don't know where to look for amusement! If I could see you for a quarter of an hour out of every twenty-four, I would be in high spirits, would work, would read, would write, and the time would pass if anything too quickly. As it is . . . but let's drop this argument because I am about to cry!

I bought the print of the Flags, and left my watch to be cleaned because—not knowing the time—I felt like a being *launched into space.* I'll leave room to answer your [letter] which I hope to get tomorrow morning! Addio for this evening.

3 January

My dear Pasticcio,

I have just this moment received your [letter] and I cannot describe my joy! I read the newspaper articles that you sent me. Mr Fougasse [Verdi's French landlord] is a man who does not arouse hatred in me, but instead true seasickness, *nausea.* Vanity, vanity, vanity! Everything under the sun is vanity! You will see one of these days that he comes from a race (of Rabbits!), that he comes down a male line straight from the Montmorencys and the Rohans! Repulsive show-off with his generous sentiments! He acted like a dog in your house, but because you are *the composer Verdi, Chevalier of the Legion of Honour*, he likes people to know that you stayed in that *palazzo . . .* of rags! *Poah*!!

I am very, very pleased that you are lost without me, and I hope you will be so bothered that you will give up your barbarous idea of leaving me alone like a saint from the Thebaid! My dear Wizard, your heart is *an angel's heart*, but your head—as far as language and certain ideas are concerned—has a skull *so thick* that if Gall were alive, he could add certain curious observations to his treatise on *Craniology*. I ask you, just by way of conversation, '*Is it true or is it not true that everybody who meddles or wants to know about other people's business takes it as an article of faith that I am in Rome?*' You will answer '*Of course. Let them think it.*' I start again (just to make conversation) '*What difference then would it make to you if your poor Pasticcio were in a room near your bedroom? Am I not here in this monk's cell, with only a little mouse to talk to?*' (I had forgotten to tell you that my fear of mice has gone, since I have got to know this night-time companion, who comes to eat the breadcrumbs that I drop at mealtime). *Now, being able to stay all, all alone, with nothing going on in the room, instead of being unhappy, I would be very, very happy if I could know that at night when you come back from the theatre, or from talking with someone, before going to bed, you would come, as you do at home, and say to me 'Good night, Pasticcio,' and in the morning, before receiving visitors in your room, 'Good morning, Pasticcio.'* It seems to me that no orator ever found arguments more convincing than mine. Since people believe that I am with you and that you are saying '*Let them think it,*' and I [would not] show myself to confirm or deny that I am there or not there, it seems to me that you could be kinder and give up playing the role of Diogenes, tyrant of Syracuse, because you are certainly too generous to keep on signing further sentences of exile!

On the day after tomorrow, I will go to Florence and if it is possible I will also go to Pisa to hear [the soprano] Piccolomini. Weren't there any letters for me [in Rome], then? I won't make any remarks about my family's silence! When I inherit 500 thousand francs, they'll all start writing me very, very warm letters again! That's the way the world is!

I hope that Penco and Goggi improve. You know that Saint Stephen is a drunken saint and a poor judge [so things go badly on 26 December, his feast day]. Addio, write me a nice letter and hurry and give *our Trovatore*. A kiss on your heart.

Peppina.[51]

On that same day, 3 January, she got another letter form Verdi. She wrote back at once, this time 'Al Sig. Maestro Giuseppe Verdi, Roma'.

Dearest,

I received your second letter and I thank you for thinking of me on the first day of the new year, the eleventh [year] of our relationship! If I didn't send you [holiday greetings] it was because I know such things do not matter to you . . . but you can imagine how much I desire you and will desire you on the first and on every day of every year of the rest of your life! (That means that God will have you close my eyes [in death]!)

Your arm hurts? I hope it is something that will pass; but in any case, stay as much as possible out of the night air and use oil of camphor. I am not well either, and my appetite is starting to fail. My dear Verdi, I confess my weakness to you; but this separation has been more painful for me than so many others. Without you, I am a body without a soul. I am (and I think you are the same) different from so many others who need frequent separations to keep their love alive. I would stay with you for years and years without being bored, or weary. On the contrary, now that we have been together a long time, not separated for a moment, I am ever more sensitive to separation, even though you give me hope that it will be short.

Tomorrow I go to Florence and I pray Heaven [*'God' crossed out*] that I will not have any worries. I will stay there a few days and, if I don't find any troubles, I will be less sad than I am here at Leghorn. I have had second thoughts about the trip to Pisa. It seems inconvenient to stay one night, just to go to the theatre *alone*. You will understand that when I too was an artist, it was a different matter: my name kept me company in a certain way, or I could ask for letters of introduction, etc. etc. Now that—thanks to God—I have disappeared from society, and after so many years that we have lived a solitary, almost primitive life together, my 'I' is like a swimmer in space, when it has to go here or there alone in the inhabited and civilized world. Like me, you can say out loud that you would like your little room at Sant'Agata! Then if you did not have the contract for the opera, we could—either at Sant'Agata or in some other deserted place—enjoy our peaceful life! enjoy our pleasures, so simple and so delightful for us! Sometimes I am afraid that the love of money will reawaken in you and condemn you to yet many more years of work! My dear Wizard, you would make a big mistake! Don't you see? we have lived a great part of our lives and you would be absolutely mad if, instead of enjoying the fruit of your glorious and honoured works in peace, you should sweat to accumulate money and make happy those who—in the sad word *Death*—see the moment when their infamous expectations are realized, in the sinful word *Inheritance*!

We will not have children (since God perhaps is punishing me for my sins in not granting me any legitimate joy before I die!) Well, then, not having any children by me, I hope you will not make me sad by having any by another woman. Now, without children you have a fortune that is more than enough to provide for your needs and even for a little luxury. We love the country, and in the country we spend very little—and have a great deal of pleasure. When I think that at Sant'Agata there are those dear rumps of [the horses] *Solfarin* and *Menafiss* who draw your little carriage so spiritedly and cost so little . . . When I think that I have my Poli-Poli, Pretin, Matt, Prevost, etc. etc. [domestic animals], who look at me with those little eyes full of affection and hunger, that cost so little and amuse me so much—our flowers and a little bit of a garden where we have as good a time as if it were Eden in the Terrestrial Paradise, I ask whether the *City* ever gave us so many pleasures, and if two or three months a year in [an] accursed *city* are not more than enough to make us feverish with desire to get back to the Country.

Don't you feel the same way? Then let me end this chatter, which is, I know, a bit too long. But you would feel sorry for me . . . if you knew what sad life I live during these days! And you haven't yet composed anything [of *La traviata*]? You see, you do not have your poor Pest in a corner of your room, tucked away in an armchair, saying to you '*This is beautiful, Wizard.—This is not. Stop. Play that again. This is original.*' Now without this poor Pest, God is punishing you, making you wait and rack your brain, before opening up the little boxes and letting your magnificent musical ideas out of them.

So Goggi does not want to go to Penco's [house] to rehearse? If I were Penco, I would go to Goggi and say to her, in a superior and slightly teasing way: '*Signora Goggi, I know that you have trouble coming to my house for the rehearsals; so I will come to you, since in this era of progress, the old theatrical customs should not prevail, excepting in a rehearsal of an opera seria by Maestro Gnecco*'! I did not think that Goggi was so mean-spirited. Good evening, *Wizard.* Tomorrow before leaving, I will finish this letter.

4 January

Good morning, Pasticcio! I have just got up, and I do not feel well. Perhaps I will see a doctor in Florence. [Dr] Frignani [in Busseto] did not want to have me bled and I think he was wrong, as he has been so many times. I hope that man won't be the cause of new worries. He makes many serious errors, [and seems unsure of himself]. The proof is in your farm manager and Signor Antonio's wife and so many others. I believe that if he had taken blood, I would be much better, but as it is I will perhaps have to be bled in Florence.

Keep sending your letters to Leghorn, because I will leave the necessary orders here [for forwarding them]. I will leave this afternoon on the fourth trip of the day, to be in Florence this evening. I cannot warn you enough about being careful, *but always* so as not to harm the première of your opera. Apparently Frezzolini with her demands and her whims drove everyone crazy here at the hotel. I'll tell you the details when I see you.[52]

On 12 January, from Florence, she wrote:

Dearest,

I got your few lines here in Florence, and without insulting your (*handwriting*) talent, I had all the trouble in the world reading them. I realize, though, that you wrote to me in a moment of bad humour, and so I don't complain about your very unkind remark addressed to me! [You think] I don't write to you out of neglect?

For reasons of etiquette? Listen, my dear Wizard, excepting for *You*, I have nothing on earth that consoles me. I (and perhaps this is bad) love you above everything else and above all others. No matter how great, how many, and how unrelenting my sorrows are, your love is for me such a good thing that it is enough to give me the courage to bear all the bitter things that torment me. So if some action, word or oversight of mine sometimes makes you unhappy with me, forgive it, thinking of all the sad and unfortunate things that I have in my life!

I stayed in Florence longer than I had expected; but the days are so short, and I get tired so easily when I walk that just to make the *required visits* I have had to take several days. You will say: '*You should have taken the carriage.*' But thinking about it, it seemed to me more convenient not to take a carriage, and not *solely* for reasons of economy, although when one travels it is hard to save money. Think that just to come here to Florence and return to Leghorn, the cost of the passport and the journey, will be more than 6 *monete*, without thinking about the hotel. Even Signor Ronzi, thinking to do me a favour, (understood, of course, to do *you* a favour), brought me the key to a box [at the theatre] and, to my great annoyance, I had to go to *Il profeta, which Frezzolini will perhaps not sing during Carnival*, and I had to spend 12 *paoli*!! Don't ask me anything about *Il profeta* and the performers. I'll keep all my critical-philosophical remarks until you get back. I also went somewhere else, which you are a thousand miles from guessing, but I say again that you will hear the story (though sad and boring) of these days of exile when you get to Leghorn.

[Stefano] Jouhaud [Ricordi's agent], is very kind to me and talks of you with incredible enthusiasm.

I will be in Leghorn on Friday evening and will take a rest after all the tumult of these days. I hope that *Il trovatore* will be staged no later than the fifteenth; in that case, you will be in Leghorn on the nineteenth, if there are boats. On Friday I hope to find your letters, having left orders that nothing be forwarded to Florence after Sunday the tenth. Don't lose any time, and hurry to be near me as soon as you finish business in Rome. Love me as I love you.

Your Peppina.[53]

Verdi evidently wrote to Strepponi that he was having trouble with the music for *La traviata*. Five days later she wrote to him again:

Dearest,

I am really desolate over what you tell me about the opera for Venice. I hope that the devil is not as ugly as you paint him, and that when you get to Leghorn you will have several sections [of the opera] finished in your trunk. Having said that, however, I don't want to refuse to do what you want: for a long time, I have not expected to have wishes!—just fancies! [*non pretendo aver volontà, ma velleità*]. Only this (and I say this frankly to you) I would be very very unhappy if you were to beg off, under any pretence whatever, take me back to Sant'Agata and leave again without me. [But] if this is what you have in mind, all you have to do was say: 'Peppina, this is a sacrifice that I ask of you, out of your affection.' I have made so many sacrifices for someone who has repaid me and repays me with immense ingratitude that I am very, very happy to agree to something that pleases you, for you, who alone in the world has never made me unhappy! Let it be as you wish, then; let's go back to Sant'Agata and may your will be done, so long as I am alive and have the strength to tell you that I love you with all my love!

Now, as I write to you, the wind is blowing from every direction. The boat could not continue its trip because the sea is very rough and it would be dangerous. I hope it will be completely calm on the day you leave. I came back from Florence the other evening, and have not tried to go back, for many reasons, one of which is the expense.

I had hoped that you would have taken care of *Il trovatore* long before this, but I see that you are doubtful even about arriving here on the twenty-fourth. If, though, you do arrive on the twenty-fourth, we can be in Genoa on the twenty-fifth, leave again on the twenty-sixth (if you want to hear [the soprano] Biscottini), and sleep at home in our own bed on the evening of the twenty-seventh. So be quick and leave Rome right away.

If I were selfish, what you tell me about Naples ought to make me advise you to sign the contract. But your health and peace of mind are worth more than all the wonders of Naples, Capri, and Sorrento! So, if I were in your shoes, I would not really commit myself at this time. I would look for a book that I liked, and I would set it to music *without a commitment and in my spare time*! If I were to finish it at a time that would not cheat nor ruin the Paris Opéra, I would then produce it [in Naples] giving them a few months' advance warning. On the other hand, I would not get into a cold sweat, thinking of the problems that the managements of Naples and Paris could create for you. Among the likely options, why would it not be convenient for you to compose for the Teatro Italiano [in Paris]? Write the music, and then you can give the nod to the theatre that is willing to agree to do what you want. Your enemy Meyerbeer (without wanting to do so) teaches you how to do this; and it is a very useful tactic. You are in a better position than he is. *Take advantage of it.*

You wrote to me about all the singers in Rome except Penco. Why? Ivanoff [the tenor], who came to see me, spoke to me pleasantly and very, very respectfully. Rossini is not as happy as he could have been. He thought that he could annihilate his heart by force of will; now his heart is demanding its rights, looking for affection that it cannot find. Sometimes the heart destroys the spirit!

Frezzolini, as I told you, will not make her début until the end of the month. I am afraid that this woman is preparing a sorry future for herself. What a pity! I don't know whether I told you that Lanari left behind an *obscene* will. I'll tell you more when I see you.

BOOK III

I won't write about myself! I am incredibly sad, and Heaven help me if I were to go on like this. In Florence I had things to do, [but had] problems, not fun. But the smoke from the boat on the twenty-fourth will announce the arrival of my Wizard, and with him will come moments of good humour and amusement. Oh! if Sant'Agata were in France, England, America . . . Who on earth, apart from you, my Joy, would ever see me again? Believe me, the loathing that I show toward society in general is much less than that I feel within myself. . . . My dearest Pasticcio, I have spent a mountain of money, without having bought anything beautiful or important for myself. It is true that the trip to Florence (all the more because I hardly ever ate alone) has thrown my accounts off balance; but as you will see from the records, I was very careful; still, the money just flies away. Oh, yes, I never even think about tasting bordeaux or champagne, as I do when I am with you; no, in Leghorn, I have not even tasted a black coffee yet! So if you don't come until the twenty-fourth, I certainly will not have the treasure of Croesus left, and I am sorry about that.

So I won't write to you again and I will await you on the twenty-fourth. For the love of God, do all you can not to delay. A kiss on your heart. Addio, addio.

Peppina.

PS If you are counting on having Bernardo come to Piacenza, wait to let Giovannino [Menta, the farm-manager] know. It is worth waiting until you know the exact day; otherwise, if the man and horses have to have their expenses covered, if you have to send the trunks on Giovannon[e]'s [*sic*] wagon, etc., it is better for you to pick up a covered carriage at Piacenza, which we can also load with our own things. I don't think that the expense will be much greater and we will arrive when no one expects us and can see with our own eyes how much we can trust [the servants], you for your affairs, and I for mine (the bird cages, for example). Do what you want, though, because I am happy, no matter what happens.[54]

He evidently did not take the route she suggested. Instead of going through Genoa and Piacenza, he passed through Bologna on the morning of 27 January, 'in a great hurry'.[55] We do not know whether she was with him or not. He left *Il trovatore* behind him in Rome, continuing to attract big audiences. More than any of his previous works except *Ernani* and *Rigoletto*, it pleased the audiences of his time and survived to become one of the world's perennial favourites.

19

January–March 1853

La traviata

The exhausting trip from Rome took its toll on Verdi, as it had before.
When he got back to Sant'Agata he was plagued with rheumatism in his
right arm, just as he faced the daunting job of finishing *La traviata*,
which—as he had confessed to Strepponi—he had found hard to compose
in Rome. The opera was behind schedule, according to Article 3 of his
original contract with the Teatro La Fenice, which stipulated that he
should be in Venice at the beginning of February 1853, finish the scoring
in time to start rehearsing on the eighth, and get the opera on stage no
later than the last Saturday of the month.[1] He was later given a week's
grace. Also troubled by reports of fiascos and near-fiascos at the theatre,
he was more convinced than ever that the company under contract was not
suited for his new opera.

The project of composing again for Venice had originated with Gallo,
who had asked his friend to give the city its fourth original work.[2] In
January 1852 Marzari had made the first formal proposal from La Fenice,
to which Verdi replied graciously, while warning that he would not sign a
contract until he knew who would sing.[3] He suggested Augusta Albertini,
a dependable, popular artist. Finding that she was not free, the theatre
management then proposed three alternatives: Sofia Cruvelli, Giuseppa
Medori, and Gazzaniga. Verdi, then in Paris, wrote back to Marzari to let
him know that Cruvelli was not available. Medori would be an acceptable
choice, he said, and if she could not be had, he would ask for Barbieri-
Nini, who had already created leading roles in three of his premières. He
rejected Gazzaniga because he had been 'unhappy' with her work in the

past and felt that she had been the chief cause of the failure of *Rigoletto* in Bergamo the year before.[4] Three other candidates were also reviewed: Carolina Alajmo, Carlotta Gruitz, and Fanny Salvini-Donatelli. Finally the choice fell to Alajmo, who was to be cast with Lodovico Graziani, the tenor, and Verdi's old colleague Varesi. But on 19 April the impresario Giovanni Battista Lasina let the directors know that Alajmo was ill.[5] At a hastily called meeting, Marzari and his team decided to invite Salvini-Donatelli, but only if Verdi would accept her. They were clearly afraid of losing the composer and were aware, as they said, that the soprano was not an artist suited to the demands of a great theatre.[6] Marzari admitted that she was no better than mediocre.

Brenna was sent to Sant'Agata in mid-April 1852 to discuss the matter with Verdi. In three days he came away with an agreement that stipulated that Verdi would compose for La Fenice, that his fee would be 8,000 Austrian lire, that the première would be postponed until the first Saturday of March 1853, that Graziani and Varesi would sing, and that 'as for the prima donna Fanny Salvini-Donatelli, engaged for the theatre, Maestro Verdi reserves unto himself the right to decide after [she sings in] her début opera [at La Fenice] whether she shall or shall not be in the opera that he today commits himself of write.'[7] Verdi also asked that the theatre engage the young soprano Maria Giani-De Vivez, who had sung a good Medora in *Il corsaro* at the Teatro Carcano in Milan. No subject for the opera had yet been chosen.

Brenna left Sant'Agata on the morning of 25 April, taking Verdi's letter-agreement back to Venice. Lanari arrived at the villa that same night, hoping to persuade Verdi to compose a new opera for the Teatro Comunale in Bologna, or, at the least, to stage *Stiffelio* there.[8] The composer did neither, although Piave came to Sant'Agata that spring to work on *Stiffelio*. Angry to hear that the opera would be given in Bologna as *Guglielmo Wellingrode*, Verdi gave up the project: 'No one ever said a word to me about *Vellingrood*, and for a very good reason, because that is not my opera,' he wrote to Lanari, denouncing the censored work as 'ridiculous' and 'senseless'.[9] In May 1852 Verdi signed a formal contract with La Fenice. The search for a usable libretto went on through the summer. Buying time, he wrote again to Marzari, asking for a second extension of the deadline for giving the theatre a scenario or first draft sketch. In his letter of 26 July Verdi said that Piave had not yet offered him an 'original' or 'provocative' subject. 'I don't want any of those everyday subjects that one can find by the hundreds.'[10] He also said that he was worried about the censors and about 'the mediocrity of the company' and asked to be allowed to deliver the libretto at the end of September. To Varesi, Verdi confessed that he had no idea what he would write for Venice because neither he nor Piave had found a suitable play. 'It's easy to find commonplace ones, and I can find fifty of them an hour; but it is difficult, very, very difficult, to find one that has all the qualities needed to make an impact, and that is also original and provocative.[11] At one time the French drama *La Juive de Costantine* was under consideration, but it, too, was put aside. Finally Verdi found something he liked— we do not know what it was—and he and Piave set to work at Sant'Agata; but September was already over, the deadline had passed again. Marzari, under pressure from the authorities, asked Verdi to deliver the libretto no later than 15 October and appealed to the librettist for help. Piave's surprising answer reveals that after the libretto chosen for Venice was completely finished, Verdi became excited about yet another subject—*La Dame aux camélias*, as everyone learned later—and that he and Piave finished the rough draft of it in about five days:

You know the landscape of Sant'Agata; and you know that no one stays here just for fun. . . . Farewell to the world! I have to stay here *a long time* (not *eternally*, thank God). When it rains here, I assure you that . . . [we] look in the mirror to see whether we still have human shape or whether we have been turned into toads or frogs! Auf! Be patient! Everything will turn out fine, and we shall have a new masterpiece from this true wizard of modern harmonies.[12]

By the end of October Piave, still at the villa, 'surrounded by water, air, and mud', begged Brenna to do what he could to get the censors' approval of the rough draft that he had sent to Venice earlier. He called the opera *Amore e morte* (Love and Death) and added that Verdi was in love with it. When Varesi heard a description of the plot, he correctly guessed that the opera was taken from 'a novel by Dumas fils called *La Dame aux camélias*, in which the main character is a kept woman or rather a common whore of our own time who died in Paris not very long ago'.[13] From a reference in Varesi's letter to changing the epoch of the opera to 'more than a hundred years in the past' we learn that even at an early date the theatre considered it safer to present the opera as a period piece. In another letter to Brenna Varesi wrote that he had read an Italian translation of the French play, and that he found it monotonous and felt that the role of the heroine was 'very unsuited to Salvini-Donatelli's figure' because she had to portray an 'ideally beautiful' woman who was in the 'flower of youth' and ridden with consumption. Varesi was convinced that Salvini-Donatelli, who was then 38, could not play 'this unhappy prostitute' but said that he did not intend to tell Verdi this.[14]

The Teatro La Fenice opened its 1852–3 season on 26 December with Pacini's *Buondelmonte*, which proved quite successful, even though Varesi had reservations about it. Although Salvini-Donatelli did well enough, someone wrote Verdi more than one letter that 'analysed and demolished not just la Salvini but *Varesi's exhaustion* and Graziani's *marmoreal, monotonous* singing', as Piave reported to the management.[15] The season soon began to falter as the première of Carlo Ercole Bosoni's *La prigioniera* ended in a fiasco and had to be taken off the programme. *Ernani* was chosen as the *opera di ripiego*, but even it did not do well. Verdi was still at home on 7 February, wretchedly unhappy about giving his new work in a seventeenth-century setting and alarmed by reports coming from Venice. He had written to Marzari at the end of January that the situation was so discouraging, especially after *Ernani*, that 'I am forced to announce that I certainly will not give the role of the Traviata to Signora Salvini!' He urged the management to find another prima donna at once and suggested Penco; Virginia Boccabadati, Varesi's sister-in-law; and Marietta Piccolomini, whose qualifications Strepponi had investigated shortly before. He then added a throw-away line that must have struck fear into the hearts of Marzari and his team. 'Penco would be better than the others because she could sing *Il trovatore* if I were not able to come to Venice.'[16] He said that he was still sick with rheumatism in his arm but hoped to be better soon. If he were not able to fulfil his obligations, he would send the necessary medical certificates. He also asked the management to send Piave back to Sant'Agata so they could do further work on the libretto.

Piave was dispatched again to do what Verdi required as the theatre started casting about for a new soprano. Faced with the threat posed by Verdi's possible defection, the house hoped that Piave could handle 'The Bear of Busseto' and bring him in to save the season. On the same day that the librettist got to the country, he wrote to Marzari that he felt Verdi could finish the opera, in spite of his rheumatism, but that the composer had stated again 'firmly' that to do *La traviata* they needed 'an elegant figure, young, who can sing passionately' and that all Piave's efforts to make Verdi change his mind had gone for nothing.[17]

Under the terms of his contract, Verdi had no legal right to ask that a substitute be found for the soprano for his deadline for making such a cast change had passed on 15 January. But he stuck to his conviction that the opera was bound for ruin. While admitting that Marzari was 'legally right', he said that he was 'artistically wrong' because the soprano and the whole company were unworthy of a great theatre. So let it be Salvini and her colleagues, but I declare that if the opera is given, I have no faith whatsoever that it will succeed, and—on the contrary—it will be a complete fiasco.'[18] Piave added that the composer was in an infernal humour because he had no confidence at all in the cast and was also opposed to the production of *Il corsaro*, which he feared, would prove more popular with the audience than the other works of the season. In fact, when *Il corsaro* was given on 12 February it did not do very well, not because of the singers, but because of the opera itself. In the theatrical journal *Teatri, arti, e letteratura*, the critic wrote that Salvini-Donatelli and Giani-De Vivez had come away triumphant but the opera did not hold up.

With Piave back in Venice with part of the opera and with Verdi still at Sant'Agata, the management of La Fenice began to rehearse *La traviata* and, one day later, sent the final draft of the libretto to the censors.[19] Costume sketches were sent for approval on 15 February. Contrary to Verdi's wishes, *La traviata* was set 'in the era of Richelieu'. From Marzari's letter to the police and censors, we learn that Verdi had delayed right down to mid-February before giving up his hope to stage the opera as a contemporary drama (as *Stiffelio* had been staged) and to dress his characters in costumes of his own time.[20] Even with the work under way, things went badly. Some time about 15 February Verdi received an anonymous letter from Venice warning him of inevitable disaster. Reporting the incident to Piave, he said that he had been warned that if he did not find substitutes for the soprano and baritone, he would have a complete fiasco. 'I know. I know. I'll show you the letter.'[21] Even at this late date he was still getting parts of the text from Piave and sending his recommendations back.

The composer got to Venice on 21 February and went to his usual suite at the Europa, where Piave had provided a good piano and a high, wooden reading-stand. He expected to begin orchestrating the same night that he arrived. Piave was in charge of rehearsals. Over the years Verdi had gathered a circle of good, loyal friends in Venice; and if he had ever needed them, this was the moment. He was fully aware of having chosen a difficult subject for the opera. In a letter to De Sanctis written in January 1853, he said:

BOOK III

In Venice I am doing *La Dame aux camélias*, which will perhaps be called *Traviata*. A subject from our own time. Perhaps someone else would not have done it because of the costumes, the period, and a thousand other awkward reservations. I am doing it with immense pleasure. Everyone protested when I put a hunchback on-stage. Well, I was happy to compose *Rigoletto*. The same thing with *Macbeth*, and so on.[22]

In the same letter he had also described his perennial search for 'new, great, beautiful' subjects that were unusual, and 'daring in the extreme with new forms'.[23] Having gone right out to the edge with *La traviata*, he faced the consequences. As he later said himself, a company can do *Rigoletto* with average singers, but for *La traviata* the artists have to match the characters. He was also fully aware that *Ernani* had turned out badly that season. The critic Tommaso Locatelli had written that Verdi was a great cook but that the salt and pepper were missing in the 'warmed-up' *Ernani*, which was not as good as he had remembered it.[24] One curious aspect of the première of *La traviata* was the fact that *La Dame aux camélias* was playing in an Italian translation at the Teatro Apollo in Campo San Luca, just a few minutes walk from La Fenice. This offered the theatre-going audience in Venice a rare choice between these two versions of Dumas's play.

Verdi directed his rehearsals as required, but he was far from happy. At the dress rehearsal he criticized the singers to their faces, letting the management know that even at that late date he was dissatisfied. With a cast he did not want, and with scenery and costumes that the theatre poster described as being from the epoch of Louis XIV, Verdi produced *La traviata* on 6 March. From all accounts, the singers—apart from Salvini-Donatelli, who sang very well—failed to understand the spirit of the opera. Varesi seemed dissatisfied with his role, which may have seemed unimportant compared to Macbeth and Rigoletto, which had been written for him. He said that he could not understand why the composer 'did not know how to use the gifts of the artists at his disposition.'[25] Graziani was ill and in bad voice. Only Salvini-Donatelli came close to satisfying Verdi's demands, and she only vocally, for, as Varesi had predicted, her age and appearance made it difficult for her to be the Violetta that Verdi wanted. One strong element in the production was Giorgio Mares, who directed the orchestra of La Fenice and had seen Verdi through tempestuous times nine years before, with *Ernani*. As *La traviata* began, the Prelude was so brilliantly played that the audience broke out in applause almost before the first notes had died away. Verdi was called out for bows. Although Graziani was somewhat hoarse, the brindisi got a round of applause and Verdi was brought forward again, as he also was after the love duet. Salvini-Donatelli sang Violetta's great aria and cabaletta marvellously and was praised by the critic Locatelli as 'a miracle'.[26] Other ovations were offered throughout the evening, during which the soprano distinguished herself among her company. But from the beginning of the second act, the première took a turn for the worse. At one point there was some laughter from the audience. Verdi's close friend and supporter Dr Cesare Vigna, a distinguished physician and alienist who was then the director of the city's mental hospital at San Servolo and became one of Italy's authorities on humane care of mental patients, was also a music critic. Writing for Ricordi's *Gazzetta musicale di Milano*, Vigna said that the poor quality of the performance kept the audience from understanding the true spirit of Verdi's work.[27] The first edition of the score of *La traviata* is dedicated to him.

Verdi was justifiably angry over the outcome. When he reached his hotel, he began to write to friends, notifying them that *La traviata* had failed.

To Muzio: '*La traviata*, last night, fiasco. Is it my fault or the singers'? Time will tell.'[28]

To Ricordi: 'I am sorry to have to give you a piece of sad news, but I cannot hide the truth from you. *La traviata* was a fiasco. Let's not ask about the causes. This is the story.'[29]

To his Roman friend Vincenzo Luccardi: 'I did not write to you after the first performance of *La traviata*: I am writing after the second. It was a *fiasco*! An absolute fiasco! I don't know who is to blame: it's better not to talk about it. I won't say anything about the music, and allow me to say nothing about the singers.'[30]

To De Sanctis: '*La traviata* was a fiasco; it is useless to ask why; it is a fiasco and that is that.'[31]

Finally, to Angelo Mariani, then the conductor at the Teatro Carlo Felice in Genoa:

La traviata was an immense fiasco, and worse, people laughed. Still, what do you expect? I am not upset over it. I'm wrong or they are wrong. As for myself, I believe that the last word on *La traviata* was not said last night. They will see it again, and we shall see! Anyway, dear Mariani, mark down the fact that it was a fiasco.[32]

The conductor wrote back to offer to save '*Il traviatissimo*' by producing it in Genoa himself in a performance that would redeem the 'Lost Woman'; but Verdi, as we shall see, chose another Venetian theatre for the task.

The composer started home, leaving Piave in charge of the ongoing performances, which were certainly not a failure, although the controversy continued. Salvini-Donatelli carried on with her role, having been praised by Locatelli (in a review that ran in parallel columns with the serialized *Uncle Tom's Cabin* in the local paper). The critic said that the soprano had ravished the audience, which deluged her with applause and delivered 'the most beautiful and most spirited melodies that have been heard in a long time. Everything not sung by her went badly.' But in spite of all that weighed against it, *La traviata* ran for nine nights. After the third performance Locatelli reported that the work was getting a steadily warmer reception. It even did modestly well at the box-office. Only the opening night of *Buondelmonte* brought in more money, as, indeed, the first evening of the season would always do. Although its disgruntled composer denounced *La traviata* as a complete fiasco, it could boast an average revenue that was more than double the average evening return for either *Ernani* or *Il corsaro*. While *La traviata* went on earning at the Teatro La Fenice, all musical Italy was reading Verdi's sentence, pronounced on it in Ricordi's *Gazzetta musicale*: 'Fiasco'.

Strepponi at Home

While in Venice, Verdi had received letters from Strepponi, who kept him up to date on life at Sant'Agata. Ill, left alone with the servants, and in the care of Dr Frignani whom she mistrusted, she was miserable; but even in this difficult moment, her spirit and humour often shine through in her letters.

My poor Wizard, how painful it has been for me to see you these recent days, working like a Negro and having the additional [burden] of seeing me ill—you cannot imagine! But I will be well again and I will try with my good humour to make you forget the troubles of the past. You are so good to your Long-Term Tenant, and I am desolate that I cannot repay you for everything you do for me! I don't even dare to speak of your generous and sensitive . . . but you see that it is not [out of] ingratitude, you feel that, you understand it! More than once I have swallowed, coughed, and so on, trying to begin my speech . . . but emotion chokes off the words in my throat; I begin to cry, my head begins to spin, and so on, and I have to give up saying those sincere phrases that I would want to say to you, and that you have every right to expect [to hear].

On the other hand, knowing your exquisite sensibility, I am sure that you would be just as confused and moved as I am! Poor Wizard! and to think that your exalted soul came to live in the body of a Bussetan! You'd need the faith of St Thomas to believe it. I still believe that some swap took place when you were an infant and that you come from some sweet error committed by two unhappy and superior beings. Write when you can; hurry up with the rehearsals; and come back to your hut.

Our youth is past; nevertheless, we are the whole world to each other! and we watch all the human puppets with pity as they get excited, run, climb, crawl, fight, hide, reappear—all so they can try to get into costume and be seen in the first ranks of the social masquerade party. In all this perpetual hurly-burly, they get to the top of the ladder, surprised that they have not enjoyed anything, that they have nothing honest and unselfish to console them in the last hour of their lives; and searching when it is too late for that peace of mind that seems to me the greatest good on earth, which they have despised all their lives because they have clung to the phantom of vanity.

So long as God leaves us our health, our simple and modest joys and desires, they will make us happy even in old age; our affection and our characters, which are so in tune with each other, will not leave room for those frequent, sharp arguments that diminish love and end up by destroying every illusion! Isn't it true, my dear Pasticcio, that I see life from an uncommon point of view? If you see it that way too, the future can still be beautiful for you and for me.[33]

Strepponi added extremely unkind remarks about one of Barezzi's sons, who had come to the villa at nine one morning, while she was still in bed ill. She had refused to see him but had heard from the servants that he was about to marry and that he had stayed at the house of one of the Cavalli women until four in the morning. She said she did not know whether he had gone away offended, but that he was an 'idiot' of 'a very bad sort'; she was unhappy that he had come at an hour that was improper for a visit to a woman.

Another letter, dated 26 February, brought news that she was better and had been consoled somewhat by letters from Verdi and Piave. She asked the composer to order Piave not to be a panderer, bringing women friends to Verdi, and asked that he stay away from men friends who shared what she called Piave's 'erotic zeal'. She lamented that she was at Sant'Agata alone in the snow, abandoned because that was the wish of 'the only person on earth who can give me orders'. The elder Barezzi had come once to visit her; and she had had letters from Jouhaud, Corticelli, and the Bolognese agent Agostino Marchesi. She showed some faint concern over Verdi's rumoured interest in the soprano Medori but dismissed it as nonsense. Writing about the Paris production of *Luisa Miller* under Roqueplan, she said that she was not surprised to learn that he had not written to Verdi and suggested that he be realistic and stop hoping to hear directly from France. She also offered advice on how Verdi might handle his French affairs and added some unkind remarks about 'the Mummy', Meyerbeer. Muzio's future was a matter of concern because of what Strepponi called his hot-headedness and instability. 'He is very, very honest, but with an extremely heated and excitable character, with an ease and openness that is too quick in making remarks, offering pronouncements, and giving unsolicited advice.'[34] She added the opinion that he offended people and kept them from helping him and that only those who knew him well realized how good, honest, decent, and loyal he was. 'Addio, I kiss you on your angel heart, which I hope will be mine forever; as for the rest of your body, I would not swear to that, not even at this moment when I am writing to you, particularly as you have Piave nearby. Addio addio.'[35] News of the house included the reassurance that the maid Tognetta [Antonia Beltrami] and the farm-manager Giovannino Menta had things in hand. She was keeping up with activity in Venice through the pages of *Il pirata*, a theatrical journal, and offered her view that Brenna was an untrustworthy gossip who was leaking information on the production to journalists.

By 2 March she was ill again and had had bad news from Florence. In a separate one-page note she revealed how troubled and lonely she was. It was snowing; Verdi had not written; Muzio had failed to send her the newspapers; she was weak. On a passionate note, concluded: 'Come soon. I desire you as I desire God. A kiss on your heart.'[36]

On 4 March she wrote another note to Verdi. 'Tell me why you have not written me, and tell me what Emanuele wrote in answer to [your letter]. I confess to you that I am very surprised at his neglect in not following up on something you recommended. . . . I hope to get a letter from you. I need some consolation and instead I have nothing but unhappy forebodings.'[37] Some of her worry was caused by the flood of theatrical gossip about Verdi that had appeared in recent issues of the periodical *Il pirata*. If she had had only one letter from Verdi, she probably did not know whether Salvini was really singing or whether Penco had been sent for. None of the Barezzis had heard from the composer either.

Although we do not know what Verdi told Strepponi about *La traviata*, we do have the version of events he gave to Demaldè.

The first act was wildly successful; the other two acts went badly, however, when Salvini was *not* singing, because neither of the other two singers was in good voice. The fact is that [Verdi], *certain that the opera would not go well . . .* protested against two of the principal singers [Salvini and Varesi] to the management; but the management insisted that the opera be produced with them. Again, at the dress rehearsal, the Maestro protested to the management, in the presence of the singers themselves; but in spite of everything the production had to go on. To blame for this half-success: *the management.*[38]

By publishing his letter to Muzio in Ricordi's *Gazzetta musicale di Milano*, Verdi had actually done some harm to his singers' reputations. Varesi wished to refute Verdi's charge that the singers had shipwrecked *La traviata*. To defend himself he offered proof of the public's enthusiasm for him in both *La traviata* and *Il corsaro*, which was substituted for the third performance of the new opera when Graziani fell ill. In *Il corsaro*, he said, he had enjoyed a notable triumph; Verdi had been unwise and inappropriate in failing to make the best use of the artists in the company. Only the first act was right for Salvini; Graziani had little or nothing of merit in his part. The baritone described the third performance, which had been a benefit for charity. It had had a poor house, with some applause for the brindisi and much for Salvini in the cavatina, which got two curtain calls. The soprano–baritone duet had got some applause; Verdi had taken two bows after the second-act finale; in the last act, no applause but a curtain-call for Verdi because the audience knew that he was leaving Venice the next day. Varesi feared being blamed for the failure.[39] According to the baritone's report, the optimism generated by the good response to the second performance would have had to be laid aside on the third night. But one of the critics, at least, hoped for a better future for the work. The Venetian critic Locatelli analysed the opera in articles in the *Gazzetta* on 7 and 12 March, concluding that *La traviata* would triumph in the end. Giovanni Ricordi, who died on 15 March, did not live to see *La traviata* vindicated.

The Redemption of *La traviata*

One year later on 8 May 1854 Locatelli reported on the opera's complete vindication in an article entitled 'Reparations'; for it was not until that year that *La traviata* was produced satisfactorily. Then, while Verdi was in Paris and Piave was in charge of the performances, it was presented by Gallo at the Teatro San Benedetto in Venice, a theatre with a long record of producing Verdi's operas.[40] Although it was not a 'Verdi house', for it offered Donizetti, Bellini, Ricci, and such local composers as Buzzolla, it had given ample proof of its loyalty to Verdi. Gallo's and Piave's love for the composer helped to further his cause there.

On 18 March 1854 Ricordi wrote to Verdi, who was then in Paris, to confirm the company: the soprano Maria Spezia; the tenor Francesco Landi, whom the management of La Fenice had refused to include in the original cast; and the baritone Coletti, one of Verdi's most trusted singers. The conductor was Carlo Ercole Bosoni, whom Verdi knew. Gallo promised many serious rehearsals, just 'as M. Verdi wants them'.[41] Verdi made a number of changes in the score, perhaps drawing lessons from the first production. Muzio helped with these and completed 'the entire edition' of *La traviata*.[42] Reassuring Verdi about Spezia, Ricordi wrote that she had sung *Rigoletto*, *Nabucco*, *I Lombardi*, and *I due Foscari*, and that she was not a mezzo-soprano, as Verdi had heard.[43] Before the première, Piave reported to Tito Ricordi:

I have overseen four great rehearsals of *La traviata* and this evening we will have the general rehearsal, more as a formality than because we need it. I have the satisfaction of telling you that Spezia is made for this opera, and that this opera seems made for Spezia; and that if nothing else happens, and the lungs of this excellent young woman do not give out, she will perform our opera as no one else on earth could ever dream of doing it. In this opera, she is a woman different from those in all the other [works], and [in] her very pallor, her exhaustion, and her entire person, everything in her comes together to make her the true incarnation of the idea of Dumas, of Verdi, and also of myself.[44]

While Gallo was in rehearsal, Verdi was kept informed of events in Venice, thanks to Vigna, Gallo himself, Piave, Coletti, and Ricordi. The enormously successful first performance took place on 6 May. News of it was sent to Verdi by Ricordi, who wrote to send the best possible news:

In a word, I have to tell you again that there was never a success in Venice like that of *La traviata*, not even in the time of your *Ernani*. Gallo tells me that on the third night there was an uproar of indescribable applause, and that the [last] act was even more effective than on the other two nights, if that is possible, and that even he (Gallo) had to take a curtain-call in the midst of all that applause from the audience—a novelty, but that is what really happened. And this gives me all the more joy, because this means not only that your fears will be allayed, but the news of the immense success will be all the more welcome to you.[45]

'Then it was a *fiasco*; now it is creating an *uproar!*' Verdi exulted, writing to De Sanctis.[46]

From that moment on, *La traviata* joined *Rigoletto* and *Il trovatore* in the permanent repertory. When the opera reached Milan, finally, at the Teatro Cannobiana in September 1856, it was again given with Louis XIV settings, as at the Teatro San Benedetto. The men in the cast wore long, curled wigs and scarlet and blue silks, gold brocades, white lace collars, white silk stockings, knee-length balloon breeches, and buckled, tasselled shoes. The first performance of the opera in contemporary dress was not given until 1906, in Milan, with Rosina Storchio, the first Madama Butterfly, as Violetta. By then, of course, 'contemporary' was the wrong word. But even then critics remarked on the novelty of seeing it in something other than the style of Louis XIV, as they always had. In southern Italy, it was given in Louis XIV settings as late as 1917.

Returning to Sant'Agata after the third performance of *La traviata*, Verdi, who was in a very bad humour, found Strepponi still ill. At the end of a cold, snowy winter, the weather was still 'atrocious', he wrote to Piave on 27 March.[47] Strepponi, adding a letter of her own, thanked the librettist for the gift he had sent her—'a very, very pretty little purse'— and referred for the first time to a new project, a proposed biography of Verdi, promised to the publisher Luzzati, who wished to add it to his series of books on famous people. An acquaintance of Piave and a member of a distinguished family of Venetian Jews that included Luigi Luzzati, later the prime minister of Italy,[48] the publisher initially had Verdi's approval, though it was nothing more than 'half-hearted' agreement as Vigna said.[49] Strepponi agreed to take care of getting the 'few biographical notes' to Piave.[50] But in an April letter to the librettist, Verdi said that 'just yesterday evening I read my biography to Peppina';[51] this sounds as if she had not had a hand in it after all. 'She had reservations about it, . . . but Luzzati will include whatever he thinks right. Besides, it is absolutely true. My only wish is that no one leave out the praises that are owed to my father-in-law and the attacks on these pricks of priests, who did not want me to be maestro here'.[52] He also asked for news of Gallo and his productions, of La Fenice and its season, the name of the new impresario, and the date on which Marzari would be replaced by a new director. The fact that Verdi says he read his biography to Strepponi strongly suggests that these 'Cenni Biografici', bearing the same name as Demaldè's manuscript biography, were written by Demaldè and Verdi together. On 17 April Verdi wrote of 'the biographical notes that the *Pasticcio-Livello* [Strepponi] did' and gave Piave and Luzzati the job of rewriting them, of setting them right.[53] He also asked Piave's advice on placing a Muzio opera, set to a Piave libretto, at La Fenice. He offered to write Marzari about it, but wanted Piave to test the waters first.

The relationship with Luzzati went from fair to bad to worse, when Luzzati wanted to make changes in the manuscript that had been sent to him. Angrily, Verdi wrote to Piave, complaining.

You know that I was not looking for biographies; you know that it was a dreadful bother for me; and, finally, you know that I don't give a shit [*cazzo*] for these kinds of honours. Maybe Signor Luzzati thinks that I am happy, [maybe he] believes that he has opened the gates of paradise for me (and I don't give a shit!!) and he writes to me in a high flown style, expressing astonishment. Asking me to tell him the name of my mother's family, he says 'I ask you to send your letter directly to me, as I am in direct communication with Italy's most famous people, whose portraits and biographies I am publishing without one [of them] using intermediaries.' What difference does it make if he is in direct correspondence with celebrated people? . . . Does he perhaps mean to say that if celebrated people write to him, I, who am just a poor devil, ought to write to him, beg him for favours, thank him, and even kiss his hand? Famous people do as they wish and rightly so: I, poor devil, will make a mistake, but I also do as I wish. As for intermediaries, who asked for them? I, or he? My mother's name was Luisa [*sic*] Uttini. But if Signor Luzzati wants to give me a marvellous gift, stripping me of the honour of including me among those illustrious biographies, I would even be willing to reimburse him for the few expenses that he will have incurred because of me. You tell him just this, and I will also be grateful to you.[54]

When the matter was not resolved, he also wrote to Vigna, asking him to approach the publisher, who by the beginning of September was claiming that Verdi had authorized the biography. Vigna cautioned Luzzati, saying that if he published what Verdi did not want in print, it would cost him his reputation.[55] This, too, was reported to Verdi in one of Vigna's letters.

Answering Vigna, Verdi exploded. Luzzati had asked for damages, which Verdi denounced as 'indecent' and 'greedy'.

So he throws himself on my honesty, to compensate him for damages! So I should perhaps thank him and be obligated to him!! For God's sake, this is too much, too much. Dear Vigna, forgive me for all this inconvenience, and let's not say anything more about that Jew. Let him do what he wants, I don't care. . . . A little bit of the blame rests with our dear Piave, who arranged for me to meet this delightful acquaintance, and then was not able to act promptly at the beginning and get the biography back when I wrote to him; it must be more than two months ago.[56]

The matter was not resolved at once. As late as 1857 Verdi was appealing to Vigna to approach Luzzati, who still had the manuscript and was editing it himself.

Praise? And who is looking for praise? I defy [everyone] to find one single person in the entire world who can say that I ever sought one word of praise. If I wished to do so, I would live in the great capitals of the world, in the great societies, I would have accepted commissions and high-level offers that were proposed to me. Instead, look: I live in the country, or rather in a deserted place where you almost never see a living soul. And I am looking for praise? Oh, for God's sake, that is strange and stupid!! I never asked to be among Signor Luzzati's Elected Ones; he asked me first, and used Piave as an intermediary, and was desperately insistent, as Piave says himself. Signor Luzzati does not know me either as a man or a composer. If he knew me, he would be convinced that I have little desire to be guided by him into the temple of immortality. The conclusion of all this is that I wish, and I authorize you, to do everything possible to get my biography back from the printers, [and I am] willing to pay whatever expenses have been incurred. With this letter, you will also find the [proof], which I have not read, not even [the one done by] Signor Luzzati with his *variations* and *corrections*, etc. Just in case Signor Luzzati should not wish to give up the idea of printing this Biography, tell me whether I can stop him in some way.[57]

Nothing more is heard of this project. Demaldè obviously went forward with his own manuscript, adding information on Verdi's triumphs that can only have come from the composer himself.

As a late spring came to Sant'Agata, the composer turned to new projects and returned to old ones, such as the *Re Lear* libretto, which he had entrusted to Cammarano; the imminent production of *Il trovatore* at La Fenice; and Muzio's second attempt to win the post of maestro di musica in Busseto. To Piave, Verdi sent an answer to the request of the soprano Barbieri-Nini, who wanted him to make changes in Leonora's music.

Give my regards to Barbieri, and tell her that I believe that the cavatina of *Trovatore* is good, and because of that I cannot and must not change it. It would be suicide! If I can express my own opinion: why is Barbieri singing that role, if it does not suit her? And, if she wishes to do *Trovatore*, there is another role, that of the Gypsy. Put tradition aside: they say it is a secondary role: No, truly: it is a leading role—even the very most important role, more beautiful, more dramatic, more original than the other one [Leonora]. If I were a prima donna (Fine thing!) I would always want to sing the role of the Gypsy in *Trovatore*.[58]

He added an invitation to Piave to come to Sant'Agata and play at *bocce* (lawn bowling) with him.

You know that an ugly room is always here: I make it a habit of not inviting anyone because I don't have a [suitable] house and servants that make it possible: also I love my freedom to run here and there, things that I could not do if I had guests: but you can always come whenever you like, because even if we were not at Sant'Agata, you can always say 'Tognetta, two sheets on the bed and dinner.' Amen![59]

His other closest friend was Muzio, who had written two operas, *Giovanna la Pazza* and *Claudia*. Both had been produced. The latter, written to Carcano's libretto, was given at the Teatro Re in Milan in February 1852. Muzio was working on a third opera, *La sorrentina*, which kept him at his table during much of the winter of 1853–4. Verdi was ready with moral support at this time, as we will see.

The composer also supported a local initiative: an appeal by the people of Busseto to the government in Parma to allow the return of instrumental music in the town's churches. That effort did bear fruit: in 1852, the Società Filarmonica was again allowed to play for religious services. Barezzi, who was put in charge, wished to resign, giving the post to Muzio, who could then stay at home, where he could be the greatest possible help to Verdi. Matters like this and the farm claimed Verdi's time as spring was about to give way to summer.

March 1853–December 1855

Re Lear

At Sant'Agata Verdi was engaged every day in overseeing his capital investment of land, buildings, livestock, and crops and dealing with his tenants. As his agricultural enterprise expanded, he bought new properties and had to hire men from other parishes to help him run it. At the outset, and for many years to come, the one-armed Giovannino Menta was Verdi's lieutenant.[1] The fields had to be worked, the seed had to be drilled. The composer experimented with breeding cattle and horses and was said to be a hard trader; he tried new strains of grapes, wheat, and corn, while establishing his slaughterhouse, from which he eventually began to sell pork products on the market. From the start he required daily or weekly reports from his farm managers, who could proceed only when he had signed them. When he was at Sant'Agata, Verdi often compiled these reports himself and asked his farm-managers to check them. The landscape garden that still surrounds the house became one of his favourite projects soon after he moved to Sant'Agata, leading him to initiate long exchanges of letters and money with nurserymen in Milan and Genoa. From the farmhouse and the stables to the back, one could see as far as the next parishes, Villanova and San Martino in Olza. It is a family tradition that Verdi marked his career by planting selected trees: a sycamore for *Rigoletto*, an oak for *Il trovatore*, and a weeping willow for *La traviata*. As the garden expanded, he became interested in more exotic strains of trees and flowers; but he never lost interest in the basics of his estate administration: the crops, the rents, and his profits. Whatever else it did, the country gave Verdi fresh energy and set new blood running in his veins; his health seemed to improve regularly from year to year. Again thinking of *Re Lear*, the project he had begun with Cammarano, Verdi asked De Sanctis to get from the librettist's widow the scenario (in Strepponi's hand) that had not been returned to him after Cammarano's death. He then turned to Antonio Somma, a poet and journalist from Udine who had first met the Strepponis in Trieste, where he had been one of the directors of the Teatro Grande. An editor of *La favilla*, he had already declared himself a supporter of Verdi and, after moving to Venice in 1848, became a member of the composer's circle there. In 1847 he had sent Verdi a sketch for a libretto called *Usca*, which had been rejected. In the spring of 1853, soon after the première of *La traviata*, he wrote again, proposing a libretto called *Sordello*, which Verdi also refused. 'To set it to music worthily, or as well as I could, would be impossible,' he said.[2] The two men did collaborate on *Re Lear*, which they had perhaps discussed even while Verdi was still in Venice. A rough sketch or scenario was soon finished. By September, after several exchanges of letters between the two men, Somma wrote that he had finished 'the third and fourth parts of *Lear*', which he sent for Verdi's approval.[3] The composer sent his payment for the work and received from the librettist his reassurance that he would do what the composer wanted. Verdi hoped to finish this opera 'for Italy' even before beginning the new work that he had promised to the Paris Opéra. 'But it was impossible,' he wrote to Somma on 6 February 1854.[4] He set it aside temporarily, promising himself to take up *Re Lear* as soon as he finished the score for Paris. 'Perhaps it is better this way,' he wrote to Somma, 'because I will be able to . . . work on it later with all my energy and make of it—I dare not say something new—but something a bit different from [my other works].' By May 1854 he had decided to 'put it off for another year'.[5] But seven months later, in January 1855, Verdi promised to work on it at once. 'The beginning of March' was the timetable he set. By that time, he hoped, he would be back at Sant'Agata.[6] At that time he considered a production of *Re Lear* at La Fenice, but he found the company of singers unsuited to such a demanding work. April found Verdi raising new objections: the opera was too long; the public would become bored. Thus all the time Verdi was in Paris, he had *Re Lear* in mind. His interest, as we shall see, continued into the later decades of his life.

Wanting to escape from Sant'Agata during the winter of 1853–4, Verdi made plans to take an apartment in Naples with Strepponi. On 9 September he wrote to De Sanctis, asking him about 'a small, comfortable, pretty little apartment in a good position, facing the sea,' the chances of getting one or two servants, and the question of whether he and 'a lady who would come with me' would be bothered by the police. 'If I come to Naples, it will be as Sig. Giuseppe Verdi, and not as M[aestro] Verdi; that means that I don't want to hear operas, subjects for operas, etc.', he wrote.[7] De Sanctis reassured him, saying that whatever Verdi wanted would be done. But the winter sojourn in the south did not materialize, for Verdi found himself forced to go to Paris instead, even though he had written on 17 August to Nestore Roqueplan of the Paris Opéra that he wanted to 'break this contract' between them.[8] He cited his reasons: he had not received the promised scenario from his librettist; he had had no news from the management; and he was completely in the dark about what was happening at the Opéra. In fact, Verdi mistrusted Roqueplan, about whom he heard regularly from the Escudiers, and was extremely unhappy about the Paris staging of *Luisa Miller* in February 1853, which had been produced against his will. Even while that production was being planned, the composer sent off an angry protest.

I am writing to you, not to complain about it, but to declare to you that this is against my every wish and my every desire. Do you want to make my name popular in France? You certainly will not do it with this translation. . . . What is absolutely certain about all this is that in my career, now long, no theatre has ever given me more trouble and more misery than the Opéra. If I could put an end to them once and for all, I would be deliriously happy![9]

Les Vêpres Siciliennes

Problems concerning this commitment dated back as far as 1850, when Roqueplan first asked Verdi to write a new work for the Opéra. Finally the contract was signed on 28 February 1852. It stipulated that Verdi would write a four- or five-act work to a libretto by Scribe alone or by Scribe with one of his collaborators; that the scenario would be sent to Verdi no later than 30 June 1852; and that if he accepted it, the complete libretto would reach him around 31 December that year. He agreed to begin rehearsing during July 1854 and finish in December. Roqueplan agreed to put the Opéra at Verdi's disposal from 15 August 1854 onward and to produce the opera no later than December. Verdi had the right to choose his singers from the company that would then be under contract. Other conditions were added to protect both parties.[10] In July 1852 Verdi let Scribe know that he wanted a subject that would be grand, impassioned, and original, so that he could create an impressive, overwhelming spectacle.

This is the contract Verdi wanted to break, even though Scribe had lived up to it by sending him a scenario in 1852 for a work called *Wlaska*, which the composer rejected.[11] Another drama, *Les Circassiens*, came under consideration in the summer of 1852. When Verdi and Strepponi left for Paris in October 1853, no final decision had yet been made. Just before leaving Italy, he had visits from both Piave and Muzio. From Paris he wrote to Piave that things were not going well. 'Scribe is writing the libretto for me, and unless some unforeseen circumstance does not save me, the opera will have to be written in French. . . . Auf! In the mean time I would have written two or three operas in Italian with more pleasure and greater financial return.'[12] He had brought Strepponi with him and had taken lodgings for them both in an apartment at 4 Rue Richer. Still unmarried, surrounded by people who were curious about whether he was married or not, he lived with Strepponi openly. To use her words, he had given up the role of Diogenes, tryrant of Syracuse and let her accompany him.

Verdi was 'angry and sad' at having to go to Paris.[13] He had just passed his fortieth birthday. His chestnut hair was greying slightly and his beard was still dark. He was famous, but not yet rich. Given his disapproval of the *Luisa Miller* production at the Paris Opéra and of what he called the 'assassination' of *Jérusalem*, he cannot have been happy. In the autumn of 1852 the latter work had been cut to three acts, the crusaders' march suppressed, a vulgar ballet added, and the last scene omitted completely, leaving the opera to end after the famous trio. Yet in a sense writing a work for the Paris Opéra was a rite of passage for Italian composers. Since the days of Louis XIV Paris had been a battleground for French and Italian theatrical figures. On this field, the honour of Italy had been defended frequently, in a country where foreign musicians were not always welcome. What had been risked by composers from Cavalli to Donizetti, Verdi would risk also.

On several occasions during his stay in France, he expressed painful homesickness. 'I am insane to go home,' he wrote, and 'I have a ferocious desire to return to my house.'[14] As we shall see, the work did not go smoothly, as the composition of the new opera stretched over months, and the months became years. At times Verdi sought excuses for breaking his contract and leaving. At the beginning of his stay, he did not have a libretto, for even the subject of the opera had not been decided upon. In

December Scribe corresponded with a librettist and colleague, Charles Duveyrier, about using an old libretto of theirs, *Le Duc d'Albe*, for Verdi.

Verdi is in Paris. I have been asked to provide an opera for him. He has a contract with the management, the piece is to be produced next year, 1854, and forty performances are guaranteed. . . . I had the happy idea of reviving that poor Duke of Alba whom everyone believed to be dead. . . . I suggested this to Verdi, making no secret of the adventures of the deceased. Many of the situations were to his liking; some things weren't. First, the fact that the piece was originally intended for Donizetti, and that we might seem to be dealing with a subject that had been deflowered, cast aside—in a word, with shopsoiled goods.[15]

Eventually *Le Duc d'Albe*, revised, became *Les Vêpres siciliennes*. Verdi's idea of setting the opera in Naples was put aside, in favour of a Sicilian locale. When Verdi protested that the Italian censors would not allow the title *I vespri siciliani*, Scribe altered the work and called it *Giovanna de Guzman*. The new setting was Portugal. As we know from Andrew Porter's study of the Scribe–Verdi correspondence, *Giovanna de Guzman* reached Italy, censored and changed, in 1855.[16] Porter also notes that Cammarano had proposed a *Vespri siciliani* to Verdi in 1848, but Verdi composed *La battaglia di Legnano* instead.

As early as 4 December Verdi was asking De Sanctis to send him details of Sicilian festas.[17] He was irritated about Scribe's foot-dragging: 'You are not ignorant of the fact that I have been in Paris for two months, and for me time is very precious,' he wrote, as he asked the librettist to deliver the two acts he had promised before the end of December.[18] Yet Scribe apparently did not respond; he delivered the complete libretto to Roqueplan's assistant on 31 December. 'I acknowledge that I have received from Mr Scribe, according to the terms for his agreement with Mr Roqueplan, the entire five acts of *Vêpres siciliennes*, with which I am very happy.'[19] Yet, as Porter points out, Verdi cannot have been very happy with it; more than six months passed before he wrote again to Scribe.

In that time he also worked on *Re Lear*. In April he decided to add to his holdings at Sant'Agata. Writing to his notary Ercolano Balestra on 8 April 1854, Verdi noted that the sale of his wheat and wine would have brought in a 'good sum' of money, that he did not need money in France, and that 'Sig.ᵃ Sivelli's property, which adjoins my property on the south' would be a desirable acquisition.[20] If Balestra did not have enough of Verdi's funds on hand after the sale of the crops and wine, Verdi would provide more. 'I only want to execute the contract as quickly as possible because I detest things that drag on.'

All through the period from December until spring Verdi continued to express his doubts about *Les Vêpres siciliennes*. 'Will I set it or not? Who knows? I hope not,' he wrote to De Sanctis. 'You will be astonished to hear that; but you may be sure that it is the pure truth.'[21] After he had begun the actual work of composition, 'I curse. Yes, I curse, and I do not compose because I do not feel well. I do not know what it can be. Is it the cold, the climate, the lack of sunshine?'[22] And to Giuseppina Appiani, one of the two or three friends from Milan with whom he still kept in touch, 'I am composing very slowly, or rather you could say that I am not writing at all. The libretto is there, where it has been all along, in the same place.'[23] And 'When I have finished, I will be glad, very glad. An opera for the Opéra is enough work to kill a bull.'[24] Yet the collaboration with Scribe ought to have proved fruitful, for the poet, with his great expertise in theatre, had a great deal to offer Verdi. He was the most important librettist in Europe then. Born in 1791, and therefore almost as old as Verdi's father, Scribe was a learned man, a scholar of jurisprudence who had early given himself to the theatre. Among his librettos were some of the great works of the time: *Robert le Diable*, *La Muette de Portici*, *Fra Diavolo*, *La Juive*, *Les Huguenots*, *La favorita*, *Le Prophète*, and *L'Étoile du nord*. The inventor of what he considered the 'well-made play', he turned out more than 400 works, ranging from musical sketches, written when Verdi was just 3, to a celebrated tragedy *Adrienne Lecouvreur*, which the Italian composer Cilea later used as the subject for his own opera.[25] He also had his 'libretto factory' of minor writers, whose work he signed or co-signed. The plot of *Les Vêpres siciliennes* Verdi chose from among various subjects offered to him—to use Porter's words—'*faute de mieux*. The opportunities it offers for spectacle are not great, even though there are multiple, contrasting choruses in the Meyerbeer manner.'[26]

From his summer home in Mandres on 7 June 1854, Verdi wrote to Scribe, asking 'a little change' in the second act and added that he would like to discuss the work with Scribe 'one of these days' in Paris.[27] The composer also had reservations about the baritone engaged by the company.[28] The librettist did meet Verdi during that summer, but after their meeting, as he confessed, Verdi worked very little.[29] Although Roqueplan was assured that the opera would be finished by 15 July and that rehearsals would begin on 1 September,[30] as late as the end of

August Verdi was still requesting more changes from Scribe. He had finished the first four acts, he said, but Scribe still had not delivered the 'lines that you promised me for Acts I and II, and also the allegro of Hélène's aria.'[31] A letter of 15 September, written while Verdi was still at Mandres, said 'Thank God, we are almost at the end;' yet the composer asked his librettist to add women to the finale of Act II.[32]

Rehearsals were finally scheduled to begin in October, with a cast that included Sophie Cruvelli, Louis Gueymard, Louis-Henri Obin, and Marc Bonnehée. The strongest and most popular of these artists was Cruvelli, Sophia Crüwell, a gifted German artist, the leading soprano of a spectacular *Ernani* produced in Paris. This was the woman Verdi had once considered for the première of his *Traviata* in Venice. 'With her, I could almost guarantee the success of my opera,' he had written to the Teatro La Fenice as that work was being written.[33] Now in 1854 he had the opportunity to work with her. Although eccentric, Cruvelli was intelligent, handsome, and a fine musician.

Verdi was chagrined when, without notice or warning, Cruvelli, this 'second Malibran', simply disappeared from Paris. On Verdi's birthday, the evening of the first performance of *Les Huguenots*, the soprano failed to come to the theatre. Verdi sent Piave the news. 'La Cruvelli has run off!! Where? The devil knows where. At first the news bothered me a lot; but now I am secretly laughing . . . This disappearance gives me the right to cancel my contract [here] and I did not let the occasion slip by; and I formally demanded [my release].'[34] But the Opéra insisted on keeping him. Even a government minister came to offer the composer 'the moon' if he would stay, proposing a contract for a new three-act opera, performances of *Il trovatore*, of *Rigoletto*—anything to fill the gap until Cruvelli could be traced. With her apartment under lock and key, her possessions sequestered, she was being sought everywhere on the continent. Her flight was looked upon as an insult to the state. While the police searched for her, the English, enjoying the uproar from across the Channel, staged a farce called *Where's Cruvelli*. Meanwhile Verdi said: 'I am headed for Sant'Agata. I will go back to great Busseto (al gran Busseto),' where he would be better off than in France. 'I used to get bored only at the opera; now—see what progress I have made—I am bored by tragedies and comedies too.'[35] He claimed not to understand what went on at the Opéra.

I went to the first performance of this *Étoile du nord*, and I understood little or nothing [of it], while this fine audience understood *everything* and found it all beautiful, sublime, divine!!! And this is the same audience which, after twenty-five or thirty years, has not yet understood *Guglielmo Tell*, and, because of that, gives the opera maimed, mutilated, in three acts instead of five, and with a wretched *mise-en-scène*! And this is the foremost theatre in the world.[36]

When it was rumoured that Verdi's long stay in Paris meant that he was establishing a permanent residence there, he wrote angrily to Clara Maffei:

Put down roots!!! Put down roots? Impossible! Why? To win glory? I don't believe in it. For money? I earn as much, or perhaps more, in Italy. And even if I wanted to do so, I repeat: it would be impossible. I love my lonely place and my sky too much. [At Sant'Agata] I don't tip my hat to anyone, not to counts, nor to marquises, nor to anyone else.[37]

Hating the machinery of the French music business, he said that he would never 'spend the few thousand francs' that he earned on 'publicity, on a claque, and filth like that', even though he thought they were necessary if one were to have a success in Paris.[38] Equally important were appearances at concerts, operas, receptions, soirees, and banquets; but both Verdi and Strepponi detested such social events. On two occasions when Count Baciocchi sent invitations to receptions given by the Emperor in the Tuileries Palace, Verdi asked a friend to deliver his regrets. He and Strepponi rarely went out, preferring to spend their evenings at home in the city or in the villa they rented at Mandres, where, Verdi said, they went to bed at ten, 'the hour when only bats are around'.[39] She was in mourning in the late summer and autumn of 1854 for her brother Davide had died in Locate on 15 August. He was 31, and the health officer and principal physician of the town.

When Verdi realized finally that the Opéra would not release him, he went on with *Les Vêpres siciliennes* while continuing to demand the return of his contract and his score. He and the Opéra were still at an impasse in mid-November, when Cruvelli returned, a month after her disappearance. She had been on the Côte d'Azur with Baron De Vigier, whom she was soon to marry. At that point rehearsals went on; Cruvelli returned to the cast of *Les Huguenots* to be rousingly greeted by a delighted audience. In the backwash of the Cruvelli affair Roqueplan had been dismissed. From then on, Verdi had yet another element to deal with, the new director François-Louis Crosnier, but the inefficiency of the Opéra, which the composer deplored, was unchanged. The long, grinding rehearsals and the orchestra's sluggishness remained the despair of his day-to-day existence. Accustomed to producing a new opera in three, four, or five weeks, he found it hard to accept that an opera already in rehearsal in September could not get on the stage before February—the projected date of the première.

Verdi had written to Roqueplan on 28 October, reviewing the proposals that had been made to him by the Minister of State; he said that he would not accept any of them. He asked the Opéra not to exact any further sacrifices from him and suggested that *Les Vêpres siciliennes* be postponed until the circumstances were more favourable.[40] In November he had to refuse an offer made him by Gennaro Sanguineti, an impresario and agent, to compose a new opera for the opening of a new theatre in Genoa.[41] In the same letter, he asked Sanguineti not to name the theatre after him. His request was honoured: the theatre was called the Teatro Paganini. From Bologna, Mauro Corticelli wrote to ask Verdi to write a new opera for the Teatro Comunale. 'Let's not discuss this now, and go ahead with your business as if I did not exist,' Verdi wrote.[42] He did, however, add a note of hope, saying that he would see later whether it would be a good step to take. He gave Corticelli some sound advice about getting his company of singers together. Cirelli's partner Boracchi wanted Verdi to write for La Scala.

Christmas passed, and on 3 January 1855 Verdi, who had been in Paris fifteen months, sent a long letter to Crosnier, putting forth his 'reflections' on *Les Vêpres siciliennes*. A list of complaints followed: Scribe had not 'taken the trouble' to make the requested changes in the fifth act; his 'sovereign indifference' offended the composer; he never came to rehearsals; further changes might be necessary. Verdi had decided that the plot of the opera was an affront to Italian honour; French dignity, too, was injured; one of the central characters, Giovanni da Procida, had been turned into a 'common conspirator' by Scribe, who had put 'the inevitable dagger' in his hand.

My God! in the history of every people there are virtues and crimes, and we [Italians] are no worse than the others. In any case, I am an Italian above everything else, and no matter what it costs, I will never become the accomplice in an injury done to my native land. I have something else to say about the rehearsals in the foyer. Here and there I hear words, remarks that, if they are not actually wounding, are at the least out of place. I am not accustomed to this, and I shall not be able to tolerate them. Possibly there may be someone who does not find my music good enough for the Grand Opéra; possibly others do not find their roles worthy of their talent; possibly I, for my part, find the performance and the kind of singing different from what I would like! . . . Without perfect agreement, no success is possible. . . . I know well that you will answer me [saying] that the Opéra has already lost time, and has undertaken some expense! but this is not an important matter compared to the year that I have lost here, and during which I would have been able to earn a hundred thousand francs in Italy.[43]

Verdi urged Crosnier to choose the lesser evil—that of cancelling the opera.

Trust, Monsieur, my experience in music: given the condition in which we find ourselves, *a success is very, very difficult!* A half-way success does not profit anyone. The best thing is to end it. Each of us will try to regain the time we have lost. Try, Monsieur, to arrange these matters quietly, and we will both perhaps have gained something.[44]

Crosnier took what was certainly the wrong tack with Verdi; he would not meet him but instead sent Verdi a letter asking him to come to a rehearsal. On 9 January Verdi let the management know that he would not attend again until the issues raised in his letter had been dealt with.[45] He asked Crosnier to solve the problems or release him from his contract. Some resolution was reached, allowing Verdi to return to rehearsals in mid-January. In March theatrical gossip circulated to the effect that Verdi and Scribe had quarrelled at the Opéra. Verdi denied this in *Europe artiste*.[46] But on 11 March the composer walked out of a rehearsal because the soprano was late, and four days later he left the theatre when Gueymard asked to be allowed to leave to do a personal errand.[47] Berlioz reported in a letter that Verdi 'was also at odds with all the people at the Opéra. He made a terrible scene at the dress rehearsal.' The Italian composer's victory was, Berlioz said, 'a success won at a terrible cost to the composer, at the cost of so many battles, so many worries, and undignified struggles against miserable, wretched people'.[48] Saint-Saëns facetiously suggested that Verdi was only capable of composing operas about wars: 'Why not *La battaglia di Pavia* and *Waterloo*?' Verdi's enemies called him 'Merdi' or 'Shits'.

Finally *Les Vêpres siciliennes* was offered as a gala on 13 June 1855 during the Universal Exhibition in Paris. Many Italians had come to Paris for the exposition and thus formed a contingent at the Opéra. But there was a certain anti-Italian sentiment abroad. 'Why not one of our own? Why not a Frenchman?' one of the newspapers demanded. As Verdi confided to Clara Maffei, he could not predict what would happen on the night of the première: 'the theatre will be filled by people the directors want and by a formidable *claque* (what a satisfaction and what glory for an artist!) . . . but it could even happen that I could enjoy the privilege of being badly received, even on the first night.'[49]

Hector Berlioz wrote of the opera:

Without taking anything away from the worth of *Il trovatore* and of so many other moving scores [by Verdi], one has to agree that in *Vêpres* the penetrating intensity of the melodic expression, the sumptuous variety and wisdom of the instrumentation, the vastness, the poetic sonority of the ensemble pieces, the colourful warmth that shines everywhere, and that passionate but deliberate force . . . that makes up one of the characteristic traits of Verdi's genius, give the entire opera a greatness, a kind of sovereign majesty that is more detectable [here] than in the previous works by this composer.[50]

On 28 June Verdi informed Clara Maffei that the opera was not going 'too badly'. Parisian journalists were 'accommodating or favourable', excepting for the three Italians Fiorentini, Montazio, and Scudo. 'My friends say: "What an injustice! What an infamous world"! But they are wrong: the world is too stupid to be infamous.'[51] He also sent news of the triumph of the actress Adelaide Ristori, who had 'wiped out' the great French tragedienne Rachel. 'The difference is that Ristori has a heart and Rachel has a piece of cork or marble where her heart should be.' Verdi added kind remarks about Bartolini's follower, the Italian sculptor Vincenzo Vela, whose work he had seen in the exposition. From this letter, it is clear that Verdi intended to return home 'within fifteen days'; but various business matters kept him in France for more than six months.

The First Parisian Production of *Il trovatore*

During the autumn and early winter of 1854–5 Verdi, at odds with the Opéra over *les Vêpres siciliennes*, agreed to stage and conduct *Il trovatore* at the Théâtre des Italiens, in spite of the fact that he had a long-standing grudge against its impresario, the Spaniard Torribio Calzado. Writing to De Sanctis at the end of November, he announced that he would 'stage it, against my will' so as to produce his music at the Italiens as he wanted it.[52] He added that he did not believe it was possible to do the opera well in a theatre that had ruined *Luisa Miller*. But, in any case, he wanted to try. Calzado had hired the tenor Lodovico Graziani, who had sung the Duke in *Rigoletto* in Venice in 1852 and Alfredo in the world première of

La traviata there in 1853. Although at least one critic had faulted him as a boring, cold singer, he had sung in many of Verdi's operas and was a hardy professional, as was the contralto engaged for Azucena, Adelaide Borghi-Mamo.

To his delight, *Il trovatore* proved to be a huge success, as Verdi confided to De Sanctis on 20 January 1855: 'Ten consecutive performances (something that never happens) and the theatre was packed, especially on the last four nights. Afterward, they gave *Linda* [*di Chamounix*] on one evening; and yesterday they put *Il trovatore* back on stage again, and it will probably stay there until Pacini's opera is produced.'[53] Later in the year a controversy arose over Tito Ricordi's handling of the libretto and score in negotiations with the management of the Italiens and other theatres. Angrily Verdi claimed that the publisher's drive to earn from his scores led Ricordi to sell them to companies that massacred them and robbed him of his royalties.[54] From Paris in October 1855 he claimed that the Italiens would have given *Il trovatore* again, and badly, had he not been in the city to try to stop it. 'As always, I bear the expense and the annoyance, while the revenue goes to someone else.' Drawing up his bill of particulars and complaining of Ricordi's lack of respect for him and his music, he added that even the editions of his music were sloppily prepared with 'endless mistakes' that could have been prevented. 'Fine words and the worst possible conduct,' he railed. 'To sum up, I have never been thought of as anything but an object, a tool to be used [by you] as long as it works.'[55] Ricordi, attempting to defend himself and his firm, declared that Verdi's indictment was more severe than those prepared by the Royal Prosecutor.

As he attempted to win better terms for himself, other composers, and librettists, Verdi also fought on the authors' rights front in England, where he went twice to prevent pirated editions of his scores from being used in productions of his operas. The threat was real: in August 1855 the English Parliament passed a law stipulating that no foreign composer could claim royalties for his works given on English soil unless his own country had a treaty with England covering such performances. When it was suggested that Verdi give up his citizenship in the Duchy of Parma and become a citizen of France or the Piedmont, countries that had such treaties with England, he refused. 'I want to remain what I am: a peasant from Roncole,' he wrote to Ercolano Balestra. 'I would rather ask my own country to make a treaty with England.'[56] He asked the notary to see what would have to be done in Parma to get a treaty signed.

As we shall shortly see, he was able to profit enormously from having Muzio settled in Paris, where he monitored all of the composer's interests and went as far as he could in assuring authentic interpretations of his works.

In Defence of Muzio

Muzio had had a stroke of very bad luck two years earlier. His new opera, *Claudia*, had its première at the Teatro Carcano in Milan in February 1853, but though it did well enough, the work was performed only once, for an uprising in Lombardy closed the theatres of Milan. Muzio, who had never enjoyed a very large return from the practice of his profession, needed help. Among his supporters the idea was then proposed that he be named the maestro di cappella at the church of San Bartolomeo in Busseto and head of the Busseto Philharmonic Society, thus bringing the two musical entities back under one director, as they had been in Provesi's time. Like a bad comedy, the affair played itself out along standard lines. Just as Verdi had been subjected to trial by public contest, so Muzio was to submit. Because of his established professional rank, Muzio asked that he be allowed time free for his theatrical career. He also asked to be spared the embarrassment of entering a competition, because Verdi himself had declared that he was fully qualified for the position. This was the third time Muzio had considered taking the local post; but this time, with Verdi's backing, it seemed that he must be named. However, the vestry of the church of San Bartolomeo demanded that he give up his theatrical career and submit to what Muzio regarded as a kind of slavery, which would leave him cut off from opera and short of funds. 'I did not have the courage to put my head under that axe,' Muzio told Barezzi. When Muzio was not chosen, Verdi penned a blast to the Bussetan authorities of the Società Filarmonica:

Signori, Many months ago some of you came to me . . . so that I would take an interest in restoring music in Busseto and get a competition for [the post of] maestro established. I accepted with pleasure. . . . There was no maestro, and I begged Emanuele Muzio to enter the competition. He was willing to do this, but after he saw the vestry, he refused, as you will see from the enclosed letter. My mission is ended. . . . In any other place, in any matter relating to music, I would have been able to get what you and I wished: in any other town, I would have had the support of the civil and ecclesiastic authorities: in my own town, it was not possible. Perhaps in other places people have a bit of esteem and respect for my name. That's all right: that is perfectly right, nor am I complaining about it. . . . In some other place, I repeat, I would have succeeded; in Busseto (it is laughable) I could not. There is an old proverb: 'Nemo propheta in patria'!!![57]

Verdi enclosed a copy of Muzio's letter to him. Even though the moment passed, Verdi remained bitter about this defeat.

Returning from Paris to Sant'Agata two years later, in December 1855, he made a special effort to stop in Alessandria, near Genoa, where Muzio was at the end of a successful run of *La traviata*—twenty-seven performances of the opera, all sold out. 'We talked of many things,' Muzio wrote to Ricordi, adding that he would follow Verdi to Sant'Agata in a few days. Verdi would come in person to Piacenza to meet him, Muzio said, and escort him back to the villa. This was the composer's way of proclaiming his loyalty to his friend; but it was also a way of showing scorn for those who had opposed him in Busseto. The little city was a real object of dislike to the composer. Coming and going to the station of Borgo San Donnino, he avoided Busseto by taking a circuitous route around its walls; he also regularly used the stations of Piacenza, Alseno, and Fiorenzuola to avoid it completely. Verdi and Strepponi welcomed Muzio to Sant'Agata, where he spent the holidays. Barezzi, too, was a guest at the year-end festivities. At that time any *rapprochement* between the composer and Busseto's authorities would have been extremely difficult to achieve. Verdi went on helping Muzio, who became solidly established in his profession as a conductor, agent, impresario, and teacher and was fully worthy of all the effort Verdi spent on him. Over decades he spent far more energy on the Signor Maestro's business than he ever spent on his own.

The effort Verdi had devoted to *Les Vêpres siciliennes* quickly began to be repaid in Italy. The Teatro Regio in Turin and the Teatro Ducale in Parma both offered the opera, under the title *Giovanna di Guzman* on the opening nights of their seasons of 1855–6. The Turin cast was headed by Gazzaniga and Fraschini, who sang under the baton of Giulio Cesare Ferrarini. In Parma the opera was sung by the soprano Caterina Goldberg Strossi, Antonio Giuglini, and Francesco Cresci, and conducted by Nicola Di Giovanni. Runs of sixteen nights attested to the opera's popularity. At La Scala a production was planned after the censors lifted their objections to it. Muzio, who attended one performance in Parma, wrote to Ricordi to say that he was quite overwhelmed by the magnificence of the work, which seemed sure to hold the stage. It was given in nine theatres in all in that season.[58]

At the end of 1855 Verdi had a visit from Alberto Mazzucato, the conductor, composer, and teacher who had taken over the reins at La Scala. He, Muzio, and Verdi discussed the critical issue of finding the right soprano for the leading role. Barbieri-Nini was among those under consideration. It was decided to try her in *Lucrezia Borgia* and, if she passed muster, give her the role as another artist was kept in reserve.[59] At the end of Mazzucato's visit Verdi, Strepponi, and Muzio celebrated New Year's Eve quietly at home.

21

January 1856–Summer 1857

Simon Boccanegra and Aroldo

Verdi stayed in Italy for the first seven months of 1856, farming, travelling to Venetia, and working on revisions of *Stiffelio* and *La battaglia di Legnano* in the hope that they could gain a foothold in the permanent repertory. With *Re Lear* still in mind, he continued to correspond with Somma in the spring. Soon after his return from Paris Verdi decided to buy a large new holding, the property called Piantadoro, lying north and east of Sant'Agata. The estate comprised the farms called Casavecchia, Casanuova, Stradello Casanuova, Pecorara, Casello, Canale, Colombarolo, and Palazzina and reached into the present Comunes of Villanova sull'Arda and Polesine, making him one of the major landowners of the region. The price, about 300,000 francs, matched the importance of what Muzio called Verdi's 'magnificent acquisition'.[1] As he developed it, rebuilding its tenant houses and farm buildings and improving the land, it became one of his most precious assets. At the end of his life, he left it in his will to 'my relatives who are descended from the brothers and sisters of my late father Carlo Verdi, and the brothers and sisters of my late mother Luigia Uttini.'[2]

On 9 February Verdi received an important decoration, the title of Cavaliere dell'Ordine di SS. Maurizio e Lazzaro, awarded to him by King Vittorio Emanuele II of the Kingdom of Sardinia. Count Cavour, the Prime Minister, engaged in a struggle with the Catholic Church, had committed himself to bringing the Piedmont (as the kingdom was called) into the European mainstream and into the modern world. His anticlerical statute, providing for the suppression of religious orders held to be parasites on society, also ordained the seizure of their property. In an angry response, Pope Pius IX claimed that nuns, friars, and priests should not be subject to all the laws of the state; that freedom of the press was not reconcilable with 'the Catholic religion in a Catholic state'; and that the State should have little or no control over the Church's provisions relating to lay matters.[3] Such a position was, of course, anathema to Cavour and others of anticlerical persuasion. When Verdi got his decoration, the Parliament in Turin had just passed the suppression and confiscation law. As George Martin pointed out in his biography of Verdi, Cavour's progressive policies helped to convert Republicans of long-standing convictions to the liberal, monarchist position of the Kingdom of Sardinia.[4] To Cavour, the engineer of that policy, Verdi wrote on 11 February, declaring his gratitude to the 'Governo Patrio', and sending his 'sincere and warm expression' of thanks for the honour.[5] His use of the term 'Government of the Country' perhaps reveals for the first time the allegiance that he felt.

In this same month a breach was healed between the composer and Ricordi, who visited Sant'Agata after Muzio urged him to come. Verdi's angry letters of July and October 1855 have already been quoted. There were persistent rumours that Verdi would seek another publisher, a step that would have damaged Ricordi, perhaps even bankrupting the firm. As the visit was planned, Muzio, who certainly took his cues from Verdi, told the publisher what tack to take and what areas of conversation to avoid. Peace was restored, at least temporarily.

Further negotiations with Paris were undertaken, as Crosnier of the Opéra wrote on 27 February proposing *Il trovatore* in French and a new work as well. In his answer to Crosnier's letter which Verdi pinned into his *Copialettere*, the composer described his purchase of Piantadoro:

As soon as I arrived in Italy, it was suggested to me that I buy a [piece of] land under very favourable conditions; I bought it, and signed the contract before a notary about twenty days ago, paying a large part of the agreed price in cash and pledging myself to pay the balance in instalments on given dates. Here I am, then, [saddled] with debts, and for that reason I am obliged to keep my agreements to write an opera for Italy this winter, or for any Italian theatre whatever. Our operas here are shorter [than those written for France. They take less time to write, less time to produce.] The profit one realizes [is] returned at once, and that is what I absolutely must have [to cover] my present business matters.[6]

Verdi did, however, propose other dates to Crosnier and accepted his terms for producing *Il trovatore* in Paris. He also agreed to direct a revival of *Les Vêpres siciliennes*. In an April letter, Verdi suggested September or October 1856 as a possible date for *Il trovatore*.

At the end of March Piave arrived at Sant'Agata to work on *Stiffelio*. The librettist had a hidden agenda as well, having been asked to use his friendship with Verdi to persuade him to write a new work for Venice. A letter from Giovanni Battista Tornielli of La Fenice to Piave said that the theatre would do almost anything to achieve this.[7] Some fourteen months earlier Mocenigo had written to Verdi in Paris with the same request. At that time the composer had declared that he could not sign any contract then, having promised himself that he would never write again to meet a fixed deadline for producing a new work.[8] Less than a month later he had restated his case to Tornielli, saying that the main obstacle was his 'unshakeable determination never to tie myself up again to a set date, neither for composing nor for staging.'[9] In Paris, exhausted by the work on *Les Vêpres siciliennes*, he had said that he was so overwhelmed that he did not know when he would ever compose again. But the management in Venice had not lost hope. Surely now Piave could get him to agree. The assignment was difficult enough, for Verdi was still ill with stomach trouble that he had brought home from Paris. Describing himself to Clara Maffei as 'this poor Bear of Busseto', he said that he was not reading nor writing. 'I go around in the fields from morning till evening and try to cure—in vain, so far—the stomach trouble that *Vespri* left me. Damned, damned operas!'[10]

Piave, who got to the villa on 28 March, stayed until mid-May and, within a few days of his arrival, approached Verdi with the proposal from La Fenice. Again Verdi refused to promise anything that involved specific dates; but he did show some interest in writing a new opera, to be given at the end of the Carnival season in 1857. Most encouraging were the discussions he had with Piave over which singers would be available. Letters flew between Piave and the management of La Fenice throughout April; and on 14 May Brenna set out for Sant'Agata. Piave could reassure Tornielli that the matter would be settled.[11] Having set forth his conditions in a letter of his own on 12 May,[12] Verdi worked with Brenna and Piave on the details of the agreement. The fact that it was signed on 15 May shows that Piave had handled the negotiations well.[13] While they were together at Sant'Agata that spring, Verdi and Piave also finished much of the work of transforming *Stiffelio* into *Aroldo*, hoping that it would not incur the censors' wrath. Verdi was also thinking again about *Re Lear*, which he discussed that year with De Sanctis and other friends.

That summer Verdi took a vacation in Bassano del Grappa and Venice as he recovered from the work on *Aroldo*, which had run longer that he had anticipated. Strepponi went with him to Venetia. They were still not married, but now her handkerchiefs were 'white trimmed with lace' and they bore the initials 'G.V.' embroidered on them,[14] proclaiming that she was Giuseppina Verdi. She had dropped one handkerchief in a gondola! The couple returned to Sant'Agata on 22 July and left nine days later for Paris. They took up their old quarters at 4 Rue Richer, then went to Enghien-les-Bains in September to take the waters, as they had the previous year. The trip to France put Verdi in touch directly with the Paris Opéra, with which he signed a contract on 22 September to produce *Il trovatore* as *Le Trouvère*.[15] Some additional work was done on *Aroldo*, as Verdi corresponded with Piave about the opera itself and the possibility that it might have its première in Rimini, under the banner of the Marzi brothers, Ercole and Luciano, the impresarios who also had the *appalto* at La Fenice. Verdi pursued his lawsuit against the impresario Calzado, whom he tried to enjoin from staging *Rigoletto* and *La traviata* in Paris. He lost; but his lawyer intended to take the suit into the Court of Appeals, where, Verdi was assured, he would win. 'No lost case ever caused so little pain', Verdi informed Piave;[16] but he denounced Calzado as a 'savage' and 'brute' all the same. The action must have cost him something, at a time when his reserves were needed to make payments on Piantadoro. To Balestra, he gave instructions: 'Please be good enough to demand 6,000 francs at the end of October from the sale of the wine, as you know. Giovannino Barezzi will give you the other 6,000 francs at the beginning of November.'[17] Some of the debt payments were already overdue; there were expenses to be paid. Verdi said that he would make up the rest of the amount needed by sending a note from Paris.

The composer's short stay, during which he had hoped—as he said—to play the role of plain Verdi, not Maestro Verdi, had turned into a longer stay and he had been thrust back into the music business, in spite of himself. Briefly, though, in October, he was the honoured guest of the Emperor Napoleon III at Compiègne, uncomfortable and looking to the moment when he could get free. He and Strepponi took a new apartment in Paris, at 20 Rue Neuve des Mathurins, settling in for the autumn. Before leaving for Compiègne, the composer had let Piave know that he would not return to Italy as he had planned. He sent the librettist a section of the *Aroldo* text; asked about the soprano Medori, whom Piave had heard in *Les Huguenots* and *Ernani*; requested a new cabaletta for the tenor; and, in a casual throw-away line, wrote: 'And how is *Simon Boccanegra* going?'[18] Here, for the first time, we learn the name of the new opera for Venice.

Simon Boccanegra

Turning to Antonio Garcia Gutiérrez, as he had for *Il trovatore*, Verdi hit upon the drama *Simon Boccanegra*, then drew up or had drawn up a prose version of it, and sent it to Piave some time before 23 August. Five days later the librettist gave it to the directors of La Fenice for their approval and that of the Venetian police.[19] This text, which is still in the archive of the Teatro La Fenice, bears the title 'SIMON BOCCANEGRA' and the words 'libretto di Francesco Mª Piave per musica del Mº Cav.ʳᵉ Giuseppe Verdi da comporsi espressamente pel Gran Teatro della Fenice nella Stagione di Carnovale e Quadregesima 1856-7.'[20] Tornielli returned it to Piave at once, saying that a 'scenario in prose' was unacceptable and could not be considered as a substitute for 'the libretto in verse'.[21] Verdi, who was under contract to deliver a libretto in verse within the month of August, was granted a one-month extension. The matter of engaging a baritone who could act well was also mentioned, for Verdi had asked the theatre to look for someone who could fill this bill. Piave passed this news on to Verdi.

Verdi replied on 12 September.

You yourself shall write again in my name to the directors [and say] that the *Simon Boccanegra* that I sent in August is not a scenario (it seems to me that scenarios are not done like that) but [is] the libretto as it should be, as it should be approved by the censors. I am under contract to give an opera for the great Teatro La Fenice in Carnival, and this time, to do something different, I plan to compose music for a prose libretto! What do you think of that?[22]

In another letter ten days earlier, he said: 'It [is] the drama, completely finished. What does it matter to you now whether it is in prose or verses? And as you remarked yourself, this *Simone* has something original about it. So the shape of the libretto, of the set pieces, has to be as original as possible.'[23]

Here are two unequivocal, straightforward statements about Verdi's intentions, from a man who rarely evaded issues and counted candour and plain speaking among the virtues. From the earlier of these two letters, both written in September, it is clear that even Piave, who knew Verdi better than most of his colleagues, did not understand what the composer planned. Whatever he had in mind, one thing is clear: he officially informed the management at La Fenice that he intended to compose to a prose libretto.[24]

The idea of a prose libretto never recurred at any other time in his career, and Tornielli may be right that it was a joke. However this might be, Verdi sent his letter from Paris on 12 September. Four days later Piave forwarded it to Tornielli, referring to 'the prose libretto',[25] and a day later Tornielli wrote to Brenna:

his libretto in prose is not a scenario, but a libretto as it should stand and as it must be approved by the censors; and he adds, I believe as a joke, that to create something new, he intends to set it to music as it is, in prose. Because the contract with Verdi does not stipulate whether the libretto should be in prose or in verses, we cannot argue with the Maestro's wish. For this reason, I conclude that we have to send it to the police to be read and approved by the censors, quite apart from the approval [needed] from the directors, Podestà, and delegate for this shapeless and incomplete work.[26]

To Piave, Tornielli wrote that he believed that Verdi was only joking when he said that he wanted to compose Piave's prose libretto. To the police, he apologized for the simple prose and said that Verdi insisted on the censors seeing it as it was. Ten days later the police returned the material from the censors, having approved the plot and reserved judgement until a libretto in verses could be produced. Verdi and Piave were given a deadline for the delivery of the complete text. On 1 October Piave 'produced the libretto in verses that Cav.^{e} Verdi will set'.[27] Discussions about finding a good baritone comprimario went on.

Verdi was by this time caught up in the preparations for *Le Trouvère* at the Paris Opéra, for which he was making a number of changes to the music. 'For now, I won't come to Italy', he said, asking Piave to send the libretto of *Simon Boccanegra* 'act by act'.[28] On 3 November Verdi returned to Paris from his visit to the Emperor and Empress and advised Piave to get ready to come to Sant'Agata 'because I hope to be there very soon'.[29] The house was ready for him; but he had to postpone his return and remain in Paris, where *Le Trouvère* was to be staged on 9 January 1857. 'I will be in Piacenza on the fourteenth',[30] Verdi wrote to Ricordi; but he was delayed by three days.

Muzio, sent to Venice by Verdi to hear some of the singers, reported unfavourably on Leone Giraldoni, the baritone to whom Verdi would entrust the role of Simon; but Luigia Bendazzi, the soprano, had a 'stupendous' voice, and Carlo Negrini, the tenor, 'is always a great artist'.[31] While he was in Paris, Verdi sought the collaboration of the Tuscan patriot Giuseppe Montanelli, who was then living in exile in France, to help rework the libretto of *Simon Boccanegra*.[32] With Piave far away, and the encounter at Sant'Agata postponed, the composer probably felt he had to find someone close at hand. He may or may not have let Piave know about Montanelli while the work was going on. Predictably, Piave was troubled about the third hand in his libretto and may have gone so far as to say he would not put his name to it. But Verdi defended himself: '*It was a necessity*,' he said.[33] Both men were under severe pressure, with Verdi detained at the Opéra and Piave busy with the critical Carnival season at La Fenice. *Le Trouvère* finally reached the stage of the Opéra on 12 January 1857. Verdi left Paris the next day and reached Sant'Agata four days later.

At the end of January and even into February Montanelli's verses for the libretto were still arriving from Paris. 'I have to have the opera finished by 15 February', Verdi advised Montanelli; but soon after he got home, he became ill, again with stomach trouble. Alarmed, Tornielli warned Piave that any delay would make it impossible to give as many performances of the new opera as La Fenice wished and wrote directly to Verdi on 6 February to ask the composer to send some of the music right away. 'On 11 February all the artists of the company will have nothing to do and [are] completely at your disposition, to study their roles.'[34] But Verdi, 'dragging myself along as best I can', found it difficult because his illness prevented him from working when he wanted. The first packet of music was to arrive in Venice on 9 February. Verdi was to follow within days, but his stomach was 'in pieces', he wrote to Piave.[35] 'I haven't done a note in four days,' he said. Strepponi wrote to Léon Escudier that he was killing himself with work. When he arrived in Venice, four days later than he had expected, Strepponi was with him. Piave and Brenna had taken the production in hand; and rehearsals were already under way. Verdi protested about the baritone engaged for Paolo and proposed another man; but he was 'very, very happy' about the rest of the cast. 'The company adores Verdi and his divine music,' Piave wrote to Ricordi.[36] Bosoni conducted the first orchestra rehearsal on 1 March. Eleven days later *Simon Boccanegra* played to an expectant audience at La Fenice. Its fine cast, which included Giraldoni and Bendazzi, did not assure its success: the opera was a 'fiasco', as Verdi wrote the next day to Vincenzo Torelli in Naples,[37] almost as bad as that of *La traviata*. I believed that I had done something passable, but it seems that I was wrong.'

No one can dispute Verdi's popularity in Venice, for in the previous Carnival season, La Fenice had staged *La traviata* while Gallo had opened with *Nabucco* and closed by giving individual acts of *Il trovatore* on separate evenings in May at the Teatro San Benedetto.[38] But Muzio, in a letter to Ricordi, wrote before the première that he had doubts about the success of *Simon Boccanegra*: 'It is a stupendous creation, moving, touching . . . perhaps the opera will be coldly received on the first evening, but in the second, in the third performance[s], it will succeed in moving everyone to tears; it is solemn, the end is great; but you need the audience of Milan or Rome to understand all its beauties on first hearing.'[39]

The failure of the première of *Simon Boccanegra* gave rise to ugly rumours: that Meyerbeer and other Jews had had a hand in the defeat; that the libretto was unacceptable and that Verdi himself had written it. Piave tried to console Verdi, declaring that those who had not understood *Simon Boccanegra* were ignorant, that the second night had gone well, although in the third performance Bendazzi had had a cold and the opening curtain of the fourth performance had been delayed because she was ill.[40] By the fifth performance, the soprano was better, the boxes were all fully sold, the audience responded about as it had to the third performance, adding 'solemn applause' after some numbers.[41] The librettist also referred to 'the usual organized opposition', and Vigna confirmed this: 'The existence of an opposition party, fully organized' was obvious. It constituted a paid claque, not just persons who gossiped and circulated malicious stories. Vigna blamed the Jews, who had gathered behind the composer Samuele Levi, and added that on 22 March one 'ugly Jew, nicknamed Rigoletto because he is deformed, raised a tremendous racket, and did not calm down until a police commissioner seriously reprimanded him'.[42] Vigna went on: 'In the midst of so much scandal and so many controversies, a curious phenomenon has been recognized, that is the conversion, the second thoughts of those who systematically oppose you, who now defend you with the same fire they used before to accuse you! Isn't the world beautiful? What a pity we can only stay on the earth such a short time!'[43]

Verdi was especially angry at the rumour that he himself had written the libretto of *Simon Boccanegra*. When he heard that even Piave said that the libretto was Verdi's, the composer unleashed his rage at the librettist. Piave's answer, dignified and noble, speaks of his shock, sorrow, and dismay: he was neither a cheat nor an imbecile, he said; he and Verdi had been friends for fourteen years; he had made their friendship 'a faith, a religion, a cult'; he could not have said that the libretto was Verdi's, for he would have known in advance that Verdi would be enraged; he had never even heard the rumour that Verdi had written the libretto. Piave expressed his fond hope that he might see Verdi, either at Sant'Agata or at Reggio Emilia, where the next production of *Simon Boccanegra* was on the schedule.[44]

Verdi, nursing his wounds, was looking for solace at Sant'Agata. 'From morning to evening, I am always out in the fields, the woods, surrounded by peasants, animals—the four-legged variety are best. Getting home tired at night, I have not found the time and the courage until now to take my pen in hand,' he wrote to Vigna.[45] Defending Piave's poetry in the same letter, he added that he wished he had the ability to write something as good. He added the news that Piave and one of the Marzis had been to Sant'Agata and that he had agreed to stage *Simon Boccanegra* himself in Reggio Emilia. 'Are the Venetians calm now? Who would ever have said that this poor *Boccanegra*, good or bad, whichever it is, would have raised such a devilish uproar?'[46] Muzio, who was living at Sant'Agata at the time, bore the brunt of moments of ill-temper.

Piave's visit on 10 April sent a sign to everyone that the librettist and composer remained friends. Both concentrated on the production in Reggio Emilia, for which Verdi made a number of amendments to the score. Verdi, Strepponi, and Piave spent an entire month there. A disastrous season was under way, with *Norma* hooted off the stage. Shortly after the curtain came down, Verdi wrote to Muzio and Ricordi, describing angry ticket-holders who had followed the Marzi brothers to their hotel and shouted protests under their windows. 'An inferno! In spite of that, these pricks have not been able to reach the only conclusion that makes sense: close the theatre for three or four days: have two or three rehearsals a day of *Boccanegra*, and reopen it with the first night of this opera.'[47] Verdi said that he had never seen a worse fiasco than *Norma* in his life. With Piave, he prepared his company, which included Bendazzi and Giraldoni, the Amelia and the Boccanegra of the Venetian première. Verdi was so busy that he could not find time to write to Barezzi, who was waiting in Busseto and planning his own trip to Reggio to see the opera.[48] Barezzi wrote to Verdi:

Please give my regards to Piave. Tell him that they don't sell good straw hats here, but they just sell ordinary ones; because of that, I will not bring it with me, for it is not a hat worthy of him, especially with that huge beard! I hope that your health is good, and that of Signora Peppina too, wishing that the two of you will share my hopes that we will all live a long time,—providing, of course, that we can find the great Secret! A thousand kisses, addio, addio, your very affectionate father-in-law Antonio Barezzi.[49]

In a postscript, he asked Verdi to provide a room at his hotel and two good seats in the theatre, for he would also bring his second wife Maddalena.

Verdi confided his and Piave's fears to Barezzi, whose next letter reveals that the composer told his father-in-law that the audience was in such a wretched humour that he feared a complete fiasco. Barezzi replied at once.

In such a situation, when factions exist, the reckless audience does not respond to the call of the music, nor the bravura of the singers, and even less to the world-wide fame of the Maestro; instead, it goes to the theatre just to whistle at the impresarios and the directors. If I were to attend a performance like that, I'm absolutely certain that I would not walk out of the theatre on my two legs, but would be carried out half-dead.[50]

Verdi was to let Barezzi know how the first night went; but he did not write, perhaps because he was overwhelmed with the production and the Marzis' problems, so Barezzi did not see *Simon Boccanegra*, at least on its first three nights, having remained in Busseto at the bedside of Giovanni Cavalli, one of his closest friends, who was dying. But he learned from people in Parma that *Simon Boccanegra* was a great success. Hearing that Verdi was coming home right away, Barezzi wrote on 13 June, which was the Feast of Sant'Antonio and his name-day, inviting Verdi and Strepponi and Piave to celebrate with him in Busseto the following Sunday, and 'eat the cake' with the family.[51] All Barezzi's letters to Verdi close with expressions of love: 'Here are a thousand kisses from my heart,' he wrote, and 'I swear that I am your very, very loving Antonio Barezzi.'

The success of *Simon Boccanegra* in Reggio Emilia raised Verdi's spirits, for the opera scored an absolute triumph with rounds of applause for all on the opening night. The second night went slightly less well; but the third night 'went very, very well',[52] as Verdi wrote to Torelli, the secretary of the Teatro San Carlo in Naples. Having heard from Ricordi that Naples wanted *Boccanegra*, Verdi advised the San Carlo that he preferred to give it during the winter of 1857–8, when he could profit from the good company under contract and the chance to direct the production himself. He suggested Coletti, Fraschini, and Penco and proposed that *Boccanegra* be staged before the new opera he was to write for the San Carlo.[53] From Sant'Agata, in another letter, he urged Torelli to give *Boccanegra* first, then follow it with one or two works by other composers, then give his new opera. 'I could be in Naples in November,' he wrote.[54] But Torelli did not rise to the bait; questioning Verdi's account of the success in Reggio, he said that he had heard from other sources that *Boccanegra* had not fared any better in Reggio than it had in Venice. He tried to get Ricordi's rental fee of 1,000 ducats reduced to 300 ducats, an offer that Verdi called 'very, very modest'; Ricordi also reported that Torelli had tried to get the score without paying at all, on the grounds that *Simon Boccanegra* was a failure and that it was in Verdi's and Ricordi's interest to have it produced. The composer's sharp reply to Torelli dealt with all these issues and with the fact that the theatre should negotiate with Ricordi; 'I think it is my duty to advise you not to count on my co-operation, because I will not come to direct it.'[55] More negotiations followed, and came to nothing. In September Verdi wrote: 'I absolutely cannot lose any more time, and there is nothing else for me to do but get busy with the new opera.'[56]

Farming was claiming an inordinate amount of Verdi's time. From Sant'Agata on 4 July, Strepponi wrote to Léon Escudier, saying that his 'love for the country has become a mania, madness, rage, fury, everything exaggerated that you can [say]. He gets up almost at dawn, to go look at the wheat, the corn, the grapevines, etc. He comes back dropping with fatigue.'[57]

Verdi had finished his work on the *Aroldo* score, perhaps with the help of Muzio, who spent part of the spring in Verdi's house, getting up early, working there, then dining with Barezzi in town and playing the piano for him, while he played his flute. In the evening Muzio returned to Sant'Agata. One of the projects he handled in Verdi's absence was the new bridge over the Arda River at Villanova; opposition to the structure arose, but Muzio was able to respond, having had instructions from Verdi. The architect and engineer was Pier Luigi Montecchini from Parma, who also designed the new theatre that would be built in Busseto in the 1860s.[58] In May, while Verdi was in Reggio, Muzio worked on the composition of his opera *La sorrentina*. Ricordi was conducting the business correspondence with the theatres, having taken over from Muzio and Verdi the negotiations with Parma and other companies. Muzio was engaged for Padua and Senigallia that summer and wished to stage and direct *Simon Boccanegra* in Alessandria in the Piedmont.[59] Writing to Verdi on 22 May, he let the composer know that the Marzis had discussed an engagement for Muzio in Trieste; perhaps Verdi could help by saying a word to Bendazzi and Giraldoni.[60] Verdi had also helped Muzio by writing to Luigi Monti about the Senigallia engagement, and Bologna. 'Certainly Bologna would be better than all the other cities,' Muzio wrote, 'and I would think that I was touching heaven with my hand [if I could conduct there].' In the same letter, sent from Padua on 28 May, Muzio let Verdi know that he should go in person to the Minister of Finance about the new bridge proposed over the Ongina River, near Verdi's house: 'a Milanese company is being formed to make a great effort to work on the Po, from Soarza to Polesine, so the house that you own on the Ongina, if converted into a tavern, can sell all the wine it wants; and it will be a very good opportunity, when the bridge is built.'[61] Muzio was also helping Verdi buy and sell horses.

Verdi surely cannot have been easy at the prospect of dealing with the Marzis again. In Muzio's letter of 31 May he wrote to Verdi:

The news of the great fiasco of *Norma* [in Reggio] reached us even in Padua; the whistles hurled at the director, and the audience's threats against Luciano Marzi made us all laugh because everyone was so afraid. . . . It seems impossible that these Marzis can stay on their feet; in Venice there are seven orders out to arrest them for unpaid promissory notes. Ercole was here a few days ago, but since, with the new law, he no longer has to surrender his passport, he laughs in his creditors' faces.[62]

Muzio had objected to Conti, the tenor in *La Traviata* in Padua, where he was also conducting *Macbeth*. On 3 June further warnings were sent about the Marzis: 'It seems impossible that after they have been so many years in the theatrical business, they are such cheats.'[63] Muzio stood his ground in Padua: the tenor was removed from the *Traviata* cast and a substitute was summoned; the opening was postponed three days. Not even the substitution saved *La traviata*: 'the [soprano] Basseggio was very badly received; the tenor Pagnoni, worse; only Guicciardi was good; we won't even discuss the secondary roles; God help us, if there had not been a concerted effort on everyone's part in the [last] act, the performance would not have been allowed to finish.'[64] The soprano, who was 'ruddy, large, and somewhat fat' had a corps of fans among the soldiers in Padua; the management of the theatre was afraid to complain about her. (Although he also complained to Ricordi about her, he later had a change of heart and conducted her elsewhere.) After Padua, Muzio went on to conduct at La Fenice in Venice.

Verdi, who had agreed to go to Rimini for the production of *Aroldo*, began to have second thoughts about his participation, probably because the Marzis were not to be trusted. Late in June, using Muzio as his agent, he let the Marzis know that he would not go. Writing to Verdi, Muzio said that Luciano Marzi was

surprised and very, very mortified, and made a long face! He says that just the idea [that you will not go] would cause a popular revolution in Rimini and cause the massacre and assassination of his brother Ercole, who is already there. 'Verdi is the foundation, the pivot of the theatre,' as Luciano says. He became the impresario [in Rimini] because of Verdi; things were made easier for him because of Verdi; after all, he could get whatever he wanted because of the magic of [Verdi's] name. . . . The city is already counting on the fact that Verdi's presence will attract people from all over.[65]

Little by little, Luciano Marzi let Muzio hear *his* side, which Muzio then referred to Verdi. His final plea—that Verdi not destroy him utterly—was also referred through Muzio. A word from Verdi assured the Marzis' future, at least for the moment, when he agreed to go to Rimini.

Muzio also received help from the conductor Angelo Mariani, who tried to get him the post of Maestro Concertatore at the Teatro Regio in Turin. The editor and agent Francesco Regli joined the effort and wrote to Muzio that it was absolutely certain that he would be named if Verdi would write a note to either Urbano Rattazzi, the Minister of the Interior, or Count Cavour. But Verdi apparently did not contact either man.[66]

Aroldo, Rimini, and Angelo Mariani

Verdi and Strepponi returned from Reggio to Sant'Agata in mid-June, spent about four weeks at the villa, and prepared to leave for Rimini. Absorbed in the composition of *Aroldo*, the individual pieces of which he sent off to Ricordi during July, Verdi also offered his views on the Marzis, who were proposing *Boccanegra* for Trieste.

Do what you want about *Boccanegra* in Trieste. The Marzis do not deserve any consideration because of the terrible *mise en scène* and because after I left they let an aria of *Lucia* be stuck into *Boccanegra*, cutting out several pieces of the opera and the very ones that the public liked best, for example the tenor's aria and the Terzetto. This is awkward and indecent![67]

But Verdi balanced his anger against the fact that Bendazzi and Giraldoni would sing in Trieste, and at the end, he told Ricordi to evaluate the situation himself and do want he thought best.

Verdi and Strepponi arrived in Rimini on 23 July, to find Piave and Mariani already there, working on *Aroldo*. This engagement proved to be an event that changed both men as Verdi's friendship with the conductor became important to him personally and professionally. Mariani was the same age as Muzio, having been born in Ravenna on 11 October 1821[68] of humble origins. Because the city of Bologna was the centre of musical activity in the Romagna, Mariani made his way there and met Rossini, who encouraged him in his study of composition.[69] His career began in earnest with contracts in Trent in 1844 and in Messina in 1844–5, where he emerged as maestro concertatore and primo violino. In his autobiographical sketch, Mariani wrote of being badly received, because of his youth and his 'foreign' origins; but he was able to conduct for the local Società Filarmonica, for which he wrote original compositions, just as Verdi had done in Busseto. At the end of the season, Mariani visited Mercadante in Naples, then returned to Bologna, where he could find theatrical agents and seek work. After a short engagement at Bagnacavallo in the Romagna, he was invited to Messina for the winter season 1845–6. Opposed again by the men in the orchestra, he worked with the Filarmonica and conducted other concerts in the city, but finally gave up and left for the north, again stopping in Naples.[70]

Working for the first time in Milan in the summer of 1846, Mariani conducted Verdi's *I due Foscari* at the Teatro Re. Probably he and Verdi met at this time. Muzio attended a performance on 1 July and reported that it was 'perfect'.[71] At the Teatro Carcano in August, Mariani conducted *Ernani* and *I Lombardi alla prima crociata*, neither of which pleased Muzio, because the cast was poor. Mariani wrote in his autobiography that he had had to play encores of the violin solo every evening in *I Lombardi*, and that his solos were the only thing in the production that had not been roundly criticized by the *Gazzetta musicale*.

From Verdi's correspondence with Lanari some scholars concluded that Verdi may have wanted Mariani to conduct his *Macbeth* in its première in Florence, but that is almost certainly incorrect.[72] Mariani returned to the Teatro Carcano in the spring of 1847, while Verdi was in Florence. The conductor's Milan repertory included Verdi's *Giovanna d'Arco*, Federico Ricci's *Michelangelo e Rolla*, and a new work, Fontana's *I Baccanti*. Because of the interference of the Austrian police, the season became a stage in the Milanese political theatre of the time. When the police commissioner Count Bolza tried to pressure Mariani into producing *I Baccanti* without sufficient rehearsals, the conductor and his baritone Ghislanzoni found a way out: Ghislanzoni did not come to the theatre on opening night, giving Mariani the chance to produce another work: *Nabucco*. The audience raised a political demonstration that so threatened the Austrian authorities that they summoned Mariani before the police officials and almost jailed him 'for having given to Verdi's music a too obvious revolutionary tint, hostile to the imperial government'. Ghislanzoni was sentenced to several days in jail.[73]

In November 1847 Mariani left for Copenhagen, where he served for two seasons as Conductor of Italian Operas at the court theatre. He also wrote the Requiem Mass for the King of Denmark. His next post was in Constantinople, the first opera he directed there being *Macbeth*. While there, he became a familiar figure in society, lived at the palace of the Russian Minister, composed several pieces, published an album of songs called *Rimembranze del Bosforo*, and composed other works. He returned to Messina in December 1851, and the following May became the conductor of the Teatro Carlo Felice at Genoa. At the end of the season, he agreed to become the permanent conductor of the city orchestra and of the opera-house. He held this post until he died, more than twenty years later.[74]

Although Verdi and Mariani probably met in 1846 in Milan, we have no correspondence between them until 1853, when Verdi, using the intimate 'tu' form, reported on the fiasco of *La traviata*. This suggests that a friendship had been established in the 1840s. In fact, Mariani was one of the first to propose a revival of *La traviata*, writing to Ricordi and to Verdi himself about it. Verdi did not accept the offer, perhaps because Mariani's cast had both Salvini-Donatelli and Graziani in it.[75] In Genoa, however, Mariani had a good orchestra of fifty-six men. One account of his rehearsals gives us a glimpse of him at work:

At the first orchestral rehearsal of a work, Mariani always took up the baton and began to read the score, pages and pages without stopping, sometimes an entire act, without ever going back. Once this first run-through was finished, he continued a more analytical reading, but before this he sometimes took the violin and played some passages, some phrases, with that expression of eloquence, so full of communication that penetrated and impressed itself even on the most closed minds. More frequently he sang the most important phrases, explaining them and colouring them with his warm and beautiful and extraordinarily suggestive voice; little by little, as he took fire, he would seize the baton and, accompanying his arm movements with the swaying of his leonine head and with the sparks from his bright, bright eyes, he transmitted to the attentive, fascinated performers all the shadings of his [interpretation], all the warmth of his vibrant, enthusiastic spirit.[76]

Mariani's physical beauty is beyond dispute. Tall, straight, with a splendid head crowned with thick black hair, the conductor wore a Mazzini beard. He was sentimental to a fault, and enjoyed many friendships that lasted from his youth until his death. Rossini, his acquaintance and supporter, signed photographs to the conductor, one of which was inscribed to 'Anzlett Mariani' with the 'huge, beautiful eyes'.[77] When Mariani and Verdi met in Rimini in July 1857, the conductor had been in Genoa for more than five years and had been decorated by King Vittorio Emanuele with the Cross of the Order of San Maurizio, which Verdi had also received. As they worked together, a close association between the two developed. Although there was hysteria in the city over Verdi's presence there, opposition to *Aroldo* was also expressed, as protests were registered against this *Stiffelio Warmed-Up*. Verdi's high fee—paid out of the city's treasury—was about one fourth of the total production costs. He was paid 1,305.5 lire, while Piave got 80.5 lire, according to the city treasurer's report of 20 March.[78] The composer had also caused the city fathers a great deal of anxiety by declaring that he would not attend the première.

The rehearsals went well, as Mariani reported to Ricordi. 'I, for my part, am working hard to see that everything goes according to [Verdi's] wishes.'[79] In another letter:

The piano rehearsals are going well and Verdi and I are taking turns with this work. . . . Give my regards to [Girolamo] Cerri and tell him that Verdi began to laugh when he read in [Cerri's] letter to me the words 'The Illustrious One' and 'The Great One'.[80]

The first orchestral rehearsal with the singers and chorus went stupendously and was run through without interruption from beginning to end. Verdi was fully satisfied with my orchestra, which he praised very eloquently several times, saying 'Bravi, bravi, e molto'. . . . As always the singers have made poor Verdi work like a dog teaching them their parts . . . Verdi is very, very happy and so am I.[81]

BOOK III

In his own letters to the publisher, Verdi expressed his impatience over delays in getting *Aroldo* staged, denounced the Marzis as 'two first-class pumpkin heads', and praised the orchestra and the chorus—men and women—as 'very, very excellent'.[82] In a postscript, he said that the rehearsals had begun well but that the tenor, Emilio Pancani, made him nervous. Mariani had had some reservations about the soprano, Marcellina Lotti, whom he described as 'a very, very beautiful voice, but lacking in artistic sentiment'. She was, however, Verdi's choice for the leading role, though a later account of his stay in Rimini says that he found her unsatisfactory.

On the night of the première, which was an enormous success, Rimini overflowed with foreigners and people from other Italian cities. Verdi took twenty-seven calls. Even Piave was called out twice. At the end of the evening, a large crowd followed the town band to Verdi's apartment at the Hotel dell'Aquila, where Strepponi awaited him. A torchlight parade and shouts of 'Evviva' and all kinds of ovations marked the triumph. '*Aroldo* created a furore,' wrote Mariani. 'There was not one piece that was not applauded; the Maestro was called out on stage countless times. He is very, very happy about it, the performance was good.' Mariani added that he was overjoyed at the responsive audience.[83] The orchestra members had honoured both Verdi and Mariani by having lithograph portraits made of them: 'the portraits are very, very beautiful and look alike', the conductor remarked.[84]

After this sojourn in Rimini, where Verdi and Strepponi also relaxed and took long walks along the Adriatic beach, the couple returned to Sant'Agata. Mariani took a few days to visit his mother in Ravenna. Verdi, writing from Bologna to Ricordi, on his way home, expressed irritation because Mariani had kept the manuscript score of the opera in Rimini beyond the three performances that Verdi attended. This meant that Muzio would be delayed in working on the reductions for the publisher. 'Mariani wanted to keep the score, and I was very, very annoyed about it. Insist that Mariani return the score to you, and keep after him. He might forget it, and I would not want some theft to happen. For your information, Mariani is longer on words than on action.'[85] Verdi need not have feared. The conductor had a musician from Parma bring the score to Sant'Agata, in a carefully sealed parcel; Verdi could inform Ricordi that 'the score is in order'.[86] He sent Mariani a French poodle pup that had just been born at Sant'Agata, the first of many gifts exchanged between the two men.

In all of Verdi's letters to Ricordi in this summer and fall, there is not one word of criticism of Mariani, save the composer's observation that the conductor was 'longer on words than on action'. Several years later, however, Verdi wrote Mariani a letter in which he said that Mariani had offended him during their stay in Rimini by declaring that Meyerbeer's music would outlive Verdi's.

When we were in Rimini, one evening when there were a lot of people around talking about music, and about mine in particular, you said 'But this is music that will not last. Talk to me about the [music] of Meyerbeer, etc. etc.'—Well! I didn't do anything and this is the first time that I mention it to you, to prove to you that you shouldn't pay attention [to what people say].[87]

Mariani answered in a letter of 6 December 1864, written from Bologna.

I do not remember having said what you remind me of, about something I said in Rimini when we were over there. It seems impossible that I should have uttered those words, for they do not express what I feel. If I had said them, I would have been a madman or a fool, and since I have never been either, someone wished to attribute to me something that I would not even want to hear from anyone else, and I would not allow anyone to blaspheme in that way.[88]

One has to believe Mariani, who was indeed neither a madman nor a fool. The incident raises the suspicion that a third party, perhaps Luigi Monti from Bologna, who was in Rimini for the production, may have suggested the remark to Verdi out of malice. There was no love lost between Monti and Mariani, as was amply proved later.

Verdi hoped that *Aroldo* would be popular, being bolstered in that hope by the success of the première and by the fact that Turin, Treviso, Venice, and other cities wished to give it. Still smarting over the failure of *Simon Boccanegra* in Venice, the composer chose Treviso. Parma, too, wished to stage it.

At Sant'Agata, where the summer harvests were in full swing, Verdi continued a transaction in which Luccardi, visiting friends in Udine and Treviso, would buy two large horses, strong enough to pull his four-wheeled carriage on long trips. The price was unimportant, he said, so long as they met his requirements. Soon he changed his mind, though. Writing on 25 August, he said that although he had considered coming to see the animals himself, he was too tired and not feeling well.

I have no desire to move. I don't doubt for a moment your judgement and that of the people you contacted. But horses are like women: they have to please the person who owns them; beyond their qualities (which must surely be excellent, since you assure me they are) they have to be attractive in the eye of their owner, especially when it is a matter of spending a rather large amount of money.[89]

Later Luccardi found a better pair in the country near Padua, and at a better price.

Verdi, alone, as Strepponi had gone to visit her mother and sister in Locate Triulzi, where they continued to live after Davide Strepponi's death, asked Ricordi to help her when she changed carriages in Milan and added that the publisher should provide her with anything she needed for the trip. Later in the summer he offered advice to Muzio about future engagements when the two were together at Sant'Agata. Muzio had been through a harrowing season in Padua in the late spring and summer, coping with the prima donna Adelaide Basseggio;

Absolutely nothing! Poor Parma! Poor Bologna! I hope she won't ruin any other opera in the future! . . . She has absolutely no voice nor talent nor style of singing! Imagine delicate, heartfelt, sentimental music such as that of *La traviata* meowed by a voice that is neither soprano nor mezzo-soprano nor contralto; add a rotund, fat body with two extraordinary tits![90]

Yet in spite of his worst fears, Basseggio did a creditable job in *Aroldo* under Muzio's baton. 'Great success! *Aroldo* triumphs' he reported to Ricordi.[91] After playing his score of *La sorrentina* for Verdi, 'because he loves me very much and he wants good things for me', Muzio left Sant'Agata to serve as *concertatore* for his own opera in Bologna.[92] *La sorrentina* went fairly well; but the directors of the Teatro Regio in Parma, where the opera was scheduled for its second production, decided not to give it. Pressure was brought on Basseggio to choose another work, which she did, even though Carlo Verdi went to Parma and offered her 30 gold *marenghi* and a bracelet if she would sing Muzio's opera.[93]

Verdi had high hopes for *Aroldo*; but, as he confided to his publisher, it had not gone as well as he had hoped in Bologna and Turin. Blaming the cast of the opera at the Teatro Comunale and the *mise-en-scène* and the minor singers in Turin, he again belaboured the Marzis:

You cannot trust the Marzis, and—whether out of laziness or something else— they are capable of ruining or letting someone else ruin any production, even the most expensive. . . . Granted that a composer is obliged to write the best [music] he can; that is his duty; but he also has to watch out that his best things are not ruined.[94]

JANUARY 1856–SUMMER 1857

Simon Boccanegra had gone badly in Florence; Gallo wanted to produce *Aroldo* at the San Benedetto in Venice. —So Verdi wrote to Ricordi during the week of his forty-fourth birthday. It was October; another summer at Sant'Agata was drawing to an end.

22

Autumn 1857–August 1859

Un ballo in maschera

With *Aroldo* behind him, Verdi turned in September 1857 to the search for a suitable subject for his new opera for the San Carlo in Naples, having negotiated a contract with the theatre in 1856, using Torelli as his intermediary. The Neapolitan critic, writing in 1841 in *L'omnibus*, had sharply criticized Verdi when *Oberto* failed at the San Carlo. 'We will not say a word about Verdi's music, [for] it is [so bad] that it makes one say twice as emphatically as before that the San Carlo is bankrupt,[1] playing the name 'Verdi' against the idiom for being bankrupt, 'ridotto al verde'. But as the composer's output grew, Torelli had muted his criticism and become a supporter, though sometimes an irascible one, of Verdi's work. In 1856 he was working as secretary of the theatre management, which was then in the hands of the impresario Luigi Alberti. Verdi's first concern was for his rights, for the San Carlo had an agreement with the publisher Cottrau that allowed him to hold world rights to all works commissioned for that theatre. Verdi wanted to grant Cottrau only the rights for the Kingdom of the Two Sicilies—even that being a big concession. But he insisted on approving the company of singers and being paid a fee of 6,000 ducats, while holding all other rights himself.[2] At this stage he was thinking of *Re Lear*. If that were the opera, they would have to engage a major artist: 'a great baritone for the part of *Re Lear*' and a prima donna soprano with much feeling for Cordelia. 'Two excellent comprimarios; a very, very good contralto; a dramatic tenor with a beautiful voice, but not a very famous man.'[3] He suggested Giuseppina Brambilla for the contralto and Marietta Piccolomini for the soprano. In

May 1856 Verdi received a contract from the San Carlo; but its terms were unacceptable. Expressing his 'honest unhappiness' over the contract, he said he could not sign until the beginning of 1857. If the management were willing to wait, 'I would absolutely give *Re Lear*. For the protagonist, a baritone *artist*—in every sense of the word—would be needed: an artist, for example, such as Giorgio Ronconi was.'[4] Verdi added that Fraschini was too important for the tenor role and that Lotti, who was 'excellent in dramatic parts', would not be a suitable Cordelia. He agreed to approach Piccolomini himself.

From Paris in August, he wrote to London, to the banker Paolo Mitrovich, asking help in his negotiations with the soprano, to whom Verdi had written about Cordelia. Piccolomini had responded with 'such kindness, such self-denial' that Verdi became apprehensive, fearing that she would later regret her generosity. He asked for assistance in determining what Piccolomini really wanted, so he could let Naples know her terms. She would make her début at the San Carlo in *La traviata* and would be engaged there from 15 October 1857 until 15 March 1858.[5] As late as November the composer had still not signed his contract: 'I would have been able to send you the signed contracts if some difficulties had not delayed me.'[6] Verdi declared that he was still not satisfied with all the conditions and that he felt that only three sopranos could be considered for Cordelia: Spezia, Boccabadati, and Piccolomini. 'All three have weak voices but great talent, soul, and feeling for the theatre.' And he concluded: 'So find a soprano to do Cordelia that will please me, and a contralto to do the Fool, and you can consider the contract signed,' he wrote, after having raised other points about the agreement, which he finally signed in February 1857. He rejected Torelli's suggestion that Penco could sing in the new opera saying:

The agreement with Penco is impossible for me. It is my habit not to let any artist be *forced* upon me, not even if Malibran were to come back from the dead. All the gold on earth would not make me give up this principle. I have all possible respect for Penco's talent, but I don't want her to be able to say to me: 'Signor Maestro, give me the part in your opera, I want it, I have the right to it.'[7]

In January 1857, during the trip from Paris, Verdi had still not budged: 'It is impossible to write *Re Lear* for a contralto and mezzo-soprano of whom I do not have a very high opinion, or for a soprano not suited to the work.'[8] His uneasiness was reflected in a letter in which he commented on the impossibility of giving a minor role to a major singer (Fraschini) and of having 'a sweet, ingenuous part sung by Penco'. To do the Fool, you need an actress, he added. 'An opera done badly or done half-heartedly is like a painting that is seen in the dark: no one understands it.'[9]

By June Verdi was writing 'I am very hesitant about *Re Lear*', because, he said, apart from the baritone, no one would be right for the roles. With a catalogue of complaints, he let the San Carlo know how unhappy he was.

Believe me, it is a great mistake to risk *Re Lear* with a company of singers who, as good as they are, are not—one might say—made to order for those roles. I would perhaps ruin an opera, and you, to some extent, would ruin your management. Let me scrounge around among other plays, and it will be fine when I finally find a subject.[10]

The subject Verdi found was *Gustave III, ou Le bal masqué*, which Verdi referred to as *Gustavo III di Svezia* in a letter to Torelli dated 19 September 1857.[11] Earlier in the month the composer had written that he was working day and night to find something and had considered *Ruy Blas*, which he put aside because it was not suitable for Coletti, and *Il tesoriere del Re Don Pedro*, which presented 'too many obstacles'.[12] Adding that he would compose *Re Lear* the following year, he proposed *Aroldo* and *Boccanegra*; but the management of the San Carlo rejected that. Both parties then settled on *Gustavo III*.

The story of the assassination of Gustavus III of Sweden was not new to the European stage. The King, whose coronation music had been composed by his court musician Francesco Antonio Uttini, was killed in 1792, shortly after Uttini left his service. Murdered at a masked ball, Gustavus III was later the protagonist of ballets, operas, and a drama that reached the stage over the next half-century. *La festa da ballo in maschera*, with choreography by Louis Henry, had been given at La Scala in 1829 and again in 1833, when Verdi, a student, was going to the theatre regularly. Choreographed by Salvatore Taglioni and composed by Mercadante, a different work with the same title was given at the Teatro Regio in Turin in February 1832. As *Gustavo III, re di Svezia*, the story of the king's assassination appeared at La Scala in March 1846.[13] On the night of its première, Verdi was in Venice; but he may have seen the ballet later, as it was given seventeen times that spring. The plot was also used in *Il reggente*, composed by Mercadante to a Cammarano libretto and given at the Regio in Turin in 1843.[14]

In September 1857, then, Verdi wrote to Torelli.

Now I am adapting a French play, *Gustavo III di Svezia*, libretto by Scribe and done at the Opéra more than twenty years ago. It is grand and vast; it is beautiful; but even it has the conventional styles of all works set to music, something that has always made me unhappy, but that I now find unbearable. I tell you again that I am desolate, because it is now too late to find other subjects, and besides, I would not know where to go to dig one out; those that I have in hand don't give me any feeling of security.[15]

He wrote at once to Somma, who replied on 13 October, saying that he would work as quickly as he could on the libretto; this he did, over the next three months.

As early as October Torelli had warned Verdi that the Neapolitan censors would require changes. Because Mercadante's *Il reggente* had been set in sixteenth-century Scotland, Verdi might have expected that such a change of period might be effected in his own work; but he postponed making a decision about it at the time. Soon, though, both the composer and his librettist had to comply with the orders of the Neapolitan censors. The King had to become a duke, ruling over a pre-Christian land in the north; the King's love for Amelia had to be pure; he had to show remorse; the conspirators had to hate their ruler because of injury to their families or patrimonies; the elegant masked ball had to be set, as the entire opera was, in a pre-Christian time! Finally, there could be no firearms. In the assassination, no gun could be used: in Hus's 1846 ballet at La Scala, the King was shot on-stage.

Somma suggested Pomerania for the setting, Stockholm becoming Stettin, and proposed that the period be the twelfth century. The title might be *Il duca Ermanno*, he said. But Verdi rejected the medieval setting and made no mention of the title. He continued to refer to the protagonist as 'Gustavo' and urged Somma to finish the libretto, adding that they could discuss the epoch of the opera later. Perhaps some of the difficulty encountered later was owed to the fact that Somma did not come to Sant'Agata as Piave often had. Instead, he said he would stay in Venice until the work was almost or completely finished and asked to be allowed to use a pseudonym on the title-page. Abbiati accounts for this odd request by recalling the many troubles Somma had had with the Austrian censors in Trieste, while he was the editor of the newspaper *La favilla*.[16] The writer may also have known the librettist of yet another version of *Gustave III*, Gaetano Rossi, who wrote the text for Gabussi's *Clemenza di Valois*, which was presented at the Teatro La Fenice in Venice in 1841. In November he wrote to Verdi to report that he was aware that the censors might raise objections to the opera. Throughout the entire correspondence, Verdi remained patient, while demanding what he needed. When Somma pleased him, Verdi let him know it. On 20 November he had received the second act of the libretto: 'Beautiful, very, very beautiful [is] the duet between Gustavo and Amelia. In it there is all the warmth and disorder that passion needs.'[17] But he did not hesitate to criticize the poetry that seemed to him impossible to set. Six days later: '[In Amelia's aria,] those two little added verses do not heighten the scene, which is still mean. There is no fire, there is no excitement, there is no disorder (and that should be at its peak at this moment).' Also on 26 November Verdi wrote that characters rendered in French style, such as Gustavo and the page Oscar, made no sense at all in a twelfth-century setting.[18] He urged his librettist to find a 'minor prince, a duke, even a devil, so long as they come from the North, have seen a bit of the world, and are familiar with the Court of Louis XIV.' In the second act, he found Somma's version of the duet between Amelia and Ankarstrom

cold, in spite of the very animated scene: in French, there is that 'Il faut mourir' that comes out from time to time, and that is very theatrical. I know perfectly well that 'prepare to die . . . ask God to protect you' ['apparecchiati alla morte . . . raccomandati al Signore'] mean the same thing, but on the stage they do not have the same power as that simple 'you must die' ['Bisogna morire'].[19]

He added criticism of the scene of the drawing of the lots: 'When Amelia enters and draws her husband's name, in the French play the situation is terrifying and extremely beautiful: in the poetry you sent me, it does not move me in the same way.' It was a very important moment in the drama, he said. Finally Somma decided to use 'Tommaso Anoni', an anagram of his name, on the title-page.[20] After making last-minute suggestions for an added scene for Amelia, he informed Verdi on 10 December that he would come to Busseto during the Christmas holidays to go over the entire libretto and make further corrections. Although he planned to arrive on the day after Christmas, Verdi argued that he should come sooner. He did.

This was not the happiest of holidays, for Antonio Barezzi had been ill in Busseto in mid-December, suffering from dysentery. In a note of 21 December to Verdi, he wrote that he had not been able to come to Sant'Agata the day before, as planned, but that he wanted to know whether Verdi, la Signora Peppina, and the poet, 'if he stays on', would be his guests in Busseto on Christmas Eve. In spite of the snow, Verdi would have no trouble, having a closed carriage and good horses, he said. He sent his regards to all, even to the 'bravo Poeta', whom, he said, he did not know.[21] The envelope bears the composer's name and titles: 'Al Celebre Maestro Cav^{re} Sig^r Giuseppe Verdi, Ufficiale della Legion d'Onore, S. Agata.' Barezzi's servant brought it to Verdi's home. The tone of his first reference to Strepponi is equally formal: she is 'Deg[nissi]ma', but in the last line of his letter, she is 'Carissima', as indeed by now she was to him.

After Christmas further letters were exchanged between Verdi and Somma, as the librettist went on making changes in the text. Having advised Torelli that he could not get to Naples before the end of the year, Verdi said that he expected to be there about 8 January. He let De Sanctis know that he would stay at the Hôtel de Rome at first then take a private apartment for himself, Strepponi (whom he referred to as his wife in at least one letter), and their domestic, Serafina Gagliardi Zilioli. Also in the company was Loulou, their pet dog. They left Sant'Agata on 5 January 1858 and were delayed a full day by a heavy snowstorm that stalled transportation so badly that it took them ten hours to travel 12 miles in such dangerous conditions that at one post-house they were refused fresh horses. When they reached Genoa, the ship *Pompei*, which Verdi had hoped to get, had already left, so he had to book on another vessel, which put him down in Naples on 14 January. It seems almost beyond belief that he, Strepponi, and their servant could have landed without being recognized; but they apparently did. Sending a note to De Sanctis, he warned his friend not to ask for him by name, but to come to room 18 at the Hôtel de Rome. Verdi wanted to learn at first hand about the 'very ugly things' he had heard about the management of the Teatro San Carlo.[22] Their trip was the subject of an article in Torelli's *L'omnibus*, which described Verdi's 'long and difficult trip', made through the snow from Sant'Agata to Genoa, and by sea from there.

But [now that he has] arrived in Naples, our wishes, promises, and contract are fulfilled, because his music is written, and it can face the challenge. . . . It has the strange, new title *Una vendetta in domino*. . . . Verdi's opera is grand and effective . . . On the very evening of his arrival, the celebrated Maestro, begged to do so by his friends, went to the theatre. When he got to his box, there was a widespread murmuring in the huge San Carlo, and every eye and lorgnette was turned in his direction.[23]

Verdi had an unpleasant surprise that evening, when he learned that sickness, real and feigned, was rife in the company. Torelli ventured the opinion that the singers were not really ill, but were reporting in sick to spite the management and the public. In spite of the rebellion in the ranks, Coletti sang an aria from *Batilde di Turenna* (Verdi's *Les Vêpres siciliennes*, in a censored version), rousing the audience to 'clamorous applause', during which Verdi had to take several bows, 'modestly and moved by emotion and gratitude'.[24] He was called up to the stage later in the performance; from there he took bows with the singers and alone. To honour him, the orchestra repeated the overture to the opera. Surrounded by Fraschini, Coletti and other friends, Verdi was seen as 'the genius of Italy, great and sublime', the master of innovation, 'simple and frank, modest and dignified, averse to insincere compliments, but grateful to those who truly esteem him, said, with few words and gestures: "I never asked for an ovation, and that is why I am all the happier over it." '[25]

All that honest pleasure was soon dissipated. On the day of his arrival, Verdi had given Torelli the libretto in verse that Somma had just completed; but he had not had a receipt for it. That must have seemed odd, for Verdi waited several days, then asked Torelli to give him a receipt. Still no one spoke to him about the opera. On 23 January, nine days after his and Strepponi's arrival in Naples, the composer wrote to Luigi Alberti, the impresario of the Teatro San Carlo, saying that he was ready to fulfil the terms of his contract and that he had chosen Penco for Amelia, Fioretti for Oscar, Ganducci for the fortune-teller Ulrica, Fraschini for the Duke, and Coletti for the Count: 'Please advise me in writing whether the artists mentioned above are free and available to me, so the rehearsals can begin as soon as possible.'[26] As we know from another of Verdi's letters on the same day, he had not even seen Alberti to discuss the cast. He had also heard that Fioretti was not willing to sing Oscar.

Then and only then did the management reveal a secret they had been hiding for almost three months: in October the Neapolitan censors had refused to approve the libretto. Alberti and Torelli had kept the news to themselves and evidently had kept it from De Sanctis as well, believing that if they told Verdi, he would not have continued composing the score.

Verdi was furious. He wrote to Luccardi in Rome:

I am in a real Hell. The censors will veto the libretto (it is almost certain). Yet in this libretto there was nothing that could undermine religion, politics, morals. They forbid it . . . and why? I do not know. Because of this, the subscribers refuse to pay two instalments [of their subscriptions] (about 30,000 ducats) and the government will not pay its subvention. The management will certainly sue everyone, and me too. What will happen? I do not know. Damn the minute I signed this contract. I don't know how to find peace of mind, because I cannot understand why this libretto has been prohibited, for it is absolutely the most innocent thing on earth.[27]

Writing to Somma, Verdi said that he was in a 'sea of troubles' because it was almost certain that the censors would forbid the libretto. He said that they had begun to take offence at certain expressions, certain words, then certain scenes, and finally to the subject itself. As a 'favour' they had proposed that the Duke become a mere lord, so that he could in no way be perceived as a ruler; Amelia should be Renato's sister, not his wife; that the scene with the soothsayer had to be changed; that the masked ball should be abandoned; that the epoch be changed; that the assassination take place off-stage; that the scene of the drawing of lots be removed; 'and more, and more, and more!!'[28]

Somma had heard of Verdi's dilemma two days before the composer's letter arrived in Venice. Offering a lawyer's view, for he had been a practising one, he also sent a colleague's sympathy. With a noble gesture, he offered to take his name off the libretto completely and let the censors rework it. 'Do whatever you wish with the poetry that is mine. Delete or patch [it] together, as the censors wish, if there is time . . . Let those Signori do everything they want.'[29] He stipulated only that someone else's name be printed on the title-page, for the libretto would no longer be his work, and that the opera not be called *Una vendetta in domino*.

Even before receiving Somma's letter, Verdi had written to Torelli, protesting at the proposed changes. 'It seems to me a joke, not to say an insult', because they stripped the opera of all its characters and every possible effect.

Move the action back five or six centuries?! What an anachronism! Take out the scene when they draw lots for the name of the killer?!—But this is the most powerful and the newest scene in the drama, and they want me to give it up?! I told you before that I cannot do the monstrous things that were done here in *Rigoletto*. They are done here because I cannot prevent them. Nor does it mean anything to tell me of the success it had: if some pieces, here and there, two or three, were applauded, that is not enough to make a music drama. In matters of art, I have my ideas, my firm convictions, which are specific, which I cannot and will not renounce.

He added that he had heard he was going to be sued by the management and that he was not afraid of the legal action, because he believed he was right. He proposed that the management cancel the contract, assigning damages to no one. 'I am from another country; my business affairs are here; I came here to Naples to fulfil the conditions of a contract; if unforeseeable obstacles,—I'll say more: obstacles that are incomprehensible, prevent this, I am not to blame. Provide the guarantees for your own rights, if you have any, and if you want to, but free me.'[30]

Verdi's score would not be wasted for Ricordi had already proposed to produce it at La Scala. But it was not at all sure that he would be free to leave Naples. The president of the Royal Theatres, who was also the censor, sued Verdi for damages and ordered his arrest. Torelli advised the president that he had spent three hours trying to persuade Verdi to meet Filippo Cirelli, one of the censors, at noon on 20 February. 'If they don't tear each other's hair out, who knows whether they may work something out.'[31] But he held out no hope whatever for the new opera; again, he advised his principal to look for another solution. 'Do you think Jesus Christ will help?' He advised against pursuing the suit. But it was too late. Verdi had asked damages, with interest, for himself; working with his lawyer Ferdinando Arpino, he prepared a document called 'Defence of Maestro Cavalier Giuseppe Verdi', in which he defended the libretto, which had been given back to him, retitled *Adelia degli Adimari*. To bolster his case, he asked Luccardi to send him a theatrical poster from Rome, proving that the Roman censors had approved *Gustavo III* in a dramatic version that was to be given in that same season. He also asked Luccardi to go to Donizetti's brother-in-law, Antonio Vasselli, to see whether the orchestra score and parts of *Simon Boccanegra* were still in his hands. Verdi confided to Luccardi that he might need them in Naples and also asked for the libretto of *Simon Boccanegra* to be sent to him.[32] The Roman sculptor did what he was asked. Shortly afterwards Verdi informed him that *Vendetta in domino* would definitely not be given in Naples and that he would prefer to produce it in Rome, 'first, to be able to spend some time happily with you and our dear Vasselli; second, to give this opera almost at the gates of Naples, and show people that even the Roman censors approved this libretto'.[33] Verdi won: the impresario Jacovacci arrived at the Hôtel de Rome, having discussed the project with Luccardi. Delighted at the opportunity, he gave Verdi all the guarantees he needed. Verdi sent him Somma's libretto.

Winter had passed, with Verdi still in Naples, where the Commercial Court was reviewing Somma's *Vendetta in domino* and the censors' *Adelia degli Adimari*. Verdi worked ahead on his ninety-page defence, which was deposited in court on 13 March, with his lawyer's text laced with his own remarks.[34] He denounced the censors for destroying his libretto, pointing out that the text called 'Vendetta in domino' had 884 lines, of which 297 had been changed in *Adelia degli Adimari*. Of the original period and setting, nothing remained. The northern city of Stettin had become Florence; the palace of the Duke had been changed into a simple house. The masked ball and the drawing of lots had been cut. Oscar, the vivacious, young page, had become a soldier, who followed the chief of a political faction (formerly the Duke). Taking up the libretto scene by scene, the composer made his case. Summing up, he wrote:

I ask, further, whether in the censored drama there exist, as in mine:

The title?	No.
The poet?	No. [It was Domenico Bolognese.]
The period?	No.
Setting?	No.
Characters?	No.
Situations?	No.
The drawing of lots?	No.
The Ball?	No.

A maestro who respects his art and himself could not and must not dishonour himself, accepting . . . these strange things that desecrate the most fundamental principles of the drama, and revile the artist's conscience.[35]

Verdi showed that he and Somma had in fact made the changes requested by the censors, after their first review of *Gustavo III*. 'Inconscionable and ridiculous,' his document concluded.

His and Arpino's effort was worth it. The Commercial Court conceded that the changes could result in damage to the music. The two parties were asked to reach a compromise, which allowed Verdi to leave Naples with his score, providing he returned to produce *Simon Boccanegra* at the San Carlo in the fall. This Verdi did at the end of November 1858 for a wildly enthusiastic audience. The house was sold out. As Verdi said, that was his test of success.

Sometime before he left Naples in the spring of 1858, Verdi inscribed a composition of his own into Melchiorre Delfico's album. 'Sgombra, o gentil', twenty-two bars long, set to verses from the third section of a chorus from Manzoni's *Adelchi*, marks the death of Ermengarda, the heroine. Discovered by Francesco Degrada in the collection of an American autograph dealer, it was on the programme of the Verdi Festival in Parma in 1989. So far as is known, it had never been performed before.

BOOK III

Un ballo in maschera in Rome

Verdi had good news from Muzio in March, when the conductor wrote to say that Lumley had engaged him as 'maître concertante, chef de tout la musique, directeur générale' at Her Majesty's Theatre in London.[36] Muzio had conducted most of the negotiations without his Maestro's help, although he had occasionally relied on Verdi for advice. He did, however, ask for letters of introduction to Paolo Mitrovich, whom Verdi had contacted about Piccolomini,[37] and later to Piccolomini herself.[38] Proudly, Muzio let Antonio Barezzi know of his appointment, writing from Bologna on the day he left for London. 'Once I went to London and was still a music student; I now return there maestro direttore, composer, and head of all the music at Her Majesty's Theatre, and without having to take an examination, as they wanted me to do to get the post of maestro in Busseto!'[39] Shortly after he got to England, Muzio let Verdi know that he had directed and conducted *Les Huguenots* with the soprano Thérèse Tietjens. The second opera on his programme was *Il trovatore*, which would be followed by *Luisa Miller*. He had taken rooms near Regent's Park.[40]

In late April Verdi and Strepponi left Naples by steamer and stopped in Genoa again to visit Mariani and Ricordi, who had come from Milan to meet them. As we learn later from Muzio, both the London and Paris newspapers had followed the composer's lawsuit almost on a day-to-day basis, and were currently reporting Verdi's voyage on the ship *Pompei* and his stay in Genoa. At the Teatro Carlo Felice, Mariani let Verdi into a fourth-tier box through a secret door, so he could hear Rossini's *Mosè* without being recognized. Behind drawn curtains, the composer heard the first two acts, then left. His friendship with Mariani, strengthened by these visits, went beyond music to their shared interests in literature, autograph collecting, and hunting. An invitation to Sant'Agata was extended. With Strepponi, Verdi made his way to Piacenza, from where he wrote to De Sanctis with the news that *Vendetta in domino* might have trouble even in Rome. If he could not present the opera as he wished, he said, he would cancel his contract.[41] Finally, after three months away, the couple returned home.

Exciting news from Muzio came in a letter of 5 May. 'Last night, [*Il trovatore*] had an enormous success, from the first piece to the last. The theatre was packed. I never saw Lumley happier than yesterday evening; the Queen and all the Court attended, something that Lumley had not had happen often.'[42] He added news of the triumph of Tietjens and of his disputes with Lumley over his contract. On 21 May Muzio sent his thanks for the letter to Piccolomini, in fact written by Strepponi, which had won him entrance to the soprano's family circle. 'It seems certain that [Piccolomini] will go to America at the end of August,' he said.[43] He reported on the 'marvellous orchestra' at Covent Garden and on the fact that on 25 May *La traviata* was being given in all three theatres on the same night: Piccolomini sang it at Her Majesty's, Angiolina Bosio at Covent Garden, Fanny Donatelli-Salvini at Drury Lane. On 9 June he wrote of the 'immense success of *Miller*; the top honours went to the music, which caused a great sensation'.[44] He described the opera's triumph, piece by piece, and added a few words about the defence of Verdi he had mounted during an orchestra rehearsal, to counter the criticism of French and German musicians playing there. Only twelve Italians were in his orchestra, fortunately all in first chairs. His dispatches continued to reach Verdi regularly.

During the summer Verdi spent most of his time in the fields at Sant'Agata, sometimes with his horses in the woods near the Po, wanting nothing more than to rest. He wrote to Clara Maffei:

Now here I am, and after the uproar of Naples, this deep silence is even dearer to me than before. It is impossible to find a place uglier than this, but on the other hand, it is impossible for me to find a place where I can live more freely; and what is more, this silence leaves me time to think: and it is a good thing, too, not even to see uniforms of any colour! . . . From *Nabucco*, you may say, I have never had one hour of peace. Sixteen years in the galleys![45]

In this letter he also asked Clara Maffei about Milan, which he said he had not visited in ten years.

Instead of taking a vacation in Venetia, Verdi and Strepponi spent time at nearby Tabiano Terme, a modest spa above Borgo San Donnino and near Salsomaggiore. Both Muzio and Mariani were then in London, the latter having gone there for a friend's wedding. The two men met and gossiped about a mangled *Don Giovanni* at Covent Garden with the tenor Mario in the title role. By August Muzio was in Dublin, where *La traviata* and *Il trovatore* had created a sensation. He was looking forward to returning to Busseto himself; but for the moment he went on conducting concerts and operas in Liverpool, Leeds, Manchester, and other English cities, sending regular reports to both Verdi and Ricordi. 'Verdi's music is hugely popular here, and it was a real disaster that the [English] rights are lost, for in all the music stores, Cremer [sic], Bosey [sic], etc., you only find Verdi's music everywhere, *corrected* by some wretched German musician who has redone the accompaniments [and] the vocal parts,' he wrote to Ricordi. Lumley held the rights on all those sales.[46] When Mariani came back to Italy that summer, he undoubtedly gave Verdi his own reports. Before leaving, he had visited the villa for more than a week, working on music and roaming the fields of what he called the 'Hermitage of the Wizard of Busseto'; and on his return Verdi urged him to come again. Expressions of mutual affection and shared interests appear in both men's letters.[47]

In July the composer became alarmed when he learned that papal censors wanted to make changes in the libretto of *Vendetta in domino*. To Somma, he wrote that 'the subject [of the opera] and the situations would be permitted; but the setting must be taken out of Europe. What would you say to North America at the time of English rule?'[48] Massachusetts was chosen. Support during this difficult time came from many quarters, Venice among them. Piave wrote from there of his outrage over the suit in Naples.

So they want other people to judge whether your music, written for one libretto, can be adapted to another? And who would be audacious enough to do it? He could only be an ass or a scoundrel; there's no other way [he could do it]. . . . I'll cut this short, because thinking about this will make me go off the deep end with rage. Good day, my Angel, adorable Bear.[49]

As Muzio had asked Verdi to think about writing a new opera for London, so Piave had a hand in discussions at the Teatro La Fenice, where Tornielli hoped the composer would honour Venice with another première. Verdi declined, saying that a sixth work would be too much. 'I believe that it is better for me to leave this honour to another, luckier person, and [one] who would be more able than I in winning the approval of the audience of La Fenice.'[50] Yet, as he said, he loved the 'magnificent city' of Venice.

From Parma, where he was then the chief of operations at the Teatro Ducale, the former baritone Antonio Superchi wrote to ask Verdi to allow a new production of *La battaglia di Legnano* there. In an amusing letter, Verdi answered, with a firm 'No'.

After I had the pleasure of seeing you at the [Hotel del]la Posta in Parma, I ate well and came home happy. That makes little difference to you, but it makes a lot of difference to me. From then on, every day I get up in the morning, I am dressed, fed, taking long walks in the garden, the fields, the woods along the Po—without falling in. That makes little difference to you, but it makes a lot of difference to me. . . . If you would like to hear more little stories like these later, I will be very happy to write them down for you, and I would have a lot of them to tell you right now; but I am at the bottom of the page, and I have to put the idea out of my head because I don't want the inconvenience of turning the page over.—All joking aside. I promise to do to *La battaglia di Legnano* what I did to *Stiffelio*; so until that work is finished, you will have to let *Battaglia* and *Aroldo* sleep on.[51]

Somma, who was again working on *Vendetta in domino*, had a chance to collaborate directly with the composer, who was in Venice for three days in July. They were joined by Vigna. After he returned to Sant'Agata, Verdi got an understanding and generous letter from Vigna, who expressed his joy at sharing those 'three, extremely pleasant days'.[52] Somma was cursing the Roman censors; but Vigna was at his side, urging common sense. The librettist changed all but two of the sixty-odd lines the censor vetoed. From Somma's letter of 11 August it is clear that Gustavus III had become Riccardo, Duke of Surrey; but even that would not pass: he became a count of Warwick.[53]

During the summer illness cut a swath in Barezzi's family, as his grandson Ciro died, and Barezzi himself suffered a stroke. Verdi, who had sent the youth a personal note during his last illness and had invited him to come to Sant'Agata and play his piano there, also consoled his father-in-law, who recovered almost at once and resumed his normal life. Muzio remained abroad, having decided to go to the United States with Piccolomini. By September Somma had finished all but a few final touches on the libretto of the new opera, which had yet another title: *Un ballo in maschera*. Verdi foresaw no further problems, with Vasselli and the impresario Jacovacci working for him. Reassuring his librettist, he asked that he get ready to come to Rome.[54] In October Verdi, who was disappointed to have missed the eruption of Vesuvius earlier that year, also prepared to return to Naples. Again, he went through Genoa and spent time with Mariani. With Strepponi at his side, he took the ship for Naples, where a group of about twenty close friends awaited the couple's arrival. De Sanctis and his wife had a new-born son, whose godparents were Verdi and Strepponi. When it was finally staged, Verdi's production of *Simon Boccanegra* enjoyed a notable success, even though illness had taken its toll of the cast.

BOOK III

A proposal to write again for the Opéra in Paris was rejected out of hand. Verdi wrote to Escudier in mid-October:

You talk to me about the theatre? . . . about writing for the Opéra!! You?!! Let's speak frankly, and please accept what I feel. I am not either rich enough or poor enough to write for your most important theatre. Not poor enough to need those meagre earnings; not rich enough to lead a comfortable life in your country, where the expenses are very, very high.[55]

Early in January 1859 Verdi and Strepponi left Naples for Rome. After nearly nineteen hours on a very rough sea, they reached Civitavecchia; but the trip had been dangerous and uncomfortable, with Strepponi very ill, the dog Loulou agitated, and Verdi himself suffering, although he had 'not given anything to the sea'. He and Strepponi remained in bed for sixteen hours, unable even to stand up as a 'furious and icy wind' buffeted the ship.[56] A hellish night, he said. Verdi sent news of the trip to De Sanctis, and asked him to look for a thermometer that had been kept in the room near his piano. He had forgotten it, and wanted his friend to bring it to him later. In Rome, the couple took an apartment that Luccardi had leased for the entire Carnival season. 'Very, very ugly', Strepponi said, describing the house at Campo di Marzio 2. She invited De Sanctis to join her and Verdi and to take meals with them; they couldn't offer him a bedroom, she said.[57] Verdi wanted only to get the opera behind him, for he was 'tired of the theatre'. She predicted that *Un ballo in maschera* would be 'not good enough, or bad'.[58] De Sanctis, with other Neapolitan friends, did come to Rome for the première and remained there until the end of February. With Verdi's help, he came to an understanding with Ricordi about being paid for some of the work he did when Gaetano Feroce, the publisher's agent in Naples, was not well.[59]

The composer had other serious concerns in early February, for *Simon Boccanegra* had failed at La Scala, where a tumultuous audience reaction reawakened unhappy memories in Verdi. With Luigia Bendazzi and Sebastiano Ronconi, it had survived for twelve performances. On 4 February, the same day that Strepponi told De Sanctis that Verdi was 'in a chaos of business matters', the composer wrote angrily to Ricordi:

The fiasco of *Boccanegra* in Milan had to happen, and it happened. A *Boccanegra* without a Boccanegra!! Cut off a man's head and then recognize him, if you can. So you are surprised at the *indecency of the audience*? It does not surprise me at all. They are always happy when they can manage to create a scandal! Yet, no matter what friends or enemies may say, *Boccanegra* is not inferior to many of my other operas that are more fortunate than it is; perhaps you need for it an execution that is more refined, and an audience that wants to listen.—A sad place, the theatre!!⁶⁰

Five days later he wrote to the critic Filippo Filippi, who had been in Milan and had written to him about the uproar at La Scala.

Scandalous behaviour in the theatre has never surprised me, and, as I wrote to Ricordi, when I was 26 years old, I knew what the [word] 'audience' meant. From that time on, successes have never gone to my head, and fiascos have never discouraged me. If I went on in this wretched career, it is because when I was 26, it was too late to do anything else, and because I was not physically robust enough to go back to my fields.⁶¹

He deplored the poor reception given by Italian audiences to the great dramatic actress Adelaide Ristori, who had returned from abroad. As to *Boccanegra*, he suggested that it might be welcomed by audiences later on. He was against a cast-change at La Scala and said that he accepted the judgement of the audience with the greatest indifference.

Verdi, who—in Strepponi's words—wanted to get his opera over at any cost, finally produced *Un ballo in maschera* at the Teatro Apollo in Rome on 17 February 1859, with a cast that included Fraschini as Riccardo; Giraldoni, Verdi's original Boccanegra, as Renato; the French soprano Eugènie Julienne-Déjean as Amelia; the contralto Zelinda Sbriscia as Ulrica; and Pamela Scotti, a light soprano, as Oscar. According to an account in Monaldi, Verdi had problems with Julienne-Déjean. When she asked him to go over her role with her, he is said to have replied that she should have come to the theatre prepared, with her music memorized. The fact that Strepponi had to make peace between them suggests that the soprano was her former protégée.⁶² In spite of the problems, the opera had a huge success, with Verdi called out to the footlights more than twenty times.⁶³ With the house completely sold out, tickets were soon being hawked at 'fabulous prices', twice or more the original cost. The ovations grew louder and longer every evening, the acclaim immensely pleasing the composer, who wrote to De Sanctis that the fourth performance went 'magnificently'.⁶⁴ Although Giraldoni became ill, the theatre was 'packed', as it had been the first night.

Many years later Verdi confided to Torelli that he had once criticized

Jacovacci, half-jokingly, for not having had a good company. Jacovacci said: 'What more do you want? The theatre is full every night. Next year you will find we have good women, and so the opera will still be new to the audience. This year, half; the other half, later.'[65]

To Piave, who had been to Paris, had visited Rossini, and had spoken on Verdi's behalf to him, the composer wrote:

I thank you for the good wishes sent from Rossini, and I am happy to have such a worthy defender; but it is certainly humiliating to need defenders always!! . . . But now it is all over! In the midst of the wilderness of Sant'Agata no one plays music, there are no singers, and no theatres, thank God, and no need for anyone to tear his guts out for me. *Ballo in maschera* was successful. Gallo will give you the details. . . . Come to see me at Sant'Agata.[66]

He was clearly thinking of home, although he was still busy at the Apollo and worried about his production. By the first week in March Fraschini was ill. 'To the devil with the theatres', Verdi wrote to De Sanctis, whom he asked to buy a book on the clarification and purification of wines, together with the 'powders or gelatines' to make the process work.[67] He and Strepponi finally left Rome for Civitavecchia, where they spent several days resting, eating, reading, and waiting for good weather and a sound ship. Reminding De Sanctis of errands he had asked him to do, the composer also invited his Neapolitan friend to Sant'Agata.[68] When they got to Genoa, where they stayed in the Hotel Croce di Malta, the couple found Jacovacci, who had left Rome after they did, and invited him to dinner, because, as Verdi said, he was curious to know what business Jacovacci had there. Torelli, who had just proposed that Verdi become director of music in Naples, also hoped to attract Jacovacci to the San Carlo or work with him in some other setting. Mariani was rehearsing *Aroldo*, for which he had high hopes. On the morning after his arrival, Verdi and the conductor took the parts of the *Ballo in maschera* score to the express office and sent them to Ricordi, who would start the process of publishing the music.

On 19 March, the Feast of San Giuseppe, their name-day, Verdi and Strepponi took the train to Piacenza, where they stayed one night in the Hotel San Marco. Verdi had several relatives who lived there, among them his first cousin Don Carlo Uttini, who was then the director of the Teachers' College, the doors of which he had recently opened to women for the first time. The city was an armed fortress, overflowing with the Austrian military force that had occupied it. Threatened by the Piedmont, Austria had selected Piacenza as a key city in its military strategy.[69]

Towards Unification with the Kingdom of Sardinia

The decade from 1848 to 1858 had been a time of ferment and resistance in the Duchy of Parma and Piacenza. In 1848, during the First War for Italian Independence, high hopes had been raised; but the Austrian army's victory had ended the patriots' dream. Many nationalists had gone underground or fled into exile; subversive activities against the occupying forces continued. On 26 March 1854 Duke Carlo III of Parma had been stabbed to death by an assassin. Three months later, following the repression of an uprising, eight patriots had been shot and others condemned to prison.

In 1852 Count Cavour had been elected president of the Council of State in the Kingdom of Sardinia—the Piedmont—thus beginning his seven-year tenure in that post. His domestic and foreign policy transformed the Kingdom of Vittorio Emanuele II and, in the end, changed the map of Europe. Cavour, convinced that Italy could never become a united nation unless the Kingdom played a larger role in European politics, committed his troops in the Crimean War, where they fought as allies of France and England. This commitment won the Piedmont a place among the victors at the peace conference that was held in Paris in 1856. Cavour was then able to raise the question of Italian nationhood among his allies. In 1858 Napoleon III assured Cavour that France would fight beside the Kingdom of Sardinia should that country be attacked by the Austrians, giving him the pledge of a strong ally.

Piacenza, *La Primogenita*

When the Piedmont began to arm, Austria responded by increasing the size of its forces in northern Italy. Piacenza, called 'the first-born daughter of Italy' because it had been the first city to vote for annexation to the Piedmont in 1848, was a post that Austria believed it had to hold at any cost. In January 1859, when war seemed inevitable, Austria began to move additional troops and supplies into the city and send patrols into the countryside. Landowners were ordered to surrender their carriages, wagons, straw, hay, wood, and wine, on threat of sequestration.[70] The campaign against Italian patriots at first took the form of confiscation of leaflets and broadsides. Later, Austria applied a heavier hand. Over Christmas and New Year, street fights between loyalists and Italian patriots resulted in arrests. Austrian officers were warned that 'the infamous Garibaldi' was infiltrating the area to recruit volunteers. Austrian troops were alerted against 'persons suspected for political reasons' and were ordered to survey the towns and villages and report on 'the public spirit' of each.[71]

By 17 January it was reported that Austria had garrisoned 6,000 troops in Piacenza, adding them to the 4,000 already there. A major nationalist demonstration took place on 9 February at the theatre in Cortemaggiore, where a play called *Vittorio Alfieri e la duchessa d'Albany* was being given; and a group of patriots held a secret conference on strategy at Villanova sull'Arda, the town whose territory included most of Verdi's property at Sant'Agata. Because the police commissioner for the entire jurisdiction of Piacenza was held to be too soft on Italian subversives, he was replaced with an officer with a reputation for cruelty, Lieutenant-Marshal Johannes Rohn, who was called 'The Killer'. One day after he took command, he ordered the people of Piacenza to quarter Austrian officials in their houses.[72] In nearby Fiorenzuola troops were sent to stop political demonstrations on the railway line which was being laid to Parma: the engineers and labourers had pinned red, white, and green rags—the Italian colours—to their signal flags.

Many of the most committed nationalists had already left for Turin, where they enrolled as volunteers in the army of the Piedmont. Of 2,365 who joined on 10 March, 576 were from Parma and Piacenza. One week later, when Verdi and Strepponi left Genoa for Sant'Agata, 404 more men from the area enlisted in Turin. By the end of March Parma and Piacenza had contributed about 3,700 soldiers to the cause. There was so much tension in Piacenza the week that Verdi stopped there that Austrian officers were ordered to evacuate their families, and further reinforcements were brought in.[73] The couple stayed only one night in the city. On 20 March they reached Sant'Agata.

If Verdi thought that by going home he could escape from the theatre, he was wrong. Eugenio Tornaghi from Casa Ricordi wrote to him five times in seventeen days in March. From America came news of Muzio, who had left England nearly six months earlier. His first engagement was at the New York Academy of Music, where he had begun to conduct in the autumn. Opened by Max Maretzek on 30 August 1858, the Academy saw Piccolomini's splendid début as Violetta in *La traviata*, under Muzio's baton. The company made a brief trip to Boston, then returned to the Academy on 10 January. Their tour began on 14 February, as Muzio told Verdi and Strepponi in his letter of 19 March, sent from New Orleans.

Here we are with another [Feast of] San Giuseppe, and I still farther from you, who occupy a large part of my heart. . . . From 14 February until now I have done nothing but travel over land and water; I arrived in this city on 14 March; in that month I saw an immense number of beautiful things, but also ugly things. The beautiful things are the forests, woods, rivers, lakes, plantations, flowers, Nature in all its beauty and all its hideousness. I went by Niagara Falls twice, and there is nothing in the world, nothing in all Europe that is a bigger spectacle, more majestic, more imposing, more dreadful and terrifying than that.

In New Orleans, Muzio had seen a slave market, where a boy cost from $300 to $400, while a strong, adult male brought between $1,500 and $2,000. The conductor asked whether Verdi and Strepponi wanted him to buy a slave. As for himself, 'I certainly will not get one.' With Piccolomini's contract with Ullman about to end, the company would go on touring for Lumley, to cities where they had not been, and could earn a lot of money.[74]

He described his conducting style, which he thought would please Verdi: 'Broad gestures, a strong forte, a piano that is not exaggerated, [and] sweetness in the instruments that tie the orchestra together make a good ensemble. I like it, and the audience does too.' Muzio had sent money to his mother, through Verdi's good offices, had paid part, or perhaps all, of his debt to Ricordi, and hoped to be able to send something to Antonio Barezzi at the end of the season.[75] When Strepponi and Verdi heard that Muzio's mother was ill, Strepponi took the ailing woman a rosary that had been blessed by the Pope.

In May Verdi heard from De Sanctis that the management of the Teatro San Carlo wanted to produce *Un ballo in maschera*, but that the censors continued their 'systematic' obstruction of the libretto.[76] He had already written that he would come to Naples to direct the work himself, provided Fraschini sang, a 'sublime' Page could be found for Oscar, *and* the censors approved the exact libretto as it was presented in Rome. 'With these three things—*Fraschini, Page, approval*—you can count on me to stage it; without these, no.'[77] He also rejected an offer to write a new opera, but talked about returning to Naples for the winter and renting a house there.

BOOK III

War

Throughout March the political situation had worsened. National Guard units, which Austria had mustered to maintain order, began to declare their patriotic sympathies and gather in the youth of the Duchy. Early in April, when Austria ordered Piedmont to break up its army, Cavour replied that 'Italy will disarm when Austria evacuates Piacenza'.[78] The response, which newspapers published, was: 'If the Italians want Piacenza, they will have to conquer it.'[79] Vittorio Emanuele II issued his call to the people of Italy late in April. And on the last day of the month Austria declared that Piacenza was in a state of siege. Austrian forces crossed the Ticino River, and war began.

When Cavour learned that the Austrians had indeed taken up his challenge, the statesman (as the poet Giovanni Prati recalled) was overcome with emotion. Rushing to the window of his study, he flung it open and sang the first lines of 'Di quella pira' from *Il trovatore* into the open air.[80]

As the war started, Verdi, like Manzoni, another national hero, was urged to leave and seek a safer sanctuary, the farm being only about 25 kilometres from the Austrian bastion at Piacenza and 18 kilometres from Cremona, the Austrian frontier city on the Po. Verdi's land ran down to the river on the Piacenza side; across the river, the fields were enemy territory. When war was declared, Mariani wrote, advising Verdi to leave and sending him news of the arrival of thousands of French troops in Genoa.[81] There was a general belief that hostilities would begin in Piacenza.[82] The fact that General Gyulai's imperial forces moved across the Ticino instead did little to change the threat to Piacenza. News of the course of war was provided by Mariani on a regular basis, as he sent Verdi newspapers when he could and copied bulletins and other information when he could not.

The flight of the Grand Duke of Tuscany and the establishment of a provisional government there was followed by the removal from Parma of the Regent, Duchess Luisa Maria, who ruled for her son Duke Roberto I. After establishing her own ministers as a governing commission, she moved her children, herself, and her household to a hotel in Mantua, in Austrian territory. Italian patriots took over the city and established a provisional junta that swore loyalty to Vittorio Emanuele II. But on 4 May the ducal governing commission declared the junta invalid and oversaw the return of the Duchess and her entourage to the Ducal Palace.[83] Her son the Duke remained in Mantua. In Piacenza, where a stage of siege was in force, the Austrian authorities ordered anyone leaving or entering the city to obtain a certificate from the police. When the labourers finally finished the stretch of track from Borgo San Donnino to Fiorenzuola, they ran the first work engine with two little Italian flags flying from it, provoking the Austrians into sending additional troops into the country. They were quartered about 12 kilometres from Sant'Agata. Piacenza was in chaos, as the commander ordered the demolition of buildings within the city. On 6 May, sparing only the historic Collegio Alberoni, which stood about 2 kilometres down the Via Emilia toward Cadeo, the destruction began.

News of the war could only be passed from one person to another, as the state of siege continued. Verdi, however, received information from Mariani, who wrote on 12 May to let the composer know that France had indeed sent 'about 100,000 men' with modern weapons through Genoa. The city, hung with decorations, awaited the arrival of Napoleon III, who reached there in mid-May. Verdi probably received all the news late, as Mariani's letters were delayed. The news he got at once was far from comforting, for the Austrians moved troops up the south bank of the Po and into the valleys west of Piacenza. One entire family was executed in the Val Tidone, just on the suspicion that one of them had given out news of Austrian troop movements. An important Austrian advance secured the entire road to Castel San Giovanni, as imperial scouts made their way even into Voghera. On 13 May fresh Austrian troops from Moravia entered Piacenza, and three days later General Urban invaded the Piedmont and began sending Italian prisoners back to the city. More than 12,000 Austrian soldiers were said to be poised at the frontier, while new forces arrived at Piacenza. On 20 May the French and the army of the Piedmont won its first important victory over Austria at Montebello. One day later a newspaper in Parma published a report on the 'complete devastation' of the 'rich, fertile outlying areas' of the 'poor city' of Piacenza. One of Verdi's neighbours and close friends, the patriot Giuseppe Manfredi of Cortemaggiore, had fled the Duchy, under sentence of death.

Writing from Sant'Agata that day, Strepponi, of course, knew something of these developments. In a letter to De Sanctis, she said:

We are at Sant'Agata. Verdi has had several letters from you and says that he has answered them promptly, so one must be lost, nor does that surprise me in these times when communications are interrupted, and the restrictions, especially concerning letters and newspapers, are immense. We thank you; and [will] you thank our friends on our behalf, for their affectionate expressions of interest. Our health is good, [we are] not afraid, but [we are] worried about the serious events that are taking place. This morning at eight the bridges were drawn up and the gates of Piacenza, which is about 32 kilometres from us, were sealed. A section of the Franco-Piemontese Army is coming down to attack that fortress; and tomorrow, perhaps this evening, we will hear the thunder of cannons. Everything is being prepared to make this a war of the giants. Verdi is serious, grave, but calm and trusting in the future. I am certainly more upset, more agitated; but I am a woman, with a more excitable temperament. Moreover, you will understand perfectly that the thought of such things is not going to make us wild with joy. Add to this the fact that although we are not on the front line, we are just [behind], in the second line, and given the swift events of a war, from one day to the next, the [second line] could become the very front . . .

PS The siege of Piacenza will not begin tomorrow, as they said, but could start in two or three—well, in a very few—days. There was a bloody battle at Santa Giustina, between Voghera and Casteggio.[85]

When Strepponi wrote this, there were Austrian soldiers just a few kilometres west of the villa, while battles were being fought in the valleys some 20 to 30 kilometres west of Piacenza. Again, on 23 May; Mariani wrote to beg Verdi to leave the 'exposed position' in which he found himself at Sant'Agata.

It is very probable that the fatal battle will take place on those plains [near Cremona]. . . . So put everything you own away safely, jewellery, silverware, linen, and other valuables. To be brief, you must bury everything, for these are most dangerous times, and you know better than I do that that horde of barbarians has no respect for anything, not fame, nor talent, nor works of art, nor men, and much less women and children. . . . Should you want to leave Sant'Agata, I warn you that you cannot go by Piacenza, for the largest part of the Austrian army is there.[86]

In this, as in all his letters, he gave Verdi the latest news of the war.

Victories were won by the Franco-Piedmontese army at Palestro on 30 May and Magenta on 4 June. The latter, though not a decisive win, did cause the Austrian evacuation of Lombardy. Mariani, writing to Verdi about Palestro, reported that Vittorio Emanuele II had fought with his troops and proved his 'immense courage', arousing the admiration of the French Zouaves at his side.[87] The war, however, went on. It was gradually becoming clear that Italy might become a nation after all. The Duchess Luisa Maria of Parma announced early in June that she was leaving the Duchy and establishing a governing commission there. The Austrians, in a last, brutal gesture, as they evacuated Piacenza, destroyed their remaining fortifications and moved to the north bank of the Po. The people of the city, free at last, tore down all signs of the Austrian and Bourbon regimes and established a council to rule and to convey to the Piedmont the citizens' request to become part of that state. One day later the Duke of Modena also fled, as did the Papal Delegate in Bologna. Also on 11 June the first ranks of the Franco-Piedmontese army entered Piacenza, where they were welcomed as saviours.[88] Among them was Giuseppe Montanelli, Verdi's friend and former collaborator on the libretto of *Simon Boccanegra*. He had entered the ranks as a simple volunteer.

Verdi learned about the evacuation of Piacenza almost at once. Writing to Mariani, he reported on the dynamiting of the fortifications and the retreat. At that moment the Austrian army was just across the Po. 'One can see them passing from Cremona to Mantua', he said.[89] At some moment during these weeks, Verdi and Strepponi had decided to marry, as she confided to De Sanctis in her letter of 21 May. Sending affectionate greetings to her godson Giuseppe De Sanctis, and to his mother, she wrote: 'Teach them to say "Peppina Verdi" this autumn.'[90]

Within a week of the Austrian retreat, Verdi had launched an appeal for contributions to help the families whose sons had volunteered for service. From Sant'Agata on 20 June, he headed the subscription list with his own appeal:

The victories won up to this moment by our valiant brothers were not won without bloodshed, and without terrible sorrow for thousands of families. In these times, everyone who has an Italian heart must contribute, according to his own means, to the holy cause that is being fought for. I propose a subscription to help the wounded and the poor families of those who died for our country.

G. Verdi.

His own name headed the list, with a contribution of 550 francs. Strepponi, signing 'Giuseppina Verdi', which she was not, contributed 88 francs, as did Antonio Barezzi. Carlo Verdi signed for 22 francs as the third contributor to the subscription. Angiolo Carrara, the notary; some of Verdi's farmers; and several of the Barezzis added their names to the list, which was endorsed by the Bussetans, rich and poor.[91]

Three days later a long letter from Verdi to Clara Maffei brought her news of Sant'Agata, of the dynamiting of Piacenza and the retreat.

Finally they have left! or at least they have withdrawn, and may our lucky star take them even further away, until—driven beyond the Alps—they go off to enjoy their own climate, their own sky, which I hope is even clearer, beautiful, [and] more resplendent than ours.—How many wonderful events in a few days! It doesn't seem that it's true. And who would ever have believed in such generosity in our allies? As for myself, I confess and say: *mea grandissima culpa*, for I did not believe that the French would come into Italy, and that, in any case, they would have shed their blood for us, without thinking of conquest. On the first point, I was misled; I hope and pray that I shall not be wrong about the second point, that Napoleon will not go back on his Milan Proclamation. Then I will adore him as I adored Washington, and even more; and, blessing the great nation [France], I will willingly put up with all their *blague*, their insolent *politesse* and the contempt they feel for everything that is not French.[92]

He added news of Montanelli, who had been seen in Piacenza, where he was still in the volunteer forces. Verdi had nothing but admiration for him, he said.

A poor priest (the only right-minded one in this part of the country) brought me Montanelli's good wishes. . . . The former professor of jurisprudence makes a noble example of himself! That is beautiful and sublime! I can only admire and envy him. Oh, if my health were better I would be with him myself! I say this to you in absolute secrecy: do not repeat it to others, for I don't want anyone to think it a vain boast. But what can I do, who am not able to complete a 3-mile march, who cannot stand five minutes of sun on my head, and a little wind or humidity gives me sore throats that send me to bed, sometimes for weeks? What a miserable nature I have! Good for nothing![93]

Montanelli was, in fact, a model patriot, having fought in 1848 at the battle of Curtatone with a troop of Tuscan university students. Wounded in the chest, he was taken prisoner and transported to the Austrian prison at Innsbruck. Now eleven years later he was back in the uniform of a common soldier, in a duchy that was not completely free of strife. Nearby Fiorenzuola, where a reactionary faction had revolted on 13 June, had a powerful pro-Bourbon party that was calling for the return of the Duchess. In Parma the *duchisti* had even more power; there it was suggested that the Duchy might continue as a neutral state, not united to Italy. From Turin, the King sent his own man as governor to Parma. On 20 June, the same day that Verdi issued his appeal for funds for the families of the wounded and dead, a platoon of eighty soldiers was sent from Piacenza to Fiorenzuola, where a pro-Austrian revolt threatened. An Austrian spy was arrested in Borgo San Donnino. Where the Italian patriots were stronger, in Cortemaggiore, a hero's welcome awaited Manfredi. Skirmishes and battles continued. At San Martino, between Peschiera and Desenzano, the Franco-Piedmontese troops were victorious; but the bloody but indecisive battle of Solferino, fought just to the south of San Martino on 24 June, led to the end of the war.

A national hymn of joy was in order; and Giulio Carcano was chosen to write the text. Asked by the Mayor of Milan to provide the music, Verdi declined, although Carcano himself wrote to the composer that he alone could provide music that would endure. Addressing 'my best friend', the poet begged Verdi in the name of their long-standing friendship to contribute to the effort; but Verdi claimed he did not have enough time to compose a score worthy of the occasion. His answer, sent also to the Marzis, who had sought his co-operation even before the Milanese authorities had written, is eloquent in its expression of love of country.[94] Verdi did not, however, compose a 'Canto per Napoleone'. Within days he had every reason to be glad that he had refused. The Treaty of Villafranca, signed by the warring nations, guaranteed that the Piedmont could add Lombardy to its territories, but that 'Venice and the fortresses of Peschiera, Pizzighetone, and Mantua' would remain under Austrian dominion. This shocking news set off demonstrations in Piacenza and led to a general denunciation of an agreement that made no mention of 'the fate of the Duchy', which was not named in the treaty, and 'abandoned Tuscany, Piacenza, Parma, Reggio Emilia, Modena, and the Papal States to the cruel judgement of Princes who are detested and cursed by the people.'[95] From Piacenza, the governing body sent letters to the mayors of every city and town, warning of possible seditious uprisings in the area. From Saint Gall, Switzerland, where the Duchess Luisa Maria and her son had taken refuge, came the news that she might return. There were rumours that Modena would again be under Austrian control, even though it too had chosen to be incorporated into the Piedmont. Noisy demonstrations in support of Vittorio Emanuele II took place in Parma and Piacenza in mid-July, as the *Gazzetta piacentina* denounced the Treaty of Villafranca. But in Paris, to the astonishment of all Italian patriots, Napoleon III had granted an audience to the Duchess and her counsellor Marquis Pallavicino. At the end of July it was by no means certain that the former Duchy of Parma and Piacenza would become part of the new Italy for the Duchess even had the support of Queen Victoria.

In this troubled time, Verdi fulminated against the unexpected turn of events.

Ah, instead of singing a hymn to glory, it seems to me more appropriate today to send up a lament to the eternal misfortunes of our country. Together with your letter I received a bulletin of the twelfth [of July] that read: '*The Emperor to the Empress*: . . . *Peace has been made* . . . *Venice remains Austrian*!!' And where, then is the independence of Italy, so long hoped for and promised? What does the Proclamation of Milan mean? What!? Venice is not Italian? After so many victories, what an outcome! How much blood shed for nothing! How many poor young people deluded! And Garibaldi, who even sacrificed his old, long-held views in favour of a king, without achieving the goals he wished! It is enough to drive one mad! I am writing under the influence of the deepest outrage, and I do not know what you will say to me. Isn't it absolutely true that we will never have anything to expect from a foreigner, no matter what nation it may be! What do you say about this? Perhaps I am wrong again. I hope so.[96]

But Italy had indeed been betrayed; and Verdi was not wrong. All the rulers, save those who had fled Milan, expected to be able to return to power; but the former duchies and the former Papal States found the power to resist. Luigi Carlo Farini, a former editor of the newspaper *Il Risorgimento*, elevated to power in Modena, took the title of dictator. Shortly, Parma united itself to his state. In Florence, Verdi's friend Baron Ricasoli held the same title. Patriotic demonstrations were called everywhere, even as a National Guard was strengthened throughout the former Duchy. Manfredi, whom Vittorio Emanuele II appointed secretary-general in the government of 'the Parma States' in August, soon became the governor-general. One of his first acts was to call electoral committees, so that a plebiscite could be held to allow Parma and Piacenza to be incorporated into the Piedmont.

The French army, holding forts in Piacenza and Cremona, was supplemented by more volunteers for the National Guard. From Turin, the King then laid his claim to the former Duchy and accepted Farini as Dictator of Modena, Reggio Emilia, Parma, and Piacenza. A small state was thus constituted along the Via Emilia. The announcement of the plebiscite in the whole territory set off reactions from pro-Austrian priests, who advised their parishioners not to vote. But the former Duchy of Piacenza registered more than 17,000 votes for annexation against 255 votes opposed. Bolstered by about 18,000 French soldiers who were part of what was then called 'The Army of Italy', the people asked for unification.

Verdi and Strepponi, who had been planning marriage since the spring, travelled to the village of Collange-sous-Salève on 29 August 1859. In the Savoy, just outside Geneva, they were married by the Abbé Charles

Mermillod, rector of the church of Notre Dame in Geneva. Before two witnesses, the coachman who had brought them there and the bell-ringer of the church, the couple took their vows. Later, Verdi said that they had chosen Collanges because Mermillod, for whom he expressed contempt, had guaranteed that the bond would be valid under religious and civil law.[97] He had sent the parish priest away, Verdi said, perhaps to be sure that his authority alone would prevail, perhaps because he wanted to keep the entire honorarium for himself.

For the first time since September 1849, Verdi returned home as a man living by the law, rather than outside it; but he and Strepponi appear to have kept their marriage a secret from almost everyone, perhaps telling only Piave and Barezzi. The fact that Strepponi's son Camillino reached his twenty-first birthday in January 1859 may have had something to do with their decision to marry.

Verdi and Strepponi returned to Sant'Agata in time for the election to choose the deputy to the Assembly of the Parma Provinces. Because he and his father were still legal residents of Busseto, Verdi voted there. The balloting was held inside the city walls, in the former Jesuit church of Sant'Ignazio, where thirty-three years before the promising youth had aroused enthusiasm with his organ concert. Then he had been the centre of a political storm. Now he was the voice of the new Italian nation. All Busseto turned out for the election. The ailing canon of the church of San Bartolomeo was borne to the polling place in a chair litter. Hours before the balloting began, the church was full, the infirm leaning against the red-brick walls or sitting on the steps outside. The town band marched down the road to meet Verdi; and when his carriage came into view, a shout went up from the crowd. The Mayor and the Provost of San Bartolomeo delivered their official greetings, which were followed by a concert of some of the best-known pieces from Verdi's operas. Grown men wept, as women covered their faces with their shawls. The crowd shouted 'Viva Verdi!' and 'Viva l'Italia!'[98]

Even before the election, it had seemed certain that Verdi would be chosen to represent Busseto in the delegation sent to Parma to vote for annexation to the Piedmont. When he won, he was offered the honour of representing his city as deputy to the Assembly of the Parma Provinces.

BOOK IV

23

September 1859–December 1860

Verdi as Deputy to the Assembly

On 5 September Verdi sent his formal letter of acceptance to Donnino Corbellini, the Podestà of Busseto:

Illustrious Signor Podestà,

The honour that my fellow-citizens wished to confer upon me, nominating me as their representative to the Assembly of the Parma Provinces, flatters me and makes me very grateful. If my few talents, my studies, the art that I profess do not make me very suited for this kind of office, at least may there be value in the great love I have borne and still bear for this, our noble and unhappy Italy. Needless to say, I shall proclaim in my name and that of my fellow-citizens:

the fall of the Bourbon dynasty;
annexation to the Piedmont;
the Dictatorship of the illustrious Italian Luigi Carlo Farini.

In annexation to the Piedmont rests the future greatness and regeneration of our native land. Anyone who feels Italian blood running in his own veins must desire this strongly and constantly; thus the day will dawn for us when we can say that we belong to a great and noble Nation.[1]

Two days later at twelve-thirty in the afternoon the first Assembly of the Parma Provinces was called to order in Parma. Excited crowds filled the streets around the building as the deputies arrived. During the session, Farini won rounds of applause for his patriotic address. The second and third sessions, both on 9 September, saw Marquis Giuseppe Mischi and Carlo Fioruzzi elected to office, the former as the vice-President, the latter as one of the body's two secretaries. Manfredi on this same day received a communication from the statesman Giuseppe La Farina, asking to have

BOOK IV

Verdi appointed to the Commission of Deputies that would present the results of the election to King Vittorio Emanuele II. The main order of business on the eleventh was the resolution that the Bourbons should be driven from the Duchy and never allowed to return. Fioruzzi proposed the act, which the deputies accepted, fifty-five votes in favour, none opposed. A decree was then promulgated to verify that annexation to the Piedmont was desired by the people. In support of it, Verdi, Manfredi, Mischi, Fioruzzi, and Enrico Stevani addressed their fellow-members, urging passage. The unanimous vote was announced at once, as the cannon of the fortress of Parma began firing to mark the event. Before the session ended, Verdi and other delegates were elected to represent the Assembly before the King. The body had also drafted a document for Napoleon III, declaring its support of unification.[2]

The Commission left Parma on the fourteenth. With Verdi were Fioruzzi, Mischi, the elderly patriot-noble Count Jacopo Sanvitale of Fontanellato and Parma, and Gian Carlo Dosi of Pontremoli. They travelled through Piacenza, Castel San Giovanni, Voghera, Tortona, and Alessandria, hailed everywhere by crowds of city officials, bands, and school children offering bouquets of flowers. Reaching Turin on 15 September, as the King had ordered, they were welcomed at the station and at the Albergo Trombetta, where they stayed. Long, noisy demonstrations took place under their windows. Early that afternoon carriages took them to the palace, where Vittorio Emanuele II received them. During their audience, the King praised the thousands of volunteers from Parma, Piacenza, and Modena who had swelled the ranks of his army. The blood they had shed, he said, gave proof of the will of their people. At the head of the Commission, Verdi presented the election results to the King. That evening a huge rally was held outside the Trombetta, where the Commission members had to appear again and again on the balcony. Verdi was given a special ovation then and on the eighteenth, when parliament entertained the members at a banquet in Palazzo Carignano.

Even before voting day, Verdi's election had been seen as inevitable by the people of his town and by the composer himself. On 3 September he had visited Parma and spoken to someone in the provisional government. He also wrote to Mariani, asking him to arrange for him to meet Cavour during the forthcoming visit to Turin of the deputies of the Assembly. The conductor assured Verdi that Cavour would indeed receive him and then asked Sir James Hudson, the English Ambassador, to arrange the meeting.

The former Prime Minister was then living in retirement at his estate at Leri, having resigned from the government after Villafranca. To his agent Giacinto Corio the statesman wrote: 'Hudson writes to me that the famous composer Verdi, author of *Trovatore*, *Traviata*, etc. is coming tomorrow on the first train to Livorno [Ferraris], intending to pay me a visit. Since he is a European celebrity, I think you will be happy to be with him.'[3] Cavour sent his own carriage to fetch Verdi, who may have been accompanied by Mariani or Hudson, and received him with open arms. They met on 17 September.

The profound impression Cavour made is reflected in the letter that Verdi sent to him.

Excellency,

May Your Excellency forgive my boldness and the annoyance that these few lines may perhaps inflict on you. For a long time I wanted to know the Prometheus of our country personally; nor did I ever give up hope of finding the opportunity to fulfill this real desire of mine. What I would not have dared to hope for, however, is the open and friendly welcome with which Your Excellency honoured me. I was very moved when I left! I shall never forget your Leri, where I had the honour of grasping the hand of the great man of State, the supreme citizen, the man whom every Italian will have to call the father of our country. Please receive kindly, Excellency, these sincere words from a poor artist who has had no other merit than that of loving and of having always loved his own native land.[4]

Cavour's answer was equally eloquent.

The letter that you wrote me when you returned to Busseto moved me very, very deeply. It is a great compensation for the hard work I have borne to be sure that I have the affectionate sympathy of a fellow citizen who contributed to keeping the name of Italy honoured in Europe. So I thank you for your visit and for the emotions you felt in Leri. I will always have this happy memory and the continuing desire to be with you again in your native land, which is now the country of both of us.[5]

Their meeting and their mutual respect and love affected Verdi in many ways. As Mariani confirmed, the atmosphere of the encounter was warm; shared interests in Italian unification and in agriculture guaranteed an understanding between the two. Cavour was surely not indifferent to the fact that of all the deputies on the Commission Verdi received the wildest acclaim.

The members of the Commission left Turin on 19 September, and all but Verdi went on to Milan, where, as in the capital, they were greeted at the station and again at their hotel by huge crowds and bands. Although they did not arrive until seven in the evening, they were expected at a gala at La Scala, where every public official and private dignitary in Milan was gathered for a welcoming ceremony. Clara Maffei, Filippo Filippi, and others of the Countess's circle had prepared a glorious welcome for Verdi, who had not been in Milan for more than ten years. Filippi wore his best evening clothes; Clara had made little bouquets with her own hands. But they, and the people of Milan, waited in vain. From the stage, it was announced that Verdi would not attend.[6]

To avoid the celebration, Verdi had gone directly from Turin to Sant'Agata. Mariani accompanied him as far as Broni, near Stradella, where the conductor stayed with the Massa family for several days, regretting the fact that he had not accepted Verdi's invitation to go home with him. In letters, the two men discussed their correspondence with Cavour and Verdi's stay in Turin. From Piave came news of the Austrian troop reinforcements in Venice. The librettist was depressed and angry over the political situation, but full of concern for Verdi, who had written him from Parma while he was there for the Assembly. Piave thanked Verdi for his

dear lines, sent from Parma on the eleventh. . . . I cannot tell you how much comfort they brought me in my present despair!!! You are always the same, and I am not, because I am becoming more and more your admirer, friend, and adorer!!! . . . Beloved soul, may heaven console you, because you are worthy, and may you always have greater comforts because your worth will always increase. The day that I consider the most solemn of the year is near, 9 [October, which Verdi considered his birthday]!!! And will I be able to be at Sant'Agata? Will I be able to share my holy joy with that of your Sweetest Creature [Strepponi], whom God has made for you, and whom you were able to find among the thousands [of others]. Who knows? Oh, if I am not at Sant'Agata on the ninth, my thoughts will be there, my vows will join them, and you will surely remember this poor old friend who will love you as long as there is life in him.[7]

Piave went on to describe Venice as a sad place; throngs of Austrian soldiers with rifles patrolled the streets; La Fenice was closed for the winter, because of the political situation; Gallo was 'close to hydrophobia' because with the theatres closed, he had no business. Sending regards from Gallo and Vigna, Piave added expressions of love for Strepponi, 'our adorable Chatelaine', and signed off: 'Addio, Verdi. Good day, good day.'[8]

Like many of Verdi's friends, Piave thought of the ninth of October as a day to honour the composer. In Genoa, Mariani performed a rite of his own. Having received a fine portrait photograph as a gift from Verdi, he had had it framed and covered with a small, green silk curtain so it would not fade. At exactly 4.20 p.m. the conductor stood before Verdi's photograph, gazed at it, and raised his glass in a toast. He hoped that the composer, who kept his watch ten minutes fast, would think of him at 4.30, Verdi's time. Barezzi and his wife Maddalena were guests at Sant'Agata that day. Clara Maffei, although not at the celebration, had been sent a large photograph of Verdi together with six smaller pictures of him in several poses, looking—Verdi said jokingly—like a hairdresser, an imbecile, and a pirate.

With the help of Giovannino Menta, Verdi carried on the work at Sant'Agata, where life was slightly more tranquil than it had been in May and June. The composer's mail was no longer being opened, censored, and sometimes confiscated; the threat of occupation of the villa by Austrian officers had been removed with the evacuation of enemy troops from the region south of the Po and from the Cremonese; and nearby families no longer feared that their property would be sequestered. Yet the autumn of 1859 was still a troubled time; unrest and uncertainty still ruled people's lives. Wrenching changes were taking place throughout the region as new codes of commercial law were adopted, new forces of order were mustered, and new rules governing postage and taxes were beginning to be enforced. Even though annexation was still not a fact, public officials were ordered to swear loyalty to the King and the laws of the Piedmont. Passports were abolished for travellers moving only in Parma, Piacenza, Modena, Tuscany, Piedmont, and Lombardy. Men from the region who had served in the Duchess's troops were invited to return from exile beyond the Po, even as the former Regent and her son Duke Roberto continued to press their absolutist claims from abroad.[9] Disorder was rife in the local military, as young soldiers were mistreated; some turned to house-breaking, assault, and robbery. Early in October a hated tyrant, the Piacentine Colonel Luigi Anviti returned to Parma, where for more than ten years he had acted brutally in the name of the Bourbon regime. Recognized at the railroad station, he was dragged to the Caffè Ravazzoni, one of his former haunts, and was decapitated by members of a mob. His body and head were carried through the streets for perhaps as much as four hours before the local authorities sent a company of soldiers to seize them. It seemed that the murderers would not be punished. The incident had repercussions in Turin, Milan, Paris, and Austria, as further disorders and even a possible uprising were feared. Hoping to assure order, Farini demanded that every citizen turn in firearms, swords, and other weapons; but only a few decorative swords and about fifty old guns were handed over, leaving Parma with 'at least 5,000 hidden guns; the common people have thousands of knives and daggers; and in certain parts of the city, no boy of 14 or 15 . . . leaves his house without one of these dangerous weapons.'[10] When arrests were made, no witnesses could be found among the frightened people of the place.

The alarm raised in France by the colonel's murder provoked Napoleon III to propose again that some of the provinces be made into a single state with the Pope at its head, with the Duchess restored to power as the ruler of Modena, in the hope of laying some of the anarchy to rest. A quick response to that proposal came with the suggestion that Cavour be made dictator of Tuscany, the Romagna, Modena, Reggio Emilia, Parma, and Piacenza. Some solution had to be found, if the disorders were to cease, for every day brought news of an uprising, a rebellion led by loyalists, or a concerted resistance to the draft. Finally Farini summoned the Assemblies back to Parma and Modena to deal with the crisis, as local militias took over protection of some communities. At the sessions of the Assembly, which met on 6 and 7 November, the future of the Parma Provinces was considered. Fioruzzi read a message from Farini, proclaiming Eugenio of Savoy, Prince of Carignano, as the regent of the new state that had been created 'in the name of the King Vittorio Emanuele.'[11] Before the end of the month Farini, driven by his passion to unite the former duchies and the Romagna, and, as he said, to establish one law and one state, dissolved the individual governments and placed Piacenza, Parma, Reggio Emilia, Modena, Bologna, and all the territory of the Romagna under one single government.[12]

With the final meeting of the Assembly, Verdi formally returned to private life; but he continued his commitment to his district. In October the commissioner in Fidenza had urged the authorities in Busseto to provide rifles for at least a part of the National Guard; but because the city treasury could not cover the cost, Corbellini, the Podestà, asked Verdi to help. With a sum of 3,500 lire, the composer acquired the weapons, although not without difficulty. At first, he contacted a man whom Sir James Hudson had mentioned, but when there was no response, he turned to Mariani. Having originally ordered one hundred guns on 1 October and seventy-two more eighteen days later, and having heard nothing further about them, he asked the conductor to investigate whether the dealer, Andrea Danovaro of Genoa, had in fact received the order.[13] Mariani responded to Verdi's appeal and undertook what the composer called a 'worthy and holy' mission. One hundred guns came from Genoa; and Busseto repaid Verdi for them. Further funds for weapons were provided by the Monte di Pietà.

Through October and November some of Verdi's time was spent in trying to help young men from Busseto and the surrounding countryside. Seeking the assistance of his former schoolmate Giuseppe Piroli who had been at Farini's side throughout the crises of 1859, Verdi asked for a commission in the new armed forces for Demaldè's son Alberto,[14] and appealed for a second chance for 'a deserter, spy, former soldier of the [Duchess] Regent' who would be 'one more soldier for our army', as he would be saved from a life of crime.[15] When it later developed that the deserter had fled from the garrison of Modena, Verdi defended him, saying that the youth of the area felt that they had been drafted illegally. He added that there unrest and unhappiness were rife in the countryside.[16]

Strepponi described her husband in this period as having taken refuge in the country because he wished to be left alone after so much travelling, so that he could enjoy the solitude that he had earned with his labour. 'I am afraid that he has unlearned [what he knows about] music', she wrote to De Sanctis.[17] Verdi described himself as having put music aside, after his return from Rome and the première of *Un ballo in maschera*. 'I have not done any more music, I have not seen any more music, I have not thought any more about music. I don't even know what colour my last opera is, and I almost don't remember it. So tell Zarlatti [the impresario of the San Carlo] that I would not know how to take my pen in hand to write down notes.'[18]

As early as 1844 and 1845 the composer had announced his decision to retire. While he was in Rome producing *Un ballo in maschera*, Verdi had declared in public that he was retiring. At a dinner on 11 March 1859, when he and Strepponi had Jacovacci and the Roman journalist Giuseppe Cencetti as their guests, he had said several times that he would not compose again. When at the end of the evening the impresario made a remark about the possibility that a stay at Sant'Agata would relax Verdi and reminded him of the woeful state of Italian opera, the composer interrupted Jacovacci and repeated his announcement: he had stopped composing. His decision was reported in Torelli's *L'omnibus* a few days later. Now it seemed that he had indeed given up music.[19]

In December Mariani again visited Sant'Agata, where he had also spent time in September. A severe winter, with 3 feet of snow in Busseto and 10 feet in the passes of the Appenines, brought hardship to a weary region. Barezzi was virtually the only other visitor to the villa, for Muzio remained in America. From there, he wrote to Verdi during the summer and autumn of 1859, sending news of the operas he conducted. In New York *I vespri siciliani*, given with opulent scenery and costumes, launched the season, while *Aroldo*, with the Parma-born baritone Gaetano Ferri, and *Rigoletto*, with Frezzolini, were scheduled later. Muzio got news of the Second War of Italian Independence from the editor of the *New York Herald*, who had sources of information on the Italian conflict. 'You can imagine how anxiously we Italians await news from Italy; up to now, we are happy and hope that the Emperors will want to let the Italians govern themselves in their own way, and according to their own wishes.'[20] Asking Verdi to pay Ricordi for some scores that he wanted shipped, he also told the composer to keep some money for himself, perhaps to pay a small debt, and to give the rest to Muzio's mother.[21] With news that *I vespri siciliani* had saved the American company from bankruptcy, Muzio sent word of the revolt in Virginia and added that he considered John Brown a madman. The slaves' emancipation could never be accomplished, he said. Piave, who wished to escape from 'Austrian warships' and 'insignia' in economically devastated Venice, hoped that Verdi and Mariani would help him. Writing on 6 December, the composer held out little hope but said he would do everything possible. He also invited Piave to Sant'Agata in spite of the snow while warning him that after Christmas he planned to spend some time in Genoa. Overwhelmed with his own problems, the librettist remained where he was, at least for the moment.[22]

It was probably Mariani who persuaded Verdi and Strepponi to live in Genoa during the winter, for he had begun his campaign in June,[23] and continued it into the autumn. In October he summed up the reasons why Naples and Paris would be unsuitable.[24] Shortly after New Year's Day in 1860, Strepponi and Verdi took up residence in the Hotel Croce di Malta, where they had stayed on previous visits to Genoa. Originally, Mariani had been asked to find a small town house or private apartment; but when nothing satisfactory became available, Verdi chose the hotel, which stood in Via Carlo Alberto near the Piazza del Banco San Giorgio, in the very heart of the busy commercial city. When Verdi lived there, a broad marble terrace lay along one side of the street and overlooked the harbour, providing a favourite promenade for the people of the neighbourhood. The docks were not far away.[25]

Verdi's operas, many of which had been given at the Teatro Carlo Felice before and during Mariani's tenure there, had made the composer's name a byword in Genoa; but because of the particular character of the Genovese, Verdi was able to lead a private life there that proved more satisfying than that he had led in Milan, Naples, or Venice. In his visits to Genoa between 1854 and 1860, he had spent time chiefly with Mariani, making few other close friends. One respected intimate was Giuseppe De Amicis, an engineer, the cousin of the novelist Edmondo De Amicis. An anecdote established their first meeting at a construction site, almost certainly in the mid-1850s. Verdi and Strepponi were taking a walk through the city, when they stopped to study a building that was under construction. De Amicis invited them to inspect the project at close reach. Verdi introduced himself as a farmer. The engineer talked of the building and, later in the conversation, added that he sometimes went to the theatre and was particularly fond of *Il trovatore*. At that point, Strepponi intervened, revealing Verdi's identity.[26] Their friendship lasted until the end of Verdi's life.

His friendship with Mariani, probably in its twelfth or thirteenth year when Verdi began to spend his winters in Genoa, had already reached the 'Tu' level before 1853; but in 1857, 1858, and 1859, the composer and conductor began to depend on each other for news and exchanges of opinion on theatrical and political matters. The composer asked Mariani to help him with countless personal matters, among them the shipment of rifles, statuary, orange trees, magnolias, furniture, works of art, and dress patterns. Errand after errand was performed by Mariani, obedient to Verdi's every request, at what must often have been a serious sacrifice of his own time and energy, as visits to gun-dealers, booksellers, newspaper offices, owners of apartments and houses, and customs officers were followed up with commitments of money (which Verdi always repaid) to nurserymen, station-masters, and shipping agents. Verdi clearly enjoyed Mariani's company immensely. In Genoa, they often were together.

News from home came from Barezzi, who answered Verdi's frequent letters. On 4 January, almost immediately after his arrival, the composer sent Barezzi troubling news about the unresolved political situation, to which the older man replied: 'What will come of us, if we have to go back to being slaves, as we were before?'[27] He sent Verdi good news of the triumph of *Il trovatore* in Lodi, Strepponi's birthplace, and attached a record of the daily weather at Busseto. All his letters included regards to Strepponi and 'the good, kind Mariani'. Jubilantly, on 20 January Barezzi commented on Napoleon's letter to the Pope, which could only benefit Parma, and, especially, the Romagna. Rumours abounded: that Prussia was sending volunteers to Rome; that 50,000 men from Central Italy would be sent to the Piedmont; that the King's army would move on Bologna and the Papal States; and that Napoleon III would sent 150,000 soldiers into Italy. 'God willing, things will go well and finish well', he said,[28] but he expressed a general fear that a new war would break out. He and Verdi had different statistics on the size of the Army of Central Italy, which included Parma, Piacenza, Modena, and the Romagna. Just from Busseto more than 100 new soldiers had enrolled, perhaps inspired by the manœuvres of the local forces of the National Guard, who were 'using your fine rifles, which I wish were 200 instead of 100', Barezzi wrote. Both he and the composer deplored a demonstration in Parma, where a drunken crowd had begun to shout 'We want Garibaldi!' 'But you will have to agree with me that they are desperate, that they are dying of hunger.'[29]

Barezzi's well-formed opinions and independence of spirit often set him against his son-in-law, for whom he was a match.

You write to me that there in nothing new in political matters, but it seems to me that there is news! The Congress [to determine the fate of Central Italy] broke up because Rome did not wish to accept the advice of the Emperor of the French; behind Rome are Naples and Austria; and as a result, Central Italy and Piedmont will probably have to get ready for war! You always write to me that there are not many soldiers in Central Italy; but I, on the other hand, have heard that there are many in Reggio [and] Modena; and at Bologna, 10,000 men. This doesn't seem like few to me, and what is more, if war were declared many will go to take part in it who are now living at home but—of course—have already been soldiers.[30]

To Genoa came requests for help from Verdi's friends, sent by Barezzi, who, immobilized by the snow and sub-zero temperatures, was staying 'home, near the fire in my shop.'[31] He prayed that the spirit of war would inspire the soldiers of Central Italy to march on Venice and drive out every Austrian soldier, and that annexation would soon become a fact. Remarks on the 'stupid' encyclical issued by Pope Pius IX were followed by: 'I hope for the best for our Italy. Long live Italy, France, Vittorio Emanuele and his ministers!'[32] In another letter, he gave Verdi news of the meeting of the eligible voters in the church of Sant' Ignazio, where a member of the provincial council and twenty members of the city council were chosen. 'The first nomination went to you, with fifty votes; and I was elected city councillor, also with fifty votes. Before 18 March all the voters will have to go to Borgo San Donnino [now Fidenza] to elect the deputy to Parliament; and I believe that you will be elected, even against your will.' Barezzi seemed certain that after the elections annexation would be inevitable. Verdi, who had written a pessimistic letter, did not have enough faith. 'I still hope for the best', Barezzi said, as he asked his son-in-law to continue to send news of political developments, 'because it is very, very dear to me.'[33]

Verdi intended to stay about three months in Genoa; but Barezzi's letter of 26 February, notifying him that he had been elected a member of the provincial council, brought about a change of plan. He returned to Sant'Agata with Strepponi during the second week in March and declined to serve in that office. A transformation had taken place during his absence, for his country had a new character and a new name: the former Parma Provinces had officially become the Royal Provinces of Emilia.[34] On Farini's orders 'all traces of the old' had been obliterated in the hope of bringing about the de facto destruction of traditional, local allegiances. 'One single government', with the dictator at its head, ruled the whole area. 'Unless they hang me and burn Parma, Modena, and Bologna, no dukes or priests will come back to rule here,' Farini declared.[35] At his right hand during this massive organization of a new state was Piroli, Verdi's intimate friend. Correspondence between the two men documents a trust that lasted almost to the end of the century. The new government could command about 200,000 members of the National Guard as 1860 began.[36] The force of such a corps helped to guarantee the survival of the Royal Provinces of Emilia, although Farini still faced pro-Austrian demonstrations at which protestors, raised yellow and black flags and shouted: 'Long Live Radetsky', summoning up the spirit of the hated commander who had ruled 'ungovernable Milan' and fought so hard to keep Lombardy and Venetia in Austrian hands, while supporting dukes and duchesses on the thrones of Parma, Modena, and Tuscany.[37] These regions were helped into the modern age in 1859 and 1860 as work on the railway system went forward. The last link of the Piacenza–San Nicolò line was opened to general traffic in January 1860, connecting the cities from Bologna on the south through Modena, Reggio Emilia, Parma, and Piacenza to Turin, the capital.

Also in January came the welcome news that Cavour had returned to power. Parma and Piacenza celebrated the statesman's nomination with band concerts and general illuminations of the cities. A rash of hand-

written posters appeared on walls throughout the Provinces urging immediate annexation to the Piedmont. Even Queen Victoria had referred to
the pacification of Italy in her address to Parliament, supporting the
exclusion of all foreign rulers and their legal structures. It was widely
rumoured that troops from the Piedmont would leave Alessandria for
Piacenza, Parma, Modena, and Bologna.

The new provincial council was to begin transacting business in the
spring; but it faced signs of rebellion. In Piacenza, the Bishop had
preached and published texts in favour of the temporal power of the Pope,
only to be confronted with angry responses coming from all quarters.
Many of the walls of the city were smeared with 'Death' and 'Traitor' and
'Betrayer of the Christian Faith', while the National Guard was summoned
to protect the Bishop's residence. Rightists raised their heads wherever
they could, secure in the knowledge that the provincial election results
were not in. New deputies were to be chosen to vote in their respective
assemblies yet once more, to endorse the annexation. Piedmont was to
lose the Savoy (the King's ancestral home) and Nice (Garibaldi's birthplace), which were to be ceded to France.[38] It seemed almost certain that
Parma, Piacenza, and Modena would be annexed; the Romagna asked
formally for annexation; but unification with Tuscany was far from sure.
Napoleon III, who received a special appeal on its behalf from one of
Cavour's emissaries in Paris, publicly expressed his wish to see the
Italian question settled. Farini asked the people of Emilia to use the
electoral process in March to choose deputies and to vote unanimously for
union with Piedmont. Although Barezzi believed that Verdi would be
elected, the deputy chosen to represent Borgo San Donnino and Pellegrino
Parmense was Giuseppe Massari, whose invaluable diary is the source of
so much information about this period. The Neapolitan patriot, a loyal
supporter of Cavour, had given up a more promising post in order to run.
Verdi, although happy not to be a deputy, was irritated at the call for
another vote, believing that Italy was being used by the Emperor for his
own purposes. He wrote to Piroli:

Why vote yet again? Napoleon treats us like children and as if we had been
joking up to now. But we have to beg and be grateful to him too. If I knew
anything about politics, I would say that he—the master—wants Savoy, Nice,
and the Duchy of Tuscany for himself; he would agree to have Piedmont
stronger, on the condition that it be his very humble servant. That is the Italy
he wants![39]

'So you didn't want to be a deputy?' Piave wrote. 'That's all right; we will make you a senator.'[40] But Verdi for the moment was pleased to be able to stay at home. The elections in March 1860 reaffirmed the wish of the people of Emilia-Romagna and Tuscany to be annexed to the kingdom of Vittorio Emanuele II. When 800,000 Italians voted 'Yes' to the question, deputies were chosen for the Parliament, which was to be convened in Turin, which, on the night of 16 March, was illuminated to celebrate the results of the elections. Because more than 426,000 people had voted for annexation, the Royal Provinces of Emilia were considered the heart of the new state. Only 756 voters were against annexation; 750 abstained. Around Bologna, where the Papal Legate had held power, fears of a pro-papal uprising were laid to rest in March, when four battalions of Vittorio Emanuele's troops marched into the city. The next day Farini was received in Turin, where he presented the results of the Emilian plebiscite to the King, who then signed the decree declaring that the Royal Provinces of Emilia were integrated into his nation. When a telegram announcing the news reached Piacenza and Parma, all the bells of the cities' churches rang; their clamour was then taken up by the country churches. People rushed into the streets, carrying lanterns and torches; banners and flags were flown everywhere; patriotic hymns were sung in the streets.

Cavour and the King had paid a high price for unification in the loss of Savoy and Nice and in the anger raised among the Pope's supporters, who resented the loss of papal territory; but Austria pledged to France that it would not attack the new nation. That provided some reassurance of peace. Further guarantees were given on 22 March, when Baron Ricasoli presented the results of the Tuscan plebiscite to the King. With this act, the former Grand Duchy of Tuscany won annexation. Almost at once, the former rulers of Modena, Parma, and Piacenza announced their opposition to annexation; but their protests were vain. The new, coherent state survived.

Villa Verdi at Sant'Agata

Verdi and Strepponi left Genoa on 11 March for Sant'Agata. One month earlier, writing to Escudier, the composer had described his life at the farm:

Now that I am not manufacturing any more notes, I am planting cabbages and beans, etc., etc., but [since] this work is no longer enough to keep me busy, I

411

have begun to hunt!!!!!!! that means that when I see a bird, *Punf!* I shoot; if I hit it, fine; if I don't hit it, good night! I have a supply of good St Etienne guns, but now I have the idea of getting a double-barrelled *Le Faucheux* with a double action; that is to say, *the old system* where you load powder and shot, together with *the system called Le Faucheux* with cartridges. Here they have these beautiful, fine Belgian guns at a reasonable price; but I have a craving to have a real one from the inventor, so long as the price is not too high. . . . Tell the manufacturer that it has to be used not for a skilled hunter but for a maestro di musica.[41]

Again declaring that he was no longer a composer, Verdi began a second remodelling of the house at Sant'Agata. In 1849, as we have seen, Carlo Verdi, the 'courageous and happy father of a son who is an honour to me and to the place where he was born', prayed to God to show his son 'the road that leads men to happiness.'[42] His prayer was answered, for at Sant'Agata Verdi found peace on the land.

He and Strepponi lived simply in the country, at first with only two servants. Later they had a household staff of about ten and fourteen gardeners. They invited only close friends to visit, among them Barezzi and his second wife Maddalena Fagnoni; Gallo, Piave, Brenna, Somma, and Vigna from Venice; Ricordi, with members of his family, from Milan; Mariani, Luccardi, and others who did not mind the unpretentious house. On one occasion, Verdi invited Donnino Corbellini, the Mayor of Busseto; but other local people were not often welcome.

Isidoro Chini from Piacenza was hired as master mason and crew manager for the remodelling, to build a stable and 'a great part of my house'.[43] At first the work went smoothly through the spring of 1860, when it seemed that everything would be completed on schedule before the first week in November; but at the end of July Chini told Verdi that he could not finish the job. Paid for his work, he left his tools for Verdi's crew. Menta, the farm-manager, was then put in charge. 'In less than three months he did what Chini could not have done in a year,' Verdi claimed.[44] Sometime while the work was in progress, Verdi invited the other deputies from the Assembly to dinner. Strepponi said that they 'dined in a kind of ante-room, a hall, where swallows that came and went tranquilly through a grille, carrying food to their babies.'[45] The house that Verdi designed in 1860 and continued to work on for more than twenty years was not the house we see today. At the end of that year Sant'Agata consisted of the present billiard-room, at the centre of the main façade; the small salon, which was then the only salon; the present library, which then served as dining room; the kitchen and stair hall; the main hall, which was at the rear of the house and faced the courtyard; and bedrooms and dressing-rooms of Strepponi and Verdi. The two wings, which now include the aviary and service rooms were not part of the 1860s restoration. The chapel was also built later.

Unlike many European houses, especially those near rivers that flood, Sant'Agata has its living- and dining-rooms, kitchen, pantries, library, main bedrooms, and billiard-room on the ground floor. The entire house, raised just three shallow steps above the ground, has French windows that open many of the rooms directly on to the garden. Sant'Agata is bound to the earth, the soil that Verdi loved. From his bedroom/sitting-room/workroom through Strepponi's bedroom to all the living-rooms and the kitchen almost all the rooms have either doors or windows in all their walls. The house was created by a man who loved air.

For himself Verdi designed the large, square room where he composed, wrote, kept his accounts, and slept. On the room's north-west wall is his piano. One door in the wall leads to his small office, where he transacted farm business and stored important papers. The other door in the north-west wall looks out to the central courtyard. Opposite his piano is his bed, flat against the wall, with a gold damask spread and a draped canopy of white lace. Over the bed is a sixteenth-century painting, *Saint Peter Weeps* (*Il pianto di San Pietro*). A bookcase is at the foot of the bed. At its head, a door leads to Strepponi's bedroom. On the north-east wall is a fireplace. The south-west wall opens into the garden, through French windows. To their right is a gun cabinet with Verdi's arms and ammunition. The middle of his room is taken up by a large walnut writing desk and a chair. At the end of the desk is a *chaise longue*; near it, an armchair stands, its long seat designed to accommodate the composer's long thigh bones. Next to his gun cabinet is his shaving stand, which is near the garden door. One chair commemorates *Aida*; and the room is well furnished with memorabilia.

Like Verdi's room, Strepponi's has a door in each wall. Her handsome poster bed, with its dark green damask bedspread and its heavy, dark green velvet hangings, has a small table at its foot, on which is placed the noble bust of the soprano that Pietro Tenerani sculpted in 1841 in Rome. Inlaid chests and an armoire stand against the walls. Beside the bed is the gold reliquary given by the Emperor of Austria to Feliciano Strepponi. On the walls are paintings of Strepponi's pets, the dog Loulou and the parrot Lorito. It has a fireplace in the north-east wall, French windows opening to the garden on the south-west wall, and access to other rooms in the house as well. The adjacent, long dressing-room, with its huge built-in wardrobes, holds some of Strepponi's books, including her little handwritten text from Conservatory days on the writing and versification of librettos. A piano also now stands in the room; a *chaise longue* is near the window, which gives onto garden. Lorito, embalmed, looks down from the top of the wardrobe.

From Strepponi's dressing-room, one steps directly into the small salon, which in 1860 was the sitting-room of the house, the large salon and dining-room having been added twenty years later, together with the terraces that are above them. The billiard-room, which occupies the centre of the front of the house, also functions as a sitting-room. To the right of it is the former dining-room, now a library, furnished with two tables, a fireplace, chairs, and floor-to-ceiling bookcases with closed cupboards below and glass doors above. Here Verdi and Strepponi, both avid readers, kept their collection of several hundred books. A small door leads from this room into the large central hall, which has two imposing staircases leading to the floor above. Beyond the hall is the huge, light kitchen with its unglazed tile floor and dishes in cupboards of polished walnut and pots and pans, many of fine copper, on racks against the wall. In the centre is a walnut work-table nearly 7 feet long. It is dwarfed by the room. Pantries and a well-head are to the left. A stair leads to servants' quarters upstairs. The house Verdi built in 1860 could probably accommodate four or five guests; later, additional bedrooms were added.

Verdi planned Sant'Agata along a number of axes, which are still apparent, even though the garden has grown in on them. The main axis runs from the front of the house to the back. In the nineteenth century, if one stood on the bridge over the Ongina River and looked toward the main façade, one could see—when the doors were open—from the centre door of the billiard-room through the main hall, courtyard, carriage-house doors, and garden, straight to the fields beyond. That one long view, through the core of the house, reached for nearly a quarter of a mile, from the Ongina to the expanse of Verdi's land between Sant'Agata and Villanova sull'Arda. Another of the axes runs from the garden to the right of the house through the dining-room, library, billiard-room, small salon, and large salon into the west garden, where a carefully placed statue is the focus of one's gaze. From just outside Verdi's and Strepponi's bedrooms, where a neat, gravel-paved area is furnished with lawn chairs and dozens of pots of blooming plants, one could see along the straight garden path and through the long *allée*, edged by trees, into the fields, in this case, almost to Villanova, about 3 kilometres away. The house is indivisible from the gardens and fields around it. In plan, it is a *corte chiusa* with its central courtyard and structures on all sides. This design, also called a *corte lombarda*, differs in almost every particular from the plan of the typical farm on the Parma side of the Ongina River;[46] but it is frequently seen on the roads between Busseto and Cortemaggiore and in the farther reaches of the Piacentino.

The main body of the house at Sant'Agata faces the bank of the Ongina. Set back from the road, it is reached through a wrought iron gate in a high brick wall; the second entrance is through a small wooden door near the caretaker's lodge. Where, in a smaller farm, the tenant-farmer's lodgings, hay-mow, and animal's stalls would be found, there are the 'wings' of Sant'Agata, housing the aviary, storage areas, chapel (built later), and carriage house. This last closes the *corte chiusa*. Access to the courtyard is through an archway cut in the wall. When its doors are closed at night, the house is a completely sealed unit. The front façade of Sant'Agata faces south-east. When Verdi and Strepponi moved there in 1851, Sant'Agata resembled many farmhouses in the area; but as Verdi realized his plans for the garden, especially after 1860, and transformed the house, it became a great country estate surrounded by acres of trees and plants. After his return from Genoa, the composer's garden grew as he canvassed nurseries in and near Genoa and solicited the help of friends in expanding his planting. Thus the house, once open to the elements on all sides, became protected. Sant'Agata is a liveable, generous, welcoming, and comfortable dwelling, where the many windows, doors, French windows, and long views within and through the structure make it impossible for one to feel closed in, winter or summer. The fireplaces and the heating system, which Verdi installed, kept it warm, no matter how cold it was outside.

The development of this estate raised the morale of many of the desperate poor of the neighbourhood and put money into their pockets at a time when the new Italy of the early 1860s faced economic and social problems that sometimes seemed beyond resolution. After the annexation to the kingdom of Vittorio Emanuele II, a crisis was generated by changing structures and ranges of authority. In rural areas, education was a priority, for about 70 per cent of the people were illiterate.[47] The entire country depended on agriculture for its prosperity; from the farms came the wealth that fed commerce and the developing industry. At Sant'Agata, as in other villages of the region, the peasant class was grouped into four fairly inflexible categories: the share farmers, called *mezzadri* or *terzaoli* who farmed the *padrone's* land and received one half or one third, respectively, of the return; the *famigli a spesa*, who received no cash pay but were given room and board in exchange for their labour; farmhands called *braccianti* because they gave their arms, or *braccia*, to the *padrone*; and the artisans or craftsmen, who might stay in one place or move from one area to another.[48] All these workers were poor; but the situation of the *famigli a spesa* and the *braccianti*, always more desperate than the other labourers, remained critical even in good times, because they were paid nothing in cash (*famigli a spesa*) or minimal daily wages (*braccianti*). In the Italy of 1860, where the old systems no longer existed and the new systems had not begun to function, disorder frequently was rife in the country, where many men had left for the army, some under the compulsory military service of the draft, others as volunteers.

One of the first concerns of the new government was roads; but while these eased problems of transportation and communication, they aggravated the condition of peasants, who in many instances, were forced to labour without pay. New levees were built to hold back the Po, which flowed and flooded across the entire peninsula. Many communities in the provinces of Parma and Piacenza had few or no elementary schools; more than half had no education whatever for women. The existing schools did not have enough classrooms for the student population, nor could the towns find enough elementary teachers to direct classes. Verdi's cousin Don Carlo Uttini, who had emerged as one of the most respected educators in the area, had already found his voice in the front ranks of modern pedagogues. A graduate of the seminary and the Collegio Alberoni in Piacenza, Uttini had become a priest in 1844 and a professor in the seminary. A liberal in the war of 1848–9, the First War for Italian Independence, he had been censured by his superiors and was a particular target of Bishop Sanvitale, who had so hated Verdi. As director of the Teachers' College in Piacenza, Don Uttini was filling one of Italy's most pressing needs in preparing men and women to be competent, professional educators. Even at the beginning of the 1860s, Uttini had already become interested in what became the central focus of his life: kindergartens and nursery schools that provided day-care. Pre-school education found in him one of its most able exponents. He found in Verdi and Strepponi two sympathetic supporters who often donated money to his causes. Don Carlo Uttini and his brother, Don Ciriaco, also a priest, were of liberal convictions. But many members of the clergy were still pro-Austrian: they supported the

Old Regime and would have been glad to see the Austrians return to the Emilia Provinces. The Bishop of Piacenza had been under fire from moderates and the left even in the months before annexation; in 1860 the Bishop of Parma was driven from his diocese by the animosity of his opponents.[49] Although a motto of the times was 'A free Church in a free Nation', many priests believed that they were worse off after 1860 than before. Acting from their partisan positions, they sometimes even took official action against priests who took part in the celebration of the National Holiday; some patriotic priests were forbidden to say Mass. As we shall see later, Verdi feared the vendettas of the local priests more than the return of Austrian troops. One of his closest friendships was with Don Giovanni Avanzi, the parish priest and canon of Vidalenzo, the hamlet where Verdi's father lived. Avanzi, a liberal and Garibaldino, shared the patriotic passion of the Uttinis and was always indentified as a man to the left of much of the rest of the clergy.

As the former deputy to the Assembly, Verdi kept his hand in the local affairs of Busseto. When the King announced that he would visit his recently annexed territories in the spring of 1860,

Verdi persuaded the City to give the King a cannon, on which '*Busseto offers*' will be engraved. He said, gruffly but with much emotion: 'illuminations and celebrations are useless and do not chase away the enemy who is still at our doors. They no longer prove our love for the King. We will prove it better by giving him the means to fight Austria and make our country stronger and more respected. It needs soldiers and weapons. We have sent off all of our youth that we could. We underwrote rifles for Garibaldi: now, instead of celebrating his trip with an illumination [of the city] or other frivolous things, let us give a cannon', and the poor Bussetans voted unanimously to give a cannon to the King.[50]

Verdi thanked the city administration for its vote, declaring that he hoped every other town would follow its example. 'We shall be able to become strong, respected, and masters of our own house, not with celebrations and illuminations, but with arms and soldiers. And we must not forget that the powerful and menacing foreigner [Austria] is still in Italy.'[51] He added that he could not write a hymn for the occasion, which would be useless in any case, because he had already refused similar requests from Milan and Turin. He also had declined the office of provincial council member, to which he had been elected.[52]

During that spring of 1860, other matters required Verdi's attention. Help in drafting letters came from Strepponi, as it certainly had in the past; but in January she began to keep the first of her Letter-books, all five of which have entries written by her, entries by her which Verdi corrected, and entries entirely in his own hand. These volumes, invaluable because of what they tell us about both the composer and his wife, are especially important because of the large gap in Verdi's *Copialettere*, which runs from October 1858 to September 1867. The first entry in Strepponi's letter books is a reproach to Ricordi for not having taken sufficient care with the score of *Un ballo in maschera*, which was still being sent out with errors Verdi had brought to the publisher's attention a year before. Matters relating to the selection of a director for a conservatory of music—almost certainly that of Parma—were referred through Verdi to Mazzucato in Milan, Piroli, and the Minister of Public Education in Modena, the seat of Farini's government. The man to be chosen director, Verdi said, must be very informed, wise, have high ideals, and be free of any particular prejudices about which school of music to follow. Strong, forceful, he must know how to impose his administration on others and command respect from both the students and the professors, the latter being more difficult to deal with than the former. This letter of 3 February was the first of many that Verdi wrote on conservatory reform.

In March letters from Piave brought the news that the librettist had fled Venice and come to Milan. On 3 March he begged Verdi for his advice and protection; five days later, he sent another letter through Filippi, who was visiting Sant'Agata and had also taken Piave's cause to heart. Verdi wrote a week later to Manzoni's son-in-law, Massimo d'Azeglio, who was then the Governor of Milan, asking him to help Piave. With characteristic common sense, Verdi advised Piave to tell d'Azeglio just what he wanted. On 20 March Piave had good news to report: d'Azeglio had 'welcomed me very, very kindly. Your letter was a golden key for me, if—as I hope— (the Governor himself led me to hope) I am successful in getting what I want, I shall owe it to you.'[53] Piave's remark about having taken a room in the house of 'old Gigia, one hundred steps above the pavement in the Galleria de Cristoforis' provides a clue to where Verdi lived after the success of *Nabucco*, for the landlady sent her regards to both Verdi and Strepponi through Piave, something she would never have done had she not known them both. Piave had also been taken under the wing of Clara Maffei, and Filippi was also helping him, as was Andrea Maffei.

On the same day that Verdi wrote to d'Azeglio he notified the Mayor of Milan that he would not compose a hymn for the city, and on 21 March he wrote to Mariani saying:

First of all, you will go to pick up my portrait [in marble] and pay for everything, as per the letter included here. Second, you will have Gambini, the musician, take you to that nursery and you will buy ten *Magnolia grandiflora* that are 1½ metres high, but in any case no shorter than 1 metre. See that they are dug up properly and packed in straw, on the actual day you leave [Genoa for Sant'Agata]. Third, you will go to Noledi and ask him whether he wants to exchange my Saint-Etienne rifle for the one he has from Liège, the one I like that has a calibre of 13–14. You know him; and I will give him 4 gold napoleons [and the old gun]. You can assure him that my rifle is—one could say—new, for I used it only for part of the month of December; and the metal and wood [still] have all the polish of a new one. Furthermore, if Noledi wants to see it first, write to me at once, and I will send it to you by rail, in a box. I want you though to try the Liège rifle, and be sure that it hits the target right, and doesn't kick. If it is not right, don't get it. You have to try it with five or six pinches of powder.

There is no more snow here. If you wait a few days, the ground will get dry and we can go out in the woods. You will bring everything with you, on the train, as baggage. Buy your ticket to Piacenza; at Piacenza you will get a supplement to Borgo San Donnino. You will leave at ten in the morning, you will arrive at Piacenza about three, stop half an hour at Piacenza, and you will be at Borgo after four. You will find a coach for Busseto, but because this coach waits for the train from Parma, you will leave Borgo very late. You can wait for that coach, having dinner in Borgo; or you can pick up a wagon that carries freight [and] that will bring you to Sant'Agata; or write to me the day before, and I will be at Borgo or send my horses there. Do you understand?[54]

Not many house guests, in the last century or any other, can have been asked to bring ten young trees, a marble statue about a yard high, and a rifle along with their own luggage. But for Verdi and Mariani, this kind of request was part and parcel of their friendship. Verdi gave orders and Mariani obeyed.

The magnolias were not available. This left the conductor with the chore of visiting all the nurseries in Genoa until he found the trees Verdi wanted. Because his visit to Sant'Agata was postponed until after Easter, Mariani got orders from Verdi to bring the statue and trees when he came. At the last moment, Verdi ordered two additional magnolias! Finally Mariani sent everything by freight train. The shipment was hardly out of Genoa when he received from Naples the large crate Verdi had expected De Sanctis to send earlier. In it was a portrait of Strepponi by the Neapolitan artist Ruo, other paintings, now on the walls at Sant'Agata, and books. Because Verdi had had it sent care of Mariani, the conductor then had to provide for its reshipment.

BOOK IV

After Easter Mariani, planning for his postponed visit, intended to bring with him the gun Verdi had given him in February. On that occasion, the composer had written to Mariani, making reference to a phrase from one of the conductor's letters: '"*Courage is the gift of God; I don't have any!*"—That is what you say!!! And so that you will get some, and also remember me, I am sending you this gun. Look at it, touch it, get to feel comfortable with it, and shoot; after all, it doesn't bite, it only kills.'[55] The letter was signed 'A deputy of Central Italy who was stupid enough to write music for many years. G. Verdi'. Among many other invitations to the conductor, Verdi wrote to say that Mariani was welcome at any time, 'and you know perfectly well that you will never be a burden to me, and you always make me happy'.[56] He also said that Mariani could stay at Sant'Agata for months and months.

Strepponi, in that spring of pressing needs, drafted in her Letter-book an appeal to the women of Busseto, asking for funds for a gift to be offered to the King by the women of Emilia. 'Poor women and rich can contribute according to their possibilities, for giving a proof of love to the King is not a privilege of the rich but the right of every good Italian.'[57] The response was not good, perhaps because there had already been too many calls on the purses of the Bussetans. Writing to De Sanctis in April, she described the solitude of Sant'Agata, saying that she and Verdi saw literally no one except Antonio Barezzi. Verdi, at the head of his work crew, had no intention whatever of writing music. The only piano in the house was out of tune. The composer described himself to Mariani as a man surrounded by bricks, cement, stone masons and workers. He got up at five, went out hunting for quails, had breakfast, checked the masons, wrote letters, took a nap from one until two, had dinner, took walks in the evening, talked about everyday things, and went to bed early, so as to get up the next day at five. To Luccardi, Verdi wrote:

Tell [Jacovacci] that the shop is closed, and that I have no desire to open it up again; that if this were to happen (and I don't see that), and if I were to write for Rome, I would always give him the first chance, on condition that I have a better company than I had the last time. . . . [In] dealing with me, you have to have the courage to spend money right.[58]

He had not sworn *not* to compose, Strepponi said, because that would place restraints on him and rob him of his prized independence. Faced with the expense of remodelling the house at Sant'Agata, Verdi had written to Ricordi in May about the project. He had lived for years in a modest, rundown shanty in the country, he said, a shack so indecent that he was embarrassed to let even his closest friends see it. Now that he was in the process of restoring it, he asked his publisher to pay a sum of 10,000 francs that was owed to him. Verdi suggested that Ricordi make four equal payments, the first at the beginning of June. Claiming that he was out of money, he also expressed concern over a proposed production of *Un ballo in maschera* in Reggio Emilia and a production in Lisbon. He feared that the latter had been more of a fiasco than a success.[59] When Ricordi said that he could not make the June payment, Verdi gave him a month's grace, stipulating that the payments should be made on the first of every month from July to October. He could make no further concessions. Yet in spite of the crisis, he wrote to Escudier that it was very unlikely that he would ever go back to the theatre.[60] At the beginning of summer he had written to Mariani to ask for help in getting the wrought-iron or cast-iron gates that he needed for the door-frames of the French windows that opened from the ground-floor rooms out into the garden. The considerable dimensions provided the air and light the composer wanted; they should be 3 metres, 10 centimetres high and 1 metre, 20 centimetres wide, with a simple design.[61] Later Verdi decided to order them in Cremona. Mariani, who had already received an offer from the Teatro Comunale in Bologna to direct the autumn season there, asked Verdi's opinion of the idea; but the only answer he got was equivocal, for Verdi said he did not feel like saying anything—good or bad—about art.

Alone at the villa while Strepponi visited her mother, who was ill in Locate Triulzi, Verdi continued his oversight of the construction. When she returned, they went together to take the waters at Tabiano. During Luccardi's visit in August, the two men hunted near the house and in the woods near the Po. Verdi wrote to Mariani, asking him to join them.

Hunting quail is the business of the day, and soon we will catch dozens in the nets and get some with our guns, if we know how to shoot straight. Anyway, every morning we come home with eight or ten birds, big and small, and without going any farther from the house than just the range of a couple of shots. . . . Come then, and arrange to stay here until the day you leave for Bologna.[62]

In later letters to the conductor, Verdi asked about hunting licences; a suitable situation for Marcellino Demaldè, one of the housemen at Sant'Agata who hoped to find work in Genoa. Obedient to Verdi's command, the conductor approached the impresario and composer Achille

Montuoro, who seemed disposed to give the young man a chance, on terms that were virtually dictated by Verdi himself. The date for Mariani's visit was set for the end of summer. Verdi let him know that a carriage would be at the station in Borgo San Donnino to bring him to Sant'Agata.

Garibaldi and the Thousand

While Verdi was farming, hunting, and overseeing the remodelling of his house, another hero of the Risorgimento, Garibaldi, was living in retirement at Caprera in Sardinia. During the war for unification, he had led his volunteers, the 'Cacciatori delle Alpi', into battle; but the armistice of Villafranca had caught him by surprise, just as he was planning to march into the Veneto and try to take Venice. When the spring of 1860 brought peace to the north, the old hero fought again. His troops, as in the past, were volunteers. On 5 May 1860 Garibaldi and his 'Thousand' sailed from the port of Quarto, near Genoa. Ten days later the general marked up his first victory in Sicily. By August he had most of the island under his control. Crossing the Strait of Messina, he and his troops—who eventually numbered more than 20,000, as more volunteers joined his forces—marched to Naples, the Bourbon king's capital. While Garibaldi and his men were making their way north through the peninsula, Vittorio Emanuele's forces, moving south, won an important engagement at Castelfidardo in September, eleven days after Garibaldi's triumphant entry into Naples. In October Garibaldi defeated troops of Francesco II at Volturno, virtually guaranteeing the victory of the Italian forces in the entire peninsula. Only a few small areas remained to be conquered, among them Rome, which remained in the Pope's hands. The parliament in Turin voted 290 to 6 in favour of the annexation of the Kingdom of the Two Sicilies to Vittorio Emanuele's kingdom. This left Venetia still in Austrian hands; but a plebiscite there confirmed the people's wish for annexation. On 26 October Garibaldi and Vittorio Emanuele II met at Taverna di Catena near Teano. 'I salute the first King of Italy'. Garibaldi was reported to have said. The last battle at Capua sealed the Italian conquest. The King and Garibaldi entered Naples together one day before Vittorio Emanuele was given the results of a plebiscite in the south, which also voted for annexation. Garibaldi bade farewell to his men and set out for Caprera.[63]

Verdi and Strepponi followed the news of the war from Sant'Agata. As he had in 1859, the composer relied on Mariani for some of his information about the war. At the end of May he expressed his unreserved admiration for the general. 'Hurrah for Garibaldi! God, he is a man before whom we truly should kneel!'[64] Later, when Cialdini and the army of Vittorio Emanuele were moving toward Rome, making their way through Ancona and Perugia, Verdi asked for news of them. 'But tell me about some other music. How are the tones and semitones of Cialdini, Garibaldi, etc.? Those are maestros! and what operas! and what finales! to the sound of cannon-fire!'[65] In the autumn, after having been publicly humiliated by the King, who failed to appear for a review of Garibaldi's assembled troops, the old soldier retired to his home in Sardinia. Strepponi praised him as 'the purest and greatest hero that has ever existed, from the creation of the world until this moment'.[66]

Although he seems not to have mentioned it to any of his closest friends, the war took its toll on Verdi's family that summer, when one of his near relatives was captured with other volunteers when a boat carrying the Thousand to Sicily was seized by Bourbon patrols. In a letter to the president of the Fund for a Thousand Rifles in Milan, Verdi asked for help in locating Pietro Scaglioni, whom he described as 'mio nipote'—'my nephew' or 'my grandson'. Perhaps ill or even dead, he had disappeared with his comrades after beng taken prisoner.[67] Scaglioni, whose mother was a Bianchi from Roncole, survived and returned to Busseto after unification.

Verdi and his Art

Piave, who had found a post as stage director and 'poet assigned to the productions' at La Scala, wrote to Verdi to send his congratulations for the composer's forty-seventh birthday in the autumn. In his reply, Verdi also referred to Piave's remarks about the enormous success of *Un ballo in maschera* at the Teatro Comunale in Bologna. He apologized for not having answered Piave's letter sooner—he had again been suffering from rheumatism in his right arm.

Now I am better, though not well; and I thank you very, very much indeed for the wishes of the ninth of October and a little less for the compliments on the success of *Ballo*. You know that I have never become very excited about this kind of business, and now I am so indifferent that you could not believe it. If people knew this, they would curse me, accuse me of being ungrateful, and of not loving my art.

Oh, no! I have adored this art and I adore it, and when I am all alone, battling with my notes, then my heart pounds, the tears stream from my eyes, and the emotions and joys are beyond description; but if I think that these poor notes of mine have to be thrown to people who have no intelligence, to a publisher who sells them to be used later to entertain the crowd or to be jeered at, oh, then I no longer love anything! Let's not talk about it![67]

Like that other Giuseppe, Verdi seemed to have left the field of battle. Garibaldi with his farm and his bag of seed-corn and Verdi with his estate and his wheat crop appeared satisfied with retirement, having put their service to their country behind them.

24

December 1860–Spring 1862

Election to the First Parliament of Italy

At the end of Mariani's visit to Sant'Agata in September he had gone on to his assignment at the Teatro Comunale in Bologna, where an exciting *Ballo in maschera*, *La favorita*, and *Gli Ugonotti* were on the programme. When the season ended he stopped again at the villa to visit the Verdis. Surprisingly, Verdi left for Genoa with him, in an apparently unplanned move. Strepponi wrote to De Sanctis that she and Verdi had intended to spend the entire winter in the country because they were low on funds, having made such extensive renovations and additions to the house. 'What is strange is that just this year, because he ought not to go away, he has a tremendous desire to go everywhere. —The whims of the human heart!'[1] Although her letter is spirited, the note of sadness and pessimism that crept in suggests that something had gone wrong. She remarked on her own poor health. 'I also have not been well for some time because of pain from stomach spasms; but I am no longer young, and if I go on to the next world, there's little harm done; one woman less, and there are so many of them.' She was 45 years old, left in what she called 'the Vale of Yawns, if not of Tears', Sant'Agata.

Before leaving, Verdi had written to Piroli to say that he expected to be away about two months. He told De Sanctis that he had 'come to Genoa because I felt the need to move around'.[2] At Sant'Agata, with the work completed, at least for the winter, there can have been little for him to do, for—as he told Fioruzzi—Menta had finished the job. Going off with Mariani freed him to lead the life of the city, attend the theatre, hear operas from the hidden fourth-tier box at the Teatro Carlo Felice, take long walks, and discuss politics with the friends of Mariani's circle. The conductor had offered Verdi the hospitality of his house. Verdi had hardly arrived in Genoa when he wrote to De Sanctis, asking for information about the political situation in Naples. 'Write me what you think, hope, and fear. I hope for the best, although I would have wished for a bit more order and calm [in the south], that kind of order and calm that was in Central Italy last year and that helped our cause so much; and I would wish for better understanding of the great idea of Italian unity.'[3] Earlier he had sent a letter to Antonio Capecelatro, refusing to compose a hymn to the King, who was visiting there.

You would like me to write a hymn, at a time when Garibaldi's men have not yet finished their job? Ohibò! The national anthem must be sung on the lagoon in Venice, in Naples, and in the Alps all at the same time. I have refused, and I will refuse to write one, until that moment; and if God helps us to break our chains, and I live long enough to see that day, it shall be the first and last hymn by G. Verdi.[4]

He deplored the 'rotten and corrupt' atmosphere that years of 'slavery' had left in Italy.

Verdi's relations with his publisher had deteriorated, as Ricordi proceeded with the Reggio Emilia production of *Un ballo in maschera* without Mariani, whom Verdi had recommended as conductor. In November the composer complained that all his operas had been massacred in Paris, except for *Il trovatore*, which he had directed himself. 'Your sale will have been good for your pocketbook, not for art. And now you give *Ballo* without my permission!'[5] Probably Strepponi had Ricordi in mind when, writing in December to Escudier, she lashed out at people who had earned 'hands full of gold' and built palaces and villas worthy of a prince with *Ernani*, *Rigoletto*, and Verdi's other works but had never had the common decency to thank the composer. 'And to think that Verdi has worked so hard, and that people think he is so rich (and they are wrong); not until now has he been able to fix up his cottage, and you know whether it needed it.'[6]

While Verdi was with Mariani in Genoa, Strepponi wrote to him regularly with news of the house and herself. These beautiful letters express her love for the composer, a love that had grown in the nearly twenty years that they had known each other. The first that has survivied, dated 4 December, in the evening, begins with a complaint about the postman and refers to a letter written that morning. It was raining in torrents. Strepponi had sent Menta to Busseto, where he had spoken with someone, perhaps Giovannino Barezzi, about a debt owed to or by Carlo Verdi. Reporting on her health and her loneliness, she said that she had eaten in the dining-room only once and had stayed in her room upstairs even for dinner because the large room was

too empty without you and that empty place at the table makes me sad. Think of me when you are falling asleep; think of the companion who has lived with you for so many years and would like to live with you for just as many centuries. Don't make an ugly face. . . . I would look for and perhaps find in my heart a way not to bother you ever, nor to be a burden to you, not even now; I'll say goodbye and I am going to bed. I hope you have a quiet night and a blue sky tomorrow morning![7]

The next day it was still raining, and the doors and windows were swollen with humidity. A leaden sky hung overhead. Strepponi, writing to Verdi again, said that she felt she even had rain in her bones. Asking Verdi's opinion about a problem with one of the servants, she put down her pen until that evening. Then she asked about Verdi's proposed visit to Turin, where he intended to visit Cavour and Hudson.

You go to visit ministers of State and ambassadors exactly as I go to visit Giovanna. Yet the thing that makes the world take off its hat to you is the quality about which I never or almost never think. I swear to you; and you won't have any trouble believing it, that I often am almost surprised that you know music! Even though this art is divine, and your genius is worthy of the art that you profess, still the quality that I find fascinating and that I adore in you is your character, your heart, your indulgence toward the mistakes of others, while you are so hard on yourself. Your charitableness, full of modesty and reserve, your proud independence, and your childlike simplicity, the qualities inherent in that spirit of yours that knows how to maintain a primitive virginity in thought and sentiment, in the midst of the sewer of humanity! O my Verdi, I am not worthy of you, and the love that you have for me is a gift, a balm to a heart that is often very sad, underneath the semblance of happiness. Go on loving me, love me even after I am dead, so that I can go before Divine Justice rich with your love and your prayers, O my Redeemer! I am rereading this sloppy letter, which I perhaps should not send you, but I don't have the courage to recopy it. Even though it is the pure expression of my feelings, I still ought to have written you in another way, and with more tranquil thoughts. Forgive this crankiness, which has plagued me for some time and is not the predominant trait of my character, although it certainly is of yours! Oh, finally I have found a defect, a failing in you! I am *delighted* to know that you have at least one, or perhaps several. I'll think about this seriously, and write a memorandum and throw it in your face the first time I have a chance.

I am so-so. I haven't had any more attacks of cramps, but just brief threats of them. Tomorrow I will be better; I hope so; I want to be, for you. These little illnesses keep me from laughing; and I just need peace of mind and good humour in order to get rid of them, so as not to show you—as I have done—the spectacle of these painful crises, which I would have wanted to hide but did not have the strength to do.

In the house, everything is all right, running smoothly. However, I have to tell you that I have been downstairs only once, and I hope you will forgive me for that because of my [poor] health. Anyway, [if the servants have done something wrong], the problem is only that they have given away a piece of bread or meat without my permission. When we are dead, there will still be cattle, wheat, and money that we will not have been able to enjoy! So let's close our eyes to these charitable violations of our rules and agree that they are a small matter compared to serious human misery. You will say: 'What a Saint Augustine!' It's true, but I am always like that. Good night, my Pasticcio, have a good time, but remember that I am at Sant'Agata.

Your Peppina.[8]

Verdi's plan to spend two months away might have marked a change in their lives. But in fact this separation ended abruptly after about ten days when Verdi changed his plans and came home, perhaps because he had not been able to see (and also help to prepare) *Un ballo in maschera* at the Teatro Carlo Felice in Genoa, where Mariani had planned to produce it as the first opera of his season. When the schedule changed, the opera was postponed. Or perhaps he became bored with the city and with the changes inevitably wrought in his well-established routine. He bought a gift for Strepponi: a fine velvet cloak that pleased her, particularly because she would not have to pay for one out of her own funds.

Sometime in December Verdi learned that he was about to be chosen to run for Parliament in the electoral district of Borgo San Donnino, which included Busseto. The seat had fallen vacant when Massari was elected by plebiscite in Bari. Just after Christmas the composer had written to Dr Giovanni Minghelli-Vaini, 'an old patriot and very experienced man of politics'[9] who had served with Verdi in the Assembly of the Parma Provinces and had gone on to Parliament. Verdi said that he might have to run, in spite of his opposition to being a candidate. On 9 January 1861 Minghelli-Vaini answered, declaring that if Verdi ran, he would withdraw his own name and throw his energies into getting Verdi elected. 'It is essential that there be no competition between [you] and me, other than that of showing how much we care for each other; and I feel that I am inferior to you in every way. . . . Answer me about your intentions regarding Parliament and be sure that my offer is absolutely sincere.'[10] They were already friends. Minghelli-Vaini was a formidable opponent, for he had been a member of the provisional government in 1848 in Modena, had voted for annexation to the Piedmont, and had been exiled by the Duke of Modena after the restoration. Moving into the Duchy of Parma, he had settled in San Secondo and had been elected first to the Assembly of the Parma Provinces and then gone on to Parliament in Turin. Soon after the annexation of the Royal Provinces of Emilia to the Piedmont, Minghelli-Vaini had been elected to Parliament from San Secondo.[11] When his letter reached Sant'Agata, Verdi was already in Turin, where he had gone to visit Cavour and Sir James Hudson. Strepponi had known Minghelli-Vaini for about fifteen years, and perhaps longer. Sometime earlier that year, perhaps during the sessions of the Assembly of the Parma Provinces, to which Minghelli-Vaini and Verdi had both been deputies, she had lent her copy of *Uncle Tom's Cabin* to the politician and his wife Countess Marianna Serra. With Verdi away, she replied to Minghelli-Vaini's letter, saying that Verdi did not want to be a candidate and that he had gone to Turin 'just to be excused from such an honour, and I hope he will succeed'.[12] But exceedingly strong pressure was being exerted on Verdi to force him to run. Cavour addressed the 'Most Esteemed Signor Cavaliere' Verdi on 10 January, sending a personal appeal that Verdi could scarcely have refused.

The electoral committees are about to meet, from the Alps to Etna. On them depend not just the fate of the ministry but truly that of Italy. Woe unto us if from their efforts there did not emerge a Chamber [of Deputies] with superlative views, daring ideas, and revolutionary proposals. The wondrous work of our Risorgimento, which is about to become reality, would be wrecked, perhaps for centuries. I believe that it is the duty of every good citizen, under these circumstances, to sacrifice every personal concern, to meet major sacrifices head on in co-operating in our mutual salvation.[13]

Although he was aware that a term in Parliament would be a burden, Cavour urged Verdi to accept because

Your presence . . . will contribute to the dignity of Parliament in and beyond Italy; it will lend credit to the great national party that wants to build the nation on the solid foundations of liberty and order; it will convince our colourful colleagues from the south of Italy, who are very much more susceptible to the influence of your artistic genius than we denizens of the cold Po Valley are. In the hope that you will surrender to my pleas, and that I will therefore soon be able to grasp your hand in Turin, I am yours, with affectionate esteem,

Your devoted C. Cavour.[14]

The day after he arrived in Turin, Verdi received a note from Cavour, sent to his hotel, asking him to come to the ministry offices at once. A meeting was arranged for the following morning, the eighteenth, at the minister's house. After it, Verdi wrote to Mariani:

Don't be surprised if you see me in Turin! You know why I am here? So as not to be a deputy. Others scheme to be one; I am doing everything possible not to be, but don't say a word about this. This morning at seven I saw Cavour, and Hudson is just now leaving me, he wanted me to go to dinner at his house, but I will go for coffee at seven. . . . Tomorrow I leave and will be home at four. Write to me. . . . I wanted to come to Genoa this evening, but now it is too late, almost five o'clock. Addio, then.[15]

In 1865, when Piave asked him for an account of his career in Parliament, Verdi answered:

What is this craziness of yours in asking me for news of and documents about my life in public and in Parliament! My life in Parliament does not exist. I am a deputy, it is true, but even I really don't know why I am, and how this is happening. I know that when it came time for the elections, I was proposed [for a seat], and I refused: when Count Cavour learned of this, I don't know how, he wrote to me, urging me to accept. Embarrassed to answer his letter (which I think you have read) I decided to go to Turin. I went to see the Count one day in the month of December [sic] at five in the morning, with [the temperature at] 12 or 14 degrees (and you, being terribly lazy will be astonished); and after quite a long conversation, I accepted, on the condition that after a few months I would resign. . . . The 450 [deputies] are really only 449 because Verdi as a deputy does not exist. Addio, addio, and believe me, yours affectionately,

G. Verdi

The original letter is clearly dated 'Busseto, Sant'Agata, 4 Feb. 1865'.[16] A week after visiting Cavour, Verdi gave Mariani further details.

I was in Turin, as you know from my other letter; and perhaps my trip was wasted. Perhaps I will be a deputy (may Heaven save me from such a disaster) but not for long, because I will hand in my resignation after a few months and I told Cavour and Hudson that. Let that stay just between us. I need to know from you as soon as possible what day Parliament opens. Find out the right date and tell me.[17]

As soon as he got home, Verdi invited Minghelli-Vaini to meet him at the Albergo dell'Angelo in Borgo San Donnino to let him know that he was going to run. Strepponi said that Verdi

brought Minghelli-Vaini up to date on everything that had happened. Hearing the announcement that Verdi found that he was forced—in spite of himself—to accept if he were nominated, his friend—a maniac politician—almost fainted, something that made the austere artist [Verdi] smile with compassion. The disappointed former deputy's distress kept him at that moment from working out a way to save himself from the danger of being shut out of Parliament; he seems to have submitted to the wounding blow.[18]

But if Minghelli-Vaini were down, he certainly was not out. As soon as he got home, he wrote to Verdi about his shock.

Yesterday the surprise you gave me, in announcing that Hudson had convinced you to run—between one glass of wine and another—was so great that—because of seeing my hopes for Parliament sunk, and because of my joy at seeing you offer the lustre of your great name to our country—I did not see any alternative to doing my double duty, of *not* withdrawing my name, so as not to let down my voters, and not to promote my own cause in any way, so as not to interfere with yours.[19]

Other politicians were confused because Minghelli-Vaini had said that Verdi would not run; now they heard that he would. To the composer, the politician proposed a scheme that would help him save face. Verdi should seek another electoral district, bringing pressure on Hudson and the ministers of state to help him. Minghelli-Vaini admitted that the proposal was unusual, but that the idea of seeing the doors of parliament closed in his face was unacceptable. He set forth all the reasons why he should be the candidate for Borgo San Donnino, why other politicians supported him, and why he was the better candidate.

A determined Verdi answered by return. 'As you sensibly advise, I will reply in a calm moment to your letter of 22 January. But here is just a line to declare, or rather to confirm, that I accept the candidacy because I am almost forced to, but that I will not offer myself nor present myself to any other electoral college.'[20]

One day later the composer answered at greater length, saying that it was not 'between one glass and another' that he had accepted to run, but over a cup of coffee. His trip to Turin had been made in the hope that he could get free from this burden. 'I did not succeed, and I am very, very unhappy about it, all the more because you are very much more suited to the battles of Parliament than the artist, who has nothing to offer of himself but his poor name.' Verdi went on to describe his own support of Minghelli-Vaini, praising the politician as a true Italian, an honest man.

I did not offer myself, I will not offer myself, nor will I take one single step to get nominated. I will accept, even though it is a terrible sacrifice for me, if I am nominated, and you know the reasons why I have been forced to do this. I am, however, firmly resolved to hand in my resignation as soon as I can do so. . . . If you succeed in winning for me the smaller number of votes, and getting yourself nominated, and freeing me from this obligation, I will not be able to find the words to thank you for such a precious service. You will do something good for the Chamber, for yourself, and something very, very big for G. Verdi.[21]

As the electoral campaign got under way, Cavour lent the weight of his name and power to Verdi's effort. Writing to a friend, Giuseppe Malmusi, a patriot from Modena, he asked for help in organizing Verdi's campaign. Malmusi then turned to General Ignazio Ribotti.

Count Cavour tells me that he has advised you that Verdi agrees to be a candidate. He also asks me to write to you at once, as I am doing, urging you to turn the whole world upside down so that this candidate will win. *'Tell the General and [Amos] Ronchei that this cannot be left to chance; Verdi must win'*, these are the Count's very words, which I have copied exactly. So set off all the bombs and do what you can.[22]

In another letter, Malmusi also said that he had been in touch with the Postal Inspector in Parma and had got his pledge to work for Verdi. Indicating other important people who should be contacted, he declared that this co-operative effort would get Verdi elected. General Ribotti also struck out on his own to help, writing to Ronchei, an influential citizen of Borgo San Donnino, urging him to campaign. 'Act energetically and don't stay too long in any one town. Send me a telegram to let me know how things are going!'[23] Posters and flyers were printed. One of them praised Verdi's character and his record as a citizen.

*To the Voters
of the College
of Borgo San Donnino*

Cavalier VERDI Giuseppe of Busseto has, in several other disciplines or social sciences, never reached nor touched that glory that the generous Spirit of the Art of Music has granted to him, more than to any other man. Nevertheless, when I look closely at his moral and civil character, I soon see that he must be a man of deep understanding and a dedicated pursuer of *the good* and *the best*. . . . That man certainly never in his long life knelt before princes or dignitaries to ask for favours, status, or fortune, nor can he have flattered them or offered adulation so that they would give him preference and honours when, attracted by his fame, they ran to him with their hands full of gold, eager to seek him out and give him money to satisfy their own needs. . . . He would enter into the arena of government with a pure and uncommitted soul, so that afterward he would be unfettered in his decisions.[24]

The author of this broadside, Dr Leonida Piletti Fanti, a distinguished patriot, closed with the declaration that he would consider it a 'crime against the *patria*' not to 'throw the name of GIUSEPPE VERDI in the ballot-box' because Italy needed to create a new nation, and Verdi was a man who could help in this great work.

Election day was 27 January 1861. In the ancient Rocca of Borgo San Donnino, the president of the Electoral Commission, Dr Giuseppe Chiarpa, oversaw the process. At that time, there were 978 registered voters in the district; of these, 350 were from Busseto and Zibello. Only 483 voters came to the polls that day; of them, 298 voted for Verdi, 185 for Minghelli-Vaini.[25] Because he had not received sufficient votes to be elected under the statutes, Verdi had to be a candidate one week later in a run-off election. One day after the first election Minghelli-Vaini received a letter with good wishes from Verdi. Replying, he reaffirmed his close friendship with the composer, but referred to 'intrigues' that had worked against him. He also confirmed that he would fight on to the end.[26] Verdi's reaction came by return.

As to the sentence in your letter [about intrigues], the word *intrigue* does not exist in my dictionary and I defy the entire world to prove that this is not so. Besides, if I had intrigued [against you], the *Gazzetta di Parma* would never have published the article [supporting you] on the twenty-second; if I had intrigued against you, the Parma committee would never have supported you with posters about your candidacy in every town; if I had intrigued against you, the article in the *Patriota* would never have appeared. Nor do I have to intrigue now, because if I had been eager to become a deputy, nothing would have prevented me from accepting the candidacy from the beginning. I was frank enough to tell you on the twenty-first the reasons that forced me to accept, if I am elected. But you have not known me long enough, so you do not know that my dignity even becomes pride, and that my hatred for certain schemes even becomes loathing! . . . I cannot, and I do not want to have a career in politics. I have said this and I say it again for the hundredth time: if I am nominated, I will accept, against my will; I will not do anything, I will not say one word to get myself elected.[27]

In the run-off of 3 February Verdi boosted his total votes to 339; Minghelli-Vaini, to 206. It was an incontestable victory for the composer, whose greatest strength came from Busseto and Borgo San Donnino. After the results were confirmed, Verdi sent his thanks to Dr Chiarpa. The election, he said, 'proves to me that I enjoy a reputation as an honest and independent man, a blessing that is dearer to me than the little glory and fortune that my art has given me.'[28] He asked Chiarpa to thank the voters on his behalf and added that although he could not bring 'the splendour of eloquence' to Parliament, he could at least bring his independent character, 'scrupulous conscience, and the solid wish to co-operate with all the energy I have for the good [of the country], for its dignity, and for the unification of this, our native land, which has been a target for so long and has been rent by internecine strife.'[29]

Preparing to serve, he wrote Mariani to let him know that he was coming to Turin early 'to rest and get over my anger [at having been elected] before putting on my white tie. Who would ever have thought it! Anyway there's no way out'.[30] He also advised Piroli, who had also been elected.

It's your good fortune and that of your voters that you are a deputy to Parliament; it's my bad luck and that of my voters that I am one. But I had to accept and believed that I did the right thing; and I'll tell you about this when we meet. In the mean time tell me when you are leaving for Turin. I am counting on being there several days before the opening of Parliament, and will need to talk to you, and ask your advice.[31]

Verdi and Piroli had been assigned seats near each other, but the composer did not accept the arrangement without questions. 'I don't know whether the seat a deputy takes in the Chamber in Turin has a political significance, as it has in France. . . . I would not want to be either White or Red, but to be independent in my views.'[32] Piroli answered that his own seat was Centre Left. 'Politically in France, and in theory here as well, [the seat] stands for the party toward which I lean, that is in support of the Prime Minister, but not automatically, and with the opposition in matters of general rules and principles when the real interest of the *patria* demands it.'[33] Piroli went on to say that he stood somewhere between those who supported the government at any cost and those who were always in the opposition. He also let Verdi know that the seat that had been chosen for him was with the Extreme Left, seat number 67; but he added that many seats were chosen at random.

Verdi and Strepponi arrived in Turin early and took an apartment at the old hotel Feder, renamed the Trombetta, where they also took a room for Strepponi's maid. Arrangements had been made for them by Arrivabene, who had been driven from Lombardy by the Austrians and was living in Turin and editing important journals, as he had in Milan before the War of 1848.

The deputies, Verdi among them, were sworn in on 18 February,

a solemn and memorable day. Less than thirteen years had passed since the day when, in that same hall [of Palazzo Carignano] the first deputies of the Kingdom of Sardinia had gathered humbly; they had had to use one of the deputies' hats as a ballot-box when they elected the first president. . . . [Now] Vittorio Emanuele II honoured the First Italian Parliament, consecrating as reality what had been our poets' dream and our martyrs' and heroes' heartfelt hope.[34]

One day later the first session opened. Strepponi, Giovannino Barezzi, and many of Verdi's supporters from Busseto attended, some in the chamber and some outside. Strepponi told Antonio Barezzi, who had not been able to come, that she had had a very good seat. 'With my opera glasses, I could easily study the faces of the King, the ministers, the ambassadors, the generals, and many others whose name and rank attracted my attention.'[35] Responding sharply to a rumour circulating in Busseto that she had not been there, she said 'If the gentlemen from Busseto were not able to give you correct information about this it is either because they could not get into the Chamber or because they do not know me personally.' Apparently they had not been able to recognize her!

To mark the opening of the parliament, the band of the National Guard from Turin offered a concert on the evening of 18 February. Three of the nine pieces were by Verdi; one was by Rossini; one by Johann Strauss; one by Mercadante; and three by minor composers. Earlier that same day Cavour had presented the King with the surrender of Gaeta, which marked the capitulation of an important stronghold in the south. Strepponi told Barezzi that when Verdi went to the Teatro Regio to hear *La favorita*, he was seated in a closed box, hoping not to be seen; but at the end of the second act, word got out that he was in the theatre.

People began to shout *Viva Verdi,* and all the people in the boxes and in the orchestra rose to salute the Great Composer from Roncole! If they only knew how well he composes *risotto alla milanese* God knows how many ovations he would have received! I have told you all these little stories, excellent Signor Antonio, because I know that . . . ovations for Verdi have always made you cry. Get out your handkerchief, because I am sure that you are crying on the spice box now.[36]

During the first sitting of the Parliament, Verdi remained in Turin and attended regularly, voting on 14 March to give Vittorio Emanuele the title of King of Italy. On 27 March he joined the vote to declare Rome the capital. 'With that act they wanted to send a message to everyone that the Eternal City was the predestined capital of Italy and that no power could prevent the Italians from making it their own and establishing the national government there.'[37] While he was a deputy, Verdi continued to fight for better musical education, and urged that three important opera-houses be given a sound economic base with government-supported choruses and orchestras. The three theatres he proposed were in Rome, Milan, and Turin. Also on his agenda were evening courses in singing, to be offered free to anyone who wished to attend. Conservatories were to work closely with opera houses; both were to have certain responsibilities towards each other.[38] Verdi believed that his programme might have been made to work. Cavour's death, however, meant that it had to be abandoned.

While they were in Turin, Verdi and Strepponi had a visit from Giovannino Barezzi, and one in early March from Mariani, who had decided not to accept an invitation to become director of music in Naples. Writing to De Sanctis, Strepponi said that the conductor was 'very, very dear to us', but she also remarked on his talkativeness.[39] Without giving any hint that Verdi might return to the theatre, she did ask for news of the 'gang of madmen' who were running the Teatro San Carlo. A week later Verdi authorized De Sanctis to act on his behalf in dealing with Torelli for a production of *Un ballo in maschera*, which he would produce in October; he could not guarantee to come to Naples in May because he had half-promised to go to London. Complaining about the nomination of Serrao as conductor, Verdi added that he would have directed his opera himself, had Serrao not been named. He also stated, in no uncertain terms, his worries over the political situation in Naples.

For God's sake, don't act like children; be quiet; keep the madmen under control; have patience; have faith in the great politician [Cavour] who controls our fates; and everything will be all right. Think that if the great idea of the unification were not to be realized, the entire fault would be yours, because no one has any doubts about the rest of Italy. If, for reasons of miserable local pride, Italy should be divided into two [nations], —and may God not want this to happen—it would always remain in the power of others and under the protection of other great Powers, and therefore weak, poor, with no freedom, and half-barbarian. Only unification can make Italy great, strong, and respected. Woe unto you if you do not join the nation confidently, openly; on your head would fall the loathing and curses of those now alive and the coming generations.[40]

He was appalled at the idea that Naples might aspire to become the capital of Italy. 'What a rotten idea!? But for God's sake, this is not patriotism!'[41] This outburst was sent just two days after the Kingdom of Italy was proclaimed in Turin.

Verdi stayed at the Chamber all day every day and was thus a witness to the events of that first session. Although political journalists called this first Parliament the 'Sleeping Chamber' and the 'Dead Men's Parliament', a good deal of activity was generated by the tension between Cavour's supporters of the Centre and Centre Right and those to the left. The Centre Left, a moderate opposition, was dominated by Urbano Rattazzi and Agostino Depretis. Garibaldi, who had been elected against his will, had not taken his seat. The General claimed that Vittorio Emanuele II was surrounded by heartless men, charlatans who were enemies of Italy and were bent on creating friction and hatred in the new nation. He also accused the government of opening a gulf between his volunteers and the regular army. Driven, finally, to appear in Turin, Garibaldi decided not to take his seat in a normal, orderly way. Instead, he waited until the session was in progress, then entered the Deputies' Gallery, dressed in his red shirt and grey poncho, as he had been on the field of war. His supporters on the left applauded, as opponents on the right protested and derided him. After two other members had spoken, Garibaldi asked for the floor to speak of his Army of the South and their heroic deeds: Shortly, though, he began to attack Cavour, accusing the Prime Minister of provoking a fratricidal war. Cavour, whom Garibaldi detested, protested at the insult, but the General shouted back at him. The session had to be interrupted for almost half an hour so order could be restored; but even after the deputies were recalled, Garibaldi and Cavour exchanged sharp words. The next day General Cialdini wrote Garibaldi a letter reproaching him for his behaviour, denouncing his address to the Chamber and accusing him of putting himself on the same level as the King and of violating the dignity of the Chamber by appearing in a wildly theatrical costume. When Cialdini's letter was published in *La perseveranza*, individuals took sides in the controversy and factions began to form. It took the intervention of the King to prevent a duel between the two generals. Finally the men shook hands; and Garibaldi was also somewhat reconciled to Cavour, to whom he wrote a respectful letter after returning to Caprera.

When De Sanctis wrote to Verdi about the incident, the composer came out soundly for Cavour. He did feel that General Cialdini's letter was violent, but Garibaldi, he said, had been wrong to act as he had.[42] Some two weeks later Verdi informed De Sanctis that he would not be able to come to Naples to produce *Un ballo in maschera* because he had lost his enthusiasm for the project. The company of singers was not good enough; there was no one to sing the Page; and he was afraid that he would have the same problems there as he had had before.[43] Strepponi, he said, had gone home, while he was still dividing his time between Sant'Agata, where more construction was under way, and Busseto, where he was temporarily staying in Palazzo Cavalli. At the end of May Verdi was still attending sessions of the Chamber, where he had served diligently and regularly for more than four months. Of this period he later said that he always watched Cavour for cues on when to rise and vote and when to remain seated. Following the Prime Minister, he knew he could never go wrong. During the spring he had discussed with Cavour the possibility that he might resign. 'I went to the Count and said to him: "Now it is time for me to go off and take care of my own affairs." "No," he said, "first we shall go to Rome." "Will we go?" "Yes." "When?" "Oh, when, when!! —Soon."'[44]

Cavour did not live to get to Rome. One evening at the end of May, he began to have a fever that was almost certainly caused by malaria. Although he recovered briefly, enough to receive the King and other ministers in his room, he was too ill to conduct business. On 6 June he died. Verdi was at home when he learned the news, getting ready to return to Turin. 'Just as I was leaving, I heard the terrible news, which kills me! I do not have the courage to come to Turin, nor could I attend that man's funeral. What a disaster, what an abyss of woes!'[45] Two days later he said that his heart was bursting at the idea of having to return to Turin, but he did ask to have his rooms at the Trombetta prepared for him. In Busseto, a Mass was celebrated 'with all the pomp that one could expect from this small town. I went to the funeral ceremony in full mourning, but the real, wrenching grief was in my heart. Between us', he confided to Arrivabene, 'I could not keep back my tears and I cried like a boy. Poor Cavour! Poor us!'[46] At the church of San Bartolomeo the clergy had celebrated without being paid; the members of the Società Filarmonica, however, did not wish to serve for nothing and asked for their fee.

Verdi continued to serve as deputy, not always regularly, for he was out of the country for long periods in the years to come. Yet he did not resign. As late as 1865 he was still the deputy from Borgo San Donnino, although he claimed that he had neither

the inclination nor the will nor the talent for it and [was] lacking in the patience, that is so necessary for being in that circle. . . . I say again that anyone wishing to or having to write my biography as a member of Parliament would not have to do anything more than print, in the centre of a fine piece of paper: 'The 450 [deputies] are really no more than 449 because Verdi as a deputy does not exist.'[47]

The sentence Verdi passed on himself was inappropriate and unduly harsh, for he proved to be a loyal, responsible public servant during the crucial first months of the life of the Kingdom of Italy, that dangerous time, when it was not even certain that the country would survive. He contributed what Cavour had asked of him: the lustre of his name and presence. Italy's good fortune lay also in the composer's fierce independence, stability, intelligence, and common sense. Given his sustained interest in politics, expressed over decades of his life, Verdi would have dignified the Chamber of Deputies under any circumstances; but his special interests in education, flood control, agriculture, music and theatre, and public services proved doubly valuable in 1861 when new programmes were the body's first concern after the two major votes of March.

La forza del destino: The Composition and the First Trip to Russia

During Verdi's self-imposed retirement, many offers to compose a new work or to produce one of his old operas had come to him, but none had tempted him to go back to the theatre. Finally in December 1860 a proposal from the Imperial Theatre in St Petersburg awakened some response, at least from Strepponi, who was alone at the farm while Verdi, in Turin, was trying to persuade Cavour to excuse him from running for

Parliament. Enrico Tamberlick, one of the most celebrated tenors of his time, had discussed the offer with Mauro Corticelli, who was on tour in Russia with the Italian actress Adelaide Ristori: 'I have heard from Corticelli, who reached here with Signora Ristori, that you might perhaps be persuaded to add another jewel to the splendid crown of your operas, which you now threaten to bring to an end.'[48] In the name of the director of the Imperial Theatres, Tamberlick appealed to Verdi to fan the spark of his genius and answer the call of the audience and the artists who were waiting for him. 'The audience that adores you without ever having seen you will be very happy to have you.'

Corticelli, who had been trying to get Verdi to compose for him as early as the mid-1850s, got a reply from Strepponi at once. Verdi would write to Tamberlick, she said, but she felt—from certain things Verdi had said—that might compose again. Even though she was a 'poor advocate' she would do what she could to persuade her husband to accept the offer and '*insist, annoy* him until we get what we want.'[49] In fact, Verdi might have been easily persuaded, given the expense of remodelling the house at Sant'Agata and the staggering costs of maintaining a hotel suite in Turin, where he entertained, kept a servant, had to dress well every day, and had even had to buy new summer clothes. Whatever other expenses he had planned for, those connected with his role as deputy were certainly not on his agenda.

Verdi, responding to the offer, proposed Victor Hugo's *Ruy Blas*, which the Imperial Theatre vetoed almost immediately. Turning to classical and contemporary plays, the composer found nothing that caught his fancy.

I cannot and do not want to sign a contract before finding a subject that is right for the singers that I would have in Petersburg and that is approved by the authorites. . . . As for myself there is nothing that could make me sign a contract that could force me later to compose some subject in a hurry that I might or might not be satisfied with. . . . If we could meet, we could have a much better understanding between us. Be sure that I will go on looking for a subject, and if I find one, I will write to you about it at once. Give me the list of the singers. Tell me whether the chorus and orchestra are good, and, if it is necessary to improve them, whether the directors would do it.[50]

Tamberlick's next move was to send Achille Tamberlick, his younger brother, to Turin, where he assured Verdi that he could indeed compose *Ruy Blas* if he wished and that he was free to choose any other drama and dictate his own terms, so long as he did not force the Tsar to proclaim a republic in Russia. By the time of young Tamberlick's visit, the composer had already set his sights on *Don Alvaro o la fuerza del sino*, a play by Angel Saavedra, the Duke de Rivas. Even as early as 1852 Verdi had discussed this work with De Sanctis, who had thought that it might have been composed then.[51] Satisfied that the Spanish drama would make a good opera, he sent to Milan for a copy of it. By that time Strepponi, almost sure that Verdi would decide to go back to the theatre, confided to Corticelli that 'there is a 90 per cent chance that Verdi will compose for Petersburg. Given this possibility, I have already begun to have someone line, change, and add fur to suits, skirts, bodices, and shirts.'[52] When Achille Tamberlick left Turin for Paris, it was taken for granted that a new opera would be written for St. Petersburg.

The honour accorded Verdi by the Imperial Theatre reflected not merely on him but on Italy as well, for the composer had gone beyond the common round of opera and become an elected representative of his nation. There is a certain irony in the fact that Verdi was chosen just at the time when Wagner's *Tannhäuser* had provoked an outcry in Paris. The opera's première at the Opéra had, of course, aroused Verdi's curiosity. Asking Escudier for precise details of the event, Verdi then remained in Turin to await news. One day after the première, Escudier wrote of the colossal fiasco of *Tannhäuser*,

this phenomenal opera. Everything that I will say to you is much, much more restrained than what actually happened. During the entire performance, which the Emperor attended, the whole audience—apart from some Prussian and Austrian shoemakers—laughed out loud, then hissed, and finally whistled. . . . So we have got rid of a madman who imagined that one could boldly write music without a trace of melody: he made a lot of noise.[53]

Even though he had been busy in Turin in April, Verdi had asked Piave to send him five plays and join him there as soon as possible. Another visitor was Mariani, who came to the capital in the summer to review the work he was doing for Ricordi's edition of *Un ballo in maschera*. He had begun to consider producing *Simon Boccanegra* at the Teatro Comunale in Bologna with Caroline Douvry Barbot and Giraldoni. When Verdi went home, it was to Palazzo Cavalli in Busseto, not to Sant'Agata, where he was having a new roof put on his house. The old guest-rooms no longer even existed, he told his librettist. Verdi went to Sant'Agata every day to oversee the work he had ordered and also put up a bell he had brought from Turin to call in his labourers.

BOOK IV

With the date set for the première of the new opera in St Petersburg, Strepponi began ordering the provisions that would be needed there, asking Corticelli to buy them for her and Verdi, as he also did for Ristori. 'In the perpetual ice-cream [snow] of Petersburg', Verdi would need tagliatelle and macaroni to keep him in good humour. For their projected three-month stay they would have to provide for themselves, two servants from Sant'Agata, and perhaps an interpreter as well. Her order covered 100 bottles of common Bordeaux for the table, twenty of fine Bordeaux, and twenty of champagne; rice, pasta, cheese, and cured ham. She had risen in the world, she told Corticelli, from the role of singer to that of housewife, which she preferred. 'You, who know me, won't have any trouble in believing this, since you know how little I liked being on the stage.'[54] During the summer, Strepponi also exchanged letters with her aunt Giovannina Strepponi who taught in the elementary school in Lodi. A cousin, whom she did not know, had come to see her and had written letters which Strepponi considered offensive. Asking to be left alone, and saying that she would not receive anyone who came without an invitation, she told her aunt that she would do anything on earth to avoid abusing Verdi's kindness toward her. She did, however, offer to visit her aunt in Lodi, provided no other relative came at the same time. At the end of the letter, which she signed 'Giuseppina Verdi', she wrote: 'From my signature you can see that you must never again address letters to "Giuseppina Strepponi", and you can thank God for me that this is so.'[55]

While preparations for the trip to Russia were in her hands, Verdi and Piave worked together on the libretto of La forza del destino, under conditions not very different from those that had prevailed in the early years of their careers. Piave was then in Milan, working as stage director for Merelli, who had once more taken over La Scala. Verdi remained at home, first in Busseto and later at Sant'Agata, fulminating against La Scala, as he had in the past.

Even Il trovatore was a fiasco the first time they gave it at La Scala! Nor should the directors of La Scala forget that two or three years ago Ricordi, at the dress rehearsal of Boccanegra, offered 5 or 6 thousand Austrian lire if they would engage another baritone. The directors refused, and the opera turned out as a scandal, indecent, as everyone knows.[56]

The librettist and composer began work at the end of July, during Piave's visit to Busseto, but Verdi was far from satisfied with the results.

For the love of God, my dear Piave, let's think this over carefully. We cannot go on like this, and it is impossible to find a way out of this mess with this drama, absolutely impossible. The style must be tighter. Poetry can and must say everything that prose says, with half the words: up to now, you are not doing it.[57]

One day later he returned to the charge, noting that eight verses in the first act could be reduced to six and that other parts of the work should be shortened as well. 'You, a poet, should still know how to say more in fewer words. Anyway, it certainly is already shortened considerably, and in this form it is more dramatic, and more correct.'[58] Accusing Piave of throwing in words just to make longer lines or proper rhymes, Verdi called on his librettist to change other verses in the first act. Piave responded with good spirit, saying that he had gone on to the second act, but did not want to range too far afield without Verdi's counsel. As to the camp scene, he would only attack it when he and the composer were together again. Piave was also told to arrange for the sketches of the scenery and costumes and to give his 'orders and suggestions' for the *mise-en-scène*.[59] By August Piave had finished the second act, except for a few of the recitatives. Verdi, who had gone ahead with the rough draft of the fourth act, asked him to be sure to include some text that would give Don Alvaro's past history. Piave, who was overwhelmed with his work, at La Scala, met Verdi's demands as best he could. He reported on the brilliant opening night at La Scala, a miracle, given the hostility of many Milanese, who accused Merelli of being pro-Austrian. In September the composer and librettist were together again in the country. Mariani also visited at the same time. The work was going well; Verdi was especially happy about Piave's suggestions for the 'Rataplan'. He also asked his librettist to bring a piano wire for his Pleyel, but vetoed Piave's offer to bring a collection of Spanish songs he had borrowed. 'Do not bring the songs, and give them back to the person who lent them to you. I am not in the habit of studying music, and so I don't keep any in the house, nor do I go looking for any from someone who has some.'[60]

Both men threw themselves fully into the opera, which Verdi finally composed in a few weeks between 20 September and the middle of November. Only the instrumentation remained to be done. The composer, who had probably not written any music in almost four years, told Fraschini that he was composing with his whole being. The play, which he had described to Escudier as powerful, unusual, and grand, drew him out of his retirement and back into the world of theatre. On 22 November

Verdi wrote to let Tito Ricordi know that he had finished everything excepting the orchestration.[61] He would leave for Russia at once.

The first stop on their journey was Piacenza, where they stayed in a hotel with Ricordi, his secretary Eugenio Tornaghi, and Mariani. While there, Verdi expressed his unhappiness with the scheduled production of *Un ballo in maschera* at La Scala, accusing Ricordi of gross mismanagement in conceding the opera to a theatre where for years all his operas had been badly produced. Verdi and Strepponi then went on to Turin to meet Piave, who turned over the revised version of last three scenes of *La forza del destino*, which he bound into the body of the libretto. In Paris, they visited friends. Verdi also picked up his new evening clothes, a frock coat, waistcoat, and trousers, ordered from his French tailor.

Travelling via Berlin and Warsaw, Verdi and Strepponi were met at a station nine hours west of St Petersburg by the baritone De Bassini and the tenor Masini. In the capital, where they arrived on 6 December, Corticelli and the members of the orchestra delivered a formal welcome. The troupe took carriages to the magnificent apartment that the director of the Imperial Theatres had leased for Verdi. The house was warm, 'like an eternal Spring', and the composer also had a carriage with 'two horses that run like lightning'.[62] The theatre, of course, was completely unfamiliar, known to Verdi only through the news brought back to France and Italy by Italians who had performed there. The tradition of Italian music at the Tsar's court was strong. Singers were engaged at high fees to sing the operas of the repertory. Often hundreds of thousands of francs were spent on settings and costumes for a single opera or ballet, for either the Emperor or members of his court were in attendance almost every night. No expense was spared. Among the artists who had prospered there were Galuppi, Paisiello, Cimarosa, and a host of lesser figures. In Verdi's own time the audience in St Petersburg had heard Rubini, Pasta, Grisi, Mario, Tacchinardi-Persiani, De Giuli-Borsi, Frezzolini, De Bassini, and Tamberlick.[63]

When Verdi reached the opera-house, he found most of his cast waiting for him, but the prima donna soprano, Emma La Grua, was ill. The 31-year-old Sicilian, then at the apex of a ten-year career, had sung in Paris, Vienna, all the Italian theatres, and South America. Her dramatic gifts were widely praised; one Viennese critic called her the greatest actress to be found on the stage in Europe. Verdi, making final changes to the opera, wrote to Piave on 14 December 1861 and again on 10 January 1862, sending his text and asking the librettist to refine it.[64] To Ricordi,

Verdi sent the news that the rehearsals were still not under way. He had discussed with his Russian publisher the release of the most popular pieces of *La forza del destino*, which Verdi wanted to have on sale within a few days of the première. He also ordered Ricordi to pay Piave for his work. Authors' rights, as always, were a concern.

Russia has no treaties with other nations, except for an unimportant, partial one with France: and it is unlikely they will have any because the Minister of Foreign Affairs has always been against them and will always oppose them, as he told me himself one day when we were having dinner with him at the home of the director of the Theatre. So there is nothing to be done about this. One day a publisher came to me and said that he had the right to print all my operas here.[65]

Ricordi wrote to Verdi about the production of *Un ballo in maschera* at La Scala, reporting that it had been something less than a success, but not a scandal. When Verdi learned just how bad the performances had been, he lashed out at his publisher, who was partly responsible for the poor production.

It's nothing new to me or to anyone else that La Scala . . . has become one of the worst theatres in Italy . . . that it thinks it has the right to lay its hands on our operas, tear them up, massacre them, and present them to the audience unattractively and foolishly. The impresarios don't make any effort to improve the choruses, the *mise-en-scène*, nor the artists, to see whether they are suitable or not for a given opera. Art is a noun without meaning: it's enough for them to be able to put up a name or the title of an opera on the poster, so long as it offers the possibility of some earnings. The directors let them do this; the Government pays; and the public judges the opera as best it can, or whistles, or doesn't care, with immense damage to the author's reputation, his interests, and those of his publisher. I have been singing the same tune for ten years, because for ten or twelve years I have seen almost all my operas massacred in that theatre (even *Il trovatore* was a failure when it was given for the first time at La Scala!!). When I was passing through Piacenza, I told you that you were wrong to give them *Ballo in maschera*. I told you why, and now you have seen that I was telling the truth, and that the opera could not have been produced more wretchedly. At a time when every Italian's effort is directed toward reaching the level of the great nations, which guarantee and respect the rights of the author, ([the work of art] is the fruit of the mind, and therefore the most legitimate property of all), it would be strange indeed if I could not manage my own music in the way that seems right for me! Some say that no one should oppose a theatre that is underwritten by the government; but I say instead that just because the government subsidizes it, we have a right to see productions given in a way that brings lustre and dignity to art. If the impresarios and directors don't want to do this, or don't know how to, then it is up to the authors to put an end to the disorder.[66]

He added that he wished to add to his contract with Ricordi a clause stipulating that *La forza del destino* should not be presented in any of the important theatres, especially La Scala, without his approval.

The Imperial Theatre in St Petersburg faced a crisis in its own house, as La Grua remained ill and Verdi searched for a replacement. Finally, he asked to have his contract cancelled, as he often did when he felt that it had been broken. When the director of the theatre refused to free him, the two men reached a compromise: the première of *La forza del destino* would be given the following winter. With that matter settled, Verdi and Strepponi set off for Moscow, to see another great Russian city.

Strepponi, reporting to Arrivabene on the events of the winter, described conditions in Russia, saying that the frightful cold had not inconvenienced them because the houses were warm, but that the poor in general and coachmen in particular were 'the most wretched people on earth.'[67] After leaving St Petersburg, she and Verdi went to Berlin and Paris, from where they planned their trip to England, where Verdi's next work was to be given.

London and *L'inno delle nazioni*

One of the few occasional pieces Verdi ever agreed to write, *L'inno delle nazioni,* was composed for the International Exhibition in London, its text provided by the 20-year-old Italian poet Arrigo Boito. The son of a Polish noblewoman and an Italian father, Boito had studied at Milan Conservatory and had been introduced by friends to Clara Maffei. When he and Verdi first met in Paris, Boito was making a grand tour of Europe with a schoolmate, Franco Faccio, who would later become one of the leading conductors of his generation. Armed with letters of introduction from Camillo Boito, his brother, and from Countess Maffei, the young musician called on Verdi at the Hotel Brittanique. Perhaps because Boito and Faccio had already made their mark in a modest way with their cantata *Le sorelle d'Italia,* presented at Milan Conservatory, Verdi commissioned Boito to write the poem for *L'inno delle nazioni,* which he had agreed to compose for the exposition. Verdi had, in fact, not been the first choice for the occasion, Rossini having been approached and having refused. As the event was planned, Auber was to represent France, Meyerbeer Germany, Sterndale Bennett England, and Verdi Italy. The compositions, scheduled for presentation in May, were to be sent to the Commission well before the date to allow for proper rehearsal.

Boito got his first draft to Verdi at the end of March, but substantial changes were made in the second version, which was published in England, and a final version, published by Ricordi.[68] The work included the national anthems of England, France, and Italy. To get a copy of *Fratelli d'Italia*, Verdi had to write to Ricordi and ask to have it sent to him.

While he was waiting for the text of the hymn, Verdi committed himself to securing the soprano Barbot to sing Leonora in *La forza del destino*. Soon after Verdi proposed her, he learned that Constance Nantier-Didiée, who was to sing Preziosilla, was trying to prevent Barbot's engagement. Hearing this, he protested to the director of the Imperial Theatres: 'This is really too much! I know that if I were director, I would set fire to the four corners of the theatre rather than put up with such demands!'[69] He then turned to Luccardi for help, asking him to approach Barbot himself to find out whether the Russian management had contacted her. Verdi proposed that the soprano make her début in *Un ballo in maschera* then sing *La forza del destino* and other repertory operas. Later, he wrote to her directly and, when her engagement was guaranteed, sent a letter of thanks to St Petersburg.

When it was time to think about going to London, Verdi sent Strepponi ahead, returned to Turin and Sant'Agata, and reached London in April. A host of problems greeted him there, for it seemed that *L'inno delle nazioni* could not be performed. Michael Costa, conductor and director of the Sacred Harmony Society, who was to conduct the works for the exposition, declared to *The Times* that Verdi's work would not be given because it was scored for voices and not just for orchestra, as the rules of the Commission stipulated. The cantata, which was for orchestra, chorus, and tenor solo, could not even be rehearsed in time because Verdi had not delivered it.

Verdi answered sharply in *The Times*.

My composition was in the hands [of the secretary of the Commission] on 5 April. . . . I did not compose a march, as agreed initially, because Auber told me in Paris that he expected to write one for this same solemn occasion. . . . I

447

thought that this change would not displease the commissioners; they, however, let it be known that twenty-five days (enough to learn a new opera) were not enough to learn this short cantata; and they refused it. I want to have the facts known, not to give importance to something that is unimportant, but merely to correct the error—that I did not send my composition.[70]

He then wrote to Ricordi, asking him to have this letter published in several other papers, and asked Escudier to do the same.

The exposition opened, with Verdi present, but without a performance of his hymn. The English press then erupted with denunciations of the Royal Commission, of Costa, and of English chauvinism, deploring the violation of international courtesy, the uncivilized action taken against Verdi, and the wrecked and perverted festivities. There was such an outcry that eventually *L'inno delle nazioni* was performed by a chorus of 260 voices, with the soprano Tietjens as the soloist, replacing Tamberlick. Costa, the director of Covent Garden, refused to release the tenor to Her Majesty's Theatre, where the cantata was finally performed on 24 May, under the baton of Luigi Arditi. The newpapers reported with satisfaction that the preparation of the work took only three days, instead of the twenty-five that the Commission had thought it would require. News of its success was duly sent to Ricordi. Verdi was particularly satisfied with the orchestra and with the reception the hymn received.

The performance of *L'inno delle nazioni* surely represented a victory for Verdi and Italy, for it got more publicity than the works of the other composers; but it was the kind of victory Verdi disliked. When it seemed that the hymn would not be performed, he said that he was very happy indeed, although he made his own wry and somewhat bitter observations on the event. To Ricordi on 24 April he wrote of his fatigue, caused by the trip to England, and of his satisfaction that the hymn would not be heard: 'So much the better! I detest pieces written for a given occasion; I have never wanted to write any for any event at all; I, who would never have agreed to write this one, had the others not already agreed,—you can imagine how happy I am that Fortune has saved me.'[71] 'I am saved,' he exulted to Escudier, 'Fortune (that is a God to whom I will build altars from now on) looked on me with favour this time, and I will not give my cantata at the exposition. . . . I, who never wrote cantatas, nor hymns, nor marches; I, who detest and despise all *pièces de circonstance*, you can imagine how happy I am to have got off so cheaply in this.'[72]

After the exposition opened, Verdi wrote a long letter to Arrivabene, returning once more to the theme of occasional pieces.

I have always thought, and I still think, that these occasional pieces are, artistically speaking, odious; and, believe me, in these enormous halls the attention [of the audience] is too distracted, and nothing makes an effect; nothing *can* be effective, and, let's face it, nothing *was* effective. Because of this, I have never wanted to write these works. . . . [The letter published in *The Times*] has been a real curse for me, for the next day it brought down on me a storm of letters invoking the Wrath of God on the Commission and on Costa; and, what's more, requests for autographs from everywhere imaginable, and written in the most extraordinary and utterly English way. In other countries, people who want autographs arrange to be introduced to you, or to present an album through the good offices of one of your friends. Not here: they write to me through the post, enclosing a stamped, postmarked envelope addressed to the person to whom I am to sign the autograph. I have no idea who the devil they are! Add to this the fact that all these letters are in English (because of that damned letter I wrote to *The Times*) and so it is a curse for Peppina, who has to translate them for me. As for Italy, our music does not need to be given at the exposition. It is given here every night in two theatres, and not just here, but everywhere. . . . Never before have there been so many Italian opera-houses as in our time; never have the publishers of every country printed and sold so much Italian music; and there is no corner in the world where—if they have a theatre and two instruments—Italian opera is not sung. When you go to the Indies and the middle of Africa, you will hear *Il trovatore*. . . . I have been to the exposition once, but everything is in such disorder that I can't tell you anything about it. Up to now, the most interesting items are broken packing-cases, rolls, bales of straw, porters whom you have to watch if you don't want to get your ribs smashed, and drops of water that drip from the glass roof to chill the noses of the curious. The [exposition hall] is absolutely wretched in all its vastness.[73]

Before leaving England, Verdi bought two new guns, which he sent home. As he described them a few weeks later to Mariani, one was a rifle like Sir James Hudson's, the other a smaller, double-barrelled gun. 'When will you come to try them?'[74] Verdi stayed a few days in Paris before leaving for Turin. Parliament had reopened on 3 June, with Rattazzi replacing Ricasoli, whose government had fallen in March. Writing from Paris, after his return from Russia, Verdi had asked Piroli for news of the situation in Italy, the tension and disorder. Garibaldi, who had been recruiting volunteers in the country around Bergamo, was suspected of planning an attack on the Trent Valley in May. Under orders from Turin, the royal troops attempted to stop him. When they encountered resistance, the troops fired, killing four people and wounding others. Garibaldi responded, not with his usual fire but with disarming calm, saying that the volunteers had come to him of their own will and that the incident was merely an exercise. But all of Italy knew that he cherished the goal of liberating Venetia and Rome. A national scandal followed, with denials, rumours, and disclaimers on all sides; almost everyone, however, believed that Garibaldi had indeed intended to invade the Trentino. After an audience with the King in Turin, Garibaldi again went home to Caprera.

Verdi returned to Parliament in the heat of this crisis. At some time during his term as deputy, he was nominated to a commission of five men who were delegated to handle special problems that had arisen in the Province of Parma. Strepponi left almost at once for Locate Triulzi, where she visited her mother and sister, who was ill. She then went on to Sant'Agata. Verdi travelled by train from Turin to Piacenza, where he was met by his carriage. After almost eight months away he was home again.

25

Summer 1862 – December 1863

Tribulations

Although he had been away from home a long time and had important work to finish, Verdi returned to Turin and Parliament at the end of June. After a short stint there, he left for Sant'Agata, but the peace he hoped to find was not to be his that summer. The remodelling project again disrupted the routine of the house, as it had in previous years. Illness struck several members of the household, as two servants and a farm agent came down with tertian fever. When Barberina Strepponi was diagnosed as having tuberculosis, Strepponi brought her from Locate to stay at the villa. Verdi, half-sick himself, decided not to try to attend sessions of the Chamber of Deputies in late July. He, his wife, and his sister-in-law were grieved by the death of Loulou, their favourite pet, whose portrait still hangs in Strepponi's bedroom. The little dog's grave in the garden, a few yards from Verdi's studio–bedroom, is marked with a monument. Because they had often taken Loulou on trips with them, carrying him like a child under Verdi's great cloak or Strepponi's shawl, he had come to be treated like a person, a member of the family, and was sorely missed.

Some of the year appeared to have been unproductive and frustrating, but Verdi had enjoyed his stay in Russia and, on his return, had continued his work on the cantata *L'inno delle nazioni*, which was to be published in England, France, and Italy. The composer promised Ricordi that he would finish it before starting back to St Petersburg. Already planning to give *La forza del destino* in Madrid, he also discussed a possible production in Rome.

Like many Italians, Verdi was concerned over the threat of civil war that summer. Garibaldi, who had remained at Caprera during part of June, sailed for Sicily on the twenty-fifth with his son and about twenty volunteers. Even now it is not certain that the government knew what he intended to do. Greeted like a hero in Palermo, he went on to Marsala, where a hysterical crowd, aroused by his rhetoric, began to shout 'Rome or Death!'—the war cry of those who wanted Rome taken by force. New volunteers joined his ranks daily, as the original force of twenty men became 3,000 strong. In Turin, the King and his cabinet seemed uncertain about a course of action. Carlo Tenca, writing to Clara Maffei, expressed the sentiments of many liberal northerners who were unsure of what the future might bring. Garibaldi 'is now in open revolt and is creating an army around himself. He is so blinded by anger and so far off the beaten path in his political views that we have everything to fear. . . . We are living in a tremendously difficult moment.'[1] Garibaldi, who may have believed that the King favoured his advance, marched on Catania and crossed the Strait of Sicily, reaching the mainland. On 25 August his men were attacked by a column of the Italian army on the road to Reggio Calabria. The General, realizing that civil war would erupt if his men returned fire, retreated into the hills of the Aspromonte. A day later a company of army sharpshooters attacked him and his Red Shirts again, wounding the General in the thigh and foot. Twelve dead and forty wounded marked a dreadful record for the new country. Some of the Garibaldini kept the war going until the beginning of October, when an amnesty was declared, allowing the prisoners to return home; but seven men were executed as deserters from the Italian army.

'Poor Italy!' Verdi wrote to Arrivabene. 'What is this ministry—so disliked by everyone—doing, that it does not hand in its resignation? And I don't understand why the King, who is so courageous, does not put himself at the head of the army and say "The nation is in danger; I am your foremost soldier; follow me." '[2] The events of summer did indeed lead to Rattazzi's fall.[3] He was replaced by Farini, the former dictator of the Royal Provinces of Emilia, whose rise to power brought Piroli close to the highest ranks of government. At that moment, Verdi, admitting to Piroli that he had neither the time nor, indeed, the patience to serve the Parliament, felt it was time for him to resign.[4] Verdi did not in fact leave but continued to return to Turin whenever he could.

The Return to Russia and the Première of *La forza del destino*

Hoping to avoid the worst winter weather, Verdi had arranged to present *La forza del destino* in the autumn; so preparations for the trip went forward at Sant'Agata during August. Mariani, who had been summoned to serve in the National Guard in Genoa during a threatened uprising of pro-Garibaldi partisans, wrote that he had been ordered to the City Hall on guard duty. When he wanted to come to Sant'Agata with Hudson, he received a letter from Verdi begging him not to bring the guest. Apart from the illness of the servants, 'my house is in utter disorder, with bricklayers, carpenters, blacksmiths, etc. etc. and not one room, not one single room is completely finished and ready to receive a gentleman.'[5] Mariani did come alone, though, on his way back to Genoa from a conducting engagement in Carpi. Verdi and Strepponi left for St Petersburg at the end of his visit, at the beginning of September, taking the same route they had taken the year before. In Turin they met Tornaghi, who returned to Verdi his original score of *La forza del destino*, which was being copied for Madrid. Ricordi also provided a sum of money in gold napoleons for Verdi's trip and gave him a score of *L'inno delle nazioni*, which Verdi hoped to give in St Petersburg with Tamberlick as the soloist. After a short time in Paris, Verdi and Strepponi went on, arriving in the Russian capital on 24 September. His first few days there were devoted to making changes in the first-act duet between the soprano and the tenor; these were duly sent back to Ricordi. At the end of September the Verdis travelled to Moscow, where *Il trovatore* was being given. Although they wished to attend the opera there without being recognized, a cry went up from the audience. Verdi was called to the stage and given a standing ovation. The next day the singers had him as guest of honour at a banquet.

From St Petersburg, Verdi kept in constant communication with Ricordi who, like the Russian publisher, was preparing to issue the best pieces from the opera. Verdi suggested that certain numbers should be published first, among them the 'romanza [of the] soprano [in] Act I; the baritone's ballata [from] the second [act]; the couplets of Preziosilla in the camp scene; the duettino between the tenor and baritone after the battle; and the 'Rataplan'.[6] Other suggestions followed. Verdi was rehearsing his cast, which included Barbot. Having had a huge success in *Un ballo in maschera*, the work Verdi had proposed for her début, she promised a second triumph as Leonora. He sent news of a good general rehearsal, with a full house and the singers in fine voice and hoped for the best for the première, scheduled for the next night.[7] Verdi had Tamberlick as Don Alvaro; Francesco Graziani as Don Carlo di Vargas; Gian Francesco Angelini, a young bass, as the Padre Guardiano; the Neapolitan bass-baritone Achille De Bassini as Fra Melitone; Verdi's familiar colleague Ignazio Marini, veteran of *Oberto* at La Scala, as the Alcalde; Nantier-Didiée as Preziosilla; and an Italian artist, Signor Meo, as the Marchese di Calatrava.

The première was given on 10 November. Because the work was four hours long, the opera began at 7.30 p.m. Verdi seemed completely satisified with its success. 'Last night the first performance of *La forza del destino*. Result: good. Performance very, very good. Settings and costumes extremely opulent.'[8] On 17 November Verdi sent news to Escudier: 'We have done three performances of *La forza del destino* with very full houses and excellent success.'[9] Strepponi, reporting to Corticelli, went even farther.

From everything I know, the opera went very, very well, in spite of the desperate efforts of the Tedesque faction, for which I feel a lot of sympathy anyway, since it has been shouting for many years that the German operas are the best, while the people are stubborn enough to leave the theatre empty when [German operas] are given and to run to the opera-house like madmen when they announce hideous trash like *Ballo in maschera*, *Forza del destino*, etc. Just think that *eight* performances of the *Forza del destino* have already been given, with the theatre packed all the time.[10]

She reported that Verdi had been handsomely paid for coming to Russia twice. A second note from Verdi to Ricordi was accompanied by a clipping from the French-language newspaper, *Le Journal de Saint-Pétersbourg*, which described the 'brilliant success won by this beautiful work', the 'magnificent score', and the 'triumph of the composer and the ovations tendered to the artists'. 'We believe that *La forza del destino* is the most complete of all Verdi's works, in the richness and inspiration of its melodies, as in its development and orchestration.'[11] Several days later a long article appeared reaffirming the success but adding that Tamberlick, 'already tired from the large number of rehearsals, perhaps did not show all the strength that he has, on that first night' and that the same could be said of the other artists as well.[12] Verdi had rehearsed his cast three or four hours every day, even when the singers had a perform-ance at night. A passing reference was made to the lugubrious and tragic story, which wore the audience down. It was a very good review, all the same. The critic predicted that many of the pieces in the opera were destined to become famous and that Verdi had never taken such pains with the orchestration, the structure of the ensembles and choruses, and the handling of all the details.

The Tsar, who had been ill, attended the opera with the Tsarina on the night of the fourth performance. They applauded generously, then—after Verdi received a long ovation and was offered wreaths and flowers—invited the composer to come to their box, where they talked with him at length about his work. Afterwards, the Tsar honoured Verdi with the Imperial and Royal Order of St Stanislaus, the cross of which was conferred on him. It was the second such decoration he had received in a year, the Italian government having awarded him the Order of St Maurizio the previous March.

It was not until later that a hint of something less than absolute triumph appeared. *L'Indépendance belge* reported that a demonstration had been mounted against *La forza del destino* by a group of Russian nationalists who were opposed to the première of this Italian work. Ricordi's *Gazzetta Musicale* took up Verdi's cause at once, while admitting that 'Russian music does exist, and Glinka was a true genius.'[13] The attempt to stage a demonstration had failed because an overwhelming majority of the audience got up and began to applaud Verdi. At least one other paper, *Le Nord*, mentioned the group of protesters, driven by national pride, and suggested that some of the audience might have expected an opera that held more closely to the style of Verdi's former works. 'Instead of a light score in the ordinary manner of Italian operas, the author of *Rigoletto* gave us . . . a production that, in its genre, is closer to Meyerbeer or Halévy.'[14] Ricordi's publication defended its composer in the strongest terms. Verdi, then as later, said that it had been a mistake to dignify the attack with a response. Explicit reservations were set forth in the article by a Russian critic in *Cyn otečestva*.

It was a success, but not nearly as enthusiastically received as certain optimists say: it is true that the composer was called out for bows, even after the first act, in which there is nothing at all; doesn't this prove that curtain-calls do not necessarily indicate an undisputed success? . . . Those who often go to the theatre know how to tell a real success from one that is forced. . . . Yes, it was a success; as the French say, a *succès d'éstime*; but there was no genuine enthusiasm at all.[15]

In spite of this, the critic found many parts of the opera very beautiful. He did, however, comment on the length of the work and on the cruel toll taken on the singers' voices. In spite of the criticism, which at its worst was moderate enough, the opera held the stage, and Verdi continued to express his satisfaction over its success. He stayed on nearly a month longer than he had intended obviously enjoying the people he had met in St Petersburg. Following a pattern set the previous year, he and Strepponi entertained and accepted invitations to dinners and soirées. The composer played at salon evenings and receptions and even listened without protest when his own music was offered. The Italian ambassador to Russia found Verdi genial, good humoured, and expansive. 'Surprise! Surprise!' the composer wrote to Clara Maffei. 'In these two months, I have gone to salons and dinners and entertainments as well. I have met people of high and low estate: men and women who are likeable and exquisitely polite, quite different from the impertinent *politesse* in Paris.'[16] On 9 December he and Strepponi had to leave behind a world that had become dear to them.

La forza del destino in Madrid

Wanting to go back to Sant'Agata, the composer had instead to travel on to Spain, where he was to produce his new opera at the Teatro Real. He stayed longer in Paris than he had intended, plagued with an attack of boils on his neck. While in France, he arranged with the Opéra to help with a production of *Les Vêpres siciliennes*, for which he agreed to coach Marie Sass himself, provided the management made the soprano available. At the same time he forbade a production of *La forza del destino* and tried to stop Calzado of the Théâtre des Italiens from giving *I Lombardi alla prima crociata*. Although he was unsuccessful in that, he counselled Escudier against suing the impresario, perhaps believing that it would be futile.

After spending Christmas 1862 and New Year's Day 1863 in Paris, Verdi and Strepponi started for Madrid, where they arrived in the second week of January after an exhausting trip that took its toll on them both. Although he had feared that rehearsals would begin without him, he was wrong. The cast learned the new work from him; but the scores sent had dozens of copyists' mistakes. He reproached Ricordi for the carelessly copied parts, saying that if those sent to Rome were as full of errors as those sent to him in Madrid, 'those poor conductors won't understand anything, then the performance will be meaningless, without dynamic contrasts, without expression, without intelligence, and therefore a fiasco'.[17] 'The music becomes just a vocal exercise.'[18] The copyists had even added notes to his score. Citing an example, he noted that in the 'Rataplan' alone he had counted fourteen wrong notes and seventy-four incorrect dynamic markings—this in a piece that has only about eighty bars!

His criticism of Ricordi's operation was more than offset by the intimation that he might return to La Scala, after an absence of decades. 'You want me to contract with La Scala to come and direct there? . . . Let the directors find singers that are suited to the opera and worthy of the theatre, and I, if I can, will come to produce *La forza del destino*.'[19] This news reached Ricordi at a difficult moment, when the publisher had asked Verdi to allow him to make only partial payments on a debt owed the composer for *La forza del destino*. Verdi replied from Madrid on 4 February:

I have received yours of 28 [January] with the accounting for the last six months. The partial payments that you would like to make are very inconvenient for me, and I would prefer that you pay me the entire amount for the opera in one single payment. In that case, I could let you keep the money for six months, paying me the usual 5 per cent interest, beginning from 5 February. If that helps you, then that will do for the 40,000 francs for the opera.[20]

This was a great favour, given the large expenses the composer had faced in the previous two years, but Verdi, as he often did, protected his own interests by dating the loan from the following day and starting the interest running at once.

As to future work, he said that he might go to London for James Mapleson's production of *La forza del destino* but that he probably would not compose a new work for Naples. He also said he would not write for the Paris Opéra. The number of options open to him—and these are but a few—show that his retirement had not diminished his popularity in any way. Verdi could probably have asked his own terms from almost any theatre at that time.

Even as rehearsals kept him busy in Madrid, Verdi kept himself informed about the production of *La forza del destino* in Rome, asking Luccardi for first-hand reports and expressing his fear that the changes made in the libretto would affect the success of the opera. In mid-

February, when Luccardi sent him a telegram with news, Verdi replied sharply.

If the opera went fairly well in Rome, it would have gone a thousand times better if Jacovacci could get it through his head that to have successes, you need both *operas suited to the artists and artists suited to the operas*. In *La forza del destino* you certainly don't have to know how to sing fancy passages, but you have to have a soul and understand the *word* and express it.

He complained about the four pieces in the opera that had not gone well. 'Four pieces are a lot, and they can make an opera's fortune! . . . Anyway, let's thank our good luck that—with so many shortcomings—they didn't kill the opera, the artists, and, above all, the impresario.'[21]

The Teatro Real had been a fortress of Italian opera from the day of its opening in 1850, though Italian singers had held forth at the Teatro de los Caños Real for more than a century before that. When Verdi reached Madrid in 1863, his major asset in his cast was the dependable, affectionate tenor Fraschini, who had visited Sant'Agata shortly before Verdi's second trip to Russia and may have been partly responsible for the composer's engagement in Spain. Fraschini had sung in the premières of five Verdi operas and was among the few singers whom the composer unstintingly praised. In Madrid, where he had an enthusiastic following, he had sung in *I vespri siciliani* in 1856–7, repeating his success of 1856 in Rome in the same opera. In 1859 he had worked with Verdi as they prepared the première of *Un ballo in maschera*. The soprano for *La forza del destino* in Madrid was Anne Caroline La Grange, a French artist who had sung in Italy since 1843 and had made a career in Vienna, Paris, and St Petersburg as well. In 1856 La Grange sang the first American Violetta in *La traviata* at the Academy of Music in New York City; in 1861 she was the prima donna soprano in two productions at La Scala.[22] With her and Fraschini were Leone Giraldoni, one of the most widely acclaimed baritones of his time, and Antonio Cotogni, younger than the veterans Fraschini and La Grange, but thoroughly competent. The Preziosilla was Emilia Méric-Lablache, daughter of the celebrated soprano Henriette Méric-Lalande.[23]

In spite of the excellent auspices this cast offered, Verdi was far from satisfied. After the second orchestral rehearsal he let Ricordi know that the production was only mediocre; the final dress rehearsal left him utterly discouraged. 'Nothing went well, and we cannot hope for a success. Chorus and orchestra and settings very, very well done; everything else is missing. Tomorrow, the performance.'[24] The composer's worst fears were not realized, for the opera was very successful, but he was still unhappy, although he admitted to Arrivabene that the opera had been well received. 'A success. Chorus and orchestra admirable, Fraschini and Lagrange good, everything else zero or bad.'[25] Yet he had enjoyed a personal triumph with the public demonstrating for him. When he sent a dispatch to Ricordi, he offered a still less optimistic picture, saying that even the leading singers had been only 'fairly good'.[26] The review in the Madrid paper *La Epoca* accused Verdi of returning to long-abandoned modes of his own and of copying Donizetti. The work violated rules of unity and harmony, the critic said; it lacked clarity; and its orchestration assaulted listeners' ears.[27] In spite of everything, the public continued to fill the theatre night after night.

Two days after the opening Verdi and Strepponi left Madrid for what proved to be an exhausting tour of Spain. On their itinerary were Toledo, Cordoba, Seville, Xeres, and other cities. Verdi later called it an 'uncomfortable, long, and tiring trip' but praised the Alhambra 'first and above all else' and the cathedrals of Toledo, Cordoba, and Seville. He disliked the Escorial, 'a pile of marble' that contained many fine works of art, among them a 'marvellously beautiful' work by Luca Giordano. 'But the whole lacks good taste. It is severe, terrible, like the ferocious ruler who built it.'[28] While he was away, the fatigued composer developed a bad cough, but in spite of it he returned to the Teatro Real, where *La forza del destino* had continued to gain in popularity. He was honoured on stage with flowers, wreaths, and compliments. 'As for the success, I can only tell you that the house is full all the time,' he told Ricordi.[29] The opera continued to attract the Madrid audience; in the fifteen years after its first performance there, *La forza del destino* was given in fifteen seasons in various theatres in the capital.[30]

Les Vêpres siciliennes at the Paris Opéra

Verdi and Strepponi left Madrid in mid-March while he was still slightly ill. He spent several days in bed in his suite at the Hotel Europa in Paris before setting off for the Opéra, where he had agreed to help prepare the revival of *Les Vêpres siciliennes*. As in the past, hd had serious reservations about the theatre and about the Théâtre des Italiens, where Calzado was still in charge. Exhausted from months of travel and from the tiring work of coaching singers, rehearsing them and the orchestra, and over-seeing the staging, he persisted in his effort to present his works as he believed they should be done. The French production came at the end of a trying period of his life. When he wrote to Arrivabene in late March, he said that he would perhaps attend a few rehearsals of *Les Vêpres siciliennes* at the Opéra;[31] but when he got into the work, he spent much more time and energy than he had thought would be necessary. In normal circum-stances, Verdi dedicated a month or less to the preparation of a première of a new opera; but he had already learned in 1855 that the Paris Opéra could take a great deal out of him. As March ran into April and April into May, Verdi grew angry over 'these damned *Vespri*'.[32] He said he wanted to leave for Turin as quickly as possible. The bass under contract fell ill and had to be replaced with Obin, who was brought from London. One anecdote should not be taken to characterize an entire season of work, but an account given in *L'Art musical* describes the end of one rehearsal, Verdi's last, which ended when he became angry and left the theatre.

To tell the truth, what happened at the Opéra is perhaps unique in the halls of this theatre. For three and a half months, Verdi has directed the rehearsals of his opera calmly and with admirable zeal. . . . The orchestra of the Opéra, or rather, one section of it, found a way to insult the maestro gratuitously. Verdi last Thursday thought it wise to call a rehearsal of the whole company; until that time he had had only two orchestral rehearsals, something which, by the way, seems like a rather modest number to us. During the first piece, the Maestro thought that he had detected a bit of ill will on the part of the strings; he made his remarks very courteously; but no one paid any attention to him. The second time, there was such exaggeration in the dynamics that Verdi had asked for that no one could doubt the players' intentions. The Maestro went over to one of these men and remarked to him, without a tinge of bitterness, that he did not understand what could be causing the orchestra's failure to co-operate. The answer was very strange: 'This rehearsal is unnecessary. We could have done without it,' said the instrumentalist.

'But if I myself asked for it, it was because I felt it was necessary,' Verdi replied.

'Well, you see, the problem is that each of us has [to take care of] his own business,' replied the artist in question.

'Ah! You have your business! I thought that your business was here; it seems that I am wrong,' said the Maestro.

Having said that, Verdi had Dietsch, the orchestra director, called and explained his astonishment at the musicians' conduct. 'I have nothing else to do here, after such a display, which I feel is extremely unseemly; and I am leaving,' he said. Verdi got his hat and really left. After that he never came back to the Opéra. He did not attend either the general rehearsal or the first performance of *Les Vêpres siciliennes*.[33]

On 1 July he confided to Arrivabene that he could not stand Paris any longer. 'On the day after the first performance, I am leaving for Italy.'[34]

In Turin it was rumoured that Verdi was about to establish his residence in France. When the report reached him, the composer declared to Arrivabene that it was false.

Give my respects to Signor Hudson and tell him that I have been, I am, and I will always be a peasant from Le Roncole. If I had wanted to become a Parisian, I would have accepted 40 thousand francs (and if I had wanted, even 50) and a quarter of the returns at the Théâtre des Italiens; I would have agreed to write an opera for that theatre, another for the Opéra, and a third for the Opéra-Comique. I refused it all; and it is true that the financial arrangements were extremely advantageous.[35]

Strepponi let De Sanctis know that a thousand projects were under consideration. 'All the directors of these theatres are lavishing all their best smiles on him, to tie him to their fiery chariots. We shall see what the Hero of Melody will do.'[36] She added, though, that Verdi would not go to Naples for *La forza del destino*. Complaining that they had lived in turmoil for two years, travelling all over Europe by train and packing and unpacking trunks, she admitted that she felt confused and could no longer even be sure where to find their clothes.

Strepponi was still in Paris with Verdi when her son Camillino died. A medical student whose official residence was Florence, he died as a charity case in the Santa Maria delle Grazie Hospital in Siena. Nowhere in Verdi's or Strepponi's surviving correspondence is there any reference to his death, which took place on 26 June. On the two certificates, his parents' names do not appear: the father is 'Camillo [Strepponi]', someone who did not even exist; the mother's name is given as 'Giuseppa N[ame not known]'.[37]

Earlier in the year Mariani had asked Verdi to help him secure a position as conductor at the Théâtre des Italiens. With Calzado dismissed from his post, Bagier was to be named director. Mariani, thinking to leave Genoa for a better situation, had hoped that Verdi could intervene directly in Paris on his behalf. At first Verdi did try to help, but he also advised Mariani to consider his move very seriously. The post in Paris would never be secure because the government gave no support whatever to the

Italiens and the conductor might be let go at any time. 'If you have now decided to leave Genoa for Paris, remember that nothing is sure here and that you have many competitors here as well.'[38] Yet he said he would do what he could, while urging Mariani to make a firm decision about his future. He also offered advice about Mariani's pension, which the City of Genoa was to have paid. 'I tell you again not to hesitate any longer, and think that this [past] hesitation has made you lose ten years, the best of your life. If the City guarantees your pension, then I advise you to stay; if not, choose the road that seems best.'[39] Mariani had also had an offer to conduct in Lima, Peru; Verdi seemed to tilt the scales against it, pointing out the advantage that Paris, a great city, would have. Soon after this letter was sent, Verdi heard from someone that Mariani had also asked for help from other quarters in seeking the post at the Italiens and that Bagier had actually made some kind of offer to him. Verdi wrote a harsh letter to Mariani:

I know that you have approached others about the post at the Théâtre des Italiens in Paris (you did the wrong thing) and I know that Bagier made some proposals about this to you. You can do what you like, but I declare from this moment that I no longer have anything to do with this affair, and if you care even a little about my friendship, you will not mention my name in this matter and even less will you talk about this letter.[40]

Whatever the conductor's reasons, he had made a serious error in not telling Verdi about his negotiations with Bagier or his agent. He seems to have waited about two weeks to answer Verdi. When he did, he offended the composer still further by asking for advice on how to reply to the man who was handling Bagier's affairs. Verdi wrote back:

You absolutely do not understand me, you have never understood me, and you don't understand anything about business. When I wrote you that from the moment you opened negotiations with Toffoli, I did not want to get mixed up any longer in a mess like that, you should have accepted or rejected those offers immediately. This is all I can tell you and am telling you again.[41]

But in spite of his bad humour, Verdi did go on helping Mariani and even offered to speak to Bagier on his behalf, provided Mariani asked him to do so in writing. Soon Verdi invited Mariani to Sant'Agata again and asked him to do the kind of favour he had so often been asked to do in the past: pay the expenses on a case of wine Verdi had bought in Xeres and sent in Mariani's care. Verdi also asked for help in getting a four-horse-power steam engine that he intended to use at the farm to pump water from the

Ongina. But the business affair involving Mariani, Bagier, and his agent claimed Verdi's attention again in July, when he declared that he could do nothing for the conductor and that Mariani would have to plead his cause himself. However, Verdi in fact did what he had originally said he would not do: he spoke to Toffoli.[42] He also reminded Mariani again that Paris would be precarious at best. 'So if Bagier accepts, *good*; if he doesn't accept (don't despair) *better*.'[43] Five days later Verdi sent Mariani a cordial letter inviting him to Turin and Sant'Agata.

I will leave tomorrow evening (Tuesday). I will arrive in Turin on Wednesday evening about midnight at the Hotel Trombetta. I will stay in Turin two days, and on Saturday morning at four I will be at Sant'Agata. Maybe you have some great idea? If heaven sends you an inspiration, pick up your bag and come to Turin, and we will leave for Sant'Agata together. You can help me unpack my suitcases. Thank Providence with your hands clasped in prayer that you did not let them make a fool of you in Paris![44]

While he and Strepponi were abroad, they acquired furniture, draperies, and works of art for the house at Sant'Agata. All through the spring and summer, Verdi had charged Arrivabene with the job of getting his packing cases through the customs in Turin. Several of these cases came from St Petersburg, the rest from France. If, as it seems, Arrivabene had only one room in Turin, the burden of storing these shipments must have been extraordinary. In one letter of 1 July, Verdi referred almost casually to the 'cases and packages that are perhaps cluttering up your room'.[45] Two weeks later:

Dear Arrivabene,

If you think and hope that you have finished with my packing cases, because you have two of them that have been dancing around in your room for three or four months, you are wrong. Yesterday I sent seven others with a total weight of about 8[00] or 900 kilos, all addressed to the Customs in Turin, and if they do not arrive while I am in Turin, I will leave you the keys, if you will be kind enough to go and get them out of the Customs for me. What do you say to that? Am I cheeky or not? What is more, since you know everbody in the world, if—in the mean time—you should by chance run into some gentleman from the Customs, you should speak to him about this, so there will not be a thorough examination. I will leave you a note signed by me Signor G. Verdi of Busseto, or rather of Roncole, in which I will declare everything old and new in there: if those gentlemen knew me even a little, they could be sure that I will not cheat the Customs out of a centesimo. Furthermore, in three or four days I will send a pianoforte from Erard, which is no longer new because I used it during the four months that I stayed here, but since I sent it back to Erard to be cleaned and tuned, it will look like new: let them say that it is, if that is what they want.[46]

Although he had been home only a short while, Verdi started back to Turin, where he had asked Arrivabene to reserve rooms for him and his wife; but they stayed only two days and then returned to Sant'Agata, where Strepponi remained as Verdi again left for Turin. He had personal and official business in the capital, among other matters the goods he had shipped from abroad and the appeal he had addressed to Piroli about his rights to the floodlands of the Po, where the fields of his Piantadoro ran down to the river. Other serious problems had arisen at the villa after a farm-agent—not Menta—absconded with funds and goods. The house was an inferno, Verdi said, with bricklayers, stonemasons, plasterers, and marble-cutters at work everywhere. When Sir James Hudson sent him a painting, the composer hung it in an empty room with unfinished walls. He still showed no inclination whatever to compose and let it be known that he was not looking for librettos. When Somma proposed a *Demetrio*, which Maffei has also called to Verdi's attention in August 1861, taken from Schiller's unfinished drama about the False Demetrius, the imperial succession, and Boris Godunov, Verdi refused it. 'It is grand, it is beautiful, it is theatrical'; but he was not interested.[47] In mid-August he and Strepponi went to Tabiano for a cure. September brought news from Clara Maffei about a duel between Filippi and the editor of a political journal, *La cicala politica*, which had carried an article Filippi considered a personal affront. Wounded by a sabre slash on the forehead and nose, Filippi fell; a doctor rushed to help him. 'Dear Verdi,' Clara wrote, 'maybe I am a primitive soul; but I confess to you that it makes me sad to think that in our so-called humanitarian century we need such barbarian disputes to bring justice.'[48]

She also brought Verdi up to date on Faccio's career. From Paris in July, Verdi had sent the young composer a piece of advice in a letter to Clara: 'Let Faccio put his hand on his heart and write whatever it tells him to, without paying any attention to anything else; may he dare to find new paths and have the courage to face those who are against him.'[49]

I often saw Boito and Faccio last year in Paris, and they certainly are two very gifted young men, but I cannot say anything about their musical talent, because I have never heard anything by Boito and have only heard those few things that Faccio came one day to have me hear. Anyway, since Faccio is going to give an opera [*I profughi fiamminghi*], the public will pass its sentence. These two young men are accused of being very warm admirers of Vagner [*sic*]. There is nothing wrong with that, so long as admiration does not degenerate into imitation. Vagner has been done, and it is useless to do him again. Vagner is not a wild animal as the purists say, nor is he a prophet as his apostles would have it. He is a man of great gifts who likes the roughest roads because he does not know how to find the easy and straightest ones. These young people should not delude themselves; many, many people make them think they have wings when, in fact, they don't have legs to stand on.[50]

Clara carried the message to Faccio, who told her that he considered Verdi's advice sacrosanct.

You recognized the genius in him and in Boito; I know that they are so good, that I call them 'my dear sons' [*i me car fieu*], do you understand Milanese dialect? So let us make a vow about their future, that they too may honour our Italy. . . . Anyway, you know perfectly well that I could never fail to remember lovingly the recollections I have of you always and everywhere; and here [at Clusone] if it is possible, more than ever [this place] is full of you. I even have that old cembalo on which you played and studied so much, and would you believe it? just that would be enough to make me never be without it; as far as the world is concerned, I am perhaps a society woman, but those who know me really well know that I truly live only the life of the heart, and in that life, my Verdi, you play a great role.[51]

She added that in her salon she was surrounded with people who loved Verdi—her 'little orchestra', she called them, of Verdi's admirers.

The news of these young artists did not awaken in Verdi the desire to compose. In a letter to Tito Ricordi in October, he admitted that he had been intending to change the end of La forza del destino but had done nothing. He did provide for Escudier to send a copy of the romanza he had written for the French production of Les Vêpres siciliennes, but he concluded on a bitter note.

Write more operas? Why? To see them always performed in the most barbarous way possible? Do you think that the *Ballo in maschera* has been—I won't say performed—but even a little interpreted, a little understood? Never. And you saw it in Milan. We will have to go back to the cavatinas, the duets, the rondos with roulades, or else teach the singers to read. That was the mission of your *Gazzetta*: to inculcate a literary culture. And now it should be the duty of the liceos and conservatories not to admit anyone to study singing who has not studied literature seriously. As for the Società del Quartetto, I beg you to leave me out of it. You know that I am an ass as far as music is concerned and that I absolutely do not understand what the scholars baptize as classical. I'll stop here because you might blush if your composer spoke all those truths that, to my honour, I will leave in my pen.[52]

This letter, written a week before Verdi's fiftieth birthday, most certainly did not raise Ricordi's hopes for a new opera. To Escudier, Verdi wrote that from being a composer, he had become a farmer.[53] Six months later he told Arrivabene that he was not writing any music, that that fact in itself was unimportant, and that while he didn't know anything about beans, he did know that his grapevines were in good condition.[54] As it had before, his career seemed to be over.

The Young Revolutionaries of the Milanese Scapigliatura

Clara Maffei's 'dear sons' stood at the core of a movement that posed a threat to both Manzoni and Verdi, the twin pillars of Italian art. The Scapigliatura (Dishevelled Artists), as the movement was called, was described by the man who fixed its terms, Carlo Righetti, whose pseudonym was Cletto Arrighi.

In all the great and rich cities of the uncivilized world, there exists a certain number of individuals of both sexes, between 20 and 35 years of age, not more, full of talent, almost always, well ahead of their times, independent as the eagles of the Alps, ready for good and evil, restless, unhappy, troubled, who because of certain terrible contradictions between their conditions and their position in life—that is, between what they have in mind and what they have in their pockets—. . . deserve to be classified in a new and special rank in the Great Family of Society as a caste unto itself, distinguished from all the rest. This caste or class, as it might better be called, [is] the true, true pandemonium of our era; the personification of madness beyond the asylum walls; a reservoir of disorder, improvidence, the spirit of revolt and opposition to all of the established order; I called it precisely the Scapigliatura. . . . The Scapigliatura is made up of individuals of every social class, every condition, every possible level on the social ladder. Proletariat, middle class, and aristocracy; [from] the law, letters, art, and commerce; unmarried or married; they will all bring their contribution. . . . [The Scapigliatura] welcomes them all with a loving embrace and binds them together in a mystic band. . . . Hope is its religion; pride is its uniform; poverty is its basic trait. My Scapigliatura has two faces . . . on the one hand, full of spirit, hope, and love . . . on the other hand, a ghastly, lined, cadaverous face, on which are written the stories of nights spent in hideous vice and gambling, on which fall the shadows of a hidden, infinite sorrow.[55]

In the ranks of the Scapigliati were Boito; his closest friend, the playwright-novelist Emilio Praga; the critic Filippi; the editor, historian, and man of letters Leon Fortis; and the novelist Giuseppe Rovani. Although they were somewhat ambiguous in their attitude toward him, the Scapigliati found in Manzoni a prime target, a man who had outlived his time, 'a statue that is still standing, without any intrinsic justification, without any value in the new literary and poetic climate.'[56] Later, the young hotheads modified their stand, claiming that they loved and revered him, his 'serene faith', and his 'absolutely pure genius'.[57] They did, however, feel that he had ruled too long. The movement gave voice to its sentiments in several publications, among them *Il pungolo*, *La cronaca grigia*, *La perseveranza*, and also *Il figaro*, which Boito and Praga began to edit, write for, and publish in January 1864. Its revolutionary tone sounded clearly when it published an article that announced that

Our generation, the fair-haired one, cries out every day that Catholicism is collapsing, that fetishism is ruinous, and that a troubling truth is growing. It cries out that God has rotted, and that Man has deified himself . . . that genius alone is the son of God, that the heresy of eighteen centuries ago is becoming truly sublime, that the Holy Spirit . . . is no longer among us, that Pentecost is no longer here, that the Virgin does not exist, that the *Resurrection* did not happen, but that some poet or farm-labourer, digging in some future time around the hill of Golgotha, that blood-soaked earth, will perhaps find the holy skull of Christ. . . . And from our cries . . . come the art that is boiling in our hearts![58]

At the end of the essay, Boito and Praga 'spit out' the word 'realism', a tenet of their new faith. Boito, perhaps deliberately, seized on the hunchback as a symbol of good fortune and an augury for the future, just as Bartolini had more than a decade before, in his own war against academicians in Italian art.

The artistic revolution had been bursting with creative energy even before Verdi left for his trip to Russia. Righetti's first cry in the wilderness preceded by more than five years the première of Praga's and Boito's drama, *Le madri galanti*; but in those five years a lot of ink was spilled in Milan. When Boito was criticized for excessive bitterness and cynicism, he defended himself and his colleagues by declaring that the wall of the future had to be penetrated by the sharp point of the intellect. He spoke of filing away the debris of ages and of pricking, wounding paring down, and escaping from the cage of tradition. Verdi, of course, was a totem of that tradition. It was perhaps inevitable that he should become a target of

the Scapigliati, yet, as we have seen, Boito and Faccio were not above
using the 'Old Man' when it suited their purposes. So when Faccio
prepared to give his opera *I profughi fiamminghi*, he approached Verdi
through Clara Maffei, as he had when he and Boito visited Verdi in Paris.
Advance publicity about the opera made it seem that Faccio would
shake the music world to its foundations; in fact, the opera lasted only
five nights at La Scala, but the polemics generated by the Scapigliati
reverberated for years.

At a banquet to celebrate the première of *I profughi fiamminghi*, which
was given on 11 November 1863, the Scapigliati flung at Verdi and at
Manzoni an insult which generated scandal in the art world of the time.
Raising a toast, after everyone had had a good deal to drink, Boito rose
from his chair and read an ode that he had written for the occasion, a long
poem, one section of which invoked hope for the future:

> Alla salute dell'Arte italiana!
> Perché la scappi fuora un momentino
> Dalla cerchia del vecchio e del cretino,
>   Giovane e sana!
>
>   .   .   .   .   .   .
>
> Forse già nacque chi sovra l'altare
> Rizzerà l'arte, verecondo e puro,
> Su quell'altare bruttato come un muro
>   Di lupanare.
> Arte italiana! tu che al tempo bello
> Stavi maestra a un nordico paese,
> Colle sante armonie di Pergolesi
>   E di Marcello,
> Forse non fu la tua nota postrema,
> Etico soffio o inavvertito esempio,
> Forse dai cori del tuo queto tempio
>   Sorge il Poema.
> Dunque si beva! e nelle tazze liete
> Sia battesimo dell'arte lo Sciampagna,
> E la folla rachitica e grifagna
>   Crepi di sete.[59]

To the health of Italian Art! May it, young and healthy, be freed from the prison
of the old, the idiotic. . . . Perhaps the man has already been born who will raise
Art, modest and pure, upon the altar that has been soiled like a whorehouse wall.
Italian Art! You, who in one fine moment in the past, taught a northern country
the holy harmony of Pergolesi and Marcello! Perhaps the Poem will come forth

from the choir of your silent temple. So drink, then! And may this Champagne baptize joyfully this [new] art; and may the rickety and scrofulous Old Crowd die of thirst.

The ode, published in *Museo di famiglia* eleven days after the première of Faccio's opera, got into Verdi's hands at once. He took it as an attack on himself, above all because other composers' names were mentioned. Boito's words were offensive then, as they would be now: 'il cretino', 'la folla rachitica e grifagna', and the phrase that seemed to injure Verdi the most, 'quell'altar bruttato come un muro di lupanare'. He remembered them for many years to come.

The first of his friends to catch the backlash from Sant'Agata was Clara Maffei, to whom Verdi wrote in December, in a letter that was an indirect answer to Faccio's letter of 16 November to him. As we know, Clara had urged Faccio to give Verdi news of his new opera *I profughi fiamminghi*. Timid and respectful, Faccio had declared that the Countess herself was committed to getting Verdi's 'indulgence' for the letter itself and for its young writer.[60] But Verdi's answer, sent to Clara Maffei, carried an unambiguous message that was typical of him.

I was running around like a madman for two weeks, accomplishing nothing, as usual, just for the joy of driving myself crazy, and driving crazy some friends I met, and so I have not answered your letter nor that of Faccio before now. I will tell you anyway, with my usual frankness, that the latter embarrasses me a bit. How can I answer him? You will say 'With a word of encouragement;' but what need is there for this word, if he has already introduced himself and has made the public his judge? Now this is a matter for them to handle; and words become useless. I know that a great deal has been said about this opera, too much, in my opinion; and I have read some newspaper articles where I found some huge words on *Art, Aesthetics, Revelations*, the *Past*, the *Future*, etc. etc.; and I confess that I (big ignoramus that I am) didn't understand a word of it. On the other hand, I am not familiar with either Faccio's talent or his opera; and I would want not to know it so as not to discuss it, not to pass judgement on it, things I detest because they are the most useless in the world. *Discussions* never convince anyone; *Judgements* are wrong most of the time. Anyway, if Faccio—as his friends say—has found new roads, if Faccio is destined to raise art on the altar that is now soiled *like a whorehouse wall*, so much the better for him, and for the Public. If he has gone astray, *Se è un* Traviato, as others suggest, let him get back on the right track, if this is what he believes he should do.[61]

When Verdi wrote to Ricordi, he was more explicit and more willing to reveal how deeply he had been hurt. 'If I, too, among others, have soiled the altar, as Boito says, let him clean it up, and I will be the first to come and light a candle.'[62] Eighteen months later, in a sarcastic observation to Piave, the composer used the phrase again:

Don't be afraid of this Babylonia (as you call it) that is the music of the future. It, too, is right; it has to be like this. These so-called apostles of the future are the creators of something great, sublime. It was necessary *to wash the altar soiled* by the pigs of the past. . . . I am looking up and waiting for the star that will show me where the Messiah has been born, so that I—like the Three Wise Men—can go and worship him.[63]

On 14 December, one day after writing to Clara, Verdi sent a note to Faccio, thanking him for news of the new work.

If the public, this sovereign judge, has looked kindly on your first work, and it was well received, as you say, go on with the career you have begun, and add to the glorious names of Pergolesi and Marcello another glorious name, your own. I wish the same for your friend Boito, to whom I ask you to give my regards.[64]

Strepponi, in a letter to Piave, sent off yet another barb.

Verdi cannot answer you, because he has an eye infected and almost closed, but it opened wide when he heard from you that Faccio, the Countess, and others were ecstatic over the responses he sent, which, as you well know, were a bit long in coming! . . . Try, however, to see them and read them carefully; then you will tell me whether they were important to [Verdi] in terms of praise, . . . the words, or frankness of the views. . . . We will have Signor Antonio, Maddalena, and the canon [Avanzi] for Christmas Eve supper and Christmas with us. It's almost a kind of grand event, and one that makes us very, very happy! We love with all our hearts those creatures who possess the rare virtue of not being devotees of Saint John of the Four Faces! Verdi has got champagne, truffles, torrone [nougat], mostarda, etc. etc. I signed the death sentence for four or five unhappy [birds], who were happy to be alive and are now keeping cold in the cellar. And something else even more extraordinary: I, who hate cooking so much, will go to the kitchen and fix something that only God knows how it will turn out.[65]

Strepponi's reference to the hypocrisy of Verdi's friends was clear: Saint John of the Four Faces was a well-known Milanese icon, with a church, a piazza, and a street dedicated to him. Cirelli's house and office had stood at the corner of the Contrada del Teatro dei Filodrammatici and the Contrada di San Giovanni delle Quattro Facce.

Verdi answered in his own way, when he refused to let Ricordi postpone payment of his royalties.

I have thought and rethought about rendering you the small service you ask, but it was absolutely impossible for me. I am one of those signori who never have any money in their pockets, and I am telling you that I live from one day to next, like a labourer; and although I have neither English, nor Turkish, nor Arabian horses, etc., etc., I do have a kind of house that is certainly very modest; I don't have fine furniture—no, I almost don't have any; and when I am forced to buy some, it will not be in *palissandre*, mahogany, or rosewood. From this description, you will understand that my money is always spent long before I receive it and that the sum that you owe me is already committed to the purse of someone else.[66]

He said that he did not yet know what he could do with *La forza del destino*, but that he did not intend to cut Friar Melitone out of the drama. 'If you think that he is an obstacle to the success of the score, it would be better to stop printing further scores.' Ricordi asked no further favours and paid 12,226.66 francs to his composer. An unexpected windfall came from France when Escudier let Verdi know that the impresario Carvalho intended to produce *Rigoletto* at the Théâtre Lyrique in a French translation by Edouard Duprez and pay royalties to Verdi, even though nothing was owed him under French law. He did not wish Verdi to be the victim of the French legal system, Escudier wrote.[67] Verdi, not certain that this arrangement was proper, continued to ask for further clarification from Escudier, who assured him that the money was indeed his under the title of *une prime personelle* and that Ricordi had no claim whatever to any portion of this *prime*. Again in March 1864 Verdi was told that the royalties were something 'created' for him and that he owed no one any accounting for them. 'So let your conscience be at rest. This *prime* belongs to you. . . . It will be the same if they give [your] other works: *Macbeth*, for example, which belongs to me, and which Carvalho wants to produce next winter in grand style.'[68] Escudier promised to demand another *prime* and to ask for double the amount that was to be paid for *Rigoletto*. These royalties, too, would belong to Verdi personally.

During December 1863, when this matter first came up, Verdi also asked Arrivabene's help in locating a draft on Rothschild's bank and in buying a veil for Strepponi. The couple had visited Turin early that month; and Verdi had returned there alone just before Christmas, perhaps to take his seat in the Chamber, where the members were about to debate the Pica Law, a statute providing for better control of brigands and the organized Camorra in the south of Italy. Arrivabene, who wrote to Verdi about the debate, also bought wallpaper for Sant'Agata, using samples the composer sent him, and offered suggestions about a new billiard-table for the villa. A young dog, Black, or Blach as Verdi called him, had been added to the household.

26

January 1864–Summer 1865

Aesthetics

The first week of the New Year 1864 saw the publication of the first issue
of Boito's and Praga's new journal *Il Figaro*, for which Boito wrote, under
the pseudonym 'Almaviva'. He also contributed to *La perseveranza* and
Museo di famiglia, which the composer read. During the months that
followed the première of *I profughi fiamminghi*, the young artists were
frequently under assault; in December 1864 Boito even fought a duel with
a man who had offended him during an argument at the Caffè Martini.
The original dispute grew out of remarks Rovani made about the corruption
of music by German influences. Giovanni Verga, who had been drinking
with Rovani, entered the discussion and blew cigar-smoke in Boito's face.
At this, Boito challenged him. Verga wounded Boito in the hand, as Piave
reported to Verdi. In the first number of *Figaro*, on 7 January 1864, its
young creators declared that criticism, not defamation, would be found
in its pages; but Praga, in the second issue, threw down what was
considered by some to be an insult to Manzoni. He declared that in
the past a blessed herd of sheep revived the epic poem, the Arcadian
idyll, and the hymn of the prophets, stimulating their hearts, adulterating
history, and brutalizing the Gospel.[1] When Boito, in a flight of fancy,
wrote of *form* and *formula*, he claimed that Italian opera from its beginning until his own time, had never possessed *form*, being saddled with
the 'diminutive, the *formula*', which had been passed from Monteverdi to
Peri, Cesti, Sacchini, Paisiello, Rossini, Bellini, and Verdi, 'gathering
strength, development, variety, (especially in the last great masters), but
always remaining *formula*, as it was born *formula*'.[2] He urged a change

of style; its hour had struck, he said. It was time to use the word 'tragedy' instead of the miserable little term 'libretto'. Quite apart from the omission of the names of Donizetti and Mercadante from the roll of Italian masters, this article was taken as an attack on Piave and Romani, among others.

Boito found another outlet for his talents in the journal of the Società del Quartetto. The organization itself, which was planned in the autumn of 1862, began to offer its concerts in 1864. Among its supporters were Giulio Ricordi, son of Tito and grandson of Giovanni; and Eugenio Tornaghi, the powerful secretary of Casa Ricordi. Praising the music of French and German composers (though not necessarily that of Wagner), the journal, like other publications of its time, followed the general line of criticism taken by Boito, Mazzucato, Filippi, and others. Some of the essays contained flowery language that Verdi and others considered ridiculous; one of Boito's efforts in the *Giornale della Società del Quartetto* declared that

the Sublime is simpler than the Beautiful. The Beautiful can come to life in many kinds of forms, the most bizarre, the most varied, the most different; regarding the Sublime, one can only point to its great form, the divine form, universal and eternal: the form of the sphere. The horizon is sublime; the sea is sublime; the sun is sublime. Shakespeare is spherical, Dante is spherical, Beethoven is spherical; the sun is simpler than a carnation, the sea is simpler than a brook, the adagio by Mendelssohn is spherical and simpler than the andante by Mozart. And because of that, also more conceivable.[3]

Almost at once, Ghislanzoni, who had once been counted in the ranks of the Scapigliatura, published a comment of his own in his *Rivista minima*:

I no longer dare to walk by a pumpkin without taking off my hat to it; and thinking of Boito's luminous idea that the Sublime is simpler than the Beautiful, and that the sun, because it is spherical, is simpler than the carnation, I am almost led to suspect that a pumpkin is more sublime than the sun. . . . A musical event, to which people want to give a certain importance, is Faccio's new opera *Amleto*. . . . The libretto is by Arrigo Boito, author of *Re Orso* and the *spherical* articles in the journal of the 'Quartetto'. . . . The whole claque went to Genoa to attend the great, solemn event; and enthusiasm for the new opera will undoubtedly take the *spherical* shape of Dante, the sun, and the watermelon.[4]

Verdi, who declared that he understood nothing of these new aesthetic expressions, wrote to Piave on 3 June 1864:

I laughed a lot over the article by Ghislanzoni, but not as much as I did over the original article [by Boito]. For God's sake! What a mess, if I, too, were one of the *spherical* ones! What an inspiration I had when I refused to be the honorary president of the Società del Quartetto! I, *spherical*? The trouble is that with the stomach I am getting, the epithet would be quite properly applied! *Spherical . . . Focal Point . . .* The sun more sublime than a carnation! What beautiful things! What a pity I don't understand them.[5]

He had heard about the success of Faccio's *Amleto* in Genoa.

I know that all the *spherical ones* were there. . . . That's all right; but I ask myself whether they couldn't do things a bit more quietly?! Whatever need is there to turn half the world upside down over an opera? Maybe this, too, is a *spherical* way of doing things? All joking apart, if Faccio has had a true success, which will last and become popular, I am afraid he will have abandoned, or will abandon, the *spherical ones* and will become an apostate. There's no middle ground. *Spherical*, *focal point*, *carnation*, are beautiful things, but to make music you need one simple thing: *Music*. What do you say? Anyway, if Faccio succeeds, I am sincerely happy; others perhaps will not believe this; but [only] others: you know me and you know that I either keep quiet or say what I feel.[6]

It is much to Verdi's credit that he ever again showed even minimal courtesy to Faccio and Boito. Yet during the months and years that followed, cordial relations were kept up, either directly or through Countess Maffei, Piave, and Ricordi. At the end of 1864 Boito sent Verdi an advance copy of his poem *Re Orso*, with a dedication that read 'To Giuseppe Verdi, so that he will remember my name.' The King Bear of Sant'Agata had not forgotten it.

For Verdi, this was a period of introspection and of a certain apparent indifference to the world of theatre. When Ricordi asked permission to give the *Inno delle nazioni* in Milan; Verdi replied: 'Give it, . . . if you can find a tenor. It will be a fiasco, as all my works are, when they are first performed in Milan.'[7] He was still rethinking *La forza del destino* and was considering the revision of *Macbeth* for Paris. Although he declared to Arrivabene that he could not understand music from the printed page, he began to review some of the classics of the past. To Arrivabene:

Ricordi never sends me music because he knows that for the ten or twelve long years that I was in Milan, I never went one single time to consult his musical archives. I cannot understand music through my eyes; and if you believed that the two compositions—because they were by Rossini—could work a miracle and clear my head, so that I would understand the beauties and the treasures of harmony that [Francesco] d'Arcais and Filippi brag so much about, you were very much misled.[8]

But in the autumn Verdi asked Ricordi to send him an album of piano music by 'old and modern composers'.

Rain, rain, rain!! Goodbye fields, goodbye walks, goodbye to the beautiful sun that we will see pale and sickly from now on; goodbye beautiful blue sky; goodbye to the endless spaces; goodbye to my desire and hope to come to Como [to Ricordi's villa]! . . . Four walls will take the place of infinity; the fire, instead of the sun; books and music will take the place of air and the sky . . . boredom, instead of pleasure. . . . So be it; we will make music so as to—so as to do what many others are doing . . . [and] be bored to death with most of the so-called classical music; with a difference, though, that when I am bored, I say 'I am bored,' while others pretend that they are in ecstasy over beauty that is not there, or that—at the very least—could be found in our [Italian] music. That is how it is. The present era talks, thrashes around, is busy, produces little, and tends to manufacture a new music for us out of the powder and bones of the dead. If, however, there should be a bit of sun in it, then long live the new music![9]

He then added that he had sworn never to pay a cent for a piece of music, and that if Ricordi had sworn never to give any away free, then the album would not be sent. The publisher sent Verdi the volume all the same. At the beginning of November Verdi sent off his praise for a piece of work well done, adding that he was especially pleased with a piece by Muzio Clementi, but that Stefano Golinelli and Giulio Ricordi, the editors of the album, had made a mistake in leaving out Scarlatti's *Fuga del gatto*. 'It was so good because it showed the clearness of the old Neapolitan school. With a very odd subject like that, a German would have created chaos; an Italian made of it something as limpid as the sun.'[10] With this letter, Verdi also confirmed that Paris had asked to be allowed to produce *Macbeth* at the Théâtre Lyrique and that he had been invited to compose the ballet music and to make some changes: 'I would like to lengthen several pieces to give the opera more character,' he said. 'I beg you to send me an orchestra score so I can see what there is to do.' Thus was begun the revision of *Macbeth*.

Verdi had not been alone at the farm that year, for he and Strepponi had had guests during the spring and summer. Mariani, who was again considering the post at the Théâtre des Italiens, visited in the spring, when workmen were still everywhere. On deliberation, the conductor decided to remain in Genoa and to return to Bologna; so Bosoni went to

Paris instead. When Mariani returned to Sant'Agata in September, he reported to Tornaghi that the villa was 'a true paradise' and that Verdi was very, very well and in fine humour.[11] Luccardi also came for a short stay. While there, he repaired a statue that had been broken during shipment from Turin. Verdi wrote to Arrivabene about what had happened:

The railways are made to drive us crazy and to smash the things we give them to carry. I had a kitchen range sent from Paris via Turin to Borgo San Donnino. Yes Sir, the administration of the railway in Turin got the idea of keeping the shipment, and so I am forced to ask you to go and get hold of it, and send it to me at Borgo San Donnino. Do me this favour, and—in addition to being grateful—I will owe you 44.5 francs and the porters' charges and the expenses.—That, to drive us crazy!! As for the other things, I found one of the three statuettes that I bought in Turin broken, and the most beautiful one, too, *Il cantastorie*. Anyway, the railway is not to blame; it is the fault of the man who packed the statuette, who did not know how to place it properly in the box, and so this poor *Cantastorie* was forced to sing and dance during the whole trip.[12]

Musical matters that kept Verdi's attention were his continuing attempt to change the finale of *La forza del destino* and his exchanges with Piave and the French poet De Lauzières, to whom he had turned when he was dissatisfied with Piave's work on the opera. Neither satisfied him, as he confided to Ricordi. 'I would say that I am still terribly tangled up in changing the ending. . . . Let me think about it for a little while longer, and then—fixed, or not fixed—you can let this damned *Forza del destino* be given in Milan.'[13] He did add that he would not be likely to come to La Scala just to direct one of his old operas. In a letter to Escudier, asking him to break the news to De Lauzières that his work was not acceptable, Verdi also expressed satisfaction that *Aroldo* would not be given in Paris. He hoped that *Simon Boccanegra* would not be produced there either: 'It is a cold opera.'[14]

Occasions honouring other composers brought down upon Verdi requests for hymns written expressly for these events. As usual, he declined but he was angry with Filippi for publishing his name as part of the commission to honour Guido d'Arezzo. In fact, he confided to Ricordi, he had received a letter that notified him that Rossini was honorary president; Pacini, the president; Mercadante, 'perhaps counsellor'; and 'afterwards of course, my respectable self, perhaps in the role of porter. If they had put two other names between Mercadante's and mine, I could modestly have said—as Dante did—"*So I was sixth among so many wise men.*"'[15] Verdi advised Ricordi to tell Filippi that he felt it was his duty to refuse 'such a high honour' because he would have been completely useless to the Commission.

But I admire this holy enthusiasm we have now, that we raise monuments to the great of the past and the present (President Pacini), and that later on I will beg him to publish a proposal of mine (without my even wanting to be president of the Commission) TO RAISE A MONUMENT TO PYTHAGORAS. If this works, we will suggest later that we raise a monument to JUBAL, and through a medium, we can evoke the spirit of Guido [d'Arezzo] so that he can write the cantata. But I am not certain that Guido knew music.

The composer also gave vent to his feelings in a forthright letter to Clara Maffei. The first draft includes a denunciation of

cities, congresses, monuments, deputations, Società del Quartetto, hymns to priests, holy archangels, thrones, powers, etc. . . . If I had accepted [them all], I would have written six hymns. Six hymns!! Better to write twelve operas, because that kind of music is not music; it is the true negation of art; and it has as much to do with art as I have to do with theology. I refused them all, that goes without saying; and friends and enemies disapproved, and will disapprove. But what do you want? I have a head that often does not agree with others. When I realize that it wants to play a trick on me, I take it in my hands, squeeze it hard, and say to it: 'Shut up and don't come out with some crazy idea that would make rats laugh.' Just think that two years ago, when the Government named me president of the commission to change the Milan Conservatory, my head wanted me to propose: Point 1—the abolition (for the love of God, don't let Mazzucato and Filippi know) of the schools of AESTHETICS and ADVANCED MUSICAL COMPOSITION. I leaped up in fear and wrote to the Minister refusing. And so I stay far away from everyone and from everything, out of fear that some idea like this kind might pop out against monuments or congresses, or against these blessed and universal quartet societies, that have no purpose, or rather only that (and it is still my head that is talking) of setting Italian music on a road that will dry up the organs of the living and the dead.[16]

A discreetly edited final copy was sent to Clara on 26 September, together with an invitation to come to Sant'Agata. Verdi added that he would return to Turin early in October, probably to take his seat in Parliament, as he did infrequently during these years.

The Revised *Macbeth*

After that he dedicated much of the winter to *Macbeth*, the revision of which did not come easily. To an anxious Escudier, Verdi wrote: 'Ah, you think that I will labour [over this] just at the last minute? No: even now I am labouring like a Negro; I won't say that I am doing a lot, but I am labouring, labouring, labouring.'[17] As he reflected on the 1847 composition, he said that he was struck with things he would not have wanted to find there, places that he called weak or lacking in character. 'You cannot imagine how boring and difficult it is to get yourself back together for something done long ago and find a thread that has been broken for so many years. Yes, it can be done quickly; but I detest mosaics in music.'[18] He begged his Parisian publisher to have patience. To Piave, who was revising the libretto, Verdi sent his own recommendations. Originally the composer had expected to follow a simple work-plan:

1. An aria for *Lady Macbeth* in Act II.
2. Redo several sections in the vision [scene] [in] Act III.
3. Redo *Macbeth's* aria [in] Act III completely.
4. Touch up the first scenes of Act IV.
5. Do the last finale again, taking out *Macbeth's* death.[19]

He also committed himself to revising the ballet.[20] As the winter wore on, Verdi also changed the first-act duet of Macbeth and Lady Macbeth and decided to write a third act that he described to Escudier as 'almost new'.[21]

As he and Piave worked together, Verdi provided raw material in prose or verse, as he often had in the past. When Piave sent verses that proved unsatisfactory, he got a familiar response:

No, no, my dear Piave, it won't do! . . . All joking aside, wouldn't it be possible to fix this by keeping most of those verses that I sent to you, saving the appropriate rhyme? For example:

> langue
> La luce è pallida . . . Il faro spegnesi
> ch'eterno scorre per gli ampi cieli.
> desiata
> Notte tremenda provvida veli
> La man colpevole che ferirà.
> Nuovo delitto?!! E' necessario!
> Compier si debba l'opra fatale. . . .

> is waning
> (The light is faint . . . The beacon that rides
> Forever across the heavens is burning out.
> longed-for
> May the dreadful, protective night hide

BOOK IV

> The guilty hand that will strike!
>   Another crime?!! It is necessary!
>   The fatal work must be done. . . .)
> Answer me at once. Ad[dio] addi[o].[22]

From Verdi's insistence came Lady Macbeth's gripping scene. In January 1865 Piave and Verdi began work on the last scene of the fourth act of the opera which the composer had plotted at Sant'Agata. To Piave:

I am about to do the last chorus, but it is one of the thousands and thousands of commonplace things that are everywhere and don't leave people either cold or hot. I have created one that could be rather exciting and that I submit for your approval. After the battle, I have the *Bards* come to sing the Victory Hymn. The Bards (you know this) followed the armies in those times. [The rhythm used] gives a terse and proud feeling, which is just right and has character. . . . The verses need you to hone them down, and you will do this; but do it right away. I also had to shorten some things, as you will see.[23]

At the end of his letter, Verdi again urged his librettist to finish the work and send the scene back as quickly as possible. Piave, who had left his furnished room over the Galleria de Cristoforis and moved to the Borgo Nuovo,[24] had also entered the competition for the post as professor of dramatic literature and recitation at Milan Conservatory. Verdi asked Piroli for help in securing the position for Piave and also gave his librettist advice on how to conduct his campaign; but not even their combined efforts brought success. The post went to Boito's friend from the Scapigliatura, Praga.

By February Verdi had asked Piave for some further changes in the finale; but the work was substantially done. He had finished the first two acts earlier and had given the third act to Ricordi, who had sent it on to France; he also offered the Parisian publisher some instructions on how the company at the Théâtre Lyrique should perform the opera. His letter is a compendium of theatrical common sense.

The act ends with a duet between Lady and Macbet [*sic*]. It doesn't seem illogical to me that Lady, always concerned with watching over her husband, should have discovered where he is. The act ends better. Make Lady appear and spare Macbet a bit of his hard, hard work. You will see that in the ballet (divertissement) there is tiny bit of action, which ties in nicely with the drama. . . . The apparition of Hecate, the goddess of the night, is fine, because it interrupts all those devils' dances and makes room for a calm, serious adagio. I don't have to tell you that Hecate should never dance, but just strike poses. I

1 (*a*) The Casa Padronale, Roncole: the Verdis' home 1790s–1830.
Photograph shows Guglielmo Veroni, Verdi's coachman's grand-
nephew, on his wedding-day.

(*b*) Roncole: the national monument 'Verdi Birthplace' with
village mill (rear) and irrigation canal gates, *c*.1910.

2 (a) Sanctuary church of La Madonna dei Prati, near Roncole.
Photograph from 1920s shows rectory (left) and 'pilgrims'
restaurant' (right) built on land once leased by the Verdis.

(b) Piazza Verdi, Busseto, showing Pallavicino fortress, La
Rocca, seen from Antonio Barezzi's shop-door.

3 (*a*) The home and shop of Antonio Barezzi, Verdi's patron and
father-in-law, Busseto.

(*b*) The salon in Barezzi's house where the Busseto Società
Filarmonica rehearsed and performed young Verdi's works.

14 (a) Verdi, photograph by Nadar (Félix Tournachon), Paris, early
1860s.
(b) Verdi, photograph by Pilotti and Troisel, Milan, 1872, pasted
on to page with engraved wreath in score of *La Forza del destino*,
revised for La Scala 1869. Score dedicated to Teresa Stolz.

(c) Arrigo Boito, librettist of *Inno delle nazioni*, the revised
Simon Boccanegra, *Otello*, and *Falstaff*.

15 (*a*) Verdi in his garden at Sant'Agata, with (standing, l. to r.)
Teresa Stolz; the lawyer Umberto Campanari; Giulio Ricordi; and
the artist Leopoldo Metlicovitz; (seated, l. to r.) Maria Filomena
Verdi, wife of Alberto Carrara; Barberina Strepponi; Verdi; and
Giuditta Ricordi; after 1897.

(*b*) Verdi playing *briscola* at Montecatini, 1898, with Stolz on his
right, mezzo-soprano Giuseppina Pasqua on his left.

(tot. G. Rossi, Milano).

ULTIMO RITRATTO DI VERDI.

16 Verdi, 1900, 'last portrait', photographed by G. Rossi, Milan,
reproduced in *Natura ed arte* (January 1901).

don't have to tell you either that that adagio must be played by the bass clarinet (as is indicated) so that the ensemble with the cello and bassoon creates a dark, austere sound, as the circumstances require. Please also ask the orchestral conductor to check the ballet [rehearsals] every once in a while, so he can indicate the tempos I marked. The dancers always change all the tempos, and, if they do this, this ballet will lose all its character and would not produce the effect that I think it possesses. Another thing, I beg you, that is to keep my instrumentation exactly as it is, to form the little orchestra that is under the stage at the moment when the eight kings appear. That little orchestra of two oboes, six clarinets in A, two bassoons, and a double bassoon make a strange, mysterious sound that is—at the same time—calm and quiet, [a sound that] other instruments could not produce. They have to be put under the stage, near a trapdoor that is open and rather large, so that the sound can get out and spread through the theatre, but in a mysterious way, and as if from afar.

Another observation for the banquet scene in the second act. I have seen this drama done several times in France, in England, and in Italy. Everywhere Banquo is made to appear in a coulisse that turns; he is agitated; he inveighs against Macbet and then goes quietly off in another coulisse. In my opinion, that doesn't suggest a vision, creates no feeling at all, and you don't even understand clearly whether it is a ghost or a man. When I staged *Macbet* in Florence, I had Banquo appear (with a large wound on his forehead) from a trapdoor beneath the stage exactly in Macbet's place. He did not move, he only raised his head at the right time. It was terrifying. The scene was laid out like this: [*Verdi added a sketch of the placement of singers and props.*]

This arrangement gives Macbet the room to move around and Lady can always stay beside him to speak to him sotto voce, as the situation demands. If you can find something better, do it; but be careful that the audience understands the ghost of Banquo perfectly.—One other observation. In the duet in the first act between Macbet and Lady, there is a first section that is always very effective and where there is a phrase that has the words:

> *Follie follie che sperdono*
> *I primi rai del dì.*

The French translator has to keep the words 'Follie follie' because perhaps the whole secret of the effect that this piece has lies in these words and in this infernal mockery by Lady.[25]

As Verdi sent Escudier instructions for the last act of the opera, he called attention to the fact that he had written a fugue for the battle scene:

You will laugh when you hear that I did a fugue for the battle scene!!! A fugue? I, who hate everything that stinks of a school, and it is almost thirty years since I last wrote one!!! But I will tell you that in this case, even that musical form can be just right. The themes and counterthemes that rush after each other, the shock of the dissonances, the racket, etc. etc. can express a battle rather well. Ah, if you only had our trumpets that are so full and so brilliant!! Those piston trumpets of yours are neither fish nor fowl. Anyway, the orchestra will have fun.[26]

Verdi added that he intended to spend the rest of the winter in Turin and Genoa and closed by warning Escudier not to let too much useless gossip about *Macbeth* be circulated, especially in the newspapers.

In February Verdi had warned Escudier about the importance of the Witches.

Take it as a rule that there are three roles in this opera, and there can only be three: *Lady Macbet*, *Macbet*, [and] the *Chorus of Witches*. The Witches rule the drama: everything comes from them: coarse and gossipy in the first act; sublime and prophetic in the third. They are truly a character, and a character of the greatest importance. No matter what you do, you will never create anything very important out of the role of Macduff. On the contrary, the more one emphasizes him, the more obvious one makes his vacuousness. He only becomes a Hero when the opera is over. However, he has enough music to make his mark if he has a beautiful voice, but there is no need to give him one extra note.[27]

During visits to the capital and in letters written from Genoa, Verdi collaborated with the parliamentary commission that was to write the authors' rights' laws for Italy. Reviewing the draft of the legislation, with Ricordi, Verdi also consulted a lawyer. Two areas of concern were librettists' rights and the right of the author to approve or prohibit productions of his work after it had been published 'in a printed edition or by other means', as one of the articles of the proposed law read. Verdi, writing in Italy, had a view that differed considerably from that of French or English authors. The article, as first written, gave the impresario the right to produce a work without the special consent of the author.

I would like to know what 'or by other means' would mean, in case of a lawsuit. If an impresario can only produce a work without the author's consent after it is printed, it seems to me that there is no serious problem in not printing the work until four, five, or ten years after its first production, until its success is assured in several theatres. Anyway, here the scores are almost never printed.[28]

Because of the delayed delivery of a letter sent from Turin to notify Verdi of a session of the Commission, he could not bring his views to bear as he wished. The Chamber voted on the first article of the law on the same day that the Commission met. 'We will still be able to do something,' he wrote to Ricordi. The article covering authors' approval of productions would say 'after the publication of the complete work in a printed edition'. But the article concerning plagiarism of composer's themes did not go far enough.

When he addressed the Chamber's Commission personally, he said that Art would speak for itself because a plagiarized work, even if it were composed by 'List'—as he wrote—would have little or no artistic worth. If they were allowed to plagiarize freely, Verdi said, pianists and other instrumentalists would find it easier to steal others' ideas than to write material of their own. 'So Art will be cheated of so many original works'.[29] The composer also declared that he would be very happy if no one ever wrote variations or fantasies on the themes from his operas. He urged the Commission to find a middle ground between the stand of those who would allow no artistic or literary rights at all and those who would give the artist full power over his creation. 'If we ask for too much, we will get nothing,' he warned Ricordi; one of the articles concerning translations would probably not be passed either. 'It is absolutely true that in the Chamber many are opposed to the idea of literary and artistic property rights.' One deputy, a former music-teacher, even believed that once a work was printed, it belonged to the general public by law. Eventually, some of Verdi's reasonable ideas were adopted, as Italy entered the European community mainstream.

The first performance of the revised *Macbeth*, given at the Théâtre Lyrique on 21 April 1865, seemed successful enough. Dispatches from Carvalho and Escudier informed Verdi that the first-act finale and the brindisi had both been encored, that the scenery was marvellous, the execution admirable, and the work itself a masterpiece. Sharing his good news with Arrivabene, Verdi sent transcriptions of the telegrams he had received; but he added that he was waiting for further information and would know more when he read the newspapers and had letters about the ongoing production.[30] When Escudier did not write as expected, the composer said he was furious at not being kept up to date. In the weeks that followed, reviews finally reached him and led him to conclude that the opera had not done as well as he had been led to believe. After all the effort that had gone into the revision, Verdi expressed his disappointment and faced the facts: 'With everything taken into consideration, everything weighed and added up, *Macbeth* was a fiasco. Amen. I have to confess, though, that I did not expect this. It seemed to me that I had not done too badly; but it seems that I was wrong.'[31] He defended himself to Escudier when he learned that the critics had claimed that he did not know Shakespeare.

Someone says that I did not know Shakespeare when I wrote *Macbet*. Oh, they are terribly wrong. Perhaps I did not realize *Macbet* fully enough; but that I do not know it, that I do not understand it, and I don't have a feeling for Shakespeare, no; by God no. He is a favourite poet of mine, whose works I had in my hands from my early youth and read and reread all the time.[32]

Perhaps Strepponi reflected a certain philosophical point of view held by the composer when she wrote to Escudier that the opera would be understood by audiences fifty years later.

The failure of *Macbeth* in Paris coincided with the first production of Meyerbeer's *L'Africaine* there and the première of Faccio's and Boito's *Amleto* in Genoa. Brilliantly conducted by Mariani and heralded by a relentless clamour in the press, this opera seemed to certain critics to signal a new era. 'In forty years, Italy has not seen such a complete opera, such a modern and refined work,' Filippi wrote, wiping the names of Verdi and Donizetti from the slate of music history. The critic also reflected the current passion for the 'interpretive' conducting of Mariani.[33]

'They want Mariani as the Great Pontifex of the Future,' Piave announced to Verdi. 'Tears of joy rained in Maffei's house; and when the Triumphant Ones return, maybe champagne will flow'.[34] In a rousing protest against the pro-German enthusiasm of the time, the librettist added that 'For God's sake, we did everything we could to kick the Germans out of Italy; yet these Germanophiles are working now to stick them back in our ears! . . . Oh, it is too much, too much!' Ghislanzoni, describing the Milanese coterie that had gone to Genoa for the première of *Amleto*, also touched upon the support that Faccio had received from Casa Ricordi and from Mariani.

Maestro Mariani never conducted before with such grand gestures of the arm, was never before so generous with his sublime smiles and his white, white teeth. AH! This time he was not joking! There, to witness his performance, were the foremost music critics of the world. . . . Mariani had prepared the way for the Apostles. . . . Faccio, during the four performances of *Amleto*, was honoured with about sixty curtain-calls.[35]

Ghislanzoni added sharp criticism of the 'travelling claque' that had gone to Genoa in support of Faccio. Yet the pungent remarks and the generally facetious tone did not hide the unescapable truth of Faccio's and Boito's success.

All this came just as the failure of *Macbeth* weighed heavily on Verdi, who was still smarting from the criticism that he did not understand

Shakespeare—this, at a time when it seemed that Faccio and Boito possessed this gift. Verdi, always attentive to box-office returns, felt that his *Macbeth* would have to meet the test of the cash box. 'The real truth will lie in the paid admissions; and success will be true and real if, after about one year, the hundredth performance of *Macbeth* will be announced, as happened with *Rigoletto*.'[36] But the figures showed that the French public was not interested.

Verdi also faced a serious personal crisis at home, with his father so ill that it seemed he might not survive. Construction had been resumed at Sant'Agata, where the small chapel was about to be completed near the garden room at the rear of the house. Verdi was also involved in a controversy over the theatre that was being built in Busseto; but that did not reach a critical stage until later. Another disappointment followed when Verdi heard that the Teatro Cannobiana in Milan had asked to be allowed to give *Macbeth* in a season that Verdi did not consider serious, as it was to include comedies and a ballet and was thus a kind of variety programme. 'Oh, if they were talking about a French opera, a Russian, Turkish, or Chinese opera, they would choose a solemn occasion for presenting it; but for an Italian work of art, any old place is good enough,' he complained to Ricordi.[37] And in another context he said, 'I, too, want the music of the future, which is to say that I believe in a music to come; and if I did not know how to write it, as I wished to do, it is not my fault.'[38]

Even a proposed French production of *La forza del destino* seemed impossible to bring into port, for the new translation and the resolution of the finale posed problems that proved difficult to solve. It had been suggested in Paris that if the end of the opera were rewritten, Leonora and Don Alvaro could be married on-stage in the last scene. The composer vetoed the idea at once. 'It would take me twenty pages to explain all my ideas; but just let me say that . . . Fate cannot accommodate both families. . . . Never, absolutely never, could a marriage take place.'[39] He was utterly dismayed that Bagier might give the opera at the Théâtre des Italiens with Bosoni as its conductor, he told Ricordi.

First of all, the opera is too spectacular. The scene in the *osteria* and the camp scene are not right for the [Italiens]. The end of the opera would also be something disgusting. Another disaster, perhaps worse than the others, is the conductor. Between us, Bosoni is an impossible conductor. Now that I've said this, you do what you want. As for myself, I want to keep myself free so that I can protest if necessary.[40]

Although he often seemed quite isolated at Sant'Agata, Verdi was not so far removed from the stage as he seemed. He had tried his best to direct *Macbeth* from Italy by sending instructions for it and seemed to be committed to revising *La forza del destino*. And although Strepponi wrote that he swore over and over again that he did not want to compose another opera, and he himself had found countless ways to state this, he finally did suggest to Clara Maffei that he might take up his pen again. In the summer of 1865 he sent her his news. 'If I were to feel the desire to compose again, [and] if *Salammbô* were offered to me, and if I were to find it good, . . . I might accept [a proposal to write another opera]. As for *Re Lear*, many people already know that poor Somma made me a libretto for it that—sooner or later—I will set to music.'[41] Later he dropped a hint to Piave. '[So] they are afraid that I will compose again? Who knows? I would do it just to infuriate them all,' he said.[42] It seemed that he had decided to return to the field of honour and prove that Italian music was not dead.

'Busseto, Busseto, Busseto!!!'

For sixteen years, by his own reckoning, Verdi had been the centre of what he called 'an investigation or, better, an inquisition' conducted by the people of Busseto.[43] Curiosity about his household, aroused in September 1849, when Strepponi joined him in Palazzo Cavalli, had never been satisfied. Even after their marriage, they invited almost no one from Busseto to visit them; the roster of local guests was restricted to Antonio Barezzi and his second wife; Angiolo Carrara, Verdi's notary and friend; Piroli's father; the engineer and architect Gaetano Balestra; and Don Avanzi. The Mayor of Busseto was invited once, and perhaps never again. Carlo Verdi, whom Piave knew and liked, was not mentioned among the guests at the villa, although he surely must have dined with his son sometime. Verdi supported him with an allowance from 1851 until the end of his life, according to the terms of their legal settlement, and lodged him in the winter in Palazzo Cavalli, their official residence. But the composer had become somewhat estranged from his brothers-in-law Giovannino and Demetrio Barezzi; from his sister-in-law Marianna Barezzi, who had lent him money and moral support when he was launching his career; and from her husband Pietro Garbi, for whom Verdi had written some of his earliest compositions. Giovannino Barezzi told his family that

Marianna and Garbi had even lodged Verdi and Margherita Barezzi in their own home when the young couple was having difficulty paying their rent. Demaldè, Verdi's staunch champion, must have visited Verdi occasionally but in Verdi's and Strepponi's correspondence he is never mentioned as a guest. Among all the members of the Società Filarmonica, only one or two seem ever to have visited Verdi in his home.

His withdrawal, perhaps understandable in a creative artist, seemed inappropriate in a deputy to Parliament who was the elected representative of the citizenry and its only voice in the important legislative body in the capital. Verdi's reclusiveness made his neighbours more and more curious about what happened in his house. Verdi himself complained that they wanted to know about 'every action and word'.[44] In their field of special inquiry were his wife and his religion. Were he and Strepponi married? On whose money did she live? Did they make Confession before a priest? Did they eat meat or fish on fast days? How much food did his servants buy in the markets of Cremona and Busseto? What did they eat at Sant'Agata, and how much?[45] This intrusion into his affairs infuriated Verdi. An exacerbated situation became worse, not better, as the 1860s wore on. The Bussetans did not understand, or perhaps did not want to understand, this testy man who described himself as being as proud as Lucifer but was so shy that he could not bear to hear anyone talk about his music or play it in his hearing. Verdi's fellow-citizens wanted an affable, gregarious man. Instead, they had to deal with a son of the place who as early as 1851 had described his existence there as 'my life as a Bear'.[46] This retreat into his lair was seen as a rejection of his own constituency. Yet he needed favours from the little city, just as it needed favours from him. What he could not get locally, he asked for, and sometimes demanded, from higher authorities. But when Busseto could not get what it sought from him, it turned on him, Strepponi, and their friends: 'and no one can come to my house without becoming the target of hatred and persecution on the part of the Bussetans', he grumbled in 1865.[47] In this small world, curiosity about whether they were married was ever rife. People in prominent families would have known a great deal about at least some of her pregnancies because she had sung until the last weeks, when the fact that she was expecting a child could not be hidden.[48] Strepponi's difficult position in her first ten years in Busseto and Sant'Agata left her sometimes bitter, depressed, and suspicious of those closest to her. Even after her husband was honoured by being elected to Parliament, her home life in the country did not change much, for Verdi wished to lead the same secluded existence that he had so prized before. The couple's social life, as they entertained and were entertained, was conducted almost entirely in cities where they went on his business; but even in Genoa, where they spent many winters, they went out infrequently and had few people in. Because of Verdi's inflexibility in sharing so little of their lives with the Bussetans, Strepponi remained lonely among 'the cretins'—as she said—long after she could proudly sign her name 'Giuseppina Verdi'.[49] Her hunger for an intellectual life and for some sort of outside social contact was expressed in many letters sent from the silent world of Sant'Agata. Among them was a letter to Escudier in which she described herself as 'baring my [claws] as wild animals do' and building up a reserve of rage to move around and to destroy things, 'to take my revenge on this endless immobility',[50] which she so resented. She was no longer young, she went on, 'but intellectual life belongs to people of all ages; and here, alas, it is completely lacking.' Even though she loved the country very much, she said that 365 days a year were 'too much, very much too much'; Verdi, on the other hand, seemed completely fulfilled there. Strepponi admitted to herself and to Don Avanzi that most of the people in the community 'detested' her, even after she had been in Verdi's house for fourteen years and had been accepted by Antonio Barezzi. Such resentment of her must have grown from the conviction that she was responsible for Verdi's withdrawal from the world and was unworthy of him.

In such a situation it was perhaps inevitable that the townspeople would find ways to get at those who offended them. In the autumn of 1861 Busseto had sent a message of its own to Sant'Agata. After the harvest, as Verdi's peasants were pressing his grapes in the courtyard of Palazzo Cavalli, they began to sing 'to pass the time',[52] as was absolutely normal among those who gather to *pigiare l'uva*. Someone in town called the National Guard, which was, after all, armed with the rifles Verdi had bought for it. The guardsmen called in the Carabinieri, who were then and are now a part of the Italian Army. The soldiers 'forced these poor devils to be quiet', Verdi reported in a fury to Piroli. Angry at this 'illegal or discourteous action', he tried to find out whether there was a national law that prevented people from singing in their own houses. 'And if such a law did exist, shouldn't they give some advance notice, using a bit of courtesy, before calling out the Armed Forces?' He was 'nauseated' over the insult, which, he said, he did not intend to swallow. It was not the first incivility he had suffered at the hands of his 'very, very lovable fellow-citizens',[53] nor was it the last. Many years later someone killed one of the black swans Teresa Stolz had given him, driving a stake through the bird.

'When I can, I avoid going into Busseto because . . . people point to me because I am an atheist, proud, etc. etc.,'[54] the composer wrote, touching on his refusal to observe the rites and strictures of the Catholic Church. In a town that he described as being pro-clerical, this was a grave matter. Busseto had a standard for comparison in Verdi's own family, for Carlo Verdi, when he was well past 80 and was suffering from heart trouble and kidney disease, got out of his sick bed whenever he could to go to daily Mass and 'say a string of Pater Nosters every day'.[55]—This, from Strepponi's own description of him. As for the couple's relations with their parish priest, Don Filippo Stecconi of Sant'Agata, they were slight, and if Verdi ever went to Mass there, apparently no one knew it. Strepponi may have attended, for she described the trip to church as uncomfortable because of the heat in summer and the wretched condition of the village road in winter.[56] For whatever reason, whether to protect his wife from the curious or to provide a place of worship for himself, his staff, or his guests, Verdi decided early in the 1860s to build a little chapel in the villa, facing the garden a few yards behind his bedroom–study. When the masons had finished, he hired an artist to decorate it and got the Bishop of Cremona—a prelate from another province—to consecrate the altar stone. Then, when he needed to have someone say Mass, he met with opposition from the clergy of his own diocese, who had to authorize a priest to come to a chapel on private property. As Verdi confided to Luccardi, he would also have to have his chapel blessed, 'and perhaps that benediction can be done by the Vicar General or someone delegated by him who will be assigned to visit. The authorization from Rome is needed.'[57] He asked the sculptor to solicit the support of the conductor Domenico Alari, who had just visited Sant'Agata, or from Donizetti's brother-in-law Antonio Vasselli, who knew his way through the maze of Rome, or even from the impresario Jacovacci. But, as he found, a very substantial effort was also needed at home. In a letter the Vicar-General claimed that Verdi was trying to create 'a parish within the parish' for his own selfish needs.[58] Verdi's reaction was typical: he appealed to a higher authority, sending the Vicar-General's letter on to Piroli and asking him to get 'the government's permission'[59] and to send it back to him as quickly as possible. Strepponi, taking a different tack, turned to Don Avanzi, although many members of the local clergy looked askance at him because of his strong pro-unification stance. He may have gone to the *Curia* himself. Permission came finally, giving Verdi the right to have Mass said in his own home; but the matter was not resolved for years.

Another project was the construction of a complicated irrigation system at Sant'Agata. With a water-gate across the Ongina and an underground conduit leading from the river, Verdi could draw off water and direct it into his garden and fields. A coal-driven four-horse-power motor, which Verdi bought abroad, was attached to a pump. Verdi even hired an English engineer to come to the villa to begin the operation. The composer's request to the authorities at Villanova sull'Arda met with resistance, chiefly because he was not the only landowner on the lower Ongina and would inevitably divert a portion of the communal water supply for his own needs. Eventually he showed how at least some of the rerouted stream would be returned to the river. This project, too, had to be cleared with the national authorities; and again Verdi appealed to Piroli, though not before he had won a favourable ruling from the chief engineer of the Province of Piacenza. Piroli spoke to the Minister of Public Works, as Verdi asked him to do in April 1865; but the needed authorization did not come as he had expected. 'I think that the business of the Ongina water-gate will never come to an end,' the composer complained.[60] Months passed as officials in Turin claimed that they had not received the relevant papers while the Prefect in Piacenza swore that he had sent them. Finally the irrigation system was able to function. Verdi guarded it as jealously as if it were a treasure hoard and, over the years, bought up parcels of land all along the Castellazzo Canal, adding the farms of Gerbida, Canale, and the far-off mill in Besenzone to his holdings so as to keep firm control over the waterway.   The summer and autumn of 1865 left the provinces boiling with political controversy at a moment when a shift to the right seemed inevitable as the pro-Austrian, anti-unification forces continued their struggle to bring back the Old Regime. Verdi feared the local clergy, which, as a body, had been almost solidly against unification; to Piroli he expressed his concern that the government was putting the new nation in danger. 'Advise the government to be less indulgent toward the country priests, so that they will stop once and for all raising the spirit of revolution among the peasants,' he wrote, declaring to his friend that he was absolutely serious and not joking.[61] Although Verdi decided not to run for election in 1865 and gave up his seat and left Parliament, Piroli was again a candidate. When, to everyone's surprise, he was defeated in October, Verdi sent him a letter of consolation and encouragement: 'I am terribly sorry that you have been defeated in the electoral battle; but if you would have had to fight with shameful weapons "as others did" I prefer to see you flat on the ground with your conscience and your political faith untainted.'[62] As far as their home town was concerned, Verdi gave voice to his own dismay, which Piroli shared, for Busseto had elected a doctor whom they did not know. Verdi complained that the 'priests knew how to manage things just right, and in secret', adding that he was furious over the unexpected outcome.[63] Again and again in his letters he expressed his mistrust of anyone who supported the clerical faction or enjoyed its endorsement. 'Ah, Busseto, Busseto, Busseto!!!', he griped.

The Teatro Verdi in Busseto

In this summer of reversals and frustrations Verdi became involved in a tangled controversy that had its roots in the earliest years of his career and was fed by the justifiable pride that the community took in his success and celebrity. Verdi had scarcely made his mark in Milan in the 1840s when his townspeople began to think about building a theatre to replace the small hall that had been used for decades in the old Rocca of the Pallavicino in the main square of Busseto. From the start Verdi opposed the project, which he considered pretentious and foolish. He wrote frankly to Barezzi about it in 1845:

In the name of the *Father*, the *Son*, and the *Holy Spirit*! Before answering your dear letter, I cross myself and put myself in the Grace of God so as not to talk absolute nonsense. The Theatre in Busseto? I don't believe it, nor will I ever believe it . . . Poor us, if it should ever happen! The world will come to an end. . . . Take courage, then, and, since these are all castles in the air, make them beautiful.[64]

He had, though, said that he might write an opera for the new house, if his commitments allowed, and that although he could not promise to have his famous friends Frezzolini and Poggi come to sing, it was 'very probable' that they might do so if he asked them. On another occasion there had been talk of having the soprano and her tenor husband visit Verdi at home and sing a charity concert while there. Nothing of this, of course, had come to pass in the intervening years. In 1857 the city fathers finally decided to build the new theatre. Verdi, reminded that he had once promised to help, responded angrily to their solicitation, denying that he had ever done so. Rancour was generated on both sides by a remark Verdi made about the site of the theatre. He had indicated a lot on the Strada Maestra; but the Bussetans, believing that the parcel of land belonged to Antonio Barezzi, accused the composer and his father-in-law of trying to turn a profit at the City's expense. After that, Verdi wanted nothing to do with the project, which went ahead without him. Those who wanted the theatre, the Mayor among them, thought that they could get Verdi to commit himself while he was still deputy to Parliament. So in 1861, when work was already under way, they appealed to him again. His sensible response, urging the City to stop the construction and put the funds to a better use, when Italy and the City itself needed money so urgently, fell on deaf ears. He then refused the City's offer of a box and would not allow the theatre to be named after him. By 1864 much of the work was done, with only the interior decoration and detailing to be completed, but the theatre still had no name and Verdi still held himself aloof from the project.

In the summer of 1865 the pressure brought to bear upon him, especially by the Mayor and Giovannino Barezzi, caused the composer to react violently. Before he answered his brother-in-law's letter, Verdi and Strepponi compiled an entire dossier on Busseto's sins against its most famous citizen. Nowhere in the Verdi documents does the composer's voice ring out more clearly than in the notes his wife took as he railed against Busseto, which had laid its claim against him because of the promise, or half-promise, he had made in the 1840s.

The worst *insult* is their having put in my mouth words and promises [that I never made], making claims in bad faith and without advance preparation to which I naturally refused [to respond]; they have made me seem to be a man who does not live up to the promise he has made. You must destroy, with a letter or by some other means, the effect created by the Commission on Sunday and lift from me that responsibility that others laid on me to protect [themselves].

The matter of Emanuele as maestro—the competition [required] of him—the nomination of someone else without a competition.

Letter that they want to write [to Muzio] in America to prove that I am a man who does not keep his word . . . Fine way [to act]—sensitive and honest.

Apart from my word (which I never gave) why would they want to demand so much from me? Is it perhaps because of those 27 francs and 50 cent[esimi] a month [of the scholarship], which they gave me and could not deny me?

If they gave them, does the credit go to them or to those who left it to them in their wills?

And such an uproar over 1,200 francs!

Haven't they paid them out, and aren't they obliged to pay them out every year in perpetuity to four young people? . . . Do they perhaps want to punish me for the name that I have made for myself and for the honour I brought to the city?

And anyway it is the town's vain and crazy obsession to want to pass itself off as a Maecenas with [the generosity] of the dead and 30 cent[esimi] from the living.

[*Here Strepponi sets down her own view.*] The scholarships were left by those who are now dead and absolutely do not belong to those people who are now screaming so much in the piazza, in the filthy bars, in the cafés, and in the shops against Verdi who, whether they like it or not, made known to the whole world that Busseto was in this country. When living people go to the theatre and spend a few cent[esimi] they think that they are helping the actors, singers, players, etc. (according to them) they have done something good for all those who have come to Busseto, even Ristori, who, without their help, would never have laid the foundation for her glory and her fortune. Enough! it is time to take off [the] blinkers and look around instead, to see how the world has made progress.

[*Here Verdi's words are again set down.*] . . . Do they expect things from me because I am rich? Aren't [others] rich?

Fofino violates my house. And this is not judged an important act, perhaps because it is directed against me.

Old [Dr] Frignani—investigates, asks a straightforward question such as how and with what means my wife is living, because the city could not understand this clearly. What right has he?

The [irrigation] machine, for water.

[The teacher Signorina] Landriani—to whom they read, but do not give, the letter of apology for what was done to her and written against her by Arfini [the school superintendent], who is none the less still in his post.

Investigation, or, rather, inquisition concerning every act or word that is spoken in my house.

That no one can come into my house without becoming the target of hatred and persecution by the Bussetans.

Giovanni[no] B[arezzi] shouts in the piazza, and, when he writes, shows a velvet paw. Two-faced, like so many others. Lacks the courage of his own convictions!

[Conflicting] opinions.

To say these words all the time: '*We made him*'—if it is ridiculous, it is also offensive. It is still the matter of the 27 francs. And why did they not 'make' others, since the raw material was just the same?

If, in this situation, I were to write a letter to be published and not budge an inch from the truth, I would make them look ridiculous everywhere in Europe.

BOOK IV

It is better to put an end to this, and to the 27 francs and 50 cent[esimi], and with this kind of inquisition that has been going on for sixteen years.

I have, one might say, withdrawn from Busseto; if I am bothered, I will withdraw from Sant'Agata; and I shall not be the one to look the worst for it.

Confession, Communion, fish, meat, novenas, etc. And so one cannot enjoy personal freedom when one is living decently in his own house and not breaking the laws or offending morality?

Remarks about how much is bought in Busseto, in Cremona, etc., and about how much we eat, etc. . . .

Our views and theirs are at the opposite poles of the earth. I am as liberal as anyone can be without being a Red. I respect others' freedom and I demand that mine be respected. The town is anything but liberal; it sometimes shows that it is, perhaps out of fear; but it leans toward the priests.[65]

Strepponi added an observation of her own.

For the modest little composer Coppola the people of Catania—as a sign of their joy at his return home after fifteen years—have struck gold medals worth 1,227 francs. As for Giuseppe Verdi, who filled the entire world with his musical glory, the Bussetans pay him back by poisoning his life with all kinds of vile actions and by throwing in his face with every word and at every step the wretched sum of 1,200 francs (which they could not refuse him because it is an old testamentary disposition)!!! With countless evil acts, lies, violent actions they aggravate him, they annoy him, and—to cap it all—they oblige him to put an end finally to these daily injuries by throwing in their faces the important sum of 10,000 francs [*for his box in the new theatre*]!!! So be it! . . . so the *so-called* [scholarship] will really be repaid 1,000 per cent! One thousand to one in the glory that shines on that filthy and unworthy town![66]

When Verdi wrote to public officials about the proposed theatre, his letters were more moderate in tone; but at least two drafts of letters to Giovannino Barezzi rang with angry reproach.

Why would [the Mayor, Donnino] Corbellini come to see me? Why come with you? What office do you hold? Why the slap at the committee with which you came to Sant'Agata? Why the slap at Angiolo Carrara and the people from the City Hall? If you want the gossip to stop, begin to talk it less yourself. Anyway, since they dare to say to me *officially* that I had promised [to help], so I believe that officially [it is time that] the truth be spoken, that is *that I have never, absolutely never promised*. I am sufficiently familiar with the system some people have who specifically say one thing in the *osterie* [and] in the cafés and say something else in public. I do not know why you are meddling in this mess, for you are not part of the city administration nor of the Commission. Perhaps under the title of friend? Truthfully you cannot say that you have been that, on this

494

occasion! *As for being against gossip, you—who should have been the only one not to create any—were the first to shout around everywhere things that are terribly false and embarrassing.* Doesn't it seem to everyone that it is time to leave me in peace?[67]

A second letter to Giovannino Barezzi was even more virulent.

First of all, how did you, who call yourself *my old friend*, have the nerve to go around in the piazzas, the cafés, the *osterie*, shouting, speaking out against, and cursing this *old friend* of yours? How could you disapprove of [my] actions, without knowing about them, condemn [me], defenceless? You know that among enemies too, when they are honest, accusations are made, but there is discussion before absolution [is given] or judgement [is passed]. And you, my old friend, acted worse than an honest enemy! You have said in your letters that I am right, and you crucified me in the piazzas.[68]

A further communication announced that Verdi had considered all aspects of this unpleasant situation and wished to make an appropriate response; but the tone of even this letter reveals how much resentment, anger, misunderstanding, and pain still existed.

You say that the Bussetans believed that I would be vain enough to let my name be given to the theatre in Busseto? Whenever did I give anyone hope about that? When did I promise? On the contrary, about three years ago I rejected this honour and a box that the Mayor and Luigi Morelli kindly offered me, in the City's name. If I refused this at that time, if at all times I have always showed that I was opposed to the construction of a theatre that is too expensive and that will be useless in the future, how could the Bussetans say that I would co-operate with them in a thing that, in my opinion, is wrong? . . . I have always been against this project of yours, so I cannot be on your side. Let's not discuss whether I am right or wrong; it is [my] view, which can and must be respected, if not shared. During the [meeting of] the Commission on Sunday, the Mayor spoke words that go too far: *that he had had the theatre built for me, just for me!! and because of my supposed request and promise* (made nine or ten years ago). It is really too improper to want to place on me the responsibility for this work! Let's talk about it: and tell me whether a good public official should lay such an expense on his commune just to satisfy the whim (if it were a whim) of an individual? And how on earth could this public official, once he had the City's approval, not send me an official letter, which I could answer and confirm the supposed promises? But he took care not to do that because my answer would have destroyed all his projects. Not only did he never do that, but he failed to speak to me about it every time [we met]. Even when he came to me with Sig. Morelli he never said a word about these promises, and that was the right moment

495

to do it. And, something odder still, they build a theatre for me, *just for me*, without ever showing me the plans, without ever consulting me about anything or for anything? You will agree that that is very, very strange. The Mayor also said that I had promised—for the opening—to have the three foremost *singers in Europe*, if I were notified three years in advance!!! What contradictions! Then you would wait for three years? All that is not worth discussing and unworthy of serious men. But the Mayor ought to know that neither I nor anyone else on earth could arrange to have the *foremost singers*, and what makes this matter absolutely ridiculous is the three years' advance notice! For example, I should say to *Adelina Patti*, to *Fraschini*, etc. 'Be sure that three years from now, even if you have an offer of 200,000 francs from America, 100,[000] from Russia, etc., you will not accept them because you will come to sing (*three years from now*) in Busseto!!' I ask you yourself, and not just someone who is experienced in matters relating to the theatre, whether this is not an exorbitant and impossible expectation, and whether it is believable that I would be such an imbecile as to promise the impossible. . . . The Mayor was vain enough to leave behind him a monument that will last beyond his tenure; he made use of the commune's money and my name, and built the theatre. He did the wrong thing. That is all. Addio, addio. Your aff[ectionate]

[G. Verdi].

I notice a word in your letter that mentions *flatterers*. First of all, I do not allow anyone to praise me to my face, and if I were vain and longing to hear praise, I would not stay at Sant'Agata. As for the evil gossip [here], no one here hardly ever talks about the town; and I, I alone, sometimes make remarks about ideas, views that I don't share; and I, I alone, sometimes complain—not about words, but about actions that affect me, about annoyances and new and old unhappiness.[69]

Another letter to Giovannino Barezzi takes up the same controversy, but from another point of view, revealing how deeply Verdi had been hurt at being left out of the planning:

But I will go beyond this; and I want for a moment to concede to you and the Mayor all the promises: promises made to the Mayor in casual conversation, on the first day of his tenure when—you might say—he hadn't even got familiar with the dust in his office. When the project was approved, he never spoke to me about it, *never ever*; he says so himself.

What! they use me, my wishes, my financial means, and without discussing it with me, without consulting me? but this is worse than a lack of courtesy: it is an insult. It is an insult because that sort of behaviour means: 'Why do we need to talk to him about it? Oh! he will do it . . . he will have to do it! What right have they to act like this?

I know perfectly well that many people, talking about me, go around whispering a phrase which is—I don't know whether more ridiculous or more undignified: '*We made him ourselves!*' Words which jumped into my ear even the last time I was in Busseto eight or ten days ago.

I repeat that this is ridiculous and undignified. Ridiculous because I can answer: 'Why don't you make others, then?' Undignified because they did nothing more for me than carry out the terms of a bequest. But if they throw this beneficence in my face, I can still answer: 'Sirs, I got four years of aid, 25 francs a month: 1,200 francs in all. Thirty-two years have passed; let us make an accounting of the capital, of the interest, and I will pay it all off.'

The moral debt will always remain. Yes. But I raise my head high and say proudly: 'Signori, I have carried your name honourably into the farthest corners of the earth. That is well worth 1,200 francs.' Sharp words, but true. Do you see where you get when people don't know how to think about what they are saying, nor to act as they should. I would not have wanted these scandals, and would have given anything to avoid them; the proof of that are the proposals of agreement that I offer through the good offices of Dr Angiolo Carrara to the Commission and the [city] administration. Whatever the outcome, it is a matter I never want to discuss again. This letter is an answer to your own; it does not deserve an answer. But if you were to decide to write to me again, since you could not tell me anything new, nor anything that I have not already answered in advance, don't be astonished if I maintain the deepest silence. I ask only one thing from you: *peace*; if you wish, even *oblivion*.[70]

The whole matter was brought to a close when Carrara, playing, as Verdi said, a good role in an ugly drama, acted as intermediary and reached a compromise between the parties. The town would let Verdi alone if he would allow the theatre to be named after him. Verdi pledged his 10,000 lire, vowing never to go in the building. He kept his vow. The Teatro Verdi in Busseto was inaugurated finally in 1868 with *Rigoletto*. Verdi and Strepponi went off to Tabiano before the opening, as we shall see, and did not return until the season had ended one month later.

The Workers' Society of Busseto

Among the democratic organizations that sprang up in the 1850s and continued to thrive after unification were the Workers' Societies or mutual assistance groups. In many cities and towns the Società Operaia became the first manifestation of independence on the part of the working class in a time of difficult transition from a predominantly agricultural society to a modestly industrial one, when thousands of farm-labourers and their families were being driven into factories, workshops, and mills. The decline of agriculture particularly affected the *braccianti* (day labourers who were paid a wage) and *famigli a spesa* (unsalaried workers paid only room and board). Seeking work in the cities, they became lost in the urban mass, where they could no longer depend on a rural family, hamlet, or community for support. In cases of illness, pregnancy, accidents, joblessness, or old age, they were defenceless. Displaced, alone, and frightened by their new world, they found some help in the Società Operaia. Men and women alike could join for a modest monthly membership fee. According to the regulations set forth in its statutes, the Società Operaia guaranteed certain material and emotional support. If a worker were ill and out of work for three days or more, benefits were paid for up to three months out of the society's treasury. If a member were ill for more than three months, a special subsidy was available. Families of members who died were assisted with cash benefits. In an attempt to shield members from pawnbrokers and usurers, the Società Operaia made six-month loans. A circulating library was free to all members; help with reading and writing was also provided. Women and men received the same benefits, although no one was covered who abused wine or liquor or indulged in 'evil habits or brawling'.[71]

Important public figures sometimes agreed to become honorary officers. Mazzini led the society in Genoa, while Garibaldi served as the president for life in Bologna. Verdi became honorary president of the Busseto Società Operaia in April 1865. Among its members were some of the Muzios, who were shoemakers, and some of the Barezzis, who were seamstresses. Many of these families lived near or in Verdi's Palazzo Cavalli, where he also lodged his father and aunt and some of his Verdi cousins, who were shopkeepers and elementary-school teachers.[72] It is not surprising, then, that he accepted this honour while fighting off the City's attempt to name the theatre after him. Offended by vanity and display, he did understand the meaning of hard work. His participation in the utilitarian and humane purpose of the Società Operaia helped local workers in their mission of bettering the living conditions of the lowest class. To that, Verdi lent both the lustre of his name and the power of his money.

27

Spring 1865–Summer 1867

Don Carlos

Late in the spring of 1865 Filippi, a champion of German music in Italy, declared in an article in *La perseveranza* that the 'so-called Italian school has now come to an end', a phrase that angered Piave and drove him to write to Verdi, denouncing this and other 'craziness' perpetrated by 'La Filippa', as Piave tagged the critic, scoring off his feminine mannerisms.[1] Verdi, too, refused to accept Filippi's verdict. To another of Piave's reports from Milan, he answered: 'So they are afraid that I will compose again? Who knows? [I might] if for no other reason than to make them angry.'[2] But he had sounder motives than that. In the summer of 1864 Émile Perrin of the Paris Opéra had approached Verdi about writing a new work for his theatre.[3] He had also kept in touch through Escudier, who often heard from both Verdi and Strepponi. In June 1865 Strepponi complained bitterly to the French publisher about the sterile intellectual life at Sant'Agata and added her own observations about her husband, who had taken the Paris offer under consideration.

For a long time, I have been hearing him sing 'I don't want to write' in every key. . . . It seems that the greatest difficulty in writing for the Opéra will be the libretto. I have faith in the librettists' imagination. I know [Verdi]. Once he is committed, the picture will change. He will leave his trees, his building projects, his hydraulic machines, his guns, etc. He will let his artistic passion take him over, as usual; he will devote his whole self to his libretto, his music; and I hope that the world will be the richer for it.[4]

Verdi sent off his own energetic answer to Escudier:

You are joking?! Write for the Opéra!!! Don't you think I would be in danger of having my eyes scratched out, after what happened two years ago at the rehearsals of *Vêpres*? Write for the Opéra now, with Madame Meyerbeer's splendid precedent of showing off with [gifts to critics of] pins, tobacco boxes, bracelets, medallions, batons, etc. etc. What a business! Even Art becomes a bank, and one has to be a millionaire, otherwise success is impossible! But putting aside these ugly little intrigues and the jokes, why would I have the nerve to face all the anger and the curses, unless I had on my side an intelligent, strong director such as M. Perrin surely is. Nothing could be easier than to reach an understanding about writing an opera, and—to be brief—we will have an agreement as soon as we have a libretto, or at least a scenario that is just right. *Re Lear* is magnificent, sublime, tragic, but it is not scenically splendid enough for the Opéra. From this point of view, *Cleopatra* is better, but the protagonists' love, their characters, and their very misfortunes evoke very little sympathy. Anyhow, to judge it, one has to know it. Everything finally depends on a libretto. A libretto, a libretto, and the opera is done!... Peppina is well and sends regards to you all. Addio addio. Write to me soon.[5]

A second letter asked Escudier to speak to Perrin directly about *Re Lear*.

If we were to choose *Re Lear*, we would have to stay close to Shaspeare [*sic*] and follow his path scrupulously. He is such a great poet that one cannot touch him without taking away that originality and character that are so powerful in him.[6]

Perrin did not hesitate. To take advantage of the door Verdi had opened, he sent Escudier to Sant'Agata in mid-July, to show the composer the *Cleopatra* libretto and a scenario of *Don Carlos*, drawn from Schiller's drama. The publisher was able to write back triumphantly to Perrin that *Don Carlos* had caught Verdi's imagination.[7] The composer himself wrote four days later:

Cleopatra is not for me. *Don Carlos* magnificent drama, but perhaps lacking a bit of the spectacular. Otherwise, excellent idea of having Charles V appear; also excellent the scene at Fontainebleau. As in Schiller, I would like a little scene between Filippo and the Inquisitor, and he blind and very, very old; Escudier will tell you why when he sees you. I would also like a duet between Filippo and Posa. As for *Re Lear*, the distribution of the roles is difficult, and it is almost impossible to find a Cordelia. This drama, too, lacks spectacle. Otherwise, it is a sublime subject that I adore.[8]

Verdi may have drafted a sketch for four pages of the music of *Re Lear* at this time, a duet for a father and his daughter who are in prison awaiting death. A Jester or Fool (Giullare) is referred to in the libretto.

Two pages of this sketch, now in the Library for the Performing Arts at Lincoln Center, were sold as Verdi's *Re Lear* to Carolyn Allen Perera in the 1950s. Two other pages were bought by a collector who sent Mrs Perera photostats of them. One of the lines in this sketch reads:

> Degnar rammentati gli anni
> quando io bambina
> [per le] farfalle a cogliere
> correa per la collina.[9]

(Remember, then, the years when I, a little girl, ran in the hills, catching butterflies.)

These lines are similar to lines in another libretto, written by Ghislanzoni for a *Re Lear* by Antonio Cagnoni, Verdi's acquaintance and contemporary. Lear and Cordelia are in prison.

> Laggiu nel prato
> cogliere farfalle e fior.[10]

(Down in the meadow, catching butterflies and picking flowers.)

The Italian translation of *King Lear* by Carlo Rusconi (1838, in prose) includes these stage directions and Lear's words in Act V:

Lear e Cordelia li seguono prigionieri. . . . LEAR: Andiamo nella nostra prigione. . . . Vi canteremo entrambi come gli uccelli prigionieri nella loro gabbia, . . . cantando, raccontandoci vecchie storie e sollazzandoci come farfalle dorate, etc.[11]

(Lear and Cordelia, taken prisoner, follow them. . . . LEAR: Let us go to our prison. . . . There we will both sing like two birds in their cage . . . singing and telling each other old tales and amusing ourselves like two golden butterflies, etc.)

The similarities between the Rusconi text; the Cagnoni *Re Lear*, the libretto of which was studied by Andrew Porter; and the Perera sketch are striking.

The best efforts of several musicologists and historians, though, were not sufficient to show that Verdi was the composer of the Perera sketch, because the words did not seem to be in his hand. Walter Toscanini, particularly, worked several months on a transcription of the text, then wrote to Mrs Perera to say that he could not decipher all the words. He did, though, provide a draft, leaving illegible words blank.[12] It shows that the principals are a king and his daughter; they are in prison, awaiting execution; he holds the Fool responsible for his misfortunes; and she whiles the time away, recalling her childhood, when she ran free in the fields, catching butterflies.

A previously undiscovered document, found in 1990 in a private collection in Italy, may shed light on the *Re Lear* sketch. It is a farm account, dated by Verdi 'Harvest of Corn, year 1867'.[13] There are many similarities between his hand here and that of the Perera sketch, particularly in several of the capital letters and whole syllables. This suggests that he may have worked on *Re Lear* at about this time, even though he found it difficult to cast and had despaired of finding the right soprano for the opera.

He was already familiar with *Don Carlos*, which had been offered to him in 1850 by the librettists Royer and Vaez.[14] He had also received Piave's own libretto on the same subject, *Elisabetta di Valois*, written for Antonio Buzzolla, a composer from Adria, and performed at the Teatro La Fenice in 1850.[15]

With negotiations for a new opera under way, Verdi needed to be in Paris. The Opéra was not his only concern, for he had also considered writing a new opera for the Théâtre des Italiens. Bosoni, however, remained an obstacle there: 'Arrange things so that the Teatro Italiano will have an orchestra director at last,' Verdi asked Escudier, adding that he did not know whether Mariani would in fact take over that post or not.[16] Both the composer and the conductor were still caught up in confusion, as Mariani was still undecided about the position, chiefly because he could not get the contractual terms he had hoped for. At one point Verdi pledged himself to get Mariani to accept, even as he sent mixed signals to both sides in the discussion. In July Mariani, who had committed himself to helping his Genoese friends, the Sauli-Pallavicinos, through a crisis, arrived at Sant'Agata about ten days after the date he had first planned to get there. His involvement with the Pallavicinos, which he considered a good and charitable act, was seen by Strepponi as an error: 'As far as I am concerned, I believe that all the characters in that near-tragedy would do well to recite an "I confess"! If they do recite it, I pray God to pardon them and set them on the right road,' she wrote to De Amicis.[17]

Mariani, writing to Verdi from Cesena, mentioned for the first time the name of Teresa Stolz, the Bohemian soprano who sang in *Guglielmo Tell* and *Un ballo in maschera* in the conductor's productions in August 1865. The prima donna 'did very, very well', Mariani wrote, describing her work in *Un ballo in maschera*. Concerned, as everyone was, about the cholera epidemic that raged in Italy that year, the conductor wrote that 'if the cholera kills me, you will write my Requiem Mass. I tell you the truth: I would be very happy to die so that Italy and the world might have such a [fine] gift from you.'[18] A few weeks after visiting Sant'Agata, Mariani was sent off to Paris with his expenses paid by the Luccas, who had entrusted to him the production of Meyerbeer's *L'Africaine*, which was to be given in Bologna in the autumn. In Paris, he also dealt with the Théâtre des Italiens, but did not secure his appointment there, a fact that brought Verdi's wrath down upon him. Apart from his failure to get a contract with the Italiens, he was also blamed for getting to Sant'Agata too late to meet Escudier, who might perhaps have helped him. Verdi wrote Mariani a 'dreadful' letter of reproach, to which the conductor replied modestly, agreeing that Verdi was right to criticize him.[19] He read it, he said, with 'resigned devotion', his love and respect for Verdi unshaken. He knew Verdi was right, he said, but wished that he had not given the composer cause to write what he had. 'Mea culpa, mea culpa, mea maxima culpa', he admitted, while defending himself by adding that he believed that even if he had come to Sant'Agata as planned, he would not have got a contract with the Italiens.

I will tell you, O my Maestro, that I was not sorry that I did not accept the offer from Paris until I learned that you yourself are going there next winter, and that you will be at the Opéra and at the Italiens. You cannot imagine how sorry I was; that I will stay in Genoa without *you*, knowing that you will be in Paris without *me*, will make me just desolate. Please believe, my Maestro, that this year it was impossible to reach an agreement with Bagier. Please do not abandon your poor Wrong Head, and be sure that everything you will do for me will be accepted without question!'[20]

The conductor's career in Genoa went on; in Bologna he conducted *L'africana* at the Teatro Comunale, where the opera was enormously successful. This important première lent additional weight to Meyerbeer's already imposing presence in Italy, where *grand-opéra* was enjoying a considerable vogue. The Italian première of *Robert le Diable* at the Pergola in Florence in 1840 had been followed by *Les Huguenots* there in 1841 (given under the title *Gli anglicani*), and *Le Prophète* in 1852. In 1855 the critic Abramo Basevi described Meyerbeer as

the true representative of today's music, without rivals among composers writing now; he is the living expression of new needs. With these words, we do not mean to diminish in any way the glory owed to Verdi . . . because although [Verdi] is not destined to go down in history as the voice of contemporary music, he undeniably co-operated in and was active in contributing to its progress.[21]

BOOK IV

In a period when Verdi himself stated that very few printed scores were available, the Florentine publisher Gian Gualberto Guidi, aided by Basevi, began to publish his pocket-sized orchestral scores, 'an authentic "first" in the publishing world of the time'.[22] He began with *Les Huguenots* in 1861 and went on after Meyerbeer's death in 1864. The Luccas were also promoting his works energetically in all the theatres where they wielded influence.

If Verdi were troubled by the publicity Meyerbeer's works were getting, he let no one know it. Because news of his possible return to the stage was being circulated, he began to receive inquiries from friends and acquaintances who wanted to know his plans. In a light-hearted mood he answered Arrivabene with a funny letter from his dog Blach to Arrivabene's Ron-Ron:

Blach to his brother Ron-Ron Greetings. My beloved brother, you were very wrong not to come to see me, for I would have received you with open paws and open jaws and my four teeth in your woolly cheeks; I would have shown you all the tenderness I, a dog, can muster. You would not have been in danger of cholera here, nor would you have met any madmen from the capitals; instead, we have a rather large number of imbeciles whom we whack with our paws every once in a while, just to get them back in line. My major-domo secretary factotum, the one who writes the little hooks on paper, provides everything for me; macaroons fall into my mouth all the time; the biggest bones go to me; when I wake up, my meal is ready. The whole house is open to me, and now that the heat is suffocating, I move from one suite and one bed to another all the time; and God help anyone who touches me! In my finest moments I am busy teaching manners to a young kitten who is doing awfully well, and if he doesn't get strangled he will make a name for himself as a first-class thief. You see, dear brother, that everything here goes marvellously smoothly, according to my own counsel, and my own important wishes and desires. And if you come, my paws, teeth, and tail will be ready to greet you as an honoured relative. My male and female secretaries send you their greetings. As far as my male secretary goes, I read in some newspaper that he is thinking about making some more little hooks. I'll enroll him in the list of madmen and send him off to the capitals. If that is what happens, I will let you know. In the mean time here is my fraternal, canine embrace. Farewell.

BLACH.[23]

Verdi's good humour may have been attributable in part to his decision to leave Parliament and to compose again; but it is likely that some joy came with his and Strepponi's growing interest in Filomena Maria Cristina

504

Verdi, the 6-year-old daughter of Verdi's cousin from Roncole. The child was the granddaughter of Marcantonio Verdi, the composer's uncle. She was born on 14 November 1859 to Giuseppe Verdi, shopkeeper and 'retailer of government monopoly commodities', and his wife Maria Romanini, seamstress, whose address was 'No. 48, Roncole'.[24] Her older brother was Carlo Alberto Verdi, born in 1857.[25] On 2 November 1862, when he was just 5, the boy was scalded to death when he pulled a pot of boiling water from the stove.[26] Shortly afterward Filomena was sent to live in Palazzo Cavalli with Carlo Verdi and his aged sister Francesca Verdi Sivelli who kept house for him. In 1865 Verdi and Strepponi began to help Verdi's father, who was overseeing her education, as she was tutored by a local woman whose fees Verdi and Carlo Verdi paid. To Don Avanzi, Strepponi expressed her concern that Filomena's 'good, open' character would be changed by 'the atmosphere in which she lives',[27] that atmosphere being conservative and pious, given Carlo Verdi's strict observance of the rites, his daily attendance at Mass, and his frequent reciting of the Pater Noster.[28] (Some of that 'atmosphere' was very likely offset by Professor Landriani, the tutor, a woman locked in conflict with Don Arfini, the overseer of public education, who was both professor and priest.) Filomena was mentioned frequently in Strepponi's letters to Don Avanzi, Cesare Finzi, and other friends after 1865. Even though she still lived under Carlo Verdi's roof, Strepponi and Verdi followed her progress regularly. Her parents, who had become a man and woman of property in their own right, kept in close touch with Carlo Verdi and his sister while continuing to live in Roncole and raise their other children there. By 1871 they had bought a house of their own, had given up their shop, and may have been living from rents.[29]

As Verdi got ready to go to Paris that autumn, a production of *Macbeth* at La Scala alarmed rather than comforted him. 'Do what you want,' he wrote to Ricordi, who

in Milan, will know better than I do at Sant'Agata whether De Bassini will be able to stand up under that role. You will know whether Stolz is a tragic actress, and magnificently tragic, so as to be able to do Lady (her *Giovanna [d'Arco]* is of no value in deciding). You will know whether the impresario has courage enough to spend money for the scenery and costumes, the intelligence to spend money well, and a commitment to Italian opera—Fie!!!—as he would have for a foreign opera, for example. They will have to perform the opera as it is, without making cuts or adding a single note, and produce the ballet well because it is important.—And then there is the music! Alas! Again yesterday I had a letter from Milan with a warning: 'The productions at La Scala are, as always, impossible.' So watch, judge, and decide.[30]

With Perrin, Verdi was reviewing a possible production of *La forza del destino* in Paris, but he was apprehensive, as he had been in the past, about the soprano who was to sing Preziosilla.

Débutante singers frighten me, and especially in that role, which needs someone who is very much at ease, enormously lively, and possessed of an extraordinary stage presence. I would be less afraid of a débutante as Leonora. As far as the singers go, to whom would we give the part of D. Carlos? If M. Faure refused the role in *Il trovatore* because it was too high, he will not be able to sing D. Carlos. And who will be Alvaro? Gueymard? But I do not know how to compose for him. I wrote *Les Vêpres* just for him, and he was not effective in it; I translated [*sic*] *Le trouvère* for him and it was the same story.[31]

He also became involved in a controversy over a new edition of Verdi's composition *Suon la tromba*, the old Mazzini hymn, which Goffredo Mameli had written. Mazzini believed that he owned all the rights to the piece; he ceded those to a well-meaning publisher in Milan. 'Mameli wrote it because I asked him to: Verdi composed the music because I asked him to. Words and music were thus given to me as my property', Mazzini had written.[32] Verdi, who asked Piave to resolve the matter for him, found himself in the uncomfortable situation of one who seems to stand in the way of a worthy project. When he hedged, the publisher offered him a less attractive option: that of writing a *pièce de circonstance* for the dedication of a monument on the battlefield of Legnano; but Verdi refused this offer as well. 'I would drop the whole matter,' Piave said; but Tornaghi suggested that Verdi write to Mazzini directly about it.[33] If he did, he apparently got no answer. The matter rested.

At about the same time, Verdi learned from Piave that Ricordi had published a text book on the art of singing by Francesco Lamperti, a professor from Milan Conservatory who denounced Verdi as a destroyer of voices. Seeing it, Piave raged:

This is truly infamous, an unspeakable and unmatched [example of] ingratitude. . . . [It says that] after having sung that first time in Venice Signora Loeve [*sic*] was no longer able to sing those very beautiful melodies that she had learned from [Lamperti] before going to Venice!—And those who print these infamous statements are at your feet, constantly adoring you, waiting for four notes to fall from your pen, so they can hoard them up, and go around bragging that they are your patrons!!! Oh, by God, it is really too much.—But wait! Of course it had to be this way, from the moment that that firm began to put out the *Giornale del quartetto*, and publish odes that lamented the decline of Italian music as it was soiling the whorehouse wall.—From this moment when all the walls of Milan are plastered with posters that announce

Macbet	*Amleto*
by	by
Verdi	Faccio

in parallel columns and in the same typeface.[34]

Verdi did not reply directly; but he did get his message across all the same. Strepponi, staying at the Hotel Passarella in Milan, found herself a short walk from her old apartment in Contrada della Cerva and only a few steps from La Scala. Although she had not planned to see Verdi's publisher, he called at her hotel. For two hours, Strepponi delivered the home truths from Sant'Agata —'fresh, clear, logical, bitter truths'—[35] to Tito Ricordi. At the end of the interview, she invited only Piave, with his wife and daughter, to have dinner with her. After Strepponi got home, she sent off a second barrage to Giulio Ricordi, declaring that she had not exaggerated the situation, that Verdi had many doubts about the publisher's conduct, and that everything that went on in Milan was known at Sant'Agata 'because this hovel is not exactly at the edge of the known world!'[36] With this salvo, she and her husband prepared to leave for Paris.

The task Verdi was about to assume was backbreaking, as he knew better than anyone. 'Write for the Opéra, where the performances last half a day? Poor me! What a lot of music, or rather, how many notes!!'[37] The writing would be the smallest part of the job; after the score was completed and the work orchestrated, a harder labour would begin: co-ordinating coaching sessions, room rehearsals, stage rehearsals with piano, orchestral rehearsals, scenery, and costumes. Shortly after he reached Paris, he expressed his usual lack of confidence to Tito Ricordi: 'I am sure that the operas will be staged badly now, just as in the past, and especially at the Théâtre des Italiens. . . . The theatres are bad, as usual.'[38] At the beginning of his visit, accommodation, too, was unsatisfactory. Verdi and Strepponi moved three times in just a few days after they arrived in France, finally settling in at 67 Avenue des Champs Elysées, where the great ballerina Fanny Cerrito lived. They tried four cooks before finding one who could meet their needs, then began to entertain, inviting friends for small receptions and intimate dinners.

Among their guests were Gaetano and Clotilde Fraschini; Enrico Delle Sedie and his wife, Margherita Tizzoni, who had been Strepponi's closest friend at Milan Conservatory; Giorgio Ronconi; and Adelina Patti and her family.

Verdi prided himself on having been enthusiastic about Patti even when she was a girl. He had heard her first in London in 1862, when she was 19. (Verdi believed that she was only 18.) She had a 'perfect balance between singer and actress', he said.

A *born* artist in every sense of the word. When I heard her for the first time in London . . . I was stunned, not only by the marvellous technique, but by several moments in the drama in which she showed that she was a great actress. I remember her chaste, modest behaviour when she sits on the soldier's bed in *La sonnambula* and when she, defiled, rushes out of the Libertine's room in *Don Giovanni*. I remember a certain action in the background during Don Bartolo's aria in *Barbiere*; and more than anything else the rec[itative] before the quartet in *Rigoletto*, when her father shows her her lover in the Tavern, saying 'And you still love him' and she answers 'I love him'. No words can express the sublime effect she achieved when she said these words. . . . She knows that . . . I judged her to be a marvellous actress and singer the first time I heard her in London. An exceptional artist.[39]

The Verdis also called on Rossini and his wife Olympe, who, Strepponi thought, seemed 'more disagreeable than usual'.[40] Just after Christmas, Rossini sent the secretary of the Imperial Conservatory of Music to Verdi, armed with a good-humoured letter of introduction, which Rossini had addressed and signed:

> to M. Verdi
> Celebrated Composer of Music
> Fifth-Class Pianist!!!
> [from]
> your *Sincere* Admirer and Affectionate Rossini
> Former Composer of Music
> Fourth-Class Pianist
> PS Tell Madame Verdi that I am her servant.[41]

While he was in Paris, Verdi heard Wagner's music played for the first time, when the *Tannhäuser* overture was offered on the programme of a popular concert. 'He is mad!' Verdi wrote to Arrivabene.[42] The composer found the new Paris exciting, with its boulevards, avenues, construction projects, and shops. He even admitted to having gone into churches. But Verdi's main business in Paris was *Don Carlos*, as he and his librettists collaborated in the hope of finishing the text before spring. He had known one of the poets, Joseph Méry, for some time. The other was Camille Du Locle, secretary of the Opéra and Perrin's son-in-law.

The Verdis gave one soirée to honour the French sculptor Dantan, who had completed a bust of Verdi for the Paris Opéra. Although he declared that he had not actually 'invited' anyone for the evening, he counted Patti, Fraschini, Delle Sedie, the Tamberlicks, Du Locle, and Ronconi among his guests. As usual, Verdi did not let his music be played or sung. On this occasion, Dantan also showed Verdi the affectionate caricature he had made of him, showing the composer as a lion, seated at the piano with one paw on the keyboard and the other writing music, his long tail curled between his hind legs. A funny, four-line poem inscribed at the bottom hailed Verdi's art. Pleased with the bust, Verdi confided to Ricordi that he thought it was very beautiful and that everyone who had seen it found it marvellous.[43] At Sant'Agata Strepponi put the caricature on the corner of a chest-of-drawers in her room.

During his three-and-a-half month stay in Paris, Verdi kept up with the news from Italy through newspapers, and journals, and letters from friends. Arrivabene had been ill for more than a month at the end of 1865; but he again began to send Verdi his bulletins after New Year's Day, writing from Florence after the capital of Italy moved there. The Chamber of Deputies was in disorder; the government under assault. Common sense had gone on vacation, as the new tax laws encountered resistance everywhere.[44] As the composer had foreseen, he would have to fight many more wars in the name of his artistic integrity, most of them in Italy. Just after New Year's Day of 1865, Piave had sent news of the 'slaughter' of *Il trovatore* at La Scala:

Who is to blame? Many people. First of all, Ricordi, who—greedy to have 40 or 50 francs of rental money—let it be mistreated in all the filthiest theatres; [then] the impresario, and even more, the directors who allowed it to be given at La Scala with impossible artists. At the end of the opera, instead of having the bell, they let someone hit a frying-pan covered with a cloth, that really made the audience jump up in terror. They let the opera finish, but it will not be given again.[45]

Piave also passed on the news that Ricordi would no longer publish the *Giornale del quartetto*, although the publication might be taken over by someone else. The intramural wars at Milan Conservatory were the common gossip of the day.

Piave also wrote to let Verdi know that his brother had been arrested in Venice: 'My poor brother Luigi has been in prison for more than a month on trial for high treason!!! A spy betrayed him. . . . Ah, God! God! God! . . . my Luigi, that *holy patriot*, in those Austrian claws! Oh Verdi, these are immense sorrows.'[46] The Venetian patriots' underground war was but an early warning of the conflict that was to come. Italy had conducted negotiations with both Prussia and Austria simultaneously, in the hope of bringing Venice and the Veneto under the Italian flag; but at the beginning of 1866, Austria still held both. In the new capital of Italy, Florence, scandal and the threat of scandal hung over the Chamber of Deputies. Piroli, who had been elected for the district of Borgo San Donnino, was to be in charge of investigations that might bring down the government.[47]

Verdi followed these events from Paris, where he completed the first act of *Don Carlos* before leaving for Italy in March. After stopping in Nice and Genoa, he stayed two nights in Piacenza before going on home: 'a few hours from now I will be at Sant'Agata, but this time my stay will be terribly hard and tiring. Five acts of an opera, of which I still have four more to do! Auf!!'[48] He had scarcely settled in when he heard news of an unusually poor performance of *La forza del destino* conducted by Mariani in Genoa. The conductor had admitted his company's weakness to Ricordi before the first night, confessing that the Preziosilla was 'about as suited to her role as I am to the Chair of Arabic Languages'.[49] Having had 'very bad news' about the singers, costumes, and sets, Verdi, boiling with indignation, denounced Ricordi, Mariani, and the theatre management in two letters written in three days.

The impresarios don't even bother to make good sets and costumes for our operas! Do you want me to copy some sentences from the letters I received? sentences that concern you, too? 'Instead of recommending two women who were unfit for their roles, at a time when he was not sure of having a company capable of performing [the opera] well, Sig. Ricordi should have refused to give this opera, or taken care that the production was at the level of a great theatre! I ask you why Sig. Ricordi does not provide for Italian composers' operas as Sig. Lucca does for foreign composers' operas? . . . It seems to me that this publisher has gone to sleep. . . . on top of his past earnings!' No, I would not want you to do what Lucca does, but I certainly would like you to act differently than you do. You see that the whole problem with *La forza del destino* is not in the ending, as you wrote to me! Anyway, it is almost impossible to change that ending, and I won't do anything else about it, because I am truly fed up with operas and theatres! I have one more opera to write! if I didn't . . . Who knows (I have faith in my lucky star) whether I won't manage to get out of my contract [in France], as I have formally asked, given the things that have changed at the Opéra. But if, through bad luck, I cannot, it is certain that our business matters will have to conducted in a different way.[50]

Two days later an even angrier Verdi wrote again:

I think that *La forza del destino* would profit from being sung and not *bayed* as it was by that gang of dogs barking in Genoa! What do you think? Do you believe that Lucca would have abandoned it in those conditions, and so close to Milan? Never! Never! Lucca is a bourgeois publisher who lowers himself so far as to take care of the merchandise he buys—ohibò—So banal! An aristocratic publisher [Ricordi] lets it be massacred, proudly whispering 'We don't pay any attention to them' then looks and walks away. What a difference![51]

He also attacked Mariani. 'If the company that was to perform *La forza del destino* was truly that bad, why did you, yes, you, work so hard for your impresario, going so far as to ask Ricordi to lower the rental fees? . . . So my operas were really made to be given to all the dogs?'[52]

The Austro-Prussian War

While Verdi was composing *Don Carlos*, Italy was again engaged in conflict with Austria, during the Austro-Prussian War, which lasted for about seven weeks from 15 June to 23 August 1866. Secret negotiations between Italy and Bismarck's government had led in April to the signing of a treaty that virtually guaranteed Italy the annexation of Venetia and Venice if a war should be fought. Just three weeks after the signing of the agreement, Verdi confided to Escudier that he expected to hear the roar of cannon at any moment. Eight Italian divisions—committed to fight under the treaty—were stationed along the Po, under Cialdini, whom Verdi knew, and twelve divisions along the Mincio near Mantua, where Austria had positioned a large number of the 100,000 men it was said to have in the region. Because Sant'Agata would be at the very front, Verdi said he would probably have to leave, but 'I don't have the heart to abandon Italy.' In this same letter, he sent Escudier the good news that the third act of *Don Carlos* was finished and that he had begun the fourth.[53] The sore throat that had plagued him for four months at the beginning of the year had gone away, at least for the summer.

'So let it be war; and may it be welcome', he wrote to Piroli.

BOOK IV

You know the temper of this neighbourhood, but to tell you the truth, the soldiers [who had been drafted] are leaving fairly willingly. Mothers and young wives cry, fathers and farmers complain, because their strongest farm-hands are being taken away, but really things are going better than one had expected. As far as the priests go, I can tell you that they are behaving decently enough. They don't dare to show their hostility. However, it is certain that if they were to see the tip of a German nose, they would run toward it, with a monstrance, a thurible, and the sacrament!! . . . If there is a war, I am truly in the front line, and I will have to pack up and move, because I surely would be the first target—not of the Germans, but of the priests![54]

By mid-May, it was rumoured that Prince Umberto, who had his general headquarters in Borgo San Donnino, would commandeer one of Verdi's houses, either Palazzo Cavalli or Sant'Agata, for his own lodging; and Verdi genuinely feared that if the Austrian troops crossed the Po, Sant'Agata would be in their path. Verdi wrote to Piroli on 9 June:

I am still here but I will leave when I hear the first cannon-shot, because just the idea that those Austrians could come here would make me run a thousand miles without stopping for breath, so as not to see those ugly mugs. I would go to Genoa for now, and stay there until the last, the very last moment before I ought to and must leave for Paris. I say 'would have to' because leaving Italy at this time weighs heavily on me. It is absolutely true that I am neither young enough nor strong enough to go to war; I am no good at giving advice; and I really am not good for anything. But I still would have stayed here, I would have tried hard, I would have done whatever small good I could, and I would have enjoyed it and suffered with my own people, as so many others have. If the Paris Opéra still belonged to the Maison de l'Empereur I would write to the Minister, asking him to leave me in Italy for now. Perhaps he would have granted me that, anyway, the Maison de l'Empereur would never have sued me. But now that the Opéra is in the hands of an impresario, it is very likely that he would sue if I stayed on here![55]

He asked Piroli for advice and sent good wishes to the statesman's son, who had volunteered to fight in the Veneto.

Among the other young men who had gone off to war were Boito and Faccio, who had volunteered in response to Garibaldi's first call to arms, leaving Milan in May and rushing to Como to join a regiment there. Boito's heroic gesture won him a letter from Victor Hugo: 'Bravo, poet! . . . You are brave. You deserve Venice. You shall have it. And you shall have Rome too. . . . While waiting for news from you, I send you my heartfelt wishes. I am a good Italian, I adore your sunlit land. I salute your noble spirit.'[56] After Garibaldi reviewed his troops, the two young men and their companions-in-arms left for Lecco, Salò, Desenzano, and the Trentino, where in July they fought the Austrians, distinguishing themselves by their courage.

Italy had entered the war on 20 June, its army under La Marmora, who had been named chief of staff. Engaged near Peschiera del Garda, where he had moved many of his troops, the general made a mistake that proved crucial to the Italian cause, underestimating the strength of the Austrian forces stationed between Mantua and Verona. The Battle of Custoza, one of two major Italian engagements, took place on 24 June. Although Austria counted about twice as many dead as Italy did, La Marmora thought that he had been defeated. Retreating with his forces back across the Mincio, he virtually left the field; Cialdini's men never reached the area at all. After Custoza, the Italian fleet faced the Austrians near the island of Lissa, in the Adriatic, only to be defeated. But on 3 July the Prussians, Italy's allies, won a decisive victory over the Austrians at Sadowa, driving Vienna to ask France to intercede to end the war. By the end of July an armistice had been arranged.

Verdi and Strepponi had stayed at Sant'Agata through June and into July, the composer working on *Don Carlos* and corresponding with his librettist Du Locle, Méry having died in 1865. As Luzio remarked in the *Carteggi verdiani*, the letters from this period show once more that Verdi was 'the *dominus*' who managed to have his way even when the libretto was in a foreign language.[57] On 5 July he and Strepponi left the farm and moved to the Hotel Croce di Malta in Genoa, where Verdi learned that Austria had ceded Venice and Venetia not to Italy, but to the Emperor of France. To Escudier he wrote:

Utterly desolate. Is this possible? And what will the Emperor do with it? . . . Will he want to give it to us? But we cannot accept it, and I hope that our ministers will refuse. You don't owe us anything and we don't owe you anything. You, who are so sensitive when it comes to honour, will understand and respect this feeling in others. No: the Emperor can not nor must not accept Venice in any way nor under any circumstances. . . . And Paris is [illuminated for the celebration]!!! No, No, peace has not been concluded and cannot be as things are.

He added that his head was about to burst, he had stopped composing, and that he 'would not know how to write a note. I am ill in a thousand ways.'[58]

BOOK IV

Eight days later, less angry, calmer, but even more determined not to go on with the opera, he wrote to Escudier again about

our situation, horrible inside the country and outside it. Anyway, it is clear to us that France and the great powers do not want to destroy Austria. Now, if Prussia makes peace, we cannot wage war alone: if Prussia refuses to make peace, what will France do? Will it side with Austria? You will say 'That's impossible'; but I add that the *force of events* could drag you in that direction and do something tomorrow that you find impossible today. . . . *Burn, sack*! that is [Austria's] civilizing mission, which it wants to carry on, no matter what the cost.[59]

And to Piroli:

Poor us! The situation is so depressing that I don't even have the strength to curse that horde of inept, stupid, wind-bag, blow-hards who have brought us to ruin. Do we hope for a victory by Cialdini? But is it possible, now that the Austrians are giving up everywhere? . . . And the future? When the Left asks: 'You Moderate Gentlemen, what were you able to do during the six years you governed? A disorganized army without commanders; a non-existent navy; and the economy ruined!'[60]

'This opera was born in fire and flames', Verdi said of *Don Carlos*.[61] Wanting to send 'all the Opéra, Perrin, Paris, and everyone' to hell and go back to Sant'Agata,[62] Verdi asked again to be released from his contract and was refused. The Opéra did not consider the war a case of *force majeure*. So even though he was 'ashamed to keep myself busy with notes in these difficult and anguish-laden moments', he had to go on.[63]

Before leaving Genoa, Verdi agreed to take two floors, a huge space that Mariani had found in Palazzo Sauli Pallavicino, at Strada San Giacomo 13. Apparently there was a verbal understanding but no contract of lease, something that seems almost beyond belief, given Verdi's passion for signed agreements, contracts, and record-keeping. It is difficult to see how this man, who kept accurate accounts on three rams at his *podere* at Casello Piantadoro and five poplars cut for firewood at Due Are could have moved into, restored, and lived for seven years in a house to which he had no legal right. He accepted Mariani's word that the house was his, asked the conductor later about a contract of lease, and then let the matter slip. Verdi paid 3,700 lire a year in rent and sublet about five rooms to Mariani for 400 lire. The house, which stands on a hill and was then surrounded by a fine garden, was the family home of the noble Saulis, whose daughter Luisa was Mariani's friend. A great beauty, she had had her bust sculpted by Bartolini; when Mariani met her, she was the wife of Marquis Pallavicino and the mother of a daughter Teresa, who was caught up in an unhappy marriage with a Marquis Negrotto. The former tenants, a family named Muller or Müller, had moved to England, leaving behind some of their own furniture, which Verdi bought, together with 600 bottles of wine and liquor. The apartment, on the *piano nobile*, had a grand salon, a large room for receptions, a dining-room, morning-room, service areas, and bedrooms for Verdi, Strepponi, staff, and guests.[64]

The First Performance of *Don Carlos*

Knowing, then, that he had a winter residence in Genoa, Verdi left for Paris, but stayed there only a few days before leaving for Cauterets, a spa in the Pyrenees where he intended to take the waters for his chronic sore throat. He went on composing the fifth act of *Don Carlos* without the libretto, which he had forgotten to bring from Paris. Writing from memory while he waited for it to arrive, he used a rented piano in the Hôtel de France, where he and Strepponi took a suite for themselves and a room for their English serving-maid, whom they had brought from Paris. The war notwithstanding, Verdi seemed in good spirits while he was there, inviting Escudier to join him. In August he paid for two expensive, heavy evening coats, which he gave to Strepponi as a gift. He even joked with the hotel maid who brought them breakfast, asking her if Cauterets produced a magic water that would fill his purse when it was empty.[65] She took him seriously and answered 'No, Monsieur, never.' He stayed at the spa until mid-September, corresponding with Du Locle about the libretto. The composer left Cauterets for Paris with the fifth act virtually finished. On the way back to the capital, Verdi and Strepponi stopped briefly in Pau to see the chateau of Henri IV, then went on to Bordeaux as guests of a family they had met in Cauterets.

Settled again in their apartment at 67 Avenue des Champs Elysées, they began to entertain at simple dinner parties, while Verdi spent much of his time at the Opéra during the day. It rained constantly. He was 'drowning in music' and 'engulfed in rehearsals', he confided to Arrivabene.[66] Hoping to get *Don Carlos* staged by mid-December, he added that he doubted that would be possible. As for Italy and her woes, he had closed his eyes, so as not to see. That France had ceded Venice and the Veneto to Italy, Verdi considered a national disgrace, for the territory had not been won in war. But for the moment, he put politics aside. From Paris, he managed his affairs at Sant'Agata through his correspondence with Paolo Marenghi, the estate manager, and his plans for future productions of his operas in his letters to Ricordi. A very poor *Un ballo in maschera* in Venice left him more discouraged than usual about the way his work was offered to the Italian public:

Ballo was new for Venice and the whole province, which has many, many theatres; and the publisher should have been very careful not to put such important matters in jeopardy. Very bad singers; musical performance even worse. To sum up: if you refuse the rights to *Don Carlos*, I will thank you; if you insist on having the rights for Italy, you will have to give me ironclad guarantees so that this opera, too, will not be massacred.[67]

Verdi felt that Ricordi should have stopped La Fenice from performing *Un ballo in maschera*. In an attempt to exercise maximum control over his music, Verdi stipulated that Ricordi might have the rights to *Don Carlos* for Italy, but that the opera would have to be performed exactly as he had written it for Paris, in five acts, with the ballet. Impresarios were free to add another ballet before or after the opera, but could not perform it between any two acts of *Don Carlos*. He insisted on two major singers for Elisabeth and Eboli, an important tenor and baritone for Don Carlos and Posa, two first-ranking basses for Filippo and the Inquisitor, and a good comprimario bass for Charles V. 'The orchestra to be enlarged by adding all the instruments mentioned in the score.' Ricordi would pay the composer the usual 40 per cent of all rental fees, not just for ten years, as the publisher had before, but 'for as long as our Law provides'. Beyond that, Verdi stipulated conditions for payment of thirty thousand francs in a flat sum and one half of the fee he had paid for the libretto and of the cost of the translation.[68] When Ricordi attempted to hold Verdi to an old agreement that gave the publisher rights for Spain and Germany, he stood his ground, arguing that Ricordi now had acquired rights to the Veneto and Venice, which made up for the loss of the two foreign countries. 'So if you can profit from Venice, then let me keep my rights in the other countries.'[69] When Ricordi pleaded for understanding because of financial problems, he got a sharp answer:

you are wrong when you tell me about your poverty and damages suffered, as if my operas were the cause of your disaster. So then why do you buy them? who forces you to buy them? . . . Allow me to say that I would not be very unhappy if my works were in the hands of someone who would pay more attention to making them successful. The matter of *Un ballo in maschera* in Venice was a scandal! Look for a moment at the way Lucca made sure that *L'africana* would always be performed well. And now when the directors of La Fenice asked him for *La Juive* and *Faust*, the first stipulation was that there should be an orchestral director. Only then, when Lucca found out that the directors were negotiating with Muzio, did he decide against his own director, because he would have someone better in Muzio. You yourself were satisfied with Faccio, whom no one knew, as orchestral director. . . . Now the damage is done, and if I were permitted to give you some advice, to make up in part for the damage done, I would say: 'Seize the first chance you have to join your interests to Lucca's, and make one, single, large firm.[70]

As December wore on, Verdi's mood deteriorated, provoking Strepponi to sit down on Christmas Eve and write in her diary: 'Dinner at Mr Du Locle's. We were not there because of Verdi's sore throat. Discussion about the furniture for Genoa. It is curious to see that every year at Christmas and during the big holidays, when all men act better toward their wives, Verdi, who is always kind, becomes difficult.'[71] Part of his irritability was surely generated by the rehearsals at the Opéra; part may have been caused by worry over affairs at home, although his father's health had seemed to improve in December. The tutor continued to teach Filomena; Marenghi managed the farm and took care of Verdi's father as well. Muzio, who had returned from the United States with a bride, a young singer named Lucy Simons, had gone on to Venice, where he was to direct the Carnival season at La Fenice. In Genoa, Mariani, busy as director of the orchestra at the Carlo Felice, had been assigned the job of decorating Verdi's new apartment, getting the old furniture dusted and polished, moving the new furniture in, hanging the draperies, laying the carpets, and seeing that the house was kept clean while Verdi and Strepponi were away. To make his life easier, Mariani slept in the apartment he was preparing for Verdi.

I have just got out of bed after having slept for the first time in [Verdi's] future home: the enchanting Palazzo Sauli [on the hill] in Carignano. What a happy coincidence! Last night *Rigoletto* opened at the Carlo Felice, with such a triumph as I have never seen in this theatre. You can imagine how happy I was to be able to walk into the winter *nest* of Maestro Verdi for the first time.[72]

The conductor was so conscientious about having everything in perfect order that he placed a stereopticon and its packet of photographs on a table in the salon with Ricordi's calling card on top of it, the gewgaw being a gift from the publisher. Mariani kept Strepponi informed about the progress of furnishing and decorating in eighteen letters, some of which run to more than twenty pages. He dismissed his own apartment in a few words: 'I will only need four or five rooms, including one for my servant, plus the kitchen; I could furnish others for my friends, if they should come, and that would make me happy, because it would seem that I had a large apartment for myself.'[73] He had not arranged definitely with Verdi how much space he would have and said he would make do with just two rooms and an entrance hall until he had been told how much of the house he could have. If Verdi and Strepponi were willing to sublet the entire top floor to him, he would pay 600 francs a year in rent to them. 'Again I tell you, O my Signora Peppina, that it is such an honour for me to be able to have my *nest* under your and Verdi's roof, to be able to live in such a lovely location and to be *the guardian of Verdi's house*, that I truly don't know how to be grateful enough to you for the enormous favour that you wished to bestow on me.'[74] He spent Christmas and New Year's Day putting the finishing touches on Verdi's new residence, even having the beds made up with new linen and blankets, then providing white cotton coverings for everything, so the place would not be dusty when Verdi got there.

Because of delay in the preparation of *Don Carlos*, Verdi stayed in Paris well into March. Plunged into a depression by Carlo Verdi's death on 14 January 1867, he stopped attending rehearsals and went into seclusion, refusing to see anyone. The old man died in Palazzo Cavalli at 11 p.m.; the next morning Filomena's father, Giuseppe Verdi of Roncole, 'man of property, age 39', officially reported the death. Because he could not leave Paris, Verdi asked Carrara to make arrangements for the funeral and for burial in the church cemetery of Vidalenzo, beside Luigia Uttini Verdi. His grief was real:

Oh certainly certainly I would have wanted to close that old man's eyes, and it would have been a comfort for him and for me! Now I cannot wait to get home and see how they are taking care of those two poor creatures left behind: an old woman of 85 [Francesca Verdi Sivelli], and a little girl of 7 [Filomena]. Imagine! in the hands of two servants who, you might say, are *masters* in the house![75]

Verdi ended this letter to Arrivabene with news that the *Don Carlos* rehearsals were going well enough, though slowly, and that he hoped to open on 22 February, but was not able to meet his schedule. Some of his worry over the situation at home was allayed when he learned that Angiolo Carrara had taken Filomena into his house. Later in 1867 she went back to her parents in Roncole.[76]

Soon after Verdi's father's death, the composer had an odd visitor in Cesare Orsini, half-brother of the Italian anarchist-patriot Felice Orsini who had been guillotined in Paris after his failed attempt to assassinate Napoleon III in 1858. It is possible that Verdi had met Felice Orsini in Rome during the uprising of 1849, when Verdi became the voice of the people with *La battaglia di Legnano* and Orsini was elected deputy under the new Roman constitution. Now, years later, Cesare Orsini sent Verdi an urgent appeal for help, as he feared that he would be deported from France by the police. Although Verdi was receiving no one, he agreed to see Orsini, who asked him for the money he needed to get safely out of France. The composer advised him to leave at once without contacting the authorities and 'opened a kind of cupboard, took out a copper canister . . . full of 20-franc pieces and said 'Take what you need.'[77] Orsini took 200 francs and left, not to be heard from again until the 1880s.

Verdi struggled on with the opera, which had eight dress rehearsals, instead of the one or two that were customary in Italian houses. During one of these, in mid-February, a journalist from *Le Figaro* hid in one of the boxes and watched the third act of *Don Carlos*. On 17 February he published his report on Verdi at work: 'that pale man who was the brain, the creator, and the poet of that great music drama'.

With the lights down, the only living things in that huge hall were the stage and that orchestra, which has been expanded just for this opera. Above the players' heads, above the violins and bright brasses, you could see Georges Hainl's tousled hair and disordered moustaches. The conductor, baton in hand, like a colonel before the attack, studied his soldiers as they crouched in the trench.

Directly in front of him, almost hypnotizing him with his flashing eyes, was Verdi, seated on a straight chair, his large white hands resting on his knees, motionless, like some Assyrian god, thoughtful, listening with his whole being, completely absorbed in that music, which had come—vibrant and alive—from his heart. He is a tall man, healthily thin, with the shoulders of Atlas, looking as if he could support mountains [on them]. His long, shaggy, thick hair, tossed across his forehead in heavy locks, his beard, mottled black, like a cock's tailfeathers, but splashed with a bit of gray at the chin. Two deep lines down his cheeks, an emaciated face, thick eyebrows, electrifying eyes; a large mouth, that is bitter and contemptuous; a proud, masculine air; and a defiant attitude. . . . Signor Perrin, restless in his box, left, went through the hall to the stage, came back to the rear of the theatre to hear from some distance away, met Sig. Du Locle, author of the libretto, made remarks, listened to others. Ah! the evening before battles! And in the midst of all this churning around, Verdi, alone, at his post, thoughtful, remained still, waiting. . . . He listened: all his being, all the power of that iron character is focused on one single thing. He hears twice as much, three times as much as others, questions everything, hears—even in that heavy score—the faintest note; he hears the chorus and the brasses together, gets up, leaps, encouraging all those groups valiantly, and exclaims, with that Italian accent that makes his voice fascinating:

'There is a rest there! Come on! Quick!'

People are singing downstage, but he is talking to two members of the chorus in the back:

'Eh! Eh! There is a mark over that note!'

Over here: 'Quick! Come on!' And over there : 'Softly! Lovingly!'

He gets up, beats the time, snaps his thumb against his middle finger; and that sharp noise, so quick, nervous, like the noise of castanets, can be heard over the orchestra and the chorus; it excites them and moves them along like the snapping of a whip. Then there are his hands, which he claps together; he is music from head to foot, fighting for his own ideals, pouring his artistic genius into those men, those women, searing them with his own flame, which burns him, too; striking the stage floor with his heels, running upstage, stopping the choristers, seeking his own true meaning in that chaos, out of which a whole world is born.

So here is a man who is rich, honoured, glorious, who from his art can only expect new tribulations, more fatigue, laurels won with the greatest difficulty, triumphs paid for with disappointments and sleepless nights, and rage. He has an income of 80,000 francs a year; his name sent a message of freedom to his country, a call to arms. . . . In the theatre, he fights for something better. So he goes on, struggles, works. He carries his burdens like an athlete. When people talk to him about his celebrity, he says 'I am just a peasant.' So be it. He is one of those peasants who win battles and discover new worlds.[78]

When, during the last rehearsals, Verdi found that the opera was too long to meet the Opéra's requirements, he cut out about fifteen minutes of music, including the introduction, with the Woodcutters' Chorus and an exchange between Elisabeth and the people. He also cut a duet for Posa and Philip in the fourth act; a duet between Elisabeth and Eboli was perhaps cut earlier.[79] The opera had its première on 11 March, conducted by Hainl, who had taken over *Les Vêpres siciliennes* for Verdi in 1855. The cast included Louis-Henri Obin as Philippe II; the tenor Jean Morère as Don Carlos; Jean-Baptiste Faure as Rodrigue, the Marquis of Posa; Marie-Constance Sass as Elisabeth de Valois; Pauline Gueymard as Eboli; and the bass David as the Grand Inquisiteur. The first night was a gala evening with the Emperor, the Empress, the Princess Matilde, ambassadors, ministers, and other court luminaries in the audience. The opera was modestly successful on the first night; four pieces were encored during the second performance; the third night went even better. Verdi, who had exhausted himself while getting *Don Carlos* on stage, viewed the event philosophically, as he wrote to Piroli: 'It did not have the success I had hoped for. Perhaps in the future my hopes will be realized, but I don't have time to wait and I am leaving tomorrow night for Genoa.[80] Muzio sent his own report to Ricordi: 'As soon as the *real* audience—that is, the audience that catches fire, cries—gets a chance to hear that music, its success will increase, becoming gigantic.'[81] Bizet, in a letter to his friend Paul Lacombe, concluded: 'Verdi is no longer Italian. He wants to do Wagner. He no longer has his own shortcomings, nor even one of his good qualities. The fight is over for him. . . . Perhaps the singers will forgive him for this unfortunate attempt . . . but the audience came to be entertained and I think they won't let him get away with this.'[82] The reviews would be poor, he thought. In fact, they were not, although the critics were not unanimous in their praise.

In the *Journal des débats*, Reyer compared Verdi's individual style to a precious possession, declaring that in *Don Carlos* he had not lost his most valuable and particular qualities. Summarizing the audience's reaction to the individual numbers, he also mentioned the 'delicacy' of Verdi's orchestration, which he found unusual and welcome.[83] Théophile Gautier wrote in *Le Moniteur* that Verdi had undergone a 'conversion' to modern music in 'building' *Don Carlos*, 'his vast and colossal structure'.[84] The composer had realized that if his work were to survive, he would have to 'gather inspiration from the newest art forms' and leave the old behind. The importance of the event for Italy was quickly perceived by Mariani, who felt that

Verdi's triumph was immense and worthy of his great genius. We Italians really needed this victory, because our government and generals did not know how to do their duty during the wretched times we lived through last year. Foreigners, too, will no longer say that we have degenerated in the field of music, too, from the time of our glorious forebears. So Viva Verdi, who knows how to raise the flag of Italian musical genius right in the heart of Europe.[85]

Don Carlos went on doing well, as the Opéra management telegraphed to Verdi after the second and third performances. In fact, it was performed forty-three times.

Verdi and Strepponi, who had left Paris on 14 March, even before the second performance, settled into their new apartment in Genoa, part of which they found in the perfect order Mariani had arranged for them. Verdi described to Arrivabene the new place he had 'rented in Carignano Palazzo Sauli Pallavicino. The apartment is magnificent and the view stupendous and I am counting on passing fifty years here.'[86] And to Escudier, after two trips to Sant'Agata to oversee the spring planting in his garden, Verdi said: 'It's true that this seems like paradise after having had so much to do for eight months at the Opéra.'[87] He had read the excerpts from the French reviews in Ricordi's *Gazzetta musicale*, but was far from pleased:

So I am an almost perfect Wagnerite! But if the reviewers had paid a bit of attention, they would have recognized that the same intent was there in the *Ernani* trio, the sleepwalking scene of *Macbeth*, and in many other pieces. But the question is not whether *Don Carlos* belongs to some system, but whether the music is good or bad. That question is neat, simple, and, above all, just.[88]

He doubted that the singers in Paris had put their all into his score, questioning whether they were enthusiastic over it, or short on inspiration, or just indifferent.

With Mariani living in the second apartment in Palazzo Sauli Pallavicino, Verdi had a direct channel to the current music business of the day that he had not had at Sant'Agata. Having denounced the anaemic, frigid Paris audience, he could now look forward to productions of *Don Carlos* on home soil, as Mariani argued that the intelligent, responsive audience in Bologna would welcome the work and the management of the Teatro Regio in Turin pleaded to have it. *Don Carlos* was also to have its first London performance in the summer of 1867. Mariani, who had been away from Bologna in 1862 and 1863, returned there in 1864 and began building on his past successes. The Teatro Comunale was about to reopen after being closed for restoration, with its excellent orchestra and chorus which, as the conductor said, gave him satisfaction and the joy of seeing works well done. He proposed two 'very fine' women,[89] the Austrian soprano Antonietta Fricci and the Italian mezzo-soprano Isabella Galletti-Gianoli for Elisabetta and Eboli respectively, Fraschini as the tenor, Cotogni or Graziani as the baritone, and Medini and Bagaggiolo for the two great bass roles. Fricci, born Frietsche, had made her Italian début in *La traviata*, had sung Leonora in *Il trovatore* many times, and was respected as one of the finest artists of her generation, not just in Italy, but in Lisbon, Moscow, and London as well. Her dramatic gifts were welcome in *Les Huguenots*, *La Juive*, and *L'Africaine*; her agility of voice made her a renowned Norma. The Bolognese Galletti-Gianoli had built her reputation in Verdi's operas in Genoa, London, Madrid, and Milan. When Mariani recommended her because she was a true mezzo-soprano, she was the best Azucena on the Italian stage. Mariani made his case in other letters to Ricordi, urging the publisher to insist on Fricci, but he also wrote: 'What news have you had about La Pascal? I know Stolz. Try everything you can to get Fricci.'[90] Again, at the end of April, 'I tell you frankly that for the role of *Elisabetta*, we have to stay with Fricci. . . . Stolz is a fairly good artist, she has enough voice to be able to come off well; but Fricci is still preferable; indeed, one of Fricci's legs is worth all of Stolz.'[91] In other letters, he passed in review a dozen or more singers who were capable of filling the major roles.

By May, with Bologna pressing for a final cast, the conductor staunchly defended Verdi's interests:

But in the name of God! can't we find a dependable tenor in Italy, for a fall season? . . . Listen, my Tito, we are talking about Maestro Verdi, the greatest, the only living composer in Italy. The artists themselves should be in glory if they are in the first performance here of his masterpiece. My God! I would die of sorrow if I were to see this sublime artistic creation threatened because of inadequate singers. . . . If Stolz is not yet under contract for Trieste, I believe we could get her for Bologna. . . . She would be the only one who could do *Elisabetta*, since we cannot get anyone any better.[92]

At this point, negotiations with other sopranos had broken down. But even at this juncture, with the production only four months off, he still asked Ricordi to find out whether the soprano singing Elisabetta in London would be available for Bologna. Stolz was clearly a last choice. Verdi gave his own instructions for the chorus and orchestra but left most of the casting to Ricordi and Mariani.

Strepponi's Meeting with Clara Maffei and Barezzi's Death

In the spring Strepponi stayed on in Genoa, overwhelmed, as she said, by the dust and rags that filled up every corner of the enormous apartment. Her days were taken up with stonemasons, drapers, carpenters, painters, and workmen whom she had to handle alone, since Verdi had decided to 'stay and plant cabbages in the Athens of Italy, that is, near Busseto'.[93] She and Verdi were thinking seriously about adopting Filomena, 'a dear little girl 7 years old', she wrote to De Sanctis who had never heard of the child before.[94] Verdi's aunt Francesca had died in April in Palazzo Cavalli.

In May, while Strepponi was on her way from Sant'Agata to Locate, where her mother and sister were still living, she took her courage in her hands, and, without announcing herself in advance, paid a social call on Clara Maffei in Milan. All the details of the visit are found in Strepponi's and Verdi's letters to Maffei that May. Courage was indeed needed, for in the previous three years Strepponi had put on a great deal of weight and had begun, she thought, to look just like a housewife. She admired the diaphanous countess for her figure and grace. She drove up to Maffei's house, handed the manservant a photograph of Verdi, said that she was the wife of the man in the photograph, and asked to see the Countess. Unorthodox, generous, and good-hearted as she was, Maffei threw her arms around Strepponi's neck and kissed her over and over again, taking her by the hand and drawing her into her salon. Strepponi, who had lived far from Milanese society for more than twenty years, scarcely knew what to say, but carried the visit off well. 'Let's go together to see Manzoni,' Maffei suggested. The two women went off together to visit 'the Saint' of Via Morone; both were able to kiss the hands of the man whom they considered a genius. Strepponi wrote an effusive letter of thanks to Maffei, declaring that she could barely believe that she had been so daring as to call as she had.

But when I glance at those precious things lying here on my writing-table, . . . my shame passes and, in spite of my rotundity, I jump up with joy, I kiss your note and the violet and the ivy; then, seeing the portrait of Manzoni, my eyes fill with tears, I am calm, but I feel such a consolation in this emotion, that is respectful tenderness, with which no worldly celebration on earth could compare.[95]

A few days later she had the joy of telling Verdi of her experience, as she wrote to Maffei:

He was waiting for me at the station in Alseno, with little Filomena; and as soon as we were in the carriage, he asked me about my family and what I had done about the furniture for Genoa in Milan. I told him that I had gone all over the city without finding anything that I wanted, that I had seen Ricordi, Piave, and . . . that if he had given me a letter for you, I, although I was short of time, would have delivered it, in spite of a certain revulsion I feel for my excess weight, which, for the last three years, has kept me from sitting among the ladies. While he, laughing, was referring to me using the fine epithet 'capricious' (you don't use that except to young women, and I have not been that for a long time), I very,

very slowly pulled your note from my purse, I threw it on his knees, and as soon as he had glanced at it, he showed me a huge row of teeth, including his wisdom teeth! As quickly as I could, I told him in a rush just how you welcomed me; how you went out with me (something extraordinary for you to do); how I was foolish to wait for so many years before meeting you; and he went on saying 'That doesn't surprise me; that doesn't surprise me; I know Clarina.' Wanting to go ahead full steam, I said, pretending to be casual, 'and then if you will go to Milan, you can introduce yourself to Manzoni. He is waiting to see you, and I was there with [Maffei] the other day.' Pouff! at this point the bomb was so big and so unexpected that I didn't really know whether I should open the windows of the carriage and give him air, or whether I should close them, afraid that in the shock of his surprise and joy he might jump out! He turned red, pale, sweaty; he took off his hat, he twisted it so much that he almost turned it into a bun. Then (and let this stay between us) the terribly severe and incredibly proud bear of Busseto had his eyes filled with tears, and both of us, overcome and shaken with emotion, kept completely silent for ten minutes.

The power of genius, of goodness, and of friendship! Thanks again, my good Clarina, from Verdi and from me.[96]

Verdi, who had written to Clara Maffei from Paris in March, let her know in May that he was open-mouthed with surprise at Strepponi's visit, although before Strepponi left Sant'Agata, he had offered to write a note of introduction to Maffei for her.

'No,' she answered, 'do you think that I, big as I am, and looking like a housewife as I do, want to introduce myself to a very elegant lady, a wisp, who lives an exciting life, etc., etc. . . . Let's not talk about it again' and I who have so little faith (forgive me, without making any exceptions for the gentle sex) believed her this time. . . . You women are awful devils! However, I do love this kind of courage, which embarrasses no one, and if you are happy, I am very, very happy; Peppina is happy, and for three days has talked only of you, with such tenderness and friendliness, as if you had known each other for twenty years. . . . How I envy my wife for her having seen that Great Man! but I don't know whether I will have the courage to introduce myself to him, even if I come to Milan. You know perfectly well how much I revere that man, who, I think, wrote not only the greatest book of our time, but one of the greatest books that has come from the human mind. It is not just a book, but a consolation for the human race. I was 16 when I read it first. Since then, I have read many books, even some of the most famous ones, about which—when I reread them—I changed or even set aside completely my original opinion; but my enthusiasm for that book is still unchanged, or rather—now that I know men better—is even greater. That is to say that it is a *true* book, as true as *truth* itself. Oh, if artists would only understand this '*true*' once and for all, there wouldn't be any more musicians *of the future* and of the past; no realist, purist, or idealistic painters; no classical and romantic poets; but just true poets, true painters, true musicians.[97]

Manzoni had sent Verdi a photograph inscribed: 'To Giuseppe Verdi, the glory of Italy, from a decrepit Lombard writer.' The composer then entrusted to Clara Maffei a photograph of himself for Manzoni. On it, he had written: 'I respect and revere you as a man, as much as anyone can respect and revere a person, both as a man and as the true honour of this, our still troubled *patria*.'[98]

After her stay in Milan, Strepponi returned to Genoa to go on supervising the renovation there. From Palazzo Sauli, she wrote again to Maffei. After a lengthy and ironical account of the joys of living in the country, she continued:

I want to let you know that you will be receiving my portrait photograph, which is the last extremely precious copy of the six made in Russia . . . I say 'precious' because after conferring with my honest friend, the mirror, I promised it not to have any more made. Accept it, then, with a kind heart, as I offer it, and put it away in a dark place so the light won't change the colours and shape of that magnificent estate manager, who has the nerve to send you her portrait. Verdi sends you his photograph, and here things change. You can put it in the brightest light! It is the portrait of a man who honours his country with his genius and his character! It is the portrait of one of your most honest friends![99]

She added that Verdi refused to send his photograph to Filippi, who has asked for it, because although he was happy to send one to friends, he refused to give them away to enemies, who could go out and buy one if they wished. Verdi had framed Manzoni's photograph and arranged the ivy from Manzoni's garden around the frame. Strepponi also added news of Filomena, who might be staying with her and Verdi in the future, and sent regards to the Ricordis. At the end of the letter, she asked Maffei, whom she had known for less than a month, to go to the upholsterers to look at and sit in the armchairs she had seen, to check on whether they were really comfortable or not. She also asked her to urge Righini, the upholsterer, to hurry the order of her bedroom furniture for Genoa, to do an especially good job, and to give it to her 'cheap' and 'at reasonable prices'.

While Strepponi stayed in Genoa, Verdi went back and forth to Sant'Agata on the train. In the country, his main concern was his irrigation system, for even while he was in Paris he had learned that some of the conduits had been damaged during the winter.

The above-mentioned maestro got the idea of building a steam engine to draw water from a little river that flows near his house: to accomplish this, he needed an underground pipe, laid 6 metres down, for a length of 25 metres, and a well almost 7 metres deep. At that depth you find a lot of water and sand that make the job extremely difficult. This illustrious maestro can be found every day at the bottom of the excavation to encourage the workers a bit, to prod them on, and, above all, to give them directions. Give them directions?!!! And this is the Signor Maestro's weak point. If you tell him that *Don Carlos* isn't worth anything, he won't give a damn, but if you say he is not a good stonemason's helper, he takes it very badly.[100]

After the middle of June Strepponi returned to Sant'Agata, while Mariani, who had begun to have symptoms of urinary tract disease, went to Montecatini to take the waters. Antonio Barezzi was ill in Busseto and was not expected to live. Clara Maffei's sympathetic letter gave Verdi a chance to share his grief with this close friend.

Oh this loss will be dreadfully sad for me! For the last three or four days he has been better, but I see that it is just temporary relief that will keep him alive for a few days, nothing more! Poor old man, who loved me so much!! And poor me, who will see him for just a short time longer and then will never see him again!!! You know that I owe him everything, everything, everything. And to him alone, and not to others, as people wanted it to seem. I can still see him (and it was many, many years ago) when I had finished my studies at the Ginnasio in Busseto [and] my father told me that he would not be able to pay my way at the University of Parma; and I decided to go back to the village where I was born. This good old man, when he heard this, said to me: '*You are born for something better, and you were not made to sell salt and be a farm-worker; Ask the Monte di Pietà for the meagre scholarship of 25 francs a month for four years, and I will do the rest; you will go to Milan Conservatory, and when you can, you will pay me back the money spent for you.*' That is what happened! You see how generous, how understanding, and how good. I have known a lot of men, but never anyone any better! He loved me as much as he loved his children, and I loved him as much as I loved my father![101]

Strepponi also wrote to Maffei about 'poor Signor Antonio', who was 'still in a pitiable state'.

The other evening they called us at midnight; we left in a rush for Busseto and found him so much worse that certain of his *inordinately concerned* relatives thought it a good idea to keep a priest there! . . . About two in the morning, his fever went down, and the dear old man recovered a bit. This morning Verdi and I went to work as drapers, fixing a green curtain so that air could circulate in the room, without his being bothered by the light. If you could see how he looks at us, with his eyes filled with love! how he seizes our hands, when we are about to leave, as if he could keep us with him by force![102]

During the first week of July Verdi was unapproachable. In a diary, which Strepponi kept for a short while that summer, she wrote:

1 July. There are certainly actions that are repellent to the conscience of an honest person, but that careful consideration would indicate that we should do; and perhaps women, who don't hesitate to use certain little tricks, do these things and are right to do them. So that being a hypocrite, a flirt, [and] simpering works more or less with all men. To devote oneself to one man alone can be admirable in theory; in practice, it is a mistake. I try to raise Verdi's spirits because of his illness, which perhaps his nerves and his imagination make him think is more serious [than it is]. He says that I do not believe him, that I laugh, etc., etc., and blames me for it. He is subject to intestinal inflammation, and his craziness, his running back and forth, and the work these days on the machine [for irrigation] and his innate restlessness cause him some stomach upsets. Many, many times he comes into my room but does not stay quietly there ten minutes. Yesterday he came and, as usual, especially these days, got up the minute after he sat down. I said to him: 'Where are you going?' 'Upstairs.' And since he usually does not go there, I answered: 'To do what?' 'To look for Plato.' 'Oh, but don't you remember that it is in the book cupboard in the dining-room?' It seems to me that the questions and answers were normal, and, as for me, I thought only about not seeing him in peace, as he needs to be, and saving him some useless steps.—If only I had not said this! It was a serious matter, planned, and almost an abuse of power!

Also he is angry against the servants and me, so that I don't know what words and what tone of voice to use if I have to speak to him, so as not to offend him! Alas! I don't know how things will end, because he is steadily becoming more restless and angry.—To have such fine qualities and to have a character that is sometimes so abrasive and difficult! The copies of some of the letters in this book prove that he sometimes has faith in my character and believes that I have some intelligence. Sometimes, recognizing the return address and handwriting of a friend, I ask him 'How is he?'—I just have to be careful not to offend him and give him the idea that I am sticking my nose in where I shouldn't! Isn't this just too much sensitivity and contentiousness?

2 July. Again this evening an uproar over a window left open and over my attempt to calm him down! He became furious saying that he wants to send all the servants away, that I take their part, that they do not do their duty, and that what he says is absolutely right. But God! he looks at these servants' faults through a magnifying glass; furthermore, they need someone to look after their interests a

bit, because, poor devils, they are not bad, given the horde of corrupt servants! May God make him calm down, because I am suffering very, very much from this and am becoming utterly confused.

3 July. The last time Marcellino [Demaldè] went to Busseto, he went to Maddalena [Barezzi] and cried desperately because he is afraid that he will not be kept on here much longer, because the master lets him know that he is dissatisfied. He does whatever he can, and if he fails, it is because he is afraid, not because he doesn't want to do right; if he were to have to leave here, he would be so desperate that he would leave town because he loves his Masters![103]

One can easily believe that Verdi was half-mad with grief. 'This is an accursed year, like 1840', he had declared, even before Barezzi became so ill.[104] Barezzi died at eleven-thirty in the morning of 21 July. At his side were his wife, Verdi, Strepponi, and Fortunato Merli, his son-in-law, from whose family Verdi had bought Sant'Agata.

The husband of Antonio and Maria Barezzi's youngest daughter Amalia, Merli went to report the death to the city authorities while Verdi and Strepponi went home. We do not know whether Verdi attended the funeral or not. Strepponi let Corticelli know about the death and also wrote to Clara Maffei, to whom she said that Barezzi had died 'in our arms' and that his 'last word, his last look were for Verdi, his poor wife, and for me' and begged her friend to 'weep with us and pray for peace for the soul of this man, whom we loved so, so much'.[105]

Verdi, writing to Arrivabene four days after Barezzi's death, said

Sorrows follow upon sorrows with terrifying speed! Poor Signor Antonio, my second father, my benefactor, my friend, the man who loved me so very, very much, has died! The fact that he was so old does nothing to lessen my grief, which is immense! Poor Signor Antonio! If there is a life after death, he will see whether I loved him and whether I am grateful for all that he did for me. He died in my arms; and I have the consolation of never having made him unhappy.[106]

He also wrote to Piroli:

He recognized me almost until the last half-hour before his death! Poor Signor Antonio! You know what he was to me and what I was to him; and you can imagine my grief. The last tie that bound me to this place is broken! I wish I were thousands of miles from here. Addio.[107]

BOOK V

28

~

August 1867–January 1870

Don Carlo in Bologna and Milan

After Barezzi's death, Verdi stayed on at Sant'Agata for about two weeks before leaving for Genoa, where he and Strepponi joined Mariani in Palazzo Sauli-Pallavicino. During the summer Mariani had been invited to become the director of the famous Liceo Musicale in Bologna and orchestra director at the Teatro Comunale; but he had refused these important offers to stay with 'that Angel Verdi', who—as he wrote to Ricordi, had 'set up his house in Genoa to be with me.' No matter what the cost, he would not leave the city when 'the Great Maestro, my precious friend' was about to move into the house they shared. He offered to go to Bologna for a short season, preferably in the autumn, or to direct the planned *Don Carlo*.[1]

This was loyalty indeed, for Verdi had reached a point in his life where he considered his career 'finished or almost finished'[2] and had not had a solid box-office success since *Un ballo in maschera*. He had turned down an offer to compose a new opera for St Petersburg. Beyond that, he needed to recover from his 'grief and the terrible effort spent on *Don Carlo*'.[3] He, Strepponi, and Mariani were planning to leave for Paris in mid-August, so that the conductor could see *Don Carlo*, which was still on at the Opéra. Stolz, who was under contract to sing in the Bologna production in the autumn, had gone to Paris herself in July to hear the opera.[4] She had sung in Parma at the Teatro Regio during the entire Carnival season of 1866–7, while Verdi was in Paris producing *Don Carlos*, and had no engagements for the summer.[5]

Verdi, in a bad humour, went ahead from Genoa to Turin, from where he sent two cantankerous letters to his farm-manager Paolo Marenghi.

BOOK V

Earlier the composer had blamed Marenghi for damage done to the large water-pipes of the irrigation system. Now, he was taking no chances:

Why did you have them run the [irrigation] machine when I gave express orders that it should not be touched until I got back? Well, I would like to know once and for all whether you want to follow my orders or not! You will never know either how to *give orders* or how *to obey*!! It is time to put an end to these disorders; and I absolutely want them to come to an end. You were wrong, and Guerino [Balestrieri], to whom I gave the keys, was wrong too, in giving them out. I am leaving for Paris and you send your letters there: *Monsieur Verdi, Poste restante, Paris*, and nothing more.[6]

A second letter one day later took an even harder line.

Everyone is working independently of everyone else: there is no co-ordination; and the management falls to pieces. I am leaving tomorrow for Paris and I repeat again the orders I gave, to see whether once and for all people will listen to me and understand.

1. You (in addition to checking) will keep an eye on the horses and the coachman, in whom I have very little faith [because] of the mess [he made]. Make him walk the horses every two days, without going to Busseto.

2. Tell Guerino that he was wrong to give away the key to the machine and that he should clean it now and close it until I give further orders.

3. Tell the gardener again what I told him. The garden is to be closed: no one is to go in it, nor shall any of the household help leave, except for the coachman for the short time that it takes to walk the horses. If anyone goes out, he has to stay out forever.

I assure you, I am not joking, and I mean now to be master in my own house.[7]

Even when Marenghi wrote to Verdi, his letters did not satisfy his master.

Let me tell you privately that such meaningless letters as you send would be better off not written; . . . you don't say anything at all about my house and my servants. Maybe they are all dead? And how is the coachman? and what is he doing? Is it true that my old coachman Carlo [Piacentini] died in Piacenza? And, by the way, how is the *cholera* around there? I think these are all important matters, and that I have a right to know about them. I will leave Paris at once. Write to me as soon as you get this letter, and answer all my questions.[8]

Some of Verdi's mistrust and irritation may have been justified. Marenghi was young to be in charge of such a large estate; he found himself at a serious disadvantage, working where many of the other employees and servants were older than he was. Guerino Balestrieri, who worked for Verdi for forty years, was a carpenter. Marenghi had watched over Carlo Verdi as well. Menta, who had worked at Sant'Agata since the early 1850s, was living in one of the houses at Piantadoro.

While Verdi was in Paris, he and Strepponi attended the International Exposition several times, until the composer was 'fed up' with it and with music, which he found 'a real torture'.[10] From Ricordi he heard some unpleasant news: the Sicilian composer Vincenzo Moscuzza threatened to sue the publisher over *Don Carlos*, which, he claimed, was taken from his *Don Carlos, infante di Spagna*, a work given in Naples five years before the première of Verdi's opera in Paris.[11]

Mariani had left Paris to start work on *Don Carlo* with the two women who had been chosen for the Teatro Comunale. Of Stolz he wrote that she would do Elisabetta 'very, very well'; Fricci, who had formerly been considered for Elisabetta but would sing Eboli instead, was in 'full command of her gifts. What a consummate artist!'[12] He reassured Verdi as best he could about the company. One of his biggest worries was personal, for he was beginning to have problems with Corticelli, who had left the Ristori troupe and come back to Bologna, where he took it upon himself to go to Mariani's apartment and wake him every morning, and had also begun to criticize the conductor for staying out too late at night. 'He really is a terrible griper; and they tell me that he is a ladies man *par excellence* and that here in Bologna he has old and young mistresses everywhere. If you should write to him, please ask him to leave me alone and to try to act more sensibly.'[13] These words were not such as to please Strepponi. She was Corticelli's close friend and advocate, and very shortly afterwards persuaded Verdi to engage him as a kind of personal secretary and overseer at Sant'Agata, where he took over at the end of October 1867.

In his fifties, 'Maurone' was a big, beefy, blustering man, one of the few people to whom Strepponi wrote confidential letters. The son of a musical and theatrical family in Bologna, he had known Strepponi there, when she, Moriani, Ronconi, Morini, and Teresa Guerrieri-Paradisi were singing together. With his theatrical agency in Bologna and a second office in Peretola, near Florence, Corticelli had even acted for a time as Moriani's agent. Leaving that career, he had become the secretary and general factotum to Ristori, with whom he toured after 1859 in Russia, France, England, Spain, and the United States. Corticelli had occasionally been involved in Verdi's affairs, indirectly through Strepponi, and had been partly responsible for getting the composer his commission to write

La forza del destino. He was one of the few people whom she carried forward into her new life as Verdi's mistress and wife. In 1866, when Corticelli had financial problems, Strepponi had offered to lend him money, telling him that Verdi's generosity toward her at that time would allow her to help him with funds from her own savings. One year later she got Verdi to hire him. The composer, although he found some of the agent's jokes amusing, did not like Corticelli much and soon began to refer to him as gutless or lacking in intelligence. He later suspected Corticelli of conniving with the servants and of trying to seduce one of them. Shortly after he came to the villa to live, Corticelli threatened to create a real scandal by courting Maddalena Barezzi, who had been a widow less than four months. Later, Verdi even believed that Corticelli had conspired with Ricordi to cheat him of his royalties. Mariani called him a thorn; but Strepponi, who claimed that she could see through people as if they were crystal, was blind to his shortcomings.

Don Carlo, as the opera was called in this Italian production, was given for the first time at the Teatro Comunale on 27 October. After years of praising foreign composers, Filippi came out in *La perseveranza* with superlatives for Verdi's new work:

Its success was immense; the execution phenomenal. . . . The first and most important credit for this marvellous triumph is owed to the conductor Angelo Mariani, for whom there are not enough words or praise or epithets: in him, the whole of Verdi's opera is incarnate, because he not only co-ordinated the music and conducted the score, but thought of everything, down to the most miniscule details of the staging. His genius flashed forth from the orchestra—and it is truly genius: one might say that he himself composed another *Don Carlo* within Verdi's *Don Carlo*, with the opulence of his coloration, his fire, and the magic of his sound.[14]

Ghislanzoni, who had become the editor of Ricordi's *Gazzetta musicale di Milano*, described the conductor in equally glowing terms, declaring that Mariani deserved the title of 'Creator' more than anyone else in Italy.[15]

Verdi, happy with this victory, wrote to Escudier about its 'enormous success', adding that 'Everyone says that the execution is marvellous and that there are very, very powerful effects in it. . . . You see that I was right to say that one, single, powerful hand can work miracles.'[16] Mariani's 'miracle' at the Teatro Comunale worked partly because he had two superior artists in the leading female roles, with Fricci as Eboli and Stolz as Elisabetta di Valois. Teresa Stolz was 33 when Mariani chose her for this production. Born in Elbekosteletz (the present-day Kostelec, on the bank of the Elbe, near Prague), she came from a family that sent six of its children to Prague Conservatory. In 1856 she became the pupil of Luigi Ricci, the husband of one of her twin sisters and lover of the other, and was introduced by him in an accademia in Trieste that year. After five seasons in Tiflis and engagements in Odessa, Constantinople, Nice, Granada, and small cities, she made her Italian opera début in Spoleto, at the opening of the new Teatro Comunale, as Leonora in *Il trovatore* in 1864. During the next few years she sang in a number of Italian cities, often under Mariani.[17] She and Mariani were merely colleagues as they were preparing *Don Carlo* in Bologna. But in the spring of 1868, when the soprano sang Amelia in Mariani's production of *Un ballo in maschera* in Genoa, they began to think about marriage. Because Verdi was in Genoa as late as 14 April that year, he may have met Stolz then.

Whatever else it did, the excellent *Don Carlo* in Bologna, with its fourteen solid performances, energized Verdi, who joked with Arrivabene about the possibility that he might even compose another opera. If he did, his librettist would not be Piave, who was struck down with apoplexy on 5 December and remained an invalid for the rest of his life. With a generous gesture, Verdi helped the librettist's wife Elisa and his daughter Adelina, who was called Didina. After asking Piroli's advice, he gave the girl 10,000 lire, a handsome sum. To cover the family's immediate expenses, Verdi also began to prepare an album of compositions by contemporary composers, whom Verdi 'bludgeoned' into contributing works that would be sold for Piave's benefit.[18] Among them were Auber, whom Verdi knew and liked; Mercadante; Ricci; Ambroise Thomas; and Antonio Cagnoni. A further conflict with a Bussetan ensued when Giovannino Barezzi, who had known Piave for twenty-three years, invited Didina to visit him and his family for part of the summer. Strepponi saw to it that the girl did not come, by letting Elisa Piave know that Verdi would disapprove of the visit,[19] perhaps as something that would put pressure on him to receive her.

Mariani's and Verdi's reunion in Genoa after *Don Carlo* was postponed beyond the date when the conductor was expected back, because he had stayed on in Bologna with the opera. He wrote to Verdi that

Whatever it costs me I shall not abandon *Don Carlo* now; it is too important to me; I am enjoying satisfaction that I never knew when I had the honour to conduct other very important productions. . . . I will tell you, too, that even here in the Romagna, if people were to know that I left, they would condemn me, and everyone would blame me, because of the way they adore you.[20]

Don Carlo in Bologna proved one of the most satisfying artistic experiences of his entire career.

I enjoy it; I feel good about it; and it makes me feel like an artist: I have suffered too much in the past; and, since I never expect to have such a good company again, I am making up now for what I could never have in the past and what I shall never have again. What a divine creation your *Don Carlo* is! What magical music! What a stupendous work as a whole! I say this to you in all truth and with the greatest sincerity in my heart![21]

Mariani made a serious mistake in sending the management of the Teatro Carlo Felice a letter in which he stated that, among other reasons, he had stayed on in Bologna so as not to abandon *Don Carlo* to a second conductor. The management responded by plastering the controversy all over the city on wall posters, bringing down on Verdi the publicity he so hated. Although Mariani was not well, and had been advised by his physician to take a few months off, he stayed in his post, declaring that he felt as if he were in Paradise, with Verdi's divine music, the excellent cast, chorus, and orchestra.[22] It was 'the most perfect theatrical season' he had ever known.[23] Verdi's disapproval of his actions was reflected in Streponni's letter to Mariani: 'It almost seems that Verdi influenced your decision to stay in Bologna, to spite the Genovese.'[24] Mariani finally got back to Genoa in early December.

When he returned to Palazzo Sauli Pallavicino, Verdi expected to stay there for the rest of the winter. Among the letters he wrote from Genoa was one to Vincenzo Torelli, who had sent portrait photographs of himself and his son, with appropriate dedications. The composer confessed that he would have blushed at reading them, had 'the sun and the air in the fields not turned my skin to leather'. He praised Achille Torelli for not having accepted a pension that had been offered him.

If there is one thing on earth we should consider important, it is earning our daily bread with the sweat of our brows. He is young: let him work. . . . He should not imitate anyone, above all the great artists; and now, just now (may the scholars forgive me) he can stop studying them; let him put his hand on his heart, listen to it, and, if he has the right stuff to be an artist, it will tell him everything. He must not let praise go to his head, nor be depressed by criticism. . . . The artist must look into the future, see new worlds in the *chaos*; and if, at the very end of that new road, he sees a tiny light, he must not be frightened by the darkness that is all around: let him keep walking; and if he sometimes stumbles and falls, let him get up at once and go straight on.[25]

On this note, but with a pessimistic view of Italian politics, Verdi closed 1867, celebrating the holidays in Genoa.

On 1 January 1868 Strepponi was far from happy, as her journal entry shows. Whatever advantages the house had brought Verdi, peace of mind was not among them. On New Year's Eve he and Strepponi had an argument over the expense of the new apartment; the cook, whom Verdi found unsatisfactory; and the 'thousand things that bother him'.[26] She did her best to make him happy, 'as he deserves to be at home', and he pleased her with a gift, although she feared that he could not afford it, given the amount that had been spent on 'the apartment, stonemasons, etc.', which he blamed on her, saying that she had gone on spending for 'the house that I wanted in Genoa'.

To begin, and as the foundation of these memoranda or notes, which I promised to keep beginning with the first of the year 1868, there is the fact that while I wanted to have a *pied-à-terre* in a place by the sea, which I love to the point of adoration, as one of the great wonders of a good God and nature, I did not, however, want gorgeous things, but just a nest with a view of the sea, to be able to stay there during the worst months of winter, which are so sad in the country. . . . So he gave me a very beautiful gift, for he is a *grand seigneur* and is generous. I was touched, as I am by all the good things he does for me and which he has always done, quietly and without throwing them in my face.

2 January. A peaceful day! He thought the dinner was good. I am happy. He is calm.

3 January. We played billiards, as we almost always have recently. He kept busy, being a carpenter, a locksmith, playing the piano. He did not find anything to complain about or blame me for! My God, it would be so easy to be happy, when one has good health and a bit of a fortune. Why isn't he always like that, instead of finding something wrong, no matter what I do, and *what I do always with the same, sole thought*, to make his life easy, pleasant, and peaceful?!

4 January. Alas! The clouds are back! Yesterday evening the Marchioness de . . . came with her husband to pay us a visit. Mariani ran on about Genoa and la Ma . . .'s bad humour. He exalts Bologna to the seventh sphere of heaven, together with all the people who live there. I took part in the conversation, expressing my opinion in terms that I thought were appropriate, but—after I had spoken for a long time—that seemed to him always wrong and inappropriate. Verdi gets irritated over the tone of people's voices, either too soft or too loud, so

that I ask myself what could be just the right atmosphere to please him! At lunch in the morning he blamed me about Mr Corticelli and Maddalena [Barezzi], [and] about what [Corticelli] said about Mariani. I played billiards badly; and, because he spoke sharply to me, I answered: 'Didn't you sleep well?' Afterwards, as he came into my room, I asked him: 'What did I say last night, to deserve your criticism?' He replied: 'It is your tone . . .' But, in the name of God! at my age, should I talk like and act like a young girl? He insists that I seem to believe that I am a perfect woman (!) and that no one can touch me, nor say a word to me about what I say and do, above all about my house! My God! if, when there is something that he doesn't like, he were to speak to me a little less brusquely! . . . And besides, is it a great crime to keep busy, as I do, very conscientiously, about matters that are, in their extreme simplicity, essentially women's affairs? How many men would want to see their wives busy in that way, especially since I keep up my artistic taste at the same time in reading, the arts, and keep up an elegance that suits my age? But having turned my back on society, on the world (and happily!) to spend my time only on what could be helpful to and necessary to him, wouldn't it be right for him to say that he is satisfied with that, *at least* once a year?! But perhaps I am at fault, for not having done as most women do when they have got the prize they wanted so badly, starting out again with a life of spending, entertainment, etc. I wanted to become a *new woman*, to repay him in a dignified way for the honour that I received in becoming his wife, and for the good that I constantly receive from this man, who could be perfect if he were only a bit sweeter and pleasant in his everyday conduct toward [me], who have no other joy than that of hearing a kind word from him! With his immense talent, he should remember that bread is a necessity of daily life, but that there is another life beyond the plain material one!

2.30 p.m. Now he is playing the piano and singing with Mariani.[27]

This shared domicile served its purpose, at least temporarily. Mariani had had to sacrifice some of his privacy, for his apartment was not completely separate. Its front door opened into a hall, but its back door, which was kept locked, opened into Verdi's guest-rooms. On call all the time, and often asked to help with errands, the conductor lived rather like a younger brother who has come home. But because he had visited Verdi and Strepponi only briefly at Sant'Agata in 1866 and 1867, he may not have known beforehand just what he had 'come home' to; in 1867 and 1868 he was a witness to the drama of a marriage that was showing serious signs of strain. Among many of his acquaintances, Verdi had the reputation of being a brusque but well-mannered gentleman; but to his wife and his employees, he sometimes showed another, much more severe face. Strepponi had lived more than twenty years with this prize who in

1857 had written to Luccardi: 'Horses are like women; they have to please the man who owns them.'[28] She had spent most of her time trying to cover the composer's every need but clearly had not succeeded. Only Strepponi's immense love for Verdi sustained her over these difficult years; and sometimes it was not enough. She had led a lonely life, sometimes going for months without speaking to anyone excepting Antonio and Maddalena Barezzi, the servants, or Verdi himself. As the years passed, Verdi was less and less the centre of attention; many people neither knew nor cared where he was. But his passion for Sant'Agata filled his days; he got physical exercise all day, every day, tramping in the fields, hunting, digging wells, laying irrigation pipes, repairing roofs, and rebuilding his tenant houses, barns, and the mill at Castellazzo. He went to Cremona, Piacenza, and Parma to market or to conduct his other affairs. Strepponi was tied down with the large house, the staff, and the correspondence.

In her loneliness, Strepponi leaned on Corticelli, a bad choice. Living in the house and eating at the table with her and Verdi, who was often critical of him, the former agent became her closest friend. At the same time Mariani was—as Strepponi said—like a brother to both her and Verdi. Their situation was aggravated by Corticelli's and Mariani's dislike and mistrust of each other, which the two men tried to gloss over as best they could. The tension inherent in the relationships among these four people added stress to their lives.

Just after New Year's Day in 1868 both Ricordi and La Scala began to put pressure on Verdi to help with a production of *Don Carlo* in Milan, a project that Verdi opposed because of his lack of faith in the management and his conviction that all of the house's resources would be needed for Boito's new *Mefistofele*, scheduled for February. By refusing to budge from Genoa, he forced Ricordi to deal with him and the theatre by post, with an occasional visit to the Palazzo Sauli Pallavicino. The letters that he wrote about this production are full of spirit and common sense.

Beginning in January, when Verdi was asked to approve Marie Löwe Destinn (the teacher of Emmy Destinn) as Eboli, he began to play his hand, writing to Giulio Ricordi:

How can I give you [my opinion] when I barely know her name? Would there be some way to hear her? As far as Squarcia and Colini are concerned, people tell me many not very favourable things about them; but do you really think that they will be able to sing Filippo and Posa? Set aside all your interests, sympathies, your desire (if indeed you have any) to see this opera now, and give me your whole opinion. Tell me about the quality and strength of their voices, intonation, style of singing, pronunciation, and, above all, how they act. Be careful, because a stupid Filippo is impossible.[29]

This letter was followed by another two days later:

What you say is fine; and maybe you are completely right, excepting that it is almost impossible for me to come to Milan to stage an opera that is already old. Let's not talk about me, and let's get on to what is important. If you can't get Fricci, it would be good to get Destin [sic] under contract right away.[30]

By February Verdi was writing again.

But let me ask a question: when will rehearsals begin? and when will the season end at La Scala? To produce *Don Carlo*, you will need no less than forty days, even if everything goes perfectly smoothly. *Don Carlo* is as long as two operas: for example, like *Il trovatore* and *La traviata* given one after another. Also it requires correct scenery, as these other two operas I mentioned above do not. Think carefully about this before rehearsals begin. We will have a tired orchestra, an out-of-breath chorus; if we were also not to have enough time, that would not be good.[31]

As to the conductor,

Don't consider Mariani. It would be better not to think about *Don Carlo* because there is not enough time. No one on earth can stage that opera in a short time . . . forty days!!! Convince yourself that you cannot do it in less time, and that you must have a person in charge who is capable, honest, and efficient.[32]

One day later he sent off a longer letter, explaining why he thought the production would not work.

You see things as an optimist does, while I (in every situation and always) see things in the worst possible light; but I don't think I am wrong in saying that there cannot possibly be enough time left to give this opera well. . . . Why extend the season? To let the audience hear a new opera? So what! . . . So let the audience digest its dinner in peace, and, now that spring is coming, go for its long walks, without seeming to force it to come to the theatre to whistle or applaud an opera. Anyway, even if the season were extended to 20 April, you still would not have enough time. . . . And it is not worth while saying that twenty days were enough in Bologna, because I call to your attention the fact that in Bologna they rehearsed twice a day, they did not have Holy Week, nor the Easter holidays. So (with your schedule) these twenty days become forty; furthermore the members of the chorus had been studying the opera for a month, and all the artists knew their roles. In spite of that, you saw that many details of the staging that are suggested and required by the music were neglected or badly done; and there was a ballet that was very badly performed.

These embarrassments must not happen in Milan. Add to this the fact that if *Mefistofele* is so difficult to learn, that means that it is badly written for voices (that does not detract in any way from the gifts of the composer: Beethoven wrote extremely poorly for voices) so after this enormous effort, after a painful period of preparation, it is natural that everyone will feel physically and spiritually exhausted, and that would make yet another great effort impossible. I know *my world* and you can be absolutely sure of what I say. . . . Now let's get to Mariani. Mariani is no longer thinking about Bologna. He is tied here hand and foot and will not go anywhere. The Carlo Felice ends 15 April and will reopen after Easter. If you were afraid of Mazzucato [as the conductor], because—as you say—he is bogged down with inertia, laziness, scepticism, etc., etc., he most certainly will hurt the opera. Let's suppose that I might come to Milan; maybe I could make the rehearsals go well, but what could I do when the battle begins?

The conclusion is that this *Don Carlo* would be given in a hurry now, *for better or worse*, with a company that is physically exhausted and even more so spiritually, to sum up: a bad situation. Even if this is satisfactory to the impresario, I believe that it will not be to the publisher; but surely, and more than surely, it will not do for me. The best thing to do now is to tell the impresario to stop thinking about *Don Carlo*.[33]

Even ten days later he was still dissatisfied with the messages he was getting from Milan:

Do you remember the scandals of my other operas at La Scala?! It is always the same story. At La Scala they think about [producing] my operas either when there are impossible casts or when there isn't time to do them well. Don't come here telling me that 'This one or that one knows his role.' I know this story: and even if it were true, there is the *mise-en-scène* that concerns singers, words, and music, all at once. I know what can be done: miracles cannot be accomplished; and you will never get on stage before 2 April. Think seriously about this.[34]

In spite of everything, it was scheduled.

When the production was well under way, Ricordi proposed that Verdi should come to conduct the opera. But Boito's *Mefistofele* had just been withdrawn after a noisy fiasco and only three performances. Again to Giulio, in a letter that spared no one:

All these letters tell me to come to Milan because *the time is right*.

The time is right?!! Imbeciles! What? Am I made to gloat over others people's ruin? I am one of those men who walk straight along the road, never looking to the right or the left, who do as much as they can, when they think they can, who don't want either *the right time* or support, or protection, or *claques*, or *publicity*, or cliques. I love art when it is presented in a dignified way, not the scandals that have just gone on at La Scala. If there is one thing on earth that I am happy about, it is that I did not come to Milan now. Ah, my heart, my instinct—whatever you want to call it—always tells me the truth; when things are a bit uncertain, I ask it what to do, and it gives me the right answer. . . . We are talking about one of my operas, and the directors at La Scala have always done or let others do everything possible to ruin them. . . . Wasn't that what happened with *Boccanegra* and so many of my other operas? Luckily now you have committed yourself; and I hope—rather, I am sure—that Mazzucato will do what a real artist should. Apart from personal likes or dislikes, or from one's love for this or that genre, there is something that is greater than us, *Don Carlo*, and all the operas, past, present, and future: Devotion to Art. Addio addio.[35]

He stood his ground and refused to conduct *Don Carlo*.

It seems useless to me. Were I to come, there would be gossip and people would pay too much attention to something that is perhaps not worth it; and that would annoy the audience, so that it would undervalue even what good there might be in it. And then I add the fact that my work, as you well know, is immense.[36]

He continued to follow news of the production almost on a day-to-day basis, worrying when he had heard nothing about the first three days of orchestra rehearsals, and giving orders for the staging. He also sent Mazzucato a six-page letter about how to handle the orchestra, while refusing an invitation to come to Milan for the general rehearsal, pointing out that he hadn't gone to Bologna either, out of fear that he might offend someone in the company with a sharp remark. To calm his nerves, he left Genoa and dug in at Sant'Agata, ordering Ricordi to send him news of the general rehearsal and of the first performance. 'It would be hard if it were to go badly in Milan.'[37] When it was all over, and the opera was a great success, he returned to Genoa. Strepponi, who visited her mother and sister in Locate at the end of March and the beginning of April, went alone to La Scala to hear *Don Carlo* and brought home a glowing report. She had been especially impressed with the fifth act, Verdi said:[38] Strepponi commented to Elisa Piave on Stolz's 'very remarkable and real worth'.[39] We do not know whether the two women met while Strepponi was in Milan. So far as we know, neither Strepponi nor Verdi had been inside La Scala since the 1846–7 season.

Shortly before La Scala closed, Verdi was caught up in a controversy that reverberated for months in Italy and abroad. The Minister of Education, Emilio Broglio, had written to Rossini in March, to interest the composer in a large music association, made up of amateurs and music-lovers who would work together to revivify Italian music. He also had a master plan for reforming musical education. Admitting that he knew very little about music, he went on to describe the situation as he saw it. 'We are reduced to music that you cannot listen to, because there is no one left who knows how to sing. After Rossini, that is, for the last forty years, what do we have? Four operas by Meyerbeer and [nothing else]. How can we cure such terrible sterility?'[40] Broglio then offered Rossini the presidency of the society, which the old composer accepted.

Verdi received a copy of Broglio's letter from Ricordi, to whom he wrote, dismissing the matter: 'I saw the minister's letter. When you want to hurt someone, and say something harmful, you should know how to do a better job of it! Rossini, too, neither did nor said anything good in his letter. If one wanted to, what a beating one could give them both! . . . But it is not worth the trouble.'[41] Verdi's measured response did him honour, for Broglio, by implication, had dismissed Bellini, Donizetti, and Verdi as being unworthy of mention. At this same time Verdi learned through friends that the Italian government had honoured him with the decoration of Commander of the Order of the Italian Crown. When he replied to Luccardi, who had congratulated him on the decoration, Verdi was in high spirits:

Right now I am like an unbridled horse that has spent the winter in the stable. I believe that if I were younger I would fly over the trees as sparrows do, but now only my thoughts can fly! How these accursed years go by! . . . As far as my Commander's Cross goes, I have heard nothing officially. I . . . certainly will never use it; if they only knew how little it means to me![42]

Happy to be back at Sant'Agata, and indifferent to Broglio's letter, Verdi might indeed have let the whole matter pass, but sometime just before the middle of May he decided to refuse the decoration and to publicize his gesture. Not wanting to write to a newspaper directly, he wrote a letter to 'Caro Mariani' and asked the conductor to pass it along to a journalist. Mariani obeyed orders: he gave one copy to *Il movimento* in Genoa and sent another to Filippi for *La perseveranza*. The letter was dated 15 May from Sant'Agata.

Dear Mariani,

Our Corticelli has given me *Il movimento* of the thirteenth, where I read that I would do well to send back the Cross of the Crown of Italy. That is exactly what I had decided to do as soon as I received the diploma. But now, without waiting any longer, I authorize you to declare that I, with or without the diploma, do not accept the Cross of Commander of the Crown of Italy. As for [Broglio's] letter and project for the rehabilitation of music, the presidency of which Rossini did not refuse, I have nothing to say, and probably never will have. I do, however, find it fine and instructive that an Italian minister should hurl anathema at an art that honours the name of Italy all over the world. In haste, addio, addio, your affectionate

Giuseppe Verdi.[43]

Within a week the matter became a national scandal, argued over by many newspapers.

The whole matter put Mariani in an untenable position. He had received an invitation from Broglio—'Mr Imbroglio', the conductor called him—to serve on the Rossini Commission. Mariani, who had known Rossini personally for many years, could scarcely refuse. At the same time, the Italian government had honoured him with the same decoration, the Commander's Cross, that Verdi was refusing to accept. If he refused the decoration, it would cause a political controversy, because he was an employee of the city of Genoa and a national figure. If he did not refuse, he would seem disloyal to Verdi. But he could hardly send the Cross back. Truly heartbroken, Mariani wrote to Verdi about his dilemma. 'I have been decorated! And you, *Verdi*? I am ridiculous, am I not?'[44] Even several days after the decoration arrived, it was still on Mariani's table in Genoa. He said he did not know what to do. The conductor blamed Corticelli for pushing Verdi into refusing the decoration: 'You have managed to create a political uproar and bring down such censure on the government that the reasonable *Opinione* in Florence has rightly accused you in public. You sinned and now you should do penance.'[45] He accused Corticelli of upsetting Verdi deliberately, just to cause trouble. From what Verdi wrote originally to Ricordi, this would seem to have been the case. By criticizing Corticelli, though, Mariani ran up a debit with Strepponi. She wrote to Giulio Ricordi in June that she felt that the whole matter of the decoration had left him looking ridiculous. Boito, too, was caught up in the controversy, writing a letter of his own to *Il pungolo*. Public opinion was in Verdi's favour; he received letters praising him for his stand and heard from friends that he had done the right thing. Arrivabene underscored his support for Verdi by refusing to serve on the Rossini Commission.

The matter was closed for Verdi when he wrote to Broglio directly:

I received the diploma that names me Commander of the Crown of Italy. This Order was founded to honour those who contribute to Italy in battle, in literature, in science, and in the arts. A letter from Your Excellency to Rossini, written even though you know nothing about music (as you yourself said, and as I believe) declares that in forty years no one has written an opera in Italy. Why, then, was this decoration sent to me? The address is surely wrong: and I send it back.[46]

Within a few weeks Verdi was in the newspapers again, as it was rumoured that he was composing a new opera: *Falstaff*. From Sant'Agata, on a steamy summer day, he let Arrivabene know that this was not true: 'I am not writing *Falstaff* or any other operas: *dolce far niente* is the best thing for my soul and my body.'[47]

Having promised Clara Maffei at the beginning of June 1868 that he would come to Milan, Verdi kept his word and returned to the city of his first triumphs, where he had not set foot in more than twenty years. She took Verdi to visit Manzoni, who had been his hero ever since the days of his youth. Home again, he sent Maffei his grateful thanks for his visit:

What can I say to you about Manzoni? How can I express the indefinable, new feeling of extreme sweetness that I got while I was in the presence of that Saint, as you call him? I would have knelt in front of him, if one could adore a man. They say that we must not do that, although on the altar we worship many [saints] who have neither Manzoni's gifts nor his virtues; instead, some of them were terrible rogues! When you see him, kiss his hand for me and tell him about all my reverence.[48]

Mariani, who had been busy in Genoa with *Un ballo in maschera* at the Teatro Carlo Felice, with Stolz as his prima donna, left the city at the end of the season to visit Sant'Agata and take the waters at San Pellegrino. Ill with the cancer that later killed him, he divided his time between the podium and spas, where he tried to recover his health. Because he was only 46, handsome, and vigorous, some people refused to believe that he was ill. 'I suffer in silence, because my acquaintances, seeing that I look well, make fun of me and say that my trouble is all in my mind.'[49] Among those who tended to minimize his illness was Streppони, who advised him to devote less time to women and wrap a flannel cloth around his midriff to keep it warm. One troubling aspect of her friendship with him was her inordinate concern over the women he knew; directly and through friends, she accused him of frivolity and infidelity. Although he was close to Elena Massa, who was probably the daughter or niece of Niccolò Massa, the Genoese composer and maestro di cappella, Mariani was widely recognized as Stolz's fiancé. At one point the soprano moved to an apartment in

Palazzo Corallo in Genoa, not far from Verdi's house, although she kept Milan as her primary residence.

At the beginning of summer, Verdi, reflecting on the controversy over his Commander's Cross, confided to Clara Maffei that he suspected that Broglio's wife, a former singer, might have been at the heart of the minister's unfortunate letter to Rossini. 'Cherchez, cherchez, et vous trouverez toujours la femme. So it is true that the Signora Ministressa has not forgiven me, after more than twenty years, for the fact that I could never like either her voice or her style of singing!'[50] To Maffei, who had visited Verdi and Strepponi at Sant'Agata for a week that spring, Verdi explained why he had written indirectly to *Il movimento* about Broglio's letter: 'You know that if it had been a matter that just concerned me, I would never have said or written a word. But, along with me, the entire art was treated badly, and so were those two [Bellini and Donizetti] who are no longer alive and cannot defend themselves.'[51] To Piroli, with whom he had corresponded over several weeks about the decoration and the controversy, he said that he considered Broglio's letter 'an insult'.[52] 'Broglio and his dogs are all mad: at least they won't accomplish anything.'[53]

Verdi turned to Piroli for advice about another matter in July, asking about the boarding-school in Turin where Piroli, a widower, had sent his daughters. 'I would like to send a poor little country girl, one of my relatives, to it; but I want a solid education, with no ideas about luxury, without any kind of foolishness at all.'[54] In August he thanked Piroli for the information he had sent about the Collegio della Provvidenza. Later in the year he confided to Piroli his plan for adopting Filomena Maria Verdi and began a long correspondence about the legal procedures involved. Verdi and Strepponi both needed their own birth certificates; he had to provide Margherita Barezzi's death certificate. Piroli went to Cortemaggiore to speak to the court officials there about an act of recognition of Verdi's and Strepponi's marriage. Carrara, Don Avanzi, and Corticelli were to stand by, in case they might be needed as witnesses. In October Verdi had to ask Piroli for advice about the legality of his marriage to Strepponi; if possible, he wanted to have that marriage confirmed, rather than be married again in Italy. By November Verdi had decided definitely to send Filomena to Turin; in December he asked Piroli to appeal personally to the woman who directed the Collegio della Provvidenza, so that Filomena would be sure to be admitted. 'The little girl is 9 years old; she is in excellent health; and she is intelligent,' he said.[55] By this time, Filomena had become like Verdi's and Strepponi's own child. On the composer's birthdays, she was called on to recite poetry that Strepponi wrote for the occasion.

> Evviva Verdi and San Donnino!
> I cry 'Evviva' to the man whom Italy honours!
> Long live my cousin. Hurrah!
> All together now, one more toast![56]

During that summer, in August, Verdi and Strepponi stayed in Genoa and Tabiano so as not to be in Busseto when the Teatro Verdi opened there. The squabbles over it had not completely died out, for, although Verdi had agreed to pay 10,000 lire for his box, he later wished to 'pay' the sum by cancelling a debt he said the city owed him for repairs he had made to the bridge at Sant'Agata. The theatre opened on 15 August, just three years and two days after the composer reached his compromise with the theatre directors. The day of the opening was a holiday in the city, which honoured its famous son by dedicating a bust of him before the performance. 'The large wreath from many Italian cities, the presence of the leading authorities of the Province, the ladies' elegance, and the good feeling that was in the air showed that everyone was happy to be able to offer a message of joy and devotion to the *Genius*,' wrote Emilio Seletti, the nephew of Verdi's former teacher and the son of the composer's former landlord in Milan.[57] Many people wore green ribbons or carried green handkerchiefs, the *verde* carrying a message of its own. The orchestra played *La capricciosa*, an overture Verdi had written when he was a boy; a respectable cast performed *Rigoletto*. The company, which included the soprano Enrichetta Berini as Gilda, also gave *Un ballo in maschera*. Later in the year a series of plays was given there by a touring company. The other great event of the winter was to have been the reopening of the 'blessed' Library of the Sacro Monte di Pietà: but that event was delayed by nearly two years.[58] Verdi stayed away again the following year when the city gave *La traviata*. Toward the end of that season, one act of *Ernani* was added to the opera to brighten up the evening.

Rossini's Death and Verdi's Proposal for the Requiem Mass

Verdi was at Sant'Agata in the autumn when he learned that Rossini had died in Paris. Four days later on 17 November he sent Ricordi a letter proposing that Italian composers collaborate in writing a Requiem Mass to honour the dead genius. Verdi wished the work to be given only once, on the first anniversary of Rossini's death in the church of San Petronio in Bologna; then the score should be sealed and donated to the Liceo Musicale in Bologna; no foreigner or person outside the circle of composers should take part in the project, which should be underwritten by the composers themselves so that no agent, impresario, or publisher could profit from it.

This Mass should not be the object of curiosity or speculation. If I were in the Holy Father's good graces, I would ask him to let women take part in the performance at least this one time; but since I am not, a person more suitable than I would have to be found to arrange this. It would be good to name a commission of intelligent men to oversee the process of this effort, and above all, to choose the composers, provide for the distribution of the pieces, and keep watch over the general lines of the work.[59]

His loss was also expressed in a letter to Clara Maffei, a week after Rossini's death: 'A great name has gone from the world! His was the most widespread, most popular reputation of our time, and was the glory of Italy! When the other one [Manzoni] who is still alive will no longer be with us, what will remain?' He added that he feared that Rossini's widow would not let her husband's body be buried in the church of Santa Croce in Florence, where a monument was to be raised to him. 'No Frenchman loves Italians, but Madame Rossini detests us more by herself than all the other Frenchmen put together.'[60]

Verdi's letter to Ricordi about the Requiem Mass for Rossini was published in the *Gazzetta musicale di Milano* on 22 November. Although many people favoured the project, some voices were raised against it, one in the music journal *Il trovatore*, which hailed Verdi as 'still one of the stars of the Italian opera theatre' but regretted the Mass, which it called 'a meatloaf', a 'mixed fish fry', and 'a pot-pourri'.[61] Verdi should have offered to compose a whole Mass himself, the editor said, and have it performed rather than locked away after just one performance.

Verdi proposed the Mass for Rossini at a time when many Italian cities faced seemingly insurmountable financial problems, and when Rossini's birthplace Pesaro was still trying to pay for a huge Rossini commemoration that had been offered to the composer in 1864. On that occasion, a large bronze statue of Rossini had been dedicated during a programme that included a cantata by Pacini, a hymn by Mercadante, and works by Rossini himself. The chorus of 250 and orchestra of 200 were conducted by Mariani, a member of the organizing committee. It was after this occasion that Rossini sent Mariani his portrait photograph with the dedication to 'Anzlett Mariani' with 'the beautiful eyes',[62] After Rossini's death, of course, both Pesaro and Bologna were planning commemorative events to honour him.

In spite of this, Verdi appeared to have the support of many members of the city government in Bologna and the prestigious Accademia Filarmonica as well. A commission was established in Milan, with Giulio Ricordi as its secretary and Mazzucato, Lauro Rossi, and Stefano Ronchetti-Monteviti in its ranks. These were the 'intelligent men' Verdi had hoped for; but the project seemed to stall even at the start. Verdi became discouraged, seeing that it was 'rejected by everyone, even friends'.[63] But three months later in March 1869 Verdi urged Ricordi to 'write to the composers, whom the Commission should choose at once, assign the parts of the Mass, and do it all as quickly as possible.

In the period since Rossini's death, many cities had already held their own commemorative services, Bologna among them, even though the city planned to produce the *Messa* Verdi proposed. Muzio, the concertatore and conductor in Bologna, kept Verdi up to date on the quality of the ensemble he was rehearsing in Rossini's *Petite Messe Solennelle:*

I believe we will give at least three performances of it. . . . It is very hard to predict whether I will have a good performance; I am working very, very hard to get one and hope to succeed. . . . The orchestration is very, very easy; the difficulty lies in getting the dynamics right in the [amateur] chorus. I am placing the orchestra on stage, and I hope it will be effective.[64]

Muzio sent Verdi good news on 24 March: The *Petite Messe* as a whole had been successful; the ensemble pieces worked best; the chorus and orchestra were good; the soloists, weak from the outset, seemed even less effective than he had expected, as they were placed within the grand framework of the whole—more than 300 people, with chorus and orchestra combined. 'They were applauded anyway, but the true, real success was for the Mass itself. . . . If the production had gone badly, I would have been blamed; but everything went really well.'[65] He added that he might go to Genoa to conduct the *Petite Messe solennelle* at the Teatro Paganini. This important celebration in Bologna was to be followed by an equally significant one in Pesaro, Rossini's birthplace, where Mariani had been named president of the Artistic Committee and general director. Later, he also agreed to conduct the collective Requiem Mass that Verdi planned for Bologna in November. As these and other memorial events were given, Verdi continued to press Ricordi to make critical decisions about the Requiem Mass; but the Commission in Milan waited until May to name the composers who had been selected. Verdi had been assigned the Libera me; his collaborators were Carlo Coccia, Raymond Boucheron, Alessandro Nini, Gaetano Gaspari, Federico Ricci, Lauro Rossi, Antonio Buzzolla, Teodulo Mabellini, Carlo Pedrotti, Antonio Cagnoni, Antonio Bazzini, and Pietro Platania.

With the Bologna *Petite Messe solennelle* behind him, Muzio stopped in Busseto, where Giuseppe Demaldè died on 11 June. Muzio sent Verdi news of his imminent engagement in Cairo as concertatore and conductor. As he assembled his company in France, he kept Verdi informed about meetings with the Khedive of Egypt and Paul Draneht, director of the Khedivial theatres. Muzio had a contract only for the important season that would mark the opening of the Opera House and of the Suez Canal. About one year earlier Verdi had received a libretto on an Egyptian subject; it was *Re Amasi*, a version of *Nitteti*, by Carmine Pini-Pisanini. We do not know that he read it.

Verdi's Return to La Scala

Torn between wanting to go back to Milan and fearing to do so, Verdi had often said that it was unlikely that he would ever work there again: But in the summer of 1868, during a visit to the Ricordis' villa at Maionica on Lake Como, the publisher and Clara Maffei, who was also a guest there, brought pressure to bear on him, encouraging him to think about the effect he might have on Italian opera by taking charge of the entire theatre for as long as it would take him to produce one of his own works. He could choose his own singers, oversee the sets and costumes, instruct the conductor, supervise as many of the rehearsals as he thought necessary, and withdraw the production from the calendar if he were not satisfied.

Rumours soon began to circulate about Verdi's return for *Don Carlo*, which was scheduled for the Carnival season of 1868–9. Quick to answer, he let Piroli know in July that it was not true. 'I will stay here in Genoa and let *Don Carlo* be given in Milan any way they want to do it. The company is certainly good enough; there will be an impressive chorus and a big, expanded orchestra; but that is not enough.'[66] Later that summer he told Ricordi that he would consider revising the finale of *La forza del destino* and would perhaps be willing to direct the rehearsals of the new parts of the score and 'of the whole opera, many parts of which will have to be rewritten.'[67] However, he did not fully commit himself. When he got home to Sant'Agata, the composer was unusually busy overseeing repair of the damage caused by the flooding of the Po, while Strepponi helped her mother and sister move from Locate to Cremona. Both had been ill. They and their maid Maria Alini, who came with them, moved to Cremona on 12 December. Corticelli also helped with the tasks of moving.

Three days later, the composer made a decision that affected all the rest of his life: he agreed to return to Milan. He may have made this choice because his visit to the city gratified him and fired his imagination; but it is also likely that he went back to the theatre because he found life in Palazzo Sauli Pallavicino boring, after a season of playing at carpentry, tinkering with locks, and complaining about the bills. In fact, it is difficult to imagine how he filled his days there, in a location so different from the busy, commercial Hotel Croce di Malta, in the centre of the city.

Having decided to work at La Scala, provided he was satisfied with the way the season went, he told Ricordi not to issue any publicity about him:

Do not stick my name on the posters of La Scala. Let's imitate the French in this, too, since we are not afraid to do so in so many other ways. At the Opéra, as you know, they never put the composer's name, even of a new opera, on the poster of the first night. If the audience wants to whistle, it whistles at a piece of paper. That is good: it is the only good thing there is at the Opéra. . . . If you have to put something on the poster, just say simply that *La forza del destino* will be given. If the changes satisfy me, it will be given with the changes; otherwise, you will give it as it stands, or substitute *Simon Boccanegra* for it, as you wish.[68]

He had begun to think about the singers he wanted and to work on the changes with Ghislanzoni, whom Giulio Ricordi had brought in as librettist. He invited the two men to Sant'Agata to change the third-act finale, and other parts of the opera. To Ricordi he wrote.

I will come to Milan myself to do the rehearsals I think necessary in *La forza del destino*, changing the last-act finale and several other parts here and there throughout the opera. I do not want to have anything to do with the impresario of La Scala; I do not want to be put on the poster; and I will not stay for the first performance, which may not be given without my permission. . . . You will own the new pieces, but you will be obliged to give a copy of them to the impresario in St Petersburg if you are asked to. In exchange for everything you will give me:

1. Author's rights, according to the law and as was done for *Don Carlos*.
2. You will pay me 15,000 lire.

If these proposals are all right with you, fine; if not, don't hesitate, write me a line, and that will be the end of it.[69]

In another letter written on the same day, he suggested that he might even compose *Giulietta e Romeo*. 'I have thought about it many, many times', he said.[70]

When La Scala finally did stage *Don Carlo*, it was not nearly as successful as it had been before, even though Stolz was again the Elisabetta. Verdi then began to have second thoughts about *La forza del destino*: 'Let's avoid scandals: either you find singers who are completely suited to their roles or else you give up the idea of presenting the opera.'[71] Christmas in Genoa left him restless, angry, and complaining about the years that flew by. One piece of good news came from Mariani, who was conducting *I vespri siciliani* at the Teatro Carlo Felice. Although Verdi was in Genoa, he stayed away from the theatre to avoid publicity; but he was pleased to hear of the excellent performance. He worked ahead on *La forza del destino*, in spite of unfavourable reports about the singers and orchestra in Milan. 'If I were to find myself in an artistic morass, it would be too humiliating for me,' he confided to Tito Ricordi, asking him to evaluate the situation. He did send orders for the chorus rehearsals, though, then considered going to the city himself to see whether the orchestra was as bad as he had been told.

As we know from his letter of 11 January 1869 to Ricordi, the trip from Genoa took eight hours and ten minutes. He planned to arrive at La Scala in time for the second act of *Don Carlo*, going directly from the station to the theatre. 'You would have to prepare a box for me that is not too high up, because in the top of the theatre there is too much resonance; and I absolutely do not want to be alone and do not want to be seen.'[72] Four days later he sent Ricordi a correction: 'I should have said "and I absolutely *want* to be alone and do not want to be seen."'[73] He said that if anyone learned that he was in the house, he would leave the theatre immediately. During this performance of *Don Carlo*, Verdi probably heard Teresa Stolz for the first time. He may have met her in Genoa the year before, but it is possible that he did not know her yet. Satisfied with the singers and the orchestra, he agreed to go back to Milan for the rehearsal of *La forza del destino* on 25 January and sent ahead his last-minute changes for the libretto.[74] Tension mounted steadily during the last weeks of January as Verdi prepared to leave for Milan and Strepponi packed Filomena's clothes so that she could enter the boarding-school in Turin.

Strepponi protested about Verdi's 'profound silence', which makes one think that he had almost stopped speaking to those around him.[75] On 31 January, a Sunday, the couple took Filomena to the Istituto della Regia Opera della Provvidenza. 'Verdi and I suffered at seeing that forbidding door close. . . . I suffered very, very much! I cry every time I think of her, and I think I can see that smiling, radiant face in every corner of the house! But she isn't here any more!'[76] Something Verdi said before he left Turin apparently offended Strepponi and made her think that she would not be welcome in Milan. In fact, her situation seems to be similar to that of the 1840s and 1850s, when the composer left her behind as he went off to produce his operas. She was hurt, although this time she was not entirely alone: Corticelli was in Genoa with her.

Verdi asked Ricordi to take an apartment for him at the Grand Hôtel de Milan, down the Corsia del Giardino from La Scala and near his old flat in Contrada del Monte. The publisher also put a piano in the suite. Verdi planned to go straight from the station to La Scala, where a rehearsal was planned, jumping into the weeks of work that had to be done. Just after the first of February he wrote to Strepponi, whom he had invited to Milan so that she could attend some of the rehearsals. After serious consideration, she decided not to go. Writing her husband on 3 February, she first gave him news of Filomena:

I have had news from Turin and I send it to you at once, convinced that even in the midst of your work and worries you will occasionally think about that dear little girl who is no longer with us. She is well. . . . I, however, read between the lines and see that she had suffered and is still suffering a great deal. But for her own good she must stay in a boarding-school; so be it. Even though I had convinced myself that I would feel this separation very much, I did not think, however, that I would feel so bitter about it. I did not let anyone know that I have come back to Genoa, because I don't want to see anyone. At the same time, these enormous rooms seem to me to be sad, abandoned places, full of ghosts.

I have thought carefully and I shall not come to Milan. So I will save you from having to come secretly to the station at night to slip me out like a bundle of contraband goods. I have *reflected* on your profound silence before you left for Genoa, the things you said in Turin, your letter of Tuesday; and my inner feelings advise me to turn down the offer you make me, to come and attend some of the rehearsals of *La forza del destino*. I feel everything that is forced in this invitation; and I think it is a wise decision to leave you in peace and stay where I am. While I am not enjoying myself, I am at least not exposing myself to further, useless, bitter remarks; and you, on the other hand, will have complete freedom. Last spring, when my heart gave me the courage to introduce myself to Maffei and Manzoni, to be able to come home to you with my hands full of welcome things—how happy I was to think of the pleasant surprise that you would have had from Clarina's visit—when we went to Milan together, the visit to Manzoni, the trip to Lake [Como], and that because of all this you returned to the city of your first success, I never thought of the strange, hard outcome that I face *of being rejected.* No, Verdi, I would not have thought in the spring that we could have been introduced together into the august presence of Manzoni, and that then in the winter it would be wise [of you] to turn your back on me this way. So please let my embittered heart find dignity in saying 'no'; and may God forgive you for the excruciating, humiliating wound that you have given me. I will find some excuse to justify my refusal, in writing to Giuditta [Ricordi] and Clarina, who write to me (I don't know why) begging me to join you in Milan. I will reply tomorrow or later. As soon as myself have further news about the little girl, I will write to you. [77]

This letter reached Verdi while he was being greeted as a hero in Milan. Tenca, writing to Clara Maffei, had read in the newspapers that the composer was warmly welcomed.

So much the better, that the public shows a bit of reverence for the art of music, though it does not have any for other things. Verdi is lucky, being able to become a millionaire without arousing the envy and malice of fools and crooks. . . . I imagine that he will come to your house every evening at the hour when the important people come, and who knows whether he may not win again at *tresette*, as he always used to do so many years ago! As I think about it, I realize how many years have passed since the time when I spent an hour with Verdi, fighting over the table, with the cards in our hands. More or less a quarter of a century. All right, if he has started playing *tresette* again, he can consider me the fourth at the table, as soon as I get there. I hope that Verdi will not leave before the end of Carnival. [78]

The composer had indeed begun to visit Clara Maffei in the evening and had taken up again with Carcano and many other Milanese friends; but he was only able to stay in the city about ten days, perhaps because Strepponi's letter troubled him, perhaps because he had done all he wished at rehearsals. By 10 February he was in Genoa, giving orders to Ricordi, the chorus-master, and the singers by post. On 15 February he went back to Milan, this time with Strepponi, who rarely went out of the hotel but did receive Clara Maffei every day. She did not visit the salon.

The première of the revised *La forza del destino* was given on 27 February 1869 to a passionately enthusiastic audience, its reception marred by a single whistle, which Verdi heard after the first act and remembered for years to come. Other than that, he seemed thoroughly satisfied, reporting to Piroli on the 'good' success, the 'excellent execution', and the orchestra and chorus that performed 'divinely'.[79] Coming from a man who rarely used adjectives like these to describe a production, this was high praise.

What a shame, what a shame that the government is abandoning this art and this theatre without pity, when it still has so many good things. You will say 'Why can't it go on without the government's help?' No: it is impossible. The Teatro alla Scala has never before been as full and as active as this year; in spite of that, if the impresarios cannot give fifteen performances of *La forza* with a box-office of more than 5,000 Lire a night, they are lost.[80]

In fact, only fourteen performances were given. He told Arrivabene that he would have to sleep for two weeks to recover from his effort, but seemed fully satisfied with the production. The orchestra and chorus played marvellously; the singers exceeded his every hope. He was so pleased that he sent Giulio Ricordi 700 lire as a contribution to expenses for a dinner that the chorus and stagehands planned to have in a trattoria.[81] Further good news came when Verdi heard that the second performance, which he did not stay to hear, had gone even better than the first.

In Genoa Verdi praised Stolz's performance to acquaintances he had made there, among them Teresina Tubino Del Signore, the wife of Carlo Del Signore, Mariani's closest friend in the city. On 11 March the soprano sent Teresina her own recollection of Verdi's triumph at La Scala.

The Milanese will certainly remember forever that wonderful evening, when they had the pleasure of applauding their celebrated maestro again. . . . If you had been there, you would have experienced indescribable emotions.—Think of me, as I had to sing, and I had tears in my eyes all the time from emotion. . . . I am happy now that it is all over, and that Maestro Verdi is quite satisfied with me.[82]

Critical reception for the opera was good. In Florence, *L'opinione* headed its article with the declaration that *Forza* was 'a colossal success. Overture and new pieces hailed. Twenty-seven bows for Verdi.'[83] Filippi's review documented such an ovation as had not been heard at La Scala in some time. 'We all felt exalted at the idea of honouring the Maestro', he said, adding that he would have to hear the opera again to pass judgement on so vast a work.[84]

The composer soon left for Sant'Agata to oversee work at the farm. Early in 1869 the whole Province of Parma had been racked by riots as peasants and small farmers revolted against the hated Tasse sul Macinato, a tax the government had imposed on grains that people took to the miller to be ground into flour. It fell particularly on the poor, whose diet was based on pasta, bread, and polenta. In Borgo San Donnino, when rioters tried to set fire to the city hall, they were fired upon by troops from the Italian army who killed two peasants and wounded a city official. The town hall in Soragna, near Roncole, was burned and private homes were sacked, as were government storehouses. During these demonstrations, the parish church was often occupied, so the bells could be rung *a stormo*, wildly, or *a martello*, like a hammer. Busseto was invaded by men and women waving pitchforks, rakes, axes, and clubs. Shouting 'Down with the *Macinato*', they seized the bell tower of San Bartolomeo and rang *a martello*, in warning, before running toward the city hall. There Angiolo Carrara and other authorities confronted and calmed them by announcing that grain could be milled in Busseto without being taxed. In spite of that, soldiers fired on the mob and arrests were made; the government then quartered men from the regular army in Busseto homes.[85]

Strepponi remained in Genoa while Verdi was away. To Maffei, she confided her feelings of joy and shock at having been in Milan and said that she spent much of her time 'meditating' and passing 'in review' the people and events from her past.[86] She also regretted having been loved by so few people in her life and thanked God that she had been able to live beside 'my Verdi, who, I hope, will close my eyes in death, when the time comes for me to go and wait for him in eternity.'[87] For every day of joy, she had lived through a hundred marked 'by sorrow'.[88]

In contrast to her moodiness, Verdi seemed to be bursting with joy. Writing to Escudier about *La forza del destino*, he described Stolz's performance as 'sublime'.[89] He had a thousand projects in his head and was considering going to Florence as a tourist, to Naples, or even back to Paris. One of his visitors to Sant'Agata that spring was Clara Maffei, whose life had changed radically when she and her husband were reconciled.[90] On her way back from Florence, where she had been nursing him in May 1869, she stopped at the villa for her first visit there. Her heart was at peace, she said.[91] While there, she got from Verdi some information on his life.

Notes on Verdi's Life, written at Sant'Agata by Clara Maffei

Verdi was absolutely refused permission to enter Milan Conservatory, the head of which was Sormani, because [they] did not recognize that he had any talent for music, after they examined him in composition and in cembalo; then, encouraged by Rolla, he studied three years in Milan under M[aestro Lavigna]. By chance, he conducted at the [Teatro] Filodrammatico, first Hayden's [*sic*] *Creazione* and afterwards everything else that they were performing in that Theatre, where they were supposed to give *Roberto* [*Devereux*], which was later given at La Scala 1839.

He lost two children and his wife, June 1840.

Pasetti did nothing to help him, and even refused to ask Merelli for a loan or an advance [against his fees] of 50 *talleri*; and Pasetti, this man who brags that he helped, created many other problems.

Nabucco 4,000 L[ire].

Lombardi 9,000 L[ire].

Verdi married at age 22.

Nabucco libretto turned down by Nicolai.[92]

This fragment is valuable as a reflection of how Verdi saw his past at this time. Pasetti, who had died in April 1868, was not alive to defend himself against this rank ingratitude. Nor was there anyone to set the record straight about the deaths of Verdi's first wife and children, who, he claimed, had all died in the same month of the same year, 1840. The notes suggest that he had been engaged as the regular conductor of the Teatro dei Filodrammatici, something that we cannot confirm. The document again confirms Verdi's bitterness toward the authorities of Milan Conservatory.

The Failure of the Requiem Mass for Rossini

The celebration of Italian art and honour, the *Festa patria*, as Verdi called it,[93] remained in the planning stage for six months after Rossini's death. As we have seen, it was not until May that the composers' names were released.[94] The final plans were announced on 13 June, with the Commission stipulating that the composers' pieces were to be submitted on or before 15 September. By that date there were serious problems for the enterprise in Bologna.[95] Both the city junta and the impresario Luigi Scalaberni, who held the *appalto* for the Teatro Comunale, were caught in a tangle of financial problems and conflicts of interest. A strong current of pro-Wagner and pro-Mendelssohn partisanship came from the periodical *L'arpa*, a voice of 'the music of the future'. This publication, in supporting the efforts of the Luccas, could only harm the Ricordis. On 21 June *L'arpa* announced that Scalaberni was planning to put on an opera by

Wagner that autumn, perhaps *Die Meistersinger, von Nürnberg*, perhaps *Lohengrin*.[96] Mariani would conduct this work; but he wrote to Verdi at the beginning of August to say that he felt the opera could not be given because the singers under contract were not good enough to perform *Lohengrin*.[97] However, the intention of the Comunale was clear enough, as it seriously considered 'an initiative that would break up the old tradition, while Ricordi was representing a project that was valuable only because it gave new life to [Italian] patriotism' under the umbrella of a new project: the Requiem Mass.[98] These two conflicting cultural currents; and the rivalry of the two publishing firms, Ricordi and Lucca, added heat to whatever controversy the *Messa* raised.

As late as July the Commission had still not named a conductor. When Mariani was chosen, at the beginning of August, he had just conducted *La forza del destino* in Vicenza with Stolz and was on his way to Pesaro, where he was in full charge of the Rossini celebration. He was to conduct a Cherubini Requiem Mass in the church of San Francesco on 21 August and Rossini's Stabat Mater in the theatre on 22 and 23 August. From there he wrote to Verdi on 17 August about the excellent chorus that was to sing the Cherubini Mass and the apprehension he felt over the quality of the chorus that would sing the Requiem Mass for Rossini in Bologna. 'Do you think that you will be able to use the chorus from the theatre? I don't believe that they are able to sing this kind of music!!! I will keep you up to date on how things are going; and however I can be of service to you, you have only to give me orders.'[99]

Verdi had written that he might decide to come to Pesaro, but was not certain. Mariani, in response:

You can imagine how happy I would be if you really were to decide to come to Pesaro. Come, come, come. . . . I am at your disposition. You won't find hotels here, but you will have the hospitality that you deserve. You will be given a place to stay in one of the most important houses; or, if you will be satisfied with it, . . . I will be very happy to give you my apartment. You have only to write to me and I will do everything to make you happy.[100]

It is hard to imagine what else Mariani could have done to please the composer; but his helpful suggestions and courteous invitation were rebuffed by an angry Verdi, who wrote from Genoa, where he had gone so as to be away from Busseto while his *La traviata* was playing at the Teatro Verdi.

Sleep in peace, for I have already answered [saying] that I cannot come to Pesaro.

I go back to your letter of yesterday because there are two sentences that I don't understand well: *What will the Commission in Milan do?* and, further on, *If I can be of service to you, give me orders.* Do you mean to say that we have to beg you to get the chorus that you have in Pesaro? First of all, you should have understood before now that my *I* has disappeared, and that I am now nothing more than a pen to write four notes as best I can and a hand to offer my contribution to make possible this *Festa patria.* I will tell you that in this situation, no one should have to beg anyone, nor be begged, because we are talking about a duty that all the artists must and should fulfil.

I never have been able to understand whether the project of the Mass for Rossini had the good luck to be approved by you or not. When one acts in the name of art and the lustre and dignity of one's own country, instead of out of special interest, a good act does not need to be approved by anyone. So much the worse for anyone who does not know that! A man, a great artist who left his name on a whole era, died: a person, anyone at all, invites the artists of his generation to honour that man, honouring our art in him; music is composed for this event and performed in the greatest temple of the city that was his musical *patria*; and because of this—so that it shall not become a place where miserable vanity and odious personal interest can feed—it is sealed in the archive of a famous Liceo after the event. The history of music will have to record the fact that 'at that time, on the occasion of the death of a famous man, all Italian art was united to perform a Mass for the Dead in San Petronio in Bologna; the music, written just for this event by many composers, is kept under seal in the Liceo in Bologna'. This becomes a fact of history and not a piece of musical charlatanry. What difference does it make if the composition lacks unity, if this man's piece or that one's is more or less beautiful? What does this composer's vanity or that performer's pretentiousness matter? We are not talking about individuals here; just let the day come; let the solemn event take place; let the *historic Fact*—understand that clearly, the *historic Fact*—exist.

Given this, everyone is obliged to do whatever he can to achieve this goal, without expecting to be begged beforehand or to get praises and thanks afterward.

If this solemn event takes place, we will certainly have done a good, artistic, patriotic work. If not, we will have proved once again that we work for something only when personal interest and vanity are rewarded; when we are shamelessly praised in articles, in biographies; when our names are cried out in the theatres, dragged through the streets, like those of charlatans in the public square; but when our personalities must disappear beneath a noble and generous idea, then we run off and hide under the cloak of our egotistic indifference, which is the plague and the ruin of our *patria*.

BOOK V

Forgive my useless chatter and believe that I am your
G. Verdi.[101]

Mariani was stunned by the letter. One cannot imagine what Verdi
thought Mariani had done to deserve such a volley. Throughout the
summer the relations between the two men had been cordial, Mariani
having visited Sant'Agata and then having accompanied Verdi part of the
way home after a trip to Genoa.

Although Mariani had been ill and Verdi was faced with personal
problems, nothing seemed to have happened between them. Mariani,
heavily committed in Vicenza and Pesaro, had travelled and conducted.
Verdi, after the accident of July, when he and Strepponi both fell into the
artificial lake he had created at Sant'Agata, appeared to be reasonably
happy. But Verdi reported to Ricordi on 5 August that Mariani was 'cold'
toward the Mass, 'perhaps because he would have wanted to be invited to
compose! He is wrong!'[102] We have no idea who put this notion into
Verdi's head; but he could not have concluded it from Mariani's letters.
When we ask ourselves who could have given Verdi information that
would turn him against Mariani and end a friendship that went back
twenty years, we have to look to Corticelli, who was Bolognese, had
information from his own sources in the Romagna, and, as we shall see,
was jealous of Mariani's career and willing later to lend his name even to
a scurrilous letter in order to harm him.

Mariani, confused and hurt, answered from Pesaro on 24 August, the
day after the triumph of the Stabat Mater.

Your last letter of the nineteenth of this month caused me a lot of suffering, and
you cannot imagine how unhappy I am that I could not answer you before this.

I did not ask you 'What will the Commission in Milan do' because I wanted to
be begged to do anything, nor, as you write, to make available the chorus that is
now here in Pesaro: I did not bring them together here; they do not depend on
me; and I would not have any power at all over them.

Since I know the chorus of the Teatro Comunale, I only asked you whether the
Commission intended to make use of it or put out a call to all the Italian music-
schools instead.

If, then, I offered my services to you, you must not believe, O my Maestro,
that I believe that I am worthy to serve you: I don't think I have to explain
anything to show you the veneration I have for you!

Since the Commission in Milan wrote me some time ago to invite me to that
solemn occasion, to which I answered that I was at its service, I believe that I
only did my duty in offering you my services, which I always offer you, not in the

name of art, because I know that I am a wretched creature, but for the devotion that I have for you and your *sacred* person.

I won't say anything more, and I am sorry that you misunderstood what I wrote.

As for the project of the Mass for Rossini in San Petronio in Bologna, if you will be good enough to think back and remember the letter that I wrote to Corticelli last year, exactly at the time that your very noble proposal was announced, you will see that I was in favour of it and felt that it was worthy of you and of your immense genius. I also spoke to you, with all the admiration that I felt over it, and if I did not bother you more about this, it was out of fear of annoying you. . . . I beg you not to write me any more letters that are so severe because you demoralize me. I won't take the liberty of writing you any more for any reason whatever; and if you wish to give me orders, you will do so as you wish.

I saw your letter answering this Rossini Committee: it is very beautiful and very finely done . . . I don't want to hide from you the fact that I have worked like the devil and that I feel as if all my bones were broken. . . . Give my regards to Signora Peppina and Mauro, and write me just a line to tell me that I [just] expressed myself badly in my previous letters. If you will let me I will come to visit you before going to Bologna. And please believe that if I do something wrong, it is not out of ill will. I kiss your hand and say again that I will always be your faithful servant.

Angelo Mariani.[103]

Verdi did not answer. We do not know where or when or if he received the letter, since he was on his way from Genoa to Sant'Agata and then to Tabiano in the week after it was written.

At the end of August, Giulio Ricordi wrote to Verdi to suggest that the performance of the Requiem Mass for Rossini should be given before 17 November; but Verdi thought this a bad idea, even though he told Ricordi he could do as he liked. Earlier in the month he had written Ricordi something that was absolutely false, in a letter of 20 August[104] that stated that Mariani had asked Verdi what the Commission in Milan would do to get *his* 'marvellous chorus' from Pesaro for the Mass in Bologna. But Mariani had referred to a 'chorus *like this* in Bologna', not *his* chorus from Pesaro; furthermore, Mariani had repeated this in his letter of 24 August to Verdi, believing that the composer had misunderstood. It is difficult to understand why Verdi deliberately misstated these matters. In Verdi's letter of 20 August, he also warned Ricordi that Mariani would not co-operate because he had not been the promoter of the event and because the Commission had not assigned him one of the pieces to compose. This, too, appears not to be so.

BOOK V

By 2 September Verdi was urging Ricordi to secure a good chorus and a good orchestra for the event, and asking the same questions Mariani had asked. Because there were financial problems, Verdi suggested that the composers and those who would perform the Mass make a money contribution, which would be paid in addition to the contribution of their time and the money to cover their trips to Bologna. 'Don't lose time because there isn't too much of it left. Clarify things with the impresario [Scalaberni] so that there won't be a mess at the end', he told Giulio Ricordi.[105] This letter was written on 2 October, less than seven weeks before this important, national *Festa patria* was to take place! It is impossible to understand why Ricordi waited so long to decide who would sing, who would play, and who would pay. With less than one month to go before the final rehearsal of the Requiem Mass, Ricordi met Scalaberni in Bologna and asked to use the orchestra and chorus of the Teatro Comunale, which was then at the beginning of its fall season, with six operas on the schedule. When he got back to Milan, the publisher let Verdi know that he had been sure that everything would work out; but after he got home, he heard from Bologna that Scalaberni would not let his orchestra and chorus be used because he was afraid to ruin his own productions at the Teatro Comunale by freeing them for the rehearsal time needed for the Mass. The city government of Bologna asked to have the Mass given in San Petronio in December, after the opera season ended; but Ricordi felt that once the company disbanded, it would difficult and extremely expensive to call it back.

The publisher wrote at once to Mariani and asked him to write to the city officials; but the conductor could not see his way clear to do that. He told Ricordi that the Comunale had announced five operas, all difficult, for its short season; that the opera season, already in trouble, with a poor box-office for *Il profeta*, had had to add Rossini's *Otello* as an extra attraction; and that the chorus was not sufficiently skilled to be able to perform the Requiem Mass. At this point, Ricordi was convinced that the city of Bologna simply did not want the Mass.[106]

The controversy over the Requiem Mass soon broke out in the newspapers in Milan and Bologna. Scalaberni defended himself with a letter to *Il monitore*, in which he claimed that he had never agreed to lend his troops for the Mass; that he did not understand why a private individual like himself should have to play Maecenas; and that the Commission in Milan ought to have understood that.[107] He said that he was forced to reflect on the fact that young composers such as Boito, Dall'Argine,

Faccio, and Marchetti had not been invited to participate. The implication, of course, was that the Old Guard had kept them out.

With this letter printed and reprinted, accusations and recriminations flew from both sides, the *Gazzetta musicale di Milano* attacking and ridiculing Scalaberni, and the *Monitore* upholding Bologna's side. The anniversary of Rossini's death passed while these polemics raged back and forth. Verdi, who had been against giving the Mass before the anniversary, also opposed the idea of giving it in December, or of presenting it in Milan or Florence, the capital. On 13 October he had written to Ricordi to say that he thought the Commission could take only one course: 'give back each of the composers pieces, with heartfelt thanks for the concern they showed. The expenses that have been incurred by the Commission up to now shall be my responsibility, of course. Send me the bill and let's not talk about it again.'[108]

He accused Mariani of not having done his duty as 'an artist and a friend' and added, chagrined, 'We, and I more than everyone else, have created a great *fiasco* in Bologna (a *fiasco* about which no one should be ashamed); let's not risk creating a second one in Milan.'[109] Usually a mine of common sense where the theatre was concerned, Verdi seemed incapable of understanding Scalaberni's problems, which were so acute that the impresario had to add a second extra opera to his schedule in order to sell seats: it was Verdi's *Un ballo in maschera*. If he failed to understand Scalaberni's dilemma, he fell even shorter in not seeing why Mariani, the impresario's employee, could not work magic just by writing to the city administration and asking to have the Mass given.

On 6 November the Commission publicly accused the junta and Scalaberni of having 'boycotted' the Mass, which they surely had not done.[110] As late as May 1870 the Commission in Milan was still trying to convince Verdi to agree to a performance, but he wrote that 'nothing is more useless than this.'[111] and did not budge in December 1870, when he dismissed the Mass project as 'a warmed-over dish'.[112] He also refused to allow the Mass to be given in Milan when a statue of Rossini was to be erected in the foyer of the Teatro alla Scala.[113] The Mass was not performed until 1988, when it was given in Stuttgart and then in the Cathedral in Parma.

The confusion and tribulations that resulted from the Rossini Requiem Mass project raised Verdi's mistrust of Mariani to such a height that their spontaneous and genuine exchange virtually ended, as the conductor was widely blamed for the failure of the *Festa patria*. Writing to Ricordi at the end of October 1869, Verdi complained that Mariani had failed in his duty as a friend and artist and that he should not be allowed to conduct the Mass if it were given in Milan: 'It cannot and must not be Mariani.'[114] He distributed the blame somewhat more evenly in assessing the failure to Arrivabene:

. . . The fault [lies] with the City of Bologna, with that impresario, and a bit also with our illustrious friend Signor Angelo. He did not do what he should have done as an artist, and as my friend; perhaps he was somewhat irritated because he was not on the list of composers, *vanitas*, *vanitas*, etc. Ah! talented men are almost always like great, big boys.[115]

Verdi apparently did not see the irony in that remark. He went on misrepresenting the situation right to the end of the year and tarnished Mariani's reputation as an honourable man within the circle of his closest friends, succeeding even in driving a wedge between the conductor and people he had known for years.

29

January 1870–Spring 1873

Aida

At the end of the Bologna season, Mariani, ill with bladder cancer, returned to Palazzo Sauli Pallavicino, where Verdi, Strepponi, and Corticelli had arrived late in November. Although he had been advised to stay clear of the *piano nobile* household, because Verdi was unwilling to speak to him, he tried to arrange a meeting all the same, by sending a letter in care of Carlino Del Signore, his closest friend in Genoa. Rather than answer directly, Verdi wrote to Del Signore, saying that he would only receive Mariani if the three of them could sit down together. Accepting even this humiliation, Mariani agreed, perhaps believing that he could explain his situation if he could just make his case in person. A careful reading of Verdi's letters indicates that this was not the case, for he had already judged Mariani guilty:

You understand, my dear Carlino, that it would be very embarrassing for me to answer Mariani's letter. What could I say to him? Blame him? Accuse him? He will go on answering: 'I didn't do anything wrong.' I don't accuse him of doing anything wrong: I accuse him of not doing anything. No one has made any insinuations against him; and anyway, words don't mean anything to me when the actions speak for themselves. He refers to my letter to Pesaro to justify his strange and unusual silence. But indeed that letter didn't mean to say anything but: '*Anyone who is a true artist must work to make this project come about*' and that implied: '*Furthermore, this will be a proof of friendship.*' If there was something about that project that he didn't like, he should have refused the post that the Commission in Milan entrusted to him. But once he accepted, he had a double burden. What did he do? Nothing! Fine: I admit this; but it is impossible to concede that he acted as an artist and a friend should have done.

BOOK V

Mariani wants to speak to me: very well: but I want you to be present when we speak.[1]

Verdi's reference to the 'strange and unusual silence' may indicate that he never saw Mariani's letter of 24 August. His siege mentality and his tone and attitude make it clear that even after nearly two months Verdi still blamed Mariani for the fiasco. Nowhere in his correspondence do we find a suggestion that he criticized Giulio Ricordi, whose dilatoriness and inefficiency in negotiations with the city of Bologna and with Scalaberni were the direct cause of many of the problems that arose. Nowhere is there a hint that Verdi himself might have acted differently, by writing, for example, to Camillo Casarini, the city councillor in Bologna who was responsible for the Requiem Mass for Rossini. Nowhere is there a suggestion that Mariani might not have been able to go over his employer's head and address the city authorities himself, because it would have been a breach of etiquette and protocol that might very well have cost him his post. Verdi, the hard and unfair judge, had condemned Mariani and made his sentence public, by passing it to the Ricordis, Arrivabene, and Clara Maffei as he aired his disappointment and frustration. Indeed, he misrepresented the situation to Maffei, writing: 'Mariani didn't move a finger for this business',[2] even denying the conductor credit for what he had done. The two men did meet on many occasions over the next two years; their interrupted correspondence was resumed, with Mariani writing fairly regularly and continuing to express love for Verdi, who replied from time to time but remained cool and critical. Strepponi and Corticelli took an ever more contemptuous attitude toward the scapegoat.

Over Christmas and the 1870 New Year Verdi spent some of his time on the *Album* for Piave; a few months before he had committed himself to another act of charity by setting up a scholarship fund to help two students in Busseto, one young man and one young woman each year. The money for the grants came from the pension that Verdi got as Cavaliere dell'Ordine del Merito Civile di Savoia, a decoration that he was awarded in June 1869.[3] Verdi, who had 'a thousand projects' in his head, was considering taking several long trips, but let Arrivabene know that it would 'all end up in a polenta at Sant'Agata'.[4] He asked both Du Locle and Ricordi to send him Wagner's complete prose works and also asked Ricordi for a score of *Tannhäuser*, as he began to show interest in Wagner, perhaps because of the excitement generated by the announcement that *Lohengrin* would be given in Bologna. However, as he confided to Arrivabene, he was not planning to work 'for the Opéra or for the Opéra-Comique, nor on Sardou's *Patrie*', which Du Locle had sent him in the autumn.[5] When Ricordi asked him to consider composing *Nerone*, to Boito's libretto, Verdi answered that he might do it, if Boito did not write the opera himself. Ricordi was to investigate further and also send Garcia Gutiérrez's *Venganza catalana* and Zorrilla's *El zapatero y el rey*. The composer also kept his finger on the pulse of such productions as *Don Carlo* in Turin, where Stolz was the prima donna; *La forza del destino* in Naples; and *Les Vêpres siciliennes* in Paris. He helped Prince Joseph Poniatowsky with advice about the production of his opera *Piero de' Medici*, which was planned for La Scala.

When Strepponi's mother died in January 1870, she went to Cremona for the funeral, then arranged for Barberina's continuing care, which Maria Alini oversaw. Again in Genoa, she, Verdi, and Mariani patched together a relationship that mixed professional and personal elements. The conductor, who had gone to Turin to hear Stolz—then his fiancée— as Elisabetta, sent Verdi news of the production on 1 March, even asking about that 'thorn', Corticelli.[6] A few weeks later he and Stolz returned to Genoa together, he to Palazzo Sauli-Pallavicino, she to Palazzo Corallo. When Mariani conducted a season of opera at the Teatro Nazionale in Genoa, Verdi, Strepponi, and Stolz sat together in a box during at least one performance. Because the soprano was free from the end of the Turin season until the beginning of July, she had a chance to be with Verdi, Strepponi, and Corticelli on a regular social basis, as they dined together in Verdi's apartment and celebrated his and Strepponi's name-days together, Ricordi—as always—sending a cake from Milan for San Giuseppe. Before the end of March the composer and his wife left for Paris.

Staying at the Hôtel de Bade on the Boulevard des Italiens, the couple visited their French publishers and friends and attended the Théâtre des Italiens, where Patti was singing *Rigoletto* and *La traviata*. Muzio, who had been in Cairo for almost seven months, left Egypt as Verdi left Genoa, so they could meet in Paris before returning to Sant'Agata. A trusted colleague and, sometimes, coach to the Pattis and Strakoschs, Muzio had also conducted *Rigoletto* for the opening of the new Cairo Opera House and had directed the music for the inauguration of the Suez Canal in November 1869. In the summer of that year Verdi had been invited to write a hymn for the canal celebrations and had refused. Although he had sent a formal letter to Paul Draneht, the Superintendent of the Khedivial Theatres, he had also asked Muzio to let the Egyptian authorities know how unsatisfactory their offer had been. Muzio had kept Verdi informed about the Cairo season all winter and had sent news of the Suez Canal opening as well. In his letters, he let Verdi know that the Cairo company would be a stable, ongoing enterprise; that the next season would begin on 11 November 1870 and continue into March 1871; that the Khedive was willing to invest an enormous amount of money in it; and that artists of the highest calibre were being engaged. Tamberlick had asked 90,000 francs for the season; Nicolini, 125,000; Tiberini and his wife, 60,000 each. While Muzio and Verdi were together in Paris, they spent whole days in the hotel, discussing these and other matters.

Muzio was also trying to bring Ricordi and the Egyptian authorities together in Italy, to speed negotiations for what they all hoped would be Verdi's next opera. Draneht, a Greek and a former pharmacist, was a good administrator who had little knowledge of opera. He had created his pseudonym by anagrammatizing the surname of his pharmacology professor. Later the Khedive named him director of the Egyptian railways, although one of his main interests was mango culture in the Nile Valley. An enthusiastic Italophile, he joined the Milanese in holidays on Lake Maggiore, where the Khedive bought the magnificent Villa La Spina and transformed its gardens into a landscaped version of the *Aida* settings, so that the lakeside village of Oggebbio became known as 'Little Cairo', a tourist attraction.[7]

Writing to Verdi, neither Muzio nor Draneht seems to have told him that Temistocle Solera had become an employee of the Khedive's government. After the rupture in the winter of 1845–6, when Solera left for Madrid with the *Attila* libretto unfinished, thus putting the première at risk, he had been in Verdi's bad graces. Several attempts to get back in the composer's favour had failed, even though Solera offered librettos and a contract for Madrid. The intervention of third parties, Regli and Mariani among them, did not help. As director of the Royal Theatres in Spain, Solera became a confidant or counsellor to Queen Isabella II; but he continued to write librettos for operas that were produced in La Scala and other important theatres. When he was destitute in 1860, Verdi contributed anonymously to a fund to help him but predicted to Clara Maffei that 'eight days later' she would have to start all over again, because of Solera's improvident ways.

In spite of Verdi's predictions, Solera became a low-level official in the new Italian government, which entrusted to him part of the job of controlling brigands in southern Italy. In 1863 he was 'the Signor Cavalier' and 'inspector of the police forces' in Palermo (as Sciascia documented in *I pugnalatori*); he had been decorated by King Vittorio Emanuele II. Later he was director of police forces in several large Italian cities. His work for two royal houses earned him a post in Egypt, where he was the Khedive's organizer and director for the celebration of the opening of the Suez Canal and was also employed in the Viceroy's security forces. When Verdi declined the invitation to write the hymn for that event, Solera composed and wrote the lyrics for the *Hymn for the Celebrations at Ismailia*. (This is perhaps the national anthem of Egypt, which was later believed to have been Verdi's composition.) Muzio conducted the music for the festivities on that occasion, when the Empress Eugénie and dozens of other invited dignitaries sailed through the Canal. By 1871 Solera, then back in Italy, had opened an antique shop in Florence.

Verdi by February 1870 was suggesting that he might accept the offer, if he could graft a drama on to a historical episode with Egypt as its setting. Even as he was considering composing again, Draneht and the Khedive believed that they had found a suitable subject. It was *Aida*, the scenario of which the Egyptologist Auguste Mariette was 'editing' that winter.[8] He said he had 'intervened' to 'give the work true local colour' and told Du Locle that *Aida* was an Egyptian name, which would normally be *Aita*. (Equally close to the title *Aida*, though, is *Aidea*, the Italian title used by Lucca when he published Auber's *L'Haydée*.) In other letters, he said that he had 'done the outline' and that the scenario was 'in effect the product of my work'[9] and that it had 'come out of my brain' and 'out of my bag'. Later, he said that an important person, the Khedive, had written it, or collaborated in its creation. Mariette had 'put the scenes in order'.

Verdi had many doubts about the authorship, expressed to Giulio Ricordi in 1870, when he said he did not believe that 'an influential person' had written it.[10] He detected what he called 'such a sure hand' and 'a very expert hand, one who knows the theatre very well' behind the scenario. Given Solera's position in Egypt, it is possible that he was the real author of the scenario, for he alone had the decades of experience in composing and writing for the theatre that were required. The original plot combines *Giovanni d'Arco* (Triumph and Judgement) and a novel by Heliodorus, where we find the following characters: a Great King; his sister, a royal princess who is in love with a Greek nobleman who is described as a 'courageous warrior'; an Ethiopian princess who is a slave and personal maid to the Egyptian princess and is also in love with the Greek hero; the

King of Ethiopia; and the usual ranks of high priests, soldiers, and messengers. As in *Aida*, the jealous royal princess discovers the secret love of the hero for her slave by watching them together. She tries to persuade him to love her by offering him his freedom, when he is imprisoned. There is a judgement scene, in which the Ethiopian princess/ slave, on trial for her life, refuses to refute the charges against her, reaffirms the accusations, and does everything possible to force the judges to condemn her to death. She is also 'almost buried alive' in an underground cavern. The lovers escape and flee up the Nile to Nubia. The triumphal scene, identical to that in *Aida*, except that it takes place in the Ethiopian king's capital, celebrates the victory of the Ethiopians over Egypt! At the end of the novel, the Ethiopian princess, no longer a slave in Egypt, is reunited with her own mother the queen. Then the two embrace. The Ethiopian princess and the 'courageous warrior', as she calls him, are married and are designated the legitimate successors to the throne, as Amneris and Radamès would have been, had he accepted her hand. One of Heliodorus' characters is named Termuthis, the name assigned to the High Priestess in the *Aida* scenario and in the early printed copies of the *Aida* libretto. Because of the countless similarities between *Ethiopian Things* and *Aida*, it is possible, at least, that this is the main source for the scenario, and for the title. The full title of Heliodorus' book is *Suntagma ton peri Theagenen kai Kharikleian Aithiopikon*.[11]

The similarities between *Nabucco* and *Aida* also suggest that Solera is the author of both: their characters are virtually identical: the King of Babylon and the King of Egypt; the two 'courageous warriors'; the leaders of the captive peoples (Zaccaria and Amonasro); Abigaille and Amneris, the two princesses who are in love with the slave's lover; Fenena, a Babylonian princess held as a slave by the enemy; and Aida, an Ethiopian princess held as a slave by the enemy.

Verdi's refusal to be reconciled with Solera, over a period of more than twenty years, would likely have caused problems, had he been told that the author of *Aida* was Solera. As for Solera's failure to claim authorship, he could not have done so without ruining Mariette's reputation and defaming the Khedive. Many years later Auguste Mariette's brother Edouard said that *he* had created the *Aida* plot; but, given the content of Auguste's letters to him, that seems impossible.

We have no proof that Solera was the author; but the fact that he and Verdi were reconciled in 1871 in Florence suggests that Verdi might have discovered that Solera was 'the sure hand' and 'the very expert hand' behind the scenario. That cordial encounter led to further contacts, although he and Verdi probably never met again. Solera died in 1878 in Milan.

It was Mariette, then, who sent the scenario to Verdi, claiming first that he was responsible for it, then that the Khedive was one of the authors. Printed in Cairo in a run of only four copies, it was forwarded to Sant'Agata by Du Locle in April 1870. By May, as we shall see, Verdi was being invited to set his own conditions, no matter what they were, for the contract to compose *Aida*.

During a visit to Paris in the spring that year, Verdi persuaded Bagier to engage Muzio as a special adviser and music director of the Théâtre des Italiens, securing for him the post to which Mariani had once aspired. With this permanent post, Muzio could refuse an offer to go back to Cairo, a city he disliked. Shortly before, Verdi had virtually despaired of finding a position for Muzio, who, he felt, was too immature, too credulous, and lacking understanding of 'himself and of the world'.[12] In the summer, after Muzio and his wife visited Sant'Agata, the composer sent his protégé some advice on how to manage his new situation:

You have won this position; and now it is up to you to know how to keep it. Make people honour you and make people esteem you. Now that you have an important post, your fortune and your future depend on you; and even if Bagier should leave, there will be ten other theatres that will ask to have you, once you are recognized as a worthy man. Respect yourself and make others respect you: never a moment of weakness: treat men of the highest rank just as you treat those of the lowest: don't favour anyone; don't have likes and dislikes; and don't be afraid to swear occasionally.[13]

Muzio was 50, with thousands of miles of touring behind him, having lived in Italy, France, Spain, England, Switzerland, Belgium, the United States, Cuba, and Egypt. He had kept up his career in America even during the Civil War and had seen a good deal more of the world in his lifetime than Verdi was ever to see. While Muzio was at Sant'Agata, Verdi made him promise to go to Egypt to conduct *Aida*.

After leaving Paris, Streponi and Verdi stopped briefly at Sant'Agata then returned to Genoa. On 1 May they again went to the theatre with Stolz, whose nephew Luigino Ricci was giving his own farce *Forosina*, which Mariani conducted. The conductor's health was steadily deteriorating, forcing him to go to Bologna and put himself under the care of physicians there. Stolz, perhaps not wanting to be burdened with a man who was looked upon as a hypochondriac, broke her engagement with Mariani at this time, but apparently continued to live with him whenever they were thrown together. Del Signore, writing to Verdi on 1 June 1870, said

the marriage absolutely will not take place; and there are several reasons why it will not happen. It seems that Signora Stolz is grateful for these two months of her stay in Genoa because, as she herself says, being near Mariani, she has had the chance to get to know him better, and, as a result, is absolutely determined to leave him.[14]

Soon after he received this letter, Verdi decided to write directly to Stolz, whose address he got from Del Signore.

That Verdi wrote directly is unusual, for he often communicated with active singers through third parties, afraid, as he was, that a letter from him would be taken as a sign of endorsement. As far as we know, he had never written to Stolz before, although it seems likely that the photograph of her dated 5 December 1867, sent from Bologna while she was singing Amelia in *Un ballo in maschera* there, was intended for Verdi.[15] It shows her as a handsome woman of commanding beauty. As the soprano's answer to Verdi's letter shows, they were already discussing two matters, one professional and one personal, the first being the engagement Verdi and Muzio offered her at the Théâtre des Italiens for October and November 1870, the second being her proposed purchase of property near Busseto. She wrote: 'As for the business (far, far from the theatre), I will tell you, dear Maestro, that I have not given up the idea of buying land in your neighbourhood, and indeed am unhappy that you were unable to seal the deal you had in mind; I mean this—that if some other reasonable business should come to your attention again, you will remember me.'[16] Verdi did not forget; Stolz later almost bought a house and land at Castione dei Marchesi and perhaps lived at 'La Codetta', adjacent to Verdi's mill in Besenzone, a house that was later owned by the famous ballerina Virginia Zucchi. She wrote to Verdi again on 18 July, following up on her 2 July letter and his answer to it. She was in Senigallia, engaged as leading soprano for the fair season and singing Elisabetta, which she had made one of her signature roles. Mariani was the concertatore and conductor. Stolz let Verdi know that she had heard from Muzio, who, she said, had assured her that Verdi would come to Paris to produce *La forza del destino* himself.

Illustrious Maestro, you understand perfectly well that your presence would make that theatre splendid and guarantee the success of the entire season. This would be the first stipulation that I would put in my contract, certain as I am that they will not deny you anything, so as to make everything worthy of your extremely beautiful opera.[17]

Although this letter reeks of prima donna, Verdi assumed automatically that Mariani was responsible for Stolz's refusal to go to Paris. 'Mariani gave her bad advice. It wasn't a bad deal, to go there in October and November and go back there in April, and then we could have done the new opera,' he wrote to Rocordi.[18]

Strepponi had been denigrating the conductor in unsubtle ways earlier that year. Writing to Del Signore, she sent a kiss to 'your Teresa', the industrialist's wife, and one to Stolz, 'the other Teresa, who ought to be Mariani's, if Mariani had a head as healthy as the rest of his body and if he were not his own enemy because of his egotism. So shake the hand of this friend [Mariani], whom we might one day consider [our enemy] . . . no, may God not want that.'[19] Writing to Teresa Del Signore in May, she referred to Mariani's health again: 'He talks of his health, *which is still very much changed*, but that is a fable that no one believes.'[20] Curiously, Verdi wrote to Del Signore on 24 June to say that he had not had any news of Mariani for a long time. Again, one suspects that he had not been given the conductor's letters, for Mariani had written Verdi on the second, the fifth, and the ninth of the month. It was not in Verdi's nature to lie about something like this. On 28 July the conductor wrote again, to answer a 'little letter' Verdi had sent him. He sent news of the season in Senigallia and of a letter he had had from the soprano Isabella Galletti-Gianoli, who hoped to be assigned one of the leading roles in the opera Verdi was composing 'for Cairo'. Although Mariani did not know the title, this was *Aida*, the scenario of which the composer had received from Paris in May. Not yet fully committed, although he was working on the opera, Verdi did not sign his contract until August, as we shall see. Mariani, not wanting to offend the composer, did not want to recommend the soprano, but merely told Verdi of her hopes. Because he was so ill, Mariani had visited the Shrine of the Blessed Virgin in Loreto: 'Yesterday I was in Loreto (don't laugh) because who knows whether the Madonna might not cure me, since the treatment for my physical suffering didn't make me any better. You will laugh; but that is what I did!'[21]

Verdi did not answer, but Strepponi and Corticelli did, the agent signing the letter that she drafted and entered in her Letter-book. This document stands as testimony to the poisoned air at Sant'Agata. In its first sentence, the references to St Ignatius Loyola stamp the conductor as a 'Jesuit' or faithful Catholic.

Just before the feast-day of the saint whose name you ought to bear [31 July, the Feast of St Ignatius Loyola], you really wanted to spit out one of the most insolent bits of stupidity that have ever been spoken in our era. And if you were only in good faith! Your unbounded vanity forces you to pose all the time and even go so far as to wish to seem to be one of the most vulgar bigots in the Papist crowd! Verdi gave me your pious letter, between a little smile and a 'pouah!' That you go to Loreto to make people talk about your faith and your devotion to the Madonna is something you can explain to the husbands of your former mistresses and to the women to whom it is no longer convenient for you to be what you wished to be, and what you found it convenient to be just a short time ago. Matters of vanity and egotism can be weighed on the scale of your Ego, for a change . . . but that you dare to make a fool of Verdi and of your beloved servant with such a display—oh, for God's sake, no! We would still rather have your vanity drag you down to the level of the ridiculous, saying boldly that Napoleon III reined in his horse and stopped to say: *'Are you Mariani? What can I do for you?'* '*Sire, save Italy!' and one hundred thousand Frenchmen ran straight to the frontier just to please you.* This charlatanry, in its immensity, is valuable for making people laugh. But that you would be such a hypocrite as to want to make people believe that you go to the Madonna so that she can heal that jewel, your bladder, the subject of your conversation with everyone! . . . Now, Mariani, if you care about keeping the relationship with Verdi that was already so damaged last autumn, watch what you say and do, and what you advise your men and women friends, who are not strictly honest, so that they will not do anything rash, will not take courses of action that are not perfectly honest, worthy, straightforward, and loyal. I know that you will not answer me, or that you will answer with a letter the size of a little book; but I have said what I want to say to you, and will not discuss this subject again. You can burn this letter so that the coming generations will not find it among those that you are keeping to add lustre to your vanity.[22]

With Verdi, Strepponi, and Corticelli still at Sant'Agata, Stolz, from Senigallia, answered the composer's third letter to her, in which he had let her know that he was not going to Paris to produce *La forza del destino*. The soprano then blamed Muzio for giving her the wrong information. Mariani, who had heard that he might perhaps be chosen to conduct the première of *Aida* in Cairo, appealed to Verdi, asking for the 'honour I would have at being invited *by you* to go to Cairo for such a solemn occasion'.[23] The composer answered brusquely:

Gianoli would do well to mind his own business and not get mixed up in mine. . . . On another occasion, you wrote me that you wanted to go with me to

Cairo: I told you that I was not going. If I had thought it a good idea to send you there in my place, I would have asked you; if I didn't, that is the proof that I didn't find it proper and that I had given the responsibility to someone else. To sum up, Gianoli's letter is ugly for him, for you, and for me.[24]

Muzio, Verdi's choice, was already pledged to go.

The composer had been working on *Aida* for months. Du Locle, when Verdi asked him who had written it, said that it had been written by a very important person, the Khedive of Egypt. Yet Verdi's instincts were strong enough to tell him that someone with a sound understanding of theatre had had a hand in it: 'someone used to writing, someone who knows the theatre very well'. It was 'splendid in its *mise-en-scène*, and there are two or three moments that, if not very new, are certainly very beautiful. . . . Let's hear the financial terms offered from Egypt, and then we will decide.'[25] On 2 June the composer stipulated his conditions: he would pay for the libretto himself; he would send someone to Cairo at his own expense to produce and conduct the opera; he would send a copy of the score to Egypt and would concede his author's rights only for the Kingdom of Egypt keeping all other rights to the libretto and the music for all the rest of the world; and he would be paid 150,000 francs, to be deposited in the Rothschild Bank in Paris at the moment the score was delivered.[26] His terms were accepted.

To Piroli, he wrote saying that 'If anyone had said to me two years ago "You will compose for Cairo," I would have treated him like a madman; but now I see that I am the madman.'[27] He summoned Giulio Ricordi and Ghislanzoni to Sant'Agata, as work began. Because the Egyptian setting was unfamiliar, he was reading Herodotus and researching Egyptian cult practices and practitioners, male and female. In at least three letters written during the summer of 1870 Verdi referred to what he called 'the theatrical word' (*la parola scenica*). Writing to Giulio Ricordi on 10 July he said that he was 'continually rereading the scenario of *Aida*' and was concerned that Ghislanzoni not overlook 'the theatrical words'. 'By *theatrical words* I mean the ones that sculpt a situation or a character, that always have enormous power over the audience. I know very well that it is sometimes hard to give them a high, poetic form.'[28] He was, though, able to get what he needed from Ghislanzoni, who collaborated with him through the summer and fall as the composition went on.

That year brought the conquest of Rome by Italian troops, marking the full unification of the country. It also brought the Franco-Prussian War, about which Verdi expressed dread in August. With September and a worsening situation, he wrote to Arrivabene of his sorrow over the catastrophe in France and of his fears for the future of Italy. 'Ah, the North! It is a land and a people that frighten me.'[29] At the end of the month he confided to Clara Maffei 'the desolation in my heart' over France.

It is true that the *blague*, the impertinence, the presumption of the French was, and is, in spite of their misery, unbearable; but in truth France has given liberty and civilization to the modern world. Let us not deceive ourselves. If she falls, all our liberty and civilization will fall. . . . If [our men of letters and politicians] were to look inside the [Germans] for a moment, they would see that the ancient blood of the Goths still flows in their veins, that they are inordinately proud, hard, intolerant, contemptuous of all that is not German, and endlessly greedy. Men of intelligence, but without hearts: a strong race, but barbarous. And that King, who always has God on his lips, and talks about providence, and, with the help of these, is destroying the best part of Europe. He believes that he is predestined to reform the habits and punish the vices of the modern world!!! What a missionary! Old Attila (another missionary of the same kind) stopped in his tracks before the majesty of the capital of the ancient world; but this one is about to bombard the capital of the modern world; and now that Bismarck wants to let people know that Paris will be spared, I am more afraid than ever that at least part of it will be ruined. Why? I wouldn't know. Maybe so that such a beautiful capital will no longer exist, since they will never be able to build another one like it! Poor Paris! that I saw last April, so happy, so beautiful, so splendid!

And what about us? I would have liked to see a more generous political policy, and see us pay a debt of recognition. One hundred thousand of our men could perhaps have saved both France and us. Anyway, I would have preferred for us to sign a treaty of peace won with the French to this inertia, which will make us despised some day. We will not escape a European war; and we will be devoured by it. It will not come tomorrow, but it will come. An excuse will always be found. Maybe Rome, the Mediterranean—and then didn't they declare that the Adriatic was a German sea?

The business in Rome is a great event, but it leaves me cold, perhaps because I feel that it could be the cause of terrible problems inside the country and beyond it; because I cannot reconcile the Parliament with the College of Cardinals; freedom of the press with the Inquisition; civil law and the *Syllabus* [*of Errors*]; and because I am afraid to see our government take chances, and hope. If tomorrow a clever, astute, really smart pope should come, one of the kind that Rome has had so often, he will ruin us. *Pope* and *King of Italy* are two words I cannot see together, not even in this letter![30]

The Franco-Prussian War delayed the signing of Verdi's contract for *Aida*, for, as he said, 'In the sad, sad time through which we are now living, I would really not have dared to talk to you about the contract with Cairo';[31] but, under pressure from Du Locle, he finally signed at the end of August, asking to be paid 150,000 francs in gold. Added to the agreement were stipulations that would affect the première of the opera if the war were to make the Cairo production impossible: 'If, because of some unforeseen event that had nothing to do with me, that is to say *that is not my fault*, this opera were not given at the theatre in Cairo during the month of January 1871, I would have the right to have it given somewhere else six months later.'[32] As he wrote this, he and Ghislanzoni had worked out many of the details of the first act and part of the second, although on 14 August the composer had asked his librettist to set aside the consecration scene for the moment, so as to be able to 'study it and give it more character and a greater theatrical importance'.[33] He said that he wanted a 'real scene' and not just a 'cold hymn'. He threw himself into the work, keeping up correspondence almost on a daily basis, even when he had to go to Genoa on business for a day or two. On 17 August, writing to Ghislanzoni about the *parola scenica*, he criticized the librettist's ornate lines and reduced them to something not far from common speech:

For example, the lines:

> In volto gli occhi affisami
> E menti ancor se l'osi:
> Radamès vive . . .

[Look straight into my eyes And lie, if you dare: Radamès is alive . . .] that is less theatrical than the words (ugly, you may say):

> . . . con una parola
> strapperò il tuo segreto.
> Guardami: t'ho ingannata:
> Radamès vive . . .

[. . . with one word I will tear your secret from you. Look at me: I deceived you Radamès is alive . . .] So also the lines:

> Per Radamès d'amore
> Ardo e mi sei rivale
> —Che? Voi l'amate? Io l'amo
> E figlia son d'un re

[I am burning with love for Radamès, and you are my rival—What? You love him? I love him And I am a king's daughter] seem less theatrical to me than the words: 'You love him? But I love him too. Do you understand? The Pharaoh's daughter is your rival!' AIDA: 'My rival? So be it: I, too am the daughter, etc.' I know perfectly well that you will say: 'And what about the verse, the rhyme, the strophe?' I don't know what to say, except that when the action requires it, I would abandon verse, rhyme, and strophe: I would write free verse, to say clearly and simply whatever the action demands. Unfortunately, in the theatre sometimes the poets and composers have to have the gift of *not* writing either poetry or music.[34]

He ploughed ahead on his own with the consecration scene and, in September the Triumphal March, although he was in despair over the French defeat at Sedan, where the Prussian army was victorious and Napoleon III was captured.

With Ghislanzoni at his side, Verdi resolved problems that could not be managed by post; and, after the librettist returned to Milan, Verdi pressed him for the third-act libretto, which he finally received at the end of September. 'Very good, although there are some things that in my opinion have to be touched up', among them Aida's aria 'O patria mia'.[35] By October he had sketched out everything he needed for the third-act confrontation with Amonasro; at that point he went back to the Aida–Radamès duet, which had not satisfied him. On 26 October he complained to Luccardi that he was 'working like an animal';[36] again he summoned Ghislanzoni to Sant'Agata, and by 12 November he was able to write to Mariette that the opera was almost finished.

By that time Mariette was trapped in Paris, where he had gone to arrange for the scenery and costumes and had been caught in the siege. A letter from Draneht, who was still in Cairo, informed Verdi that the première could not be given as scheduled, forcing Verdi to revise his plans for giving *Aida* at La Scala, where he had expected to produce it himself in February 1871. From Genoa, where he and Strepponi had gone in mid-December, he wrote to Draneht that he would 'give up my hope of giving my opera in Cairo and at La Scala this season'.[37]

The casting and choice of conductors for these two important productions were worked out with the two theatres, although the postponement of the première created serious problems. Verdi wanted Stolz for Milan, but asked the Ricordis to negotiate with her. At the end of December Giulio Ricordi went to Venice, where Stolz was singing Elisabetta in *Don Carlo*. In Genoa, Verdi approached Mariani, who was conducting his own season, about the soprano's engagement and learned that the conductor was in favour of Stolz singing at La Scala. Ricordi had confirmation of his own directly from the soprano. Writing to Verdi from the station in Bologna, as he was on his way back to Milan, Ricordi said that the soprano had definitely accepted the proposal, 'having had a telegram from our friend Mariani.—But really, are they married? yes or no?'[38]

During Ricordi's interview with Stolz, whom he saw on 3 January 1871, he apparently did not settle the final terms of her contract for La Scala. On that same day or on the fourth Stolz wrote to Mariani to let him know what she wanted, certain that the conductor would act just as he did, showing the letter to Verdi. Outraged, Verdi complained to Ricordi that if all singers asked for what Stolz wanted, the impresario would go bankrupt.

40,000 L[ire] in gold and three performances!!! They would have to shut up shop half way through the season! . . . I would be very unhappy indeed to be in the hands of an impresario that could not get through the season. Something else: who will conduct the orchestra next year? I would like to know something about that. Mariani told me that he is marrying Stolz in the spring. I don't believe it.[39]

One day later Ricordi himself had a letter from Stolz, outlining her conditions:

The first condition would be to have my pay guaranteed either by the City or by a solid banking house. Secondly, 40,000 francs, net, without my having to pay agents' fees or any taxes. Thirdly, all the operas, as we agreed (and, if it is possible) to have the right to perform Maestro Verdi's new opera Aida. Fourthly, to sing not more than three performances a week. Fifthly, to be the leading prima donna. Sixthly, to have the right to take the usual eight sick days. Here are all my conditions, stated. You, good Signor Giulio, do all you can now to get them accepted, and especially the first; and I shall be ready to sign the contract.[40]

Ricordi took a hard line at once. He accused her of bad faith, of breaking the verbal agreement they had had, and of demanding terms that he could not possibly get from the management. To Verdi he raged: 'This business with Signora Stolz is really filthy: I see Mariani's paw in this! and if he were here right now I would kick him in the a[ss] and treat him like a dog! He is even ruining Signora Stolz's career!'[41] Verdi agreed that Stolz's terms were extravagant and confided to the publisher that he, on his own, had begun to investigate the chances of engaging either Antonietta Pozzoni Anastasi, or the daughter of Teresa De Giuli Borsi. He added that he did not see how he could make any kind of arrangement with Mariani, because everything that he had proposed to the conductor came out badly: it was, though, important to make major decisions about the conductor for La Scala. 'If Stolz can't be got, the world will not fall apart just because of that. . . . Get information yourself about Pozzoni and De Giuli. They are young (fine for a role like Aida) and if they have voice and heart, I will take care of making them sing and act well.'[42] Later, worried that even Pozzoni might not satisfy the demanding audience in Milan, he demanded that he be left completely free to give *Aida* or not give it at La Scala; it would be safer to withdraw the opera than to risk it with a poor cast.

Stolz asked for an even larger fee when she was invited to sing in Cairo, pushing Draneht to complain to Verdi about her extraordinary demands. Verdi, too, had a hand in the Cairo season, as it became certain that Muzio, his first choice to conduct the première of *Aida*, could not go to Egypt because of other commitments. Desperate to have a responsible person control this important production, the composer turned again to Mariani, to whom he had denied the post earlier. The conductor, who always had a hard time making up his mind about anything, faced many problems at that time: he was much sicker than he had been the year before; he had commitments of his own in Genoa, and would have to get a *laisser passer* from the mayor of the city, whose employee he was; and he was still involved with Stolz, whom he still expected to marry in the spring of 1871. Instead of telling Verdi outright that he could not go, he seems to have said initially that he would accept the responsibility, then to have asked for time to think it over, then, after asking for an extra day, to have refused the offer at the end of April. Disappointed and angry, Verdi opened his heart to Del Signore: 'Ah, c'est vraiment trop fort! trop fort! trop fort!'[43] Mariani tried to defend himself, writing Verdi a pathetic letter on 18 June:

I didn't write to you because I did not have the courage to do it. I hope, though, that Carlino's letter will have convinced you that I have always believed that I did not fail in any way in my responsibility toward you. If, without knowing it, this is what happened to me, I beg your forgiveness; and be absolutely certain that I am very, very sorry that you even thought that this was the case. I know the goodness of your noble heart, so that I hope you will want to relieve me of the anguish I feel at not ever having news from you, nor from the excellent Signora Peppina. I won't say anything to you about myself and my health, for fear that you might believe that I want to make myself sound interesting. I live a quiet life and try to get well. I confess to you, though, that this condition is beginning to cause so much trouble that I cannot go on. That's enough: it is my fate![44]

Mariani turned to the artist Serafino De Avendaño, one of his and Verdi's acquaintances in Genoa, in another attempt to reach Verdi through a third party; but he could hardly have made a worse choice, for the artist was the lover of Strepponi's Genovese friend Nina Ravina, whom Verdi did not especially like.[45] Seeing that Verdi would not answer his letter, Mariani then asked Del Signore to set up a meeting in Genoa. This too failed, perhaps because the two men's schedules did not mesh, perhaps because Verdi could not bring himself to start anew with Mariani. It is to Verdi's credit, though, that even when he suspected that Mariani might not go to Cairo, he still pushed Draneht to engage him: 'If, as you say, you want an orchestra conductor with a *recognized* and *sure* gift, there is absolutely no one but Mariani. There is no other man better.'[46] When Draneht went ahead on his own and hired Giovanni Bottesini, an apostle of the Music of the Future and founder of an avant-garde circle in Tuscany, Verdi registered his chagrin and disappointment.

Planning his own production at La Scala, he had finally secured Stolz as Aida and Francesco Pandolfini as Amonasro; both Giuseppe Fancelli and Giuseppe Capponi were being considered for Radamès. Still searching for an Amneris, Verdi advised Ricordi to get Maria Waldmann under contract without promising her a role in *Aida*, so that she could be heard in performances in the house—the only place, he said, to judge a singer. Waldmann, too, asked a high fee, leading Verdi to protest. Corresponding with Ricordi, he also asked that the orchestra at La Scala be placed out of sight, for the first time in Italy: 'This idea is not mine. It is Wagner's. It is excellent. How can we bear the sight of those wretched frock coats and white ties in the midst of Egyptian, Assyrian and Druid costumes?' [. . .] you will see that I shall become a rabid Wagnerian![47]

Mariani, too, was studying Wagner that July, with *Lohengrin* announced for the Teatro Comunale's autumn season. For the conductor, the production would mean an exceptional amount of extra work. Initially opposed to the project, he gradually came to accept it and to admire the opera, a fact that was set down at Sant'Agata as being anti-Verdi, anti-Ricordi, and anti-Italian. Verdi, Strepponi, and Corticelli received a first-hand account of the city officials' meeting at which it was decided that *Lohengrin* should be given, their source of information being Luigi Monti, the Ricordi agent in Bologna. In Monti's report, he even sent a summary of what Mariani had *said* at the meeting: '*Lohengrin* must be given' and 'the company had already been chosen for the impresario who had the Comunale, and the company was Blume, Capponi, Destin' and these artists had been sent 'telegrams because he knew that Signora Lucca was satisfied with them.' This 'Chameleon', Mariani, as Monti called him, was an artist worthy of respect, but as a man, he was 'the vilest in existence . . . I never thought that he was such a scoundrel; I have always said that as a man he is a clown, a terrible talker, but I would never have thought him so two-faced and scheming.'[48] Mariani's sin was to have proposed *Lohengrin* and *L'Africaine* rather than a revival of *Don Carlo*.

Strepponi, in one of her bursts of rage, set down a bill of accusations against Mariani in her Letter-book, under the rubric 'Copyist's Notes'. The words may be Verdi's or even Corticelli's; but they sound very much like her own.

And the masquerade about going to Cairo to conduct *Aida* when Galletti was there and people thought it could be given in that season?

And the Mass in Bologna?

And the *ibis* and *ridibis* (in the bad sense, I mean) over the engagement of Stolz in Milan, under the pretext of having his rights as a future husband?

And the tricks and lies (unknown to the public, but none the less infamous and vile) to the old and new mistresses and the continuous cheating on Stolz?

And the lies he tells every day, every hour? And his sordid greed, when his vanity is not on the line?

And the evil things said about Luisa Pallavicino, when she has moments of impatience, being bored with his endless and false stories?

And the lies to la Frugoni?

And the way he acts toward Carlino Del Signore and his family, whether there are people present or not?

And la Massa?

And the business with the Mayor of Bologna, before whom he cut the filthiest and vilest figure on earth?

And the figure he cut with Verdi, *after having accepted* [the invitation] to go to Cairo for the opera, which is surely going to be given this year?

This man's words are filth, like his soul, and he tries to pass as the most *chaste* person.[49]

Stolz, who was invited to Sant'Agata for a visit that lasted from 23 September until the second week in October, perhaps heard some of these charges aired while she was there. Mariani himself learned from De Avendaño that no one in Verdi's house was allowed to mention the conductor's name, and that if anyone dared to do so, everything possible was done to change the subject. 'But I don't believe that the thought of me should be so odious that they feel revulsion simply on hearing my name.'[50] Mariani, who had been with Stolz in Florence for ten days in late summer, returned there when he heard that she was going to Sant'Agata and kept her company on the train as far as Bologna. During the trip he told her that her visit put him in an awkward position, for he felt he could not even write her there. When the soprano left Verdi, after studying the role of Aida with him, she again saw Mariani in Bologna, while her train stopped there. Their conversation lasted only fourteen minutes before Stolz went on to Florence. From there two days later she wrote Mariani a letter that he found cold and even scornful; when he reserved a box for her for the first night of *Lohengrin*, she told him that she would stay in Bologna just that one evening, but that she was no longer his fiancée and would not marry him. 'A simple friendship between artists' was what she wanted. 'That is the gratitude and comfort that I got at that moment from the woman to whom I had consecrated all my love and my whole future.'

'Who would ever have said that my friends, the two people I revered and loved [. . .] would have acted together to treat me as they have done!!!'[51] Mariani, then suffering excruciating pain from a recurrence of his illness, dragged himself to the theatre for the rehearsals and four performances a week of *Lohengrin*, which engaged him fully during much of the autumn, because the work and its composer, new to Italy, raised problems no one south of the Alps had had to solve before 1871. Musicians claimed they could not play the notes; singers claimed they could not sing them. Everything required enormous investments of money, time, and energy as the scenery, costumes, stage action, arrangement of the orchestra, phrasing, enunciation, and style were studied. The very fact that the work was being given represented a triumph of the House of Lucca over Ricordi, and of Bologna over Milan; and the clamour raised over the opera sealed this double victory. The Luccas went to Munich with a corps of experts to study the German production, while Wagner himself followed the progress of preparations.

In Bologna, Mariani bore the full burden of concertatore at a time when he was so ill that he stayed in bed most of the time when he was not in the theatre. Had Wagner been at his side, as the composer wished to be, the conductor's task would have been easier. Late in October Wagner wrote to Mariani from Triebschen to compliment him on his effort and to beg the conductor to pay special attention to the chorus because it had such a large role to play in the opera. 'In *Lohengrin*,' Wagner wrote, 'the chorus is not put there just to sing pieces that are more or less set, as in most of the other operas; they *act* just as the principal characters do in the work. Indeed, in the second act a broad *movement* by the chorus on stage is necessary.[52] Asking Mariani to mind his markings in the score, he also called attention to the tempos, then closed with a sly remark about the impresario in Bologna, who had invited 'almost everyone in the world' but had not invited him. To Wagner's satisfaction and to Mariani's, the production went very well, being acclaimed by Italians and foreigners alike as one of the landmarks of Italian theatre history.

On 19 November Mariani, who had gone to the railway station to meet someone, found Verdi alone on the station platform. He had come to hear *Lohengrin*. When the conductor tried to help the composer with his bag, Verdi seized it from him and rebuffed any attempt to start a conversation. Ordering Mariani not to tell anyone that he was in the city, he said that he wanted to remain incognito. Mariani promised to say nothing; the two men parted. That night Box 23 at the Teatro Comunale held three men: Corticelli and Monti seated in full view of the audience, Verdi behind a curtain at the rear. The composer had a score of *Lohengrin*, in which he made marginal notes during or just after the performance. At the end of the second act, Monti stood up in the box and shouted 'Viva il Maestro Verdi', just as applause for the artists was dying down, thus setting off a fifteen-minute ovation for Verdi. He refused to come forward, take a bow, or be seen, even when the Mayor of Bologna appealed to him to do so; but Monti and Corticelli bowed and preened themselves at the front of the box. Verdi, who detested such exhibitions, must have been as unhappy as Mariani was over this vulgar demonstration. When the opera ended, at three in the morning, Verdi went to the Hotel Brun. Sometime during the day, he had a chance to speak briefly to Boito, who was also in Bologna to see *Lohengrin*. It is likely that he never saw Mariani again.

Verdi's score of *Lohengrin* is among his books at Sant'Agata, with his notations on many pages. These run from 'too loud', a criticism of the orchestra in the first bars of the Prelude, to 'beautiful', 'a great deal of interest in this scene', 'bad', 'too fast', 'ugly', 'terribly noisy', 'flat', 'vast', 'a mess', 'the scene is cold', 'empty, dead action', and,—for the Wedding Chorus—'perhaps a bit too fast, so that it does not have the calmness and the poetry that it should have'.[53] In his summary he wrote:

Mediocre impression. Beautiful music; when it is clear, it is thought-out. The action runs slowly, as do the words. From that, boredom. Beautiful effects in the instruments. Abuse of notes held too long, and that makes it heavy. Execution mediocre. Much *verve*, but lacking in poetry and finesse. In the crucial moments, bad all the time.[54]

Verdi was completely absorbed with the two productions of *Aida*, the première being planned for the Opera House in Cairo at the end of December 1871; the opening at La Scala scheduled for late January or early February 1872. Another production in Parma was also being planned, but Verdi frequently refused offers from other theatres because he was determined to give the work only where it could be performed well. Under pressure from Ricordi, he wrote an overture for the Milan version and sent it to Ricordi on 28 December with the ink wet, but withdrew it during rehearsals. (It has been performed in this century, notably by Toscanini.) The composer also considered putting in a ballet, which was to be called *La figlia dei faraoni*, but this idea too was set aside. In the months before the Milan opening, he worried about the fact that the opera was getting too much publicity, which he dreaded, and that people were being shown the score. When Ricordi let both Boito and Filippi see *Aida*, Verdi protested to his publisher:

You were wrong to show *Aida* to outsiders. Judgements made in advance are of no value at all and no good to anyone . . . Always mistrust these judgements, whether they come from friends or enemies. Also, I absolutely do not want *publicity*. Let the public judge on the first night, for better or for worse. . . . I beg you in all seriousness, do not let anyone talk about *Aida* any more; let no one look at it; and let no one judge it. Be calm yourself: either *Aida* will succeed, then we will not need publicity, or it will go badly, and these premature views will just add to the fiasco.[55]

From this letter it is clear that Boito talked about *Aida* in Bologna, and not about uncomfortable trains, as the *Gazzetta musicale di Milano* had reported.

Verdi left *Lohengrin* in Bologna for *Aida*, which he was preparing in Genoa, criticizing costume sketches and drawings of the scenery. Having coached Stolz at Sant'Agata and in Genoa, he then turned to the others. Only Waldmann, who had other commitments, could not study the work in advance with him, although he did coach her in Milan. Fearful that rehearsal time at La Scala was being cut short, he preached to Ricordi: 'Theatre managements never know what they are doing'[56] and 'Listen now, and pay absolute attention to these two matters: *ensemble scenes* and *on-stage movement*.'[57] Verdi had turned over to Ricordi the production of *La forza del destino* that was to precede *Aida* at La Scala.

When Verdi was most concerned about the effect that advance publicity might have on *Aida*, he got a long letter from Filippi, who had been invited to Cairo by the Khedive. The critic, asking whether he could do anything for Verdi while he was there, and whether he could serve as a kind of personal representative, got an angry answer. Verdi, already out of sorts because the critic had been shown a copy of the score, wrote:

BOOK V

Dear Sig. Filippi,

What I am about to say will seem strange, very strange, but forgive me if I cannot hide from you what is in my heart.

You in Cairo! And this is one of the most important *réclames* that anyone could imagine for *Aida*! It seems to me that art like this is no longer art, but rather a trade, a game played for pleasure, a hunting party, a commonplace thing that everyone runs to see, a thing to which people want to bring—if not success—at least notoriety, no matter what the cost! The emotion that I feel is disgust, humiliation!

I remember happily my first years, when, almost without friends, without anyone who talked about me, without advance preparations, without influence of any kind, I went before the audience with my operas, ready to *be shot*, and enormously happy if I could at least manage to get some favourable response. Now what an apparatus for an opera!! Journalists, artists, chorus people, directors, professors, etc., etc., and all of them have to bring their stone to help build the *publicity* palace, thus creating a frame of little miseries that add nothing to the worth of the opera,—indeed, they hide its real value! That is deplorable, absolutely deplorable!

Thank you for your courteous offer about Cairo. I wrote the other night to Bottesini about everything that concerns *Aida*. I only want this opera to have a good, and above all, *intelligent* vocal, instrumental [performance] and *mise-en-scène*; as for everything else, *the grace of God* that is how I began and that is how I want to end my career.[58]

Further, to Ricordi,

Just now I feel so disgusted, so nauseated, so irritated that I would put the score of *Aida* in the fire a thousand times, without a single regret. Do you want to do it? Do we still have time? . . . But if this poor opera has to exist anyway, for the love of heaven, no *publicity*, no apparatus, which is the most humiliating of all humiliations for me. Oh everything that I saw in Bologna and see now in Florence [where Mariani was conducting *Lohengrin*] is nauseating! No no . . . I don't want anything like *Lohengrin* [for *Aida*]. Better [to throw it on] the fire.[59]

He confided to Clara Maffei that he was desperate over the publicity: 'Publicity . . . is always humiliating and useless. Now I am so ill at ease, so irritated about these filthy theatrical matters that I may feel like doing something rash!'[60]—The 'something rash' was a threat that he might indeed prevent the production from being staged. He was very angry when news came from Cairo that the première of *Aida* would only be seen by invited guests: no tickets could be sold. Verdi erupted: 'What a pleasure for an artist, to study so long, work so hard [. . .] and then be applauded politely, as if in an *Accademia*! What a joke!! And to think that I am a part of it, and a victim of this!!!!'[61]

The première, given at the Cairo Opera House on 24 December 1871, had Antonietta Pozzoni Anastasi in the title role; Pietro Mongini as Radamès; Francesco Steller as Amonasro; Tommaso Costa as the King; Paolo Medini as Ramfis, the High Priest; and Eleanora Grossi as Amneris. After the opening, a telegram sent to Genoa announced: 'VERDI— Genova—*Aida* enthusiastic success culminating in second finale all artists celebrating—orchestra excellent—great ovation Viceroy applauded.'[62] Verdi took it philosophically: 'We'll see what happens later, because one should not put too much faith in telegrams sent after the first performance. It seems, though, that the piece that got the most applause was the second-act finale. So much the better, if that huge piece was effective, performed by an inadequate company.'[63]

He had some doubts about the company he had in Milan, where he kept strict control over the production at every step. At the beginning of the season, though, *La forza del destino* at La Scala proved disappointing, leading Verdi to hope that some of the problems it raised might be solved as the season continued. He was afraid that the tenor and the mezzo-soprano might not be good enough. About Waldmann, he said:

She has some odd things, such as her accent, her pronunciation, and her unevenness of tone, which can only make for bad effects. . . . If *La forza del destino* were to be a fiasco, what would the management do? They cannot fill the time until *Aida* [is staged], and they will have to find another opera right away, a repertory opera to fall back on, using the leading company of singers. As for me, I favour *Poliuto*. That would delay *Aida*, but there's nothing we can do about it. *Macbeth* given with the first company; *Poliuto* with the second company. Think about this, and make the management consider it, because I will not give in and under no circumstances will I let them strangle *Aida*.[64]

Verdi got to Milan on 2 January 1872 and began preparing *Aida* with Faccio, its conductor. From the outset he ordered all rehearsals closed, even the final dress rehearsal, which by tradition had been open to invited guests. Every moment was dedicated to his production, especially to Waldmann and to the tenor Fancelli. With the shortcomings of the company that the early performances revealed, he was not even sure that he could get *Aida* staged before the end of the month. This he confided to Du Locle, as he asked the French impresario to send Stolz's stage jewellery from Paris. Shortly after Verdi got to Milan, he heard that

Mariani had taken a turn for the worse. To Arrivabene, he wrote: 'Mariani was very sick and still is. I hope that he gets well and hope that everything goes well for him, but . . . he acted toward me . . . I won't say anything else.'[65] When the conductor sent New Year's greetings, Verdi apparently did not answer.

Aida, which had its first performance at La Scala on 8 February 1872, proved to be a gratifying personal triumph for the composer, who was called out thirty-two times during the evening and given a magnificent ovation. On the occasion of this, his 'official' return to Milan, the city gave him a gold and ivory sceptre. To it, as to the critics, Verdi showed typical indifference, although he did rouse himself to protest against the 'stupid reviews, and praise that is even more stupid: not one elevated or artistic concept; not one critic who was willing to present my ideas and intentions . . . just stupidity. . . . No one, no one [was] willing to take note of the extraordinary execution and the *mise-en-scène*. Not one who said to me: "*Thanks, Dog.*"'[66] When Ricordi offered to answer those who criticized *Aida* and Verdi, the composer begged his publisher not to say anything more, and 'do not defend me any further. Say instead that *Aida* is an abortion, a rag-bag of borrowed scraps, the worst opera in existence. . . . It won't matter. No one will suffer, nothing will be damaged, excepting the composer's reputation!'[67]—And the composer's feelings, he might have added, for he considered *Aida* one of the best operas he had composed. At the box-office it earned a great deal of money for La Scala and other theatres. One impresario said it was a gold mine. Quite beyond that, it gave Ricordi a weapon against the Luccas, who, together with Mariani, were producing Meyerbeer's *L'Africaine* with Marie Sass in Reggio Emillia,[68] while Verdi was staging *Aida* in Parma, the next city. Writing to Ricordi, Verdi said: 'Avenging Jove wants to turn us all to ashes; and we all are supposed to be honoured by God's bolts of lightning.'[69] From Strepponi's Letter-books one learns that she, too, had begun to refer to Mariani as Jove; but she made remarks about the 'deity' and his sexual exploits:

The Bolognese may be decent people; and let us suppose that the scandalous, wretched scenes that were put on [after *Lohengrin*] were staged by people from outside the city . . . As for the God [Mariani], who is too revered by his coterie, the newspapers, and also by [the *Gazzetta musicale di Milano*], the many apotheoses have caused him to lose not the right road, which he never knew how to find, but that kind of half-modest way of his that he used as he tried to hide, as if in a cloud, like Father Jove, when he was committing his Olympian obscenities against Juno. Now the God, injured, perhaps because some mortal has refused to perfume his altar with incense, has been stripped nude; and, alas! nudity does not really enhance the beauty of his body.[70]

She mentioned Mariani's 'challenge' to Verdi, observing that her husband would not deign to answer it. Verdi had responded to some inner call, though: 'As far as I am concerned, if I meant in the past to do the work of ten men, now I will do the work of twenty', he declared to Ricordi on 21 February.[71] With *Aida*, he, not quite 60, had begun a new life.

First, Parma. Then Naples. The first of these seemed as taxing as Milan, for the chorus of the Teatro Ducale had to be reorganized; the conductor, unsure of himself, led an orchestra that included young, inexperienced musicians; the impresario, sensing a great box-office, wanted to put on sixteen performances of this huge, demanding opera in thirty-six days, something the company could not do. Among the production's greatest assets were Girolamo Magnani's sets and costumes, which later contributed to the triumphant American tour of *Aida*. Verdi, agreeing to prepare the opera himself, went with Stolz from the Milan *Aida* to Parma just as he had with Strepponi and *Nabucco* in 1843. Although decades had passed, the composer seemed healthier and more vigorous than he had at the start of his career, when ill health had frequently plagued him. He used trains, which were operating more and more efficiently, to hurry from Genoa to Milan to Sant'Agata, first one task, then another, juggling the many areas of his life: a dozen newspapers to scan, as he always did on the train; a score of singers to be monitored; journalists to be controlled; contracts to be negotiated; investments to be tended carefully; the estate at Sant'Agata to be checked; and his own operas to be protected. These were new years of drudgery, but Verdi seemed not to notice how much he had undertaken. Dozens of letters went off from his writing-desk, covering every subject from aesthetics to politics to the local recipe for cooking pork shoulder: 'To take away the salt before cooking, soak it for two hours in warm water. Then put it on the fire in a pot. It has to boil for six hours over a slow fire, then let it cool in its own broth. When it is cold, that is, twenty-four hours later, take it out of the pot, dry it, and eat it.'[72] The recipe was sent to Arrivabene and Stolz; to the former, he wrote: '*Aida* went well. Theatre packed.'

He had begun rehearsals in Parma on 2 April and staged his production eighteen days later. Stolz and Waldmann remained from the original cast;

Faccio had been replaced by the permanent conductor in Parma, Giovanni Rossi. *Aida* proved a stunning success for Verdi in home territory. The event, however, was marked by an incident that, for all its humour, proves that Verdi was not above using publicity for his own purpose when he wished to. In early May, while he was at Sant'Agata, the composer received an angry note from a disgruntled opera lover, Prospero Bertani, who had come from Reggio Emilia to Parma to hear *Aida* and had disliked it. Feeling that he had been cheated, Bertani asked Verdi to reimburse him for the price of his ticket, his train travel and his supper. Verdi ordered Ricordi to pay the bill—27 lire and 80 centesimi—but not the supper.

Pay for the supper too? No. Not that. He could very well have eaten at home. Let it be clearly understood that he will give us a receipt for the amount and that he will agree to one little condition: to promise not to go ever again to hear my operas, so that he will be spared the threat of further nightmares, and I the bad joke of having to pay for another trip for him.[73]

In a postscript, Verdi instructed Ricordi to publish the exchange in 'as many papers as you like, as soon as you have an answer from Reggio.' Even if he cannot be located, publish it, he ordered. It was done. The furies of hell fell on Prospero Bertani, who could not leave his house, could not go to the theatre. Letters from all over Italy poured into his house. An anonymous letter from Parma threatened him with decapitation— no one in Parma had forgotten the fate of Captain Anviti of the Bourbon regime—if he were ever seen in that city. Bertani raged against Verdi and Ricordi.

Verdi's next commitment to produce *Aida* was at the Teatro San Carlo in Naples, where it seemed to be a matter of cleaning the stables. Because of his mistrust of Antonio Musella, the impresario, he expected the worst. Writing to Torelli, he said:

As for the chorus, adding twenty-one chorus-members makes me laugh. With so many bad ones, what do you think twenty-one more will do!!! And a hundred are not enough for *Aida*! They have to be good—as good as Milan, and as the contract stipulates. . . . I shall go to Naples, and, if the [various] elements are good, I will throw myself into everything and handle everything as I did in Milan and Parma, so long as we can get a good performance. If not, I will leave with my score, even on the day of dress rehearsal!!![74]

Fulminating, he wrote from Sant'Agata on 17 October to 'Cara Teresa' Stolz about Musella's attempt to persuade her to arrive in Naples on

1 November and his insulting offer to pay for her food at the hotel for two weeks, if she would come. He added that he was about to leave for Genoa, where she was staying at the Albergo Italia.[75] And to Tito Ricordi, after he and Stolz had met in Genoa: 'You can imagine Stolz's blue eyes! I think she answered saying that she did not need anyone to pay for her meals and that she will be in Naples on the date stipulated in the contract.'[76] He and Streppони left Genoa early in November and settled into the apartment they had rented in Naples in the hope of getting some rest during breaks in the production schedule. They had had a difficult summer, although a long visit from Stolz, after the Parma *Aida*, had been welcome; but bad news had come from Clara Maffei, who had broken off her twenty-five-year relationship with Tenca. Manzoni had been ill. The patriot-novelist Guerrazzi had attacked Verdi over an artistic and political controversy. Filomena, now called 'Maria' by everyone, had visited during her vacation from school.

The composer's worst fears about the San Carlo were soon to prove reality. He confided to Ricordi that as far as that 'poor theatre' was concerned, no one cared what happened and everything was going wrong. Stolz, ill and unable to sing, was but one element in a crisis that was 'fatal' to the house.[77] As he grew unhappier and more frustrated, he even accused Ricordi of not caring about the production. 'The situation here could not be any worse,' he complained. 'The management's and governing council's improvidence and stubbornness have been so marked that we cannot go on. . . . It is no longer right to stay on here. Unless something unexpected happens, or something like a miracle, I will give up on Naples very quickly.'[78] He confided to Arrivabene that things were going 'to ruin', between the bad luck of having singers ill and the ignorance and poor planning, he was merely 'waiting, rather enjoying the disorder, the crisis' so that he could flee.[79] He feared that the theatre would have to close, with *Don Carlo* taken off the schedule, creditors closing in with bills, and the audience angry. Writing to Clara Maffei, he talked of the indescribable ignorance, the inertia, the apathy, the disorder, and the lack of control that he found everywhere and in everyone.

It is beyond belief; it makes me laugh when, in a moment of quiet, I think about all the problems I am causing for myself, and all the agitation I feel over my bull-headedness in *wanting and wanting* at any cost. It seems that everyone is looking at me, laughing, and saying: 'Is this man mad?'[80]

In spite of his disappointment, though, Verdi had not given up on opera, though he certainly was bitter about it. Writing to Tito Ricordi on 3 January 1873, he let flow a torrent of bad feeling:

Let's not say anything more about this *Aida*, which, although it had earned me a fine sack of money, has brought me problems without end and immense artistic disillusionment! If I had only never written it, or if I had never published it! If, after the first productions, it had stayed in my briefcase, and if I had had it produced only under my direction, where and when I wished, it would not have become a feeding trough for the evil [and] curious, to be analysed by your critics and wretched little maestros, who don't understand anything about music, excepting its basics, and those badly. Speculators would have lost something; but art would have gained enormously.[81]

In this moment of anger, Verdi and Strepponi, living in Naples, which she called 'a terrestrial paradise populated by thieves',[82] decided to try to evict Mariani from Palazzo Sauli-Pallavicino. In Bologna for his usual autumn season at the Teatro Comunale, Mariani had directed yet another Wagner opera, *Tannhäuser*, which had had a baptism by fire, attacked by demonstrators who were probably organized by Luigi Monti and Casa Ricordi. On 11 November 1872 the conductor, after the first three performances of the opera, wrote to Del Signore that there had even been whistling before the performance began; but the overture had been so successful that it had to be repeated every evening. He had never had such ovations and such applause, he said. In the third performance, always considered important for the survival of any opera in the repertory, the whole evening had gone smoothly, with both the overture and the baritone aria encored. 'Many curtain-calls and immense ovations. So I tell you that it was a beautiful thing.'[83]

When he left Bologna at the end of the season, Mariani returned to Palazzo Sauli Pallavicino, where he spent much of his time in bed,

suffering all the time, so that I am by now fed up with this miserable life. With great difficulty, I get up to take a carriage to the theatre because, as you know, I would rather die than fail to do my duty. I know that [Dr] Loreta spoke about me for some time a few evenings ago. Ah, if he only had some drug to give me, to spare me a bit of the torture that is killing me! Unfortunately, though, I understand that he won't have anything to help; and I will have to suffer my fate, and, I assure you [. . .] that it is truly awful.[84]

He had gone so far as to lease another apartment and had learned that Verdi and Strepponi planned to put her friend Nina Ravina in his place after he moved.

Even though Verdi had assured Del Signore on 5 December that Mariani could come and go as he liked, he sent orders to Corticelli ten days later to go to Genoa, pay the rent, and

go to Carlino and arrange amicably how and when Mariani will leave the house free. I want, as I said, this matter to be handled *amicably*; but if you cannot reach a decision with Mariani, then you will evict him in the shortest time allowed under the law. . . . You shall get the information, and do whatever the law allows, but only when all the amicable negotiations have achieved nothing, as I told you before.[85]

Earlier in the year when the issue of getting Mariani out of Palazzo Sauli Pallavicino had first come up, Stolz had contributed her mite to the controversy, writing:

So the *Illustrious One* really is not thinking about looking for an apartment? Probably he thinks *He* is the *padrone* of the house!!! because of the old and recently renewed affection poured on him by the owner of the *palazzo*!!! That's enough! May he live in peace!! but may he let others live without disturbing them with his presence![86]

By this time stories about the conductor's failing health were being printed in theatrical papers; but that did not prevent Stolz from getting in another shot, when she declared that he would have a hard time getting forgiveness for his sins. Mariani, too ill to move, stayed where he was. Stolz, as usual, came to Sant'Agata where Strepponi, perhaps already trying to protect her marriage, warned her that no one should be too intimate with Verdi, because he was 'unlike other mortals and, because of that, had to be treated differently'.[87]

Verdi, still hopeful of producing *Aida* in Naples in 1873, was conducting negotiations for other productions of the work, all to be directed by him, in Germany and Austria. During the first week in February, the management of the San Carlo let him know that the vocal parts for the opera were to be given out and that rehearsals were to begin. By the middle of the month Verdi was coaching singers, directing the orchestra, and managing the scenery and props, worrying about the costume sketches, and complaining about the Egyptian trumpets that had been shipped from Milan, dirty and in a shoddy packing case. His orchestra rehearsals began during the second week in March, leading him to hope for an opening around the twenty-second; but when Waldmann became ill, there were delays. When it finally opened, he could write to Clara Maffei:

Aida [enjoyed a] straightforward, decisive success, unsoiled by *ifs* and *buts* and such cruel phrases as *Wagnerism*, the *Future*, and the *Art of Melody*, etc., etc. The audience surrendered to its feelings and applauded. That is all! It applauded and even gave itself up to excesses that I do not approve of; but in the end it showed openly what it felt, without second thoughts. And do you know why? Because here there are no critics who pose as apostles; no mob of maestros who know about music only what they study in the *scores* of *Mendelssohn, Schumann, Wagner*, etc.; there are no aristocratic dilettantes who, just to be in style, get carried away by what they do not understand, etc., etc.[88]

Genuinely gratified, Verdi left the city after sending the Mayor a letter about reforming the San Carlo. Having earlier refused an offer to direct the Naples Conservatory, he perhaps thought he could leave the city officials with some fresh ideas about modernizing an old, tradition-bound theatre.

Verdi and his ensemble might have gone on to yet another production in Rome, had Verdi not mistrusted Jacovacci so profoundly. Strepponi and Ricordi were co-ordinating the *Aida* tour to Weimar, Berlin, and Vienna, which would include both Stolz and Waldmann, if they could be engaged. When serious negotiations got under way, though, Verdi had to consider other singers for both Aida and Amneris. The German tour, as we shall see, could be arranged only later; but these early exchanges about dates and artists prove that Verdi had gained high ground with his three productions of *Aida* and was willing to take his own music theatre on to German soil.

A Postscript to Naples: *Il quartetto per archi*

'Yes, in Naples I composed a quartet, in the hours when I had nothing to do,' Verdi admitted to Arrivabene.[89] The work, written while Stolz and Waldmann were ill, was presented by the composer himself on 1 April, just after the opening of *Aida*; but Verdi did not wish to have it performed in public, preferring to give it before a handful of invited guests and singers. In the grand salon of the Hotel delle Crocelle, where he and Strepponi had moved when their lease on the apartment expired, he had had two double music stands set up. Because there was no music on them, his guests felt he was playing a joke on them, for he had held to an ironclad rule that prevented anyone from performing his own music in his house. Yet as the evening wore on, four musicians from the orchestra of the San Carlo took their places and played his quartet. It was such a surprise and such a success that the guests demanded to hear it again. Verdi agreed to the encore, but refused to let it be played anywhere else or be published. 'He has given the world of art a new masterpiece', wrote a music correspondent for the *Gazzetta Musicale di Milano*.[90] Verdi only said: 'I don't know whether it is beautiful or ugly. I only know that it is a quartet.'[91]

Yet another work of art was created during this winter in Naples: the superb bust of Verdi done by the 20-year-old sculptor Vincenzo Gemito, whom Domenico Morelli and Filippo Palizzi had presented to Verdi. The artist, poor and facing compulsory military service, was trying to raise 2,000 lire to buy a substitute to take his place in the army. Verdi agreed to help, provided Gemito also do a bust of Strepponi. The two busts in terracotta are very fine; that of Verdi in bronze has become one of the most familiar portraits of him. During his stay, the composer gave his wife an object that she considered precious all her life: a gold bracelet, inscribed 'To my dear Peppina, 1872.'

Rumours

After the first performance of *Aida* in Naples, Verdi was escorted back to his hotel by a torchlight parade, complete with bands that played his music underneath his windows late into the night. Full houses on the evenings that followed attested to the solid victory he had won at the San Carlo, where, in the past, he had often faced daunting difficulties. He and Strepponi left the city on 9 April.

If his professional triumph was complete, though, the engagement in Naples raised spectres in Verdi's private life. Even as Mariani lay in his apartment in Genoa, Strepponi heard the ugly rumours that were circulating about Verdi's passion for Stolz. Had she not been isolated by her depression, by Corticelli, and by her personal situation, she might have heard them a year earlier, as the conductor had. Her suspicions were certainly raised after the Milan and Parma productions, when Stolz wrote to Verdi so often that Strepponi, on a packet of the soprano's letters, wrote: 'Sixteen letters!! In a short time!! What activity!'[92] The correspondence reflected the affection that had developed between Verdi and Stolz. When the soprano was near Milan or Florence, where her sister lived, she visited Sant'Agata often, sometimes staying for weeks. Her letters, filled with theatrical gossip, and sometimes with acerbic criticism of her colleagues, gush with compliments to 'dear Signora Peppina' and 'dear, naughty Maestro'. Whatever else she was, she was determined: secure within Verdi's orbit, she intended to stay there. Stolz asked Verdi about her investments, solicited his opinion of the new apartment she was thinking of taking in Via dell'Agnello in Milan, and looked to him for advice on whether to come to Sant'Agata for the summer; at the same time, she hoped Strepponi would help her decide about the intentions of a certain gentleman who appeared to be courting her. Stolz's plan to buy a house near Busseto was aired.

Faced with rumours that were rife about the soprano's affair with Verdi, Strepponi got at this subject through a third party, Cesarino De Sanctis, whom she loved and trusted perhaps more than any of Verdi's other friends. Shortly after the trip to Naples, she sent him a note, asking him to find out whether Stolz knew that people were saying she was Verdi's mistress. 'I would be curious to know whether S . . . has heard the gossip about that matter that you told me people were talking so much about in Naples. If, by chance, conversation should centre on these infamous and stupid rumours, and, if you find out something about it, just answer on a scrap of paper: "She knows that." '[93] She asked De Sanctis to write the words in English. Strepponi intended to let the soprano know that she had heard the gossip about Verdi. After so many years during which few rumours had tainted his image, in the theatre or out of it, his attitude toward Stolz finally had given malicious tongues something to wag about. His assiduous concern for the soprano after the Milan production of *Aida*, had not changed during their long association.

That there was something special about his interest was seemingly evident to everyone around them. Stolz was with Verdi and Strepponi as often as possible; and Verdi, to all appearances, was in love with her. Mariani clearly believed that he had stolen the soprano from him. If, as some of Strepponi's letters and diaries suggest, she and Verdi had not had an active love life since about 1860, when she was 45, then he may have been pleased to find a young, responsive partner. At the same time, Stolz could give the composer what he needed on the stage to guarantee his operas' success: a powerful, luminous voice and an imposing dramatic presence.

30

Spring 1873–Autumn 1876

The *Messa da Requiem* and Mariani's Death

'Peppina is well but is terribly sad', Verdi confided to De Sanctis soon after he and his wife got to Sant'Agata;[1] but he painted a somewhat more discouraging picture for Ricordi, saying that she was slightly ill all the time.[2] Strepponi was waiting for De Sanctis to let her know the outcome of his conversation with Stolz; but because he did not have the courage to ask the soprano about the gossip, no answer came. Verdi's wife's unhappiness did not deter him from writing again to 'Donna Teresa', as he called her. To be sure that she got his letter, Verdi asked De Sanctis to tell Stolz that it would be waiting for her in Ancona, where she was engaged for *Aida*. Stolz also heard from Strepponi, whose mid-April letter was full of suggestive phrases and veiled warnings.

'Your affectionate words are so genuine that they really did my heart good; and if I, in spite of my eternal mistrust of people and situations, could surrender to . . .', she began, then broke off.[3] A day later she went on:

From the thirteenth to the twenty-first without getting an answer [to your letter to me]! This must have made you wonder. Alas! It is human nature to torture ourselves by guessing when we do not know how to judge certain things and how they seem. I myself did this and sometimes still do it, so I would find it quite natural if you had done it now because of me. Don't be severe toward me, seeing the *chaos* of work that I have faced recently, with a country girl passing under the title of housemaid, [with] my health not really good, and with a grey humour, like the weather we have had most of the time at Sant'Agata. If you suffered from being separated from me, I, too, suffered a great deal; and since I cried, in spite of my unfortunate inability to cry, it means that I was truly suffering! I really need people to love me, [need] you to love me! But let's understand each other, just for myself and myself alone, for my good qualities and shortcomings, spontaneously.

The garden, in spite of the cloudy skies, is beautiful and in full bloom. You could cut flowers and row on the pond, even though there are no grapes; and later there will be some fruit; but after Ancona you will have such a lot of splendid projects that you will not want even to think about burying yourself for a while in this hole in the ground before going to Cairo to get *that money*. If, though, you find that you can make the *sacrifice* for the creator of *Aida* and for his wife, your room will be made up right away and you and Corticelli can shout over [games of] *briscolin*, more or less well played.[4]

She also conveyed her usual messages about honesty among friends.

When the soprano sent news of her success in Ancona,[5] Strepponi wrote to her again. Stolz gave Verdi details of the performances and let him know that she planned to go to Milan, Prague, and Vienna but would visit Sant'Agata or Genoa before leaving for Cairo. If Verdi met her anywhere else, we do not know it. Local tradition around Busseto places their rendezvous in Cremona at the Albergo Cappello, which stood in the Contrada della Zuecca, which was later renamed Via Verdi because the composer was such a frequent guest at the hotel.[6] The librettist Luigi Illica, a native of nearby Castell'Arquato, writing to Lina Mascagni in 1916 or 1917 about Mascagni's infidelity, treated Verdi's meetings with Stolz as if they were accepted fact, saying that

Verdi went from Sant'Agata to the market in Cremona every Saturday. He stopped at the Cappello, a modest hotel. A lady, who was said to be the owner of a cloth factory, also came to the same hotel every Saturday, wearing clothes that were anything but gaudy. . . . The famous lady who owned the cloth factory [was] Teresa Stolz.[7]

Illica's letter suggested that Strepponi accepted a situation over which she had little control, managing it as skilfully as she could. One anecdote in the letter, about Verdi losing his wallet in Stolz's suite, later appeared in print, as we shall see. Such gossip would not be worth noting, had Illica not cited a very reliable source, Verdi's lawyer in Milan. '[Umberto] Campanari is still alive and can confirm this for you', Illica said.[8] Whatever the truth of the situation, it is clear that in 1872 and 1873, many people believed that Verdi and Stolz were lovers.

Bursting with energy, Verdi was often away from home that spring. He had just come back from seeing *La forza del destino* in Parma when he got a telegram from Clara Maffei with news that Manzoni had died on 22 May.[9] Verdi reacted somewhat as he had to Cavour's death, saying that he would not attend the funeral or official ceremonies. Sharing his grief with Clara Maffei, he said: 'I was not there, but few people can have been sadder or more moved than I was, even though I am far away. Now it is finished! and with him dies the purest, holiest, and highest of our glories.'[10] He promised to come to Milan, alone and unobserved, to visit Manzoni's grave confiding to Giulio Ricordi that 'maybe (after further consideration and after having weighed my strength)' he would 'propose something to honour his memory'.[11] Ten days after Manzoni's death, the composer, Clara Maffei, and Ricordi went together to the cemetery, where Verdi stood silently beside the tomb. Writing from his suite at the Grand Hôtel de Milan, he let Ricordi know that he wanted to compose a Requiem Mass for Manzoni, a vast work requiring a large orchestra and chorus and several leading singers; he wanted it performed on the first anniversary of the writer's death.[12] Even though some details of Verdi's plan recalled his ambitious intentions for the Rossini Requiem Mass, it was basically more practical, involving only one composer: himself. He also opened the door for commercial use of the score after its first production. The planned première in Milan offered Verdi many guarantees, for he and Ricordi could exercise complete control over the production.

His determination to write a Requiem Mass is somewhat surprising, given the fact that many people considered him an atheist. Less than one year earlier Strepponi had described to Cesare Vigna her despair over the state of her husband's soul. He was an unbeliever, she said, —an 'atheist' in the first draft of her letter, which she revised in its final version.

And yet this *pirate* lets himself be—I won't say an atheist, but certainly not much of a believer, and that with an obstinacy and a calm that makes you want to thrash him. I go on talking to him about the wonders of the heavens, the earth, the sea, etc., etc. He laughs in my face and freezes me in the midst of my burst of utterly divine enthusiasm, saying: 'You are mad!' and unfortunately he says it in good faith.[13]

When comparing Manzoni and Verdi, Strepponi described the writer as one of those virtuous men who needed to believe in God and the composer as one of the equally perfect people who are 'happy not believing in anything' but follow every precept of a strict moral code.[14] After Verdi's death, Boito wrote to Camille Bellaigue that 'in the ideal, moral, and social sense he was a great Christian; but one must be very careful not to depict him as a Catholic in the political and narrowly theological sense of the word: nothing could be further from the truth.'[15]

The first suggestion that Verdi write a Requiem Mass dated back to the summer of 1865, when Mariani, alarmed over the cholera epidemic that was sweeping Italy, had written to the composer: 'If the cholera kills me, you will write my Requiem Mass. I will tell you the truth: I would be very, very happy to die so that Italy and the whole world might have *such a gift* from you. A Requiem Mass by Verdi.'[16] Four years later Verdi proposed the Mass for Rossini; he later conceived the final scene in *Aida* as a 'Requiem and an Egyptian De Profundis' for Amneris to sing at Radamès' tomb.[17] Now, in 1873, with Manzoni dead and Mariani not expected to live more than a few days, Verdi decided to write the Mass.

We do not know much about how the composer felt about Mariani's suffering, but it is possible he was affected by it. After failing to evict the conductor from Palazzo Sauli Pallavicino, Verdi had let Del Signore know that Mariani could 'come and go' as he wished.[18] Strepponi, though, had ordered Corticelli to find another house for herself and Verdi who had 'written and said a thousand times: "[Mariani] won't have to pay [the whole year's rent]; he can do what he wants, so long as he gets out and people don't talk about him any more." Now he can stay forever because we don't care at all', she wrote, in a letter written on Christmas Eve, that includes one more insult: 'He is still a fool in everything he does.'[19] Mariani had planned to take his new flat in May; but by Christmas he was too ill to move, wracked with pain and haemorrhaging. On 4 May he wrote to Landoni that he had been suffering 'like a dog' for four months, 'without a shadow of a hope of getting better'.[20] He began yet another treatment; but at the end of the month he reported that his suffering had become unbearable: 'I have been suffering too long', he said. 'I have lost all hope.'[21] On 4 June, again to Landoni:

I am failing every day, abandoned by everyone. . . . For a month, I have been suffering like a dog with no one to help me. . . . And to think that Loreta never wrote to me again!! So I have to die alone, like a dog; and I will die. I understand they don't want me in Bologna, and I would never have decided to go there, were it not for this circumstance of being abandoned by everyone. Now that I under-stand the situation, I won't bother anyone else there. Loreta, instead of answering [my letter], sent word that he does not think I am well enough to travel, which means I will die here alone like a dog, and I shall die alone. The pain I am suffering is so terrible that I truly do not have the strength to bear it any longer. I leave it to you to imagine what condition I am in, without any consolation at all. It is true that I am resigned, but my death is truly too horribly agonizing.—That's enough; this is how it had to be.[22]

Mariani died on 13 June 1873.

Shortly afterward Giulio Ricordi mentioned the death in a letter to Verdi: 'You, Illustrious Maestro, will have been touched by this death, in spite of the last exchanges between you and Mariani.'[23]

Ten days after Mariani died Verdi and Strepponi left Sant'Agata for Paris, where they found Muzio recovering from a series of personal and professional losses, with the failure of his marriage to Lucy Simons and the collapse of his hopes for the Théâtre des Italiens. Caught in a legal tangle, he had kept Verdi informed, writing to him at least twice in April, then visiting Sant'Agata. With Max Strakosch, Muzio had gone to Ancona in May to try to persuade Stolz to join their planned season in America: 'We signed the contract for the scenery and props for *Aida*...[and] offered Stolz a contract for the New York season 1874–5. The offer was 200,000 francs for six months. She has not decided.'[24] As late as 29 May they were still courting the soprano, whom they had heard in a superb *Aida*: 'She received magnificent flowers, wreaths, bouquets; one among others, was a pyramid of flowers; another, the Sphinx.'[25] Strakosch, he said, was so 'enthusiastic [over the opera] that he will spend any amount to produce it well' in America.[26] Leaving Ancona, he had gone on to Forlì and Parma, to conduct further negotiations with Magnani for the scenery for the American tour. At that time, Muzio, believing that Strakosch and Merelli would form a partnership to manage the Théâtre des Italiens, also expected to conduct for them. Having been in Milan when Verdi announced his 'noble offer' to compose the Requiem Mass for Manzoni, he told Verdi he was sure his ears had been burning 'as they say, because people in the city were saying the most beautiful things that you can imagine.'[27] Muzio left almost at once for Venice, then went on to Paris to wait for Verdi. Disappointed over Strakosch's decision not to take over the Italiens at that time, he continued to teach his corps of loyal voice pupils. Verdi reassured his former protégé, though, urging him to go to America, 'make a lot of money and come home to us'.[28] Verdi worked on the *Messa da Requiem* using his suite at the Hôtel de Bade as a studio. Muzio, staying with Escudier at the time, visited him every day; Escudier and Du Locle came less often. The composer had vowed not to go to the theatre and not to listen to any music. 'A strange thing, I did not get bored,' he wrote to Piroli. Indeed, not having anything to do with theatres and music, I had a good time seeing so many beautiful things and listening to so much foolishness. Paris is a big, beautiful city, and the Parisians are even crazier than before![29] All through his visit, Verdi corresponded with Ricordi about his plans for the *Messa da Requiem* for which he wanted both Stolz and Waldmann. The mezzo-soprano, already under contract to Florence for the following spring, was willing to rearrange her schedule in order to sing. Ricordi also tried to get Verdi to commit himself to producing *Macbeth* at la Scala, something he was unwilling to do. He did, though, authorize the publisher to let *Aida* be performed wherever he wished.

One of the offers Verdi received while in Paris brought forth a burst of indignation: 'I have had a letter from the president [of the Teatro Grande] in Trieste inviting me to go there for the first performance of *Aida*!!! By Holy God, do they consider me a charlatan, a clown who loves to show off like a *Tom Thumb*, a *Miss Baba*, an orangutang, or some other wretch!! Poor me! Poor me! . . . A curse on the theatre!'[30] But in spite of this tirade, he was in good humour, as Muzio reported to Ricordi. No one bothered him, and he was 'working on the *Messa* happily; he is in good form'.[31] He took long walks, slept like a stone, ate well, and played cards with Muzio and Strepponi. At the end of the visit, they returned to Italy by train, passing through the new Fréjus tunnel, which Verdi found 'sensational', 'three thousand metres' underground.[32]

He took up the *Messa da Requiem* as soon as he got back to Sant'Agata and studied a cantata by Alessandro Scarlatti that he had ordered from Florimo in Naples. As before, one of his main concerns was securing Stolz and Waldmann for the Mass. Writing to the mezzo-soprano, he had emphasized the importance of the event:

You won't earn anything, either in money or in reputation; but because it is something that will be a landmark—not because of the music, but because of the man to whom it is dedicated—it seems to me beautiful to have history say some day: 'On 22 May there was a great Funeral Mass in [Milan] for Manzoni's anniversary, performed by . . . etc.' [So] try to manage to be free at that time.[33]

He also brought pressure on Ricordi to get Waldmann released from her contract in Florence, but the matter was not easily resolved. As late as February 1874 the impresario and agent Luigi Ronzi, with whom Verdi had crossed swords before, did not want to let Waldmann go to Milan in time for the rehearsals of the *Messa*. He suggested that Verdi change the date of the commemoration, something the composer refused to do. When Ronzi then stood *his* ground, Verdi asked the Mayor of Milan to get the Mayor of Florence to intervene.

Verdi, Strepponi, and Corticelli spent Christmas at Sant'Agata, but before New Year's Day on 1874 they were back in Genoa, where, by agreement with Marchioness Luisa Sauli Pallavicino, Verdi had given up one of the two floors he had leased, consolidating his household in the *piano nobile* apartment. This was on the *second* floor, as we know from the Marchioness's letter outlining the terms of the agreement.[34] Because Mariani had died before signing his will, which he made on the day he died, his estate had not been settled. His apartment in the *mezzarie* of the house was under court seal. This may perhaps account for Verdi's uneasiness in Palazzo Sauli-Pallavicino: 'We have only been in Genoa three days, and, to tell you the truth, I am still not happy over having abandoned my nest [at Sant'Agata] and my fields, even though they are covered with ice. After a few more days I will settle in here too; but in the mean time this house bothers me, and so does this beautiful Genoa.'[35] He followed theatrical news through letters, among them those from the mezzo-soprano and Stolz from Cairo, where they were engaged for a season that included *La forza del destino*, *Aida*, *Un ballo in maschera*, and *La favorita*. As in the previous year, Bottesini was the conductor. The two women had negotiated enormous fees for themselves; according to Strepponi's calculations, Stolz was earning 23,000 lire a month, a 'respectable amount'.[36]

Muzio, who had gone back to America in the autumn of 1873, telegraphed Verdi about the immense success of *Aida*. Muzio toured his company to Cincinnati, Saint Louis, Chicago, Milwaukee, Boston, Toledo, Detroit, and New York before Easter 1874, and had the satisfaction of seeing his engagement extended: four performances were added in Washington; thirteen in Philadelphia; and twenty in New York.[37] Fearful that Verdi might be apprehensive about the popularity of Wagner's operas, he reassured his maestro, saying that *Lohengrin*, which he had conducted, had not stolen any glory from *Aida*, the most popular opera of the repertory.

Verdi's greatest burden at this time was surely his wife's depression, aggravated by what seems to be an almost complete loss of faith. Once a devout Catholic, she had become suspicious and sceptical. Her rage surfaced only occasionally, when she was writing about Mariani or the Bussetans; but it was there, and amply attested to in the 1860s and

1870s. She tried many manœuvres to protect herself and her husband against Stolz, ranging from trying to discourage the soprano from visiting Sant'Agata to encouraging her to find a fiancé and get married. At Christmas 1873 she sent Stolz a note of advice:

I take the opportunity [offered] by the coming holidays and New Year to wish that you may go on enjoying those good things that only true happiness can bring— health, wealth, the affection and esteem of everyone, and, a woman's essential partner, a gentleman to be your husband, on whose arm you can lean, certain that he will be your faithful companion and follow you to the end of the road that God had laid out for you.[38]

Stolz stayed single; her name continued to be mentioned in connection with the dead Mariani and with Verdi, and no one else.

In one letter, to Clara Maffei in March 1874, Strepponi wrote of her unhappiness.

In a few days I think Verdi really will make another of his trips to Milan, but I will stay in Genoa. . . . It is true: when we reach a certain age, we live a lot on memories. We all have some of them that are pleasant, sad, and dear, but alas! not all of us are lucky enough to be able to keep unchanged the affections and friendships of those that are still alive, or at least [preserve] the illusion of having these good things that make life precious. Lucky you, who believe, possess, and deserve to possess the love of your old and new friends!

I tell you that I, profoundly discouraged, almost no longer believe in anything or anyone. I have suffered so many and such cruel disillusionments that I am disgusted with life. You will say that everyone has suffered disenchantments, but that means that [others], stronger than I am, have kept alive some hope and some trace of faith in the future. I, on the other hand, now laugh, when someone says that they love me. Even my religious convictions have disappeared and I hardly believe in God when I look at the marvels of creation![39]

The rough draft of this letter has an even stronger declaration: 'A grey veil has been laid over my spirit, and I no longer believe in anything.'[40] Her true cross, as she confided to De Sanctis, was 'dishonest and treacherous friends',[41] and at least some of her despair came from watching Verdi dedicate himself to Stolz during what Strepponi later called his 'spells of assiduousness and solicitude that no woman could possibly [fail to] interpret favourably'.[42] The matter of her loss of faith and struggle to return to what Walker calls more 'orthodox' beliefs is set forth brilliantly in his *The Man Verdi*, in a chapter where Walker also describes his detective work in proving that letters published by Lorenzo Alpino on this subject are forgeries.[43]

By the beginning of March Verdi could relax in the knowledge that most of the work on the *Messa da Requiem* was finished: 'I have done nothing but write note after note, to the greater glory of God. . . . Now the music is done, and I am happy to have written it.'[44] As the final touches were added, alarms began to be raised about the whole project. At a meeting of the city council in Milan, some members protested that the *Messa da Requiem* would cost the City too much money; others said the authorities should not underwrite a religious event. Boito, then a city councillor, defended Verdi and the Mass and won the day. At the same time, though, it seemed the Catholic hierarchy might not allow women to sing in church. When Mariani had faced the same opposition in Pesaro, he had been forced to give part of his Rossini celebration in church and part in the opera house, but now Verdi would not bend. Having conceived the work from the outset as a Requiem for two men and two women, he also demanded that it be sung in church. To give the première in an opera-house or hall would reduce the Mass to a mere performance, which he would not permit. As he said of himself, he felt that with the *Messa da Requiem* he had become a serious composer and 'am no longer a clown serving the audience, beating a huge drum and shouting "Come on! Come on! Step up!"'[45] Finally, he got his way; the church of San Marco was made available.

When the soloists were chosen, Verdi decided to coach them himself and not let them see their music until he could go over it with them. This long work, with one and three-quarters hours of music—almost as much as *Norma*, he said—made demands on the participants that no opera did, bringing more than 200 artists together. On 2 May the composer went to Milan alone, leaving Strepponi in Cremona with her sister; he took his usual apartment at the Grand Hôtel de Milan and began rehearsals two hours after his arrival, plunging into twenty days of exhausting coaching. Just before the first performance, Strepponi joined him. The *Messa da Requiem* was sung on 22 May 1874, the first anniversary of Manzoni's death, by Stolz, Waldmann, the tenor Giuseppe Capponi, and the bass Ormondo Maini. Verdi conducted, before an invited audience of Italian and foreign dignitaries. Three days later the work was given at La Scala, again under Verdi's baton. A third and fourth performance were entrusted to Faccio. Although most reviews were favourable, some criticism was raised by those who found the music too theatrical. Hans von Bülow, who was in Milan for the season, sent an acerbic article to the *Allgemeine Zeitung*, mocking Verdi, who had written the work to 'sweep away the last shreds of Rossini's immortality, which he found embarrassing'.[46] Yet the success of the *Messa da Requiem* was such that its composer could take it to Paris immediately after the Milan première and mount it at the Opéra-Comique in collaboration with Escudier and Du Locle, who engaged the same soloists Verdi had used in Milan. With the *Messa da Requiem* given in two major theatres in the same month, there was no talk of a national commemoration or of locking the sacred score away: this was box-office. 'It seems it is a real success.' Verdi informed Ricordi. 'We will see how much it earns later, although it is so hot that when the theatre is full you absolutely cannot stand it.'[47] Strakosch and Muzio were sent ahead to London to try to arrange performances there, but when a Handel festival made them impossible, Verdi began to think about giving the work one year later and made a quick trip to England, where he heard some of the Festival performances. After stopping again in Paris, he, Strepponi, and Muzio left for Sant'Agata.

The first order of business was the farm, but Verdi had hardly settled in when Ricordi began to write to him about the many impresarios who were asking for permission to perform the *Messa da Requiem*. Somewhat brusquely the composer told his publisher to place it wherever he thought best, but soon he was to regret his words. Muzio, who went back to Milan, reported that in Bologna a company wanted to present the *Messa* with a piano accompaniment, 'and it seems the law will allow it'.[48] Verdi, who sent Corticelli to Bologna at once, learned the performance would be given with four pianos, while in Ferrara it had been done in a sports arena with a band instead of an orchestra. 'Can you imagine a worse monstrosity?! A Mass for the Dead—by a *Band*—in an *Arena*!!'[49] He appealed to Piroli for legal advice while denouncing the 'Killer Band-Leader' who had arranged the *Messa* for military band. At issue was one clause of the authors' rights' law that specified that a work must be given as a 'complete composition'. He claimed:

Now an arrangement for piano is not my composition and is not the *complete composition*. What do you say about it? . . . . But really can't we save ourselves from these vultures that suck our blood and show us to the audience so barbarously mutilated? And then others can make use of what is mine, and [is] the product of my studies, and of my gifts, whatever they are! It is absolutely infamous and a profanation.[50]

The matter reached the ministerial level in Rome as Verdi urged his publisher to sue and protested because not enough was being done to stop such mutilations of his works. Among these was an *Aida* that had been given in 1874 in Naples without the last act, not once but several times, provoking Verdi to inveigh against Casa Ricordi for turning him into 'a common labourer, a day labourer who brings his produce to the Casa, so that the Casa can exploit it wherever and however it wishes.'[51] On other occasions, inappropriate ballets were inserted in the middle of productions, sometimes in place of whole acts of his operas. Even such a distinguished artist as Fricci was not above making changes to suit her whims. In a performance of *Don Carlo* in Reggio Emilia, she dropped an aria from the score and inserted part of *Les Huguenots* on one evening and part of *Macbeth* on another. Verdi had hoped that Ricordi would help him put a stop to such violations of his artistic purpose but had been disappointed. 'What did I succeed in doing? I have nothing but trouble and, when you feel like it, a whack on the head from Casa [Ricordi] itself. Art has stayed exactly where it was; only the rental fees have gone up outrageously.'[52]

Verdi relaxed at Sant'Agata, where, as he told Piroli, he could finally 'breathe and, above all, *not talk*. Do you understand that I am not joking? It is truly a consolation to be able to say nothing after two solid months of chatter.[53] He told Clara Maffei that he tramped the fields from morning till night and did nothing else: 'I don't read, I don't write, nothing, nothing,' he wrote, after what he thought was his sixtieth birthday.[54] It was really his sixty-first. Even in his isolation, the composer monitored events through Muzio, his most faithful correspondent, who by the end of August 1874 was back in Paris, from where he sent Verdi practical information on the opening of the Opéra:

I assure you it is worth the price of a ticket to see the *great staircase* that leads from the entrance to the orchestra. It is impossible to conceive of anything more sumptuous or grand; [but] I don't like the hall, and no one can yet say whether it will be acoustically sound. In my opinion it has many shortcomings. The proscenium opening is small, the stage immense, and the wings too big. The auditorium has too many decorations, and there are too many openings for it to be good for the voice.[55]

By November Muzio was writing from New York, where he was conducting an opera season that included *Rigoletto*, *Ernani*, and seven other operas, two of them by Wagner. He was also supposed to popularize the *Messa da Requiem* in the United States, where churches were giving it 'every Sunday' and charging a dollar a seat for tickets. On 18 November he wrote to Verdi:

Yesterday we performed the *Messa*, and it was truly a good success; out of modesty, I won't say 'great'. The priests are selling it in two churches, and that cannot be stopped, because there is no author's rights agreement with Italy. The Archbishop [of New York] wants to have a performance of it in the Cathedral; if he will pay, we shall do it.[56]

The company went on to Boston, from where the conductor sent Verdi 2,500 francs, which he asked to have set aside until he could add more to it and have Verdi invest it for him.

Strepponi and Verdi stayed in the country well into the autumn. Having given up the apartment in Palazzo Sauli Pallavicino, she had to oversee a move early that autumn. Their new winter-quarters were in the magnificent Palazzo Doria at Porta Principe, one of Genoa's most famous buildings. The couple's twenty-room apartment, above the *piano nobile* on the second floor, overlooked the huge terrace garden and the developing section of the new port. Among its famous former guests were Emperor Charles V, the Spanish prince who would later become Philip II, and Napoleon Bonaparte. Then at the very edge of the city, it proved more convenient than Palazzo Sauli Pallavicino, because it was near the new railway station, which had become all-important to Verdi as he travelled more and more frequently; but getting to the old port area, banks, and business houses took some effort. The area around Palazzo Doria Principe was then in a stage of development that continued for decades. In this neighbourhood, as in the quarter around San Giacomo di Carignano, Verdi became a familiar figure because of his long walks and shopping expeditions.

On 13 November the composer and his wife left for Genoa, stopping briefly in Piacenza on their way. They stayed in Palazzo Doria much of the winter, with Verdi making his usual short trips to Sant'Agata and Milan. On 15 November he was honoured by being included in the list of men named senator of the Kingdom of Italy. Writing to Piroli, whom he considered responsible for his nomination, he said: 'I am enormously moved by this high honour that they wished to give me; but what did I ever do to deserve it? And then . . . what a poor senator!'[57] Although he had been invited to the swearing-in, he decided not to go because he did not wish to become involved in the *Aida* that was then in rehearsal at the Teatro Apollo in Rome. Within days, even his nomination raised embarrassing problems, as it seemed that he had been included on the honours list because of the high taxes he paid—in other words, because of his wealth. The secretary of the Senate wrote to ask him for a list of his qualifications, the *titoli* that might normally include university degrees or conservatory diplomas. 'My qualifications?' he exploded to Piroli, 'the whole world knows I have never done anything but write music. . . . You will understand I don't know now whether I can refuse [the nomination], after having written to the Minister that I accepted it; but I know I will never set foot in the Senate, not even to be sworn in.'[58] Yet Strepponi did send a complete list of Verdi's decorations. With his *titoli* on record, he was confirmed as senator, because of his wealth and because of his documented service to his country; but he did not go to be sworn in at this time.

Much of Verdi's correspondence concerned the planned European tour of the *Messa da Requiem* and possible performances of *Aida* with the same soloists. As before, he hoped to have Stolz and Waldmann in his company. The soprano had had a particularly difficult year. After leaving Paris, she had gone to take the waters at Recoaro and spent further time off in her apartment in Milan. She then went on to Venice, where she sang under Gallo's flag. In the autumn season, she had gone back to her well-tested role of Elisabetta in *Don Carlo* at the Teatro della Concordia in Cremona, where she sang with Rosa Vercolini, a mezzo in whom Verdi had shown some interest earlier that year. Capponi, Napoleone Verger, and Paolo Medini completed the cast. This may be the time of Verdi's meetings with Stolz at the Albergo Cappello, for Strepponi was in Genoa, overseeing the move to the Palazzo Doria. She wrote to the soprano from there, to congratulate her on the 'glory and money' she was getting, remarking—not without some bitterness—that she was slaving like a porter and working for nothing while the move was going on.[59] Stolz also visited Barberina Strepponi in Cremona and gave her an autographed photograph of herself that later passed into the hands of Barberina's maid Maria Alini.[60] At the end of the season, Stolz visited Strepponi and Verdi at Sant'Agata. After she left, Verdi, who was again at the Albergo Cappello, telegraphed her in Milan about her role in the Paris performances of the *Messa da Requiem* giving the handwritten draft of the telegram to Achille Zoboli, a porter who often served him.[61] Stolz stayed in Milan until December, then visited her sister in Florence and went on to Rome, where she was under contract to sing *La forza del destino* in January 1875 at the Apollo. Here she faced the first serious humiliation of her career when her voice failed during the second scene of the second act. 'I became aware that she was not in perfect voice', Luccardi wrote to Verdi on 21 January, describing Stolz's collapse during the prayer 'La

Vergine degli angeli'.[62] She apologized to the audience, then left the stage in tears. Soon afterward, the tenor, too, announced that he could not go on. After an announcement, the management staged a ballet, which gave listeners time to call their carriages, then refunded the price of tickets and sent the audience home. This fiasco in the capital of Italy, where Luccardi, Piroli, and even the Mayor of Busseto were going to the opera, proved to be an embarrassment for the composer and the company, even though a later *Aida* was scheduled. Both Stolz and the tenor, Angelo Masini, asked to be released from their contracts because of illness. When substitutes were found, Verdi fumed as *Aida* in March was massacred by 'a mediocre *Aida*!! A soprano who is doing Amneris!! And a conductor who lets them change the tempos!!! . . . Well, and you talk to me about *composing*!!! About *Art*, etc. Is this Art?'[63] This to Ricordi. Four days later he mounted another attack:

You talk to me about *results achieved*!!!!!!!!!! Which ones? I will tell you which ones. After being away from La Scala for twenty-five years, I heard a whistle after the first act of *La forza del destino*. After *Aida*, endless chatter: that I was no longer the Verdi of *Ballo* (that *Ballo* that was whistled the first time it was given at La Scala); that the end of the world would come if we were not able to get through the fourth act (that is what d'Arcais said); that I had not *known how to compose* for singers; that there was something passable in the second and fourth acts (nothing in the third), and that after all I was an imitator of Wagner!!! What a fine result after twenty-five years, to end up as an *Imitator*!!!

It is certain that this senseless chatter does not make me budge at all from what I wanted to do, and never did, because I always knew what *I wanted*; but, having got where I am—whether high or low— I certainly can say: 'If this is how it is, go ahead,' and when I want to write music I can do that perfectly well in my own room, without listening to the pronouncements of wise men and imbeciles.

I can only take as a joke your sentence 'The whole salvation of the theatre and of art lies in you'!! Oh, no: there will always be composers around; and I, too, will repeat what Boito said in a toast to Faccio after his first opera: '*and perhaps the man has been born who will clean up the altar*'. Amen.[64]

Although more than eleven years had passed since the night Boito read his insulting *Ode*, the offence still festered. Verdi had heard the single whistle at the end of the first act of *La forza del destino* more than five years before. The passage of time seemed not to lessen the pain.

Just after he wrote these two April letters to Ricordi, the composer began rehearsals for the European tour, first in Stolz's apartment in Via dell'Agnello, where Verdi invited the tenor Masini and the bass Medini to join him and the soprano. Because he was unconvinced that Masini could match the power of the other singers, he gave him special attention, wanting, as he said, to let the tenor hear how he sounded against the others: 'He knows his part well but will be somewhat shocked to hear the others' music.[65] The tenor passed muster and prepared to leave for France with the rest of the company.

The year before, Verdi had taken Strepponi to Paris with him in spite of the fact that she wanted to stay at home. Then she had confided to Barberina Strepponi that she was so confused and exhausted, 'physically and spiritually,' that she hardly knew how to speak. 'I never have a day of peace, and with the noise outside and the chattering inside, I go to bed so prostrated that I seem to age a year every single day. . . . Will God give me the strength to live?'[66] As she had toured with Verdi then, so she did in 1875. The couple left Sant'Agata for Milan on 10 April, went on to Turin two days later, and got to Paris on the fourteenth. As usual, they stayed at the Hôtel de Bade, where Stolz also took a suite. The soprano had not sung in public since leaving Rome; Waldmann had just come from the Cairo season, as Medini had; Masini, like Stolz, had been resting for months. Verdi's most frequent visitors were Muzio, who had returned from the United States a few weeks before, Escudier, and Du Locle. As Muzio observed, the Paris audience also had had a chance to judge another Requiem, that of Brahms, which he found 'confused and very badly written for the voices, which are not well blended'.[67] Now it was the Italians' turn.

Verdi conducted his *Messa da Requiem* at the Opéra-Comique on 19 April, in a brilliant performance that was the first of seven given in Paris. After the third performance, the French Minister of Public Education honoured him with the Cross of the Commander of the Legion of Honour, a decoration that the composer mentioned in a letter to Piroli. 'Leaving aside the symbols of honour, . . . the *Messa* is going really well in every way. The quartet of singers is much better this year, because we have a tenor who has a delightful, perfect voice. Oh, if he were only an artist!'[68] The troupe went on to London, where Verdi and his wife stayed at the Sackville Hotel. The composer himself had chosen the Albert Hall, which he believed he could perhaps almost fill, in spite of its size. The great risk proved not justifiable, as the audiences were much smaller than Verdi had hoped; artistically, though, the *Messa da Requiem* was successful. The threat of financial catastrophe set off alarms at Casa Ricordi in Milan, where there already were problems with contracts for the German performances of the tour. Writing from London on 25 May, Verdi asked Ricordi to send him all contracts for the German engagement, because when he had glanced through them in Milan in April, he had the impression that they had not been correctly written—'At that time it did not seem to me they were done according to the spirit of my contracts [with you].'[69] This is the first reference in Verdi's letters to his suspicion that something was wrong with Ricordi's accounting of his fees. In this same letter, the composer asked his publisher to make his and Stolz's hotel reservations in Vienna: he and Strepponi would need a suite with a salon, two bedrooms, and other, smaller rooms; Stolz needed a salon, one bedroom, and a room for her personal maid. Verdi said that he, his wife, and the soprano would take all their meals in his suite, where 'dinner and supper for three' would have to be served every day. This is the first documentation of what Strepponi later called the 'menage à trois' that had been forced upon her; but it seems likely that Verdi had insisted on the same arrangement in Naples and Paris.[70]

The company arrived in Vienna on 3 June, going directly to the Hotel Munsch; Waldmann took advantage of the chance to visit her family but returned to the city for the first rehearsals of the *Messa da Requiem* and *Aida*. After a week of preparation with the Viennese orchestra and chorus, Verdi presented his *Messa da Requiem* at the Hofoperntheater. The next day he could send good news to Piroli. 'The success was solid, better than in other places, and the execution was a great deal better than anywhere else. What a good orchestra and what good choruses! and how manageable they are, and they let themselves be led correctly. To sum up, a performance that, all things considered, will never be heard again!'[71] On 19 June he produced *Aida* in the same theatre, where it was repeated on the twenty-first.[72] During the engagement, the *Messa* had to be given an extra performance, because there was so much enthusiasm for it. While in Vienna, Verdi was received and decorated by Emperor Franz Josef. To the composer's immense disappointment, however, the projected German performances of the tour were cancelled, because of Ricordi's fear of financial loss. Verdi, Strepponi, and the company left Vienna on 26 June for Venice, where the composer stayed one or two days but did not conduct the *Messa*. The Venetian performances were in the hands of Gallo, who had decided to give it in the Teatro Malibran (the old Teatro San Giovanni Grisostomo). There the work was staged by Pietro Bertoja, who had designed a Byzantine setting for it, with a replica of the great wooden choir of Santa Maria Gloriosa dei Frari in the middle of the stage.

The chorus, brought from La Scala and expanded with Venetian singers, was supported by the best instrumentalists in the Veneto; Faccio was brought from Milan to conduct.[73] Gallo's strategy was amply rewarded at the box office, where all five performances of the *Messa da Requiem* were sold out. The receipts totalled more than 82,000 lire.[74] Muzio, who had overseen the Venetian season after Verdi left, reported in person to Sant'Agata: the success had been so great that even Gallo himself had been called out time and time again for curtain-calls and bows. After learning the details from Muzio, the composer wrote to Gallo to express his fear that too much effort had been spent to guarantee the extravagant outcome.

I heard the news of the 82,000, and that is fine! Muzio has just now (12 o'clock) got here from Bologna, and brought me the hot, hot, hot news. But everything was too exaggerated. We [Italians] fall short in always going too far! Manzoni said: *'It is not hard to strike a bit low and a bit high; but it is very hard to strike right on the mark.'* And we are always a bit too high or too low, especially in the theatre!

And don't you feel that the crowns [given to the artists] are too much? And silver crowns, too? But why? . . . you know how many times I said 'Immense *Charlatan*' to a poor soul [Mariani] who is dead and who certainly was worth much more than all the others together. . . . Bouquets of flowers are alright; and curtain-calls for you are alright (if there had been just one, it would have been better), because after all you had faith and courage. And a lot of courage, . . . but with the 82,000 you will have covered everything, as I see, in spite of the fact that you did not want to tell me the *net income*.

Please note that if you had told me, you would have made me truly happy, because there is nothing that satisfies me more than to hear publishers and impresarios say: 'I did very well'!—A consolation that my publisher in Paris has given me many times, telling me and everyone that he owed his fortune to me! A consolation that my Italian publisher [Ricordi] has never given me; instead [he has] always cried poverty, not to me, but to others, as if I had skinned him alive.

'And to think that I gave [Ricordi] *Aida* for only 60,000 lire and the *Messa* for 39,000!! I knew perfectly well that they were worth more, but I wanted to seem generous! Imbecile!!'[75]

Its five sold-out performances in Venice proved the viability of the *Messa da Requiem* beyond all doubt.

A Public Scandal over Stolz

Mistrust of Ricordi had been building in the disgruntled composer for some time, exacerbated by Verdi's disappointment over the cancelled Berlin engagement. 'This was not the time to count up a few thousand francs, more or less . . . but merchants are always merchants,' he wrote to Piroli from Venice in June.[76] Whatever conversations he had had over the contracts for the German performances had not satisfied him. Home again after the tour, he began to check his own accounts, which seemed not to tally. On 11 July Corticelli was sent to Milan to pick up all of Verdi's contracts for all his operas from Ricordi, as Strepponi promised Giulio Ricordi to try to calm the waters of the 'very troubled sea' at Sant'Agata[77] and to do everything she could to pacify an angry Verdi.[78] Her promise was vain. The composer spent more than a month going over every figure and date. He then turned to Piroli for legal advice, having found that Ricordi had defrauded him of part of his royalties. When the publisher, desperate, approached Clara Maffei in the hope that she might intervene, Verdi warned her off and asked her to stay out of this 'very unpleasant dispute'.[79] Ricordi, claiming there were merely some irregularities in the accounts, tried to blame Tornaghi, but Strepponi insisted the head of the firm be held accountable. Later, the publisher also intimated that some-one in Verdi's house—Corticelli, perhaps—had misled the composer. This suggestion, too, was rejected: 'Understand this clearly: there is no one, here or anywhere else, who has influenced Verdi against you by saying evil things. And anyway, he is not a man to let himself be influenced. In this sorry affair, he had to be convinced by the evidence.'[80] At one point, Verdi even refused to meet Tito Ricordi; he did not write to the firm for many weeks. Finally an agreement was reached, Verdi accepting a token 50,000 lire in settlement. As he himself said 'It is not what I ought to have'.[81] The problem of rebuilding trust was quite another matter. Verdi proved how generous he was when he accepted a small sum of money and declined to sue. When Casa Ricordi later faced a major financial crisis, he lent it 200,000 lire, even though he knew he had been cheated over many years.

Long before the problems with Ricordi were solved, Verdi suffered through a mortifying public airing of his relationship with Stolz. *La rivista indipendente*, a periodical with editorial offices in Florence, promised on 22 August to publish what it called the 'STORY' of the career of 'Signora TERESINA STOLZ, Singer; the late Maestro M[ariani] of Bologna; Maestro

Verdi of Busseto; and the Signori Ricordi and Tornaghi of Milan', including '[her] intimacy with Maestro M.—cruelty to the same Maestro M.—Favours and intimacy with Maestro Verdi—a wallet lost and found in Signora Stolz's room, etc., etc.'. The actual articles began on 4 September and continued through four later issues, running into November. 'TERESINA STOLZ Singing Actress' ran at the beginning of a paragraph in which the newspaper declared its independence and objectivity.

Teresa Stolz, of German origin, now about 48, with a haughty face, a proud way [about her], [and] extremely uncivil manners, made her début abroad, where she stayed about ten years without anyone learning of her accomplishments, which must be undistinguished, given the fact that she and the press buried them in utter oblivion. In about 1866 this soprano reached Italy and tried to begin a career in our theatres, perhaps having failed abroad. . . . [Her Elvira in opera *Ernani* at Bologna failed] so disgracefully that directors of the Teatro Comunale in Ferrara, where Stolz was to sing the following spring, protested, . . . And so the proud soprano was quietly packing her suitcases [and] getting ready to go back to Austria, when a lucky star again lit up her path; and this star . . . was the never sufficiently mourned Maestro Mariani. He, with his magic wand, and his unmatched artistry then directed the orchestra of the Comunale in Bologna, and with . . . his kindly heart, honoured the cunning German woman. . . . Proposing that she stay, he was generous with his advice [and] with daily coaching, . . . and became her most intimate and most passionately committed friend. . . . As if by magic, that Illustrious Maestro, who loved Stolz, passed on to her the spark of his overwhelming genius, teaching her the role of Matilde in *Guglielmo Tell*. . . . Stolz was utterly transformed when she appeared again before the audience. Love and Art helped each other—Mariani had brought about a miracle. Happy with each other, Mariani and Stolz were again engaged by the Comunale in Bologna in 1867. That theatre was to give *Don Carlo*, a work that was to be presented in Italy for the first time, even though a faint, barely audible, but correct rumour circulated that it was a minor opera by Verdi and that in Paris it had left few good memories behind and had perhaps been a kind of fiasco. Good Fortune had the orchestra led, as usual, by the tireless and unmatched Mariani, who, overcoming every problem, gave Verdi's opera the colour it lacked, or that no one had known how to perceive in Paris. . . . And Verdi and Stolz saw in that Maestro [Mariani] an Angel [Angiolo]; they proclaimed their eternal devotion to him, their undying gratitude; but Stolz, this Temptress Eve, directed too many covetous glances toward the Author of *Ernani*, who, in a moment of desire, fell at the feet of [the God of Love]. [*Here the first instalment ended*].

From this regrettable incident a coldness arose in the relationship between Mariani and Stolz; and the latter, a courtesan from the official roster [of prostitutes], began to worship the more splendid star, Maestro Verdi. . . . And so there they are, Philemon and Baucis [Verdi and Stolz] right in the middle of their honeymoon! Here is Verdi and [here is] Stolz, who pretends to adore green [*verde*], a green that is no longer green [young]; and [here is] Verdi, who becomes small [in spite of] his reputation, becomes like a baby, and—poor little love-struck heart—lets himself be led around by the nose by Teresina.—[He] indeed acts like a boy who asks his teacher for permission [to urinate]. His *alter ego* schemes, has her own way, and gives orders. And Verdi obeys. Poor reputation, and poor name, how tiny have you become! . . . Mariani, sensitive, was struck by this ungrateful behaviour and indeed complained about it to his closest friends, who saw that this shock had brought about obvious changes in Mariani, both emotionally and physically. [The friends] wrote a letter on his behalf to the proud soprano, so that she would at least keep up the appearance of consoling the afflicted Mariani with some affectionate note; but this *fine* lady deigned to answer that Mariani (her benefactor) mattered little to her [and that] Verdi mattered a great deal (because he is rich). The fact is that poor Mariani, afflicted by this suffering, became ill; and this star, that was then still shining in the Italian sky, disappeared from the firmament and shall never shine again.

And Verdi and Stolz never moved from where they were, and are not moving now, save to perform *Aidas*, Masses for the living and Masses for the dead, so long as the money comes in. . . . As for Stolz, who Verdi says is necessary to him, and everyone knows why, we are told that she has folded her wings and her singing, and that her voice is hoarse or strident. . . . [*Here the second instalment ended.*]

And here we are with our soprano's comical adventures. The first act begins in the classical, beautiful city of Milan. Maestro Verdi, the writer of the *Messa da Requiem* written for Manzoni, or for whoever will leave orders for his heirs to pay for it, and the celebrated (according to her and to him) Teresa Stolz are living there; we do not know whether by chance or by design.—See how proper these little people were! they were not living in the same hotel; but that did not stop Maestro Verdi from hurrying to honour the plump, appealing soprano with a visit, which we believe was platonic. Verdi was received with all the honours and dignity required on such a visit; and soon the amorous couple lay down, or rather, did not lie down—they made themselves comfortable, they relaxed, they stretched out on a soft sofa. We really do not know what odd things they did on that sofa, what struggles went on, or what discussions, as they thrashed around, because they were in the room, and the door was closed. The adventure lies in the fact that in the heat of the encounter neither Stolz nor Verdi was aware of anything; Verdi's wallet, containing 50,000 lire, fell out of his pocket. [Verdi was compared to Don Basilio, 'teaching the young girl' in *Il barbiere di Siviglia*.] Unnoticed by the two wrestlers, the wallet slid on to the sofa. When the two wrestlers calmed down, Verdi went back home, and Stolz stayed at home to tend to her business. Soon afterward Verdi realized that he had lost his wallet and began to rave about it to all the staff in the hotel; but he had failed to take the owner into consideration. Among those honest devils on his staff, there was one who knew as rumour or as a fact where Verdi was spending his happy or sad moments (according to how he was feeling) so this [man] ran, flew to Stolz, and asked for the wallet in Verdi's name. It was news to the signora [Stolz]; but while the porter was looking around the room, his eyes called to Stolz's attention the wallet, which she had not seen, lying on the sofa. Stolz made a face; the porter laughed. —At what? Figure it out for yourself. And Verdi, who had raged at the help, was criticized in turn; and the episode gave rise to odd remarks and made people laugh like mad. [*Here the third instalment ended.*]

[Stolz, in Florence for the *Messa da Requiem*, often sang flat, and aroused the anger of the audience.] We believe that the fourth act of *Faust* is worth more than your *Mass*. Amen! But to get back to the proud soprano and to her comical adventures and platonic love affairs, we shall tell how, once she knew Verdi, she wanted to be introduced to his dear Other Half, Signora Strepponi, who kindly welcomed Stolz and was gracious to her, [because] she was the one whom Verdi proclaimed to be the interpreter of his works; but when this good lady became aware that Stolz, in addition to interpreting Verdi's works, was also showing him her intimate charms, she thought it wise to leave her in the dirt on the stage floor; and then *Anger* came. And in this way Verdi wretchedly lost his peace at home, although Stolz was *guilty* of nothing more than loving too platonically this Maestro Verdi, who had made her so famous. —[This is] blindness on Signora Strepponi's part, for she believes that a soprano might allow herself to indulge in love affairs that are something other than platonic. . . . But Signora Stolz, profiting from Maestro Verdi's good-heartedness, took too much advantage [of him] and began to boss him around, (if I can be permitted a vulgar expression) taking off his trousers. And if you want a proof of that, look at her on the stage in Ancona where she is [running the season], accepting and refusing singers and orchestra players, and with the blessing of Verdi, who is letting himself be led around by the nose and wants everyone to bow before the Goddess soprano . . . [*Here the fourth instalment ended.*]

Maestro Verdi's intimacy with Signora Stolz struck Verdi's wife, who saw in it something that injured her to the heart, so that blessed peace that reigned between Verdi and [his wife] was in fact diminished. And in fact when the usual *Messa da Requiem* was being sung in Vienna—no longer for Manzoni, but for the impresario's box-office—there was the indispensable (as Verdi believed) Stolz; Strepponi went there to be with her husband; and she could see with her own eyes that the intimacy, if not more intense, was not less than it had been; so Strepponi's friendship with Stolz cooled; but Stolz needed Verdi's support, so as not to lose the prestige she had won in the shadow of such a famous name, and not to fall from the pedestal where she [looked like] a giant, but from which, because of her already lost vocal gifts, she would soon have been pulled down. . . . It is lucky for her that the elderly Verdi has placed her under his eternal protection; otherwise, what would have happened to her, now that so many young stars have eclipsed her? She would have to lower herself to the infamous level of mediocrity. And if Verdi were to open his eyes, what would happen then?

The newspaper promised further revelations about the 'soprano in whom we are so interested'; but nothing further appeared.[82]

With the publication of these articles in September, October, and November 1875, Verdi reached the very nadir of indignity in his public life. Later another newspaper, *Il presente*, observed that what went on behind Verdi's closed doors was his own affair, but that it was 'a scandal' that any man would carry 50,000 lire in his wallet at a time when hunger was rife in Italy and unarmed, starving farm-hands were defying armed government troops in a desperate bid to get their pay raised by a few centesimi a day.[83] The fact that the composer could afford to lose such an amount was the occasion for outrage, the editors said. In fact, at the very time when Verdi was reported to have had such a large sum in his pocket, a gift of 30 or 40 lire to the family of a destitute agricultural labourer was considered enough to carry it through six months, until the next rent cycle.

Quite naturally, Strepponi was among those injured by the scandal. Her feeling of despair and her fear that her husband would indeed abandon her are reflected in the draft of a letter she wrote to him in 1875:

I am happy and not surprised to hear that your slight indisposition disappeared as soon as you get beyond the mountains [and away from Genoa]. Perhaps you will remember that I have recently mentioned several times that we need to discuss some of the questions involving both of us; and it would be a good thing to resolve these quickly, since time is pressing in on us. The chance has offered itself, and I am seizing it, as I am able to [write] a letter, since a perfect quiet lets me do so. It is certain that the climate of Genoa is wrong for you. The coal smoke that now reaches us from the new commercial complexes has, one may say, made worse the climate of this place and made very likely—indeed, almost inevitable—the need for a move, sooner or later. It is true that you have not done anything to become familiar with it, but you do not like Genovese society. So we shall have the inconvenience of moving, we shall have to move far from the sea, the light, the fresh air, and not have company to compensate us for these sacrifices. Listen carefully, my Verdi, listen to me with a tiny bit of patience; and believe that what

I am about to tell you is the result of long consideration, which I am setting forth for you with complete sincerity in my heart. You love Milan; and its climate is not harmful to you. You like the company there; in that city you have your old friends, the memories of your early triumphs, and—to use a modern noun—in Milan there is the ambience that is right for an artist. I propose that we go to Milan. The climate cannot be harmful to me, since it is my native climate; in the evening at least, you can have a little company, and if there were no one around, once in a while you could pay an occasional visit to the theatre or to a café to spend a pleasant hour. As you know, I do not need society, and it is enough for me to have some good person to whom I can speak from time to time. I love to stay in the house; I ask you only for an apartment with light and air, and that you not abandon me completely in these last years of our lives; by that I mean to say do not desert our house completely. In that flat city I can take an occasional walk, visit [someone] occasionally, and have the chance to spend a bit of money myself, something I have never had the chance or the desire to do in Genoa.

If this proposal suits you, we together could make the arrangements necessary for an apartment, etc. . . . Think about it and decide. But Genoa has become a constant anguish for me, since staying there is not right for you, either physically or spiritually.[84]

If Verdi reached a low point in his life in 1875, acting toward Stolz in ways that led journalists to drag his name, his wife's, and the soprano's through the mud, Strepponi had clearly reached the crisis point herself. This pathetic letter, with its stab at common sense and its shopping list of options offered, suggest their marriage was in serious trouble. After twenty-eight years it had come to this: 'I ask of you only an apartment with light and air, and that you do not abandon me completely in these last years of our lives; by that I mean that you should not desert our home completely.' Stolz, of course, would often be 'around' in Milan. As we have seen, Verdi's wife had been writing of her problems for almost ten years. In her diary notes of 1867, Strepponi had described an angry, driven Verdi, restless, suspicious, and unable to control his bad temper. Her diary notes of January 1868, with their mention of the 'thousand things that set him off', his 'brusque' way, and his complaints about such minor matters as her tone of voice in casual conversation reveal a household where the wife was doing everything in her power to anticipate her husband's every whim and cover every eventuality in the hope of shielding herself and the servants from a man who was not able to express his satisfaction with her even once a year. The next year he had clearly used psychological and verbal violence to discourage her from joining him in Milan during the early rehearsals of *La forza del destino* at La Scala, refusing to speak to her while they were in Genoa and treating her harshly in Turin and in his letter from Milan. Yet when he needed her to sit in a box during the dress rehearsal and on opening night, he had gone back to Genoa and accompanied her back to Milan.

From the moment of the *Forza* rehearsals, Stolz had been a third party in their lives. By the spring of 1872 when Strepponi, in her desperation, suggested to Verdi that he have Stolz buy a villa in Castione dei Marchesi, within easy reach of Sant'Agata, Verdi's wife had—by her own account— watched her husband devote more and more constant attention to the soprano. From Verdi's arrangements for his and the soprano's hotel suites, as we have seen, he had contrived a way to be with Stolz even at meals, during the tour of the *Messa da Requiem* and *Aida*. Strepponi's situation was such that even her courtesy to the soprano was repaid with Verdi's 'hard, violent, and heart-rending words'.[85] The record of their verbal and emotional exchange in the house and out of it goes beyond ordinary marital discord, painting the picture of a steadily deteriorating relationship, with Strepponi buying time from year to year by trying to keep everything under control in Verdi's professional and family life and even trying to arrange matters so that her husband could be nearer Stolz, whether in Milan or at 'La Codetta' in Besenzone, in the house adjacent to the mill Verdi bought in December 1875. This is not to deny that a powerful and enduring love united them from 1843 onward; but one simply must face the fact of the composer's dissatisfaction, anger, and restlessness and his wife's amply documented suffering.

When the articles appeared in *La rivista indipendente*, Verdi and Strepponi were at Sant'Agata and Stolz was singing, first in the Florence *Messa da Requiem* then in the Trieste *Aida*. Strepponi wrote to her:

If you are angry, be calm. Understand that I would have answered you right away, as I wanted to do, and as I would have done, if I had not been pulled to and fro, without a minute to sit down quietly at my writing-desk. Now you have got to Florence, where I think it wise to send my letter. I know—or, rather, we know—that you love us very much, we believe that, we are happy to believe it, and we have faith that we will never suffer disillusionment because of you. You know, you believe, and you are happy in believing that we love you; and you may be sure that we will never change so long as we live. So, my dear Teresa, your fear of being *unwelcome* because you detected a hint of unhappiness in me is a fear to be put aside, with that fear of yours of disturbing us that made you go to your room at an hour when the chickens go to roost, uttering your famous sentence: '*If you will let me, I will go to bed.*' You will never be unwelcome in our house so long as you and we remain those honest, straightforward souls that we now are. With this and a kiss, I end my sentence.[86]

A heroic effort to buy Verdi's and Stolz's goodwill, in the very year when Strepponi feared he might abandon her, this letter stands as a milestone on the road to an anguished confrontation that came seven months later. Keeping him happy and at home was his wife's mission in life at this time, when no sacrifice was too great, if that end were achieved. Strepponi's real view of the soprano is buried in a set of diary notes entitled 'A Philosopher's Remarks about a Woman's Heart, written down by him as Guidelines for Men':

1. Between 20 and 30 years of age, a woman takes courtship and everything else as a joke—no danger, or almost none.
2. Between 30 and 40, it is more serious: at that critical age, a woman has dangerous moods! She dreams of sin and is concerned with debating about the question of the remorse that . . . she wants!!! When a woman of that age shows you some kindness—she is showing off her remorse for what she feels and says that she is afraid of sin—oh! She is very much inclined to commit it! She really needs a bit of scandal so that people will pay attention to her! Let the man stay far, far away!
3. The woman of 40 to 50 is left. Oh! Oh! With her one has to act with the greatest discretion imaginable! Beautiful or ugly, her heart is like an Aeolian lyre that throbs and sighs in every wind; if he lets even the slightest amorous intention barely, barely show, the man is lost! With women of this age, he has to limit himself to talking of love in general terms—not risk either a glance or a sigh.[87]

When Verdi first began to pay serious attention to Stolz, the soprano was in her thirties; when the articles appeared in *La rivista indipendente*, she was 41, as she was when Strepponi wrote these lines in her Letter-book. We have no way of knowing whether Verdi ever saw them.

By October 1875 Stolz was writing from Trieste, reporting to Verdi on the *Aida* production and replying directly to Strepponi's letter of several weeks before. She also had sent Verdi a telegram from Trieste after the first performance. Her act-by-act report on the opera brought Verdi good and bad news: the audience had not been as enthusiastic as everyone in the company had expected; some encores were demanded and delivered; she had sung well; the chorus were a disgrace because they had drunk too much before the curtain—it was Sunday; the tenor had had almost no applause; the bass sang flat; Faccio, who conducted, was 'a bit mortified' because he had not got the ovations he had expected.[88] In her letter to

Strepponi, written two days after the letter to Verdi, she claimed that she had never been 'angry' and that she was glad to hear that Strepponi was not unhappy over her.

Now that I have received your dear letter, where you tell me that I was mistaken in what I believed, I am happy, and I thank you for all the affectionate words that you sent me to lift any doubt from my mind. Oh! I hope that the moment of disillusionment will never come in our friendship; and to make sure that does not happen, let us always stay just this honest and sincere, and let's enjoy pleasure and suffer sorrow together; it is so unusual to find hearts that are good and unselfish!!![89]

She added remarks about Verdi's failure to appear in Rome for the swearing-in at the Senate: 'In general, many think that the Maestro despises his nomination as senator and that it is just for that reason that he has not yet appeared to swear his oath'. Verdi settled that matter on 15 November, when he went to Rome to be sworn in a year late.

Stolz again proclaimed her loyalty to Verdi and his wife just before leaving for St Petersburg, while declaring that she could not wait to get back, so that they could all meet again in Paris, where performances of *Aida* and the *Messa da Requiem* were scheduled for the spring of 1876. She sent news of the rest of the Trieste season, where the management had earned a great deal of money from the eleven *Aidas* and the seven Requiems. The box-office for the *Messa* had been especially good, she said. From Vienna she had heard that the *Messa* was going well there, even though it could not be compared to the performances Verdi had directed. Conveying good wishes from her brother and sister in Trieste, she also sent compliments to both Strepponi and Verdi, remarking that she was enormously fortunate to know them both.[90] Verdi, to whom she had conveyed an offer to go to St Petersburg for a fee of 24,000 roubles, decided to stay at home: he also refused an offer to return to Vienna.

While Stolz, Faccio, and their company were holding the Verdi fort in Trieste, Muzio, who had visited Sant'Agata in the autumn, had coached the artists for a French tour of excerpts from the *Messa da Requiem* which he conducted himself. The composer followed the fortunes of the tour through Muzio's letters, which reached him at Sant'Agata and Genoa. The performance schedule, exhausting for both conductor and singers, included Lille, Angers, Tours, Poitiers, Bayonne, and Pau before the end of 1875. The work created 'an immense sensation' at Lille, Muzio wrote on 16 November, although not all the soloists had lived up to the level of their performance during rehearsals in Milan; the soprano, Caruzzi, who had sounded fine with the piano, could not make her voice carry over the orchestra. A substitute would have to be found, Muzio reported, while assuming full responsibility for the problems he faced.[91] Verdi lost no time in letting Escudier know how angry he was:

It certainly is deplorable, . . . but to tell you the truth, when I heard what their fees were, I had many doubts about the outcome. If you recall, I told you to take French artists, because I knew perfectly well that with the artists that could be dug up in the provinces, you would have had a difficult time finding Italian singers of any merit.[92]

After Christmas and New Year's Day of 1876, Verdi learned from an exhausted Muzio about performances in Montpellier, Marseille, Saint-Etienne, Toulon, Nice, Cannes, Menton, and Monte Carlo. The company was stranded in a blizzard near Narbonne, after which Nice seemed like 'a terrestrial paradise', Muzio said.[93] The company, which won its greatest victories in Nantes and Nice, began to turn a profit after the beginning of 1876. In Avignon, when the mezzo-soprano refused to sing the second half of the evening, Muzio had to call in the Mayor and the police commissioner to persuade her to go on; in fact, Barlani had caused an uproar even in large cities, dressing as a man, smoking cigars in hotel dining rooms, and cooking her dinner in her hotel room over a spirit stove: 'a demon', Muzio called her.[94] When the tour ended, he retreated to Paris to help prepare *Aida*. Verdi was slightly off his regular schedule during that winter, having stayed on at Sant'Agata until early January 1876, chiefly because Strepponi had been ill with bronchitis. Even when they went to Genoa, he left almost at once; by 20 January he was back at Sant'Agata. Then, as in many years past, he had to have his say about the controversy over Busseto and its theatre. To Arrivabene, who had written asking for information about a young singer named Barezzi who had sung a concert in Busseto, he answered, saying that he had no idea who she might be:

You know that I am a kind of pariah in that town. I have committed so many sins against them!!! They have never forgiven me because I did not write an opera just for the opening of their Theatre; because I gave them 10,000 lire then (which they accepted none the less); and because I did not have Patti, Fraschini, Graziani, etc. come to sing (this is history!). How in the devil should I have gone and grabbed those artists by the collar and forced them to sing in Busseto!!! You will understand from this that I have absolutely nothing to do with Busseto's business, and when they scream, I let them scream; when they sing, give plays, and dance, I let them sing and dance as they wish; and if they do something that is good and useful, I send my contribution and that's that.[95]

This letter probably represents Verdi's reality, his version of the truth. In fact, he was still in contact with Giovannino Barezzi and had sent him complimentary tickets to hear the *Messa da Requiem* at La Scala, as correspondence at Sant'Agata proves.[96] He also heard occasionally from Demetrio Barezzi but complained that they sought him out only when they needed something.

Verdi kept up with major productions abroad through Stolz, who telegraphed from St Petersburg and Moscow, and Waldmann, who was again in Cairo. News from Stolz was especially encouraging: the theatre seemed a 'holy temple', she said, as the Russian audience filled it to capacity. The Emperor's family came to the opening night; the Emperor and Empress attended the third performance.[97] In *Aida* and the Requiem, Annie Louise Cary was the mezzo:

[she sang] very well; with that rich, even voice she brought forward certain effects that even Waldmann could not do because of her voice, [which was] not always even and was sometimes unmanageable; while this American woman, with her calmness and her unspoiled voice, was more effective in the *Messa* than in the *Aida*. . . . When the *Messa* ended, the public seemed to have gone mad.[98]

She added that an additional four performances of the *Messa* would have to be scheduled in St Petersburg. 'This *Messa* was a California gold mine for the management, which only thinks of making money.' She found the Moscow audience less intelligent than that of St Petersburg, but added that it was more passionate. 'The *Messa* and *Aida* caused a revolution in the theatre,' she said, adding extremely unkind remarks about Patti, who was also in the company.

Dina [Adelina] was furious and was going around saying 'You can go and hear [*Aida*] once, but no one will make me go back a second time.' I cannot tell you in mere words what intrigues this dear diva set in motion to prevent further performances of *Aida*! She is acting the coquette with [the tenor Ernesto] Nicolini and made people believe that she would lose her voice if she went around singing *Aida*: 'That impossible music!!!' Those are her words. Like an *ass*, Nicolini agreed to play his role in this comedy and was singing that he would never sing *Aida* again because it was ruining his voice and that he preferred light operas . . . that he was singing with Patti. After singing with the diva in *I diamanti della corona* (a work no one liked), he thought it was a good idea to come back to sing in *Aida*; and the diva, with all her gossip, was just talking into thin air and letting everyone see she was more jealous than usual.

To let the audience know that she is good and fine in all kinds of music, she is now singing concerts of dramatic pieces: the Inflammatus from the Stabat [Mater] and 'Casta Diva' [from *Norma*]. What a pity that this artist, who is good—or rather, unique—is so evil and jealous. When we meet, I will tell you all the goodies!!! My greatest satisfaction is to be able to say I don't know anyone. I don't contrive intrigues, and the audience loves me and above all, packs the theatre.[99]

When she left St Petersburg, Stolz stayed a few days in Berlin before settling in at the Hôtel de Bade in Paris, where she waited for Verdi and Strepponi.

Waldmann, in Cairo, sent news she was leaving the theatre to marry Count Galeazzo Massari from Ferrara, who had been courting her for some time. Verdi sent his congratulations on New Year's Day 1876, together with news of a discouraging season in Italy. He would see her in France, he said.[100] When Arrivabene asked him his opinion of several other opera composers, Verdi answered that of those he knew, 'the one who can do the best is Ponchielli; but, alas! he is no longer young, I think he is about 40 and has seen and *heard* too much. You know my views on *hearing too much*, I told you about that in Florence.' As for the younger ones, he went on, they should not look for enlightenment in Mendelssohn, Chopin, or Gounod.

Gounod is a very great musician, the foremost maestro in France, but he does not have any dramatic substance. Stupendous music, likeable, magnificent details, with the word almost always conveyed well . . . let's understand this clearly, the word, not the situation; the characters [are] not well delineated; and [he] does not stamp the drama [with his own character] or give it colour. . . . At the Opéra, the *mise-en-scène* is splendid, superior to all the other theatres in the correctness of the costumes and [its] good taste, but the music is the very worst. The singers always very mediocre (except for Faure some years), orchestra and chorus out of sorts and undisciplined. In that theatre I have heard hundreds of performances, but never, absolutely never, a good musical execution. . . . In Germany the orchestras and choruses are more alert and conscientious; they perform correctly and well; in spite of that, I saw deplorable spectacles in Berlin. The orchestra is huge and plays *huge*. The choruses not good, the *mise-en-scène* lacking character and taste. Singers . . . oh, singers that are bad, absolutely bad.[101]

In Vienna, even though the situation was better, he had still found a mediocre *mise-en-scène*; a drowsy, indifferent audience, and no excellent singers. The idea of repertory opera, as opposed to the *stagione* system practised in Italy, would never work south of the Alps, he felt.

Even during the winter Verdi had let Escudier know his intentions for the Paris production of *Aida*, sending orders for the settings and costumes and urging his publisher to mind the musical preparation as carefully as the stage. With Muzio already in charge of some of the coaching and under contract to conduct all the orchestra rehearsals except the final dress rehearsal, the composer could be reasonably sure his wishes would be carried out. He and Strepponi left Genoa for Sant'Agata during the first week in March. On 5 March Piave died in Milan, at the end of years of paralysis and despair. Verdi and his wife, neither or whom went to Milan at this time, left Italy on the twentieth and arrived in Paris two days later. Like Stolz, they stayed at the Hôtel de Bade.

Verdi's first concern was a debt owed to him by Camille Du Locle, which he had tried to collect for more than five months. In the hope of recovering the 48,000 francs owed him, he wrote to Perrin, Du Locle's father-in-law, but got no satisfaction. This meant that a very large sum from his fee for the Cairo *Aida* seemed lost to him—an inauspicious way, certainly, to begin his stay in France. Yet with thirty full days to prepare the opera, and with a cast that knew the work, he would seem to have been in an almost ideal situation. By the fifteenth he was threatening to walk out, because he could not get the scenery for the last act fixed. He needed an extra complete rehearsal, he said. The final dress rehearsal, which Verdi conducted himself, was held on 21 April with an invited audience made up mostly of journalists. Its resounding success was reported in the newspapers the next day. The first night was 22 April, a Saturday. One day later Strepponi could report to Corticelli that Verdi was the centre of an adoring Paris audience and that his triumph was complete.[102] The cast was made up of Stolz, Waldmann, Masini, Medini, Francesco Pandolfini, and Edouard De Reszke, who made his début as the King. Matched by an excellent orchestra and supported through the first week by Verdi himself as conductor, these artists more than did justice to *Aida*.

In this moment of professional achievement, Verdi and Strepponi faced one of the gravest personal crises of their lives. One day, probably 30 April, Strepponi apparently reached the limits of her emotional endurance at the moment when her husband decided to go to Stolz's apartment. Her diary entry first refers to 'V[erdi]' in the third person;[103] but she changed it into a letter to him. The text of her letter follows.

'It did not seem to me to be a proper day to visit a Signora who is neither your wife, nor your daughter, nor your sister . . .' The remark slipped out; and I realized at once that you were unhappy over it. Naturally this bad humour of yours hurts me, because, since she is not ill and there is no performance, it seems to me that you could go twenty-four hours without seeing this signora; and—all the more—because I had taken the trouble to ask about her myself, so as not to seem unconcerned about her; I told you as soon as I got back here.

I do not know whether she is or is not . . . I know that since 1872 you have had spells of assiduousness and solicitude that no woman could possibly interpret more favourably. I know that I am always ready to love her frankly and honestly.

You know how you have thanked me! With hard, violent, heart-rending words! You cannot control yourself.

If she is . . . Let's end this once and for all. Be honest and say so, without making me suffer the humiliation of these attentions of yours [to her].

If she is not . . . be calmer in your concern, be natural and not exclusive. Think sometimes that I, your wife, loathing the gossip of the past, am also living à trois at present, and I have the right at least to your respect, if not to ask for your caresses. Is this too much?

How peaceful and happy my spirit was during the first twenty days; and it was that way because you were cordial.[104]

Although Strepponi's letter says 'Let's end this once and for all', no resolution was reached. The *ménage à trois* at the Hôtel de Bade remained intact.

After the first week of performances of *Aida*, Muzio took over the baton from Verdi. Writing of the triumph to the Milanese theatrical agent Katinka Evers Lampugnani, Muzio exulted:

The success of *Aida* is immense, unprecedented; Stolz and Waldmann were better received yesterday (the second performance) than on the first night; and they really sang like two angels; Masini was more successful on the first night than on the second; he is an uneven artist who lacks *rhythm*, and to accompany him—as Verdi says—'You have to have a bottle of Holy Oil in your pocket.' Pandolfini had an immense success; Medini did well, although his voice has suffered and he always sings flat. The box-office on the opening night was 18,223 francs; the second night, 17,750 francs. The theatre is almost all sold out through the sixth performance; and they are selling tickets for the seventh and eighth performances.[105]

The fourth and fifth performances brought in even more money than the first night, with a box office of 18,233 and 18,896 francs. But not even this artistic and financial triumph could save Escudier from bankruptcy.

Regretfully, Verdi wrote to Ricordi on 28 April that he had concluded that the theatre might even have to close in 1877. 'I hope I am wrong,' he added.[106]

While in Paris, Verdi oversaw the French translation of *Aida* that Du Locle and Nuitter were preparing, rehearsed and conducted the *Messa da Requiem*, which his company sang at the Théâtre des Italiens under his baton on 30 May; and indulged himself a bit by having his *Quartetto* played to a small audience of one hundred invited guests at the Hôtel de Bade. Among the artists was Paganini's famous pupil Camillo Sivori, whom Verdi had first met more than thirty years before. The work's success led the composer to consider having it published, so that it could be available for commercial use. In France it would be handled by Escudier, in spite of the fact that Verdi had come to mistrust him and suspect that he, like Ricordi, had not paid him all the royalties that were due. An ominous note was sounded on 19 May, when the composer asked Escudier to discuss this matter with him in the presence of 'two trusted persons', so that he would have witnesses to the review of his affairs.[107] Verdi's confidant was Muzio, who was also Escudier's employee. When Verdi left Paris, at the end of the first week in June, he entrusted his affairs to Muzio, who carried on with *Aida* until 20 June and could report to the Milanese theatrical agent and publisher Giuseppe Fassi that the opera had broken all records and exceeded everyone's expectations for it.[108] On the last night of the season, the impresario had personally offered large bouquets to both Stolz and Waldmann, who stood on stage at the end of the third act in a sea of flowers that Escudier had had spread on the boards. From Sant'Agata, Verdi let Escudier know that he was 'very happy' that the season had gone so well. 'Oh! you are very lucky! Twenty-six consecutive performances without a hitch, without anyone getting sick and making you lose a performance—this is a bit of good fortune that will never happen again![109] Verdi stayed at Sant'Agata with Strepponi and Corticelli in June, then welcomed Muzio there in July. Soon after their return, they began to make large contributions to the Asilo Infantile or nursery school in Cortemaggiore, establishing a pattern of philanthropy that continued until their deaths and (in Verdi's case) even after. In 1877 his donation was 300 lire, Strepponi's 200, gifts so large as to earn them the town's gratitude for such 'splendid acts of charity'.[110]

In August Filomena Maria Verdi took the final examinations at her boarding-school in Turin, becoming eligible for her diploma, which gave her the right to teach in any public elementary school. An arrangement for her to take these examinations well ahead of schedule had been made by Piroli at Verdi's request, because Filomena Maria was about to be engaged to young Alberto Carrara, the son of Angiolo Carrara and Caterina Demaldè. Solidly in the clan, he was the grandson of Verdi's ardent supporter Giuseppe Demaldè of the Società Filarmonica. At the end of the term Verdi and Strepponi went to Turin together to bring the girl back to Sant'Agata. Soon Strepponi and the girl went to Tabiano to join Stolz, who had been there since the first week in August. It is entirely possible that Verdi had met the soprano there.[111] The fact that Stolz chose Tabiano, a small, unfashionable spa, over other more popular Italian spas speaks for itself. It was about 25 kilometres from Verdi's estate, about two hours by carriage.

Strepponi, drafting a letter to the soprano, who was then close by, indeed too close by, wrote: 'and I would like to be completely at peace with God so that I could pass on to the other world to rest and get well.'[112] Omitted from the final version, this phrase reveals Verdi's wife's wish that death might free her from a life of pain.

On 4 September Verdi, apparently indifferent to the gossip and his wife's suffering, went to Tabiano and brought Strepponi, Stolz, and Filomena Maria back to Sant'Agata. Muzio was already back in Paris at the time. Earlier in the year it had been rumoured widely that Stolz would leave the stage that summer. She herself had confided to Muzio in June that she did not intend to sing again: 'She wants to come to Milan, find a beautiful apartment, and live quietly,' the conductor had written to Verdi.[113] Verdi himself had told Clara Maffei that Stolz really did want to give up her career. The news of her retirement reached print in the *Gazzetta musicale* on 2 July. Given this, her visits to Tabiano and Sant'Agata and, perhaps, had stays at 'La Codetta', constituted an even greater threat to Strepponi, seeming like the first actions in a well-planned scenario that would give Verdi and Stolz ample time to be together.

Stolz stayed at least three weeks and perhaps even longer, although some evidence would lead us to believe that her visit caused further tension and conflict between Verdi and Strepponi. Illica, in his letter to Lina Mascagni, referred to a final confrontation during which 'Strepponi, so good and so much in love, drove Verdi to the edge of suicide' with her jealousy over Stolz.[114] A story that is common currency around Busseto has Strepponi ordering Verdi to send the soprano away and Verdi threatening to kill himself if Stolz left. Strepponi then left the villa herself and stayed away until the soprano had gone back to Milan.[115] There is no certain evidence for this. If it did take place, it can have happened only in these days of late summer and early autumn in 1876, when Strepponi had borne the situation *à trois* for almost three months in Paris, then had confronted Verdi with her ultimatum, only to have him arrange for Stolz to come to Tabiano and Sant'Agata for yet another long visit. Strepponi did leave Verdi at the villa, although we do not know whether Stolz was with him or not. On 19 October Strepponi was in Cremona with her sister. By that time Stolz had already made a major decision about her own life, having chosen not to retire, but to go to St Petersburg after all. It is entirely possible that the soprano's hasty decision to return to the stage, made just a few weeks after she announced her well-considered retirement, was prompted by a desire to break off with Verdi and his wife, rather than just the pleasure of earning '140,000 gold francs'[116] offered by the Russian engagement. Stolz made this decision at Sant'Agata.

Several subsequent developments support the conclusion that a traumatic confrontation took place at the villa that year. First, in the correspondence between Strepponi and Stolz between October 1876 and March 1877, there are no references to the tearful farewells that had marked their previous parting. Indeed, there are no references to any farewells at all. This suggests that one or the other of the women had left the villa abruptly or in unusual circumstances. Second, the tone and frequency of Stolz's letters to Verdi and Strepponi changed at this time. The 128 Stolz letters at Sant'Agata follow a fairly predictable pattern until the autumn of 1876, when the soprano interrupted her regular correspondence with Verdi and suspended communication with the couple entirely from the time of her departure from Sant'Agata until December 1876. This alone arouses suspicion, for Stolz had been one of Verdi's main lifelines to the theatre for years. Strepponi's letter to Stolz of 18 October went unanswered until 13 December, when Stolz wrote to *both* Verdi and Strepponi from Russia. Strepponi's letter of 16 December was not answered until Stolz got back to Milan in March 1877. These letters, portions of which are reproduced below, are the screens behind which the personal drama was played. Because these famous people knew that their papers were often read by servants, secretaries, agents, or even friends, much was implied rather than stated outright. Strepponi, a superlative letter-writer, used an arsenal of double meanings, allusions, and hints in her correspondence. Third, when Stolz did write, she clearly made Verdi so happy that it is easy to believe he did indeed love her. The few examples we have of his letters to her ring with joy. The tone is extraordinary, indeed, almost unique in his correspondence, which is often marked with scepticism, cynicism, or complaint.[117] Fourth, Strepponi herself wrote Verdi a letter just after Stolz's visit to Sant'Agata, beginning 'Since fate has decreed that everything that made up my bliss in this life has been irreparably lost'.[118] She can only have been referring to the loss of his love; with it gone, she was condemned to a life of 'suffering'. Fifth, Stolz herself referred in many subsequent letters to her fear that her visits to Sant'Agata would cause trouble.

This later correspondence, in the period after Stolz left Sant'Agata and Strepponi went to Cremona, was preceded by Strepponi's October letter to Verdi, the draft of which, with its many crossed-out words and added phrases, is very difficult to read:

Since fate has decreed that everything that made up my bliss in life [*crossed out*: and made it seem enhanced by eternal youth] has been irreparably lost, may my soul's torments be lessened by my suggestion and the good [act] that you can do, and, I am sure, will do, chiefly for those who are of your blood and have, or will have your name. ['*I therefore propose*' *crossed out*] The trial that you thought you had lost . . . [against] your ['*old*' *crossed out*] lost *friend*, who was once your friend and who did you [harm] by not listening to you [about] the amount that you thought irreparably lost, thanks to this—hoped-for solution . . . [you will receive]. . . . .

I would want to give [the money] in a savings-bank book or in some other way to [Filomena] Maria's parents (the sum, for example, 500 lire in one single payment) for clothing for her little sister so as to be free once and for all of their not probable, but possible, begging.[119]

Strepponi's calculations of the annual total gifts follow. The whole of her domestic tragedy is summed up in the first sentence of the letter, the confused state of her mind reflected in the almost illegible page.

On 19 October Strepponi wrote to Stolz from Cremona, counselling the soprano to retire while the audiences still loved her rather than go on singing until everyone was tired of hearing her.

In any case, even if you were not to feel like giving up the theatre, I am convinced you will go on living your quiet life, which is right for an artist who has an honest and scrupulously clean conscience like yours. . . . I hope you will never have to struggle with the sorrows of life, especially the delusions and sorrows of the heart. . . . Yes, my dear Teresa, in joy and in misfortune (may God save you from it) say a Sunday prayer and, while saying it, think of me sometimes and beg for me the mercy of God, that God that the beautiful souls refuse to believe in, because they do not want to look at their own consciences.[120]

Because Strepponi lived with Verdi, who did not believe in God and laughed at those who did, we have to think that this is a reference to him.

Stolz's reply, addressed to both Verdi and Strepponi, reported on her début in *La Juive*, which was not as successful as the *Aida* of the year before. As always, the soprano sent news of Patti and Nicolini, together with all the current gossip about *that ménage à trois*, as the diva prepared to sue her husband the Marquis de Caux for divorce. Patti had sung *Aida* in Moscow, Stolz said, but had not been received as enthusiastically as she had expected.[121] After asking where Verdi and his wife would be spending Christmas and New Year, Stolz called herself a 'Poor Gypsy' who could not wait to get back to her house in Milan.

Strepponi took a different tack as she sent Christmas greetings to Stolz on 16 December, sharply reproving the soprano for complaining at a time when she was earning a fortune from an engagement she had chosen to accept. She could 'have a dress made out of thousand-franc notes', Strepponi said. As for the coming holiday: 'Here is Christmas: the Man-God appears to redeem the human race and teach by his example the greatest virtue: that of not only forgiving offences but also of loving the offender. I hope you achieve everything that you can wish for, certain that you will only want honest and good things.'[122] Just in case the soprano did not get the message, Strepponi followed the word 'offender' with the words 'I hope you', in a text that suggests a referential judgement passed on Stolz. The letter also contained further advice: 'Dry your tears, have someone serve you a good dinner, and drink a glass of champagne to the health of your old friends.'

The three months of silence that followed were Stolz's own answer to Strepponi's note. At this point, it seemed that Verdi's wife had won her battle, having driven Stolz off. By the middle of February, when no further word had come from the soprano, Strepponi wrote her again. This letter seems to have reached Stolz in Milan when she got back from Russia. Then, and only then, did the soprano answer, with a reference to Strepponi's 'good-natured castigation' of her.[123] She had been very ill in Russia, she said, suffering from insomnia, depression, overwork, and bronchitis. She had lost weight. None the less, Stolz was always ready to make remarks about Patti, Nicolini, De Caux, and their domestic problems. Because of the divorce, she said, even Patti's most loyal supporters had deserted her 'so as not to be compromised' by being seen at her performances. The diva had 'lost her head and much of her prestige' by abandoning her husband to take up with the tenor, who in turn had walked out on his wife and five children. 'She must be a perverse woman', Stolz concluded.[124]

When both Verdi and Strepponi answered this letter, Stolz prudently addressed her reply to both of them, including her remarks about a disastrous *La forza del destino* at La Scala with news about her nephew Luigino Ricci, and about her new apartment, which was in the fine building on Corsia del Giardino (now Via Manzoni) that later became the Hotel Continental and is now a bank. Further gossip about Patti ended with a judgement: 'This woman has no heart. She never loved her husband and does not love her lover. The stupid Nicolini was just useful so she could get rid of the Marquis [de Caux]; she said this herself to her closest friends.[125]

Stolz did not write a letter to Verdi alone until May 1877; and in it she apologized for not being able to send any news of the theatre. Living in retirement, she spent her days quietly, 'monotonously, without excitement but also without interest'.[126] The only phrase that might have raised alarm in Strepponi was a reference to Stolz's planned visit to Tabiano during the summer. Even this letter, though, was covered when Stolz also wrote to Strepponi on the same day. It seemed she did all she could to avoid giving the impression that she was concerned about Verdi as a man or as a composer. In 1878 the soprano addressed only two of her letters to Verdi alone; in 1879 three; in 1880 only one, although Verdi continued to write to her. Stolz often sent him her regards in letters addressed to Strepponi. Other letters were sent to the couple, as the soprano resolutely showed more concern for Strepponi than for her husband. The two women developed a sisterly relationship as they sent lace, hats, furniture, and advice back and forth, traded coats and furs, paid each other's small bills, and settled their petty-cash accounts. Whatever else had happened, Strepponi had put an end to what she called Verdi's exclusive attention to the soprano. The semblance of propriety was restored. The situation may not have been resolved, though, for Stolz may have bought or rented, through a third party, the small villa at 'La Codetta' in Besenzone, adjacent to the mill that Verdi owned there. Local tradition holds that the house was hers.[127]

31

Autumn 1876–Spring 1880

Normality

After Stolz left Sant'Agata in the autumn of 1876, Verdi went back to farming and digging wells. In a letter to Clara Maffei, he used a phrase that has frequently been cited since: 'Invent the truth'. When Maffei asked him about young Achille Torelli's play *Color del tempo*, which Verdi had seen in Genoa, he replied:

It has great qualities, above all a *liveliness* that is particularly French; but there is basically very little there. To copy the truth can be a good thing, but to *invent the truth* is better, much better. It seems there is a contradiction in these three words: *invent the truth*; but ask Papa [Shakespeare] about it. Maybe he, Papa, encountered some Falstaff, but he would have had a hard time finding a villain as villainous as Iago, and never—absolutely never—[could he have found] angels like Cordelia, Imogen, Desdemona, etc., and yet they are so true!

To copy the truth is a beautiful thing; but it is a photograph, not a painting.[1]

Discouraged over the scant harvest and the 'solemn fiasco' of his artesian well,[2] Verdi followed the decline of the Théâtre des Italiens through letters coming from Paris, where Muzio was handling some of Patti's affairs, following the career of the baritone Victor Maurel, teaching pupils, and sending articles about the theatre to several publications. Again engaged at the Italiens, he had little or no faith in Escudier's ability to manage the company. Against Verdi's wishes, *La forza del destino* was scheduled to open the season on 31 October. It was a failure, partly because the story was too unbelievable, partly because the singers were not equal to such demanding roles. Three different Preziosillas took the stage during the opera. At moments the audience found preposterous, there was laughter. The *Aida* that followed was modestly successful, although the soprano Singer, the mezzo Guéymard, and the tenor Carpi could not be compared to Stolz, Waldmann, and Masini. Muzio reported to Fassi that the orchestra and chorus were superb; there had been a good turnout; bouquets had been thrown; and the artists had been brought out many times for curtain calls.[3] When Nicolini was brought in to sing Radamès, the audience began to demand encores so enthusiastically that the entire second-act finale was repeated; Muzio heard them shouting to hear it yet a third time. Yet only a few weeks later, artistic bankruptcy was at hand, Escudier having engaged a soprano, Madame Eyre, who was rumoured to have paid the impresario 5,000 francs to hire her. Having bought 2,400 francs worth of tickets, she had elegant, new costumes made at her own expense then exposed herself to the ridicule of critics and the public. *Rigoletto*, which opened in January 1877 with the baritone Pandolfini in the title role and Albani as Gilda, was completely successful. Escudier, though, had already fallen behind and had failed to pay Verdi the 4,000 francs owed him that month. One of his problems was the number of complimentary tickets he gave out; this practice had aroused Verdi's anger even the year before. In spite of his precarious financial position, Escudier muddled on, keeping *Rigoletto* on the boards and postponing a *Sonnambula* indefinitely, while adding *Linda di Chamounix* and *Don Giovanni* to his programme, making use of Singer and Pandolfini. The success of the Mozart work made it possible for the impresario to pay Verdi the money he owed. A brief appearance by Masini, who had lost some of his voice and 'all the good lessons' Verdi had taught him,[4] failed to save the season, which went from bad to worse as Escudier hired the ninth tenor that year. Muzio predicted that the impresario would be in debt as much as 150,000 francs by spring; Escudier still owed him fees from the previous year, yet gave no sign he might pay his bills. 'A huge catastrophe' was certain to follow.[5]

Verdi had his own say about the shameful course of events at the Italiens, where even so celebrated a tenor as Masini had lost his way in 'La donna è mobile'. To Escudier he wrote:

I wanted the Théâtre des Italiens to rise again, and because of this I was willing to make any sacrifice; but now I no longer have the hopes I once had. I know that at the moment you are successful (I won't speak of the *Aida* that you prostituted to your experiments with your singers making their débuts, something that you—you above all—never should have done). . . . I, as an Italian, and as an

Italian *composer*, wanted above all else to see our theatre live again. You can have half-successes and some good evenings, but, forgive me, . . . I dare to tell you that you will not save the Italiens and, in the long run, you will lose your entire fortune in it.[6]

Eventually he saw his prediction come true.

During the winter of 1876–7, while he was in Genoa, Verdi's career took a new turn when the German composer and pianist Ferdinand Hiller invited him to come to Cologne to conduct the *Messa da Requiem* there during the city's spring festival. The first letter of the Hiller–Verdi correspondence dates from 20 January 1877: establishing a tone of shared interests and respect, it is the first of many letters exchanged between the two composers over a period of almost eight years. Honoured to be asked to conduct performances of the German Concert Society, Verdi agreed to direct the rehearsals and performances of the Mass and suggested in a later letter that Cologne also perform his *Quartetto* with an expanded orchestra. That, too, he was willing to direct.[7] When Muzio learned of the engagement, he asked for time off from the Italiens to help Verdi with the preparation, then made the eleven-hour train trip from Paris to Cologne for the Festival. Strepponi contributed her mite by beginning German lessons from self-help texts. The couple left for Cologne during the second week in May and, on arrival, found that Verdi would be honoured in the German city with admirers, 'invitations, visits, dinners, suppers', and high praise.[8] He conducted a choir of 500 and an orchestra of 200 in an 'excellent' performance of the *Messa da Requiem* that was marred only by the poor quality of the four soloists. Presented with an ivory-and-silver baton set with a 'V' in diamonds, and a 'magnificent crown of silver and gold', he also received a 'magnificent' album with 'splendid' views of the Rhine executed by some of the city's finest artists. The Quartet Society also performed his *Quartetto* to the composer's complete satisfaction: on it he bestowed another 'magnificently'.[9] At the end of his visit, a group of 500 invited guests shared a banquet in his honour. Muzio returned to Paris alone to await Verdi and Strepponi there, while they travelled through Holland and Belgium. They found the canals filthy and stinking, the cities depressing, the Great Dike at Scheveningen frightening, and the Rembrandts impressive. In France, Verdi heard Gounod's *Cinq Mars* and Massenet's *Le Roi de Lahore* at the Opéra. He also saw a performance of Sardou's play *Dora*. While there, the composer and Muzio discussed Muzio's decision to leave the floundering Théâtre des Italiens and go on with his teaching.

When Verdi got back to Sant'Agata, he closed the piano 'hermetically' for three or four months and joined his crew of stonemasons for the annual season of repairs to outbuildings and tenant houses on the estate.[10] He heard regularly from Waldmann, now Countess Massari. Stolz's letters of November and December 1877 were addressed to Strepponi, who was asked to convey the soprano's regards to 'il Maestro'. As she had declared in her 22 March letter, she had not come for a visit because she feared it might be 'annoying'.[11] To Verdi, in May Stolz said that she did not write to him directly 'only out of fear of annoying you'.[12] A year later on 27 June 1878 her letter included a more pointed remark. She had not written, she told Verdi, because she was afraid of causing problems for him.[13] Discretion was still the watchword.

Verdi, claiming he had no serious obligations, worked on the farm until late November, then accompanied Strepponi to Genoa, only to return almost at once to Sant'Agata. In December they moved again, from the second-floor apartment at Palazzo Doria to the *piano nobile*, where they could have more space and fewer stairs to climb. The salon and his and Strepponi's bedrooms faced the sea and had access to one of the *palazzo*'s two huge terraces. Verdi's had the clock-tower guarding it. All the other rooms faced east and north. Part of the furniture, in Turkish style, had been ordered by Stolz at Strepponi's request and sent from Milan. The effort of moving, though, proved too much for Strepponi, who spent Christmas in bed while Benedetto Mami, their cook-houseman, covered Verdi's needs. An air of depression lay over the household. The composer, who had written a 'kind letter' to Stolz, received the soprano's greetings only indirectly, as they were tucked in the middle of a paragraph in a letter to Strepponi.[14]

Before Christmas Verdi had the satisfaction of hearing from the impresario Max Maretzek that *Il trovatore* had saved the Wagner–Meyerbeer–Beethoven season in Boston from certain bankruptcy. An account in *Dwight's Journal of Music* records the 'thin houses' for *Les Huguenots*, *Lohengrin*, and *Robert le Diable*, and the 'wretchedly small' audience for *Freyschutz* (*sic*) and *Fidelio*, then:

On Thursday night! Oh! what a fall was there, my countrymen—this high and haughty ultra-German opera became Italian, and came down to *Trovatore*,— Italian of the trashiest, most hackneyed, barrel-organ type! And that night the theatre was crowded, and so it was again, and yet again the following week. But from *Fidelio* to—*Trovatore*!! . . . Beethoven's divine masterpiece with half a house, and Verdi's sensational affair hailed three times by eager crowds! . . .

BOOK V

When lovers of the best in music neglect the best, the appeal has to be made to the popular crowd; and none can blame the manager, who acts from instincts of self-preservation.[15]

Strepponi learned just after Christmas that Giovannina Strepponi, her aunt, had died in Lodi on Christmas Eve 1877 after a long illness. The former teacher left her niece 'a pair of diamond-studded buckles; the only valuable pieces I own', perhaps in recognition of the gifts of money Giuseppina had sent her over the years. Barberina was left a small purse full of holy relics, while other Strepponi nieces and nephews and one of Giovannina's former students got bequests of money out of the interest on government bonds.[16]

At the end of 1877 and the beginning of 1878, some of Verdi's concern about music was centred on Patti, whose news he got chiefly through Muzio. The soprano's broken marriage, her affair with Nicolini, the charges, counter-charges, lawsuits, and settlements were the talk of all Europe. To add to the tangle of the family's affairs, one of the Strakoschs had acquired all European rights to 'the Bell talking equipment, [which,] according to the newspapers, is the most marvellous discovery of our time.'[17] Muzio wrote to Verdi about the concerts that had been given in Philadelphia and heard in a hall in New York City, '90 English miles' away, as the telephone had its official baptism. Patti's brother-in-law had also signed contracts with her for tours in America, Germany, Holland, and Italy. These saved her from certain embarrassment, for she had been scheduled to sing at the Théâtre des Italiens with the company—'a pack of dogs'.[18] Even the legendary Tamberlick had been scored off there as 'this ancient artist'.

When Patti crossed the Alps, she aroused the same delirious enthusiasm in Italy as she had everywhere else. Impresarios in Florence, Rome, Genoa, and Milan could boast of sold-out houses and noble families fighting each other for extra tickets for her performances. Inevitably, Ricordi and others began to put pressure on Verdi to appear with her, to conduct for her, or to write a new opera for her. One of the publisher's projects was a production of the *Messa da Requiem* in Milan Cathedral; another was Verdi's appearance on the podium at the soprano's *Aida* at La Scala. There she was to appear under the banner of the agent-impresario Carlo D'Ormeville, husband of the soprano Ericlea Darclée.

During her engagement in Genoa, Patti was invited to Palazzo Doria, where she and Verdi discussed the forthcoming *Aida*. Verdi did not want to be drawn into the diva-centred maelstrom and advised her to make all her arrangements with Ricordi and D'Ormeville. But when he heard that a cut was planned for the third act of the opera, he protested to his publisher. At the same time, he again reminded everyone of his long-standing loyalty to the great soprano. He did not need new operas or a production of *Aida* to convince him of her worth, and had not waited for her to 'be baptized' by the audience before joining the ranks of her admirers because he had been her staunch supporter even when Patti was still a teenager.

What a marvellous actress-singer she was at 18, when I heard her for the first time in *Sonnambula*, *Lucia*, *Barbiere*, and *Don Giovanni*! She was then what she was now, except for some change in her voice, especially in the low notes, which were then a bit empty and childlike, and are now extremely beautiful. But the talent, the instinct for the theatre, the singing are the same, the same, the same.[19]

Verdi continued to oppose her making a cut in *Aida*.

This poor third act, which in the opinion of the Milanese audience wasn't worth anything, is destined to suffer! But there is nothing to cut, not even the ugly cabaletta of the tenor–soprano duet. It is part of the situation, and it must, or should, stay; otherwise, there is a *hole* in the fabric. You know I am the worst enemy of *cuts* and *transpositions*. It is better not to perform the operas; and if Patti finds this role tiring, why is she doing it? Why does she need to do *Aida*?

Her hope of persuading Verdi to write a new work for her came to nothing, when he refused, saying: 'Why a new opera when you have so many old ones to choose from?'[20]

Patti created a furore in Milan, where she sang *Faust*, *Il barbiere di Siviglia*, *Il trovatore*, *La sonnambula*, *Aida*, and *La traviata* with Nicolini at La Scala between November 1877 and March 1878. The disorder of her personal life spilled over when Nicolini and Strakosch attacked each other with canes in her apartment. The soprano suffered an injury to her arm trying to separate them. Stolz, who heard Patti, reported to Verdi that *Aida* had 'worked miracles' but that although she sang some parts of the opera very well, she either 'did not like' or 'cannot interpret' other parts.[21] Stolz also found her high notes forced.

Verdi had a different view. After hearing Patti in Genoa, he wrote to Arrivabene that she was greeted there with an 'undescribable enthusiasm' that was deserved because her artistic nature [is] so complete that perhaps there has never been anyone to equal her! Oh! Oh! And Malibran? Very, very great, but not always even! Sometimes sublime and sometimes exaggerated! Her singing style was not very pure, her acting was not always right, her voice shrill in the top notes! In spite of everything, a very great artist, marvellous. But Patti is more complete. A marvellous voice, an extremely pure singing style; stupendous actress with a charm and a naturalness that no one else has![22]

An unprecedented event took place in Verdi's and Strepponi's lives when they took Filomena Maria to Monte Carlo in March. Verdi, a sworn enemy of gambling, even played (and lost) 15 gold napoleons and his wife lost 5. The principality was a paradise, but the Casino 'an inferno. Nothing is more horrible to me than those gambling rooms, real regions of the damned', he told Waldmann.[23] And to Piroli: 'Horrible! Horrible!'[24] He also expressed his revulsion to Arrivabene. After the experience Verdi and Strepponi returned to Genoa then went on to Sant'Agata, where they faced a desolate countryside where hungry farm-labourers roamed the roads, begging for 'a crust of bread'.[25]

Charity

Umberto I, the new king of Italy, began his reign on 9 January 1878. The unexpected death of Vittorio Emanuele II brought a young sovereign to the throne in a country where post-unification prosperity had elevated the upper and middle classes—royalty, nobility, industrialists, large land-owners, and men of commerce, chiefly—while driving the poor into ever deeper despair. Conditions in rural areas had been deteriorating steadily for nearly twenty years, a period when taxes needed for the Italian army and public-works projects depleted the assets of every family that owned property. At the same time, the upper and middle classes had diverted funds from the rural areas when they invested in government bonds rather than their farm property. Outside towns and cities, the general situation worsened as young men who were needed for field work were called into obligatory military service. Finally, the 1869 tax on milling flour had taken a heavy economic and social toll, provoking riots and bloodshed at the outset, nurturing class hatred, and aggravating the bad feeling that already existed between the clergy and pro-unification patriots. All through the last quarter of the century, the poor in the countryside suffered constant degradation, convinced that the ruling class was lining its pockets, corrupting the government, and abandoning the destitute to their fate. The ever building rage found release in farm-workers' strikes and riots that were the models for those Bernardo Bertolucci depicted in his film *1900*. Shot at the farm Le Piacentine near Roncole and using many people from Roncole and Busseto as its extras, conceived and directed by a native of Parma, *1900* recreates vividly the conditions that prevailed in the last decades of Verdi's life, although it opens on the day Verdi died in 1901.

Against this backdrop of neglect and decay, Verdi fought his own battles to save his farm and help his people. Although he had built a virtual empire in land, and had become a true *latifondista* or large estate-owner, with acreage not only at Sant'Agata but all over the area, he remained near his tenants and peasants, chiefly because he spent so much of his time and physical energy with them. Severe and sometimes even tyrannical, he still managed to be close at hand, accessible not just to his farm-managers but to his day-labourers, carpenters, stonemasons, stable-hands, marble-cutters, gardeners, coachmen, carters, butchers, bakers, tile-factory workers, dairymen, house servants, and their families. Their appeals to him filled his files. His proximity to his many cousins and their collateral families is clear from the register of the Mappa Catastale, the land map of the Provinces of Parma and Piacenza, which records property rights from Napoleon's era through unification. Side by side with the names of dozens of absentee landowners are 'Cristoforo Verdi, boatman' of Sant'Agata; 'Luigi Verdi, son of Angelo' of Sant'Agata, with his little farm; 'Pietro Verdi, son of Luigi', smallholder from Ongina; 'Giovanni Verdi, son of the late Carlo', born in Villanova; and, at Roncole, Verdi's uncles Giulio and Isidoro Sivelli.[26] These modest people are set down in the midst of the large holdings of 'Cavaliere Count Giovanni Bonaventura Porta of Parma', 'Count Giacomo Costa of Piacenza', 'Marchese Vidoni of Cremona', 'Countess Margherita Patellani of Casalmaggiore', and many clergymen—abbots and various reverends—who were also absentee land-lords. In the Stato di Classificamento delle Proprietà Costrutte, the roll of houses,[27] Verdi's next-door neighbours between the villa and Sant'Agata village were the faithful Guerino Balestrieri, the Bocelli cousins, and the Bassinis. In the next house to the north, between the villa and the village of Ongina and the Po, were Maria Luigia Verdi, daughter of Giovanni, a small farmer, living with relatives. Then came tenants who tilled Verdi's lands; they lived side by side with day-labourers and farm-hands—the *giornalieri* and *braccianti*—who were followed by two more Verdis, both smallholders, and other cousins scattered through the two riverside hamlets. Over the decades, as Verdi bought land at Roncole and Madonna dei Prati, then Sant'Agata, Piantadoro, Gerbida, Bosco, Castellazzo, Canale, Il Giardino, Possessione, and Possessioncella, he was always surrounded by his people, as he bought most of his ancestors' farms.

He and his wife took heroic measures to help the poor, sick, abandoned, and desperate people nearby. The complete record of their acts of charity would make up a true Golden Book of its kind. Because Verdi was so famous, he received dozens upon dozens of letters from men and women he knew and many he had never seen, asking for help. In some cases he and Strepponi sent money even though it was not requested. Piave is a well known example. But Piave was someone Verdi loved, someone he might have been expected to aid. Even more praiseworthy were Verdi's and Strepponi's gifts to the needy poor and ill, no matter whether they were staying at home or living in Genoa or Milan. All those sums—30, 50, 100, 300, 500 lire or more—added up to an extraordinary act of moral and civil generosity. They supported the old and the young, singers, conductors, instrumentalists, stagehands, agents, and even actors. Among those Verdi did not help was Ruggiero Leoncavallo, who wrote several times and appealed to Verdi on an urgent basis in April 1876 and March 1877. One actor Verdi helped was Antonio Bucciotti, the son of the former *capocomico* and last surviving member of Vestri's great Reale Sarda theatre company, whom Verdi helped over and over again. But the overwhelming majority of those receiving Verdi's and Strepponi's charity were relatives and the poor of the neighbourhood. Their gifts to individuals and institutions were made through third parties, such as Don Avanzi and Maddalena Fagnoni Barezzi. Other gifts were made directly to Don Carlo Uttini, one of the founders of the nursery-school movement in Italy, and his brother, sister, and nieces, all of whom taught and several of whom were priests. They also gave to Francesco Pedrini, head of the nursery-school and day-care centre in Cortemaggiore, where he took care of fifty children every day. Sometimes Strepponi helped people under her mother's maiden name, signing herself 'G. Cornalba'. Money, food, and clothing also passed through local institutions in Sant'Agata, Villanova, Vidalenzo, Cortemaggiore, Busseto, Roncole, Bersano, Alseno, Parma, Milan, Genoa, Piacenza, and villages along the Po. Often Verdi helped others with personal recommendations to government offices, universities, and conservatories. At one time, he ordered that free polenta be given away every day at noon from the kitchen at Sant'Agata. He also tried to influence public policy, chiefly through Piroli and Arrivabene. To the former he wrote:

There is a lot of misery; it is a serious matter that could become extremely serious, even threatening public order. We are talking about hunger!!! In the big cities, even in the richest ones, such as Genoa, Milan, etc., commerce has shrunk a lot; there are frequent bankruptcies, so there is no work.

In our small cities, such as Parma, Piacenza, Cremona, the property-owner has no money, and if he has even a bit, he keeps it right in his pocket, because he is afraid of the future; and so he does only the biggest and most essential jobs, because he is loaded down with taxes; his funds shrink; and the general wealth decreases.

My dear Piroli, if you see how many poor people there are in our neighbour-hood, and many of them are robust young men who ask for work and, when they do not find any, ask for charity—a bread crust! And the government should be aware of that, too, because—just to mention the places near us—in Zibello, Soragna, Busseto, etc., etc., the Prefects have sent reinforcements of mounted Carabinieri, Sharpshooters, etc., to prevent any demonstrations. So the poor people say: 'We ask for work and bread. They send us soldiers and handcuffs.' This is what they say.

I won't talk about industry, of important commerce; but, being a peasant, I will talk to you just about agriculture. The land around us surely is not producing what it should. This is as plain as the sun. And yet the government closes the Ministry of Agriculture!! . . .

Unfortunately the future is very dark, no matter where you look, whether in [Italy] or outside it. And do you know that poverty is growing at a terrifying rate?[28]

Conditions in rural areas had been deteriorating for so long that it seemed that no one knew what measures might be effective.

This was the countryside to which Verdi and Strepponi returned in the spring of 1878. As in the past, he had continued to provide work for local labourers and craftsmen, as he continued to make improvements, which his wife sometimes criticized as being too expensive or too time-consuming. We are so accustomed to reading letters that reflect Verdi's need to dominate others that it is somewhat surprising to read one that shows him in the role of harassed husband. On 12 May 1878 he ordered Corticelli to get the house ready for his and his wife's homecoming.

Unless you get other instructions, send the big carriage to Borgo for me on Thursday, as we three will arrive on the usual train. You will have two extra days to put in good enough order our two rooms, the salon, and the dining-room. As I wrote to you, I hope that you will have had [the south foundation of the house fixed]. I hope that the painter will have finished all the doors of Peppina's dressing-room and will have painted the trim with the blue as the other is done with gold. I also hope that Guerino will not forget to see to it that the keys, the iron grilles, and the bronze handles on the big french window in the salon are in place, for when Peppina gets there, I want her to see that it is done right and that she will not have to say 'Such a lot of time, such effort, and so much money just for this'!

To sum up, take care and, in your wisdom, see to it that everything is clean in the parts of the house that are finished. Open the windows just before we get there, so that we can see things easily. Open the door to the little staircase as well and . . . and . . . and then provide for a good little supper with our asparagus on the day we arrive. Let's get this straight: not too much food, so that we are suffocated by it!!!!

Tell Pietro [Tosi] that the garden must be tidy two hours before we get there, and not two hours afterward, as usual! Don't take Piroletto and Majone away from the work I ordered, but hire someone for a day, if necessary.

Oh, if the painters, after having fixed the wallpaper in the dining-room,—something that should already be finished—could paint the façade of the house [just the east side], that would make me very happy.

I hope the stonemasons have finished, and that they have not forgotten the fireplace in the room where I was sleeping.

We have already agreed that the workmen must now leave our part of the house. The carpenters will be working only in the garden-room. The furniture varnishers only in the office. Do you understand? Until Thursday, then!

Thanks for the telegram, but I have already got four others . . .

So take care of everything and addio. . . . A case of wine will also arrive with the little wagon and you will easily be able to see what it is and have it put in the cellar right away but without taking the bottles out.[29]

Some of this effort was part of Verdi's annual reconstruction and improvement of the house, but some was probably undertaken because Filomena Maria, who was by this time called 'Maria Verdi' and was nicknamed 'Fifao', was to be married that autumn. In May Verdi and Strepponi had a visit from the Austrian Prince Guglielmo of Montenuovo, on his way to visit his Sanvitale cousins in Fontanellato. Verdi wrote to Maria Waldmann, whom the two men had discussed, letting her know how much pleasure the conversation had given him. He confided to her that Alberto Carrara, Filomena Maria's fiancé, was

not, as they say, brilliant, but he is serious and honest; and he belongs to the most honoured family that you could possibly imagine. Maria, born into the most humble condition, as I was, could not ask for more; and I believe she will be completely happy in the comfortable, not very rich condition in which she is going to find herself.[30]

The wedding, which Verdi described as very simple, took place on 11 October 1878. The couple was married in the oratorio at the villa, with Don Avanzi officiating. Maria walked to the altar on Verdi's arm as a handful of guests, including some of Verdi's and her closest relatives, watched. Avanzi delivered his sermon, then dissolved in tears as he blessed the couple.[31] For Avanzi, who had risen from poverty himself and had served in the lowest ranks of the clergy in Busseto before being assigned to the parishes of San Giuliano Piacentino and Vidalenzo, had suffered for his pro-unification and patriotic stance. Having known the Verdis all his life, and having been Maria's confessor, he participated almost as a member of the family. After the ceremony, Maria Verdi and Alberto Carrara left for a honeymoon in Venice. Immediately after the wedding, Verdi left for Genoa, where he stayed at the Albergo d'Italia rather than open Palazzo Doria for a short visit. On his return to Sant'Agata, he helped establish the newlyweds in a house he had remodelled for them just outside the old city walls of Busseto, near the Carrara villa Il Paradiso.

In mid-November Verdi and Strepponi left for Genoa together then set off for Paris, where they spent eight days visiting the International Exposition. They were not able to see Muzio, who the previous month had sailed for Havana. Muzio had served Verdi well, as always, during the year. He had been drawn into a controversy involving the Authors' Rights' Society, which was trying to help Verdi collect his royalties from Escudier. The impresario retaliated by spreading odious gossip about Muzio among their close colleagues. Earlier in the year news of the preparations for the exposition had come from Muzio, together with the news that Escudier might be forced to leave the Théâtre des Italiens. 'He lets everyone sing who comes to the door and pays him something; and tonight Manrico in *Il trovatore* will be a modestly gifted painter called Paul Vernon.'[32] Finally, Escudier was named director and impresario of the Théâtre Lyrique, where the government assigned a commission to oversee his management. Small wonder, for at the end of his tenure at the Italiens, the theatre was shut for more than a week and the company went unpaid. At this point, according to Muzio, Verdi had not even been paid for his participation in the 1875 season and had been cheated out of some of his royalties from Belgium.

BOOK V

With the complete collapse of all Muzio's hopes for the Italiens, he helped as agent and conductor for a season in Havana and also attended the highly praised concerts given by the orchestra of the Teatro alla Scala under Faccio's baton in the Orangerie of the Tuileries. These raised in Verdi a surge of patriotic pride, which led him to write enthusiastic letters to Muzio, Faccio, Clara Maffei, and other friends. Details of the engagement were sent to Verdi by Muzio and by Faccio himself: the overture to *La forza del destino* held its own during the second concert between Beethoven's *Egmont* Overture and works by Rossini, Coronaro, Boccherini, and others. At the opening event, the overture to *I vespri siciliani* had to be encored. The Cuban season was not financially successful, because of theft and other peculation. Muzio returned to Europe after stopping off in New York, where he met Strakosch. Soon he was back in Paris, happy to have escaped from Havana with even a modicum of dignity.

The year 1879 began quietly enough for Verdi, who divided his time between Genoa and Sant'Agata; but the spring floods of the Po and its tributaries turned parts of the provinces of Piacenza, Parma, Mantua, and Ferrara into a disaster area. The composer informed Piroli that

our misfortunes are not as serious as those around Mantua and Ferrara, but anyway the harvest is almost all lost. The mulberries lost, the hay almost lost: first or even second planting of wheat [lost]; corn coming up badly and rotting. Almost no grapes. This winter there will be famine and people dying of hunger. I know perfectly well that grain crops will arrive from abroad. But how will we buy these products? And at the same time the government is thinking about raising taxes, building railways that are not very much needed, under the pretext of making work for people? It really is a slap in the face. For God's sake, if you have millions, spend them for all the work on the rivers, before everyone is flooded out.[33]

To help the flood victims, Verdi organized a relief concert at La Scala, having persuaded Stolz, Waldmann, Barbacini, and Maini to contribute their services as his soloists. He agreed to conduct the *Messa da Requiem* himself for the benefit, which took place on 30 June. The orchestra and chorus were placed on stage with Verdi and the four soloists before them. Both the fugue of the Sanctus and the Agnus Dei had to be repeated, as the ovations of a 'delirious' audience went on to cries of 'Bis! Bis!'[34] When he lifted his baton to attack the encore of the fugue, the composer turned to his company with 'a happy and eloquent smile'. At the end of the performance, which the critic Filippi went on to describe as 'marvellous' and 'stupendously executed', there was a 'colossal demonstration' with flowers raining down from the boxes and the *paradiso*. Filippi said that he had never heard Stolz sing with such pure style; he added that her high notes were still limpid and perfectly on pitch. Waldmann, who came back for the event, was praised for her 'warm, resonant voice and her broad, expressive phrasing'.[35]

By the time Verdi got back to the Grand Hôtel de Milan, the Corsia del Giardino was boiling with people, who called him out on to the balcony of his salon. Even the hotel itself was filled with flowers; in the lobby, the owner had placed a huge floral arrangement that read 'Long live Verdi' in its centre. Soon the orchestra of La Scala came down the street, with Faccio at its head. Its serenade began with the *Nabucco* Overture, then continued with the Prelude to Act III of *La traviata* and other Verdi works. The concert raised 37,000 lire for the flood victims.

The 'Chocolate Project'

While Verdi and Strepponi were in Milan, they entertained Giulio Ricordi and other guests at a dinner during which 'by coincidence' the conversation centred on *Othello* and how Rossini's librettist had bungled his operatic version of it, rendering it unpoetic and undramatic.[36] Verdi's own recollection of this evening was summed up in a letter that he wrote to Ricordi on 4 September (misdating the letter 'August').

You know how this *Chocolate* project was born. You were dining with me, together with some friends. We spoke of *Otello*, of Sheaspeare [*sic*], of Boito. The next day Faccio brought Boito to me at the hotel. Three days later, Boito brought me a sketch of *Otello*, which I read and found good. Do the poetry, I said to him; it will always be good for you, for me, for someone else, and and . . .[37]

But he urged the publisher and Boito not to come to the villa because he felt that their visit would put pressure on him to commit himself to the project, which he did not wish to do. Boito went on working on the libretto throughout July and most of August while Verdi went on putting his house in order. By 24 August the librettist was ready to tackle the last act and was hoping he could get everything done quickly, but Verdi's reluctance to have him and Ricordi visit at Sant'Agata marked his unwillingness even to begin talking about the new opera. Ricordi acknowledged that perhaps some concern was due to his mistrust of Boito, whom Giulio wished Verdi might get to know better. As Clara Maffei had tried in 1862 to establish a bond of trust between Verdi and Boito, pressing him and Faccio on the older composer,[38] so Ricordi tried to bring the two men together in 1879.

BOOK V

If my memory does not fail me, I know that Boito did you some wrong [with his ode]; but I am sure that he did not know that he was doing it, with his nervous, odd character, or that [he] never found a way to make it up to you. . . . I find Boito an honest, loyal sort, indeed a perfect gentleman. . . . Boito, from the day you left [Milan], stopped everything else he was doing and worked only on the libretto.[39]

But Verdi had other things on his mind, many of them connected with Muzio's three-week visit to Sant'Agata in August. As ordered, he had brought Verdi the complete works of Johann Sebastian Bach. When Muzio got to Milan after his visit to the villa, he found everyone there speculating on whether Verdi would or would not compose another opera. Back in Paris, he carried out several of Verdi's commissions and investigated all aspects of the proposed *Aida* during several interviews with Vaucorbeil, who was planning to go to Italy and hoping to see Verdi there. Muzio also wrote Verdi about his recollection of the first day Strepponi came to Busseto:

It seems like yesterday, yet thirty years have passed since the famous triumphal entry. I remember that I came to meet you, almost out to the [Oratorio of the] Trinità on the road to Borgo San Donnino, and that your wife said 'Emanuele can walk'. I had good legs, and they are not bad even now. Tell your wife that none of her friends is happier than I over the anniversary celebrated and that I hope to be there for the fiftieth, and that I am inviting myself to that as of today. We will all three be a bit old; but our feelings will be the same as now, just the same.[40]

Verdi was concerned about Waldmann's proposed visit to Sant'Agata and the imminent birth of Maria Verdi's and Alberto Carrara's first child. Giuseppina Carrara, whom Verdi called 'Pepèn', was born on 5 October. Another major problem was the projected new railway line from Borgo San Donnino to Cremona, which would have to cross Verdi's fields. He wrote to Piroli:

If it is, though, a useful—really useful—thing, I will not raise any kind of issue about it, about my lands, not even a word. A railway that runs from Busseto directly to Cremona will have to cross my land, unless they want to make it 6 or 7 kilometres longer, going through Cortemaggiore, Monticelli [d'Ongina], etc. No matter what happens, when this [rail]way is decided upon, it will be very hard for me to stay on at Sant'Agata Indeed, it is almost sure that I will leave here; who knows where I will go?[41]

Although the line cut a huge swathe across his estate, from the mill at Castellazzo to the edge of Villanova, he did not move. The passing locomotives, burning coal, and the cars carrying freight and passengers changed the landscape for the worse and constituted an invasion of his privacy but did not deter Verdi from his grand plan of improving his farm buildings and tenant houses.

By 8 November Ricordi could write to Strepponi that Boito was still working on his 'hot chocolate', which was 'boiling, boiling, boiling'.[42] Ten days later the libretto of *Otello* was in the composer's hands: 'I have just this moment received the chocolate. I will read it tonight, because my head is spinning now with business matters.[43] Quite naturally, everyone treated Verdi with absolute reverence during the gestation of *Otello*. Yet in spite of all precautions, some things did set him off. Only a few weeks before he got the libretto of the new opera, the composer took offence at an article in Ricordi's *Gazzetta musicale* about a book by the sculptor Dupré, where it was implied that Verdi was incapable of writing a comic opera.

But look at this!! . . . For twenty years I looked for a libretto of a comic opera, and now that—you might say—I have found one, you have planted in the audience a crazy desire to hiss my opera even before it is written, thus wrecking my interests and your own. But don't worry. If, by chance, by misfortune, or by fate, in spite of the Grand Sentence, my evil genie should persuade me to write this comic opera, I say again, don't worry. I will ruin some other publisher.[44]

Although Verdi did not say what he had in mind, he may have been considering writing a comic opera on Goldoni's *La locandiera*, having agreed to read a libretto from it written by the young Piacentine journalist and poet Carlo Mascaretti, who was later the author of an eleven-volume work on Italian literature.[45]

Although Verdi was the soul of courtesy when Vaucorbeil visited Sant'Agata that year, he was unhappy over having been persuaded to give *Aida* in Paris. He confided to Muzio that he felt his consent had been wrung from him: 'Either I will not come to Paris, and the opera will be given in a flaccid, lifeless, ineffective way; or I will come and will destroy my soul and my body.'[46] Yet Vaucorbeil apparently did not sense the composer's uneasiness, for he wrote Muzio to say that he had been cordially received and that Verdi had surprised him by playing his two new compositions, the Pater Noster and the Ave Maria, which, up to then, only Muzio had heard. 'We are all happy over your consent to the *Aida*', Muzio wrote, after the impresario returned to France.[47] Vaucorbeil proved his good will by beginning rehearsals during the third week in October, nearly five months before the actual opening night, having asked Muzio to help coach the company.

In November Verdi and Strepponi went to Milan, where they discussed *Otello* in confidential conversations with the publisher. Verdi postponed his initial meeting with Boito because he was slightly ill. He did, however, acquire the rights to the libretto. He also arranged to have the Pater Noster and Ave Maria performed at La Scala in the spring. After their short stay, they went back to Sant'Agata to confront the serious problems Corticelli had created in their home. He had continued to court Maddalena Barezzi, whom he had by then known for more than twenty years; at the same time, though, he seemed to have misused some of her money. Verdi, puzzled, remarked on the 'continuing, endless intimacy' between the two,[48] asking Carrara to investigate the matter further. The composer had never fully trusted Corticelli. By 1879, when the agent had taken it upon himself to receive *and answer* correspondence that Ricordi had addressed to Verdi, the composer accused him of being 'out of order'.[49] In November, though, a far graver situation arose when Antonia (Tognetta) Belforti, the cook from Sant'Agata, who had entrusted some of her savings to Corticelli, was not able to get her money back. The bonds he had bought, he said, were in Bologna.[50] Nearly two days passed before he agreed to get them. On 23 November, after giving the cook back her funds, he left Sant'Agata for ever and took a room at the Albergo dell'Agnello in Milan because his relatives in Bologna refused to take him in.[51] He received help, though, from Strepponi, Stolz, and Ristori's brother.

Although Verdi appeared unwilling to do anything with *Otello*, he did go to Paris during the second week of February 1880 to oversee rehearsals of *Aida*. Between October and the day he left Italy, he had been kept informed by Muzio on the progress of the production, which had the Austrian soprano Gabrielle Krauss in the title role, with Rose Bloch as Amneris, the French tenor Henri Sellier as Radamès, and Victor Maurel as Amonasro, all coached by Muzio, who had spent Christmas with Verdi in Genoa discussing the production. As always, Paris took a heavy toll on him; but he had the support of both Strepponi and Stolz. The soprano, who had established regular contact with Verdi again at the time of the flood-relief benefit performance of the *Messa da Requiem*, was again staying at the Hôtel de Bade. Verdi arranged for her to accompany Strepponi to the otherwise closed final dress rehearsal.[52] Verdi conducted this rehearsal and the *anteprova generale* as well, although he had exhausted himself in the preparation. Because Maurel came down with a sore throat, the opening night was delayed from the fifteenth to the twenty-second of March. '[N]ot too bad', Verdi reported to Waldmann on the morning after the opening. 'The tenor is good. *Mise-en-scène*, chorus, and orchestra superlatively good.'[53] Sending his news to Clara Maffei on 24 March, he had something better to say: '*Aida* is a success. . . . Krauss and Maurel were stupendous; the tenor good: Amneris mediocre: chorus and orchestra excellent: *mise-en-scène* beyond comparison with anything else. This is the truth.'[54] Strepponi sent an emotion-laden letter to her sister, saying that the event had proved 'a triumphal march' for Verdi and that she was so excited over it that she was almost ill.[55] Decorated with the honours of Grand Officier of the French Foreign Legion, Verdi was also given a gold crown by the Italian colony in Paris. It was presented at the end of the third performance, after a fifteen-minute ovation. Muzio called the evening 'an apotheosis' for Verdi.[56] Gloriously fulfilled, Verdi and Strepponi left Paris for Genoa on 4 April. Stolz went back to Milan to await Verdi's visit. Muzio, left behind in Paris, said goodbye to Verdi, got into a carriage, and broke down in tears. Soon he was able to send the astonishing box office figures, as *Aida* surpassed almost every record set at the Opéra. The profits for the first two weeks were owed in part to the fact that Verdi had agreed to conduct five performances instead of three, to satisfy the subscribers.

The city government in Milan had been planning for some time to make Verdi an honorary citizen and offer him a tribute at La Scala. Although he usually tried to prevent such celebrations, he could not avoid this one. The King of Italy decorated him on 11 April as Cavaliere of the Great Cross of Italy. The next day Verdi began rehearsing a chorus of 370 and an orchestra of 130 for the concert, which Faccio was to conduct on 18 April. For the occasion Verdi offered the première of two of his compositions, a Pater Noster and an Ave Maria, both sung in Dante's Italian translation. The soprano soloist for the Ave Maria was Teresa Singer, Muzio's artist from Paris. At the end of the evening, the Mayor presented the parchment of Honorary Citizenship. Ricordi's *Gazzetta musicale di Milano* dedicated ten pages to the event.

Verdi and Strepponi left for Genoa two days after the concert, then he went on to Sant'Agata, where she sent a letter about his recent successes.

My dearest Verdi, . . .

This enthusiasm in the wake of *Aida* and the *Messa* must arouse in your mind some strange reflections about the human spirit; and, at the same time must make 'Enough! Enough!' rush to your lips. Still, you are not only the same man of genius that you were six months ago, but you are the same one I saw at the time of *Nabucco* and the artistic battles. The difference is this: Then the crowd needed good glasses to see the star that was rising in the sky; now this star casts its light wherever it appears—everyone wants to be in its light, to make themselves seen, and everyone would like to gather more light than the others, to be seen to be favoured, to say of himself 'I am the most important!'—*Vanity of vanities! Everything under the sun is vanity*!

I may be anything you like, but I am a bit different from everyday people. One has to take off one's sandals before going into the temple to contemplate the Highest One, [and lie] prostrate on the ground! It is a profanation to shout hosanna all the time, and it takes away from every profound feeling that mysterious tint that transports us into infinity. But I am truly wrong, and I will put that error with the many others that I have committed against God and His creatures! So let the staircase of ovations stretch right up to heaven, so long as you take me with you. You will see that I shall not bother you, and I will just tell you—deeply moved, and in a quiet voice—how much I love you and revere you, when the others shall have fallen silent . . . to gather their breaths and *blow their noses*! God . . . 'and little green peas', as poor Maggioni would say, if he were alive!

I got up more tired than yesterday and absolutely unable to say a word. I am happy, though, that at least for today the deep stillness of this Wednesday 21 April will not be broken into, excepting by the donkeys that are now braying. If the weather is good, I will keep busy from tomorrow onward with the furs and the winter things that have to be put in pepper and camphor . . .

Don't work too hard, my dear Pasticcio, and think that even if little money remains, it will still be too much for the merit of your heirs!—that the glory of your art 'except for a *comic opera*' can go no higher. Try to arrange it so you can live to the age of Methuselah (966 years), if for no other reason than to please the one who loves you, in spite of the French composers, not excluding the best ones! If Fetid, that is: Fétis, were still alive, he would die of rage, seeing how things have gone!

Now I salute you, I kiss you, and I embrace you. I hope you have a good appetite and hope to see you come soon, very, very soon, because I still love you like mad, and sometimes when I seem out of sorts, it is a kind of *love fever* that no doctor (including Todeschini) has ever heard about.

What a lot of stupid things I have written! I'll see you soon then . . .

Peppina.[57]

She and Verdi attended the Italian Exposition in Turin, where his eye was particularly caught by the modern paintings, which, he said, showed that Italian artists were making remarkable progress. By 11 May they had settled into Sant'Agata, where Verdi again threw himself into the farm-work and, as he said, began to breathe again. By June he was calculating the yield from the first crop and engaged in planting the second, boasting of 'a fair cutting of hay, the promise of a good harvest of wheat, fodder crops, and beans. And I have reason to hope for the best with the corn. . . . We haven't a lot of wine, but there is enough,' he wrote to Arrivabene.[58] He wrote to him again in September, saying he was surrounded by 'cows, oxen, horses' and working like a 'peasant, bricklayer, carpenter, . . . master stonemason, blacksmith', and repairing many of his old tenant houses and building new ones. He had said goodbye to 'books [and] music. It looks as if I have forgotten it and no longer recognize the notes.' And as for 'treacherous Iago, I have not written a note.'[59]

32

~

Summer 1880–Spring 1889

The 'Old Dog', *Simon Boccanegra*

The question of whether Verdi was or was not working on *Otello* came up
so frequently between 1879 and 1885 that both Verdi and his wife seem
to have prepared standard answers to it. In December 1879 Strepponi had
written to Giuseppina Negroni Prati Morosini that the opera had been put
away with 'Somma's *Re Lear*, which has been in a deep and untroubled
sleep for thirty years in his portfolio.'[1] But at the beginning of 1880 Verdi
had suggested to the Neapolitan painter Domenico Morelli that he do a
series of sketches of 'a scene from *Otello*', perhaps the suffocation scene
or the scene when the Moor, 'destroyed by jealousy, faints, and Iago looks
at him and, with an infernal smile, says: "Work, my medicine." What a
character Iago [is]!!! Well, what do you say about it?'[2] Morelli answered to
say that he had indeed found a priest who had the villain's face: 'Iago,
with the face of a righteous man',[3] a revelation that sent Verdi into a
transport of enthusiasm.

Good, very good, wonderfully good, marvellously good! Iago with a gentleman's
face! You've got it! Oh, I knew it! I was sure of it. I can see this *priest*, this Iago
with the face of a righteous man! Hurry, then: a few brush-strokes. And send me
this hasty sketch. Do it. Do it. Hurry, hurry, [acting from] your inspiration, just
as it comes to you . . . don't do it for artists . . . do it for a musician! . . . Do this
sketch![4]

When Morelli did not answer as quickly as Verdi had hoped he would, he
was pressed again to find 'a Iago face'.[5] Later, 'Have you found this
brigand with the face of a righteous man?'[6] But no matter how urgently

Verdi seemed to need the sketch, Morelli could not satisfy him. The matter was dropped for more than a year.

Muzio had confided to Ricordi that Verdi had begun to compose the opera before the end of February 1880[7] and had reaffirmed that in March, while Verdi was still working with him in Paris.[8] It is strange, then that Verdi told Arrivabene that he had not written a note of the opera, for if he said to Muzio that he had begun to write *Iago* (as the opera was then called), he surely had, for he would have had no reason to lie to this trusted friend. It seems, though, that nothing was done on it in the summer. Early in August Boito sent his revised libretto of the opera and, in response to Verdi's suggestions, set about reworking the third act, which the composer thought needed a 'theatrical piece'.[9] As it stood, there was no place for it. By mid-October he was more than satisfied with Boito's new work, which was 'divinely well done.'[10] Boito then described his own uneasiness over the finale of the act, which, he thought, had been weakened. 'We wanted to rework *Perfection* and we destroyed it.'[11] He again reviewed the doubts that Verdi had expressed earlier about the scene, while expressing his confidence that the atmosphere that had been destroyed could be recaptured with eight bars of music, which 'are enough to bring a feeling to life again; a rhythm can reconstruct a character; music is the most omnipotent of the arts, it has a logic all its own, [which is] quicker and freer than the logic of the spoken thought and a good deal more eloquent.'[12] When Verdi replied from Genoa on 2 December, he praised Boito's finale again and said that he liked the idea of Otello fainting, as Boito had placed it in his new version; but they would have to deal with the new opera later as he was under pressure to get on with another project, the revision of *Simon Boccanegra*, which Ricordi had proposed several times.[13] In November 1880 Verdi had been offered the chance to produce it at La Scala, with Anna D'Angeri, Francesco Tamagno, Victor Maurel, and Edouard De Reszke.[14] Even this cast did not satisfy Verdi, who, when he replied to Ricordi by return, recalled an old theatrical saying: 'Either [you choose] the operas for the singers [under contract] or [engage] the singers for the operas [on the schedule]—an old proverb that no impresario ever knew how to follow, and without which no success is possible in the theatre. You have a good company for La Scala, but it is not suited to *Boccanegra*.'[15] When he had asked Ricordi to suggest someone to rework the second act of the libretto, Boito was proposed and work began. Verdi then set down his terms for the production. In January 1881 he confided to Arrivabene that he was about to 'straighten the legs of an old *dog* that was beaten up badly in Venice [in 1857] and is called *Simon Boccanegra.*'[16] The revision was completed in about six weeks, between 8 December 1880 and 15 February 1881, with Verdi in Palazzo Doria in Genoa and Boito in Milan. So far as is known, they met only once during this important collaboration, when Verdi attended a performance at La Scala, hidden, seated in a box with Tornaghi and another Ricordi employee. Verdi's and Boito's letters are included in two valuable books, one in Italian, the other in English, both fully annotated: the *Carteggio Verdi—Boito* and Hans Busch's *Verdi's 'Otello' and 'Simon Boccanegra' (revised version) in Letters and Documents.* By far the most significant change originated with Verdi, who, in a letter to Giulio Ricordi in November 1880, had proposed the finale of Act I, set in the Council Chamber of the palace.[17] There Boccanegra, the Doge, has summoned his council members and confronts a mob. His plea for peace and love, addressed to patricians and the common people alike, was particularly appropriate in the strife-torn Italy of the time.

After he returned to Genoa, Verdi sent his publisher the first act of the opera, then posted the second act two days later. On 18 February he could telegraph the good news that the last act was in the post, registered; but within days he threatened to withdraw the work because not enough time had been allowed. 'I told you in person, and I repeat now *formally*, that I will give the opera only if a series of performances can be presented. . . . Watch out, for I will not make any further concessions; I have already done a lot on this opera, and I regret it. I demand thirty days, and the time to do eight or ten performances if the audience wants them.'[18] He added a postscript to say that the whole project might go up in smoke anyway, because he was not satisfied with Maurel. Complaining until the last minute, Verdi, accompanied by his wife, left for Milan on 24 February. As usual, they stayed at the Grand Hôtel de Milan.

The next evening the company was in an uproar as two of the singers— the soprano D'Angeri and the tenor Tamagno—protested at their roles, claiming they lay too high and were not sufficiently important. 'It is the most monstrous thing I have ever had happen in my life,' Giulio Ricordi declared, writing to say that he would come over to the Hôtel Milan as soon as he calmed down.[19] Mortified and angry, he feared that Verdi would take his score and leave; but that did not happen. Peace was restored within days. Verdi remained anxious and unconfident, though, and wrote Muzio just before the opening night about his fears. Muzio answered by return:

I found your letter, which surprised me so very, very much that I read it several times to convince myself that it was not a joke. . . . But I hope and have faith that [the performances] will not turn out as your letter suggests.—The new finale will not be effective? The revolt, the dramatic recitative of the Doge? The prologue? The last act? It must have been a false alarm, and maybe the audience [at the dress rehearsal] has let itself be influenced by the tragedy in Nice [*where an explosion in a gas-pipe in the opera-house started a fire that resulted in many deaths*]; and the artists too may be feeling this, and perhaps they are not all wildly enthusiastic; but I cannot believe that this will bring on a failure.[20]

The depth of Verdi's pessimism implied that the opening would be a disaster. It was not.

The whole company could rejoice in the success of the revised *Simon Boccanegra*, given at La Scala on 24 March with Maurel, D'Angeri, De Reszke, Tamagno, and Federico Salvati under Faccio's baton. The production, described by the composer himself as 'excellent', encouraged him to believe that the opera would enter the repertory 'as so many of its sisters have done, although the subject is terribly sad'.[21] As in the past, he followed the box-office figures and, when they proved disappointing, wrote frankly to Ricordi:

Everything is fine! Ovations [and] encores don't mean anything unless the cash box is full. When the cash box is full, it means a lot of people are going to the theatre. If many people go to the theatre, it means the work is *worth while*. . . . The fact is that the ten performances of *Boccanegra* brought in very little, and that is what makes me unhappy.[22]

But Ricordi assured his composer that the last three performances had indeed sold out, that the singers had outdone themselves, and that the work was considered a huge success; he began at once to try to sell it to other theatres.

After the production, Verdi, depressed by Cesarino De Sanctis's death, divided his time between Genoa and Sant'Agata until the first week in May, when he and Strepponi moved back to the country for the summer, having provided for the Milanese newspaper *Corriere della sera* and the Florentine *Fanfulla* to be sent every day for six months. Problems with Escudier's contracts had to be resolved with the help of Muzio, Ricordi, and Peragallo, while an important production of *Il trovatore* in French was being offered at the Théâtre Château d'Eau in Paris, under the aegis of the publisher Benoit, who had acquired the rights to it and was trying to acquire rights to the other works that the bankrupt Escudier had once owned. Muzio kept Ricordi and Verdi informed on a regular basis, as he tried to prevent what the composer most feared: the acquisition of his works by several publishers rather than by one alone. Again keeping busy with his tenant houses, mills, dairy barns, walls, and wells, Verdi showed few signs of being interested in music, although he did ask Ricordi to send him a low F-sharp wire for his Erard piano. As an act of charity toward the employees, he sent 500 lire in his own name and his wife's to the Mutual Assistance Fund that Casa Ricordi's workers had founded.

The political implications of the French occupation of Tunisia in 1881 led Muzio to fear war between France and Italy and Verdi to declare that he would not allow *Simon Boccanegra* to be given in Paris because of the offence to Italian honour; but, he said,

the fault is ours, all ours! It is impossible that there has been, is, or shall be in the future a government so . . . you fill in the epithet . . . [as ours]! I am not talking about *Reds*, *Whites*, or *Blacks*. I care very little about the shape or colour. Again, I say that I don't care; but I do demand that those who rule be *Citizens* with great ingenuity and impeccable honesty. [23]

While he railed about the imminent ruin of Italy, the composer made his own meaningful contribution to public order by keeping 200 people busy at Sant'Agata, an effort that became a matter of pride to him. 'People are earning and no one emigrates from my village,' he wrote to Arrivabene at the end of 1881. [24] Muzio, who had come to Milan in June to assemble a company of singers for Max Strakosch to take to New Orleans, spent a few days at the villa before returning to Paris, where he was again monitoring Verdi's business interests. Léon Escudier's unexpected death, almost at the moment when Ricordi had filed a suit against him, had led all the publisher's creditors to besiege his widow and son. At Muzio's urging, Verdi began for the first time to insist on having monthly reports of all French performances of his operas and monthly royalty payments made; but the stipulation came after Verdi had been cheated out of much of the money owed to him. By July the entire Escudier enterprise was in ruins. In September a receiver was named. Ricordi, whose French lawyer had attempted to sequester all the scores and acquire rights to Verdi's works, became caught in the tangle of the publisher's family's affairs. Armed with Verdi's power of attorney, Muzio began to review all the composer's French and Belgian royalty accounts. His suspicions raised, he uncovered further fraud. Verdi sued Peragallo, transferred his accounts to the French agent Roger, and kept Muzio as his personal representative.

Verdi appeared to take all these problems lightly enough. He seemed much more concerned about the embarrassment caused by his agreement to let a statue of him be placed in the foyer of La Scala. Having authorized the statue a year before the première of the revised *Simon Boccanegra*, he soon had had second thoughts and had asked Ricordi to get the project cancelled. Verdi also appealed to Boito in 1881 for advice on how to handle his contribution to the fund to erect a statue to Bellini at the same time, asking Boito to 'tell the directors I will put my *name on the list of donors for the Bellini statue*, offering the amount that is lacking, so it can be erected, on condition, though, that my statue not be erected at this time nor be erected in the future without my permission.'[25] The ruse did not work. Both statues were executed by the sculptor Francesco Barzaghi.

While Boito prepared his *Mefistofele* for La Scala, working throughout April 1881 and into the third week in May, Verdi stayed in Genoa, then settled again at Sant'Agata, where he planted 50 kilos of seed and ordered 50 kilos of fireproof clay for bricks for a new farmhouse on the estate. He also ordered payments of money to Piave's widow and daughter and to the families of the trumpeter Serafino Cristiani and the violinist Eugenio Cavalli, both of whom had died recently.[26] Giulio Ricordi and Boito came for a long-postponed visit in July, discussing *Otello* and a proposed production of *Simon Boccanegra* in Barcelona, to which Verdi was resolutely opposed. A month earlier Boito had sent Verdi his ideas for the Act II scene of Desdemona and the women, children, and sailors, together with the poetry he had written for it. 'It will do very well,' Verdi said,[27] as he encouraged his librettist to go ahead with the troublesome finale of the third act, which Boito tackled again in August.

Verdi went to Milan with Strepponi in August to visit the Industrial Exposition Milan itself was transformed for the celebration, which was intended to mark Italy's emergence into the modern era. With Boito's *Mefistofele*, La Scala offered a special series of performances that included the extravagant, imaginative ballet *Excelsior*, choreographed by Luigi Manzotti to a Marenco score. With its exaltation of science, it depicted Alessandro Volta as he invented the battery and the dynamiting of the railway tunnel under the Alps. At the same time visitors to Milan were stunned and delighted at the Galleria Vittorio Emanuele, the building of which Verdi had followed with much interest. With its soaring iron frame and glass vaulted ceilings, it stood just a step from Milan Cathedral and housed about thirty elegant shops and restaurants—as it does today—

providing apartments and offices in its upper reaches. Illuminated by gas in 1881, it was a scheduled stop on every visitor's itinerary, a symbol of the triumph of industry. Another important building under construction was the Hotel Continentale. Before it was begun, Stolz was forced to leave her huge apartment in the Palazzo Loria. She chose a place in Via Bigli 15, just down the street from Clara Maffei. She established herself as one of the reigning queens of Milan society, with her Monday evening receptions in her 'Egyptian salon', decorated 'with bright coloured fabrics, carpets, and ornaments in Arabian style, and divans in the proper style'—all this as a homage to *Aida*.[28] Famous singers, retired and still active, improvised impromptu concerts at the request of the diva, the 'celebrated artist, unmatched interpreter of *Aida*, *Don Carlos*, [and] *La forza del destino* [who] now reaps the harvest of her fortune: that of knowing how to make herself loved and respected, offering proof of her exquisite discretion as she receives [guests] in her home with the charm, the courtesy, the splendour of a true lady'.[29] It was said that the concerts she organized were the equal of those staged by the city's great impresarios, for Stolz numbered among her guests such as Gazzaniga, Spezia, Varesi, and Gustave Moriami. The soprano had resumed her intimacy with Verdi and his wife, their reconciliation having come gradually at the end of the 1870s and been officially certified when Stolz joined them at the Hotel de Bade in Paris during the rehearsals for the Paris Opéra *Aida* in March 1880. She had become a regular visitor in Genoa and again began to spend part of the summers at Tabiano before making her annual visit to Sant'Agata.

When Verdi expected her there in September 1881, he asked Ricordi to entrust to her 16,892 francs from the royalties paid by Peragallo, so that she could bring them to the villa. 'If they should pay it in gold, have it changed into paper to make it easier [for her] to bring the money here,' the composer asked.[30] Stolz probably stayed during Verdi's birthday. Later in October Verdi went to Genoa on business but stopped at the Hotel Italia rather than have his apartment in Palazzo Doria opened up for a two-day visit. Ricordi then wrote him at Sant'Agata, to ask him to consider a revival of *Simon Boccanegra* at La Scala with Mattia Battistini in the title role. Having stayed away from Milan because the statue of him had been dedicated in the foyer of La Scala on 25 October, Verdi conducted his affairs with the publisher by post, declaring that he was not opposed to *Boccanegra*, provided either Battistini or Giuseppe Kaschmann could be engaged for the title role.

My dear Giulio,

Does this seem right? . . . Have pity! . . . If you are giving *Boccanegra*, why give *Nabucco*, [which was also on the calendar]? The Old Testament, beside the New Testament! One testament is enough!! And anyway, *Nabucco* is not so easy. The role of Abigaille is enormously difficult to play. Soul and feelings are not enough; you need a true actress.[31]

He was also concerned about lighting, for the small oil-lamps that had been used in *Boccanegra* were to be replaced that year with gas. Verdi wanted to meet Ricordi, Boito, and Faccio in Milan to discuss the proposed reorganization of the orchestra of La Scala, but his visit was postponed temporarily when Strepponi fell ill with a stomach ailment just after they moved to Genoa for the winter. They made the trip during the second or third week in December. Not surprisingly, given the fact that they had so many friends there, Strepponi felt she was better off in Milan, that she and Verdi would do well to look for a sun-filled apartment 'and come to Milan'.[32]

The couple celebrated Christmas at the Palazzo Doria with Stolz, Muzio, De Amicis, and the conductor Giovanni Rossi and his wife. Rossi, born in 1828 in Borgo San Donnino into a family that had known Verdi even when he was a boy, had appealed successfully to the composer to help him get Mariani's post at the Teatro Carlo Felice. He became one of the Verdis' close friends in Genoa, even though Verdi often voiced his disapproval of the opera seasons there.[33] With his wife Erminia Giani Rossi, he was a frequent visitor in Verdi's house and was present when the composer cut into Ricordi's Christmas gift: a Milanese panettone with a little dark-chocolate Moor on top. The allusion to *Otello* was not lost on either the host or his guests, who laughed when they discovered that the littler figure 'was a girl' because the confectioner had failed to give it a penis.[34] Muzio, laughing, told Verdi he should 'make it a man, dress it, and get it to its feet';[35] but the composer pretended he had no idea what they were all talking about.

To celebrate New Year's Day 1882, the Verdis again invited De Amicis and the Rossis to dine with them, Stolz, and Muzio. All were curious to know whether Verdi was working again on *Otello*. But, according to a letter Strepponi wrote to Ricordi on 5 January, 'the wood was right, but the desire to set fire to it' was simply not there.[36] Verdi had other matters on his mind, she said; he got offended at stories about him in the newspapers, and at 68 thought that he had earned a rest. Yet if he were let alone, he might 'deliver the new-born, complete with the [penis] that was missing from the *Little Black Baby*' on the panettone.

Soon after the holidays Muzio returned to Paris, where his main mission was the conduct of Verdi's affairs with the Escudiers, Peragallo, and the legal advisers who had been retained. At the turn of the year, Strepponi undertook an act of charity on her own. In 1875 she had bought Palazzo Cavalli from Verdi for 18,000 lire, with the idea of having it restored and placing a marble plaque on it. But perhaps because it became a burden to her, she sold it to the Sivellis and decided to establish several perpetual annuities for the poor from money made from the sale.[37]

Although Verdi gave no sign of wanting to work on *Otello*, he did continue to press Morelli for the sketch. 'And Iago? What have you done about him? Have you thought about him? . . . I am afraid of your answer, but tell me anyway.'[38] He fended off Ricordi's suggestions about the new opera and followed the rehearsals of *Boccanegra* at La Scala through the publisher's letters, resolutely staying away.

The Revision of *Don Carlos*

In February came the first hint of pressure on Verdi to revise *Don Carlos*, when Muzio wrote 'Oh, if you would just be willing to shorten *Don Carlos*, what a lot of money you could make in France, Germany, and Italy.'[39] We do not know whether Verdi had written to Muzio earlier about this project. Again in February Muzio suggested that Verdi rework the opera to help Ricordi. It was a difficult time, for Peragallo, hounded by lawyers and suits, had killed himself. Verdi, not wishing to seem cruel, was relying on Muzio and the lawyer Dubost for counsel. At the same time he suggested that he might indeed revise the opera, writing to Muzio that he would 'need a poet close by, and naturally this would be the original author [Du Locle]. That is impossible.'[40] But Muzio swore not to give up until the work was under way; to that end he began to investigate on his own to find a librettist acceptable to the composer, approaching Nuitter first. The collaborator in the *Macbeth* translation of the 1860s, he had helped Du Locle with *La forza del destino* and *Aida* and had served as archivist of the Opéra.[41] It seemed that he would do. Muzio confided to Ricordi: 'When Verdi comes to Paris, I hope no later than the end of April, I will have him assaulted from all sides so that he will shorten [*Don Carlos*] and make out of it an opera that will travel all over the world.'[42]

Verdi and Strepponi stayed in Genoa during the winter, entertaining occasionally and going out very infrequently. They did, though, see Sarah Bernhardt, who was in the city for three performances—'truly an artist', the composer wrote to Clara Maffei. 'She is herself, herself, and always herself, even in the defects that some think they find in her.'[43] Kept informed about La Scala, he followed the fortunes of *Simon Boccanegra*, although he declined to help rehearse the production. The opera ran for ten nights with Maurel and a fair supporting cast, which was a good result. By spring Verdi was making his usual trips to Sant'Agata, where he had begun an important undertaking: the building of the Villanova Hospital. He had originally considered contributing the funds for the hospital in 1878, when he asked the Mayor of Villanova sull'Arda to get an architect to provide drawings as he himself searched for a site. At that time the Cremonese architect Vincenzo Marchettti executed two designs for the building.[44] A year later Verdi became a member of the town council, on which he sat from 1879 until 1884. During the spring and summer of 1882 he again turned his attention to the hospital, news about which reached the Italian newspapers just before Christmas. Because much of what was published was incorrect, Verdi considered releasing another story but finally decided against it, believing it would feed the journalists' mills and generate more publicity.

With the spring thaw, planting, building, and restoration at Sant'Agata went on, again employing about 200 men, whom the composer oversaw whenever he was at home. At the end of March, though, Muzio appealed to Verdi to come to Paris, where the confused affairs of the Escudier and Peragallo estates threatened the interests of both the composer and Ricordi. When Escudier's property was to be sold at public auction, Ricordi transferred to Muzio a sum that the publisher thought would cover the purchase of *Don Carlos*, *Simon Boccanegra*, the *Messa da Requiem*, and *Aida*; but the lawyer Dubost, authorized to bid, could acquire only the first three. *Aida*, which everyone expected to be sold for about 54,000 francs, went for 100,000. During this same period, Muzio had to contact some of the translators of Verdi's works to be sure they had no claims; and when some of the old contracts could not be found, new negotiations had to be opened. As accountants discovered that Peragallo apparently had owed about a million francs in royalties and other fees and personal debts, Muzio urged Verdi to bring his original contracts to France with him, so they could go over them together.

Again at the Hôtel de Bade, which had been their residence in Paris for a decade, Verdi and Strepponi rested for two days before tackling the jumble of legal matters. Also under discussion were planned performances of *La forza del destino* in France. Meetings with Nuitter, whom Muzio had approached about the revision of *Don Carlos*, settled some of the initial problems relating to the shortening of that opera, a task that Verdi predicted would be long and boring, a task that would take months. When Verdi was approached by a representative of the Vienna Opera, he authorized a production of *Simon Boccanegra* but refused to allow *Don Carlos* to be given until the short version could be used. During this sixteen-day stay in Paris, Verdi attended the Opéra twice but also worked on the French translation of *La forza del destino*, making changes that Muzio described as affecting the settings and the music. 'Some cuts; some short, new recitatives; the pistol shot taken out.'[45]

Leaving Paris on 18 May, Verdi and Strepponi stopped one day in Turin before going on to Sant'Agata. They spent about two weeks in June at the spa at Montecatini, from where Verdi wrote to Waldmann with news of his stay in Paris. Stolz was also at Montecatini, he said. Strepponi was taking the waters and going to the Grotto of Monsumano for 'the vapours'; he was taking a simpler cure, 'just drinking the water'.[46] Waldmann, with whom he exchanged letters several times a year, had visited the Verdis at Palazzo Doria during the previous winter. Living in a splendid palace in Ferrara, which Stolz described after her visit there, Waldmann had had a son in 1878; she now had the title of duchess.

Before his trip to Montecatini, Verdi had written to Nuitter about the revision of *Don Carlos*. Home again, he faced the work. It was a 'big' job, Muzio said, 'and it is not a matter of small details, for if one act is taken out, the others will have to be redone, or at least some parts of them.'[47] It was July, the weather was stifling, and Verdi refused to commit himself to any fixed schedule. During Muzio's long visit that year, the two men discussed *Don Carlos* at some length.

He says there is much work to be done, a big prelude, then a recitative that will come before Don Carlos' romanza and will explain what is said in the existing first act; then the various pieces will have to be coordinated, tied together. The Maestro assures me the changes will be as important as those for *La forza del destino* and *Boccanegra*.[48]

Verdi and Muzio also considered possible singers for *Otello*, the composer showing some interest in having Erminia Borghi-Mamo as Desdemona,

Maurel as Iago, and Tamagno—rather than Masini—in the title role. Nothing, however, was said about the actual composition.

In August Boito relayed a request from Baron Blaze de Bury to translate *Otello* into French whenever the Italian version was ready. 'Why talk about an opera that does not exist?' Verdi wrote, although he did dignify his answer to Boito with considerations about free verse, rhyme, and the requirements of the Opéra.[49] With Muzio back in Paris, the composer followed details of productions of his operas, among them *Il trovatore*, which had been given in eighteen French theatres that year. A performance of the Requiem at the Trocadéro with Krauss, Richard, Sellier, and Boudouresque was being considered, together with *Rigoletto*, which Verdi was invited to give at the Opéra. Vaucorbeil also wanted the revised *Don Carlos* as soon as it was ready. In spite of the general enthusiasm for the opera, Verdi confided to Piroli in December that he felt his work was 'almost useless'.[50] The revision took the whole winter, from October until March 1883.

At Christmas Muzio was again the Verdis' house guest at Palazzo Doria, while De Amicis was invited for dinner. Everyone expected to see another panettone arrive from Ricordi; but as the day passed, Verdi began to joke about it: 'It hasn't come yet!' he said. 'It will come,' Muzio declared. The two men went out for a walk. When they returned, Verdi again remarked: 'You see it has not come.' And Muzio: 'It will come.' Because dinner was always at six, the dessert course was about to be served when the bell rang. Verdi and Muzio exclaimed together: '*Il panetton!*' But both Streponi and De Amicis swore it could not be. The composer and conductor bet them one centesimo that it was indeed the gift. Then

the butler announced the famous crate. The Maestro saw it and exclaimed 'There is a statue,' and everyone said 'It is the statue of Otello.' When the crate was opened very carefully, the *monster* was put on the table; Verdi untied the knots, lifted the cover, and found *half of Otello*. Everyone shouted with amazement, [and] we rose and drank a toast so that one year from now he will get to his feet and have legs.[51]

Muzio added that he hoped that he would be present in 1883 for the 'great ceremony of *Otello* in chocolate and in music'.

Muzio had reason to hope for the opera, for just after Christmas, when he and Verdi read together a letter that had come from Ricordi,

At first he said nothing, then he wanted to talk, and finally he added: 'Nothing has been done, and I am not thinking about it now.' I answered him, saying that

667

he ought to finish *Otello*, and that it was a great way to cover the expense of the hospital he wants to build, and even of providing it with an endowment. He then did some calculations, and afterwards said nothing more about it until this morning, when I saw some sheets of music on the piano and others with the poetry of *Otello* that were not there last year.[52]

After New Year's Day 1883 Verdi and Strepponi were again left alone while Muzio was in Milan, tending to his own business and that of his pupil and protégé, the tenor Eugène Durot. While sitting in a café with a friend, he was robbed of some letters he had received from famous singers and composers. Believing that some English or Americans at the next table had taken them, Muzio described the theft to Verdi on 11 January, but he did not suggest that any of the composer's letters to him were stolen.[53] After Muzio and Durot left for Nice, news came from Paris of Ricordi's victory in his suit against the Escudiers' heirs, who were now subject to a judgement including all royalties from 6 January 1846 to the day of Léon's death. Muzio congratulated Verdi on the outcome as Ricordi praised Muzio for having made this legal victory possible. No one could have accomplished more, he said. By February Muzio was again on his way to Genoa for a two-day visit with the Verdis.

Earlier in 1883 Verdi had another opportunity to give advice about the reorganization of musical education in Italy, when Guido Baccelli, the Minister of Public Education, asked him to be a member of a new commission for music and theatre. In several drafts and letters, the composer discussed conservatory reform while declining to serve on the commission, which—he told Piroli—could not solve the problems. Off the record he confided to his friend that 'Germanism is invading us': the conservatory professors themselves were 'following the trend', because they 'no longer believe in Italian art and no longer know how to compose in an Italian style. So our theatre is dying; and it is also dying because the theatre cannot live without a government subsidy. If it wished, the government could provide this; as for everything else, they could do nothing.'[54] The composer's formal reply to Baccelli was written on 4 February. It carried Verdi's hope that some young genius, untainted by the influence of 'schools', would burst on to the Italian scene.[55]

The young genius would not necessarily be a man. From 1869 onwards Verdi had shown interest in Carlotta Ferrari, a woman who composed operas and other works that she struggled to get produced. Ferrari, born in Lodi in 1827, studied with Francesco Strepponi, Giuseppina's uncle, before entering Milan Conservatory in 1844. There she was trained under

Mazzucato, who was her early supporter. Ferrari produced her opera *Ugo* at the Teatro Santa Radegonda in Milan in 1857. *Sofia* followed in Lodi's Municipal Theatre in 1866. Other works were *Eleonora d'Arborea*, which Ferrari gave in Cagliari in 1871, and a Requiem Mass that was first heard in Turin in 1868. From the correspondence at Sant'Agata, it seems that Ricordi also helped her.[56] She at least filled Verdi's requirement for Italian composers in her interest in the theatre, because he was convinced that was the only important outlet for Italian music. Unlike German works, he said, it could not live in 'symphony halls' or in the 'apartments' where quartets were offered.[57]

During the second week in February Wagner died in Venice. Writing to Giulio Ricordi two days later, Verdi thanked his publisher for ruled paper he had received and added his remarks about the German composer.

The paper is very, very good, perhaps the lighter R. B. [is] better. Be careful when you have it ruled so the ink is not too dark.

———————

Sad! Sad! Sad!

Wagner is dead!!

Reading the dispatch yesterday, I was, I can say, terrified by it!

Let's not talk about it! A great individualist [has] disappeared! A name that leaves a very powerful mark on the history of Art!!! Add[io] add[io].[58]

Soon afterward Verdi got a letter that the agent Giuseppe Lamperti had written on 10 February, inviting him to compose a new work for the opening of the Metropolitan Opera in New York, which was scheduled for November 1883. Although no document survives, Verdi may have answered, declining. He and Strepponi stayed on in Genoa, although he visited Sant'Agata briefly in February and March. Verdi went back to the country again in April and was there when he got a letter from Boito asking him to conduct a commemorative concert of the Requiem Mass that was planned for 22 May 1883 in Milan. 'The event is certainly solemn', Verdi admitted, 'but it would be an encore. I detest encores. You are an artist and will understand me.'[59]

Although he seemed to be in excellent health, in spite of having worked steadily for more than five months on *Don Carlos*, Verdi had a slight stroke or heart attack in April, while he and Strepponi were at the Grand Hôtel in Milan. One morning she found him unconscious on his bed, where he had suffered dizziness and fainted. He believed that his problem was heart trouble. The news was kept within a very small circle of intimates, Muzio among them. When Verdi left again for Sant'Agata, Strepponi and Muzio were at his side; in the country, Muzio helped as best he could; and within a few weeks Verdi was again in the fields and overseeing the repairs on farm buildings and tenant houses. It seemed that the hospital Verdi wanted to build would become reality, for on 23 February Angiolo Carrara had executed the documents for the purchase of the land where it would be built, in Villanova sull'Arda, on a parcel of 1 hectare lying between the town and Verdi's farm called Piantadoro. Almost at once, the town council formally agreed to help with the expenses of maintaining the hospital with an annual contribution of 2,500 lire. It was also decided that the municipal health officer, a doctor, would help at the hospital. Verdi also began to oversee the construction of the hospital, which began that spring.[60] He paid the workers himself every Saturday.

Otello seemed to be completely forgotten. Earlier that spring Verdi had written to Arrivabene to say he had not thought about it, was not thinking about it, and did not know when he would think about it.[61]

Verdi, Strepponi, and Stolz spent almost three weeks together in Montecatini in June and July, then stopped in Florence on their way home. In the Biblioteca Laurenziana, which they were visiting with a professional guide, they met the orientalist Italo Pizzi, an archivist there. He described Verdi as 'a handsome man, already well along in years but still thin and vigorous-looking', who studied the gallery's treasures carefully and asked many questions. When Pizzi found out that the visitor was Verdi, he also showed him rare manuscripts and volumes that were not on display. The composer mentioned his interest in a particularly fine illuminated medieval office of the Madonna that he had seen once in Cava dei Tirreni, perhaps when he visited there with Barezzi. He also examined all the autographs that Pizzi brought out. He was, the archivist said, a man of 'uncommon culture in both literature and art'.[62] Stolz also recalled their pleasant, relaxing stay; Strepponi, 'the strongest of all', went off quietly in the mornings to do her shopping, the soprano said.[63] One cannot help wondering whether she also visited her daughter Giuseppa Faustina, then known as Stefani, who was unmarried and 44 years old, living with her adoptive parents in Florence.

During the third week in July Stolz returned to Milan while Verdi and Strepponi went back to Sant'Agata, from where the composer wrote at once to Stolz. His wife too sent her good wishes as she recalled the heat, stairs, statues, churches, chapels, Syrian, Hebrew, and Persian manuscripts, and the 'madness' of playing the tourist in July.[64] On the occasion of Verdi's seventieth birthday, Stolz came back to Sant'Agata, as she always did in the autumn.

Newspapers, full of gossip about him, irritated Verdi mightily and drove him to protest in the strongest possible terms to Ricordi, from whose shop and offices much of the news came. He had promised *Simon Boccanegra* to Paris and *Don Carlo* to Milan but regretted both commitments:

I never loved publicity and now I detest it to the point where it makes me sick. . . . It may be all right for others; it is wrong for me, absolutely wrong. . . . If I had not promised [them], I would not now promise either *Boccanegra* for Paris or *Don Carlos* for Milan. . . . Let me get my breath, and do me the favour of not talking any more about scenery, costume sketches, *D. Carlo*, or theatres. I really cannot stand it any longer.[65]

Yet Verdi was deeply involved with La Scala and with the Théâtre des Italiens, which was about to open again under a new management and with new investors. Nuitter, charged with the French translation of *Simon Boccanegra*, with which it would open, was working with Muzio, who, having become the composer's only personal representative in France, was charged with negotiating author's rights and royalties and monitoring as many of the performances as he could.

Verdi was shaken in October when Carlo Tenca died in Milan after a five-year battle with what seemed to be congenital spinal-cord disease. Clara Maffei, who had stayed beside her friend during the last weeks of his life, heard from Verdi more than a month after Tenca's death. To Clara, Verdi said:

I know all about it: I admired your courage and I can understand perfectly all your depression, now that the first nervous excitement is over. There are no words that can bring comfort during this kind of misfortune. And I will not say just the stupid word 'Courage' to you: a word that always made me angry when it was spoken to me. Something else is needed. You will find comfort only in the strength of your soul and in the firmness of your mind. . . . Ah, health, health! For many years, I thought nothing about it; but I don't know what will happen in the future. Really, my years are beginning to be too many, and I think . . . I think that life is the stupidest thing and—worse still—useless. What do we do? What have we done? What will we do? When you get right down to it, the answer is humiliating and very, very sad:

NOTHING!

Addio, my dear Clarina. As much as we can, let us stay away from sad things and keep them at bay, and let us love each other as long as we can.[66]

Verdi, Muzio, and Ricordi were all confronted with problems that arose when the soprano engaged for Paris, Fidès Devriès, insisted on singing a cabaletta that Verdi had written for the first version of *Simon Boccanegra*. Swearing that he had taken it out because he did not like it, the composer also said he had probably burned the original, because he cut out the old pages from the score as he reworked it. He also declared he would not write a new orchestration for it. Muzio, writing from Paris, then admitted that he remembered the instrumentation because he 'did the piano–vocal reduction in Venice, and because I heard the rehearsals and the first three performances, and then at Sant'Agata went on with the reduction for four hands';[67] nevertheless, he urged Verdi to score it himself. But the composer was in a bad humour that autumn, responding angrily to Ricordi's letters and leaving the publisher apprehensive and depressed over his threats to withhold all co-operation from La Scala while *Don Carlo* was in rehearsal. 'Don't abandon this poor Scala!! It would really mean ruin! The whole season is founded on *Don Carlo*! Don't make it collapse!' the publisher begged.[68]

Ricordi's eloquence finally won the day. After a brief stay in Genoa, during which Verdi swore that he would not help with *Don Carlo*, he finally agreed to come to Milan; but he made his publisher live through some very painful moments. When Verdi saw an article in the *Corriere della sera* announcing that he *would* direct the rehearsals of *Don Carlo*, he wrote to Ricordi to say that he felt that the report was an attempt to force him to come. He would not set a date for the first night of the opera; he did not believe the singers knew their roles; and he refused to discuss the matter further unless an announcement was published saying he *would not* be in Milan. As soon as the announcement was made, he would come, but only for 'the most important rehearsals of the new pieces'.

Verdi made one of his frequent trips to Sant'Agata during the second week in December and wrote to Streponi from there. Unfortunately, only a part of the letter remains:

Dearest Peppina,

It's done! So Angiolino [Carrara] would say. The people to execute the deed were here, and so everything is done and everything paid. Amen. I had a good trip. A little snow has fallen here, but no more of it is left. It is cold, but at least there is no wind! Ah, that wind! That wind! How hellish yesterday when I left [Genoa]! All the Carraras send you greetings. The children are fine, and Pepèn [Peppina Carrara], who wanted to show me all her dresses and hats, sends you a *big kiss*. Maria is rather resigned. It is a bit late, and I am going to see what they have done outside. I am still planning for Thursday, but if everything goes right, I will get there earlier. I also send you a big kiss and some great . . . [*letter breaks off here*].[69]

For Christmas Ricordi sent the usual panettone from Milan to Palazzo Doria, but in 1883 the little Moor had legs and was made of darker chocolate than usual. Muzio, who had been the Verdis' guest at Christmas in 1881 and 1882, stayed on in Paris to oversee the rehearsals of *Simon Boccanegra*, which Faccio was preparing at the Théâtre des Italiens. His bulletins on the production kept Verdi informed almost on a day-to-day basis. Although the opening-night curtain had been delayed for almost an hour, the performance had gone exceptionally well. Maurel, though hounded by creditors, had sung the title role to the satisfaction of the audience and critics. Ominously, hints of financial problems were soon whispered about, reminding everyone of the collapse of the previous company.

Verdi and Strepponi left Genoa for Milan after Christmas, taking their usual apartment at the Grand Hôtel de Milan. They were joined there by Muzio, who was on his way to Verona, where Durot was to sing *L'africana* at the Teatro Filarmonico. There he heard from Verdi that the *Don Carlo* had gone well, but not well enough to satisfy its composer. Writing in *Fanfulla della domenica*, Filippi remarked on the new electric lighting in the theatre and congratulated Verdi on *Don Carlo*, which was

reduced to human proportions. [The composer] directed the rehearsals with a surprisingly youthful energy, good humour, and with the most severe scrupulousness in instilling in his artists the interpretation of one of his favourite operas; they all fell under the spell of his words, [which were] passionate, few, helpful, and also of his not infrequent reproaches. . . . [At the end of the opera Verdi] appeared on the stage. . . . The evening was a bit odd [with moments of] rapture, warm enthusiasms, together with periods of quiet and sometimes of chilliness.[70]

The critic described the soprano Abigaille Bruschi-Chiatti and the mezzo Giuseppina Pasqua as affected by panic, while Tamagno, the Don Carlo and Paul Lhérie, the Rodrigo, distinguished themselves. Yet Filippi criticized the work as 'dark, sombre, monotonous, and—horrible to say— political' although Verdi knew how to make this 'unfortunate political aspect effective and even interesting'. The article, rich in praise for Verdi's genius, ended with the observation that the duet between Filippo and Rodrigo, composed for the second act of the 1884 production, revealed a Verdi who was travelling down 'a new road with his flag flying', toward 'a new artistic direction'. The critic concluded that in it Verdi 'shows that he is accommodating himself to Wagner's concepts of *music drama*'.[71] This was perhaps the piece Verdi had worked hardest on over the years. Another critic, writing anonymously in the musical publication *Il trovatore*, regretted the loss of the Fontainebleau scene, because it alone made the work less heavy and boring.[72]

Verdi confided his own feelings to both Clara Maffei and Arrivabene when he wrote from Genoa on 29 January 1884. To her, he complained about

that prison that other people call the theatre [where artists were] slaves to an audience that most of the time is ignorant (so much the better), fickle, and unfair. It makes me laugh to think that I too once was sentimental . . . I was 25 . . . but it did not last; one year later I saw the light; and afterwards, when I had to deal with [the audience], I wore armour, and, ready to be shot, cried: 'Let's fight.' And they were truly battles always! Battles that never left me satisfied, even when I won!! Sad! Sad![73]

The composer told Arrivabene that the welcome offered him by the Milanese audience was not for *Don Carlo*, not even for the composer of so many other operas, but was a kind of work order: 'That clapping meant: "You, who are still alive, even though you are so old, kill yourself with exhaustion, if you have to, but make us dance one more time . . ."—Go on, Clown, and Long Live Glory!'[74] In fairness, he did admit that the opera was well performed and very well staged; the cuts improved the work.

Otello

Resting in Genoa after the effort of *Don Carlo*, Verdi had a visit from Boito late in January. The composer seems to have asked for further changes in the libretto of *Otello* that were made almost at once. Encouraged by his visit to Palazzo Doria, Boito wrote to Tornaghi to let the Ricordis know that 'Verdi this time has thought seriously about getting to work.'[75] But to Muzio, who had returned to Paris, from where he was sending his usual reports on the anarchy at the Théâtre des Italiens, Verdi wrote that he had no desire whatever to get busy with the opera.[76] He may, though, have composed some in February or March, for Boito, after another visit, noted 'the Maestro is writing; indeed, he has already written a good part of the beginning of the first act and seems to me to be excited.'[77] The fact that Verdi had decided to rent out all of his lands may indicate that he was about to compose the opera rather than dedicate so much of his time to farming.[78] Yet at this moment, when some hope was raised, Verdi almost abandoned the *Otello* project, when he became upset over a remark that Boito was reported to have made while he was in Naples producing *Mefistofele* at the Teatro San Carlo. A journalist for the newspaper *Roma* claimed that during a banquet Boito had declared that although he had originally written the libretto of *Otello* almost against his will, he was sorry, now that it was finished, that he could not compose it himself. Verdi read the story after it had been picked up by two other papers and took offence at once. Rather than write to Boito directly, he addressed Faccio in a letter of 27 March, admitting that although something said at a banquet could not be taken too seriously, the remark would generate unfortunate comment because it might convince people that he had forced Boito to write the libretto. Furthermore, it looked as if Boito would never be satisfied with what Verdi would write.

I fully acknowledge this, I acknowledge it completely, and because of that, I turn to you, Boito's oldest, closest friend, so that when he returns to Milan, you will tell him personally, not in writing, that I, without a trace of resentment, without any kind of rancour, give his manuscript back to him intact.

Verdi added that he, the owner of the libretto, offered it as a gift 'in the hope of contributing something to the Art we all love'.[79]

In a letter that was a masterpiece of tact, Faccio tried to calm the waters, a task that was extremely difficult, for this was the second time in their professional relationship that Boito had offended Verdi with remarks made at a banquet. Boito, though, handled the problem rather badly at first. He learned of the article about the banquet while he was reading *Roma* on the train between Naples and Genoa and realized its importance at once but believed wrongly that no one in the North would see it. His first impulse was to write to the editor of *Roma*; but he thought the better of that and decided to ask Verdi's permission to write. In Genoa, when he had an excuse to visit the Verdis to deliver a photograph Morelli had given him, Boito lost courage when he saw Strepponi and never mentioned it. Not until he met Faccio at a rehearsal of a cantata in Turin did he learn that Verdi was ready to give the *Otello* libretto back to him. Stunned, he wrote to Verdi to explain that he had been misquoted by the reporter and that he could not accept Verdi's offer to return the libretto.

For heaven's sake, do not abandon *Otello*, do not abandon it; it is predestined for you, you had already begun to work on it, and I was truly comforted, and I already was hoping to see it finished some day soon. You are healthier than I, stronger than I; we tested each other's strength and my arm bent beneath yours; your life is peaceful and tranquil, take up your pen again and wrote soon to me: '*Dear Boito, do me the favour of changing these lines*' etc., etc., and I will change them joyfully, and will know how to work for you, I, who do not know how to work for myself, because you live the true and real life of Art; I, in the world of hallucinations.[80]

This letter struck just the right note and won Verdi's forgiveness and understanding, but it did not get the project back on track. The composer wrote at once:

Too much has been said about [*Otello*]! Too much time has passed! I am too old! Too many YEARS OF SERVICE!!! May the audience not say '*Enough!*' too clearly! The result is that all this has spread something cold over this *Otello*, and has stiffened my hand, which had begun to sketch some measures! What will happen afterward? I don't know! Anyway, I am very happy about this explanation, which, though, would have been better had it come just after you got back from Naples.[81]

Boito's handling of this delicate situation kept this precious friendship alive. Thanking Verdi for his letter, he sent a new section of the *Otello* libretto, Iago's Credo, satisfying the composer's wish for a dramatic scene at that point in the opera. He struck just the right note, for Verdi invited Boito for a visit. It did seem, though, that *Otello* was stalled again. Writing to Faccio, Verdi said that he regretted that the newspapers had printed anything about the controversy; but 'what is done, is done. Now, according to you, should I really finish this *Otello*? But why? For whom? I don't care about it. The public, even less.'[82]

Verdi and Strepponi visited the International Exposition in Turin and went on to Montecatini Terme, where they stayed until mid-July. Stolz also took cures there and at Tabiano, where Strepponi stayed in August, while Verdi worked on the farm and helped execute the plans for the Villanova Hospital as the project became larger than had been expected. Muzio, who stayed in Paris that summer, had toasted the fortieth anniversary of his first trip to Milan with Verdi and his first meeting with Strepponi in the summer of 1844.

At the end of September Boito, accompanied by the librettist Giuseppe Giacosa, visited Verdi and Strepponi at Sant'Agata, where they stayed more than a week. The composer, though saddened by the death of his old friend Carcano, who had died in Milan in August, welcomed the two men to the quiet villa. His exquisite hospitality made them feel as if they had 'lived there for ten years'. The composer told them how he had transformed the original four or five rooms into the important country house of 1884; showed them his collection of paintings, old prints, antique furniture, rare books, and album of autographs; treated them to the best his larder could provide; told stories about early performances; played billiards and cards; and sat on the steps outside his room with Strepponi as they watched Boito, Giacosa, and Stolz, who was there at the same time, sing and act scenes from *Ernani* in the twilight.[83] In the afternoons the composer and Boito discussed *Otello*, some of the music for which Verdi ran through on the piano as they talked.

Sometimes Verdi seized the rough draft of the drama and read sections from it out loud—Boito and I exchanged glances that showed our admiration—His voice, emphasis, intonation, violence, anger expressed during that reading betrayed such an intense fire in his soul [and] enhanced the meaning of the words so we clearly could see in them the source of his musical idea—One might say that we saw with our own eyes the flower of the melody and the words carried to their highest power and transformed into waves of sound, overwhelming the infinite anguish that the human soul is capable of feeling.[84]

During the year Verdi had followed the careers of other, younger musicians, among them Giacomo Puccini, whose first opera *Le Villi* had been given at the Teatro Dal Verme in Milan at the end of May 1884. To Arrivabene, Verdi had written:

I have heard a lot of good things said about the musician Puccini. . . . He follows modern trends, and that is natural, but he is attached to melody, which is neither modern nor old. It seems, though, that a symphonic element predominates in him! Nothing wrong there! Just that one has to be careful with this. Opera is opera; symphony is symphony, and I do not think it is good to do a symphonic section in an opera, just for the joy of making the orchestra dance. I am talking just for the sake of talking, without being important, without being certain of having said anything right; rather, being certain of having said something that is contrary to modern tendencies. All eras have their trademarks. Later history will say which era is good and which is bad.[85]

BOOK V

Good feelings abound in the composer's letter to Ricordi, whom he congratulated on having found, 'finally, after thirty years, a real maestro, Puccini, who, it seems, has unusual qualities'.[86] Although he had never met the younger composer, he had once been approached by one of his cousins, Antonio Puccini of Lucca, who proclaimed himself the descendant of a family of musicians and asked for financial aid. Verdi also showed an interest in the brothers Italo and Cleofonte Campanini, whom Muzio had been promoting for some time. Cleofonte, then in his mid-twenties, was chosen to conduct the orchestra of the Teatro Ducale of Parma at the Turin Exposition. In the orchestra in the autumn of 1884 was the young cellist Arturo Toscanini. Part of the Turin programme had been planned by Muzio, who sent music from Paris for the orchestra.

Verdi gave no sign of going on with *Otello* in the early autumn, being—as he told Clara Maffei—busy with unpoetic matters such as 'business, figures, accounts with peasants and shepherds'.[87] A drought had damaged the crops; the harvest was thin.[88] From Sant'Agata, he wrote to Strepponi shortly after he got to the villa, where, evidently, the staff did not expect him:

Dearest Peppina,

Surprise everywhere! '*The Master! The Master!*' and Giovanna very excited. But I have to say that everything was in order and that, because it is a beautiful day, even all the windows of the apartment[s] downstairs and upstairs were open. Bavagnoli told me in Fiorenzuola that the wife of Checco [Francesco Carrara] had died, and that the doctor [Angiolo Carrara] had gone to Rome! He was counting on having the body brought here. He also told me that because of this, the wedding of Mariuccia [Carrara] will be postponed still further. Well, this sentiment is too much! Because of this, I will not give [her] the bracelet now. I am going to see how things are, and I will finish the letter this evening.

I have just come back from the Carraras. Adelaide, the one from Lugagnano, is there. The doctor, as I told you, is in Rome. I gave the letter to Pepèn [Peppina Carrara], who, sitting on my knee, began to read your letter with a certain solemn air. It seemed to her that she had become someone important! She read it all, of course, spelling it out and without missing a syllable. Afterward, she handed the letter to Marietta [her grandmother] and told her in a deep, solemn voice to keep that letter with the other precious things that she is taking care of for her. I gave her a kiss and left.

I have nothing else to tell you and have nothing else to do, other than give you a kiss and say that I am your 71!!!

Addio, addio.

I will write to you in a quiet moment as soon as I have something to say. Write to me because I will not be able to come to Genoa before Monday at the earliest. Stay well and keep going. I am not bad. Moving around is positively good for me. You understand, [I mean] travelling.

Again addio.[89]

At the end of November he joined his wife at the Palazzo Doria.

This lively 71-year-old *padrone* began to work seriously on the new opera almost as soon as he got to Genoa. On 9 December he sent good news to Boito: 'It seems impossible, yet it is true!!! *Mah*!!!! [But!!!] I am busy and I am writing!! I am writing . . . because I am writing without a goal, without worries, without thinking of *afterward* . . . really with a marked dislike of the *afterward*.[90]

The 'afterward'—the exhausting work of producing the opera; the hated publicity; and the confrontation with the audience and critics—was always in his mind though, as Boito reminded the composer that so many hopes were fixed on him and Faccio declared that he must finish *Otello* 'for the glory of Italian art'.[91] Offers to produce the opera reached Verdi from Europe and America, while the whole music world waited for this idol to turn out his latest score. In spite of the pressure brought to bear on him, he composed in fits and starts. At the end of that same December Verdi told Arrivabene that he was not spending any time on music or the theatre.[92] He preached to Clara Maffei about the breakdown of professionalism in all the arts, the craze for novelty, the odd, the unfamiliar, while denouncing 'journalism, the curse of our era' and the ignorant crowds that accepted everything the critics wrote. 'Art that does not have simplicity and naturalness is not art! Inspiration can only be found in simple things.'[93]

As in the past, the composer and his wife spent Christmas and New Year's Day in Genoa, although Verdi spent a few days in Busseto just before the holidays. Muzio came from Paris to be with them. From Milan, where he stopped on his way back to Paris, he sent the composer a report on *Mefistofele*, which he did not much like, and on the excellent chorus and orchestra that had performed it.

By January 1885 Verdi was besieged by singers, publishers, and impresarios, all of whom sought a commitment from him for *Otello*. Both Eugène Ritt and Pierre Gailhard, the new directors of the Paris Opéra, came to Genoa to discuss future productions. Neither Verdi nor his wife was well: she had been suffering from bronchitis, he from headaches and stomach trouble. In spite of this, he went on with *Otello*, working with

Boito, who came to Palazzo Doria from his winter home at the Hotel Eden in Nervi, just 12 kilometres outside Genoa. The two men continued to correspond, as Boito made necessary changes in the libretto. In May Verdi and Strepponi spent two days in Milan, where he had five teeth pulled by an American dentist who was practising in the city. He also received Ponchielli at the Grand Hôtel de Milan, where the two men discussed Puccini and plans for Ponchielli's new opera *Marion Delorme*, the libretto of which Verdi had read while he was in Genoa. His interest in Ponchielli dated back over many years, Verdi having first asked to have some of Ponchielli's music sent to him in 1871, when Corticelli had organized a little music-school at Sant'Agata for local girls and boys and mustered a respectable chorus out of their ranks.[94]

When Ponchielli sought Verdi out in 1885, Verdi gave him advice on how to handle the libretto that had been made out of Hugo's *Marion Delorme*, a drama Verdi had once considered himself. Verdi thought the second and third acts of the libretto were 'a pastiche', Ponchielli wrote to his wife, the soprano Teresina Brambilla,

and advised me to cut and rewrite pitilessly. And I said: 'Even the role of Lelio?' And he, at once: 'Oh, yes, yes!' . . . Then we spoke of Puccini's opera, the kind of music we do not like, because it follows the footsteps of Massenet, Wagner, etc. . . . Then he deplored the situation the theatres find themselves in, because of having to pay too much to certain artists, so that he does not think that the impresarios will make money even in Carnival.[95]

Verdi and his wife left Milan for Sant'Agata during the first week in May; during the summer they also took cures at Montecatini and Tabiano. Muzio, who had visited them at the Palazzo Doria in the spring, came from Paris again in August and stayed a month at the villa, bringing Verdi up to date on the many productions of his operas that he monitored, either in person or through correspondence. At Verdi's request, Muzio sent him the scores of *Die Meistersinger* and *Parsifal* from Lucca's shop in Milan. While in the city, Muzio also warned Verdi about possible future problems with Casa Ricordi, which was rumoured to be foundering under the burden of its debts.

In September Verdi had a welcome visit from Boito, whom he warned in advance that he had written nothing on *Otello* the whole summer, partly because he was busy with the farm, partly because he had stayed too long in the spas, partly because it had been too hot to work. 'Let's say this, too', Verdi added, 'my incredible laziness.'[96] Yet after Boito's visit he threw himself into the work and could write in early October that he had finished the fourth act 'and I can breathe'![97] Both he and his librettist went on labouring over the 'ultra-terrible' scene of Desdemona's murder and Otello's suicide when Boito returned to the villa in mid-October.[98]

Verdi had celebrated his seventy-second birthday that year, lamenting to Clara Maffei that his life had flown by, 'in spite of so many unhappy and happy events and so many worries and labours'.[99] His forty-year friendship with her notwithstanding, the composer did not write his condolences at once when Andrea Maffei died. In fact, he rarely wrote messages of condolence soon after the death of someone he knew, perhaps because of his stated conviction that condolences caused additional pain to the survivors. The poet suffered a stroke in his room at the Hotel Bella Venezia in Milan at the end of November.[100] After two weeks Verdi, from Genoa:

I am very, very grateful for the letter you wrote me, but at the same time I am very mortified! Mortified because I should have written you as soon as I got here: instead you beat me to it. Ah, I am really a big . . . (you baptize me). The fact is that although I have been on the earth such a long time, and have seen everything, I have learned very little, and the peasant's hide is still there, and often the old country fellow from Roncole comes out, in all his greatness.[101]

The composer had been in Milan in mid-November to have his new dentures fitted and to shop with Strepponi. He admitted to Arrivabene that he was battered and utterly exhausted by 'treacherous Iago' who had kept him in slavery for months. Yet he said he had had a good time, had his spirits lifted, and even known great joy from this most recent effort.[102] Astonishingly, he observed that Andrea Maffei, who had lived a troubled life, had never known 'sorrow, a real sorrow throughout his existence',[103] a remark that shows little comprehension for the lonely survivor of the 1846 separation from his wife, the patriot who had to defend his reputation against the accusation of pro-Austrian sympathies, the father who had buried his only daughter.

In Genoa for the winter, Verdi and Strepponi entertained Muzio, who came from Paris for Christmas, as he was by now expected to do. Corti and Ricordi visited in mid-January 1886 to find Strepponi plagued with her chronic bronchitis and a persistent cough. Both the composer and his wife were distressed at her illness. When Ponchielli died that same month, Verdi sent his condolences through Ricordi, not wishing, he said, to send letters and telegrams of condolence, since they are, by my standards, a cruel custom that exacerbates the injury to a heart that is already suffering too much, repeating a thousand times (to console someone) the heartbreaking cause of the sorrow! Maybe my way is a strange way of feeling; but I believe that silence is the only comfort for great sorrows.[104]

In answer to questions that had been raised about *Otello* during the interview with Ricordi and Corti, Verdi declared the opera was not finished, adding that he did not know whether he would ever finish it. 'No, absolutely no formal commitment', he swore.[105] Gailhard of the Paris Opéra had been given the same information, as had Maurel, who had written to Verdi at the end of 1885 to ask about the role of Iago. It was in January 1886 that Verdi formally baptized the opera *Otello*, because, as he told Boito, 'It is Otello who acts, *loves, is jealous, kills*, and *kills himself*. As for me, it seems hypocritical not to call it *Otello*. I would rather people say: "*He wanted to fight with the giant* [Rossini] *and was crushed*" rather than "*He wanted to hide behind the name Iago.*"'[106]

Discussions about singers, scenery, and costumes in 1886 fixed the historical period of the opera. Alfredo Edel, a native of the Province of Parma, was asked to execute costume sketches, as he had done for other important Verdi productions at La Scala, using the period 1520–5 as his frame of reference, after Boito and Verdi determined that the action took place just before the Sack of Rome in 1527. To assure authenticity, Edel was sent to Venice to do special studies in the libraries and museums there. The paintings of Carpaccio and Gentile Bellini served as models. Early in the year Verdi discouraged both Tamagno and Masini, who were hoping to be assigned the title role; Boito was asked to evaluate other singers, especially sopranos, as the composer, librettist, and Ricordi tried to cast the female lead in the opera. Human passions played their own part, as Giulio Ricordi fought to have his favourite, Gemma Bellincioni, whom Boito did not like; Faccio, D'Ormeville, and Stolz promoted the cause of Romilda Pantaleoni, Faccio's mistress.[107] Muzio, who had heard Pantaleoni in Forlì, when she sang the season there with Durot, thought she was worse than mediocre. As he often did, Verdi decided to hear Bellincioni himself, going to La Scala in mid-February. While he was in the city, Stolz, as she had promised Pantaleoni she would, discussed her merits with Verdi, who did indeed choose her over Bellincioni. Triumphantly, Pantaleoni could report to her brother that she would be Desdemona.[108]

Muzio, who had gone back to his apartment in Nice for the winter, came to Genoa again in March to help his maestro. Verdi, who had let Muzio hear many parts of the opera as he was composing it, played pieces from the third act of *Otello* and the 'Willow Song', which made Muzio tremble and brought tears to his eyes.[109] Muzio hoped, he said, to live until the spring of 1887, so he could run back and forth from Verdi's apartment to the offices of Ricordi's copyists, as he had done when *Giovanna d'Arco* was being produced. Because Muzio had warned Verdi several times about Maurel's vocal problems, the composer, with Muzio and Strepponi, went to Paris in March to hear the baritone in performance. They stayed at the Hôtel de Bade, went to hear plays or operas almost every night, and visited the Italian-born painter Giovanni Boldini, one of Muzio's closest friends in the city. Muzio had often tried to persuade Verdi to sit for Boldini; in 1886 he was responsible for bringing them together. After a two-week stay, the composer, his wife, and his friend returned to Italy through the great Saint Gotthard tunnel, Verdi having taken the precaution of writing to Piroli to see that their luggage would not be ransacked at the customs in Chiasso. Exercising the substantial prerogative that his name gave him, he asked that an Italian official telegraph the director of the customs office in Chiasso to 'have pity' on their luggage.[110] According to Muzio, Verdi was happy with what he heard in Paris: 'He is no longer worried, his face is again tranquil, he is in a very good humour, and sings and sings over again and recites some parts of the role of Iago, which, he says, will be wonderfully played.'[111] It was clear that he was satisfied with Maurel.

The Verdis and Muzio stayed a few days in Milan, where they saw the Ricordis and Stolz. The soprano, who had gone to Genoa to promote Pantaleoni in February, welcomed them to her new apartment. After seeing their physician Dr Todeschini, who also treated Stolz, they picked up their prescriptions and left for Genoa. Muzio returned to Paris, again as Verdi's personal representative, charged with the job of negotiating Maurel's fees and arranging his schedule. To Ricordi, Muzio declared that Verdi would not give *Otello* without the celebrated baritone. In Milan he had acted as a third party in arranging the conditions under which Verdi would let the Ricordis have *Otello*. Muzio, who had researched the matter, set a fee of 250,000 francs and composed the letter of agreement between composer and publisher. Back in Paris at the end of April, Muzio also negotiated for a new production of *La battaglia di Legnano*, which had been translated into French under the title *Pour la Patrie*, and helped to arrange for the French translation of *Otello*, acting as intermediary between Verdi, Boito, Nuitter, and Du Locle. He also monitored a production of *Il trovatore* at the Théâtre de Montmartre, where the house was regularly sold out.

The composition of *Otello* kept Verdi busy in April in Genoa and in the summer at Sant'Agata, as he and Boito corresponded about translators' versions of one of Iago's lines in the first act. 'I am going on, very slowly, but I am going,' Verdi wrote his librettist in May.[112] In May he added the tenor's entrance 'Esultate!' Verdi and his wife lived quietly that spring, for she had had surgery in Genoa in April. Her surgeon Azzio Caselli, a native of Reggio Emilia, had met Verdi when he was serving as a country doctor in a city nearby. Once, when Caselli stopped at the villa and found only Verdi at home, he was treated like a member of the family. Verdi went to the kitchen, fixed a meal himself and served it in the dining room. In 1887, when Caselli was an important physician in Genoa, Strepponi was entrusted to his care. She recovered quickly and left for Sant'Agata with Verdi at the end of May. They spent late June and the beginning of July at Montecatini, where they were taking the waters when they learned that Clara Maffei, ill with meningitis in Milan, was not expected to live. The composer telegraphed to Velleda Ferretti, the Countess's close friend, who urged him to come at once. Without waiting for Strepponi, Verdi set out on the first train and got to Maffei's house just after dawn on 13 July, to find that she had died a few moments earlier. Ferretti left an unforgettable account of him, 'leaning against the doorjamb, his beautiful head bowed in desolate grief, with his whole body shaken and trembling with his suppressed sobs!'[113] Strepponi joined him almost at once, then went back to Sant'Agata with him. They did not attend the funeral, where a eulogist praised Maffei's strength of character and reminded the mourners of her important role in the struggle for Italian independence. Verdi, in letters to Piroli and Giuseppina Negroni Prati Morosini, recalled Maffei's goodness, her noble character, and her heart, as he lamented the end of this forty-four-year friendship. 'And so they are all dying, one after another', he wrote to Morosini. 'Almost everyone I knew in Milan when I was young has gone. Two or three are left, at the most. Poor Clarina! . . . A loyal friend; and with her, you could be sure; you did not have to think twice! Poor Clarina! I will not soon forget her!'[114]

At home he found his garden at the peak of bloom, cared for and cultivated by the sixteen men and two women who worked on it. As his pay records for the gardeners for 1886 and 1887 show, Verdi employed four or six men every week. Extra hands were brought in as needed. Most of this staff worked six full days a week; all worked full time in spring and summer; the highest paid earned 8 lire and 40 centesimi a week most of the summer and about 5½ or 6 lire a week in winter. As the records show, Verdi employed as many as fifteen or sixteen hands even in December and February. In January 1887 he had eighteen employees working in the garden, although most of them were putting in four days a week in the middle of the winter.

Because Verdi had rented out so much of his land, he may have been freer that summer than he usually was. That, at least, was what Muzio thought. Keeping in touch with Boito, Verdi showed concern for something that apparently had rarely, if ever, interested him before: the actual appearance of the printed pages of the libretto. He wanted, he said, to be sure that the audience 'could see and understand everything' of the finale of the third act 'at one glance', and asked that it appear as he transcribed it in the middle of his letter. He wanted Desdemona's 'solo, [to be] printed at the bottom of the page before [the finale]. Then, turning the page, one will see the whole Uproar of the concertato' laid out there.[115] Not surprisingly, Boito was astonished that Verdi should devote such careful attention to such minute details, though he agreed to study the matter.

Further additions to the opera were made to the score, while Ricordi was taking the cure at Levico, near Trent. In August Faccio visited Sant'Agata to discuss the singers with Verdi and to promote Pantaleoni's cause. She, too, had come to seek Verdi's advice about her vocal problems. At the end of summer Verdi asked Boito to make further changes in the third act, even as he took a week off because of problems with his eyes.[116] Satisfied with what he had written for the three main roles, which he had rechecked for his own peace of mind. 'They work!', he exulted, 'but all this won't mean anything if the notes don't please the eminent [audience].'[117] By 29 October he could say that the instrumentation would be finished before the end of the month; and on 1 November he could write to Boito: 'It is finished! Cheers for us . . . (and for [Otello] too!!) Addio.'[118]

Muzio, who had spent August at Sant'Agata, had been sent to Paris to coach Maurel. Faccio was teaching Desdemona to Pantaleoni in Milan. Ricordi, following Verdi's orders, was negotiating conditions with La Scala that guaranteed the composer's absolute control over the production: the poster advertising Otello would carry Verdi's and Boito's names but would have no date for the first night; all rehearsals would be closed; and

Verdi would have the right to withdraw the opera even after the dress rehearsal, if he did not like the way it was being performed. The entire company, including the conductor, orchestra, chorus, and stage-director, would work under his command. The première could not take place without his permission; if anyone should try to stage the opera without it, Ricordi would have to pay him a fine of 100,000 lire.[119] As everyone expected, La Scala accepted Verdi's conditions unconditionally. The furore over *Otello* was so great that even in Paris the fight for a seat for the opening was a matter of everyday gossip. One of those seats was to be reserved for Boldini, who had sent Verdi the portrait for which he had done the sketches earlier that year.

With the Opéra begging to be allowed to produce the work, Muzio was given the responsibility of negotiating with its management, while Verdi, in Milan in November, planned the ballet that would be added there. A near-disaster occurred at the end of November, when Maurel—whose furniture was about to be sequestered by a bailiff to pay his debts—was almost arrested for co-habitation and adultery, as he had been accused of concubinage. When the police knocked at the front door of his apartment, the baritone escaped down the service stairs, leaving his wife and Muzio to answer to the authorities. She claimed she lived there alone with her mother; Muzio stated *he* was the baritone whom the police had heard singing as they stood outside the door. It was undoubtedly Maurel's creditors who had set the police on him, after they learned that his marriage to her—a divorcée—had taken place in Switzerland and thus was not valid in France. Muzio had to register the baritone and his son in a hotel under an assumed name and settle matters with the police so that Maurel could travel to Milan. Muzio took him to the station and sent him off on his nineteen-hour trip, to be sure nothing else went wrong.[120] Shortly after arriving in Milan, he went to Genoa, where Verdi coached him at the Palazzo Doria. Muzio joined them there, spent the holidays, and helped his maestro with last-minute preparations for the opera.

Verdi was now dissatisfied with Maurel and convinced that no one would ever sing Iago as he wanted to hear it. On 15 December he declared to Ricordi that he was sorry he had ever written the role. 'And the opera, too!!'[121] Three days later, regretfully, he handed the last-act orchestrations to a Ricordi employee who had been sent to Genoa to pick them up. To Boito, Verdi wrote: 'Poor Otello! He will not come here again!!!'[122] And Boito answered: 'The great dream has become a reality.'[123]

The Production of *Otello*

Just after Christmas, Verdi arranged with Ricordi to publish an engraving taken from one of Boldini's portraits of him, as agreed by the artist in December 1886. He also hurried to Sant'Agata, then returned to Genoa to celebrate New Year's Day 1887. The year began badly, with the death of Arrivabene, to whom Verdi had last written in November with news that *Otello* was finished. 'Courage', he had said to his friend of fifty years.[124] Now, with the première of *Otello* imminent, Verdi wrote to Count Silvio Arrivabene, the nephew and heir, that the loss was 'enormously sad, irreparable', for he had counted the journalist 'dear, among my dearest friends'.[125]

On 4 January Verdi and Strepponi set off for Milan, where he began to rehearse at once. Through his correspondence with Ricordi had run the thread of his uncertainty about Pantaleoni, whom he coached privately. At the Grand Hôtel de Milan, the Verdis' apartment had just had electric wiring installed; a little upright piano had been placed in the salon. After just three days there Verdi could confide to Waldmann, who was coming for the première, that he hoped to be ready by the end of the month. He had got Ricordi to pay 1,200 lire for her box for opening night;[126] when she sent her cheque, by return, he wrote to set a tentative date for the opening.

During the piano rehearsals, which ran from noon until five in the afternoon, Verdi was helped by Boito, Faccio, Ricordi, and the assistant conductor Gaetano Coronaro. On the first day, he began with the Act III ensemble, then took his soloists aside in a separate studio, where Ricordi had had an Érard grand piano moved. The composer wanted 'to unite the singing to the action' right away; he 'recommended the greatest naturalness' to them and pointed out the gestures and movements that seemed to him 'the truest [and] most natural',[127] showing them how to stand, fall, embrace, and address each other. Rehearsals of the complete company began on 27 January; the final dress rehearsal was scheduled for 3 February. Throughout the month Verdi, at 73, often seemed the most energetic person in the theatre. Strepponi wrote to Marietta Calvi Carrara, Angiolo Carrara's wife, about the composer's strength: 'he is well, he is holding up, he eats with a good appetite, and he sleeps soundly for hours and hours.'[128]—All this, although he was besieged by well-wishers, overwhelmed by embraces and kisses, asked 'discreet and indiscreet' questions, and forced to stand and listen to praise that embarrassed him.

BOOK V

A great artistic event like *Otello* was also seen in Italy as an occasion for a national, patriotic celebration, with Verdi treated like a hero returning to home soil from a major victory. The Mayor of Milan ordered all the streets and squares around La Scala closed to traffic on 5 February, the morning of the première. The crowds flooding the area had made the Via Manzoni (the old Corsia del Giardino) impassable even before dawn. Around noon it was rumoured that Tamagno was ill; a doctor was sent to his hotel. Word went around at four that his wig would not fit, and that another had been sent for. Every window and balcony within blocks of La Scala was filled with people; bright tapestries and cloths of gold and scarlet damask hung from windows nearby. In spite of the bitter cold, many windows were open, and the crowds kept shouting 'Viva Verdi!' all along the Via Manzoni from the Grand Hôtel de Milan to the theatre.

The world première of *Otello*, given on 5 February 1887, was one of the most important productions in the history of Italian opera. Verdi's first new work since *Aida* in 1871 marked an apotheosis for its creator, who had been dignified on 27 January by King Umberto I, who decorated him with the Great Cross of the Order of Saints Maurizio and Lazzaro. Three days later Verdi sent his thanks in a telegram:

I am deeply grateful that His Majesty Our King has deigned to remember my poor name. The honour that he wished to bestow on me is a great compensation for that little I have been able to accomplish in my long, now too long, artistic career. This high honour will be a precious memory for me in the years that are still left to me to live in the stillness of my village.[129]

Before the opera began, Boito and Strepponi took their seats together in their box, while Verdi remained backstage. From the first moment, *Otello* was received with continuous enthusiasm, the chorus 'Fuoco di gioia' and the 'Willow Song' being encored. Dozens of curtain-calls ended the evening; during one of them, Verdi asked Boito to come to the stage, where he generously took the librettist's hand and drew him out to the footlights, a gesture the younger man never forgot. When Verdi, Strepponi, and Boito left the theatre, the mob at the stage door nearly tore Verdi's clothes off. His carriage had moved only a few feet when the crowd began to shout 'Take away the horses' and unharnessed the team. More than a dozen men tried to lift the carriage on to their shoulders; finally it was drawn to the Grand Hôtel de Milan by man-power. Verdi, Boito said, was pale with emotion. At the entrance to the hotel, the three tried to get out but could not. Verdi then left the carriage alone, entrusting Strepponi to

Boito. As he fought to reach the door, the crowd, which Boito described as 'insane', surrounded him. Verdi, his librettist, and his singers came out on to the balcony facing Via Manzoni, where they were greeted with waves of applause and shouting. Music was played under his windows until five o'clock in the morning.

Strepponi wrote to Marietta Calvi Carrara that the ovation was

deafening, and reached the point of delirium . . . but I confess to you that I was moved by it, because this admiration, this passionate demonstration, comes from a high esteem, an affection that is heavy with understanding, that has never been denied [by anyone] during all of Verdi's long career! In Milan he gave the first proofs of his immense gift; and he wanted to give Milan the last fruit of his genius! Verdi's genius is tied to the Resurrection of Italy.[130]

The composer's own memories of the night of the première reflect his sadness at reaching what he thought was the end of his career. He wrote to Faccio eleven months after the first night of *Otello* that he remembered

that first night, and even more the third night, when, as I was leaving the theatre in the midst of the affectionate good wishes on-stage, I met—on the staircase— the orchestra players, who, affected, without saying a word, grasped my hand; and on their faces were engraved these words: 'Maestro, we will never see each other again here, never again!!' Never again is a phrase that tolls like a bell for the dead.[131]

Verdi stayed with his company through that third performance; then, having been interviewed by many journalists, he left for Genoa. Muzio stayed on at La Scala, from where he sent the composer reports on the rest of the season, which was threatened by Maurel's sore throats and colds. At every performance, though, the audience showed a greater under- standing of and enthusiasm for Verdi's opera. In mid-March Muzio joined his maestro and Strepponi in the Palazzo Doria.

Verdi's first gesture on reaching Genoa was to donate 1,000 francs to earthquake victims; out of her own purse, Strepponi gave 500 francs. Beset by impresarios who begged him to produce *Otello* in Rome, Venice, Parma, Naples, and Brescia, Verdi refused all offers, though he had agreed to go to Paris for the first French production, which was to cause the composer a good deal of grief as the casting proceeded, and as he tried to remedy some of the problems he had perceived at La Scala. An *Otello* at the Royal Albert Hall in London was under consideration as well. For three months after the première, he had to devote almost as much time to the opera as he had before it was produced. One of the most important matters at hand was the French translation, which was being done by Boito and Du Locle, with whom Verdi conferred at the Hotel Eden in Nervi in March. Muzio, who had gone on to Paris, returned to visit Verdi and Strepponi again in April, as they were still dealing with what Strepponi called an 'avalanche'[132] of letters, cards, eulogies, poems, and books. Ricordi pushed to get the orchestral score printed, putting pressure on Verdi to compose the ballet for the French production, leading him to examine old Venetian dances and other music that might be useful, although Verdi denounced the idea of including the ballet in the printed score because, 'artistically speaking, it is a monstrosity', for it broke into the action.[133]

The search for satisfactory Desdemonas for the many proposed productions of the opera caused friction between the composer and several colleagues, among them Faccio, Muzio, and Pantaleoni. Verdi's doubts about Pantaleoni's suitability for the role surfaced again and again that spring. Yet he rejected Adalgisa Gabbi, who later proved a popular Desdemona, and went on searching for someone who would do. One candidate was Eva Tetrazzini, whom Muzio had recommended, after hearing about her from a young cellist from Parma—Toscanini, who had played in the orchestra on opening night at La Scala. As the composer lingered in Genoa long beyond the time of his usual departure for Sant'Agata, he confided to Ricordi that he was sorry *Otello* had been done. The success made no difference to him at all. Just before leaving for the country with Strepponi, who had had surgery that spring, Verdi sent Ricordi some of his revisions for the score. As before he continued to exercise as much control as he could over this new and exceedingly difficult work.[134]

Help, as usual, was offered by Muzio, who had been sent to Rome from Genoa, so he could report on the production at the Teatro Costanzi, where the opera scored a huge success and earned the impresario a small fortune. He then went to oversee the opera at the Teatro La Fenice in Venice, where there was a competent cast and the opera was well staged. But because the management had not lowered prices, as the impresario had in Rome, and as La Scala had, after the first three performances of the opera, the houses in Venice were poor, a fact Verdi deplored: 'As for me, I am extremely unhappy about the outcome in Venice! The first, only, and sole thermometer of success is the box-office! By God, [even] with the precedents of Milan and Rome, they were not able to fill the house in Venice!'[135] The composer got a first-hand report about Venice when

Muzio came to Sant'Agata in May; he also heard about it from Vigna, who was helping him plan the Villanova Hospital. The production in Brescia went ahead without Tamagno and Maurel, who were not available, and Pantaleoni, who, afflicted with professional and personal problems, had refused to sing there. 'Well! *Otello* can make it even without creators?!! . . . [T]his Moor can succeed even without stars! Is it possible?'[136] Verdi, writing this to Faccio, congratulated the conductor on keeping the opera, 'this wreck of a boat' on course, although he remarked on the fact that the audiences at the Teatro Grande, like those in Venice, were not very large. Unlike *Aida*, which had already been given more than a hundred times in Paris, *Otello*, at least at the start, did not seem certain to become a standard part of the repertory. Verdi continued to monitor the box-office in several cities while recommending singers and even making suggestions for the English translation. Occasionally he fulminated about the 'damned, damned Moor' and the worry the opera caused him, cursing the day he had let the score escape from his desk.[137] Boito, who had visited Sant'Agata in the summer, came again in September, a difficult month.

The Hospital at Villanova sull'Arda

As construction of the Villanova Hospital neared completion, the composer spent more time there, especially after he left Strepponi in Genoa in November. In the middle of that month he complained to Piroli about the 'many details' he had to take care of for 'my little shanty called the Hospital' and about the 20 centimetres of snow.[138] After another short stay in Genoa, he was back at Sant'Agata at the beginning of December, in 'rain, fog, cold, and worse . . . figures', as he went over his accounts to be sure that there would be enough money to cover the institution's needs.[139] At this same time Verdi was trying to decide whether he could afford to lend Casa Ricordi the very large sum of 200,000 lire to help with its merger with the firm of Carlo Erba (Giulio Ricordi's father-in-law and Luchino Visconti's grandfather) and its acquisition of Casa Lucca. Just after Christmas he took an overnight trip to Milan to deliver personally the funds that would make it possible for Ricordi to carry out its plans. The publisher had a note of indebtedness drawn up and ready for him.

Strepponi, who had not been well for several years, stayed in the house most of the time, no matter where they were. In 1884, when she had described her 'solitary life' to Don Avanzi, she had also expressed her distrust of Italy's rulers and her suspicion of most of the human race.

In almost everyone, there is a hypocrisy, a corruption that is growing, and threatens to drown—with an immense flood—the little that is elevated and good remaining still in humanity. . . . I'll stop here, because in spite of a splendid day, [and] that immense sea that seems to join the sky joyfully at the horizon in a divine embrace, my soul is sad and my spirit filled with gloomy thoughts.[140]

Two years later she had lamented that she had 'nothing new or beautiful' to write to the priest, that she was always in the house, and that she did not even feel well enough to see the people who came to visit.[141] The 'uproar' caused by *Otello* added a great deal to her burden, causing 'work, disorder, near-confusion' that wore her out, annoyed and irritated her, and made her pray for the 'silence' that she needed, given her age—she was 72—and her love of a tranquil life.[142] She drew courage, she said, from Verdi's strength.

Verdi's feelings about blood ties and loyalty to one's family are expressed in a letter to his foster-daughter in January 1888. Maria, then the mother of four children, had tried to help a brother who was in trouble; she had also been seeing her own parents and other brothers and sisters, some of whom were living in Busseto, just a few yards from the Carrara house. Verdi wrote:

This being the case, neither your husband nor the Carraras can love and respect that family [the Verdis]; and you had an obligation to keep them as far away as possible and to avoid their disagreeable bickering and terrible sorrows. I know you will say: 'But *my Parents*', '*my blood relatives*', etc. etc. For the love of God, this is sick and stupid sentimentality, which can never produce anything good. Your husband adores you; your grandfather *loves* you. But you should never trust emotions too much.[143]

Because his powerful personality and his need to dominate others sometimes overrode other considerations, he usually got his way. Maria, though, had nothing to be ashamed of, for her grandparents and parents were respected taverners, and her brothers and sisters were farmers, taverners, grocers, teachers, and even members of local government.

By Christmas 1887 Verdi was again in Genoa, waiting for Muzio to arrive with his baggage of theatrical gossip and news. Ricordi, Stolz, and De Amicis were invited for their usual visits; in Milan, Strepponi and Verdi had seen Boito, Giacosa, and Pantaleoni, who was preparing to sing

La Gioconda at the Carlo Felice in Genoa. After Muzio returned from a trip to Rome, Verdi wrote to Tornaghi at Ricordi about a production of *Otello* in Germany, where he feared the impresarios would not be able to provide 'three good singers' instead of artists 'who once were famous and no longer have any voice left'.[144] Also of concern were a pirated production in Amsterdam, where the impresario had had an orchestration made from the vocal score, and a proposed unauthorized production in South America. A proposed English *Otello* had to be abandoned.

The year 1888 brought further deaths, with the Verdis' physician Dr Fedeli, whom they had met at Montecatini, dying in March, as did the Neapolitan writer and librarian Francesco Florimo. When Muzio learned of the death of Margherita Tizzoni Delle Sedie, he withheld the news from Strepponi, who was ill herself in Genoa. All in all, it was a depressing spring. Verdi and Strepponi did not leave for Sant'Agata until the beginning of May.

Things seemed to improve at the villa; and the Verdis took an active role in furnishing the Villanova Hospital, which was nearly ready to open. They went to Montecatini with Stolz and De Amicis for their usual two-week stay in July. Later that month Verdi met Muzio briefly in Milan then returned to Sant'Agata to await him there. In September everyone in Verdi's circle was saddened when Tito Ricordi died, setting off a family squabble that shook the firm. Giulio Ricordi, one of Tito's eight children, was named his father's executor but could not keep peace in his strife-ridden family, whose behaviour he described to Verdi as monstrous. Early in October, Giulio and his wife visited the Verdis at Sant'Agata, where the composer celebrated his seventy-fifth birthday on 9 October. Boito, who was to have come, postponed his visit.

The Villanova Hospital opened on 5 November with the simplest inauguration imaginable, as Verdi and the five members of his administrative commission read the statute and regulations while the secretary took notes. Dr Giuseppe Torre, the local physician, and Sister Maria Broli, who headed the staff, listened.[145] Verdi had had the help of Don Carlo Uttini and the Marchioness Caggiati in choosing the three nuns, who were from the Piccole Figlie dei Cuori Santissimi di Gesù e Maria.[146] The president of the commission was Salvatore Boriani, Mayor of Villanova. The spiritual counsellor was Don Luigi Mari, parish priest. On opening day six patients were admitted; by the end of the week all ten beds were full. Seeing that the hospital was a success, Strepponi described Verdi's act of charity as 'great, humane, and very holy'.[147] The institution's usefulness has increased; it has always been needed, and now has forty beds.

'The Hospital is open and full of patients', Verdi wrote to Piroli, also referring casually to 'the project you know about',[148] his plan to build a rest-home for aged musicians. It was to be patterned on a home for sick and disabled singers that Rossini and his wife had planned. At the end of 1888 Verdi took the first steps in planning his own Casa di Riposo, but it and the construction and maintenance of the Villanova Hospital did not seem be interfere with his other charitable activities. He and his wife went on contributing to the relief efforts for victims of natural disasters and such catastrophes as the fire at the Opéra-Comique in Paris, while helping the local poor with money and gifts of clothing, school-books, hams and sausages, coffins, and circulating libraries. He also sometimes reduced rents significantly or did not collect them. Their support for the nursery-school movement went on as well. By the 1870s Don Carlo, Don Ciriaco, and Egidia Uttini had enlisted their nieces Guglielmina and Giulia in day-care and kindergartens, an enterprise dominated by this family in Parma and Piacenza. Pedrini in Cortemaggiore also continued enjoying the Verdis' dependable and substantial support of the nursery school there. Even twenty years earlier they had been honoured for their assistance to the Asili Centrali in Genoa. It is obvious that Verdi's and Strepponi's gifts to the poor and disadvantaged sometimes proved a burden. She tried to keep some of the Uttinis' letters from Verdi and, on at least once occasion, warned one of the Uttini cousins not to write again for help with their school. To Don Avanzi she confided in November 1888 that Verdi's relatives came up out of the ground like mushrooms after a thunderstorm and that they would like to have the occasional gifts of money become a regular income; but she and her husband continued to give the small gifts to individuals that they had been contributing for years. Don Carlo Uttini had won recognition for his work beyond the frontiers of Italy. In 1880 his *Sillabario intuitivo* was awarded the nation's highest honours at the Rome Exposition.

Among Verdi's many attempts to help individuals with letters of recommendation, that on behalf of the son of his coachman Luigi Veroni ranks high, not because Verdi was successful but because of his long record of employing Veroni and the subsequent history of the family. Veroni worked for the composer for thirty-two years and carried most of the composer's guests, many of them very famous indeed, back and forth

between the railway station at Fiorenzuola and Sant'Agata. As master of
the horse that Verdi fondly called 'my Bucephalus', in a joking reference
to the charger of Alexander the Great, Veroni was one of several employees
who remained with the composer and his wife for decades. Verdi waged
a two-year campaign to have Guglielmo Veroni admitted to Parma Conservatory.[149] The Veroni family now live in the Casa Padronale in Roncole,
where they moved more than sixty years ago. This is the house that
Verdi's grandparents and father leased from the church of La Madonna
dei Prati from 1791 to 1830.[150] As we have seen, Verdi was probably
born here. Among the family's memorabilia is one of Verdi's canes, which
he gave to Luigi Veroni for more than thirty years' service at Sant'Agata.
What Verdi did for this family, and dozens of others who asked for his
help, is the merest token when weighed against the immense picture of
his and his wife's charity, offered over more than half a century. As the
condition of the poor worsened in the 1880s and 1890s, and the revolts of
agricultural labourers continued to rend the fabric of rural society, their
charitable donations became ever more important over the years.

It was not in Verdi's nature to abandon any effort he launched, so he
remained diligent in his oversight of the Villanova Hospital, with which
he was directly involved all the rest of his life. Before and after the
opening, he and Strepponi frequently visited there. Just before Christmas
they moved to Genoa to wait for Muzio and the other year-end regulars as
he fought off a depression that Muzio hoped to be able to dispel. 'Why
can't you be happy? It makes me sad to read about you. You have
everything: domestic happiness, health, honours, money. I hope your
letter of the fourteenth [of December] was just a passing black cloud. On
the evening of the twenty-second we will begin our merry games of
briscola, as I will get there too late to sit down for dinner.'[151] Muzio also
sent news of his niece, whom Verdi and Piroli had helped to place in a
teaching post in Greece, where several other acquaintances of theirs were
living, among them Giorgio Verdi, one of the composer's cousins, and
Livia Zanobini's sister, who had gone to Athens. Verdi's mood was
perhaps influenced by his wife's continuing depression. Four years earlier
she had described her life to Don Avanzi, saying that she lived a lonely
existence and often thought about her earliest years; she wished that the
following decades might have been lived the same way because she was
afflicted by her conclusions about herself and about society which, she
said, she knew far too well. Her soul was sad, dreadfully sad. She often

expressed similar sentiments to other friends. Verdi, on the other hand, seemed absorbed in 1888 with the hospital and in January 1889 with his new enterprise, the Casa di Riposo. He engaged the architect Camillo Boito, brother of the librettist, to help with the purchase of land on which he would later build the Casa. An initial contract between him and Camillo was drawn up by the lawyer Alessandro Dina, one of Verdi's legal advisers.[152] At the same time, the composer was setting to rights some of the problems in the Villanova Hospital. To Boriani on 16 January he said he had heard that the patients were not getting enough food and wine; that the milk, oil, and rice were of poor quality; and that even the destitute were being forced to pay for their relatives' funeral expenses.

This news makes me terribly sad, thinking that I have not achieved the goal that I set for myself when I dedicated a part of my fortune to build this charitable institution. I believed the hospital was well provided for, and there was no need to make rigid economies; but I will tell you the truth: rather than suffer this unhappiness, I would prefer the Hospital be closed and people not talk about it anymore.[153]

He was also trying to stop Boito, Ricordi, and others who were planning a jubilee celebration for him to mark the fiftieth anniversary of *Oberto, conte di San Bonifacio* in November 1889 and a planned revival of *Otello* at La Scala. A controversy had erupted while the revival of *Otello* was still in the planning stage, when the impresario at La Scala suggested the opera needed to be changed. To Ricordi, Verdi wrote: 'Tell Signor Corti that if *Otello* needs *important changes*, he can make them!'[154] And when journalists began to have a field day with the story: 'It wouldn't be so bad if there were not an implication here: that *Otello* needs major changes, and that I, poor schoolboy, bowed before the judgement of the wise men and the infallibility of the Audience! Poor souls! Poor souls! And poor me, too!'[155] He urged Ricordi to monitor rehearsals and sent Muzio to Milan to do what he could; but the illness of the tenor and the shortcomings of the soprano combined to create a mediocre performance, which Verdi did not hesitate to call 'a disaster'.[156] He had foreseen the 'scandal', he said. He had heard that 'It did not seem like the same music'[157] as the *Otello* of the première, perhaps from Muzio, who sent him a report on it. Verdi advised Ricordi and the management to keep the opera off the boards, but La Scala put it back on the calendar after giving Giuseppe Oxilia, the tenor, a two-week sick leave. When another fiasco ensued, Verdi raged to Ricordi: 'Poor *Otello*! Destined this year to experiments by ripped-up throats and the worst provincial screamers!'[158] Boito, who had gone to see *Otello* in March, declared he would not go back again, because the cast was made up of 'cretins' and the tenor Oxilia—'the most wretched beast' he had ever seen in opera—was 'a mad dog'. 'That ass has a good voice, but what an ass! The [soprano] is a well-fed, rotund nonentity, a nothing!'[159]

Verdi also discussed this and future productions of the opera with Muzio, who had been in Naples to hear Durot sing Otello. The two men left Genoa at the end of March, Muzio bound for Paris, Verdi for Sant'Agata. Earlier in the month, while Verdi was with Boito in Milan, the two men began to work on a musical puzzle that the Bolognese musician Adolfo Crescentini had published in the *Gazzetta musicale di Milano*; but Verdi, by mistake, had thrown part of his work on this *scala enigmatica* (enigmatic scale) into the fire. Writing from Genoa, he asked Boito to send him another copy.

You will say that it is not worth the trouble to take time for such foolishness, and you are absolutely right. But what do you expect? When we are old, we become boys again, they say. . . . And furthermore, I believe that this puzzle [*scala*] could be made into a piece with words, for example: An Ave Maria. . . . Another Ave Maria! It would be my fourth! So I could hope to be beatified after I die.[160]

Boito, sending the puzzle, remarked that 'A lot of Ave Marias will be needed so you can get the Holy See to forgive you for Iago's "Credo"'.[161] Out of what seemed a light-hearted exercise came the first piece of Verdi's *Quattro pezzi sacri*.

In April Verdi and Strepponi moved back to Sant'Agata. As the composer had predicted, hunger and desperation afflicted most of the poor in rural areas. Riots in Borgo San Donnino had led to the revocation of civil liberties there in 1886, when carabinieri had been brought in to restore order. Officials in Rome, asked when the measures would be lifted, replied that unrest in the Bassa made the extraordinary controls necessary. Many small worker and farm-labourer organizations were taking part in demonstrations; and when men were arrested in protests, further rage was aroused in peasant homes. Among the many new groups—the Sons of Labour, the Peace League, the Workers League, and the Democratic Circle—members were asking themselves why they had to go on in servitude, why they could not own land, buildings, farm-tools, and the means of production. Property-owners held even their questions to be dangerous and radical. Verdi, too, had come to mistrust the parties of the

BOOK V

left; but compared to many other landlords, he was generous and fair. The estate at Sant'Agata was no Garden of Eden, nor could it be in such critical times; but in the midst of so much misery, Verdi lived by compassion and love, guiding the overseers of his new hospital and planning his next ambitious philanthropic effort.

33

Summer 1889–November 1897

Falstaff

Even though Verdi and Strepponi had been supporting charitable institutions for many years, the Villanova Hospital posed new problems for them, involved, as they were, in the administration. Particularly vexing was the conflict between Boriani, the president, and Don Mari, the parish priest, who provoked gossip by his too frequent visits to the patients and the nuns charged with their care. When the head of their order, Monsignor Agostino Chieppi, complained about mistreatment of his 'little daughters', Verdi wrote to tell Piroli about it: 'Really, he should not have anything to do with this, but the priests stick their noses in everywhere.'[1] At the end of summer, Verdi restored order himself, introducing new regulations at the meeting of his hospital commission. A few minutes before they all sat down, Sister Maria Broli spoke to Verdi about Boriani's meddling. He reassured her, saying he wanted 'only peace and charity' to prevail. At the table, he seated her beside him. Sister Maria reported to Chieppi that Verdi 'always spoke very sweetly' and 'seemed like a father surrounded by his children'.[2] The situation improved when Boriani was replaced by Giacomo Persico, with whom Verdi corresponded for more than ten years.

Keeping abreast in the music business as he oversaw farm operations, the composer often heard from Muzio, who was helping Ricordi by gathering additional evidence to be used in the ongoing litigation between the Italian publisher and his French counterpart, Benoit, over the French rights to *Il trovatore*. At the same time, Ricordi asked Muzio to handle negotiations with Sardou, intended to secure for the firm the operatic rights to his play *Tosca*. Verdi was also kept informed of plans for a London production of *Otello*, which Faccio was to conduct at the Lyceum Theatre. Sceptical over its outcome, he had virtually opposed the idea, although Tamagno and Maurel were in the cast. Verdi also continued to complain about the planned jubilee production of *Oberto, conte di San Bonifacio* at La Scala and other celebratory events. When Ricordi wrote him in May about adding several of his early operas to the popular score series that Casa Ricordi was publishing, the composer said he was against it and protested that he did not even know where the score of *Stiffelio* was. He declared that he would burn all his old scores in an *auto-da-fé* and compose 'hearty' funeral music for them.[3]

In Milan at the end of June, he met Boito and discussed the possibility of writing an opera based on the comic character of Falstaff. As we know from a later article in Ricordi's *Gazzetta musicale di Milano*, the idea of writing a comic work had been in the back of Verdi's mind for years and had occasionally been discussed with friends. In Milan in the summer of 1889, Boito suggested Shakespeare's Falstaff should be the central character and, when Verdi did not discourage him, lost no time in getting a sketch ready.[4] Just after the composer and his wife reached Montecatini, Boito's draft scenario of *Falstaff* reached him, at a moment when Verdi had, with apparent interest, reread *The Merry Wives of Windsor*, *Henry IV, Parts I and II*, and *Henry V*. He cheered his librettist with encouraging words: '*Benissimo*! Benissimo!... No one could have done better than you.'[5] The next day he raised a serious question:

In sketching *Falstaff*, did you ever consider the very large number of years in my age? I know perfectly well that you will answer me exaggerating the state of my health, [saying it is] good, excellent, robust. And that is true. All the same, you will agree with me that I could be accused of great rashness in taking on such a job!—And what if I were not to hold up under the work?!—And if I were not to finish the music? Then you would have wasted so much time and effort for nothing. I would not want that for all the gold in the world.[6]

He was also worried that the new opera would distract Boito from his own *Nerone*, which Verdi often exhorted the younger man to finish. Yet Verdi could not hide his delight at the idea of writing another opera: 'What a joy! To be able to say to the Audience: "WE ARE HERE AGAIN!! COME AND SEE US!!"'[7] In the euphoria of the moment, he then wrote to Boito

Amen; so be it! So let's do *Falstaff*! For now, let's not think of the obstacles, of age, of illnesses! I also want to keep the deepest *secrecy*: a word that I underline three times to tell you that no one must know anything about it!—But wait a minute . . . Peppina knew about it before we did, I think! Don't worry! She will keep the secret. When women have this trait, they have more of it than we do. . . . Anyway, if you are in the mood, then start to write.[8]

At Montecatini, Verdi also encouraged another composer, the Sicilian Giuseppe Auteri De Cristoforo, a young admirer with whom he had begun to correspond in 1885. Originally limiting his advice to remarks about imitating other composers, Verdi had also sent Auteri a musical quotation from *Otello*, in answer to his request for an autograph.[9] He extended a warm invitation to visit Palazzo Doria and seemed genuinely upset when Auteri, who came to Genoa in 1888, did not call on him. 'I know that I have the reputation of being a bear. In spite of that, I have not eaten anyone yet. Let that be a guarantee of security to you.'[10] By then Auteri, overcome with pride at getting letters from 'my Verdi' and 'my maestro', sent one of his own compositions, which Verdi carried in his luggage from Genoa to Sant'Agata without reading. After glancing at it, he wrote to Auteri: 'It seems to me (I always say "It seems to me") that the beginning is better than the rest, which seems a bit loose. Don't pay any attention to these words, which are of no value. I close by again saying that old phrase: don't imitate anyone.'[11]

By mid-July Verdi had news of the London *Otello*, which proved enormously successful. Writing to Faccio, he said he was pleased,

although at my age, and with the present conditions of our music, a success does no good at all. You speak of *the triumph of Italian art*!! You are wrong!! Our young composers are no longer good patriots. If the Germans, starting from Bach, get to Wagner, they are working as good Germans; and that is fine. But we descendants of Palestrina commit a musical crime by imitating Bach, and do something that is useless and even harmful. I know they have spoken very well of Boito, and this gives me the greatest pleasure: praise bestowed upon *Otello* in Shakespeare's native land is worth a great deal.[12]

The composer did pay his own tribute to German music, though, by allowing his name to be added to the honours list of the Beethoven birthplace in Bonn as a festival was being planned. The president of the Beethoven Haus was the violinist Joseph Joachim, whom Verdi may have met in Genoa during his Italian tour several years earlier. To Joachim's letter, the composer answered: 'I cannot refuse the honour that is offered to me. We are talking about Beethoven! Before such a name, we all prostrate ourselves reverently.'[13]

BOOK V

Verdi and his wife returned to Sant'Agata during the third week in July. There they received unsettling news from abroad. Faccio, still in London, was rumoured to be losing his memory and behaving oddly. In Paris, the old comprimario baritone Giacomo Vercellini, the Paolo of the *Simon Boccanegra* première in 1857, had been forced to enter the Réfuge Rossini, after having been helped by Verdi for years.[14] Earlier, one of his and Verdi's mutual acquaintances, Raffaele Scalese, the first Baron Kelbar in *Un giorno di Regno* at La Scala, had died in abject poverty, even though he too received regular subsidies from Verdi.[15] Their desperate plight weighed on the composer as he was considering how to organize his own Casa di Riposo.

It was not until August that Verdi proposed to Boito a solution to Faccio's troubles: 'Help me to do a good act. You know that the post of the director of Parma Conservatory is open. I thought of Faccio.'[16] The previous director, Giovanni Bottesini, had died earlier that year. The stipend of 6,000 lire, supplemented by a housing allowance, would help to cover the conductor's expenses if, as it seemed, he would have to leave La Scala. He could also assume the title of orchestra director at the Teatro Regio and realize an additional 4,000 lire per year. Faccio would be entitled to a pension. Having written to the conductor directly about it, Verdi hoped Boito, 'the oldest and dearest of his friends', would urge him to accept.[17]

Even as he sent this appeal, Verdi reassured Boito that he was composing: 'I hope you are working. More strange still is that I too am working. I am having a great time writing fugues! Yes, Sir! A fugue . . . and a *buffa* fugue . . . that could go very nicely in *Falstaff*. What, a *buffa* fugue you will say? I do not know *how*, nor *why*, but it is a *buffa* fugue.'[18]

Boito, who assured the composer that a comic fugue was just right and that they would find a place to put it, also agreed to try to persuade Faccio to accept the Parma post. Faccio was planning a visit to Sant'Agata, where Verdi could bring his logic to bear, for he believed that the conductor would be dismissed from La Scala that autumn or winter .

In October Verdi went to Milan to sign the contract of sale for a large parcel of land outside Porta Magenta in what is now the northwest part of the city. The purchase was a well-kept secret in a small circle that included Verdi, Camillo Boito, the attorney Dina, and the notary Stefano Allocchio. With this deed, the Casa di Riposo moved one step further toward realization.

Muzio, who had been ill with jaundice in Milan, came to Sant'Agata in

October. Boito brought the first two acts of *Falstaff* to the villa in November. The first act was finished, he said, the second still a work in progress: 'That [second] act has the devil on its back; and when you touch it, it burns,' he had written to Verdi just before his visit.[19] Librettist and composer spent about a week on the opera then and may have met in Milan later that autumn, as Verdi was trying his best to flee the fiftieth anniversary jubilee events that were planned in Busseto, Milan, and Genoa. He and Strepponi moved to Genoa for the winter during the first week in December. As usual, they were joined by Muzio at Christmas, although the trip was an effort for him, as he had just travelled to Paris and back on Ricordi's and Verdi's affairs. Muzio had stopped tinting his hair and moustache with weekly applications of hair dye and had given up smoking. At the end of his visit, he wrote to apologize for not being a livelier companion and again expressed his love for Verdi and Strepponi.[20]

With him gone and Stolz and Ricordi ill in Milan, the composer and his wife fell into 'a black, black, black' depression and were slightly ill.[21] The New Year of 1890 came in with 'complaints and disasters everywhere', Verdi wrote to Ricordi. 'Later there will be abject poverty!! What an ugly year we have begun! And how wretchedly we ended last year!!!'[22] He took a very dim view of two projected productions of the *Messa da Requiem*: 'In Berlin there will be mediocre singers but a good chorus and orchestra. In Verona both will probably be bad.'[23] Yet however dark his mood, he did go on with the new opera.

As 1890 began, Faccio's health was a matter of concern to all who knew him, for he was showing ever more disturbing symptoms of what was later diagnosed as the dementia of latent syphilis. He had prepared *Die Meistersinger* scrupulously but sometimes lost his place in the score. During the third performance he put on his coat and started to leave La Scala before the opera was over and had to be convinced that he had one more act to conduct. In February, when he asked for a two-week leave, the management turned the podium over to Coronaro, the assistant conductor, as the news of Faccio's illness was widely reported in the newspapers, one of which Verdi sent on to Boito.[24] Though he could no longer conduct, Faccio sometimes seemed better, as Boito confided to Verdi.[25] Seeking a cure in the Kraft-Ebbing clinic in Graz, the conductor left Milan, just as Todeschini, the physician who also treated Verdi, Strepponi, and Stolz, let Boito know that Faccio was beyond help. It was rumoured that Faccio had even attacked Boito and had tried to kill himself. Sent home, he soon was in Milan. 'It is better to die', Boito lamented to Verdi.[26] 'It is better to die', Verdi agreed.[27] In mid-April Boito went to Parma to pick up the money owed to Faccio, who had been named director of the Conservatory. He also confided to the institution's authorities the true state of the conductor's health. Verdi, in Genoa with Muzio, offered his own advice in the matter, and, when Boito agreed to serve in Faccio's place, accepting the title of honorary director of the Conservatory and giving the salary to Faccio, praised him: 'You have done very, very well! You will help Art [and] the poor, sick man and have saved the institute from a bad situation.'[28] By filling in, Boito made it possible for Faccio's stipend and benefits to continue.

In spite of the strain on them all, Verdi went on with *Falstaff*, completing the first act before 17 March.[29] At that point, he slowed his pace, although Boito visited him at Sant'Agata in May. The Verdis spent part of the summer with Stolz, who had also been with them at Palazzo Doria that spring and had taken an apartment in Genoa to be able to spend more time there.[30] With her usual visits in December, January, summer, and autumn, she was spending about two months a year with the composer, who also called on her during his visits to Milan. When Stolz went back to Milan after holidaying with them in Montecatini, Verdi sent her and Ricordi two pork shoulders from Sant'Agata, asking her to choose one and give the publisher the other. With them he sent his recipe for cooking them:

1. Put it in lukewarm water for about 12 hours to get the salt out of it.

2. Afterward put it in cold water and boil it over a slow fire, so it will not fall apart, for about three and a half hours, maybe four for the bigger one. To know whether it is fully cooked, stick it with a toothpick and if it goes in easily, the 'shoulder' is cooked.

3. Let it cool in its own broth and serve it. Watch the cooking especially; if it is tough, it is no good; if it is overcooked, it is dry and stringy.[31]

The cheerful humour of August ended when Verdi learned that Muzio was ill in Paris. With a diagnosis of liver trouble, probably caused by chemicals in the hair dye he had used for about twenty years, the conductor expected to recover soon; but his hopes proved vain. Plagued with dropsy, he entered a hospital but asked Verdi to find a nursing home for him in Pisa, where he expected to arrive late in the autumn. The composer replied by return, after having conferred with the surgeon who had operated on Strepponi. He was busy at the same time with the

Villanova Hospital, where Boriani, although no longer mayor, was still the president. Hoping Boriani would resign, Verdi adopted a wait-and-see attitude. He also intervened personally to get a certificate-of-need for a woman from Gaetano Uttini's family, for whom he provided in other ways.[32] From 1890 onwards Persico, the new mayor, to whom Verdi wrote more than 100 letters and notes, remained his trusted mediator and confidant in many of the crises that followed.

When Boito visited in October, he brought bad news about Faccio. Boito himself, ill at ease in his own professional life, with the burden of Parma Conservatory laid on him, was also almost at the end of his four-year affair with Duse.[33] Verdi, in spite of his many worries, had 'accomplished something' on the opera: 'The sonnet in the third act was bothering me; and to get it out of my head, I set the second act aside and, beginning with that sonnet, little by little, one note after another, I got to the end. It is nothing but a sketch! and who knows how much will have to be rewritten! We'll see later on.'[34]

The composer's philosophy of life often led him to believe that little good could ever happen on this earth. 'Whatever is life? When we are young, everything is pleasant, we are carefree, impertinent, proud, and it seems that the world should exist [just] for us. When we are old . . . But never mind these miseries.'[35] So he wrote to Stolz. Piroli was ill; Faccio was mad; Muzio was in a serious condition. Piroli died on 14 November.

Nevertheless, when Strepponi and Verdi visited Milan that month, he seemed happy enough. While there, they invited Boito, Giulio and Giuditta Ricordi, their daughter Ginetta, and their son-in-law to dinner.

Verdi was in a cheerful humour, and . . . has never seemed younger and in better spirits; in his appearance, words, [and] manner he looked like a contented man. When the champagne was served, when everyone was in excellent spirits, Boito rose and, showing that he wanted to propose a toast, said: 'I drink to the health and victories of the Big Belly!' Everyone was surprised; no one understood what Boito was referring to. Ricordi was the most surprised of all. Then Boito went on: 'I drink to the health of *Falstaff*!' Again surprise on Ricordi's part, [for he] still did not understand. But Signora Giuditta Ricordi, who was sitting opposite Signora Giuseppina Verdi, understood, or rather had an intuition about the revelation and, leaning toward Signora Verdi's ear, asked her: 'A new opera?' And Signora Verdi nodded yes.[36]

The next day the news that Verdi was composing another opera was reported in the *Corriere della sera* and in Ricordi's *Gazzetta musicale di Milano*. Verdi, Strepponi, and Boito had kept their secret for almost a year and a half. Even the composer's music-paper had been sent from Paris by Muzio, who may have had some idea of what his maestro was planning: 'It really wouldn't scare me if the paper were to be used for an opera; I would clap my hands with joy,' he had written at the end of January.[37]

The good spirits of the moment were soon dispelled when news came that Muzio had died on 26 November. Verdi was notified by Ricordi's agent in Paris and by Maurel's wife, who had visited him in hospital just a few days earlier. In his will, he left a scholarship for young people to be administered by the Busseto Monte di Pietà, because he wished to follow 'Maestro Verdi's good example'. At the end of the will, a copy of which Verdi received in January 1891, the conductor left a moving last message to his maestro:

I will soon go on to the other world, filled with love and friendship for you and your good, dear wife. I have loved you both, and remember that my faithful friendship never flagged from 1844 until now. Remember me sometime, and goodbye, until we meet—as late as possible—in the other world. Kisses and kisses from your faithful and very loving friend E. Muzio.[38]

Muzio also provided for the destruction of all the letters that Verdi had written to him.

Verdi confided his own sadness to Maria Waldmann, whose letters, he said, were always a consolation for him.

In about fifteen days I have lost my two oldest friends! Senator Piroli, a learned, honest, sincere man, of unmatched rectitude. A faithful friend, steadfast over sixty years! *Dead*!! Muzio, whom you knew when he was the orchestra/director in Paris for *Aida*. A sincere friend, devoted for about fifty years. *Dead*! And both were younger than I!! Everything ends!! Life is a sad thing! I leave it to you to imagine what I felt and what I am feeling! And so I have very little desire to write an opera I have begun but not got very far with. Don't pay any attention to the newspaper gossip. Will I finish it? Or will I not finish it? Who knows! I am writing without any plan, without a goal, just to pass a few hours of the day.[39]

Verdi, who was with Strepponi in Genoa as he wrote this, did not attend Muzio's funeral, which took place in Busseto on 9 December. It is likely that Christmas and New Year's Day 1891 were spent at Palazzo Doria with De Amicis and his wife; Stolz and Ricordi may also have come for a visit. On New Year's Eve Boito wrote from Milan and forwarded to Verdi a humorous letter that he had received from Count Andrea Zorzi,

asking about *Falstaff*. A nobleman from Vicenza, Zorzi had met Verdi in
Venice in 1843 during the rehearsals and performances of *Ernani* at La
Fenice. Although few letters from Zorzi to Verdi survive at Sant'Agata,
their friendship lasted over decades.[40] In 1844 Zorzi had had the handle
of a fine cane engraved with the word *Ernani* and had added all Verdi's
subsequent works to it.[41] At the end of 1890 he had asked Boito for news
of *Falstaff*, leading the librettist to send the letter along to Genoa.

'We have to begin the year smiling', Boito wrote to Verdi, as he
forwarded Zorzi's letter.[42] But Verdi's answer was not likely to encourage
the librettist, Zorzi, Ricordi, or anyone else that was waiting for the new
opera: 'The Big Belly is not moving on. I am upset and distracted. The
terribly sad recent months, the cold now, the holidays, and, and . . . have
thrown me off balance.'[43] He explained to Ricordi that even with the best
will in the world he could not finish in 1891 and admitted that he could
not work as easily as he had years before:

When I was young, I could stay at the desk for ten or even twelve hours, even
when I was slightly ill!! working steadily, and more than once I sat down at work
from four in the morning to four in the afternoon with nothing more than a simple
coffee in my stomach . . . and working right through, without a break. Now I
cannot. Then I was in command of my body and my time. Alas, now I am not.[44]

Boito, who planned to come to Nervi for part of the winter, may have
visited the composer in January.

In spite of his seventy-seven years and the cold, Verdi continued to
travel from Genoa to Milan and Sant'Agata during the winter. Legal
matters relating to the French litigation over *Il trovatore* still claimed his
attention, the situation perhaps being made more complicated because
Muzio's death removed a helpful party from the action. There was a
visit in March from the celebrated poet Giosue Carducci and his young
companion Annie Vivanti. On the day they came to Palazzo Doria,
Strepponi was writing to Marietta Calvi Carrara: 'I'll break off, because
Carducci is just coming in with another poet . . . and, being very curious,
I am running to see him . . . and the young woman poet as well!' He was
small and ugly, Strepponi reported, unpretentious, and almost shy.
'He had extremely expressive eyes that alone indicate his enormous
intelligence! He is Tuscan and naturally speaks Tuscan, very rapidly, in
short bursts. The woman poet is 22, Carducci has given her the passport
to Parnassus; and, as you will understand, this passport is of enormous
value!!'[45]

BOOK V

Annie Vivanti, the London-born daughter of an Italian political exile and his German wife, had sung in Italy and the United States. In 1890 she published her first volume of poetry, for which Carducci wrote a preface.[46] Her own recollections of Verdi, published two years later, portrayed the composer as a lean, restless man who walked back and forth in the grand salon of his apartment 'with long strides', impatiently pushing back locks of his thick, grey hair that fell across his lined forehead. When asked about *Falstaff*, he declared that he was composing it only for his own pleasure, and that it was his last opera. He would have preferred to keep the work a secret but had forgiven 'that Mefistofeles, Boito' for his indiscretion. Ushered into his little studio, which was furnished only with his grand piano, a desk, a reading-stand, and a single chair, Vivanti and Carducci heard a few bars of music, which Verdi played at the young woman's request. Throwing open the french windows that gave on to the grand terrace, he led them outside. The garden below was overgrown and 'abandoned'; the moss-covered fountain had no water in it. Verdi had pots of geraniums and camellias everywhere, though they too seemed neglected. Apparently self-conscious over their straggly condition, the composer went back into the house and brought a pitcher of water for one of them.[47] Carducci seems to have said almost nothing while they were in the house. Asked by Vivanti how he felt about his music taken up by the common people, Verdi declared that it made him very happy. He then turned to Carducci to ask how he would feel if his poetry were to be massacred during public readings in the streets. The poet admitted that he loved the people, though in an idealized way. Verdi, he said, was lucky that his music had become a part of everyday life—the 'nation's life', Carducci said—in Italy. At that moment the composer recalled a moment during the rehearsals of *Nabucco* in 1842, when the theatre carpenters were rebuilding a piece of stage scenery. 'The soloists were singing as badly as they could', Verdi said, although one of those 'soloists', Strepponi, was standing beside him. When the chorus began to run through 'Va, pensiero', though, the theatre became as still as a church, after the first five or six bars. One by one, the stage-hands stopped what they were doing and sat on the steps and sets. Waves of cheers and applause shook the theatre when the chorus ended, as the labourers beat on the stage with their tools to contribute to the ovation.[48]

Vivanti said that when he described this memorable scene, 'his sharp, blue eyes took on a kindly look for a moment, one that we rarely see in them. Usually Verdi looks at the world from beneath his bushy, grey eyebrows with a severe, austere expression, and he rarely speaks of himself. Even with friends, he avoids all gestures that could allow one to have any contact with him that is not formal.'[49] Although she and Carducci also met Strepponi that day, the young poet mentions her only to say that she spoke of the composer's passion for his flowers.

By 1891 Strepponi was plagued with pains and stiffness in her legs from arthritis. He, on the other hand, was in good health and—as Strepponi described him—'younger and quicker on his feet' than a lot of men half his age.[50] While she sometimes had to be carried in a chair in Genoa, he was still taking his daily strolls in the city, with his soft, wide-brimmed black hat on his head and his topcoat thrown over his shoulders. Once in 1889, when the journalist Leone Fortis met him by chance in Genoa station, a Frenchman in the compartment mistook Verdi for the composer's son or young relative. It is to Fortis that we owe a description of his youthful face, good colour, pink cheeks, flashing eyes, smile, and 'kind, calm air' and—traits that almost every writer mentioned—his lively step and decisive movements.[51]

In the spring of 1891 Verdi spent part of his time at Sant'Agata, then brought Strepponi back there at the end of April. Falstaff, he said, was pale and wan: 'Let's hope we can find some good capon to fill up his paunch again! Everything depends on the doctor! Who knows! Who knows!'[52] Addressing Boito, who came to the villa during the third week in May, Verdi seemed to hold out some small hope for the opera; and after the visit, things took a decided turn for the better, even though Verdi and Strepponi had a sick guest, Barberina Strepponi, staying with them. In June Verdi wrote to Boito again: 'The Big Belly is on the road to madness. There are some days when he does not move, he sleeps, and is in bad humour; at other times he shouts, runs, jumps, and tears the place apart; I let him act up a bit, but if he goes on like this, I will put him in a muzzle and straitjacket.'[53]

An overjoyed Boito answered:

Great! Let him do it, let him run; he will smash all the glass and furniture in your room; it doesn't matter much; you will buy more; he will break up the piano; it doesn't matter much; you will buy another one. Let everything be wrecked, so long as the *great scene* gets done. Hurrah!

> *Hit him! Hit him! Hit him! Hit him!!*
> *What pandemonium!!*

But it is a pandemonium that is as bright as the sun and as crazy as a madhouse!! I already know what you are going to do. Hurrah.[54]

709

BOOK V

True to his philosophy that moving around was good for him, Verdi took Stromponi to Milan at the end of June, when an official announcement was made that the composer would order the building of 'an Institute for a home for poor musicians who are old and infirm'.[55] At the beginning of July they went to Montecatini again, almost certainly with Stolz.

At home again in late July, Verdi read of Faccio's death, which moved him to write a magnificent letter of condolence to Boito, whom he praised for his extraordinary loyalty to the conductor. Ever concerned for his maestro, Boito had sent Verdi a telegram to Montecatini but had had it returned, as the composer had already left. Faccio was resting in peace, Boito said, and had 'returned to the eternal normality of souls and things. Only death could cure him; and death truly has cured him.'[56] With Faccio dead, the City of Parma tried to persuade Boito to remain as director of the Conservatory, but he was no longer willing to occupy the position. Armed with a letter from Boito, the composer Giuseppe Gallignani visited Verdi at Sant'Agata in September, hoping for support in his own campaign for the post. With Boito declaring that he would be a good man for the Conservatory, Verdi helped the candidate as much as he could, and Gallignani was appointed.

Denying a report that he had finished the opera, Verdi simply told Boito that he was still working on it and would tackle the first part of Act III next. Boito may have come to Sant'Agata in October; in any case he and the composer met again in November, for the regular pattern of the Verdis' lives was changed when they spent a month at the Grand Hôtel de Milan. Before leaving the villa, Verdi had had the satisfaction of seeing some of the problems of the Villanova Hospital resolved. Boriani had resigned as president, and the physician had been replaced, opening the door to the 'silence, peace, and harmony' that the institution's founder so ardently desired.[57] In May Persico, whom Verdi trusted, was named president. Verdi was 'happy and contented' with the nuns, whom he had praised to the Mayor during one of his visits to Villanova that spring.[58] When Persico tried to resign as Mayor at the end of 1891, Verdi persuaded him to stay on.

Arriving in Genoa in mid-December, Verdi and Strepponi planned to stay for the winter. On New Year's Day 1892 they were both ill, she confined to bed with nausea and chest congestion, he kept in the house with a severe cough. More than three weeks passed before the composer felt comfortable enough to write to Persico and say he was finally able to leave the house for carriage-rides. The peace won the year before in

710

Villanova had not lasted, the parish priest having provoked a fresh crisis. He was also about to ask for a fourth nun to be added to the staff, an idea Verdi vetoed, asking Persico to 'rein in' the trouble-maker.[59] Determined to keep control of the situation, he promised to come to the country, even in the middle of winter, while still recovering from a three-week illness. When he wrote this, he was 78 years old and busy with drafting additional rules: the priest should 'go to the Hospital when he is called there on religious duties . . . and nothing more'.[60]

Lamenting that he had lost almost two months of work in Genoa, Verdi wrote to Boito, who had also had influenza, that he and Strepponi were still feeling the after-effects of a sickness that left him too weak to work for more than a half-hour at a time. He also complained about the hated wind in Genoa, which 'smashes my brain and drives thorns into my throat'.[61] He said he would settle for an even worse climate, just to get away from it. Yet he kept at the task of scoring the first act of *Falstaff*, which, he wrote to Boito, was finished in mid-April.

Verdi surprised the music world that spring by agreeing to conduct the Prayer from Rossini's *Mosè* at a concert for the Rossini Commemoration, although it was an ungrateful task that he said he wanted to refuse. Among members of the Committee whom he knew were Count Zorzi; the conductor Edoardo Mascheroni, who had taken Faccio's place at La Scala; and Muzio's former colleague Carlo D'Ormeville.

'Unflagging admirer of Rossini's genius, I have accepted the invitation extended by this Committee, even though my presence here were to be as useless as Donizetti's was useful, when he conducted the première of the Stabat [Mater] in Bologna. Happy, none the less, to have paid this tribute of admiration,' he wrote, as he asked Ricordi to send him *another* copy of the score and the printed edition of the Prayer.[62] Yet he did not stop complaining.

No greater sacrifice could have been asked of me. This exhibition of myself (prettied up as much as you like) is still a theatrical stunt, a really stagy thing that repels me very, very much! But I swear, counter-swear, and swear again that (since there are not two Rossinis) I will never [again] make this kind of sacrifice for anyone, not for anything in the world, not for any country.[63]

He got ready for two rehearsals in Milan and ordered four harps—'at least'—for the orchestra. The piece, he said, was 'sublime' and had to be performed 'sublimely'. Because Strepponi was ill, she had to stay in Genoa—'weak, tired all the time, exhausted, . . . lonely, in a very sad mood'.[64] But her energetic husband conducted his part of the concert at La Scala on 10 April and was back at Palazzo Doria the next day, complaining of nothing more serious than a bit of fatigue.

From his writing-desk there, Verdi had to reply to a letter from the German conductor Hans von Bülow, who had inveighed against him in the past and was now apologetic and repentant; Bülow explained that he had been blinded by his fanaticism, his 'ultra-Wagnerian' stance. He had begun to study *Aida*, *Otello*, and the *Messa da Requiem*; a performance of the Mass had moved him to tears. 'Now I admire you, I love you! Will you forgive me, will you use the sovereign's right to grant pardon?' He ended: 'Long live VERDI, the Wagner of our dear allies!'[65]

'He is decidedly mad,' Verdi confided to Ricordi,[66] although he sent the German musician a courteous note of thanks, which Boito praised as 'extremely noble and very beautiful'. To his maestro, the librettist remarked on Verdi's gift for sounding 'the right note at the right moment', which he described as 'the great secret of art and life'.[67]

Streamponi and Verdi moved back to Sant'Agata in May, then spent time at Tabiano in June, visited Milan for three days on the way to Montecatini and took the waters there in July. Stolz was with them, as usual; and on 10 July they were joined by the mezzo-soprano Giuseppina Pasqua, who had sung Eboli in the revised *Don Carlo* at La Scala in 1882 and was being considered for the role of Quickly in *Falstaff*. Verdi read her the entire text and asked her to sing some of her part. After the reading, he seemed favourably impressed with this 'intelligent' woman, for whom he was disposed to steal some of the lines belonging to Alice Ford and Meg Page, so as to flesh out her part a bit. As he considered Masini for the role of Fenton, Tetrazzini was suggested for Alice, but by 14 July the composer was leaning toward Emma Zilli, whom he proposed to coach himself for her audition. Seemingly tireless, he notified Ricordi of his schedule:

We will stay here until the middle of the next week; then we will go to Sant'Agata, where we will stay two or three days. I could then go to Genoa for my business matters and come back through Milan, where I could hear Zilli. I could confer with Boito, and we could decide whether it will be possible to give [*Falstaff*]. Is that all right with you?[68]

Supposedly on 'holiday' at Montecatini, Verdi wrote to Casa Ricordi on 12 and 14 July about Pasqua, Masini, and other singers under consideration, and he promised to write again on the fifteenth. (He wrote himself to

Maurel about the title role.) Again at home, he wrote on the third, fifth, fourteenth, seventeenth, twenty-second, and twenty-third of August.— Just to the publisher! He also expressed his concern over Boito's *Nerone* again, after young Pietro Mascagni, confident after the huge success of his *Cavalleria Rusticana* at the Teatro Costanzi in Rome in 1890, stated publicly that he was thinking about writing a *Nerone* himself: 'Yes, *Nerone*, for which the respected M[aestro] Boito is giving me a lot of time.'[69] When Verdi read his remarks in a Genoese newspaper, he sent the clipping to Boito, urging him to reply to the 'impertinent' declaration by announcing that his own opera would be ready for La Scala in 1894;[70] but nothing, it seemed, could speed Boito's creative process. Verdi's greatest worry grew from the pressure being exerted on all sides concerning performances. La Scala claimed to have the 'right' to give the première, and Maurel and his wife made unreasonable demands based on their belief that the role 'belonged' to the baritone, and that he should be paid royally for singing it. At the end of August the composer stood his ground, frightening Ricordi by ordering the firm to suspend all negotiations with the artist.

And he! Who is he? Nothing like this ever happened to me before in fifty years of life in the theatrical galleys! . . . You must not hesitate and really must publish Maurel's demands, with my telegram [to you], and add *because of that, Falstaff cannot be given.* . . . Cards on the table. No concessions! When we are pushed to this point, we have to break off everything.[71]

And the next day:

Don't hesitate a moment in breaking off the negotiations. My self-respect has been too injured by Maurel's proposals. What? A singer, no matter who, will come into my study and grab an opera of mine that is not yet finished and say to me, 'I will perform your opera, but afterward I want to be the first one to sing it in the major theatres . . . London, Madrid, etc.' I don't even agree to his terms for the money. One can say that this is not my business, [but] I don't want people to say that the management lost money on a new opera of mine. . . . I won't even allow the 10,000 lire for the rehearsals!! It is too, too much!! What a precedent!! . . . This is horrible.[72]

On 1 September Verdi sat down and drafted a set of conditions governing the production, entering them into his letter-book. A slightly modified final version of the terms was sent off to Ricordi the same day: he was not obligated to give *Falstaff* anywhere that 'others' wanted to produce it; the artists should not be paid exorbitant fees nor be paid for the rehearsals. If he decided to make changes in the score, he would not allow the baritone to put pressure on him, saying 'I don't have time to wait, and I *want* to do the opera in Madrid and London.' In conclusion, 'I simply demand to be the master of my own stuff and not ruin anyone. If anyone were to create a dilemma, [saying] "Either accept this condition or burn the score," I would light the fire right away, and I myself would put Falstaff and his big belly on the pyre.'[73]

Worse followed, when Maurel's wife retreated to France and wrote to Verdi, claiming that Luigi Piontelli, the impresario of La Scala, of whom the composer disapproved, had agreed to give Maurel forty performances in Milan, Rome, and Florence. 'If this is true,' Verdi wrote to Ricordi, 'I have nothing else to say to you, except send me back the first act of *Falstaff* and never mention it again. . . . I will never, never, never accept these conditions.'[74]

Within hours Mme. Maurel was in full retreat, and her husband was on his way to Sant'Agata to speak to Verdi directly. 'I am expecting the god right away!', Verdi said; then: 'It is four o'clock, and the god has got here. Anyway, to avoid the annoyance of talking about the score, I will tell him that it is no longer in the Maestro's hands, but is at the publishers.'[75] Verdi confided to Stolz that he had 'spent a week in hell' because of Maurel.

His demands were so outrageous, exorbitant, [and] incredible that there was nothing else to do but stop the entire project. Four thousand lire a night! Fee of 10,000 lire for the rehearsals! And he to have the sole right to perform *Falstaff* in Florence, Rome, Madrid, America, etc. Then I unsheathed my claws and said, 'The opera is mine, and I do not permit anyone to have rights over my property. I am not willing to agree that you should be paid for the rehearsals, something that has never been done before; I don't want an impresario, not even Piontelli, to be ruined because of an opera of mine.'[76]

Secure in his rights and—as he said—'in my own house', he won.

On 13 September, as he was on a routine business trip to Piacenza, he met Ricordi's representative in the railway station and handed over the score of the third act. Back home, he checked the proofs of the libretto, while planning the scenery according to the way he had imagined it as he was composing. 'I won't approve anything unless I am absolutely convinced about it all.'[77] His sole concession was to agree to give *Falstaff* at La Scala in the Carnival season of 1892–3, provided the company suited him. Although a tentative date of early February was mentioned by the composer, he stipulated that the entire theatre would have to be available to him for rehearsals from 2 January 1893 until the first night, and that he could withdraw the opera even after the dress rehearsal: 'I will leave the theatre, and [Ricordi] will have to take the score away.'[78]

Just before his seventy-ninth birthday, Boito and Giulio Ricordi brought models of the sets and props to Sant'Agata for Verdi's approval. Prepared by the La Scala designer Adolf Hohenstein according to Boito's and Verdi's recommendations, the miniature of the entire production had been planned to accommodate the action as Verdi, its director, envisaged it. He set *Falstaff* up on the billiard-table in the great central room at Sant'Agata and satisfied himself that it worked. After both Boito and Ricordi had gone, Verdi celebrated his birthday with members of his family, then accompanied Streponi to Cremona, left her for her usual autumn visit with her sister, and went on to Milan for a three-day stay that was dedicated at least in part to making last-minute changes in the libretto and score. Knowing that he would be in the opera-house for the whole of January, he and Streponi went to Genoa at the end of October that year. But not even the work on *Falstaff* kept the composer from monitoring his rent receipts—all rents were payable on 11 November, the Feast of St Martino (traditionally the worst day of the year for the poor)—and the management of the Villanova Hospital, where for the first time everything was running smoothly. In a moment of sentiment he defended the nuns to Persico and claimed no harm was done if they were 'even a bit too much attached to religion'. He found them 'disciplined, sweet, mild-mannered, [and] full of love for the ill'.[79]

Suffering from a sore throat in Genoa, he protested against the weakest member of his *Falstaff* cast, the tenor Edoardo Garbin, whom he was coaching at Palazzo Doria, and about whom he had almost nothing good to say. He authorized the German translation of the libretto, while reminding his publisher that he retained the rights to the French translation.

The schedule of La Scala, announced on 7 December, thoroughly offended Verdi when he saw the words 'either a revival of *Tannhäuser* or *Falstaff*'. Denouncing both his publisher and the management, he said: 'Bad . . . bad . . . bad . . . bad. No, no, either one or the other! Decide at once!' And of the proposed date for the première, which coincided with the anniversary of the world première of *Otello*: 'Never, never! I don't want these anniversaries: they are real circus acts!' 'Everything else' was 'bad'—he used the adjective eight times in the letter.[80]

As he was coaching Garbin, Zilli, and Antonio Pini-Corsi in Genoa,

BOOK V

Verdi warned Ricordi that 'the Bear', his *alter ego*, might spring out at any time and attack someone, perhaps his singers. Zilli, he said, had a 'ferocious drive' to learn; but Garbin, always happy to get out of rehearsing, 'doesn't know anything and will know very little [more]'.[81]

Christmas and New Year's Day 1893 were spent in Genoa, where Verdi and Strepponi made their way through a panettone that Ricordi had sent. They then took the train to Milan, where Giuseppe Spatz, the opera-loving owner of the Grand Hôtel de Milan, had prepared their suite, which Verdi later described as 'the most expensive' in the building.[82] Just down Via Manzoni, Patti had taken a suite at the Grand Hôtel Continental and was preparing to sing *La traviata* at La Scala while *Falstaff* was in rehearsal.

These were exciting weeks in Milan. Tickets for *La traviata* and *Falstaff* were being sold on the black market at exorbitant prices as groups of fans followed Patti from the Continental to La Scala and spied on Verdi as he left the Grand Hôtel de Milan. At the end of a rehearsal on 25 January, Verdi paid a call on the soprano, who had enjoyed a triumph as Violetta and was signing her letters 'the Queen of Milan'. She wrote to a colleague in England that Verdi 'is such a *wonderful* man, 80 years of age and only looks 60, he is *much* younger looking than Gladstone, and is as jolly and gay as a lad.[83] Her success in *La traviata* generated so much demand for it that she had to cancel a planned performance of *Il barbiere di Siviglia* and add another evening of the Verdi work. Out of gratitude, 'dear, darling Verdi' gave her his portrait just before she left for Nice, inscribing it 'To the marvellous artist Adelina Patti'.[84] Fifteen years later she proudly published the photograph in the *Strand Magazine* with her reminiscences.[85]

Verdi rehearsed *Falstaff* from 4 January, when he began piano rehearsals with the full cast, into February. According to accounts in Milanese newspapers, orchestra rehearsals began in the theatre either 22 or 23 January. Many changes and corrections made by him are found in a bound set of proofs that Ricordi sent for use during these rehearsals. They are now in Milan Conservatory, having come from Mascheroni's collection.[86] Strepponi wrote to Barberina about the 'letters, requests of all kinds, . . . pests, admirers, friends, and enemies, the real musicians, who would like to convince others that that is what they are, [and] evil-tongued windbags'. She also remarked on the extraordinary demand for tickets. After hearing a rehearsal, she said: 'If I must make a judgement using my head and my impression [of the opera], it seems to me to be a new kind of event, indeed, the date of a new art, music, and poetry!

We shall see what the great consensus, the respectable audience, will say!'[87] Boito too was convinced that *Falstaff* was 'an extremely new art form'.[88]

Verdi's comic masterpiece was finally staged on 9 February 1893, after closed dress rehearsals, from which he excluded even Europe's most respected music critics. His cast included Maurel as Falstaff; Pini-Corsi as Ford; Garbin as Fenton; Zilli as Alice; Adelina Stehle as Nannetta; Virginia Guerrini as Meg; Pasqua as Quickly; and Giovanni Paroli, Paolo Rossetti, and Vittorio Arimondi as Caius, Bardolfo and Pistola. Mascheroni conducted it before a distinguished audience that included Princess Letizia Bonaparte; Carducci; the Minister of Public Education, Ferdinando Martini; all the city councillors of Milan; critics from Europe and the United States; Puccini, who had just come from the successful world première of his *Manon Lescaut* at the Teatro Regio in Turin; Mascagni, who was still enjoying his triumph with *Cavalleria rusticana*; the librettists Boito and Giacosa; famous singers such as Stolz and Waldmann; and the artist Boldini, who had come from Paris, as he also had for *Otello*. The evening, a grand gala, celebrated Verdi in his eightieth year. Two encores were demanded, the quartet of the four women in the first act and Maurel's 'Quand'ero paggio del duca di Norfolk', which the baritone later recorded. Ovations for Verdi, his conductor, and his cast lasted for almost half an hour. The Minister of Education presented the composer with greetings from King Umberto I, to whom Verdi wrote:

Majesty!

With my heart deeply touched, I, artist and citizen of Italy, send Your Majesties the King and Queen of Italy my feelings of gratitude for the very high and unexpected honour that the royal Word brings me.

Your very devoted Giuseppe Verdi.[89]

At the end of the evening, after he, his artists, and Boito had taken curtain-calls, Verdi, Strepponi, and the librettist slipped out a side door of La Scala into Via dei Filodrammatici, where a carriage was waiting; but when they got to the Grand Hôtel de Milan, they were greeted by the same pandemonium that had reigned after *Otello*. Dignitaries waited inside the lobby; the flower-decked salon of the composer's suite was decorated with a bronze wreath, a gift of Spatz, who had had many of its leaves engraved with the names of Verdi's operas but had left some of them blank! To satisfy the mob outside, Verdi and Boito had to make appearances on the balcony. An unidentified writer who was with them reported that the composer was 'happy and satisfied: his beautiful face was bright with a smile. Verdi gladly received the congratulations of his friends, and did not forget anyone who was there. He was overjoyed to see Carducci and spent time talking with him.'[90] Nowhere is there a hint that the composer ever showed fatigue or exasperation during the taxing month before the *Falstaff* première. Instead, several men of science published articles on his extraordinary physical strength, energy, and soundness of mind.

According to his old custom, Verdi stayed with his opera until the end of the third performance, when he said goodbye to them all. Several months later he wrote to the soprano Zilli about his sorrow and regret that evening:

Do you remember the third *Falstaff*?!!! . . . I took my leave of you all; and you were all somewhat moved, especially you and Pasqua. Imagine what my greeting implied, since it meant: '*We will never meet again as artists*!!' . . . It is true that we saw each other after that, in Milan, in Genoa, in Rome; but memory carried us back always to that third evening, which meant: '*Everything is finished*!!' Lucky you who still have such a long career ahead.[91]

In the days after the première, he and his wife were inundated with 'letters, telegrams, photographs to be signed, French and Italian business-men, etc.'.[92] Predictably, the unsolicited librettos began to roll in too, for Verdi sometimes got so many of them that he considered them 'an avalanche, a flood' and kept them stored in a bag apart from his other mail.[93] During his stay in Milan he was honoured by an art organization called the Famiglia Artistica, which invited him to an exhibition of paintings and sculpture, where Giacosa presided over the reception for him. Two newspapers printed a story saying that he was about to be named the marquis of Busseto, a prospect so appalling that he telegraphed the Minister of Public Education to ask him to do everything possible to prevent it. It was not true, the minister assured him, adding that when the King saw the item in the papers, he laughed about it, although he regretted the embarrassment it had caused. 'The man who is the King of Art in the world today cannot become the marquis of Busseto in Italy,' Verdi was told.[94]

When Verdi sent the complete copy of his autograph score to Casa Ricordi, he inserted in it a little note that he had written on his letter-paper:

Le ultime note del *Falstaff*
Tutto e finito!

718

> Va, va, vecchio John . . .
> Cammina per la tua via
> finche tu puoi . . .
> Divertente tipo di briccone
> Eternamente vero, sotto
> maschera diversa, in ogni tempo,
> in ogni luogo!!
> Va, cammina, cammina
> Addio![95]

(The last notes of *Falstaff*. Everything is finished! Go on, go on, old John . . . Go on down your road as far as you can . . . Entertaining sort of rascal eternally true, beneath different masks, all the time, everywhere!! Go, go on, go on Addio!)

As he and his wife left Milan on 2 March, it seemed this was truly farewell. Dreadful regret, which, he confessed to Ricordi as he wrote from Genoa, was so painful that he could not even think about it:

Otherwise, I will fly to Milan in a balloon to beg my dear Merry Wives and Big Belly and the Men to start rehearsing again!! It was just exactly two months ago today, the third, that we had the first rehearsal!!! Everything ends!! Alas, alas! too sad!! This thought is too sad!! . . . It is all Big Belly's fault! . . . What madmen!! Everyone . . . He, You, You, You, You. Everything on earth is a joke.[96]

But, Verdi admitted, the excitement was not over, as Boito joyously proclaimed that all the Milanese were becoming citizens of Windsor, with La Scala registering notable box-office figures.

From this transfusion of happiness, strength, truth, light, [and] intellectual health shall come a great good for art and the public. . . . Giulio and I are convinced that this time your presence [in Rome] is essential for many reasons. . . . A very new art form such as *Falstaff* must not be abandoned by its creator after the first experiment, even though this produced prodigious results.[97]

Verdi arrived at the Hotel Quirinale in Rome with a grand entourage that included Strepponi, Stolz, Boito, and Giulio and Giuditta Ricordi. On 14 April King Umberto received him in audience; on the same day, the City Council voted to give him honorary citizenship of Rome. A day later *Falstaff* was given at the Teatro Costanzi, again under Mascheroni, who had brought his leading singers to the capital two weeks before. As the performance began, Queen Margherita was seated in a box near the stage. Unannounced, the King arrived; and at the end of the second act, he called Verdi into the royal box, took his hand, asked him to stand on his right, and then presented him to the audience, which honoured the composer with a long ovation. The King then walked with Verdi to the Queen's box and presented him to her. During the interval Verdi was also given the parchment of Roman citizenship, which the Mayor awarded. With the sovereigns, dozens of royal and noble families, and all Rome's national government and city officials in the audience, this grand gala at the Teatro Costanzi represented a national recognition and apotheosis of Verdi that had never been tendered him before. On the following evening, the orchestra of the Costanzi, under Mascheroni's baton, gave a concert in his honour on the terrace above the entrance to the theatre; thousands of people crowded the streets around the opera house and Verdi's hotel, to get a glimpse of him, as he appeared to thank the musicians and his admirers. At the end of this homage, a human touch: when Verdi, Strepponi, and Stolz got to the railway station on their way home, Mascheroni had to lend Verdi 100 lire to buy his tickets! Later he and the conductor laughed together over the incident. Verdi's high spirits are reflected in his letter of 23 April to Mascheroni.

Ah! Ah! Ah! Ah! Ah! Ah! When I read your letter, I, too, sang as the Merry Wives sang! Poor Farfarello! In addition to all the irritations and work, the danger of losing 100 lire as well! Ah! Ah! Ah! Ah! I telegraphed right away to Giulio, who telegraphed right away to Nuti, who will perhaps already have settled the debt.

So be it! . . . And we? And art? What 'we', what 'art!' . . . We? Poor supers with the job of beating the bass drum until they say to us 'Shut up over there'.

Tutto nel mondo è burla! [All the world's a jest!]

Ah! Ah! Ah!

Give my greetings to everyone on-stage who asks about me! . . . maybe you won't give my greetings to anyone.

I won't pay you any compliments, because I already have done so. I won't say 'Thanks' because I hope to make more trouble for you in the future. Forgive me.[98]

At the end of April Verdi confided to Giulio Ricordi that he was glad to have put the chaos of Rome behind him; but he still was following the fortunes of his new opera almost daily.

An Integrated Life

'I am at Sant'Agata, and I can draw a deep breath,' Verdi wrote to Mascheroni on 7 May. 'But what am I saying? I will have so much to do here, too, before getting things in order. It is fate! Every man has a destiny: one to stay on the breast all his life; one to be a cuckold; one to be rich; one to be poor; I, with my tongue [hanging out] like a mad dog, to work all the time until the last blow falls.'[99] Nearing 80, he seemed as energetic as ever, driven, as before, by his need for action. The company from Rome had gone on to Venice, where it performed at the Teatro La Fenice in May. A report on the company, and on arguments over casting, came from Pini-Corsi, whose wife was about to be replaced with a soprano whom Verdi called 'a big chunk of meat'.[100] Both Verdi and Ricordi may have intervened in the matter. Verdi, apologizing for answering with such a short letter, said that he was overwhelmed with work.

For the last four months I . . . I really did not sing, but I have been dancing the tarantella every minute, and the performance is not over yet. [The disputes between singers] are foolish enough to make the chickens laugh! Oh, singers are *Great Big Babies*!! Or should I say 'We are'? But I have the good luck to be 80 years old![101]

Even at Sant'Agata he was not left in peace, for two men from Trieste brought Verdi a gift of poems written in his honour and an album signed by thousands of admirers. Mascheroni reported that the performances of *Falstaff* at the Teatro Grande were a 'great triumph',

not what they call a success, but a delirium, an unbelievable enthusiasm, an apotheosis of your (for the moment) last work. I don't know how to describe last evening's gala to you. . . . My orchestra accomplished miracles and it, too, enjoyed a huge success. Encores for the quartet, Ford's monologue, and 'Quand'ero paggio' was repeated four times.[102]

With good reason, Verdi was hardly ever in better humour than after *Falstaff*, when his letters burst with laughter, and remarks like his phrase to Mascheroni: 'What marvellous comedies are born all the time in the theatre and outside it too.'[103] And in mid-May jokingly: 'Now I am terribly busy with an opera that has twelve acts and a prologue and an overture as long as all Beethoven's nine symphonies together; and another prelude for each act with all the cellos and double basses . . . playing a modern melody that doesn't have either a beginning or an end and hangs in the air like Mohammed's tomb.'[104] He said he was looking for a way to have the singers imitate the sound of cymbals being banged together. Later in May he approved a production of *Otello* in Italian in Monte Carlo, with the soprano Ericlea Darclée as Desdemona, and followed the fortunes of the

Falstaff tour, which went on to Vienna and Berlin. 'After the fifth or sixth performance, send me some information about the box-office,' he asked.[105]

The time was not without its sorrows, for neither Strepponi nor her sister was well. Both Vigna and his young son had died just before *Falstaff* went into rehearsal; Catalani and Ghislanzoni died shortly after Verdi got back to the country. Having followed Catalani's carreer, Verdi had had him as his guest in Genoa while Catalani was producing *La Wally* at the Teatro Carlo Felice in the season of 1892–3. Now he expressed his regret over the young musician's untimely death, writing to Mascheroni in August 1893: 'Poor Catalani! A fine man! an excellent musician! What a pity! What a pity!'[106] When he was told about Ghislanzoni's fatal illness in July, Verdi ordered Ricordi to send him 200 lire 'as quickly as possible'.[107] In the summer he, Strepponi, and Stolz went to Montecatini; then Verdi, after a short trip to Genoa, had Mascheroni as his guest at Sant'Agata. There they discussed several proposed productions, among them a *Falstaff* in Paris and another tour of the opera, an *Otello* planned for Belgium, and the new season at La Scala, where Mascheroni was to prepare *Die Walküre*. By early September Boito was ready to bring his French translation of *Falstaff* to the villa, where he wanted to go over it surrounded by what Verdi called 'the mad pleasures of Sant'Agata'.[108] Ricordi was already pressing Verdi to go to France, but Verdi protested that he was too old to go back to France again: 'Seriously, I also add that I do not feel able to start out on huge projects! People will say that others can help me. No, no, this is not possible, especially in France. . . . So don't count on me.'[109]

Verdi celebrated his eightieth birthday at Sant'Agata in October, again honoured by his King, as Umberto I praised the 'glorious and flawless life' of his famous subject.[110] In reply, the composer expressed his gratitude to the King and acknowledged that 'The grateful old artist bows and thanks Your Majesty.'[111] As greetings came from all over the world, Verdi tended to the farm and the Villanova Hospital, where order reigned, thanks largely to Persico. '[Verdi] would write letters of recommendation to generals and ministers on behalf of him and his relatives, as when he turned to Di Rudini, then the head of the government, to ask for the decoration of Cavalier for him. On his side, Persico showed his devotion by sending flowers, plants, and wild game frequently.'[112] Turning to the project of the Casa di Riposo, Verdi asked Boito to get information from his brother Camillo on the actual cost of maintaining a healthy man or woman in institutions like the Pio Albergo Trivulzio in Milan, which had been the city's most famous poor house and hospital since the 1100s. The cost, like that of the poor house in Genoa, was 345 lire per year.[113]

While he was still at Sant'Agata, Verdi heard from one of his regular correspondents, the composer Marco Enrico Bossi, who had been a friend of Muzio as well. Sending his greetings at the beginning of October, Bossi enclosed one of his compositions, a violin sonata that he had dedicated to the young violinist Teresina Tua, whom Verdi knew. Swearing, as always, that he had no faith at all in individuals' judgements about music, Verdi did admit that he and Boito had looked at the piece together and that they 'admired' it, although he felt that there was too much dissonance in it. 'You could answer me, saying "Why not? Dissonance and harmony are [both] essential elements in music; out of personal preference I use the former, etc." And you would be right. On the other hand, why should I be wrong?'[114] Another composer who benefited from Verdi's advice was Auteri di Cristoforo, to whom he had written twice in May, to say that he was 'half-dead with fatigue' after the *Falstaff* productions.[115] In spite of that, Verdi sent his opinion of a work that Auteri had asked him to review:

The orchestration has very beautiful timbres. There is too much emphasis on the harps, which play from the beginning to the end and could become monotonous. The harmony is a bit contorted and those semitonal progressions go on for too long. The sung passages with the chorus are fine. At the thirty-fifth bar, it would be better to take out those three 'si' for the second soprano and write it like this: [*Here Verdi offered his own version of the line*].[116]

When he heard again from Auteri in mid-September, Verdi firmly criticized the Ave Maria that the Sicilian composer had sent:

What can I tell you? I don't like religious things treated that way. The solos for the instruments disturb, distract, and take away the right colour . . . Surely I am wrong. Famous composers have done what I should not want to do. So I am wrong! I saw my name written at the end of your piece. Thank you, but be careful that this is not a dedication, if you were to print the work. For thirty or forty years now I have not accepted dedications.[117]

With Strepponi, he moved to Genoa during the first week in November, and from there he tackled the question of the concealed orchestra, about which Mascheroni had asked him.

The invisible orchestra! It is such an old idea that everyone, or almost everyone, has dreamed about it. I, too, would like the theatres' orchestras to be invisible, but not [just] by half. I would like it *completely out of sight.* . . . But if the *completely invisible* orchestra is not possible, as is demonstated by not just the Opéra, [but] many German theatres, even Munich and Bayreuth (I repeat *completely*) all the changes that you will make are childish, they have nothing to do with art; and, alas, I think that in thirty years people will laugh at our discoveries.[118]

If followed to their logical conclusion, he said, some of these changes would lead to the complete elimination of the conductor. Mascheroni, whom Verdi called his 'dear Farfarello', laughed with Ricordi over the letter, as he was preparing *Die Walküre* at La Scala, where the opera was staged on 26 December. Reports about it reached Verdi from both Boito and Ricordi.[119]

A planned visit from Boito was postponed from Christmas Eve to New Year's Eve, and then was cancelled completely as the librettist became involved in a controversy that almost ended in a duel. The protagonists of the drama were the English composer Frederic Cowen; the music-publisher Edoardo Sonzogno, an enemy of Ricordi and publisher of Mascagni and Leoncavallo; and Boito himself, who was attacked by Sonzogno over a letter that he wrote to Cowen. In it, Boito said that Sonzogno represented neither the courtesy, the intellectual range, nor the good faith of the Italian people.[120] Foolishly, Cowen published the letter in England, provoking Sonzogno to call Boito 'a coward' in a newspaper. On 12 December Boito went to Naples, where Sonzogno was staying, to engage him in a duel, leaving his brother and friends behind. Camillo Boito followed at once, though, on another train. In Genoa, Verdi waited anxiously for the news. The duel was delayed initially because Sonzogno's seconds refused to meet with Boito's seconds. When new seconds were named, they reached an agreement among themselves, signing a document that stated that Boito's letter and Sonzogno's telegram were not worth duelling over; the resolution may have so infuriated Boito that he smashed everything he could in his hotel room and fell exhausted on the sofa afterwards. The next day he started back to Nervi; but when he got off the train in the Genoa station, Verdi was waiting for him. He invited Boito to come to Palazzo Doria—a few yards away—to recover his calm, but after a five-minute visit in the station Boito went on to Nervi, from where he wrote Verdi that same day, in part to answer a telegram that the older composer had also sent him. When he got to his hotel, he learned that Verdi had *also* gone to the station the day before in the hope of finding him, believing that Boito would arrive on the twentieth. 'Yes, [you say,] *be calm and be calm.* I am,' the librettist wrote, apologizing for the inconvenience Verdi had suffered.[121] Begging off for Christmas Eve, he went on to Milan and was not with Strepponi and Verdi on the last night of the year. Along with the worry caused by Boito's challenge to Sonzogno came the news that Verdi's lawyer in Paris was owed 403 francs as a final payment of his fee. With a wry remark about his fears for the future of Italy—it would be dismembered by France and Austria, he said, and would become the great innkeeper for the world's tourists—he ordered Ricordi to send the funds from his account 'quickly, quickly, quickly . . . quickly, quickly', so that 'these Frenchmen' would not be able to 'say that we [Italians] don't pay our bills right away'.[122] With this remittance, he freed himself from the aggravations of the suit in Paris. As he himself and his attorney Pouillet had predicted years before, he had lost. In June 1893 he had 'shouted' to Ricordi 'Free me from Benoit.'[123] Now that matter, at least, was behind him.

The French translation of *Otello*, which several French opera houses wished to produce, claimed both Boito's and Verdi's attention in January 1894. Boito had allowed Du Locle to translate part of the text. When further changes were requested by Gailhard, who expected to give it at the Paris Opéra, Verdi complained that the matter had got out of hand and that no changes could be made without the express permission of Boito and Du Locle 'and no one else'.[124] While in Genoa, Verdi also helped Rachele Bossola Massa, the young widow of the composer Niccolò Massa, although, protesting his age, he declined to attend the *Messa da Requiem*.[125] He asked Ricordi to help the family in getting Massa's operas produced.[126]

Much of the year 1894 was taken up with the French productions of *Falstaff* and *Otello*. In January he questioned Gailhard about plans to give *Otello* at the Opéra in Italian, saying that he could not imagine this great national theatre not performing the work in French: 'There is something astonishing and shocking in this *mélange*.'[127] Equally concerned about the quality of the productions, he asked Du Locle to make discreet inquiries about the Opéra-Comique, so that the 'artistic reputation' of Italy would be protected along with 'personal dignity'.[128] But Carvalho of the Opéra-Comique, hoping that the composer would come to France, wrote to ask Verdi to oversee the production himself.

But you all have forgotten one very small, small detail. You have forgotten my eighty years!! At this age, one needs peace, rest; and although I am quite well, all things considered, I can no longer bear either the work or the fatigue or the annoyances that are inevitable in the theatre. . . . But anyway, I can say again to you the words that I said to Maurel: *If my health, my strength, and my eighty years allow me, I shall come to Paris.*[129]

And with that he began to plan his trip, even though he protested to Ricordi that he would 'do more bad than good', and reminded his publisher that although he had managed the *Falstaff* production and the trip to Rome in 1893, his legs were bothering him and he could not get around as easily as he formerly had. 'My strength had diminished every day since I got back from Rome.'[130] Nevertheless, he said that he and Strepponi would leave after the first of April, perhaps in one of the new sleeping-cars; although Verdi said he did not know what they were, he agreed that if he could get some sleep on the train, he would begin rehearsing the day of his arrival. What he would not do, though, was put himself on exhibition 'like Martin the Bear'. 'Tell me', he asked Ricordi, 'is this a dignified thing for an old man of 80?'[131]

Settled in Paris in a suite of four or five rooms in the Grand Hôtel, the composer was besieged from the second day by journalists asking about the French arrangement of the orchestra, the merits of his singers, and his opinion of several composers, Verdi extricated himself tactfully and got on with his business. On 18 April *Falstaff* had its opening at the Opéra-Comique, where it was welcomed by an enthusiastic audience. Verdi, pleased, wrote to Stolz immediately: 'I have finished! Performance on stage good; excellent for Maurel and Quickly. Marvellous orchestra. Completely effective! . . . Fine, fine, fine! But oh, what a lot of bother and work!'[132]

Much-needed rest was sought at Sant'Agata, where Verdi suffered through part of May with a cold. Boito, who had planned a visit early that month, postponed his trip and then gave it up altogether when Gailhard arrived in Milan and Verdi decided to go there. Although the cast and date of the Paris Opéra *Otello* was under discussion, more attention had to be paid to *Falstaff* at the Opéra-Comique, where, it was reported, Maurel was wilfully making unauthorized cuts in his part. Furious, Verdi wrote to Ricordi, telling him to protest.

He takes away a bit here or there, according to his whim, as if to experiment with or judge which parts are fit to be tolerated and which should be forgotten! And then they talk about art! . . . about great art!! What a joke!! Done like this, the operas become nothing more than exercises to show off either a voice or a way of singing, or the gesture (mannered, of course) of any artist at all.[133]

The affair was monstrous and humiliating; he did not care whether Maurel sang or not: let the management get a substitute, but 'ALL OF FALSTAFF MUST BE PERFORMED OR THE PERFORMANCES MUST BE STOPPED'. I formally demand this of my publisher.'[134] But action was taken too late: and Maurel continued to do what he liked with the music.

During his stay in Montecatini, Verdi tried to write the ballet music for the Paris Opéra *Otello*, promised to Gailhard during their June meeting in Milan; but inspiration did not come, even though Ricordi sent several scores for review. Among them were Greek pieces, a Bizet *farandole*, a *furlana* from the Veneto, and *Le Désert*, a symphonic work by Felicien David, who had fired Muzio's enthusiasm decades earlier. Verdi, defeated by the July heat and by Strepponi's persistent stomach trouble, told his publisher that perhaps it was better to do nothing. The words, though, were scarcely on paper when he suggested an even more drastic solution: have some other composer write the ballet segment. Then: 'No, not that! Let's think about this a while longer,' he said.[135] When he and his wife started home, they stopped over in Milan, and during their stay Verdi and Ricordi discussed the problem. From Sant'Agata the composer promised to try once more, after he had rested a bit. By 21 August the ballet score was finished and sent off with a high-spirited letter:

Your Doctors of Music couldn't find anything for me . . . but I found a Greek song of 5,000 years before Christ! . . . If the world didn't exist then, so much the worse for it! Then I found a *muranese* that was written 2,000 years ago for a war between Venice and Murano, and the people of Murano won. Never mind if Venice did not exist them. After this discovery, I composed my fine ballet.[136]

The seven pieces, according to Verdi's precise instructions, were to run for 5 minutes and 59 seconds! Verdi also made various musical changes to *Otello* for the Paris performances.

Rehearsals for *Otello* got under way in Paris as he prepared to go there himself, writing to get customs clearance and making his own and Strepponi's hotel reservations for the same suite they had had earlier that year. With yet one more show of extraordinary strength, Verdi ordered piano rehearsals with the soprano Rose Caron, the tenor Albert Saleza, and Maurel for one and three in the afternoon of the day he arrived, 26 September. He had left Genoa the day before and got to the Gare de Lyon at seven in the morning!

Boito stood by him throughout his visit and took part in the composer's eighty-first birthday celebration. *Otello* was presented under the best possible circumstances on 12 October, the same day that Jean Casimir-Périer, the President of France, decorated Verdi with the Grand Cross of the Legion of Honour. While in Paris, Verdi went to *Falstaff* at the Comique and sent Ricordi good news about its success; and, accompanied by Ambroise Thomas, he attended a commemoration to mark the second anniversary of the death of Gounod. On 18 October Verdi and Strepponi were invited to the Elysée Palace, where their host, President Casimir-Périer, welcomed them as his guests of honour at a luncheon. They left France that evening. Even after he arrived in Genoa, Verdi was fêted when the city offered its tribute of a concert under the portico of Palazzo Doria, forcing him to make a public appearance. The next day he paid visits to the Mayor of Genoa, the Prefect, and the French consul, all the while complaining that he had no time to relax and remarking on his and Strepponi's health, which was rather good, he said. Irrepressible, he was also planning to make a short trip to Sant'Agata, where he had to attend to matters at the Villanova Hospital and monitor the 11 November rents and the annual hog-killing, which provided meat for the winter. Watching his purse he discussed the nuns' request for additional funds then decided he could do no more than he was then doing.[137] Once again, the staff's feathers were ruffled, this time by an aggressive young doctor, Francesco Belloni, who did not hesitate to write to the founder when he felt like it. Another source of irritation was Parma Conservatory's rejection of Guglielmo Veroni, the son of Verdi's coachman, one year after Verdi had originally asked to have him admitted. In June 1894 the composer had written to Gallignani, who had followed Boito as head of the Conservatory, reminding him of his request for help for young Veroni; he wrote again in October, after the trip to Paris, and sent his coachman directly to Parma. There, Luigi Veroni was told that his son was a few months too old to be admitted! Learning that, Verdi let off steam to Gallignani: 'NEMO PROPHETA IN PATRIA . . . If I had been born a Turk, perhaps I would have succeeded! Nevertheless, I bow before the minister's elevated wisdom! How lucky we are! Ruled so severely, we shall become a nation of perfect beings! Forgive me, and addio.'[138] The boy got into the conservatory, as we have seen, and became a player in ship's orchestras on the trans-atlantic runs from Italy.

Verdi was gratified by the large box-office *Otello* had earned in Paris and by the news of *Falstaff* in Berlin, where—contrary to the composer's expectations—it did well. As usual, Verdi entertained very few friends at Palazzo Doria. Among them were Ricordi's daughter and son-in-law and

Massenet, all of whom came to Genoa in November. Recalling his visit, Massenet described reaching the door of the composer's apartment and finding a simple calling card reading 'VERDI' attached to the door. The huge entryway and the vast rooms, the former habitat of 'rich Genoese nobility', were so large that an entire apartment could have been set down in the middle of one of them. The two men talked for about half an hour in Verdi's study, as he questioned Massenet about French theatre and young composers then active. They then went out on to the terrace to see the 'unforgettable spectacle' of the port below. What impressed Massenet most, though, were

Verdi himself and his attitude. His head [was] bare and held erect under the sun that beat down. . . . He showed me the changing colours of the city and the golden sea below, with a gesture that was proud, like his genius, and simple, like his beautiful artist's soul. And he was like the evocation of one of the great doges of the past who reaches across Genoa with his powerful and gentle hand.[139]

When Massenet got ready to leave, he went for his briefcase, which was full of papers and scores; but Verdi seized it and helped him, walking with him downstairs and ushering him into his carriage.

Although he was not composing an opera based on the figure of Count Ugolino of Pisa, as rumoured,[140] Verdi was working on an Agnus Dei, which, as Boito said, was to be offered as 'an act of charity' for earthquake victims in Sicily and southern Italy. In the librettist's Italian text, this became *Pietà Signor*; it was published in a special number of *Fata Morgana*.[141] Verdi and Strepponi stayed in Genoa over Christmas and New Year's Day of 1895. Again Ricordi had an extravagant panettone delivered, one so big that Verdi said it would last until Easter. While he was in the city, he got very bad news from the Teatro Carlo Felice, where, under Piontelli's management, *Falstaff* had been a fiasco—'but really a fiasco with ribbons', Verdi admitted. 'No one is going to the theatre! And the beautiful part is that they say that such a perfectly performed and co-ordinated opera has never been heard before! That must mean that the music is truly accursedly bad!'[142] By the second week in January the impresario had lowered the price of his tickets, every management's act of desperation; still the house remained empty. Verdi declared ironically to Ricordi that Piontelli should take out all the seats, set up a big table just behind the orchestra pit, and open a beer hall to serve the operagoers. A hawker out front should shout: 'Signori, come in, come in! Free admission, free show, free chorus and orchestra, all free!! You pay only for the beer, 5 centesimi a glass!! Come on, Signori, come on!! Great fun.'[143]

A few months earlier they had again considered giving up their apartment in Palazzo Doria and leaving Genoa, but after the city's mayor appealed personally to ask them to stay, they did not move. They did, though, spend more than a month at the Grand Hôtel de Milan in 1895 between the end of January and the first week in March, while they consulted Camillo Boito and others about the Casa di Riposo per Musicisti. From there, Verdi sent Persico advice about the Villanova Hospital, where Dr Belloni had brought down another crisis. 'Resign yourself,' he counselled; 'the only cure is to give this poor soul, who is sick with rotten temper, a good beating every eight days and even more frequently, if he needs it. You are not afraid to apply this remedy, which won't accomplish much.'[144]

On 17 February Verdi read his testamentary provisions for the Casa di Riposo to Ricordi and Emilio Seletti, the son of his former landlord and one-time nemesis Giuseppe Seletti.[145] More than two weeks later, they could all study Camillo Boito's first drawings for the project, as Verdi went on gathering information from De Amicis about a similar institution in Genoa. At this time Verdi and Strepponi did not plan to be buried there, as they eventually were, for even as work on the Casa di Riposo went forward, the composer appealed to the Prefect of Piacenza for permission for him and his wife to be buried in the chapel of the villa at Sant'Agata. They were perhaps concerned about her health; for Verdi, in letters to friends, mentions her poor appetite, which had plagued her for six months, her weakness, and a severe weight loss. He himself was slow, he said, and bored. He tired easily.[146] He had not given up composing, in spite of his age. In March, soon after he and Strepponi returned to Genoa, Verdi turned again to his study of the text of the *Te Deum*, which he had begun to examine earlier that winter in a 'little book of Canto Fermo' that a priest, one of Gallignani's friends, had provided.[147] Later that spring, when Mascheroni visited at Palazzo Doria and saw some music manuscripts in Verdi's hand lying on his writing-desk, Verdi admitted that he 'wanted to do a Te Deum!! *Giving thanks* not for myself, but for the public for being freed, after so many years, of hearing more works by me!!'[148]

As winter ended Verdi had to give orders for work to repair damage done at Sant'Agata by the flooding of the Ongina. He also planned for a review of business with the Carraras.

I wrote to you from Milan that my *affairs and my obligations make it necessary for me to know to the last centesimo what I can count on from income.* I now repeat the same words, all the more since I no longer have, and will not have in the future, the large, extra sums from new operas! When people deal with me, no one takes the trouble to be exact in paying, under the pretense that: *I have a lot of money!!* It is not true! A modest property owner with an income of 3,000 lire a year and a well-balanced *budget* is more comfortable than I am, with new expenses all the time that are huge and unforeseen; and I never know exactly the figures for my income! This state of affairs must end.[149]

He asked the notary to get ready a balance sheet with the renter's debts, with 'the assurance that the rents will be paid when they are due'. Carrara had written to say that he would get the record ready and that he hoped it would be correct. This, too, set Verdi off: '"*I hope*" is frightening in this situation! So why did I make the sacrifice of reducing the rents to such a large extent?'[150] At the end of March he went to Sant'Agata himself to see what his situation was. When he got back to Genoa, Verdi let Camillo Boito know that he had 'examined' his conscience and that his financial situation was not 'brilliant', partly because of poor harvests and high expenses. 'In spite of that, I would, as I told you, like to begin the work on the Casa di Riposo.'[151] The original estimates, though, had been set aside and new, much higher figures had been submitted. 'I was a bit frightened by that, for I would not want to begin the work and then bring it to a halt because of the lack of money,' he said, as he asked for a 'sure' figure, the lowest estimate possible; then he began to make his own suggestions for lowering the costs, by having one window in each two-resident room instead of two. He had already refused to consider the architect's original plans for dormitories, which Verdi considered too institutional.

In the spring Verdi and Strepponi returned to Sant'Agata. Just before leaving Genoa, he had declined to write a composition for the twenty-fifth anniversary of the liberation of Rome, as he had declined a year earlier to write for the three-hundredth anniversary of Palestrina's death. He did, though, often send small contributions to such events and to the committees constructing monuments to public figures. In 1894 he contributed funds towards a monument to the Genoese Nicolò Barabino, with whom Verdi had corresponded in the 1880s.[152] And in 1895 he helped Marco Enrico Bossi, who was applying for a post at the conservatory in

Pesaro, although Verdi did not offer an opinion on his compositions, as Bossi hoped he would. Privately, he told Bossi that his works were 'masterfully done'.[153] While he was in the country, Verdi also had a hand in establishing a new physician at Villanova, Dr Emilio Cesaroni, a former student of Dr Pietro Grocco, who had treated Verdi for years at Montecatini. Verdi, with his passion for detail, wanted to know whether Cesaroni was too young and too sophisticated for the job, whether he would be able to stand the peasant folk of 'a town with four villages' full of 'poor, rough, and ignorant' people, and whether they would be able to understand the doctor's Tuscan accent.[154] Appointed in October 1895, Cesaroni took care of Verdi at the end of his life and remained in Villanova until his own death in 1951. Another appointment in which Verdi had an interest was that of president of Parma Conservatory, which he urged the Mayor, Giovanni Mariotti, to accept.[155] Throughout all this, Verdi still kept control over farm matters and engaged an engineer from Milan to help with water control, which concerned him for fifty years.[156]

The annual visit to Montecatini, where the Verdis were under Dr Grocco's care, found the composer 'not bad' and Strepponi perhaps a bit better than the previous year, though her appetite was still poor and she had trouble walking. While there, Verdi agreed to receive an Italian musicologist and music librarian, Arnaldo Bonaventura. An account of his acquaintance with Verdi, in honour of whom Bonaventura had written and published an ode earlier that year, describes their meeting on 5 July in Verdi's hotel. A smiling, courteous Maestro welcomed the young guest, with whom he discussed ancient music, aesthetics, history, and literature, leaving Bonaventura somewhat surprised at the range of the composer's knowledge. Verdi could recite 'whole scenes of plays' and poems by Shakespeare, Dante, and Homer. The composer declared that: 'Art and systems are opposed to each other, and those who adhere to a systematic preconceived idea are wrong for they sacrifice their imagination and their gifts. For that reason, the influence of the colossal, very great Wagner was harmful. Let us follow our own instincts and our directions honestly, without becoming slaves to systems.'[157] Verdi expressed some optimism over the new initiatives in Italian music and said that he hoped young composers would stay on the right road, rather than 'fall back into the baroque'. Like others, Bonaventura remarked on Verdi's physical beauty in his old age; he was especially impressed by the expressive eyes and the 'austere yet sweet face'. As in other years, Verdi had an entourage of friends with him, including Stolz, Pasqua and her husband Leopoldo

Mugnone, Dr Grocco, and the violinist Federico Consolo, who cor-responded with Verdi from his home in Florence about old music and other topics of mutual interest.[158] The heat was suffocating that summer; but it did not keep Verdi from leaving for Sant'Agata on the evening of 31 July after spending three weeks happily, surrounded by friends.

Another writer who engaged Verdi that summer was Eugenio Checchi, who was then the journalist 'Tom', a contributor to *Fanfulla*. In an article addressed to Mascagni, Checchi criticized his manners, dress, and work-habits so severely that Mascagni was forced to reply, especially because the writer had warned him that another young composer—Puccini—might beat him in the race for fame. In the exchange of published letters that followed Checchi mentioned Verdi, and then wrote to him to apologize. Verdi answered that there was no harm done because he never paid any attention to what was written about him, good or bad, and that he was now 'out of the battle'.[159] That was not quite true, for he was still working on his Te Deum. Boito, who had visited Sant'Agata in June, sent his good wishes for Verdi's eighty-second birthday in October, hoping that the composer would remain 'happy and contented' and that the two men would go on working together.[160] The librettist was bound for the villa of Giuseppina Negroni Prati Morosini, where, with a delegation from Poland, he was to be given the heart of the Polish patriot Tadeusz Kosciuszko, which had been placed in the Morosini mausoleum after 1817. While in Vezia on this nationalist effort, Boito obtained photographs of the tomb that were later given to Verdi and placed in the great Album at Sant'Agata. At the end of September Verdi and Strepponi welcomed Camillo Boito and his wife Madonnina Malaspina to Sant'Agata, where the Casa di Riposo was the main topic of discussion. Barberina Strepponi made her annual visit; and Boito himself returned in late October. By November the Verdis were ready to leave for Genoa; earlier in the autumn they had also gone to Milan for a stay at the Grand Hôtel. Neither age nor infirmity, it seemed, would force them to change their way of life. Just before Christmas, Boito sent news of a dress rehearsal of *Falstaff* that he had heard Mugnone conduct at the Teatro Dal Verme in Milan. Praising the 'newest, newest opera of all the operas', the librettist said that the singers were 'all dogs'.[161] One of them, Ada Giachetti, the Alice, was the mistress of Caruso, who, recently launched, had scored a notable success in Giordano's *Andrea Chénier*. The Nanetta and the Quickly were the well-tested Stehle and Guerrini; the Fenton was Garbin. Given their competence and reputations, Boito's remark is surprising. Three days later he went to

Genoa to spend Christmas Eve and Christmas with Verdi and Strepponi, whose only other guest was De Amicis.

Just after New Year's Day 1896 another trip to Milan was planned. The couple stayed almost a month to attend to matters relating to the Casa di Riposo, the final plans and estimates for which Camillo Boito had shown them during his visit to Palazzo Doria in December; the beginning of the work was imminent. Verdi also met Ermanno Wolf-Ferrari, who had written to him after the *Falstaff* at the Dal Verme. By mid-February the couple were again in Genoa, where Verdi again began to express interest in versions of the Te Deum. He wanted to find one composed in the 1700s by Francesco Antonio Vallotti, a priest and organist at the basilica of Sant'Antonio in Padua. There was no question of using Vallotti's work as a model for his own, as Verdi made clear when he reminded Boito that his Te Deum had been finished before 14 February: 'just in case I should be accused'.[162] In his correspondence with Giovanni Tebaldini over the Vallotti work, Verdi recorded his own conception of the piece:

This is usually sung at great, solemn, noisy celebrations, for a victory or for a coronation, etc.

The beginning is right for that, for Heaven and Earth exult . . . 'Sanctus sanctus Deus Sabaoth' but half-way through it changes in colour and expression. 'Tu ad liberandum' it is Christ who is born of the Virgin and opens the *regnum coelorum* to Humanity. Humanity believes in the 'Judex venturus', it invokes him 'Salvum fac' and ends with a prayer 'Dignare Domine die isto', which is moving, sad to the point of terror!

All this has nothing to do with victories and invocations: and so I wanted to know whether Vallotti, who lived in a time when he could make use of an orchestra and of a rather rich harmony, had found the expressions, colours, and meanings that were different from those of many of his predecessors.[163]

His attempt to get a copy of Vallotti's works and to study them went on into the late spring.

During a trip to Milan at the end of March, Verdi again attended to business relating to the Casa di Riposo. A major concern was Strepponi's continuing illness. Having had an operation for an abdominal cyst in the 1880s, she was again plagued with nausea that kept her from eating. Both Boito and Ricordi suggested remedies that Verdi said she probably would not agree to use; and hopes were raised in late April and early May, when her health improved. As always she and Verdi left Genoa for Sant'Agata. On 30 May, the composer went to Milan alone to provide for the transfer of funds for the construction of the Casa di Riposo and, to his surprise, met Maria Waldmann in the station for a joyful and unexpected reunion. 'It was a bolt of lightning . . . a dream that brought back our much-loved moments in Art! Now it is all over! You have become a duchess! I am nothing more than a decrepit person! And don't think that I can do anything more.'[164] Yet he accomplished the remarkable feat of depositing 400,000 lire, realized from the sale of some of his Azioni Meridionali stocks, in the Banca Popolare. He had already put 150,000 lire there. The account was to guarantee 'the continuing work'[165] at the Casa di Riposo, where the Fratelli Noseda, a construction firm, had begun their task.

At home, Verdi found Strepponi out of bed and better. He wrote to Boito that the Te Deum needed only a bit of scoring. When it was finished, he would 'put it together with the Ave Maria and they will sleep together without ever seeing sunlight. Amen.'[166] Gatti said that Verdi told Maria Verdi Carrara that he wished to have the Te Deum put under the pillow beneath his head in his coffin.[167]

Seeing his wife better, Verdi planned their usual July cure at Montecatini. On the way there they spent several days in Milan, visiting the construction site of the Casa di Riposo with the Boitos, Ricordi, Seletti, and other friends, then went on with Stolz to the spa. They stayed at the Locanda Maggiore, as they always did, sometimes eating in the dining-room, sometimes having their meals served in their suite. The other regular guests there included the Mugnones (Pasqua and her husband), all of whom were part of Verdi's closest circle of colleagues. The Verdis returned to Sant'Agata and stayed there until October, when Strepponi went to spend a few days in Cremona with her sister. The composer, who turned 83 on 10 October, did not even mention his birthday as he wrote to Boito the day before which he usually celebrated as his birthday. Within a few days the librettist was at the villa himself. The Stabat Mater, Verdi's new composition, must have been discussed at that time, for Boito was asked to look for the text of a Stabat Mater Speciosa, which Verdi called the 'Stabat Mater di letizia'. It was attributed to the Franciscan friar Jacopone da Todi. Even though Boito found almost the entire text and sent it along, it was never set, although Verdi went on with the Stabat Mater Dolorosa. He and Strepponi left for Genoa in mid-November and were followed later by Maria Verdi Carrara. Among other guests were the ever-constant De Amicis and Mascheroni, who was conducting the regular season at the Teatro Carlo Felice. Umberto Giordano and Olga Spatz, who had married in Milan in November, paid a call on Verdi at Palazzo Doria as they were honeymooning on the Riviera. Encouraged by the success of his *Andrea Chénier*, which had had its première at La Scala earlier that year, Giordano and his bride presented their visiting-cards and were welcomed by an ebullient Verdi and Strepponi, plump, short, unsteady on her feet, and wearing a dark brown wig. Describing the afternoon visit to his father in a letter, Giordano left an unforgettable account of the Verdis, their house, and its furnishings. Before they left Verdi gave the young composer sound advice about his career.[168]

On 6 January 1897 Verdi wrote cheerfully to Boito over some event that he had reported in a letter which has not survived. One morning during the following week Verdi had a stroke while he was still in bed. He was discovered, mute and immobile, by Strepponi. When she spoke to him, he could not answer. He did, though, indicate that he wanted to write something on paper: 'Coffee'. After taking sips of the strong espresso that had got him started every morning for about eighty years, he began to show signs of recovery. Strepponi sent at once for Mascheroni, who rushed to Verdi's bedside then wrote to Ricordi and Boito. No telegrams were sent, for fear that the news would get out; and it was agreed among the composer's family and staff, Boito, Ricordi, and Mascheroni that nothing would be made public. Within about ten days Verdi was better and Strepponi had taken to bed herself with her usual stomach problems. By 25 January Verdi was able to write to Ricordi. He mentioned only that he was 'not well', and added that both Strepponi and the maid were ill.[169] He would have to put off his proposed visit to Milan. Less than four weeks later he and Strepponi did recover enough to travel, although he was still 'a bit ill, hoarse, and almost without a voice'.[170] Yet this octogenarian, who was still getting over a stroke and had laryngitis, was planning to coach Caron so that she could sing Desdemona in the Italian-language *Otello* for which she had been engaged in Paris. Tamagno was to be her Otello in the production, which was scheduled for the Opéra. Protesting that his doctor had warned him not to get overtired and that he was not well enough to accompany the soprano during the rehearsals, Verdi none the less moved himself, his wife, and his servant to Milan, trained Caron, checked the progress of the Casa di Riposo, and worried over a proposed *Don Carlo* at La Scala which he strenuously opposed.

Even though he had had a stroke just a few weeks before, Verdi seemed well, as the Austrian composer and pianist Heinrich Ehrlich attested after a visit with Verdi at the Grand Hotel de Milan. Typically up early, he sent a note to Ehrlich at 8.40 a.m., telling him to come over at once. Ehrlich found Verdi younger and healthier looking than he had been some five years earlier, when the two men first met. 'His head was held straight upright on his shoulders, like a soldier's, and his vigorous manner made one think more of a man of 70 than of a man born in 1813! As he first began to speak, one could notice [he was] somewhat slow, but soon he picked up [speed] and became ever more lively.'[171] Verdi even joked about his one trip to Monte Carlo and the money he had lost there. The two men then discussed the growing power of orchestral conductors, with Verdi complaining about the 'changes of tempo' that they made as they tried to get effects that no composer ever intended. Ehrlich mentioned Richard Strauss, who had sent Verdi a score of his *Guntram*, together with an effusive letter, in 1895;[172] but Verdi apparently did not tell his guest about the gift or about his own answer to Strauss.[173] When Ehrlich was about to leave, Verdi gave him 'spirited' advice about how to spend his day—at the Certosa in Pavia. 'He walked with me to the stair; his step was firm and sure, almost as springy as that of a vigorous 50-year-old.'[174]

Ehrlich testified eloquently to Verdi's good health. Apparently his secret was still safe: everyone assumed that he was as well as he had been for decades. The rest of his three-week visit to Milan went smoothly; and the Verdis went back to Genoa in March. Yet the composer, ever restless, visited Milan again in April.[175] He also corresponded with Boito, sounding a note of high good spirit: 'So! Let's be happy! Amen!'[176] They were perhaps rejoicing over the success of the Paris *Otello*. One performance had been offered as a benefit for the French Children's League, and in a generous gesture, Verdi too donated his royalties for that performance to the charity.[177] While he was still in Genoa, Verdi confided to Boito that the Stabat Mater was at a standstill:

If I think about it, I am repelled at showing myself to the public again. Really, why face judgements, useless gossip, criticisms, praise, hates, loves that I do not believe in? Just now, I don't know what I want to do! Everything that I would like to do seems useless! Just now I cannot make up my mind about anything. If I should finish the scoring, I will write to you![178]

Verdi sent this from Genoa just a month before he and Strepponi left for Milan and Sant'Agata. In the city he again visited the Casa di Riposo, where the builders hoped to finish the side walls by June. Satisfied, he and his wife went on to the country on 17 May. Boito joined them there about two weeks later. He hoped to persuade the composer to let some organization perform the works that were later to be called the Quattro pezzi sacri: the 'Ave Maria su scala enigmatica', the 'Laudi alla Vergine Maria', which Verdi called the *'Paradiso* Prayer', recalling its source in Dante's *Divina commedia*; the Te Deum; and the Stabat Mater dolorosa.[179] Although he said he did not wish to release them for performance, Ricordi and Boito were not willing to give up, although they did desist, at least for a while. At the beginning of July Strepponi and Verdi stopped in Milan on their way to Montecatini, where they again had Stolz with them. While in the city, they visited the Casa di Riposo with Camillo Boito, the lawyer Umberto Campanari, Giulio Ricordi, and his son Tito. When their carriage drew up in Piazzale Michelangelo, the couple saw the building with its roof on. They spent two hours walking through the whole structure, from the cellar to the top floor.[180]

In Montecatini, Verdi again granted an interview, this time to Corrado Ricci, who was then 39 years old and was directing Parma's most important art collection, the Royal Gallery.[181] As they talked, Verdi preached against perfectionism and praised spontaneity in art, saying that creative people who re-worked their original ideas over and over again destroyed their beauty. Ricci described a Verdi who was 'still energetic' and natural in his speech, with a memory that called up 'events, names, dates' and let him express his ideas with complete lucidity.[182] Verdi's liveliness was evident to all when he travelled from Montecatini to Milan to Sant'Agata to Milan and Genoa, then back to Milan in about six weeks in July, August, and September of 1897. In August Verdi helped the city of Busseto achieve equal status with larger cities in the designation of its upper school as a royal *ginnasio*. He also reviewed the situation of the Villanova Hospital, where the problem of overstaffing had again come up in 1896. Verdi felt that five nuns were too many for just twelve patients. In a letter to Persico, he had written:

So tell the sisters to be happy with the three. Let them waste less time by going to church less often. You can give glory to God by doing your own duty and staying at home, too. So let's agree: (1) the staff that has been there until now will have to manage; (2) they must obey the rules and not admit the chronically ill. . . . If, in hospitals with 1,000 patients, they had the staff we have, there would be about 400 people! An army!! Oh, oh, it is too much!![183]

But the nuns apparently did not accept the founder's decree. Very soon Verdi had written to Persico to say that if the sisters would not obey, he would look for another order to run the hospital.

And if, even with these, we were not able to accomplish something worth while, then THE HOSPITAL WILL BE CLOSED. I have done everything I could, I have spent a lot of money, and now, at 82 years of age, I have the right to have a little peace before I die! So show my letters to the nuns . . . and tell them straight out what I intend to do.[184]

The nuns were told that they should go to the village church only on Sundays and Holy Days. Verdi endorsed the rule and denounced the nuns as 'disrespectful' and their actions as 'not very civil and even less Christian'.[185] He authorized Persico to replace the Piccole Figlie with the Sisters of Saint Vincent de Paul, who served at the Villanova Hospital until 1973.[186]

34

November 1897–January 1901

Strepponi's Last Illness and Death

Ill through much of the summer, claiming that the sight of food nauseated her, Strepponi was able to get out of bed for a few hours a day. Verdi went to Genoa and Milan on his own affairs; and when he got back on 19 September, he found her somewhat improved, so that she was able to stay up several hours. Still, she was so weak that she did not feel like talking. The villa was silent, because neither she nor Verdi could stand the sound of voices. To make his wife more comfortable, Verdi ordered a new coal stove sent from Milan and had it set up in her room.[1] At the beginning of October birthday wishes for him began to arrive, with Verdi answering them as best he could. To Auteri, he sent a brief note on 2 October: 'May it be as you say. May the good wishes come true. I thank you and pray for your health and happiness.'[2]

On his eighty-fourth birthday, Verdi again invited Boito to come to the villa, although he warned him of what he would find. Strepponi was still weak, listless, unhappy, and closed in her silence.

I, although I am not very sick, have a thousand little ailments. My legs barely hold me up and I hardly walk any more: my sight is poor and I cannot read for very long: furthermore, I am a bit deaf. All in all, a thousand ailments. So you will understand that if Sant'Agata was boring in the past, it is now terribly, terribly sad! If you will come and have the courage to face so much illness, you will always be welcome and will perform one of the Acts of Charity: 6. *Visit the sick*.[3]

In spite of her condition, Strepponi recovered enough to plan a short trip to Cremona to see her sister. Verdi expected to go with her, for he still shopped and did errands in the city, now using the Albergo Italia as his headquarters. One of his and his wife's favourite charities was the Cremona Children's Hospital, to which Verdi had donated two of his scores—*Otello* and *Falstaff*—in 1894. With 'noble inspiration' he had signed both with dedications to the 'poor children of the hospital' on the occasion of the institution's annual flower show.[4] He also helped with regular support to the building fund when remodelling was planned. The city library was another of his haunts on such trips. In mid-October, as he wrote to Boito, he planned to take Strepponi to Barberina's and go back for her later. When the moment came, though, she seemed too ill to go, so Barberina came to Sant'Agata. As he waited for Boito, Verdi put the last touches on the *Quattro pezzi sacri* which he sent off to Ricordi in two packets, the 'Ave Maria su scala enigmatica' and the Te Deum first, the 'Laudi alla Vergine Maria' and the Stabat Mater on 25 October. With the latter he sent a letter.

I am sending, alas, these two other pieces too, the '*Paradiso* Prayer' and the Stabat . . . with immense sorrow. As long as they were on my writing-desk, I looked at them every so often with pleasure and they seemed to be mine! Now they are no longer mine!! You will say that they are not yet published. That is true: but they no longer exist just for me and I no longer see them on my writing-desk!! It is truly sad![5]

With this letter in the Ricordi files is a note on which he asked to be advised when the music arrived in Milan. 'Peppina is not getting better! Ah, that is very, very sad.' he wrote.

The next day, when his wife was worse, Verdi asked Ricordi to confirm the details of his arrangement with the Milan city administration to have two graves in the Cimitero Monumentale, for he and Strepponi planned to be buried in the Casa di Riposo, if possible. Boito had come and gone, finding Verdi suffering from fatigue, and a failing memory. He stayed with Strepponi throughout her illness, supported by Barberina Strepponi, whom at the last he sent back to Cremona, and by Maria, her children, and the Carraras. Strepponi died of pneumonia on Sunday, 14 November 1897, at four-thirty in the afternoon.

As family and friends gathered, telegrams were sent to the Ricordis, Stolz, and others. Boito, who had gone to Paris to arrange for the première of the *Quattro pezzi sacri*, started back to Italy as soon as he heard the news. Strepponi had left instructions for her funeral, asking that the rite be conducted at dawn and that there be no flowers, no remarks, and no speeches: 'I came into the world poor and without pomp; and without pomp I want to go down into the grave.'[6] Dressed by the women of the household, she was laid on her bed, under the dark, emerald velvet canopy. On the wall near her head was the reliquary that the Emperor of Austria had given to Feliciano Strepponi. Verdi continued to sleep in his own room, a few feet away. Shortly after her death he remembered her desire to be buried with the little envelope she had sealed in October 1846. According to family tradition, Verdi and Maria looked for it in vain; and Strepponi's coffin was closed before it was found. Later, it was discovered among her papers.

When Amilcare Martinelli, her lawyer from Cremona, got to the villa, he was at first told that Verdi did not want to talk to anyone, but when asked, he went to the composer's room.

He was standing upright in front of his armchair. . . . The desk was covered with papers and the piano was closed. . . . His chin was down on his chest, and his cheeks were bright with a purplish colour. He stammered a few words. 'I don't feel like talking. Tell Barberina that it was better that she obeyed me and left yesterday. It was better.'[7]

When Martinelli begged Verdi to take care of himself, the suggestion was shrugged off.

Verdi left the villa at 6.30 in the morning of 16 November and walked behind his wife's coffin to the parish church of the village of Sant'Agata, where a crowd awaited him. Next to the local dignitaries were the villa's peasant families and the servants. Attending the funeral were the mayors and city council members of Villanova, Busseto, Parma, and Cortemaggiore, with the entire faculty of the Busseto schools, honouring the woman who had been their benefactor for decades. The heads of the nursery school and day-care centre, the hospital, and the Monte di Pietà of Cortemaggiore also came, as did a provincial deputation from Parma. Officers and soldiers of the Carabinieri of Fiorenzuola stood at attention, as Maria and the Carraras helped Verdi through the ceremony. When it was over, they went back to the villa with him as Strepponi's coffin was taken to Fiorenzuola, where it was put on the train. There, too, honours of the city were offered, as they also were in Piacenza, where city officials greeted Lino and Alberto Carrara, the escorts for Strepponi on this last trip. At their side was Benedetto Mazzacurati, the stationmaster, with whom Verdi corresponded over many years. In Milan the Mayor and city council members were at the station with Arrigo Boito, who had just arrived from Paris. When the cortège reached the Cimitero Monumentale, it was met by several senators; Camillo Boito and his wife; the Ricordi family and Casa Ricordi employees; Countess Giuseppina Negroni Prati Morosini; Toscanini; the Spatz-Giordano family; Pantaleoni; Martinelli, who had come from Cremona; and Verdi's lawyer Umberto Campanari. After a brief ceremony, Strepponi was buried, honoured in her death for her husband's dignity and her own.[8]

Giuditta Ricordi and Stolz, who were not at the ceremony, had already gone to Sant'Agata to be with Verdi. In the week after Strepponi died, her will was read. She named Verdi her universal heir and Martinelli and Lino Carrara her executors. It was her wish that gifts of money from her estate be given every year to fifty poor families of Sant'Agata and that 12,000 lire be given to the poor of Villanova. She left 24,000 lire to Barberina Strepponi; 12,000 lire to the children of her Strepponi uncles in Lodi; 4,000 lire to her first cousin Carolina Strepponi; and 2,400 lire to her cousin Angela Cornalba, for whom she also provided a lifelong pension. To Teresa Stolz, she left a watch framed with small diamonds, a gold chatelaine with green enamel, and a bracelet of Roman work with the word 'Souvenir' in small diamonds. Strepponi gave Verdi a special commission: 'With tears in my eyes, I beg him to keep one single thing with him until his death and then leave it to my sister Barberina, if she is alive, or to Maria Verdi Carrara, that they will keep it as a sacred memory! It is my gold bracelet, given to me in Naples, that bears the inscription "To my dear Peppina 1872"'. Her will invoked God's protection for Verdi 'in life and death' and asked that He 'reunite him to me for all eternity in a better world'. Her last words to her husband were: 'And now, addio, my Verdi. As we were united in life, may God rejoin our spirits in Heaven.'[9]

The Widower

After Strepponi died, Verdi was rarely left alone. Maria Verdi Carrara and Stolz, relieved occasionally by Giuditta Ricordi and Peppina Carrara, also called on Angiolino Carrara, then 16, who helped with errands, correspondence, and companionship. Early in December Verdi wrote to Boito that his hands trembled so that he could barely write, that he was half-deaf, half-blind, and unable to focus on anything.[10] But by mid-month, somewhat recovered, he wrote to De Amicis with a steady enough hand, scolding him for not having answered an earlier letter Verdi had sent him about some important matter: 'We should not let time pass. So make me happy by answering at once. My health is so-so, and I shall spend Christmas here.'[11] On Christmas Eve, with the house overflowing with people, he sent Veroni to Fiorenzuola to pick up Boito at the station. It was the time of year that Verdi loved best, Boito said: 'Christmas Eve reminded him of the holy wonders of childhood, the enchantments of faith, which is truly celestial only if it reaches upward as far as belief in miracles. Alas, like all of us, he had lost that credulity early, but, perhaps more than us, he kept a poignant regret for it all his life.'[12] Sometime during that period Verdi gave Stolz his autograph score of the *Messa da Requiem*. Signed 'To Teresa Stolz the first interpreter of this composition. G. Verdi. Sant'Agata, December 1897', this gift honoured the woman, then 63, who had consecrated more than twenty-five years to her idol.[13]

Boito, who stayed at the villa until New Year's Day 1898, described Verdi to Bellaigue: 'He is better, his health has not suffered, and every day he is getting back a bit more of his emotional equilibrium.'[14] On Epiphany Verdi and Stolz followed Boito to Milan, perhaps accompanied by Maria, although she, if there, did not stay long. Verdi settled into his usual apartment at the Grand Hôtel de Milan; Stolz was in her new apartment in Via Borgonuovo 14, just a block away. How Verdi felt about being there is clear from a letter he wrote in May of that year to Maria, who was at Sant'Agata: in Milan there were no farm-managers

who want to make me believe things that I do not believe; no cook to give me bad food; no Guerino [Balestrieri] and others to bother me. Worries about money are lethal, unbearable to me. Here, on the other hand, I have no business matters to trouble me; no farm-manager; no cook who is poisoning me; instead, I have a rich, splendid menu; one hundred servants to tear themselves apart for me; and not one complaint directed to anyone!! What do you say? Isn't this better?[15]

In fact, Verdi got much of his spirit back early in 1898 and continued to live quite independently. For part of that year, at least, he even left Giuseppe Gaiani, his valet, at Sant'Agata. At the age of 84, Verdi got up early, as he always did; went for long carriage-rides in the park; entertained friends at lunch; rested until three in the afternoon; took care of his business; drove to the Casa di Riposo to watch the construction; had friends in for supper; played *tresette* or *briscola* with anyone he could corner; and went to bed about midnight. As always, his regular visitors were Stolz, the Ricordis, the Boitos, and Camillo Boito's wife. He also had occasional visits from Gallignani and other conservatory professors and from young Mascagni, who had moved into the suite next to Verdi's on the same floor and was even allowed to make use of Verdi's apartment when the older composer was away.

The most important business needing attention was the printing and imminent première of the *Quattro pezzi sacri*, which Boito had arranged in Paris the previous November. To be performed by the Société des Concerts in the spring of 1898, they became three pieces, not four, when Verdi decided to allow the 'Ave Maria su scala enigmatica' to be printed but withdrew it from the concert programme. Writing to Paul Taffanel, the conductor who also headed the Société des Concerts, he asked to have a firm date on which the publisher should send the scores. He also said that if his eighty-four years allowed it, he would leave for Paris himself at the end of March.[16] After mid-February he finally decided to go to Genoa, although Maria was ill with influenza in Busseto, but even this trip was postponed as he worried about her health and criticized her plan to send the servants ahead from Sant'Agata to Palazzo Doria.

It is not a good idea to send the servants to Genoa on Saturday! What would they do there? If two days [in advance] were enough on other occasions, why now advance their departure by so many days? What is the benefit? unless there is some advantage in keeping three houses open—*Sant'Agata, Genoa, Milan*—*instead of two*! You have not recovered, and if the *influenza* was severe enough, it will take some time before you can risk leaving your own house and starting on a trip! And what if you were to become ill while travelling? Either in Genoa or in Milan? Get completely well, and don't risk anything. I, too, am not completely over my sore throat and stuffy chest, nor do I want to risk anything for myself, all the more because the trip to Paris is becoming ever more urgent! I see clearly that you have let the servants' talk soften you up. Peppina's wish to go off and sigh in Linda's arms in Genoa; the *laziness* of the cook, who will get tired of the country; the restlessness and hysteria of Giuseppe [Gaiani], who can never stay in one place, and when he is in Genoa wants to go to Sant'Agata and, vice versa, when he is at Sant'Agata wants to go to Genoa—[all these things] have generated in all of them the wish to leave Sant'Agata. So this way they are the masters and can do whatever they like.

To end this: without useless chatter, if you think it is right to send all three of them to Genoa on Saturday, go ahead and send them, and may God bless them! I will tell you later when I will go. If they do go, De Amicis has to be told of their arrival.

I am glad you are better: but take care: when influenzas go on for a long time, they have a long, difficult recovery, and be careful not to get sick again. Take care of yourself, take care of yourself, take a lot of care of yourself, a lot, a lot.[17]

Yet even with these plans in place, Verdi stayed in Milan, complaining about the fog and rain, but enjoying his 'great carriage-rides' and the evening visits of friends. His only problem, he told Barberina Strepponi, was that he often didn't sleep well.[18]

The move to Genoa came in mid-March, even as Ricordi was printing bulletins about Verdi's forthcoming visit to Paris. But less than a week later his physician absolutely forbade the trip, saying that he would not be responsible for what might happen if he went. Dismayed, Verdi told Ricordi that if there were time to withdraw the scores, it 'would be better to burn everything'!![19] Yet within a day Boito had rushed into the breach and agreed to go to Paris himself, leaving the composer relieved and satisfied. Verdi ordered Ricordi to pay out of his own funds for the trip as he asked to have 'the three scores, or at least the printed reductions' brought to him in Genoa so he could mark his instructions in them.[20] He conveyed his ideas to Boito during a two-day session in Palazzo Doria at the end of the month, but continued to send him careful directions for performance.

The première of the *Pezzi sacri*—three of them—took place on 7 April at the Paris Opéra under Taffanel's baton, as Verdi, Maria, and Stolz waited in Genoa to hear how they were received. The composer had registered every tone on the anxiety scale as Boito sent him the hard truths about the chorus he had to deal with. 'Now I don't hope for much! But we have gone to the ball and we have to dance', Verdi said.[21] Good news came after the general rehearsal, in a telegram from Boito, who laid some of the composer's fears to rest. One piece, the 'Laudi alla Vergine Maria', sung by the sopranos Ackté and Granjean and the mezzos Heglon and Delna, was encored, during the première, and the entire programme was repeated on 8 April. The composer's gratitude to Boito was expressed in particularly moving terms when Verdi wrote that instead of offering some precious object as a gift, he would simply shake his hand when the two men met in Genoa: 'and for this handshake, you will not say a word nor say "thanks" to me'. They were 'true friends', Verdi said, 'I to you, and you to me.'[22] Their meeting took place as planned. But when Boito got back to Milan he learned that his sister-in-law Madonnina Malaspina was ill with cancer.

While Verdi was still in Genoa, he agreed to discuss the *Pezzi sacri* with Toscanini, who was about to conduct them for the new exhibition in Turin. Although he was 'tired and not in perfect health', he said that the conductor and two colleagues could call on him at Palazzo Doria any afternoon.[23] Even before they got there, Verdi had let them know that the chorus of 200 voices was too large; he urged them to reduce it to 120 voices. During the interview Toscanini sat at the piano in Verdi's study and played parts of the score as the chorus-master Aristide Venturi listened to the composer's remarks. 'His voice, hoarse at first, became clear and commanding again; his eyes flashed; no detail of the performance escaped him,' recalled Giuseppe Depanis, a critic and journalist who was also there. 'He explained his own meanings in short, precise, vivid phrases, yet they said a great deal more than a long commentary would have. I particularly remember one remark that made everyone smile, including Verdi himself.'[24] Verdi fell back on a Piedmontese accent as he described the distant, other-worldly voice of the woman's solo in the Te Deum, which, he said, should sound like the voice of 'humanity that is frightened of hell' ('l'umanità che ha paura dell'inferno')—as 'the old people' used to speak in Turin. As the three men were leaving, they invited the composer to Turin, but he declined, saying he was 'old, old'. And in fact he did not hear the *Pezzi sacri*, which Toscanini conducted on 26 May. By that time Verdi was back in Milan, where he had gone at the end of April. For a moment it seemed that he and Boito might go to Turin together for one of the rehearsals, but Verdi refused, leading Boito to conclude that he might have been afraid that too much excitement might bring on a heart attack.[25] Earlier in the year there had even been reports in newspapers about his heart trouble.

The Turin rehearsals were going on during a time of upheaval in Milan and other cities, as the riots that had wracked Italy during the winter of 1897–8 provoked ever more severe reactions from the government. Between the sixth and tenth of May, while Verdi was living at the Grand Hôtel de Milan, the troops, under the command of General Bava Beccaris, killed about 80 Milanese and wounded 450 others. Umberto I decorated the officer with the Grand Cross of the Order of Saints Maurizio and Lazzaro (which Verdi had received in 1887) and named him a senator-for-life after the action. The poor commemorated their dead, wounded, and imprisoned with a popular song, 'Il feroce monarchico Bava', denouncing the hated 'ferocious royalist Bava', who 'fed lead bullets to the starving people' to allay their hunger.[26] Boito reassured

BOOK V

Bellaigue about his and Verdi's safety, saying that the composer was 'managing both his body and spirit marvellously' just ten days after the massacre. He declared that the riots were not caused by hunger because the people were 'stuffed' with bread in rich Milan, where there was plenty of work. The people wanted 'sweets', he said—cake, not bread—and the government had acted properly in sending in the troops. 'We are still in a state of siege, a condition that is not without charm for it offers an illusion of being in the Middle Ages. We come home before midnight; you find patrols, bicycles and cars have disappeared altogether; as for me, I am delighted and have become four centuries younger.'[27] Boito feared 'social revolution' and was satisfied that the prisoners were locked away where they belonged, in the dank dungeons of the Sforza Castle.

Soon after the riots Verdi left for Sant'Agata, where Barberina Strepponi visited in June. Maria and Peppina Carrara came occasionally from Busseto for dinner. Stolz, who had been taking the cure at Salsomaggiore, a spa just a few kilometres from Busseto that had become fashionable in the early 1880s, got to the villa on the twenty-fourth and stayed until she and Verdi left for Montecatini in July. The composer, his family, and his circle of friends were shocked to hear that Madonnina Malaspina Boito had died in Milan. Generously, Verdi offered the hospitality of Sant'Agata and sent his condolences to both Camillo and Arrigo.

While he was in Montecatini, Verdi was sometimes followed by a young journalist who left a record of that summer, remarking on the composer's 'robust' old age and daily habits.

Not at all expansive, severe in appearance, stingy with words, [he] stayed very much to himself. He wore black [suits] and his soft, wide-brimmed hat, and went in the morning to drink the waters at the springs of Regina or Savi more often that of Tettuccio, which has a bigger flow and attracts more people. He sipped them very slowly. In the afternoon he walked to the spring of Il Rinfresco. When he became aware that he was the target of stares of the too-curious, he moved or left. He spent almost all day in his apartment: he took lunch there, but for dinner he came down to the round table of the Locanda [Maggiore], sharing the meal, sitting at the head of the table, a place that everyone respectfully kept for him. In the evening he went upstairs early, and before going to bed he enjoyed himself for an hour or so playing card games, *tresette* or *briscola* [and other four-player games] that always put him in a good humour right away. He prided himself on being very skilful at these games.[28]

Stolz and Pasqua were his inseparable companions there, and when he left, Stolz went back to Sant'Agata with him. Although he told Boito in

August that he felt the burden of his age and that life was slipping away, his humour had not left him. Inviting the Boitos to the villa, he warned them that his cook was an 'assassin'.[29] He was also expecting Giuditta and Giulio Ricordi; Barberina Strepponi was already there.

At the end of September Verdi and his family faced a crisis, when Angiolino Carrara, then 17, accidentally killed Giuseppina Belli, a young woman of 26 who was a maid in the house. Her brother was a houseman there. Because she was shot in the neck, and at very close range, Angiolino's account—that he had been cleaning his gun in the house after three days of hunting and visiting with the Persico family in Soarza—was held to be scarcely believable. He said that he had forgotten to empty his gun after the shoot, had ridden 14 kilometres on his bicycle over dirt-roads with his loaded gun over his shoulder, had forgotten to empty it when he got home, and had laid it on the hall table. He had asked Giuseppina Belli to clean it for him, and, when she did not do so at once, had begun to clean it himself. He pulled the trigger accidentally, he said.

The police and three judges who heard the case brought a charge of culpable homicide against him; in the community, and perhaps in court, it was suspected that he was the scapegoat for someone else, perhaps his father. His defence was so shaky that the President of the Court wrote 'What more!' in the final sentence. Angiolino, sentenced to thirty-eight days in prison and a fine of 41 lire, court costs, and damages, appealed at once; but his appeal was denied.

The King of Italy reversed the sentence on 12 March 1899, with a royal decree. Verdi's letter of thanks reads:

Your Majesty, May Your Majesty allow me to offer my kindest and most humble thanks for the lofty act of clemency in favour of my unfortunate nephew. With reverence, I offer my humble homage to Your Majesty and my deep feeling of devotion. I have the honour of declaring myself your most devoted servant,
G. Verdi.[30]

After the killing, Giuseppina Belli's brother Alfonso was, according to the family's account, given funds so that he could emigrate. He later returned to Busseto. Because the account of the killing had appeared in newspapers, friends wrote to Verdi, offering sympathy. To Giulio Ricordi he said that life was like that: a rare moment of joy, then misery, sorrow, disenchantment. He added that his whole family had been thrust into utter despair. In the same letter, Verdi dealt with the transfer of his stocks, bonds, and author's rights to the Casa di Riposo which, he said, was 'now almost finished' and asked Ricordi to send Campanari to Sant'Agata for a day or two. Verdi was 85 on 10 October, having celebrated one day before, with Stolz, Maria Verdi Carrara, and Peppina Carrara beside him. Boito arrived three days later and stayed until early November, leaving Verdi still at the villa, where he stayed all through the autumn.

Several important business matters had to be taken care of in Milan in December, as Verdi and Campanari worked to draft the document that established the foundation for the Casa di Riposo. He also tried to persuade Boito and Giulio Ricordi to stop a planned performance of the *Pezzi sacri* in the 1898–9 season at La Scala. Boito, who had suggested the performance at the start, was encouraged also by the successful performance of all four of the works in Vienna in November; but Verdi was absolutely opposed to the presentation, saying he wanted 'those poor pieces left in peace' because 'I do not believe that those pieces will be effective at La Scala, given the exaggeration [about them] and the actual conditions' and because 'my name is too old and boring! Even I get bored when I hear it!'[31] In spite of his best efforts, the directors for La Scala kept the *Pezzi sacri* on the programme as the opera-house planned to reopen after being closed for a year. Under its new management, Giulio Gatti-Casazza was named the general manager and Toscanini became the orchestral director. The new team's first-season schedule included *Die Meistersinger*, *Les Huguenots*, Mascagni's *Iris*, *Guglielmo Tell*, and *Falstaff*. Toscanini, in spite of his already considerable reputation, met stiff opposition from some singers, his orchestra, and even the press because of his strict tempos and tight control. Verdi, reading some of Ricordi's critical articles in *La gazzetta musicale*, agreed with his publisher that the conductor had gone too far:

If things are as you say, it is better to go back to the modest conductors of old times. . . . When I began to scandalize the music world with my sins, we had the calamity of the prima donnas' rondos, now there is the tyranny of the orchestra directors! Bad, bad!! But the former is the lesser of two evils.[32]

After Christmas in Milan, spent with Stolz and the Ricordis, Verdi had his usual New Year's Eve supper at the hotel, again with friends, as he welcomed 1899. He went on to Genoa on 9 February as he nursed a sore throat and laryngitis. Apprehensive about the *Falstaff* scheduled at La Scala, he agreed that the protagonist, Antonio Scotti, might be good enough, but that the Alice was weak: 'And note that the main character in

Falstaff is not Falstaff but Alice.'[33] At the end of the season Verdi again begged Boito and Ricordi to withdraw the *Pezzi sacri* but his plea fell on deaf ears. The works were scheduled on 16 April, an evening that also included a Schumann symphony and a Schubert march. Although the soloists were excellent, there was a very small audience. The 'Laudi alla Vergine Maria' had to be repeated; the Te Deum was better received than the Stabat Mater. Boito, in a long letter, tried to explain the apparent failure of the evening, citing the late date, the weary public, the tired chorus, and the badly organized concert. But Verdi was not consoled. Hard on himself as he always had been, he thanked Boito for his warm words but added: 'As for myself, I believe and have always believed that when the public does not run to a new production, it is already a failure. Some charitable applause, some indulgent criticism, as a comfort to the Old Man cannot soften me up. No no: neither indulgence nor pity. It is better to be whistled.'[34] When he went back to Milan at the beginning of May, he and Boito could meet, he said, but they should not discuss music. A rumour circulated that spring to the effect that Verdi was composing *Re Lear*, which he denied as he replied to an unidentified admirer who had written to him about it. 'There is no truth in what has been said about *Re Lear*. Boito will be able to confirm this as the truth.'[35] But the librettist, who had described Verdi in January 1899 as being in good health, playing the piano, singing, taking walks, engaging in lively conversations, eating well, and seeming to be very happy indeed, may have suspected that his old master was working in secret. Verdi's sole concession to his age that year was noticed by Spatz at the Grand Hôtel de Milan, where Verdi was taking the elevator rather than climbing the stairs to his suite. One constant worry was the financing of the Casa di Riposo. When Boito and Verdi met in Milan in May, they inspected the nearly finished building. The composer then went on to Sant'Agata, where all the aggravations of estate life awaited him.

It was perhaps during this stay in the country that Verdi received a package of music by the composer-priest Don Lorenzo Perosi, whose *Risurrezione di Cristo* had been given at Sant'Ambrogio in Milan the preceding January. Highly critical of an interview with Perosi in *Il Figaro*, Verdi had said that he wanted to study his scores. To Ricordi, he complained about Perosi's pretensions: 'He acts as if he were a Messiah! So welcome *Don Perosi Messiah!*'[36] A family tradition reported by Abbiati concerns a note that Don Perosi wrote to Verdi. When Angiolino Carrara brought it to the composer's study at Sant'Agata, Verdi is said to have torn it up and thrown it out, ordering the boy to stay away from priests: 'Sta lontan dai pret!'[37] The incident almost certainly took place in the spring of 1899, when Perosi would have had the chance to hear the *Pezzi sacri* in Milan. Stolz was also at Sant'Agata that spring, on her way to the spa at Tabiano. In July she and Verdi went to Montecatini together. There, as always, they met Pasqua and other colleagues from the music business; Verdi got his annual check-up from Dr Grocco, who gave him a clean bill of health. From the spa, Verdi also took care of some matters relating to the Villanova Hospital, where he hoped to get the former Mother Superior back as its manager. She knew all the shopkeepers of the town, he said, and knew how to get them to deal honestly. That was what was needed. At the beginning of August Verdi found that he had almost run out of money and had to send an SOS letter to Giulio Ricordi, asking to have 4,000 lire delivered to him care of the Banca d'Italia.

In August and September Stolz and Barberina Strepponi were with Verdi, who showed very little desire to slow down. By the middle of the month, he was off to Milan, where he stayed briefly before going for a two-day stay in Genoa. Again to the train, and back to Milan for four days there to oversee some of the work on the interior of the Casa di Riposo. On Sunday 24 September he had to get back to Sant'Agata, for he was expecting Italo Pizzi for his annual visit. Described by *La gazzetta musicale di Milano* as 'activity personified', he remained an energetic old man.[38] To Pizzi, who persisted in discussing the rumours that Verdi was writing his memoirs, the composer emphatically denied that he would write about himself. Five days later he appealed to Guido Baccelli, one of the King's ministers, to get further information about the published rumour that he would be granted the Collar of the Annunziata on his next birthday: 'I am not a man of politics', he protested, 'just a simple artist who never had such high aspirations.' There was, though, one favour the government could grant him: to be buried together with 'my poor wife' in the oratorio of the Casa di Riposo per Musicisti in Milan. 'Can I hope for that?' he asked, as he appealed to Baccelli to grant him 'the only request that I still have to make in my very old age'.[39] His request was granted as the government officially authorized burial in the chapel.

Verdi had Stolz and the Carraras as his guests on his eighty-sixth birthday. In late October and early November Boito stayed for almost three weeks. In November Giulio and Giuditta Ricordi came, to join other guests, who included their son Tito II and his wife. Verdi exulted in having so much company: 'Oh, joy joy of all joys!!! . . . We will be a little brigade. . . . The air of Sant'Agata did you a lot of good the other time and I am absolutely sure that it would help now.'[40] His carriage would be waiting for them at Fiorenzuola, he said. At this point, his only concession to his age seemed to be the massages that Dr Cesaroni gave him twice a day, for, as he said over and over again, he needed legs. Boito, joking, offered to exchange his younger legs for Verdi's head, if the composer was willing: 'But I think your horses' legs are already very useful to you during your morning carriage-rides.'[41] His purpose on the carriage tours was to keep abreast of work being done on his estate. He even went from farm to farm to decide which animals should be sent to slaughter and which should be moved from worn pastures to fresher ones.

With Sant'Agata shut down for the winter, Verdi left for Milan in early December. His legal advisers were drawing up the final documents concerning the Casa di Riposo, the official act of founding and the regulations, which he signed in his notary's office just before Christmas 1899. The next day he summoned the members of his administrative council to the hotel, where he discussed his wish to have the institution recognized by the national government as a 'charitable entity'. That status was granted at the end of the year. Verdi spent Christmas in Milan with his closest friends, who also came on New Year's Eve.

The new year, 1900, was ushered in by the Mayor of Milan and the city council, who paid Verdi a visit on 1 January, to inform him officially that 'charitable entity' status had been decreed for the Casa di Riposo. Slightly infirm, he was confined to his rooms only because of the bad weather. His doctor also feared the influenza epidemic that had struck both the Boitos. At the beginning of March he left for Genoa, where, in the station, he met Arrigo Boito, Peppina Carrara, and her husband, Italo Ricci, whom he took with him to Palazzo Doria. There, as Verdi said, they spent a pleasant evening together.—Not a word about fatigue or about the exhausting trip by train, although he did note that the train was on time. In fact, he had slept well and declared that his 'old carcass' did not have much to complain about. It *would* complain, though, 'because I have been complaining all the time, as long as I have been in the world. It is one of my great qualities.'[42] Boito was his guest at Easter, while Maria Verdi Carrara and her son and daughter remained with him at Palazzo Doria that spring. Verdi declared late in March that he was eating little, sleeping little, writing little, and thoroughly bored. 'Ah, idleness! What a horror!'[43] But discontented as he was, he kept informed of the work at the Casa di Riposo, where a new heating system was being installed. He wanted, he said, 'to settle all my business affairs and, afterward, be in peace a bit', for he wanted to arrange things so that 'I will not be needed any longer'.[44] If it were all 'clean and clear', he would not be so burdened with 'this business, which is a real torment for me! Furthermore, I am not forgetting that I am almost 87 years old, and I am worried at the sad idea that I might not be able to govern my affairs well!'[45]

The Will

One step toward peace of mind was taken in Milan on 14 May, when Verdi signed his will, naming 'my cousin Maria Verdi' his universal heir and her husband and father-in-law, Alberto and Angiolo Carrara respectively, as his exeutors. His will reconfirmed many of the legacies he had indicated earlier in a letter to Maria. Verdi's first items provide for sums of 20,000 lire to the central nursery schools (day-care centres) in Genoa; and 10,000 each to the hospitals for rickets patients, the deaf and dumb, and the blind of Genoa. Items 5 and 6 and 15 to 20 provided legacies for Guerino Balestrieri (10,000 lire); his gardener Basilio Pizzola (3,000); his maid and his valet, Teresa Nepoti and Giuseppe Gaiani (4,000 each); his servants who had been with him for ten years (4,000 each); other servants (1,000 each); and Giovanna Macchiavelli and her children Alessandro, Marcellina, Geltrude and Vittoria (4,000 to Giovanna; 1,000 to Alessandro and Marcellina; and 500 each to Geltrude and Vittoria). Giovanna had lived in the gatehouse at Sant'Agata for decades; her children worked in the house and garden. Verdi was particularly fond of Alessandro Macchiavelli. He stipulated that all these legacies must be paid within six months of his death but that Basilio Pizzola should be paid at once.

To Angelo Carrara, Verdi left his gold pocket-watch and chain; to Alberto Carrara, his guns, the cupboard where they were stored, and his gold shirt buttons. These were the only personal items mentioned in the will.

The Villanova Hospital was given 'all the properties at Castellazzo', including Cornocchio nuovo, Cornocchio vecchio, Cornochietto, Stradazza, Colombara, Casello, Provinciale, Pergolo, and Casavecchia, with the provision that the nursery school of Cortemaggiore, which Verdi had helped to found and had supported with large gifts for a quarter of a century, receive 1,000 lire a year out of the income from these farms. He also stipulated that the hospital should pay 20 lire a year to each of 100 poor people in Villanova, so that they could have help in paying their rents, which fell due on 11 November. Verdi ordered that these sums be paid on 10 November.

Verdi left the Monte di Pietà in Busseto a legacy of three farms at Sant'Agata: Cipella, Scandolara, and Casanuova, which are behind his house. Out of this legacy, the Monte was to pay 2,000 a year to the Busseto Hospital, which Verdi helped to found; 1,000 a year to the nursery school of Busseto which his cousin Giulia Uttini had been directing since 1897; and 30 lire a year to each of 50 poor people in Roncole. These sums, too, were to be paid on 10 November. He also provided for two scholarships—one to a student from Busseto, one from Villanova—to help these young people in 'the study of the theory and practice of agriculture'. If no candidates applied, these funds, too, were to be paid to the poor of Villanova and Roncole.

To his cousin Carolina Uttini Lotteri, Verdi left the little farm called La Pavesa in Bersano, the profits from which he had passed to her for 'many years'. His other Verdi and Uttini cousins, 'descendants of the brothers and sisters of my late father Carlo Verdi and . . . my late mother Luigia Uttini', were left two very large properties, Piantadoro and Bosco, including the farms at Due Are Casavecchia, Due Are Casanuova, Stradello Casavecchia, Stradello Casanuova, Pecorara, Casello, Canale, Colombarolo, and Palazzina.

Barberina Strepponi was left the income from the farm called Canale, 'Which I bought from Signor Francesco Pedrini of Cortemaggiore', the director of the nursery school there. The property itself was left to Peppina Carrara, Maria's oldest child.

The Comune of Villanova was left the title to the Hospital and the land around it, together with all its furnishings. The Casa di Riposo in Milan was given the title to various Rendita Italiana bonds and all Verdi's author's rights and royalties 'in Italy and Abroad, from all my operas'; it was further provided for with 200,000 lire that Casa Ricordi owed to Verdi and the amount that the City of Milan would pay to the estate for the plots Verdi had acquired in the Monumental Cemetery in Milan. This was to be reimbursed when he and Strepponi could be buried in the chapel of the Casa di Riposo. He also gave the Casa his Erard piano, which was in Genoa; his spinet, which his father had given him in 1821; all his decorations and medals; and other memorabilia. The two instruments and the memorabilia were to be displayed in a salon at the Casa di

Riposo. In a specific clause, he expressed his 'strong wish' to be buried in the chapel of the building. If he could not be buried there, he asked Maria Verdi to leave his body in the Milan cemetery and erect a monument, 'not to exceed 20,000 lire in cost'.

'I lay on my heir the duty of keeping the garden and my house at Sant'Agata exactly as they are now, asking her to keep the fields around the garden as they are now. This duty extends also to her heirs.' He even provided a safe, ongoing water supply for the garden, for in the legacies to the Villanova Hospital and the Monte di Pietà of Busseto, Verdi ordered that the Castellazzo canal, which he had protected for decades by buying many of the farms along it, kilometre after kilometre, not be included in the deeds of conveyance. It was to remain part of his estate.

For his funeral, he ordered 'extremely modest rites', to be conducted at dawn or in the evening, when the Ave Maria of the last canonical hour is observed. 'No singing and no music to be played.' 'I do not want any of the usual rituals after my death.'

With this business behind him, he left Milan on 22 May for Sant'Agata. Stolz followed shortly after, then went on to Tabiano, while Verdi stayed at the villa, writing to her very frequently. His letters to her speak volumes for the passionate bond that remained, even when he was 87 and she was 66. He wrote the first of them just after she left Sant'Agata for Tabiano:

Dearest,

Delightful hours but [they were] too short! And who knows when even ones as short as those will come again! Oh an old man's life is truly unhappy! Even without real illness, life is a burden and I feel that vitality and strength are diminishing, each day more than the one before. I feel this within myself and I don't have the courage and power to keep busy with anything . . . Love me well always, and believe in my [love], great, very, very great, and very true.[46]

As the week went on:

We will write to each other again and see what we shall be able to do. I am feeling a moment of good humour, and I give you not one kiss but two. Addio, addio, addio.[47]

Dearest,

I am answering you with two words to say that I am happy over your words that are so comforting. So if the Ricordis come on Saturday, I will send our little carriage to Borgo [San Donnino]; if they don't come, I will send the two-horse [carriage] at whatever time you wish. Anyhow, Saturday . . . Happy! Until we meet again.[48]

Two days later:

'So everything is set for Saturday morning at nine; I will send a carriage to Borgo [San Donnino] to bring you to Sant'Agata. If I can, I will also send the wagon for your luggage. If, by chance, the Ricordis should also come, I would send the red coach. The morning is better, to avoid the heat. If you approve, just send me a word: 'All right!' Oh! Joy! Joy! I am truly happy, even though my health is a bit off.'[49]

Stolz's reply, dated 22 June from Tabiano, confirmed the arrangements:

Your letter received yesterday evening. Thanks. It is settled. I will be in Borgo [San Donnino] tomorrow Saturday at nine in the morning. What joy!! What happiness!! Your very affectionate [Teresa].[50]

Reading these notes, few will doubt that this man and woman were in love.

Stolz stayed at the villa for about a week before Verdi left for Milan at the beginning of July. He then returned to the country and started for Montecatini with her. They stayed a month. Boito, who had seen the composer, reported that he was quite well.

All Italy was stunned on 20 July when Umberto I was assassinated in Monza, killed by the Tuscan anarchist Gaetano Bresci. Immediately after his death, Queen Margherita wrote a noble, simple prayer for her husband. Verdi, who was at Sant'Agata, soon received two letters from Countess Giuseppina Negroni Prati Morosini, who asked him to set it to music. Boito, she said, could revise the text, if necessary. To make her point quite clear, she copied the entire prayer at the end of her second letter. But 'The King of Music', as the Countess called him, could not do as she asked. He was, he said, 'terrified by the infamous tragedy' and had lacked the strength and the courage to answer her first letter. He confessed that he had wanted to compose music for the Queen's text; but he was 'half-sick' and could not do it.

In its elevated simplicity the Queen's prayer seems written by one of the first Fathers of the Church. She, inspired by a profound religious feeling, found words that are so honest, [and] of such a primitive tint that it is impossible to match them and translate [them] through our music, which is so recherché and inflated. One would have to go back three centuries . . . to Palestrina. I hope you will forgive me. I am sorry about it . . . but it is impossible!

He added that he was perhaps more than 'half-sick' and that he might be truly sick. During his stay at Montecatini Dr Grocco had advised him not to take the usual cure; other doctors called in for consultation agreed. He was, though, ordered to go on with the massages. All the doctors and 'ferocious nurses' at the spa had told him to do nothing, think about nothing, not keep busy, and not to change 'ever ever ever'![51]

The eternally loyal Countess sent his letter on to the Queen, who would, she said, be gratified to read his opinion of her prayer. Not willing to give up, she hoped that when he was more rested, Palestrina would inspire him to set it to music. As for herself, she was enjoying playing some Beethoven and a four-hand arrangement of the *Messa da Requiem*, which had 'so many truly divine moments'. It left her and her English friend weeping with emotion and praising the 'Dear Angel' who had written it.[52] Just after Verdi's eighty-seventh birthday, which he celebrated at the villa with Maria and her family and Stolz, she sent him a humorous poem in Milanese dialect, pretending that it had come from 'a friend', although she had written it herself. It was called 'EL GRAN MAESTER VERDI E LA CA DI CAN' (the great MAESTRO VERDI and the dog-house).[53]

Although he told the Countess that he had not written any music for the Queen's prayer, he had, in fact, sketched it out on music-paper, including the line that read: 'Sagrificò la vita al dovere ed al bene della Patria'[54] 'He sacrificed his life to duty and the good of the *patria*'.

On 1 October Verdi was in Genoa, where he transferred his entire financial operations to Milan. He answered the protests of his bankers and brokers, who lamented the loss of his large accounts, by saying that he had to simplify his life. At that time, his fortune was estimated to be worth about 6,000,000 lire. Calculated with the 1990 coefficients provided by ISTAT, it proves to be worth about 29,278,064,112 Italian lire, or 13,325,170 pounds sterling, or 23,071,760 American dollars. His annual income from his farms, investments, and author's rights was estimated at 200,000 lire, a very conservative figure. A substantial amount in cash, stock certificates, and bonds was kept in drawers and small safes in the house at Sant'Agata and in Palazzo Doria. Its value is not known.[55]

While he was in Genoa, Verdi visited Giuseppe De Amicis, who was then living in Via Balbi. For the first time, he had to be carried up the stairs to the apartment, a sign of his failing physical strength. Even so, he still had good days and bad. He returned to Sant'Agata, where he was expecting Boito at the end of October. He also had a visit from Mugnone. Verdi said that he was not seriously ill but felt so weak that he could not move easily and found it difficult to focus on anything. Pizzi, who had come to the villa at the beginning of September, said that he found Verdi very prostrated. The day before he had had to send a guest away because he was too ill to receive anyone. At the moment of Pizzi's visit, a thunderstorm was raging outside; the wind was howling through the poplars; and the house was cold, almost chilly. Although it was midday, a time when Verdi was normally at his very best, Pizzi found him 'melancholy and sad', although he smiled warmly and welcomed his guest with genuine kindness. The conversation centred on Verdi's health, for he complained that he did not feel at all well. 'I don't talk any more, I don't read any more; I don't write any more; and I don't play any more! . . . What a season! It is the seasons that depress me! . . . My legs won't carry me any longer!' As Pizzi started toward the door, Verdi walked beside him, leaning heavily on the younger man's arm and taking slow, short, painful steps. As Pizzi remarked that Verdi's doctor in Busseto claimed he was blessed with a healthy, strong constitution, Verdi said: 'I know, I know, and if I were not, I would never have got to 87 years of age. But it is the eighty-seven years that are a burden to me!'[56]

Late in October Verdi received a large number of guests, when the Conservatory orchestra and Tebaldini came from Parma for a concert in Busseto and were invited to Sant'Agata. Among the men was Ildebrando Pizzetti, who would later become a famous composer in his own right. Although he did not speak to Verdi, he and other players watched as the Mayors of Parma and Busseto, the Prefect of Borgo San Donnino, and Tebaldini himself entered the house. When they came out, 'behind them, He . . . Verdi. The Maestro cut a majestic figure, with marvellous simplicity in his movements. . . . Serene and solemn with his white hair, his white beard; a biblical figure, grand, an apparition from a dream.'[57] On the day that the musicians were there, Verdi could at least manage the shallow steps that led from the billiard-room out into the garden before the house. Five days later Tebaldini, again at the villa, found him 'extraordinarily cordial and open', with a 'very, very lucid mind' and a flawless memory. When Verdi asked him who among his students showed the most promise, the professor named Pizzetti. 'Well', Verdi said, 'tell him to keep looking straight ahead and upwards and ever upwards: above all, to remember that he is an Italian.' After lunch Verdi went out in the garden, dressed only in a black velvet suit. He was hatless, although it was cold. As some of the peasants armed with axes were attacking one of the giant magnolias in front of the house, Verdi sat down to watch them. 'I planted that magnolia with my own hands when I first came to Sant'Agata. And now it is in the way and smells too much. I am having it taken out!' He stayed where he was until the tree came down.[58]

One of his main concerns was to provide for the destruction of the two wooden crates that contained his early compositions, which he had gathered in over many years. At the end of 1900 he asked Maria to take care of this for him. Satisfied to know that the hospital, too, was functioning smoothly, he left it in Persico's hands.

Verdi, Maria, and their personal maid and valet left Sant'Agata on 4 December, intending to spend some time in Milan and then go on to Genoa in February or March. He seemed well, as Stolz reported to Waldmann; he had a good appetite, slept soundly, went out in his carriage almost every day, walked a bit, and complained because he could no longer take the long strolls that he loved. 'Anyway, he is good humour, he loves company, and every evening many of his friends gather in his house.'[59] Just after he got to Milan, Verdi wrote to Auteri, who had sent him some music: 'I haven't read for some time; I no longer write, and even less can I look at musical compositions, no matter what they are. It is not my fault. It is my age. Forgive me and believe that I am still your old friend, G. Verdi.'[60] He did write regularly to Barberina Strepponi, although his letters were short. All of his Milanese friends were on hand as the holidays approached; and Verdi and Maria entertained as they always had. He and Camillo Boito drove out to the Casa di Riposo together on the day after Christmas.

On New Year's Day 1901 the Roman poet Cesare Pascarella was among the guests. Because of the cold, Verdi stayed inside from about the third of January until the eighteenth, when he wrote to Barberina Strepponi.

I am quite well, as in the past, but, as I am absolutely attached to my chair and am not moving. . . . Let us hope that beautiful days like this one will go on, and then we will also be free of the cold. I am writing only a little because writing tires me, but you, with your firm hand, write to me. I know that Maria gives you my news. She is fine and sends her regards. With my whole heart, [and] I grasp your hands.[61]

In his last letter to De Amicis, Verdi said he was vegetating, not living, and did not know why he was still on the earth.

Death

He was felled by a stroke in the morning of 21 January, just after a visit from his doctor. Sitting on the edge of the bed, he began to tremble as he tried to button his vest. When the maid spoke to him, he said: 'One button more, or one button less' and fell back senseless. The maid's cries brought Maria, who called the hotel physician while they waited for Verdi's own man to return. Their diagnosis was a paralysis of the right side.[67] Dr Grocco, who rushed to Milan from Florence to be with his famous patient, could do nothing. Although Verdi's eyes showed no reaction to light, there was some movement in the arms and hands. For several days his breathing was regular and his colour good. Boito, shocked and desolate, later described this last week to Bellaigue:

He died magnificently, like a formidable, silent fighter. One week before he died, the silence of death fell on him. Do you know the admirable bust of the Maestro done by Gemito? . . . This bust, sculpted forty years ago, is the exact image of the Maestro as he was on the fourth day before the end. His head bowed on his chest and his eyebrows drawn together, he looked down and seemed to weigh with his look an unfamiliar and redoubtable adversary and calculate in his mind the strength needed to fight him.

He also mounted a heroic resistance. . . . Poor Maestro, how courageous and handsome he was, right up to the last moment.[63]

From the day Verdi became ill, the Grand Hôtel and the City of Milan made special efforts to control the noise and traffic around the hotel. Some vehicles were rerouted; carriages were ordered to move at the slowest possible speed; tram conductors were told not to ring the bell as they passed. Spatz, who closed the hotel to incoming guests, kept a special press office on the ground floor of the building for nearly a week. Bulletins on Verdi's condition were regularly posted on a board to the right of the hotel's main entrance. Some even gave his heart and respiration rates, as the end neared. The King and Queen of Italy were sent a telegram every hour. News of Verdi's illness was overshadowed briefly by the death of Queen Victoria; but within a day he was again the focus of the news.

Don Adalberto Catena, who had given last rites to Manzoni, came twice to call and administered extreme unction shortly before Verdi died. By the morning of 26 January it was believed that he would not live through the day. Bulletins were issued at 10:15 and 10:30, then again at 3:45 p.m. At 4:00 the physicians said no further bulletins would be issued.

BOOK V

Two hours later he stopped breathing, but then began again. Gathered in the hotel were Boito, Giacosa, Stolz, Campanari, Maria and Peppina Carrara, Alberto Carrara, and the Ricordis. No one was admitted to the building, for Spatz closed the doors, with the journalists inside. The shutters were all drawn; all lights on the outside of the hotel were turned off. The doctors told the family at eleven that night that Verdi was in an irreversible coma. About three hours later Stolz fainted and had to lie down on a bed in another room of the suite. Ill herself, she died one year later.

Verdi died at 2:50 a.m. on 27 January 1901. Dr Grocco, with tears on his face, turned to Maria and made a sign, then bent over the bed and kissed Verdi's forehead.[64] Spatz left the suite and, standing at the head of the staircase, pale and speechless, threw open his arms then began to cry. Journalists below then left the building. Within minutes a crowd had begun to gather in the street, standing in respectful silence. By dawn, the flags of the city and those in the churches had been draped with mourning ribbons. For the next three days most of the shops in Milan were closed. On their shutters and on the doors of houses were hung signs that read, in large black letters: 'FOR NATIONAL MOURNING'. These, like all the newspapers, bore black mourning borders. The first papers to carry the news were *Il corriere italiano*, *Il telegrafo* of Leghorn, and *Il càffaro* of Genoa, which came out with three editions and a supplement. All the theatres and music halls in Milan closed, as many cities prepared for memorial concerts.

The Italian Senate met on Sunday 27 January, when Verdi had been dead only a few hours. Eulogies by senators and the Minister of Internal Affairs, who was also president of the Council of Ministers, mourned the loss of 'that shining star who filled the whole civilized world with its glory'. Antonio Fogazzaro declared that Verdi

deserved, more than anyone, to be the symbol of the heroic era of our Risorgimento, because of the mystic fusion of his music [and] the longed-for, prayed-for unity of the nation around the throne of its first king. Verdi was our great unifier, when the wave of his passionate music, something that the enemy could not seize, embodied the idea of the nation, which swept freely from the Alps to the sea, setting our hearts on fire.

The Chamber of Deputies devoted most of Monday to a commemoration of its former member, who was hailed as 'one of the highest expressions of

762

the national genius, our brightest, purest, and most favoured glory'. The people, one orator said, had understood from the start that Verdi was the apostle, the faithful expression of the desire for national unity. The people seized on his art and loved him and his music, just as they loved his character—the modesty, the simplicity, the humility, the reserve, the industriousness. Of him, one could not say that he lived in the nineteenth century, but that the nineteenth century lived in him, because of the extraordinary concordance between his work and nature and the sixty years of national emergence and foundation. Every orator mentioned Verdi's generosity and philanthropy, and the fact that he had left so much of his estate to charitable institutions.

Evoking his music, one speaker recalled his personal experiences when 'before and after 1848 we heard the majestic music that accompanied the hymn to the *patria* . . . or the cry of pain of a people in chains.' He was, it was said, the artist who made the squalid desert of pre-unification Italy flower, who preached the resurrection of Italy to a people stunned by generations of foreign occupation. 'He felt and sought the patriotic mission of his art. . . . We could turn to him in pride; because of him we felt that we were all Italian, and brothers.'[65]

One measure of the nation's emotion can be taken from the fact that the Chamber of Deputies voted to keep the rostrum and the flags draped with mourning bands for seven days beyond the mourning observance that had been decreed for the King of Italy. The Senate voted to commission a bust of Verdi by the sculptor and senator Giulio Monteverde. The government announced that it would oversee an official commemorative ceremony, to be held later. It was to be a time of national mourning.

Rites

In his will and in instructions given to Maria and the Carraras, Verdi ordered 'two priests, two candles, and one cross' for the 'extremely modest' service that he wanted.[66] Because he also said that he wanted no flowers when he died, Maria and Peppina Carrara laid palm fronds beside his body and an ebony cross on his chest. He was dressed in his best evening clothes and laid on his bed. A second-class hearse was ordered for the morning of 30 January. Verdi's friends and family began to gather in his suite about four that morning. All traffic in downtown Milan had been stopped as a crowd estimated at 200,000 people blocked the streets. The hearse came at 6:00 a.m.; priests and acolytes from the church of San Francesco di Paola followed a few minutes later. At 6:55 a.m. Giuseppe Gaiani, Verdi's valet, walked down the stairs ahead of the coffin; when the cortège began to move, Angiolo Carrara, two senators, Demetrio Barezzi, and Campanari were to the right of the hearse; to the left were Giulio and Tito Ricordi, Arrigo Boito, Giacomo Persico, and Emilio Seletti. Puccini, Mascagni, Leoncavallo, Giordano, Gallignani, and Platania were with the family. Fewer than 200 people made up the official funeral party, which walked to the church of San Francesco di Paola; dawn was still more than an hour away. Don Modesto Gallone, the parish priest, accompanied by his acolytes and assistant, led the way. Mounted cavalry officers stood at every intersection; the Royal Savoia Honour Guard stayed near the hearse. The crowds on the pavements were silent, although many people fell to their knees and wept. The simple ceremony of absolution in the church lasted less than twenty minutes, according to one account. Then the funeral cortège made its way out through the gates and along the great circle of the ring road as many of the city's electric trams were pressed into service to carry mourners to the cemetery.

'The white road along the outside of the city walls, broad and lined with huge horse chestnut tress, was boiling with a restless throng that was obviously struck with emotion. Many people were running. . . . At Porta Garibaldi, the crowd packed the whole area. . . . A wave of silence moved ahead [of the procession]. Then the ranks of the Savoia cavalry filled the entire street. At the sides, [soldiers] and carabineri formed a great, empty open square space. In the middle was the priest: two candles at the sides. Then the hearse with a narrow, black coffin on it. Then another rank of troops closed the open area at the rear and kept back the crowd that was pressing from behind. . . . The people moved together in a strange, disorderly way, like ocean waves. . . . At the cemetery, where the whole square before the gate was sealed off, the crowd stood, motionless, silent. . . . Formality, the ancient, classical Italian evil, was conquered that day by the grand will of the Old Man, wise and provident maestro, even after death. No apotheosis for the dead was ever more magnificent than that silence, which he commanded from his simple bier.'[67]

Verdi was laid beside Strepponi in the Cimitero Monumentale, not far from the graves of Piave and Clara Maffei. When the Senate and Chamber of Deputies passed resolutions decreeing that they could be buried in the chapel of the Casa di Riposo, the Italian government planned a ceremony with full honours.

La Scala, which had been closed, opened two days after the funeral with a programme that included the overtures to *Nabucco* and *I vespri siciliani*; the chorus from *I Lombardi*, which in Verdi's time had been sung as a patriotic hymn; the prelude to Act IV of *La traviata*; the quartet from *Rigoletto*, with Enrico Caruso as the Duke; duets from *Un ballo in maschera* and *La forza del destino*; and the Act II finale from *Forza*. Toscanini conducted an ensemble of 100 members of the chorus and 100 in the orchestra. The event was a benefit for the monument to Verdi that was to be raised in front of the Casa di Riposo.

The official memorial service took place on 27 February, when Verdi's and Strepponi's bodies were moved from the Monumentale and buried in the Casa di Riposo. More than 300,000 people paid reverence to him on that day; the funeral car, towering more than 4 metres above the street, looked like a black and gold boat sailing on a sea of humanity. It was drawn by six horses, draped in black. Six carriages with wreaths and floral displays followed. Before the cortège left the cemetery, Toscanini conducted a chorus of 820 voices in 'Va, pensiero' from *Nabucco*. After it reached the Casa di Riposo, the Miserere from *Il trovatore* was sung. In the procession were a royal prince, the Count of Turin, representing the King and Queen; consuls from several European governments; the presidents of the Italian Senate and Chamber of Deputies; many members of Parliament; the Mayor and city officials of Milan; delegates from every other major Italian city; several cabinet ministers; Puccini, Mascagni, Leoncavallo, Giordano, and scores of other professional colleagues; the Conservatory faculty and student body; a squadron of lancers; a band; a large corps of mounted police; the entire city fire department; and, immediately behind the funeral car, members of the Verdi, Carrara, Barezzi, and Strepponi families. *L'illustrazione italiana* noted that no priest accompanied the coffins. All along the route, tapestries, flags with mourning ribbons, and coloured silk hangings were displayed from windows and balconies. People everywhere were leaning from rooftops and clinging to the branches of trees. At the Casa, Verdi and Strepponi were buried, according to his wishes, in the tomb lying just off the garden and below the Casa's own chapel. The walls of the tomb are decorated with mosaics that Stolz commissioned from the Venezia-Murano Company in Venice before her own death. A plaque honours Margherita Barezzi. In 1905 Puccini composed a Requiem to be performed at the Casa di Riposo in Verdi's memory.

Few heads of state have been tendered higher honours than Verdi,

BOOK V

universally hailed as an artist, a model citizen, and a philanthropist. To the world, as to the nation he helped to found, he left an enduring legacy of music, charity, patriotism, honour, grace, and reason. He was and remains a mighty force for continuing good.

Notes

Note: I have referred everywhere to Palazzo Cavalli, which Verdi bought from Contardo Cavalli; in other books about Verdi, it is referred to as Palazzo Dordoni (from the original owner) or Palazzo Orlandi (from the present owners, the Barezzi-Orlandis). Strepponi referred to it as Casa Verdi in her letters. It became Palazzo Sivelli briefly, when she sold it to one of the Sivellis. The house is now a museum, called Palazzo Orlandi. My references to the Monte di Pietà all refer to the historic institution of Verdi's time. The correct name of the Busseto Library now is Biblioteca della Cassa di Risparmio di Parma e Monte di Credito su Pegno di Busseto. It is owned by the Parma bank. The Monte di Pietà Archive is in this library. In these notes I have indicated many archives where the original documents are located. This does not mean that the public or even scholars may gain access to them, for access is severely restricted. This is particularly true of private collections and municipal archives (Stato Civile and Archivio Storico del Comune).

BOOK I

Chapter 1

1. Original Parish Registers (Baptisms, Marriages, Deaths), at Sant'Agata and Saliceto di Cadeo (1769–1813), and Busseto and Roncole (1781–1813).

The Verdis' move is proved by the baptisms of children at Sant'Agata before 1784 and at Roncole from 1784 onward. At Roncole were baptized Carlo Verdi, the composer's father, 1785; Maria Maddalena Rosa Antonia, 1788; Anna Maria Maddalena, 1790; and Marcantonio IV, 1791. (Three previous Marcantonios had been born and died at Sant'Agata.) The Uttinis' emigration to Busseto is traced in baptisms of 1805, 1806, and 1807. The Uttinis do not appear in the Status Animarum, 1800, of the Collegiate Church of San Bartolomeo, Busseto, although one of the Verdis of Sant'Agata does; Vincenzo Verdi, son of Vincenzo, a taverner, was the only Verdi baptized in Busseto between 1777 and 1807. I am very grateful to my benefactor and friend, Mgr. Stefano Bolzoni, Provost of the Collegiate Church of San Bartolomeo in Busseto, and his brothers Don Tarcisio Bolzoni and Mgr. Giacomo Bolzoni for their help in this long, difficult, research. Lino Baratta of Busseto provided invaluable insight on the lives of the Verdis and Uttinis in the Duchy of Piacenza.

2. Some, but not all, of the taverners' records are available in the Archivio di Stato, Parma and Piacenza and in parish registers.

3. These families can be traced year to year in two exceptionally fine archives: the historic archive of the Collegiate Church of Santa Maria delle Grazie (which includes the Parish Registers and the Status Animarum from the 1600s onwards) and the Archivio Storico del Comune, Cortemaggiore (which includes the civil Stato della Popolazione for 1824). Some census folios are also available for the years after 1866. Arturo Toscanini's grandfather owned a silk-mill there. The Respighis lived there for centuries. I am grateful to Don Gian Carlo Biolzi and Mgr. Giovanni Ferrari of the Collegiate Church of Santa Maria delle Grazie; and Vittorio Susani, the former Segretario Comunale of Cortemaggiore, and his staff in the town hall for help in finding these documents.

4. See n. 1, above.

5. Stato della Popolazione, 1820s, Archivio Storico del Comune, Cadeo; Stato Civile, 1806 through 1865, Archivio di Stato, Piacenza. See also E. Gallarati, 'Sintesi salicetana', typescript history of Saliceto di Cadeo in the Parish Archive, church of San Pietro, Saliceto di Cadeo (n.d.).

6. Don A. Rossi, *Roncole Verdi* (Fidenza, 1969), 26 ff. I am grateful to Don Rossi and Don Ugo Uriati, the parish priest at La Madonna dei Prati for many years and the author of privately printed essays on La Madonna dei Prati.

7. Original Parish Registers (Baptisms), Collegiate Church of San Bartolomeo, Busseto, 1777–1807. Proof of the Uttinis' connection to the Barezzi–Carrara clan is found in the baptismal record of Verdi's first cousin Maria Margherita Uttini, daughter of Gaetano Uttini and Rosa Malvisi, born in 1806. Her godmother was Donna Margherita Carrara, who was also the

godmother of Antonio Barezzi (Verdi's future patron and father-in-law) and of Margherita Barezzi (Verdi's future wife). Both Margherita Uttini and Margherita Barezzi were named for Donna Margherita Carrara. On 7 June 1806 (baptism of Giulio Uttini, son of Antonio), Verdi's grandparents Carlo Uttini and Angela Villa are described as 'of this parish'; however, they did not stay long in Busseto, for they reappear almost immediately in Saliceto records.

8. Parish Archive (records of the sacred societies), church of San Michele Arcangelo, Roncole. See also leases and payments in Archivio Diocesano, Fidenza.

9. Status Animarum, 1800, Collegiate Church of San Bartolomeo, Busseto. See also *Mappa Catastale*, Archivio Storico del Comune, Busseto; and Matricola della Mappa Catastale, Archivio di Stato, Parma. I am grateful to Dr Marzio Dell'Acqua, director of the archive in Parma, and Emilio Casali in Busseto for help with the history of the Casalis in Roncole and Parma. Verdi's godfather Pietro Casali died in 1830. He was 67.

10. Original Parish Registers (Marriages), Collegiate Church of San Bartolomeo, Busseto, 30 Jan. 1805. Gatti (1931, i. 5) errs in dating this marriage 1812.

11. For the records of the Uttinis in the Duchy of Piacenza in the first half of the 18th cent.: Collegiate Church of Santa Maria delle Grazie, Cortemaggiore, 1705 ff.; church of San Vitale, Besenzone, 1708 (marriage of Francesco Uttini of Cranna Superiore, Parish of Crusinallo, Diocese of Novara, to Maria Francesca Avanzini of Besenzone); church of San Pietro, Saliceto di Cadeo, 1734 ff.; Church of Santa Maria delle Grazie, Chiavenna Landi, 1744 (death of Carlo Uttini, born in Crusinallo, widower of Caterina De Nobili). For the Uttinis in Bologna in the 17th and 18th cents.: Biblioteca dell'Archiginnasio: Carrati's extracts of baptismal registers, 1600–1750; Archivio della Curia Vescovile: Parish Registers and Status Animarum of the churches of SS. Cosma e Damiano, S. Lorenzo Porta Stiera, S. Biagio, Santa Maria Baroncelli; Archivio di Stato: Feudi e Registri Parziali (Cittadinanza); records of the Ufficio Bollette (Entrata e Uscita Stranieri); Senato/Partiti Partitorum: Uttini records 1630–1740; Senato/Delibere, filza 19, 1688–9, fol. lll, request for citizenship by Antonio, Giovanni Battista, Pietro Antonio, and Alberto Uttini, sons of Giacomo Uttini, all of whom had come to Bologna in 1656. For records of the Uttinis in Omegna and Crusinallo in the 17th and 18th cents.: Collegiate Church of Sant'Ambrogio, Omegna; and church of San Gaudenzio, Crusinallo, which has the Status Animarum from 1642 onwards and the Original Parish Registers (Baptisms) from the 1500s to 1750. Using the Status Animarum in Crusinallo and Cortemaggiore, we can trace the emigration to the Po Valley, the trips back to the Alps, and the eventual settlement in Cortemaggiore year by year.

Verdi's great-grandfather Lorenzo Uttini was baptized in Crusinallo on 13 Aug. 1708; he was the son of Giacomo Antonio Uttini and Anna Maria Bracco of the hamlet of Cranna Superiore, Parish of Crusinallo. His godmother was the wife of Carlo Uttini, who emigrated to Cortemaggiore in 1705. Only one of these early emigrants to Cortemaggiore married a woman from that area; and it was this marriage—of Francesco Uttini to Maria Francesca Avanzini of Besenzone—that provided the clue to the Uttinis' origins in the Alps. I am grateful to Don Primo Ruggieri and to Mario Concari for their help in finding this marriage record in Besenzone. The composer Francesco Antonio Uttini was Verdi's first cousin in the ascendancy, three times removed. He was born in Bologna on 7 July 1724, son of Giacomo Maria Uttini and Vittoria Corticelli. A student of Perti and Sandoni, he was admitted in 1743 to the Accademia Filarmonica in Bologna; he became its head (Principe) in 1751, when the sopranos Elisabetta and Brigida Uttini were already singing professionally. Elisabetta Uttini was later at the Court of Queen Isabella [Elisabetta Farnese of Parma] in Madrid. (See my article 'Generations: A Work in Progress', *Opera News* (30 Jan. 1988), 26 ff.) Francesco Antonio Uttini married Rosa Scarlatti, the daughter of Tommaso Scarlatti and the niece of Alessandro. The couple went on to Germany and Scandanavia, where Uttini became Master of the King's Music in Stockholm in 1767. He composed the funeral music for King Adolphus Frederik and the coronation music for King Gustavus III. See *Grove*, xix. 480. There is no record of Verdi mentioning Francesco Antonio Uttini; but he almost never wrote of anyone in his family.

I am very grateful to Kathleen Hansell of the Svenskt Musikhistoriskt Arkiv in Stockholm for locating the Uttini and Scarlatti vital records and Francesco Antonio Uttini's estate settlement and inventories; to Dr Giuseppe Vecchi of the Accademia Filarmonica in Bologna; to Dr Mario Fanti of the Archivio della Curia Vescovile in Bologna; and to the staffs of the Archivio di Stato and the Biblioteca dell'Archiginnasio in Bologna for helping to put the pieces of this puzzle together. I owe special thanks to Don Arturo Melloni, the busy parish priest of Crusinallo, who gave me three full days to work in the archive of the church of San Gaudenzio and also accompanied me to all the villages where the Uttinis had lived.

12. *Nuovo dizionario biografico piacentino, 1860–1960* (Piacenza, 1987), 270–1.

13. Original Parish Records (Baptisms), church of San Pietro, Saliceto di Cadeo. I am grateful to two parish priests of Saliceto, Don Enrico Gallarati and Don Oreste Bionda, and to Don Amos Aimi, the archivist of the Diocese of Fidenza, for their help in making the Saliceto records available.

14. Gallarati, 'Sintesi salicetana'.

15. Stato Civile, Archivio Storico del Comune, Busseto.

16. Will of Carlo Uttini, 20 Nov. 1821, Archive of the Notary Giovanni Coppellotti of Pontenure, Archivio di Stato, Piacenza. This will was found by Count Carlo Emanuele Manfredi, director of the Biblioteca Passerini-Landi in Piacenza, to whom I am grateful for referring it to me. The will states that Carlo's son Lorenzo had lent him money on several occasions from his military pension.

17. See n. 1, above.

18. Status Animarum, 1800, Collegiate Church of San Bartolomeo, Busseto. No. 26 is occupied by Vincenzo Verdi, son of Vincenzo of Sant'Agata, who is living with his wife, 7 children, 1 servant, and an unidentified girl. No. 16 is Marcantonio Barezzi, who was the mayor. No. 2 is Dominus Francesco Carrara. All are in the quarter called Il Paradiso.

19. Original Parish Registers (Baptisms), parish church of Sant'Agata. From the beginning of records to 1840. The properties owned by the Verdis at Sant'Agata at the beginning of the 19th cent. are shown on the Mappa Catastale, Archivio Storico del Comune (for Villanova sull'Arda). I am grateful to Dr Adelfo Fragni for making it available.

20. Original Parish Registers (Deaths), parish church of Sant'Agata.

21. Handwritten note by an unidentified parish priest of Sant'Agata, perhaps from 1920s or 1930s.

22. *C*, 48–9, 48 n. 1. Verdi later also bought all of his ancestors' lands to the north of the Cittadella and other farms, among them Gerbida, which is half in Villanova sull'Arda and half in Cortemaggiore (San Martino in Olza). It belonged originally to the Sichels, who had married into the Uttinis.

23. Filomena Maria Cristina was the granddaughter of Marcantonio Verdi and Giuditta Piccelli (or Pizzelli) and the daughter of Giuseppe Verdi and Maria Romanelli. All were from Roncole, although Marcantonio Verdi moved briefly to Besenzone and ran the tavern in Bersano in the 1830s, as the Stato Civile in Besenzone shows. Later the family returned to Roncole.

24. Inventories of the property owned in and around Roncole and La Madonna dei Prati by the sanctuary church of La Madonna dei Prati; plot maps of the houses and property; and Carlo Verdi's lease contract and rent payment records. All in Archivio Diocesano, Fidenza. These documents were discovered by Don Amos Aimi. The inventory of 15 May 1729 describes these properties and refers to decoration of the main house (Casa Padronale) in 1690, when an image of the Madonna and a coat of arms were painted on the front of its portico. It even describes the hinges and locks that are still

in the house today. Carlo Verdi's contract of lease of 1827 (9 May) describes the same house: 'a cultivated piece of land with trees, meadow, and hemp field with a farmhouse provided with the necessary facilities and service area, with an area of 19 *biolche* and 1 *pertica*, situated in Roncole near the church, bordering on the east with the town road which is called Church Road, to the south with the property of Signora Catterina Ghirardelli Biazzi and that of Signor Pietro Vitali, and on the north with that of the said Signor Vitali and that of Giulio Sivelli [Verdi's uncle] and of the Diocesan Seminary of Borgo San Donnino, with a road nearby that is also part of it'. Note in margin: 'To the west with the property of the said Signora Biazzi', initialled by the notary. Because this property is numbered on the lot map that is in the Diocesan Seminary, and because the numbers correspond to the numbers on the Mappa Catastale and its Matricola, this property can be identified beyond any dispute as the Osteria Vecchia of Roncole, where Carlo Verdi and his wife were living with his mother on the day that she died here, as both the church records and civil records confirm. Carlo Verdi went on leasing this property, as his parents had, until 11 Nov. 1830. The house itself has a direct connection to Verdi: it belongs to the descendants of his trusted coachman, whose son Verdi fought to get admitted to Parma Conservatory. I am grateful to Mr Veroni and his daughter and to Romano Bergamaschi, who arranged for me to examine the house from attic to stall and cellar, comparing it with the descriptions of it from 1729, 1827 and 1830. The inventories are so detailed that even the number of planks on the feeding trough is given.

Bergamaschi, born in Roncole, the son of taverners who operated the Osteria in Roncole and, later, that in La Madonna dei Prati, was particularly helpful with his knowledge of these villages. One of his aunts, Rosa Verdi, was a blood cousin of the composer. Like many others in this family, she was a schoolteacher. Her brother Giuseppe Verdi, called 'Peppino', was the podestà of Busseto.

25. See n. 24, above. The Sivelli property is clearly shown on the Mappa Catastale, together with Isidoro and Giulio Sivelli's other acreage.

26. Parish Archive (records of the sacred societies), church of San Michele Arcangelo, Roncole.

27. Ibid.

28. Carlo Verdi's invoices and records of service, and receipts, Archivio Diocesano (Fidenza).

29. T. Lombardi, *I Francescani a Busseto* (Bologna, 1963), 37 ff.

30. Original Parish Registers (Deaths), church of San Michele Arcangelo, Roncole.

31. Original Parish Registers (Baptisms, Deaths), church of San Michele Arcangelo, Roncole.

32. Information from Don Amos Aimi and from lease contracts, Archivio Diocesano, Fidenza. See also G. Drei, 'Notizie e documenti verdiani', *Aurea Parma* (1941), 1–2: 21–5.

33. Drei, 'Notizie'.

34. The fine photograph of the church and Osteria discovered by Dalmazio Besagni probably dates from around 1920.

35. Drei, 'Notizie'.

36. See n. 10, above.

37. Status Animarum, 1800, Collegiate Church of San Bartolomeo, Busseto.

38. The Uttinis' residence in Chiavenna Landi is well-proved by their records there. The fact that Carlo Uttini, the taverner of Saliceto, lived there (two of Verdi's aunts were born here) suggests that he may indeed have had this ancient, beautiful inn. I am grateful to Don Alceo Frepoli, parish priest of the church of Santa Maria delle Grazie in Chiavenna Landi for information on the inn. In the 1730s marriages, it is surprising to see the records of men from Poland, Germany, Switzerland, and even Portugal in this crossroads hamlet.

39. Original Parish Registers (Deaths), 1807, church of San Michele Arcangelo, Roncole. The act states that she lived in the house leased from the sanctuary church of La Madonna dei Prati: 'in domo juris Ven[eran]di Oratorii Pratorum'. In the Stato Civile, Archivio Storico del Comune, Busseto, the record shows that her son and she lived in this house together. This makes it absolutely clear that the Verdis were living in the Osteria Vecchia in Roncole, the Casa Padronale described in their lease. I am grateful to Don Amos Aimi and Don Rino Guerreschi for a correct reading of the Roncole document and to Gianfranco Viglioli of Busseto and his staff for making the Stato Civile available.

40. Gatti (1931), i. 5.

41. Walker, 1.

42. (Florence, 1869), 296 ff; see also 1873 edn., 287 ff.

43. Mappa Catastale, in Archivio Storico del Comune, Busseto and in Archivio di Stato, Parma; Matricola in Archivio di Stato, Parma. The Matricola of open lands and the Matricola of plots with buildings are not always available in the same place that has the actual map. The Matricola of open lands in Roncole shows that Verdi's father and his two uncles controlled a great deal of land in the village through purchase or leasehold.

44. M. Accarini, 'Ercolano Balestra notaro e i suoi rapporti con Giuseppe Verdi', *Parma nell'Arte*, 2 (1972), 87–101.

45. P. L. Spaggiari, *L'agricoltura negli Stati Parmensi dal 1750 al 1859* (Milan, 1966), 60.

46. Ibid. 59.

Chapter 2

1. Original Parish Registers (Marriages), Church of San Michele Arcangelo, Roncole, 1813. I thank Don Amos Aimi and Don Rino Guerreschi for information about the music and the clergy there.

2. Original Parish Registers (Baptisms), Church of San Michele Arcangelo, Roncole, 11 Oct. 1813.

3. The Bersani–Uttini ties are found in the Stato Civile, Archivio Storico del Comune, Besenzone.

4. See Demaldè, 'Cenni biografici' and notes and drafts for it. Demalde, whose family owned property in Roncole, was 17 on the day of Verdi's baptism. Demaldè's sister, born in 1798, was the godchild of one of the Casalis. Giuseppe Demaldè was the son of Giovanni Demaldè and Agata Carrara. He is also the ancestor of many surviving descendants in the Busseto area, for his daughter Caterina Demaldè married Angiolo Carrara, Verdi's notary. This tangle provides a fine example of how these clans kept their property in the family.

5. Ibid.

6. See n. 1, above.

7. I had the good fortune to know some of this family before they left Roncole, where many of their cousins still live.

8. Verdi's claim was reported by a reliable source in Busseto who said that Angiolo Carrara recalled Verdi making this statement. As for the present national monument, the 'Verdi Birthplace', it was also different at one time: the front entrance was on the west, as is clearly shown in the Mappa Catastale, and as one can see on the façade, where the former door has been bricked-up and the old house number remains. The stairway rose out of the hall, in reverse position to the present stair. Its shape was notably different.

9. See Ch. 1, n. 24. I have not been able to place the Verdi family in the 'Verdi Birthplace' any earlier than 1833, when Verdi's sister died there, in the tavern leased from the Pallavicinis. It is absolutely certain that they kept the Osteria Vecchia (the Veroni house) until 11 Nov. 1830; it was leased to the Tabloni family on 29 Nov.

10. Original Parish Registers (Baptisms), Church of San Michele Arcangelo, Roncole, 1813; and Stato Civile, Archivio Storico del Comune, Busseto, 1813.

11. Gatti (1951), 13.

12. [17 or 18] Oct. 1876 (Di Ascoli, 330−1).

13. Demaldè.

14. Cavalli, 7. Cavalli has the year right and the month wrong.

15. The legend of the wandering musicians is told in Abbiati, i. 27−8. He and other biographers follow Demaldè, who was the source for early accounts of Verdi's life. It is likely that they were hired for the celebration of the marriage and baptism.

16. Demaldè.

17. Although the story of the violence in Roncole was told by Verdi to his friend Giuseppe De Amicis (see F. Resasco, *Verdi a Genova: ricordi aneddoti e episodi* (Genoa, 1901), 45), Verdi did not have it put in Pougin, when he could have done so, as he reviewed the notes for the Italian edn.

18. M. Conati, *Interviste e incontri con Verdi* (Milan, 1980), 147. The German writer is identified by Conati (p. 141) as A. von Winterfeld, who published his *Unterhalten in Verdis Tuskulum* in *Deutsche Revue*, 12 (1887).

19. Original Parish Registers (Deaths), Church of San Michele Arcangelo, Roncole, 1813−14. Contrary to what Verdi's biographers say about Russians killing villagers, a local legend is that the people of Roncole killed several Russian soldiers and buried them at night near the roadside oratory of Bassa de' Mai. Farmers around Roncole still said 'There's a Russian buried there' even in the 1960s, when a fruit tree bore heavily.

20. L. Grazzi, *Parma romantica* (Parma, 1964), 63 ff. See also E. Seletti, *La città di Busseto* (Milan, 1883), ii, *passim*.

21. E. Seletti, *Busseto*, ii. 228.

22. Ibid. See also Grazzi, *Parma*, 63 ff.

23. Demaldè. See also 'Raccolta ricordanze roncolesi', unpublished MS, parish archive, church of San Michele Arcangelo, Roncole. Parts of it were written by men who went to school with Verdi.

24. Demaldè.

25. 'La famiglia', *Facchino* (15 Nov. 1845), Antonaldo Conforti Collection, Busseto.

26. Ibid.

27. Parish Archive, Church of San Michele Arcangelo, Roncole. The parish's concern for the organ and the acoustics of the building are reflected in

records going back to 1736 and continuing up to Verdi's time. See Don A. Rossi, *Roncole Verdi* (Fidenza, 1969), 43-4.

28. Original Parish Registers (Baptisms), Church of San Michele Arcangelo, Roncole, 20 Mar. 1816. In the Stato Civile, Archivio Storico del Comune, Busseto, Verdi's sister is registered as a 'child of male sex', Giuseppe Francesco. Not until Giuseppa died did some unidentifiable clerk note in the margin that 'this must be a female' and counter-reference the death document. She is also entered as 'Verderi'.

29. Verdi Family Records, compiled *c*. 1831 by Giuseppe Demaldè, (Manuscript Collection, Biblioteca Civica, Busseto).

30. Stato Civile (Registers and Indexes, 1833), Archivio Storico del Comune, Busseto.

31. 'Raccolta ricordanze roncolesi'.

32. Demaldè.

33. Original Parish Registers (Deaths), Church of San Michele Arcangelo, Roncole, 1817.

34. Demaldè.

35. Ibid.

36. G. Verdi, Will, 14 May 1900, *C*, 724 ff.

37. On the instrument, Museo Teatrale alla Scala, Milan, the original inscription can still be read. Verdi's remarks are cited in Conati, *Interviste*, 145. The writer, von Winterfeld, also copied the inscription as Verdi showed him the spinet. A scholar from the University of Edinburgh, Dr Grant O'Brien, has recently identified the 'spinet' as a Venetian virginal, made by Marco Jadra. O'Brien has also raised some serious doubts about the hand that wrote the famous inscription. My brief study of documents of the period shows that it cannot have been written by Carlo Verdi or Don Arcari. The word 'Verdi' in the inscription is very similar to the carved signature 'Giuseppe Verdi' on the church organ in Roncole, which is believed to have been carved by Verdi himself. (See photograph in 'Verdi', special issue of *Natura ed arte* (1901), 91.)

38. I am indebted to Giuseppe Godi for taking me to the organ loft and showing me the instrument in Soragna.

39. The established family tradition, as told to me in 1956 during a visit, is mentioned in Abbiati, iv. 642. A letter to Verdi from the priest-composer Don Lorenzo Perosi is said to have set Verdi off.

40. Accounts of this incident appear in several biographies, including Gatti, and in I. Pizzi's *Ricordi verdiani inediti* (Turin, 1901), 94-5. It is part of

the family tradition in several local families, who re-tell this story in conversations about the composer.

41. The dead appear in Original Parish Registers (Deaths), Church of San Michele Arcangelo, Roncole, 14 Sept. 1828.

42. G. Bragagnolo, and E. Bettazzi, *La vita di Giuseppe Verdi* (Milan, 1905), 8-9. The passage cited is from Giuseppe De Amicis's memoirs.

43. Photograph of the broadside entitled 'AVVENIMENTI FUNESTI', 15 Sept. 1828, in Abbiati, i., facing page 128.

44. Bragagnolo and Bettazzi, *Vita*. Gatti (1931), i. 14 n. 6, states that Verdi had stopped to eat with the Michiaras. Don Ugo Uriati's research, done in the 1950s and 1960s, revealed that this family, of Austrian origin, had been given the farm 'La Separata' by Archduchess Marie Louise, widow of Napoleon I and ruler of the Duchy of Parma.

45. Original Parish Registers (Deaths), Church of San Michele Arcangelo, Roncole, 1820-5.

46. Carlo Uttini, Will: see Ch. 1 n. 16. This document is important in identifying Verdi's uncles and aunts, some of whom had roles in his later life. Among the witnesses was Don Michele Villa, Archpriest of Saliceto di Cadeo, a relative of Verdi's grandmother. One of the Capra family from Crusinallo is another witness; he printed his name with some evident difficulty.

47. D. Soresina, Dario, *Enciclopedia diocesana fidentina* (Fidenza, 1961), i. 269. See also E. Seletti, *Busseto*, ii. 274, and Pougin, 11 n. 2. Pougin states that Verdi taught Mingardi later, when he was in Busseto. Mingardi was only one year older than Verdi and was Barezzi's protégé.

48. Conati, *Interviste*, 146.

49. Demaldè, notes for 'Cenni biografici'.

50. Conati, *Interviste*, 146.

51. See n. 44, above.

52. Conati, *Interviste*, 146.

53. Account of Verdi's life, given to Onorato Roux by Verdi and published by him in 'Omaggio a Verdi', special issue of *Farfalla* (1896), 16.

54. C. Bellaigue, *Verdi* (Milan, 1913), 4.

Chapter 3

1. Stato Civile (Births), Archivio Storico del Comune, Busseto, 1820-36.

2. T. Lombardi, *I Franciscani a Busseto* (Bologna, 1963), 188 ff. See also L.

Di Stolfi, 'I Francescani di Busseto e Giuseppe Verdi', *Frate Francesco* 6: 2 (1959).

3. Di Stolfi, 'Francescani'. After the Napoleonic suppression, the Franciscan monastery in Busseto remained empty for several years. After Waterloo and the Congress of Vienna, the Pallavicino family asked to have the order brought back; in 1816 the Franciscans returned. Terzorio's school was located in one of the ground-floor rooms off the cloister, to the right of the main entrance.

4. Demaldè.

5. Cavalli, 10–11. Pougin stated that Verdi came to live in Busseto 'in the company of another village boy called Michiara' (Pougin, 6).

6. S. Pignagoli, *Il Comune di Busseto* (Busseto, 1926), 39 ff.

7. E. Seletti, *Busseto* (Milan, 1883), ii. 218.

8. Ibid. 218 ff. See also M. Bensa, *Busseto dal secolo vii al xx* (Parma, 1911), 110 ff.

9. E. Seletti, *Busseto*, ii. 247 ff.

10. Ibid.

11. M. J. Phillips-Matz, 'José Verdi, Hercules Cavalli, and the Florence *Macbeth*', in A. Porter and D. Rosen (eds.), *Verdi's Macbeth: A Sourcebook* (New York, 1984), 129 ff.

12. A. Alessandri, 'Un gravissimo fallo di Ferdinando Provesi', *Parma per l'arte*, 3 (1959), 112 ff., 143 ff.; 10 (1960), 93 ff., 11 (1961) 67 ff.; 12 (1962), 188 ff.; 19 (1969), 123 ff.

13. Ibid.

14. Manuscript Collection, BMP-B. A large collection of documents about this rivalry was donated to the library in 1980.

15. E. Seletti, *Busseto*, ii. 259 ff.

16. Salone Barezzi, restored in the 1980s, is the recital hall of the Amici di Verdi, an organization with about 500 members.

17. Register List of Members (Manuscript Collection, BMP-B).

18. Lombardi, *Francescani*, 190–1.

19. Among Verdi's schoolmates, Gaetano Zilioli became a civil engineer and professor of mathematics at the University of Parma; Ireneo Riva became a lecturer in philosophy and theology; Luigi Balestra became a physician, poet, and translator; Gaetano Balestra became the Chief Lawyer at the Ducal Court and Special Counsellor to the Supreme Court in Parma and, later, Minister of Finance to the King of Italy; Casimiro Frondoni was later

a Doctor of Law and professor; and Carlo Fontana became a priest and professor of theology at the Diocesan Seminary in Borgo San Donnino.

20. Letter of Recommendation for Verdi, written by Canon Giuseppe Demaldè, inspector of the city schools in Busseto, 9 Jan. 1832 (Manuscript Collection, BMP-B). This Giuseppe Demalde was a priest.

21. Pougin, 10–11, n. 1. See also Gatti (1931), i. 24.

22. Pougin, 10–11, n. 1.

23. Ibid. In the parish registers and vestry records, Soncini is identified as a gentleman, landowner, born in 1766, and a standard-bearer in religious processions and rites.

24. Verdi, facs. letter in L. Broglio *et al.* (eds.), *Nel primo centenario di Giuseppe Verdi, 1813–1913: numero unico illustrato* (Milan, 1913).

25. Demaldè, 'Cenni biografici' and notes.

26. Ibid.

27. Ibid.

28. A very early note from Verdi to Francesco Silva refers to the ode *Il cinque Maggio*: 'Dear Silva, I have very, very slowly come to the end of the Manzoni ode. When you have half an hour, come to listen to it, and if you also bring the magistrate, you would do me a favour, because, just between us, I would like to hear what you think of the music in this private situation before putting the final touches to it.' (Anthony Schippers Collection, New York.)

29. 24 May 1867 (Di Ascoli, 161–2).

30. L. O. Kuhns, *The Great Poets of Italy* (Boston, 1904), 262.

31. Demaldè.

32. Cited in Gatti (1931) i. 26.

33. At the end of his life, Verdi asked his foster-daughter Filomena Maria Verdi, then the wife of Alberto Carrara, to take the box of his early works out of the house and burn it at Sant'Agata. Gatti felt, however, that several of Verdi's earliest compositions were still in the Music Archive of the BMP-B. In June 1989, together with Dino Rizzo, the organist of the Collegiate Church of San Bartolomeo in Busseto, I began to try to identify some of these, beginning with compositions from the 1830s that are clearly assigned in the catalogue to men who were not composers but were either Verdi's soloists or instrumentalists. Foremost among these are the tenors Luigi Macchiavelli and Giovanni Arduzzoni, and the clarinettist Eugenio Arduzzoni, Provesi's former pupils, who played or sang with Verdi's orchestra. These

were selected because of Verdi's documented ties to them: he wrote many works for Machiavelli and lived with one of the Arduzzonis in Milan during his student days. At this writing, several works have been identified from his 1830s calligraphy (especially the capital 'L') and from his distinctive rests. This work is still in progress.

34. See n. 28, above.

35. L. Molossi, *Vocabolario topografico dei Ducati di Parma, Piacenza, e Guastalla* (Parma, 1832–4), 44.

36. See n. 17, above.

37. As listed on concert programmes in collections in Busseto.

38. Provesi's invitation to a concert on 18 Feb. 1830 proves that Barezzi's salon was being used even then. Collection of the Museo Civico, Busseto.

39. Status Animarum, 1800, Collegiate Church of San Bartolomeo, Busseto. The Status animarum of 1865 shows the Demaldès still there.

40. (SAA).

41. 2 Nov. 1828 (SAA).

42. 2 Nov. 1828 (SAA).

43. 11 July 1828 (SAA).

44. Verdi to Clara Maffei, 30 June 1867 (Di Ascoli, 167).

45. Parish Archive. This letter, which the parish priest kindly allowed me to have microfilmed for the American Institute for Verdi Studies, is the earliest example we have of Verdi's handwriting, save for one early signature in a textbook.

46. Ferdinando Provesi to the Podestà of Busseto, 18 Feb. 1830, Museo Civico, Busseto.

47. Cited in Gatti (1931), i. 31.

48. Sketch from the Gallini Collection, Milan, cited in Abbiati, i. 14–15.

49. E. Seletti, *Busseto*, ii. 307.

50. Demaldè.

51. Contract of Lease for the Osteria Vecchia of Roncole to the Tabloni family, dated 29 Nov. 1830, Archivio Diocesano, Fidenza. See also Don A. Aimi, 'Vi vuol dunque tutta l'energia col Verdi', *Corriere di Parma* (summer 1991), 88–90.

52. Stato Civile (Births), Archivio Storico del Comune, Besenzone, 1831–2. The index dates the first birth from May 1831, but the original record is dated June.

53. (Manuscript Collection, BMP-B).

54. F. Botti, *La forca d'Bretta* (Parma, 1958), 47–9. Mezzadri, 'of Sant'Agata di Cortemaggiore', was hanged on 25 Mar. 1833.

55. Photograph of room in Gatti, *Verdi nelle immagini* (Milan, 1941), 15.

56. 14 Dec. 1831 (Manuscript Collection, BMP-B).

57. Barezzi, note, 13 Jan. 1832 (Manuscript Collection, BMP-B).

58. [Antonio Accarini to Antonio Barezzi], note, (Manuscript Collection, BMP-B).

59. Minutes of the meeting of the administrative council of the Monte di Pietà (Manuscript Collection, BMP-B).

60. Carlo Verdi to [Accarini, the Podestà of Busseto], 18 Feb. 1832; and Antonio Barezzi to [Accarini, the Podestà of Busseto], 18 Feb. 1832 (Manuscript Collection, BMP-B).

61. [Spring 1832] (SAA).

62. Verdi's passport, issued 20 May 1832 (Museo Teatrale alla Scala).

Chapter 4

1. See Ch. 3 n. 62.

2. A. Calderini and R. Paribeni, *Milano* (Rome, 1951), 167 ff., 203 ff.

3. A. Bosisio, *Storia di Milano* (Milan, 1964), *passim*.

4. E. Seletti, *Busseto*, ii. 254 ff., The neighbourhood around the Casa dei Borromei was heavily bombed during the Second World War, leaving only the façade and a few inside walls of the Borromeo palace and little else of the 15th-cent. buildings that once surrounded it. Seletti's house in Via Santa Marta (formerly no. 19) was levelled. Before the war it was marked: 'In this house | Guest of the Bussetan Giuseppe Seletti | lived | GIUSEPPE VERDI | when for the first time | he came to our city | to learn the rudiments of that art | that has made him immortal | On the first centenary of his birth | the Comune [of Milan] laid this stone.' Cited in Gatti (1951), 42.

5. E. Seletti, *Busseto*, i. 255–7.

6. Giuseppe Seletti to Antonio Barezzi, 27 Aug. 1832 (SAA).

7. (SAA).

8. Giuseppe Seletti to Antonio Barezzi, 4 July 1832 (SAA).

9. Ibid.

10. Verdi's account, in Pougin, 140–1.

11. Giuseppe Seletti to Antonio Barezzi, 7 July 1832 (SAA).

12. (SAA).

13. E. Seletti, *Busseto*, ii. 307–8.

14. 3 Oct. 1883 (Museo Teatrale alla Scala).

15. A. Ghislanzoni, excerpt from his *Libro serio*, cited in Abbiati, i. 116.

16. Demaldè, note (Manuscript Collection, BMP-B).

17. C. Schmidl *Dizionario universale dei musicisti* (Milan, 1887), 259.

18. Verdi to Francesco Florimo, 9 Jan. 1871 (Library of the Conservatory of San Pietro a Majella, Naples).

19. Giuseppe Seletti to Antonio Barezzi, 8 Aug. 1832 (SAA).

20. See n. 18, above.

21. M. Mila, *La giovinezza di Verdi* (Turin, 1974), 30.

22. Dates of birth, professions, and street addresses of Angelo Boracchi, Leopoldo Robbia, Camillo Cirelli, and Vincenzo Merighi from Stato Civile (Rubrica del Ruolo della Popolazione, Milano, 1835), Archivio Storico Civico, Milan. I am grateful to Dr Camilla Gavazzi for helping with this area of research and for providing *Milano numerizzato ossia guida numerica della Regia Città di Milano*, Archivio Storico Civico, Milan and other relevant directories and maps of the period 1830–47.

23. Giuseppe Seletti to Antonio Barezzi, 18 Dec. 1832 (SAA): receipts.

24. Giuseppe Seletti to Antonio Barezzi [Nov. 1832] (SAA).

25. Giuseppe Seletti to Antonio Barezzi, 10 and 22 June 1833 (SAA).

26. 26 July 1833, cited in Gatti (1931), i. 190 n. 41.

27. Original Parish Registers (Deaths), Church of San Michele Arcangelo, Roncole, 1833; and Stato Civile, 1833, Archivio Storico del Comune, Busseto. The church record is the earliest document that places the Verdi family in the 'Birthplace' in Roncole, the Osteria that belonged to the Marquis and Marchioness Pallavicino. Curiously, the civil record states that she was a male child; this error was rectified when she died. (See Ch. 2, note 28.) The Verdis lived '*in domo juris Marchionis Romae*'. This is the only document placing them in the 'national monument birthplace'.

28. 22 June 1833 (SAA).

29. (SAA).

30. The description of the 1834 masked ball is in *Magnifico passeggio con ballo e maschere che ebbe luogo nella Galleria de Cristoforis la notte del 10 febbraio 1834*, published by Paolo Ripamonti Carcano, whose bookshop was at 20 Galleria de Cristoforis. See also *Gazzetta privilegiata di Milano*, 16 Feb. 1833, for the rules and orders governing the masked ball that year. Descriptions of these and other celebrations are in A. Blanche, *Sui Margini della storia: vecchia Milan*, 2 vols. (Milan, 1931).

31. Pougin, 40.

32. Stato Civile (Rubrica del Ruolo della Popolazione, Milano, 1835), Archivio Storico Civico, Milan.

33. Schmidl, *Dizionario dei musicisti*, i. 142. For further information on the Belgioiosos, see R. Barbiera's *La Principessa Belgioioso* (Milan, Treves, 1902); and B. A. Brombert's *Cristina* (New York, 1977). Princess Cristina Belgioioso had a long acquaintance with Giuseppina Strepponi, her mother Rosa Cornalba, and her sister Barberina Strepponi. In the 1830s they lived next to Palazzo Belgioioso in 105 Contrada della Guastalla, Milan; and in the 1850s they lived in Princess Cristina's Palazzo Salazar in Locate Triulzi, near Pavia. One of the most outrageous stories circulated about Princess Cristina concerned her lover Gaetano Stelzi, whose body she was said to have had embalmed and kept in a wardrobe in Palazzo Salazar. The Original Parish Registers (Deaths) of Locate Triulzi, show that Stelzi was indeed buried *one year after* he died, although it does not show where his body was kept all that time. Before becoming Princess Cristina's tenants, the Strepponis lived in another, simpler house in Locate, as one can see from the Status Animarum for the years of their residence there.

34. Verdi's account to Ricordi, in Pougin, 40.

35. Information about Massini's 'new school of singing' was first mentioned in *Barbiere* on 28 Mar. 1833; a performance of the first act of *Don Giovanni* was reviewed that year. In April the organization gave Vaccai's *Romeo e Giulietta*, which was also reviewed (24 Apr. 1833). Although Verdi is not mentioned until 1834, he may have been familiar with this company during the first year of its existence. I am grateful to Marcello Conati for calling these reviews to my attention.

36. J. N. Black ('The Libretto of *La creazione del mondo*, Milan, April 1834', *Studi verdiani* 2 (1983), 147 ff.) reproduces the title-pages and pages showing the cast of the two performances of this work. He notes that there was a change of cast, the first Adamo being Gaetano Nulli, the second being Luigi Valli, a student at Milan Conservatory.

37. R. L. Parker, 'Verdi and the *Gazzetta privilegiata di Milano*', *Research Chronicle*, 18 (1982), 60–1 (pub. by Royal Music Association, 1984). The work was described in the *Gazzetta* as a canzone, 'set to music by Maestro Verdi'. In the appendix of Parker's article the complete title is: 'Cantata pel dì natalizio di S[ua] M[aestà] Ferdinando Primo Imperatore e Re'. The singers were from Massini's Società Filarmonica.

38. A biographical sketch of Don Ballarini's life is in D. Soresina, *Enciclopedia della diocesena fidentina* (Fidenza, 1961), iii. 418.

39. The Bishop of Guastalla to Don Gian Bernardo Ballarini, 4 Nov. 1833 (G. Marchesi, *Verdi, merli, e cucù* (Busseto, 197S), 81).

40. Giuseppe Seletti to Antonio Barezzi, 25 July 1834 (SAA).

41. Giuseppe Seletti to Antonio Barezzi, 16 June 1834 (SAA).

42. Ibid.

Chapter 5

1. Record of meeting of the vestry, Collegiate Church of San Bartolomeo, Busseto, 16 June 1834. See also records of vestry meeting of 18 June 1834. Both documents are in the Parish Archive and are also reproduced in G. Marchesi, *Giuseppe Verdi: l'uomo, il genio, l'artista* (Milan, 1981), 91–3.

2. Demaldè.

3. Luigi Sanvitale, Bishop of Borgo San Donnino, to Francesco Cocchi, 9 July 1834 (Marchesi, *Verdi*, 102–3). Sanvitale, born in Parma in 1772, died in Piacenza in 1848. During the last years of his life, he became the enemy of Verdi's first cousin, Don Carlo Uttini.

4. Demaldè.

5. Sanvitale to Cocchi, 10 July 1834 (ibid. 104).

6. 22 June 1834 (SAA).

7. After Provesi's death, Demaldè acquired the collection. Before the Second World War, Carlo Gatti and local historians catalogued it.

8. 23 May 1833 (Marchesi, *Verdi*, 78–9).

9. Cited in F. T. Garibaldi, *Giuseppe Verdi nella vita e nell'arte* (Florence 1904), 43–4.

10. Giuseppe Seletti to Antonio Barezzi, 25 July 1834 (SAA). Verdi later also conducted one of his compositions, also a Mass, at the parish church of Croce Santo Spirito near Cremona on 11 Oct. 1837. See R. L. Parker's 'Verdi and the *Gazzetta privilegiata di Milano*', *Research Chronicle*, 18 (1982), 62.

11. Demaldè to Martini, 3 July 1834 (Marchesi, *Verdi*, 99).

12. Demaldè to Martini, 11 July 1834 (ibid. 105).

13. Demaldè to Martini, 17 July 1834 (ibid. 106).

14. Demaldè to Martini, 9 Aug. 1834 (ibid. 109–11).

15. Demaldè to Martini, 21 Sept. 1834 (ibid. 120–1). This letter is interesting in identifying the gifted Savazzini as one of Verdi's early supporters. He seems to have directed Carnival festivities in Piacenza from 1820 to 1823 and later was the organist in Busseto. Many of his compositions are in the

music archive of the BMP-B. The letter also names a Respighi who was a former music student at this time. The Respighis, Uttinis, and Verdis later intermarried, more than a century after they were first living in and near Cortemaggiore.

16. E. Santoro, *I teatri di Cremona* (Cremona, 1970), ii. 223 ff., see also 301–2. On 13 Oct. 1834, Antonio Barezzi sent out an appeal for funds to cover Morganti's fee, so that the Società Filarmonica could add this 'experienced professor of violin and extremely capable orchestra director' to its roster. Morganti had worked in Busseto for four years at the beginning of his career and had been orchestra director, maestro concertatore, and conductor for many orchestras in Lombardy. See L. A. Garibaldi, *Giuseppe Verdi nelle lettere di Emanuele Muzio ad Antonio Barezzi* (Milan, 1931), 380–2.

17. Demaldè to Martini, 18 Oct. 1834 (Marchesi, *Verdi*, 124–5).

18. [Luigi Seletti] to [Antonio Accarini, Podestà of Busseto], 7 Nov. 1834 (ibid. 134–5).

19. Francesco Silva to Antonio Accarini, 8 Nov. 1834 (ibid. 135–7).

20. Accarini to the Director-General of the Police Headquarters, Parma (ibid. 137–8).

21. Demaldè to Martini, 7 Nov. 1834 (Abbiati, i. 170–1). See also letters of 2, 3, and 6 Nov. (excerpts only, ibid.).

22. Ferrari to the Monte di Pietà, 15 Oct. 1834 (Marchesi, *Verdi*, 123).

23. Lorenzo Molossi to Demaldè, 11 Dec. 1834 (ibid. 145).

24. Demaldè to Martini, 29 Dec. 1834 (ibid. 146). See also Demaldè to Martini, 8 [Jan.] 1835 (ibid. 157).

25. A. Barezzi, page from Day-Book, 'in occasione di aver condotto Verdi e Martelli a Milano 5 January 1835', (C. Gatti, *Verdi nelle immagini* (Milan, 1941), 32). The page notes payments for transportation, tips, meals, theatre tickets in Lodi, and at La Scala, the Teatro Carcano, and the Teatro Cannobiana in Milan. Barezzi also bought 3 teaspoons. The trip from Lodi to Milan took as much as twelve hours in bad weather.

26. Strepponi's concerts in Lodi on 31 Oct. and 17 Nov. 1834 and the date of her arrival in Trieste are in Walker (Eng. edn.), 52.

27. It seems that Barezzi did indeed go directly to the new apartment with Verdi and Martelli, for had he lodged at Seletti's, he would not have paid for the dinners. De Capitani's father had been a court official.

28. 13 Jan. 1835 (Marchesi, *Verdi*, 159–62).

29. 5 Aug. 1834 (ibid. 109). The name 'Massini' has been misread by other biographers as 'Nicolini'. See Gatti (1951), 75, corrected by Walker (Eng.

edn.), 17 n. 2. The recent discovery of a large collection of Tasca's private papers may lead to further exploration of Verdi's relationship to this librettist, if it existed. The fact that Tasca wrote of Verdi's successes in *Nabucco* and *I Lombardi alla prima crociata* in 1843, signing himself 'O.T.' may indicate that he knew Verdi fairly well, given the tone of the poem, 'Brindisi d'un Imparziale a Quanti Figurarono nel Teatro alla Scala durante la Stagione Carnevalesca del 1842–3'.

30. Verdi to Demaldè, 24 Apr. 1835 (SAA). The Francesco Mingardi mentioned in this letter lived in Milan and served as intermediary between Verdi and Barezzi.

31. Ferdinando Galluzzi to Antonio Barezzi, 22 Aug. 1834 (transcription of original letter, Marchesi, *Verdi*, 114 ff.).

32. 31 Mar. 1835 (ibid. 213 ff.).

33. Luigi Bassetti, of the Ducal Dragoons, to the Commissario Territoriale of Borgo San Donnino, 14 Mar. 1835 (ibid. 200–1).

34. Sanvitale to Cocchi, 11 Mar. 1835 (ibid. 197).

35. 20 July 1835 (ibid. 252–3).

36. n.d. (SAA). From Barezzi's letter to Verdi of 15 July (SAA), we may conclude that Martelli's appeal to Verdi was probably written in June or early July.

37. Antonio Barezzi to Verdi, 15 July 1835 (SAA).

38. Verdi to Opprandino Arrivabene, 27 Dec. 1877 (A. Alberti, *Verdi intimo* (Milan, 1931), 205–6). See also Verdi to Brenna, 5 Oct. 1850 (Archive of TLF-V; ISV-P) and Verdi to Torelli, 7 Dec. 1856 (Biblioteca Nazionale, Naples, Biblioteca Lucchesi-Pallini; ISV-P).

39. Postscript to letter of 5 July 1835 (SAA).

40. Pougin, 41.

41. Review cited in Walker (Eng. end.), 24.

42. Demaldè to Martini, 21 Apr. 1835 (Marchesi, *Verdi*, 220).

43. Verdi to Demaldè, 24 Apr. 1835 (SAA).

44. Demaldè to Martini, 27 Feb. 1835 (Marchesi, *Verdi*, 182–3).

45. See n. 43, above.

46. Ibid.

47. Pougin, 41.

48. Verdi to Emilio Seletti, 14 May 1871 (Museo Teatrale alla Scala).

49. Lavigna, Certificate, 15 July 1835 (Manuscript Collection, BMP-B).

50. Sanvitale to the President for Internal Affairs, Parma, 3 June 1835 (Marchesi, *Verdi*, 231–2).

51. Demaldè to Martini, 28 July 1835 (ibid. 257).

52. 29 Aug. 1835 (ibid. 275).

53. 28 July 1835 (Biblioteca dell'Istituto G. Donizetti, Bergamo). Verdi wrote: 'Io scrivo l'opera (come tu sai)'.

54. Demaldè to Martini, 24 Sept. 1835 (Marchesi, *Verdi*, 309–10).

55. Seletti to Antonio Barezzi, 6 Nov. 1835 (SAA).

56. Verdi, Application to the Vestry of the Basilica Collegiata di San Giovanni, Monza, 11 Oct. 1835 (G. Riva, *La Cappella del Duomo di Monza (sec. XVII–XIX) e il Concorso di G. Verdi* (Monza, 1907), plate III; also in Marchesi, *Verdi*, 310).

57. Seletti to Antonio Barezzi, 28 Nov. 1835 (SAA).

58. Seletti to Antonio Barezzi (SAA).

59. [Between 3 and 11 Dec. 1835] (SAA).

60. 15 Dec. 1835 (Riva, *Cappella del Duomo*, plate V; also in Marchesi, *Verdi*, 317–18).

61. 18 Dec. 1835 (Riva, *Cappella del Duomo*, 29–30; also in Marchesi, *Verdi*, 318–19).

62. Demaldè to Martini, 7 Jan. 1836 (Marchesi, *Verdi*, 323). Barezzi wrote in his Day-Book about the same concert: 'Il concorso è stato immenso, in particolare dopo pranzo, e l'incontro è stato generale, anche dalla parte avversa' (see Gatti (1931), i. 118).

63. Antonio Accarini, Announcement of Competition, 23 Jan. 1836 (L. Carrara (ed.), *Verdi: rivista per l'anno giubilare* (Bologna, 1926); also in Marchesi, *Verdi*, 325–7).

64. Antonio Barezzi to Antonio Accarini, 26 Jan. 1836 (Marchesi, *Verdi*, 328–30).

65. Demaldè to Martini, 23 Feb. 1836 (ibid. 331–2). 'We are on the eve of finding out whether the Philharmonic hit the target straight in the middle regarding Verdi's ability.'

66. Verdi to Antonio Barezzi, 29 Feb. 1836 (facsimile in L. Carrara (ed.), *Verdi: rivista per l'anno giubilare*, 14–15). Part of the letter seems to have been written by Verdi and Molossi to Barezzi and part by Ferdinando Accarini to his father. Young Accarini was a painter, then working in Parma. The original is perhaps in the collection at Villa Paradiso, Busseto.

67. Molossi to Antonio Barezzi. See n. 66, above.

68. Ibid.

69. Ferdinando Accarini to Antonio Accarini. See n. 66, above.

70. I am grateful to Marcello De Angelis for calling my attention to the Paganini material which is in LAN-BN-F.

Chapter 6

1. Minute, President for Internal Affairs, 5 Mar. 1836 (Gustavo Marchesi, *Giuseppe Verdi: l'uomo, il genio, l'artista* (Milan, 1981), 339). See also Antonio Accarini to Antonio Barezzi, 12 Mar. 1836 (ibid. 342).

2. Luigi Sanvitale, Bishop of Borgo San Donnino, to the President for Internal Affairs, 23 Aug. 1835 (ibid. 272). He pressed to have the ban extended 'forever' so that 'there will be no further profanation of a Holy Place'.

3. 14 Mar. 1836 (ibid. 342–3).

4. 21 Dec. 1835 (ibid. 321–2).

5. Declaration of Intention to Wed, 16 Apr. 1836, Stato Civile, Archivio Storico del Comune, Busseto.

6. Agreement between Verdi and the City of Busseto, 20 Apr. 1836 (Marchesi, *Verdi*, 352–4).

7. See n. 5, above.

8. Don Andrea Pettorelli, manuscript poem *Gli uccelli accademici*, in BMP-B. Born in 1779, Pettorelli became provost of San Bartolomeo after Verdi left the city. He also taught in the schools there and was a prolific writer. Among his works is a poem *Il sogno di Nabucco*, with which Verdi may have been familiar. It, too, is in BMP-B. See D. Soresina, *Enciclopedia diocesana fidentina* (Fidenza, 1961), i. 351.

9. Cavalli, 19.

10. 25 Apr. 1836 (SAA).

11. The Tedaldis, a noble family, had other business dealings with Barezzi, sometimes serving as witnesses or depositing bonds for his purchases of real estate. (See Barezzi's deeds, with Andrea Tedaldi's signatures, Collection of Gianfranco Stefanini, Busseto.) The Marquis and Marchioness Tedaldi occupied the main floor or *piano nobile* of the house; Verdi and Margherita probably lived on the second floor, where a spacious apartment with a fine salon remained intact until the recent restoration. With its beautiful frescoes, which decorated even the bedroom walls, this was a fine residence for the young couple; Gigia, their servant; and their children.

12. The two charcoal portraits, one of Verdi and one of Margherita Barezzi, were done by Stefano Barezzi, perhaps on their honeymoon, perhaps on

their wedding-day. The original portrait of Verdi is in the collection of Gianfranco Stefanini, to whom I am grateful for permission to open the back of the frame to identify the artist. Anna Faroldi helped in the search for it. The portrait of Margherita was formerly in the collection of Luigi Agostino Garibaldi of Quarto, Genoa, whose family was given many of the most important Barezzi documents and some of Margherita's jewellery, together with portraits of her, one of which was reproduced in L. A. Garibaldi's *Giuseppe Verdi nelle lettere di Emanuele Muzio ad Antonio Barezzi* (Milan, 1931). The portrait of Margherita was found in November 1992 in the collection belonging to the heirs of Amalia Barezzi (Margherita's youngest sister) and Fortunato Merli (from whom Verdi bought the farm at Sant'Agata). A partial inventory of the collection, provided below, was given to me in Busseto in 1964. It included: 4 vols. of Barezzi's Day-Books; 3 vols. of Barezzi's *Copialettere* Letter-Books; autographed letters from Margherita Barezzi; 9 letters from Strepponi to Antonio Barezzi and his second wife; the entire collection of Muzio's letters to Barezzi; Margherita Barezzi's wedding-ring; her locket and a lock of her hair; and 2 portraits of her executed by her uncle, Stefano Barezzi. The catalogue of the exhibition organized by *La stampa* in Turin in Apr. 1941 also lists the silver box in which Verdi kept Margherita's wedding-ring; the portrait of Verdi by Stefano Barezzi; Boldini's portrait of Emanuele Muzio; 6 letters from Giovanni Barezzi to his father (1844), one also signed by Verdi; a receipt signed by Provesi; a receipt for a carriage trip from Piacenza to Genoa, from Genoa to Pisa, from Florence to Rome, made out to Verdi (1849); receipt for trip to Porta Romana, Milan, signed by Verdi (1839); a hotel bill (Verdi) (1849); 2 letters from Giovanni Barezzi (Jan. and Dec. 1841) about *Nabucco* and Strepponi; Barezzi's notes on his trip with Verdi to Naples in 1849; letter from Barezzi to his daughter Marianna Barezzi Garbi; draft of letter from Barezzi written after the Battle of Novara; 4 letters from Piave to Giovannino and Antonio Barezzi; note in Verdi's hand with his address in Genoa and an itinerary of a trip from Fiorenzuola to Genoa; printed announcement of the opera *Violetta* at the Teatro Regio, Parma, 1855; tickets issued to Verdi by the management of the Royal Academy in Paris for the first and second performances of *Jérusalem*; invitation from Napoleon III to Verdi for a reception at the Tuileries; memorandum in Verdi's hand with the expenses for travel and lodging in Rome and Naples (no date); copy of a letter from Verdi to his farm-manager asking him to persuade all the people in the country to vote for annexation to the Piedmont; 9 letters from Francesco Silva to Antonio Barezzi; and 2 letters from Stefano Barezzi to his brother. This important collection has been lost for almost fifty years. It was apparently never returned to the Garibaldis, as Luigi Agostino Garibaldi's heir has stated on more than one occasion. The fact that at least one of these items (and perhaps more than one) is in Busseto may suggest that this entire collection was divided among Amalia Barezzi's heirs, some of whom now live in Milan and Rome.

13. 'Giuseppe Verdi: nuovi particolari inediti ed interessanti', *Il pensiero di Nizza* (29, 30, and 31 Dec. 1876 and 4 Jan. 1877). Parts of these articles are cited in Pougin, 18 ff. In his *José Verdi*, Cavalli gives a slightly different version of this story.

14. Carlo Verdi to the President for Internal Affairs, 25 Sept. 1836 (Marchesi, *Verdi*, 370–1). See also Barezzi to the Monte di Pietà, 26 Jan. 1836 (ibid. 328–30).

15. Minutes of the administrative council of the Monte di Pietà, 'Informazione e parere del Podestà Presidente del Monte di Pietà [etc.]', 19 Dec. 1836, (ibid. 375–7).

16. 15 Oct. 1836 (Biblioteca dell'Istituto G. Donizetti, Bergamo).

17. Ibid.

18. Demaldè; in *La città di Busseto* ((Milan, 1883), ii. 308) Emilio Seletti also remarked on Verdi's friends' efforts to 'get him out of Busseto'.

19. Gasparo Tavelli to Verdi, 14 Feb. 1884 (SAA).

20. 2 Nov. 1837 (cited in Abbiati, i. 241).

21. 3 Nov. 1837 (Biblioteca dell'Istituto G. Donizetti, Bergamo). From Verdi's previous letter to Massini, dated 9 Oct. 1837, we have confirmation that Massini was then living at Contrada del Lauro 1810, the address that in the Stato Civile (Rubrica del Ruolo della Popolazione, Milano, 1835) is given as No. 1810, annex of the Teatro dei Filodrammatici. The Rubrica is in the Archivio Storico Civico, Milan.

22. Programmes of these and other concerts of the Philharmonic are in the Museo Civico, Busseto.

23. Molossi to Giuseppe Demaldè, 14 Apr. 1838 (SAA).

24. Ibid.

25. Concert programmes in Museo Civico, Busseto.

26. The edn. included a fine portrait of Verdi, commissioned by Canti, who also commissioned a portrait of Don Ruggero Manna of Cremona in the same format. In Aug. and Sept. 1838, Manna was composing music for Giuseppina Strepponi, the leading soprano of the Teatro della Concordia in Cremona. She may have met Manna in Trieste, when they were both living there. Manna was a protégé of Princess Elisa Bonaparte Baciocchi, whose son-in-law Count Filippo Camerata dei Passionei was one of Strepponi's lovers in 1841. Strepponi sang the music Manna composed for her in

concerts at the Concordia in the autumn season of 1838. Because the Selettis, Barezzis, and Verdi went to opera often in the cities around Busseto, and because they were very frequently in Cremona, it is entirely possible that Verdi heard some of Strepponi's performances at the Concordia, where both Manna and Morganti were very much at home. Cirelli was the impresario for this autumn season. According to Elio Santoro, Strepponi's first performance was 15 August, which probably means that she did not sing in Leghorn in *Caterina di Guisa* by Fabio Campana on 14 Aug., as reported by Walker. (See Walker (Italian edn.), 70.) This important season in Cremona was honoured by the presence of the Emperor of Austria, Ferdinand I, his Empress, and many members of their Court; they and their entourage arrived on 23 Sept. and heard Strepponi in *Norma* that night. (See E. Santoro, *I teatri di Cremona* (Cremona, 1970) ii. 231–2, 305–6.) Manna was also the head of the Società Filarmonica in Cremona, and thus held the corresponding position to Barezzi's in Busseto, Molossi's in Parma, Francesco Strepponi's in Lodi, and Massini's in Milan.

27. A. Alberti (*Verdi intimo*, 333), cites a letter from Opprandino Arrivabene to Verdi, [31] Oct. 1886: 'Retroceduto talvolta sino ad 1837 oppure 1836 che sia, m'è tornato in mente quando a Milano sedevamo accanto "Al Leoncino". Alla stessa tavola sedeva pure il Vaccai, non presago che l'amico che mi stava al lato, modesto e taciturno, ne avrebbe presto oscurata la fama!'

28. Stato Civile, (Births), Archivio Storico del Comune, Busseto, 14 Aug. 1838, birth of Icilio Romano Carlo Antonio Verdi.

29. 5 Sept. 1838 (Bonini Collection, Busseto).

Chapter 7

1. E. Colombo, *Scenografie Sormani*, tr. by M. J. Phillips-Matz (Milan, 1988), 2. Still flourishing, the firm, now more than 150 years old, belongs to Anthony Stivanello of New York, who acquired it from Ercole Sormani, its founder's descendant.

2. Gatti (1931), i. 145.

3. Verdi to Antonio Barezzi [11 Sept. 1838] (Bonini Collection, Busseto).

4. Verdi to Antonio Barezzi, 16 Sept. 1838 (Bonini Collection, Busseto).

5. Stato Civile (Rubrica del Ruolo della Popolazione, Milano, 1835), Archivio Storico Civico, Milan. Pasetti and his sister lived in the Parish of Santa Maria della Passione, the Strepponis' parish; he later moved to 1812 Piazza del Teatro dei Filodrammatici, next to Cirelli and Massini.

6. Verdi to [Giuseppe Demaldè?], 6 Oct. 1838 (Bonini Collection, Busseto).

7. Conversation of Margherita Barezzi, described by Ballarini; see Ch. 5 n. 32.

8. 28 Oct. 1838 (Museo Civico, Busseto).

9. Pougin, 41.

10. Verdi to Emilio Seletti, 14 May 1871 (Museo Teatrale alla Scala).

11. Demaldè.

12. For further discussion of *Rocester*, see M. Conati, '*L'Oberto, conte di San Bonifacio* in due recensioni straniere poco note e in una lettera inedita di Verdi', in *Atti del I congresso internazionale di studi verdiani* (Parma, 1969), 67–92. See also C. Sartori, '*Rocester*, la prima opera di Verdi', *Rivista musicale italiana*, 43: 1 (1939), 97–104; Walker, 26; Budden, i. 46 and n., 48–9, 59, 66; and D. R. B. Kimbell, 'Poi . . . diventò l'*Oberto*', *Music and Letters*, 52 (1971), 1–7. The fact that Demaldè spells the name of the opera right (*Rochester*) makes one think that he might have seen a libretto or the score itself. It is entirely possible that Verdi himself read Demaldè's 'Cenni biografici' and read them aloud to Strepponi in Apr. 1853, as he said he would do in a letter to Piave of [1 Apr.] 1853 (cited in Abbiati, i. 240). See also Strepponi (postscript of Verdi's letter to Piave, dated 27 Mar. 1853) (Abbiati, i. 239–40). Had there been a serious error, he would perhaps have corrected it, as he wrote to Piave that the sketch represented 'the whole truth'—'tutta la verità'. Because Amalia Massini, Pietro Massini's daughter, lived in Brescia at the end of her life, other papers of the impresario may be found there.

13. (ISV-P).

14. Cited in Walker, 32.

15. 22 Apr. 1839 (SAA).

16. Pougin, 41.

17. *Enciclopedia dello spettacolo* (Rome, 1954–62), vii. 844–6.

18. Ibid. viii. 1187–8.

19. Stato Civile (Rubrica del Ruolo della Popolazione, Milano, 1835), Archivio Storico Civico, Milan.

20. M. De Angelis, *Le carte dell'impresario* (Florence, 1982), 163. The complete record from the orphanage (1839–41) gives the names of wet-nurses and foster-families to whom this baby was assigned and of the couple who finally claimed falsely that they were her 'true and legitimate parents'. I am also indebted to Dr Rosalia Manno-Tolù, Sovrintendente per i Beni Archivistici of Tuscany and of the Archivio di Stato in Florence for helping me find the police documents relating to official suspicions that Strepponi and Lanari had broken the law by concealing the birth, which was officially

represented as 'stomach trouble' and 'sore throat'. The description of the birth, described in Antonio Gazzuoli's letter to Lanari on 9 Feb. 1839, is in the BN-F. (See M. J. Phillips-Matz, '*José Verdi*, Hercules Cavalli, and the Florence *Macbeth*', in A. Porter and D. Rosen (eds.) *Verdi's 'Macbeth': A Sourcebook* ((New York, 1984), 133.) The authorities apparently believed that a miscarriage or stillbirth had taken place, as I reported in 1977, in the Danville, Kentucky, Fifth International Verdi Congress. I am indebted to De Angelis for the discovery of what actually happened in 1839, for his understanding of the procedures that followed the abandonment of a baby at the orphanage and for collaboration in further research.

21. Camillo Cirelli to Alessandro Lanari, 26 Jan. 1839 (De Angelis, *Carte*, 156–7).

22. Cirelli to Lanari, 22 and 24 Apr. 1839 (ibid. 164). This letter, bearing two dates, was written from Milan just after Strepponi's début there in *I Puritani*.

23. C. Gatti, *Il Teatro alla Scala* (Milan, 1964), ii. 41.

24. *Enciclopedia dello spettacolo*, viii. 1187. Domenico Ronconi died on 11 Apr., while rehearsals for *I Puritani* were in progress.

25. 24 Apr. 1839 (BN-F).

26. Ibid.

27. 20 May 1839 (BN-F).

28. Ibid.

29. Pougin, 41.

30. Merelli to Lanari, 25 May 1839 (BN-F).

31. Ibid.

32. Strepponi to Lanari, 23 June 1839 (BN-F).

33. When *Oberto* was staged at La Scala, Strepponi was singing under Lanari's banner at the Teatro alla Pergola in Florence. She then went on to Verona, where she stayed until the beginning of Mar. She was again ill and wished to withdraw from the Verona season; her request for a period of rest led to an acrimonious controversy with Lanari.

34. Pougin, 41.

35. Ibid.

36. Ibid.

37. Neuschel to Michele Pazzoni 14 Feb. 1839 (Marchesi, *Verdi*, 399).

38. Neuschel to Michele Pazzoni, 9 Mar. 1839 (ibid. 400–1).

39. Neuschel to Marie Louise of Parma, 12 Apr. 1839 (ibid. 401–2).

40. Pougin, 41–2.

41. Ibid.

42. Abbiati, i. 310–12. Abbiati provides a veritable guide to the quarter, describing the old Osteria della Scala at Teatro Grande and the Caffè Martini, the De Marchi *palazzo*, and the theatrical people who lived in the area.

43. Pougin, 42.

44. Gatti (1951), 138. The street is now Via Cesare Correnti, which runs into the Carrobbio.

45. (Bonini Collection, Busseto).

46. Ibid.

47. Abbiati, i. 316.

48. 20 Oct. 1839 (Gatti (1951), 138).

49. Pougin, 43. Here, in his own account of his life, Verdi misrepresents the circumstances of the death of his daughter Virginia, saying that she died 'a few days' after Icilio Romano.

50. Ibid. 42.

51. F. T. Garibaldi, *Giuseppe Verdi nella vita e nell'arte* (Florence, 1904), 52.

52. Cited in Gatti (1951), 140.

53. Cited in Gatti (1951), 140–1.

54. See Conati, '*L'Oberto*', 81 ff. Another review, from the *Corriere delle dame*, is mentioned and excerpts from it are reproduced in pp. 84–5 n. 45.

55. Pougin, 42.

56. Tito Ricordi to Giovanni Morandi, 9 Nov. 1839 (G. Radiciotti, *Lettere inedite di celebri musicisti* ((Milan, [1892]), 109).

57. M. J. Phillips-Matz, 'Casa Ricordi', *Opera News*, 15 Dec. 1958. All material for this article was provided by Casa Ricordi from their archive in Milan during my visit there in 1956.

58. *Verdi Newsletter*, 13 (American Institute for Verdi Studies, New York, 1985), 6–20.

59. J. Rosselli, *The Opera Industry in Italy from Cimarosa to Verdi: The Role of the Impresario* (Cambridge, 1984), 129–30.

60. Conati, '*L'Oberto*', 83–7; see n. 54, above. The review from *Allgemeine Musikalische Zeitung* is reproduced in the illustration following p. 88.

Chapter 8

1. (SAA).

2. M. Engelhardt, 'Nuovi dati sulla nascita dell'opera giovanile di Verdi, *Un giorno di regno*', *Studi Verdiani* 4 (1986–7), 13–16.

3. Pougin, 42.

4. '*Un giorno di regno* from Romani's Libretto to Verdi's Opera', *Studi Verdiani* 2 (1983), 38 ff.

5. Pougin, 42–3.

6. Register of Deaths, Congregazione Municipale della Regia Città di Milano, June 1840, Archivio di Stato, Milan.

7. (Cited in Gatti (1931), i. 171).

8. Pougin, 43.

9. Barezzi, Day-Book, entry by unidentified shop clerk (cited in Gatti (1931), i. 171).

10. Demaldè.

11. Pougin, 43.

12. Inventory of furniture shipped by Verdi, 9 Nov. 1840, Bonini Collection, Busseto.

13. (Museo Teatrale alla Scala, Milan).

14. Demaldè.

15. Review in *Il Figaro* (cited in Abbiati, i. 352–3).

16. Reviews from *La moda* and *Glissons, n'appuyons pas* (ibid. i. 353–4).

17. Verdi's support of Scalese is documented in letters (1883) from the bass to Verdi and in Muzio's letters describing the conditions in which the Scalese family lived at the time when he delivered Verdi's donations himself.

18. Review in *La fama* (cited in Abbiati, i. 353).

19. Ibid.

20. Review in *Il Figaro* (Abbiati, i. 353).

21. Verdi to Tito Ricordi, 4 Feb. 1859 (*C*, 556).

22. Verdi to Filippo Filippi, 9 Feb. 1859 (*C*, 557–8).

23. A. Pettorelli, *Gli uccelli accademici* (Manuscript Collection, BMP-B).

24. Pougin, 43.

25. These items were given back to the Barezzis after Verdi's death. One

of Antonio Barezzi's heirs gave them to the Garibaldi family. (Ch. 6, n. 12.)

26. Stato Civile (Rubrica del Ruolo della Popolazione, Milano, 1835), Archivio Storico Civico, Milan. The Galleria De Cristoforis, destroyed during the Second World War, stood where the present Galleria del Toro is. A 'new' 1950s Galleria De Cristoforis is farther along, toward the Duomo. Later Verdi lived at 860 and Muzio at 866 Contrada Del Monte, with Merelli sandwiched in between.

27. Pougin, 43–5.

28. M. Lessona, *Volere è potere* (Florence, 1876), 296–7.

29. 7 Mar. 1874 (A. Alberti, *Verdi intimo* (Milan, 1931), 166–76). Alberti also gives the Lessona text.

30. Demaldè.

31. Cavalli, 23–4.

32. Verdi to Dr Luigi Balestra, 12 Jan. 1841, in Gatti (1951), 131. See also Conati, '*L'Oberto*', 67–92.

33. [4] Apr. 1841, SAA.

34. Pougin, 45–6; see also 25 n. 1 on Verdi's collaboration with Solera and the librettist's career at La Scala.

35. 11 Feb. 1873 (SAA). Saporiti wrote to Verdi on other occasions, always from Angera on Lago Maggiore.

36. Maria Negri to Verdi, 15 Dec. 1876 (SAA). The daughter of a cabinet minister in the Italian government, she lived in Turin.

37. Pougin, 45.

Chapter 9

1. Verdi's account to Ricordi (Pougin, 45).

2. Cited in L. Carrara, 'Modeste origini', in id. (ed.), *Verdi: rivista per l'anno giubilare* (Bologna, 1926), 8–9. The letter itself was in the Verdi exhibition mounted by the newspaper *La stampa* in Turin in 1941, where it was catalogued.

3. *Volere è potere* (Florence, 1869), 298.

4. Demaldè.

5. Statement by Tito Barezzi, reported in *Il presente*, in an article (31 Aug. 1913). Although not documented elsewhere, this matter is alluded to in other documents, some in Verdi's own hand, and some having his indirect approval or endorsement.

6. Verdi's account to Ricordi (Pougin, 45).

7. See n. 5, above.

8. Verdi's account to Ricordi (Pougin, 46).

9. A. Cavicchi, 'Verdi e Solera, considerazioni sulla collaborazione per *Nabucco*', in *Atti del I congresso internazionale di studi verdiani* (Parma, 1969), 44–58.

10. 4 Mar. 1842 G. Zavadini, *Donizetti: vita, musiche, epistolario* ((Bergamo, 1948), 579–80).

11. See n. 5, above. Tito Barezzi also recalled the episode of the overture to *Nabucco*. See I. Pizzi, *Ricordi verdiani inediti* (Turin, 1901), 96.

12. *Giuseppe Verdi: 'Nabucodonosor'*, critical edn. (Chicago, 1987), introd. *passim*.

13. See n. 5, above.

14. Pougin, 35.

15. Ibid.

16. (10 Mar. 1842).

17. (10 Mar. 1842).

18. (15 Mar. 1842).

19. *Volere*, 299.

20. Verdi's account to Ricordi (Pougin, 34–5).

21. For further information on the Strepponis' musical activities, see G. Oldrini, *Storia musicale di Lodi* (Lodi, 1883), *passim*; and C. Schmidl, *Dizionario universale dei musicisti* (1887; Milan, 1926), ii, under 'Strepponi'.

22. Original Parish Registers (Baptisms, Marriages, and Status animarum), cathedral and church of Santa Maria del Sole, Archivio del Duomo, Lodi. When Strepponi's parents married, her father was still a student in Milan. Their other children were: Davide Carlo Cristoforo, born 1817; Maria Teresa, born 1818; Maria Antonietta, born 1819; and Barberina, named for her mother's Barberini ancestors, born in Monza in 1828. Francesco, Giuseppina's uncle, was, as we have seen, the head of the Philharmonic Society in Lodi. He also taught Carlotta Ferrari, Italy's only woman composer of professionally performed operas in the nineteenth century.

23. Gatti (1951), 133.

24. Report from the Royal Provincial Delegation in Lodi to the Imperial Royal Government in Milan, 27 June 1834. Dr Barblan kindly sent me a photocopy of this document, which is in the Milan Conservatory Archives.

25. Walker (Eng. edn.), 49.

26. Stato Civile (Rubrica del Ruolo della Popolazione, Milano, 1835), Archivio Storico Civico, Milan.

27. Walker (Eng. edn.), 52–6 gives a compilation of many of Strepponi's performances in this period.

28. [Alessandro Lanari] to Cirelli, 17 Apr. 1837 (M. De Angelis, *Le carte dell'impresario* (Florence, 1982), 141).

29. A partial reconstruction of the career of Francesco Luigi Morini, a Bolognese tenor, has been made possible from examination of the annals of the theatres of Bologna and Leghorn, notices in theatrical papers, and letters in the Lanari Archive (under Carteggi vari), which I had the opportunity to identify correctly and re-collate in the BN-F in 1975–7. I have believed for years that Morini might have been the father of Giuseppa Faustina, the daughter of Strepponi whose paternity was in question during the pregnancy. *The seducer was in Florence while Lanari and Moriani were in Venice together.* (See Cirelli to Lanari, 26 Jan. 1839: 'In a word, I believe that I am the F[ather], that the Sergeant could leave nothing behind him but a vile stain [and not a pregnancy]. If you only knew how he is behaving!!! Of course, we should have expected it of him.') Abbiati frequently spoke in the 1950s of his conclusion that Moriani was the father of the child Strepponi was expecting and wrote of their relationship in 1959 in his biography of Verdi. (See Abbiati, i. 296, 297 ('il frutto della sua debolezza umana'), 369 ('Strepponi e l'inseparabile Moriani'), 378–9 ('un "vile M...", non pero di Verona, bensi, opiniamo, di Firenze.... Pare che costui—Moriani—abbia messa a sua volta la primadonna nei pasticci')).

30. Original Parish Registers (Baptisms), Church of San Eusebio, Parish of San Filippo, Turin. I am grateful to Don Maurizio Bottasodi, who helped me find this document in 1977 and made a legalized copy of it for me, and to Pietro and Bruna Fanchin, who assisted in this research. In the Stato Nominativo or Stato Civile (Births) for 1838, Camillino is entered under the name 'Sterponi', in Turin records.

31. *Enciclopedia dello spettacolo* (Rome, 1954–62), ix. 1621–3. Feliciano Strepponi may have used one of Vestri's plays as a source for one of his operas. Vestri's son Gaetano later translated *Stifelius*, from which *Stifelio* was taken.

32. Antonietta Dupin married the Bergamasque tenor Domenico Donzelli at a time when several members of her family were choreographers and dancers.

33. [Jan. 1839] (cited in Walker, 65). See also Gazzuoli to Lanari, 9 Feb. 1839 (LAN-BN-F) in which Lanari's aide gives the impresario a detailed account

of the costume fitting before *Il giuramento*. Romani, writing on that same day, 9 Feb., was much more circumspect.

34. Registro di Introduzione 1839, segnato A, Part I, no. 209, entry for Sinforosa Cirelli, abandoned on 28 Feb. 1839, Ospedale degli Innocenti, Florence (cited in De Angelis, *Carte*, 163). She was known as Sinforosa Cirelli until Jan. 1841, when a couple came to the Innocenti to declare that she was their legitimate child and that her name was Giuseppa Faustina. Sostegno Stefani and his wife Luisa Albizi were obviously sent by Strepponi or Cirelli or someone acting for them, for they produced the child's original baptism certificate, from the church of San Giovanni. (See ibid. 138–9.) This child grew up with the Stefanis in a house just a few steps from the Arno and died in Florence in the San Bonifazio Hospital for the Insane in 1919. She was unmarried and was a charity patient.

35. Lanari, documents relating to litigation with Strepponi, 1840 (ibid. 173).

36. Letters of 1 and 3 Mar. 1840 (ibid. 183–4).

37. Stato Civile (Births, 1840, Milan), Parish of Santa Maria della Passione, record of female child born dead on 22 Mar. 1840. Neither parent is identified. I am grateful to Don Attilio Cavalli of Santa Maria della Passione in Milan for letting me examine the baptismal registers of his church, so they could be checked against the Stato Civile in the Archivio Storico Civico.

38. See Strepponi chronology in Walker, 55.

39. W. Ashbrook, *Donizetti* (London, 1965), 250–1.

40. See n. 36, above, for Boracchi's reference to Monti, the fiancé. The 'father of a family' is referred to in Strepponi's letter of 16 Aug. 1841 to Lanari (see Abbiati, i. 380–1; original in (LAN-BN-F).

41. Strepponi's first reference to 'Count C—' of Ancona is found in her letter to Lanari dated 20 Aug. 1841, but she could have met him during the season she sang under Lanari in Senigallia in 1839 (July and Aug.), for Camerata was on the theatre council and gave Lanari an apartment and office in his palazzo during the season. (See Camerata's correspondence with Lanari, BN-F)

42. 16 Aug. 1841 (LAN-BN-F).

43. 25 Sept. 1841 (LAN-BN-F).

44. Original Parish Registers (Baptisms), church of Santa Maria Maggiore, Trieste, 5 Nov. 1841. Adelina's godmother was Teresa Guerrieri-Paradisi, a singer.

45. Original Parish Registers (Deaths), church of Santa Maria Maggiore, Trieste,

4 Oct. 1842. The house in which Adelina died is shown in an 1865 lithograph of 'Die Kirche der Evangelische gemeinde A.B. in Triest', in A. Seri, *Trieste nelle sue stampe* (Trieste, 1979).

46. Strepponi, undated portrait with dedication (SAA).

47. 3 Feb. 1842 (LAN-BN-F).

48. See n. 10, above.

49. 14 Mar. 1842 (LAN-BN-F).

50. Report of Milanese physicians (Stefano Moro, Alessandro Vandoni, Gaetano Ciceri) attesting to Strepponi's illness, 3 Mar. 1842. See also Strepponi to Lanari, 14 Mar. 1842 (Both in LAN-BN-F).

51. 23 Mar. 1842 (LAN-BN-F).

52. 26 Mar. 1842 (LAN-BN-F).

53. 23 Mar. 1842 (LAN-BN-F).

54. A. Mazzucato, Review (13 Mar. 1842).

55. Review reproduced in part in Abbiati, i. 415–16, where the reviewer, G. Romani, is incorrectly identified as Felice Romani. Walker (Eng. edn., 92) was the first to note and correct the error.

56. G. J. Pezzi, review of *Nabucco* in *Glissons, n'appuyons pas*, repr. in *Teatri, arti e letteratura* (24 Mar. 1842). See also Parker (ed.), *Giuseppe Verdi: 'Nabucodonosor'*, introd. nn. 50–3.

57. A. Mazzucato, Review in *Gazzetta musicale di Milano* (20 Mar. 1842).

BOOK II

Chapter 10

1. A. Calderini and R. Paribeni, *Milano* (Rome, 1951), 205; see also 203.

2. Memoir, cited in R. Barbiera, *Il salotto della Contessa Maffei* (Milan, 1895), 126.

3. Cavalli, 26.

4. In a letter Verdi wrote to Clara Maffei's biographer Raffaele Barbiera on 14 June 1892, he said that he had met her in the first months of 1842. Two studies of her and her circle are Barbiera's *Salotto*, and Di Ascoli. Although it has many errors of transcription, Di Ascoli documents the activities of the Maffeis, Verdi, Strepponi, Tenca, and their friends more thoroughly than any other book. A corrected copy of it is in the Istituto di Studi Verdiani, Parma.

5. M. S. Tronca, 'Il Maffei politico: un cosmopolita nell'Europa dell'800', in *L'Ottocento di Andrea Maffei* (Riva del Garda, 1987), 75.

6. Calderini and Paribeni, *Milano*, 205 ff., 280–1.

7. Clara Maffei's resistance to pressure to visit Austrian authorities and sympathizers is documented in her correspondence.

8. Evocations of 'Verdi and Victory' and to Verdi's position as 'the Glory of Italy' are in *Strenna teatrale europea*, ix. (Milan, 1846), 55–7, 281–2 and in earlier *Strenne*.

9. *Enciclopedia italiana*, iv. 597.

10. (Milan, 1877), *passim*.

11. Arrivabene to Verdi, 31 Oct. 1886 (A. Alberti, *Verdi intimo* (Milan, 1931), 333–4; see also pp. ix–xiii).

12. Abbiati, i. 415–16.

13. Among contributors to it and *Rivista italiana* were Cantù, Achille Mauri, G. Romagnosi, Tenca, Count Giulio Püllé, Carcano, Abramo Basevi, Andrea Maffei, Arrivabene, and Giacinto Battaglia.

14. *Enciclopedia italiana*, vii. 979. See also Barbiera, *Salotto*, 21, 96 ff.

15. See W. Weaver, 'The Shakespeare Verdi Knew', in A. Porter and D. Rosen (eds.), *Verdi's 'Macbeth': A Sourcebook* (New York, 1984), 144–5.

16. *Enciclopedia italiana*, xvii. 994.

17. Ibid. xxii. 77.

18. Carlo Tenca to Clara Maffei, 31 Jan. 1869 (Di Ascoli, 197).

19. *Enciclopedia italiana*, xxxiii. 483. See also Tenca's letters and the biographical information on him in Di Ascoli. He lived with Count Porro at Contrada del Monte di Pietà 15.

20. Sonnet to Clara Maffei (Barbiera, *Salotto*, 134). Tommaso Grossi, writing in Milanese dialect, described Clara Maffei's cleverness, personal magnetism, sweet voice, and intelligence (see ibid. 16–17). For Maffei's poem to his wife, 'Tu mi guardi', see ibid. 15.

21. Ibid. 101–2.

22. Fondo Presidenza del Governo, ccli 'Conti del Sandrini'; and ccxl/v 'Sandrini che è quello di cui sono la più parte degli atti segreti per parte del Governo (Conti di pagamento)', Archivio di Stato, Milan. The record reads: 'nel 1848 fu cacciato; nel 1859 si amicò i Piemontesi'.

23. *Milano numerizzato ossia guida numerica della Regia Città di Milano*, Archivio Storico Civico, Milan.

24. Two of the letters (Sept.–Oct. 1842 and Paris 1847) were published by A. M. Cornelio in 'Giuseppe Verdi, sue memorie e la sua Casa di Riposo per Musicisti', *Rassegna nazionale*, 122 (1903), 594–8. Abbiati published

one from 1842 in Abbiati, i. 422–3. Those of 21 July 1842 and Sept.–Oct. 1842 appear in A. Oberdorfer, *Giuseppe Verdi: autobiografia dalle lettere* (3rd edn. ed. by Marcello Conati, Milan, 1981), 125–7, in Biblioteca Universale Rizzoli. The Museo Teatrale alla Scala has 13 of Verdi's letters to Donna Emilia, dating from 21 July 1842 to 9 Mar. 1848. All the letters quoted at length here are from La Scala.

25. C. Castellaneta, and S. Corradeschi, *L'opera completa di Hayez* (Milan, 1971), 126–7. Catalogue nos. are as follows: Gina Della Somaglia, 130; Giuseppina Appiani, 184; Emilia Zeltner Morosini, 282 and 286; Giuseppina Negroni Prati Morosini, 291 and 355; Clara Carrara Spinelli Maffei, 309.

26. Strepponi to Giovanna Lucca, 17 Aug. 1844 (Casa Ricordi; ISV-P).

27. M. Conati, *La bottega della musica* (Milan, 1983), 21–8 for a documented reconstruction of this time.

28. Ibid. See also Walker, 122–3.

29. Demaldè.

30. Abbiati, i. 420–1.

31. Verdi to Donna Emilia Zeltner Morosini, 21 July 1842 (Museo Teatrale alla Scala).

32. Ibid.

33. Cavalli, 26–7.

34. Verdi to Donna Emilia Zeltner Morosini, [Sept.–Oct.] 1842 (Oberdorger, *Verdi* (1981), 126–7).

35. H. Weinstock, *Rossini* (New York, 1968), 196 ff., 220 ff.

36. See n. 34, above.

37. C. Gatti, *Il Teatro alla Scala* (Milan, 1959), i. 118.

38. Cavalli, 26.

39. Pougin, 37.

40. Ibid. n. 2.

41. Ibid. 47.

42. G. Bragagnolo and E. Bettazzi, *La vita di Giuseppe Verdi* (Milan, 1905), 74 n. 2. See also A. Colombani, *L'opera italiana nel secolo XIX* (Milan, 1900), 77 ff.

43. Pougin, 45–6.

44. Verdi to Lorenzo Molossi, 2 July 1842 (*Gazzetta di Parma* (3 Feb. 1901)).

45. Cavalli, 27.

46. Barbiera, *Salotto*, 104.

47. Ibid. 105.

48. G. Monaldi, *Le opere di Verdi al Teatro alla Scala* (Milan, 1914), 35.

49. Pougin, 47 n. 2.

50. Ibid.

51. Ibid.

52. F. Regli, *Dizionario biografico* (Turin, 1860), 211.

53. Pougin, 49.

54. Cited in Monaldi, *Le opere di Verdi*, 38–9. Excerpts from other reviews are in Abbiati, i. 447.

55. Pougin, 47 n. 2.

56. (27 Mar. 1847). I am grateful to Marcello Conati for making photocopies of this and other early sketches for me.

57. Unsigned articles 'Giuseppe Verdi', *Fuggilozio*, 3: 1 (Jan. 1857), 13–16; 3: 6 (Feb. 1857), 92–6; 3: 9 (Mar. 1857), 139–44. Account of *I Lombardi* on p. 95.

58. 31 Jan. 1843 (original in BMP-B). This letter was written from Busseto during Verdi's winter visit there.

59. 13 Feb. 1843 (original in BMP-B).

60. 25 Feb. 1843 (SAA).

61. See Abbiati, i. 431.

62. See n. 60, above.

63. 'Brindisi d'un imparziale a quanti figurano nel Teatro alla Scala durante la stagione Carnevale 1842–1843' (Milan, 1843). This *scherzo poetico* is signed 'O.T.' and correctly identified as Tasca's in the New York Public Library catalogue in the Library for the Performing Arts at Lincoln Center.

Chapter 11

1. 25 Feb. 1843 (SAA).

2. Donizetti to Antonio Vasselli, 19 Feb. 1843 (G. Zavadini, *Donizetti: vita, musiche, epistolario* (Bergamo, 1948), 659). When the schedule was changed to accommodate the prima donna, *Linda* was given first.

3. 12 Apr. 1843 (Museo Teatrale alla Scala).

4. Walker, 111 n. 1.

5. (Zavadini, *Donizetti*, 718–19).

6. Verdi to Count Alvise Francesco Mocenigo, 9 Apr. 1843, (M. Conati, *La bottega della musica* (Milan, 1983), 39).

7. E. Benassi, 'Giacomo Tommasini, medico di Giuseppina Strepponi', *Aurea Parma* (Jan.–Mar. 1951), 40–2.

8. M. Conati, 'Verdi e Il Teatro Regio di Parma', in *Omaggio al Regio nel 150° anniversario dell'apertura* (Parma, 1979), 46.

9. Marianna Orlandini to Verdi, 20 Feb. 1872 (SAA).

10. 'Relazione del Buon Governo', in Conati, 'Verdi e il Teatro Regio di Parma', 46.

11. Ibid. 48–9. Antonio Barezzi's mother-in-law was a Baroncini.

12. Verdi to Isidoro Cambiasi, [end of Apr. 1843], (L. G. Broglio, C. Vanbianchi, G. Adami, *et al.* (eds.), *Nel primo centenario di Giuseppe Verdi* (Milan, 1913), 23).

13. Cited in Conati, 'Verdi e il Teatro Regio di Parma', 54–7.

14. (Conati, *Bottega*, 46).

15. (Ibid. 48–9).

16. Strepponi to Verdi, 3 Jan. 1853 (SAA).

17. Review of *Nabucco* in *Il Figaro*, cited in Abbiati, i. 456.

18. Verdi to Luigi Toccagni 18 May 1843 (Abbiati, i. 458).

19. Ibid.

20. M. De Angelis, *Le carte dell'impresario* (Florence, 1982), *passim*.

21. Count Filippo Camerata dei Passionei to Lanari (Carteggi Vari, LAN-BN-F).

22. Conati, *Bottega*, 64 ff.

23. Review in *Teatri, arti, e letteratura* 40 (1843), 46–7. Before vol. 35, this periodical, published in Bologna, was called *Cenni storici intorno alle lettere, invenzioni, arti, al commercio ed agli spettacoli teatrali*. Vol. 34 was the last to have this title.

24. (LAN-BN-F).

25. See D. Valeri, *Verdi e La Fenice* (Venice, 1951), 11–13.

26. Ibid. 13. See also Conati, *Bottega*, 35.

27. Verdi's letters to Mocenigo, dated 9 and 28 April and 3 May (Conati, *Bottega*, 39, 42, 44, respectively).

28. Verdi to Mocenigo, 25 May 1843 (ibid. 48–9).

29. Verdi to Mocenigo, 6 June 1843 (ibid. 52–3).

30. Verdi to Mocenigo, 29 June 1843 (ibid. 57).

31. Verdi to Guglielmo Brenna, 4 July 1843 (ibid. 58–9).

32. 5 Sept. 1843 (ibid. 74–5).

33. Verdi to Mocenigo, 6 June 1843 (ibid. 52–3).

34. B. Cagli, ' "Questo povero poeta esordiente", Piave a Roma', in '*Ernani* ieri e oggi' *Bollettino dell'ISV*, 10 (1987), 1–18. Cagli provides a reliable bibliography on Piave on pp. 2–4 and important unpublished material on Ferretti. See also A. Cametti, *Un poeta melodrammatica romano* (Milan, 1898), *passim*.

35. Cattaneo, for the Austrian Office of Censorship, to the Presidenza of the Teatro la Fenice, 27 Oct. 1843 (Conati, *Bottega*, 99).

36. A. Maurois, *Olympio*, trans. G. Hopkins (New York, 1956), 132 ff.

37. Verdi to Mocenigo, 18 Sept. 1843 (Conati, *Bottega*, 77).

38. See n. 35, above.

39. Verdi to Brenna, 15 Nov. 1843 (Conati, *Bottega*, 102–3).

40. Ibid.

41. Verdi to Donna Giuseppina Appiani, 12 Dec. 1843 (*C*, 424).

42. Verdi to Mocenigo, 21 Dec. 1843 (Conati, *Bottega*, 108). The incident took place in the Fontana house.

43. Verdi to Mocenigo, 29 Dec. 1843 (ibid. 109–10).

44. Verdi to Donna Giuseppina Appiani, 26 Dec. 1843, 'one hour after midnight' (*C*, 424).

45. 26 Dec. 1843 (*CV* ii. 355–6, original in Deutsche Staatsbibliothek, Berlin).

46. See n. 43, above.

47. Verdi to Mocenigo, 8 Jan. 1844 (Conati, *Bottega*, 116).

48. [beginning of 1844] (Abbiati, i. 481–2).

49. 31. Jan. 1844 (Conati, *Bottega*, 118–19).

50. Valeri, *Verdi e La Fenice*, 18.

51. Giovannino Barezzi to Antonio Barezzi, 26 Feb. 1844 (Garibaldi, 66–8).

52. Giovannino Barezzi to Antonio Barezzi, 29 Feb. 1844 (ibid. 68–71).

53. Giovannino Barezzi to Antonio Barezzi, 9 Mar. 1844 (ibid. 72).

54. 10 Mar. 1844 (ibid. 73–4).

55. Ibid.

56. 9 Mar. 1844 (*C*, 425).

57. Verdi to Piave, 15 Mar. 1844 (private collection). Verdi to Piave, 2 Apr. 1844 and 25 Mar. 1851 (Morgan Library). Thomas Kaufman helped to compile records on the careers of Bortolotti, Montenegro, Sofia Peruzzi, Angiolina Cignozzi, and other singers of the period. The Valmaranas, like

the Zorzis, who were also Verdi enthusiasts, were originally from Vicenza. Countess Valmarana, born Giuseppa Valier, belonged to a family that had given Venice two seventeenth-century doges and many diplomats as well. I am grateful to Mario Valmarana for his help in establishing his ancestors' connections to Verdi.

58. (Private collection).

59. Deed of Sale, 8 May 1844 (Archivio Notarile, Parma).

60. See Garibaldi, 13–14.

61. Ibid. 17–20.

Chapter 12

1. 12 May 1858 (Di Ascoli, 110).

2. Verdi to Antonio Lanari, 22 July 1844, (*C*, 8).

3. M. Conati, '*Ernani* di Verdi: le critiche del tempo. Alcune considerazioni', in '*Ernani* ieri e oggi', *Bollettino dell'ISV*, 10 (1987), 261 ff.

4. Verdi to Piave, 9 May 1844 (Morgan Library).

5. 18 Apr. 1844 (Museo Teatrale alla Scala). See also Verdi to Giacomo Pedroni, [May 1844], (G. Zavadini, *Donizetti: vita, musiche, epistolario* (Bergamo, 1948), 926). Verdi wrote to Donizetti at once in May to express his confidence that *Ernani* would be correctly executed. On 20 May 1844 Muzio wrote to Barezzi about the exchange of letters between Verdi and Donizetti (see Muzio to Antonio Barezzi, 20 May 1844 (Garibaldi, 158–60)). Earlier, Donizetti had written graciously of Verdi to Giuseppina Appiani: 'I speak the highest praise of Verdi's talent everywhere, quite apart from the friendship that binds me to him.' (See Donizetti to Giuseppina Appiani (Zavadini, *Donizetti*, 735)).

6. Muzio to Antonio Barezzi, 20 May 1844 (Garibaldi, 158–60). See also Garibaldi's remarks at 49–50, 65.

7. '*Ernani* di Verdi', 208–9.

8. Muzio to Antonio Barezzi, 24 June 1844 (Garibaldi, 166–7).

9. Muzio to Barezzi, 30 June 1844 (ibid. 169–71). See also letter of 12 Jan. 1845 (ibid. 181–2).

10. Verdi to the Società de' Nobili, 10 July 1844 (*C*, 6). For Muzio's account, see Garibaldi, 169.

11. Verdi to Felice Romani, 10 July 1844, (*C*, 7). The next day Verdi asked Emilia Morosini to tell Count Barbò that he had received one of the three parts of the cantata *Flavio Gioja* from Romani the day before and that he found that there were six pieces just in the first part of the work. He said

that he had already informed the members of the Nobile Società that because of the 'short time, my obligations, and, above all, my health, I cannot let myself do such an imposing work.' Further: 'I would have been able to compose only one part of this Cantata that I would have chosen from among the last numbers.' He added that he was extremely sorry about the whole affair but 'absolutely would not have been able to do' the job (see Verdi to Emilia Morosini, 11 July 1844 (Museo Teatrale alla Scala)).

12. 14 July 1844 (Di Ascoli, 26).

13. Muzio to Antonio Barezzi, 30 June 1844 (Garibaldi, 169–70).

14. *Enciclopedia italiana*, xxii. 77. Other collections with important material on Manara are the Museo del Risorgimento, Milan and the Archivio Storico Civico, Barzanò (Como).

15. See *C*, 442 n. 1.

16. (Garibaldi, 31–2, 157–8).

17. 20 May 1844 (ibid. 159–60).

18. Ibid.

19. Muzio to Antonio Barezzi, 29 May 1844 (ibid. 160–3).

20. Ibid.

21. 11 June 1844 (ibid. 164–5).

22. (Letters at SAA).

23. 5 Feb. 1844 (SAA).

24. 9 May 1844 (Morgan Library).

25. Verdi to Piave, 14 May 1844 (Morgan Library).

26. Muzio to Antonio Barezzi, 24 June 1844 (Garibaldi, 166–9). Muzio refers to Cannetti's *Saul* in his letter of 13 Oct. 1845 (ibid. 222).

27. 17 Aug. 1844 (Casa Ricordi; ISV-P). Verdi, writing from Bergamo to Emilia Morosini on 12 Aug., said that *Ernani* 'went on stage last evening and turned out very, very mediocre' (Museo Teatrale alla Scala).

28. Muzio to Antonio Barezzi, 16 Nov. 1844 (Garibaldi, 173). Muzio also quotes *La rivista dei Teatri* of 4 Nov. 1844.

29. Muzio to Antonio Barezzi, 16 Nov. 1844 (Garibaldi, 173–4). Muzio reported that the work created a huge furore after the undistinguished first-night performance. The singers, chorus, and orchestra 'disfigured' it, he said.

30. 22 July 1848 (G. Morazzoni, *Lettere inedite di G. Verdi* (Milan, 1929), 28–9).

31. 26 Nov. 1844 (Abbiati, i. 528).

32. Muzio to Antonio Barezzi, 16 Nov. 1844 (Garibaldi, 173).

33. Solera to Giovanni Ricordi, n.d. (cited in Abbiati, i. 534).

34. Muzio to Antonio Barezzi, 22 Dec. 1844 (Garibaldi, 177–8).

35. Ibid.

36. Muzio to Antonio Barezzi, 29 Dec. 1844 (ibid. 179).

37. Muzio to Antonio Barezzi, 6 Feb. 1845 (ibid. 182–3).

38. Ibid.

39. Muzio to Barezzi, 17 Mar. 1845 (ibid. 190; see also Abbiati, i. 533).

40. Muzio to Antonio Barezzi, 10 Apr. 1845 (Garibaldi, 194–5).

41. 25 Mar. 1845 (cited in B. Gasperini, 'Per una lettera inedita di Giuseppe Verdi sulla *Giovanna d'Arco*' from an unidentified publication in the ISV, Parma).

42. 2 April 1845 (private collection).

43. Muzio to Antonio Barezzi, 27 Feb. 1845 (Garibaldi, 183). See also Muzio to Barezzi, 14 Apr. 1845 (ibid. 195); and Muzio to Barezzi, 17 Apr. 1845 (ibid. 196).

44. Muzio to Antonio Barezzi, 10 Mar. 1845 (ibid. 186–7).

45. Cited in Muzio to Antonio Barezzi, 13 June 1846 (ibid. 247–8).

46. [June 1845] (*C*, 14–15).

47. The deed of sale for Carlo Verdi's field is dated 3 Mar. 1846; Ercolano Balestra drew it up. Original of deed in Archivio Notarile, Parma.

48. 28 Apr. 1845 (Garibaldi, 198).

49. [May 1845] (*C*, 10).

50. 14 May 1845 (*C*, 11). See also Verdi to Flaùto, 25 and 26 Apr. 1845 (*C*, 9–10).

51. Muzio to Antonio Barezzi (Garibaldi, 200).

52. Muzio to Antonio Barezzi, 9 June 1845 (ibid. 203–4).

53. Muzio to Antonio Barezzi, 9 July 1845 (ibid. 207–8).

54. See n. 52, above.

55. 12 July 1845 (F. Schlitzer, *Mondo teatrale dell'ottocento* (Naples, 1954), 135; I am grateful to Fausto Fiorentino for calling this book to my attention).

56. Cited in Walker, 138.

57. Schlitzer, *Mondo teatrale*, 137.

58. 17 Aug. 1845 (Casa Ricordi, ISV-P).

59. 14 Aug. 1845 (private collection).

60. 21 Apr. 1845 (SAA).

61. M. Conati, *Interviste ed incontri con Verdi* (Milan, 1980), 7–9. On 26 May 1845 Muzio wrote to Barezzi that 'Signor Escudier, the editor of the *Gazzetta musicale di Francia*, has been to visit the Signor Maestro; and he wanted a statuette [of Verdi] to take to Paris and put in his office between Rossini and Bellini' (see Garibaldi, 202–3).

62. 30 July 1845 (*C*, 432).

63. 5 Nov. 1845 (*C*, 432).

64. Ibid.

65. n.d. (*C*, 432).

66. Muzio to Antonio Barezzi, 13 Aug. 1845 (Garibaldi, 215).

67. Verdi and Muzio to Antonio Barezzi, 26 Aug. 1845 (ibid. 211–12). This letter is incorrectly dated July.

68. Ibid.

69. Report on Merelli, filza no. 250, in Presidenza del Governo, 1847. Archivio di Stato, Milan.

70. See n. 67, above.

71. Stato Civile (Births, Marriages, Busseto and San Secondo Parmense), Archivio di Stato, Parma.

72. Muzio to Antonio Barezzi, 13 Oct. 1845 (Garibaldi, 222).

73. Muzio to Antonio Barezzi, 18 Oct. 1845 (ibid. 223–4).

74. 7 Nov. 1845 (cited in Abbiati, i. 589).

75. Verdi to Benjamin Lumley, 9 Apr. 1846 (*C*, 19–20). See also Verdi to Lumley, 22 May 1846 (*C*, 22).

76. 2 Sept. 1845 (private collection).

77. 27 Nov. 1845 (*C*, 17).

78. Verdi to Piave, 24 Nov. 1845 (Morgan Library).

79. 18 Oct. 1845 (Garibaldi, 223–4).

80. 27 Dec. 1845 (Di Ascoli, 45).

81. Verdi to Carlo Marzari, 5 Dec. 1850 (*C*, 108–9).

82. 25 Jan. 1846 (Casa Ricordi Archive; ISV-P).

83. 24 Feb. 1846 (Casa Ricordi; ISV-P).

84. 18 Mar. [1846] (Gallini Collection, Milan; ISV-P).

85. *Fama* (30 Mar. 1845), 103 (cited in M. Conati, *La Bottega della musica* (Milan, 1983), 173).

86. 7 June 1881 (D. Valeri, *Verdi e La Fenice* (Venice, 1951), 35).

87. 23 Mar. 1846 (Garibaldi, 236).

88. R. Barbiera, *Il salotto della Contessa Maffei* (Milan, 1895), 133–7.

89. Ibid. 139.

90. 24 June 1846 (Di Ascoli, 53).

91. Ibid.

92. Muzio to Antonio Barezzi, 17 June 1846 (Garibaldi, 248–9).

93. Muzio to Antonio Barezzi, 4 June 1846 (ibid. 246–7).

94. Muzio to Antonio Barezzi, [between 22 April and 6 May 1846] (ibid. 241).

95. Cited in Muzio's letter to Antonio Barezzi, 4 June 1846 (ibid. 246).

96. Muzio to Antonio Barezzi, 11 May 1846 (ibid. 244).

97. Muzio to Antonio Barezzi, 22 June 1846 (ibid. 250–1). Verdi and Maffei finally left on 3 July.

98. Muzio to Antonio Barezzi, 9 July 1846 (ibid. 252–3).

99. Muzio to Antonio Barezzi, 22 July 1846 (ibid. 254–6).

100. Muzio to Barezzi, 13 Aug. 1846 (ibid. 258–9). This letter is particularly interesting for its reference—the first in Muzio's correspondence—to the 'very beautiful anagram' on the Pope's name; in it the letters were rearranged to read: 'Gratia nomi Amnistia e Ferrata Via'—'Welcome words Amnesty and Railway'—two symbols of freedom for Italians. The development of the railways proved a major factor in unification.

101. Muzio to Antonio Barezzi, 26 [Aug.] 1845 (Garibaldi, 211–12). If Verdi was in the house to say 'No' to Merelli's messenger, this letter is misdated in Garibaldi as 26 July, a date on which Verdi was still in Naples preparing *Alzira*.

102. Muzio to Antonio Barezzi, 26 Oct. 1846 (ibid. 286–7).

103. Ibid.

104. 29 Dec. 1846 (*C*, 34–5 (draft) and in A. Porter and D. Rosen (eds.), *Verdi's 'Macbeth': A Sourcebook* (New York, 1984), 28). This is the earliest surviving letter from Verdi to Giovanni Ricordi in the Casa Ricordi Archive in Milan.

105. L. Anelli, *La storia d'Italia* (Milan, 1864), i. 353.

106. Ibid. ii. 44–5.

107. *Storia di Milano, 1836–1848* (Lecco, [1870]) 30.

108. Anelli, *Storia*, ii. 45.

109. Muzio to Antonio Barezzi, 24 Aug. 1846 (Garibaldi, 260–1). See also

Muzio to Barezzi, 10 Apr. 1845 (ibid. 194-5) for an earlier reference to the popularity of street organs.

110. ix (Milan, 1846), 55-7.

111. 19 Mar. 1847 (SAA).

112. *Strenna teatrale europea* (Milan, 1843), 139.

Chapter 13

1. Muzio to Antonio Barezzi, 6 May 1846 (Garibaldi, 241-2).

2. 23 Nov. 1846 (ibid. 298-9).

3. (SAA).

4. (A. Basso, *Autografi di musicisti* (Turin, 1962), documenti aggiunti, p. 3, ISV-P).

5. Verdi to Lanari, 17 May 1846 (LAN-BN-F).

6. Review of *Macbeth*, 27 Mar. 1847, by Enrico Montazio (cited in A. Porter and D. Rosen (eds.) *Verdi's 'Macbeth': A Sourcebook* (New York, 1984), 381).

7. P. Weiss, 'Verdi and the Fusion of the Genres', *Journal of the American Musicological Society*, 35: 1 (spring 1982), 141-2.

8. Ibid.

9. 13 Aug. 1846 (Garibaldi, 258-9).

10. 19 Aug. 1846 (*C*, 25-6).

11. 25 Aug. 1846 (*Verdi's 'Macbeth': A Sourcebook*, 6; original in Accademia Chigiana, Siena).

12. 4 Sept. 1846 (Morgan Library).

13. Muzio to Antonio Barezzi, 24 Sept. 1846 (Garibaldi, 274).

14. 26 Sept. 1846 (Di Ascoli, 63-4).

15. 22 Sept. 1846 (Morgan Library).

16. *Teatri, arti, e letteratura*, 21: 39 (1843-4), 197.

17. Walker (It. edn.), 217-18.

18. Rubrica del Ruolo della Popolazione, Milano, 1835, Archivio Storico Civico di Milano.

19. (SAA).

20. (SAA).

21. [22 Oct. 1846] (Abbiati, i. 653-4).

22. Verdi to Benjamin Lumley, 11 Nov. 1846 (*C*, 30). See also Verdi to Lucca, 9 Nov. 1846 (*C*, 30).

23. Muzio to Barezzi, 23 Nov. 1846 (Garibaldi, 298–9).

24. 15 Oct. 1846 (Abbiati, i. 650–1).

25. Muzio to Antonio Barezzi, 22 Oct. 1846 (Garibaldi, 285).

26. 26 Oct. 1846 (*C*, 444–5).

27. 9 Nov. 1846 (G. Piccini, [pseud. Jarro], *Memorie d'un impresario fiorentino* (Florence, 1892), 95–6).

28. Muzio to Antonio Barezzi, 2 Nov. 1846 (Garibaldi, 289–90).

29. Varesi to Lanari, 15 Nov. 1846 (LAN-BN-F).

30. 3 Dec. 1846 (Morgan Library).

31. 10 Dec. 1846 (Morgan Library).

32. 19 Dec. 1846 (Garibaldi, 302–3).

33. 22 Dec. 1846 (*C*, 446–7).

34. 21 Jan. 1847 (*C*, 447–8).

35. Verdi to Ricordi, [mid-Jan. 1847] (*C*, 448).

36. 21 Jan. 1847 (Morgan Library).

37. [24 Jan. 1847] (Private collection).

38. 14 Feb. 1847 (Morgan Library).

39. 7 Jan. 1847 (*Verdi's 'Macbeth': A Sourcebook*, 30–2; original in Accademia Chigiana, Siena).

40. 31 Jan. 1847 (*Verdi's 'Macbeth': A Sourcebook*, 39–40).

41. 24 Jan. 1847 (LAN-BN-F).

42. Muzio to Antonio Barezzi, 28 Jan. 1847 (Garibaldi, 308–9).

43. 14 Feb. 1847 (M. Tinti, *Lorenzo Bartolini* (Rome, 1936), i. 124 n. 2).

44. *Lorenzo Bartolini: mostra delle attività di tutela*, published by the Committee for the Bartolini Commemoration (Florence, 1978), 158–9. With documents, ed. Anna Maria Petrioli Tofani. See also M. J. Phillips-Matz, 'Statue Maker', *Opera News* (29 Feb. 1992), 13 ff.

45. Ibid. See also A. Maffei, '*La Fiducia in Dio* scolpita da Lorenzo Bartolini', in *Poesie scelte ed inedite*, (Florence 1869), 118. Giusti had written a sonnet on the same statue in 1836.

46. [Feb. 1847.] (Biblioteca Labronica, Leghorn. I am grateful to Dr Luca Badaloni for help in using this collection and Dr Vera Durbè of the Civica Pinacoteca.)

47. N. Ginzburg, *The Manzoni Family*, trans. Marie Evans (New York, 1987), 213–7.

48. Ibid. 218.

49. Verdi to Clara Maffei, 20 Feb. 1847 (Di Ascoli, 71).

50. Muzio to Antonio Barezzi, 28 Jan. 1847 (Garibaldi, 308–9).

51. L. Pinzauti, 'Verdi's *Macbeth* and the Florentine Critics', in *Verdi's 'Macbeth': A Sourcebook*, 139.

52. [c.18 Feb. 1847] (*C*, 449). An earlier letter about the lodging is missing.

53. 23 Feb. 1847 (*CV* iv. 252–3; original in Biblioteca Queriniana, Brescia).

54. Rubrica del Ruolo della Popolazione, Milano, 1835, Archivio Storico Civico, Milan.

55. M. De Angelis, *Le Carte dell' impresario* (Florence, 1982), 163. The phrase appears in a report on the foster-parents dated 4 Jan. 1841.

56. Muzio to Antonio Barezzi, 25 Feb. 1847 (Garibaldi, 311).

57. R. Piatti, *Racconti di una donna* (2nd edn., Florence, 1872), in Rare Books and Manuscripts, Biblioteca Carducci, Spoleto.

58. Giulio Piatti to Niccolo Puccini (letters in Manuscript Collection, Biblioteca Forteguerriana, Pistoia).

59. See M. J. Phillips-Matz, 'José Verdi, Hercules Cavalli, and the Florence *Macbeth*', in *Verdi's 'Macbeth': A Sourcebook*, 129–36.

60. G. Dupré, *Pensieri sull'arte e ricordi autobiografici* (Florence, 1879), 166–8.

61. Collection of Gian Carlo Menotti, Yester House, Gifford, East Lothian, Scotland. Dr Annarita Caputo-Calloud was helpful in examining the photographs of both the portraits from the Menotti collection and the Gallini miniatures in Florence in the spring of 1977. She is an authority on Piatti and his contemporaries.

62. Sepia drawing of the Witches' Cavern (SAA).

63. 9 Mar. 1847 (Garibaldi, 262–3).

64. [11 Mar. 1847] (Di Ascoli, 72).

65. Barbieri-Nini, recollections of the *Macbeth* première, taken from biographies of Verdi by Gino Monaldi (1899) and Eugenio Checchi (1926), in *Verdi's 'Macbeth': A Sourcebook*, 49 ff.

66. Varesi to Ranzanici, 17 Mar. 1847 (*Verdi's 'Macbeth': A Sourcebook*, 54–6).

67. 27 Mar. 1847, in *La rivista di Firenze*, cited in *Verdi's 'Macbeth': A Sourcebook*, 381 ff.

68. Anonymous correspondent to *Gazzetta musicale di Milano*, letter dated 24 Mar. 1847, published 4 Apr. 1847, cited in *Verdi's 'Macbeth': A Sourcebook*, 381.

69. 19 Mar. 1847 (SAA).

70. 27 Mar. 1847 (Museo Teatrale alla Scala).

71. 25 Mar. 1847 (Alba Caraffini Collection, Fidenza, in Archive of the Amici di Verdi, Busseto).

72. Cavalli, 31.

73. [end Mar. 1847] (*Verdi: rivista per l'anno giubilare* (Bologna, 1926), 20); original may be in the Lino Carrara Collection, Busseto.

74. 1901 (Abbiati, i. 685).

75. J. Rosselli, 'Verdi e la storia della retribuzione del compositore italiano', *Studi verdiani*, 2 (1983), 21–2.

Chapter 14

1. Muzio to Antonio Barezzi, 14 Apr. 1847 (Garibaldi, 314–5).

2. 6 June 1846 (SAA).

3. Muzio to Antonio Barezzi, 24 Sept. 1846 (Garibaldi, 274–6).

4. Muzio to Antonio Barezzi, 17 May 1847 (ibid. 318).

5. Verdi to Francesco Lucca, 10 Apr. 1847 (Casa Ricordi; ISV-P).

6. (London, 1864), 159–60.

7. Muzio to Antonio Barezzi, 4 June 1847 (Garibaldi, 325–7).

8. Muzio to Antonio Barezzi, 4 June 1847 (ibid. 325–7).

9. Ibid.

10. Muzio to Antonio Barezzi, 29 June 1847 (ibid. 332–8).

11. Muzio to Antonio Barezzi, 16 June 1847 (ibid. 327–32).

12. Muzio to Antonio Barezzi, 29 June 1847 (ibid. 332–8).

13. Lumley, *Reminiscences*, 171.

14. R. M. Marvin 'Verdi's Artistic Concerns and Practical Considerations in the Composition of *I masnadieri*: A Newly Discovered Version of "Tremate, o miseri"', paper presented 2 Feb. 1991 to the American Institute for Verdi Studies and the Greater New York Chapter of the American Musicological Society, New York University.

15. Muzio to Antonio Barezzi, 29 June 1847 (Garibaldi, 332–8).

16. Muzio to Antonio Barezzi, 16 June 1847 (ibid. 327–32).

17. (*C*, 457–8).

18. Ibid.

19. 29 June 1847 (Garibaldi, 332–8).

20. See n. 17, above.

21. Ibid.

22. Lumley, *Reminiscences*, 171. Superchi was from Parma. His descendants live in Busseto in the summer.

23. Muzio to Antonio Barezzi, 17 July 1847 (Garibaldi, 338–40).

24. Muzio to Antonio Barezzi, 23 July 1847 (ibid. 344–9).

25. Lumley, *Reminiscences*, 193.

26. Ibid.

27. 29 July 1847 (Di Ascoli, 82–3).

28. Muzio to Antonio Barezzi, 29 June 1847 (Garibaldi, 332–8).

29. 30 July 1847 (Museo Teatrale alla Scala).

30. Giulia Tillet-Torriglioni to Tenca, 1 July 1847 (Di Ascoli, 80–1). She was the wife of one of the artists who sang with Strepponi in the concert.

31. (*C*, 457–8).

32. 29 July 1847 (Di Ascoli, 82–3).

33. See n. 29, above.

34. Muzio to Antonio Barezzi, 8 Aug. 1847 (Garibaldi, 349–50).

35. 22 Aug. 1847 (*C*, 462).

36. Ibid.

37. Verdi to Clara Maffei, 6 Sept. 1847 (Di Ascoli, 83).

38. 1 Aug. 1847 (ibid. 84).

39. (*C*, 42–3).

40. Transcription of slide of page from Verdi's autograph score of *Jérusalem*, transcribed in A. Porter, 'Life, 1843–1880', in *The New Grove Masters of Italian Opera* (London, 1983), 249. This material was discovered by Ursula Günther in Paris and first shown during an International Congress for Verdi Studies.

41. Muzio to Antonio Barezzi, 23 Aug. 1847 (Garibaldi, 351–3).

42. Muzio to Antonio Barezzi, 13 Sept. 1847 (ibid. 355).

43. Verdi to Clara Maffei [9 June 1847] (*C*, 457).

44. 16 Oct. 1847 (Garibaldi, 357–9).

45. 15 Oct. 1847 (*C*, 44–5).

46. Verdi to Donna Giuseppina Appiani, 22 Sept. 1847 (*C*, 463–4).

47. 3 Dec. 1847 (Di Ascoli, 84).

48. 31 Jan. and 3 Feb. 1848 (SAA).

49. Ibid.

50. (*C*, 454–5).

Chapter 15

1. 24 Jan. 1848 (formerly in Biblioteca Comunale, Palermo; ISV-P).

2. 14 Jan. 1848 (M. Conati, *La Bottega della musica* (Milan, 1983), 180; original in Deutsche Staatsbibliothek, Berlin; see also Abbiati, i., 736).

3. 3 Mar. 1848 (Casa Ricordi; ISV-P).

4. 17 Feb. 1848 (Garibaldi, 361).

5. 12 Feb. 1848 (*C*, 47).

6. 6 Oct. 1848, in programme for concert version of *Il corsaro*, directed by David Lawton, Town Hall, New York City, 1981. Originally published in 'Una lettera di Giuseppe Verdi', *Nuova antologia*, 124 (1906), 322–3. Author not identified.

7. 9 Mar. 1848 (*C*, 464–5).

8. R. Barbiera, *Il salotto della Contensa Maffei* (Milan, 1895), 148–9.

9. See also Verdi's letters to her as follows: 28 Jan. 1848, 18 Feb. 1848, and an undated letter from Feb. or Mar. (all in Museo Teatrale alla Scala, Milan).

10. H. Weinstock, *Rossini* (New York, 1968), 242–3.

11. Ibid.

12. (Private collection).

13. See V. Alfieri, *Tragedie* (Cremona, 1823), i., *Filippo* and *Virginia*.

14. Barbiera, *Salotto*, 142–59. Clara Maffei was a declared Mazzinian.

15. B. Brombert, *Cristina* (New York, 1977), 179–80.

16. Verdi, pro-memoria, 1 May 1848 (*C*, 48). The pro-memoria is dated 1 May, but the contract of sale is dated 8 May. See *C*, 48, n. 1. Fortunato Merli, whose family owned the farm at Sant'Agata, was Antonio Barezzi's son-in-law.

17. Verdi to Piave, 22 July 1848 (*CV*, iv. 217–8). The Toscanini Collection, Library for the Performing Arts at Lincoln Center, has this letter on microfilm.

18. Muzio was in Mendrisio as early as 4 Feb. 1849. See his letter of 4 Feb. 1849 to Barezzi (Garibaldi, 362).

19. Ibid.

20. 24 Aug. 1848 (*C*, 467–8).

21. F. T. Garibaldi, *Giuseppe Verdi nella vita e nell'arte* (Florence, 1904), 119 ff.

22. *CV*, iv. 217 ff.

23. See n. 17, above.

24. *Enciclopedia italiana*, xviii, 211.

25. 20 Apr. 1848 (*CV*, ii. 59; original in SAA).

26. Letters of 15 and 18 Sept. 1848, (*C*, 52–4).

27. Verdi to Cammarano, 24 Sept. 1848 (*C*, 55–6).

28. 27 July 1848 (Abbiati, i. 753–4; original in SAA).

29. Petition, Verdi, Aleardi, Guerrieri-Gonzaga, Trivulzi, and others, 8 Aug. 1848, to General Cavaignac and other French officials (*C*. 466–7).

30. See n. 20, above.

31. Ibid.

32. (Abbiati, i. 758).

33. 18 Oct. 1848 (*C*, 469–70).

34. (Di Ascoli, 92).

35. 30 Jan. 1848 (Casa Ricordi; ISV-P).

36. 18 Sept. 1848 (*C*, 53–4).

37. [Nov. 1848] (*C*, 63).

38. 21 Nov. 1848 (*C*, 63–4; see also Abbiati, i. 775–6 for complete transcription from original in Gallini Collection; original in the Morgan Library).

39. G. Martin, *Verdi: His Music, Life, and Times* (New York, 1963), 238–40.

40. At that moment, Verdi condemned the Pope for his weakness, but later he forgave him. In a letter to Clara Maffei, dated 12 Feb. 1878, he wrote: 'Dear Clarina, But now everyone is dying! Everyone! Now the Pope! I am not in sympathy with the Pope of the Syllabus, but I am for the Pope of the Amnesty, the Pope who cried: "Great God, bless Italy!" Without him, who knows where we would be now? They accused him of having turned back to reaction, of having lacked courage, of not knowing how to wield the sword of Julius II. Fortunately!! Even admitting that in 1848 he might have been able to drive the Austrians out of Italy, what would we have now? A government of priests! And anarchy, probably, and dismemberment. Better that it turned out this way. Every good that he did, and everything bad, too, turned out for the good of this country; and in his heart he was good natured, and a good Italian, better than so many who just shout "Patria!

Patria!" And ... so may this poor Pope rest in peace.' (See Di Ascoli, 358).

41. I. Bonomi, *Mazzini, triumviro della Repubblica Romana* (Turin, 1936), 38 ff.

42. 4 Feb. 1849 (Garibaldi, 362). Nearly forty years later Muzio could report to Verdi on the triumph of *La battaglia di Legnano*, rebaptized *Pour la Patrie* in France: it 'was having a great deal of success in the provinces and also in Paris, in modest theatres with audiences [that are] not blasé, because the music of that opera is rhythmic, clear, and full of motifs; the last act, particularly, is very effective' (See *CV*, iv. 219).

43. (Casa Ricordi; ISV-P). Muzio's incorrect date of '1848' has misled scholars; but in Feb. 1848 Verdi was *not* hurrying back to Paris and taking a detour, backtracking from Pontremoli to avoid 'German lines' that stood between him and Busseto.

44. Ricordi to Muzio [spring 1849] citing Verdi's words in an earlier letter from Verdi to Ricordi (Abbiati, i. 788).

45. See also Verdi to Roqueplan and Duponchel, 25 Nov. 1848 (*C*, 65 and n. 1).

46. 14 Feb. 1849. (Dated 1 Feb. in G. Morazzoni, *Lettere inedite di G. Verdi* (Milan, 1929), 29-30; microfilm in the Toscanini Collection, Library for the Performing Arts, New York Public Library). I am grateful to Warren Michon for help in correcting the date.

47. Ibid.

48. Cammarano to Verdi, 14 Apr. 1849 (*C*, 71-2; see also *CV*, iv. 217 ff).

49. 14 July 1849 (*C*, 474-5).

50. Verdi to Flaùto (*C*, 80).

51. Memorandum, 5 June [1849] (*C*, 81).

52. 15 May 1849 (Abbiati, ii. 9; original in SAA).

53. 15 May 1849 (Abbiati, ii. 9; original in SAA).

54. 1 May 1849 (*C*, 75, n. 2).

55. A. Mauroner, in *Il costituzionale* (29 Oct. 1848), cited in G. Stefani, *Verdi e Trieste* (Trieste, 1951), 38. One would like to see the 'incandescent' letter from Giovannina Lucca to Lodovico Corio about the fiasco of *Il corsaro* and its subsequent withdrawal from the repertory.

56. Cited in Stefani, *Verdi e Trieste*, 38-9.

57. (N. Perfetti, *Giuseppe Verdi a Como nel primo centenario della nascita, 1813-1913* (Como, [1913]), 12, facsimile of first page of Verdi's letter,

with musical illustrations). Neither this letter nor the one that precedes it is in Zanon's list of Verdi's letters to the Ricordis.

58. 2 June 1848 (Biblioteca Civica, Forlì; ISV-P).

BOOK III

Chapter 16

1. Strepponi to Verdi, 3 Sept. 1849 (SAA). Although she does not mention Bartolini by this letter, it is clear from her letter of 18 May 1851 to Verdi (also in SAA) that he is the man who had charge of Camillino's education.

2. Strepponi's payments to the Zanobini-Pagliais are recorded in her Letterbooks, (which are at SAA) and in Verdi's correspondence with Ricordi. He later asked Piroli's help in getting Pagliai a position with the Italian government. Only a few letters from this family are at Sant'Agata. From Strepponi's letter to Lanari of 31 Aug. 1849 and Lanari's payment records in LAN-BN-F, we see that Strepponi and Cirelli were paying the Zanobinis in the 1840s and that she contacted Livia Zanobini almost as soon as she got to Florence in 1849. Further research into this family, particularly in the Status Animarum of their parish, is indicated.

3. It was Strepponi's mention of young Palagi (*sic*) in her correspondence with Corticelli that led me to ask Dr Rosalia Manno-Tolù to search the Stato Civile Toscano for Camillino's death. See Strepponi, Memorandum to Corticelli, 17 Feb. 1864 (Museo Teatrale alla Scala).

4. Verdi to Giovanni Ricordi, 22 Oct. 1851 and 1 Nov. 1851 (Casa Ricordi; ISV-P). Just before asking for this loan, Verdi had Ricordi pay Livia Zanobini a sum of money that may have gone for Camillino Strepponi's room and board or for Zanobini's wages for caring for him or some other child (see Abbiati, ii. 144). See also the payment of 113½ *paoli* in Verdi to Ricordi, 11 Oct. 1851 (Casa Ricordi; ISV-P).

5. Verdi acknowledged the 'kind loan' in his letter of 1 Nov. to Ricordi and promised to repay it in a year. Almost the entire amount was paid immediately to one of Verdi's creditors against the mortgage for the farm at Sant'Agata. As Muzio informed the publisher, the composer and Strepponi left for Paris on 10 Dec. (Muzio to Ricordi, 6 Dec. 1851 (Abbiati, ii. 148)).

6. The nature of her investments is suggested in her letter of 18 May 1851 to Verdi (SAA).

7. (SAA).

8. (Gatti (1951), 202–3); in the 1951 and in the first (1931) edition (i. 256),

Gatti dated this letter 1845. Marcello Conati dated it correctly in his edition of A. Oberdorfer, *Giuseppe Verdi: autobiografia dalle lettere* (1951; 3rd edn., Milan, 1981), 253, n. 14.

9. (Private collection).

10. Muzio to Verdi, 14 Sept. 1879 (Napolitano).

11. 29 May 1850 (Morgan Library).

12. 6 Oct. 1849 (Abbiati, ii. 35-6). This and all subsequent references to the Verdi–Escudier correspondence have been checked with Stephen Casale's master's thesis 'A Catalogue of Letters from Verdi and Giuseppina Strepponi Verdi to the Escudiers' (New York, 1983). I am grateful to Mr Casale for letting me make a photocopy from his original and to the Istituto di Studi Verdiani, Parma, for use of their photographs of the Verdi–Escudier letters and for letting me copy J.-G. Prod'homme, 'Lettres inédites de G. Verdi à Leon Escudier', *Rivista musicale italiana*, 35 (1928).

13. 19 Apr. [1849] (*C*, 72-4). See also record of payment to 'Rosa Strepponi of Pavia' at the end of vol.ii. of the autograph *C* at Sant'Agata.

14. (Garibaldi, 378-80).

15. Verdi to Flaùto, 1 Nov. 1849 (*C*, 85-6).

16. n.d. (Abbiati, ii. 42).

17. List of possible subjects for operas, facsimile in *C*, plate XI, preceding p. 423. Although scholars believed that this dated from 1843-4, Conati correctly dated it 'not before February 1849' in *La bottega della musica* (Milan, 1983), 256, n. 10. In his introduction to the new edn. of *Rigoletto*, Martin Chusid also mentions a *Guzmán el Bueno* by Zarate. See *The Works of Giuseppe Verdi*[1], vol. xvii. *Rigoletto* (Chicago, 1983), p. xii, n. 12.

18. 28 Feb. 1850 (private collection). He wrote: 'I will read your [libretto of] *Elisabetta* this evening.' It was composed by Antonio Buzzola and presented at the Teatro La Fenice. Microfilm of Buzzola's autograph score, Mary Jane Phillips-Matz Collection. I am very grateful to Emanuele De Checchi of TWA in Milan for obtaining this microfilm for me in 1980 and grateful to the Teatro La Fenice in Venice for allowing a Venetian microfilmer to copy it from the archive of that theatre.

19. (*C*, 478).

20. Verdi to [Marie Escudier], 7 Mar. 1850. See also Verdi to Escudier, 20 May 1850 (BN-P; ISV-P).

21. Angelo Vivante, president of the Teatro Grande, Trieste, to Domenico Ronzani, impresario of the theatre, n.d., in *La passione verdiana di Trieste* (Trieste, 1951), 57, n. *a*.

22. Muzio to Giovanni Ricordi, 13 July 1850 (Casa Ricordi; ISV-P).

23. Verdi to Antonio Barezzi, 10 May 1850 (Garibaldi, 364–5).

24. Trezzini, *Due secoli di vita musicale* (Bologna, 1966), i. 12, ii. 70–1. *Macbeth* was given on 2 Oct. 1850, *Luisa Miller* on 10 Oct. 1850.

25. Verdi to Giovanni Ricordi, 13 Oct. 1850 (Casa Ricordi; ISV-P). See also Walker 324–5 and C. Schmidl, *Dizionario universale dei musicisti* (Milan, 1887), 415–16 for further information on Luigi and Federico Ricci.

26. Cited in G. Stefani, *Verdi e Trieste* (Trieste, 1951), 46.

27. 15 Feb. 1850 (ibid. 47).

28. See n. 22, above.

29. Stefani, *Verdi e Trieste*, 60. A longhand copy of Michele Buono's Ode to Verdi is in Demaldè's files at the BMP-B together with other documents brought from Trieste in 1850.

30. Stefani, *Verdi e Trieste*, 60. Poiret's lithograph portrait is also published in this vol.

31. Ibid. 65. The manuscript is in the Museo Teatrale of the Teatro Grande (now the Teatro Verdi) in Trieste. It is curious that Felice Romani, in his unpublished manuscript notes on Verdi's operas (now in xerox in Special Music Collections, Library for the Performing Arts at Lincoln Center) confuses Severi with the tenor Raffaele Monti, whom he lists as having sung Arvino in the world première of *I Lombardi* at La Scala. Monti seems to have sung Arvino only in the second production at La Scala. He also sang it at the Regio in Turin.

32. Ibid. 48.

33. Article of 17 Nov. 1850 (cited in Stefani, *Verdi e Trieste*, 48. Hermet describes 'un verbale' sealing the fate of *Stiffelio* with an 'assoluto divieto di più rappresentare lo *Stiffelio*'.

34. In *Passione verdiana di Trieste*, 57, n. *b.*

35. For a complete record of the censors' actions to prevent or mutilate Verdi's operas in Trieste, even into the twentieth century, see Mario Nordio's essay 'Verdi e l'Anima Italiana di Trieste', in *Passione verdiana di Trieste*, 7–9. *Ernani* came under fire for nearly seventy years, having been taken off the stage in 1888 in Trieste because it provoked patriotic, anti-Austrian demonstrations. When it was produced again in 1903 one of the choruses was encored so many times that the police closed it down again. The Triestini even turned pigeons loose in the theatre, attaching Italian tricolour flags (red, white, and green) to their bodies. *Ernani* was kept off the stage there until after the first World War.

36. See *Passione verdiana di Trieste*, 54 ff. for further analysis of the changes made. The play *Stifellius* had actually been allowed on stage, produced by the Rossi-Leigheb Company at the Filodrammatico in Trieste. This fine old theatre, which stands across the street from the Hotel Città di Parenzo, has recently been closed. Gaetano Vestri translated the play.

37. Verdi to Giovanni Ricordi, 5 Jan. 1851 (Abbiati, ii. 79). This letter is not in Zanon's *Elenco*.

38. F. Hermet, article of 20 Nov. 1850 (cited in *Passione verdiana di Trieste*, 54).

39. (Review cited in *Passione verdiana di Trieste*, 60).

40. See n. 37, above.

Chapter 17

1. *C*, plate XI (facsimile). See also M. Conati, *La Bottega della musica* (Milan, 1983), 256-7 n. 10, for dating of this list.

2. Verdi to Flaùto, 7 Sept. 1849 (*C*, 84-5).

3. 10 Mar. 1850 (private collection).

4. 16 Mar. 1850 (private collection).

5. 9 March 1850 (*C*, 96-7).

6. Verdi to Marzari, 14 Mar. 1850 (*C*, 97-8).

7. Verdi to Brenna, 31 Mar. 1850 (Conati, *Bottega*, 191).

8. Ibid.

9. 31 Mar. 1850 (ibid. 191-2).

10. Verdi to Marzari, 18 Apr. 1850 (*C*, 102). Marzari's and Brenna's letters of 10 Apr. are in *C*, 100-1 and are inserted into Verdi's original vol.

11. Verdi to Piave, 28 Apr. 1850 (Morgan Library).

12. 6 May 1850 (Morgan Library).

13. 14 May 1850 (Abbiati, ii. 63-4; original in SAA).

14. See Conati, *Bottega*, 200, 260 n. 43.

15. [29 May 1850] (Morgan Library).

16. 3 June 1850 (Morgan Library).

17. Conati, *Bottega*, 260 n. 47.

18. 14 June 1850 (Conati, *Bottega*, 202).

19. 30 July 1850 (ibid. 205).

20. Ibid. 205-6.

21. 15 Aug. 1850 (ibid. 207-8).

22. Ibid.

23. (*C*, 106–7).

24. Brenna to Verdi, 27 Aug. 1850 (*C*, 106 n. 1). Questions about the date of this letter are reviewed in Conati, *Bottega*, 209, 261 n. 55.

25. 5 Oct. 1850 (Conati, *Bottega*, 219).

26. 15 Oct. 1850 (Abbiati, ii. 69–70; original in Casa Ricordi; ISV-P).

27. 22 Oct. 1850 (Morgan Library).

28. Marzari to Verdi, 11 Nov. 1850 (*C*, 485–6).

29. Verdi to Brenna, 15 Nov. 1850 (Conati, *Bottega*, 225).

30. (Ibid. 226).

31. (Morgan Library).

32. (Morgan Library).

33. (*C*, 486–7).

34. Luigi Martello, director, central office for public order, Venice, 21 Nov. 1850, to the head of the directors of the Teatro La Fenice (*C*, 487).

35. Verdi to Marzari, 5 Dec. 1850 (*C*, 108–9).

36. 5 Dec. 1850 (Conati, *Bottega*, 230).

37. 6 Dec. 1850 (ibid. 230; original in Casa Ricordi; ISV-P).

38. Marzari to Verdi, 9 Dec. 1850 (Conati, *Bottega*, 231–2).

39. (*C*, 109–11).

40. (*C*, 111).

41. Piave to the Director of La Fenice [Marzari], 19 Dec. 1850 (Conati, *Bottega*, 234).

42. Written report of meeting between Dr Adolfo Benvenuti and Dr Carlo Marzari, 27 Dec. 1850 (ibid. 237–8).

43. Marzari to Verdi, 23 Dec. 1850 (*C*, 488–9).

44. See n. 42, above.

45. (Private collection). This letter, which bears no postmarks, must have been delivered directly to Piave's hotel in Cremona.

46. Agreement: Verdi, Piave, and Brenna, Busseto, 30 Dec. 1850 (Conati, *Bottega*, 240–1).

47. Marzari to Verdi (*C*, 490).

48. Ibid.

49. 14 Jan. 1851 (*C*, 490–1).

50. 14 Jan. 1851 (Morgan Library).

51. (Morgan Library).

52. (*C*, 491–2).

53. (SAA).

54. Undated memorandum (Morgan Library).

55. 24 Jan. 1851 (Morgan Library).

56. (*C*, 492–3).

57. 26 Jan. 1851 (*C*, 114–15).

58. (*C*, 494).

59. 31 Jan. 1851 (Morgan Library).

60. (Morgan Library). Verdi wrote '5 del 1851', which would be Jan., but the letter is clearly from Feb.

61. 21 Jan. 1851 (*C*, 113).

62. 31 Jan. 1851 (Abbiati, ii. 93).

63. Ibid. 94.

64. (SAA).

65. (Morgan Library).

66. (Morgan Library).

67. Verdi to Ercolano Balestra (Abbiati, ii. 94).

68. 8 Feb. 1851, drawn up by Ercolano Balestra (Abbiati, ii. 95–6). Only a part of the agreement was published.

69. n.d. (ibid. 96).

70. Pietro Allegri had just sold the house across the road to Antonio Barezzi.

71. Piave to Verdi, 9 Feb. 1851. (SAA).

72. 20 Jan. 1851 (*C*, 491–2).

73. 30 Oct. 1854 (Private collection).

74. See Conati, *Bottega*, 253.

75. Anonymous critic (12 Mar. 1851), in A. Della Corte, 'Saggio di bibliografia delle critiche di *Rigoletto*', *Bollettino dell'ISV*, 3: 9 (1982), 1640–2.

76. Anonymous critic (13 Mar. 1851). The complete file of this newspaper is in the Biblioteca Statale, Cremona. On 11 Mar., under the headline 'THE ABANDONMENT OF CHILDREN' it ran a front-page article on the 'terrifying' increase in the number of infants that were left in orphanage turnstiles by parents, many married, who 'abandon their children like miserable garbage to be thrown on the mercy of the public'. The statistics indicated that in Cremona there was one abandoned child to every 327 inhabitants, while in Milan there was one abandoned child to every 76 inhabitants.

77. Anonymous critic in *Il vaglio* (15 Mar. 1851) (cited in M. Conati, 'Appendix to the Bibliography of Critical Writings on *Rigoletto*', in *Bollettino dell'ISV*, 3: 9 (1982), 1700-1). See also anonymous critic in *L'Italia musicale* (19 Mar. 1851) (ibid.).

78. M. Conati, 'Saggio di cronologia delle prime rappresentazioni di *Rigoletto*', *Bolletino dell'ISV*, 3: 9, pp. 1853 ff. See also Conati, 'Appendix'.

79. 2 Aug. 1852, letter published on 15 Aug. 1852 (Conati, 'Appendix').

80. Melchiorre Balbi, 6 Aug. 1852, letter published on 15 Aug. 1852 (ibid.).

81. 25 Mar. 1851 (Morgan Library).

82. Abbiati, ii. 128.

83. Verdi to Antonio Barezzi, 21 Jan. 1852 (*C*, 128-31).

84. (Private collection).

85. (Private collection).

86. Registro [degli] Esposti, 1848-1872, Comune di Cremona, No. 35, sheet 207 and facing page in Archivio di Stato, Cremona. See also my article 'A Time of Stress', *Opera News* (5 Jan. 1991), 11 ff.

87. Original Parish Registers (Baptisms), Parish of Santa Maria della Pietà (Ospedale Maggiore), Cremona, 15 Apr. 1851. Baptismal record of 'Streppini Santa, abandoned in the turnstile on 14 Apr. 1851 at nine-thirty in the evening, a female, recently born, and she was baptized on the fifteenth day of the same month by the priest Sartori Pietro, Senior Adjutant; illegitimate. Name and domicile of the mother: [unknown]. Name and domicile of the father: [unknown]. If married, the date of their marriage and the parish in which it was celebrated: [unknown]. Religion and legal status of both: [unknown]. Godparent: Domenica Ghio, hospital worker.' I am particularly grateful to Father Pio Daprà, the present parish priest of Santa Maria della Pietà, which is still inside the Cremona City Hospital. He made an extraordinary effort to find this baptismal record in a locked cabinet of the lowest storage cellar of the hospital. I am grateful, too, to Ms Donata Fioni, Archivist of the Hospital, and Ms Giovanna Pegoiani, her assistant. Ms Adriana Cerati of the Archivio Diocesano in Cremona helped me locate the building where she thought these registers might have been stored.

88. Stato della Popolazione, Cortemaggiore, Chiavenna Landi, e San Martino in Olza, 1824, in Archivio Storico Civico, Cortemaggiore. The Uggeris are shown as living on their own land in the house at La Rabbiosa where Santa Streppini was brought up: Parcel no. 605, sect. 3, of the Mappa Catastale. I am grateful to Dr Massimo Gaudenzi of the Ufficio Tecnico of the Comune

of Cortemaggiore for his help in locating the original map. The Register is in the Archivio di Stato, Piacenza.

89. Vacchet[t]a per lo Stato dell'Anime, 1834–1859, Parish of San Martino, San Martino in Olza, Comune of Cortemaggiore. I am very grateful to Don Luigi Galluzzi and his family for their help with this and other parish registers.

90. Registro [degli] Esposti, 1848–1872, Comune di Cremona, see n. 86, above. This document gives the residence of Zilioli and Brigida Uggeri as 'Cortemaggiore', referring to the Comune; but they always lived at San Martino in Olza, as Santa's marriage certificate proves.

91. Chierici confirmed by telephone in 1989 that he had been given this information by a family in Cortemaggiore. In his novel *Quel delitto in Casa Verdi* he uses the information in a fictional rendering of one of his incidents. Walker was also told this same story.

92. Chierici believed that Verdi had been the victim of attempted extortion on the part of 'the carpenter from San Pietro in Cerro', whom he, like Gatti, believed to be Strepponi's son.

93. Barberina Strepponi to Giuseppina Strepponi, 4 Mar. 1873 (SAA). Zeffirina Braibanti, who was born in Busseto, was treated very well by Strepponi, even though she was dismissed from the staff. It seems that Strepponi found her a position with Verdi's friends, the Zorzis from Vicenza, and corresponded with her for years.

94. 4 Apr. 1840 (LAN-BN-F).

95. (SAA).

96. Verdi to Piroli, in Carteggi Verdiani, iii. 165 (6 Dec. 1883).

97. 25 Mar. 1851 (Morgan Library).

98. Settlement between Giuseppe and Carlo Verdi, 29 Apr. 1851. I am grateful to three private collectors who made available the widely scattered documents relevant to this period.

Chapter 18

1. Verdi to Paolo Marenghi, 16 Aug. 1867 (*C*, 549; original in RAI—Radiotelevisione Italiana Archive).

2. *Pro-Memoria* on purchase of Sant'Agata, 1 May 1848 (*C*, 48–9). The total area was originally '350 *biolche* circa'. On 4 Apr. [1859] Verdi, writing to Ercolano Balestra, said that the total area was 400 *biolche* (see G. Cenzato, *Itinerari verdiani* (Parma [1949]), 76–7). In the Battaglia *Grande dizionario della lingua italiana*, a *biolca* is defined as the area that one ploughman with two oxen could plough in one work-day.

3. G. F. Scognamiglio and G. Macellari, *Valdarda e Valchero* (Piacenza, 1975), 229–30.

4. Verdi to Clara Maffei, 12 May 1858 (*C*, 572).

5. Verdi to Carlo Antonio Borsi, 8 Sept. 1852, postscript (*C*, 497–8). The word 'bovi' has been misread by scholars as both 'voci' and 'vacche'.

6. L. Grazzi, 'Documenti inediti della giovinezza di Verdi', *Gazzetta di Parma* (3 July 1950). Photocopies of Verdi's farm accounts have been provided by Dr Francesco Cafasi and the Machiavelli family in Busseto.

7. (SAA).

8. [2 June 1851] (Deutsche Staatsbibliothek; ISV-P).

9. Muzio to Giovanni Ricordi, 29 June 1851 (Casa Ricordi; ISV-P).

10. Ibid.

11. This stone was transferred from the original grave in the old cemetery at Vidalenzo and placed in the church wall. When Carlo Verdi died, the parish priest Canon Don Avanzi, Verdi's friend, had a new stone prepared: 'Here lie Carlo Verdi and Luigia Uttini, to whom was born Giuseppe Verdi, Honour of Italian Music'. There is a discrepancy between the date of Verdi's mother's death on the stone and that given in Muzio's letter to Ricordi announcing her death.

12. See n. 8, above. 'I will write to you about the life we have here, so that you will not be too uncomfortable'.

13. 11 Oct. 1851 (Casa Ricordi; ISV-P).

14. Verdi to Francesco Regli, 28 July 1851 (*C*, 121).

15. Verdi to Antonio Gallo, n.d. [Sept. 1851] (*C*, 124).

16. 22 Oct. 1851 (Casa Ricordi; ISV-P).

17. 26 Oct. 1851 (SAA).

18. (*C*, 128–31). Barezzi seems to have reproached Verdi for not spending Christmas and New Year's Day at home. The composer had left Sant'Agata about 40 days before this was written.

19. Strepponi to Verdi, 17 Jan. 1853 (SAA).

20. 19 Mar. 1852 (Casa Ricordi; ISV-P).

21. Verdi to Lanari, 26 Apr. 1852 (Abbiati, ii. 164–5).

22. 9 May 1852 (Di Ascoli, 99).

23. 29 Mar. 1851 (*CV* i. 4–5).

24. Ibid.

25. (Abbiati, ii. 122–3).

26. Ibid.

27. Ibid.

28. Ibid.

29. Ibid.

30. Ibid.

31. (*C*, 118-21).

32. Ibid.

33. 1 Oct. 1851 (*C*, 127-8).

34. Verdi to De Sanctis, 20 Feb. 1852 (*CV* i. 5).

35. 7 Mar. 1852 (*CV* i. 6).

36. 2 May 1852 (Casa Ricordi; ISV-P).

37. Verdi to De Sanctis, 3 May 1852 (*CV* i. 6).

38. Verdi to Jacovacci, [June 1852] (Abbiati, ii. 167).

39. (*CV* i. 6).

40. 5 Aug. 1852 (*CV* i. 9-10).

41. Ibid.

42. De Sanctis to Verdi, 23 Oct. 1852 (Abbiati, ii. 172).

43. *Enciclopedia dello spettacolo* (Rome, 1954-62), i. 1497.

44. 5 Nov. 1852 (Morgan Library).

45. Demaldè manuscript notes (Monte di Pietà Archive, BMP-B).

46. Ibid.

47. 22 Jan. 1853 (*CV* i. 18).

48. 29 Jan. 1853 (Di Ascoli, 100).

49. 2 May 1862 (A. Alberti, *Verdi intimo* (Milan, 1931), 15-17).

50. (SAA).

51. (SAA).

52. (SAA).

53. (SAA).

54. (SAA).

55. Notice in *Teatri, arti e letteratura* (3 Feb. 1853), 193, cited in M. Conati, *La Bottega della musica* (Milan, 1983), 312.

Chapter 19

1. Contract between Verdi and the Teatro La Fenice, [4] Mar. 1852, in M. Conati, *La Bottega della musica* (Milan, 1983), 290-2.

2. Verdi to Gallo, [Sept. 1851] (*C*, 124).

3. 4 Feb. 1852 (Conati, *Bottega*, 272–3).

4. 20 Feb. 1852 (ibid. 273).

5. (Ibid. 279–80).

6. Minutes of Directors' Meeting, Teatro La Fenice, 19 Apr. 1852 (ibid. 280–4). The minutes clearly state that the management chose Alajmo because they had had 'very, very bad reports' on Salvini-Donatelli. 'An artist of Donatelli's quality can be engaged whenever we want.' She was 'not suitable to our production' and 'not able to meet the demands of a great theatre', although she had a beautiful, flexible voice.

7. Agreement between Verdi and Brenna, 25 Apr. 1852 (ibid. 286–7).

8. Muzio to Giovanni Ricordi, 26 Apr. 1852 (Casa Ricordi; ISV-P).

9. 4 Aug. 1852 (Ditta Pietro Cuneo, Chiavari; ISV-P).

10. 26 July 1852 (Conati, *Bottega*, 297).

11. 5 Aug. 1852 (ibid. 298).

12. 20 Oct. 1852 (ibid. 301).

13. Varesi to Brenna, 10 Nov. 1852 (ibid. 303).

14. 24 Nov. 1852 (ibid.).

15. Piave to Marzari, 4 Feb. 1853 (ibid. 315–16).

16. [Postmarked Cremona, 30 Jan. 1853] (ibid. 312–13).

17. 3 Feb. 1853 (ibid. 314–15).

18. Piave to Marzari, 4 Feb. 1853 (ibid. 315). Piave sums up Verdi's statements to him. One paragraph gives Verdi's exact words.

19. Marzari to the Director of the Police, 14 Feb. 1853 (ibid. 322–3).

20. [Marzari] to the Director of the Police, 15 Feb. 1853 (ibid. 323). Given the length of time needed for the preparation of an important première, it is surprising to learn from this letter that the rehearsals of *La traviata* began on 14 Feb. and that the costume sketches were being submitted for the censors' approval on 15 Feb., leaving less than three weeks for the wardrobe to prepare them.

21. 16 Feb. 1853 (G. Morazzoni, *Lettere inedite di G. Verdi* (Milan, 1929), 36; original in the Toscanini Collection).

22. 1 Jan. 1853 (*CV* i. 16–17).

23. Ibid.

24. Article in *Gazzetta privilegiata di Venezia*, 18 Jan. 1853 (Biblioteca Marciana, Venice).

25. Varesi to Francesco Lucca, 10 Mar. 1852 (F. Schlitzer, *Mondo teatrale dell'Ottocento* (Naples, 1954), 157–8.

26. Article in *Gazzetta privilegiata di Venezia*, 7 Mar. 1853 (Biblioteca Marciana, Venice).

27. (9 Mar. 1853).

28. 7 Mar. 1853 (Gatti (1951), 305; see also *C*, 533).

29. 7 Mar. 1853 (*C*, 533).

30. 9 Mar. 1853 (*C*, 533).

31. 12 Mar. 1853 (*CV* i. 18–19).

32. 7 Mar. 1853 (G. Monaldi, *Verdi, il maestro della rivoluzione italiana* (Milan, 1913), 90).

33. 23 Feb. 1853 (SAA).

34. (SAA).

35. (SAA).

36. 2 Mar. 1853, postmarked 4 Mar. 1853 from Borgo San Donnino. The single, undated page that was sent with this letter was probably written on 3 Mar. The delay is due to the snow (SAA).

37. (SAA).

38. Demaldè. (BMP-B).

39. See n. 25, above.

40. G. Pavan, *Il Teatro San Benedetto (ora Rossini)* (Venice, 1917), 48–53. The Gallo theatres, including the historic Teatro Malibran (formerly the Teatro San Giovanni Grisostomo) were bought by the Marigonda family in Venice; as late as 1972 family members still held part of the Gallo archives. The San Benedetto had staged *Nabucco* in 1844, 1846, and 1849; *Ernani* in 1844, 1845, 1849, 1850, 1851, and 1852; *I due Foscari* in 1845, 1849, 1851 (twice), and 1854; *I Lombardi alla Prima Crociata* in 1846, 1847, 1849, and 1850; *Attila* in 1851 and 1853; *I masnadieri* in 1851; *Macbeth* in 1851 and 1853; and *Luisa Miller* in 1852.

41. (*C*, 535).

42. Ricordi to Verdi, 13 Apr. 1854 (*C*, 536).

43. Ibid.

44. [End of April 1854] (Abbiati, ii. 271).

45. 22 May 1854 (*C*, 537).

46. 26 May 1854 (*CV* i. 24–5).

47. (Deutsche Staatsbibliothek, Berlin; ISV-P).

48. *Encyclopedia judaica* (New York, 1971), xi. 595.

49. Vigna to Verdi, 6 Sept. 1853 (SAA). Vigna said that Verdi agreed to the project when he was distracted and busy with other, much more important matters.

50. Strepponi to Piave, 27 Mar. 1853 (Abbiati, ii. 239).

51. [Early Apr. 1853] (Morazzoni, *Lettere*, 35; original in the Toscanini Collection).

52. Ibid.

53. Verdi to Piave, 17 Apr. 1853 (private collection).

54. 14 July 1853 (Istituto per la Storia del Risorgimento Italiano, Rome; ISV-P).

55. See n. 49, above.

56. [After 26 Aug. 1853], (G. Bongiovanni, *Dal carteggio inedito Verdi–Vigna* (Rome, 1941), 43).

57. [Summer 1857] (Abbiati, ii. 244).

58. See n. 53, above.

59. See n. 53, above.

Chapter 20

1. Stato della popolazione, Villanova sull'Arda, in Archivio Civico Storico, Villanova.

2. 22 Apr. 1853 (A. Pascolato, *'Re Lear' e 'Un ballo in Maschera'*; *Lettere di Giuseppe Verdi ad Antonio Somma* (Città di Castello, 1902), 45–8.

3. 22 Sept. 1853 (SAA).

4. 19 Nov. 1853 (Pascolato, *'Re Lear'*, 58–62). See also Verdi to Somma, 6 Feb. 1854 (ibid. 62–4).

5. 17 May 1854 (ibid. 66–7).

6. Verdi to Somma, 4 and 8 Jan. 1855 (ibid. 68–74).

7. (*CV* i. 20).

8. (*C*, 151–2).

9. Verdi to Roqueplan, 10 Nov. 1852 (*C*, 150–1).

10. Contract between Verdi and Roqueplan, 28 Feb. 1852 (*C*, 139–40).

11. Verdi to Escudier, 18 Aug. 1852 (Toscanini Collection; trans A. Porter, in id., *'Les Vêpres siciliennes*: New Letters from Verdi to Scribe', *Nineteenth-Century Music*, 2: 2 (Nov. 1978), 97).

12. 1 Dec. 1853 (Toscanini Collection; on microfilm in Library for the Performing Arts at Lincoln Center, Music Special Collections).

13. Verdi to Vigna, 1 Dec. 1853 (G. Bongiovanni, *Dal carteggio inedite Verdi–Vigna* (Rome, 1941), 26–7).

14. Verdi to Clara Maffei, 2 Mar. 1854 (Di Ascoli, 69–70).

15. 3 Dec. 1853 (trans. Porter in id., '*Vêpres siciliennes*', 99–100).

16. Ibid. 100–1.

17. 4 Dec. 1853 (*CV* i. 21–2).

18. 18 Dec. 1853 (trans. Porter in id., '*Vêpres siciliennes*', 101).

19. Verdi to Eugène Deligne, 31 Dec. 1853 (*C*, 152).

20. (*C*, 152–3).

21. 4 Dec. 1853 (*CV* i. 21–2).

22. Verdi to De Sanctis, 16 Feb. 1854 (*CV* i. 23–4).

23. 20 Feb. 1854 (Abbiati, 263–4).

24. Verdi to De Sanctis, 9 Sept. 1854 (*CV* i. 26).

25. *Enciclopedia dello spettacolo* (Rome, 1954–62), viii. 1766 ff.

26. 'The Grand Operas', in 'Giuseppe Verdi', in *The New Grove Masters of Italian Opera* (London, 1983), 264.

27. (Trans. Porter, in id., '*Vêpres siciliennes*', 101–2).

28. Ibid. 102.

29. Verdi to Scribe, 29 Aug. 1854 (trans. Porter, in id., '*Vêpres siciliennes*', 102–3).

30. Ibid. 102.

31. Ibid. 102–3.

32. (trans. Porter, in id., '*Vêpres siciliennes*', 104–5).

33. Verdi to Marzari, 20 Feb. 1852 (M. Conati, *La Bottega della musica* (Milan, 1983), 273). It is not clear that Verdi asked Cruvelli to sing Violetta, but it is likely that he knew her.

34. 30 Oct. 1854 (private collection).

35. Verdi to Piave, 6 Jan. 1854 (private collection).

36. Verdi to Clara Maffei, 2 Mar. 1854 (Di Ascoli, 69–70).

37. Ibid.

38. Ibid.

39. Verdi to J. B. Benelli, 2 Sept. 1854 (Abbiati, ii. 277). A baritone whom Benelli had introduced to the composer had dared to pay a visit to Verdi's

villa at Mandres at ten at night. Verdi said he was 'not very kind' to the singer, but excused himself because he had 'retired to a very remote place in the country just to have tranquillity'. The baritone's visit was 'a very crazy thing', Verdi said.

40. (*C*, 154–5).

41. Verdi to Gennaro Sanguineti, 18 Nov. 1854 (*C*, 156).

42. 18 Nov. 1854 (*C*, 157).

43. 3 Jan. 1855 (*C*, 157–9).

44. Ibid.

45. Verdi to Crosnier (*C*, 160).

46. *C*, 160 n. 1.

47. Porter, in id., '*Vêpres siciliennes*', 105.

48. Berlioz to [?] Belloni [June 1855] (Abbiati, ii. 293).

49. 4 Feb. 1855 (Di Ascoli, 72).

50. *La France musicale* (7 Oct. 1855). See J. Budden, *The Operas of Verdi* (London, 1973–81), ii. 187 n. Abbiati (ii. 300) states that Berlioz's essay appeared originally in the *Journal des débats*.

51. 28 June 1855 (Di Ascoli, 105–6).

52. 29 [Nov.] 1854 (*CV* i. 27; see also 27 n. 1). The letter is incorrectly dated 'Sept.', but postmarks confirm the date.

53. (*CV* i. 28–9).

54. Verdi to Tito Ricordi, 8 July 1855 (Casa Ricordi; ISV-P).

55. 24 Oct. 1855 (*C*, 166–9).

56. 21 Oct. [1855] (*C*, 169–70).

57. 27 Sept. 1853 (G. Carrara Verdi, 'Giuseppe Demaldè e il Maestro di Cappella della Collegiata', *Biblioteca 70*, (1970), 9–10; see also Abbiati, ii. 256).

58. Budden, *Operas*, ii. 239.

59. Muzio to Tito Ricordi, 19 Jan. 1856 (Casa Ricordi; ISV-P).

Chapter 21

1. Muzio to Tito Ricordi, 10 Feb. 1856 (Casa Ricordi, ISV-P).

2. Verdi, Last Will and Testament, 14 May 1900, clause 11, (Gatti (1951), 793–5).

3. 'Allocution', cited in G. Martin, *Verdi: His Music, Life, and Times* (New York, 1963), 329.

4. Martin, *Verdi*, 331.

5. (Abbiati, ii. 346–7).

6. [After 27 Feb. 1856] (ibid. 351–3).

7. 23 Mar. 1856 (M. Conati, *La bottega della musica* (Milan, 1983), 342–3).

8. Verdi to Mocenigo, 13 Jan. 1855 (ibid. 336).

9. 16 Feb. 1855 (ibid. 356–7).

10. 1 Apr. 1856 (Di Ascoli, 108).

11. 13 May 1856 (Conati, *Bottega*, 364).

12. 12 May 1854 (ibid. 363–4). Draft dated 10 May 1856 (*C*, 190–1).

13. Scrittura Teatrale, 15 May 1856, in *C*, 191 (summary only); Conati gives the complete contract in *Bottega*, 365–7.

14. Verdi to Vigna, 22 July 1856 (G. Bongiovanni, *Dal carteggio inedite Verdi–Vigna* (Rome, 1941), 58).

15. Contract with the Paris Opéra, in U. Günther, 'Documents inconnus concernant les relations de Verdi avec l'Opéra de Paris', in *Atti dei III Congresso Internazionale di studi verdiani*' (Parma, 1974), 569.

16. 21 Oct. 1856 (Morgan Library).

17. 23 Oct. 1856 (Abbiati, ii. 373).

18. 23 Aug. 1856 (Morgan Library).

19. See Conati, *Bottega*, 380.

20. Title on cover of libretto, see ibid. 381. See also ibid. 414 n. 26.

21. 28 Aug. 1856 (ibid. 381).

22. 12 Sept. 1856 (ibid. 383; TLF-V; ISV-P).

23. 3 Sept. 1856 (Museo Teatrale alla Scala; ISV-P).

24. J. Budden believes that Verdi was not serious. See *The Operas of Verdi* ii (New York, 1979), 246–7.

25. (Conati, *Bottega*, 383).

26. 17 Sept. 1856 (ibid. 384).

27. Protocollo 604, Teatro La Fenice (ibid. 387).

28. [7 Oct. 1856, postmark] (Museo Teatrale alla Scala).

29. (G. Morazzoni, *Lettere inedite di G. Verdi* (Milan, 1929), 43; original in Museo Teatrale alla Scala).

30. 2 Jan. 1857 (Casa Ricordi; ISV-P).

31. Muzio to Tito Ricordi, 4 Jan. 1857 (Casa Ricordi; ISV-P).

32. F. Walker, 'Verdi, Giuseppe Montanelli, and the Libretto of *Simon Boccanegra*', *Bollettino dell'ISV*, 1: 3 (1960), 1373–90.

33. [Feb. 1857] (Morazzoni, *Lettere inedite*, 38; original in Museo Teatrale alla Scala).

34. (Conati, *Bottega*, 399–400).

35. 9 Feb. 1857. Deutsche Staatsbibliothek, Berlin, (ISV-P).

36. 2 Mar. 1857 (Conati, *Bottega*, 407).

37. 13 Mar. 1857 (Abbiati, ii. 393).

38. G. Pavan, *Il Teatro San Benedetto ora Rossini*) (Venice, 1917), 54.

39. 22 Feb. 1857 (Casa Ricordi, ISV-P).

40. 18 Mar. 1857 (SAA).

41. Piave to Verdi, 20 Mar. 1857 (SAA).

42. Vigna to Verdi, 23 Mar. 1857 (Bongiovanni, *Verdi–Vigna*, 43; original in SAA).

43. Ibid.

44. 1 Apr. 1857 (SAA).

45. 11 Apr. 1857 (Bongiovanni, *Verdi–Vigna*, 54–5).

46. Ibid.

47. Verdi to Tito Ricordi, 29 May 1857 (Casa Ricordi; ISV-P).

48. Antonio Barezzi to Verdi, 28 May 1857 (SAA).

49. Ibid.

50. 8 June 1857 (SAA).

51. (SAA).

52. [Early July 1857] (Abbiati, ii. 417–18).

53. Verdi to Torelli, 14 May 1857 (*C*, 554). Original in Biblioteca Nazionale, Naples, in Biblioteca Lucchesi-Palli (ISV-P). See also *C*, 484.

54. (see n. 52, above).

55. Ibid.

56. Verdi to Torelli, 9 Sept. 1857 (*C*, 555).

57. (Paris Opéra Archive; ISV-P).

58. Muzio to Verdi, 12 May 1857, (Napolitano).

59. Muzio to Tito Ricordi, 20 May 1857 (Casa Ricordi; ISV-P).

60. (Napolitano) See also Muzio to Verdi, 14 May 1857 (ibid.).

61. (Ibid.).

62. (Ibid.).

63. (Ibid.).

64. Muzio to Verdi, 17 June 1857 (ibid.).

65. 29 June 1857 (ibid.).

66. Ibid.

67. Verdi to Tito Ricordi, 25 June 1857 (Casa Ricordi; ISV-P).

68. U. Zoppi, *Angelo Mariani, Giuseppe Verdi e Teresa Stolz* (Milan, 1947), 27.

69. T. Mantovani, *Angelo Mariani* (Rome, 1921), 7 ff.

70. A. Mariani, Autobiographical Sketch, manuscript, Biblioteca Comunale Classense, Ravenna.

71. Muzio to Antonio Barezzi, 2 July 1846 (Garibaldi, 252). See also letter of 24 Aug. 1864 (ibid. 200–1).

72. Verdi to Antonio Lanari, 19 Aug. 1846 (*C*, 25–6). The letter almost certainly refers to Napoleone Moriani, not to Angelo Mariani.

73. A. Ghislanzoni from unidentified personal account. See Walker (It. edn.), 358.

74. See n. 70, above.

75. Mariani to Verdi, 25 Sept. 1853 (SAA).

76. Mantovani, *Mariani*, 23–4.

77. Zoppi *Mariani*, 94.

78. G. Bottoni, *Giuseppe Verdi a Rimini*, (Rimini, 1913), 6–11.

79. [July 1857] (Abbiati, ii. 425).

80. [July 1857] (ibid).

81. [Aug. 1857] (ibid. 426).

82. [July 1857] (Casa Ricordi; ISV-P).

83. Mariani to Ricordi, night of 16–17 Aug. 1857 (Abbiati, ii. 426–7).

84. Ibid.

85. [22 Aug. 1857] (Casa Ricordi; ISV-P).

86. 28 Aug. 1857 (Casa Ricordi; ISV-P).

87. [Dec. 1864] (*C*, 256–7 n. 1). Verdi himself says that this story was *reported about* Mariani: 'I'll tell you a story told about you!' He does not say who told him. Verdi's letter is strongly supportive of Mariani.

88. (SAA).

89. Verdi to Luccardi, (Morgan Library).

90. Muzio to Girolamo Cerri, 17 June 1857 (Casa Ricordi, ISV-P).

91. Muzio to Tito Ricordi, 5 Oct. 1857, '1/2 hour after midnight' (Casa Ricordi; ISV-P).

92. Muzio to Tito Ricordi, 14 Nov. 1857 (Casa Ricordi; ISV-P).

93. Muzio to Tito Ricordi, 11 [Jan.] 1858 (Casa Ricordi; ISV-P).

94. 9 Oct. 1857 (Casa Ricordi; ISV-P).

Chapter 22

1. *C*, 189 n.1.

2. Verdi to Torelli, 22 Apr. 1856 (*C*, 189–90).

3. Ibid.

4. Verdi to Torelli, 16 May 1856 (*C*, 190–1).

5. (*C*, 194–5). Abbiati correctly identified Mitrovich as the recipient, although the *C* identified the recipient as Ercolano Balestra, and correctly dated the letter from the orignial in Gallini's collection. See Abbiati, ii. 338–9.

6. Verdi to Torelli, 11 Nov. 1856 (*C*, 196–7).

7. 6 Dec. 1856 (*C*, 197–8).

8. Verdi to Torelli, 15 Jan. 1857 (*C*, 483–4).

9. Verdi to Torelli, 14 May 1857 (*C*, 484).

10. Verdi to Torelli, 17 June 1857 (ibid.).

11. 19 Sept. 1857 (*C*, 561–3).

12. Verdi to Torelli, 9 Sept. 1857 (*C*, 561).

13. Ballet librettos of *La festa da ballo in maschera* and *Gustavo III, re di Svezia*, (Library for the Performing Arts at Lincoln Center, Dance Collection).

14. Libretto of *Il reggente*, (Library for the Performing Arts at Lincoln Center, Dance Collection).

15. 19 Sept. 1857 (*C*, 561–3).

16. Abbiati, ii. 450–1.

17. 20 Nov. 1857 (A. Pascolato, *'Re Lear' e 'Un ballo in maschera; Lettere di Giuseppe Verdi ad Antonio Somma* (Città di Castello, 1902), 81–4).

18. (Ibid. 85–8; see also *CV* i. 228–30).

19. See n. 18, above.

20. Somma to Verdi, 6 Dec. 1857 (SAA).

21. (SAA).

22. 14 Jan. 1858 (*CV* i. 39).

23. n.d. (Abbiati, ii. 467).

24. Ibid.

25. Ibid.

26. *C*, 565.

27. 7 Feb. 1858 (Morgan Library).

28. 7 Feb. 1858 (Pascolato, '*Re Lear*', 90–1).

29. 13 Feb. 1858 (SAA).

30. 14 Feb. 1858 (*C*, 566–7).

31. Torelli to Antonio Monaco, [20 Feb. 1858] (Abbiati, ii. 473). See also F. Walker, 'Unpublished letters', *Bollettino dell'ISV*, 1: 1 (Apr. 1960), 28 ff.

32. 18 Feb. 1858 (*C*, 568).

33. 27 Feb. 1858 (*C*, 570–1).

34. *CV* i. 241–75. Verdi gave the document to De Sanctis before he left Naples, asking De Sanctis not to let anyone see it.

35. *CV* i. 269.

36. 27 Mar. 1858 (Napolitano).

37. Ibid.

38. 14 Apr. 1858 (Napolitano).

39. 28 Mar. 1858 (Garibaldi, 369–71).

40. See n. 38, above.

41. 29 Apr. 1858 (*CV* i. 41–2).

42. 5 May 1858 (Napolitano).

43. (Napolitano).

44. (Ibid.).

45. 12 May 1858 (Di Ascoli, 110–12).

46. 24 Aug. 1858 (Casa Ricordi; ISV-P).

47. Mariani's surviving letters to Verdi are in SAA; almost all Verdi's to Mariani are in the Biblioteca Beriana, Genoa; the Biblioteca Comunale Classense, Ravenna; and in draft form in Strepponi, Letter-books, SAA.

48. 8 July 1858 (Pascolato, '*Re Lear*', 92).

49. 14 Apr. 1858 (SAA).

50. 16 May 1858 (Conati, *La Bottega della musica* (Milan, 1983), 419).

51. '29 or rather 30 June 1858' (G. Micheli, 'Tre lettere di Verdi ad Antonio Superchi', *Aurea Parma*, 1–2 (1941), 64–6).

52. [July 1858] (SAA).

53. 11 Aug. 1858 (*CV* i. 238–9); original in (SAA).

54. 11 Sept. 1858 (Pascolato, '*Re Lear*', 94–7).

55. 20 Oct. 1858 (Bibliothèque de l'Opéra, Paris; ISV-P). Strepponi added her postscript to the letter.

56. Verdi to De Sanctis, 12 Jan. 1859 (*CV* i. 51).

57. 4 Feb. 1858 (*CV* i. 52).

58. Strepponi to De Sanctis, 11 Feb. 1859 (*CV* i. 52–3).

59. Verdi to De Sanctis, 2 Mar. 1859 (*CV* i. 54).

60. (*C*, 556–7). A major gap at Casa Ricordi is from Dec. 1857 to May 1860.

61. (*C*, 577–8).

62. G. Monaldi, *Verdi aneddotico* (L'Aquila, 1926), 75–6.

63. *Gazzetta musicale di Milano*, cited in Abbiati, ii. 528–9.

64. 28 Feb. 1859 (*CV* i. 53–4).

65. [end of 1872–beginning 1873], in a special issue, *San Carlo* (Naples, 1913). See also Abbiati, ii. 529.

66. 25 Feb. 1859 (private collection).

67. 7 Mar. 1859 (*CV* i. 55–6).

68. 14 Feb. 1859 (*CV* i. 57–8).

69 S. Maggi, 'La provincia piacentina nella cronaca risorgimentale, 1859–1860', *Studi piacentini sul Risorgimento*, 11 (1961), 210.

70. Ibid. 211.

71. E. Nasalli-Rocca (ed.), *Piacenza 1859* (Piacenza, 1960), 43.

72. Ibid. 44–5.

73. Ibid.

74. 19 Mar. 1859 (Napolitano).

75. Ibid.

76. 21 May 1859 (*CV* i. 58–9).

77. 30 Apr. 1859 (*CV* i. 59–60).

78. Nasalli-Rocca (ed.), *Piacenza 1859*, 46.

79. Ibid. The article from the *Gazzetta austriaca* was reprinted in the *Piccolo corriere d'Italia*.

80. G. Monaldi, *Verdi: il maestro della rivoluzione italiana* (Milan, 1913), 104. Monaldi says that he heard the story told by Prati himself.

81. 26 Apr. 1859 (SAA).

82. Giuseppe Massari, diary note, 28 Apr. 1859 (cited in Nasalli-Rocca (ed.), *Piacenza 1859*, 46.

83. Nasalli-Rocca (ed.), *Piacenza 1859*, 47.

84. 12 May 1859 (SAA).

85. (*CV* i. 61–2).

86. (SAA).

87. 4 June 1859 (SAA).

88. Nasalli-Rocca (ed.), *Piacenza 1859*, 52–3.

89. 12 June 1859 (Biblioteca Beriana, Genoa; ISV-P).

90. (*CV* i. 61–2).

91. Verdi, Subscription for funds for the wounded and families of the dead, 20 June 1859 (Museo Civico, Busseto).

92. 23 June 1859 (Di Ascoli, 112–3).

93. Ibid.

94. Verdi to the Marzi brothers, n.d. (Abbiati, ii. 547). See also Giulio Carcano to Verdi, 10 July 1859 (SAA).

95. Don Vincenzo Molinari, in *Gazzetta Piacentina*, 16 July 1859, cited in Nasalli-Rocca (ed.), *Piacenza 1859*, 58. Molinari was a classmate and friend of Don Carlo Uttini.

96. Verdi to Clarina Maffei, 14 July 1859 (Di Ascoli, 113).

97. Verdi to Giuseppe Piroli, 3 Nov. 1868 (*CV* iii. 58). See also Verdi to Piroli, 27 Oct. 1868 (ibid. 57–8), and Strepponi to Avanzi, 26 Dec. 1868 (BMP-B).

98. P. Dotti, personal recollection cited in Gatti (1951), 371. See also N. Musini, 'Giuseppe Verdi, patriota', in *Archivio Storico per le Provincie Parmensi*, (1941), 31–60.

BOOK IV

Chapter 23

1. (*C*, 580).

2. E. Nasalli-Rocca (ed.), *Piacenza 1859* (Piacenza, 1960), 68–9.

3. 16 Sept. 1859 (*C*, 582).

4. 21 Sept. 1859 (*C*, 582).

5. 24 Sept. 1859 (*C*, 583).

6. Filippo Filippi to Verdi, [end of Sept. 1859] (Abbiati, ii. 551–2).

7. 19 Sept. 1859 (SAA).

8. Ibid.

9. Nasalli-Rocca (ed.), *Piacenza 1859*, 70–3.

10. Report in *The Times*, London, cited in Nasalli-Rocca (ed.), *Piacenza 1859*, 73.

11. Nasalli-Rocca (ed.), *Piacenza 1859*, 76.

12. Ibid. 78.

13. 25 Oct. 1859 (*C*, 584).

14. 27 Oct. 1859 (*CV* iii. 8).

15. 15 Nov. 1859 (*CV* iii. 9–10).

16. [16 Nov. 1859] (*CV* iii. 10).

17. 15 Oct. 1859 (*CV* i. 65–6).

18. Verdi to De Sanctis, 17 Dec. 1859 (*CV* i. 66).

19. C. Osborne, *Verdi: A Life in the Theatre* (New York, 1987), 159–60.

20. 11 May 1859 (Napolitano).

21. 29 Nov. 1859 (ibid. 113).

22. (Abbiati, ii. 565).

23. 2 June 1859 (SAA).

24. 21 Oct. 1859 (SAA).

25. G. Monleone, *Le dimore genovesi di Giuseppe Verdi* (Genoa, 1941), 4.

26. F. Resasco, *Giuseppe Verdi, cittadino genovese* (Rome, 1918), 5.

27. 5 [Jan.] 1860 (SAA).

28. (SAA).

29. 28 [Jan.] 1860 (SAA).

30. Ibid.

31. 5 Feb. 1860 (SAA).

32. Ibid.

33. 13 Feb. 1860 (SAA).

34. Nasalli-Rocca (ed.), *Piacenza 1859*, 78.

35. Ibid.

36. Ibid. 79.

37. Id., *Piacenza 1860*, 47.

38. Ibid. 50–6.

39. 3 Feb. 1860 (*CV* iii. 10–11).

40. 10 Apr. 1860 (SAA).

41. 10 Feb. 1860 (Bibliothèque de l'Opéra, Paris; ISV-P).

42. Carlo Verdi to Ricordi, 1 May 1849 (*C* 75 n. 2).

43. Verdi to Carlo Fioruzzi, n.d. (E. Ottolenghi, 'Nel XXV anniversario della morte di G. Verdi: due lettere inedite del Maestro', in *Bollettino storico piacentino*, 21 (1926), 21.

44. Ibid.

45. Strepponi to Clara Maffei, 14 June 1867 (Di Ascoli, 162–4; see also Conati's notes to his edn. of A. Oberdorfer, *Giuseppe Verdi: autobiografia dalle lettere* (1951; Milan, 1981), 228 nn. 2, 3, 4).

46. S. C. Ghizzoni, 'Tipi di case rurali nella zona di Busseto', *Biblioteca 70*, 4 (1975), 213 ff.

47. G. Berti, *Trasformazioni interne della società parmense–piacentino 1860–1900* (Piacenza, 1972), 14.

48. Ibid. 18. The figure given is for 1880, but Berti makes it clear that the conditions in 1860 were even worse. See also id., 'Ideologie politiche e sociali negli ex-ducati di Parma e Piacenza durante il primo decennio dell'unità italiana', in *Archivio Storico per le Provincie Parmensi* (1960–1), xiii. 121–57.

49. Id., *Trasformazioni*, 21.

50. Strepponi to Escudier, 30 Apr. 1860 (Strepponi, Letter-books, SAA).

51. Verdi to the Comunale Rappresentanza of Busseto, 26 Apr. 1860 (*C*, 586).

52. Verdi to the Consiglio Provinciale, 16 Mar. 1860 (Strepponi, Letter-books, SAA).

53. (SAA).

54. 21 Mar. 1860 (*C*, 544–5).

55. 7 Feb. 1860 (*C*, 543).

56. 20 Aug. 1860 (Biblioteca Beriana, Genoa; ISV-P).

57. [Mar. 1860] (SAA).

58. 12 May 1860 (Morgan Library).

59. 4 May 1860 (Casa Ricordi; ISV-P).

60. June 1860 (Strepponi, Letter-books, SAA).

61. 23 June 1860 (*C*, 545).

62. 9 Aug. [1860] (*C*, 546).

63. I. Montanelli, *L'Italia del Risorgimento* (6th edn., Milan, 1972), 604–84, *passim*. See also Denis Mack Smith, *Italy: A Modern History* (Ann Arbor, 1959), *passim*.

64. Verdi to Mariani, 27 May 1860 (*C* ii. 204). See also T. Mantovani, *Angelo Mariani* (Rome, 1921), 73.

65. Verdi to Mariani, 7 Oct. 1860 (*CV* ii. 204; original in Biblioteca Beriana, Genoa; ISV-P).

66. Strepponi to Antonio Capecelatro, note added to Verdi's letter to Capecelatro (*CV* i. 74 n. 1).

67. Verdi to Agostino Bertani, 11 July 1860 (private collection).

68. Verdi to Piave, 3 Nov. 1860 (*CV* ii. 353-4; Deutsche Staatsbibliothek, Berlin; ISV-P).

Chapter 24

1. 14 Dec. 1860 (*CV* i. 75).

2. 6 Dec. 1860 (*CV* i. 74).

3. Ibid.

4. [Nov. 1860] (*CV* i.74 n.1).

5. (*CV* ii. 16).

6. n.d. (*CV* ii. 16). The draft in her Letter-books is dated 14 Dec. 1860.

7. (SAA).

8. (SAA).

9. N. Musini, 'Giuseppe Verdi, deputato', in *Archivio Storico per le Provincie Parmense* (1941) vi. 46-7.

10. Musini, 'Giuseppe Verdi, deputato', 46.

11. Musini, 'Giuseppe Verdi, deputato', 45 n. 1.

12. 16 Jan. 1861, (Strepponi, Letter-Books, SAA).

13. (SAA).

14. Ibid.

15. 18 Jan. 1861 (*C*, 589).

16. (Private collection). This letter is incorrectly dated 8 Feb. in *C*, 601-2, and in an old handlist from a private collection, where it was dated 4 Jan. Abbiati, ii. 601 has the correct date. The actual letter differs slightly from the version in *C*; the date on the original is clear.

17. 25 Jan. 1861 (*C*, 590; original in Biblioteca Beriana, Genoa; ISV-P).

18. Note described by Musini as a *foglietto* at Sant' Agata (Musini, 'Giuseppe Verdi, deputato' 49-50).

19. 21 Jan. 1861 (*C*, 590-2).

20. 22 Jan. 1861 (*C*, 593).

21. 23 Jan. 1861 (*C*, 593).

22. (Musini, 'Giuseppe Verdi, deputato', 52). Malmusi's letter is presumably dated 19 Jan.

23. 19 Jan. 1861 (ibid).

24. Electoral broadside, written by Leonida Piletti Fanti (*C*, 594–5). See also Musini, 'Giuseppe Verdi, Deputato', 53–4.

25. Musini, 'Giuseppe Verdi, Deputato', 53–4.

26. 28 Jan. 1861 (595–6).

27. 29 Jan. 1861 (*C*, 597).

28. 6 Feb. 1861 (*C*, 597).

29. Ibid.

30. 12 Feb. 1861 (*C*, 597).

31. 5 Feb. 1861 (*CV* iii. 14).

32. Verdi to Piroli, 11 Feb. 1861 (ibid. 16).

33. 12 Feb. 1861 (ibid. 17).

34. Musini, 'Giuseppe Verdi, deputato', 56.

35. 19–25 Feb. 1861 (Strepponi, Letter-books, SAA).

36. Ibid.

37. Musini, 'Giuseppe Verdi, deputato', 58.

38. Verdi to Arrivabene, 15 Mar. 1876 (*C*, 598; see also A. Alberti, *Verdi intimo* (Milan, 1931), 188–9).

39. 12 Mar. 1861 (*CV* i. 77–8).

40. 19 Mar. 1861 (*CV* i. 78–9).

41. Verdi to De Sanctis, 26 Apr. 1861 (*CV* i. 79).

42. Ibid.

43. 3 May 1861 (*CV* i. 79–80).

44. Verdi to Piave, 4 Feb. 1865 (Private Collection).

45. Verdi to Arrivabene, [7 June 1861] (Alberti, *Verdi intimo*,8).

46. 14 June 1861 (ibid. 9–10).

47. See n. 44, above.

48. 23 Dec. 1860 (SAA).

49. 17 Jan. 1861 (Museo Teatrale alla Scala).

50. Verdi to Tamberlick, 5 Mar. 1861 (original in George Martin Collection). See also *Bollettino dell'ISV*, 2: 5, (1962), 1089–90.

51. De Sanctis to Verdi, 22 Oct. 1852 (*CV* i. 11–14).

52. 17 Apr. 1861 (Museo Teatrale alla Scala).

53. 14 Mar. 1861 (SAA).

54. 17 July 1861 (Museo Teatrale alla Scala).

55. 19 July 1861 (Strepponi, Letter-books, SAA).

56. Verdi to Piave, 5 Aug. 1861 (Morgan Library).

57. Ibid.

58. 6 Aug. 1861 (Morgan Library).

59. 13 Aug. 1861 (Morgan Library).

60. 10 Oct. 1861 (Morgan Library).

61. (Casa Ricordi; ISV-P).

62. Verdi to Piave, [7 Dec. 1861] (Abbiati, ii. 673; original formerly in Gallini Collection).

63. *Enciclopedia dello spettacolo* (Rome, 1954–62), vi. 1377 ff.

64. (Morgan Library).

65. 7 Jan. 1862 (Casa Ricordi; ISV-P).

66. 17 Jan. 1862 (Casa Ricordi; ISV-P).

67. 1 Feb. 1862 (Alberti, *Verdi intimo*, 13–14).

68. Abbiati, ii. 690–2.

69. Verdi to General Sabouroff, 19 Mar. 1862 (*CV* iv. 229).

70. 23 Apr. [1862] (Gatti (1951), 416). Verdi lived at 43 Alpha Road, Regent's Park.

71. (Casa Ricordi; ISV-P).

72. 24 Apr. 1862 (Bibliothèque de l'Opéra, Paris; ISV-P).

73. 2 May 1862 (Alberti, 15–17).

74. 19 June 1862 (Biblioteca Beriana, Genoa; ISV-P). In the letter, Verdi said that he was on the train between Turin and Genoa as he wrote.

Chapter 25

1. 10 Aug. 1862 (Di Ascoli, 125–6).

2. 28 Aug. 1862 (A. Alberti, *Verdi intimo* (Milan, 1931), 21–2).

3. I. Montanelli, *L'Italia del Risorgimento* (6th edn., Milan, 1972), 70–2.

4. Verdi to Piroli, 21 July 1862 (*CV* iii. 20–1).

5. 1 Aug. 1862 (original in Biblioteca Beriana, Genoa, has only the first page; the envelope and other pages are missing; ISV-P).

6. 11 Oct. 1862 (Casa Ricordi; ISV-P).

7. Verdi to Tito Ricordi, 11 Nov. 1862 (Casa Ricordi; ISV-P).

8. Ibid.

9. 17 Nov. 1862 (Bibliothèque de l'Opéra, Paris; ISV-P).

10. 3 Dec. 1862 (Museo Teatrale alla Scala).

11. 9 Nov. 1862 (Western calendar) (cited in G. Barblan, 'Up po' di luce sulla prima rappresentazione della *Forza del Destino* a Pietroburgo', *Bollettino dell'ISV*, 2: 5 ((1962), 843–5).

12. Summary of review in *Le Nord*, from *Gazzetta musicale*, 23 Nov. 1862 (ibid. 838).

13. 7 Dec. 1862 (ibid. 839–41).

14. Summary of review in *Le Nord*, from *Gazzetta musicale*, 7 Dec. 1862 (ibid. 840).

15. 13 Nov. 1862 (ibid. 859–62).

16. 17 Sept. 1862 (Di Ascoli, 127–8).

17. 17 Jan. 1863 (Casa Ricordi; ISV-P).

18. 21 Jan. 1863 (Casa Ricordi; ISV-P).

19. Ibid.

20. (Casa Ricordi; ISV-P).

21. 17 Feb. 1863 (*C*, 612).

22. *Enciclopedia dello spettacolo* (Rome, 1954–62), vi. 1154.

23. G. Gualerzi, 'Il cammino dell'opera', *Bollettino dell'ISV*, 2: 5 (Jan.–Dec. 1962), 165.

24. 21 Feb. 1863 (Casa Ricordi; ISV-P).

25. 22 Feb. 1863 (Alberti, *Verdi intimo*, 24). Verdi mistakenly wrote '1862'.

26. 13 Mar. 1863 (Casa Ricordi; ISV-P).

27. Cited in Gualerzi, 'Cammino', 163.

28. Verdi to Arrivabene, 22 Mar. 1863 (Alberti, *Verdi intimo*, 24).

29. See n. 26, above.

30. Gualerzi, 'Cammino', 148 n. 3.

31. See n. 28, above.

32. Verdi to Arrivabene, 25 May 1863 (Alberti, *Verdi intimo*, 26–7).

33. L. Escudier, 'L'orchestre de l'Opéra', *L'Art musicale*, 3: 30 (23 July 1863), 271–2 (cited in M. Conati, *Interviste ed incontri con Verdi* (Milan, 1980), 39–41; the same anecdote is told in Pougin, 27).

34. (Alberti, *Verdi intimo*, 27).

35. See n. 32, above.

36. 12 Apr. 1863 (*CV* i. 87–9).

37. Stato Civile Toscano (Deaths, 1863), Archivio di Stato, Florence; and Stato Civile (Deaths, 1863), Archivio del Comune, Siena. Dr Rosalia Manno-Tolù found the first of these in Florence in the early 1970s, following a lead in Strepponi's Pro memoria of 19 Feb. 1864 to Corticelli, which is in the Museo Teatrale alla Scala. The second document, found in Siena in 1990, shows that Camillino was a medical student, a resident of Florence. These documents tell a story of their own, for the omission of Strepponi's surname and Cirelli's baptismal name is unusual, making it appear that Camillino had been a foundling or 'child of the turnstile', which he was not. One cannot help reflecting on the fact that Giuseppa Faustina (Sinforosa) was also misrepresented in 1839, when she was abandoned in the turnstile. Falsification of vital records was and is illegal. A particular acknowledgement is made to the staffs of the Ufficio Stato Civile and the Archivio di Stato, Siena. The archivist of the latter institution helped search for the death record when her office was closed for the August holiday. She proved that Camillino was a charity case, a *gratuito*.

38. 2 Apr. 1863 (Biblioteca Beriana, Genoa; ISV-P).

39. Ibid.

40. 14 Apr. 1863 (Biblioteca Comunale Classense, Ravenna; ISV-P).

41. 3 May 1863 (Biblioteca Comunale Classense, Ravenna; ISV-P).

42. Verdi to Mariani, 15 July 1863 (Biblioteca Comunale Classense, Ravenna; ISV-P).

43. Ibid.

44. 20 July 1863 (Biblioteca Comunale Classense, Ravenna; ISV-P).

45. Verdi to Arrivabene (Alberti, *Verdi intimo*, 27).

46. 15 July 1863 (ibid. 27–8).

47. 17 Dec. 1863 (in A. Pascolato, '*Re Lear*' e '*Un ballo in maschera*'; *Lettere di Giuseppe Verdi ad Antonio Somma* (città di cantello, 1902), 97–8). See also Maffei to Verdi, 31 Aug. 1861 (Abbiati, ii. 656).

48. 3 Sept. 1863 (Di Ascoli, 134–5).

49. 31 July 1863 (Di Ascoli, 131).

50. Ibid.

51. 3 Sept. 1863 (Di Ascoli, 134–5).

52. 3 Oct. 1863 (Casa Ricordi; ISV-P).

53. 2 Oct. 1863 (ISV-P). See also Verdi to Escudier, 28 Oct. 1863 (ISV-P).

54. 9 Apr. 1864 (Alberti, *Verdi intimo*, 41–2).

55. G. Mariani, *Storia della Scapigliatura* (Palermo, 1967), 11–12.

56. Ibid. 90.

57. Ibid. 92.

58. Ibid. 93–4.

59. *Ode all'Arte Italiana*, in *Museo di Famiglia*, 22 Nov. 1863 (reproduced in Abbiati, ii. 762).

60. Franco Faccio to Verdi, 16 Nov. 1863 (Di Ascoli, 136).

61. 13 Dec. 1863 (ibid. 136–8).

62. 3 May 1865 (Casa Ricordi; ISV-P).

63. 21 May 1865, (P. Nardi, *Boito* (Milan, 1944), 131). A draft of this is in the SAA.

64. (R. De Rensis, *Franco Faccio e Verdi: carteggi e documenti inediti* (Milan, 1934), 30–1).

65. [23 Dec. 1863] (Strepponi, Letter-books, SAA). I am grateful to Camilla Gavazzi of the Archivio Storico Civico in Milan for helping to locate the references to San Giovanni delle Quattro Facce in *Milano numerizzato* and other city directories of the last century.

66. 13 Dec. 1863 (Casa Ricordi; ISV-P).

67. 9 Dec. 1863 (SAA).

68. 13 Mar. 1864 (SAA).

Chapter 26

1. Editorial, 14 Jan. 1864 (cited in Abbiati, ii. 749).

2. In *Perseveranza* [Sept. 1863] (ibid. 765–6).

3. (Cited in P. Nardi, *Boito* (Milan, 1944), 162).

4. (Cited in Abbiati, ii. 774).

5. (Catalogue of the Biblioteca Antiquariana Vinciana, 2, p. 12, lot 99 (ISV-P); see also Abbiati, ii. 777.) Conati suggests that this letter may have been written in 1865.

6. Ibid.

7. 12 June 1864 (Casa Ricordi; ISV-P).

8. 9 Apr. 1864 (A. Alberti, *Verdi intimo* (Milan, 1931), 41–2).

9. 22 Oct. 1864 (Casa Ricordi; ISV-P).

10. 2 Nov. 1864 (Casa Ricordi; ISV-P).

11. 22 Sept. 1864 (Abbiati, ii. 799).

12. 30 July 1864 (Alberti, *Verdi intimo*, 42–3).

13. 2 July 1864 (Casa Ricordi; ISV-P).

14. 29 July 1864 (Bibliothèque de l'Opéra, Paris; ISV-P).

15. 8 Sept. 1864 (Casa Ricordi; ISV-P). The reference is to Dante's *Inferno*, iv. 102.

16. Sept. 1864 (Di Ascoli, 138).

17. 2 Dec. 1864 (Bibliothèque de l'Opéra, Paris; ISV-P).

18. 13 Dec. 1864 (Bibliothèque de l'Opéra, Paris; ISV-P).

19. Verdi to Escudier, 22 Oct. 1864 (Bibliothèque de l'Opéra, Paris; ISV-P).

20. Ibid.

21. 13 Dec. 1864 (Bibliothèque de l'Opéra, Paris; ISV-P).

22. 20 Dec. 1864 (Morgan Library).

23. 28 Jan. 1865 (Morgan Library).

24. Verdi wrote to Ricordi about his worry that he had got the address wrong.

25. 23 Jan. 1865 (The text in *C*, 452–4 is taken from a draft at SAA; original in Bibliothèque de l'Opéra, Paris; ISV-P).

26. 3 Feb. 1865 (Bibliothèque de l'Opéra, Paris; ISV-P).

27. 8 Feb. 1865 (Bibliothèque de l'Opéra, Paris; ISV-P).

28. Verdi to Tito Ricordi, 8 Feb. 1865 (Casa Ricordi; ISV-P).

29. Verdi to Tito Ricordi, 18 Feb. 1865 (Abbiati, ii. 820–2; original in Gallini Collection).

30. 25 Apr. 1865 (Alberti, *Verdi intimo*, 51–2).

31. Verdi to Escudier, 3 June 1865 (Bibliothèque de l'Opéra, Paris; ISV-P).

32. 28 Apr. 1865 (Bibliothèque de l'Opéra, Paris; ISV-P).

33. Remarks by Filippo Filippi, in a letter from Piave to Verdi, 2 June 1865 (SAA).

34. Piave to Verdi, 2 June 1865 (SAA).

35. Article in *Rivista minima* (cited in Abbiati, iii. 25–6).

36. Verdi to Arrivabene, 28 Apr. 1865 (Alberti, *Verdi intimo*, 52–4).

37. 3 May 1865 (Casa Ricordi; ISV-P).

38. Ibid.

39. Verdi to Escudier, 29 July 1864 (Bibliothèque de l'Opéra, Paris; ISV-P).

40. 18 Dec. 1864 (Casa Ricordi; ISV-P).

41. 3 July 1865 (Di Ascoli, 139–40).
42. [July–Sept. 1865] (Abbiati, iii. 54).
43. Notes transcribed by Strepponi from Verdi's conversation (Strepponi, Letter-books [July 1865], SAA, another version in French is in her file on servants).
44. Ibid.
45. Ibid.
46. Verdi to Luccardi, 18 Mar. 1851 (Accademia Nazionale dei Lincei, Rome; ISV-P).
47. See n. 43, above.
48. Gatti reported a family anecdote that had been told him in Busseto: that Verdi himself told Marianna Barezzi (the wife of Pietro Garbi) that Strepponi had had a child by 'Merelli'. They were at La Scala at the time, perhaps during the *Nabucco* run of 1842, when we know that a Busseto contingent had gone to hear the opera. See Gatti (1951), 134.
49. Strepponi to Escudier (draft) [20–2] June [1865] (Strepponi Letter-books, SAA).
50. Ibid.
51. 19 Apr. 1863 (BMP-B).
52. Verdi to Piroli, 12 Oct. 1861 (*CV* iii. 18).
53. Ibid.
54. Verdi to Filippo Coletti, 11 Feb. 1866 (Strepponi, Letter-books, SAA).
55. Strepponi to Avanzi, 4 Feb. 1866 (BMP-B).
56. Strepponi to Avanzi, 24 July 1865 (BMP-B).
57. 19 June 1865 (A. Oberdorfer, *Giuseppe Verdi: autobiografia dalle lettere* ed. M. Conati (Milan, 1981 edn.), 243–4 (see also ed.'s note about Alari, 244 n. 26); original in Morgan Library).
58. Strepponi to Avanzi, 24 July 1865, wrote of her reaction to a letter from the Vicar General to Verdi: 'If he is as hard and stiff as his style, he really must look like a man who walks around with a ramrod down his back! This *Reverend* must love *thunderstorms* passionately, and maybe, just maybe, he also wants to go back to the time [of Austrian rule].' She also added an unkind remark about the Holy Office (BMP-B).
59. 30 July 1865 (*CV* iii. 30).
60. Verdi to Piroli, 30 May [1865] (*CV* iii. 29–30).
61. See n. 59, above.
62. 30 Oct. 1865 (*CV* iii. 34).

63. Verdi to Piroli, 22 [Oct.] 1865 (*CV* iii. 33).

64. Verdi to Barezzi, 12 June 1845 (Strepponi, Letter-books, SAA; transcribed in 1865). See also *C*, 14–15 (undated letter).

65. (Strepponi, Letter-books [July 1865] SAA).

66. (Strepponi, Letter-books, SAA).

67. [summer 1865] (draft in Strepponi, Letter-books, SAA).

68. Ibid.

69. Ibid. See also 434–5

70. Undated draft (*C*, 436–7).

71. Statutes and Regulations of the Società Operaia of Busseto. The membership book in the BMP-B belonged to Celestina Barezzi, seamstress. *Statuto: Regolamento della Società Operaia di Busseto* (Parma, 1865).

72. *Registro della Popolazione, Anagrafe*, Busseto, in Archivio Storico del Comune, Busseto. The register shows Verdi's and Carlo Verdi's legal residence at Strada Maestra 14. At No. 12 lived Angelo Verdi, son of Giuseppe. At No. 13 lived Telesforo Verdi, shopkeeper, who was also Tito Barezzi's father-in-law, Giovannino Barezzi's son Tito having married Telesforo Verdi's daughter. At No. 15 lived Pietro Verdi's son Giuseppe, an elementary-school-teacher. Emanuele Muzio's brother Giulio, a shoemaker, lived at No. 16. No. 29 was later the residence of Maria Romanini, widow of the composer's first cousin Giuseppe and mother of Filomena Maria Verdi, the composer's foster-daughter. Next-door to her were Giovannino and Demetrio Barezzi, 'shopkeepers and men of property'. Angelo Orlandi, the present occupant of Palazzo Cavalli (1989), is a descendant of Giovannino Barezzi and his wife Adele Cavalli. He is also descended from the Verdis, through Tito Barezzi's marriage to Telesforo Verdi's daughter.

Chapter 27

1. Article cited by Piave in his letter to Verdi, 4 June 1865 (see Abbiati, iii. 21; Piave's original letter in SAA).

2. Phrase from a letter from Verdi to Piave, cited in Piave's letter to Verdi dated 23 Sept. 1865 (SAA). Piave read the phase in Verdi's letter of 18 Sept.

3. Verdi to Perrin, 12 Sept. 1864 (cited in A. Porter, 'The Making of *Don Carlos*', *Proceedings of the Royal Music Association*, 98 (1971–2), 75).

4. [20–2] June [1865] (in *CV* ii. 21–2; draft in Strepponi, Letter-books, SAA).

5. 19 June 1865 (Bibliothèque de l'Opéra, Paris; ISV-P).

6. 30 June 1865 (Bibliothèque de l'Opéra, Paris; ISV-P).

7. 17 July 1865 (U. Günther, 'La Genèse de *Don Carlos*', *Revue de Musicologie*, 58 (1972), 24).

8. Verdi to Perrin, 21 July 1865 (ibid. 30).

9. Musical sketch, represented as Verdi's *Re Lear* (New York Public, Music Special Collections, Library for the Performing Arts at Lincoln Center, Perera Collection; photostats of two additional pages from the sketch in my collection, together with Walter Toscanini's letter and transcriptions of the text).

10. Notes made by Andrew Porter from Ricordi edn. I am grateful to Porter for making these and the Rusconi translation available.

11. (Padua, 1838), 89. Verdi's copy of this translation is in the bookshelf beside his bed at Sant'Agata.

12. Letter from Walter Toscanini to Carolyn Allen Perera, 4 July 1960, with partial text of transcription in pencil on reverse. A separate, typed sheet has a somewhat more complete draft, which he gave to Mrs Perera later (both in my collection).

13. (Private collection, Italy; photocopy in my collection).

14. A. Royer and G. Vaez to Verdi, 7 Aug. 1850 (*C*, 104–5).

15. Verdi to Piave, 28 Feb. 1850 (see Ch. 16. n.18).

16. See n. 5, above.

17. 31 July 1865 (Strepponi, Letter-books, SAA).

18. 15 Aug. 1865 (SAA).

19. 26 Sept. 1865 (SAA).

20. Ibid.

21. 'La musica di Meyerbeer', *Gazzetta musicale di Firenze* (22 Feb. 1855) (cited in F. Nicolodi, 'Meyerbeer e il grand-opéra a Firenze', *Quaderni di Teatro*, 4: 36 (May 1987), 80 ff.).

22. Ibid.

23. 28 Aug. 1865 (A. Alberti, *Verdi intimo* (Milan, 1931), 58).

24. Stato Civile (Births, 14 Nov. 1859) Archivio Storico del Comune, Busseto.

25. Stato Civile (Births, 31 July 1857), Archivio Storico del Comune, Busseto.

26. Stato Civile (Deaths, 2 Nov. 1862), Archivio Storico del Comune, Busseto.

27. 4 Feb. 1866 (BMP-B).

28. Ibid.

29. Stato Civile (Births), Archivio Storico del Comune, Busseto: Torquato Verdi, 1867; Ormsida Verdi, 1869; Ines Verdi, 1871; and Marco Verdi, 1874, all children of Giuseppe Verdi (son of Marcantonio) and Maria Romanini. See also death record of Giuseppe Verdi (son of Marcantonio) 18 Nov. 1891. This Giuseppe was with Carlo Verdi when he died.

30. 23 Sept. 1865 (Casa Ricordi; ISV-P).

31. Verdi to Perrin, 29 Sept. 1865 (Strepponi Letter-books, SAA; see also *CV* ii. 24).

32. Mazzini to Paolo di Giorgi, 22 June [1865], cited in Piave's letter to Verdi, 23 Sept. 1865 (SAA).

33. Piave to Verdi, 23 Sept. 1865 (SAA).

34. 13 Sept. 1865 (SAA).

35. Piave to Verdi, 4 Oct. 1865 (SAA).

36. 17 Oct. 1865 (Abbiati, iii. 60–1; draft in Strepponi, Letter-books, SAA).

37. Verdi to Arrivabene, 30 Sept. 1865 (Alberti, *Verdi intimo*, 59).

38. 4 Dec. 1865 (Casa Ricordi; ISV-P).

39. Verdi to Giulio Ricordi, 6 [Oct.] 1877 (*C*, 624; see also Conati's notes in his 1981 edn. of Oberdorfer, *Giuseppe Verdi*, 348–9).

40. Note (Letter-book, SAA). Muzio offered his own scathing portrait of Olympe Pélissier in an early letter to Barezzi: 'La Pélissier was a whore who took on anyone willing to pay her with his small change. [She was] living in Paris. . . . She has an income of 30,000 francs, which she earned by moving her thighs back and forth. Rossini, by his own confession, says that he never gave her any money.' See letter of 27 Aug. 1846 from Muzio to Antonio Barezzi (Garibaldi, 261–5).

41. 27 Dec. 1865 (SAA). See also G. Carrara Verdi, 'Le lettere di Rossini a Verdi', *Biblioteca 70*, 3 (1973), 9–16.

42. 31 Dec. 1865 (Alberti, *Verdi intimo*, 61).

43. 28 Jan. 1866 (Casa Ricordi; ISV-P). In this short letter, Verdi expressed his concern over the publisher's health and his regret that Tito Ricordi left Paris before seeing the Dantan bust, which Verdi described as 'absolutely beautiful' and a work of art admired by all.

44. 1 and 3 Jan. 1866 (Alberti, *Verdi intimo*, 62–5).

45. 4 Jan. 1866, continued on 5 Jan. (SAA).

46. 4 Feb. 1866 (SAA).

47. Arrivabene to Verdi, 9 [Jan.] 1866 (Alberti, *Verdi intimo*, 65–8).

48. Verdi to Arrivabene, 24 Mar. 1866 (ibid. 69–70).

49. n.d. (Abbiati, iii. 76).

50. Verdi to Tito Ricordi, 14 Apr. 1866 (Casa Ricordi; ISV-P).

51. Verdi to Tito Ricordi, 16 Apr. 1866 (Casa Ricordi; ISV-P).

52. 8 Apr. 1866 (Draft in Strepponi, Letter-books, SAA; see also Abbiati, iii. 77–8 and *CV* ii. 25).

53. 6 [June] 1866 (ISV-P). Verdi wrote 'May' by mistake.

54. 10 May 1866 (*CV* iii. 38).

55. 9 June 1866 (*CV* iii. 39).

56. 16 May 1866 (P. Nardi, *Boito* (Milan, 1944) 207–8). Arturo Toscanini's father Claudio was also a volunteer in the Trentino.

57. 'G. Verdi e suoi editori di Francia e d'Italia' (*CV* iv. 163).

58. 6 July 1866 (*CV* iv. 165; ISV-P).

59. 14 July 1866 (*CV* iv. 165–6; original in Bibliothèque de l'Opéra, Paris; ISV-P).

60. 14 July 1866 (*CV* iii. 41).

61. Verdi to Escudier, 18 June 1866 (Bibliothèque de l'Opéra, Paris; ISV-P).

62. Strepponi to Corticelli, 13 July 1866 (Museo Teatrale alla Scala).

63. Verdi to Escudier, 6 July 1866 (Bibliothèque de l'Opéra, Paris; ISV-P).

64. Strepponi to Avanzi, 26 Dec. 1868 (BMP-B).

65. Verdi to Escudier, 20 [Aug.] 1866 (Bibliothèque de l'Opéra, Paris; ISV-P).

66. 28 Sept. 1866 (Alberti, *Verdi intimo*, 72).

67. Verdi to Tito Ricordi, 12 Nov. 1866 (Casa Ricordi; ISV-P).

68. Verdi to Tito Ricordi, 18 Nov. 1866 (Casa Ricordi; ISV-P).

69. 27 Nov. 1866 (Casa Ricordi; ISV-P).

70. 12 Dec. 1866 (Casa Ricordi; ISV-P).

71. (Letter-books, SAA).

72. Mariani to Ricordi, 9 Dec. 1866 (Abbiati, iii. 113).

73. 9 Sept. 1866 (SAA).

74. 28 Nov. 1866 (SAA).

75. 8 Feb. 1867 (Alberti, *Verdi intimo*, 74).

76. Strepponi to Avanzi, 7 Dec. 1867 (BMP-B).

77. Cesare Orsini to Verdi, 25 July 1883 (*CV* iv. 37).

78. J. Claretie, 'Une répétition de "Don Carlos"—Verdi', *Le Figaro*, (M. Conati, *Interviste e incontri con Verdi* (Milan, 1980), 59–62; See also Conati's notes, pp. 55 ff.).

79. These parts of the opera, restored for the Metropolitan Opera production in the 1980s, were translated by me for the Schirmer libretto published at that time and again in 1991 for the Metropolitan Opera libretto.

80. 12 Mar. 1867 (*CV* iii. 43).

81. 19 Mar. 1867 (Casa Ricordi; ISV-P).

82. (Abbiati, iii. 129). See also Conati, '*Don Carlo*: dramma dell'incomunicabilità; in *Don Carlo*, house programme of the Teatro Comunale di Bologna (Bologna, 1987).

83. [Mar. 1867] (cited in Alberti, *Verdi intimo*, 75 n. 1).

84. (Ibid. 77 n. 1).

85. Mariani to Tornaghi, n.d. (Abbiati, iii. 128).

86. 16 Mar. 1867 (Alberti, *Verdi intimo*, 76–7).

87. 24 Mar. 1867 (Bibliothèque de l'Opéra, Paris; ISV-P).

88. Verdi to Escudier, 1 Apr. 1867 (Bibliothèque de l'Opéra, Paris; ISV-P).

89. Mariani to Ricordi, 6 Apr. 1867 (Abbiati, iii. 133).

90. [Apr. 1867] (ibid. 133–4).

91. 28 Apr. 1867 (ibid. 134).

92. Mariani to Ricordi, [end of May 1867] (ibid. 136).

93. Strepponi to Ricordi, 29 Mar. 1867 (Letter-books, SAA).

94. 25 May 1867 (*CV* ii. 100–1).

95. 17 May 1867 (Di Ascoli, 157–8; see also Strepponi, Letter-books, SAA).

96. [21 May 1867] (Di Ascoli, 160–1, where it is dated 23 May; see also Strepponi, Letter-books, SAA).

97. 24 May 1867 (Di Ascoli, 161).

98. Inscriptions: Manzoni to Verdi (SAA); Verdi to Manzoni (cited in Abbiati, iii. 142).

99. 14 June 1867 (Di Ascoli, 162–4).

100. Verdi to Arrivabene, 16 June 1867 (Alberti, *Verdi intimo*, 78–9).

101. 30 June 1867 (Di Ascoli, 167; ISV-P). Luzio in *C*, 521–2 and Abbiati (iii. 116) both assign this letter to an earlier period.

102. 6 July 1867 (Di Ascoli, 168).

103. (Letter-books, SAA).

104. Verdi to Clara Maffei, 6 Feb. 1867 (Di Ascoli, 146–7).

105. 22 July 1867 (ibid. 170).

106. 25 July 1867 (Alberti, *Verdi intimo*, 79).

107. n.d. (*CV* iii. 46).

BOOK V

Chapter 28

1. 9 July 1867 (Abbiati, iii. 151).

2. Verdi to Sir Michele Costa, 4 July 1867 (Strepponi, Letter-books, SAA; see also *CV* ii. 26). Final draft dated 6 July (Harvard University Library Theatre Collection).

3. Strepponi to De Sanctis, 26 July 1867 (*CV* i. 101–2).

4. *Gazzetta musicale di Milano*, 4 Aug. 1867 (Walker, (It. edn.), 410–11).

5. List of Stolz's engagements (ibid. 367 ff).

6. 15 Aug. 1867 (*C*, 547).

7. 16 Aug. 1867 (*C*, 549).

8. 4 Sept. 1867 (*C*, 550).

9. Stato della popolazione, Villanova sull'Arda, Frazione di Sant'Agata, in Archivio Storico del Comune, Villanova Sull'Arda. I am grateful to Adelfo Fragni for helping me locate these documents.

10. Verdi to Tito Ricordi, 18 Sept. 1867 (Casa Ricordi; ISV-P).

11. Verdi to Giulio Ricordi, 17 Sept. 1867 (Casa Ricordi; ISV-P).

12. Mariani to Tornaghi [Sept. 1867] (Abbiati, iii. 153–4).

13. Mariani to Verdi [14 Aug. 1867] (SAA).

14. (Cited in Gatti (1931), ii. 157). See also Mazzucato's review (ibid. 157–8).

15. (Ibid. 156–7).

16. 30 Oct. 1867 (Bibliothèque de l'Opéra, Paris; ISV-P).

17. *Enciclopedia dello spettacolo* (Rome, 1954–62), ix. 390–1.

18. Martin, *Verdi: His Music, Life and Times*, (New York, 1963), 435.

19. 11 Apr. 1868 (Strepponi, Letter-books, SAA).

20. Mariani to Verdi, 4 Nov. 1867 (SAA).

21. 6 Nov. 1867 (SAA).

22. Mariani to Verdi, 21 Nov. 1867 (SAA).

23. Mariani to Faccio, [6 Dec. 1867] (R. De Rensis, 'A proposito del *Lohengrin*', in *Giornale d'Italia*, (26 Jan. 1927) (cited in Walker (It. edn.), 418).

24. 24 Nov. 1867 (Strepponi, Letter-books, SAA).

25. 23 Dec. 1867 (*C*, 618–9).

26. Strepponi, diary notes, 1 Jan. 1868 (Strepponi, Letter-books, SAA).

27. Ibid.

28. 25 Aug. 1857 (Morgan Library).

29. 11 Jan. 1868 (Casa Ricordi; ISV-P).

30. 14 Jan. 1868 (Casa Ricordi; ISV-P).

31. 9 Feb. 1868 (Casa Ricordi; ISV-P).

32. 16 Feb. 1868 (Casa Ricordi; ISV-P).

33. 17 Feb. 1868 (Casa Ricordi; ISV-P).

34. 29 Feb. 1868 (Casa Ricordi; ISV-P).

35. 13 Mar. 1868 (Casa Ricordi; ISV-P).

36. Verdi to Giulio Ricordi, 18 Mar. 1868 (Casa Ricordi; ISV-P).

37. 21 Mar. 1868 (Casa Ricordi; ISV-P).

38. Verdi to Camille Du Locle, 8 Apr. 1868 (Bibliothèque de l'Opéra, Paris; ISV-P).

39. 11 Apr. 1868 (Strepponi, Letter-books, SAA).

40. 29 Mar. 1868 (cited in A. Alberti, *Verdi intimo* (Milan, 1931), 88 n. 1).

41. 12 May 1868 (Casa Ricordi; ISV-P).

42. 8 May 1868 (Morgan Library).

43. 15 May 1868 (draft in Strepponi, Letter-books, SAA); see also *CV* ii. 28).

44. 26 May 1868 (SAA).

45. 24 May 1868 (SAA).

46. [May 1868] (Alberti, *Verdi intimo*, 88 n. 1). Casa Ricordi has a one-page draft in Verdi's hand.

47. 28 July 1868 (Alberti, *Verdi intimo*, 93).

48. 7 July 1868 (Di Ascoli, 184–6).

49. Mariani to Gaetano Grilli [summer 1868]. I am grateful to the Conservatorio Rossini in Pesaro for giving me photocopies of this entire correspondence.

50. 7 June 1868 (Di Ascoli, 183–4).

51. Ibid.

52. 30 May 1868 (*CV* iii. 53–4).

53. 28 June 1868 (*CV* iii. 54).

54. 28 July 1868 (*CV* iii. 55–6).

55. 17 Dec. 1868 (*CV* iii. 61).

56. Toast to Verdi, written for Filomena Maria Verdi (Strepponi, Letter-books, SAA).

57. E. Seletti, *Busseto*, ii. 343–5.

58. *La Rocca di Busseto* (Cremona, 1869), 146 ff.

59. 17 Nov. 1868 (Casa Ricordi; ISV-P).

60. 20 Nov. 1868 (Di Ascoli, 193).

61. C. M. Mossa, 'Una Messa per la storia', in *'Messa per Rossini*: la storia, il testo, la musica', *Quaderno dell'ISV*, 5 (1988), 15–16. The citation is from the 29 Nov. 1868 issue of the theatrical journal *Trovatore*.

62. T. Mantovani, *Angelo Mariani* (Rome, 1921), 84 ff.

63. Verdi to Giulio Ricordi, 14 Dec. 1868 (Casa Ricordi; ISV-P).

64. 15 Mar. 1869 (Napolitano).

65. 24 Mar. 1869 (ibid.).

66. 14 July [1868] (*CV* iii. 55).

67. 26 Aug. 1868 (Casa Ricordi; ISV-P).

68. 24 Nov. 1868 (Casa Ricordi; ISV-P).

69. Verdi to Tito Ricordi, 15 Dec. 1868 (*C*, 208; original in Casa Ricordi).

70. Verdi to Giulio Ricordi, 15 Dec. 1868 (Casa Ricordi; ISV-P).

71. Verdi to Giulio Ricordi, 28 Dec. 1868 (Casa Ricordi; ISV-P).

72. (Casa Ricordi; ISV-P).

73. 15 Jan. 1869 (Casa Ricordi; ISV-P).

74. Verdi to Giulio Ricordi, 22 Jan. 1869 (Casa Ricordi; ISV-P).

75. Strepponi to Verdi, 3 Feb. 1869, draft (Strepponi, Letter-books, SAA).

76. Strepponi to Avanzi, 2 Feb. 1869 (BMP-B).

77. See n. 75, above.

78. 31 Jan. 1869 (Di Ascoli, 197).

79. 1 Mar. 1869 (*CV*, iii. 62).

80. Ibid.

81. Verdi to Arrivabene, 1 Mar. 1869 (Alberti, *Verdi intimo*, 99–100). See also Verdi to Giulio Ricordi, [*c*.1 Mar. 1869] (ISV-P).

82. (U. Zoppi, *Angelo Mariani, Giuseppe Verdi e Teresa Stolz* (Milan, 1947), 111).

83. (Cited in Alberti, *Verdi intimo*, 99).

84. *La perseveranza* (ibid. 99–100).

85. *La Rocca di Busseto* (Cremona, 1870), chronology of the riots against the tax on milling grain 134 ff.

86. 9 Mar. 1869 (Di Ascoli, 197–8).

87. Ibid.

88. 15 Mar. 1869 (Di Ascoli, 200–1).

89. 1 Mar. 1869 (Bibliothèque de l'Opéra, Paris; ISV-P).

90. Laura Scaccabarozzi d'Adda, account (Di Ascoli, 194–5).

91. Clara Maffei to Tenca, 29 Nov. 1868 (ibid. 195).

92. (Ibid. 212–14). These notes were made on 21 May 1869.

93. Verdi to Mariani, 19 Aug. 1869 (*C*, 210–13).

94. List of Composers, in *Gazzetta musicale di Milano* (9 May 1869) (cited in Mossa, '*Messa per Rossini*', app. 7, pp. 64–5).

95. Mossa, '*Messa per Rossini*', 36.

96. 21 June 1869 (cited in Mossa, '*Messa per Rossini*', 43, n. 112).

97. 6 Aug. 1869 (SAA).

98. Mossa, '*Messa per Rossini*', 45.

99. (SAA).

100. 19 Aug. 1869 (SAA).

101. 19 Aug. 1869 (*C*, 210–13).

102. (Casa Ricordi; ISV-P).

103. (SAA). Abbiati examined this letter in the early 1950s and published it in 1959 in his vol. iii. pp. 298–300. When I looked at the original, I could not help wondering whether Verdi might never have seen it, given the circumstances of his life in the week after it was sent. In his letters after 24 Aug, he does not indicate that he ever saw it—quite the contrary, he goes on accusing Mariani of 'sins' that Mariani had clearly explained away in this letter.

104. (Casa Ricordi; ISV-P).

105. 2 Oct. 1869 (Casa Ricordi; ISV-P).

106. Giulio Ricordi to Verdi, 15 Oct. 1869 (SAA).

107. (Cited in *C*, 215).

108. (*C*, 214–15).

109. Verdi to Giulio Ricordi, 27 Oct. 1869 (*C*, 216).

110. Article in *Pungolo* (4 Nov. 1869) (cited in Mossa, '*Messa per Rossini*', app. 10, p. 67, from an article originally published in *Monitore* (6 Nov. 1869)).

111. Verdi to Giulio Ricordi, 26 May 1870 (Casa Ricordi; ISV-P).

112. Verdi to Giulio Ricordi, 17 Dec. 1870 (Casa Ricordi; ISV-P).

113. Verdi to Giulio Ricordi, 3 Jan. 1871 (Casa Ricordi; ISV-P).

114. 27 Oct. 1869 (*C*, 216).

115. 30 Dec. 1869 (Alberti, *Verdi intimo*, 114–15).

Chapter 29

1. 11 [Jan.] 1870 (*C*, 223–4). The controversy surrounding the *Messa per Rossini* and the rupture with Mariani were covered in Mantovani's *Angelo Mariani* (1921), Zoppi's *Angelo Mariani, Giuseppe Verdi e Teresa Stolz* (1947), and Abbiati's *Verdi* (1959), iii. Zoppi reproduced the complete or nearly complete texts of Mariani's letters to Carlino Del Signore in the section 'Documenti Epistolari' (63–361), together with some of Mariani's letters to Verdi, Ricordi, and other colleagues, and some of the Stolz–Mariani and Stolz–Verdi correspondence. In 'Ultime note biografiche' (362–87) he covers Mariani's correspondence with Gaetano Grilli and Teodorico Landoni. Abbiati, writing while Zoppi was working on this book and in the decade after it was published, added dozens of other documents, in full or in part, including the Stolz letters at Sant'Agata. Walker published many documents that had appeared in Zoppi's and Abbiati's books, together with other letters that he transcribed during his own research. Gatti also covered much of this ground in his first and second editions of *Verdi*. He also dealt with Verdi's relations with Mariani in 'Verdi contro i creatori', in *Revisioni e rivalutazioni verdiani* (Milan, 1951), 62 ff; which he gave me in May 1956, together with Zoppi.

2. Verdi to Clara Maffei, 14 Nov. 1869 (Di Ascoli, 227–8).

3. Verdi to [P. Prayer Galletti], 10 Oct. 1869 (*C*, 213–14).

4. 30 Dec. 1869 (A. Alberti, *Verdi intimo* (Milan, 1931), 114–15).

5. Ibid.

6. 1 Mar. 1870 (SAA).

7. E. Caballo, *La nuova guida del Lago Maggiore e dei Laghi Prealpini* (Genoa, 1967), 130.

8. Auguste Mariette to Du Locle, 27 Apr. 1870 (H. Busch, *Verdi's 'Aida': The History of an Opera in Letters and Documents* (1978; 2nd edn. (Minneapolis, 1979), 11–12).

9. Mariette to Paul Draneht, 19 July 1871 (ibid. 186–7).

10. 25 June 1870 (ibid. 27–8).

11. For further examination of the origins of *Aida*, see 'Aida's roots', *Opera News* (21 Dec. 1991), 20–3. *Re Amasi*, which Pini-Pisanini sent to Verdi, is a version of *Nitteti*.

12. Verdi to Clara Maffei, n.d. (*C*, 226 n. 2).

13. 20 June 1870 (*C*, 226).

14. (SAA).

15. (Robert Tuggle Collection, New York City). Another photograph of the soprano, acquired at the same time as this, is autographed to Barberina Strepponi.

16. 7 July 1870 (SAA). The house at 'La Codetta' was sold on 28 February 1878 to Girolamo Lombardi; its deed was executed by Dr Gaetano Arati, who had lent money for the purchase of Verdi's house at Sant'Agata. Verdi bought the adjacent mill from Arturo Toscanini's uncles on 29 December 1875. 'La Codetta' has been associated with Stolz for three generations.

17. 18 July 1870 (SAA).

18. [c.1–10 Aug. 1870] (Casa Ricordi; ISV-P).

19. May 1870 (Strepponi, Letter-books, SAA).

20. 20 May 1870 (Strepponi, Letter-books, SAA).

21. 28 July 1870 (SAA).

22. (SAA).

23. 18 Nov. 1870 (SAA).

24. 19 Nov. 1870 (Strepponi, Letter-books, SAA).

25. 26 May 1870 (J.-G. Prod'homme, 'Unpublished Letters from Verdi to Camille Du Locle, 1866–1876', trans. Theodore Baker, *Musical Quarterly*, 7:4 (1921), 88.

26. Verdi to Du Locle (*C*, 224–5).

27. 16 July 1870 (*CV* iii. 71).

28. [10 July 1870] (H. Busch, 'Verdi's *Aida*', 31).

29. 13 Sept. 1870 (Alberti, *Verdi intimo*, 121).

30. 30 Sept. 1870 (Di Ascoli, 245–6).

31. Verdi to Du Locle, 25 Aug. 1870 (*C*, 227–8).

32. Ibid.

33. 14 Aug. 1870 (*C*, 639).

34. 17 Aug. 1870 (*C*, 641–2).

35. 28 Sept. 1870 (*C*, 645).

36. (*C*, 662; original in Morgan Library).

37. 5 Jan. 1871 (Abbiati, iii. 406–7).

38. 4 Jan. 1871 (ibid. 416–7; original in SAA).

39. 6 Jan. 1871 (Casa Ricordi; ISV-P).

40. 6 Jan. 1871 (*CV* iv. 190–1).

41. [7 Jan. 1871] (*CV* iv. 192).

42. Verdi to Giulio Ricordi, 7 Jan. 1871 (Casa Ricordi; ISV-P).

43. 3 July 1871 (Zoppi, *Mariani*, 225–6).

44. 18 June 1871 (SAA).

45. In his collection, Gatti had a packet of letters from Strepponi to Nina Ravina from this period. Much of Gatti's collection is in the Archivio Storico del Comune, Asti.

46. 14 Apr. 1871 (*C*, 259).

47. 10 July 1870 (*C*, 263–5; original in Casa Ricordi).

48. Monti to Ricordi, 5 Aug. 1871 (see Luzio's commentary in *CV* ii. 34–5).

49. (SAA).

50. Mariani to Del Signore, 14 Nov. 1871 (Zoppi, *Mariani*, 278–83).

51. Ibid.

52. 23 Oct. 1871 (Zoppi, *Mariani*, 267). The letter was written by Cosima Liszt and sent to Mariani through Giovannina Lucca.

53. *Lohengrin* score annotated by Verdi (SAA; see also *CV* ii. 216 ff).

54. Ibid.

55. 23 Nov. 1871 (Casa Ricordi; ISV-P).

56. 2 Dec. 1871 (Casa Ricordi; ISV-P).

57. 6 Dec. 1871 (Casa Ricordi; ISV-P).

58. 8 Dec. 1871 (*C*, 272–3).

59. 9 Dec. 1871 (Casa Ricordi; ISV-P).

60. 11 Dec. 1871 (Di Ascoli, 262).

61. Verdi to Giulio Ricordi, 24 Dec. 1871 (Casa Ricordi; ISV-P).

62. Bottesini telegram to Verdi [24 Dec. 1871] cited in Verdi's letter to Ricordi, 25 [Dec. 1871] (Abbiati, iii. 526–7).

63. Verdi to Giulio Ricordi [25 Dec. 1871] (Casa Ricordi; ISV-P).

64. Verdi to Giulio Ricordi, 26 Dec. 1871 (Casa Ricordi; ISV-P).

65. 13 Jan. 1872 (Alberti, *Verdi intimo*, 137).

66. Verdi to Tito Ricordi, 3 Jan. 1873 (Casa Ricordi; ISV-P). (Dated 2 Jan. in *C*.)

67. [15–31 July 1872] (Casa Ricordi; ISV-P).

68. Ibid.

69. 21 Feb. 1872 (Casa Ricordi; ISV-P).

70. Strepponi to Giuditta Ricordi, 16 Nov. 1872 (SAA).

71. See n. 69, above.

72. 27 Apr. 1972 (Alberti, *Verdi intimo*, 144–5).

73. 10 May 1872 (Casa Ricordi; ISV-P).

74. 22 Aug. 1872 (*C*, 681–2).

75. (Antiquarian Catalogue of Gian Carlo Griffoni, Bologna, summer 1991, item 527, p. 22.)

76. Verdi to Ricordi [Oct. 1872], in Abbiati, iii. 607.

77. 12 Dec. 1872 (Casa Ricordi; ISV-P).

78. 26 Dec. 1872 (Casa Ricordi; ISV-P).

79. 29 Dec. 1872 (Alberti, *Verdi intimo*, 152–3).

80. 29 Dec. 1872 (Di Ascoli, 288–9).

81. See n. 66, above.

82. See n. 70, above.

83. 11 Nov. 1872 (Zoppi, *Mariani*, 354–5).

84. Mariani to Teodorico Landoni, 31 Dec. 1872 (ibid. 373).

85. (Museo Teatrale alla Scala).

86. Stolz to Strepponi, 8 Mar. 1872 (Abbiati, iii. 576).

87. Stolz to Verdi, reporting Strepponi's remark, 20 July 1872 (SAA).

88. 9 Apr. 1873 (Di Ascoli, 290–1).

89. 16 Apr. 1873 (Alberti, *Verdi intimo*, 156–7).

90. Apr. 1873 (cited in Abbiati, iii. 624–5).

91. See n. 87, above.

92. Strepponi's longhand note, written across the corner of Stolz's letter to Verdi dated 15 Aug. 1872. Gatti first called my attention to this note in May 1956.

93. 12 Apr. 1873 (*CV* i. 162–3).

Chapter 30

1. 15 Apr. 1873 (*CV* i. 163).

2. 11 May 1873 (Casa Ricordi, ISV-P).

3. 20 Apr. 1873 (Strepponi, Letter-books, SAA).

4. Ibid.

5. Stolz to Verdi, [spring 1873], marked 'Introito di *Aida*' (SAA).

6. Cremona City Directories, Archivio di Stato, Cremona. Those from the end

of the century note that old Contrada della Zucca was renamed because of Verdi's stays at the Cappello.

7. Letter of 1916 or 1917, in Mario Morini, corrected galley proofs for an unidentified newspaper article (Gianfranco Stefanini Collection, Busseto).

8. Ibid.

9. N. Ginzburg, *The Manzoni Family*, trans. Marie Evans (New York, 1987), 336.

10. 29 May 1873 (Di Ascoli, 296).

11. 3 June 1873 (Casa Ricordi; ISV-P).

12. Ibid.

13. 9 May 1872 (*CV* iv. 286). Vigna replied on 12 May.

14. Strepponi to Clara Maffei, 7 Sept. 1872 (Di Ascoli, 282–3).

15. n.d. (C. Bellaigue, *Verdi* (Paris, 1912), 88–91). 'Dans le sens idéal, moral, social, c'était un grand Chrétien, mais il faut bien se garder de le presenter . . . strictement Catholique', Boito wrote, adding that nothing could be more contrary to the truth.

16. 15 Aug. 1865 (SAA).

17. Verdi to Giulio Ricordi, [*c*.11–14 Nov. 1870] (Casa Ricordi; ISV-P).

18. 5 Dec. 1872 (Strepponi, Letter-books, SAA),

19. 24 Dec. 1872 (Museo Teatrale alla Scala).

20. (Biblioteca dell'Archiginnasio, Bologna).

21. Mariani to Landoni, 28 May 1873 (Biblioteca dell'Archiginnasio, Bologna).

22. 4 June 1873 (Biblioteca dell'Archiginnasio, Bologna).

23. 16 June 1873 (SAA).

24. [May 1873] (Napolitano).

25. 29 May 1873 (ibid.).

26. 2 June 1873 (ibid).

27. [June 1873] (ibid.).

28. Phrase from a letter from Verdi to Muzio, cited in Muzio to Verdi, 8 Nov. 1873 (ibid).

29. 17 Sept. 1873 (*CV* iii. 98).

30. Verdi to Giulio Ricordi, [6 Sept. 1873] (Casa Ricordi; ISV-P).

31. 9 Aug. 1873 (Casa Ricordi; ISV-P).

32. Verdi to Du Locle, 13 July 1873 (Bibliothèque de l'Opéra, Paris; ISV-P).

33. 23 Aug. 1873 (*C*, 285 n. 3). Luzio and Cesari incorrectly dated this letter

23 Oct., noting that it was written from Paris. Verdi, who had been in Paris from late June until late in Aug., was not in Paris in Oct. See also *CV* iii. 227. Waldmann replied 27 Aug. from Ottakring, Austria.

34. Luisa Sauli Pallavicino to Verdi, 11 Sept. 1873 (SAA).

35. Verdi to Waldmann, 3 Dec. 1874 (*CV* ii. 229).

36. Strepponi to Waldmann, 16 Jan. 1874 (Biblioteca del Conservatorio G. B. Martini, Bologna; ISV-P).

37. Muzio to Verdi, 24 Mar. 1874 (Napolitano).

38. 14 Dec. 1873 (Strepponi, Letter-books, SAA).

39. 5 Mar. 1874 (Di Ascoli, 304).

40. (Strepponi, Letter-books, SAA).

41. 9 Jan. 1874 (*CV* i, 167).

42. Strepponi, diary notes and draft of letter to Verdi, [Apr. 1876] (Strepponi, Letter-books, SAA).

43. Walker (Italian edn., 484–7), gives the original texts of all documents.

44. Verdi to Piroli, 7 Mar. 1874 (*CV* iii. 100–1).

45. Verdi to Du Locle, 24 Feb. 1874 (Bibliothèque de l'Opéra, Paris; ISV-P).

46. (21 May 1874) (cited in Abbiati, iii. 690).

47. 10 June 1874 (Casa Ricordi; ISV-P).

48. Muzio to Verdi, 27 July 1874 (Napolitano).

49. Verdi to Piroli, 4 Aug. 1875 (*CV* iii. 112).

50. Ibid.

51. Verdi to Ricordi, 11 Mar. 1874 (*C*, 291).

52. Verdi to Tornaghi, 8 Sept. 1874 (*C*, 294).

53. 14 July 1874 (*CV* iii. 102).

54. 2 Nov. 1874 (Di Ascoli, 310–12).

55. 20 Aug. 1874 (Napolitano).

56. (Ibid. 171).

57. 21 Nov. 1874 (*CV* iii. 106).

58. 5 Dec. 1874 (*CV* iii. 107).

59. 14 Sept. 1874 (Strepponi, Letter-books, SAA).

60. Signed photograph from Teresa Stolz to Barberina Strepponi. In her 14 Sept. 1874 letter Strepponi thanked Stolz for inviting Barberina to a rehearsal at the Teatro della Concordia. Although many items from Barberina's collection of photographs were donated by her maid Maria Alini

to the Diocesan Seminary in Cremona, this photograph made its way into the hands of private collectors. In the 1970s and 1980s it was in the Robert Tuggle Collection in New York.

61. Achille Zoboli to Verdi, 9 Mar. 1888, and Antonio Molla to Verdi, 29 Jan. 1882 and 23 Aug. 1884 (SAA).

62. 21 Jan. 1875 (SAA).

63. 25 Mar. 1875 (Casa Ricordi; ISV-P).

64. 4 Apr. 1875 (Casa Ricordi; ISV-P).

65. Ibid.

66. 15 May 1874 (A. Martinelli, *Verdi: raggi e penombre* (Genoa, 1926), 11–12).

67. Muzio to Verdi, n.d. (Napolitano).

68. 6 Mar. 1875 (*CV* iii. 110–11).

69. 25 [May] 1875 (Casa Ricordi; ISV-P). The photograph shows that Verdi wrote '25 giugno' and 'da Londra'.

70. Strepponi to Verdi, draft of letter [30 Apr. 1876] (Strepponi, Letter-books, SAA).

71. 12 June 1875 (*CV* iii. 111–12).

72. M. Conati, 'Cronologia delle prime rappresentazioni dal 1871 al 1881', in 'Genesi dell'*Aida*', in *quaderno dell'ISV*, 4 (1971), 161 gives the date of an *Aida* at the Vienna Opera on 19 June 1875 with Stolz, Waldmann, Masini, and Medini, with Verdi as maestro concertatore and director of the orchestra.

73. P. Faustini, 'Il Requiem del Maestro Verdi a Venezia al Teatro Malibran nel luglio 1875', in N. Mangini, *I teatri di Venezia* (Milan, 1974), 209 n. 9.

74. Ibid.

75. [Aug. 1875] (Abbiati, iii. 764–5).

76. 27 June 1875 (*CV* iii. 11–12).

77. 11 July 1875, writing as Verdi dictated (draft in Strepponi, Letter-books, SAA; ISV-P). 'Verdi mi incarica di dirLe che si sorprende si ricorra a Lui per definire l'affare di Trieste', she said.

78. [7] Aug. 1875 (draft in Strepponi, Letter-books, SAA).

79. 17 Oct. 1875 (Di Ascoli, 324).

80. See n. 77 above.

81. Verdi to Piroli, 29 Dec. 1875 (*CV* iii. 115–16).

82. 'Teresa Stolz, attrice cantante' in *Rivista indipendente*, 8 (4 Sept.–9 Nov. 1875) (ISV-P).

83. Editorial comment (cited in M. Chierici, *Quel delitto in Casa Verdi* (Milan, 1981), 98).

84. 1875 (Strepponi, Letter-books, SAA).

85. Strepponi to Verdi, draft of letter [30 Apr. 1876] (Strepponi, Letter-books, SAA).

86. 15 Sept. 1875 (*CV* ii. 46).

87. (Strepponi, Letter-books, [1876], SAA).

88. 4 Oct. 1875 (SAA).

89. 6 Oct. 1875 (SAA).

90. Stolz to Strepponi, 8 Nov. 1875 (SAA).

91. 16 Nov. 1875 (Napolitano).

92. 28 Dec. 1875 (Bibliothèque de l'Opéra, Paris; ISV-P).

93. 19 Jan. 1876 (Napolitano).

94. Muzio to Katinka Evers Lampugnani, 10 Feb. 1876 (BMP-B).

95. 5 Feb. 1876 (Alberti, *Verdi intimo*, 185–7).

96. Giovannino Barezzi to Verdi, note (SAA).

97. Stolz to Verdi and Strepponi, 2 Dec. 1875 (SAA).

98. Stolz to Verdi and Strepponi, 2 Jan. 1876 (SAA).

99. Stolz to Verdi and Strepponi, 8 Feb. 1876 (SAA).

100. (*CV* ii. 241–2).

101. 5 Feb. 1876 (Alberti, *Verdi intimo*, 185–7).

102. 22 and 23 Apr. 1876 (Museo Teatrale alla Scala).

103. (Strepponi Letter-books, SAA).

104. [30 Apr. 1874] (Strepponi, Letter-books, SAA).

105. 26 Apr. 1876 (Biblioteca Civica, Busseto).

106. (Abbiati, iii. 798).

107. 19 May 1876 (ISV-P).

108. 8 June 1876 (Napolitano).

109. 20 June 1876 (ISV-P).

110. Records of Strepponi and Verdi donations to the Asilo Infantile of Cortemaggiore, 21 Aug. 1877 (Verdi 300 lire, Strepponi, 200 lire); see also 1878 and all years following. See also correspondence of Francesco Pedrini, director of the Asilo, 10 Sept. 1882 and 22 Mar. 1887 and printed acknowledgement of gratitude (SAA).

Stefano Fermi, who wrote about Verdi's ties to the Province of Piacenza in many publications between 1913 and 1950, said: 'Verdi was also extraordinarily attached to Cortemaggiore, where he visited every autumn; and Boito's beautiful epigraph, inscribed [on the commemorative marker] in the wall of the Asilo Infantile [nursery school and day-care centre], to which the Maestro—after having made other generous donations—allotted an annual gift in perpetuity that bears his name. Because of that [generosity to the Asilo], Verdi was elected provincial councillor in 1889–91, though there is no proof that he ever came to Piacenza to fill that office. . . . It seems that he guessed that the area around Cortemaggiore might be rich in [gas and oil] resources, for in a letter to his notary Ercolano Balestra just after 1860 he mentioned his concern about a certain property [Gerbida] that he owned in that neighbourhood, because "they tell me that under the soil there is a gas that could catch fire".' (See Fermi, 'Verdi e Piacenza', *Regione Emilia-Romagna*, 1: 9–12 (1950): special nos. entitled 'Giuseppe Verdi nel primo cinquantenario della morte', 86 ff.)

111. Strepponi to Stolz, 8 Aug. 1876 (Strepponi, Letter-books, SAA).

112. [8 Aug. 1876], cancelled from draft (Strepponi, Letter-books, SAA).

113. [June 1876] (Napolitano).

114. See n. 7 above.

115. Many people in Busseto have told this story, which I first heard from Luigi Grandini, who had worked at Verdi's side as a stone mason's helper and knew many other men and women who had worked at the villa. Frank Walker said that he was told the story at Sant'Agata; he mentions Basilio Pizzola as a possible source. In the Registro della Popolazione, Archivio Storico Civico in Villanova sull'Arda, Pizzola is listed as having been born there in 1857. His wife Clara Tessadri, also born in 1857, is listed as a ward of the orphanage in Cremona, where her records appear in Registro Generale degli Esposti, Archivio di Stato, Cremona. She was from Rivarolo del Re, near Casalmaggiore; placed with a family from Besenzone, she married Pizzola, who was then living in Busseto, in 1882. In February 1886 Pizzola was on Verdi's payroll as a gardener. In the 1870s he was not at the villa but his Mainardi cousins were.

116. Verdi to Clara Maffei, 20 Oct. 1876 (Di Ascoli, 330–1).

117. G. Cenzato, 'Giuseppe Verdi e Teresa Stolz in un carteggio inedito', *Corriere della sera* (30 Oct. 1932), 3. In these excerpts from Verdi's letters to Stolz words like 'joy', 'happy', 'contented', 'very, very happy', and 'delightful' are often found. Cenzato later published an account of a letter he received from one of Stolz's former servants, who swore that Verdi and Stolz had been lovers.

118. [Oct. 1876] draft (Strepponi, Letter-books, SAA).

119. Ibid.

120. (Cenzato, 'Giuseppe Verdi e Teresa Stolz'.)

121. 13 Dec. 1876 (SAA).

122. 16 Dec. 1876 (Cenzato, 'Giuseppe Verdi e Teresa Stolz').

123. 2 Mar. 1877 (SAA).

124. Ibid.

125. 18 Mar. 1877 (SAA).

126. 3 May 1877 (SAA).

127. See also p. 860 n. 16. Many circumstances point to a probable connection between Stolz and this house: the time frame; the fact that Stolz's letters to Verdi and Strepponi virtually stop after 1878, when the deed was executed by Dr Arati of Cortemaggiore, one of Verdi's former creditors; the fact that the next owner was Virginia Zucchi, a famous ballerina who danced in the Teatro Verdi in Busseto on opening night and performed in the major theatres of Europe before becoming director of the Imperial School of Ballet in St. Petersburg; and the persistent local tradition that Stolz lived here.

Chapter 31

1. 30 Oct. 1876 (Di Ascoli, 331–2). On 30 Jan. 1876, when Verdi was going to see *Color del tempo*, he sent Clara Maffei a letter about the dangers an artist faced if he were too successful early in his career (ibid. 326).

2. Verdi to Clara Maffei, [17 or 18] Oct. 1876 (ibid. 330–1).

3. 15 Nov. 1876 (BMP-B).

4. Muzio to Verdi, 28 Feb. 1877 (Napolitano).

5. Muzio to Evers Lampugnani, n.d. (ibid.).

6. [Jan. 1877] (*C*, 299–300).

7. 18 Apr. 1877 draft (Strepponi, Letter-books, SAA; see also *CV* ii. 47 and 317 ff).

8. Verdi to Arrivabene, 22 May 1877 (A. Alberti, *Verdi intimo* (Milan, 1931), 203–4).

9. Ibid.

10. Verdi to Waldmann, 16 Oct. 1877 (*CV* ii. 246).

11. (SAA).

12. 3 May 1877 (SAA).

13. (SAA).

14. 31 Dec. 1877 (SAA).

15. (Boston, 10 Nov. 1877), p. 126, col. 3. See also *New York Tribune* (14 May 1897), Maretzek obituary; and (17 May 1897), 'Musical Comment', for the account of Maretzek sending Verdi the cable telling him that *Il trovatore* had 'saved a company of Wagnerian singers from starvation'. I am grateful to William Seward for finding this material and making it available.

16. Ignazio Pietrabissa to Strepponi, 28 Jan. 1878 (SAA).

17. Muzio to Verdi, 12 Apr. 1877 (Napolitano).

18. Muzio to Fassi, 13 Oct. 1877 (ibid.).

19. Verdi to Giulio Ricordi, 12 Mar. 1878 (Casa Ricordi; ISV-P).

20. Ibid.

21. Stolz to Verdi and Strepponi, 18 Mar. 1878 (SAA).

22. 27 Dec. 1877 (Alberti, *Verdi intimo*, 205–6).

23. Verdi to Waldmann, 19 Mar. 1878 (*CV* ii. 246).

24. 19 Mar. 1878 (*CV* iii. 134–5).

25. Verdi to Piroli, 12 Mar. 1878 (*CV* iii. 134).

26. Matricola della Mappa Catastale: for Busseto and Roncole, in Archivio di Stato, Parma; for Villanova sull'Arda, in Archivio Storico del Comune; for Cortemaggiore, in Archivio Storico del Comune; for San Martino in Olza, in Archivio Storico del Comune, Cortemaggiore, and in Archivio di Stato, Piacenza.

27. Archivio Storico del Comune, Villanova sull'Arda. Dr Adelfo Fragni provided invaluable help with these very fragile materials and with research on the hospital that Verdi built at Villanova.

28. 12 Mar. 1878 (*CV* iii. 134).

29. (A. Basso, *Autografi di musicisti* (Turin, 1862)). Incorrectly dated 1 July 1879 in Basso's catalogue.

30. 25 Aug. 1878 (*CV* ii. 248). See also Verdi to Waldmann, 27 Oct. 1878 (*CV* ii. 249). Verdi also wrote Stolz about the engagement.

31. G. Avanzi, 'Agli onorevoli e gentili sposi Alberto Carrara e Maria Verdi per le nozze contratte a dì 17 ottobre 1878' (Parma, 1878), 1–9 (Manuscript collection, BMP-B).

32. 24 Mar. 1878 (Napolitano).

33. 11 June 1879 (*CV* iii. 139–40).

34. Review in *La perseveranza* (1 July 1879) (cited in Alberti, *Verdi intimo*, 238 n. 1).

35. Ibid.

36. Strepponi to Giuseppina Negroni Prati Morosini, 18 Dec. 1879 (Museo Teatrale alla Scala).

37. (*Carteggio Verdi–Boito*, ed. M. Medici and M. Conati (Parma, 1978), vol. i, p. xxvii).

38. Clara Maffei to Verdi, 18 July 1863 (Di Ascoli, 134–5).

39. 5 Sept. 1879 (*Carteggio Verdi–Boito*, vol. i, p. xxviii).

40. 14 Sept. 1879 (Napolitano).

41. 17 July 1879 (*CV* iii. 140–1).

42. (SAA).

43. Verdi to Giulio Ricordi, 18 Nov. 1879 (*Carteggio Verdi–Boito*, vol. i, p. xxix).

44. Verdi to Giulio Ricordi, 26 Aug. 1879 (*C*, 308–9).

45. C. Mascaretti, 'Come nacque il *Falstaff*', in *Strenna piacentina* (Piacenza, 1928), 25–9, in Biblioteca Passerini-Landi, Piacenza. Mascaretti, born in Piacenza in 1855, managed to get a personal interview with Verdi to discuss *La locandiera*. During a long walk the two men took in Genoa, the composer agreed to read the libretto, which the young journalist said he would send to Verdi. Although nothing came of the project, Mascaretti did refer to it in his poem 'Generazioni diverse', which was published in several newspapers after *Falstaff* had its première. The poem, dedicated to Verdi, reads:

> You were writing *Otello*!
> You remember that I, a crazy and indecisive young man,
> Under your spell, chasing unreachable rainbows,
> Wanted to set in rhyme, in a comic libretto,
> Goldoni's sublime comedy. . . .

Like Verdi, Mascaretti was a leading figure in political and artistic circles in the Province of Piacenza. In Rome, he directed the National Library.

46. 7 Oct. 1879 (*C*, 312–13).

47. 13 Oct. 1879 (Napolitano).

48. Verdi to Piroli, 8 Nov. 1879 (*CV* iii. 141–2).

49. 9 Apr. 1879 (*C*, 307–8).

50. Verdi to Piroli, 12 Nov. 1879 (*CV* iii. 142).

51. Verdi to Piroli, 24 Nov. 1879 (*CV* iii. 143).

52. Stolz to Evers Lampugnani, 25 Mar. 1880 (Museo Teatrale alla Scala; cited

in Busch, *Verdi's 'Aida': The History of an Opera in Documents and Letters* (Minneapolis, 1979), 442).

53. 20 Mar. 1880 (*CV* ii. 251–2).

54. 24 Mar. 1880 (Di Ascoli, 382).

55. 11 Apr. 1880 (G. Mondini, *Nel cinquantennio della morte di Giuseppe Verdi* (Cremona, 1952), 81–2). This letter, from the files of the lawyer Amilcare Martinelli, who counted both the Strepponi sisters among his clients, was also published by Aldo Martinelli. Mondini published a series of articles in *La provincia* in Cremona.

56. Muzio to Ricordi, 25 Mar. 1880 (Napolitano).

57. 21 Apr. 1880 (SAA).

58. 24 June 1880 (Alberti, *Verdi intimo*, 258–9).

59. 14 Sept. 1880 (ibid. 259–60).

Chapter 32

1. 18 Dec. 1879 (*CV* ii. 47–8).

2. 6 Jan. 1880 (*C*, 692–3).

3. 8 Jan. 1880 (SAA).

4. 7 Feb. 1880 (*C*, 693–4).

5. 19 Apr. 1880 (*C*, 694).

6. 12 May 1880 (*C*, 694).

7. 25 Feb. 1880 (Casa Ricordi; ISV-P).

8. 4 Mar. 1880 (Casa Ricordi; ISV-P).

9. Verdi to Boito, 15 Aug. 1880 (*Carteggio Verdi–Boito*, ed. M. Medici and M. Conati (Parma, 1978), i. 1–2).

10. 14 Oct. 1880 (ibid. 3).

11. [18 Oct. 1880] (ibid. 4–6).

12. Ibid.

13. 2 De[c.] 1880 (ibid. 6).

14. Giulio Ricordi to Verdi, 19 Nov. 1880 (*Carteggio Verdi–Ricordi 1880–1881*, ed. P. Petrobelli, *et al.* (Parma, 1988), 68–9).

15. 20 Nov. 1880 (ibid. 69–71).

16. 6 Jan. 1881 (A. Alberti, *Verdi intimo* (Milan, 1931), 268–71).

17. See n. 15, above.

18. 21 Feb. 1881 (*Carteggio Verdi–Ricordi*, 135–6).

19. 25 Feb. 1881 (ibid. 144 n. 1).

20. 25 Mar. 1881 (Napolitano).

21. Verdi to Arrivabene, 2 Apr. 1881 (Alberti, *Verdi intimo*, 285–6).

22. [14 Apr. 1881] (*Carteggio Verdi–Ricordi*, 152–3).

23. Verdi to Arrivabene, 27 May 1881 (Alberti, *Verdi intimo*, 288–9).

24. 28 Dec. 1881 (ibid. 294).

25. 2 Apr. 1881 (*Carteggio Verdi–Boito*, i. 48–9).

26. See *Carteggio Verdi–Ricordi, 1880–1881*, 168 n. 2, 169 n. 1.

27. 23 June 1881 (*Carteggio Verdi–Boito*, i. 57).

28. Filippo Filippi, description of Stolz's apartment (Gatti (1931), ii. 356).

29. Ibid.

30. 17 Sept. 1881 (*Carteggio Verdi–Ricordi*, 173–4).

31. 5 Nov. 1881 (ibid. 185–6).

32. Strepponi to Giuditta Brivio Ricordi, 19 Dec. 1881 (ibid. 198–9).

33. See Rossi's letters to Verdi (SAA).

34. Muzio to Ricordi, 22 Dec. 1881 (*Carteggio Verdi–Ricordi, 1880–1881*, 200 n. 1).

35. Ibid.

36. (Abbiati, iv. 189–90).

37. Verdi to Arrivabene, 5 Jan. 1882 (Alberti, *Verdi intimo*, 295).

38. 5 Jan. 1882 (*C*, 697).

39. 6 Feb. 1882 (Napolitano).

40. Cited in Muzio to [Tito] Ricordi, 22 Feb. 1882 (Casa Ricordi; ISV-P).

41. J. Budden, *The Operas of Verdi*, iii. (London, 1981), 32.

42. 22 Feb. 1882 (see n. 40, above).

43. 23 Apr. 1882 (Di Ascoli, 389–90).

44. C. Mingardi, *Verdi e il suo ospedale, 1888–1988* (Piacenza, 1988), 10.

45. Muzio to Giulio Ricordi, 19 May 1882 (Casa Ricordi; ISV-P).

46. 25 June 1882 (*CV* ii. 255; original in Conservatorio G. B. Martini, Bologna).

47. Muzio to [Tito] Ricordi, 15 July 1882 (Casa Ricordi; ISV-P).

48. Muzio to Giulio Ricordi, 10 Aug. 1882 (Casa Ricordi; ISV-P).

49. 16 Aug. 1882 (*Carteggio Verdi–Boito*, i. 65).

50. 3 Dec. 1882 (*CV* iii. 158–9).

51. Muzio to [Tito] Ricordi, 25 Dec. 1882 (Casa Ricordi; ISV-P).

52. Muzio to Giulio Ricordi, 29 Dec. 1882 (Casa Ricordi; ISV-P).

53. 11 Jan. 1883 (Napolitano).

54. 21 Jan. 1883, draft (*C*, 319 n. 1; final version in *CV* iii. 160–1).

55. (*C*, 321–2).

56. Carlotta Ferrari, letters to Verdi, 1869 and subsequent years; see also notes, clippings (SAA).

57. Verdi to Piroli, 2 Feb. 1883, draft (*C*, 319–20; final version in *CV* ii. 162).

58. [14 Feb. 1883] (*C*, 323, see also plate VII). Original in Casa Ricordi is dated 15 Feb.

59. 7 Apr. 1883 (*Carteggio Verdi–Boito*, i. 68).

60. Mingardi, *Verdi e il suo ospedale*, 15–16.

61. 15 Mar. 1883 (Alberti, *Verdi intimo*, 300).

62. Pizzi, *Ricordi verdiani inediti* (Turin, 1901), 9–13.

63. Stolz to Verdi, 19 July 1883 (SAA).

64. 18 July 1883 (Strepponi, Letter-books, SAA).

65. 27 Oct. 1883 (Casa Ricordi; ISV-P).

66. 11 Oct. 1883 (Di Ascoli, 398).

67. Muzio to Verdi, 30 Oct. 1883 (*CV* iv. 224).

68. 28 Sept. 1883 (SAA).

69. 10 Dec. 1883 (SAA).

70. 6: 3 (20 Jan. 1884) (cited in Gatti (1953), 679–80).

71. Ibid.

72. (17 Nov. 1884) (cited in Gatti (1953) 681).

73. 29 [Jan.] 1884 (Di Ascoli, 399).

74. 29 [Jan.] 1884 (Alberti, *Verdi intimo*, 305).

75. 13 [Feb. 1884] (*Carteggio Verdi–Boito*, ii. 318).

76. Muzio to Carlo D'Ormeville, 9 Mar. 1884 (BMP-B).

77. Boito to Ricordi [20 Mar. 1884] (*Carteggio Verdi–Boito*, ii. 318).

78. Muzio to Verdi, 4 Feb. 1884 (Napolitano).

79. 27 Mar. 1884 (*C*, 324–5).

80. [19 Apr. 1884] (*Carteggio Verdi–Boito*, i. 69–73).

81. 26 Apr. 1884 (*C*, 325–6).

82. 6 May 1884 (Abbiati, iv. 244).

83. G. Giacosa, *Verdi in Villa*, published in *Gazzetta musicale di Milano* (11 Nov. 1889) (cited in M. Conati, *Interviste ed. incontri con Verdi* (Milan, 1980), 152–8).

84. Ibid.

85. 16 Nov. 1884 (Alberti, *Verdi intimo*, 316).

86. Cited in Muzio to Giulio Ricordi, 27 June 1884 (Casa Ricordi; ISV-P).

87. 16 Nov. 1884 (Di Ascoli, 404).

88. Verdi to Arrivabene, 24 Dec. 1884 (Alberti, *Verdi intimo*, 317).

89. [end of Nov. 1884] (SAA).

90. 9 Dec. 1884 (*Carteggio Verdi–Boito*, i. 28–9).

91. 29 Apr. 1884 (SAA).

92. 24 [Dec.] 1884 (Alberti, *Verdi intimo*, 318–19).

93. 17 Dec. 1884 (Di Ascoli, 404–5).

94. Verdi to Giulio Ricordi, 13 Jan. 1871 (Casa Ricordi; ISV-P).

95. [end of Apr. or early May 1885] (Abbiati, iv. 261–2).

96. 19 Sept. 1885 (*Carteggio Verdi–Boito*, i. 84–5).

97. Verdi to Boito, 5 Oct. 1885 (ibid. 85–9).

98. Ibid. See also Verdi to Boito, 11 Oct. 1885 (*Carteggio Verdi–Boito*, i. 91).

99. 9 Oct. 1885 (Di Ascoli, 410–12).

100. M. S. Tronca, 'Il Maffei politico: un cosmopolita nell'Europa dell'800', in *L'Ottocento di Andrea Maffei* (Riva del Garda, 1987), 75 ff.

101. 11 Dec. 1885 (Di Ascoli, 413–14).

102. 20 Nov. 1885 (Alberti, *Verdi intimo*, 326–7).

103. Verdi to Arrivabene, 11 Dec. 1885 (ibid. 329–30).

104. Verdi to Giulio Ricordi, 20 Jan. 1886 (Casa Ricordi; ISV-P).

105. Verdi to Boito, 21 Jan. 1886 (*Carteggio Verdi-Boito*, i. 99–100).

106. Ibid.

107. Romilda Pantaleoni to Alceo Pantaleoni, 27 Feb. 1886 (*Carteggio Verdi-Boito*, ii. 344). See also Stolz to Romilda Pantaleoni [Feb. 1886] (Abbiati, iv. 291–2).

108. Ibid.

109. Muzio to [Giulio] Ricordi, 28 Jan. 1886 (Casa Ricordi; ISV-P).

110. Verdi to Piroli, 7 Apr. 1886 (*CV* iii. 176).

111. Muzio to Giulio Ricordi, Apr. 1886 (Casa Ricordi; ISV-P).

112. 8 May 1886 (*Carteggio Verdi–Boito*, i. 103).

113. (Di Ascoli, 486).

114. 23 July 1886 (Museo Teatrale alla Scala; ISV-P).

115. 17 Ju[ly] 1886 (*Carteggio Verdi–Boito*, i. 108 ff; the exact format Verdi used is shown on pp. 109–10).

116. Verdi to Boito [9 Sept. 1886] (ibid. 115–16).

117. Ibid.

118. (*Carteggio Verdi–Boito*, i. 117).

119. Pro Memoria, Verdi to Giulio Ricordi [3 Oct. 1886] (Casa Ricordi; ISV-P). Ricordi had just visited Verdi at Sant'Agata; Verdi left for Milan around the middle of the month.

120. Muzio to Verdi, 26 Nov. 1886 (Napolitano).

121. (Casa Ricordi; ISV-P).

122. (*Carteggio Verdi–Boito*, i. 118).

123. [21 Dec. 1886] (ibid. 119).

124. 4 Nov. 1886 (Alberti, *Verdi intimo*, 334).

125. 21 Jan. 1887 (ibid. 335).

126. 7 Jan. 1887 (*CV* iv. 261).

127. U. Pesci, 'Le prove dell'*Otello*', in 'Verdi e *Otello*', special issue of *Illustrazione italiana* (1887).

128. 12 Feb. 1887 (Abbiati, iv. 325–6).

129. Verdi to the Minister of the Interior, 30 Jan. 1887 (Archivio di Stato, Turin, Biblioteca Reale).

130. See n. 128, above.

131. [Jan. 1888] (R. De Rensis, *Franco Faccio e Verdi: Carteggi e documenti inediti* (Milan, 1934), 248–9).

132. Strepponi to Giuseppe De Sanctis, 21 Mar. 1887 (*CV* i. 205).

133. Verdi to Giulio Ricordi, 25 Mar. 1887 (Casa Ricordi; ISV-P).

134. Verdi to Giulio Ricordi, 29 Apr. 1887 (*CV* iv. 87–8).

135. Verdi to Giulio Ricordi, 19 May 1887 (Casa Ricordi; ISV-P).

136. 19 Aug. [1887] (*C*, 701). The letter is misdated 1884 in *C*.

137. See n. 135, above.

138. 19 Nov. 1887 (*CV* iii. 185–6).

139. Verdi to Giulio Ricordi, 5 Dec. 1887 (Casa Ricordi; ISV-P).

140. 11 Apr. 1884 (BMP-B).

141. 5 Feb. 1886 (BMP-B).

142. See n. 128, above.

143. [11 Jan. 1888] (SAA).

144. 13 Feb. 1888 (Abbiati, iv. 352–3). See also Verdi to Tornaghi, 23 Feb. 1888 (ibid. 353).

145. Mingardi, *Verdi e il suo ospedale*, 79.

146. Verdi to Marchioness Caggiati, n.d. (cited in Mingardi, *Verdi e il suo ospedale*, 23).

147. Strepponi to Avanzi, 11 Nov. 1888 (BMP-B).

148. 15 Nov. 1888 (*CV* iii. 190).

149. The Macchiavelli Collection in Busseto includes a fine photograph of Veroni, with his full moustaches and his coachman's jacket, shown with the other servants, among them Alessandro, Giuseppina, Marcellina, Giovanna, and Vittoria Macchiavelli, with Guerino Balestrieri in the centre of the front row.

150. See Bk. i, Ch. 2 n. 8.

151. 16 Dec. 1888 (Napolitano).

152. See Verdi to Camillo Boito, 14 Jan. 1889, and Verdi to Alessandro Dina, 14 Jan. 1889 (*C*, 349).

153. (*C*, 350).

154. 6 Jan. 1889 (*C*, 348; original in Casa Ricordi; ISV-P).

155. 7 Jan. 1889 (Casa Ricordi; ISV-P).

156. Verdi to Faccio, 24 Feb. 1889 (F. De Rensis, *Franco Faccio e Verdi: carteggi e documenti inediti* (Milan, 1934), 256).

157. Verdi to Giulio Ricordi, 3 Mar. 1889 (Casa Ricordi; ISV-P).

158. 28 Mar. 1889 (Casa Ricordi; ISV-P).

159. Boito to Verdi [13 Mar. 1889] (*Carteggio Verdi–Boito*, i. 140–1).

160. 6 Mar. 1889 (ibid. 138).

161. [7 Mar. 1889] (ibid. 139).

Chapter 33

1. 28 Aug. 1889 (*CV* iii. 195).

2. (C. Mingardi, *Verdi e il suo ospedale 1888–1988* (Piacenza, 1988), 29–33).

3. 10 May 1889 (Casa Ricordi; ISV-P).

4. 'Un opera nuova di Giuseppe Verdi' (30 Nov. 1890) (cited in *Carteggio Verdi–Boito*, ed. M. Medici and M. Conati' (Parma, 1978), ii. 383).

5. 6 July 1889 (ibid. i. 142).

6. 7 July 1889 (ibid. 143).

7. Ibid.

8. 10 July 1889 (ibid. 147).

9. 18 May 1888 (F. Botti, 'Inediti verdiani', *Ecclesia*, 2 (Feb−Mar. 1954), 125).

10. Ibid.

11. 12 July 1889 (Botti, 'Inediti Verdiani', 125).

12. 14 July 1889 (*C*, 702).

13. 7 May 1889 (*C*, 353).

14. Giacomo Vercellini to Verdi, letters (SAA).

15. Raffaele Scalese to Verdi, letters (SAA).

16. 18 Aug. 1889 (*Carteggio Verdi−Boito*, i. 152−3).

17. Ibid.

18. Ibid.

19. 30 [Oct. 1889] (*Carteggio Verdi−Boito*, 155−6).

20. Muzio to Verdi, 4 Jan. 1890 (Napolitano).

21. Verdi to Giulio Ricordi, [1 Jan. 1890] (Casa Ricordi; ISV-P).

22. Ibid.

23. Ibid.

24. [15 Feb. 1890] (*Carteggio Verdi−Boito*, i. 157−8). The article is from *Il pungolo*.

25. 1 Mar. [1890] (*Carteggio Verdi−Boito*, i. 158).

26. 15 Apr. [1890] (ibid. 169−70).

27. [17 Apr. 1890] (ibid. 170).

28. 23 May [18]90 (ibid. 175).

29. Verdi to Boito, 17 Mar. 1890 (ibid. 163).

30. Verdi to Giulio Ricordi, 9 Apr. 1890 (Casa Ricordi; ISV-P).

31. 12 Aug. 1890 (Cenzato, 'Giuseppe Verdi e Teresa Stolz in un Carteggio inedito', *Corriere della sera* (30 Oct, 1932), 3).

32. Verdi to Giacomo Persico, 16 Nov. 1890 (Mingardi, *Verdi e il suo ospedale*, 33−4).

33. W. Weaver, *Duse* (New York, 1984), 85.

34. Verdi to Boito, 6 Oct. 1890 (*Carteggio Verdi−Boito*, i. 176−7).

35. 9 Sept. 1890 (Cenzato, 'Giuseppe Verdi e Teresa Stolz', 3).

36. Account from *Teatro illustrato*, Milan (Dec. 1890) (cited in M. Conati, *Interviste e incontri con Verdi* (Milan, 1980), 224-6).

37. 28 Jan. 1890 (Napolitano).

38. Archivio Notarile Carrara.

39. 6 Dec. 1890 (*CV* ii. 264).

40. Letters of Zeffirina Braibanti to Strepponi (SAA).

41. *Carteggio Verdi–Boito*, ii. 403-4.

42. 31 Dec. 1890 (*Carteggio Verdi–Boito*, i. 178).

43. 1 Jan. 1891 (ibid. 179).

44. 1 Jan. 1891 (Casa Ricordi; ISV-P).

45. 14 Mar. 1891 (Abbiati, iv. 417).

46. Conati, *Interviste*, 221 ff.

47. Ibid. 233.

48. Ibid. 230.

49. Ibid. 231.

50. Strepponi to Giuseppe De Sanctis, 20 Mar. 1891 (*CV* i. 211).

51. Conati, *Interviste*, 224-6.

52. Verdi to Boito, 1 May 1891 (*Carteggio Verdi–Boito*, i. 186).

53. 12 June 1891 (ibid. 190).

54. 14 June [1891] (ibid. 191).

55. Article from *Gazzetta musicale di Milano*, 5 July 1891 (ibid. ii. 412-13).

56. 24 July 1891 (ibid. i. 193).

57. Verdi to Salvatore Boriani, 22 Apr. 1891 (Mingardi, *Verdi e il suo ospedale*, 34-6).

58. Sister Serafina to the Mother Superior of the Piccole Figlie, 19 May 1891 (ibid. 41-5).

59. 23 Jan. 1892 (ibid. 45-6).

60. Verdi to Persico, 15 Mar. 1892 (ibid. 49).

61. 12 Feb. 1892 (*Carteggio Verdi–Boito*, i. 203-4).

62. 2 Apr. 1892 (Casa Ricordi; ISV-P).

63. Verdi to Giulio Ricordi, 4 Apr. 1892 (Casa Ricordi; ISV-P).

64. Strepponi to Giulio Ricordi, 14 Apr. 1892 (Casa Ricordi; ISV-P).

65. 7 Apr. 1892 (SAA). See also *C*, 375-6.

66. 11 Apr. 1892 (Casa Ricordi; ISV-P).

67. [17 Apr. 1892] (*Carteggio Verdi–Boito*, i. 205).

68. 12 July 1892 (Casa Ricordi; ISV-P).

69. Remarks quoted in *Il secolo XIX*, article attached to Verdi's letter to Boito of 6 Aug. 1892 (*Carteggio Verdi–Boito*, i. 208–9).

70. 6 Aug. 1892 (ibid. 207–8).

71. 30 Aug. 1892 (Casa Ricordi; ISV-P).

72. 31 Aug. 1892 (Casa Ricordi; ISV-P).

73. 1 Sept. 1892 (Casa Ricordi; ISV-P).

74. 5 Sept. 1892 (Casa Ricordi; ISV-P).

75. Verdi to Giulio Ricordi [7 Sept. 1892] (Casa Ricordi; ISV-P).

76. 9 Sept. 1892 (Cenzato, 'Giuseppe Verdi e Teresa Stolz', 3).

77. Verdi to Giulio Ricordi, 18 Sept. 1892 (Casa Ricordi; ISV-P).

78. Ibid.

79. 9 Dec. 1892 (Mingardi, *Verdi e il suo ospedale*, 49–50).

80. 7 Dec. 1892 (Casa Ricordi; ISV-P).

81. 21 Dec. 1892 (Casa Ricordi; ISV-P).

82. Verdi to Giulio Ricordi, 7 Nov. 1896 (Casa Ricordi; ISV-P).

83. Patti to Edward Hall, 25 Jan. 1893 (Library for the Performing Arts at Lincoln Center, Music Special Collections). I am grateful to William Seward for calling these letters to my attention.

84. Patti to Hall, 8 Feb. 1893 (Library for the Performing Arts at Lincoln Center, Music Special Collections).

85. (May 1908), 706–15 (William Seward Collection).

86. Printer's proof of piano reduction made for Verdi's use (collection of the Conservatorio Giuseppe Verdi, Milan).

87. n.d. (A. Martinelli, *Verdi: raggi e penombre* (Genoa, 1926), 11–12).

88. 19 Mar. [1893] (*Carteggio Verdi–Boito*, i. 215–16).

89. (Cited in Gatti (1951) 737).

90. Conati, *Interviste*, 234 n. 19. The anonymous writer's article was in *Gazzetta dell'Emilia* (10 Feb. 1893).

91. 15 Dec. 1893 (*C*, 721). See also A. M. Cornelio, 'Giuseppe Verdi, sue memorie e la sua Casa di Riposo per Musicisti', *Rassegna nazionale*, 122 (1903), 609–10.

92. Strepponi to Barberina Strepponi, 11 Feb. 1893 (A. Martinelli, *Verdi*, 12–13).

93. C. Mascaretti, 'Come nacque il *Falstaff*, in *Strenna Piacentina* (Piacenza, 1928), in Biblioteca Passerini-Landi, Piacenza. Although Mascaretti stated that he saw *Attila* at the Teatro Regio in Turin in 1879 or 1880, he appears to have been mistaken about the theatre. He did, however, publish his poem 'Generazioni diverse', dedicated to Verdi, during the composer's lifetime.

94. 12 Feb. 1893 (SAA).

95. Note sent with the last revisions of the *Falstaff* score. These lines, drafted as if they were part of a letter, may have been sent to Ricordi on 23 May 1893, where Verdi actually uses the same words 'le ultime note del Falstaff' that he does in this note. See Abbiati, iv. 509 for text of Verdi's letter to Ricordi dated 23 May 1893. The phrase 'Pace all'anima sua!!' strongly suggests that the envoy was written on the same day. I am grateful to the late Wally Toscanini, Countess Castelbarco, for her help in understanding how her father discovered this text and for giving me his copy of it.

96. 3 Mar. 1893 (Casa Ricordi; ISV-P).

97. Boito to Verdi, 19 Mar. 1893 (*Carteggio Verdi–Boito*, i. 215–16).

98. (*Omaggio di Siena a Verdi con la Messa da Requiem* (Siena, 1913), 48–9. Eight of Verdi's letters to Mascheroni were published here from Mascheroni's collection, with the conductor's permission.)

99. (*C*, 717–18).

100. Verdi to Giulio Ricordi, 21 May 1893 (cited in A. Frizzi, 'Echi di un soggiorno genovese di Giuseppe Verdi', *Rapallo*, 40 (July–Aug. 1964), 6; original in Casa Ricordi; ISV-P).

101. Verdi to Antonio Pini Corsi, 5 May 1893 (Frizzi, *Echi*, 5).

102. Mascheroni to Verdi, 12 May 1893 (SAA).

103. 7 May 1893 (*C*, 717–18).

104. Verdi to Mascheroni, 15 May 1893 (Houghton Library, Harvard University; ISV-P).

105. Verdi to Mascheroni, 16 Aug. 1893 (*C*, 720).

106. 10 Aug. 1893 (*C*, 719–20).

107. 21 May 1893 (Casa Ricordi; ISV-P).

108. Verdi to Boito, 15 Sept. 1893 (*Carteggio Verdi–Boito*, i. 218).

109. 2 Oct. 1893 (Casa Ricordi; ISV-P).

110. Umberto I of Italy to Verdi (cited in Gatti (1951) 745).

111. (Ibid.).

112. Mingardi, *Verdi e il suo ospedale*, 50.

113. Boito to Verdi, 1 Nov. [1893] (*Carteggio Verdi–Boito*, i. 219).

114. 26 Oct. 1893 (*C*, 401 n. 1). Verdi wrote to Bossi again in 1895. Bossi's correspondence with Verdi covers 1889–1900.

115. 1 May 1893 (Botti 'Inediti verdiani', 126).

116. 6 May 1893 (ibid. 126).

117. 20 Sept. 1893 (ibid. 126–7).

118. 8 Dec. 1893 (*C*, 690–1; original in Houghton Library, Harvard University; ISV-P).

119. See Conati, *Interviste*, 259 n. 8.

120. Quoted in Giacosa to Verdi, 13 Dec. 1893 (SAA; see also Abbiati, iv. 523–5).

121. [21 Dec. 1893] (*Carteggio Verdi–Boito*, i. 220–1).

122. 11 Jan. 1894 (Casa Ricordi; ISV-P).

123. 7 June 1893 (*C*, 710). The original in Casa Ricordi is dated 8 June.

124. Verdi to Boito, 19 Jan. 1894 (*Carteggio Verdi–Boito*, i. 223).

125. 31 Jan. 1894 (*C*, 387).

126. 13 Jan. 1894 (Casa Ricordi; ISV-P).

127. 31 Jan. 1894 (*C*, 388).

128. 6 Feb. 1894 (*C*, 389).

129. 11 Feb. 1894 (*C*, 390).

130. 17 Mar. 1894 (Casa Ricordi; ISV-P).

131. 31 Mar. 1894 (Casa Ricordi; ISV-P).

132. 19 Apr. 1894 (Cenzato, 'Giuseppe Verdi e Teresa Stolz', 3).

133. 1 June 1894 (Casa Ricordi; ISV-P).

134. 9 June 1894 (*C*, 195–6).

135. 12 July 1894 (Casa Ricordi; ISV-P).

136. (Casa Ricordi; ISV-P).

137. Verdi to Persico, 23 Nov. 1894 (Mingardi, *Verdi e il suo ospedale*, 53).

138. 4 Nov. 1894 (*C*, 404 n. 1).

139. Conati, *Interviste*, 266–8; Jules Massenet, in *Gaulois du Dimanche* (9–10 Oct. 1897). Massenet stated that the interview took place in Jan. 1896. Conati correctly established the meeting as having taken place in Dec. 1894.

140. The story of Count Ugolino was told by Dante in canto xxxiii of the *Inferno*. Verdi was seeking Vincenzo Galilei's *Canto del Conte Ugolino* in the library of the Florence Conservatory.

141. See *Carteggio Verdi–Boito*, ii. 459–60, notes for Letter 228.

142. Verdi to Giulio Ricordi, 30 Dec. 1894 (Casa Ricordi; ISV-P).

143. 11 Jan. 1895 (Casa Ricordi; ISV-P).

144. 5 Feb. 1895 (Mingardi, *Verdi e il suo ospedale*, 53).

145. G. Cenzato, *La Casa di Riposo per Musicisti* (Milan, 1937), 13.

146. Verdi to Giulio Ricordi, 23 Jan. 1895 (Abbiati, iv. 567–8).

147. Verdi to Gallignani, 31 Jan. 1895 (*C*, 411 n. 1).

148. 21 Apr. 1895 (Houghton Library, Harvard University; ISV-P).

149. Verdi to Angiolo Carrara, 23 Mar. 1895 (*C*, 396–7).

150. Ibid.

151. 3 Apr. 1895 (*C*, 398). Letter is misdated 1893 in *C*.

152. Verdi to the Mayor of San Pier d'Arena, 30 Apr. 1894 (*C*, 395).

153. 21 June 1895 (*C*, 402).

154. Verdi to Dr Pietro Grocco, 1 Sept. 1895 (Mingardi, *Verdi e il suo ospedale*, 54–5).

155. 27 Aug. 1895 (G. Micheli, 'Sei lettere di Verdi a G. Mariotti', *Aurea Parma* 1–2 (1941), 42–3; 403–4 for Verdi's draft; original in collection of Giuseppe Micheli, Fidenza).

156. Verdi to Engineer [?] Ronchetti of Milan, [summer 1895] (Abbiati, iv. 575–6). See *C*, 368 n. 1, for information on the lawyer Ronchetti, also of Milan, who was on the City Commission for reorganization of La Scala.

157. Conati, *Interviste*, 270 ff. Arnaldo Bonaventura's personal memoir was published in *Scena illustrata* in Nov. 1900.

158. Ibid.

159. 5 Sept. 1895 (*C*, 406). See also Checchi to Verdi, 3 Sept. 1895 (*C*, 405).

160. 9 Oct. [1895] (*Carteggio Verdi-Boito*, i. 240).

161. 20 Dec. [1895] (ibid. 241).

162. 18 Feb. 1896 (ibid. 243).

163. 1 Mar. 1896 (*C*, 411 n. 1. Verdi added the word 'cupo' (dark) to his description of 'Domine', as we can see from the facsimile (ISV-P).

164. 23 Dec. 1896 (*CV* ii. 268). He also wrote to her on 21 Mar. 1896 about her son (see *CV* ii. 267–8).

165. Verdi to Giulio Ricordi, 8 May 1896 (*C*, 407–8).

166. 11 June 1896 (*Carteggio Verdi–Boito*, i. 245–6).

167. Gatti (1951), 762.

168. Umberto Giordano to his father Ludovico Giordano [late Nov. or eary Dec. 1896] (P. Alverà, *Giordano* (Milan, 1986), 42-4).

169. 25 Jan. 1897 (Casa Ricordi; ISV-P).

170. Verdi to Giulio Ricordi, 20 Feb. 1897 (Casa Ricordi; ISV-P).

171. Conati, *Interviste*, 284. Heinrich Ehrlich's article about Verdi was published in *Deutsche Revue* in 1897. See also Conati's notes, 278 ff.

172. Richard Strauss to Verdi, 18 Jan. 1895 (SAA).

173. Verdi to Strauss, 27 Jan. 1895 (Conati, *Interviste*, 283; see also 288 n. 13).

174. Ehrlich article, cited in Conati, *Interviste*, 286.)

175. *Carteggio Verdi—Boito*, ii. 477.

176. 15 Apr. 1897 (*Carteggio Verdi—Boito*, i. 250).

177. Verdi to Gustave Roger, 19 June 1897 (*C*, 410).

178. 17 Apr. 1897 (*Carteggio Verdi—Boito*, i. 250).

179. Verdi to Giulio Ricordi, 11 June 1897 (Casa Ricordi; ISV-P).

180. Article in *Gazzetta musicale di Milano* (8 July 1897) (*Carteggio Verdi— Boito*, ii. 479).

181. See *Carteggio Verdi-Boito*, ii. 458.

182. Memoir of Verdi (cited in Abbiati, iv. 612).

183. 15 Jan. 1896 (Mingardi, *Verdi e il suo ospedale*, 56).

184. 21 Jan. 1896 (ibid. 57).

185. Verdi to Persico, 12 Mar. 1896 (ibid. 58).

186. (Ibid. 61).

Chapter 34

1. Verdi to Giulio Ricordi, 22 Sept. 1897 (Casa Ricordi; ISV-P).

2. (F. Botti, 'Inediti verdiani', *Ecclesia*, 2 (Feb—Mar. 1954), 127).

3. Verdi to Boito, 10 Oct. 1897 (*Carteggio Verdi—Boito*, ed. M. Medici and M. Conati) (Parma, 1978), i. 251.

4. A. Mandelli, President of the Cremona Children's Hospital Executive Committee, to Verdi, 20 May 1894 (SAA).

5. (Casa Ricordi; ISV-P).

6. Orders for burial (SAA).

7. (Cited in G. Mondini, *Nel cinquantennio della morte di Giuseppe Verdi* (Cremona, 1952), 83-4).

8. A. Martinelli, in *Gazzetta musicale di Milano* (18 Nov. 1897).

9. Last Will and Testament, Cremona, 24 May 1897; and list of legatees and personal items, 18 and 20 June 1897. After Strepponi's death, Verdi wrote an undated memorandum, sometime between 14 and 21 Nov. 1897, titled 'Expenses to be paid to others' ('Spese da farsi a altri') to remind the lawyers and notaries of the exact amounts and the names of the legatees. He even drew up the total: 54,000 lire (SAA).

10. 6 Dec. 1897 (*Carteggio Verdi-Boito*, i. 252).

11. 17 Dec. 1897 (Phillips-Matz Collection).

12. Boito to Camille Bellaigue, Easter, 1901 (C. Bellaigue, *Echos de France e d'Italie* (Paris, 1919), 301–2; see also R. De Rensis, *Lettere di Arrigo Boito* (Rome, 1938), 329–31.

13. Verdi, dedication to Teresa Stolz, original holograph score, Requiem Mass (Museo Teatrale alla Scala).

14. 29 Dec. 1897 (*Carteggio Verdi–Boito*, ii. 482).

15. 13 May 1898 (A. Oberdorfer, *Giuseppe Verdi: autobiografia dalle lettere* (Milan, 1981 edn.), ed. M. Conati, 241.

16. 24 Jan. 1898 (*C*, 413).

17. 23 Feb. 1898 (Oberdorfer, *Giuseppe Verdi*, 240–1).

18. 4 Feb. 1898 (A. Martinelli, *Verdi: raggi e penombre* (Genoa, 1926), 50).

19. 20 Mar. 1898 (Casa Ricordi; ISV-P).

20. 21 Mar. 1898 (Casa Ricordi; ISV-P).

21. 2 Apr. 1898 (*Carteggio Verdi–Boito*, i. 258–9).

22. 8 Apr. 1898 (ibid. 264–5).

23. M. Conati, *Interviste e incontri con Verdi* (Milan, 1980), 291. Giuseppe Depanis's memoir originally appeared in *I concerti popolari ed il Teatro Regio di Torino* (Turin, 1914–15), ii. 234–40.

24. Conati, *Interviste e incontri*, 296.

25. Boito to Toscanini, [May 1898] (*Carteggio Verdi–Boito*, ii. 491).

26. The song was released on the Dischi del Sole label. In the summer of 1988 the Milan city administration was considering erecting a monument to Bava-Beccaris's victims.

27. 19 May 1898 (*Carteggio Verdi–Boito*, ii. 492).

28. Conati, *Interviste*, 310–11. Conati identifies the anonymous 'Z' as Jacopo Zennari.

29. 10 Aug. 1898 (*Carteggio Verdi–Boito*, i. 268).

30. 15 Mar. 1899 (Museo Centrale del Risorgimento, Rome; ISV-P).

31. 15 Dec. 1898 (*Carteggio Verdi–Boito* i. 270).

32. 18 Mar. 1899 (Casa Ricordi; ISV-P).

33. Verdi to Giulio Ricordi, 27 Feb. 1899 (Casa Ricordi; ISV-P).

34. 20 Apr. 1899 (*Carteggio Verdi–Boito*, i. 275).

35. Verdi to an unidentified correspondent, 4 Apr. 1899 (cited in M. J. Phillips-Matz and C. A. Perera, 'The Search for *King Lear*', *Opera News* (20 Jan. 1958), 12 ff., facsimile of letter, p. 12. Formerly in Carolyn Allen Perera Collection; now in Library for the Performing Arts at Lincoln Center, Music Special Collections).

36. 25 Mar. 1899 (Casa Ricordi; ISV-P).

37. Anecdote told to Abbiati while he was gathering material for his biography of Verdi in the 50s.

38. (28 Sept. 1899) (cited in *Carteggio Verdi-Boito*, ii. 501).

39. Draft [29 Sept. 1899] (Abbiati, iv. 649). The final version of the letter is dated 1 Oct. 1899 (see *Carteggio Verdi–Boito*, 503).

40. Verdi to Giulio Ricordi, 9 Nov. 1899 (Casa Ricordi; ISV-P).

41. 8 Oct. [1899] (*Carteggio Verdi–Boito*, i. 276–7).

42. Verdi to Giulio Ricordi, 2 Mar. 1900 (Casa Ricordi; ISV-P).

43. Verdi to Giulio Ricordi, 29 Mar. 1900 (Casa Ricordi; ISV-P).

44. Verdi to Giulio Ricordi, 27 Apr. 1900 (Casa Ricordi; ISV-P).

45. Verdi to Giulio Ricordi, 29 Apr. 1900 (Casa Ricordi; ISV-P).

46. 12 June 1900 (G. Cenzato, *Itinerari verdiani* (Parma [1949]), 159).

47. 14 June 1900 (ibid. 160).

48. 18 June 1900 (ibid.).

49. 20 June 1900 (ibid.).

50. (SAA).

51. 16 Aug. 1900 (Museo Teatrale alla Scala).

52. 25 Aug. 1900 (SAA).

53. Poem included with letter, 11 Oct. 1900 (SAA).

54. Verdi's sketch of the line from Queen Margherita's prayer is reproduced in *C*, plate xii.

55. I am particularly grateful to Dr Maurizio Marchetti and Cristina Lavezzini of the Cassa di Risparmio di Parma, Filiale di Busseto, for calculating the value of Verdi's estate in 1991 lire, dollars, and pounds sterling. They and the staff of this bank, which Dr Marchetti then directed, have been unfailingly helpful over decades in matters of Verdi research.

56. I. Pizzi, *Per il centenario della nascita di Giuseppe Verdi* (Turin, 1913), 18–20.

57. I. Pizzetti, in *Gazzetta musicale di Milano*, 8 Nov. 1900 (cited in a memoir by Giovanni Tebaldini that appears in Conati, *Interviste*, 359–60). When I interviewed Pizzetti in Rome, he spoke of Verdi's great dignity, erect posture, and warmth. He had been impressed especially by the composer's smile. During the two visits that Tebaldini described, Verdi seemed to be in good health, as Boito said he was. Perhaps Pizzi, who found him 'prostrated' had simply come on a bad day. The thunderstorm that raged outside cannot have improved Verdi's humour. See also I. Pizzetti, 'Giuseppe Verdi, maestro di teatro', *Quaderno dell'Accademia Nazionale dei Lincei*, (1952), 12–3.

58. Tebaldini memoir (cited in Conati, *Interviste*, 360–1).

59. [Dec. 1900] (Abbiati, iv. 666).

60. 9 Dec. 1900 (Botti, 'Inediti Verdiani', 127).

61. (A. Martinelli, *Verdi*, 56).

62. Account of Verdi's stroke, in G. Bragagnolo and E. Bettazzi, *La vita di Giuseppe Verdi* (Milan, 1905), 326; also cited in Conati, *Interviste*, 365.

63. See n. 12, above.

64. G. Giacosa, article in *Corriere della sera* (27–28 Jan. 1901) (cited in Conati, *Interviste*, 366).

65. Proceedings, Senato del Regno, 27 Jan. 1901 and Camera dei Deputati, 28 Jan. 1901 (*Nuova antologia*, 1 Feb. 1901, no. 175, fasc. 699, pp. 538–51).

66. Verdi, Last Will and Testament, 14 May 1900, and codicils (SAA).

67. A. Panzini, 'Tra la folle', in 'Verdi', special issue of *Natura ed arte* (Milan, 1901), 78–80.

APPENDIX

THE VERDIS' PROPERTY

1695–6 Giovanni Verdi of Sant'Agata leased four properties from Marquis Pallavicino of Busseto (Possessioncella, Sant'Agata; Colombarone, and San Bernardino, Busseto; farm, Bersano).

1700s Cristoforo Verdi of Sant'Agata leased farms from Marquis Pallavicino and owned farm at Sant'Agata. Vincenzo, Marcantonio, and Giuseppe Antonio, the composer's direct ancestors, owned farms at Sant'Agata and Bersano (1690s–1770s).

1791 Giuseppe Antonio Verdi of Roncole leased a master's house (Casa Padronale), tenant house, and eighteen small properties from the Church of La Madonna dei Prati at a 'burned candles' auction. He, his wife, and his sons were taverners.

1796 Verdi family paid for pew, Church of San Michele Arcangelo, Roncole.

1800 Francesca Bianchi Verdi, widow of Giuseppe Antonio, renewed lease on properties from Church of La Madonna dei Prati at a 'burned candles' auction.

1809 Carlo Verdi renewed lease after his mother's death; renewed again in 1818.

1813 (10 Oct.) Giuseppe Verdi was born.

1819 Land map of Sant'Agata shows 'Possessione dei Verdi', a large holding adjacent to the Bianchis' land, and the 'Casa dei Verdi' in centre of village.

1821 Carlo Uttini, Verdi's grandfather, died, leaving money to Verdi's mother. Carlo Verdi and Luigia Uttini bought a spinet for Verdi.

1823 Verdi, age 10, moved to Busseto to study, covering part of room and board with earnings as organist of Roncole.

1827 Carlo Verdi, seriously in arrears in rent, renewed lease on one house (Casa Padronale) and land.

1830 (5 Feb.) Eviction notice against Carlo Verdi, ordering him and his family to surrender the Casa Padronale and land on 11 Nov. 1830.

APPENDIX

Family moved to tavern leased from Marquis Pallavicino of Busseto. New tenants moved into Casa Padronale on 29 Nov.

1832–6 Verdi's studies in Milan paid by grant, Barezzi, Carlo Verdi.

1836 Verdi won post of municipal music master, married Margherita Barezzi, and moved into Palazzo Rusca-Tedaldi; apartment paid for by Barezzi.

1838 Carlo Verdi bought land in Roncole. Verdi's daughter died.

1839 Verdi's son died.

(17 Nov.) *Oberto, conte di San Bonifacio*, première at Teatro alla Scala, Milan.

1840 (18 June) Verdi's wife died.

(5 Sept.) *Un giorno di regno*, première at Teatro alla Scala, Milan.

1842 (9 Mar.) *Nabucco*, première at Teatro alla Scala, Milan.

1843 (11 Feb.) *I Lombardi alla prima crociata*, première at Teatro alla Scala, Milan.

1844 (9 Mar.) *Ernani*, première at Teatro La Fenice, Venice.

(Apr.) Verdi agreed to buy farm, Il Pulgaro, near La Madonna dei Prati, Roncole. Carlo Verdi, with power of attorney from Verdi, bought Il Pulgaro from Sabatino Sacerdoti of Parma at 'burned candles' auction.

(8 May) First payment on farm: 8,000 lire in gold. Other payments due: Nov. 1844, Dec. 1845, Dec. 1846.

(3 Nov.) *I due Foscari*, première at Teatro Argentina, Rome.

1845 (15 Feb.) *Giovanna d'Arco*, première at Teatro alla Scala, Milan.

(12 Aug.) *Alzira*, première at Teatro San Carlo, Naples.

(6 Oct.) Verdi bought Palazzo Cavalli in Busseto from Contardo Cavalli. First payment: 10,000 lire. Other payments due: Dec. 1845, May 1846.

(Dec.) Verdi paid Cavalli but fell behind on payment for Il Pulgaro, which was due the same week.

1846 (30 Jan.) Carlo Verdi wrote to creditor Sacerdoti about debt.

(3 Mar.) Carlo Verdi sold a field in Roncole for 1,000 lire.

(17 Mar.) *Attila*, première at Teatro La Fenice, Venice.

(May) Verdi paid 4,000 lire, final payment for Palazzo Cavalli.

1847 (14 Mar.) *Macbeth*, première at Teatro della Pergola, Florence.

(22 July) *I masnadieri*, première at Her Majesty's Theatre, London.

(July) Verdi rented apartment in Paris.

(20 and 30 Sept.) Carlo Verdi wrote to Sacerdoti about debt.

(26 Nov.) *Jérusalem*, première at Académie Royale de Musique, Paris.

APPENDIX

1848   (Apr.–May) Verdi made short trip to Milan, Busseto.

(8 May) Verdi signed agreement to purchase land and houses at Sant'Agata from Rosa Guindani and her sons Pietro, Giacomo, Paolo, and Fortunato Merli, his brother-in-law, surrendering Il Pulgaro to them and agreeing to cover many debts and liens against this heavily mortgaged property.

(31 May) Carlo Verdi, in his son's name, repaid 7,000 lire to notary Gaetano Arati of Cortemaggiore.

(1 July) Carlo Verdi, in his son's name, paid 20,000 lire in gold to Annunciata Morosoli and her son Carlo Bonini of Piacenza, against a debt of 42,646 lire plus expenses. Other debts still unpaid.

(July–Aug.) Verdi rented villa in Passy, living there with Giuseppina Strepponi.

(25 Oct.) *Il corsaro*, première at Teatro Grande, Trieste. Verdi remained in Paris and did not attend.

1849   (27 Jan.) *La battaglia di Legnano*, première at Teatro Argentina, Rome.

(12 May) Carlo Verdi and Luigia Uttini moved from Palazzo Cavalli to farmhouse at Sant'Agata.

(29 July) Verdi left Paris for Busseto, taking up residence in Palazzo Cavalli and giving up rented apartment in Paris.

(14 Sept.) Strepponi joined Verdi in Busseto.

(4 Dec.) Carlo Verdi received 2,900 lire from sale of a house and land in Roncole (Querino Finetti, seller, to Gianantonio Allegri and his brothers).

(8 Dec.) *Luisa Miller*, première at Teatro San Carlo, Naples.

(12 Dec.) Carlo Verdi gave his son the proceeds from the Finetti sale and those from the 1846 sale of land in Roncole.

(15 Dec.) Carlo Verdi, in his son's name, paid 4,600 lire to creditors Morosoli and Bonini, further reducing mortgages against Sant'Agata.

(29 Dec.) Another payment was made, perhaps one year late.

1850   Part of this mortgage was renegotiated.

(16 Nov.) *Stiffelio*, première at Teatro Grande, Trieste.

1851   (Jan.) Friction between Verdi and his father.

(Feb.) Proposed legal settlement between father and son.

(11 Mar.) *Rigoletto*, première at Teatro La Fenice, Venice.

(20 Apr.) Verdi lent his father 1,000 lire for advance on rent on Pietro Allegri's tenant house in Vidalenzo, so his parents would move from Sant'Agata. (Antonio Barezzi had just bought adjacent property from Allegri.) Carlo Verdi and Luigia Uttini left Sant'Agata, moved to Vidalenzo.

APPENDIX

1851   (30 Apr.) Signed agreement between Carlo Verdi and Verdi. Verdi was repaid 1,000 lire he had lent his father in April. Final settlement: Verdi paid his father the 2,305.25 lire he owed him. Agreement signed.

(1 May) Verdi and Strepponi moved to Sant'Agata.

(28 June) Luigia Uttini died in Vidalenzo.

(summer) Verdi began to remodel farmhouse, took full charge of land, livestock, and tenants.

(13 Aug.) Verdi paid 1,500 lire on renegotiated mortgage and made payment to Merli family. Money to the Levi family of Soragna still owed.

(25 Oct.) Strepponi, sent to Milan by Verdi, negotiated loan from Ricordi of 10,000 lire at 5 per cent interest.

(11 Nov.) Verdi paid 10,000 lire to Isacco Levi of Soragna, further reducing principal on debt.

1852   (11 Nov.) Verdi paid 500 lire to Isacco Levi.

1853   (19 Jan.) *Il trovatore*, première at Teatro Apollo, Rome.

(6 Mar.) *La traviata*, première at Teatro La Fenice, Venice.

(10 Oct.) Verdi's accounts showed that he owned 46 animals and large holdings of grain. His three tenants farmed the land.

1855   (13 June) *Les Vêpres siciliennes*, première at Opéra, Paris.

1857   (12 Mar.) *Simon Boccanegra*, première at Teatro La Fenice, Venice.

(15 Apr.) Verdi bought huge estate called Piantadoro, adjacent to Sant'Agata, from Countess Sofia Bulgarini of Parma. Property included nine farms, a smaller property in Villanova sull'Arda, and a house now called Osteria Ongina, with house and land in Comune of Polesine Parmense. Verdi may have obtained a licence to sell wine in the tavern.

(16 Aug.) *Aroldo*, première at Teatro Nuovo, Rimini.

1858   *Un ballo in maschera*, written for Naples, rejected by censors.

1859   (17 Feb.) *Un Ballo in maschera*, première at Teatro Apollo, Rome.

(29 Aug.) Verdi and Strepponi married in Collonges-sous-Salève in the Savoy.

(4 Sept.) Verdi was elected to the Assembly of the Parma Provinces.

1861   (27 Jan.) Verdi was elected to the first Parliament of Italy. He rented a hotel suite in Turin.

(Dec.) Planned première of *La forza del destino* in St Petersburg cancelled.

1862   (24 May) *Inno delle nazioni*, première at Her Majesty's Theatre, London.

APPENDIX

(10 Nov.) *La forza del destino*, première at Imperial Theatre, St Petersburg.

1863   (summer) Verdi planned for irrigation and water control rights at Sant'Agata.

1864   Work on house at Sant'Agata completed.

1865   (21 Apr.) *Macbeth* (revised) given at Théâtre Lyrique, Paris.

1867   (14 Jan.) Carlo Verdi died in Palazzo Cavalli in Busseto. Verdi began to oversee education of Carlo Verdi's ward, Filomena Maria Verdi (age 7).
(Jan.) Verdi's new winter home ready in Palazzo Sauli-Pallavicino in Genoa.
(11 Mar.) *Don Carlos*, première at Opéra, Paris.
(14 Mar.) Verdi moved into new apartment in Genoa.
Purchase of material for steam engine, pump, well and irrigation channels at Sant'Agata. Orders of trees and plants for garden.
(21 July) Antonio Barezzi died in Busseto.

1868   Purchases of trees, plants.

1869   (27 Feb.) *La forza del destino*, first performance of revised opera at Teatro alla Scala, Milan, Verdi directing. Dedicated to Teresa Stolz, soprano.

1870   (spring) Verdi bought farm in Lombardy, at Gerre del Pesce near Cremona, and farm La Pavesa in Bersano.

1871   (24 Dec.) *Aida*, première at Opéra, Cairo.

1872   (8 Feb.) *Aida*, first European performance at Teatro alla Scala, Milan, Verdi directing.
(spring) Verdi bought large farm Colombarola in Fiorenzuola.
(Apr. and Nov.–Dec.) Verdi directed productions of *Aida* in Parma and *Don Carlo* in Naples.

1873   (30 Mar.) *Aida*, first perfomance at Teatro San Carlo, Naples, Verdi directing.
(1 Apr.) *Quartetto per archi*, première in Verdi's suite in Albergo delle Crocelle, Naples.

1874   (22 May) *Messa da Requiem*, première in church of San Marco, Milan, Verdi conducting.
(Sept.) Verdi signed lease for new apartment in Palazzo Doria Principe in Genoa, giving up Palazzo Sauli-Pallavicino.
(15 Nov.) Verdi was named Senator of Kingdom of Italy.

1875   (Feb.–June) European tour of *Messa da Requiem*, Verdi conducting.
(Aug.) Verdi sold Palazzo Cavalli to Strepponi for 18,000 lire.
(8 Nov.) Verdi bought farm from Giuseppe Guarnieri of Sant'Agata.

APPENDIX

1875   (29 Nov.) Verdi bought Castellazzo mill and farm Gerbida from Serafina Sichel, with houses and land in Sant'Agata and San Martino in Olza (Cortemaggiore).
(3 Dec.) Verdi bought farm from Luigi Borlenghi of Sant'Agata.
(16 Dec.) Verdi bought large estate Castellazzo from 17 heirs of Ugo Testa. (Adjacent to Sant'Agata, formerly the property of Baron Profumo.)
(29 Dec.) Verdi bought land, house, and mill at Besenzone (Cortemaggiore) from Dr Luigi Parmigiani and Domenico Sidoli, a relative of the Toscanini family. House on next property said to have been leased by Teresa Stolz; the notary was Dr Arati of Cortemaggiore, who had lent Verdi money to buy Sant'Agata.

1876   (Mar.–June) *Aida* and *Messa da Requiem* at Théâtre des Italiens, Paris, conducted by Verdi.
(7 Dec.) Verdi bought farm from Carlo Merli of Sant'Agata.
(date unknown) Verdi bought farm La Bosella, San Martino in Olza.

1877   (21 May) *Messa da Requiem* in Cologne, Verdi conducting.

1878   (11 Oct.) Filomena Maria Verdi, Verdi's foster daughter, married Alberto Carrara of Busseto.

1879   (30 June) *Messa da Requiem* at Teatro alla Scala, Milan, Verdi conducting. Benefit for flood victims.

1880   (22 Mar.) *Aida* in French at Opéra, Paris, Verdi conducting.
(18 Apr.) Pater noster and Ave Maria, première at Teatro alla Scala, Milan. Verdi attended.
(21 Dec.) Verdi bought land from Dr Giuseppe Boriani, Villanova sull'Arda.

1881   (24 Mar.) *Simon Boccanegra*, first performance of revised opera at Teatro alla Scala, Milan, Verdi directing.

1882   (29 Apr.) Verdi bought farm from Dr Giuseppe Scarabelli of Piacenza.
(27 July) Verdi traded the farm Gerbida to the Monte di Pietà, Busseto, for another farm.
(13 Dec.) News story about the hospital Verdi was having built in Villanova sull'Arda.

1883   (27 Feb.) Verdi bought land from Callisto Boriani of Villanova sull'Arda.
(24 Aug.) Verdi bought farm from Giuseppe, Arone, and Moise Vigevani of Cortemaggiore.

1884   (10 Jan.) *Don Carlo*, first performance of revised opera at Teatro alla Scala, Milan, Verdi conducting.

APPENDIX

1885   (15 Apr.) Verdi bought farm from Francesco Pedrini of Cortemaggiore, a relative of the Toscanini family.
(5 Nov.) Verdi bought farm Prato di Gargoni from Giuseppe Parizzi.

1887   (5 Feb.) *Otello*, première at Teatro alla Scala, Milan, Verdi directing.
(15 Oct.) Verdi bought farm from Francesco Pedrini.

1888   (July) Verdi bought railroad stock and Banca Nazionale bonds.
(6 Nov.) Inauguration of hospital built by Verdi in Villanova sull'Arda.

1889   Verdi acquired railroad stock and land in Milan for site of Casa di Riposo per Musicisti.

1890   (summer) Verdi founded company to sell pork products at Sant'Agata, under the 'GV Brand' name.

1891   (30 Nov.) Verdi bought farm from Tancredi Menta of Sant'Agata.

1893   (9 Feb.) *Falstaff*, première at Teatro alla Scala, Milan, Verdi directing.

1895   (Jan.) Verdi arranged for building the Casa di Riposo in Milan.

1896   Verdi deposited large sum of money for construction.

1897   (Oct.) Verdi authorized Ricordi to publish the *Quattro pezzi sacri* and supervised publication (1898).
(14 Nov.) Strepponi died at Sant'Agata.

1898   (7 Apr.) Stabat mater, 'Laudi alla Vergine Maria', and Te Deum première at Opéra, Paris.

1899   (16 Dec.) Verdi signed a document founding the Casa di Riposo.

1900   (14 May) Verdi signed his will in Milan.

1901   (27 Jan.) Verdi died in Milan.

Note: I owe particular thanks to Angelo Lodigiani of Besenzone, the staffs of the Archivio Notarile and Archivio di Stato, Parma; the Archivio di Stato, Piacenza; the Archivio del Comune, Busseto, Besenzone, Cortemaggiore, Fiorenzuola, San Pietro in Cerro, Villanova sull'Arda; and the Archivio di Stato in Cremona. Gabriella Carrara Verdi provided much information about contracts to purchase and deeds; and Dr Francesco Cafasi of Reggio Emilia helped by determining the size and value of these properties. Dr Giorgio Fiori, Piacenza, provided invaluable information on the notarial archives. For many details not related to the purchase of land, I am indebted to Elvidio Surian's 'A Chronological Timetable of Verdi's Life and Works', in W. Weaver and M. Chusid (eds.), *The Verdi Companion* (New York, 1979) 255 ff.

Bibliography

I am particularly grateful to Marcello Conati; the Istituto di Studi Verdiani, Parma; and Corrado Mingardi, director of the Biblioteca della Cassa di Risparmio e del Monte di Credito sul Pegno di Busseto for help in compiling this bibliography.

ABBIATI, FRANCO, *Giuseppe Verdi*, 4 vols. (Milan, 1959).

L'Accademia Filarmonica di Verona e il suo teatro (Verona, 1982).

ACCARINI, MARIO, 'Ercolano Balestra notaro e i suoi rapporti con Giuseppe Verdi', *Parma nell'arte*, 2 (1972), 87–101.

AFFÒ, IRENEO, and PEZZARA, A., *Memorie degli scrittori e letterati parmigiani* (Parma, 1789–97 and 1825–33).

AIMI, [Don] AMOS, 'L'adolescenza di Giuseppe Verdi', *Gazzetta di Parma* (5 Jan. 1970).

—— 'Vi vuole dunque tutta l'energia col Verdi', *Corriere di Parma* (summer 1991), 88–90.

—— and ALDO, COPELLI, *Giuseppe Verdi, deputato di Borgo San Donnino* (Fidenza, 1988).

AJELLO, RAFFAELE, *et al.*, *Il Teatro di San Carlo* (Naples, 1987).

ALBERTI, ANNIBALE, *Verdi intimo. Carteggio di Giuseppe Verdi con il conte Opprandino Arrivabene 1861–86* (Verona, 1931).

ALCARI, CESARE, *Parma nella musica* (Parma, 1931).

ALESSANDRI, ASCANIO, 'Ferdinando Provesi', *Parma per l'arte*, 3 (1953), 137–43.

—— 'Un gravissimo fallo di Ferdinando Provesi', *Parma per l'arte*, 9 (1959), 112 ff., 143 ff.; 10 (1960), 93 ff.; 11 (1961), 67 ff.; 12 (1962), 188 ff.; 19 (1969), 123 ff.

—— 'Processo, condanna e fuga di Ferdinando Provesi', *Parma per l'arte*, 12 (1962), 168–70.

ALFIERI, VITTORIO, *Vita di Vittorio Alfieri scritta da esso* (Florence, 1853).

ALVERÀ, PIERLUIGI, 'Luna di Miele in Casa Verdi', in id., *Giordano* (Milan, 1986).

AMOROSO, GIUSEPPE, *Voci borghesi e tensione romantica* (Rome, 1973).

ANELLI, LUIGI, *La storia d'Italia*, 4 vols. (Milan, 1864).

'Archivio musicale del Sig^r Demaldè Giuseppe', catalogue of scores, Manuscript Collection, BMP-B.

ARMANI, FRANCO, and BASCAPÈ, G., *La Scala* (Milan, 1951).

Atti del I congresso internazionale di studi verdiani (Parma, 1969).

Atti del II congresso internazionale di studi verdiani (Parma, 1971).

BIBLIOGRAPHY

Atti del III congresso internazionale di studi verdiani (Parma, 1974).

AVANZI, [Don] GIOVANNI, *Agli onorevoli e gentili sposi Alberto Carrara e Maria Verdi per le nozze contratte a dì 17 ottobre 1878* (Parma, 1878), Manuscript Collection, BMP-B.

BACCHINI, MAURIZIA BONATTI, 'Scenografia e teatralità nell'opera di Girolamo Magnani', in ead. (ed.) *Il Teatro di Girolamo Magnani* (Fidenza: 1989).

BAKER, EVAN, 'Lettere di Giuseppe Verdi a Francesco Maria Piave 1843–1865', *Studi verdiani*, 4 (1986–7), 136–66.

BALDACCI, LUIGI, 'Verdi e Solera', in *40° Maggio Musicale Fiorentino* (Florence, 1977).

BALDINI, GABRIELE, *Abitare la battaglia: la storia di Giuseppe Verdi* (Milan, 1970); trans. in English as *The Story of Giuseppe Verdi* (Cambridge, 1980).

BALESTRA, LUIGI, 'Ritratto fisico e morale del Maestro Giuseppe Verdi', sonnet in Manuscript Collection, BMP-B.

BANTI, ALBERTO MARIO, *Terra e denaro, una borghesia padana dell'Ottocento* (Venice, 1989).

BARBIERA, RAFFAELLO, *La Principessa Belgioioso* (Milan, 1902).

—— *Il salotto della Contessa Maffei* (Milan, 1895).

BARBIERI, C., *Don Carlo Uttini, pedagogista* (Rome, 1913).

BARBLAN, GUGLIELMO, 'Un po' di luce sulla prima rappresentazione della *Forza del destino* a Pietroburgo', *Bollettino dell'ISV*, 2: 5 (1962).

BARRILI, A. G., *Giuseppe Verdi, vita e opere* (Genoa, 1892).

—— *Voci del passato* (Milan, 1909).

BASSO, ALBERTO, *Autografi di musicisti*, a catalogue for exhibition sponsored by RAI (Turin, 1962).

BASSO, MAURIZIO, *Giuseppe Verdi, la sua vita, le sue opere, la sua morte* (Milan, 1901).

BELFORTI, ADOLFO, *Emanuele Muzio, l'unico allievo di G. Verdi* (Fabriano, 1895).

BELLAIGUE, CAMILLE, *Echos de France et d'Italie* (Paris, 1919).

—— *Les Musiciens célèbres* (Paris, 1927).

—— *Verdi* (Paris, 1912; Milan, 1913).

BENSA, MARIA, *Busseto dal secolo VII al XX* (Parma, 1911).

BERMANI, EUGENIO, *Schizzi sulla vita e le opere di G. Verdi* from *Gazzetta musicale di Milano* (Milan, 1846).

BERTI, GIUSEPPE, 'Ideologie politiche e sociali negli ex-ducati di Parma e Piacenza durante il primo decennio dell'unità italiana', in *Archivio Storico per le Province Parmensi*[4] (1960–1), 121–57.

—— 'Transformazioni interne della società parmense–piacentina, 1860–1900' (Piacenza, 1972).

Biblioteca 70, ed. Corrado Mingardi, 1–4 (1970–5), publication of the Biblioteca della Cassa di Risparmio di Parma e del Monte di Pietà di Busseto.

BIBLIOGRAPHY

BLACK, JOHN, N., *Donizetti's operas in Naples, 1822–1848* (London, 1982).

—— 'The Libretto of *La creazione del mondo*, Milan, April 1834', *Studi verdiani*, 2 (1983), 147–9.

—— 'Salvatore Cammarano's Programma for "Il trovatore" and the Problems of the Finale', *Studi verdiani*, 2 (1983), 78–107.

BLANCHE, ALBERTO, *Sui margini della storia: vecchia Milan*, 2 vols. (Milan, 1931).

BONAVENTURA, ARNALDO, *L'avventura della musica* (Pisa, 1888).

—— *Ode a Giuseppe Verdi* (Pisa, 1895).

BONGIOVANNI, GIANNETTO, *Dal carteggio inedito Verdi–Vigna* (Rome, 1941).

BONI, ORESTE, *Verdi: l'uomo, le opere, e l'artista* (Parma, 1901).

BONOMI, IVANOE, *Mazzini, triumviro della Repubblica Romana* (Turin, 1936).

BOSISIO, ALFREDO, *Storia di Milano* (Milan, 1964).

BOTTI, [Don] FERRUCCIO, *La forca d'Bretta* (Parma, 1958).

—— *Giuseppe Verdi* (Alba, 1941).

—— 'Giuseppe Verdi, il contadino delle Roncole', *Parma economica*, 11 (Nov. 1969).

—— 'Inediti verdiani', *Ecclesia*, 2 (Feb.–Mar. 1954).

—— *Spigolature d'archivio*, 5 vols. (Parma, 1952–66).

—— 'Spigolature verdiane', *Biblioteca 70*, 3 (1973), 63–6.

—— *Verdi e l'ospedale di Villanova d'Arda* (Parma, 1952).

BOTTI, RENATA PESCANTI, *Donne nel Risorgimento italiano* (Milan, 1966).

BOTTONI, GIROLAMO, *Giuseppe Verdi a Rimini* (Rimini, 1913).

BOUQUET, MARIE THÉRÈSE, GUALERZI, VALERIA, and TESTA, ALBERTO, *Storia del Teatro Regio di Torino* (Turin, 1988).

BRAGAGNOLO, G., and BETTAZZI, E., *La vita di Giuseppe Verdi* (Milan, 1905).

BROGLIO, L., VANBIANCHI, C. ADAMI, G. *et al.* (eds.), *Nel primo centenario di Giuseppe Verdi 1813–1913* (Milan, 1913).

BROMBERT, BETH ARCHER, *Cristina* (New York, 1977).

BRUNIALTI, ATTILIO, *Giuseppe Verdi al Parlamento*, pamphlet in *Verdi di autori vari*, bound vol. in BMP-B.

BUDDEN, JULIAN, *The Operas of Verdi*, 3 vols. (London, 1973–81; revised paperback edition, Oxford, 1992).

BUSCH, HANS, *Verdi's 'Aida': The History of an Opera in Letters and Documents* (Minneapolis, second printing 1979).

—— *Verdi's 'Otello' and 'Simon Boccanegra' (revised version) in Letters and Documents*, 2 vols. (Oxford, 1988).

CAGLI, BRUNO, ' "Questo povero poeta esordiente", Piave a Roma', in *'Ernani' ieri e oggi'*, 1–18.

CALDERINI, A., and PARIBENI, R., *Milano* (Rome, 1951).

CAMBIASI, POMPEO, *La Scala, note storiche e statistiche* (Milan, 1888).

CAMETTI, ALBERTO, *Jacopo Ferretti e i musicisti del suo tempo* (Milan, 1897).

BIBLIOGRAPHY

CAMETTI, ALBERTO, *Il Teatro di Tordinona poi di Apollo*, 2 vols. (Tivoli, 1938).

CANNIZZARO, TOMMASO, 'Per Giuseppe Verdi', in *Verdi di autori vari*, bound vol. in BMP-B.

CAPRA, MARCO, 'Girolamo Magnani, scenografo: cronologia annotata', in Bacchini (ed.), *Teatro di Girolamo Magnani*, 113–34.

CAPRI, ANTONIO, *Verdi, uomo e artista* (Milan, 1939).

CARCANO, GIULIO, *Emilio Dandolo* (Turin, 1861).

CARRARA, ENRICO, '*Gli uccelli accademici*, commento ad un poema inedito del Can. Andrea Pettorelli', in L. Carrara and L. Rizzi (eds.), *Falstaff*.

CARRARA, L[ino], 'Modeste origini', in id. (ed.), *Verdi: rivista per l'anno giubilare*.

—— (ed.), *Verdi: rivista per l'anno giubilare* (Bologna, 1926).

—— and RIZZI, LINO (eds.), *Falstaff, periodico illustrata delle celebrazioni de cinquantenario verdiano* (Cremona, 1951).

CARRARA-VERDI, GABRIELLA, 'Giuseppe Demaldè e il M° di cappella della Collegiata', *Biblioteca 70*, 1 (1970), 5–10.

—— 'Le lettere di Rossini a Verdi', *Biblioteca 70*, 3 (1973), 9–16.

—— 'O il Senato o la chiesa di San Siro', *Biblioteca 70*, 4 (1975), 171–80.

—— 'Preliminari di *Aida*', *Biblioteca 70*, 2 (1971), 9–22.

Le carte degli archivi piemontesi (Turin, 1881).

CASA, EMILIO, *Parma da Maria Luigia Imperiale a Vittorio Emanuele II, 1847–1860* (Parma, 1901).

CASALE, STEPHEN, 'A Catalogue of Letters from Verdi and Giuseppina Strepponi to the Escudiers', Master's Thesis (New York, 1983).

CASINI, CLAUDIO, *Verdi* (Milan, 1981).

CASSI, P., 'Girolamo Magnani e il suo carteggio con Verdi', in *Vecchie cronache di Fidenza* (Milan, 1941).

CASTELLANETA, CARLO, and CORRADESCHI, SERGIO, *L'opera completa di Hayez* (Milan, 1971).

CASTIGLIONI, CARLO, *L'ultima dominazione austriaca di Milano, 1841–1859* (Milan, 1959).

CATELANI, BICE PAOLI, *Il Teatro Comunale del Giglio di Lucca* (Pescia, 1941).

CATTANEO, CARLO, *L'insurrezione di Milano e le considerazioni sul 1848* (Milan, 1949).

CAVALLI, HERCULES, 'Giuseppe Verdi: nuovi particolari inediti ed interessanti', *Pensiero di Nizza* (29, 30, and 31 Dec. 1876 and 4 Jan. 1877).

—— *José Verdi, maestro de musica* (Madrid, 1867).

CAVALLI, [Don] TEOFILO, *Busseto: storia, arte, guida del museo, episodi inediti verdiani, Roncole* (Parma, n.d.).

—— *Verdi, a Roncole, a Busseto, a S. Agata* (Parma, 1974).

CELLA, FRANCA, 'Il carteggio Verdi–Morosini', *Gazzetta del Museo teatrale alla Scala*, 2: 5 (winter 1986–7), 47–51.

BIBLIOGRAPHY

—— and PETROBELLI, PIERLUIGI (eds.), *Giuseppe Verdi–Giulio Ricordi, corrispondenza e immagini, 1881–1890* (Milan, 1981), catalogue of exhibition.

CELLETTI, RODOLFO, 'On Verdi's Vocal Writing' in Weaver and Chusid (eds.), *Verdi Companion.*

CELLI, TEODORO, '*Va pensiero*' (Milan, 1951).

CENZATO, GIUSEPPE, *La Casa di Riposo per Musicisti* (Milan, 1937).

—— 'Giuseppe Verdi e Domenico Morelli', *Corriere della sera* (14 Dec. 1934).

—— 'Giuseppe Verdi e Teresa Stolz in un carteggio inedito', *Corriere della sera* (30 Oct. 1932).

—— *Itinerari verdiani* (Parma, [1949]).

—— 'Luzio e il Verdi definitivo', *Corriere della sera* (1 Feb. 1935).

—— 'La Strepponi, Ricordi e Piave', *Corriere della sera* (11 Aug. 1934).

—— *L'universalità di Giuseppe Verdi* (Milan, 1939).

CESARESCO, EVELYN MARTINENGO, *Cavour* (London, 1898).

—— *The Liberation of Italy, 1815–1870* (London, 1902).

CESARI, GAETANO, and LUZIO, ALESSANDRO (eds.), *I copialettere di Giuseppe Verdi* (Milan, 1913).

CHECCHI, E., *Giuseppe Verdi: il genio e le opere* (Florence, 1887).

—— 'I librettisti di Verdi', *Nuova antologia*, 1004 (Oct. 1913), 529–42.

CHIERICI, MAURIZIO, *Quel delitto in Casa Verdi* (Milan, 1981).

CHORLEY, HENRY, *Thirty Years' Musical Recollections* (New York, 1926).

CHUSID, MARTIN (ed.), *The Works of Giuseppe Verdi*, xvii. *Rigoletto*, with introduction (Chicago, 1983).

—— 'Verdi's Own Words: His Thoughts on Performance with Special Reference to *Don Carlos, Otello*, and *Falstaff*' in Weaver and Chusid (eds.), *Verdi Companion*, 144–92.

COLOMBO, ERMINIA, *Scenografie Sormani*, tr. Mary Jane Phillips-Matz (Milan, 1988).

COLQUHOUN, ARCHIBALD, *Manzoni and his Times* (London, 1954).

Commemorazione del pittore Stefano Barezzi di Busseto (Milan, 1859).

CONATI, MARCELLO, 'Appendix to the Bibliography of Critical Writings on *Rigoletto*', *ISV Bollettino, Studi Verdiani*, 3: 9 (1982), 1700–1.

—— *Autobiografia dalle lettere* (see Oberdorfer.)

—— *La bottega della musica* (Milan, 1983).

—— '*Don Carlo*: dramma dell'incomunicabilità', in *Don Carlos* (house programme of the Teatro Comunale, Bologna, 1987).

—— '*Ernani* di Verdi; le critiche del tempo', in '*Ernani' ieri e oggi*'.

—— 'Giuseppina Strepponi in Paris, with a review by Berlioz', *Verdi Newsletter*, 6 (American Institute for Verdi Studies, 1979).

—— *Interviste e incontri con Verdi* (Milan, 1980).

—— 'Le lettere di Giuseppe Verdi e Giuseppina Verdi a Giuseppe Perosio', *Nuova rassegna di studi musicali*, 1 (1977).

BIBLIOGRAPHY

CONATI, MARCELLO, 'Saggio di cronologia delle prime rappresentazioni di *Rigoletto*', *ISV Bollettino*, 3: 9 (1982).

—— 'Verdi e il Teatro Regio di Parma', in *Omaggio al Regio nel 150° anniversario dell'apertura* (Parma, 1979).

—— and PAVARANI, MARCELLO, Orchestre in Emilia-Romagna nell'Ottocento e Novecento (Parma, 1982).

COPERTINI, GIOVANNI, 'Riconoscimento iconografico di un Grande di corte del ducato parmense [Soldati]', *Parma per arte*, 4 (1954), 143–4.

CORNELIO, A. M., 'Giuseppe Verdi, sue memorie e la sua Casa di Riposo per Musicisti', *Rassegna nazionale*, 122 (1903), 593–620.

CORRADI-CERVI, MAURIZIO, *Cronologia del Teatro Regio di Parma, 1928–1948* (Parma, 1955).

—— *Il Teatro Regio* (Parma, 1962).

CORSI, MARIO, *Tamagno, il più grande fenomeno canoro dell'Ottocento* (New York, 1977).

Cortemaggiore, alla vigilia del suo cinquecentesimo anno di fondazione: 11 ottobre 1479–11 ottobre 1979 (Cortemaggiore, 1975).

COSTANTINI, TEODORO, *Sei lettere di G. Verdi a Giovanni Bottesini* (Trieste, 1908).

COTARELO Y MORI, E., *Origines de la opera en España* (Madrid, 1917).

CRISPOLTI, CESARE, 'Cronologia della vita di Giuseppe Verdi', *Verdi: studi e memorie a cura del Sindacato Nazionale Fascista Musicisti* (Rome, 1941), 483–527.

Cultura dell'Ottocento a Pistoia: la collezione Puccini (Florence, 1977).

DACCI, GIUSTO, *Cenni storici e statistici intorno al Reale Scuola di Musica in Parma* (Parma, n.d.).

DALLA LIBERA, SANDRO, 'Cronologia delle opere', in *La Fenice*.

DA MARETO, FELICE, *Bibliografia generale delle antiche province parmensi*, 2 vols. (Parma, 1973–4).

DANDOLO, EMILIO, *I volontari e i bersaglieri lombardi* (Turin, 1849).

DE ANGELIS, MARCELLO, *Le carte dell'impresario* (Florence, 1982).

—— *Le cifre del melodramma* (Florence, 1982).

—— *La musica del Granduca: vita musicale e correnti critiche a Firenze, 1800–1855* (Florence, 1978).

DE GIOVANNI, ETTORE, *Giuseppe Nicolini e Sebastiano Nasolini* (Piacenza, 1927).

—— *Piacentini alunni della R. Scuola di Musica di Parma, 1818–1888* (Piacenza, 1927).

—— *Studi sull '800 musicale piacentino* (Piacenza, 1927).

DEGRADA, FRANCESCO, *Il palazzo incantato*, 2 vols. (Fiesole, 1979).

DELLA CORTE, ANDREA, 'Saggio di bibliografia delle critiche al *Rigoletto*', *ISV Bollettino* 3: 9 (1982), 1640–2.

DELL'OLIO, [Don] ENRICO, 'Trebbiatura dei tempi andati', *Qui Parma*, suppl. to *Gazzetta di Parma* (24 Aug. 1989).

BIBLIOGRAPHY

DEMALDÈ, GIUSEPPE, 'Cenni biografici del Maestro Giuseppe Verdi', Manuscript Collection, BMP-B; English trans. by Mary Jane Phillips-Matz and Ernesto Macchidani in *Verdi Newsletter* (originally titled *AIVS Newsletter*), 1, 2, and 3 (American Institute for Verdi Studies; May 1976, Dec. 1976, and June 1977). Notes for Demaldè's 'Cenni' are also in the Busseto collection.

DEMALDÈ, VALERIANO, 'Verdi a Busseto', *Corriere della sera* (16 Feb. 1886).

DEPANIS, GIUSEPPE, *I concerti popolari ed il Teatro Regio di Torino*, 2 vols. (Turin, 1914–15).

DE RENSIS, RAFFAELLO, *Franco Faccio e Verdi: carteggi e documenti inediti* (Milan, 1934).

—— *Lettere di Arrigo Boito* (Rome, 1938).

DEVOTO, G., and GIACOMELLI, G., *I dialetti delle regioni d'Italia* (Florence, 1972).

DI ASCOLI, ARTURO [pseud.], *Quartetto milanese ottocentesco: lettere di G. Verdi, G. Strepponi, C. Maffei, C. Tenca e di altri personaggi del mondo politico e artistico dell'epoca* (Rome, 1974).

DI MANZANO, FRANCESCO, *Cenni biografici dei letterati ed artisti friulani* (Udine, 1887).

DREI, [Don] GIOVANNI, 'Il concorso di Verdi a Busseto secondo nuovi documenti', *Aurea Parma* (1939), 3–4: 119–32.

—— 'Una contravvenzione all'oste delle Roncole' and 'Notizie e documenti verdiani', *Aurea Parma* (1941), 1–2: 9–25.

DUPRÉ, GIOVANNI, *Pensieri sull'arte e ricordi autobiografici* (Florence, 1879).

Enciclopedia dello spettacolo, 9 vols. and suppl. (Rome, 1954–62).

ENGELHARDT, MARKUS, 'Nuovi dati sulla nascita dell'opera giovanile di Verdi, *Un giorno di regno*', *Studi verdiani* 4 (1986–7), 11–7.

'*Ernani' ieri e oggi*' (Atti del Convegno Internazionale di Studi, Modena; Teatro San Carlo, 9–10 December 1984), pub. in *Bollettino dell'Istituto di Studi verdiani*, 10 (1987).

ESCUDIER, LEON, *Mes souvenirs* (Paris, 1863).

'Esposizione dei bambini', editorial commentary in *Il Lombardo–Veneto* (11 Mar. 1851).

'La famiglia', *Facchino* (15 Nov. 1845), Antonaldo Conforti Collection, Busseto.

FAUSTINI, P., 'Il Requiem del Maestro Verdi a Venezia al Teatro Malibran nel luglio 1875' in Mangini, *Teatri di Venezia*.

La Fenice, a vol. of the series *I teatri del mondo* (Milan, 1972).

FERMI, STEFANO, 'Ancora della madre di Verdi e di alcuni membri della famiglia Uttini', *Bollettino storico piacentino*, 36 (1941), 72–6.

—— 'Per uno studio sul pedagogista Carlo Uttini', *Rollettino storico piacentino*, 35 (1940) 77–86.

FERRARI, [Mgr.] GIOVANNI, *La singolare storia di Cortemaggiore* (Piacenza, 1986).

BIBLIOGRAPHY

FERRARI, LUIGI, *Onomasticon: repertorio bibliografico degli scrittori italiani dal 1501 al 1850* (Milan, 1947).

FERRARI, PAOLO EMILIO, *Spettacoli drammatico-musicali e coreografici in Parma dall'anno 1628 all'anno 1883* (Parma, 1884).

FÉTIS, FRANÇOIS-JOSEPH, *Biografie universelle des musiciens et bibliografie générale de la musique* (Brussels, 1835–44, and Paris, 1860–5).

—— *La musica accomodata all'intelligenza di tutti*, 2 vols. (Turin, 1858).

FIORENTINO, E. F., 'Carlo Uttini, uno dei maggiori educatori', in *Personaggi piacentini dell'ultimo secolo* (Piacenza, 1972).

FLISI, GIUSEPPE (ed.), *Cesare Vigna, psichiatra e musicologo nel primo centenario della morte* (Viadana, 1992).

FORBES, ELIZABETH, *Mario and Grisi* (London, 1985).

FORCANI, MARIA GIOVANNA, *Il Teatro Municipale di Piacenza, 1804–1984* (Piacenza, 1985).

FRIZZI, ANITA, 'Echi di un soggiorno genovese di Giuseppe Verdi', *Rapallo*, 40 (July–Aug. 1964).

FULCINI, [Don] GIOVANNI, 'Memorie della commemorazione centenaria del grande musicista Giuseppe Verdi', manuscript in Parish Archive, church of San Michele Arcangelo, Roncole [1913].

FURLOTTI, ARNALDO, 'Inediti verdiani', in *La regione Emilia-Romagna: Giuseppe Verdi nel primo centenario della morte* (Bologna, 1950).

GAJOLI, A., *Monsignor Carlo Uttini e la sua opera pedagogica* (Intra, 1914).

GALLARATI, [Don] ENRICO, 'Sintesi salicetana', typescript in Parish Archive, church of San Pietro, Saliceto di Cadeo [n.d.].

GANDINI, ALESSANDRO, *Cronistoria dei teatri di Modena* (Modena, 1873).

GARA, EUGENIO, 'La misteriosa giovinezza di Giuseppina Strepponi', *Corriere della sera* (27 Jan. 1951).

GARAVELLI, GIOVANNI, 'Monsignor Carlo Uttini e la sua carriera', manuscript on deposit in the home of Prof. Garavelli, San Nazzaro d'Ongina.

GARIBALDI, FRANCO TEMISTOCLE, *Giuseppe Verdi nella vita e nell'arte* (Florence, 1904).

GARIBALDI, LUIGI AGOSTINO, *Giuseppe Verdi nelle lettere di Emanuele Muzio ad Antonio Barezzi* (Milan, 1931).

GASPERINI, GUIDO, 'Per una lettera inedita di Giuseppe Verdi sulla *Giovanna d'Arco*', in Articles File, ISV, Parma (original pub. not identified).

GATTI, CARLO, *Revisioni e rivalutazioni verdiani* (Milan, 1951).

—— *Il Teatro alla Scala*, 2 vols. (Milan, 1964).

—— *Verdi*, 2 vols. (Milan, 1931; 2nd edn. 1951).

—— *Verdi nelle immagini* (Milan, 1941).

'Genesi dell'Aida', *Quaderno dell'ISV*, 4 (1971).

GHISLANZONI, ANTONIO, *Reminiscenze artistiche ed artisti di teatro* (Milan, 1871/2–80).

BIBLIOGRAPHY

—— *In chiave di baritono* (Milan, 1882).

—— *Storia di Milano, 1836–1848* (Lecco, [1870]).

GHIZZONI, SANDRA CAVAZZINI, 'Tipi di case rurali nella zona di Busseto', *Biblioteca 70*, 4 (1975), 213–30.

GINZBURG, NATALIA, *The Manzoni Family*, trans. Marie Evans (New York, 1987).

Giornale cremonese per l'anno 1851 (Cremona, 1851).

GIOVANELLI, PAOLA D., 'La storia e la favola dell'*Oberto*', *Studi verdiani*, 2 (1983), 29–37.

'Giuseppe Verdi', *Fuggilozio*, 3: 1 (Jan. 1857), 13–16; 3: 6 (Feb. 1857), 92–6; 3: 9 (Mar. 1857), 139–44.

Giuseppe Verdi: edizione commemorativa in occasione delle rappresentazioni verdiane al Teatro di Busseto dirette da Arturo Toscanini (Busseto, [Sept.] 1926).

Giuseppe Verdi (Accademia Chigiana, Siena, 1951).

GOLDIN, DANIELA, 'Il *Simon Boccanegra* da Garcia Gutiérrez a Verdi', in *Simon Boccanegra* (house programme of the Teatro Comunale, Florence, season 1988–9), 265–71.

GOSSETT, PHILIP, 'La fine dell'età borbonica, 1838–1860', in *Il Teatro di San Carlo* (Naples, 1987).

GRANDI, ANGELO, *Descrizione dello stato fisico, politico, statistico, storico, biografico della provincia e diocesi di Cremona* (Cremona, 1858).

GRAZZI, [Don] LUIGI, *Parma romantica* (Parma, 1964).

—— 'Documenti inediti della giovinezza di Verdi', *Gazzetta di Parma* (3 July 1950).

GUALERZI, GIORGIO, 'Il cammino dell'opera', *Bollettino dell'ISV*, 2: 5 (1962).

GUERRAZZI, F. D., *Manzoni, Verdi e l'albo rossiniano* (Milan, 1874).

Guida storico e sacro della R[eale] città e sobborghi di Cremona (Cremona, 1818).

GÜNTHER, URSULA, 'Documents inconnus concernant les relations de Verdi avec l'Opéra de Paris', in *Atti del III congresso internazionale di studi verdiani*.

—— 'L'edizione integrale del *Don Carlos* di Giuseppe Verdi', pref. to the critical edn. (Milan, 1977).

—— 'La Genèse de *Don Carlos*', *Revue de musicologie*, 58 (1972).

Gustavo III, re di Svezia, azione coreografica in cinque atti di Augusto Hus (Milan, 1846).

HALE, E. E. Y., *Mazzini and the Secret Societies* (London, 1956).

—— *Pio Nono: A Study in European Politics and Religion* (London, 1956).

HEPOKOSKI, JAMES A., *Giuseppe Verdi: 'Otello'* (Cambridge, 1987).

HERMET, FRANCESCO, reviews and commentary on *Stiffelio* in *La passione verdiana di Trieste* (Trieste, 1951).

HOPKINSON, CECIL, *A Bibliography of the Works of Giuseppe Verdi, 1813–1901*, 2 vols. (New York, 1978).

HUSSEY, DYNELEY, *Verdi* (London, 1940).

BIBLIOGRAPHY

Indicatore delle contrade di Cremona (Cremona, 1868).

In memoria di Carlo Uttini (Piacenza, 1902).

ISSARTEL, CHRISTINE, *Les Dames aux camélias de l'histoire et à la légende* (Paris, 1981).

JARRO (See Piccini, Giulio.)

JENSEN, LUKE, *Giuseppe Verdi and the Publishers of his Music from 'Oberto' to 'La traviata'* (Ann Arbor, Mich., 1988).

KIMBELL, DAVID R. B., 'Poi . . . diventò l'*Oberto*', *Music and Letters*, 52 (1971).

—— *Verdi in the Age of Italian Romanticism* (Cambridge, 1981).

KING, BOLTON, *A History of Italian Unity, 1814–1871*, 2 vols. (London, 1899).

LAWTON, DAVID, '*Le Trouvère*: Verdi's revision of *Il trovatore* for Paris', *Studi verdiani*, 3 (1985), 78–119.

LESSONA, MICHELE, *Volere è potere* (Florence, 1876).

—— 'Una lettera di Giuseppe Verdi', *Nuova antologia*, 214: 5 (1906), 322–3.

LEVI, PRIMO, *Domenico Morelli nella vita e nell'arte* (Turin, 1906).

—— *Verdi* (Rome, 1901).

LOMBARDI, [Friar] TEODOSIO, *I Francescani a Busseto* (Bologna, 1963).

LONGYEAR, R. M., *Schiller and Music* (Chapel Hill, 1967).

LOPEZ, GUIDO, *La Casa di Riposo per Musicisti, Fondazione Giuseppe Verdi di Milano* (Milan, 1988).

LUALDI, ADRIANO, *Viaggio musicale in Italia* (Milan, 1927).

LUMLEY, BENJAMIN, *Reminiscences of the Opera* (London, 1864).

LUZIO, A., (ed.), *Carteggi verdiani*, i, ii (Rome, 1935); iii, iv (Rome, 1947).

—— 'Epistolario verdiano', *Lettura* (Feb. 1904–Mar. 1905).

—— *Profili biografici e bozzetti storici* (Milan, 1927).

MACK SMITH, DENIS, *Cavour and Garibaldi* (Cambridge, 1954).

—— *Garibaldi* (London, 1957).

—— *Italy: A Modern History* (Ann Arbor, Mich., 1959).

MAFFEI, ANDREA, '*La Fiducia in Dio* scolpita da Lorenzo Bartolini', in *Poesie scelte ed inedite* (Florence, 1869).

—— 'A Giuseppe Verdi, gloria d'Italia', *Strenna teatrale europea* (Milan, 1846).

MAGGI, SERAFINO, 'La provincia piacentina nella cronaca risorgimentale, 1859–1860', *Studi piacentini sul Risorgimento*, 11 (1961).

Magnifico passeggio con ballo e maschere che ebbe luogo nella Galleris De Cristoforis la notte del 10 febbraio 1834 (Milan, 1834).

MAISEN, PIETRO, *Cremona illustrata* (Milan, 1866).

MANCINELLI-CORA, LUISA, *Giuseppe Verdi, ricordi personali* (Genoa, 1936).

MANCINFORTE-SPERELLI, FILIPPO, *Elenco delle famiglie nobili anconetane compilato sull'archivio del Marchese Benincasa* (Ancona, n.d.).

MANFREDI, CARLO EMANUELE, and DI GROPELLO, GUSTAVO, *Le antiche famiglie di Piacenza* (Piacenza, 1979).

MANGINI, NICOLA, *I teatri di Venezia* (Milan, 1974).

BIBLIOGRAPHY

Mantovani, Tancredi, *Angelo Mariani* (Rome, 1921).

Marchesi, Gustavo, *Giuseppe Verdi: l'uomo, il genio, l'artista* (Milan, 1981).

—— *Verdi* (Milan, 1978).

—— *Verdi e il Conservatorio di Parma* (Parma, 1976).

—— *Verdi, merli, e cucù* (Busseto, 1979).

Marescotti, E. A., 'Una visita a Verdi', *Aurora*, suppl. to 104 (Milan, 1901).

Mariani, Gaetano, *Storia della Scapigliatura* (Palermo, 1967).

Marinetti, F. T., 'Les Funerailles d'un Dieu', *Vogue* (French edn.) (15 Feb. 1901).

Marmottan, P., *Elisa Bonaparte* (Paris, 1898).

Martin, George, *Aspects of Verdi* (New York, 1988).

—— *The Red Shirt and the Cross of Savoy* (New York, 1969).

—— 'Verdi and the Risorgimento', in Weaver and Chusid, *Verdi Companion*, 13–42.

—— *Verdi: His Music, Life and Times* (New York, 1963).

Martinelli, Aldo, *Verdi: raggi e penombre* (Genoa, 1926).

Mascaretti, Carlo, 'Come nacque il *Falstaff*', in *Strenna piacentina* (Piacenza, 1928), in Biblioteca Passerini-Landi, Piacenza.

Masseangeli, Masseangelo, *Catalogo della collezione di autografi lasciata alla R. Accademia Filarmonica di Bologna* (Bologna, 1881).

Matz, Mary Jane (See Phillips-Matz.).

Medici, Mario, and Conati, Marcello, with Casati, Marisa, *Carteggio Verdi– Boito*, 2 vols. (Parma, 1978).

Memorie dell'I.R. Accademia di Scienze, Lettere, ed Arti degli Agiati in Rovereto, per commemorare il suo centocinquantesimo anno di vita, 2 vols. (Rovereto, 1901–5).

Menarini, Piero, 'Antonio Garcia Gutiérrez, in *Simon Boccanegra* (house programme of the Teatro Comunale, Florence, season 1988–9), 273– 82.

Mensi, Luigi, *Dizionario biografico piacentino* (Piacenza, 1899).

'Messa per Rossini': la storia, il testo, la musica, ed. Michele Girardi and Pietroluigi Petrobelli (Parma, 1988).

Micheli, Giuseppe, 'Tre lettere di Verdi ad Antonio Superchi', *Aurea Parma* (1941), 1–2: 64–6.

—— 'Sei lettere di Verdi a G. Mariotti', *Aurea Parma*, (1941), 1–2: 35–46.

Mila, Massimo, *La giovinezza di Verdi* (Turin, 1974).

—— *L'arte di Verdi* (Turin, 1980).

—— *Il melodramma di Verdi* (Bari, 1931).

Milano e laghi (Milan, 1956).

Milano numerizzato, ossia guida numerica alla Regia Città di Milano (Milan, 1854).

Mingardi, Corrado, 'Composizioni giovanili di Giuseppe Verdi in quattro programmi inediti della Filarmonica Bussetana del 1838', *Biblioteca 70*, 1 (1970), 39–44.

—— *Con Verdi in Casa Barezzi* (Busseto, 1985).

—— *Con Verdi nella sua terra* (Cremona, 1989).

—— 'Una nuova terribile lettera di Verdi contro i bussetani', *Biblioteca 70*, 2 (1971), 27–30.

—— *Verdi e il suo ospedale 1888–1988* (Piacenza, 1988).

MOLOSSI, LORENZO, *Vocabolario topografico dei Ducati di Parma, Piacenza e Guastalla* (Parma, 1832–4).

MONALDI, GINO, *Le opere di Giuseppe Verdi al Teatro alla Scala* (Milan, 1914).

—— *Verdi aneddotico* (L'Aquila, 1926).

—— *Verdi e le sue opere* (Florence, 1887).

—— *Verdi: il maestro della rivoluzione italiana* (Milan, 1913).

MONDINI, GIULIO, *Nel cinquantennio della morte di Giuseppe Verdi* (Cremona, 1952).

MONLEONE, GIOVANNI, *Le dimore genovesi di Giuseppe Verdi* (Genoa, 1941).

MONTANELLI, INDRO, *L'Italia del Risorgimento* (6th edn., Milan, 1972).

MORAZZONI, G. *Lettere inedite di G. Verdi* (Milan, 1929).

MORINI, NESTORE, *La Reale Accademia Filarmonica di Bologna* (Bologna, 1930).

MORINI, UGO, *La R. Accademia degli Immobili e il suo teatro La Pergola* (Pisa, 1926).

MOSSA, CARLO MATTEO, 'Una *Messa* per la storia', in *'Messa per Rossini'* (Parma, 1988).

Mostra di autografi musicali di Giuseppe Verdi, catalogue of exhibition at the Museo teatrale alla Scala (Milan, 1951).

MUNDULA, MERCEDE, *La moglie di Verdi* (Milan, 1938).

La musica e il cuore d'Italia: Giuseppe Verdi, Giuseppina Strepponi, Edmondo De Amicis, nelle loro lettere (Imperia, 1976).

MUSINI, LUIGI, *Da Garibaldi al socialismo* (Milan, 1960).

MUSINI, NULLO, 'Giuseppe Verdi, deputato', in *Archivio Storico per le Province Parmensi*, vi (Parma, 1941), 31–41.

—— 'Giuseppe Verdi, patriota', in *Archivio Storico per le Province Parmensi*, vi (Parma, 1941), 43–61.

—— 'Il primo sfortunato concorso di Giuseppe Verdi', *Aurea Parma*, 1 (1937).

NAPOLITANO, ALMERINDO, *Un'antica famiglia, i Casali* (Parma, 1969).

—— *La Biblioteca del Monte di Pietà di Busseto* (Parma, 1965).

—— 'La devozione di Emanuele Muzio a Verdi', *Biblioteca 70*, 1 (1970).

—— 'La famiglia Muzio-Delfanti', *Biblioteca 70*, 1 (1970).

—— 'Emanuele Muzio e Giuseppe Verdi', typescript, SAA.

—— *Il Teatro Verdi di Busseto e le sue origini* (Parma, 1969).

NARDI, PIETRO, *Boito* (Milan, 1944).

NASALLI-ROCCA, EMILIO (ed.), *Piacenza 1859* (Piacenza, 1960).

BIBLIOGRAPHY

—— *Piacenza 1860* (Piacenza, 1960).

NATALUCCI, MARIO, *Ancona attraverso i secoli*, 3 vols. (Città di Castello, 1961).

NICOLODI, FIAMMA, 'Meyerbeer e il grand-opéra a Firenze', *Quaderni del teatro*, 4: 36 (May 1987).

NORDIO, MARIO, VALEI, DIEGO, *et al.*, *Verdi e La Fenice* (Venice, 1951).

—— 'Verdi e l'anima italiana di Trieste', in *La passione verdiana di Trieste* (Trieste, 1951).

NOSKE, FRITS, *The Signifier and the Signified* (The Hague, 1977; paperback, Oxford, 1990).

Nuovo dizionario biografico piacentino, 1860–1960 (Piacenza, 1987).

OBERDORFER, ALDO, *Giuseppe Verdi: autobiografia dalle lettere* (Milan, 1951; 3rd edn. ed. Marcello Conati, Milan, 1981).

OLDRINI, GASPARE, *Storia musicale di Lodi* (Lodi, 1883).

Omaggio di Siena a Verdi con la 'Messa da Requiem' (with Verdi's letters to Mascheroni) (Siena, 1913).

ORSINI, LUIGI, *Giuseppe Verdi* (Turin, 1958).

OSBORNE, CHARLES, *Verdi: A Life in The Theatre* (New York, 1987).

OTTOLENGHI, EMILIO, 'La madre di Verdi', *Bolletino storico piacentino*, 35 (July–Dec. 1940), 65–77.

—— 'Nel XXV anniversario della morte di G. Verdi: due lettere inedite del Maestro', *Bolletino storico piacentino*, 21 (1926), 15–22.

PAGANUZZI, E. and BOLOGNA, A. *La musica a Verona* (Verona, 1976).

PALLAVICINO, PAOLO, *Notizie sulla illustre e nobilissima famiglia del Pallavicino dell'Emiliano* (Florence, 1911).

PANZINI, ALFREDO, 'Tra la folle', in 'Verdi', special issue of *Natura ed arte* (Milan, 1901).

PARKER, ROGER L., *The Genesis of 'Aida'* (London, 1980).

—— '*Un giorno di regno* from Romani's Libretto to Verdi's Opera', *Studi verdiani*, 2 (1983), 38–58.

—— 'Verdi and the *Gazzetta privilegiata di Milano*', *Research Chronicle*, 18 (1982), 51–65.

—— (ed.), *Giuseppe Verdi: 'Nabucodonosor'*, critical edn. with introduction (Chicago, 1987).

PARRIS, JOHN, *The Lion of Caprera: A Biography of Garibaldi* (London, 1962).

PASCOLATO, A., *'Re Lear' e 'Un ballo in maschera'; Lettere di Giuseppe Verdi ad Antonio Somma* (Città di Castello, 1902).

La passione verdiana di Trieste (Trieste, 1951).

PAVAN, GIUSEPPE, *Il Teatro degli Immobili in V. della Pergola* (Milan, 1901).

—— *Il Teatro San Benedetto ora Rossini* (Venice, 1917).

PERAZZOLI, B., *Ricordando Carlo Uttini* (Piacenza, 1973).

PERFETTI, A., *Il Maestro Verdi e Carlo Uttini* (Piacenza, 1926).

PERFETTI, NINO, *Giuseppe Verdi a Como nel primo centenario della nascita*,

BIBLIOGRAPHY

1813–1913 (Como, [1913]).

PEROSIO, GIUSEPPE, *Ricordi verdiani* (Pinerolo, 1928).

PESCI, UGO, 'Le prove dell'*Otello*', in 'Verdi e Otello' special issue of *Illustrazione italiana* (1887).

PETROBELLI, PIERLUIGI, Marisa Di Gregorio Casati, and Carlo Matteo Mossa (eds.), *Carteggio Verdi–Ricordi, 1881* (Parma, 1988).

PETTORELLI, [Don] ANDREA, Gli uccelli *accademici*, manuscript collection, BMP-B.

—— 'Antonio Barezzi', unpublished sonnet in *Poesie varie*, BMP-B.

PHILLIPS-MATZ, MARY JANE, '*Aida* without Tears', *Opera News* (25 Nov. 1957).

—— 'An Ancestor for *Aida*', *Opera News* (26 Dec. 1955).

—— 'Chatelaine to the End: New Light on Giuseppina Strepponi', *Opera News* (27 Jan. 1979).

—— '*Aida*'s Roots', *Opera News* (21 Dec. 1991), 20–3.

—— 'La famiglia Barezzi di Busseto', in *Con Verdi in Casa Barezzi* (Busseto, 1985).

—— 'The [Verdi] Family Tree', in Weaver and Chusid (eds.), *Verdi Companion*.

—— 'Generations: A Work in Progress [on the Uttinis]', *Opera News* (30 Jan. 1988).

—— 'José Verdi, Hercules Cavalli, and the Florence *Macbeth*', in Porter and Rosen (eds.), *Verdi's 'Macbeth': A Sourcebook*.

—— 'Magnani e l'America', in Bacchini (ed.), *Teatro di Girolamo Magnani*, 105–12.

—— 'New Verdi Documents', *Verdi Newsletter*, 4 (American Institute for Verdi Studies, 1978).

—— 'Public Sinners', *Opera News* (Nov. 1988).

—— 'Statue Maker', *Opera News* (29 Feb. 1992), 13 ff.

—— 'A Time of Stress: Backdrop to *Rigoletto*', *Opera News* (5 Jan. 1991).

—— 'The Truth about *Traviata*', *Opera News* (11 Jan. 1964).

—— 'Verdi e la lotta contro la ragione', in *Atti del II congresso internazionale di studi verdiani*.

—— 'The Verdi Family of S. Agata and Roncole', in *Atti del I congresso internazionale di studi verdiani*.

—— 'Verdi's Gardener', *Opera News* (20 Mar. 1965).

—— 'Verdi, Salsomaggiore e Tabiano', in Bacchini (ed.), *Salsomaggiore: Art Déco Termale* (Parma, 1989).

—— 'Verdi, Vigna and Madness', in *Cesare Vigna, psichiatra e musicologo nel primo centenario della morte* (ed.) Giuseppe Flisi (Viadana, 1992).

PICCINI, G. [pseud. Jarro], *Memorie d'un impresario fiorentino* (Florence, 1892).

PICCINNINI, GUGLIELMO, 'Due lettere di Verdi e una di Giuseppina Verdi', in *Strenna degli Artigianelli* (Reggio Emilia, 1942).

PIGNAGOLI, SILVIO, *Il Comune di Busseto* (Busseto, 1926).

BIBLIOGRAPHY

Pighini, Giacomo, *La personalità di Giuseppe Verdi* (Parma, 1951).

Pigorini-Beri, Caterina, 'Giuseppe Verdi e Jacopo Sanvitale', *Gazzetta di Parma* (8 Feb. 1901).

—— 'Verdi intimo', in 'Verdi', special issue of *Natura ed arte* (1901), 19–26.

—— 'Una visita a Verdi', *Illustrazione italiana*, 44 (1881), repr. in Conati, *Interviste*.

Pinzauti, Lorenzo, 'Verdi's *Macbeth* and the Florentine Critics', in Porter and Rosen (eds.), *Verdi's 'Macbeth': A Sourcebook*.

Pizzetti, Ildebrando, 'Giuseppe Verdi, maestro di teatro', *Quaderno dell'Accademia Nazionale dei Lincei*, 26 (1952).

—— *Giuseppe Verdi nel cinquantenario della morte* (Milan, 1951).

Pizzi, Italo, *Per il centenario della nascita di Giuseppe Verdi* (Turin, 1913).

—— *Ricordi verdiani inediti* (Turin, 1901).

Porter, Andrew, 'The Grand Operas', in 'Giuseppe Verdi' *The New Grove Masters of Italian Opera* (London, 1983).

—— '*Les Vêpres siciliennes*: New Letters from Verdi to Scribe', *Nineteenth-Century Music*, 2: 2 (Nov. 1978), 101 ff.

—— 'Life: 1843–1880', in 'Giuseppe Verdi' *The New Grove Masters of Opera* (London, 1983).

—— 'The Making of *Don Carlos*', *Proceedings of the Royal Musical Association*, 98 (1971–2).

—— 'Observations on *Don Carlos*', *World of Opera*, 1: 3 (1978).

—— 'A Selected Bibliography', in Weaver and Chusid (eds.), *Verdi Companion*.

—— and Rosen, D. (eds.) *Verdi's 'Macbeth': A Sourcebook* (New York; 1984).

Pougin, Arthur, *Giuseppe Verdi: vita aneddotica con note e aggiunte di Folchetto* (Milan, 1881).

Prod'homme, Jean-Gabriel, 'Lettres inédites de G. Verdi à Léon Escudier', *Rivista musicale italiana*, 38 (1928).

—— 'Unpublished Letters from Verdi to Camille Du Locle, 1866–1876, trans. Theodore Baker, *Musical Quarterly*, 7: 4 (1921).

Pullé, Leopoldo [pseud. Leo di Castelnuovo], *Penna e spada* (Milan, 1899).

Raccolta ricordanze roncolesi, manuscript in the Parish Archive, church of San Michele, Roncole [1907?].

Radiciotti, G., *Lettere inedite di celebri musicisti* (Milan, [1892]).

—— 'Teatro e musica in Roma nel secondo quarto del secolo xix'. in *Atti del congresso italiano di scienze storiche, Roma aprile 1903* (Rome, 1905).

Radius, Emilio, *Verdi vivo* (Milan, 1951).

Regli, Francesco, *Dizionario biografico* (Turin, 1860).

Resasco, Ferdinando, *Giuseppe Verdi, cittadino genovese* (Rome, 1918); originally pub. in *Nuova antologia*, 251 (1913), 221–44.

—— *Verdi a Genova: ricordi, aneddoti ed episodi* (with other essays by Giuseppe De Amicis and E. A. De Albertis) (Genoa, 1901).

BIBLIOGRAPHY

RIBERA, ALMERICO, I combattenti (*Il Risorgimento italiano*, 5; Rome, 1943).

—— *Giuseppe Verdi: note biografiche, 1813–1913* (Milan, 1913).

RICCI, CORRADO, *Giuseppe Verdi e l'Italia musicale all'estero* (Bologna, 1889).

RIGILLO, M., 'Carlo Uttini educatore', *Libertà* (9 Jan. 1922).

—— 'Carlo Uttini, grande educatore', *Libertà* (27 Nov. 1925).

—— 'Carlo Uttini', in *Strenna piacentina* (Piacenza, 1937).

RINALDI, MARIO, *Due secoli di musica al Teatro Argentina*, 3 vols. (Florence, 1978).

—— *Gli 'anni di galera' di Giuseppe Verdi* (Rome, 1969).

RIVA, GIUSEPPE, *La Cappella del Duomo di Monza (sec. XVII–XIX) e il concorso di G. Verdi* (Monza, 1907).

La Rocca di Busseto (Cremona, 1869).

La Rocca di Busseto (Cremona, 1870).

ROLANDI, ULDARICO, 'Libretti e librettisti verdiani dal punto di vista storico-bibliografico', in *Verdi: studi e memorie a cura del sindacato nazionale fascista musicisti* (Rome, 1941), 183–232.

ROMAGNOLI, SERGIO, and GARBERO, ELVIRA, *Teatro a Reggio Emilia*, 2 vols. (Florence, 1980).

RONCAGLIA, GINO, *Ascensione creatrice di Verdi* (Florence, 1951).

'Roncole, memorie storiche', collection of documents, including rental and lease contracts, loans, and benefices, in Parish Archive, Church of San Michele Arcangelo, Roncole.

ROOSEVELT, BLANCHE, *Verdi, Milan, and 'Otello'* (London, 1887).

ROSCIONI, CARLO MARINELLI, *Il Teatro di San Carlo in cronologia 1737–1987* (Naples, 1987).

ROSSELLI, JOHN, *The Opera Industry in Italy from Cimarosa to Verdi: The Role of the Impresario* (Cambridge, 1984).

—— 'Register of Italian Theatrical Agents and Managers', computerized print-out in the author's collection.

—— 'Verdi e la storia della retribuzione del compositore italiano', *Studi verdiani*, 2 (1983), 11–28.

ROSSI, [Don] ADOLFO, *Roncole Verdi* (Fidenza, 1969).

ROTA, E., *L'Austria in Lombardia e la preparazione del movimento democratico cisalpino* (Milan, 1911).

—— *Questioni di storia risorgimentale e dell'unità d'Italia* (Milan, 1915).

SALVADORI, MASSIMO, *Cavour and the Unification of Italy* (Princeton, 1961).

SANTORO, ELIA, *I teatri di Cremona*, 4 vols. (Cremona, 1969–70).

SARTORI, CLAUDIO, 'Rocester, la prima opera di Verdi', *Rivista musicale italiana*, 43: 1 (Jan.–Feb. 1939).

SCHLITZER, FRANCO, 'Il Carteggio inedito Verdi–Florimo', in *Rassegna d'Italia*, 1: 8 (Aug. 1946).

—— *Mondo teatrale dell'Ottocento* (Naples, 1954).

BIBLIOGRAPHY

SCHMIDL, CARLO, *Dizionario universale dei musicisti* (Milan, 1887; 2-vol. edn. Milan, 1926).

SCIACCA, MICHELE FEDERIGO, *Il pensiero italiano dell'età del Risorgimento* (Milan, 1963).

SCOGNAMIGLIO, G. F., and MACELLARI, GINO, *Valdarda e Valchero* (Piacenza, 1975).

SECCHI, ALBERTO, *Roncole* (Busseto, 1934).

SELETTI, EMILIO, *La città di Busseto*, 3 vols. (Milan, 1883).

SELETTI, GIUSEPPE, 'La vera patria del Maestro Giuseppe Verdi', *Gazzetta privilegiata di Milano* (6 Mar. 1843).

SERI, ALFIERI, *Trieste nelle sue stampe* (Trieste, 1979).

SIMONI, C., 'Giuseppe Verdi: lettere al tenore Mario di Candia', *Nuova antologia*, 375 (1 Oct. 1934).

SMITH, J. PATRICK, *The Tenth Muse* (New York, 1970).

SORESINA, DARIO, *Enciclopedia diocesana fidentina*, 3 vols. (Fidenza, 1961).

SPADA, MARCO, '*Ernani* e la censura napoletana', *Studi verdiani*, 5 (1988–9), 11–34.

Statuto regolamentare della Società Operaia di Busseto (Parma, 1865).

STEFANI, GIUSEPPE, *Verdi e Trieste* (Trieste, 1951).

Storia di Piacenza, L'Ottocento (Piacenza, 1980).

SURIAN, ELVIDIO, 'A Chronological Timetable of Verdi's Life and Works', in Weaver and Chusid (eds.), *Verdi Companion*, 255–324.

TASCA, [Count] OTTAVIO, 'Brindisi d'un imparziale a quanti figurano nel Teatro alla Scala durante la stagione Carnevale 1842–1843' (Milan, 1843).

Teatro Massimo Bellini, special suppl. of *SM: Sicilia* (Palermo, 1989).

TEBALDINI, G., 'Giuseppe Verdi nella musica sacra', *Nuova antologia* (16 Oct. 1913), 561–73.

TEGANI, ULDERICO, *Accademia dei Filodrammatici di Milano* (Milan, 1923).

'Teresa Stolz, attrice cantante', *Rivista indipendente*, 8 (4 Sept.–9 Nov. 1875).

THAYER, W. R., *The Life and Times of Cavour*, 2 vols. (Boston, 1911).

—— *The Dawn of Italian Independence*, 2 vols. (Boston, 1894).

TINTI, MARIO, *Lorenzo Bartolini*, 2 vols. (Rome, 1936).

TINTORI, GIAMPIETRO, *Due cento anni di Teatro alla Scala: opere—balletti—concerti* (Milan, 1979).

—— *Palco di proscenio: il melodramma* (Milan, 1980).

—— 'Verdi in Milan', in Weaver and Chusid (eds.) *Verdi Companion*, 43–66.

TIRINCANTI, GIULIO, *Il Teatro Argentina* (Rome, 1971).

TOFANI, ANNA MARIA, et al., *Lorenzo Bartolini, mostra delle attività di tutela* (Florence, 1978).

TOSCANINI, WALTER, '*Gustavo III, azione coreografica*', *Bollettino dell'ISV*, 1: 3 (1960), 125.

TOYE, FRANCIS, *Giuseppe Verdi* (London, 1931).

BIBLIOGRAPHY

TREVELYAN, GEORGE M., *Garibaldi*, 3 vols. (London, 1911).

TREVES, GIULIANA ARTOM, *The Golden Ring: The Anglo-Florentines 1847–1862*, trans. Sylvia Sprigge (London, 1956).

TREZZINI, LAMBERTO, *Due secoli di vita musicale*, 2 vols. (Bologna, 1966).

TRONCA, MARIA SERENA, 'Il Maffei politico: un cosmopolita nell'Europa dell'800', in *L'Ottocento di Andrea Maffei* (Riva del Garda, 1987).

URIATI, [Don] UGO, *Giuseppe Verdi e il Santuario di Madonna Prati* (Busseto, n. d.), one of several privately printed and privately circulated works on Verdi.

UTTINI, [Don] CARLO, *Compendio di pedagogia e didattica ad uso delle scuole normali e magistrali femminili* (Piacenza, 1864).

—— *'Educhiamo': scritti vari di Carlo Uttini*, 2 vols. (Florence, 1874).

—— *Sillabario ordinato secondo i principi della didattica* (Piacenza, 1871).

VANBIANCHI, CARLO, *'Nel 1° centenario di Giuseppe Verdi: saggio di bibliographia verdiana: 1813–1913* (Milan, 1913).

VANNUCCI, ATTO, *I martiri della libertà italiana* (Milan, 1877).

—— *Ricordi della vita e delle opere di G. B. Niccolini* (Florence, 1866).

VAUSSARD, MAURICE, *Daily Life in Eighteenth-Century Italy* (New York, 1963).

Verdi: studi e memorie a cura del sindacato nazionale fascista musicisti (Rome, 1941).

VETRO, GASPARE NELLO, 'Un padre e un figlio, Carlo e Giuseppe Verdi', *Archivio Storico per le Province Parmensi*[4], 39 (1987).

VIALE FERRERO, MERCEDES, *Storia del Teatro Regio di Torino*, iii, *La scenografia dalle origini al 1936* (Turin, 1980).

VISCONTI VENOSTA, GIOVANNI, *Ricordi di gioventù, cose vedute e sapute* (Milan, 1906).

WALKER, FRANK, *The Man Verdi* (London, 1962); trans. in Italian as *L'uomo Verdi* (Milan, 1964).

—— 'Mercadante and Verdi', *Music and Letters* 33 (1952) and 34 (1953).

—— 'Premessa per uno studio biografico verdiano: deputato a Torino, operista a Pietroburgo', *Bollettino dell'ISV*, 2: 4 (1962).

—— 'Unpublished letters', *Bollettino dell'ISV*, 1: 1. (1960).

—— 'Verdi, Giuseppe Montanelli, and the Libretto of *Simon Boccanegra*', *ISV Bollettino*, 1: 3 (1960).

—— 'Verdian forgeries', *Music Review*, 19: 4 (Nov. 1958); 20: 1 (Feb. 1959).

—— 'Verdi a Vienna', in *Giuseppe Verdi* (Accademia Chigiana, Siena, 1951).

—— 'Vincenzo Gemito and his Bust of Verdi', *Music and Letters*, 30: 1 44 (1949).

WALL, BERNARD, *Alessandro Manzoni* (New Haven, Conn., 1954).

WEAVER, WILLIAM, 'Aspects of Verdi's Dramaturgy', in id. and Chusid (eds.), *Verdi Companion*.

—— *Duse* (New York, 1984).

—— *Verdi: a Documentary Study* (London, 1977).

BIBLIOGRAPHY

—— 'Verdi and his Librettists', in id. and Chusid (eds.), *Verdi Companion*.

—— and CHUSID, MARTIN (eds.), *The Verdi Companion* (New York, 1979).

WEINSTOCK, HERBERT, *Rossini* (New York, 1968).

WHYTE, A. J., *The Evolution of Modern Italy* (New York, 1965).

—— *The Political Life and Letters of Cavour, 1848–1861* (London, 1930).

WILLIAMS, STEPHEN, *Verdi's Last Operas* (London, 1950).

ZANON, MAFFEO, 'Elenco delle lettere di Verdi e Giuseppina Strepponi nell'archivio di Casa Ricordi, Milan', typescript in Ricordi Archive, Milan; ISV-P (1950).

ZAVADINI, GUIDO, *Donizetti: vita, musiche, epistolario* (Bergamo, 1948).

ZOPPI, UMBERTO, *Angelo Mariani, Giuseppe Verdi e Teresa Stolz* (Milan, 1947).

Index of Verdi's works

INDEX OF VERDI'S WORKS

INDEX OF VERDI'S WORKS

General Index

GENERAL INDEX

GENERAL INDEX

GENERAL INDEX

GENERAL INDEX

GENERAL INDEX

GENERAL INDEX

GENERAL INDEX

GENERAL INDEX

GENERAL INDEX

GENERAL INDEX

GENERAL INDEX

GENERAL INDEX